Business Mathematics

11TH EDITION

Charles D. Miller

Stanley A. Salzman
AMERICAN RIVER COLLEGE

Gary Clendenen
SIENA COLLEGE

PEARSON
Addison Wesley

Boston San Francisco New York London Sydney
Tokyo Singapore Madrid Mexico City Paris
Cape Town Hong Kong Montreal

Editorial Director: Christine Hoag
Editor in Chief: Maureen O'Connor
Project Editor: Katie Nopper DePasquale
Assistant Editor: Caroline Case
Senior Managing Editor: Karen Wernholm
Senior Production Supervisor: Sheila Spinney
Photo Researcher: Beth Anderson
Media Producer: Michelle Small
Software Development: Janet Wann, Math XL, and Marly Wright, TestGen
Marketing Manager: Michelle Renda
Marketing Coordinator: Nathaniel Koven
Senior Author Support/Technology Specialist: Joe Vetere
Manufacturing Manager: Evelyn Beaton
Production Coordination, Composition, and Illustrations: Pre-Press PMG
Interior Design: Sandy Silva
Cover Design: Diane Ernsberger
Cover Photo: Cityscape/©Getty Images

For permission to use copyrighted material, grateful acknowledgment is made to the copyright holders listed in the Acknowledgments on the second-to-last page of this book. These materials are used by permission. All existing copyrights relating to these materials remain in effect and are the exclusive property of the corporations named.

Library of Congress Cataloging-in-Publication Data

Miller, Charles David, 1942–1986
Business mathematics/Charles D. Miller, Stanley A. Salzman, Gary Clendenen. —11th ed.
p. cm.
Includes index.
ISBN 0-321-50012-1; ISBN 978-0-321-50012-0 (Student Edition)

1. Business mathematics. 2. Business mathematics—Programmed instruction. I. Salzman, Stanley A. II. Clendenen, Gary. III. Title.

HF5691.M465 2007
650.01′513—dc22 2007060122

1 2 3 4 5 6 7 8 9 10 WC 11 10 09 08

Contents

Preface

The eleventh edition of *Business Mathematics* has been extensively revised to maximize student involvement in each chapter of the text. More than ever, real-life examples from today's business world have been incorporated; new examples from actual companies and the people who run them are woven throughout the book to serve as applications of the concepts presented. Many new photographs, news clippings, and graphs have been added to increase the relevance of chapter content to the world students know. The globalization of our society is emphasized through examples and exercises that highlight foreign countries and international topics.

The new edition reflects the extensive business and teaching experience of the authors, as well as the suggestions of many reviewers nationwide. Providing solid, practical, and up-to-date coverage of business mathematics topics, the text begins with a brief review of basic mathematics and goes on to introduce key business topics, such as bank services, payroll, business discounts and markups, simple and compound interest, stocks and bonds, consumer loans, taxes and insurance, depreciation, financial statements, and business statistics. The text is accompanied by a greatly enhanced supplements package that provides many avenues—both print and other media—for students to further practice and explore the concepts discussed in the chapters. (Please see pages xvii–xviii of this preface for full descriptions of the student and instructor supplements available.)

New Content Highlights

Chapter 3, "Percent," has additional examples and exercises showing the applications of percent in our daily lives. The topics included are "what first-time buyers are paying for new homes," "the affordability of homes across the nation," and "how Americans plan to enhance the exterior of their homes."

The material in Chapter 4, "Bank Services," has been updated in keeping with the latest banking trends and practices. The statistics showing the use of banking services, today's banking charges, and currently used credit card deposit slips reflect the latest available information. Also covered are the latest technologies in banking, electronic funds transfer (EFT), automated teller machines (ATM), and the most recent trends in the use of online banking.

In Chapter 5, "Payroll," all wages and salaries have been updated along with FICA, Medicare, and tax-withholding rates. The chapter looks at American workers and their jobs, the average annual earnings for various occupations, the work schedules of U.S. women, and the percent of women in the workforce around the world. Average hourly pay for workers around the world, Social Security rates for employees and employers in major countries, today's new jobs, the minimum wage landscape across the country, and the fastest growing career fields are also included.

Chapter 6, "Mathematics of Buying," introduces e-commerce and the resulting changes in business operations. A new tool to help students remember the number of days in each month of the year has been added.

In Chapter 7, "Mathematics of Selling," holiday shopping patterns, retail merchandising methods, and where shoppers shop are included.

Chapter 8, "Simple Interest," has been updated to reflect current interest rates. A graph with both housing starts and prime interest rates is used to show the general relationship between interest rates and housing.

Chapter 9, "Compound Interest and Annuities," shows the benefits of compounding interest over periods of time. Inflation is defined and examples are included to show the effect of inflation on earning power.

Chapter 10, "Annuities, Stocks, and Bonds," uses both examples and exercises to emphasize the value of long-term saving for students and includes descriptions of the basic types of retirement accounts. It also explains how companies use long-term savings to their advantage. The stock and bond data has been updated.

Chapter 11, "Business and Consumer Loans," now has a greater emphasis on debt and student debt in particular. All interest rates have been adjusted to current rates. The sections on Installment Loans and Real Estate Loans will be of special interest to students. A discussion of FICO score has been added and tips are given to help students improve their own score, and therefore their ability to obtain credit.

In Chapter 12, "Taxes and Insurance," all personal income tax applications have been updated using the most current tax laws. The rates for motor vehicle insurance and life insurance have been updated to more accurately reflect today's rates.

The most recent federal laws and guidelines are used in Chapter 13, "Depreciation." This coverage helps students who will be studying accounting in the future.

The company highlighted in Chapter 14, "Financial Statements and Ratios," has been changed to a company every student knows, The Hershey Company, which manufactures many different chocolate products. Students can learn about financial statements using a company whose products they enjoy.

Many of the problems in Chapter 15, "Business Statistics," have been changed, and graphs from the business world that interest students have been added.

Appendix A, "Equations and Formulas," includes many of the basic algebra concepts needed to work business math problems. Appendix B, "The Metric System," contains the conversions needed to work with the metric system. Appendix C, "Basic Calculators," presents detailed coverage of basic calculators for professors who allow students to use calculators. Appendix D, "Financial Calculators," reviews the basic functions of financial calculators using present value and future value.

New Features

Quick Check Exercises and Answers Each example throughout the text is followed by a related exercise called a Quick Check. Designed to reinforce understanding of the specific concept, it will give immediate feedback to the student. The answer to each Quick Check is given at the bottom of the same page.

Larger Format (size) and Larger Type Size The larger format of the eleventh edition allows the material to be spread out over a larger page and a larger type size to be used, resulting in easier reading. Additional photos have been added to attract student interest.

Classroom Lectures and Case Studies on DVD-ROM The NEW Classroom Lectures and Case Studies on DVD-ROM, included with each new text, offer students a comprehensive lecture for each section of the text, along with case study videos that profile real companies from the in-text Case Studies.

Additional Features

Chapter Openers Many chapters introduce a new or popular business—such as SUBWAY®, The Home Depot, The Hershey Company, Bank of America, General Motors, Citigroup, Century 21, and Mattel—to capture students' interest. These chapter openers, identified as "Case in Point," present the owner, manager, or employee of the business, and that person is discussed throughout the chapter in the context of the company he or she represents. Exercises marked with a Case in Point icon continue to support the application of the chapter topic.

Enhanced Treatment of Real-World Applications The eleventh edition places greater emphasis on real-world applications. Application problems have been updated throughout to be as relevant as possible to today's students, and they reference well-known companies such as SUBWAY, The Home Depot, Jackson and Perkins Company, REI, Ford Motor Company, Bank of America, General Motors, Citigroup, Century 21, The Hershey Company, and Mattel.

Art Program The art program of the eleventh edition includes not only new and larger color photographs, but also graphs and charts that utilize current data from a variety of recognized sources. Rendered to draw students' attention while emphasizing the data itself, the graphs and charts, entitled Numbers in the News, help students see that the mathematics of business is inherent to the world around them.

Here & Now Many of the newspaper clippings, magazine articles, and other media items in the text are flagged with a Here & Now icon in the margin. By drawing students' eyes to these real media sources, the Here & Now icon helps emphasize the practical, everyday relevance of business mathematics.

Numerous Exercises Mastering business mathematics requires working through many exercises, so we have included more than 2850 in the eleventh edition. They range from simple drill problems to application exercises that require several steps to solve. All problems have been independently checked to ensure accuracy. A comprehensive Index of Applications appears at the beginning of this text.

Graded Application Exercises All application exercises are arranged in pairs and increase progressively in difficulty. This arrangement prepares students to work the more difficult exercises as they proceed through the exercise set. Each even-numbered application exercise is the same type of problem as the previous odd-numbered exercise. This allows students to solve an odd-numbered exercise, check the answer in the answer section, and then solve the following even-numbered exercise.

Supplementary Exercises Additional sets of supplementary exercises occur throughout the book to help students review and synthesize difficult concepts. For example, two sets in Chapter 3 require students to distinguish among the different elements of a percent problem and decide upon the correct method of solution. The set in Chapter 7 includes exercises in both markup on cost and markup on selling price. This will help the student distinguish between these two types of markup. A set in Chapter 8 gives practice in distinguishing simple interest from simple discount; a set in Chapter 10 helps students understand annuities and sinking funds, and another set in Chapter 13 combines methods of calculating depreciation.

Case in Point Found throughout each chapter and flagged by the C icon, the Case in Point application is tied to the business introduced in the chapter opener. This approach demonstrates to the student how specific topics are used by those operating the business.

Newspaper and Magazine Articles A wide selection of current newspaper and magazine articles from various news media sources appears within each chapter to emphasize the "Here & Now" of these topics. These current, eye-catching items are tied to examples within the chapter sections and are a constant reminder to students of the relevance of the chapter content to current business trends and topics.

Calculator Solutions Calculator solutions, identified with the calculator symbol, appear after selected examples. These solutions show students the keystrokes needed to obtain the example solution.

Cumulative Reviews Four Cumulative Reviews, found at the end of Chapters 3, 7, 9, and 11, help students review groups of related chapter topics and reinforce understanding.

Investigative Questions The Investigate feature now appears at the end of every chapter's Summary Exercise. The Investigate questions require higher-level thinking skills and encourage students to apply the chapter material in a practical way or go outside the classroom to seek additional knowledge. Many of these questions are ideal for collaborative assignments.

Metric System The metric system has been added to Appendix B.

Basic Calculator Appendix This edition includes an appendix (Appendix C) containing extensive coverage of basic calculators. A number of exercises are provided to help students develop their calculator skills.

Financial Calculators Financial calculators are presented in Appendix D, along with exercises that may be solved by students using the financial calculator of their choice.

Cautionary Remarks Common student difficulties and misunderstandings appear as Quick Tips. This feature is given a special graphic treatment to help students locate them.

Quick Start Solutions to Exercises Selected exercises in the exercise sets—usually the first of each type of exercise—are denoted by a Quick Start head and include answers with solutions to help students get started. This on-the-spot reinforcement gives students both the confidence to continue working practice problems and the knowledge of which topics may require additional review.

Quick Review with Chapter Terms The end-of-chapter Quick Review feature begins with a list of key terms from the chapter and the pages on which they first appear. The Quick Review uses a two-column format (Concepts and Examples) to help the student review all the main points presented in the chapter.

Writing Exercises Designed to help students better understand and relate the concepts within a section, these exercises require a written answer of a few sentences. They are flagged in the Annotated Instructor's Edition by the icon and often include references to a specific learning objective to help students formulate an answer.

Summary Exercises Every chapter ends with a Summary Exercise that has been designed to help students apply what they have learned in the chapter. These problems require students to synthesize most or all of the topics they have covered in the chapter in order to solve one cumulative exercise. Ending with a feature labeled Investigate, these exercises offer the student an opportunity to further develop problem-solving skills beyond the classroom. The Investigate questions may be worked out as a group or individual activity, depending on the instructor's preference.

Example Titles Each example has a title to help students understand the purpose of the example. The titles can also help students work the exercises and study for quizzes and exams.

Flexibility After basic prerequisites have been met, the chapters in this text can be taught in any order to give instructors maximum freedom in designing courses. Chapter prerequisites are as follows:

Chapter	Prerequisite	Chapter	Prerequisite
1	None	9	Simple interest
2	None	10	Simple interest
3	Arithmetic	11	Simple interest
4	Percent	12	Percent
5	Percent	13	Percent
6	Percent	14	Percent
7	Percent	15	Percent
8	Percent		

Pretest A business mathematics pretest is included in the introduction of the book. This pretest can help students and instructors identify individual and class strengths and weaknesses.

Chapter Tests Each chapter ends with a chapter test that reviews all of the topics in the chapter and helps evaluate student mastery.

Equations and Formulas A review of equations, business applications of equations, and ratios and proportions is included in Appendix A. Instructors may find it appropriate to introduce this material to lay the groundwork for an alternative approach to the mathematics of buying and selling (Chapters 6 and 7), interest (Chapters 8 and 9), annuities (Chapter 10), and consumer loans (Chapter 11).

Glossary A glossary of key words, located at the back of the book, provides a quick reference for the main ideas of the course.

Summary of Formulas The inside back cover of *Business Mathematics* provides a handy summary of commonly used information and business formulas from the book.

Walkthrough

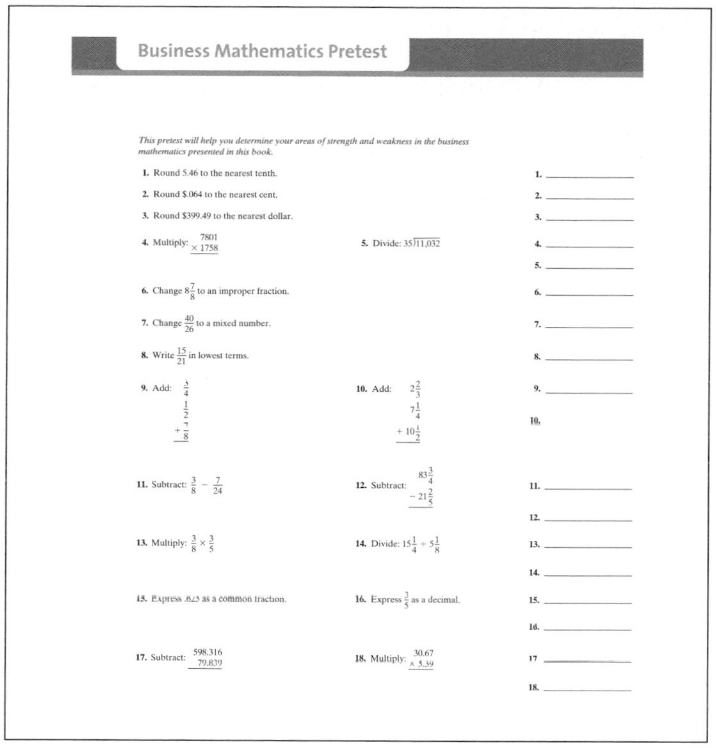

Business Mathematics Pretest

This pretest will help you determine your areas of strength and weakness in the business mathematics presented in this book.

1. Round 5.46 to the nearest tenth. **1.** ______

2. Round $.064 to the nearest cent. **2.** ______

3. Round $399.49 to the nearest dollar. **3.** ______

4. Multiply: 7801×1758 **5.** Divide: $35\overline{)11{,}032}$ **4.** ______ **5.** ______

6. Change $8\frac{7}{8}$ to an improper fraction. **6.** ______

7. Change $\frac{40}{26}$ to a mixed number. **7.** ______

8. Write $\frac{15}{21}$ in lowest terms. **8.** ______

9. Add: $\frac{3}{4} + \frac{1}{2} + \frac{7}{8}$ **10.** Add: $2\frac{2}{3} + 7\frac{1}{4} + 10\frac{1}{2}$ **9.** ______ **10.**

11. Subtract: $\frac{3}{8} - \frac{7}{24}$ **12.** Subtract: $83\frac{3}{4} - 21\frac{2}{5}$ **11.** ______ **12.** ______

13. Multiply: $\frac{3}{8} \times \frac{3}{5}$ **14.** Divide: $15\frac{1}{4} \div 5\frac{1}{8}$ **13.** ______ **14.** ______

15. Express .625 as a common fraction. **16.** Express $\frac{3}{5}$ as a decimal. **15.** ______ **16.** ______

17. Subtract: $598.316 - 79.839$ **18.** Multiply: 30.67×5.39 **17** ______ **18.** ______

Pretest

A business mathematics pretest is included before the first chapter to help students and instructors identify individual and class strengths and weaknesses.

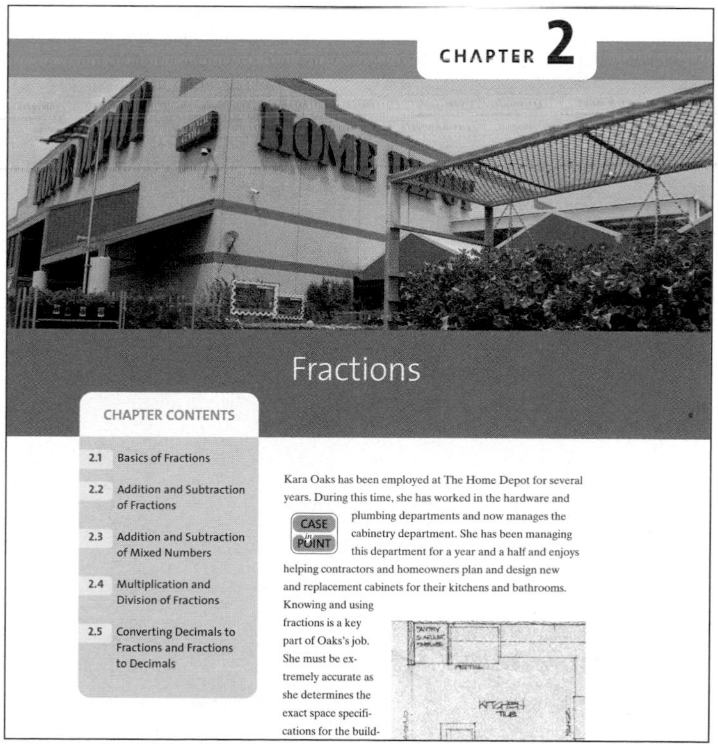

CHAPTER 2

Fractions

CHAPTER CONTENTS

CASE in POINT

Kara Oaks has been employed at The Home Depot for several years. During this time, she has worked in the hardware and plumbing departments and now manages the cabinetry department. She has been managing this department for a year and a half and enjoys helping contractors and homeowners plan and design new and replacement cabinets for their kitchens and bathrooms. Knowing and using fractions is a key part of Oaks's job. She must be extremely accurate as she determines the exact space specifications for the build-

Chapter Openers

Each chapter begins by introducing a particular business, which is revisited throughout the chapter as a Case in Point.

Case in Point

Introduced in the chapter opener, the Case in Point highlights a specific business that is revisited throughout the chapter, and incorporated into the exercises.

CASE in POINT Kara Oaks must use fractions on a daily basis as she works with contractors and homeowners at The Home Depot. The measurements of cabinets, trim pieces, and room sizes never seem to be even numbers of inches—they always have fractions of an inch.

OBJECTIVE 4 Divide fractions. T… tiply the first fraction by t… ator and the denominato… *multiplying*.

QUICK TIP Only the second fraction (divisor) is inverted when dividing by a fraction. Cancellation is done *only after inverting*.

Quick Tips

Cautionary remarks to help students avoid common difficulties and misunderstandings appear throughout the book in special boxes.

Here & Now

Many clippings from newspapers, magazines, and other media appear throughout the text, and are flagged with a Here & Now icon, emphasizing the practical, everyday relevance of business mathematics.

HERE & NOW

Housing Slump Deepens

Two major companies report big drops in new orders and weaker quarterly results.

By Deborah Yao

ASSOCIATED PRESS

PHILADELPHIA – In a sign of a deepening housing slump, two major home builders on Tuesday reported steep declines in new orders and weaker fourth-quarter results.

Luxury home builder Toll Brothers Inc. of Horsham, Pa., said home-building revenue fell by 10 percent and signed contracts were down by 55 percent compared with a year ago. The company, which released its quarterly outlook ahead of earnings, also said it will incur a hefty charge against profits as it pares down the number of lots it controls.

Beazer Homes USA Inc. of Atlanta reported a 44 percent decline in profit as higher revenue was offset by squeezed margins. The company said there was "significant" discounting in most markets.

New orders for Beazer fell by 58 percent to 2,064 homes from 4,937 last year, as the housing market continued to slow. It has cut 1,000 jobs, or 25 percent of its work force.

"We think it's a loss of confidence in the buyers," Toll Brothers Chief Executive Robert Toll said during a conference call with analysts Tuesday. "Nobody wants to buy something that they think will cost less two weeks later."

Quick Check Answer

2. 1280 took exam

45. COMPUTER ASSEMBLY When installing a printer cable to a computer, Ann Kuick must be certain that the proper type and size of mounting hardware are used. Find the total length of the bolt shown.

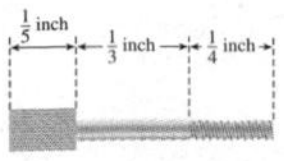

45. ____________

46. CABINET INSTALLATION When installing cabinets for The Home Depot, Sarah Bryn must be certain that the proper type and size of mounting screw are used. Find the total length of the screw.

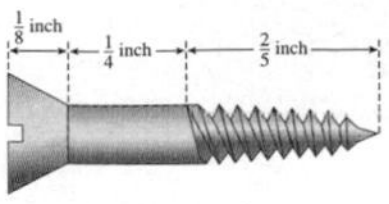

46. ____________

47. PETROLEUM TRANSPORT Ken Faulk drives a tanker truck for Wonder Transport. He leaves the refinery with his tanker filled to $\frac{7}{8}$ of capacity. If he delivers $\frac{1}{4}$ of the tank's contents at the first stop and $\frac{1}{3}$ of the tank's contents at the second stop, find the fraction of the tanker's contents remaining.

47. ____________

Graded Application Exercises

Numerous application exercises, highlighting both established and new actual businesses, are available in the exercise sets.

Calculator Solutions

These examples are identified with a calculator icon, and show students the keystrokes needed to obtain the example solution.

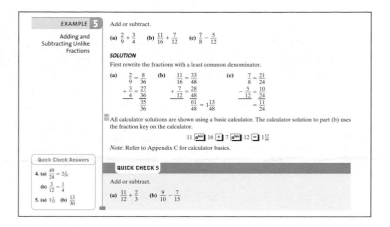

EXAMPLE 5

Adding and Subtracting Unlike Fractions

Add or subtract.

(a) $\frac{2}{9} + \frac{3}{4}$ **(b)** $\frac{11}{16} + \frac{7}{12}$ **(c)** $\frac{7}{8} - \frac{5}{12}$

SOLUTION

First rewrite the fractions with a least common denominator.

(a) $\frac{2}{9} = \frac{8}{36}$, $+\frac{3}{4} = \frac{27}{36}$, $\frac{35}{36}$ **(b)** $\frac{11}{16} = \frac{33}{48}$, $+\frac{7}{12} = \frac{28}{48}$, $\frac{61}{48} = 1\frac{13}{48}$ **(c)** $\frac{7}{8} = \frac{21}{24}$, $-\frac{5}{12} = \frac{10}{24}$, $= \frac{11}{24}$

All calculator solutions are shown using a basic calculator. The calculator solution to part (b) uses the fraction key on the calculator.

11 [a b/c] 16 [+] 7 [a b/c] 12 [=] $1\frac{13}{48}$

Note: Refer to Appendix C for calculator basics.

Quick Check Answers

4. (a) $\frac{49}{24} = 2\frac{1}{24}$
(b) $\frac{3}{12} = \frac{1}{4}$
5. (a) $1\frac{7}{12}$ (b) $\frac{13}{30}$

QUICK CHECK 5

Add or subtract.

(a) $\frac{11}{12} + \frac{2}{3}$ **(b)** $\frac{9}{10} - \frac{7}{15}$

QUICK CHECK 5

A plumber needs 68 pieces of 1-inch-diameter copper tubing. If each piece of tubing must be $28\frac{1}{2}$ inches long, how many total inches of tubing are needed?

NEW—Quick Checks

Quick Check exercises follow each example in the text and allow students to immediately reinforce the concepts explained in the example.

Writing Exercises

These exercises, often referencing a specific objective, are designed to help students better understand and relate to concepts within a section. Writing exercises are flagged in the *Annotated Instructor's Edition* for instructor convenience.

39. What does it mean when a fraction is expressed in lowest terms? (See Objective 4.)

40. Eight rules of divisibility were given. Write the three rules that are most useful to you. (See Objective 5.)

SUPPLEMENTARY APPLICATION EXERCISES ON BASE AND PART 111

SUPPLEMENTARY APPLICATION EXERCISES ON BASE AND PART

Solve the following application problems. Read each problem carefully to determine whether base or part is being asked for.

1. SHAMPOO INGREDIENTS Most shampoos contain 75% to 90% water. If there are 12.3 ounces of water in a bottle of shampoo that contains 78% water, what is the size of the bottle of shampoo? Round to the nearest whole number. 1. ________

2. HOUSEHOLD LUBRICANT The lubricant WD-40 is used in 82.3 million U.S. homes, which is 79% of all homes in the United States. Find the total number of homes in the United States. Round to the nearest tenth of a million. (***Source:*** WD-40.) 2. ________

3. PROPERTY INSURANCE Thomas Dugally of Century 21 Real Estate sold a commercial building valued at $423,750. If the building is insured for 68% of its value, find the amount of insurance coverage. 3. ________

4. FLU SHOTS In a survey of 3860 people who were 18–49 years old, 16.3% had received an influenza vaccination (flu shot). How many of those surveyed received the vaccination? Round to the nearest whole number. (***Source:*** National Health Interview Survey.) 4. ________

5. CAMAROS AND MUSTANGS The Chevrolet Camaro was introduced in 1967. Camaro sales that year were 220,917, which was 46.2% of the number of Ford Mustangs sold in the same year. Find the number of Mustangs sold in 1967. Round to the nearest whole number. 5. ________

6. CHILD SUPPORT Sean Eden has 12.4% of his earnings withheld for child support. If this amounts to $396.80 per month, find his annual earnings. 6. ________

7. CALORIES FROM FAT Häagen-Dazs vanilla ice cream has 270 calories per serving. If 60% of these calories come from fat, find the number of calories coming from fat. (***Source:*** Häagen-Dazs.) 7. ________

8. BLOOD-CHOLESTEROL LEVELS At a recent health fair, 32% of the people tested were found to have high blood-cholesterol levels. If 350 people were tested, find the number having a high blood-cholesterol level. 8. ________

Supplementary Exercises

Additional sets of supplementary exercises occur throughout the book to help students review and synthesize difficult concepts.

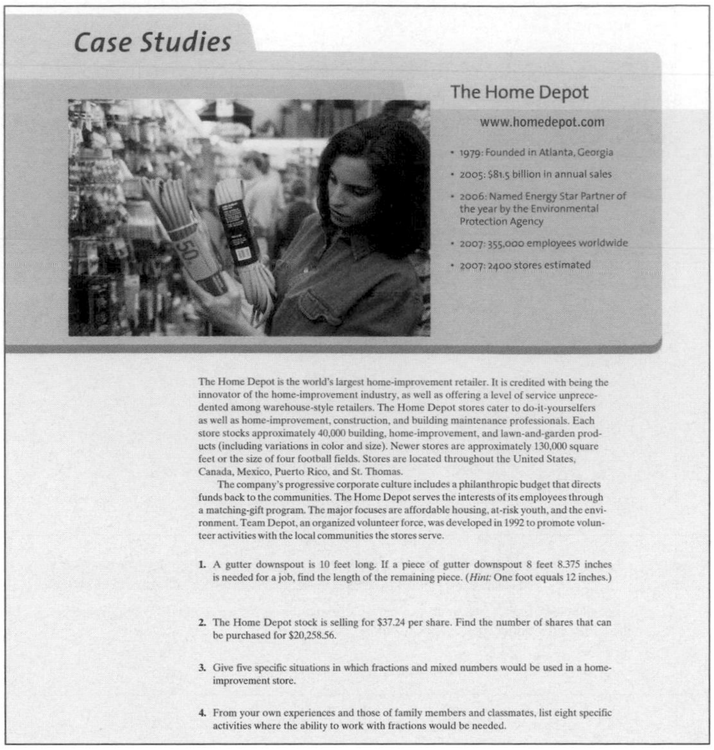

Case Studies

The Home Depot

www.homedepot.com

- 1979: Founded in Atlanta, Georgia
- 2005: $81.5 billion in annual sales
- 2006: Named Energy Star Partner of the year by the Environmental Protection Agency
- 2007: 355,000 employees worldwide
- 2007: 2400 stores estimated

The Home Depot is the world's largest home-improvement retailer. It is credited with being the innovator of the home-improvement industry, as well as offering a level of service unprecedented among warehouse-style retailers. The Home Depot stores cater to do-it-yourselfers as well as home-improvement, construction, and building maintenance professionals. Each store stocks approximately 40,000 building, home-improvement, and lawn-and-garden products (including variations in color and size). Newer stores are approximately 130,000 square feet or the size of four football fields. Stores are located throughout the United States, Canada, Mexico, Puerto Rico, and St. Thomas.

The company's progressive corporate culture includes a philanthropic budget that directs funds back to the communities. The Home Depot serves the interests of its employees through a matching-gift program. The major focuses are affordable housing, at-risk youth, and the environment. Team Depot, an organized volunteer force, was developed in 1992 to promote volunteer activities with the local communities the stores serve.

1. A gutter downspout is 10 feet long. If a piece of gutter downspout 8 feet 8.375 inches is needed for a job, find the length of the remaining piece. (*Hint:* One foot equals 12 inches.)
2. The Home Depot stock is selling for $37.24 per share. Find the number of shares that can be purchased for $20,258.56.
3. Give five specific situations in which fractions and mixed numbers would be used in a home-improvement store.
4. From your own experiences and those of family members and classmates, list eight specific activities where the ability to work with fractions would be needed.

NEW—Case Studies

In each chapter, a one-page feature on a particular business provides some background, and poses related questions. Video material for several of these case studies is available on the new Classroom Lectures and Case Studies DVD-ROM.

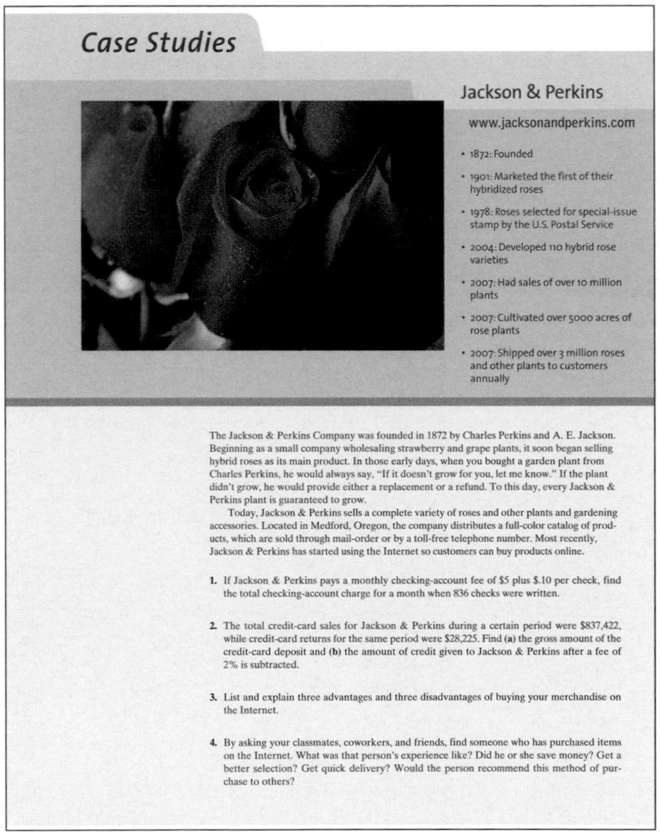

Case Studies

Jackson & Perkins

www.jacksonandperkins.com

- 1872: Founded
- 1901: Marketed the first of their hybridized roses
- 1978: Roses selected for special-issue stamp by the U.S. Postal Service
- 2004: Developed 110 hybrid rose varieties
- 2007: Had sales of over 10 million plants
- 2007: Cultivated over 5000 acres of rose plants
- 2007: Shipped over 3 million roses and other plants to customers annually

The Jackson & Perkins Company was founded in 1872 by Charles Perkins and A. E. Jackson. Beginning as a small company wholesaling strawberry and grape plants, it soon began selling hybrid roses as its main product. In those early days, when you bought a garden plant from Charles Perkins, he would always say, "If it doesn't grow for you, let me know." If the plant didn't grow, he would provide either a replacement or a refund. To this day, every Jackson & Perkins plant is guaranteed to grow.

Today, Jackson & Perkins sells a complete variety of roses and other plants and gardening accessories. Located in Medford, Oregon, the company distributes a full-color catalog of products, which are sold through mail-order or by a toll-free telephone number. Most recently, Jackson & Perkins has started using the Internet so customers can buy products online.

1. If Jackson & Perkins pays a monthly checking-account fee of $5 plus $.10 per check, find the total checking-account charge for a month when 836 checks were written.
2. The total credit-card sales for Jackson & Perkins during a certain period were $837,422, while credit-card returns for the same period were $28,225. Find **(a)** the gross amount of the credit-card deposit and **(b)** the amount of credit given to Jackson & Perkins after a fee of 2% is subtracted.
3. List and explain three advantages and three disadvantages of buying your merchandise on the Internet.
4. By asking your classmates, coworkers, and friends, find someone who has purchased items on the Internet. What was that person's experience like? Did he or she save money? Get a better selection? Get quick delivery? Would the person recommend this method of purchase to others?

NEW—Classroom Lectures and Case Studies on DVD-ROM

The NEW Classroom Lectures and Case Studies on DVD-ROM, included with each new text, offer students a comprehensive lecture for each section of the text, along with case study videos that profile real companies from the in-text Case Studies.

Quick Review

At the end of each chapter, students will find a quick review to help them review the entire chapter. The quick summary includes an indexed list of key terms from the chapter, and goes through important concepts and examples from the chapter in a two-column format.

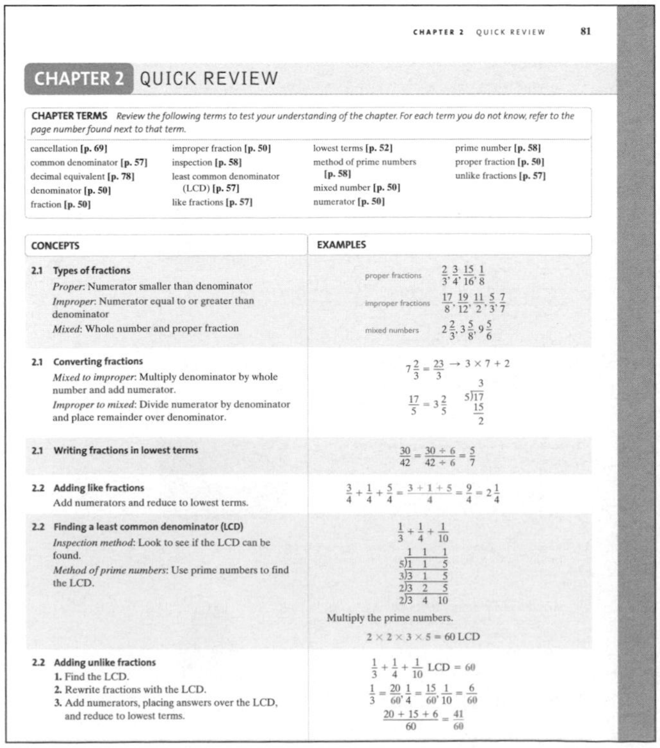

CHAPTER 2 QUICK REVIEW 81

CHAPTER 2 QUICK REVIEW

CHAPTER TERMS *Review the following terms to test your understanding of the chapter. For each term you do not know, refer to the page number found next to that term.*

cancellation **[p. 69]**	improper fraction **[p. 50]**	lowest terms **[p. 52]**	prime number **[p. 58]**
common denominator **[p. 57]**	inspection **[p. 58]**	method of prime numbers **[p. 58]**	proper fraction **[p. 50]**
decimal equivalent **[p. 78]**	least common denominator (LCD) **[p. 57]**	mixed number **[p. 50]**	unlike fractions **[p. 57]**
denominator **[p. 50]**	like fractions **[p. 57]**	numerator **[p. 50]**	
fraction **[p. 50]**			

CONCEPTS	EXAMPLES
2.1 Types of fractions *Proper:* Numerator smaller than denominator *Improper:* Numerator equal to or greater than denominator *Mixed:* Whole number and proper fraction	proper fractions $\frac{2}{3}, \frac{3}{4}, \frac{15}{16}, \frac{1}{8}$; improper fractions $\frac{17}{8}, \frac{19}{12}, \frac{11}{2}, \frac{5}{3}, \frac{7}{7}$; mixed numbers $2\frac{2}{3}, 3\frac{5}{8}, 9\frac{5}{6}$
2.1 Converting fractions *Mixed to improper:* Multiply denominator by whole number and add numerator. *Improper to mixed:* Divide numerator by denominator and place remainder over denominator.	$7\frac{2}{3} = \frac{23}{3} \to 3 \times 7 + 2$; $\frac{17}{5} = 3\frac{2}{5}$ ($17 \div 5 = 3$, remainder 2)
2.1 Writing fractions in lowest terms	$\frac{30}{42} = \frac{30 \div 6}{42 \div 6} = \frac{5}{7}$
2.2 Adding like fractions Add numerators and reduce to lowest terms.	$\frac{3}{4} + \frac{1}{4} + \frac{5}{4} = \frac{3+1+5}{4} = \frac{9}{4} = 2\frac{1}{4}$
2.2 Finding a least common denominator (LCD) *Inspection method:* Look to see if the LCD can be found. *Method of prime numbers:* Use prime numbers to find the LCD.	$\frac{1}{3} + \frac{1}{4} + \frac{1}{10}$; divide 3, 4, 10 by primes: 2 → 3, 2, 5; 2 → 3, 1, 5; 3 → 1, 1, 5; 5 → 1, 1, 1. Multiply the prime numbers. $2 \times 2 \times 3 \times 5 = 60$ LCD
2.2 Adding unlike fractions 1. Find the LCD. 2. Rewrite fractions with the LCD. 3. Add numerators, placing answers over the LCD, and reduce to lowest terms.	$\frac{1}{3} + \frac{1}{4} + \frac{1}{10}$ LCD = 60; $\frac{1}{3} = \frac{20}{60}, \frac{1}{4} = \frac{15}{60}, \frac{1}{10} = \frac{6}{60}$; $\frac{20 + 15 + 6}{60} = \frac{41}{60}$

CHAPTER 3 SUMMARY EXERCISE

Investment Gains and Losses

Understanding the stock market can be an important part of financial planning. Looking toward retirement, you may invest a portion of your savings by buying stock in various companies. Every day the changes in stock prices are shown in most major newspapers. Listed below are some well-known companies along with stock price information for this year and last year. Find the stock price last year, the percent of change from last year, or the stock price this year, as necessary. Round dollar amounts to the nearest cent and percents to the nearest tenth.

The Ups and Downs of Last Year

Company Name	Stock Symbol	Stock Price Last Year	Stock Price This Year	% Change from Last Year
Amazon.com	AMZN	\$25.76	\$39.26	____
Daimler LG	DCX	\$45.98	____	28.6%
Gateway Computer	GTW	____	\$1.30	− 58.6%
Krispy Kreme	KKD	\$4.78	\$10.39	____
McDonald's	MCD	\$31.73	\$41.97	____
Merck	MRK	____	\$43.12	54.1%
Pepsi Bottling	PBG	\$27.99	____	14.0%
NetFlix Inc.	NFLX	____	\$29.38	62.1%
Wal Mart	WMT	\$52.15	____	− 10.9%
Yahoo	YHOO	\$22.65	\$27.39	____

Summary Exercises

This cumulative exercise set, at the end of each chapter, requires students to synthesize most or all of the topics covered in the chapter.

Investigative Questions

Found at the end of each chapter's summary exercise, investigative questions require higher-level thinking skills and encourage students to develop concepts beyond what they have already learned. This feature is ideal for collaborative assignments.

INVESTIGATE

Find the New York State Exchange (NYSE) listing in a newspaper. Select five stocks that you have heard of and list their closing prices. Find the cost of 10 shares of each of these stocks, and round each of these costs to the nearest dollar.

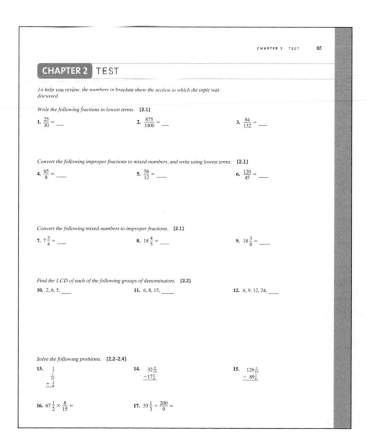

CHAPTER 2 TEST

To help you review, the numbers in brackets show the section in which the topic was discussed.

Write the following fractions in lowest terms. **[2.1]**

1. $\frac{25}{30} =$ ___ **2.** $\frac{875}{1000} =$ ___ **3.** $\frac{84}{132} =$ ___

Convert the following improper fractions to mixed numbers, and write using lowest terms. **[2.1]**

4. $\frac{65}{8} =$ ___ **5.** $\frac{56}{12} =$ ___ **6.** $\frac{120}{45} =$ ___

Convert the following mixed numbers to improper fractions. **[2.1]**

7. $7\frac{3}{4} =$ ___ **8.** $18\frac{4}{5} =$ ___ **9.** $18\frac{3}{8} =$ ___

Find the LCD of each of the following groups of denominators. **[2.2]**

10. 2, 6, 5, ___ **11.** 6, 8, 15, ___ **12.** 6, 9, 12, 24, ___

Solve the following problems. **[2.2–2.4]**

13. $\frac{1}{5} + \frac{3}{10} + \frac{3}{8}$ **14.** $32\frac{5}{16} - 17\frac{1}{4}$ **15.** $126\frac{3}{16} - 89\frac{7}{8}$

16. $67\frac{1}{2} \times \frac{8}{15} =$ **17.** $33\frac{1}{3} \div \frac{200}{9} =$

Chapter Tests

Each chapter ends with a test reviewing all of the topics in the chapter.

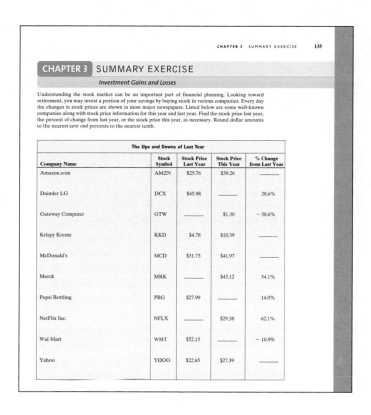

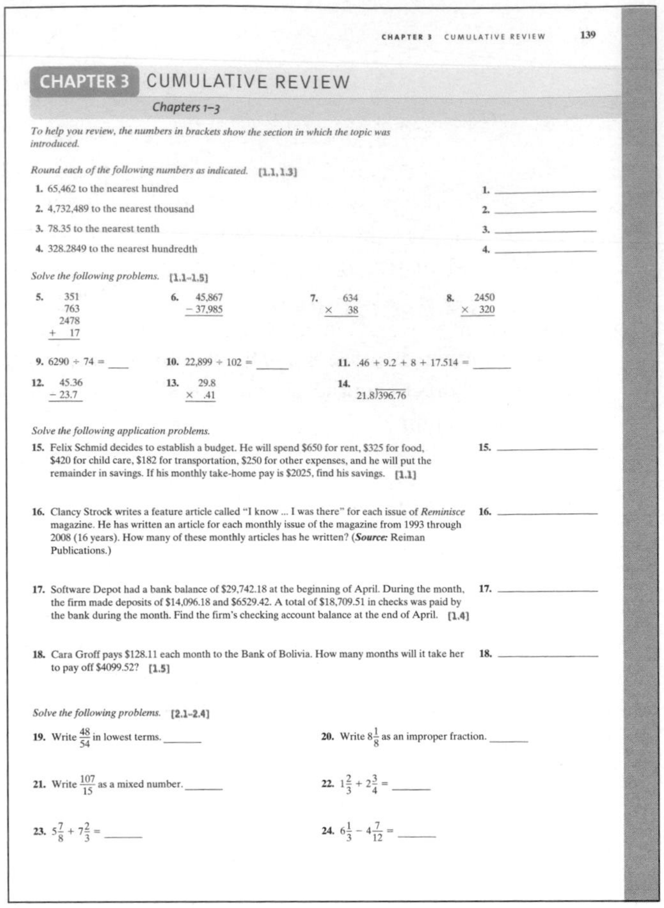

CHAPTER 3 CUMULATIVE REVIEW

Chapters 1–3

To help you review, the numbers in brackets show the section in which the topic was introduced.

Round each of the following numbers as indicated. [1.1, 1.3]

1. 65,462 to the nearest hundred — 1. ______
2. 4,732,489 to the nearest thousand — 2. ______
3. 78.35 to the nearest tenth — 3. ______
4. 328.2849 to the nearest hundredth — 4. ______

Solve the following problems. [1.1–1.5]

5. 351 + 763 + 2478 + 17
6. 45,867 − 37,985
7. 634 × 38
8. 2450 × 320
9. 6290 ÷ 74 = ______
10. 22,899 ÷ 102 = ______
11. .46 + 9.2 + 8 + 17.514 = ______
12. 45.36 − 23.7
13. 29.8 × .41
14. 21.8)396.76

Solve the following application problems.

15. Felix Schmid decides to establish a budget. He will spend $650 for rent, $325 for food, $420 for child care, $182 for transportation, $250 for other expenses, and he will put the remainder in savings. If his monthly take-home pay is $2025, find his savings. [1.1] — 15. ______

16. Clancy Strock writes a feature article called "I know ... I was there" for each issue of *Reminisce* magazine. He has written an article for each monthly issue of the magazine from 1993 through 2008 (16 years). How many of these monthly articles has he written? (*Source:* Reiman Publications.) — 16. ______

17. Software Depot had a bank balance of $29,742.18 at the beginning of April. During the month, the firm made deposits of $14,096.18 and $6529.42. A total of $18,709.51 in checks was paid by the bank during the month. Find the firm's checking account balance at the end of April. [1.4] — 17. ______

18. Cara Groff pays $128.11 each month to the Bank of Bolivia. How many months will it take her to pay off $4099.52? [1.5] — 18. ______

Solve the following problems. [2.1–2.4]

19. Write $\frac{48}{54}$ in lowest terms. ______
20. Write $8\frac{1}{8}$ as an improper fraction. ______
21. Write $\frac{107}{15}$ as a mixed number. ______
22. $1\frac{2}{3} + 2\frac{3}{4} =$ ______
23. $5\frac{7}{8} + 7\frac{2}{3} =$ ______
24. $6\frac{1}{3} - 4\frac{7}{12} =$ ______

Cumulative Reviews

At the end of selected chapters, these exercise sets help students retain previously learned material.

Student Supplements

Business Math Review Card

ISBN 0–321–33670–4

A 6-page foldout that covers basic math topics. The card also covers specific business math topics such as gross earnings, markup and markdown, and finding gross profit and gross income, insurance, taxes, simple and compound interest, present value, annuities, sinking funds, stocks and bonds, depreciation, financial statements, and business statistics.

Student's Solutions Manual

ISBN 0–321–54303–3/978–0–321–54303–5

This supplement contains the complete, worked-out solutions to all of the odd-numbered exercises in the text.

Classroom Lectures and Case Studies on DVD-ROM

The NEW Classroom Lectures and Case Studies on DVD-ROM, included with each new text, offer students a comprehensive lecture for each section of the text, along with case study videos that profile real companies from the in-text Case Studies.

Instructor Supplements

Annotated Instructor's Edition

ISBN 0–321–51805–5/978–0–321–51805–7

The Annotated Instructor's Edition provides immediate access directly on the page to the worked-out answers to all exercises. In addition, an answer section at the back of both the Student's and Instructor's Editions gives answers to odd-numbered section exercises and answers to all chapter test exercises. Writing exercises are marked with the icon exclusively in the AIE so that instructors may use discretion in assigning these problems.

Printed Test Bank/Instructor's Resource Guide

ISBN 0–321–54298–3/978–0–321–54298–4

This extensive supplement contains teaching suggestions; two pretests—one in basic mathematics and one in business mathematics; six different test forms for each chapter (four short answer and two multiple choice); two final examinations; numerous application exercises (test items) for each chapter; answers to all test materials; suggested answers to the writing questions in the text, and a selection of tables from the text.

TestGen® with QuizMaster

ISBN 0–321–53804–8/978–0–321–53804–8

TestGen enables instructors to build, edit, print, and administer tests using a computerized bank of questions developed to cover all the objectives in the text. TestGen is algorithmically based, allowing instructors to create multiple, but equivalent, versions of the same question or test with the click of a button. Instructors can also modify test bank questions or add new questions. Tests can be printed or administered online.

Media Supplements

MyMathLab®

MyMathLab is a series of text-specific, easily customizable online courses for Pearson Education's textbooks in mathematics and statistics. Powered by CourseCompass™ (our online teaching and learning environment) and MathXL® (our online homework, tutorial, and assessment system), MyMathLab gives you the tools you need to deliver all or a portion of your course online, whether your students are in a lab setting or working from home. MyMathLab provides a rich and flexible set of course materials, featuring free-response exercises that are algorithmically generated for unlimited practice and mastery. Students can also use online tools, such as video lectures, animations, and a multimedia textbook, to independently improve their understanding and performance. Instructors can use MyMathLab's homework and test managers to select and assign online exercises correlated directly to the textbook, and they can also create and assign their own online exercises and import TestGen tests for added flexibility. MyMathLab's online gradebook—designed specifically for mathematics and statistics—automatically tracks students' homework and test results and gives the instructor control over how to calculate final grades. Instructors can also add offline (paper-and-pencil) grades to the gradebook. MyMathLab also includes access to the **Pearson Tutor Center** (*www.pearsontutorservices.com*). The Tutor Center is staffed by qualified mathematics instructors who provide textbook-specific tutoring for students via toll-free phone, fax, email, and interactive Web sessions. MyMathLab is available to qualified adopters. For more information, visit our Web site at *www.mymathlab.com* or contact your sales representative.

MathXL

MathXL is a powerful online homework, tutorial, and assessment system that accompanies Pearson Educationís textbooks in mathematics or statistics. With MathXL, instructors can create, edit, and assign online homework and tests using algorithmically generated exercises correlated at the objective level to the textbook. They can also create and assign their own online exercises and import TestGen tests for added flexibility. All student work is tracked in MathXLís online gradebook. Students can take chapter tests in MathXL and receive personalized study plans based on their test results. The study plan diagnoses weaknesses and links students directly to tutorial exercises for the objectives they need to study and retest. Students can also access supplemental animations and video clips directly from selected exercises. MathXL is available to qualified adopters. For more information, visit our Web site at *www.mathxl.com*, or contact your sales representative.

Value Packaging Options: Which package is right for your program?

The eleventh edition package options provide you with a variety of levels of involvement with electronic tools beyond classroom teaching. Here are a few notes to help you identify the best package to fit your needs. Please contact your representative to learn more about our tools and packaging options.

- **Traditional classroom with little need for online instructor involvement**

The book package including **MathXL Tutorials on CD,** packaged with the student textbook and the Classroom Lectures and Case Studies on DVD-ROM, is ideal for this setting. The MathXL tutorials on CD offer tutorials and practice sets that require no online interaction from the course instructor. Order package (ISBN: 0-321-54069-7/978-0-321-54069-0)

- **Traditional classroom with online homework and quizzes that automatically feed an Instructor Gradebook**

The book package including online access to **MathXL,** packaged with the student textbook and the Classroom Lectures and Case Studies on DVD, is ideal for this setting. MathXL allows you to set up homework assignments and quizzes for students and easily monitor student performance at any time. Order package (ISBN: 0-321-55734-4/978-0-321-55734-6)

- **Traditional classroom or fully online course with a need for the full range of classroom management, assessment tools, and course content, including an interactive ebook**

The book package including **MyMathLab,** packaged with the student textbook and the Classroom Lectures and Case Studies on DVD-ROM, is ideal for this setting. MyMathLab provides you with all of the content, classroom management tools, and diagnosis and assessment options you might need in this course. Order package (ISBN: 0-321-54302-5/978-0-321-54302-8)

The **Printed Student Solutions Manual** (ISBN: 0-321-54303-3/978-0-321-54303-5) and the **Quick Reference Tables** (ISBN: 0-13-513693-8) can be packaged with any of these options on demand.

Acknowledgments

We would like to thank the many users of the tenth edition for their insightful observations and suggestions for improving this book. We also wish to express our appreciation and thanks to the following reviewers for their contributions.

Julia Angel, *North Arkansas College*
Kathy Blondell, *St. Johns River Community College*
Yvonne Block, *College of Lake County*
Jesse Cecil, *College of the Siskiyous*
Vittoria Cosentino, *Metropolitan Community College*
Ron Deaton, *Grays Harbor College*
Jacqueline Dlatt, *College of DuPage*
Chris Howell, *New Mexico Junior College*
Chuck Lyons, *Hibbing Community College*
Krista Mahan, *Walla Walla Community College*
Frederick Reed, *Eastern New Mexico University–Ruidoso*
Bob Reese, *Illinois Valley Community College*

Our appreciation goes to Cheryl Davids, John Garlow, Ellen Sawyer, and Gary Williams, who checked all of the exercises and examples in the book for accuracy. We would also like to express our gratitude to our colleagues at American River College and Siena College who have helped us immeasurably with their support and encouragement: Vivek Pandey, Robert Gonzalez, Meg Pollard, James Bralley, Henry Hernandez, and Rob Diamond.

The following individuals at Addison-Wesley had a large impact on this eleventh edition of *Business Mathematics,* and we are grateful for their many efforts: Greg Tobin, Maureen O'Connor, Ron Hampton, Katie Nopper DePasquale, Caroline Case, Michelle Renda, Nathaniel Koven, Sheila Spinney, Beth Anderson, Joe Vetere, Evelyn Beaton, and Michelle Small. Thanks are due as well to Pre-Press PMG, and Tracy Duff in particular, for adeptly handling the production of this eleventh edition.

As an author team, we are committed to providing the best possible text to help instructors teach and students succeed. As we continue to work toward this goal, we would welcome any comments or suggestions you might have via e-mail to *millersalzman@yahoo.com*.

Charles D. Miller
Stanley A. Salzman
Gary Clendenen

About the Authors

Stan Salzman has taught Business Math, Marketing, and Real Estate courses at American River College in Sacramento for 35 years. He says, "Some of my greatest moments in teaching have been seeing the look on the face of a student who understands a business math concept or idea for the first time." Stan and his wife have four children and six grandchildren. The grandchildren (all 6 years old and younger) enjoy playing "math class," where they practice simple arithmetic using chocolate raisins. Stan likes outdoor activities, exercising, and collecting antique toy trains.

Gary Clendenen received bachelor's and master's degrees in mathematics before going into business for himself in the oil industry. He returned to academia and earned his Ph.D. in Business Management in 1993 and has been a faculty member since that time. Dr. Clendenen's business experience includes working as an actuary for an insurance company and owning commercial real estate. He has published papers in numerous refereed journals. His hobbies include bike riding, traveling, and reading on diverse topics such as the history of the Apache Indians of the Southwest, economics, and energy-related issues. He has two sons and four grandchildren.

Learning Tips for Students

Success in Business Mathematics

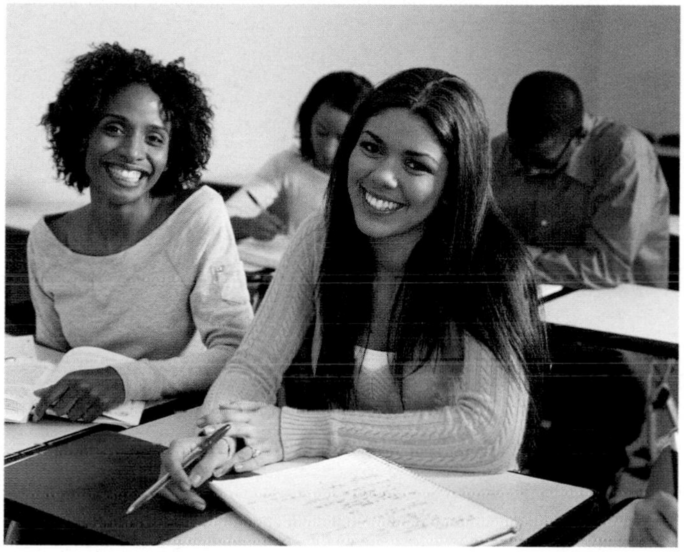

With a growing need for keeping records, establishing budgets, and understanding finance, taxation, and investment opportunities, mathematics has become a greater part of our daily lives. This text applies mathematics to daily business experiences. Your success in future business courses and pursuits will be enhanced by the knowledge and skills you will gain in this course.

Studying business mathematics is different from studying subjects like English or history. The key to success is *regular practice*. This should not be surprising. After all, can you learn to ski or play a musical instrument without a lot of regular practice? The same is true for learning mathematics. Working problems nearly every day is the key to becoming successful. Here are some suggestions to help you succeed in business mathematics.

1. **Attend class regularly. Pay attention to what your instructor says and does in class, and take careful notes.** In particular, note the problems the instructor works on the board, and copy the complete solutions. Keep these notes separate from your homework to avoid confusion when you review them later.

2. **Don't hesitate to ask questions in class.** It is not a sign of weakness, but of strength. There are always other students with the same question who are too shy to ask.

3. **Read your text carefully.** Many students read only enough to get by, usually only the examples. Reading the complete section will help you solve the homework problems. Most exercises are keyed to specific examples or objectives that will explain the procedure for working them.

4. **Before you start on your homework assignment, rework the problems the teacher worked in class.** This will reinforce what you have learned. Many students say, "I understand it perfectly when you do it, but I get stuck when I try to work the problem myself."

5. **Do your homework assignment only after reading the text and reviewing your notes from class.** Check your work against the answers in the back of the book. If you get a problem wrong and are unable to understand why, mark that problem and ask your instructor about it. Then practice working additional problems of the same type to reinforce what you have learned.

6. **Work as neatly as you can using a pencil, and organize your work carefully.** Write your symbols clearly, and make sure the problems are clearly separated from each other. Working neatly will help you to think clearly and also make it easier to review the homework before a test.

7. **After you complete a homework assignment, look over the text again.** Try to identify the main ideas that are in the lesson. Often they are clearly highlighted or boxed in the text.

8. **Use the chapter test at the end of each chapter as a practice test.** Work through the problems under test conditions, without referring to the text or the answers until you are finished. You may want to time yourself to see how long it takes you. When you finish, check your answers against those in the back of the book, and study the problems you missed.

9. Keep all quizzes and tests that are returned to you, and use them when you study for future tests and the final exam. These quizzes and tests indicate what concepts your instructor considers to be most important. Be sure to correct any problems on these tests that you missed so you will have the corrected work to study.

10. Don't worry if you do not understand a new topic right away. As you read more about it and work through the problems, you will gain understanding. Each time you review a topic, you will understand it a little better. Few people understand each topic completely right from the start.

Business Mathematics Pretest

This pretest will help you determine your areas of strength and weakness in the business mathematics presented in this book.

1. Round 5.46 to the nearest tenth. **1.** ______

2. Round $.064 to the nearest cent. **2.** ______

3. Round $399.49 to the nearest dollar. **3.** ______

4. Multiply: $\begin{array}{r} 7801 \\ \times\ 1758 \\ \hline \end{array}$

5. Divide: $35\overline{)11,032}$

4. ______

5. ______

6. Change $8\frac{7}{8}$ to an improper fraction. **6.** ______

7. Change $\frac{40}{26}$ to a mixed number. **7.** ______

8. Write $\frac{15}{21}$ in lowest terms. **8.** ______

9. Add: $\begin{array}{r} \frac{3}{4} \\ \frac{1}{2} \\ +\ \frac{7}{8} \\ \hline \end{array}$

10. Add: $\begin{array}{r} 2\frac{2}{3} \\ 7\frac{1}{4} \\ +\ 10\frac{1}{2} \\ \hline \end{array}$

9. ______

10. ______

11. Subtract: $\frac{3}{8} \quad \frac{7}{24}$

12. Subtract: $\begin{array}{r} 83\frac{3}{4} \\ -\ 21\frac{2}{5} \\ \hline \end{array}$

11. ______

12. ______

13. Multiply: $\frac{3}{8} \times \frac{3}{5}$

14. Divide: $15\frac{1}{4} \div 5\frac{1}{8}$

13. ______

14. ______

15. Express .625 as a common fraction.

16. Express $\frac{3}{5}$ as a decimal.

15. ______

16. ______

17. Subtract: $\begin{array}{r} 598.316 \\ -\ 79.839 \\ \hline \end{array}$

18. Multiply: $\begin{array}{r} 30.67 \\ \times\ 5.39 \\ \hline \end{array}$

17. ______

18. ______

19. Divide: $1.2\overline{)309.6}$

20. Express $\frac{7}{8}$ as a percent.

19. ____________

20. ____________

21. Intelnet spent 5.2% of its sales on advertising. If sales amounted to \$864,250, what amount was spent on advertising?

21. ____________

22. What annual rate of return is needed to receive \$930 in one year on an investment of \$18,600?

22. ____________

23. Home Entertainment Systems offers a 42-inch LCD HDTV at a list price of \$2459 less trade discounts of 20/10. What is the net cost?

23. ____________

24. A department head at Old Navy is paid \$16.80 per hour with time and a half for all hours over 40 in a week. Find the employee's gross pay if she worked 43 hours in one week.

24. ____________

25. How long will it take an investment of \$12,500 to earn \$125 in interest at 4% per year? (*Hint:* Use Bankers Interest, i.e., assume 360 day year.)

25. ____________

26. An invoice from Collier Windows amounting to \$20,250 is dated October 6 and offers terms of 3/10, n/30. If the invoice is paid on October 14, what amount is due?

26. ____________

27. Find the percent of markup based on selling price if some home exercise equipment costing \$1584 is sold for \$1980.

27. ____________

28. Find the single discount equivalent to a series discount of 30/20.

28. ____________

29. Using the straight-line method of depreciation, find the annual depreciation on a Bobcat loader that has a cost of \$18,750, an estimated life of six years, and a scrap value of \$750.

29. ____________

30. Whiting's Oak Furniture sells a dining room set for \$1462.98 after deducting 26% from the original price. Find the original price.

30. ____________

Index of Applications

BUSINESS EQUIPMENT

CONSTRUCTION

DOMESTIC

EDUCATION

EMPLOYMENT/EMPLOYEE BENEFITS

ENTERTAINMENT/SPORTS

ENVIRONMENT

FAMILY

FOOD SERVICE INDUSTRY

FOREIGN AFFAIRS

GENERAL INTEREST

GOVERNMENT

HEALTH CARE

INSURANCE

REAL ESTATE

SALES/MARKETING

SCIENCE/TECHNOLOGY

STOCKS/INVESTMENTS

TAXES

CHAPTER 1

Whole Numbers and Decimals

CHAPTER CONTENTS

CASE in POINT

Steve Edwards began working part time for SUBWAY® when he was a community college student, and after graduation he was selected to attend the management class offered by the company. Upon completion of this training, he was promoted to store manager. He has between 15 and 20 employees at his store, and he must continually recruit and train new people to replace the employees who go on to college or other careers. Each day, Edwards works with whole numbers and decimals as he does scheduling and payroll, computes sales and sales taxes, and orders and pays for inventory.

Often, the most difficult part of solving a problem is knowing how to set the problem up and then deciding on the procedure that will work best to solve it. The first two chapters of this book review the mathematical concepts of whole numbers, decimals, and fractions. The rest of the chapters then apply these concepts to actual business situations.

1.1 WHOLE NUMBERS

OBJECTIVES

1. Define whole numbers.
2. Round whole numbers.
3. Add whole numbers.
4. Round numbers to estimate an answer.
5. Subtract whole numbers.
6. Multiply whole numbers.
7. Multiply by omitting zeros.
8. Divide whole numbers.

CASE in POINT The employees at SUBWAY must be cross-trained so that they can perform several tasks. Food preparation, cash-register operation, and all beverage-preparation tasks require basic mathematical skills.

After observing an employee give a customer too much change, Steve Edwards, the manager, began giving a short math test without the use of a calculator to all employee applicants. All employees are expected to know how to read numbers, round whole numbers, add, subtract, multiply, and divide. With this knowledge, Edwards and his employees can work more accurately and better serve the customers.

OBJECTIVE 1 Define whole numbers. The standard system of numbering, the **decimal system**, uses the ten one-place **digits** 0, 1, 2, 3, 4, 5, 6, 7, 8, and 9. Combinations of these digits represent any number needed. The starting point of this system is the **decimal point** (**.**). This section considers only the numbers made up of digits to the left of the decimal point—the **whole numbers**. The following diagram names the first fifteen places held by the digits to the left of the decimal point.

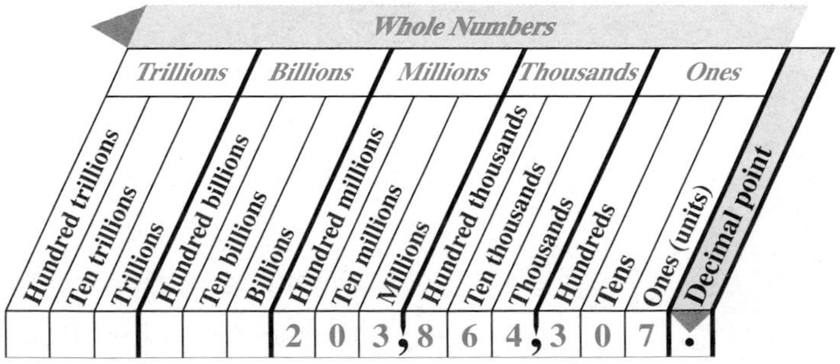

According to the Transportation Department, there are 203,864,307 motor vehicles in the United States. To help in reading this number, a **comma** is used at every third place, starting at the decimal point and moving left. An exception to this is that commas are frequently omitted in four-digit numbers, such as 5892 or 2318.

QUICK TIP Commas are not shown on most calculators.

The number 203,864,307 is read "two hundred three million, eight hundred sixty-four thousand, three hundred seven." Notice that the word *and* is **not** used with whole numbers. The word *and* represents the decimal point and is discussed in **Section 1.3**.

EXAMPLE 1

Expressing Whole Numbers in Words.

Write the following numbers in words.

(a) 7835 **(b)** 111,356,075 **(c)** 17,000,017,000

SOLUTION

(a) seven thousand, eight hundred thirty-five
(b) one hundred eleven million, three hundred fifty-six thousand, seventy-five
(c) seventeen billion, seventeen thousand

QUICK CHECK 1

Write 6,702,045,318 in words.

OBJECTIVE 2 **Round whole numbers.** Business applications often require **rounding** numbers. For example, money amounts are commonly rounded to the nearest cent. However, money amounts can also be rounded to the nearest dollar, hundred dollars, thousand dollars, or even hundreds of thousands of dollars and beyond.

Use the following steps for **rounding whole numbers**.

Rounding Whole Numbers

STEP 1 Locate the **place** to which the number is to be rounded. Draw a line under that place.

STEP 2A If the first digit to the *right* of the underlined place is **5 or more, increase** the digit in the place to which you are rounding by 1.

STEP 2B If the first digit to the right of the underlined place is **4 or less, do not change** the digit in the place to which you are rounding.

STEP 3 **Change** all digits to the right of the underlined digit to zeros.

EXAMPLE 2

Rounding Whole Numbers

Round each number.

(a) 368 to the nearest ten
(b) 67,433 to the nearest thousand
(c) 5,499,059 to the nearest million

SOLUTION

(a) STEP 1 Locate the **place** to which the number is being rounded (the tens place). Draw a line under that place.

3<u>6</u>8
↑ place to which number is rounded

STEP 2 The *first digit to the right* of that place is 8, which is **5 or more,** so **increase** the tens digit by 1.

STEP 3 Change all digits to the right of the tens place to zero: 368 rounded to the nearest ten is 370.

(b) STEP 1 Find the place to which the number is being rounded (the thousands place). Draw a line under that place.

6<u>7</u>,433
↑ place to which number is rounded

STEP 2 The *first digit to the right* of the underlined place is 4, which is **4 or less,** so **do not change** the thousands digit.

STEP 3 Change all digits to the right of the thousands place to zero: 67,433 rounded to the nearest thousand is 67,000.

Quick Check Answer

1. six billion, seven hundred two million, forty-five thousand, three hundred eighteen

(c) STEP 1 Find the place to which the number is being rounded (the millions place). Draw a line under that place.

5,499,059
↑ place to which number is rounded

STEP 2 The *first digit to the right* of the underlined place is 4, which is 4 or less, so do not change the millions digit.

STEP 3 Change all digits to the right of the millions place to zero: 5,499,059 rounded to the nearest million is 5,000,000.

QUICK TIP When rounding a number, look at the first digit to the right of the digit being rounded. Do not look beyond this digit.

QUICK CHECK 2

Round each number.

(a) 653,781 to the nearest ten thousand
(b) 6,578,321 to the nearest million

The four basic **operations** that may be performed on whole numbers—**addition**, **subtraction**, **multiplication**, and **division**—are reviewed in this section.

OBJECTIVE 3 Add whole numbers. In **addition**, the numbers being added are **addends**, and the answer is the **sum**, or **total**, or **amount**.

8	addend
+ 9	addend
17	sum (answer)

QUICK TIP **Checking answers** is important in problem solving. The most common method of checking answers in addition is to re-add the numbers from bottom to top.

Add numbers by arranging them in a column with units above units, tens above tens, hundreds above hundreds, thousands above thousands, and so on. Use the decimal point as a reference for arranging the numbers. If a number does not include a decimal point, the decimal point is assumed to be at the far right.

85 no decimal point indicated; decimal point assumed to be at far right

85. with decimal point shown

EXAMPLE 3

Adding with Checking

To find the one-day total amount of purchases at the SUBWAY that he manages, Steve Edwards needed to add the following amounts and check the answer.

	\$4028
Problem (add down) ↓	\$738 ↑
	63
	125
	2617
+	485 **Check** (add up)
	\$4028

By adding down and then adding up, you should arrive at the *same* answer.

Adding from the top down results in an answer of \$4028. Check for accuracy by adding again—this time from the bottom up. If the answers are the same, the sum is most likely correct. If the answers are different, there is an error in either adding down or adding up, and the problem should be reworked. Both answers agree in this example, so the sum is correct.

QUICK CHECK 3

Find the total of the following expenses.

\$2805 + \$871 + \$28 + \$169 + \$1196

Quick Check Answers

2. **(a)** 650,000
(b) 7,000,000
3. \$5069

OBJECTIVE 4 Round numbers to estimate an answer. **Front-end rounding** is used to estimate an answer. With front-end rounding, each number is rounded so that all the digits are changed to zero, except the first digit, which is rounded. Only one nonzero digit remains.

EXAMPLE 4

Using Front-End Rounding to Estimate an Answer

With the information in the following graphic, use front-end rounding to estimate the total number of millions of barrels of oil produced.

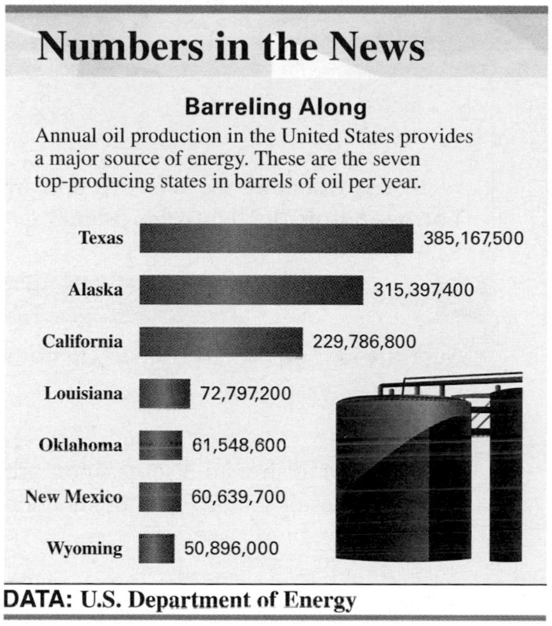

SOLUTION

$$\begin{array}{rcr}
385{,}167{,}500 & \rightarrow & 400{,}000{,}000 \\
315{,}397{,}400 & \rightarrow & 300{,}000{,}000 \\
229{,}786{,}800 & \rightarrow & 200{,}000{,}000 \\
72{,}797{,}200 & \rightarrow & 70{,}000{,}000 \\
61{,}548{,}600 & \rightarrow & 60{,}000{,}000 \\
60{,}639{,}700 & \rightarrow & 60{,}000{,}000 \\
+\ 50{,}896{,}000 & \rightarrow & +\ 50{,}000{,}000 \\
\hline
 & & 1{,}140{,}000{,}000
\end{array}$$

all digits changed to zero except first digit, which is rounded

estimated answer

The estimate is 1,140,000,000 barrels of oil.

QUICK TIP In front-end rounding, only one nonzero digit (first digit) remains. All digits to the right are zeros.

QUICK CHECK 4

Use front-end rounding to estimate the total of the following numbers.

621,150; 38,400; 9682; 27,451; 435,620

OBJECTIVE 5 Subtract whole numbers. A **subtraction** problem is set up much like an addition problem. The top number is the **minuend**, the number being subtracted is the **subtrahend**, and the answer is the **difference**.

$$\begin{array}{rl}
23 & \text{minuend} \\
-\ 7 & \text{subtrahend} \\
\hline
16 & \text{difference}
\end{array}$$

Subtract one number from another by placing the subtrahend directly under the minuend. Be certain that units are above units, tens above tens, and so on. Then begin at the right column and subtract the subtrahend from the minuend.

When a digit in the subtrahend is larger than the corresponding digit in the minuend, use **borrowing**, as shown in the next example.

Quick Check Answer

4. 1,080,000

EXAMPLE 5

Subtracting with Borrowing

Subtract 2894 SUBWAY drink cups from 3783 SUBWAY drink cups in inventory. First, write the problem as follows.

$$\begin{array}{r|l} 378 & 3 \\ -\ 289 & 4 \\ \hline \end{array}$$

In the ones (units) column, subtract 4 from 3 by borrowing a 1 from the tens column in the minuend to get 1 ten + 3, or 13, in the units column with 7 now in the tens column. Then subtract 4 from 13 for a result of 9. Complete the subtraction as follows.

$$\begin{array}{rrrr} 2 & 16 & 17 & 13 \\ \not{3} & \not{7} & 8 & \not{3} \\ -\ 2 & 8 & 9 & 4 \\ \hline & 8 & 8 & \mathbf{9} \end{array} \quad \text{drink cups}$$

In this example, the tens are borrowed from the hundreds column, and the hundreds are borrowed from the thousands column.

QUICK CHECK 5

Subtract 7832 customers from 9511 customers.

Check an answer to a subtraction problem by adding the answer (difference) to the subtrahend. The result should equal the minuend.

EXAMPLE 6

Subtracting with Checking

Subtract 1635 from 5383, and check the answer.

	Problem		Check	
Problem (subtract down) ↓	5383	minuend	5383	This result should equal the minuend.
	− 1635	subtrahend	+ 1635	
	3748	difference	3748	Check (add up)

QUICK CHECK 6

Subtract 2374 from 4165, and check the answer.

QUICK TIP The symbol used for multiplication is × or • between two numbers. Also, two or more numbers within parentheses that are next to each other ( )( ) means to multiply. With a computer, the * means to multiply.

Multiplication is actually a quick method of addition. For example, 3 × 4 can be found by adding 3 a total of 4 times, since 3 × 4 means 3 + 3 + 3 + 3 = 12. However, it is not practical to use the addition method for large numbers. For example, 103 × 92 would be found by adding 103 a total of 92 times; instead, find this result with multiplication.

OBJECTIVE 6 **Multiply whole numbers.** The number being multiplied is the **multiplicand**, the number doing the multiplying is the **multiplier**, and the answer is the **product**.

$$\begin{array}{rl} 3 & \text{multiplicand} \\ \times\ 4 & \text{multiplier} \\ \hline 12 & \text{product} \end{array}$$

When the multiplier contains more than one digit, **partial products** must be used, as in the next example, which shows the product of 25 and 34.

Quick Check Answers

5. 1679 customers
6. 1791

EXAMPLE 7

Multiplying Whole Numbers

On a recent trip, a Ford Escape averaged 25 miles per gallon while using 34 gallons of gasoline. To find the total number of miles traveled, multiply 25 miles traveled per gallon of gasoline by 34 gallons of gasoline used.

25	multiplicand
× 34	multiplier
100	partial product (4 × 25)
75	partial product (3 × 25, one position to the left)
850	product

Find the product of 25 and 34 by first multiplying 25 by 4. (The 4 is taken from the units column of the multiplier.) The product of 25 and 4 is 100, which is a partial product. Next multiply 25 by 3 (from the tens column of the multiplier) and get 75 as a partial product. Since the 3 in the multiplier is from the tens column, write the partial product 75 one position to the left so that 5 is under the tens column. Finally, add the partial products and get the product 850.

QUICK TIP If the multiplier had more digits, each partial product would be placed one additional position to the *left*.

QUICK CHECK 7

Multiply 18 telemarketers by 36 phone calls to find the total number of calls.

OBJECTIVE 7 Multiply by omitting zeros. If the multiplier or multiplicand or both end in zero, save time by first omitting any zeros at the right of the numbers and then replacing omitted zeros at the right of the final answer. This shortcut is useful even with calculators. For example, find the product of 240 and 13 as follows.

24~~0~~	Omit the zero in the calculation.
× 13	
72	
24	Replace the omitted zero at the right of 312 for a final answer (product) of 3120.
3120	

EXAMPLE 8

Multiplying, Omitting Zeros

In the following multiplication problems, omit zeros in the calculation and then replace omitted zeros to obtain the product.

(a)

150	15	
× 70	× 7	
	105	attach 2 zeros
	10,500	answer

(b)

300	3	
× 90	× 9	
	27	attach 3 zeros
	27,000	answer

QUICK CHECK 8

Multiply 400 by 50. Omit zeros in the calculation and replace them in the product.

QUICK TIP A shortcut for multiplying by 10, 100, 1000, and so on is to just attach the number of zeros to the number being multiplied. For example,

33 × 10 = 33 and 1 zero = 330
56 × 100 = 56 and 2 zeros = 5600
732 × 1000 = 732 and 3 zeros = 732,000

Quick Check Answers

7. 648 phone calls
8. 20 attach 3 zeros = 20,000

OBJECTIVE 8 Divide whole numbers. Various symbols are used to show **division**. For example, ÷ and $\overline{)\quad}$ both mean "divide." Also, a — with a number above and a number below, as in a fraction, means division. In printing, or when seen on a computer screen, the bar is often written /, so that, for example, 24/6 means to divide 24 by 6.

The **dividend** is the number being divided, the **divisor** is the number doing the dividing, and the **quotient** is the answer.

Write "15 divided by 5 equals 3" in any of the following ways.

$$15 \div 5 = 3$$

dividend, divisor, quotient (answer)

$$\begin{array}{r} 3 \\ 5\overline{)15} \end{array}$$

divisor: 5; quotient (answer): 3; dividend: 15

$$\frac{15}{5} = 3$$

dividend: 15; divisor: 5; quotient (answer): 3

EXAMPLE 9 Dividing Whole Numbers

To divide 1095 baseball cards evenly among 73 collectors, you must divide 1095 by 73. Write the problem as follows.

$$73\overline{)1095}$$

Since 73 is larger than 1 or 10, but smaller than 109, begin by dividing 73 into 109. There is one 73 in 109, so place 1 *over the digit 9* in the dividend as shown. Then multiply 1 and 73.

$$\begin{array}{r} 1 \\ 73\overline{)1095} \\ \underline{73} \\ 36 \end{array} \qquad 1 \times 73 = 73$$

Then subtract 73 from 109 to get 36. The next step is to bring down the 5 from the dividend, placing it next to the remainder 36. This gives the number 365. The divisor, 73, is then divided into 365 with a result of 5, which is placed to the right of the 1 in the quotient. Since 73 divides into 365 exactly 5 times, the final answer (quotient) is exactly 15.

$$\begin{array}{r} 15 \\ 73\overline{)1095} \\ \underline{73} \\ 365 \\ \underline{365} \\ 0 \end{array}$$

QUICK CHECK 9

Divide $7506 evenly among 18 winners. How much will each receive?

Often, part of the quotient must be expressed as a remainder, or as a **fraction part** or **decimal part**, of the quotient. The fraction part of the quotient is discussed in the next chapter. The decimal part of the quotient, most commonly used, is discussed later in this chapter.

EXAMPLE 10 Dividing with a Remainder in the Answer

Divide 126 by 24. Express the remainder in each of the three forms.

Remainder ↓

$$\begin{array}{r} 5\text{ R}6 \\ 24\overline{)126} \\ \underline{120} \\ 6 \end{array}$$

Fraction ↓

$$\begin{array}{r} 5\tfrac{6}{24} \\ 24\overline{)126} \\ \underline{120} \\ 6 \end{array}$$

Decimal ↓

$$\begin{array}{r} 5.25 \\ 24\overline{)126.00} \\ \underline{120} \\ 6\,0 \\ \underline{4\,8} \\ 1\,20 \\ \underline{1\,20} \\ 0 \end{array}$$

Quick Check Answer

9. $417

In the first form, the answer 5 R6 is usually difficult to work with. The second form, $5\frac{6}{24}$, defines the remainder as $\frac{6}{24}$. The third form, 5.25, is also precise in its meaning. For the time being, write remainders as fractions, using the remainder as the top number (numerator) and the divisor as the bottom number (denominator). After studying decimals, express the quotient in the manner most useful in the problem being solved. After studying fractions, write fractional remainders in lowest terms, $\frac{6}{24} = \frac{1}{4}$.

QUICK CHECK 10

Divide 315 by 36. Write the remainder in each of three forms.

QUICK TIP The shortcut of dropping zeros from the divisor and moving the decimal point the same number of places to the left in the dividend saves time and eliminates errors that may result from using larger numbers.

If a divisor contains zeros at the far right, as in 30, 300, or 8000, first drop the zeros in the divisor. Then move the decimal point in the dividend the same number of positions to the left as there were zeros dropped from the divisor. For example, divide 108,000 by 900 by letting

$900\overline{)108{,}000}$ becomes $9\overline{)1080}$

Drop 2 zeros. Move decimal point 2 places left.

Divide 7320 by 30 by letting

$30\overline{)7320}$ become $3\overline{)732}$

EXAMPLE 11

Dropping Zeros to Divide

For each of the following, first drop zeros, and then divide.

(a) $40\overline{)11{,}000}$ **(b)** $3500\overline{)31{,}500}$ **(c)** $200\overline{)18{,}800}$

SOLUTION

(a)
$$\begin{array}{r} 275 \\ 4\overline{)1100} \\ \underline{8} \\ 30 \\ \underline{28} \\ 20 \\ \underline{20} \\ 0 \end{array}$$

(b)
$$\begin{array}{r} 9 \\ 35\overline{)315} \\ \underline{315} \\ 0 \end{array}$$

(c)
$$\begin{array}{r} 94 \\ 2\overline{)188} \\ \underline{18} \\ 8 \\ \underline{8} \\ 0 \end{array}$$

QUICK CHECK 11

First drop zeros, and then divide 19,200 ÷ 300.

Quick Check Answers

10. 8 R27; $8\frac{27}{36}$; 8.75

11. 64

EXAMPLE 12

Checking Division Problems

In a division problem, check the answer by multiplying the quotient (answer) and the divisor. Then add any remainder. The result should be the dividend. If the result is not the same as the dividend, an error exists and the problem should be reworked. Check the following division problems.

(a) $19\overline{)418}$ = 22
38
38
38
0 match

(b) $716\overline{)26,492}$ = 37
2148
5012
5012
0

(c) $418\overline{)35,536}$ = 85 R6
3344
2096
2090
6 remainder

QUICK TIP When checking a division problem that has a remainder, be sure to add the remainder to get the check answer. Also, when an answer is rounded, know that the check answer will not be the same. The rounded answer does not allow a perfect check.

SOLUTION

(a)
$$\begin{array}{r} 19 \\ \times\ 22 \\ \hline 38 \\ 38 \\ \hline 418 \end{array}$$
correct

(b)
$$\begin{array}{r} 716 \\ \times\ 37 \\ \hline 5012 \\ 2148 \\ \hline 26,492 \end{array}$$
correct

(c)
$$\begin{array}{r} 418 \\ \times\ 85 \\ \hline 2090 \\ 3344 \\ \hline 35,530 \\ +\ \ 6 \\ \hline 35,536 \end{array}$$
remainder
correct

QUICK CHECK 12

Divide 9897 by 215. Check the answer by multiplying the quotient (answer) by the divisor.

Quick Check Answer

12. 46 R7

1.1 EXERCISES

FOR EXTRA HELP

MyMathLab

MathXL PRACTICE

WATCH

DOWNLOAD

READ

REVIEW

The QUICK START *exercises in each section contain solutions to help you get started.*

Write the following numbers in words. (See Example 1.)

QUICK START

1. 7040 seven thousand, forty
2. 5310 five thousand, three hundred ten
3. 37,901 ______
4. 11,222 ______
5. 725,009 ______
6. 218,033 ______

Round each of the following numbers first to the nearest ten, then to the nearest hundred, and finally to the nearest thousand. Go back to the ***original number*** *before rounding to the next position. (See Example 2.)*

QUICK START

	Nearest Ten	*Nearest Hundred*	*Nearest Thousand*
7. 2065	2070	2100	2000
8. 8385	8390	8400	8000
9. 46,231			
10. 55,175			
11. 106,054			
12. 359,874			

13. Explain the three steps that you will use to round a number when the digit to the right of the place to which you are rounding is 5 or more. (See Objective 2.)

14. Explain the three steps that you will use to round a number when the digit to the right of the place to which you are rounding is 4 or less. (See Objective 2.)

C indicates an exercise that is related to the Case in Point feature.

Add each of the following. Check your answers. (See Example 3.)

QUICK START

15.	75	16.	57	17.	875	18.	135
	63		26		364		594
	45		43		171		415
	+ 27		+ 18		+ 776		+ 276
	210						

19.	750	20.	371	21.	311,479	22.	803,526
	91		45		77,631		759,991
	8		839		+ 594,383		+ 36,024
	540		3				
	+ 7		+ 47				

Subtract each of the following. Check your answers. (See Examples 5 and 6.)

23.	896	24.	757	25.	3715	26.	6215
	− 228		− 286		− 838		− 767

27.	65,198	28.	445,193	29.	7,025,389	30.	9,807,943
	− 43,652		− 62,785		− 936,490		− 959,489

Solve the following problems. To serve as a check, the vertical and horizontal totals must be the same in the lower right-hand corner.

31. PRODUCT PURCHASES The following table shows Circuit City's monthly purchases by product for each of the first six months of the year. Complete the totals by adding horizontally and vertically.

QUICK START

Product	Jan.	Feb.	Mar.	Apr.	May	June	Totals
Software	$49,802	$36,911	$47,851	$54,732	$29,852	$74,119	**$293,267**
Computers	$86,154	$72,908	$31,552	$74,944	$85,532	$36,705	
Printers	$59,854	$85,119	$87,914	$45,812	$56,314	$91,856	
Monitors	$73,951	$72,564	$39,615	$71,099	$72,918	$42,953	
Totals							

32. DEPARTMENT SALES The following table shows Delta Manufacturing's expenses by department for the last six months of the year. Complete the totals by adding horizontally and vertically.

Department	July	Aug.	Sept.	Oct.	Nov.	Dec.	Totals
Office	$29,806	$31,712	$40,909	$32,514	$18,902	$23,514	
Production	$92,143	$86,599	$97,194	$72,815	$89,500	$63,754	
Sales	$31,802	$39,515	$58,192	$32,544	$41,920	$48,732	
Warehouse	$15,746	$12,986	$32,325	$41,983	$39,814	$20,605	
Totals

Multiply each of the following. (See Example 7.)

QUICK START

33. 218 × 43 = 654, 872, 9374	34. 672 × 56	35. 1896 × 62	36. 7318 × 38
37. 6452 × 263	38. 7143 × 295	39. 1109 × 7311	40. 9503 × 3411

Estimate answers by using front-end rounding. Then find the exact answers. (See Example 4.)

QUICK START

41.

Estimate		Exact
8000	← rounds	8215
60	← to	56
700	←	729
+ 4000	←	+ 3605
12,760		12,605

42.

Estimate		Exact
	←	2685
	←	73
	←	592
+	←	+ 7183

43.

Estimate		Exact
	←	783
−	←	− 238

44.

Estimate		Exact
	←	942
−	←	− 286

45.

Estimate		Exact
	←	638
×	←	× 47

46.

Estimate		Exact
	←	864
×	←	× 74

Multiply, omitting zeros in the calculation and then replacing them at the right of the product to obtain the final answer. (See Example 8.)

QUICK START

47. 370 × 180

37 × 18 = 666; 2 zeros → 66,600

48. 520 × 400

49. 3760 × 6000

50. 7200 × 1300

Divide each of the following. Use fractions to express any remainders. (See Examples 9 and 10.)

QUICK START

51. $4\overline{)4965}$ = $1241\frac{1}{4}$

4
09
8
16
16
05
4
1

52. $7\overline{)13,214}$

53. $43\overline{)19,715}$

54. $93\overline{)81,452}$

55. Explain why checking the answer is an important step in solving math problems.

56. In your personal and business life, when is it most important to check your math calculations? Why?

Divide each of the following, dropping zeros from the divisor. Express any remainder as a fraction. (See Examples 10 and 11.)

QUICK START

57. $180\overline{)429,350}$

$$\begin{array}{r} 2\,385\ \tfrac{5}{18} \\ 18\overline{)42,935} \\ \underline{36} \\ 6\,9 \\ \underline{5\,4} \\ 1\,53 \\ \underline{1\,44} \\ 95 \\ \underline{90} \\ 5 \end{array}$$

58. $320\overline{)360,990}$

59. $1300\overline{)75,800}$

60. $1600\overline{)253,100}$

Rewrite the following numbers in words. (See Example 1.)

61. TOTAL BUSINESSES There are 24,375,300 business enterprises in the United States. (***Source:*** A. G. Edwards.)

62. WOMEN IN BUSINESS There are 8,534,350 businesses owned by women in the United States. (***Source:*** A. G. Edwards.)

63. PARACHUTE JUMPS There are 3,200,000 parachute jumps in the United States each year. (***Source:*** History Channel.)

64. GROSS NATIONAL PRODUCT The annual gross national product for the United States (the sum of all goods and services produced) was $13,625,400,000,000. (***Source:*** U.S. Department of Commerce.)

Rewrite the numbers from the following sentences using digits. (See Example 1.)

QUICK START

65. JELL-O SALES The average number of boxes of Jell-O gelatin sold each day is eight hundred fifty-four thousand, seven hundred ninety-five. (***Source:*** Kraft Foods.)

65. 854,795 boxes

66. CRAYON SALES The Binney & Smith Company makes about two billion Crayola Crayons each year. (***Source:*** Binney & Smith Company.)

66. ____________

67. SALVATION ARMY During the past year, the Salvation Army served fifty-five million, five hundred seventy-two thousand, six hundred thirty-three meals to hungry men, women, and children. (***Source:*** The Salvation Army National Annual Report.)

67. ____________

68. HURRICANE KATRINA At a New Orleans pumping station, one of the pumps designed by Alexander Baldwin Wood pumped six hundred forty-eight million gallons of flood water (7500 gallons per second) in one day. (***Source:*** Modern Marvels, Hurricane Katrina, History Channel.)

68. ______________

Solve the following application problems.

QUICK START

69. HERSHEY MINI CHIPS There are approximately 5000 Mini Chips semisweet chocolate chips in 1 pound. How many chips are in 40 pounds? (***Source:*** Hershey Foods Corporation.)

$5 \times 4 = 20$ 4 zeros

↙

200,000

69. 200,000 chips

70. HERSHEY KISSES Each day 33,000,000 Hershey Kisses can be produced. Find the number of Hershey Kisses that can be produced in 30 days. (***Source:*** Hershey Foods Corporation.)

70. ______________

71. CAMPUS VENDING MACHINES On a normal weekday, the vending machines at American River College dispense 900 sodas, 400 candy bars, 500 snack items, and 200 cups of coffee. If it takes Jim Wilson four hours to restock the vending machines, how many items does he restock each hour?

71. ______________

72. TELEMARKETING TEAMWORK In a recent week (Monday through Friday), a telemarketing team sold 380 residential carpet-cleaning jobs, 92 commercial carpet-cleaning jobs, 208 upholstery-cleaning jobs, and 120 drapery-cleaning jobs. How many jobs were sold each day?

72. ______________

RECREATION EQUIPMENT RENTAL *American River Raft Rentals lists the following daily raft rental fees. Notice that there is an additional $2 launch fee payable to the park system for each raft rented. Use this information to solve Exercises 73 and 74.*

American River Raft Rentals

Size	Rental Fee	Launch Fee
4 persons	$ 36	$2
6 persons	$ 48	$2
10 persons	$ 90	$2
12 persons	$100	$2

(***Source:*** American River Raft Rentals.)

73. On a recent Tuesday, the following rafts were rented: 6 4-person rafts, 15 6-person rafts, 10 10-person rafts, and 5 12-person rafts. Find the total receipts including the $2-per-raft launch fee.

73. ______________

74. On the 4th of July, the following rafts were rented: 38 4-person rafts, 73 6-person rafts, 58 10-person rafts, and 46 12-person rafts. Find the total receipts including the $2-per-raft launch fee.

74. ______________

ORGANIC ACREAGE *The following pictograph shows the states with the most organic cropland. Use this information to answer Exercises 75–78.*

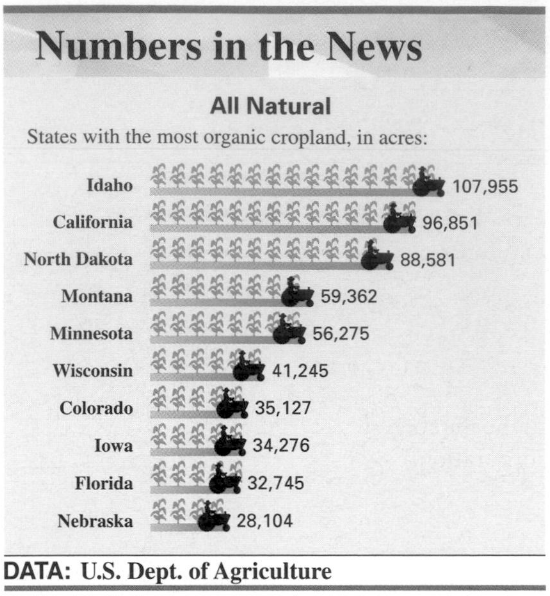

75. Find the total number of organic cropland acres in Idaho, California, and North Dakota.

75. ______

76. What is the total number of organic cropland acres in Iowa, Florida, and Nebraska?

76. ______

77. How many more acres of organic cropland are there in Montana than in Colorado?

77. ______

78. How many more acres of organic cropland are there in Idaho than in Nebraska?

78. ______

RETAIL GIANTS *The following pictograph shows the number of retail stores worldwide for the seven companies with the greatest number of outlets. Use the pictograph to answer Exercises 79–84.*

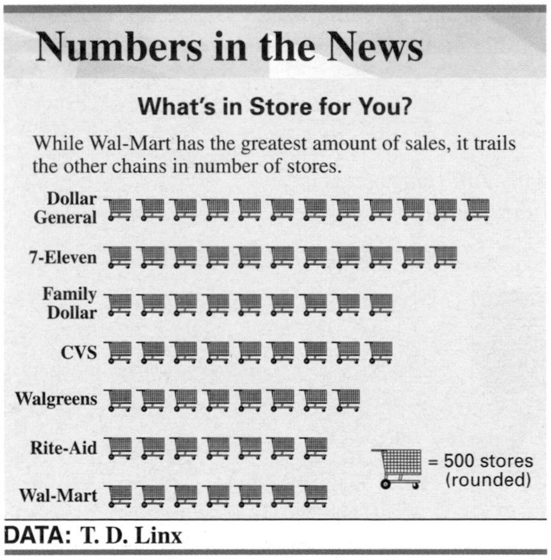

QUICK START

79. Find the number of Family Dollar retail stores.

9 × 500 = 4500 stores

79. 4500 stores

80. Approximately how many retail stores does 7-Eleven have?

80. ______

81. Which company has the greatest number of retail stores? How many stores does it have?

81. ______

82. Which companies have the least number of retail stores? How many stores do they have?

82. ______

83. How many more retail stores does Walgreens have than Wal-Mart?

83. ______

84. How many more stores does Dollar General have than Family Dollar?

84. ______

1.2 APPLICATION PROBLEMS

OBJECTIVES

1. Find indicator words in application problems.
2. Learn the four steps for solving application problems.
3. Learn to estimate answers.
4. Solve application problems.

CASE *in* POINT When Steve Edwards became a manager at a SUBWAY store, he had to brush up on his math skills. He remembered that certain words indicate addition, subtraction, multiplication, and division. He and his employees got together and listed some of these words.

Many business-application problems require mathematics. You must read the words carefully to decide how to solve the problem.

OBJECTIVE 1 **Find indicator words in application problems.** Look for **indicator words** in the application problem—words that indicate the necessary operations: addition, subtraction, multiplication, or division. Some of these words appear below.

Addition	Subtraction	Multiplication	Division	Equals
plus	less	product	divided by	is
more	subtract	double	divided into	the same as
more than	subtracted from	triple	quotient	equals
added to	difference	times	goes into	equal to
increased by	less than	of	divide	yields
sum	fewer	twice	divided equally	results in
total	decreased by	twice as much	per	are
sum of	loss of			
increase of	minus			
gain of	take away			
	reduced by			

OBJECTIVE 2 **Learn the four steps for solving application problems.**

QUICK TIP Be careful not to make the mistake that some students do. They begin to solve a problem before they understand what the problem is asking. Be certain that you know what the problem is asking before you try to solve it.

Solving Application Problems

STEP 1 Read the problem carefully, and be certain that you understand what the problem is asking. It may be necessary to read the problem several times.

STEP 2 Before doing any calculations, work out a plan and try to visualize the problem. Know which facts are given and which must be found. Use word *indicators* to help determine your plan.

STEP 3 Estimate a *reasonable answer* using rounding.

STEP 4 *Solve* the problem by using the facts given and your plan. Does the answer make sense? If the answer is reasonable, *check* your work. If the answer is not reasonable, begin again by rereading the problem.

OBJECTIVE 3 **Learn to estimate answers.** Each of the steps in solving an application problem is important, but special emphasis should be placed on step 3, estimating a reasonable answer. Many times an answer just *does not fit* the problem.

What is a *reasonable answer*? Read the problem and estimate the approximate size of the answer. Should the answer be part of a dollar, a few dollars, hundreds, thousands, or even millions of dollars? For example, if a problem asks for the retail price of a shirt, would an answer of \$20 be reasonable? \$1000? \$.65? \$65?

Always make an estimate of a reasonable answer. Always look at the answer and decide if it is reasonable. These steps will give greater success in problem solving.

EXAMPLE 1

Using Word Indicators to Help Solve a Problem

At a group yard sale, the total sales were $3584. The money was divided equally among the boys soccer club, the girls soccer club, the boys softball team, and the girls softball team. How much did each group receive?

SOLUTION

After reading the problem and understanding that the four groups equally divided $3584, work out a plan. The word indicators *divided equally* suggest that $3584 should be divided by 4. A reasonable answer would be slightly less than $900 each ($3600 ÷ 4 = $900). Find the actual answer by dividing $3584 by 4.

$$4\overline{)3584} = 896$$ Each group should get $896.

The answer is reasonable, so check the work.

$$\begin{array}{r} 896 \\ \times \quad 4 \\ \hline \$3584 \end{array}$$ The answer is correct.

QUICK CHECK 1

A library budget surplus of $13,280 is divided evenly by four branch libraries. How much did each receive?

OBJECTIVE 4 **Solve application problems.** To improve your accuracy, use the four steps and estimate answers when solving application problems.

EXAMPLE 2

Solving an Application Problem

One week, Steve Edwards decided to total his sales at SUBWAY. The daily sales figures were $2358 on Monday, $3056 on Tuesday, $2515 on Wednesday, $1875 on Thursday, $3978 on Friday, $3219 on Saturday, and $3008 on Sunday. Find his total sales for the week.

SOLUTION

The sales for each day are given, and the total sales are needed. The word indicators *total sales* tell you to add the daily sales to arrive at the weekly total. Since the sales are about $3000 each day for a week of 7 days, a reasonable estimate would be around $21,000 (7 × $3000 = $21,000). Find the actual answer by adding the sales for each of the 7 days.

$$\begin{array}{r} \$20{,}009 \\ \hline \$2358 \\ \$3056 \\ \$2515 \\ \$1875 \\ \$3978 \\ \$3219 \\ + \ \$3008 \\ \hline \$20{,}009 \end{array}$$

Check ↑

$20,009 sales for the week

The answer $20,009 is reasonable.

QUICK CHECK 2

The numbers of visitors to a war veterans' memorial during one week are 5318, 2865, 4786, 1898, 3899, 2343, and 7221. First estimate the total attendance for the week; then calculate exactly.

Quick Check Answers

1. $3320
2. 28,000; 28,330 visitors

EXAMPLE 3

Solving an Application Problem

Use the information in the following bar graph to answer each question.

(a) Find the difference in annual earnings between a high-school graduate and a person with an associate of arts degree.

(b) In one year, a person with a bachelor's degree will earn how much less than a person with a professional degree?

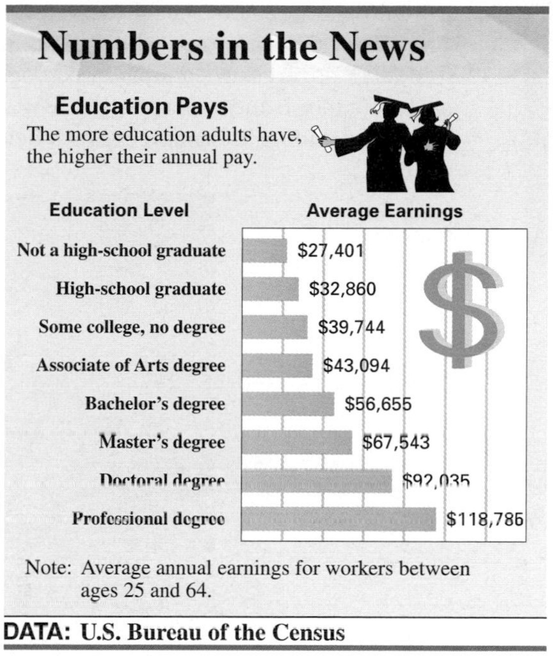

SOLUTION

The word indicator in part **(a)** is *difference,* and the word indicators in part **(b)** are *less than.* These words indicate that we must subtract.

(a)

$43,094	Associate of Arts degree
− 32,860	high-school graduate
$10,234	difference in annual earnings

(b)

$118,785	professional degree
− 56,655	Bachelor's degree
$62,130	less than a person with a professional degree

QUICK CHECK 3

From the bar graph, how much more each year does a person with a bachelor's degree earn than a person who is a high-school graduate?

EXAMPLE 4

Solving a Two-Step Problem

In May, the landlord of an apartment building received $940 from each of eight tenants. After paying $2730 in expenses, how much money did the landlord have left?

SOLUTION

STEP 1 The amount of rent is given along with the number of tenants. Multiply the amount of rent by the number of tenants to arrive at the monthly income. Since the rent is about $900 and there are eight tenants, a *reasonable estimate* would be around $7200 ($900 × 8 = $7200).

$940	
× 8	
$7520	monthly income (this is reasonable)

STEP 2 Finally, subtract the expenses from the monthly income.

$7520	
− 2730	
$4790	amount remaining

Quick Check Answer

3. $23,795

QUICK CHECK 4

A homeowner's association collected \$385 from each of 62 homeowners. If the association paid \$18,280 in expenses, how much remained?

SUBWAY promotes healthy, low-fat food choices and fresh vegetables. The chain offers eight sandwiches that are low in fat, containing 6 grams of fat or less. Perhaps you have seen the SUBWAY advertising featuring Jared Fogle. As a college student, he weighed 425 pounds. By eating just two (a 6-inch and a foot-long) SUBWAY sandwiches each day, he lost 225 pounds in one year.

The nutritional information shown below is printed on all SUBWAY napkins.

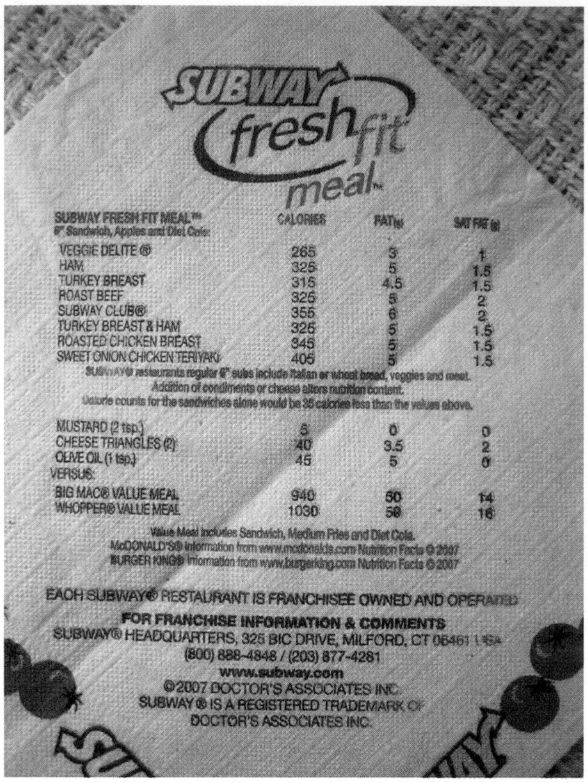

EXAMPLE 5 Solving Application Problems

Using the nutritional information shown for SUBWAY, answer each question.

(a) How many fewer calories and grams of fat are in a 6-inch Veggie Delite sandwich than a Big Mac?

(b) How much less calories and fat are in a 6-inch Turkey Breast and Ham sandwich than in a Whopper?

SOLUTION

The word indicator in part **(a)** is *fewer,* and the word indicator in part **(b)** is *less.* These words indicate that we must subtract.

(a)

560 Big Mac	30
− 230 Veggie Delite	− 3
330 fewer calories	27 fewer fat grams

(b)

670 Whopper	39
− 290 Turkey Breast and Ham	− 5
380 less calories	34 less fat grams

QUICK CHECK 5

From the SUBWAY nutritional information, how many fewer calories and grams of fat are in a Sweet Onion Chicken Teriyaki sandwich than in a Whopper?

Quick Check Answers

4. \$5590

5. 300 less calories; 34 less fat grams

1.2 EXERCISES

FOR EXTRA HELP

MyMathLab

MathXL PRACTICE

WATCH

DOWNLOAD

READ

REVIEW

Solve the following application problems.

1. SUBWAY SANDWICHES Last week, SUBWAY sold 602 Veggie Delite sandwiches, 935 ham sandwiches, 1328 turkey breast sandwiches, 757 roast beef sandwiches, and 1586 SUBWAY Club sandwiches. Find the total number of sandwiches sold.

1. ______________

2. COMPETITIVE CYCLIST TRAINING During a week of training, Rob Andrews rode his bike 80 miles on Monday, 75 miles on Tuesday, 135 miles on Wednesday, 40 miles on Thursday, and 52 miles on Friday. What is the total number of miles he rode in the five-day period?

2. ______________

3. CRUISE SHIP TRAVEL A cruise ship has 1815 passengers. When in port at Grand Cayman, 1348 passengers go ashore for the day while the others remain on the ship. How many passengers remain on the ship?

3. ______________

4. SUV SALES In a recent three-month period, there were 81,465 Ford Explorers and 70,449 Jeep Grand Cherokees sold. How many more Ford Explorers were sold than Jeep Grand Cherokees? (***Source:*** J. D. Power and Associates.)

4. ______________

5. WORLD WAR II VETERANS World War II veterans, part of what is now called "the greatest generation," are dying at the rate of 1400 each day. How many World War II veterans are projected to die in the next year of 365 days? (***Source:*** Department of Veterans Affairs.)

5. ______________

6. TOTAL WORLD WAR II VETERANS There are an estimated 3,520,000 World War II veterans alive today. If only 1 in 5 is still alive, find the total number of people who were World War II veterans. (***Source:*** Department of Veterans Affairs.)

6. ______________

7. FISHING BOAT A fishing boat weighs 8375 pounds. If its 762-pound engine is removed and replaced with a 976-pound engine, find the weight of the boat after the engine change.

7. ______________

8. PRESCHOOL MANAGER Miss Bobbi has $2324 in her preschool operating account. After she spends $734 from this account, the class parents raise $568 in a rummage sale. Find the balance in the account after the money from the rummage sale is deposited.

8. ______________

C indicates an exercise that is related to the Case in Point feature.

9. FORD MUSTANG In 1964, its first year on the market, the Ford Mustang sold for $2500. In 2008, the Ford Mustang sold for $32,044. Find the increase in price. (***Source:*** eBay.) **9.** ________

10. WEIGHING FREIGHT A truck weighs 9250 pounds when empty. After being loaded with firewood, the truck weighs 21,375 pounds. What is the weight of the firewood? **10.** ________

11. LAND AREA There are 43,560 square feet in 1 acre. How many square feet are there in 140 acres? **11.** ________

12. CHECK PROCESSING Bank of America processes 40 million checks each day. Find the number of checks processed by the bank in a year. (Use a 365-day year.) (***Source:*** Bank of America.) **12.** ________

13. HOTEL ROOM COSTS In a recent study of hotel–casinos, the cost per night at Harrah's Reno was $45, while the cost at Harrah's Lake Tahoe was $99 per night. Find the amount saved on a seven-night stay at Harrah's Reno instead of staying at Harrah's Lake Tahoe. (***Source:*** Harrah's Casinos and Hotels.) **13.** ________

14. LUXURY HOTELS A hotel room at the Ritz-Carlton in San Francisco costs $645 per night, while a nearby room at a Motel 6 costs $74 per night. What amount will be saved in a four-night stay at Motel 6 instead of staying at the Ritz-Carlton? (***Source:*** Ritz-Carlton; Motel 6.) **14.** ________

15. PHYSICALLY IMPAIRED The Enabling Supply House purchased 6 wheelchairs at $1256 each and 15 speech compression recorder-players at $895 each. Find the total cost. **15.** ________

C **16.** KITCHEN EQUIPMENT Find the total cost if SUBWAY buys 32 baking ovens at $1538 each and 28 warming ovens at $887 each. **16.** ________

17. YOUTH SOCCER A youth soccer association raised $7588 through fund-raising projects. There were expenses of $838 that had to be paid first, and the remaining money was divided evenly among the 18 teams. How much did each team receive? **17.** ________

18. EGG PRODUCTION Feather Farms Ranch collects 3545 eggs in the morning and 2575 eggs in the afternoon. If the eggs are packed in flats containing 30 eggs each, find the number of flats needed for packing. **18.** ________

19. THEATER RENOVATION A theater owner is remodeling to provide enough seating for 1250 people. The main floor has 30 rows of 25 seats in each row. If the balcony has 25 rows, how many seats must be in each row of the balcony to satisfy the owner's seating requirements? **19.** ________

20. PACKING AND SHIPPING Nancy Hart makes 24 grapevine wreaths per week to sell to gift shops. She works 30 weeks a year and packages six wreaths per box. If she ships equal quantities to each of five shops, find the number of boxes each shop will receive. **20.** ________

1.3 BASICS OF DECIMALS

OBJECTIVES

1. Read and write decimal numbers.
2. Round decimal numbers.

OBJECTIVE 1 **Read and write decimal numbers.** A **decimal number** is any number written with a decimal point, such as 6.8, 5.375, or .000982. Decimals, like fractions, can be used to represent parts of a whole. These parts are "less than 1." **Section 1.1** discussed how to read the digits to the *left* of the decimal point (whole numbers). Read the digits to the *right* of the decimal point as shown here.

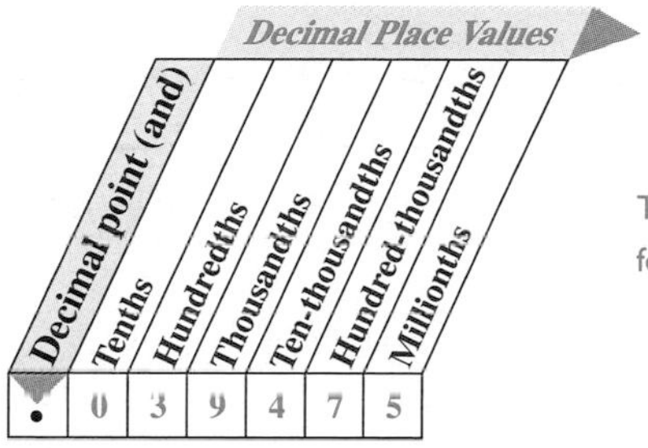

The decimal .039475 is read as thirty-nine thousand, four hundred seventy-five millionths.

QUICK TIP The word *and* is used only to separate a whole number and a fraction or a whole number and a decimal. Also, notice that all decimals end in *ths*.

The decimal 9.7 is read as "nine and seven tenths." The word *and* represents the decimal point. Also, 11.59 is read as "eleven and fifty-nine hundredths," and 72.087 is read as "seventy-two and eighty-seven thousandths."

EXAMPLE 1

Reading Decimal Numbers

Write the following decimals in words.

(a) 19.08 **(b)** .097 **(c)** 7648.9713

SOLUTION

(a) nineteen **and** eight hundredths
(b) ninety-seven thousandths
(c) seven thousand, six hundred forty-eight **and** nine thousand, seven hundred thirteen ten-thousandths

QUICK CHECK 1

Write 310.6218 in words.

OBJECTIVE 2 **Round decimal numbers.** It is important to be able to round decimals. For example, Walgreens sells two candy bars for \$.79, but you want to buy only one candy bar. The price of one bar is \$.79 ÷ 2, which is \$.395, but you cannot pay part of a cent. So the store rounds the price up to \$.40 for one bar.

Use the following steps for **rounding decimals**.

Quick Check Answer

1. three hundred ten and six thousand, two hundred eighteen ten-thousandths

QUICK TIP Do not move the decimal point when rounding.

Rounding Decimals

STEP 1 Find the **place** to which the number is to be rounded. Draw a vertical line after that place to show that you are cutting off the rest of the digits.

STEP 2A Look at only the first digit to the right of your cut-off line. If the first digit is **5 or more, increase** the digit in the place to which you are rounding by 1.

STEP 2B If the first digit to the right of the line is **4 or less, do not change** the digit in the place to which you are rounding.

STEP 3 **Drop** all digits to the right of the place to which you have rounded.

EXAMPLE 2

Rounding Decimal Numbers

Round 98.5892 to the nearest tenth.

SOLUTION

STEP 1 Locate the tenths digit and draw a vertical line to its right.

98.5|892
↑ tenths digit

The tenths digit here is 5.

STEP 2 Locate the *first digit to the right* of the line.

98.5|892
↑ first digit to the right of the line

The first digit to the right of the line is 8. The digit is **5 or more,** so **increase** the digit found in Step 1 by 1.

STEP 3 Drop all digits to the right of the tenths place: 98.5892 rounded to the nearest tenth is 98.6.

98.6
↑ increase 5 by 1

QUICK CHECK 2

Round 72.8499 to the nearest tenth.

EXAMPLE 3

Rounding to the Nearest Thousandth

Round .008572 to the nearest thousandth.

SOLUTION

Locate the thousandths digit and draw a vertical line.

.008|572
↑ thousandths digit

Since the digit to the right of the line is 5, increase the thousandths digit by 1. The number .008572 rounded to the nearest thousandth is .009.

QUICK CHECK 3

Round .003498 to the nearest thousandth.

Quick Check Answers

2. 72.8
3. .003

EXAMPLE 4

Rounding the Same Decimal to Different Places

QUICK TIP The answer to part **(c)** may be surprising because of the answer in part **(b)**. However, **always round a number by going back to the *original number* instead of a number that *has already been* rounded.**

Round 24.6483 to the nearest

(a) thousandth. **(b)** hundredth. **(c)** tenth.

SOLUTION

Use the method just described.

(a) 24.6483 to the nearest thousandth is 24.648.
(b) 24.6483 to the nearest hundredth is 24.65.
(c) 24.6483 to the nearest tenth is 24.6.

QUICK CHECK 4

Round 518.4464 to the nearest **(a)** thousandth, **(b)** hundredth, and **(c)** tenth.

EXAMPLE 5

Rounding to the Nearest Dollar

Preparing for a SUBWAY training session, Steve Edwards wants to round each of the following to the nearest dollar.

(a) \$48.69 **(b)** \$594.36 **(c)** \$2689.50 **(d)** \$.61

SOLUTION

(a) Locate the digit representing the dollar and draw a vertical line.

\$48.|69
↑ dollar digit

Since the digit to the right of the line is 6, increase the dollar digit by 1. The number \$48.69 rounded to the nearest dollar is \$49.

(b) \$594.36 rounded to the nearest dollar is \$594.
(c) \$2689.50 rounded to the nearest dollar is \$2690.
(d) \$.61 rounded to the nearest dollar is \$1.

QUICK CHECK 5

Round each of the following to the nearest dollar.

(a) \$1875.49 **(b)** \$.50

Quick Check Answers

4. (a) 518.446
(b) 518.45
(c) 518.4
5. (a) \$1875
(b) \$1

1.3 EXERCISES

FOR EXTRA HELP

MyMathLab

MathXL PRACTICE

WATCH

DOWNLOAD

READ

REVIEW

The QUICK START *exercises in each section contain solutions to help you get started.*

Write the following decimals in words. (See Example 1.)

QUICK START

1. .38 thirty-eight hundredths
2. .91 ninety-one hundredths
3. 5.61 ____
4. 6.53 ____
5. 7.408 ____
6. 1.254 ____
7. 37.593 ____
8. 20.903 ____
9. 4.0062 ____
10. 9.0201 ____
11. "My answer is right, but the decimal point is in the wrong place." Can this statement ever be correct? Explain. (See Objective 1.)

12. In your own words, explain the difference between thousands and thousandths.

Write the following decimals, using numbers.

QUICK START

13. four hundred thirty-eight and four tenths 438.4
14. six hundred five and seven tenths 605.7
15. ninety-seven and sixty-two hundredths ____
16. seventy-one and thirty-three hundredths ____
17. one and five hundred seventy-three ten-thousandths ____
18. nine and three hundred eight ten-thousandths ____
19. three and five thousand eight hundred twenty-seven ten-thousandths ____
20. two thousand seventy-four ten-thousandths ____

GROCERY SHOPPING *Alan Zagorin is grocery shopping. The store will round the amount he pays for each item to the nearest cent. Write the rounded amounts. (See Examples 2–4.)*

21. Claim Jumper apple pies are two for \$11.99. So one pie is \$5.995. Zagorin pays ____.

22. Four 12-packs of soda cost \$11.90. So one 12-pack costs \$2.975. Zagorin pays ____.

23. Muffin mix is three packages for \$1.75. So one package is \$.58333. Zagorin pays ____.

24. Candy bars are six for \$2.99. So one bar is \$.4983. Zagorin pays ____.

C indicates an exercise that is related to the Case in Point feature.

25. Barbeque sauce is three bottles for \$3.50. So one bottle is \$1.1666. Zagorin pays _____.

26. Tony's Pizzas are five for \$9.98. So one pizza is \$1.996. Zagorin pays _____.

Round each of the decimals to the nearest tenth, the nearest hundredth, and the nearest thousandth. Remember to use the original number each time before rounding. (See Examples 2–4.)

QUICK START

	Nearest Tenth	Nearest Hundredth	Nearest Thousandth
27. 3.5218	3.5	3.52	3.522
28. 4.836	4.8	4.84	4.836
29. 2.54836			
30. 7.44652			
31. 27.32451			
32. 89.53796			
33. 36.47249			
34. 58.95651			
35. .0562			
36. .0789			

Round each of the dollar amounts to the nearest cent.

QUICK START

37. \$5.056 \$5.06 **38.** \$16.519 \$16.52 **39.** \$32.493 _____

40. \$375.003 _____ **41.** \$382.005 _____ **42.** \$12,802.965 _____

43. \$42.137 _____ **44.** \$.846 _____ **45.** \$.0015 _____

46. \$.008 _____ **47.** \$1.5002 _____ **48.** \$7.6009 _____

49. \$1.995 _____ **50.** \$28.994 _____ **51.** \$752.798 _____

Round each of the dollar amounts to the nearest dollar (nearest whole number).

QUICK START

52. \$8.58 \$9 **53.** \$26.49 \$26 **54.** \$.57 _____

55. \$.49 _____ **56.** \$299.76 _____ **57.** \$12,836.38 _____

58. \$268.72 _____ **59.** \$395.18 _____ **60.** \$666.66 _____

61. \$4699.62 _____ **62.** \$11,285.13 _____ **63.** \$378.59 _____

64. \$233.86 _____ **65.** \$722.38 _____ **66.** \$8263.47 _____

67. Explain what happens when you round \$.499 to the nearest dollar. (*See Objective 2.*)

68. Review Exercise 67. How else could you round \$.499 to obtain a result that is more helpful? What kind of guideline does this suggest about rounding to the nearest dollar?

1.4 ADDITION AND SUBTRACTION OF DECIMALS

OBJECTIVES

1. Add decimals.
2. Estimate answers.
3. Subtract decimals.

CASE in POINT As manager of a SUBWAY, Steve Edwards is responsible for making bank deposits to the company checking account. These banking activities require the ability to accurately add and subtract decimal numbers.

OBJECTIVE 1 Add decimals. Decimals are added in much the same way whole numbers are added. The main difference with adding decimals is that the decimal points must be kept in a column.

EXAMPLE 1

Adding Decimals and Checking with Estimation

Add 9.83, 6.4, 17.592, and 3.087, or

$$\begin{array}{r} 9.83 \\ 6.4 \\ 17.592 \\ +\ 3.087 \\ \hline \end{array}$$

by first lining up decimal points.

$$\begin{array}{r} 9.83 \\ 6.4 \\ 17.592 \\ +\ 3.087 \\ \hline 36.909 \end{array}$$

Line up decimal points.

Add by columns, just as with whole numbers. One way to keep the digits in their correct columns is to place zeros to the right of each decimal, so that each number has the same number of digits following the decimal point. Attaching zeros to this example gives

$$\begin{array}{r} 9.830 \\ 6.400 \\ 17.592 \\ +\ 3.087 \\ \hline 36.909 \end{array}$$

All numbers now have three places after the decimal point.

QUICK TIP Placing zeros after any digits to the right of the decimal point does not change the value of a number. For example, 4.21 = 4.210 = 4.2100, and so on.

QUICK CHECK 1

Add 3.8, 14.604, 5.76, and 27.152.

OBJECTIVE 2 Estimate answers. Check that digits were not added in the wrong columns by estimating the answer. For the numbers just added, estimate by using front-end rounding.

Problem		Estimate
9.830	⟶	10
6.400	⟶	6
17.592	⟶	20
+ 3.087	⟶	+ 3
36.909		39

The answer is reasonable.

QUICK TIP The estimate shows that the answer is reasonable and that the decimal points were lined up properly.

Quick Check Answer

1. 51.316

EXAMPLE 2

Adding Dollars and Cents

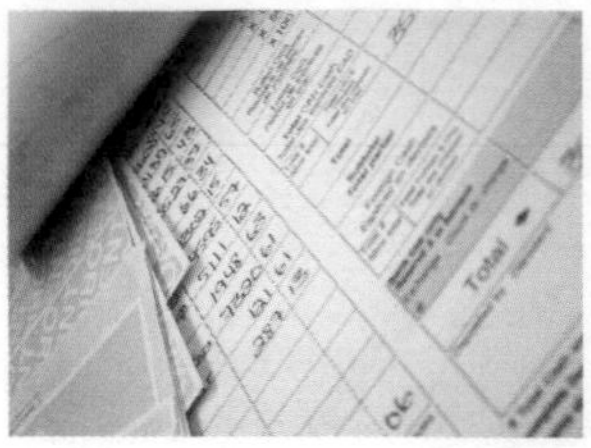

During a recent week, Steve Edwards made the following bank deposits to the SUBWAY business account: $1783.38, $4341.15, $2175.94, $896.23, and $2562.53. Use front-end rounding to estimate the total deposits and then find the total deposits.

SOLUTION

Estimate		Problem
$ 2000	⟵	$ 1783.38
4000	⟵	4341.15
2000	⟵	2175.94
900	⟵	896.23
+ 3000	⟵	+ 2562.53
$11,900		$11,759.23

The total deposits for the week were $11,759.23, which is close to our estimate.

QUICK CHECK 2

The following bills were paid by SUBWAY last week; $1268.72, $228.35, $2336.19, $176.68, and $1560.75. Use front-end rounding to estimate the total amount of the bills paid, and then find the total bills paid.

OBJECTIVE 3 **Subtract decimals.** Subtraction is done in much the same way as addition. Line up the decimal points and place as many zeros after each decimal as needed. For example, subtract 17.432 from 21.76 as follows.

$$\begin{array}{r} 21.760 \\ -\ 17.432 \\ \hline 4.328 \end{array}$$ Place one zero after the top decimal.

EXAMPLE 3

Estimating and Then Subtracting Decimals

First estimate using front-end rounding and then subtract.

(a) $\begin{array}{r} 11.7 \\ -\ 4.923 \\ \hline \end{array}$ **(b)** $\begin{array}{r} 39.428 \\ -\ 27.98 \\ \hline \end{array}$

SOLUTION

Attach zeros as needed and then subtract.

(a)

Estimate		Problem
10	⟵	11.700
− 5	⟵	− 4.923
5		6.777

(b)

Estimate		Problem
40	⟵	39.428
− 30	⟵	− 27.980
10		11.448

QUICK CHECK 3

First estimate using front-end rounding, and then subtract 5.32 from 26.952.

Quick Check Answers

2. $5400; $5570.69

3. 25; 21.632

1.4 EXERCISES

FOR EXTRA HELP

MyMathLab

MathXL PRACTICE

WATCH

DOWNLOAD

READ

REVIEW

The **QUICK START** *exercises in each section contain solutions to help you get started.*

First use front-end rounding to estimate and then add the following decimals. (See Examples 1 and 2.)

QUICK START

1. Estimate		Problem	2. Estimate		Problem	3. Estimate	Problem
40	←	43.36	**600**	←	623.15		6.23
20	←	15.8	**700**	←	734.29		3.6
+ **9**	←	+ 9.3	+ **700**	←	+ 686.26		5.1
69		**68.46**	**2000**		**2043.70**		7.2
							+ 1.69

4. Estimate	Problem	5. Estimate	Problem	6. Estimate	Problem
	12.79		2156.38		1889.76
	2.15		5.26		21.42
	16.28		2.791		19.35
	4.39		+ 6.983		+ 8.1
	+ 7.61				

7. Estimate	Problem	8. Estimate	Problem	9. Estimate	Problem
	6133.78		743.1		1798.419
	506.124		3817.65		68.32
	18.63		2.908		512.807
	+ 7.527		4123.76		643.9
			+ 21.98		+ 428.

Place each of the following numbers in a column and then add. (See Example 1.)

QUICK START

10. 45.631 + 15.8 + 7.234 + 19.63 = **88.295**

11. 12.15 + 6.83 + 61.75 + 19.218 + 73.325 = **173.273**

12. 197.4 + 83.72 + 17.43 + 25.63 + 1.4 =

13. 27.653 + 18.7142 + 9.7496 + 3.21 =

14. 73.618 + 19.18 + 371.82 + 355.125 =

15. It is a good idea to estimate an answer before actually solving a problem. Why is this true? (See Objective 2.)

16. Explain why placing zeros after any digits to the right of the decimal point does not change the value of a number. (See Objective 1.)

Solve the following application problems.

17. SUBWAY SALES Sales for each day of the week at the SUBWAY managed by Steve Edwards were $1815.79, $2367.34, $1976.22, $2155.81, $1698.14, $2885.26, and $2239.63. Find the total weekly sales.

17. ______________

C indicates an exercise that is related to the Case in Point feature.

18. STAFF-MEETING COST During the holiday season, Paul Burke has made the following 18. _____
purchases of SUBWAY sandwiches for his office staff: $78.83, $125.48, $165.83, and $108.89.
Find the total amount of these purchases.

19. BEEF/TURKEY COST The average cost of T-bone steak is $6.71 per pound, while the average 19. _____
cost of turkey is $.98 per pound. How much more per pound is the price of T-bone steak than
turkey? (*Source:* U.S. Bureau of the Census.)

20. CHILD DAY CARE The number of hours spent in day care by 20. _____
an infant averages 30.5 hours a week, while the number of
hours spent in day care by four-year-olds averages 27.75
hours a week. How much more time is spent in day care each
week by infants than by four-year-olds?

First use front-end rounding to estimate the answer and then subtract. (See Example 3.)

QUICK START

21. Estimate	**Problem**	**22. Estimate**	**Problem**	**23. Estimate**	**Problem**
20	19.74	40	35.86		51.215
− 7	− 6.58	− 8	− 7.91		− 19.708
13	**13.16**	32	**27.95**		

24. Estimate	**Problem**	**25. Estimate**	**Problem**	**26. Estimate**	**Problem**
	27.613		325.053		3974.61
	− 18.942		− 85.019		− 892.59

27. Estimate	**Problem**	**28. Estimate**	**Problem**	**29. Estimate**	**Problem**
	7.8		27.8		5
	− 2.952		− 13.582		− 1.9802

 *CHECKING-ACCOUNT RECORDS Steve Edwards, manager of SUBWAY, had a bank balance of $5382.12
on March 1. During March, Steve deposited $60,375.82 received from sales, $3280.18 received as credits
from suppliers, and $75.53 as a county tax refund. He paid out $27,282.75 to suppliers, $4280.83 for rent
and utilities, and $12,252.23 for salaries. Find each of the following.*

QUICK START

30. How much did Edwards deposit in March? 30. $63,731.53

$60,375.82 (sales) + $3280.18 (credits) + $75.53 (refund) = $63,731.53

31. How much did he pay out? 31. _____

32. What was his final balance at the end of March? 32. _____

1.5 MULTIPLICATION AND DIVISION OF DECIMALS

OBJECTIVES

1. Multiply decimals.
2. Divide a decimal by a whole number.
3. Divide a decimal by a decimal.

CASE in POINT Managing a business requires the ability to multiply and divide decimal numbers. Steve Edwards, the manager at SUBWAY, applies these skills in many ways; some examples include payroll, purchasing, and sales.

OBJECTIVE 1 Multiply decimals. Decimals are multiplied as if they were whole numbers. (It is not necessary to line up the decimal points.) The decimal point in the answer is then found by using the following steps.

Positioning the Decimal Point

STEP 1 Count the total number of digits to the *right* of the decimal point in each of the numbers being multiplied.

STEP 2 In the answer, count from *right to left* the number of places found in step 1 and write the decimal point. It may be necessary to attach zeros to the left of the answer in order to correctly place the decimal point.

EXAMPLE 1
Multiplying Decimals

Multiply each of the following.

(a) 8.34 × 4.2 **(b)** .032 × .07

SOLUTION

(a) First multiply the given numbers as if they were whole numbers.

```
    8.34   ←— 2 decimal places
 ×   4.2   ←— 1 decimal place
    1668
   3336
  35.028   ←— 3 decimal places in answer
```

There are two decimal places in 8.34 and one in 4.2. This means that there are 2 + 1 = 3 decimal places in the final answer. Find the final answer by starting at the right and counting three places to the left:

35.028 3 places to the left

(b) Here, it is necessary to attach zeros at the left in the answer:

```
    .032   ←— 3 decimal places
 ×   .07   ←— 2 decimal places
  .00224   ←— 5 decimal places in answer
   ↑
   └———— Attach 2 zeros.
```

QUICK CHECK 1

Multiply each of the following

(a) 6.7 × 4.32 **(b)** .086 × .05

Quick Check Answers

1. (a) 28.944
(b) .0043

The next example uses the formula for determining the gross pay (the pay before deductions) of a worker paid by the hour.

Gross pay = Number of hours worked × Pay per hour

EXAMPLE 2

Multiplying Two Decimal Numbers

Find the gross pay of a SUBWAY employee working 31.5 hours at a rate of $8.65 per hour.

SOLUTION

Find gross pay by multiplying the number of hours worked by the pay per hour.

$$\begin{array}{rl} 31.5 & \longleftarrow \text{1 place} \\ \times\ 8.65 & \longleftarrow \text{2 places} \\ \hline 1575 & \\ 1890 & \\ 2520 & \\ \hline 272.475 & \longleftarrow \text{3 places in answer} \end{array}$$

This worker's gross pay, rounded to the nearest cent, is $272.48.

QUICK CHECK 2

A college student earns $9.28 per hour. How much is earned for 26.5 hours of work?

The following graph shows the price for 30 seconds of advertising time during these Super Bowl games.

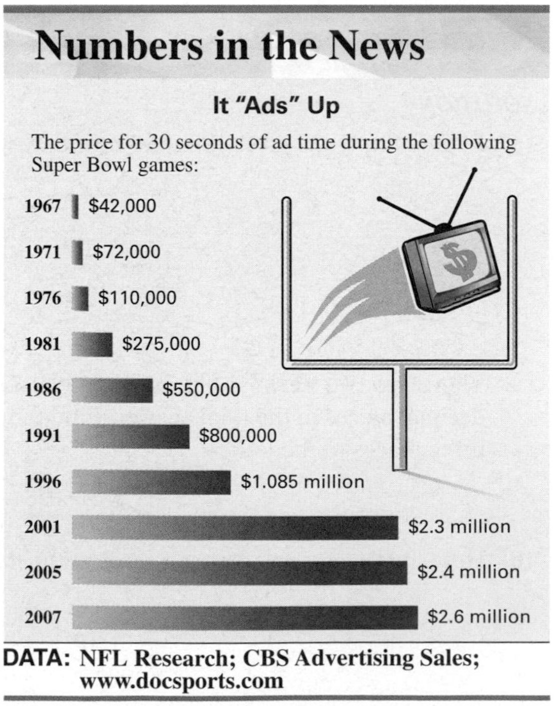

Quick Check Answer

2. $245.92

EXAMPLE 3

Applying Decimal Multiplication

If there were 60 advertising spots of 30 seconds each during the 2007 Super Bowl, find the total amount charged for advertising during the game.

SOLUTION

Find the total amount charged for advertising during the 2007 Super Bowl by multiplying the number of 30-second advertising spots during the game by the charge for each advertisement.

$$\begin{array}{r l} 2.6 & \leftarrow \text{1 place} \\ \times\ 60 & \leftarrow \text{0 places} \\ \hline 00 & \\ 156 & \\ \hline 156.0 & \leftarrow \text{1 place} \end{array}$$

The total amount charged for advertising during the 2007 Super Bowl was \$156 million (\$156,000,000).

QUICK CHECK 3

If there were 58 advertising spots during the 2005 Super Bowl, find the amount charged for advertising during the game?

OBJECTIVE 2 Divide a decimal by a whole number. Divide the decimal 21.93 by the whole number 3 by first writing the division problem as usual.

$$3\overline{)21.93}$$

Place the decimal point in the quotient directly above the decimal point in the dividend and perform the division.

Place a decimal point directly above dividend's decimal point.

$$\begin{array}{r} 7.31 \\ 3\overline{)21.93} \end{array}$$

Check by multiplying the divisor and the quotient. The answer should equal the dividend.

$$\begin{array}{r l} 7.31 & \\ \times\quad 3 & \\ \hline 21.93 & \leftarrow \text{matches dividend} \end{array}$$

Sometimes it is necessary to place zeros after the decimal point in the dividend. Do this if a remainder of 0 is not obtained. Attaching zeros *does not change* the value of the dividend. For example, divide 1.5 by 8 by dividing and placing zeros as needed.

Problem **Check**

$$\begin{array}{r} .1875 \\ 8\overline{)1.5000} \\ 8 \\ \hline 70 \\ 64 \\ \hline 60 \\ 56 \\ \hline 40 \\ 40 \\ \hline 0 \end{array} \qquad \begin{array}{r} .1875 \\ \times\quad 8 \\ \hline 1.5000 \end{array}$$

By the check, $1.5 \div 8 = .1875$

matches

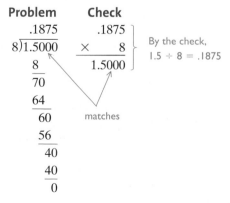

A remainder of 0 might not be obtained even though extra zeros are placed after the dividend. For example, when 4.7 is divided by 3, a remainder of 0 is never obtained. The digit 6 repeats indefinitely. In such a case, round to the nearest thousandth, although different problems might require rounding to a different number of decimal places. Rounding to the nearest thousandth gives 4.7 ÷ 3 = 1.567. Round to the nearest thousandth by carrying out the division to four places and then rounding to three places. Check by multiplying 1.567 by 3. The answer will be only approximately equal to the dividend, because of the rounding. Here is the division.

$$\begin{array}{r} 1.5666 \\ 3\overline{)4.7000} \\ \underline{3} \\ 1\,7 \\ \underline{1\,5} \\ 20 \\ \underline{18} \\ 20 \\ \underline{18} \\ 20 \\ \underline{18} \\ 2 \end{array}$$

QUICK TIP When rounding an answer, be certain to carry the answer one place further than the position to which you are rounding.

EXAMPLE 4

Dividing a Decimal by a Whole Number

Divide the following, then check by using multiplication.

(a) 27.52 ÷ 32 **(b)** 153.4 ÷ 8

SOLUTION

Problem (a)

$$\begin{array}{r} .86 \\ 32\overline{)27.52} \\ \underline{25\,6} \\ 1\,92 \\ \underline{1\,92} \\ 0 \end{array}$$

Check

$$\begin{array}{r} .86 \\ \underline{\times\ 32} \\ 172 \\ \underline{258} \\ \mathbf{27.52} \end{array}$$

Problem (b)

$$\begin{array}{r} 19.175 \\ 8\overline{)153.400} \\ \underline{8} \\ 73 \\ \underline{72} \\ 1\,4 \\ \underline{8} \\ 60 \\ \underline{56} \\ 40 \\ \underline{40} \\ 0 \end{array}$$

Check

$$\begin{array}{r} 19.175 \\ \underline{\times\qquad 8} \\ \mathbf{153.400} \end{array}$$

QUICK CHECK 4

Divide the following, then check by using multiplication.

(a) $15\overline{)823.26}$ **(b)** 78.562 ÷ 4

OBJECTIVE 3 **Divide a decimal by a decimal.** To divide by a decimal, first convert the divisor to a whole number. For example, to divide 27.69 by .3, convert .3 to a whole number by moving the decimal one place to the right. Then move the decimal point in the dividend, 27.69, one place to the right so that the value of the problem does not change.

$.3.\overline{)27.6.9}$

First, convert the decimal to a whole number.

Then move the decimal point in the dividend the same number of places to the right as done in the divisor.

QUICK TIP Sometimes it is necessary to place zeros after the dividend. As before, attach zeros and divide until the quotient has one more digit than the desired position, and then round.

After moving the decimal point, write the original problem as 276.9 ÷ 3, and then divide as follows:

$$\begin{array}{r} 92.3 \\ 3\overline{)276.9} \\ \underline{27} \\ 06 \\ \underline{6} \\ 0\,9 \\ \underline{9} \\ 0 \end{array}$$

Quick Check Answers

4. (a) 54.884
(b) 19.6405

EXAMPLE 5

Dividing a Decimal by a Decimal

Divide and check the following.

(a) 17.6 ÷ .25 **(b)** 5 ÷ .42

SOLUTION

(a)

```
         70.4
.25.)17.60.0
     17 5
        10
         0
        100
        100
          0
```

Check

```
  70.4
× .25
  3520
 1408
17.600
```

(b)

```
       11.9047
.42.)5.00.0000
     4 2
       80
       42
       38 0
       37 8
          200
          168
           320
           294
            26
```

Rounding the answer to the nearest thousandth gives 11.905.

Check

```
  11.905
×    .42
  23810
 47620
 5.00010
```

(The check is off a little due to rounding.)

QUICK TIP For an answer that has been rounded, the check answer will not be exactly equal to the original dividend.

QUICK CHECK 5

Divide, then check by using multiplication.

(a) 22.5 ÷ .8 **(b)** 8.6 ÷ .32

Quick Check Answers

5. (a) 28.125
(b) 26.875

1.5 EXERCISES

FOR EXTRA HELP

MyMathLab

MathXL PRACTICE

WATCH

DOWNLOAD

READ

REVIEW

The QUICK START *exercises in each section contain solutions to help you get started.*

First estimate using front-end rounding and then multiply. (See Example 1.)

QUICK START

1. Estimate 100 ← × 4 ← = 400 **Problem** 96.8 × 4.2 = 406.56

2. Estimate 20 ← × 4 ← = 80 **Problem** 16.6 × 4.2 = 69.72

3. Estimate **Problem** 34.1 × 6.8

4. Estimate **Problem** 70.35 × 8.06

5. Estimate **Problem** 43.8 × 2.04

6. Estimate **Problem** 69.3 × 2.81

Multiply the following decimals.

QUICK START

7. .532 × 3.6
.532 ← 3 decimals
× 3.6 ← 1 decimal
1.9152 ← 4 decimals

8. .259 × 6.2
.259 ← 3 decimals
× 6.2 ← 1 decimal
1.6058 ← 4 decimals

9. 21.7 × .431

10. 76.9 × .903

11. .0408 × .06

12. 2481.9 × .003

CALCULATING GROSS EARNINGS *Find the gross pay for each SUBWAY employee at the given rate. Round to the nearest cent. (See Examples 2 and 3.)*

QUICK START

13. 18.5 hours at $8.25 per hour
18.5 × $8.25 = $152.63 — **13.** $152.63

14. 36.6 hours at $9.85 per hour — **14.** ________

15. 27.9 hours at $11.42 per hour, and 6.8 hours at $14.63 per hour — **15.** ________

16. 11.4 hours at $8.59 per hour, and 23.9 hours at $10.06 per hour — **16.** ________

C indicates an exercise that is related to the Case in Point feature.

Divide the following, and round your answer to the nearest thousandth. (See Examples 4 and 5.)

17. $6\overline{)48.45}$

18. $5\overline{)62.38}$

19. $411.63 \div 15$

20. $2.43\overline{)9.6153}$

21. $.65\overline{)37.6852}$

22. $15.62 \div .28$

23. In your own words, write the rule for placing the decimal point in the answer of a decimal multiplication problem. (See Objective 1.)

24. Describe what must be done with the decimal point in a decimal division problem. Include the divisor, dividend, and quotient in your description. (See Objectives 2 and 3.)

Solve the following application problems:

QUICK START

25. REAL ESTATE FEES Robert Gonzalez recently sold his home for \$246,500. He paid a sales fee of .06 times the price of the house. What was the amount of the fee?

\$246,500 × .06 = \$14,790

25. \$14,790 ____________

26. CROWN MOLDING Mazie Chauvin bought 9.5 yards of crown molding to complete her bathroom remodeling. If she paid \$5.68 per yard for the trim, what was her total cost?

26. ____________

27. GAS MILEAGE The SUBWAY company van used 18.5 gallons of gas and traveled 464 miles. How many miles per gallon (mpg) did the van get? Round to the nearest tenth.

27. ____________

28. MANAGERIAL EARNINGS A SUBWAY assistant manager earns \$2528 each month for working a 48-hour week. Find **(a)** the number of hours worked each month and **(b)** the assistant manager's hourly earnings (1 month = 4.3 weeks). Round to the nearest cent.

(a) ____________
(b) ____________

29. BIG RIMS AND TIRES Henry Barnes has a loan balance of \$2872.26 on the new 23-inch rims and tires he bought for his SUV. If his payments are \$106.38 per month, how many months will it take to pay off the balance? (***Source:*** Less Schwab Tire.)

29. ____________

30. MEDICINE DOSE Each dose of a medication contains 1.62 units of a certain ingredient. Find the number of doses that can be made from 57.13 units of the ingredient. Round to the nearest whole number.

30. ______________

31. U.S. PAPER MONEY The thickness of one piece of paper money is .0043 inch.

(a) If you had a pile of 100 bills, how high would it be?

(b) How high would a pile of 1000 bills be?

(a) ______________
(b) ______________

32. (a) Use the information from Exercise 31 to find the number of bills in a pile that is 43 inches high.

(b) How much money would you have if the pile was all $20 bills?

(a) ______________
(b) ______________

Use the information from the Look Smart online catalog to answer Exercises 33–36.

Knit Shirt Ordering Information		
43–2A	Short sleeve, solid colors	$14.75 each
43–2B	Short sleeve, stripes	$16.75 each
43–3A	Long sleeve, solid colors	$18.95 each
43–3B	Long sleeve, stripes	$21.95 each
XXL size, add $2 per shirt.		
Monogram, $4.95 each. Gift box, $5 each.		

Total Price of All Items (excluding monograms and gift boxes)	Shipping, Packing, and Handling
$0–25.00	$3.50
$25.01–75.00	$5.95
$75.01–125.00	$7.95
$125.01+	$9.95
Shipping to each additional address add $4.25.	

33. Find the total cost of ordering four long-sleeve, solid-color shirts and two short-sleeve, striped shirts, all size XXL and all shipped to your home.

33. ______________

34. What is the total cost of eight long-sleeve shirts, five in solid colors and three striped? Include the cost of shipping the solid shirts to your home and the striped shirts to your brother's home.

34. ______________

35. (a) What is the total cost, including shipping, of sending three short-sleeve, solid-color shirts, with monograms, in a gift box to your aunt for her birthday?

(b) How much did the monogram, gift box, and shipping add to the cost of your gift?

(a) ______________
(b) ______________

36. (a) Suppose you order one of each type of shirt for yourself, adding a monogram on each of the solid-color shirts. At the same time, you order three long-sleeve, striped, size-XXL shirts to be shipped to your father in a gift box. Find the total cost of your order.

(b) What is the difference in total cost (excluding shipping) between the shirts for yourself and the gift for your father?

(a) ______________
(b) ______________

Case Studies

SUBWAY

www.subway.com

- 1965: First location in Bridgeport, Connecticut
- 1968: Fifth shop is opened
- 1974: First franchised shop is opened
- 1989: SUBWAY shops in all 50 states
- 1995: Becomes supporter of American Cancer Institute and Produce for Better Health
- 2002: Becomes national sponsor of American Heart Association Heart Walk
- 2007: Over 28,400 SUBWAY restaurants in 86 countries

In 1965, seventeen-year-old Fred DeLuca had just graduated from high school. DeLuca and a family friend, Dr. Peter Buck, opened the first SUBWAY sandwich shop with a total investment of $1000. From the beginning, the freshest ingredients were used, with DeLuca driving many miles in his Volkswagen bug to purchase vegetables directly from the produce mart. Hard work resulted in 16 stores in the state of Connecticut. In 1974, to further expand, they decided to franchise. Today SUBWAY is the largest submarine sandwich chain in the world. The company operates more stores in the United States, Canada, and Australia than McDonald's does.

SUBWAY restaurants is a national sponsor of the American Heart Association Heart Walk and a supporter of the American Cancer Institute and Produce for Better Health.

1. An employee slices 23.6 pounds of turkey breast from a carton containing 50 pounds. Find the number of pounds remaining.

2. A measuring scoop holds .0335 pound of baker's yeast. How many measuring scoops are in 2.2 pounds of baker's yeast? Round to the nearest whole number.

3. Based on your knowledge of SUBWAY restaurants, the products that it sells, and the company advertising, what kind of statement do you think the company is trying to make about itself?

4. In addition to using decimals when baking, name six additional applications of decimals in a SUBWAY store.

CHAPTER 1 QUICK REVIEW

CHAPTER TERMS *Review the following terms to test your understanding of the chapter. For each term you do not know, refer to the page number found next to that term.*

addends [**p. 4**]	decimal system [**p. 2**]	indicator words [**p. 17**]	quotient [**p. 8**]
addition [**p. 4**]	difference [**p. 5**]	minuend [**p. 5**]	rounding [**p. 3**]
amount [**p. 4**]	digits [**p. 2**]	multiplicand [**p. 6**]	rounding decimals [**p. 23**]
borrowing [**p. 5**]	dividend [**p. 8**]	multiplication [**p. 4**]	rounding whole numbers [**p. 3**]
checking answers [**p. 4**]	dividing decimals [**p. 35**]	multiplier [**p. 6**]	subtraction [**p. 4**]
comma [**p. 2**]	division [**p. 4**]	multiplying decimals [**p. 33**]	subtrahend [**p. 5**]
decimal number [**p. 23**]	divisor [**p. 8**]	operations [**p. 4**]	sum [**p. 4**]
decimal part [**p. 8**]	fraction part [**p. 8**]	partial products [**p. 6**]	total [**p. 4**]
decimal point [**p. 2**]	front-end rounding [**p. 5**]	product [**p. 6**]	whole numbers [**p. 2**]

CONCEPTS	EXAMPLES
1.1 Reading and writing whole numbers The word *and* is not used. Commas help divide thousands, millions, and billions. A comma is not needed with a four-digit number.	795 is written as "seven hundred ninety-five." 9,768,002 is written as "nine million, seven hundred sixty-eight thousand, two."

1.1 Rounding whole numbers

Rules for rounding:

1. Identify the position to be rounded. Draw a line under that place.
2. If the digit to the right of the underlined place is 5 or more, increase by 1; if the digit is 4 or less, do not change.
3. Change all digits to the right of the underlined digit to zero.

Round:

726 to the nearest ten

5 or more, so add 1 to tens position

tens position

So, 726 rounds to 730.

1, 498,586 to the nearest million

4 or less, so do not change

millions position

So, 1,498,586 rounds to 1,000,000.

1.1 Front-end rounding

Front-end rounding leaves only the first digit as a nonzero digit. All other digits are changed to zero.

Round each of the following, using front-end rounding.

76 rounds to 80
348 rounds to 300
6512 rounds to 7000
23,751 rounds to 20,000
652,179 rounds to 700,000

1.1 Addition of whole numbers

Add from top to bottom, starting with units and working to the left. To check, add from bottom to top.

$$\begin{array}{r} 1140 \\ 687 \\ 26 \\ 9 \\ + \ 418 \\ \hline 1140 \end{array}$$

Problem (add down) Check (add up)

1.1 Subtraction of whole numbers

Subtract the subtrahend from the minuend to get the difference, borrowing when necessary. To check, add the difference to the subtrahend to get the minuend.

Problem
$$\begin{array}{r} 621 \\ 4738 \\ - \ 649 \\ \hline 4089 \end{array}$$

Check
$$\begin{array}{r} 4089 \\ + \ 649 \\ \hline 4738 \end{array}$$

CONCEPTS	EXAMPLES

1.1 Multiplication of whole numbers

The multiplicand is multiplied by the multiplier, giving the product. When the multiplier has more than one digit, partial products must be used and then added.

```
   78   multiplicand
×  24   multiplier
  312   partial product
 156    partial product (one position left)
 1872   product
```

1.1 Division of whole numbers

÷ and $\overline{)\ \ }$ mean divide.

A —, as in $\frac{25}{5}$, means divide 25 by 5.

Also, the /, as in 25/5, means to divide 25 by 5.

Remainders are usually expressed as decimals.

```
           44   quotient
divisor  2)88   dividend
           88
            0
```

If answer is rounded, the check will not be perfect.

1.2 Application problems

Follow these steps.

1. Read the problem carefully.
2. Work out a plan, using *indicator words* before starting.
3. Estimate a reasonable answer.
4. Solve the problem. If the answer is reasonable, check; if it is not, start over.

Shauna Gallegos earns $118 on Sunday, $87 on Monday, and $63 on Tuesday. Find her total earnings for the three days.
Total means to add.

```
   $268   Check
   $118
  $  87
+ $  63
   $268   total earnings
```

1.3 Reading and rounding decimals

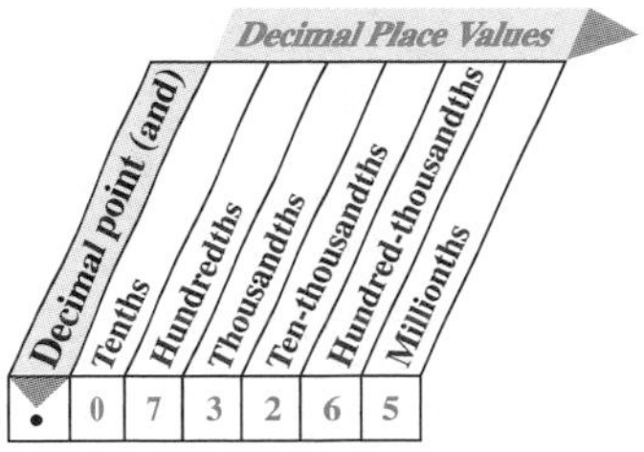

1.3 is read as "one and three tenths."
Round .073265 to the nearest ten-thousandth.

.0732|65 (ten-thousandth position)

Since the digit to the right is 6, increase the ten-thousandths digit by 1 and drop all digits to the right; .073265 rounds to .0733.

1.4 Addition and subtraction of decimals

Decimal points must be in a column. Attach zeros to keep digits in their correct columns.

Add: 5.68 + 785.3 + .007 + 10.1062
Line up the decimal points.

```
     5.6800  ←
   785.3000  ← Attach zeros.
      .0070  ←
+   10.1062
   801.0932
```

1.5 Multiplication of decimals

Multiply as if decimals are whole numbers. Place the decimal point as follows.

1. Count digits to the right of decimal points.
2. Count from right to left the same number of places as in step 1. Zeros must be attached on the left if necessary.

Multiply: .169 × .21

```
   .169   3 decimal places
 ×  .21   2 decimal places
    169
   338
 .03549   5 decimal places in answer
 ↑
 Attach one zero.
```

1.5 Division of decimals

1. Move the decimal point in the divisor all the way to the right.
2. Move the decimal point the same number of places to the right in the dividend.
3. Place a decimal point in the answer position directly above the dividend decimal point.
4. Divide as with whole numbers.

Divide 52.8 by .75

```
         70.4          Check
 .75.)52.80.0            70.4
      52 5            ×   .75
         30              3520
         00             4928
         30 0           52.800
         30 0
            0
```

CHAPTER 1 SUMMARY EXERCISE

The Toll of Wedding Bells

The Wedding Report recently released statistics showing the average wedding costs in the United States in 2007. In 2004, the cost of the average wedding was $24,168. This cost has increased as the average number of wedding guests has grown to over 200. The graph gives most of the costs involved in a wedding. Use this information to answer the questions that follow.

Numbers in the News

'Til Debt Do You Part

With over 200 guests, the cost of an average wedding has continued to grow. Most of the money is spent on the following:

DATA: The Wedding Report, Shane McMurray

(a) What is the total of the costs shown in the graph? **(a)** ______________

(b) How much more expensive was a wedding in 2007 compared with 2004? **(b)** ______________

(c) If you decide to spend $11,000 for your wedding reception, and the cost per guest is $54, how many guests can you invite? How much of your budgeted amount will be left over? **(c)** ______________

(d) If 150 guests are invited to the wedding and $11,000 is budgeted for the reception, find the amount that can be spent per person. Round to the nearest cent. **(d)** ______________

(e) If you budget $6000 for the wedding reception and the cost per person is $37, how many guests can you invite and how much of your budgeted amount will be left over? **(e)** ______________

(f) If you budget $1000 for the wedding reception and the cost per person is $15, how many guests can you invite and how much of your budgeted amount will be left over? **(f)** ______________

(g) The bridal party will need five bouquets that cost $36.25 each and five boutonnieres, each costing $7.50. If a total of $863 is budgeted for flowers, find the amount that remains to be spent for other floral arrangements. **(g)** ______________

INVESTIGATE

List six expenses associated with a wedding that are not mentioned. List six things that could be changed to bring the cost of the wedding down. What are some costs associated with a wedding where you live? You may have to ask some friends or relatives who recently have been involved in wedding planning.

CHAPTER 1 TEST

To help you review, the bracketed numbers indicate the section in which the topic is discussed.

Round as indicated. **[1.1]**

1. 844 to the nearest ten — **1.** ________

2. 21,958 to the nearest hundred — **2.** ________

3. 671,529 to the nearest thousand — **3.** ________

Round each of the following, using front-end rounding. **[1.1]**

4. 50,987 — **4.** ________

5. 851,004 — **5.** ________

6. One week, Katie Nopper earned the following commissions: Monday, \$124; Tuesday, \$88; Wednesday, \$62; Thursday, \$137; Friday, \$195. Find her total amount of commissions for the week. **[1.2]** — **6.** ________

7. A rental business buys three airless sprayers at \$1540 each, five rototillers at \$695 each, and eight 25-foot ladders at \$38 each. Find the total cost of the equipment purchased. **[1.2]** — **7.** ________

Round as indicated. **[1.3]**

8. \$21.0568 to the nearest cent — **8.** ________

9. \$364.345 to the nearest cent — **9.** ________

10. \$7246.49 to the nearest dollar — **10.** ________

Solve each problem. **[1.4 and 1.5]**

11. 9.6 + 8.42 + 3.715 + 159.8 = ________

12.
$$\begin{array}{r} 2.715 \\ 32.78 \\ 426.3 \\ +\ 37 \\ \hline \end{array}$$

13.
$$\begin{array}{r} 341.4 \\ -\ 207.8 \\ \hline \end{array}$$

14. 3.8 − .0053

15.
$$\begin{array}{r} 21.98 \\ \times\ .72 \\ \hline \end{array}$$

16.
$$\begin{array}{r} 218.6 \\ \times\ .037 \\ \hline \end{array}$$

17. $21.8\overline{)252.008}$

18. $57.358 \div 2.41 =$_____

19. $79.135 \div 18.62 =$_____

C **20.** SUBWAY wants to find the total cost of 24.8 pounds of sliced turkey at $1.89 a pound and 38.2 pounds of provolone cheese at $2.05 a pound. **[1.4 and 1.5]**

20. ____________

21. Roofing material costs $84.52 per square (10 ft × 10 ft). The roofer charges $55.75 per square for labor, plus $9.65 per square for supplies. Find the total cost for 26.3 squares of installed roof. Round to the nearest cent. **[1.4 and 1.5]**

21. ____________

22. A federal law requires that all residential toilets sold in the United States use no more than 1.6 gallons of water per flush. Prior to this legislation, conventional toilets used 3.4 gallons of water per flush. Find the amount of water saved in one year by a family flushing the toilet 22 times each day (1 year = 365 days). **[1.4 and 1.5]**

22. ____________

23. Steve Hamilton bought 135.5 meters of steel rod at $.86 per meter and 12 meters of brass rod at $2.18 per meter. How much change did he get from eight $20 bills? **[1.4 and 1.5]**

23. ____________

24. The Capital Hills Supermarket in Washington, DC, sells bananas for $1.74 per kilogram (2.2 pounds). Find the price of bananas per pound. Round to the nearest cent. (***Source:*** Associated Press.) **[1.5]**

24. ____________

25. A concentrated fertilizer must be applied at the rate of .058 ounce per seedling. Find the number of seedlings that can be fertilized with 14.674 ounces of fertilizer. **[1.5]**

25. ____________

CHAPTER 2

Fractions

CHAPTER CONTENTS

Kara Oaks has been employed at The Home Depot for several years. During this time, she has worked in the hardware and

CASE *in* POINT

plumbing departments and now manages the cabinetry department. She has been managing this department for a year and a half and enjoys helping contractors and homeowners plan and design new and replacement cabinets for their kitchens and bathrooms. Knowing and using fractions is a key part of Oaks's job. She must be extremely accurate as she determines the exact space specifications for the building and placement of new cabinets.

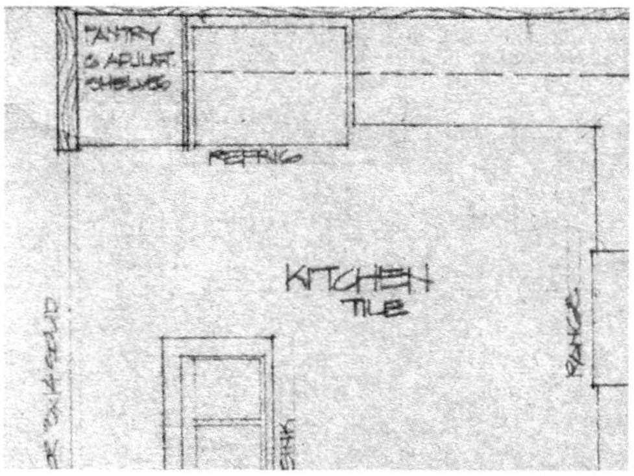

Chapter 1 discussed whole numbers and decimals. This chapter looks at *fractions*—numbers, like decimals, that can be used to represent parts of a whole. Fractions and decimals are two ways of representing the same quantity. Fractions are used in business and our personal lives.

2.1 BASICS OF FRACTIONS

OBJECTIVES

1. Recognize types of fractions.
2. Convert mixed numbers to improper fractions.
3. Convert improper fractions to mixed numbers.
4. Write a fraction in lowest terms.
5. Use the rules for divisibility.

A **fraction** represents part of a whole. Fractions are written in the form of one number over another, with a line between the two numbers, as in the following.

$$\frac{5}{8} \quad \frac{1}{4} \quad \frac{9}{7} \quad \frac{13}{10} \quad \begin{array}{l} \longleftarrow \text{numerator} \\ \longleftarrow \text{denominator} \end{array}$$

The number above the line is the **numerator**, and the number below the line is the **denominator**. In the fraction $\frac{2}{3}$, the numerator is 2 and the denominator is 3. The denominator is the number of equal parts into which something is divided. The numerator tells how many of these parts are needed. For example, $\frac{2}{3}$ is "2 parts out of 3 equal parts," as shown in the figure.

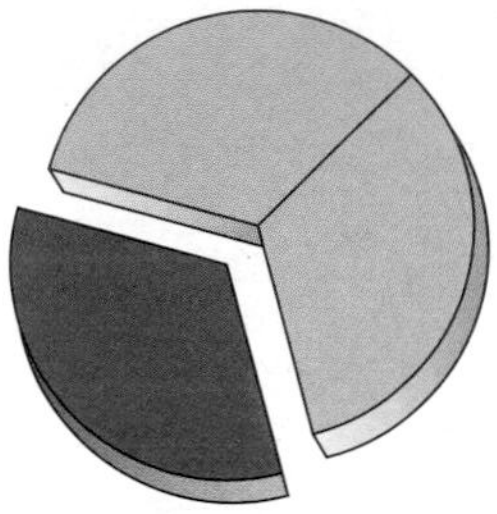

$\frac{2}{3}$ means 2 parts out of 3 equal parts

OBJECTIVE 1 Recognize types of fractions. If the numerator of a fraction is smaller than the denominator, the fraction is a **proper fraction**. Examples of proper fractions are $\frac{2}{3}$, $\frac{3}{4}$, $\frac{15}{16}$, and $\frac{1}{8}$. A fraction with a numerator greater than or equal to the denominator is an **improper fraction**. Examples of improper fractions are $\frac{17}{13}$, $\frac{19}{12}$, and $\frac{5}{5}$. A proper fraction has a value less than 1, while an improper fraction has a value greater than or equal to 1.

To write a whole number as a fraction, place the whole number over 1; for example, $7 = \frac{7}{1}$ and $12 = \frac{12}{1}$. The sum of a fraction and a whole number is a **mixed number**. Examples of mixed numbers include $5\frac{2}{3}$ (a short way of writing $5 + \frac{2}{3}$), $3\frac{5}{8}$, and $9\frac{5}{6}$. A mixed number can be converted to an improper fraction as shown next.

OBJECTIVE 2 Convert mixed numbers to improper fractions. To convert the mixed number $4\frac{5}{8}$ to an improper fraction, first multiply the denominator of the fraction part (in this case, 8) and the whole number part (in this case, 4). This gives $8 \times 4 = 32\left(4 = \frac{32}{8}\right)$. Then add the product (32) to the numerator (in this case, 5). This gives $32 + 5 = 37$. This sum is the numerator of the new improper fraction. The denominator stays the same.

$$4\frac{5}{8} = \frac{37}{8} \longleftarrow (4 \times 8) + 5$$

The opening in the kitchen cabinet to the left is for a microwave oven and measures $25\frac{3}{4}$ inches wide by $16\frac{1}{2}$ inches high. These are both mixed numbers. The thickness of the oak wood used for the cabinet is $\frac{7}{8}$ inch, which is a proper fraction.

EXAMPLE 1

Converting Mixed Numbers to Improper Fractions

The width and height of the opening in the cabinet shown on the previous page are both expressed as mixed numbers. Convert these mixed numbers to improper fractions.

(a) $25\frac{3}{4}$ **(b)** $16\frac{1}{2}$

SOLUTION

(a) First multiply 4 (the denominator) by 25 (the whole number), and then add 3 (the numerator). This gives $(4 \times 25) + 3 = 100 + 3 = 103$. The parentheses are used to show that 4 and 25 are multiplied first.

$$25\frac{3}{4} = \frac{103}{4} \leftarrow (4 \times 25) + 3$$

(b) $16\frac{1}{2} = \frac{(2 \times 16) + 1}{2} = \frac{33}{2}$

QUICK CHECK 1

Convert to improper fractions.

(a) $15\frac{1}{3}$ **(b)** $21\frac{3}{8}$

OBJECTIVE 3 Convert improper fractions to mixed numbers. To convert an improper fraction to a mixed number, divide the numerator of the improper fraction by the denominator. The quotient is the whole-number part of the mixed number, and the remainder is used as the numerator of the fraction part. The denominator stays the same. For example, convert $\frac{17}{5}$ to a mixed number by dividing 17 by 5.

$$5\overline{)17} = 3 \text{ R } 2 \quad (15 \text{ subtracted, remainder } 2) \qquad \frac{17}{5} = 3\frac{2}{5}$$

The whole-number part is the quotient 3. The remainder 2 is used as the numerator of the fraction part. Keep 5 as the denominator.

$$\frac{17}{5} = 3\frac{2}{5}$$

EXAMPLE 2

Converting Improper Fractions to Mixed Numbers

Convert the following improper fractions to mixed numbers.

(a) $\frac{27}{4}$ **(b)** $\frac{29}{8}$ **(c)** $\frac{42}{7}$

SOLUTION

(a) Convert $\frac{27}{4}$ to a mixed number by dividing 27 by 4.

$$4\overline{)27} = 6 \text{ R } 3 \quad (24 \text{ subtracted, remainder } 3) \qquad \frac{27}{4} = 6\frac{3}{4}$$

The whole-number part of the mixed number is 6. The remainder 3 is used as the numerator of the fraction. Keep 4 as the denominator.

$$\frac{27}{4} = 6\frac{3}{4}$$

Quick Check Answers

1. (a) $\frac{46}{3}$ (b) $\frac{171}{8}$

(b) Divide 29 by 8 to convert $\frac{29}{8}$ to a mixed number.

$$8\overline{)29}\quad \frac{29}{8} = 3\frac{5}{8}$$

$$\begin{array}{r} 3 \\ 8\overline{)29} \\ \underline{24} \\ 5 \end{array}$$

QUICK TIP A proper fraction has a value that is less than 1, while an improper fraction has a value that is greater than or equal to 1.

(c) Divide 42 by 7 to convert $\frac{42}{7}$ to a mixed number.

$$\begin{array}{r} 6 \\ 7\overline{)42} \\ \underline{42} \\ 0 \end{array}\quad \frac{42}{7} = 6$$

QUICK CHECK 2

Convert to mixed numbers.

(a) $\frac{73}{4}$ **(b)** $\frac{32}{5}$

OBJECTIVE 4 **Write a fraction in lowest terms.** If both the numerator and denominator of a fraction cannot be divided without a remainder by any number other than 1, then the fraction is in **lowest terms**. For example, 2 and 3 cannot be divided without a remainder by any number other than 1, so the fraction $\frac{2}{3}$ is in lowest terms. In the same way, $\frac{1}{9}$, $\frac{4}{11}$, $\frac{12}{17}$, and $\frac{13}{15}$ are in lowest terms.

When both numerator and denominator *can* be divided without a remainder by a number other than 1, the fraction is *not* in lowest terms. For example, both 15 and 25 may be divided by 5, so the fraction $\frac{15}{25}$ is not in lowest terms. Write $\frac{15}{25}$ in lowest terms by dividing both numerator and denominator by 5, as follows.

$$\frac{15}{25} = \frac{15 \div 5}{25 \div 5} = \frac{3}{5} \quad \text{lowest terms}$$

Divide by 5.

EXAMPLE 3 Writing Fractions in Lowest Terms

Write the following fractions in lowest terms.

(a) $\frac{15}{40}$ **(b)** $\frac{33}{39}$

SOLUTION

Look for a number that can be divided into both the numerator and denominator.

(a) Both 15 and 40 can be divided by 5.

$$\frac{15}{40} = \frac{15 \div 5}{40 \div 5} = \frac{3}{8} \quad \text{lowest terms}$$

(b) Divide by 3.

$$\frac{33}{39} = \frac{33 \div 3}{39 \div 3} = \frac{11}{13} \quad \text{lowest terms}$$

QUICK CHECK 3

Write in lowest terms.

(a) $\frac{36}{45}$ **(b)** $\frac{48}{66}$

Quick Check Answers

2. (a) $18\frac{1}{4}$ **(b)** $6\frac{2}{5}$

3. (a) $\frac{4}{5}$ **(b)** $\frac{8}{11}$

OBJECTIVE 5 Use the rules for divisibility. It is sometimes difficult to tell which numbers will divide evenly into another number. The following rules can sometimes help.

Rules for Divisibility

A number can be evenly divided by

2	if the last digit is an even number, such as 0, 2, 4, 6, or 8
3	if the sum of the digits is divisible by 3
4	if the last two digits are divisible by 4
5	if the last digit is 0 or 5
6	if the number is even and the sum of the digits is divisible by 3
8	if the last three digits are divisible by 8
9	if the sum of all the digits is divisible by 9
10	if the last digit is 0

EXAMPLE 4

Using the Divisibility Rules

Determine whether the following statements are true.

(a) 3,746,892 is evenly divisible by 4.
(b) 15,974,802 is evenly divisible by 9.

SOLUTION

(a) The number 3,746,892 is evenly divisible by 4, since the last two digits form a number divisible by 4.

$$3,746,8\underbrace{92}$$

92 is divisible by 4.

(b) See if 15,974,802 is evenly divisible by 9 by adding the digits of the number.

$$1 + 5 + 9 + 7 + 4 + 8 + 0 + 2 = \underbrace{36}$$

36 is divisible by 9.

Since 36 is divisible by 9, the given number is divisible by 9.

QUICK TIP Testing for divisibility by adding the digits works for only 3 and 9.

The rules for divisibility help determine only whether a number is evenly divisible by another number. They cannot be used to find the result. You must carry out the division to find the quotient.

QUICK CHECK 4

Determine **(a)** whether 628,375,210 is evenly divisible by 5, and **(b)** whether 825,693,471 is evenly divisible by 3.

Quick Check Answers

4. (a) 628,375,210 is evenly divisible by 5
(b) 825,693,471 is evenly divisible by 3

Case Studies

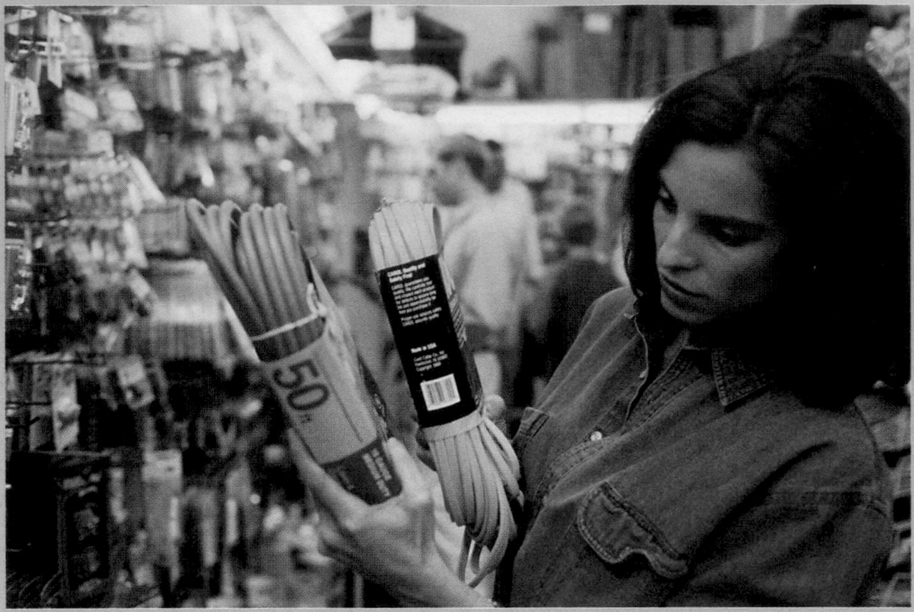

The Home Depot

www.homedepot.com

- 1979: Founded in Atlanta, Georgia
- 2005: $81.5 billion in annual sales
- 2006: Named Energy Star Partner of the year by the Environmental Protection Agency
- 2007: 355,000 employees worldwide
- 2007: 2400 stores estimated

The Home Depot is the world's largest home-improvement retailer. It is credited with being the innovator of the home-improvement industry, as well as offering a level of service unprecedented among warehouse-style retailers. The Home Depot stores cater to do-it-yourselfers as well as home-improvement, construction, and building maintenance professionals. Each store stocks approximately 40,000 building, home-improvement, and lawn-and-garden products (including variations in color and size). Newer stores are approximately 130,000 square feet or the size of four football fields. Stores are located throughout the United States, Canada, Mexico, Puerto Rico, and St. Thomas.

The company's progressive corporate culture includes a philanthropic budget that directs funds back to the communities. The Home Depot serves the interests of its employees through a matching-gift program. The major focuses are affordable housing, at-risk youth, and the environment. Team Depot, an organized volunteer force, was developed in 1992 to promote volunteer activities with the local communities the stores serve.

1. A gutter downspout is 10 feet long. If a piece of gutter downspout 8 feet 8.375 inches is needed for a job, find the length of the remaining piece. (*Hint:* One foot equals 12 inches.)

2. The Home Depot stock is selling for $37.24 per share. Find the number of shares that can be purchased for $20,258.56.

3. Give five specific situations in which fractions and mixed numbers would be used in a home-improvement store.

4. From your own experiences and those of family members and classmates, list eight specific activities where the ability to work with fractions would be needed.

2.1 EXERCISES

FOR EXTRA HELP

MyMathLab

MathXL PRACTICE

WATCH

DOWNLOAD

READ

REVIEW

The **QUICK START** *exercises in each section contain solutions to help you get started.*

Convert the following mixed numbers to improper fractions. (See Example 1.)

QUICK START

1. $3\frac{5}{8} = \frac{29}{8}$

$\frac{(8 \times 3) + 5}{8} = \frac{29}{8}$

2. $2\frac{4}{5} = \frac{14}{5}$

$\frac{(5 \times 2) + 4}{5} = \frac{14}{5}$

3. $4\frac{1}{4} =$ ____

4. $3\frac{2}{3} =$ ____

5. $12\frac{2}{3} =$ ____

6. $2\frac{8}{11} =$ ____

7. $22\frac{7}{8} =$ ____

8. $17\frac{5}{8} =$ ____

9. $7\frac{6}{7} =$ ____

10. $21\frac{14}{15} =$ ____

11. $15\frac{19}{23} =$ ____

12. $7\frac{9}{16} =$ ____

Convert the following improper fractions to mixed or whole numbers and write in lowest terms. (See Examples 2 and 3.)

QUICK START

13. $\frac{13}{4} = 3\frac{1}{4}$

$$\begin{array}{r} 3 \\ 4\overline{)13} \\ \underline{12} \\ 1 \end{array} \quad 3\frac{1}{4}$$

14. $\frac{9}{5} = 1\frac{4}{5}$

$$\begin{array}{r} 1 \\ 5\overline{)9} \\ \underline{5} \\ 4 \end{array} \quad 1\frac{4}{5}$$

15. $\frac{8}{3} =$ ____

16. $\frac{23}{10} =$ ____

17. $\frac{38}{10} =$ ____

18. $\frac{56}{8} =$ ____

19. $\frac{40}{11} =$ ____

20. $\frac{78}{12} =$ ____

21. $\frac{125}{63} =$ ____

22. $\frac{195}{45} =$ ____

23. $\frac{183}{25} =$ ____

24. $\frac{720}{149} =$ ____

25. Your classmate asks you how to change a mixed number to an improper fraction. Write a couple of sentences explaining how this is done. (See Objective 2.)

C indicates an exercise that is related to the Case in Point feature.

26. Explain in a sentence or two how to change an improper fraction to a mixed number. (See Objective 3.)

Write the following in lowest terms. (See Example 3.)

QUICK START

27. $\frac{8}{16} = \frac{1}{2}$

$\frac{8 \div 8}{16 \div 8} = \frac{1}{2}$

28. $\frac{15}{20} = \frac{3}{4}$

$\frac{15 \div 5}{20 \div 5} = \frac{3}{4}$

29. $\frac{25}{40} =$ ___

30. $\frac{36}{42} =$ ___

31. $\frac{27}{45} =$ ___

32. $\frac{112}{128} =$ ___

33. $\frac{165}{180} =$ ___

34. $\frac{12}{600} =$ ___

UNDERSTANDING GOLD KARATS The fineness (purity) of gold is regulated by law and is the same in all parts of the world. The scale below shows the fineness in 24-kt., 18-kt., 14-kt., and 10-kt. gold. Write each fraction in lowest terms. (***Source:*** Costco Wholesale.)

QUICK START

35. 24 kt. = (24 parts gold, no alloy) $\frac{24}{24} = 1$

36. 18 kt. = (18 parts gold, 6 parts alloy)

37. 14 kt. = (14 parts gold, 10 parts alloy)

38. 10 kt. = (10 parts gold, 14 parts alloy)

35. 1

36. ___

37. ___

38. ___

39. What does it mean when a fraction is expressed in lowest terms? (See Objective 4.)

40. Eight rules of divisibility were given. Write the three rules that are most useful to you. (See Objective 5.)

Put a check mark in the blank if the number at the left is evenly divisible by the number at the top. Put an X in the blank if the number is not divisible. (See Example 4.)

QUICK START

	2	3	4	5	6	8	9	10
41. 32	√	X	√	X	X	√	X	X
42. 45	X	√	X	√	X	X	√	X
43. 60	_	_	_	_	_	_	_	_
44. 72	_	_	_	_	_	_	_	_
45. 90	_	_	_	_	_	_	_	_
46. 105	_	_	_	_	_	_	_	_
47. 4172	_	_	_	_	_	_	_	_
48. 5688	_	_	_	_	_	_	_	_

2.2 ADDITION AND SUBTRACTION OF FRACTIONS

OBJECTIVES

1. Add and subtract like fractions.
2. Find the least common denominator.
3. Add and subtract unlike fractions.
4. Rewrite fractions with a common denominator.

CASE in POINT Kara Oaks must use fractions on a daily basis as she works with contractors and homeowners at The Home Depot. The measurements of cabinets, trim pieces, and room sizes never seem to be even numbers of inches—they always have fractions of an inch.

OBJECTIVE 1 Add and subtract like fractions. Fractions with the same denominator are called **like fractions**. Such fractions have a **common denominator**. For example, $\frac{3}{4}$ and $\frac{5}{4}$ are *like* fractions with a common denominator of 4, while $\frac{4}{7}$ and $\frac{4}{9}$ are *not like* fractions. Add or subtract like fractions by adding or subtracting the numerators, and then place the result over the common denominator.

EXAMPLE 1 Adding and Subtracting Like Fractions

Add or subtract.

(a) $\frac{3}{4} + \frac{1}{4} + \frac{5}{4}$ **(b)** $\frac{11}{15} - \frac{4}{15}$

SOLUTION

The fractions in both parts of this example are like fractions. Add or subtract the numerators and place the result over the common denominator.

(a) $\frac{3}{4} + \frac{1}{4} + \frac{5}{4} = \frac{3+1+5}{4}$ ← Add the numerators. ← Write the common denominator.

$= \frac{9}{4} = 2\frac{1}{4}$ ← Write the answer as a mixed number.

(b) $\frac{11}{15} - \frac{4}{15} = \frac{11-4}{15} = \frac{7}{15}$

QUICK CHECK 1

Add or subtract.

(a) $\frac{5}{8} + \frac{7}{8} + \frac{1}{8}$ **(b)** $\frac{17}{21} - \frac{4}{21}$

OBJECTIVE 2 Find the least common denominator. Fractions with different denominators, such as $\frac{3}{4}$ and $\frac{2}{3}$, are **unlike fractions**. Add or subtract unlike fractions by first writing the fractions with a common denominator. The **least common denominator (LCD)** for two or more fractions is the smallest whole number that can be divided, without a remainder, by all the denominators of the fractions. For example, the LCD of the fractions $\frac{3}{4}$, $\frac{5}{6}$, and $\frac{1}{2}$ is 12, since 12 is the smallest number that can be divided evenly by 4, 6, and 2.

Quick Check Answers

1. (a) $\frac{13}{8} = 1\frac{5}{8}$ **(b)** $\frac{13}{21}$

Notice that the fractions shown in the shelf-end base drawing below are *like fractions*, $23\frac{3}{16}$, $10\frac{9}{16}$, and $11\frac{3}{16}$. However, in the drawing of the shelf-end peninsula base, the fractions are *unlike fractions*, $22\frac{7}{16}$, $11\frac{3}{32}$, and $11\frac{5}{8}$.

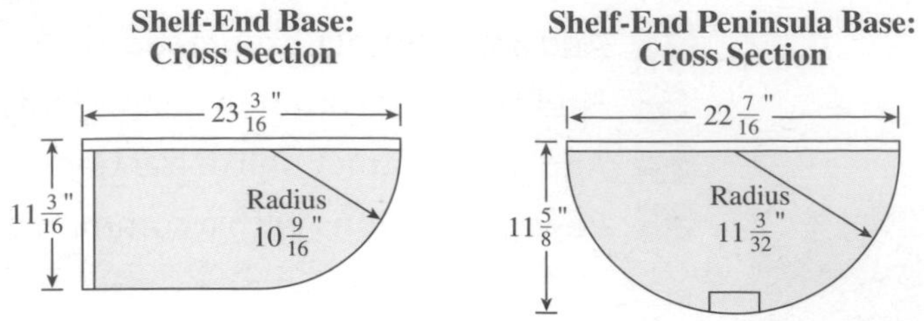

There are two methods of finding the least common denominator.

Inspection. With small denominators, it may be possible to find the least common denominator by inspection. For example, the LCD for $\frac{1}{3}$ and $\frac{1}{5}$ is 15, the smallest number that can be divided evenly by both 3 and 5.

Method of prime numbers. If the LCD cannot be found by inspection, use the method of prime numbers, as explained in the next example.

QUICK TIP All prime numbers other than 2 are odd numbers. Not all odd numbers, however, are prime numbers. For example, 27 is the product of 3 and 9.

A **prime number** is a number that can be divided without a remainder by exactly two distinct numbers: itself and 1. Prime numbers are 2, 3, 5, 7, 11, 13, 17, and so on. (1 is *not* prime because it can be divided evenly by only *one* number: the number 1.)

EXAMPLE 2

Finding the Least Common Denominator

Use the method of prime numbers to find the least common denominator for $\frac{5}{12}$, $\frac{7}{18}$, and $\frac{11}{20}$.

SOLUTION

First write the three denominators: 12 18 20

Begin by trying to divide the three denominators by the smallest prime number, 2. Write each quotient directly above the given denominator as follows.

$$\begin{array}{r|rrr} & 6 & 9 & 10 \\ \hline 2 & 12 & 18 & 20 \end{array}$$

This way of writing the division is just a handy way of writing the separate problems $2\overline{)12}$, $2\overline{)18}$, and $2\overline{)20}$. Two of the new quotients, 6 and 10, can still be divided by 2, so perform the division again. Since 9 cannot be divided evenly by 2, just bring up the 9.

$$\begin{array}{r|rrr} & 3 & 9 & 5 \\ \hline 2 & 6 & 9 & 10 \\ \hline 2 & 12 & 18 & 20 \end{array}$$

Just bring 9 up.

None of the new quotients in the top row can be divided by 2, so try the next prime number, 3. The numbers 3 and 9 can be divided by 3, and one of the new quotients can still be divided by 3, so the division is performed again.

$$\begin{array}{r|rrr} & 1 & 1 & 5 \\ \hline 3 & 1 & 3 & 5 \\ \hline 3 & 3 & 9 & 5 \\ \hline 2 & 6 & 9 & 10 \\ \hline 2 & 12 & 18 & 20 \end{array}$$

Since none of the new quotients in the top row can be divided by 3, try the next prime number, 5. The number 5 can be used only once, as shown.

$$\begin{array}{r|rrr} & 1 & 1 & 1 \\ \hline 5 & 1 & 1 & 5 \\ \hline 3 & 1 & 3 & 5 \\ \hline 3 & 3 & 9 & 5 \\ \hline 2 & 6 & 9 & 10 \\ \hline 2 & 12 & 18 & 20 \end{array}$$

QUICK TIP It is not necessary to start with the smallest prime number as shown in Example 2. In fact, no matter which prime number we start with, we will still get the same least common denominator.

Now that the top row contains only 1's, find the least common denominator by multiplying the prime numbers in the left column.

The least common denominator is $2 \times 2 \times 3 \times 3 \times 5 = 180$.

QUICK CHECK 2

Use prime numbers to find the least common denominator for $\frac{3}{5}, \frac{5}{6}$, and $\frac{3}{20}$.

EXAMPLE 3

Finding the Least Common Denominator

Find the least common denominator for $\frac{3}{8}, \frac{5}{12}$, and $\frac{9}{10}$.

SOLUTION

Write the denominators in a row and use the method of prime numbers.

$$\begin{array}{r|rrr} & 1 & 1 & 1 \\ 5 & 1 & 1 & 5 \\ 3 & 1 & 3 & 5 \\ 2 & 2 & 3 & 5 \\ 2 & 4 & 6 & 5 \\ 2 & 8 & 12 & 10 \end{array}$$

Start here → $2\overline{)8 \quad 12 \quad 10}$

The least common denominator is $2 \times 2 \times 2 \times 3 \times 5 = 120$.

QUICK TIP Sometimes it is tempting to use a number that is not prime when solving for the least common denominator. This should be avoided because the result is often something different from the least common denominator.

QUICK CHECK 3

Find the least common denominator for $\frac{4}{9}, \frac{5}{24}$, and $\frac{3}{4}$.

Unlike fractions may be added or subtracted using the following steps.

Adding or Subtracting Unlike Fractions

STEP 1 Find the least common denominator (LCD).

STEP 2 Rewrite the unlike fractions as like fractions having the least common denominator.

STEP 3 Add or subtract numerators, placing answers over the LCD and reducing to lowest terms.

OBJECTIVE 3 Add and subtract unlike fractions. To add or subtract unlike fractions, rewrite the fractions with a common denominator. Since Example 2 shows that 180 is the least common denominator for $\frac{5}{12}, \frac{7}{18}$, and $\frac{11}{20}$, these three fractions can be added if each fraction is first written with a denominator of 180.

STEP 1 $\quad \frac{5}{12} = \frac{\ }{180} \quad \frac{7}{18} = \frac{\ }{180} \quad \frac{11}{20} = \frac{\ }{180}$

OBJECTIVE 4 Rewrite fractions with a common denominator. To rewrite the preceding fractions with a common denominator, first divide each denominator from the original fractions into the common denominator.

STEP 2 $\quad 12\overline{)180} = 15 \quad 18\overline{)180} = 10 \quad 20\overline{)180} = 9$

Next multiply each quotient by the original numerator.

$15 \times 5 = 75 \quad 10 \times 7 = 70 \quad 9 \times 11 = 99$

Now, rewrite the fractions.

$$\frac{5}{12} = \frac{75}{180} \quad \frac{7}{18} = \frac{70}{180} \quad \frac{11}{20} = \frac{99}{180}$$

Quick Check Answers

2. 60 **3.** 72

Add the fractions.

STEP 3

$$\frac{5}{12} + \frac{7}{18} + \frac{11}{20} = \frac{\mathbf{75}}{\mathbf{180}} + \frac{\mathbf{70}}{\mathbf{180}} + \frac{\mathbf{99}}{\mathbf{180}} = \frac{\mathbf{75 + 70 + 99}}{\mathbf{180}}$$

$$= \frac{244}{180} = 1\frac{64}{180} = 1\frac{16}{45}$$

Write the answer as a mixed number with the fraction in lowest terms.

EXAMPLE 4

Adding and Subtracting Unlike Fractions

Add or subtract.

(a) $\frac{3}{4} + \frac{1}{2} + \frac{5}{8}$ **(b)** $\frac{9}{10} - \frac{3}{8}$

SOLUTION

(a) Inspection shows that the least common denominator is 8. Rewrite the fractions so each has a denominator of 8. Then add.

$$\frac{3}{4} + \frac{1}{2} + \frac{5}{8} = \frac{\mathbf{6}}{\mathbf{8}} + \frac{\mathbf{4}}{\mathbf{8}} + \frac{\mathbf{5}}{\mathbf{8}} = \frac{\mathbf{6 + 4 + 5}}{\mathbf{8}} = \frac{15}{8} = 1\frac{7}{8}$$

(b) The least common denominator is 40. Rewrite the fractions so each has a denominator of 40. Then subtract.

$$\frac{9}{10} - \frac{3}{8} = \frac{\mathbf{36}}{\mathbf{40}} - \frac{\mathbf{15}}{\mathbf{40}} = \frac{\mathbf{36 - 15}}{\mathbf{40}} = \frac{21}{40}$$

QUICK CHECK 4

Add or subtract.

(a) $\frac{2}{3} + \frac{5}{8} + \frac{3}{4}$ **(b)** $\frac{11}{12} - \frac{2}{3}$

Fractions can also be added or subtracted vertically, as shown in the next example.

EXAMPLE 5

Adding and Subtracting Unlike Fractions

Add or subtract.

(a) $\frac{2}{9} + \frac{3}{4}$ **(b)** $\frac{11}{16} + \frac{7}{12}$ **(c)** $\frac{7}{8} - \frac{5}{12}$

SOLUTION

First rewrite the fractions with a least common denominator.

(a)
$$\begin{array}{rcl} \frac{2}{9} &=& \frac{8}{36} \\ +\frac{3}{4} &=& \frac{27}{36} \\ \hline && \frac{35}{36} \end{array}$$

(b)
$$\begin{array}{rcl} \frac{11}{16} &=& \frac{33}{48} \\ +\frac{7}{12} &=& \frac{28}{48} \\ \hline && \frac{61}{48} = 1\frac{13}{48} \end{array}$$

(c)
$$\begin{array}{rcl} \frac{7}{8} &=& \frac{21}{24} \\ -\frac{5}{12} &=& \frac{10}{24} \\ \hline &=& \frac{11}{24} \end{array}$$

All calculator solutions are shown using a basic calculator. The calculator solution to part (b) uses the fraction key on the calculator.

11 [a b/c] 16 [+] 7 [a b/c] 12 [=] $1\frac{13}{48}$

Note: Refer to Appendix C for calculator basics.

Quick Check Answers

4. (a) $\frac{49}{24} = 2\frac{1}{24}$

(b) $\frac{3}{12} = \frac{1}{4}$

5. (a) $1\frac{7}{12}$ **(b)** $\frac{13}{30}$

QUICK CHECK 5

Add or subtract.

(a) $\frac{11}{12} + \frac{2}{3}$ **(b)** $\frac{9}{10} - \frac{7}{15}$

2.2 EXERCISES

FOR EXTRA HELP

MyMathLab

MathXL PRACTICE

WATCH

DOWNLOAD

READ

REVIEW

The QUICK START *exercises in each section contain solutions to help you get started.*

Convert each fraction so that it has the indicated denominator. (See Objective 3.)

QUICK START

1. $\frac{4}{5} = \frac{16}{20}$

   $20 \div 5 = 4$

   $4 \times 4 = 16$

2. $\frac{3}{4} = \frac{12}{16}$

   $16 \div 4 = 4$

   $4 \times 3 = 12$

3. $\frac{9}{10} = \frac{\quad}{40}$

4. $\frac{7}{8} = \frac{\quad}{56}$

5. $\frac{6}{5} = \frac{\quad}{40}$

6. $\frac{7}{8} = \frac{\quad}{64}$

7. $\frac{6}{7} = \frac{\quad}{49}$

8. $\frac{11}{15} = \frac{\quad}{120}$

Find the least common denominator for each group of denominators using the method of prime numbers. (See Example 2.)

QUICK START

9. 3, 8, **24**

```
   1 1
3)3 1
2)3 2
2)3 4
2)3 8
```

   $2 \times 2 \times 2 \times 3 = 24$

10. 18, 24, **72**

```
   1   1
3) 3   1
3) 9   3
2) 9   6
2) 9  12
2)18  24
```

   $2 \times 2 \times 2 \times 3 \times 3 = 72$

11. 12, 18, 20, _____

12. 18, 20, 24, _____

13. 15, 24, 32, _____

14. 6, 8, 10, 12, _____

15. 10, 35, 50, 60, _____

16. 5, 18, 25, 30, 36, _____

17. 3, 5, 8, 12, 18, _____

18. Prime numbers are used to find the least common denominator. Write the definition of a prime number in your own words. (See Objective 2.)

19. Explain how to write a fraction with an indicated denominator. Give the example of changing $\frac{3}{4}$ to a fraction having 12 as a denominator. (See Objective 4.)

C indicates an exercise that is related to the Case in Point feature.

Add or subtract. Write answers in lowest terms. (See Examples 4 and 5.)

QUICK START

20. $\frac{2}{5} + \frac{1}{5} = \frac{3}{5}$

$\frac{2+1}{5} = \frac{3}{5}$

21. $\frac{2}{9} + \frac{4}{9} = \frac{2}{3}$

$\frac{2+4}{9} = \frac{6}{9} = \frac{2}{3}$

22. $\frac{5}{8} + \frac{7}{12} =$ ______

23. $\frac{11}{12} - \frac{5}{12} =$ ______

24. $\frac{5}{7} - \frac{1}{3} =$ ______

25. $\frac{5}{12} - \frac{1}{16} =$ ______

26. $\frac{2}{3} - \frac{3}{8} =$ ______

27. $\frac{3}{4} + \frac{5}{9} + \frac{1}{3} =$ ______

28. $\frac{1}{4} + \frac{1}{8} + \frac{1}{12} =$ ______

29. $\frac{3}{7} + \frac{2}{5} + \frac{1}{10} =$ ______

30. $\frac{5}{6} + \frac{3}{4} + \frac{5}{8} =$ ______

31. $\frac{7}{10} + \frac{8}{15} + \frac{5}{6} =$ ______

32. $\frac{3}{10} + \frac{2}{5} + \frac{3}{20} =$ ______

33. $\frac{3}{4} + \frac{2}{3} + \frac{8}{9}$

34. $\frac{7}{12} + \frac{5}{8} + \frac{7}{6}$

35. $\frac{8}{15} + \frac{3}{10} + \frac{3}{5}$

36. $\frac{1}{6} + \frac{5}{9} + \frac{13}{18}$

37. $\frac{7}{10} - \frac{1}{4}$

38. $\frac{4}{5} - \frac{2}{3}$

39. $\frac{5}{8} - \frac{1}{3}$

40. $\frac{19}{24} - \frac{5}{16}$

41. Where are fractions used in everyday life? Think in terms of business applications, hobbies, and personal finance. Give three examples.

42. With the exception of the number 2, all prime numbers are odd numbers. However, not all odd numbers are prime numbers. Explain why these statements are true. (See Objective 2.)

Solve the following application problems.

43. GARDENING Zalia Todd is planting her flower bed and has ordered $\frac{1}{4}$ cubic yard of sand, $\frac{3}{8}$ cubic yard of mulch, and $\frac{1}{3}$ cubic yard of peat moss. Find the total cubic yards that she has ordered.

43. ______

44. AUTO REPAIR Chuck Manly has used his savings to repair his car. He spent $\frac{1}{4}$ of his savings for new tires, $\frac{1}{6}$ of his savings for brakes, $\frac{1}{10}$ of his savings for a tune-up, and $\frac{1}{12}$ of his savings for new belts and hoses. What fraction of his total savings has he spent?

44. ______

45. COMPUTER ASSEMBLY When installing a printer cable to a computer, Ann Kuick must be certain that the proper type and size of mounting hardware are used. Find the total length of the bolt shown.

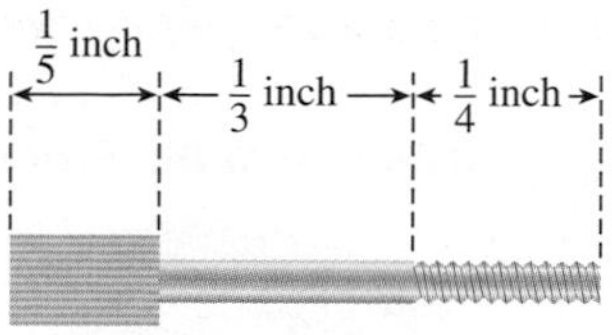

45. ________

46. CABINET INSTALLATION When installing cabinets for The Home Depot, Sarah Bryn must be certain that the proper type and size of mounting screw are used. Find the total length of the screw.

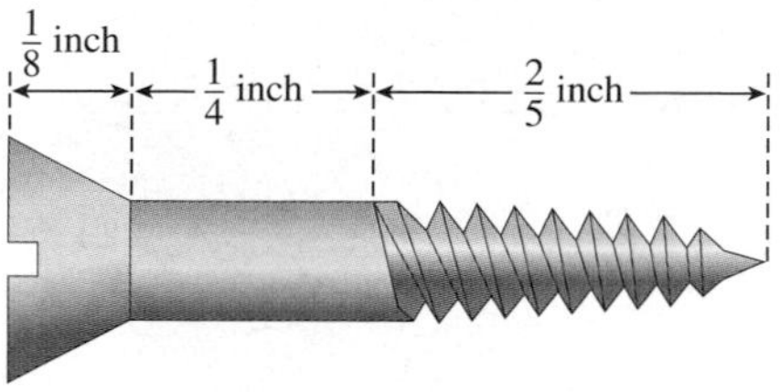

46. ________

47. PETROLEUM TRANSPORT Ken Faulk drives a tanker truck for Wonder Transport. He leaves the refinery with his tanker filled to $\frac{7}{8}$ of capacity. If he delivers $\frac{1}{4}$ of the tank's contents at the first stop and $\frac{1}{3}$ of the tank's contents at the second stop, find the fraction of the tanker's contents remaining.

47. ________

48. HYDRAULIC SYSTEM The hydraulic system on a fork lift contains $\frac{7}{8}$ gallon of hydraulic fluid. A cracked seal resulted in a loss of $\frac{1}{6}$ gallon of fluid in the morning and another $\frac{1}{3}$ gallon in the afternoon. Find the amount of fluid remaining.

48. ________

49. DEBT REDUCTION Dave Chwalik paid $\frac{1}{8}$ of a debt in January, $\frac{1}{3}$ in February, $\frac{1}{4}$ in March, and $\frac{1}{12}$ in April. What fraction of the debt was paid in these four months?

49. ________

50. NATURAL-FOODS STORE Joan McKee wants to open a natural-foods store and has saved $\frac{2}{5}$ of the amount needed for start-up costs. If she saves another $\frac{1}{8}$ of the amount needed and then $\frac{1}{6}$ more, find the total portion of the start-up costs she has saved.

50. ________

51. CABINET INSTALLATION Find the diameter of the hole in the mounting bracket shown. (*Hint:* Diameter is the distance across.)

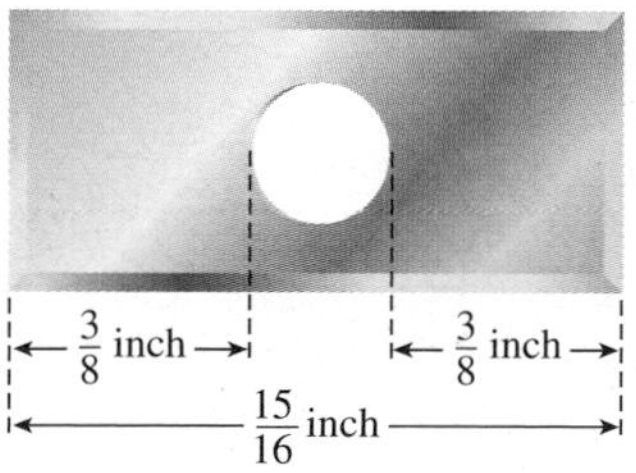

51. ________

52. SWIMMER TRAINING Sheri Minkner will swim $\frac{7}{8}$ of a mile in a five-day period. If she swims $\frac{1}{8}$ of a mile on both Monday and Wednesday, $\frac{1}{6}$ of a mile on both Tuesday and Thursday, and the balance on Friday, find the distance she must swim on Friday.

52. ________

STUDENT TIME MANAGEMENT *Refer to the circle graph to answer Exercises 53–56.*

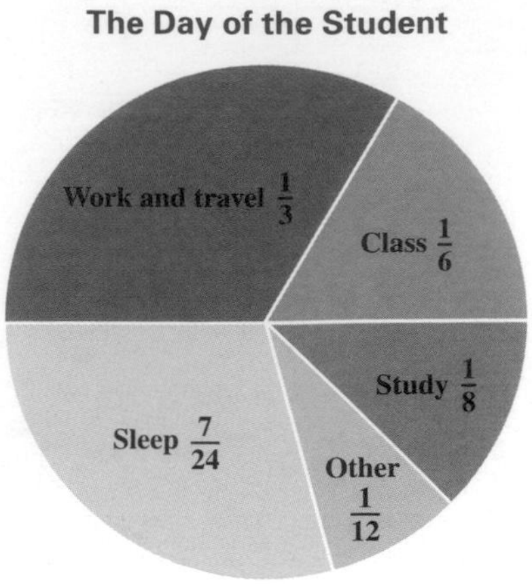

53. What fraction of the day was spent in class and study? **53.** ____________

54. What fraction of the day was spent in work and travel and other? **54.** ____________

55. In which activity was the greatest amount of time spent? What fraction of the day was spent on this activity and class time? **55.** ____________

56. In which activity was the least amount of time spent? What fraction of the day was spent on this activity and study? **56.** ____________

Use the newspaper advertisement for this four-piece chisel set to answer Exercises 57 and 58. (***Source:*** Harbor Freight Tools.)

57. Find the difference in the cutting-edge width of the narrowest chisel and the second to widest chisel. The symbol " is for inches. **57.** ____________

58. Find the difference in the cutting-edge width of the two chisels with the narrowest blades. The symbol " is for inches. **58.** ____________

59. PERIMETER OF FENCING A hazardous-waste site will require $\frac{7}{8}$ mile of security fencing. The site has four sides, three of which measure $\frac{1}{4}$ mile, $\frac{1}{6}$ mile, and $\frac{3}{8}$ mile. Find the length of the fourth side. **59.** ____________

60. NATIVE-AMERICAN JEWELRY Chakotay is fitting a turquoise stone into a bear-claw pendant. Find the diameter of the hole in the pendant. (The diameter is the distance across the center of the hole.) **60.** ____________

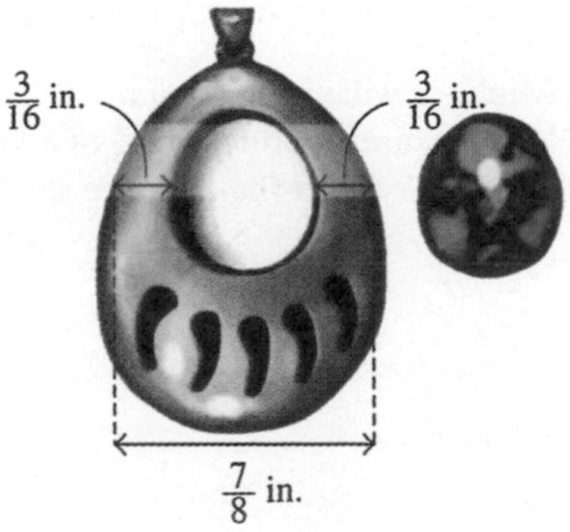

2.3 ADDITION AND SUBTRACTION OF MIXED NUMBERS

OBJECTIVES

1. Add mixed numbers.
2. Add with carrying.
3. Subtract mixed numbers.
4. Subtract with borrowing.

CASE in POINT Total customer satisfaction is important to Kara Oaks and The Home Depot. Complete accuracy is just as important in the small jobs in hardware and trim as it is in the large jobs in cabinets and installation. To achieve this accuracy, Oaks knows that mixed numbers must be added and subtracted carefully and that all calculations must then be checked to make sure they are correct.

OBJECTIVE 1 Add mixed numbers. To add mixed numbers, first add the fractions. Then add the whole numbers and combine the two answers. For example, add $16\frac{1}{8}$ and $5\frac{5}{8}$ as shown.

sum of fractions

$$\mathbf{16\frac{1}{8}} + \mathbf{5\frac{5}{8}} = \mathbf{21\frac{6}{8}}$$

sum of whole numbers

Write $\frac{6}{8}$ in lowest terms as $\frac{3}{4}$, so that $16\frac{1}{8} + 5\frac{5}{8} = 21\frac{3}{4}$.

To add mixed numbers, change the mixed numbers, if necessary, so that the fraction parts have a common denominator.

EXAMPLE 1 Adding Mixed Numbers

Add $9\frac{2}{3}$ and $6\frac{1}{4}$.

SOLUTION

Inspection shows that 12 is the least common denominator. Write $9\frac{2}{3}$ as $9\frac{8}{12}$, and write $6\frac{1}{4}$ as $6\frac{3}{12}$. Then add. The work can be organized as follows.

$$\begin{array}{rcr} 9\frac{2}{3} & = & 9\frac{8}{12} \\ +\,6\frac{1}{4} & = & 6\frac{3}{12} \\ \hline & & 15\frac{11}{12} \end{array}$$

QUICK CHECK 1

Add $5\frac{3}{4}$ and $8\frac{3}{8}$.

OBJECTIVE 2 Add with carrying. If the sum of the fraction parts of mixed numbers is greater than 1, carry the excess from the fraction part to the whole number part.

EXAMPLE 2 Adding with Carrying

A rubber gasket must extend around all four edges (perimeter) of the dishwasher door panel shown on the following page before it is installed. Find the length of gasket material needed. Add $34\frac{1}{2}$ inches, $23\frac{3}{4}$ inches, $34\frac{1}{2}$ inches, and $23\frac{3}{4}$ inches.

Quick Check Answer

1. $13\frac{9}{8} = 14\frac{1}{8}$

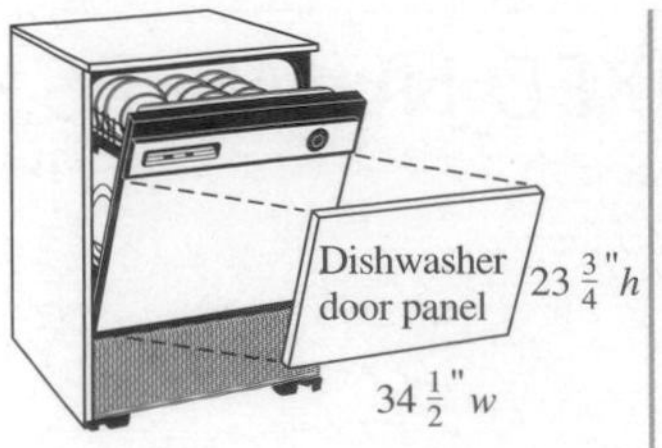

SOLUTION

$$34\frac{1}{2} = 34\frac{2}{4}$$
$$23\frac{3}{4} = 23\frac{3}{4}$$
$$34\frac{1}{2} = 34\frac{2}{4}$$
$$+\ 23\frac{3}{4} = 23\frac{3}{4}$$

$$114\frac{10}{4} = 114 + \frac{10}{4} = 114 + 2\frac{2}{4} = 116\frac{2}{4} = 116\frac{1}{2} \text{ inches}$$ length of gasket needed

QUICK TIP When adding mixed numbers, first add the fraction parts. Then add the whole-number parts. Finally, combine the two answers.

QUICK CHECK 2

The four sides of a vegetable garden are $15\frac{1}{2}$ feet, $18\frac{3}{4}$ feet, $24\frac{1}{4}$ feet, and $30\frac{1}{2}$ feet. How many feet of fencing are needed to go around the garden?

OBJECTIVE 3 Subtract mixed numbers. To subtract two mixed numbers, change the mixed numbers, if necessary, so that the fraction parts have a common denominator. Then subtract the fraction parts and the whole-number parts separately. For example, subtract $3\frac{1}{12}$ from $8\frac{5}{8}$ by first finding that the least common denominator is 24. Then rewrite the problem as shown.

$$8\frac{5}{8} - 3\frac{1}{12}$$

use 24 as a common denominator

$$8\frac{15}{24} - 3\frac{2}{24}$$

$$\begin{array}{r} 8\frac{15}{24} \\ -\ 3\frac{2}{24} \\ \hline 5\frac{13}{24} \end{array}$$

Now subtract the fraction parts and subtract the whole-number parts.

Subtract fractions.

Subtract whole numbers.

OBJECTIVE 4 Subtract with borrowing. The following example shows how to subtract when borrowing is needed.

EXAMPLE 3

Subtracting with Borrowing

(a) Subtract $6\frac{3}{4}$ from $10\frac{1}{8}$. **(b)** Subtract $15\frac{7}{12}$ from 41.

SOLUTION

Start by rewriting each problem with a common denominator.

(a)

$$\begin{array}{r} 10\frac{1}{8} = 10\frac{1}{8} \\ -\ \ 6\frac{3}{4} = \ \ 6\frac{6}{8} \\ \hline \end{array}$$

Subtracting $\frac{6}{8}$ from $\frac{1}{8}$ requires borrowing from the whole number 10.

$$10\frac{1}{8} = 9 + 1 + \frac{1}{8}$$
$$= 9 + \frac{8}{8} + \frac{1}{8} = 9\frac{9}{8} \quad 1 = \frac{8}{8}$$

Rewrite the problem as shown.
Check by adding $3\frac{3}{8}$ and $6\frac{3}{4}$.
The answer should be $10\frac{1}{8}$.

$$\begin{array}{r} 10\frac{1}{8} = 9\frac{9}{8} \\ -\ \ 6\frac{6}{8} = 6\frac{6}{8} \\ \hline 3\frac{3}{8} \end{array}$$

(b)

$$\begin{array}{r} 41 \\ -\ 15\frac{7}{12} \\ \hline \end{array}$$

To subtract the fraction $\frac{7}{12}$ requires borrowing 1 whole unit from 41.

$$41 = 40 + 1 = 40 + \frac{12}{12} = 40\frac{12}{12} \quad 1 = \frac{12}{12}$$

Rewrite the problem as shown.
Check by adding $25\frac{5}{12}$ and $15\frac{7}{12}$.
The answer should be 41.

$$\begin{array}{r} 41 \ \ = 40\frac{12}{12} \\ -\ 15\frac{7}{12} = 15\frac{7}{12} \\ \hline 25\frac{5}{12} \end{array}$$

The calculator solution to part (a) uses the fraction key.

10 [a b/c] 1 [a b/c] 8 [−] 6 [a b/c] 3 [a b/c] 4 [=] $3\frac{3}{8}$

QUICK CHECK 3

Subtract **(a)** $5\frac{2}{3}$ from $12\frac{3}{8}$ and **(b)** $17\frac{5}{9}$ from 73.

Quick Check Answers

2. $87\frac{8}{4} = 89$ feet

3. (a) $6\frac{17}{24}$ **(b)** $55\frac{4}{9}$

2.3 EXERCISES

FOR EXTRA HELP

MyMathLab

MathXL PRACTICE

WATCH

DOWNLOAD

READ

REVIEW

The QUICK START *exercises in each section contain solutions to help you get started.*

Add. Write each answer in lowest terms. (See Examples 1 and 2.)

QUICK START

1. $82\frac{3}{5} + 15\frac{1}{5}$ $82\frac{3}{5} + 15\frac{1}{5} = 97\frac{4}{5}$

2. $25\frac{2}{7} + 14\frac{3}{7}$ $25\frac{2}{7} + 14\frac{3}{7} = 39\frac{5}{7}$

3. $41\frac{1}{2} + 39\frac{1}{4}$

4. $28\frac{1}{4} + 23\frac{3}{5} + 19\frac{9}{10}$

5. $46\frac{3}{4} + 12\frac{5}{8} + 37\frac{4}{5}$

6. $26\frac{5}{8} + 17\frac{3}{14} + 32\frac{2}{7}$

7. $32\frac{3}{4} + 6\frac{1}{3} + 14\frac{5}{8}$

8. $16\frac{7}{10} + 26\frac{1}{5} + 8\frac{3}{8}$

9. $46\frac{5}{8} + 21\frac{1}{6} + 38\frac{1}{10}$

Subtract. Write each answer in lowest terms. (See Example 3.)

QUICK START

10. $16\frac{3}{4} - 12\frac{3}{8}$ $16\frac{6}{8} - 12\frac{3}{8} = 4\frac{3}{8}$

11. $25\frac{13}{24} - 18\frac{5}{12}$ $25\frac{13}{24} - 18\frac{10}{24} = 7\frac{3}{24} = 7\frac{1}{8}$

12. $9\frac{7}{8} - 6\frac{5}{12}$

13. $374 - 211\frac{5}{6}$

14. $19 - 12\frac{3}{4}$

15. $71\frac{3}{8} - 62\frac{1}{3}$

16. $6\frac{1}{3} - 2\frac{5}{12}$

17. $72\frac{3}{10} - 25\frac{8}{15}$

18. $23\frac{1}{2} - 18\frac{3}{4}$

19. $5\frac{1}{10} - 4\frac{2}{5}$

20. $15\frac{3}{18} - 12\frac{8}{9}$

21. In your own words, explain the steps you would take to add two large mixed numbers. (See Objective 1.)

22. When subtracting mixed numbers, explain when you need to borrow. Explain how to borrow using an example. (See Objective 4.)

Solve the following application problems.

QUICK START

C **23.** WINDOW INSTALLATION A contractor who installs windows for The Home Depot must attach a lead strip around all four sides of a custom-made stained glass window. If the window measures $34\frac{1}{2}$ by $23\frac{3}{4}$ inches, find the length of lead stripping needed.

$34\frac{1}{2} + 23\frac{3}{4} + 34\frac{1}{2} + 23\frac{3}{4} =$
$34\frac{2}{4} + 23\frac{3}{4} + 34\frac{2}{4} + 23\frac{3}{4} = 114\frac{10}{4} = 116\frac{1}{2}$ inches

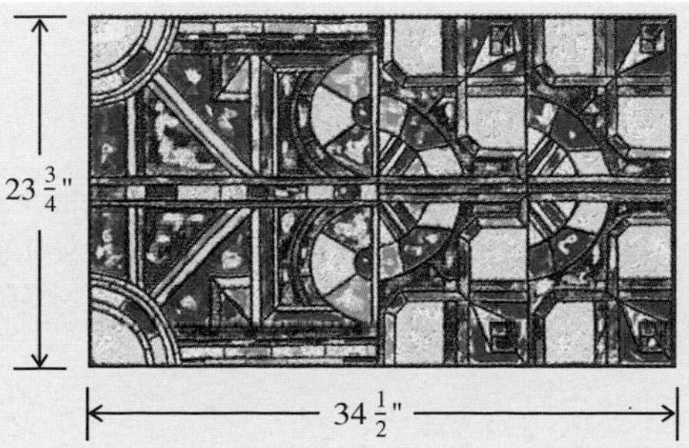

23. $116\frac{1}{2}$ inches

C indicates an exercise that is related to the Case in Point feature.

24. MEASURING BRASS TRIM To complete a custom order, Kara Oaks of The Home Depot must find the number of inches of brass trim needed to go around the four sides of the lamp base plate shown. Find the length of brass trim needed.

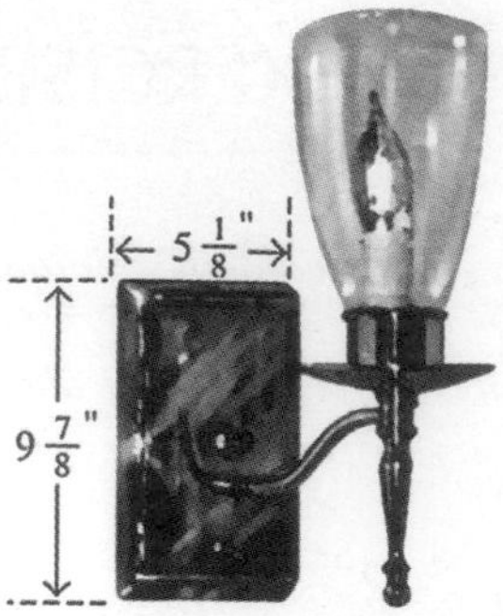

24. ______________

25. SECURITY FENCING The exercise yard at the correction center has four sides and is enclosed with $527\frac{1}{24}$ feet of security fencing around it. If three sides of the yard measure $107\frac{2}{3}$ feet, $150\frac{3}{4}$ feet, and $138\frac{5}{8}$ feet, find the length of the fourth side.

25. ______________

26. PARKING LOT FENCING Three sides of a parking lot are $108\frac{1}{4}$ feet, $162\frac{3}{8}$ feet, and $143\frac{1}{2}$ feet. If the distance around the lot is $518\frac{3}{4}$ feet, find the length of the fourth side.

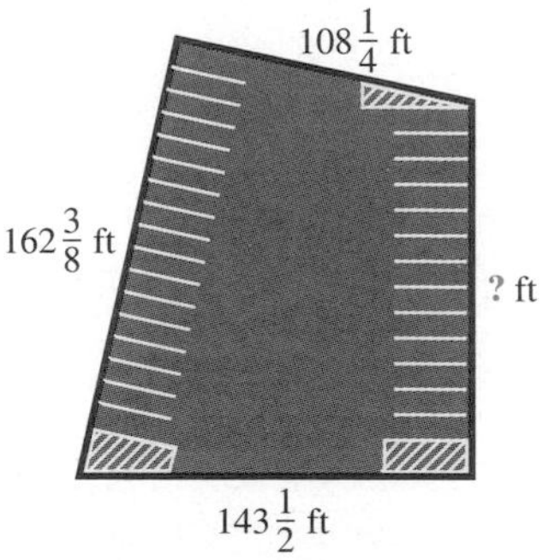

26. ______________

27. DELIVERING CONCRETE Chuck Stone has $8\frac{7}{8}$ cubic yards of concrete in a truck. If he unloads $2\frac{1}{2}$ cubic yards at the first stop, 3 cubic yards at the second stop, and $1\frac{3}{4}$ cubic yards at the third stop, how much concrete remains in the truck?

27. ______________

28. TAILORED CLOTHING Marv Levenson bought 15 yards of Italian silk fabric. He made two tops with $3\frac{3}{4}$ yards of the material, a suit for his wife with $4\frac{1}{8}$ yards, and a jacket with $3\frac{7}{8}$ yards. Find the number of yards of material remaining.

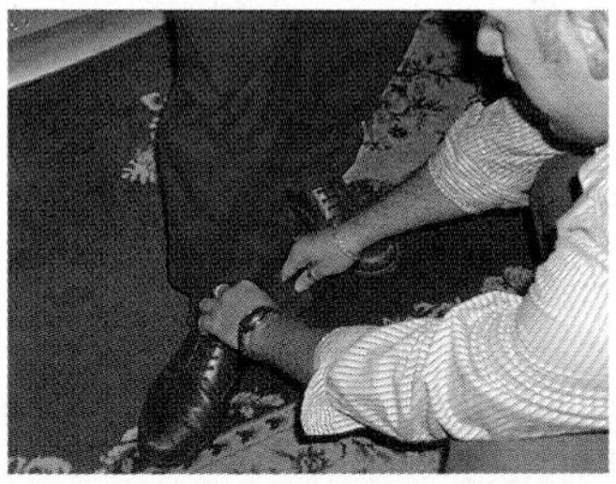

28. ______________

29. PART-TIME WORK Loren Kabakov, a college student, works part time at the Cyber Coffeehouse. She worked $3\frac{3}{8}$ hours on Monday, $5\frac{1}{2}$ hours on Tuesday, $4\frac{3}{4}$ hours on Wednesday, $3\frac{1}{4}$ hours on Thursday, and 6 hours on Friday. How many hours did she work altogether?

29. ______________

30. TRAILER LOAD A truck trailer is to be loaded with plasma televisions weighing $2\frac{5}{8}$ tons, DVD players weighing $6\frac{1}{2}$ tons, personal computers weighing $1\frac{5}{6}$ tons, and computer monitors weighing $3\frac{1}{4}$ tons. If the truck weighs $7\frac{3}{8}$ tons empty find the total weight after it has been loaded.

30. ______________

2.4 MULTIPLICATION AND DIVISION OF FRACTIONS

OBJECTIVES

1. Multiply proper fractions.
2. Use cancellation.
3. Multiply mixed numbers.
4. Divide fractions.
5. Divide mixed numbers.
6. Multiply or divide by whole numbers.

CASE in POINT Most of the cabinets sold by The Home Depot are standard size units and modules that can be combined to satisfy varied applications and room sizes. However, all too often, Kara Oaks finds that various components and trim pieces must be custom sized. In order to custom size items, she must multiply and divide fractions.

OBJECTIVE 1 Multiply proper fractions. To multiply two fractions, first multiply the numerators to form a new numerator and then multiply the denominators to form a new denominator. Write the answer in lowest terms if necessary. For example, multiply $\frac{2}{3}$ and $\frac{5}{8}$ by first multiplying the numerators and then the denominators.

Multiply numerators.

$$\frac{2}{3} \times \frac{5}{8} = \frac{2 \times 5}{3 \times 8} = \frac{10}{24} = \frac{5}{12} \quad \text{in lowest terms}$$

Multiply denominators.

OBJECTIVE 2 Use cancellation. This problem can be simplified by **cancellation**, a modification of the method of writing fractions in lowest terms. For example, find the product of $\frac{2}{3}$ and $\frac{5}{8}$ by cancelling as follows.

$$\frac{\overset{1}{\cancel{2}}}{3} \times \frac{5}{\underset{4}{\cancel{8}}} = \frac{1 \times 5}{3 \times 4} = \frac{5}{12}$$

Divide 2 into both 2 and 8. Then multiply the numerators and, finally, multiply the denominators.

EXAMPLE 1

Multiplying Common Fractions

Multiply.

(a) $\frac{8}{15} \times \frac{5}{12}$ **(b)** $\frac{35}{12} \times \frac{32}{25}$

SOLUTION

Use cancellation in both of these problems.

(a) $\frac{\overset{2}{\cancel{8}}}{\underset{3}{\cancel{15}}} \times \frac{\overset{1}{\cancel{5}}}{\underset{3}{\cancel{12}}} = \frac{2 \times 1}{3 \times 3} = \frac{2}{9}$

Divide 4 into both 8 and 12.
Divide 5 into both 5 and 15.

(b) $\frac{\overset{7}{\cancel{35}}}{\underset{3}{\cancel{12}}} \times \frac{\overset{8}{\cancel{32}}}{\underset{5}{\cancel{25}}} = \frac{7 \times 8}{3 \times 5} = \frac{56}{15} = 3\frac{11}{15}$

Divide 4 into both 12 and 32.
Divide 5 into both 35 and 25.

QUICK TIP When cancelling, be certain that the numerator and the denominator are both divided by the same number.

QUICK CHECK 1

Multiply using cancellation.

(a) $\frac{7}{8} \times \frac{4}{21}$ **(b)** $\frac{36}{15} \times \frac{45}{24}$

Quick Check Answers

1. (a) $\frac{1}{6}$ **(b)** $\frac{9}{2} = 4\frac{1}{2}$

QUICK TIP Mixed numbers must always be changed to *improper fractions* before multiplying. When multiplying by mixed numbers, do not multiply whole numbers by whole numbers and fractions by fractions.

OBJECTIVE 3 Multiply mixed numbers. To multiply mixed numbers, change the mixed numbers to improper fractions, use cancellation, and then multiply them. For example, multiply $6\frac{1}{4}$ and $2\frac{2}{3}$ as follows.

$$6\frac{1}{4} \times 2\frac{2}{3} = \underbrace{\frac{25}{4} \times \frac{8}{3}}_{\text{Change to improper fractions.}} = \frac{25}{\underset{1}{\cancel{4}}} \times \frac{\overset{2}{\cancel{8}}}{3} = \frac{\mathbf{25 \times 2}}{\mathbf{1 \times 3}} = \frac{50}{3} = 16\frac{2}{3}$$

EXAMPLE 2 Multiplying Mixed Numbers

Multiply.

(a) $3\frac{3}{4} \times 8\frac{2}{3}$ **(b)** $1\frac{3}{5} \times 3\frac{1}{3} \times 1\frac{3}{4}$

SOLUTION

(a) $\frac{\overset{5}{\cancel{15}}}{\underset{2}{\cancel{4}}} \times \frac{\overset{13}{\cancel{26}}}{\underset{1}{\cancel{3}}} = \frac{\mathbf{5 \times 13}}{\mathbf{2 \times 1}} = \frac{65}{2} = 32\frac{1}{2}$

(b) $\frac{\overset{2}{\cancel{8}}}{\underset{1}{\cancel{5}}} \times \frac{\overset{2}{\cancel{10}}}{3} \times \frac{7}{\underset{1}{\cancel{4}}} = \frac{\mathbf{2 \times 2 \times 7}}{\mathbf{1 \times 3 \times 1}} = \frac{28}{3} = 9\frac{1}{3}$

The calculator solution to part (b) uses the fraction key.

1 [a b/c] 3 [a b/c] 5 [×] 3 [a b/c] 1 [a b/c] 3 [×] 1 [a b/c] 3 [a b/c] 4 [=] $9\frac{1}{3}$

QUICK CHECK 2

Multiply.

(a) $3\frac{3}{5} \times 1\frac{2}{3}$ **(b)** $2\frac{2}{3} \times 1\frac{5}{9} \times 3\frac{3}{4}$

The recipe shown next is easy to follow using proper measuring cups and spoons. Sometimes you may want to double or triple a recipe, or perhaps, cooking for a small group, you need to cut the recipe in half. To double the recipe, multiply each ingredient by 2. To triple the recipe, multiply by 3. To halve the recipe you'll need to divide by 2.

Chocolate/Oat-Chip Cookies

1 cup (2 sticks) margarine or butter, softened
$1\frac{1}{4}$ cups firmly packed brown sugar
$\frac{1}{2}$ cup granulated sugar
2 eggs
2 tablespoons milk
2 teaspoons vanilla
$1\frac{3}{4}$ cups all-purpose flour
1 teaspoon baking soda
$\frac{1}{2}$ teaspoon salt (optional)
$2\frac{1}{2}$ cups uncooked oats
One 12-ounce package (2 cups) semi-sweet chocolate morsels
1 cup coarsely chopped nuts (optional)

Heat oven to 375°F. **Beat** margarine and sugars until creamy.
Add eggs, milk, and vanilla; beat well.
Add combined flour, baking soda, and salt; mix well. **Stir** in oats, chocolate morsels, and nuts; mix well.
Drop by rounded measuring tablespoonfuls onto ungreased cookie sheet.
Bake 9 to 10 minutes for a chewy cookie or 12 to 13 minutes for a crisp cookie.
Cool 1 minute on cookie sheet; remove to wire rack. Cool completely.
MAKES ABOUT 5 DOZEN

Quick Check Answers

2. (a) 6 **(b)** $15\frac{5}{9}$

EXAMPLE 3

Multiplying a Mixed Number by a Whole Number

(a) Find the amount of uncooked oats needed if the preceding recipe for chocolate/oat-chip cookies is doubled (multiplied by 2).

(b) How many cups of all-purpose flour are needed when the recipe is tripled (multiplied by 3)?

SOLUTION

(a) $2\frac{1}{2} \times 2 = \frac{5}{\underset{1}{\cancel{2}}} \times \frac{\overset{1}{\cancel{2}}}{1} = \frac{5 \times 1}{1 \times 1} = \frac{5}{1} = 5$ cups

(b) $1\frac{3}{4} \times 3 = \frac{7}{4} \times \frac{3}{1} = \frac{7 \times 3}{4} = \frac{21}{4} = 5\frac{1}{4}$ cups

QUICK CHECK 3

(a) Find the amount of brown sugar needed if the preceding recipe is tripled.

(b) How many teaspoons of salt are needed if the recipe is multiplied 15 times?

OBJECTIVE 4 Divide fractions. To divide two fractions, invert the second fraction (divisor) and then multiply the first fraction by the inverted second fraction. (Invert a fraction by exchanging the numerator and the denominator.) For example, divide $\frac{3}{8}$ by $\frac{7}{12}$ by *inverting* the second fraction and then *multiplying*.

QUICK TIP Only the second fraction (divisor) is inverted when dividing by a fraction. Cancellation is done *only after inverting*.

invert second fraction

$$\frac{3}{8} \div \frac{7}{12} = \frac{3}{8} \times \frac{12}{7} = \frac{3}{\underset{2}{\cancel{8}}} \times \frac{\overset{3}{\cancel{12}}}{7} = \frac{3 \times 3}{2 \times 7} = \frac{9}{14}$$

multiply

EXAMPLE 4

Dividing Common Fractions

Divide.

(a) $\frac{7}{8} \div \frac{1}{4}$ **(b)** $\frac{25}{36} \div \frac{15}{18}$

SOLUTION

Invert the second fraction and then multiply.

(a) $\frac{7}{8} \div \frac{1}{4} = \frac{7}{\underset{2}{\cancel{8}}} \times \frac{\overset{1}{\cancel{4}}}{1} = \frac{7 \times 1}{2 \times 1} = \frac{7}{2} = 3\frac{1}{2}$ **(b)** $\frac{25}{36} \div \frac{15}{18} = \frac{\overset{5}{\cancel{25}}}{\underset{2}{\cancel{36}}} \times \frac{\overset{1}{\cancel{18}}}{\underset{3}{\cancel{15}}} = \frac{5 \times 1}{2 \times 3} = \frac{5}{6}$

QUICK CHECK 4

Divide.

(a) $\frac{2}{3} \div \frac{1}{2}$ **(b)** $\frac{12}{21} \div \frac{18}{24}$

OBJECTIVE 5 Divide mixed numbers. To divide mixed numbers, first change all mixed numbers to improper fractions, then invert the second fraction, use cancellation, and multiply.

invert

$$3\frac{5}{9} \div 2\frac{2}{5} = \frac{32}{9} \div \frac{12}{5} = \frac{\overset{8}{\cancel{32}}}{9} \times \frac{5}{\underset{3}{\cancel{12}}} = \frac{8 \times 5}{9 \times 3} = \frac{40}{27} = 1\frac{13}{27}$$

Quick Check Answers

3. (a) $3\frac{3}{4}$ cups
(b) $7\frac{1}{2}$ teaspoons

4. (a) $\frac{4}{3} = 1\frac{1}{3}$ **(b)** $\frac{16}{21}$

OBJECTIVE 6 Multiply or divide by whole numbers. To multiply or divide a fraction by a whole number, write the whole number as a fraction over 1.

Multiply: $3\frac{3}{4} \times 16 = 3\frac{3}{4} \times \frac{16}{1} = \frac{15}{4} \times \frac{16}{1} = \frac{15}{\cancel{4}_{1}} \times \frac{\cancel{16}^{4}}{1} = 15 \times 4 = 60$

(whole number over 1)

Divide: $2\frac{2}{5} \div 3 = \frac{12}{5} \div \frac{3}{1} = \frac{\cancel{12}^{4}}{5} \times \frac{1}{\cancel{3}_{1}} = \frac{4 \times 1}{5 \times 1} = \frac{4}{5}$

Base-End Panel

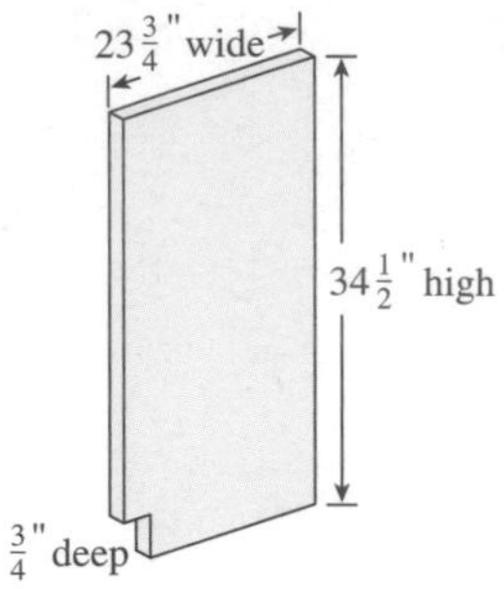

Mills Pride manufactures cabinets for kitchens and baths. The specifications for base-end panels are shown in the diagram. The lumber used is $\frac{3}{4}$ inch deep and is cut down from 24 inches to a $23\frac{3}{4}$-inch width. The panel is then cut to a height of $34\frac{1}{2}$ inches. The materials used in the manufacture of cabinets, solid oak in this case, are very expensive. Every precaution is taken to ensure a minimum of wasted material.

EXAMPLE 5

Multiplying a Whole Number by a Mixed Number

A cabinet maker will need 80 base-end panels to complete a job. If each panel is $34\frac{1}{2}$ inches long, how many inches of oak material are needed?

SOLUTION

Multiply the number of panels needed by the length of each panel: $34\frac{1}{2}$, or $\frac{69}{2}$.

$$80 \times \frac{69}{2} = \frac{\cancel{80}^{40}}{1} \times \frac{69}{\cancel{2}_{1}} = \frac{\mathbf{40 \times 69}}{\mathbf{1 \times 1}} = \frac{2760}{1} = 2760 \text{ inches}$$

The length of material needed by the cabinet maker is 2760 inches.

QUICK TIP It is often best to change a fraction or mixed number to a decimal number. This procedure is discussed in **Section 2.5**.

QUICK CHECK 5

A plumber needs 68 pieces of 1-inch-diameter copper tubing. If each piece of tubing must be $28\frac{1}{2}$ inches long, how many total inches of tubing are needed?

EXAMPLE 6

Dividing a Whole Number by a Mixed Number

To complete a custom-designed cabinet, oak trim pieces must be cut exactly $2\frac{1}{4}$ inches long so that they can be used as dividers in a spice rack. Find the number of pieces that can be cut from a piece of oak that is 54 inches in length.

SOLUTION

To divide the length of the piece of oak by $2\frac{1}{4}$, or $\frac{9}{4}$, invert and then multiply.

$$54 \div 2\frac{1}{4} = 54 \div \frac{9}{4} = \frac{\cancel{54}^{6}}{1} \times \frac{4}{\cancel{9}_{1}} = \frac{\mathbf{6 \times 4}}{\mathbf{1 \times 1}} = \frac{24}{1} = 24$$

The number of trim pieces that can be cut from the oak stock is 24.

QUICK CHECK 6

A welder needs angle iron pieces that are $3\frac{1}{3}$ inches long. Find the number of pieces that can be cut from a piece of angle iron that is 70 inches in length.

Quick Check Answers

5. 1938 inches
6. 21 pieces

2.4 EXERCISES

FOR EXTRA HELP

MyMathLab

MathXL PRACTICE

WATCH

DOWNLOAD

READ

REVIEW

The QUICK START *exercises in each section contain solutions to help you get started.*

Multiply. Write each answer in lowest terms. (See Examples 1–3.)

QUICK START

1. $\frac{3}{4} \times \frac{2}{5} = \frac{3}{10}$

$\frac{3}{\cancel{4}_2} \times \frac{\cancel{2}^1}{5} = \frac{3}{10}$

2. $\frac{2}{3} \times \frac{5}{8} = \frac{5}{12}$

$\frac{\cancel{2}^1}{3} \times \frac{5}{\cancel{8}_4} = \frac{5}{12}$

3. $\frac{9}{10} \times \frac{11}{16} =$ ____

4. $\frac{2}{3} \times \frac{3}{8} =$ ____

5. $\frac{9}{22} \times \frac{11}{16} =$ ____

6. $\frac{5}{12} \times \frac{7}{10} =$ ____

7. $1\frac{1}{4} \times 3\frac{1}{2} =$ ____

8. $1\frac{2}{3} \times 2\frac{7}{10} =$ ____

9. $3\frac{1}{9} \times 3 =$ ____

10. $\frac{3}{4} \times \frac{8}{9} \times 2\frac{1}{2} =$ ____

11. $\frac{1}{4} \times 6\frac{2}{3} \times \frac{1}{5} =$ ____

12. $\frac{2}{3} \times \frac{9}{8} \times 3\frac{1}{4} =$ ____

13. $\frac{5}{9} \times 2\frac{1}{4} \times 3\frac{2}{3} =$ ____

14. $3 \times 1\frac{1}{2} \times 2\frac{2}{3} =$ ____

15. $5\frac{3}{5} \times 1\frac{5}{9} \times \frac{10}{49} =$ ____

Divide. Write each answer in lowest terms. (See Example 4.)

QUICK START

16. $\frac{1}{4} \div \frac{3}{4} = \frac{1}{3}$

$\frac{1}{\cancel{4}_1} \times \frac{\cancel{4}^1}{3} = \frac{1}{3}$

17. $\frac{3}{8} \div \frac{5}{8} = \frac{3}{5}$

$\frac{3}{\cancel{8}_1} \times \frac{\cancel{8}^1}{5} = \frac{3}{5}$

18. $\frac{13}{20} \div \frac{26}{30} =$ ____

19. $\frac{9}{10} \div \frac{3}{5} =$ ____

20. $\frac{7}{8} \div \frac{3}{4} =$ ____

21. $2\frac{1}{2} \div 3\frac{3}{4} =$ ____

22. $1\frac{1}{4} \div 4\frac{1}{6} =$ ____

23. $5 \div 1\frac{7}{8} =$ ____

24. $3 \div 1\frac{1}{4} =$ ____

C indicates an exercise that is related to the Case in Point feature.

25. $\frac{3}{8} \div 2\frac{1}{2} =$ ____

26. $1\frac{7}{8} \div 6\frac{1}{4} =$ ____

27. $2\frac{5}{8} \div \frac{5}{16} =$ ____

28. $5\frac{2}{3} \div 6 =$ ____

29. In your own words, explain the rule for multiplying fractions. Make up an example problem of your own showing how this works.

30. A useful shortcut when multiplying fractions involves dividing a numerator and a denominator before multiplying. This is often called cancellation. Describe how this works and give an example of cancellation. (See Objective 2.)

Find the time-and-a-half pay rate for each of the following regular pay rates. (See Example 5.)

QUICK START

31. \$8 **\$12**
$\$8 \times 1\frac{1}{2} = \$12$

32. \$17 ____________

33. \$12.50 ____________
(*Hint:* $\$12.50 = \$12\frac{1}{2}$)

34. \$9.50 ____________

35. Your classmate is confused about how to divide by a fraction. Write a short explanation telling how this should be done.

36. If you multiply two proper fractions, the answer is smaller than the fractions multiplied. When you divide by a proper fraction, is the answer smaller than the numbers in the problem? Show some examples to support your answer.

Solve the following application problems.

37. ELECTRICITY RATES The utility company says that the cost of operating a hair dryer is $\frac{1}{5}$¢ per minute. Find the cost of operating the hair dryer for 30 minutes. (***Source:*** Pacific Gas and Electric Company.)

37. ____________

38. ELECTRICITY RATES The cost of electricity for brewing coffee is $\frac{2}{5}$¢ per minute. What is the cost of brewing coffee for 90 minutes? (***Source:*** Pacific Gas and Electric Company.)

38. ____________

39. PRODUCING CRAFTS Matthew Genaway wants to make 16 holiday wreaths to sell at the craft fair. Each wreath needs $2\frac{1}{4}$ yards of ribbon. How many yards does he need?

39. ____________

40. EARNINGS CALCULATION Jack Horner worked $38\frac{1}{4}$ hours at \$10 per hour. How much money did he make?

40. ____________

41. FINISH CARPENTRY The Home Depot estimates that a certain design for a kitchen and bathroom needs $109\frac{1}{2}$ feet of cabinet trim. How many homes can be fitted with cabinet trim if there are 1314 feet of cabinet trim available?

41. ________________

42. COMMERCIAL FERTILIZER For 1 acre of a crop, $7\frac{1}{2}$ gallons of fertilizer must be applied. How many acres can be fertilized with 1200 gallons of fertilizer?

42. ________________

43. A manufacturer of floor jacks is ordering steel tubing to make the handles for this jack. How much steel tubing is needed to make 135 of these jacks? (The symbol for inch is ".) (*Source:* Harbor Freight Tools.)

43. ________________

44. A wheelbarrow manufacturer uses handles made of hardwood. Find the amount of wood that is needed to make 182 handles. The longest dimension shown is the handle length. (*Source:* Harbor Freight Tools.)

44. ________________

45. STEEL FABRICATION A fishing boat anchor requires $10\frac{3}{8}$ pounds of steel. Find the number of anchors that can be manufactured with 25,730 pounds of steel.

45. ________________

46. COMMERCIAL CARPETING The manager of the flooring department at The Home Depot determines that each apartment unit requires $62\frac{1}{2}$ square yards of carpet. Find the number of apartment units that can be carpeted with 6750 square yards of carpet.

46. ________________

47. FUEL CONSUMPTION A fishing boat uses $12\frac{3}{4}$ gallons of fuel on a full-day fishing trip and $7\frac{1}{8}$ gallons of fuel on a half-day trip. Find the total number of gallons of fuel used in 28 full-day trips and 16 half-day trips.

47. ____________

48. MAKING JEWELRY One necklace can be completed in $6\frac{1}{2}$ minutes, while a bracelet takes $3\frac{1}{8}$ minutes. Find the total time that it takes to complete 36 necklaces and 22 bracelets.

48. ____________

49. DISPENSING EYEDROPS How many $\frac{1}{8}$-ounce eyedrop dispensers can be filled with 11 ounces of eyedrops?

49. ____________

50. CONCRETE FOOTINGS Each building footing requires $\frac{5}{16}$ cubic yard of concrete. How many building footings can be constructed from 10 cubic yards of concrete?

50. ____________

51. FIREWOOD SALE Alison Romike has a small pickup truck that can carry $\frac{2}{3}$ cord of firewood. Find the number of trips needed to deliver 40 cords of wood.

51. ____________

52. WEATHER STRIPPING Bill Rhodes, an employee at The Home Depot, sells a 200-yard roll of weather stripping material. Find the number of pieces of weather stripping $\frac{5}{8}$ yard in length that may be cut from the roll.

52. ____________

2.5 CONVERTING DECIMALS TO FRACTIONS AND FRACTIONS TO DECIMALS

OBJECTIVES

1. Convert decimals to fractions.
2. Convert fractions to decimals.
3. Know common decimal equivalents.

OBJECTIVE 1 Convert decimals to fractions. A common method of converting a decimal to a fraction is by thinking of the decimal as being written in words, as in Chapter 1. For example, think of .47 as **"forty-seven hundredths."** Then write this in fraction form as

$$.47 = \frac{47}{100}$$

In the same way, .3, read as **"three tenths,"** is written in fraction form as

$$.3 = \frac{3}{10}$$

Also, .963, read **"nine hundred sixty-three thousandths,"** is written in fraction form as

$$.963 = \frac{963}{1000}$$

Another method of converting a decimal to a fraction is by first removing the decimal point. The remaining number is the numerator of the fraction. The denominator of the fraction is 1 followed by as many zeros as there were digits to the right of the decimal point in the original number.

EXAMPLE 1

Converting Decimals to Fractions

Convert the following decimals to fractions.

(a) .3 **(b)** .98 **(c)** .654

SOLUTION

(a) There is one digit following the decimal point in .3. Make a fraction with 3 as the numerator. For the denominator, use 10, which is 1 followed by one zero.

$$.3 = \frac{3}{10}$$

(10: 1 followed by 1 zero)

This fraction is in lowest terms.

(b) There are two digits following the decimal point in .98. Make a fraction with 98 as the numerator and 100 as the denominator.

$$.98 = \frac{98}{100} = \frac{49}{50} \text{ (lowest terms)}$$

(100: 1 followed by 2 zeros)

(c) There are three digits following the decimal point in .654.

$$.654 = \frac{654}{1000} = \frac{327}{500} \text{ (lowest terms)}$$

(1000: 1 followed by 3 zeros)

QUICK CHECK 1

Convert the following decimals to fractions. **(a)** .75 **(b)** .64 **(c)** .875

Quick Check Answers

1. (a) $\frac{3}{4}$ **(b)** $\frac{16}{25}$ **(c)** $\frac{7}{8}$

OBJECTIVE 2 Convert fractions to decimals. Convert a fraction to a decimal by dividing the numerator of the fraction by the denominator. Place a decimal point after the numerator and attach one zero at a time to the right of the decimal point as the division is performed. Keep going until the division produces a remainder of zero or until the desired degree of accuracy is reached.

EXAMPLE 2

Converting Fractions to Decimals

Convert the following fractions to decimals.

(a) $\frac{1}{8}$ **(b)** $\frac{2}{3}$

SOLUTION

(a) Convert $\frac{1}{8}$ to a decimal by dividing 1 by 8.

$$8\overline{)1}$$

Since 8 will not divide into 1, place a 0 to the *right* of the decimal point. Now 8 goes into 10 once, with a remainder of 2.

$$\begin{array}{r} .1 \\ 8\overline{)1.0} \\ \underline{8} \\ 2 \end{array}$$

Be sure to move the decimal point up.

Continue placing zeros to the *right* of the decimal point and continue dividing until the remainder is 0.

$$\begin{array}{r} .125 \\ 8\overline{)1.000} \\ \underline{8} \\ 20 \\ \underline{16} \\ 40 \\ \underline{40} \\ 0 \end{array}$$

Keep attaching zeros.

remainder of 0 Therefore, $\frac{1}{8} = .125$.

(b) Divide 2 by 3.

$$\begin{array}{r} 0.6666 \\ 3\overline{)2.0000} \\ \underline{1\,8} \\ 20 \\ \underline{18} \\ 20 \\ \underline{18} \\ 20 \\ \underline{18} \\ 2 \end{array}$$

Keep attaching zeros.

This division results in a repeating decimal and is often written as $.\overline{6}$, $.6\overline{6}$, or $.66\overline{6}$. Rounded to the nearest thousandth, $\frac{2}{3} = .667$.

The calculator solution to this example is

2 [÷] 3 [=] 0.666666667

QUICK CHECK 2

Convert the following fractions to decimals. **(a)** $\frac{4}{5}$ **(b)** $\frac{5}{8}$

Decimal Equivalents

$\frac{1}{16} = .0625$
$\frac{1}{10} = .1$
$\frac{1}{9} = .1111$ (rounded)
$\frac{1}{8} = .125$
$\frac{1}{7} = .1429$ (rounded)
$\frac{1}{6} = .1667$ (rounded)
$\frac{3}{16} = .1875$
$\frac{1}{5} = .2$
$\frac{1}{4} = .25$
$\frac{3}{10} = .3$
$\frac{5}{16} = .3125$
$\frac{1}{3} = .3333$ (rounded)
$\frac{3}{8} = .375$
$\frac{2}{5} = .4$
$\frac{7}{16} = .4375$
$\frac{1}{2} = .5$
$\frac{9}{16} = .5625$
$\frac{3}{5} = .6$
$\frac{5}{8} = .625$
$\frac{2}{3} = .6667$ (rounded)
$\frac{11}{16} = .6875$
$\frac{7}{10} = .7$
$\frac{3}{4} = .75$
$\frac{4}{5} = .8$
$\frac{13}{16} = .8125$
$\frac{5}{6} = .8333$ (rounded)
$\frac{7}{8} = .875$
$\frac{9}{10} = .9$
$\frac{15}{16} = .9375$

OBJECTIVE 3 Know common decimal equivalents. Some of the more common **decimal equivalents** of fractions are listed in the margin. These decimals appear from least to greatest value and are rounded to the nearest ten-thousandth. Sometimes decimals must be carried out further to give greater accuracy, while at other times they are not carried out as far and are rounded sooner.

Quick Check Answers

2. (a) .8 **(b)** .625

2.5 EXERCISES

FOR EXTRA HELP

MyMathLab

MathXL PRACTICE

WATCH

DOWNLOAD

READ

REVIEW

The QUICK START *exercises in each section contain solutions to help you get started.*

Convert the following decimals to fractions, and write each in lowest terms. (See Example 1.)

QUICK START

1. .75 = $\frac{3}{4}$

$\frac{75}{100} = \frac{3}{4}$

2. .55 = $\frac{11}{20}$

$\frac{55}{100} = \frac{11}{20}$

3. .24 = ____

4. .64 = ____

5. .73 = ____

6. .33 = ____

7. .85 = ____

8. .68 = ____

9. .34 = ____

10. .288 = ____

11. .444 = ____

12. .125 = ____

13. .625 = ____

14. .875 = ____

15. .805 = ____

16. .791 = ____

17. .096 = ____

18. .012 = ____

19. .0375 = ____

20. .0875 = ____

21. .1875 = ____

22. .9845 = ____

23. .0016 = ____

24. .0085 = ____

25. A classmate of yours is confused about how to convert a decimal to a fraction. Write an explanation of this for your classmate, including changing the fraction to lowest terms. (See Objective 1.)

26. Explain how to convert a fraction to a decimal. Be sure to mention rounding in your explanation. (See Objective 2.)

Convert the following fractions to decimals. If a division does not come out evenly, round the answer to the nearest thousandth. (See Example 2.)

QUICK START

27. $\frac{1}{4}$ = .25

$$\begin{array}{r} .25 \\ 4\overline{)1.00} \\ 8 \\ \hline 20 \\ 20 \\ \hline 0 \end{array}$$

28. $\frac{7}{8}$ = ____

29. $\frac{3}{8}$ = ____

30. $\frac{5}{8} =$ ____________ **31.** $\frac{2}{3} =$ ____________ **32.** $\frac{5}{6} =$ ____________

33. $\frac{7}{9} =$ ____________ **34.** $\frac{1}{9} =$ ____________ **35.** $\frac{7}{11} =$ ____________

36. $\frac{8}{25} =$ ____________ **37.** $\frac{22}{25} =$ ____________ **38.** $\frac{14}{25} =$ ____________

39. $\frac{181}{205} =$ ____________ **40.** $\frac{1}{99} =$ ____________ **41.** $\frac{148}{149} =$ ____________

42. GAMBLING WITH HEALTH A hospital study of 1521 heart-attack patients found that 1 out of 8 quit taking the life-saving drugs prescribed to them. **(a)** What fraction stopped taking their medicine? **(b)** Convert this fraction to a decimal. **(c)** How many patients in the study quit taking their medicine? Round to the nearest whole number. (***Source:*** Associated Press.)

(a) ____________
(b) ____________
(c) ____________

43. BAD MEDICINE A study was made of 185 patients visiting their doctors. In two-thirds of these visits, doctors failed to mention a new drug's side effects or how long to take the drug. **(a)** Convert this fraction to a decimal. Round to the nearest thousandth. **(b)** How many patients in the study did not receive this information? Round to the nearest whole number. (***Source:*** Associated Press.)

(a) ____________
(b) ____________

CHAPTER 2 QUICK REVIEW

CHAPTER TERMS *Review the following terms to test your understanding of the chapter. For each term you do not know, refer to the page number found next to that term.*

cancellation **[p. 69]**
common denominator **[p. 57]**
decimal equivalent **[p. 78]**
denominator **[p. 50]**
fraction **[p. 50]**
improper fraction **[p. 50]**
inspection **[p. 58]**
least common denominator (LCD) **[p. 57]**
like fractions **[p. 57]**
lowest terms **[p. 52]**
method of prime numbers **[p. 58]**
mixed number **[p. 50]**
numerator **[p. 50]**
prime number **[p. 58]**
proper fraction **[p. 50]**
unlike fractions **[p. 57]**

CONCEPTS	EXAMPLES
2.1 Types of fractions *Proper*: Numerator smaller than denominator *Improper*: Numerator equal to or greater than denominator *Mixed*: Whole number and proper fraction	proper fractions $\frac{2}{3}, \frac{3}{4}, \frac{15}{16}, \frac{1}{8}$ improper fractions $\frac{17}{8}, \frac{19}{12}, \frac{11}{2}, \frac{5}{3}, \frac{7}{7}$ mixed numbers $2\frac{2}{3}, 3\frac{5}{8}, 9\frac{5}{6}$
2.1 Converting fractions *Mixed to improper*: Multiply denominator by whole number and add numerator. *Improper to mixed*: Divide numerator by denominator and place remainder over denominator.	$7\frac{2}{3} = \frac{23}{3} \rightarrow 3 \times 7 + 2$ $\frac{17}{5} = 3\frac{2}{5}$ $\begin{array}{r} 3 \\ 5\overline{)17} \\ \underline{15} \\ 2 \end{array}$
2.1 Writing fractions in lowest terms	$\frac{30}{42} = \frac{30 \div 6}{42 \div 6} = \frac{5}{7}$
2.2 Adding like fractions Add numerators and reduce to lowest terms.	$\frac{3}{4} + \frac{1}{4} + \frac{5}{4} = \frac{3+1+5}{4} = \frac{9}{4} = 2\frac{1}{4}$
2.2 Finding a least common denominator (LCD) *Inspection method*: Look to see if the LCD can be found. *Method of prime numbers*: Use prime numbers to find the LCD.	$\frac{1}{3} + \frac{1}{4} + \frac{1}{10}$ $\begin{array}{r} 1\ \ 1\ \ 1 \\ 5\overline{)1\ \ 1\ \ 5} \\ 3\overline{)3\ \ 1\ \ 5} \\ 2\overline{)3\ \ 2\ \ 5} \\ 2\overline{)3\ \ 4\ \ 10} \end{array}$ Multiply the prime numbers. $2 \times 2 \times 3 \times 5 = 60$ LCD
2.2 Adding unlike fractions 1. Find the LCD. 2. Rewrite fractions with the LCD. 3. Add numerators, placing answers over the LCD, and reduce to lowest terms.	$\frac{1}{3} + \frac{1}{4} + \frac{1}{10}$ LCD = 60 $\frac{1}{3} = \frac{20}{60}, \frac{1}{4} = \frac{15}{60}, \frac{1}{10} = \frac{6}{60}$ $\frac{20 + 15 + 6}{60} = \frac{41}{60}$
2.2 Subtracting fractions 1. Find the LCD. 2. Subtract numerator of subtrahend, borrowing if necessary. 3. Write the difference over the LCD and reduce to lowest terms.	$\frac{5}{8} - \frac{1}{3} = \frac{15}{24} - \frac{8}{24} = \frac{7}{24}$

CONCEPTS	EXAMPLES
2.3 Adding mixed numbers 1. Find the LCD, then add fractions. 2. Add whole numbers. 3. Combine the sums of whole numbers and fractions. Write the answer in simplest terms.	$9\frac{2}{3} = 9\frac{8}{12}$ $+\,6\frac{3}{4} = 6\frac{9}{12}$ $15\frac{17}{12} = 16\frac{5}{12}$
2.3 Subtracting mixed numbers 1. Find the LCD and subtract fractions, borrowing if necessary. 2. Subtract whole numbers. 3. Combine the differences of whole numbers and fractions.	$8\frac{5}{8} = 8\frac{15}{24}$ $-\,3\frac{1}{12} = 3\frac{2}{24}$ $5\frac{13}{24}$
2.4 Multiplying proper fractions 1. Multiply numerators and multiply denominators. 2. Reduce the answer to lowest terms if cancelling was not done.	$\frac{6}{11} \times \frac{7}{8} = \frac{\overset{3}{\cancel{6}}}{11} \times \frac{7}{\underset{4}{\cancel{8}}} = \frac{21}{44}$
2.4 Multiplying mixed numbers 1. Change mixed numbers to improper fractions. 2. Cancel if possible. 3. Multiply as proper fractions.	$1\frac{3}{5} \times 3\frac{1}{3} = \frac{8}{\underset{1}{\cancel{5}}} \times \frac{\overset{2}{\cancel{10}}}{3} = \frac{8}{1} \times \frac{2}{3}$ $= \frac{16}{3} = 5\frac{1}{3}$ Always reduce to lowest terms.
2.4 Dividing proper fractions Invert the divisor, multiply as proper fractions, and reduce the answer to lowest terms.	$\frac{25}{36} \div \frac{15}{18} = \frac{\overset{5}{\cancel{25}}}{\underset{2}{\cancel{36}}} \times \frac{\overset{1}{\cancel{18}}}{\underset{3}{\cancel{15}}} = \frac{5}{2} \times \frac{1}{3} = \frac{5}{6}$
2.4 Dividing mixed numbers Change mixed numbers to improper fractions. Invert the divisor, cancel if possible, multiply numerators, and multiply denominators.	$3\frac{5}{9} \div 2\frac{2}{5} = \frac{32}{9} \div \frac{12}{5} = \frac{\overset{8}{\cancel{32}}}{9} \times \frac{5}{\underset{3}{\cancel{12}}}$ $= \frac{40}{27} = 1\frac{13}{27}$
2.5 Converting decimals to fractions Think of the decimal as being written in words and write in fraction form. Reduce to lowest terms.	Convert .47 to a fraction. Think of .47 as "forty-seven hundredths." Then write as $\frac{47}{100}$.
2.5 Converting fractions to decimals Divide the numerator by the denominator. Round if necessary.	Convert $\frac{1}{8}$ to a decimal. $\begin{array}{r} .125 \\ 8\overline{)1.000} \\ \underline{8} \\ 20 \\ \underline{16} \\ 40 \\ \underline{40} \\ 0 \end{array}$ $\quad \frac{1}{8} = .125$

CHAPTER 2 SUMMARY EXERCISE

Using Fractions with Statistics

It is often said that a picture is worth a thousand words. Visual presentation of data is often used in business in the form of graphs. A commonly used graph that shows the relationships of various data is the circle graph, also called a pie chart. The circle, which contains 360 degrees, is divided into slices, or fractional parts. The size of each slice helps to show the relationship of the various slices to each other and to the whole.

The annual operating expenses for Woodline Moldings and Trim are shown below. Use this information to answer the questions that follow.

Woodline Moldings and Trim	**(Operating Expenses)**		
Expense Item	**Monthly Amount**	**Annual Amount**	**Fraction of Total Expenses**
Salaries	\$5000	______	______
Rent	\$3000	______	______
Utilities	\$1000	______	______
Insurance	\$ 750	______	______
Advertising	\$ 750	______	______
Miscellaneous	\$1500	______	______
Total Expenses		______	

(a) Find the total annual operating expenses for Woodline Moldings and Trim. **(a)** ______________

(b) What fraction should be used to represent each expense item as part of the total expenses? **(b)** ______________

(c) Draw a circle (pie) graph using the fractions you found in part (b) to represent each expense item. Approximate the fractional part of the circle needed for each expense item. Label each segment of the circle graph with the fraction and the expense item.

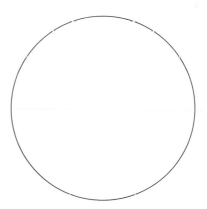

(d) Since there are 360 degrees in a circle, find the number of degrees that would be used to represent each expense item in the circle graph. **(d)** ______________

(e) In **Chapter 15, Statistics**, you will learn more about using graphs in business. Add all of the answers found in part (d). What is the total number of degrees? Why is this the answer? **(e)** ______________

CHAPTER 2 TEST

To help you review, the numbers in brackets show the section in which the topic was discussed.

Write the following fractions in lowest terms. **[2.1]**

1. $\frac{25}{30} =$ ___ **2.** $\frac{875}{1000} =$ ___ **3.** $\frac{84}{132} =$ ___

Convert the following improper fractions to mixed numbers, and write using lowest terms. **[2.1]**

4. $\frac{65}{8} =$ ___ **5.** $\frac{56}{12} =$ ___ **6.** $\frac{120}{45} =$ ___

Convert the following mixed numbers to improper fractions. **[2.1]**

7. $7\frac{3}{4} =$ ___ **8.** $18\frac{4}{5} =$ ___ **9.** $18\frac{3}{8} =$ ___

Find the LCD of each of the following groups of denominators. **[2.2]**

10. 2, 6, 5, ___ **11.** 6, 8, 15, ___ **12.** 6, 9, 12, 24, ___

Solve the following problems. **[2.2–2.4]**

13.
$$\begin{array}{r} \frac{1}{5} \\ \frac{3}{10} \\ + \frac{3}{8} \\ \hline \end{array}$$

14.
$$\begin{array}{r} 32\frac{5}{16} \\ -17\frac{1}{4} \\ \hline \end{array}$$

15.
$$\begin{array}{r} 126\frac{3}{16} \\ -\ 89\frac{7}{8} \\ \hline \end{array}$$

16. $67\frac{1}{2} \times \frac{8}{15} =$

17. $33\frac{1}{3} \div \frac{200}{9} =$

EXAMPLE 4

Writing Fractions as Percents

A marketing manager is given the following data in fraction form and must change the data to percents.

(a) $\frac{1}{4}$ **(b)** $\frac{3}{8}$ **(c)** $\frac{4}{5}$

SOLUTION

First write each fraction as a decimal, and then write the decimal as a percent.

(a) $\frac{1}{4} = .25 = 25\%$ **(b)** $\frac{3}{8} = .375 = 37.5\%$ **(c)** $\frac{4}{5} = .8 = 80\%$

QUICK CHECK 4

Change the fractions to percents.

(a) $\frac{3}{4}$ **(b)** $\frac{2}{5}$ **(c)** $\frac{5}{8}$

A second way to write a fraction as a percent is by multiplying the fraction by 100%. For example, write the fraction $\frac{4}{5}$ as a percent by multiplying $\frac{4}{5}$ by 100%.

$$\frac{4}{5} = \frac{4}{5} \times 100\% = \frac{400\%}{5} = 80\%$$

OBJECTIVE 3 **Write a percent as a decimal.** To write a percent as a decimal, ***move the decimal point two places to the left and drop the percent sign.*** For example, 50% becomes .50 or .5, 100% becomes 1, and 352% becomes 3.52.

Converting Percents to Decimals

Change a percent to a decimal by moving the decimal point two places to the left and dropping the percent sign (%).

25%	original percent
.25.%	Move decimal point 2 places to the left.
.25	Drop the percent sign.

EXAMPLE 5

Writing Percents as Decimals

To calculate some insurance claims, an insurance agent must change the following percents to decimals.

(a) 35% **(b)** 50% **(c)** 325% **(d)** $37\frac{1}{2}\%$ (*Hint:* $37\frac{1}{2}\% = 37.5\%$.)

SOLUTION

Move the decimal point two places to the left and drop the percent sign.

(a) .35 **(b)** .5 **(c)** 3.25 **(d)** .375

QUICK TIP In Example 5(d), change $37\frac{1}{2}\%$ to 37.5%. It is usually best to change fractional percents to the decimal percent form and then change the percent to a decimal.

QUICK CHECK 5

Change the percents to decimals.

(a) 75% **(b)** 40% **(c)** 280%

Quick Check Answers

4. (a) 75% **(b)** 40% **(c)** 62.5%
5. (a) .75 **(b)** .4 **(c)** 2.8

OBJECTIVE 4 Write a percent as a fraction. To write a percent as a fraction, first change the percent to a decimal, then write the decimal as a fraction in lowest terms.

EXAMPLE 6

Writing Percents as Fractions

The following bar graph shows how Americans enhance the exteriors of their homes. The bars show the percent of the owners surveyed that would add each of the improvements. Convert each percent to a fraction. When possible, reduce each fraction to its lowest term.

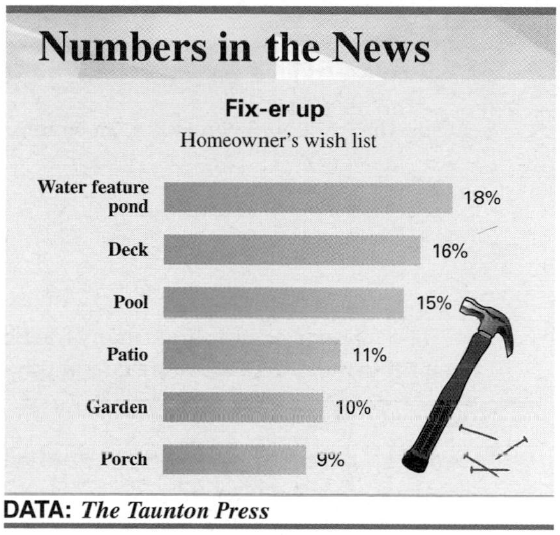

SOLUTION

First write each percent as a decimal, and then write the decimal as a fraction in lowest terms.

(a) $18\% = .18 = \frac{18}{100} = \frac{9}{50}$ **(b)** $16\% = .16 = \frac{16}{100} = \frac{4}{25}$

(c) $15\% = .15 = \frac{15}{100} = \frac{3}{20}$ **(d)** $11\% = .11 = \frac{11}{100}$

(e) $10\% = \frac{10}{100} = \frac{1}{10}$ **(f)** $9\% = .09 = \frac{9}{100}$

QUICK CHECK 6

Change the percents to fractions. Reduce to lowest terms.

(a) 35% **(b)** 22% **(c)** 88%

OBJECTIVE 5 Write a fractional percent as a decimal. A fractional percent such as $\frac{1}{2}\%$ has a value less than 1%. In fact, $\frac{1}{2}\%$ is equal to $\frac{1}{2}$ of 1%. Write a fractional percent as a decimal by first changing the fraction to a decimal, leaving the percent sign. For example, first write $\frac{1}{2}\%$ as .5%. Then write .5% as a decimal by moving the decimal point two places to the left and dropping the percent sign.

$$\frac{1}{2}\% = .5\% = .005$$

↑ written as a decimal with percent sign remaining

Quick Check Answers

6. (a) $\frac{7}{20}$ **(b)** $\frac{11}{50}$

(c) $\frac{22}{25}$

EXAMPLE 7

Writing Fractional Percents as Decimals

QUICK TIP When writing a fractional percent as a decimal, first change the fraction to a decimal, leaving the percent sign. Then move the decimal point two places to the left and drop the percent sign.

The following percents appear in a newspaper article. Write each fractional percent as a decimal.

(a) $\frac{1}{5}\%$ **(b)** $\frac{3}{4}\%$ **(c)** $\frac{5}{8}\%$

SOLUTION

Begin by writing the fraction as a decimal percent.

(a) $\frac{1}{5}\% = .2\% = .002$ **(b)** $\frac{3}{4}\% = .75\% = .0075$ **(c)** $\frac{5}{8}\% = .625\% = .00625$

QUICK CHECK 7

Write the fractional percents as decimals.

(a) $\frac{1}{2}\%$ **(b)** $\frac{1}{4}\%$ **(c)** $\frac{7}{8}\%$

The following chart shows many fractions as well as their decimal and percent equivalents. **It is helpful to memorize the more commonly used ones.**

Fraction, Decimal, and Percent Equivalents

$\frac{1}{100} = .01 = 1\%$	$\frac{9}{16} = .5625 = 56.25\%$ or $56\frac{1}{4}\%$
$\frac{1}{50} = .02 = 2\%$	$\frac{3}{5} = .6 = 60\%$
$\frac{1}{25} = .04 = 4\%$	$\frac{5}{8} = .625 = 62\frac{1}{2}\%$
$\frac{1}{20} = .05 = 5\%$	$\frac{2}{3} = .666\overline{6} = 66\frac{2}{3}\%$
$\frac{1}{16} = .0625 = 6.25\%$ or $6\frac{1}{4}\%$	$\frac{11}{16} = .6875 = 68.75\%$ or $68\frac{3}{4}\%$
$\frac{1}{12} = .083\overline{3} = 8\frac{1}{3}\%$	$\frac{7}{10} = .7 = 70\%$
$\frac{1}{10} = .1 = 10\%$	$\frac{3}{4} = .75 = 75\%$
$\frac{1}{9} = .111\overline{1} = 11\frac{1}{9}\%$	$\frac{4}{5} = .8 = 80\%$
$\frac{1}{8} = .125 = 12.5\%$ or $12\frac{1}{2}\%$	$\frac{13}{16} = .8125 = 81.25\%$ or $81\frac{1}{4}\%$
$\frac{1}{7} = .1428 = 14\frac{2}{7}\%$	$\frac{5}{6} = .833\overline{3} = 83\frac{1}{3}\%$
$\frac{1}{6} = .166\overline{6} = 16\frac{2}{3}\%$	$\frac{7}{8} = .875 = 87\frac{1}{2}\%$
$\frac{3}{16} = .1875 = 18\frac{3}{4}\%$	$\frac{9}{10} = .9 = 90\%$
$\frac{1}{5} = .2 = 20\%$	$\frac{15}{16} = .9375 = 93.75\%$ or $93\frac{3}{4}\%$
$\frac{1}{4} = .25 = 25\%$	$1 = 1.00 = 100\%$
$\frac{3}{10} = .3 = 30\%$	$1\frac{1}{10} = 1.1 = 110\%$
$\frac{5}{16} = .3125 = 31.25\%$	$1\frac{1}{4} = 1.25 = 125\%$
$\frac{1}{3} = .333\overline{3} = 33\frac{1}{3}\%$	$1\frac{1}{3} = 1.1333\overline{3} = 133\frac{1}{3}\%$
$\frac{3}{8} = .375 = 37\frac{1}{2}\%$	$1\frac{1}{2} = 1.5 = 150\%$
$\frac{2}{5} = .4 = 40\%$	$1\frac{2}{3} = 1.6666\overline{6} = 166\frac{2}{3}\%$
$\frac{7}{16} = .4375 = 43.75\%$ or $43\frac{3}{4}\%$	$1\frac{3}{4} = 1.75 = 175\%$
$\frac{1}{2} = .5 = 50\%$	$2 = 2.00 = 200\%$

Quick Check Answers

7. (a) $\frac{1}{2}\% = .5\% = .005$

(b) $\frac{1}{4}\% = .25\% = .0025$

(c) $\frac{7}{8}\% = .875\% = .00875$

3.1 EXERCISES

FOR EXTRA HELP

MyMathLab

MathXL PRACTICE

WATCH

DOWNLOAD

READ

REVIEW

The QUICK START *exercises in each section contain solutions to help you get started.*

Write the following decimals as percents. (See Examples 1–3.)

QUICK START

1. .25 = **25%** **2.** .4 = **40%** **3.** .72 = ______

4. 1.3 = ______ **5.** 2.034 = ______ **6.** .625 = ______

7. 3.625 = ______ **8.** 4.6 = ______ **9.** .875 = ______

10. .005 = ______ **11.** .0005 = ______ **12.** .0012 = ______

13. 3.45 = ______ **14.** .2108 = ______ **15.** .0308 = ______

Write the following as decimals. (See Examples 4–6.)

QUICK START

16. $\frac{1}{5}$ = **.2** **17.** $\frac{5}{8}$ = **.625** **18.** 64% = ______

19. 65% = ______ **20.** $\frac{1}{100}$ = ______ **21.** $\frac{1}{8}$ = ______

22. $8\frac{1}{2}\%$ = ______ **23.** $12\frac{1}{2}\%$ = ______ **24.** $\frac{1}{200}$ = ______

25. $\frac{1}{400}$ = ______ **26.** $50\frac{3}{4}\%$ = ______ **27.** $84\frac{3}{4}\%$ = ______

28. $3\frac{3}{8}$ = ______ **29.** $1\frac{3}{4}$ = ______ **30.** 350% = ______

Determine the fraction, decimal, or percent equivalents for each of the following, as necessary. Write fractions in lowest terms.

QUICK START

	Fraction	*Decimal*	*Percent*
31.	$\frac{1}{2}$	**.5**	**50%**
32.	**$\frac{3}{50}$**	.06	**6%**
33.	______	.875	______
34.	$\frac{4}{5}$	______	______
35.	______	______	.8%
36.	______	.00625	______
37.	$10\frac{1}{2}$	______	______
38.	______	______	675%
39.	______	.65	______
40.	$4\frac{3}{8}$	______	______

	Fraction	*Decimal*	*Percent*
41.	________	.005	________
42.	________	________	$\frac{1}{8}\%$
43.	$\frac{1}{3}$	________	________
44.	________	________	12.5%
45.	________	2.5	________
46.	$\frac{7}{20}$	________	________
47.	________	________	$4\frac{1}{4}\%$
48.	________	.7	________
49.	$\frac{3}{200}$	________	________
50.	________	5.125	________
51.	________	________	1037.5%
52.	________	________	$\frac{3}{4}\%$
53.	________	.0025	________
54.	$\frac{5}{8}$	________	________
55.	________	________	$37\frac{1}{2}\%$
56.	________	________	$6\frac{3}{4}\%$

57. Fractions, decimals, and percents are all used to describe a part of something. The use of percents is much more common than fractions and decimals. Why do you suppose this is true?

58. List five uses of percent that are or will be part of your life. Consider the activities of working, shopping, saving, and planning for the future.

59. Select a decimal percent and write it as a fraction. Select a fraction and write it as a percent. Write an explanation of each step of your work. (See Objectives 2 and 3.)

60. The fractional percent $\frac{1}{2}\%$ is equal to .005. Explain each step as you change $\frac{1}{2}\%$ to its decimal equivalent. (See Objective 4.)

3.2 FINDING PART

OBJECTIVES

1. Know the three components of a percent problem.
2. Learn the basic percent formula.
3. Solve for part.
4. Recognize the terms associated with base, rate, and part.
5. Calculate sales tax.
6. Learn the standard format of percent problems.

CASE in POINT As a real estate agent with Century 21 Real Estate, Thomas Dugally is paid on a commission plan. When he produces income for the company as a result of a sale, a sale of his listing by someone else, or a rental agreement that is completed, he is paid a portion of this income. Currently, Dugally is looking for a home in the \$210,000 price range for Scott and Andrea Abriani, a couple he met at an open house.

OBJECTIVE 1 Know the three components of a percent problem. Problems in percent contain three main components. Usually, two of these components are given, and the third component must be found. The three key components in a percent problem are as follows.

QUICK TIP *Percent* and *part* are different quantities. The stated percent in a given problem is always the rate (R). The part (P) is the product of the base (B) and the rate (R). Thus, the part is a quantity and never appears with *percent* or % following it.

1. **Base:** The whole or total, starting point, or that to which something is being compared.
2. **Rate:** A number followed by % or **percent**.
3. **Part:** The result of multiplying the base and the rate. The part is a *part* of the base, as sales tax is a part of the total sales, or as the number of hybrid cars is part of the total number of cars.

OBJECTIVE 2 Learn the basic percent formula. The base, rate, and part are related by the basic **percent formula**.

$$P = B \times R \qquad P = R \times B$$

Part = Base × Rate or Part = Rate × Base

OBJECTIVE 3 Solve for part. If Thomas Dugally finds a \$210,000 home for the Abrianis and is paid a 6% commission, use the formula $P = B \times R$ to find 6% of \$210,000. Multiply the base, \$210,000, by the rate, 6%. The rate must be changed to a decimal before it is multiplied.

$$P = B \times R$$
$$P = \$210{,}000 \times 6\%$$
$$P = \$210{,}000 \times .06 \quad \text{or} \quad \begin{array}{r} \$210{,}000 \\ \times \quad .06 \\ \hline \$12{,}600 \end{array}$$

Finally, 6% of \$210,000 is \$12,600.

EXAMPLE 1

Solving for Part

Solve for part, using $P = B \times R$.

(a) 4% of 50 **(b)** 1.2% of 180 **(c)** 140% of 225 **(d)** $\frac{1}{4}$% of 560 $\left(\textit{Hint: } \frac{1}{4}\% = .25\%.\right)$

SOLUTION

(a) $\begin{array}{r} 50 \\ \times\ .04 \\ \hline 2.00 \end{array}$ **(b)** $\begin{array}{r} 180 \\ \times\ .012 \\ \hline 2.160 \end{array}$ **(c)** $\begin{array}{r} 225 \\ \times\ 1.4 \\ \hline 315.0 \end{array}$ **(d)** $\begin{array}{r} 560 \\ \times\ .0025 \\ \hline 1.4000 \end{array}$

QUICK CHECK 1

Solve for part.

(a) 6% of 200 **(b)** 1.8% of 150 **(c)** 210% of 310 **(d)** $\frac{1}{2}$% of 1300

EXAMPLE 2

Finding Part

The following bar graph shows that 56% of the housing units in the United States have a dishwasher. Out of 18,000 households, how many are expected to have a dishwasher?

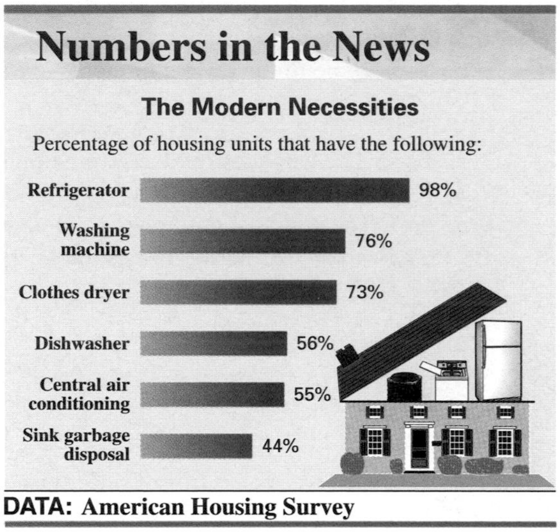

SOLUTION

The number of households, 18,000, is the base. The rate, 56%, is the percent of the total households that have a dishwasher. Since the number of households that have a dishwasher is part of the total number of households, find the number of households that have a dishwasher by using the formula to find part.

$$P = B \times R$$
$$P = 18{,}000 \times 56\%$$
$$P = 18{,}000 \times .56$$
$$P = 10{,}080$$

The number of households expected to have a dishwasher is 10,080.

The calculator solution to this example is

18000 [×] 56 [%] [=] 10080 or 18000 [×] .56 [=] 10080

Note: Refer to Appendix C for calculator basics.

QUICK CHECK 2

The bar graph above shows that 98% of the 18,000 households have refrigerators. How many have refrigerators?

Quick Check Answers

1. **(a)** 12 **(b)** 2.7 **(c)** 651 **(d)** 6.5
2. 17,640 households

OBJECTIVE 4 Recognize the terms associated with base, rate, and part. Percent problems have certain similarities. For example, some phrases are associated with the base in the problem. Other phrases lead to the part, while % or *percent* following a number identifies the rate. The following chart helps distinguish between the base and the part.

Words and Phrases Associated with Base and Part

Usually indicates the base (B)		Usually indicates the part (P)
Sales	→	Sales tax
Investment	→	Return
Savings	→	Interest
Value of bonds	→	Dividends
Retail price	→	Discount
Last year's anything	→	Increase or decrease
Value of real estate	→	Rents
Old salary	→	Raise
Total sales	→	Commission
Value of stocks	→	Dividends
Earnings	→	Expenditures
Original	→	Change

OBJECTIVE 5 Calculate sales tax. Calculating **sales tax** is a good example of finding part. States, counties, and cities often collect taxes on retail sales to the consumer. The sales tax is a percent of the sale. This percent varies from as low as 3% in some states to 8% or more in other states. The formula used for finding sales tax is as follows.

$$P = B \times R$$
$$\text{Sales tax} = \text{Sales} \times \text{Sales tax rate}$$

EXAMPLE 3

Calculating Sales Tax

Real Estate Supply sold $2857.50 worth of merchandise. If the sales tax rate was 8%, how much tax was paid? Find the total cost including the tax.

SOLUTION

The amount of sales, $2857.50, is the starting point or base (B), and 8% is the rate (R). Since the tax is a *part* of total sales, use the formula $P = B \times R$ to find part.

$$P = B \times R$$
$$P = \$2857.50 \times 8\%$$
$$P = \$2857.50 \times .08 = \$228.60$$

The tax, or part, is $228.60.

To find the total amount of sales and tax, the amount of sales ($2857.50) is added to the sales tax $228.60. The total sales and tax is $3086.10 ($2857.50 + $228.60).

QUICK CHECK 3

The Lock Shop had sales of $1485 and charged a sales tax of 6%. Find the sales tax and the total sales including the tax.

Quick Check Answer

3. $89.10 sales tax; $1574.10 total

Identify the rate, base, and part with the following hints.

> **Base** tends to be preceded by the word *of* or *on*; tends to be the *whole*.
> **Rate** is followed by a percent sign or the word *percent*.
> **Part** is in the same units as the base and is usually a portion of the base.

OBJECTIVE 6 Learn the standard format of percent problems. Percent problems often take the following form.

% of something is something

For example,

5% of the automobiles are red
4.2% of the workers are unemployed
20% of the income is income tax
74% of the students are full time

> **QUICK TIP** **Rate** is identified by % (the percent sign); the word *of* means × (multiplication); the multiplicand, or number being multiplied, is the **base**; the word *is* means = (equals); and the product, or answer, is **part** of the base.

When expressed in this standard form, the components in the percent problem always appear in this order.

R	×	*B*	=	*P*
Rate	×	Base	=	Part
%	of	something	is	something

The following survey results show that 14.7% of the 1582 people surveyed buy Breyers brand ice cream.

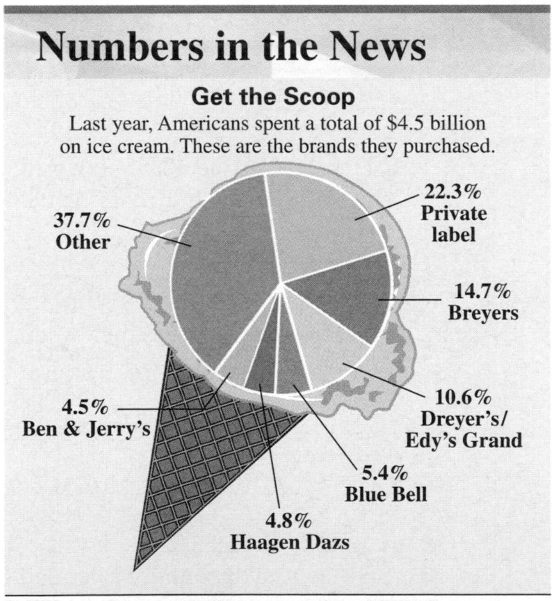

DATA: *Information Resources Inc; NPD Group*

The rate is the percent selecting Breyers, 14.7%. The base, or number of people in the survey, is 1582; and the number of people who buy Breyers ice cream is the part. Find part, the number of people in the survey who buy Breyers ice cream.

$$14.7\% \times 1582 = 232.554 = 233 \text{ people (rounded)}$$

EXAMPLE 4

Identifying the Elements in Percent Problems

Identify the elements given in the following percent problems and determine which element must be found.

(a) During a recent sale, Stockdale Marine offered a 15% discount on all new recreation equipment. Find the discount on a jet ski originally priced at \$3895. First arrange this problem in standard form.

%	of	something	is	something
%	of	price	is	discount
15%	of	\$3895	=	discount
R	×	*B*	=	*P*

At this point, check that the rate and base are given, so the part must be found. Find the discount by multiplying 15%, or .15, by \$3895.

$$.15 \times \$3895 = \$584.25$$

The amount of the discount is \$584.25.

(b) Round Table Pizza spends an amount equal to 5.8% of its sales on advertising. If sales for the month were \$28,500, find the amount spent on advertising. First arrange this problem in standard form.

%	of	something	is	something
%	of	sales	is	advertising
5.8%	of	\$28,500	=	advertising
R	×	*B*	=	*P*

Rate is given as 5.8%, base (sales) is \$28,500, and part (advertising) must be found. Find the amount spent on advertising by multiplying .058 and \$28,500.

$$.058 \times \$28{,}500 = \$1653$$

The amount spent on advertising is \$1653.

QUICK CHECK 4

A video game is priced at \$280 less a 15% discount. First identify the elements in the problem, then find the amount of the discount.

Quick Check Answer

4. $B = \$280$; $R = .15$;
P = discount amount = \$42 discount

3.2 EXERCISES

FOR EXTRA HELP

MyMathLab

MathXL PRACTICE

WATCH

DOWNLOAD

READ

REVIEW

The QUICK START *exercises in each section contain solutions to help you get started.*

Solve for part in each of the following. Round to the nearest hundredth. (See Example 1.)

QUICK START

1. 10% of 620 homes = **62 homes**
2. 25% of 3500 Web sites = **875 Web sites**

3. 75.5% of \$800 = ________
4. 20.5% of \$1500 = ________
5. 4% of 120 feet = ________
6. 125% of 2000 products = ________
7. 175% of 5820 miles = ________
8. 15% of 75 crates = ________
9. 17.5% of 1040 cell phones = ________
10. 52.5% of 1560 trucks = ________
11. 118% of 125.8 yards = ________
12. 110% of 150 apartments = ________
13. $90\frac{1}{2}$% of \$5930 = ________
14. $7\frac{1}{2}$% of \$150 = ________

15. Identify the three components in a percent problem. In your own words, write one sentence telling how to identify each of these three components. (See Objective 1.)

16. There are words and phrases that are usually associated with base and part. Give three examples of words that usually identify the base and the accompanying word for the part. (See Objective 4.)

Solve for part in each of the following application problems. Round to the nearest cent unless otherwise indicated. (See Examples 2 and 3.)

QUICK START

17. WEDDING PREFERENCES In a recent survey of 480 adults, 55% said that they would prefer to have their wedding at a religious site. How many said they would prefer the religious site? (***Source:*** National Family Opinion Research.)

$P = B \times R$
$P = 480 \times .55 = 264$ adults

17. **264 adults**

18. ICE CREAM SALES In a poll of 1582 people, 4.5% said that they prefer to purchase Ben and Jerry's brand ice cream. Find the number of people who said they prefer Ben and Jerry's ice cream. Round to the nearest whole number. (***Source:*** Information Resources Inc., NPD Group.)

18. ________

19. SALES TAX A real estate broker wants to purchase a Palm i705 with a built-in radio modem priced at \$399. If the sales tax rate is 7.75%, find the total price including the sales tax. (***Source:*** Real Estate Technology.)

19. ________

C indicates an exercise that is related to the Case in Point feature.

20. Thomas Dugally of Century 21 Real Estate is working with a mortgage company that charges borrowers $350 plus 2% of the loan amount. What is the total charge to get a home loan of $95,000?

20. ______________

21. WOMEN IN THE NAVY The navy guided-missile destroyer USS *Sullivans* has a 335-person crew of which 13% are female. Find the number of female crew members. Round to the nearest whole number. (***Source:*** U.S. Navy.)

21. ______________

22. SUPERMARKET SHOPPING The Point of Purchase Advertising Institute says that 55% of all supermarket shoppers have a written list of their needs. If 3680 shoppers enter the supermarket that you manage in one day, what number of shoppers would you expect to have a written shopping list?

22. ______________

23. BAR SOAP A bar of Ivory Soap is $99\frac{44}{100}$% pure. If the bar of soap weighs 9 ounces, how many ounces are pure? Round to the nearest hundredth.

23. ______________

24. CANNED-MEAT SALES According to Hormel Foods Corporation, Spam® and Spam Lite together held 62.2% of the $148-million canned lunchmeat category over a 52-week period (the entire year). Find the total annual sales of these Hormel products. Round to the nearest hundredth of a million.

24. ______________

25. DRIVING DISTRACTIONS It is estimated that 29.5% of automobile crashes are caused by driver distractions, such as mobile communications devices. If there are 16,450 automobile crashes in a study, what number would be caused by driver distractions? Round to the nearest whole number. (***Source:*** National Conference of State Legislatures.)

25. ______________

26. WORKPLACE REQUIREMENTS A study of office workers found that 27% would like more storage space. If there are 14 million office workers, how many want more storage space? (***Source:*** Steelcase Workplace Index.)

26. ______________

27. FEMALE LAWYERS There are 1,094,751 active lawyers living in the United States. If 71.4% of these lawyers are male, find **(a)** the percent of the lawyers who are female and **(b)** the number of lawyers who are female. Round to the nearest whole number. (***Source:*** American Bar Association.)

(a) ______________
(b) ______________

28. SMALL DOWN PAYMENTS According to the National Association of Realtors, 56% of first-time buyers make down payments of less than 5% of the purchase price. If 2.6 million first-time home buyers bought homes, find **(a)** the percent who had down payments of 5% or more and **(b)** the number of buyers having down payments of less than 5%. (***Source:*** NAR Research.)

(a) ______________

(b) ______________

29. DIGITAL CAMERA A Sony 6.0 megapixel digital camera priced at $319 is marked down 25%. Find the price of the camera after the markdown. (***Source:*** RC Willey.)

29. ______________

30. HOSPITAL STAFFING In a survey of 245 small- to medium-size hospitals, 45% said that they do not have enough radiologists. How many of these hospitals do have enough radiologists? Round to the nearest whole number. (***Source:*** U.S. Radiology Partners Incorporated.)

30. ______________

31. NEW PRODUCT FAILURE Marketing Intelligence Service says that there were 15,401 new products introduced last year. If 86% of the products introduced last year failed to reach their business objectives, find the number of products that did reach their objectives. Round to the nearest whole number.

31. ______________

32. FAMILY BUDGET A family of four with a monthly income of $5150 spends 90% of its earnings and saves the balance for the down payment on a house. Find **(a)** the monthly savings and **(b)** the annual savings of this family.

(a) ______________

(b) ______________

33. GM SALES IN CHINA General Motors auto sales in China were 36.7% greater than last year's sales of 629,778 units. Find this year's sales. Round to the nearest whole number. (***Source:*** General Motors Corporation.)

33. ______________

34. SUPER BOWL ADVERTISING The average cost of 30 seconds of advertising during the Super Bowl 6 years ago was $2.3 million. If the increase in cost over the last 6 years has been 17%, find the average cost of 30 seconds of advertising during the Super Bowl this year. Round to the nearest tenth of a million. (***Source:*** NFL Research.)

34. ______________

35. SALES-TAX COMPUTATION As the owner of a copy and print shop, you must collect $6\frac{1}{2}\%$ of the amount of each sale for sales tax. If sales for the month are $48,680, find the combined amount of sales and tax.

35. ______________

36. TOTAL COST A NuVac 3200 is priced at $524 with an allowed trade-in of $125 for an old unit. If sales tax of $7\frac{3}{4}\%$ is charged on the price of the new NuVac unit, find the total cost to the customer after receiving the trade-in. (*Hint:* Trade-in is subtracted last.) 36. ______

37. REAL ESTATE COMMISSIONS Thomas Dugally of Century 21 Real Estate sold a home for $174,900. The commission was 6% of the sale price. However, Dugally receives only 60% of the commission, while 40% remains with his broker. Find the amount of commission received by Dugally. 37. ______

38. BUSINESS OWNERSHIP Jimmy Ruiz has an 82% ownership in a company called Jimmy's Cell Phones. If the company has a value of $98,400 and Ruiz receives an income of 45% of the value of his ownership, find the amount of his income. 38. ______

CONSUMER INTERNET SALES *Country Store has a unique selection of merchandise that it sells by catalog and over the Internet. Use the shipping and insurance delivery chart below and a sales tax rate of 5% to solve Exercises 39–42. There is no sales tax on shipping and insurance.* (***Source:*** Country Store catalog.)

Shipping and Insurance Delivery Chart

Up to $15.00	add $3.95
$15.01 to $25.00	add $5.95
$25.01 to $35.00	add $6.95
$35.01 to $50.00	add $7.95
$50.01 to $70.00	add $8.95
$70.01 to $99.99	add $9.95
$100.00 or more	add $10.95

39. Find the total cost of 6 Small Fry Handi-Pan electric skillets at a cost of $29.99 each. 39. ______

40. A customer ordered 5 sets of flour-sack towels at a cost of $12.99 each. What is the total cost? 40. ______

41. Find the total cost of 3 pop-up hampers at a cost of $9.99 each and 4 nonstick minidonut pans at $10.99 each. 41. ______

42. What is the total cost of 5 coach lamp bird feeders at a cost of $19.99 each and 6 garden weather centers at $14.99 each? 42. ______

3.3 FINDING BASE

OBJECTIVES

1. Use the basic percent formula to solve for base.
2. Find the amount of sales when tax amount and tax rate are both known.
3. Find the amount of investment when expense and rate of expense are known.

CASE in POINT Thomas Dugally of Century 21 Real Estate helps buyers select properties that they can afford. Real estate lenders have strict guidelines that determine the maximum loan that they will give a buyer. Usually, the lender will limit the borrowers' monthly house payment to no more than 28% to 36% of their monthly income.

OBJECTIVE 1 **Use the basic percent formula to solve for base.** In some problems, the rate and part are given, but the base, or starting point, must be found. The formula $P = B \times R$ can be used to get the **formula for base**. The following diagram illustrates the formula $P = B \times R$. To find the formula for base, cover B. Now the letter P is left over the letter R. Think of this as meaning $\frac{P}{R}$, or part ÷ rate.

$$\text{Base} = \frac{\text{Part}}{\text{Rate}} \quad \text{or} \quad B = \frac{P}{R}$$

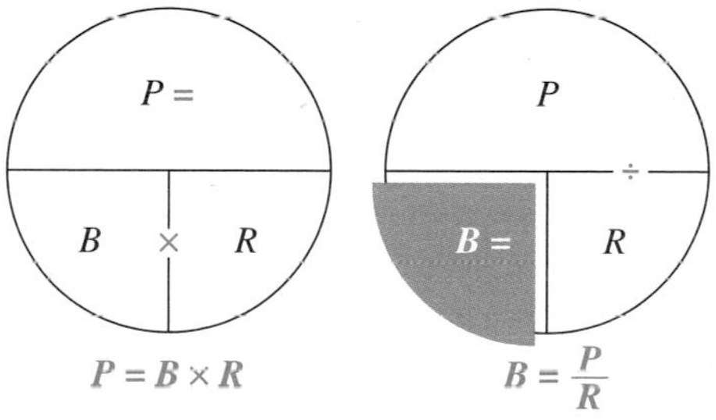

QUICK TIP In this formula, P (part) is always on top.

Suppose that Scott and Andrea Abriani told Thomas Dugally that they are able to make a monthly payment of $1386. If this is 28% of their monthly income, how can Dugally find the amount of their monthly income? The key word here, indicating that the amount of monthly income is the base, is the word *of*. To find the amount of their monthly income, insert the rate (28%) and the part ($1386) into the formula.

$B = \frac{P}{R}$ Replace P with 1386 and R with .28 to get

$B = \frac{1386}{.28} = 4950$ The amount of their monthly income is $4950.

EXAMPLE 1 Solving for Base

Solve for base, using the formula $B = \frac{P}{R}$.

(a) 8 is 4% of ______. **(b)** 135 is 15% of ______. **(c)** 1.25 is 25% of ______.

SOLUTION

(a) $\frac{8}{.04} = 200$ **(b)** $\frac{135}{.15} = 900$ **(c)** $\frac{1.25}{.25} = 5$

QUICK CHECK 1

Solve for base, using $B = \frac{P}{R}$.

(a) 15 is 10% of ______. **(b)** 62 is 1% of ______. **(c)** 1.6 is 40% of ______.

Quick Check Answers

1. (a) 150 **(b)** 6200 **(c)** 4

OBJECTIVE 2 Find the amount of sales when tax amount and tax rate are both known. In business problems involving sales tax, the amount of sales is always the base.

EXAMPLE 2

Finding Sales When Sales Tax Is Given

The 5% sales tax collected by Famous Footwear was \$780. What was the amount of total sales?

SOLUTION

Here, the rate of tax collection is 5%, and taxes collected are a part of total sales. The rate in this problem is 5%, the part is \$780, and the base, or total sales, must be found. Arrange the problem in standard form.

R	$\times$	B	$=$	P
%	of	something	is	something
5%	of	total sales	is	\$780 (tax)

Using the formula $B = \frac{P}{R}$, we get

$$B = \frac{780}{.05} = \$15{,}600 \text{ total sales}$$

The calculator solution to this example is

780 ÷ .05 = 15600

QUICK TIP It is important to consider whether an answer is reasonable. A common error in a base problem is to confuse the base and the part. In Example 2, if the taxes, \$780, had been mistakenly used as the base, the resulting answer would have been \$39 (\$780 × 5%). Obviously, \$39 is not a reasonable amount for total sales, given \$780 as sales tax.

QUICK CHECK 2

The number of people who passed the real estate license exam was 832. If this was a 65% pass rate, how many took the exam?

The following newspaper clipping states that new orders for Beazer Homes fell by 58% compared to last year. In these calculations, the number of sales last year is the base, or starting point. It is the number to which this year's sales is being compared.

HERE & NOW

Housing Slump Deepens

Two major companies report big drops in new orders and weaker quarterly results.

By Deborah Yao

ASSOCIATED PRESS

PHILADELPHIA – In a sign of a deepening housing slump, two major home builders on Tuesday reported steep declines in new orders and weaker fourth-quarter results.

Luxury home builder Toll Brothers Inc. of Horsham, Pa., said home-building revenue fell by 10 percent and signed contracts were down by 55 percent compared with a year ago. The company, which released its quarterly outlook ahead of earnings, also said it will incur a hefty charge against profits as it pares down the number of lots it controls.

Beazer Homes USA Inc. of Atlanta reported a 44 percent decline in profit as higher revenue was offset by squeezed margins. The company said there was "significant" discounting in most markets.

New orders for Beazer fell by 58 percent to 2,064 homes from 4,937 last year, as the housing market continued to slow. It has cut 1,000 jobs, or 25 percent of its work force.

"We think it's a loss of confidence in the buyers," Toll Brothers Chief Executive Robert Toll said during a conference call with analysts Tuesday. "Nobody wants to buy something that they think will cost less two weeks later."

Quick Check Answer

2. 1280 took exam

OBJECTIVE 3 Find the amount of investment when expense and rate of expense are known. When solving problems involving investments, the amount of the investment is the base.

EXAMPLE 3

Finding the Amount of an Investment

The yearly utility cost of an apartment complex is $3\frac{1}{2}\%$ of its value. If the utility cost is $73,500 per year, find the value of the apartment complex.

SOLUTION

First set up the problem:

R	$\times$	B	$=$	P
$3\frac{1}{2}\%$	of	value	is	utility cost
$3\frac{1}{2}\%$	of	value	is	$73,500

Find the value of the apartment complex, the base, with the formula $B = \frac{P}{R}$.

$$B = \frac{73{,}500}{.035} = \$2{,}100{,}000 \text{ value of complex}$$

QUICK TIP When working with a fraction of a percent it is best to change the fraction to a decimal. In Example 3, $3\frac{1}{2}\%$ was changed to 3.5%, which equals .035.

QUICK CHECK 3

The income earned on an investment is $8\frac{1}{2}\%$ of the amount invested. If the income is $12,750, find the amount of the investment.

The prices of homes vary dramatically across the nation. The bar graph below shows what percent of first-time home buyers are purchasing homes in different price ranges.

Numbers in the News

First-time Cost

Prices of homes purchased by first-time buyers:

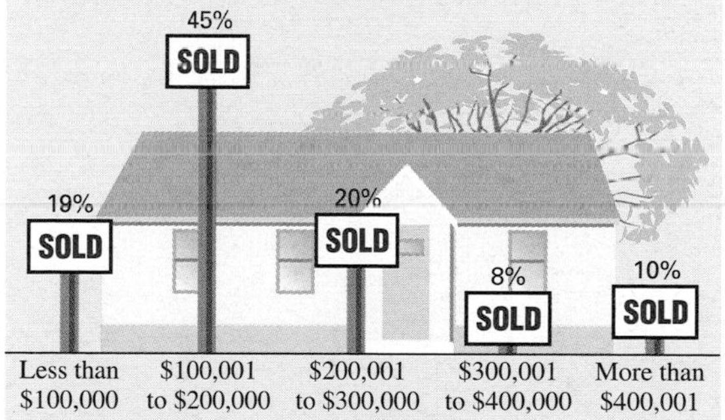

Note: *Total doesn't add up to 100 due to rounding.*

DATA: National Association of Realtors Profile of Home Buyers and Sellers

Quick Check Answer

3. $150,000

3.3 EXERCISES

FOR EXTRA HELP

MyMathLab

MathXL PRACTICE

WATCH

DOWNLOAD

READ

REVIEW

The QUICK START *exercises in each section contain solutions to help you get started.*

Solve for base in each of the following. Round to the nearest hundredth. (See Example 1.)

QUICK START

1. 530 firms is 25% of **2120** firms.

2. 240 letters is 80% of **300** letters.

3. 130 salads is 40% of ________ salads.

4. 32 shipments is 8% of ________ shipments.

5. 110 lab tests is 5.5% of ________ lab tests.

6. \$850 is $4\frac{1}{4}$% of ________.

7. 36 students is .75% of ________ students.

8. 23 workers is .5% of ________ workers.

9. 66 files is .15% of ________ files.

10. 54,600 boxes is 60% of ________ boxes.

11. 50 doors is .25% of ________ doors.

12. 39 bottles is .78% of ________ bottles.

13. \$33,870 is $37\frac{1}{2}$% of ________.

14. \$8500 is $27\frac{1}{2}$% of ________.

15. $12\frac{1}{2}$% of ________ people is 135 people.

16. $18\frac{1}{2}$% of ________ circuits is 370 circuits.

17. 375 crates is .12% of ________ crates.

18. 3.5 quarts is .07% of ________ quarts.

19. .5% of ________ homes is 327 homes.

20. 6.5 barrels is .05% of ________ barrels.

21. 12 audits is .03% of ________ audits.

22. 8 banks is .04% of ________ banks.

23. The basic percent formula is $P = B \times R$. Show how to find the formula to solve for B (base). (See Objective 1.)

24. A problem includes amount of sales, sales tax, and a sales-tax rate. Explain how you could identify the base, rate, and part in this problem. (See Objective 2.)

Solve for base in the following application problems. (See Examples 2 and 3.)

QUICK START

25. HOME OWNERSHIP The number of U.S. households owning homes last year was 72.6 million—a record-setting 67.8% of all households. What is the total number of U.S. households? Round to the nearest tenth of a million. (***Source:*** *Habitat World.*)

$B = \frac{P}{R} = \frac{72.6}{.678} = 107.07 = 107.1$ million (rounded)

25. **107.1 million households**

26. EMPLOYEE POPULATION BASE In a large metropolitan area, 81% of the employed population is enrolled in a health maintenance organization (HMO). If 700,650 employees are enrolled, find the total number of people in the employed population.

26. ________

27. COLLEGE ENROLLMENT This semester there are 1785 married students on campus. If this figure represents 23% of the total enrollment, what is the total enrollment? Round to the nearest whole number.

27. ________

C indicates an exercise that is related to the Case in Point feature.

28. VOTER REGISTRATION Registered voters make up 13.8% of the county population. If there are 345,000 registered voters in the county, find the total population in the county.

28. ________

29. LOAN QUALIFICATION Thomas Dugally found a home for Scott and Andrea Abriani that will require a monthly loan payment of $1350. If the lender insists that the buyer's monthly payment not exceed 30% of the buyer's monthly income, find the minimum monthly income required by the lender.

29. ________

30. PERSONAL BUDGETING Jim Lawler spends 28% of his income on housing, 15% on food, 11% on clothing, 15% on transportation, 11% on education, 7% on recreation, and saves the balance. If his savings amount to $266.50 per month, what are his monthly earnings?

30. ________

31. DIABETES SURVEY In a telephone survey, 749 people said that diabetes is a serious problem in the United States. If this was 71% of the survey group, find the total number of people in the telephone survey. Round to the nearest whole number. (***Source:*** Hoffman-La Roche Company.)

31. ________

32. DRIVING TESTS In analyzing the success of driver's license applicants, the state finds that 58.3% of those examined received a passing mark. If the records show that 8370 new driver's licenses were issued, what was the number of applicants? Round to the nearest whole number.

32. ________

33. MAN'S BEST FRIEND In a recent survey of dog owners, it was found that 901 or 34% of the owners take their dogs on vacation with them. Find the number of dog owners in the survey who do not take their dogs on vacation. (***Source:*** American Animal Hospital Association.)

33. ________

34. COMMUNICATIONS INDUSTRY LAYOFFS Telecommunications equipment maker Nortel Networks says it will lay off 4000 workers globally. If this amounts to 4% of its total workforce, how many workers will remain after the layoffs? (***Source:*** Nortel Networks.)

34. ________

35. GAMBLING PAYBACK An Atlantic City casino advertises that it gives a 97.4% payback on slot machines, and the balance is retained by the casino. If the amount retained by the casino is $4823, find the total amount played on the slot machines.

35. ________

36. SMOKING OR NONSMOKING A casino hotel in Barbados states that 45% of its rooms are for nonsmokers. If the resort allows smoking in 484 rooms, find the total number of rooms.

36. ________

SUPPLEMENTARY APPLICATION EXERCISES ON BASE AND PART

Solve the following application problems. Read each problem carefully to determine whether base or part is being asked for.

1. SHAMPOO INGREDIENTS Most shampoos contain 75% to 90% water. If there are 12.5 ounces of water in a bottle of shampoo that contains 78% water, what is the size of the bottle of shampoo? Round to the nearest whole number. 1. ________

2. HOUSEHOLD LUBRICANT The lubricant WD-40 is used in 82.3 million U.S. homes, which is 79% of all homes in the United States. Find the total number of homes in the United States. Round to the nearest tenth of a million. (***Source:*** WD-40.) 2. ________

3. PROPERTY INSURANCE Thomas Dugally of Century 21 Real Estate sold a commercial building valued at $423,750. If the building is insured for 68% of its value, find the amount of insurance coverage. 3. ________

4. FLU SHOTS In a survey of 3860 people who were 18–49 years old, 16.3% had received an influenza vaccination (flu shot). How many of those surveyed received the vaccination? Round to the nearest whole number. (***Source:*** National Health Interview Survey.) 4. ________

5. CAMAROS AND MUSTANGS The Chevrolet Camaro was introduced in 1967. Camaro sales that year were 220,917, which was 46.2% of the number of Ford Mustangs sold in the same year. Find the number of Mustangs sold in 1967. Round to the nearest whole number. 5. ________

6. CHILD SUPPORT Sean Eden has 12.4% of his earnings withheld for child support. If this amounts to $396.80 per month, find his annual earnings. 6. ________

7. CALORIES FROM FAT Häagen-Dazs vanilla ice cream has 270 calories per serving. If 60% of these calories come from fat, find the number of calories coming from fat. (***Source:*** Häagen-Dazs.) 7. ________

8. BLOOD-CHOLESTEROL LEVELS At a recent health fair, 32% of the people tested were found to have high blood-cholesterol levels. If 350 people were tested, find the number having a high blood-cholesterol level. 8. ________

9. RETIREMENT ACCOUNT Erin Joyce has 9.5% of her earnings deposited into a retirement account. If this amounts to \$308.75 per month, find her annual earnings. 9. ________

10. SAVINGS ACCOUNT INTEREST The Northridge PTA received \$50.75 in annual interest on its bank account. If the bank paid $3\frac{1}{2}\%$ interest per year, how much money was in the account? 10. ________

AIDING DISABLED EMPLOYEES The bar graph below shows how companies have accommodated their employees with disabilities. The data were collected from personnel directors, human resource directors, and executives responsible for hiring at 501 companies. Use this information to solve Exercises 11–14. Round to the nearest whole number. (***Source:*** Heldrich Work Trends Survey.)

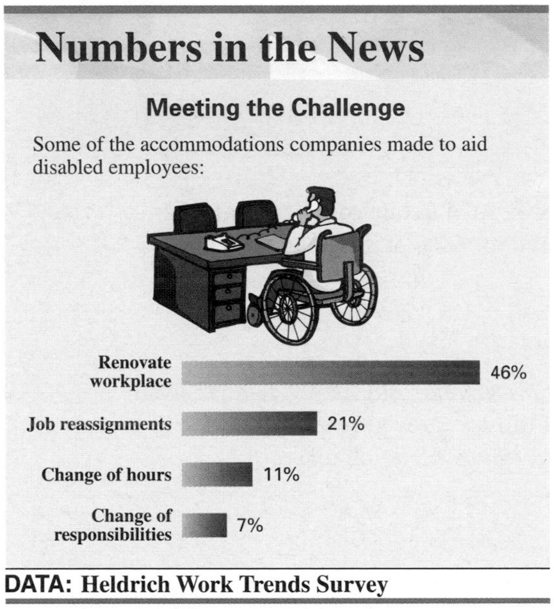

11. How many companies have renovated the workplace to aid employees with disabilities? 11. ________

12. How many companies changed worker responsibilities to aid employees with disabilities? 12. ________

13. Find the number of companies that changed worker hours to aid employees with disabilities. 13. ________

14. Find the number of companies that made job reassignments to aid employees with disabilities. 14. ________

3.4 FINDING RATE

OBJECTIVES

1. Use the basic percent formula to solve for rate.
2. Find the rate of return when the amount of the return and the investment are known.
3. Solve for the percent remaining when the total amount and amount used are given.
4. Find the percent of change.

CASE in POINT At Century 21 Real Estate, where Thomas Dugally is a real estate broker, all of the expenses of running the real estate office are compared to the income generated from sales and leasing activities. The most meaningful way of making these comparisons is by calculating all expense items as a percent of income. Dugally often calculates those percents as he makes decisions on how to run his business.

OBJECTIVE 1 Use the basic percent formula to solve for rate. In the third type of percent problem, the part and base are given, and the rate must be found. The **formula for rate** is found from the formula $P = B \times R$. The diagram shows that to find the formula for rate, cover R to get $\frac{P}{B}$, or part ÷ base.

$$\text{Rate} = \frac{\text{Part}}{\text{Base}} \quad \text{or} \quad R = \frac{P}{B}$$

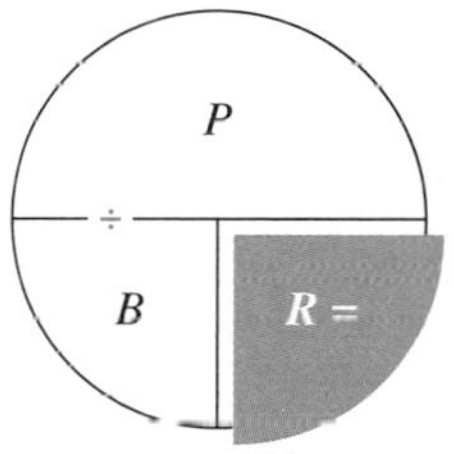

$R = \frac{P}{B}$

QUICK TIP In this formula, *P* (part) is always on top.

The formula $P = B \times R$ can be used to find either P, B, or R as long as the values of two of the components are known. When either B or R must be found, the known value must be divided into P, on the other side of the equal sign.

Find B:	Find R:
$P = B \times R$	$P = B \times R$
$B = \frac{P}{R}$	$R = \frac{P}{B}$

See why this works by using numbers.

$10 = ? \times 2$	$10 = 5 \times ?$
$? = \frac{10}{2}$	$? = \frac{10}{5}$
$? = 5$	$? = 2$

After the division, the known numbers are on one side of the equal sign and the unknown number is on the other side of the equal sign. Refer to Appendix A, Equation and Formula Review, for additional discussion of this topic.

The rate is identified by % or ***percent***. For example, what percent of 32 is 8? Use the formula $R = \frac{P}{B}$.

$$R = \frac{8}{32} = .25 = 25\%$$

Thus, 8 is 25% of 32 or, in other words, 25% of 32 is 8.

EXAMPLE 1

Solving for Rate

Solve for rate.

(a) 26 is _____% of 104. **(b)** _____% of 300 is 60. **(c)** 54 is _____% of 12.

SOLUTION

(a) $\frac{26}{104} = .25 = 25\%$ **(b)** $\frac{60}{300} = .2 = 20\%$ **(c)** $\frac{54}{12} = 4.5 = 450\%$

QUICK TIP When finding rate, be sure to change your decimal answer to a percent.

QUICK CHECK 1

Solve for rate.

(a) 63 is_______ % of 84. **(b)** _______% of 128 is 544.

OBJECTIVE 2 **Find the rate of return when the amount of the return and the investment are known.** The rate of return in an investment problem may be found using the basic percent formula.

EXAMPLE 2

Finding the Rate of Return

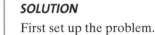

Thomas Dugally invested a total of $2010 in a cell phone, a Palm Pilot, a Compaq Presario notebook, and a portable DVD player. As a result of having this equipment, he had additional income of $1820 in the first year. Find the rate of return.

SOLUTION

First set up the problem.

R	$\times$	B	$=$	P
%	of	something	is	something.
What %	of	investment	is	income?
What %	of	$2010	is	$1820?

The amount of investment, $2010, is the base, and the return, $1820, is the part. The return is part of the total investment. In the formula $R = \frac{P}{B}$, let $P = 1820$ and $B = 2010$.

$$R = \frac{1820}{2010} = .9054 \text{ or } 90.5\%$$ Rounded to the nearest tenth of a percent.

QUICK CHECK 2

An investment of $40,500 resulted in a profit of $2632.50. What was the rate of return?

OBJECTIVE 3 **Solve for the percent remaining when the total amount and amount used are given.** In some problems, the total amount of something and the amount used are given and the percent remaining must be found.

Quick Check Answers

1. (a) 75% **(b)** 425%

2. 6.5%

EXAMPLE 3

Solving for the Percent Remaining

QUICK TIP Remember that base is always 100%, the whole or total.

A hot-water heater is expected to last 10 years (its total "life") before it needs replacement. If a water heater is 8 years old, what percent of the water heater's life remains?

SOLUTION

The total life of the water heater (10 years) is the base. Subtract the amount of life used, 8 years, from the total life, 10 years, to find the number of years remaining. In other words, 10 years (total life) − 8 years (life used) = 2 years (life remaining). The life remaining is part of the entire life.

$$R = \frac{P}{B} = \frac{2}{10} = .2 = 20\%$$

If the age of the water heater (8 years) had been used as part, the resulting answer, 80%, would be the percent of life used. Find the percent of remaining life by subtracting 80% from 100%. Therefore, the remaining life is 20%, which is the same answer.

QUICK CHECK 3

The distance around Lake Tahoe is 65 miles. If Lino Delgadillo has completed 39 miles of the Lake Tahoe run, what percent of the run remains?

OBJECTIVE 4 **Find the percent of change.** The basic percent formula is used to find the **percent of increase** and the **percent of decrease**.

EXAMPLE 4

Finding the Percent of Increase

QUICK TIP Remember, to find the percent of increase, the first step is to determine the *amount of increase*. The base is *always* the original amount, such as last year's or last month's amount, and the amount of increase is the part.

Due to an advertising campaign, sales of radio-controlled cars, boats, and planes at RC Country climbed from \$36,600 last month to \$113,460 this month. Find the percent of increase.

SOLUTION

The sales last month, \$36,600, is the base. Subtract the sales last month, \$36,600, from the sales this month, \$113,460, to find the increase in sales volume.

$$\$113{,}460 - \$36{,}600 = \$76{,}860 \text{ increase in sales volume (part)}$$

Since the increase in sales volume is the part, solve for rate. Use the formula $R = \frac{P}{B}$.

$$R = \frac{\$76{,}860}{\$36{,}600} = 2.1 \text{ or } 210\%$$

The percent of increase in sales volume is 210%.

The calculator solution to this example is

(113460 − 36600) ÷ 36600 = 2.1

QUICK CHECK 4

Attendance at the company picnic this year was 234 people, while attendance last year was 120 people. Find the percent of increase.

Quick Check Answers

3. 40%
4. 95%

The following map of the United States and the accompanying chart show that homes are becoming less affordable in many parts of the country.

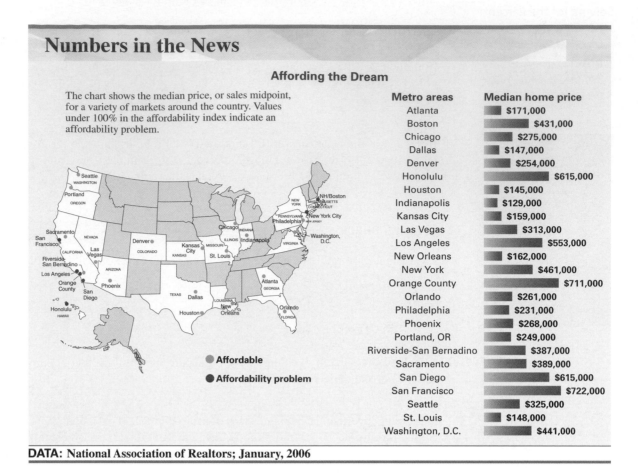

Numbers in the News

Affording the Dream

The chart shows the median price, or sales midpoint, for a variety of markets around the country. Values under 100% in the affordability index indicate an affordability problem.

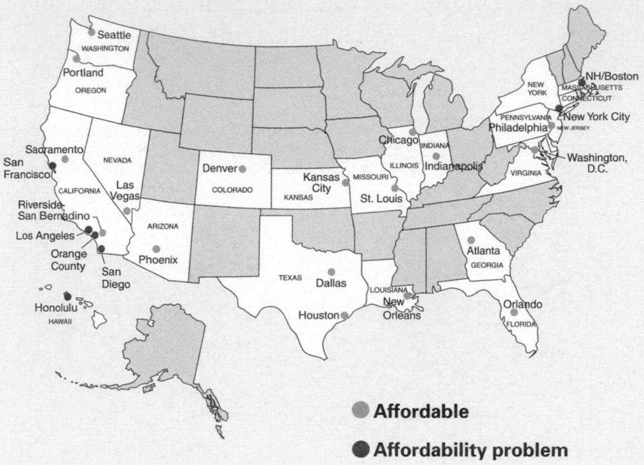

DATA: National Association of Realtors; January, 2006

EXAMPLE 5

Finding the Percent of Decrease

As a result of lower mortgage interest rates, Scott and Andrea Abriani will be able to decrease their monthly mortgage payment from \$1386 to \$1266. Find the percent of decrease.

SOLUTION

The base is the previous payment, the old monthly payment of \$1386. Subtract the new monthly payment, \$1266, from the old payment, \$1386, to find the decrease in the monthly payment.

$$\$1386 - \$1266 = \$120 \text{ decrease in monthly payment (part)}$$

Use the formula $R = \frac{P}{B}$:

$$R = \frac{120}{1386} = .0866 = 8.7\% \text{ (rounded)}$$

The percent of decrease is 8.7%.

The calculator solution to this example is to subtract to find the difference and then divide.

1386 [−] 1266 [=] 120 [÷] 1386 [=] 0.0866 = .087 (rounded)

QUICK TIP To find the percent of decrease, the first step is to determine the *amount of decrease*. The amount of decrease is the part in the problem, and the base is *always* the original amount, such as last year's, last month's, or last week's amount.

QUICK CHECK 5

The gas usage in a hybrid car decreased from 48 miles per gallon in the city to 32 miles per gallon on the highway. Find the percent of decrease.

Quick Check Answer

5. .3333 = 33.3% (rounded)

3.4 EXERCISES

FOR EXTRA HELP

MyMathLab

MathXL PRACTICE

WATCH

DOWNLOAD

READ

REVIEW

The QUICK START *exercises in each section contain solutions to help you get started.*

Solve for rate in each of the following. Round to the nearest tenth of a percent. (See Example 1.)

QUICK START

1. __10__ % of 2760 listings is 276 listings.

2. __40__ % of 850 showings is 340 showings.

3. 35 rail cars is ______ % of 70 rail cars.

4. 144 desks is ______ % of 300 desks.

5. ______ % of 78.57 ounces is 22.2 ounces.

6. ______ % of 728 miles is 509.6 miles.

7. 114 tuxedos is ______ % of 150 tuxedos.

8. $310.75 is ______ % of $124.30.

9. ______ % of $53.75 is $2.20.

10. ______ % of 850 liters is 3.4 liters.

11. 46 shirts is ______ % of 780 shirts.

12. 5.2 vats is ______ % of 28.4 vats.

13. ______ % of 600 acres is 7.5 acres.

14. ______ % of $8 is $.06.

15. 170 cartons is ______ % of 68 cartons.

16. ______ % of 425 orders is 612 orders.

17. ______ % of $330 is $91.74.

18. ______ % of 752 employees is 470 employees.

19. The basic percent formula is $P = B \times R$. Show how to find the formula to solve for R (rate). (See Objective 1.)

20. A problem includes last year's sales and this year's sales and asks for the percent of increase. Explain how you would identify the base, rate, and part in this problem. (See Objective 4.)

Solve for rate in the following application problems. Round to the nearest tenth of a percent. (See Examples 2–5.)

QUICK START

C **21.** ADVERTISING EXPENSES Thomas Dugally of Century 21 Real Estate reports that office income last month was $315,600, while advertising expenses were $19,567.20. What percent of last month's income was spent on advertising?

$$R = \frac{P}{B} = \frac{19{,}567.20}{315{,}600} = .062 = 6.2\%$$

21. __6.2%__

22. JOB CUTS Beutler Heating and Air Conditioning will lay off 45 of its 1215 workers. What percent of the workers will be laid off? (***Source:*** Beutler Heating and Air Conditioning.)

22. ______

C indicates an exercise that is related to the Case in Point feature.

23. WOMEN IN THE MILITARY A recent study by Rand's National Defense Research Institute examined 48,000 military jobs, such as Army attack-helicopter pilot or Navy gunner's mate. It was found that only 960 of these jobs are filled by women. What percent of these jobs are filled by women?

23. ________

24. VOCABULARY There are 55,000-plus words in *Webster's Dictionary*, but most educated people can identify only 20,000 of these words. What percent of the words in the dictionary can these people identify?

24. ________

25. ADVERTISING EXPENSES Advertising expenditures for Bailey's Roofers are as follows.

25. ________

Newspaper	\$2250	Television	\$1425
Radio	\$954	Yellow Pages	\$1605
Outdoor	\$1950	Miscellaneous	\$2775

What percent of the total advertising expenditures is spent on radio advertising?

26. ANTIQUE SALES Barbara's Antiquery says that of its 3800 items in inventory, 3344 are just plain junk, while the rest are antiques. What percent of the total inventory is antiques?

26. ________

27. WOMEN MOTORCYCLISTS Today there are 635,000 women motorcyclists in the United States, up from 467,400 just eight years ago. Find the percent of increase in the number of women motorcyclists. (***Source:*** Motorcycle Industry Council.)

27. ________

28. STARTER-HOME PRICE The average selling price of a starter home in the United States last year was \$186,500, while the average selling price this year was \$193,400. What is the percent of increase? (***Source:*** National Association of Realtors.)

28. ________

29. FALLING PHONE BILLS Long-distance phone bills plummeted to an average of \$24.40 a month from last year's monthly average of \$30.50. What was the percent of decrease? (***Source:*** J.D. Power.)

29. ________

30. SOLAR POWER In the past five years, the cost of generating electricity from the sun has been brought down from 24 cents to 8 cents per kilowatt hour (less than the newest nuclear power plants). Find the percent of decrease.

30. ________

SUPPLEMENTARY APPLICATION EXERCISES ON BASE, RATE, AND PART

Solve the following application problems. Read each problem carefully to determine whether base, part, or rate is being asked for. Round rates to the nearest tenth of a percent.

1. VACATION MISTAKES When 571 employees were interviewed, 17% said they made the mistake of thinking about work while on vacation. How many people felt that they had made this mistake? (***Source:*** Office Team survey.) **1.** ______

2. AMERICAN CHIROPRACTIC ASSOCIATION There are 50,000 licensed chiropractors in the United States. If 30% of these chiropractors belong to the American Chiropractic Association (ACA), find the number of chiropractors in the ACA. **2.** ______

3. MOTORCYCLE SAFETY Only 20 of the 50 states require motorcycle riders to wear helmets. What percent of the states require motorcycle riders to wear helmets? (***Source:*** National Highway Traffic Safety Administration.) **3.** ______

4. DANGER OF EXTINCTION Scientists tell us that there are 9600 bird species and that 1000 of these species are in danger of extinction. What percent of the bird species are in danger of extinction? **4.** ______

5. LOST OVERBOARD In a recent insurance company study of boaters who had lost items overboard, 88 boaters or 8% said that they lost their cell phones. Find the total number of boaters in the survey. (***Source:*** Progressive Groups of Insurance Companies.) **5.** ______

6. LIGHTS OUT There are still 100,000 households in the United States that do not have electricity. If this is .08% of the homes, find the total number of households. (***Source:*** *Time* magazine.) **6.** ______

7. COST AFTER MARKDOWN A fax machine priced at $398 is marked down 7% to promote the new model. If the sales tax is also 7%, find the cost of the fax machine including sales tax. **7.** ______

8. BOOK DISCOUNT College students are offered a 6% discount on a dictionary that sells for $18.50. If the sales tax is 6%, find the cost of the dictionary including the sales tax. **8.** ______

9. WOMEN'S COATS A "60%-off sale" begins today. What is the sale price of women's wool coats normally priced at $335? **9.** ______

10. APPLIANCES What is the sale price of a $769 Sear's Kenmore washer/dryer set with a discount of 25%? **10.** ______________

A weekly sales report for the top four salespeople at Active Sports is shown below. Use this information to answer Exercises 11–14.

Employee Commission	Sales	Rate of Commission	
Strong, A.	$18,960	3%	______
Ferns, K.	$21,460	3%	______
Keyes, B.	$17,680	______	$707.20
Vargas, K.	$23,104	______	$1152.20

11. Find the commission for Strong. **11.** ______________

12. Find the commission for Ferns. **12.** ______________

13. What is the rate of commission for Keyes? **13.** ______________

14. What is the rate of commission for Vargas? **14.** ______________

15. BIKER HELMET LAWS There were 2.48 million motorcycle riders in the country who supported biker helmet laws. If this was 62% of the total motorcycle riders in the country, what is the total number of motorcycle riders? (***Source:*** National Highway Traffic Safety Administration.) **15.** ______________

16. AVERAGE HOME PRICE According to the National Association of Realtors, the median national sales price of a house was down 1.4%, or $2085, from last month. Find the median national sales price this month. Round to the nearest dollar. **16.** ______________

17. WOMEN MOTORCYCLE OWNERS There are 6.6 million motorcycle owners in the United States. If 635,000 of the motorcycle owners are women, find the percent who are women. (***Source:*** Motorcycle Industry Council.) **17.** ______________

18. LAYOFF ALTERNATIVE Instead of laying off workers, a company cut all employee hours from 40 hours a week to 30 hours a week. By what percent were employee hours cut? **18.** ______________

NATIONWIDE HOME SALES *The numbers of existing single-family homes sold in four regions of the country in the same month of two separate years are shown in the figure below. Use the figure to answer Exercises 19–22.*

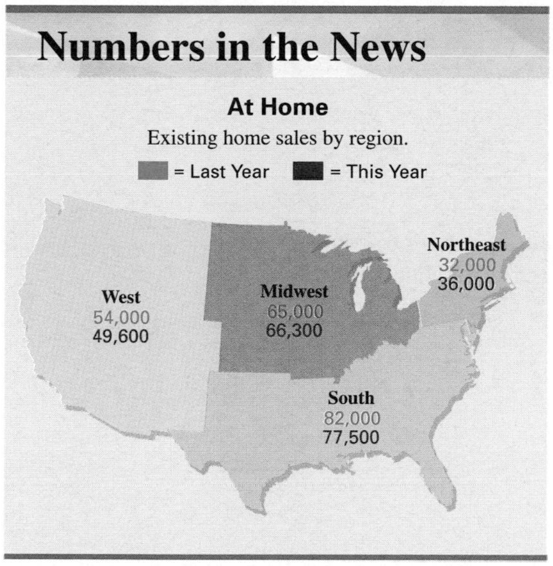

19. Find the percent of increase in sales in the northeastern region. **19.** ______

20. Find the percent of increase in sales in the midwestern region. **20.** ______

21. What is the percent of decrease in sales in the southern region? **21.** ______

22. What is the percent of decrease in sales in the western region? **22.** ______

23. HEALTH IN A MACHINE Vending machines on campus must include healthy food choices such as fruits, fruit juices, and healthy snacks. Of the total items sold in the machines this past month, 1440 or 25% have been in the healthy foods group. Find the total number of items sold in the vending machines. **23.** ______

24. TOTAL SALES If the sales tax rate is $7\frac{1}{2}\%$ and the sales tax collected is \$942.30, find the total sales. **24.** ______

25. FAMILY BUDGETING Scott and Andrea Abriani established a budget allowing 25 percent of their total income for rent, 22 percent for food, 12 percent for clothing, 24 percent for travel and recreation, and the remainder for savings. Scott takes home \$2350 per month and Andrea takes home \$31,200 per year. How much will the couple save in one year for the down payment on a home? **25.** ______

26. CHICKEN NOODLE SOUP In one year, there were 350 million cans of chicken noodle soup sold (all brands). If 60% of this soup is sold in the cold-and-flu season (October through March), find the number of cans sold in the cold-and-flu season. **26.** ______

27. SOCIAL SECURITY BENEFITS The Social Security Administration reported that in the last three years the average monthly benefit to single retirees has increased from $903 to $1008. Find the percent of increase. (***Source:*** Social Security Administration.)

27. ______________

28. BENEFIT INCREASE The average monthly Social Security benefit to couples will be increased to $1559. If the current monthly benefit is $1492, what is the percent of increase? (***Source:*** Social Security Administration.)

28. ______________

29. SIDE-IMPACT COLLISIONS Automobile accidents involving side-impact collision resulted in 9000 deaths last year. If automobiles were manufactured to meet a side-impact standard, it is estimated that 63.8% of these deaths would have been prevented. How many deaths would have been prevented?

29. ______________

30. NEW-HOME PRICES The average price of a new home dropped 9.6%. If the average price of a new home was $240,000, find the average price after the decrease.

30. ______________

31. U.S. PATENT RECIPIENTS Among the 50 companies receiving the greatest number of U.S. patents last year, 18 were Japanese companies. **(a)** What percent of the top 50 companies were Japanese companies? **(b)** What percent of the top 50 companies were not Japanese companies?

(a) ______________
(b) ______________

32. BLOOD-ALCOHOL LEVELS In the United States, 15 of the 50 states limit blood-alcohol levels for drivers to .08%. The remaining states limit these levels to .10%. **(a)** What percent of the states have a blood-alcohol limit of .08%? **(b)** What percent have a limit of .10%?

(a) ______________
(b) ______________

3.5 INCREASE AND DECREASE PROBLEMS

OBJECTIVES

1. Learn to identify an increase or decrease problem.
2. Apply the basic diagram for increase word problems.
3. Use the basic percent formula to solve for base in increase problems.
4. Apply the basic diagram for decrease word problems.
5. Use the basic percent formula to solve for base in decrease problems.

CASE *in* POINT Thomas Dugally of Century 21 Real Estate knows that real estate values are always changing, usually going up, occasionally going down, but never staying the same. Dugally needs to keep track of the market and must be able to calculate increases and decreases in value on a regular basis.

OBJECTIVE 1 Learn to identify an increase or decrease problem. Businesses commonly look at how amounts change, either up or down. For example, a manager might need to know the percent by which sales have **increased** or costs have **decreased**, while a consumer might need to know the percent by which the price of an item has changed. Identify these **increase** and **decrease** problems as follows.

Identifying Increase and Decrease Problems

Increase problem. The base (100%) *plus* some portion of the base gives a new value, which is the part. Phrases such as *after an increase of, more than,* or *greater than* often indicate an increase problem. The basic formula for an increase problem is

Original + Increase = New value
(base) (part)

Decrease problem. The part equals the base (100%) *minus* some portion of the base, giving a new value. Phrases such as *after a decrease of, less than,* or *after a reduction of* often indicate a decrease problem. The basic formula for a decrease problem is

Original − Decrease = New value
(base) (part)

QUICK TIP Base is always the original amount, and both increase and decrease problems are *base* problems. Base is always 100%.

EXAMPLE 1

Using a Diagram to Understand an Increase Problem

The value of a home sold by Thomas Dugally this year is $203,500, which is 10% more than last year's value. Find the value of the home last year.

SOLUTION

Use a diagram to help solve this problem. Remember that base is the starting point, or that to which something is compared. In this case the base is last year's value. Call base 100%, and remember that

Original + Increase = New value

OBJECTIVE 2 Apply the basic diagram for increase word problems.

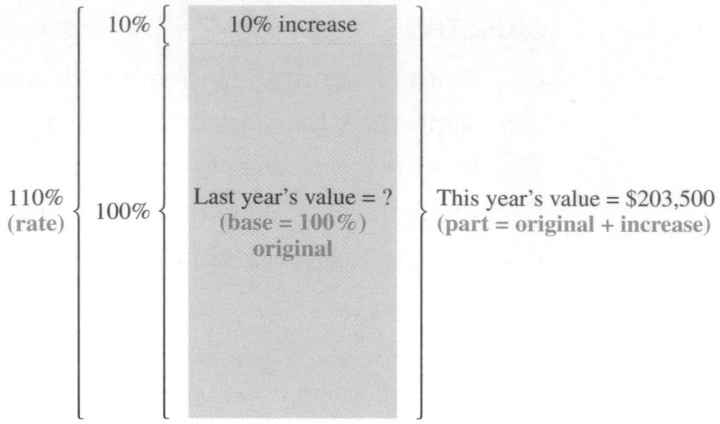

This diagram shows that the 10% increase is based on last year's value (which is unknown) and not on this year's value of $203,500. To get this year's value, 10% of last year's value was added to the amount of last year's value.

OBJECTIVE 3 Use the basic percent formula to solve for base in increase problems.

Original	+	Increase	=	New value
100%	+	10%	=	**110%**

This year's value is all of last year's value (100%) plus 10% of last year's value (or 100% + 10% = 110%). Since this year's value is 110% of last year's value, find last year's value, which is the base. The formula $B = \frac{P}{R}$ gives

$$B = \frac{\$203{,}500}{\mathbf{110\%}}$$ ← an amount that is all of base plus 10% of base; ← 100% + 10%

$$B = \frac{\$203{,}500}{\mathbf{1.1}}$$ ← 110% changed to 1.1 (change % to decimal)

$$B = \$185{,}000$$ ← last year's value

Now check the answer.

	$185,000	← last year's value
+	18,500	← 10% of $185,000
	$203,500	← this year's value

QUICK TIP The common error in solving an increase problem is thinking that the base is given and that the solution can be found by solving for part. Remember that the number given in Example 1, $203,500, is the result of having added 10% of the base to the base (100% + 10% = 110%). In fact, $203,500 is the part, and the base must be found.

QUICK CHECK 1

The total sales at Office Products this year are $713,340, which is 35% more than last year's sales. What is the amount of last year's sales?

Quick Check Answer

1. $528,400

The following graphic lists the rates of world population growth over many decades and the length of time that it takes for the population to double at various rates of growth. Population growth rates are an example of increase problems because each year's rate of growth (increase) is based on the previous year. Similarly, last year's rate of growth was based on the year prior to that.

Numbers in the News

On the Grow

The rate of world population growth, although lower than the 1960s, is still high enough to double the world's population in under 100 years.

Decade	Growth rate	Years to double
1960s	2.0%	36
1970s	1.8%	40
1980s	1.7%	42
1990s	1.4%	50
2000s*	1.2%	59
2010s*	1.0%	71

*projected

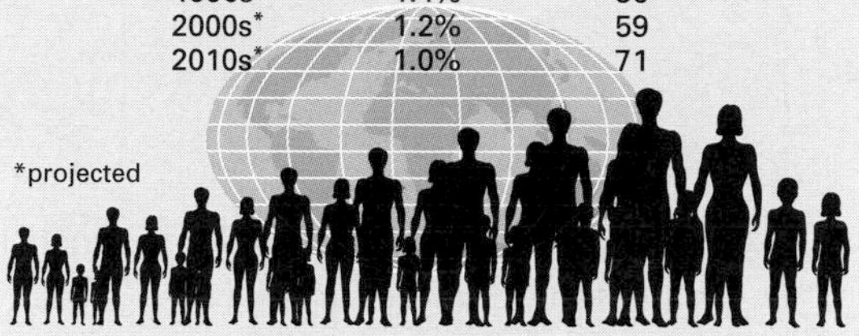

DATA: U.S. Bureau of the Census

The next example shows how to handle *two* increases.

EXAMPLE 2

Finding Base after Two Increases

At Builders Doors, production last year was 20% more than the year before. This year's production is 93,600 doors, which is 20% more than last year's. Find the number of doors produced two years ago.

SOLUTION

The two 20% increases cannot be added together because the increases are from two different years, or two separate bases. The problem must be solved in two steps. First, use a diagram to find last year's production.

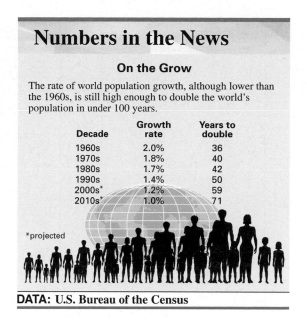

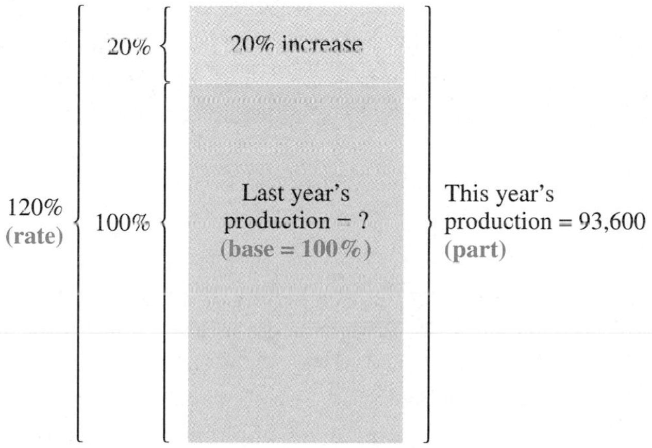

The diagram shows that last year's production plus 20% of last year's production equals this year's production. If $P = 93{,}600$ and $R = 100\% + 20\% = 120\%$, the formula $B = \frac{P}{R}$ gives

$$B = \frac{93{,}600}{120\%} = \frac{93{,}600}{1.2} = 78{,}000 \quad \text{last year's production}$$

Production last year was 78,000 doors. Production for the preceding year (two years ago) must now be found. Use another diagram.

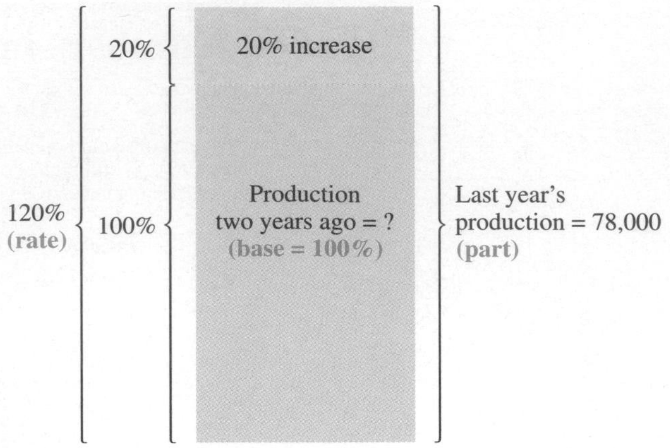

Thus, production two years ago added to 20% of production two years ago equals last year's production. Use the formula $B = \frac{P}{R}$ with P equal to 78,000 and R equal to 120%.

$$B = \frac{78{,}000}{120\%} = \frac{78{,}000}{1.2} = 65{,}000 \quad \text{production 2 years ago}$$

Check the answer.

65,000	production 2 years ago
+ 13,000	20% increase
78,000	production last year
+ 15,600	20% increase
93,600	production this year

The calculator solution to this example is done by dividing in a series.

93600 ÷ 1.2 ÷ 1.2 = 65000

QUICK TIP It is important to realize that the two 20% increases cannot be added together to equal one increase of 40%. Each 20% increase is calculated on a different base.

QUICK CHECK 2

The number of scholarships and grants offered last year was 10% more than the year before. The number of scholarships and grants offered this year is 1815, which is 10% more than last year. How many scholarships and grants were offered two years ago?

EXAMPLE 3

Using a Diagram to Understand a Decrease Problem

After Fleetfeet deducted 10% from the price of a pair of competition running shoes, Katie Small paid $135. What was the original price of the shoes?

SOLUTION

Use a diagram again, and remember that base is the starting point, which is the original price. As always, the base is 100%. Use the decrease formula.

Original	−	Decrease	=	New value
100%	−	10%	=	90%

Quick Check Answer

2. 1500 scholarships and grants offered

OBJECTIVE 4 **Apply the basic diagram for decrease word problems.**

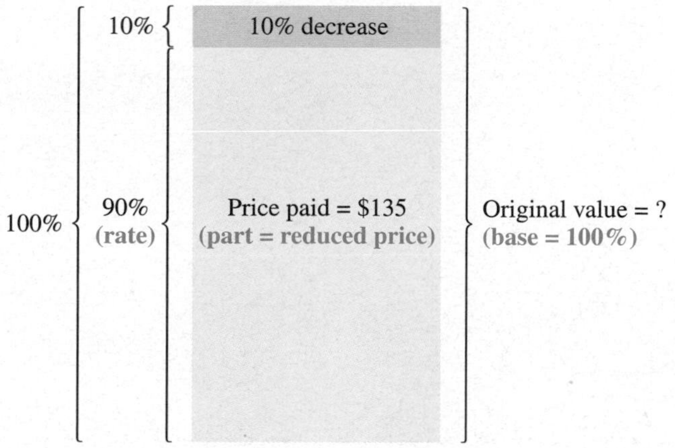

OBJECTIVE 5 **Use the basic percent formula to solve for base in decrease problems.** The diagram shows that 10% was deducted from the original price. The result equals the price paid, which is 90% of the original price. Since the original price is needed, and the diagram shows that the original price here is the base, use the formula $B = \frac{P}{R}$.

But what should be used as the rate? The rate 10% cannot be used because the original price is unknown (the price to which the 10% reduction was applied). The rate 90% (the difference, 100% − 10% = 90%) must be used, since 90% of the original price is the $135 price paid. Now find the base.

$$B = \frac{P}{R}$$

$$B = \frac{135}{90\%} = \frac{135}{.9} = \$150 \quad \text{original price}$$

Check the answer.

$150	original price
− 15	10% discount
$135	price paid

QUICK TIP The common mistake made in Example 3 is thinking that the reduced price, $135, is the base. The original price is the base, while the reduced price, $135, is a result after subtracting 10% from the base. The reduced price is the part or 90% *of the base* (100% − 10% = 90%).

QUICK CHECK 3

A 40-inch HD LCD television is discounted 25% from the original price. If the discounted price is $1799.99, what was the original price of the television?

Quick Check Answer

3. $2399.99 (rounded)

Case Studies

CENTURY 21

www.century21.com

- 2007: Headquarters in Parsippany, New Jersey
- 7800 independently owned and operated offices
- Over 143,000 brokers and sales professionals worldwide
- Operations in 42 countries and territories

Century 21 Real Estate Corporation is the franchiser of the world's largest residential real estate sales organization. It provides comprehensive training, management, administrative, and marketing support for more than 7800 independently owned and operated offices in more than 42 countries and territories worldwide.

The Century 21 System is the number-one consumer brand in the real estate industry. It consists of the largest broker network and has greater global coverage than any other real estate brand. Century 21 is dedicated to providing buyers and sellers of real estate with the highest-quality services possible.

1. A report by Century 21 says that home values in a certain area have increased by 8.2% since last year. Find the value of a home today that was valued at $195,000 last year.

2. Total property sales in a Century 21 office this month were $4.76 million. If total sales last month were $4.25 million, find the percent of increase.

Phone or visit a Century 21 office in your community and introduce yourself as a student before asking the following questions:

3. In what kinds of applications does the real estate industry use percent? Describe a minimum of six.

4. What are the advantages of working at Century 21? Ask for five positive characteristics of a career in real estate. Do you think that a career in real estate is for you? Why or why not?

3.5 EXERCISES

FOR EXTRA HELP

MyMathLab

MathXL PRACTICE

WATCH

DOWNLOAD

READ

REVIEW

The QUICK START *exercises in each section contain solutions to help you get started.*

Solve for base in each of the following. Round to the nearest cent. (Hint: Original + Increase = New value.) (See Examples 1 and 2.)

QUICK START

Part (after increase)	Rate of Increase	Base
1. \$450	20%	\$375
2. \$800	25%	________
3. \$30.70	10%	________
4. \$10.09	5%	________

Solve for base in each of the following. Round to the nearest cent. (Hint: Original − Decrease = New value.) (See Example 3.)

QUICK START

Part (after decrease)	Rate of Decrease	Base
5. \$20	20%	\$25
6. \$1530	15%	________
7. \$598.15	30%	________
8. \$98.38	15%	________

9. Certain words or word phrases help to identify an increase problem. Discuss how you identify an increase problem. (See Objective 1.)

10. Certain words or word phrases help to identify a decrease problem. Discuss how you identify a decrease problem. (See Objective 1.)

C indicates an exercise that is related to the Case in Point feature.

Solve the following application problems. Read each problem carefully to decide which are increase or decrease problems, and work accordingly. (See Examples 1–3.)

QUICK START

11. HOME-VALUE APPRECIATION Thomas Dugally of Century 21 Real Estate just listed a home for $205,275. If this is 5% more than what the home sold for last year, find last year's selling price.

$B = \frac{P}{R} = \frac{205,275}{1.05} = \$195,500$

11. $195,500

12. DEALER'S COST Cruz Electronics sold an Xbox 360 Gaming and Entertainment System for $345, a loss of 8% of the dealer's original cost. Find the original cost.

$B = \frac{P}{R} = \frac{345}{.92} = \$375$

12. $375

13. FAMILY RESTAURANT Santiago Rowland owns a small restaurant and charges 8% sales tax on all orders. At the end of the day he has a total of $1026 including the sales and sales tax in his cash register. **(a)** What were his sales not including sales tax? **(b)** Find the amount that is sales tax.

(a) ________
(b) ________

14. SALES TAX Tom Dugally of Century 21 Real Estate purchased a Tom Tom GO 910 Navigation System for $639 including $6\frac{1}{2}$% sales tax. Find **(a)** the price of the navigation system and **(b)** the amount of sales tax. (***Source:*** Office Depot.)

(a) ________
(b) ________

15. EATING OUT There are 177,000 fast-food restaurants in the United States. If fast food represents 21% of the total restaurants, find the total number of restaurants. Round to the nearest whole number. (***Source:*** Contra Costa Times/Knight Ridder Newspapers.)

15. ________

16. ANTILOCK BRAKES In a recent test of an automobile antilock braking system (ABS) on wet pavement, the stopping distance was 114 feet. If this was 28.75% less than the distance needed to stop the same automobile without the ABS, find the distance needed to stop without the ABS.

16. ________

17. POPULATION GROWTH In 2007, the population of Rio Linda was 10% more than it was in 2006. If the population was 26,620 in 2008, which was 10% more than in 2007, find the population in 2006.

17. ________

18. DELI SALES Sara Rasic, owner of Sara's Deli, says that her sales have increased exactly 20% per year for the last two years. Her sales this year are $170,035.20. Find her sales two years ago.

18. ________

19. DVD RENTALS Netflix, a DVD-rental company, has 5,700,000 subscribers, an increase of 338.5% from three years ago. Find the number of subscribers three years ago. Round to the nearest whole number. (***Source:*** Netflix.)

19. ________

20. FARMLAND PRICES The value of Iowa farmland increased 4.3% this year to a statewide average value of $1857 per acre. How much per acre did Iowa farmland increase this year? Round to the nearest dollar. (***Source:*** Iowa State University.)

20. ______________

21. FAST-FOOD SALES Fast-food sales in the United States are projected to be $163.22 billion in 2008. If this is an increase of 35.4% in the last five years, find fast-food sales five years ago. Round to the nearest tenth of a billion. (***Source:*** Contra Costa Times/Knight Ridder Newspapers.)

21. ______________

22. EXPENSIVE RESTAURANTS Among New York City's 20 most expensive restaurants, the average per-meal cost, excluding drinks, increased 5.5% to $90.13 in the last year. Find the price of this meal before the increase.

22. ______________

23. SURPLUS-EQUIPMENT AUCTION In a three-day public auction of Jackson County's surplus equipment, the first day brought $5750 in sales and the second day brought $4186 in sales, with 28% of the original equipment left to be sold on the third day. Find the value of the remaining surplus equipment.

23. ______________

24. COLLEGE EXPENSES After spending $3450 for tuition and $4350 for dormitory fees, Edgar Espina finds that 35% of his original savings remains. Find the amount of his savings that remains.

24. ______________

25. PAPER PRODUCTS MANUFACTURING The world's largest paper-manufacturing company reported a 16% drop in third quarter earnings. If earnings had dropped to $122 million, find the earnings before the drop. Round to the nearest hundredth of a million.

25. ______________

26. NATIONAL HOME SALES Sales of existing homes decreased 7.4% to an annual number of 4.87 million units. Find the annual number of homes sold before the decrease. Round to the nearest hundredth of a million. (***Source:*** National Association of Realtors.)

26. ______________

27. WINTER-WHEAT PLANTING Even though wheat prices rose during the planting season, farmers planted only 50.2 million acres of winter wheat varieties. If this is 2% fewer acres than last year, find the number of acres planted last year. Round to the nearest tenth of a million.

27. ______________

28. CHIQUITA BRANDS INTERNATIONAL Shares of Chiquita Brands stock fell 14%, to close at $13.35 per share. What was the value of the stock before the fall? Round to the nearest cent. (***Source:*** Associated Press.)

28. ______________

29. COMMUNITY COLLEGE ENROLLMENT In 2007, the student enrollment at American River College was 6% more than it was in 2006. If the enrollment was 33,708 students in 2008, which was 6% more than it was in 2007, find the student enrollment in 2006.

29. ______________

30. UNIVERSITY FEES Students at one state university are outraged. The annual university fees were 30% more last year than they were the year before. If the fees are $3380 per year this year, which is 30% more than they were last year, find the annual student fees two years ago.

30. ______________

31. CONE ZONE DEATHS This year there were 1181 deaths related to road construction zones in the United States. If this is an increase of 70% in the last five years, what was the number of deaths five years ago? Round to the nearest whole number. (***Source:*** American Road and Transportation Builders Association.)

31. ______________

32. MINORITY LOANS A large mortgage lender made 52% more loans to minorities this year than last year. If the number of loans to minorities this year is 2660, find the number of loans made to minorities last year.

32. ______________

33. NEW-HOME SALES New-home sales this year in the Sacramento, California, area were 36% fewer than last year. If the number of new homes sold this year was 11,645, find the number of new homes sold last year. (***Source:*** Sacramento Association of Realtors.) Round to the nearest whole number.

33. ______________

34. STOCK VALUE The stock value of drugstore operator CVS dropped 7.4% to close at $29.06 per share. Find the value of each share of stock before the drop. Round to the nearest cent. (***Source:*** *Sacramento Bee.*)

34. ______________

CHAPTER 3 QUICK REVIEW

CHAPTER TERMS *Review the following terms to test your understanding of the chapter. For each term you do not know, refer to the page number found next to that term.*

base **[p. 95]**	hundredths **[p. 88]**	percent formula **[p. 95]**	percents **[p. 88]**
decrease problem **[p. 123]**	increase problem **[p. 123]**	percent of decrease **[p. 115]**	rate **[p. 95]**
formula for base **[p. 105]**	part **[p. 95]**	percent of increase **[p. 115]**	sales tax **[p. 97]**
formula for rate **[p. 113]**	percent **[p. 88]**		

CONCEPTS	EXAMPLES
3.1 Writing a decimal as a percent Move the decimal point two places to the right and attach a percent sign (%).	$.75(.75.) = 75\%$
3.1 Writing a fraction as a percent First change the fraction to a decimal. Then move the decimal point two places to the right and attach a percent sign (%).	$\frac{2}{5} = .4$ $.4(.40.) = 40\%$
3.1 Writing a percent as a decimal Move the decimal point two places to the left and drop the percent sign (%).	$50\% \ (.50.\%) = .5$
3.1 Writing a percent as a fraction First change the percent to a decimal. Then write the decimal as a fraction in lowest terms.	$15\% \ (.15.\%) = .15 = \frac{15}{100} = \frac{3}{20}$
3.1 Writing a fractional percent as a decimal First change the fraction to a decimal, keeping the percent sign. Then move the decimal point two places to the left and drop the percent sign (%).	$\frac{1}{2}\% = .5\%$ $.5\% = .005$
3.2 Solving for part, using the percent formula Part = Base × Rate $P = B \times R$ $P = BR$	A company offered a 15% discount on all sales. Find the discount on sales of $1850. $P = B \times R$ $P = \$1850 \times 15\%$ $P = \$1850 \times .15 = \$277.50$ discount
3.2 Using the standard format to solve percent problems Express the problem in the format $R \times B = P$ _____% of _____ is _____ where % of something is something. Notice that *of* means × and *is* means = .	A shop gives a 10% discount on all repairs. Find the discount on a $175 repair. $R \times B = P$ % of something is something 10% of repair is discount. $.1 \times \$175 = \$17.50$ discount

CONCEPTS	EXAMPLES

3.3 Using the percent formula to solve for base

Use $P = B \times R$.

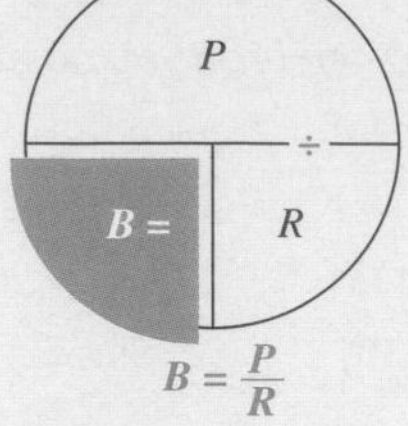

If the sales tax rate is 4%, find amount of sales when the sales tax is \$18.

$$R \times B = P$$

% of something is something
4% of sales is \$18 (tax).

$$B = \frac{18}{.04} = \$450 \text{ sales}$$

3.4 Using the percent formula to solve for rate

Use $P = B \times R$.

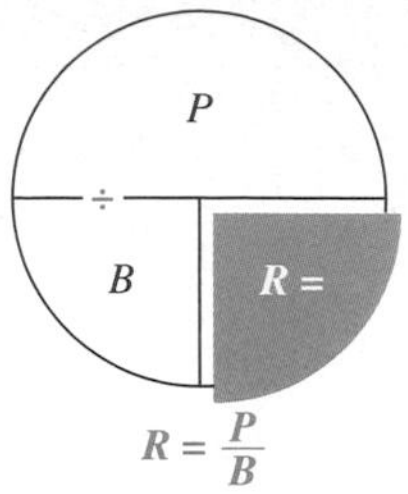

The return is \$307.80 on an investment of \$3420. Find the rate of return.

$$R \times B = P$$

% of something is something
What % of investment is return?
What % of \$3420 is \$307.80?

$$R = \frac{307.8}{3420} = .09 = 9\%$$

3.4 Finding the percent of change

Calculate the change (increase or decrease), which is the part. The base is the amount before the change.

$$R = \frac{P}{B}$$

Production rose from 3820 units to 5157 units. Find the percent of increase.

$$5157 - 3820 = 1337 \text{ change (increase)}$$

$$R = \frac{1337}{3820} = .35 = 35\%$$

3.5 Drawing a diagram and using the percent formula to solve increase problems

Solve for the base when given the rate (110%) and the part (after increase).

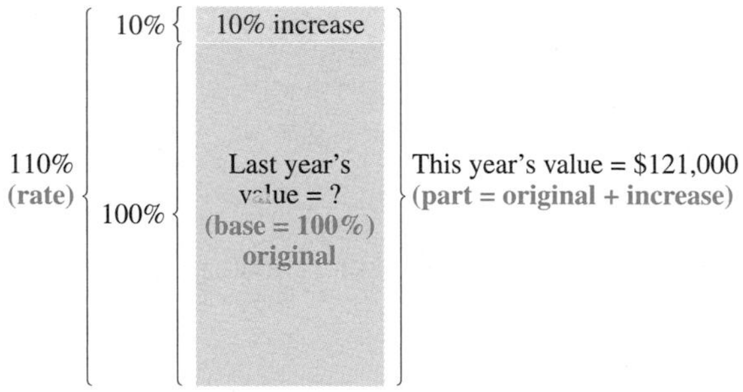

This year's sales are \$121,000, which is 10% more than last year's sales. Find last year's sales.

Original	+ Increase	= New value
100% +	10% =	110%

Use $B = \frac{P}{R}$.

$$B = \frac{\$121{,}000}{110\%} = \frac{\$121{,}000}{1.1}$$
$$= 110{,}000 \text{ last year's sales}$$

Check:

	\$110,000	last year's sales
+	11,000	10% of \$110,000
	\$121,000	this year's sales

3.5 Drawing a diagram and using the percent formula to solve decrease problems

Solve for the base when given the rate (90%) and the part (after decrease).

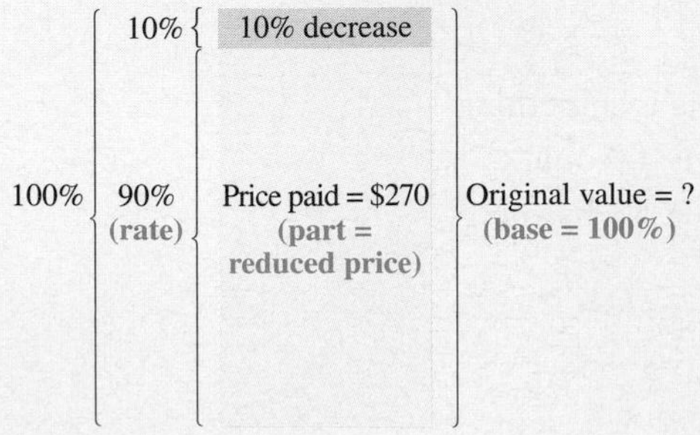

After a deduction of 10% from the price, a customer paid \$270. Find the original price.

Original	− Decrease	= New value
100%	− 10%	= 90%

Use $B = \frac{P}{R}$.

$$B = \frac{270}{.9} = \$300 \text{ original price}$$

Check:

	\$300	original price
−	30	10% discount
	\$270	price paid

CHAPTER 3 SUMMARY EXERCISE

Investment Gains and Losses

Understanding the stock market can be an important part of financial planning. Looking toward retirement, you may invest a portion of your savings by buying stock in various companies. Every day the changes in stock prices are shown in most major newspapers. Listed below are some well-known companies along with stock price information for this year and last year. Find the stock price last year, the percent of change from last year, or the stock price this year, as necessary. Round dollar amounts to the nearest cent and percents to the nearest tenth.

The Ups and Downs of Last Year

Company Name	Stock Symbol	Stock Price Last Year	Stock Price This Year	% Change from Last Year
Amazon.com	AMZN	$25.76	$39.26	______
Daimler LG	DCX	$45.98	______	28.6%
Gateway Computer	GTW	______	$1.30	− 58.6%
Krispy Kreme	KKD	$4.78	$10.39	______
McDonald's	MCD	$31.73	$41.97	______
Merck	MRK	______	$43.12	54.1%
Pepsi Bottling	PBG	$27.99	______	14.0%
NetFlix Inc.	NFLX	______	$29.38	62.1%
Wal-Mart	WMT	$52.15	______	− 10.9%
Yahoo	YHOO	$22.65	$27.39	______

INVESTIGATE

Find the New York State Exchange (NYSE) listing in a newspaper. Select five stocks that you have heard of and list their closing prices. Find the cost of 10 shares of each of these stocks, and round each of these costs to the nearest dollar.

CHAPTER 3 TEST

To help you review, the numbers in brackets show the section in which the topic was discussed.

Solve the following problems. **[3.1–3.4]**

1. 36 home sales is 12% of what number of home sales? **1.** ________

2. What is 5% of 240 open houses? **2.** ________

3. 33 shippers is 3% of what number of shippers? **3.** ________

4. 36 accounts is what percent of 1440 accounts? **4.** ________

5. What is $\frac{1}{4}$% of \$1260? **5.** ________

6. Find the fractional equivalent of 24%. **6.** ________

7. 48 purchase orders is $2\frac{1}{2}$% of how many purchase orders? **7.** ________

8. Change 87.5% to its fractional equivalent. **8.** ________

9. \$141.10 is what percent of \$1660? **9.** ________

10. What is the fractional equivalent of $\frac{1}{2}$%? **10.** ________

11. One share of Bank of America stock sells for \$54.21 and pays a 4.2% dividend. Find the dividend per share. Round to the nearest cent. **[3.2]** **11.** ________

12. A supervisor at Barrett Manufacturing finds that cabinet door hinge rejects amount to 1120 units per month. If this amounts to .5% of total monthly production, find the total monthly production of door hinges. **[3.3]** **12.** ________

13. A Cadillac Escalade is offered at 18% off the manufacturer's suggested retail price. Find the discount and the sale price of this Escalade, originally priced at $50,500. **[3.2]**

13. ____________

14. There are 40 million Americans 65 or older, and they make up 13 percent of the U.S. population. What is the total population of the United States? Round to the nearest tenth of a million. (***Source:*** AARP.) **[3.2]**

14. ____________

15. A retail store with a monthly advertising budget of $3400 decides to set up a media budget. It plans to spend 22% for television advertising, 38% for newspaper advertising, 14% for outdoor signs, 15% for radio advertising, and the remainder for bumper stickers.
(a) What percent of the total budget do they plan to spend on bumper stickers?
(b) How much do they plan to spend on bumper stickers for the entire year? **[3.2]**

(a) ____________
(b) ____________

16. Americans lose about 300 million golf balls each year, and about 225 million of these are recovered and resold in what has become a $200-million annual business. What percent of the lost golf balls are recovered and resold? (***Source:*** *USA Today*.) **[3.4]**

16. ____________

17. A Zune 30 GB Digital Media Player is marked "Reduced 20%, Now Only $224.40." Find the original price of the media player. **[3.5]**

17. ____________

18. Last year's backpack sales were 10% more than they were the year before. This year's sales are 1452 units, which is 10% more than last year. Find the number of backpacks sold two years ago. **[3.5]**

18. ____________

19. The local real estate board reports that the number of condominium listings last month was 379. If 357 condominiums were listed in the same month last year, find the percent of increase. Round to the nearest tenth of a percent. (***Source:*** Sacramento *Realtor*.) **[3.4]**

19. ____________

20. Proctor & Gamble, the maker of Tide detergent, Pampers diapers, and Clairol hair-care products, had quarterly earnings that rose 20% to $1.76 billion. Find the earnings in the previous quarter. Round to the nearest hundredth of a billion. (***Source:*** Proctor & Gamble.) **[3.4]**

20. ____________

CHAPTER 3 CUMULATIVE REVIEW

Chapters 1–3

To help you review, the numbers in brackets show the section in which the topic was introduced.

Round each of the following numbers as indicated. **[1.1, 1.3]**

1. 65,462 to the nearest hundred **1.** ________

2. 4,732,489 to the nearest thousand **2.** ________

3. 78.35 to the nearest tenth **3.** ________

4. 328.2849 to the nearest hundredth **4.** ________

Solve the following problems. **[1.1–1.5]**

5. $351 + 763 + 2478 + 17$

6. $45{,}867 - 37{,}985$

7. 634×38

8. 2450×320

9. $6290 \div 74 =$ ____

10. $22{,}899 \div 102 =$ ____

11. $.46 + 9.2 + 8 + 17.514 =$ ____

12. $45.36 - 23.7$

13. $29.8 \times .41$

14. $21.8\overline{)396.76}$

Solve the following application problems.

15. Felix Schmid decides to establish a budget. He will spend $650 for rent, $325 for food, $420 for child care, $182 for transportation, $250 for other expenses, and he will put the remainder in savings. If his monthly take-home pay is $2025, find his savings. **[1.1]** **15.** ________

16. Clancy Strock writes a feature article called "I know ... I was there" for each issue of *Reminisce* magazine. He has written an article for each monthly issue of the magazine from 1993 through 2008 (16 years). How many of these monthly articles has he written? (***Source:*** Reiman Publications.) **16.** ________

17. Software Depot had a bank balance of $29,742.18 at the beginning of April. During the month, the firm made deposits of $14,096.18 and $6529.42. A total of $18,709.51 in checks was paid by the bank during the month. Find the firm's checking account balance at the end of April. **[1.4]** **17.** ________

18. Cara Groff pays $128.11 each month to the Bank of Bolivia. How many months will it take her to pay off $4099.52? **[1.5]** **18.** ________

Solve the following problems. **[2.1–2.4]**

19. Write $\frac{48}{54}$ in lowest terms. ____

20. Write $8\frac{1}{8}$ as an improper fraction. ____

21. Write $\frac{107}{15}$ as a mixed number. ____

22. $1\frac{2}{3} + 2\frac{3}{4} =$ ____

23. $5\frac{7}{8} + 7\frac{2}{3} =$ ____

24. $6\frac{1}{3} - 4\frac{7}{12} =$ ____

25. $8\frac{1}{2} \times \frac{9}{17} \times \frac{2}{3} =$ ______

26. $3\frac{3}{4} \div \frac{27}{16} =$ ______

Solve the following application problems.

27. The size of a prison cell at Alcatraz Prison in the San Francisco Bay is 5 feet by 9 feet. The average size of a shark cage is 5 feet by $6\frac{1}{2}$ feet. How many more square feet are there in the prison cell than in the shark cage? (***Source:*** Discovery Channel, Monster Garage Factoid.)

27. ______

28. To prepare for the state real estate exam, Mia Dawson studied $5\frac{1}{2}$ hours on the first day, $6\frac{1}{4}$ hours on the second day, $3\frac{3}{4}$ hours on the third day, and 7 hours on the fourth day. How many hours did she study altogether? **[2.3]**

28. ______

29. The storage area at American River Raft Rental has four sides and is enclosed with $527\frac{1}{24}$ feet of security fencing around it. If three sides of the yard measure $107\frac{2}{3}$ feet, $150\frac{3}{4}$ feet, and $138\frac{5}{8}$ feet, find the length of the fourth side. **[2.3]**

29. ______

30. Play-It-Now Sports Center has decided to divide $\frac{2}{3}$ of the company's profit-sharing funds evenly among the eight store managers. What fraction of the total amount will each receive? **[2.4]**

30. ______

Solve the following problems. **[2.5]**

31. Change .65 to a fraction.

31. ______

32. Change $\frac{2}{3}$ to a decimal. Round to the nearest thousandth.

32. ______

Solve the following problems. **[3.1–3.4]**

33. Change $\frac{7}{8}$ to a percent. ______

34. Change .25% to a decimal. ______

35. Find 35% of 6200 home loans. ______

36. Find 134% of $80. ______

37. 275 sales is what percent of 1100 sales? ______

38. 375 patients is what percent of 250 patients? ______

Solve the following application problems.

39. Analysts say that during the next three years, about 15,000 of the United States' 39,000 theater (movie) screens will be shut down. What percent of the screens will be shut down? Round to the nearest tenth of a percent. (***Source:*** *USA Today.*) **[3.4]**

39. ____________

40. A Bose Home Theater System normally priced at $899.99 is on sale for 15% off. Find the amount of discount and the sales price. Round to the nearest cent. **[3.2]**

40. ____________

41. Bookstore sales of the *Physicians' Desk Reference*, which contains prescription drug information, rose 13.7% this year. If sales this year were 111,150 copies, find last year's sales. Round to the nearest whole number. **[3.5]**

41. ____________

42. After deducting 11.8% of total sales as her commission, George-Ann Hornor, a salesperson for Marx Toy Company, deposited $35,138.88 to the company account. Find the total amount of her sales. **[3.5]**

42. ____________

43. Tumaro's Gourmet Tortillas saw sales increase 450 times in the past few years. What percent increase did they experience? Show your work, explaining how you arrived at your answer. (***Source:*** *Los Angeles Times.*) **[3.1]**

43. ____________

44. The value of a stock used to be 6 times what it is worth today. The value today is what percent of the past value? Round to the nearest tenth of a percent. Show your work, explaining how you arrived at your answer. **[3.1]**

44. ____________

WHERE'S THE BEEF? *The United States exported 2.3 billion pounds of beef. Use the circle graph below to solve Exercises 45–48.* **[3.2]**

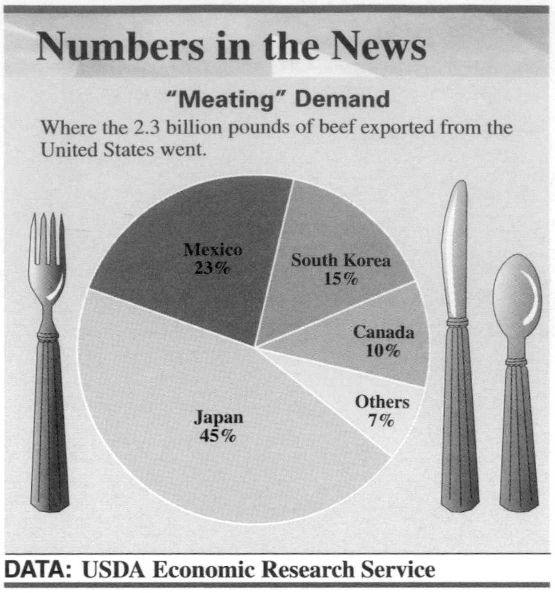

45. **(a)** What percent of the exported beef was shipped to Japan, Mexico, and South Korea combined? **(b)** Find the total number of pounds exported to these three countries.

(a) ______

(b) ______

46. **(a)** What percent of the exported beef was shipped to countries other than Japan, Mexico, and South Korea combined? **(b)** Find the total number of pounds exported to these three countries.

(a) ______

(b) ______

47. How much more beef was exported to Japan than to South Korea?

47. ______

48. How much more beef was exported to Mexico than to Canada?

48. ______

CHAPTER 4

Bank Services

CHAPTER CONTENTS

The outdoors, lots of fresh air, and nature's growing plants have always been special to Barbara Wiffy. Today, she owns and operates a small nursery, Green Giant Nursery. The nursery sells outdoor trees and shrubs, vegetable plants and fruit trees, indoor plants, and gardening accessories.

CASE in POINT

As her business has grown, one of the most important decisions made by Barbara Wiffy was selecting a bank that would offer her the services to help her operate the business profitably and with the greatest efficiency. Knowing about each service that a bank offers can help anyone who owns or operates a business.

Modern banks and savings institutions offer many services. They are more than just places to deposit savings and take out loans. Today, many types of savings accounts and a variety of checking accounts are offered. Additional services offered are online banking at home and business banking, automated teller machines (ATMs), credit cards, debit cards, investment securities services, collection of notes (covered in Chapter 8), and even payroll services for the business owner.

This chapter examines checking accounts and check registers and how to use them. It also discusses business checking-account services, the depositing of credit-card transactions, and, finally, bank reconciliation (balancing a checking account).

4.1 CHECKING ACCOUNTS AND CHECK REGISTERS

OBJECTIVES

1. Identify the parts of a check.
2. Know the types of checking accounts.
3. Calculate the monthly service charges.
4. Identify the parts of a deposit slip.
5. Identify the parts of a check stub.
6. Complete the parts of a check register (transaction register).

CASE in POINT One of the first bank services that Green Giant Nursery needed was a business checking account. Barbara Wiffy knew that she would be receiving checks from customers and that she would be using checks as well as electronic payments to pay her suppliers and all of the other expenses of operating her business. Example 1 shows how the monthly service charge for her checking account is determined.

OBJECTIVE 1 **Identify the parts of a check.** Even with the growth in **electronic commerce (EC)**, where goods are purchased and sold electronically, the majority of business transactions today still involve checks.

A small business may write several hundred checks each month and take in several thousand, while large businesses can take in millions of checks in a month. This heavy reliance on checks makes it important for all people in business to have a good understanding of checks and checking accounts. The various parts of a check are explained in the following diagram.

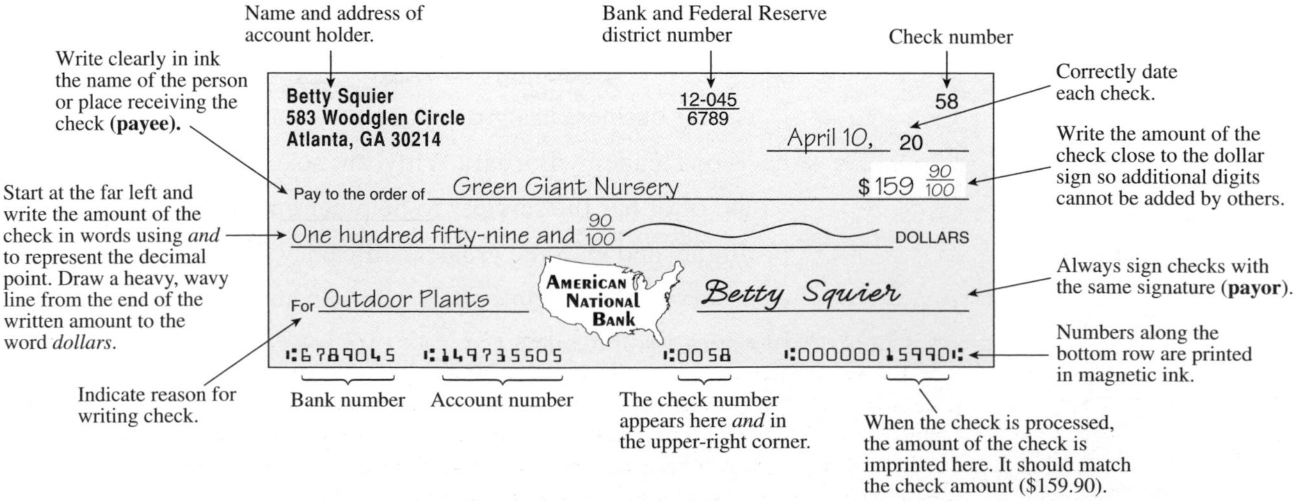

OBJECTIVE 2 **Know the types of checking accounts.** Two main types of checking accounts are available.

Personal checking accounts are used by individuals. The bank supplies printed checks (normally charging a check-printing fee) for the customer to use. Some banks offer the checking account at no charge to the customer, but most require that a minimum monthly balance

Checking Facts

- Three of every four families have a checking account.
- The average adult writes 100 checks each year.
- Checks became common after World War II.
- Checks represent about one-third of all consumer spending.
- The average check amount is $1070.
- Each year 188.6 million checks are returned for insufficient funds (bounced).

QUICK TIP Those on vacation in Europe, Canada, Mexico, and many other countries can often obtain cash in the local currency using ATM machines.

QUICK TIP When using your ATM card, remember to keep receipts so that the transaction can be subtracted from your own account records. Be certain to subtract any service charges made for using the ATM card.

Transaction Costs

The cost to banks of different payment transactions.

Bank branch	$1.07
U.S. mail	$0.73
Telephone	$0.54
ATM	$0.27
Internet	$0.01

Data: Jupiter Communication, *Home Banking Report*

remain in the checking account. If the minimum balance is not maintained during any month, a service charge is applied to the account. Today, the **flat-fee checking account** is common. For a fixed charge per month, the bank supplies the checking account, a supply of printed checks, a bank charge card, an ATM card, a debit card, and a host of other services. **Interest paid** on checking-account balances is common with personal checking accounts. These accounts are offered by savings-and-loan associations, credit unions, and banks and are available to individuals as well as to a few business customers.

Business checking accounts often receive more services and have greater activity than do personal accounts. For example, banks often arrange to receive payments on debts due to business firms. The bank automatically credits the amount to the business account.

A popular service available to personal and business customers is the **automated teller machine (ATM)**. Offered by many banks, savings and loans, and credit unions, an ATM allows the customer to perform a great number of transactions. The ATM card and **electronic banking** allow cash withdrawals and deposits, transfer of funds from one account to another, including the paying of credit-card accounts or other loans, and account-balance inquiries at *any* time. In addition, through several networking arrangements, the customer may make purchases and receive cash advances from hundreds, and in some cases thousands, of participating businesses nationally and often worldwide.

ATM cards are like **debit cards**, not credit cards. When you use your debit card at a **point-of-sale terminal**, the amount of your purchase is instantly subtracted from your bank account, and credit is given to the seller's bank account. When you use a credit card, you usually sign a receipt. However, when using a debit card, you enter your **personal identification number (PIN)**, your special code that authorizes the transaction. Cash can also be obtained from many ATM machines using credit cards such as Visa and MasterCard, even in other countries. The bar graph below shows additional services that adults would like to see offered at the ATMs.

Numbers in the News

Not Just Cash

A recent survey of men and women indicated ATMs should offer the following additional services.

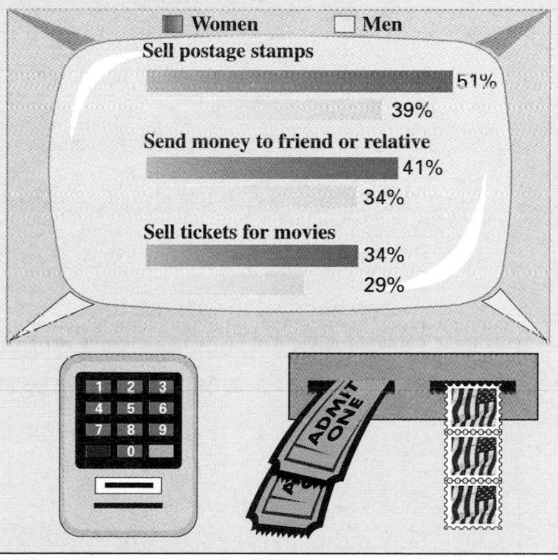

DATA: Survey of 2000 ATM users conducted by Harris Poll interactive

The use of **electronic funds transfer (EFT)** is a popular alternative to paper checks because EFT saves businesses money. The box at the side shows the cost to the company receiving payment with the use of each payment method. It is estimated that electronic payment transactions will double in volume from 2005 to 2010. **Home banking (Internet banking)** is becoming very popular for its convenience and cost savings. A recent study found that 44% of Internet users bank online. Home banking allows a customer to pay bills, check balances, and move funds, all over the Internet from home. The following visual shows how online banking customers use the service.

OBJECTIVE 3 Calculate the monthly service charges. Service charges for business checking accounts are based on the average balance for the period covered by the statement. This average balance determines the **maintenance charge per month**, to which a **per-debit charge** (per-check charge) is added. The charges generally apply without regard to the amount of account activity. The following table shows some typical bank charges for a business checking account.

QUICK TIP Companies may reduce or even eliminate charges by paying bills electronically.

Average Balance	Maintenance Charge Per Month	Per-Check Charge
Less than $500	$12.00	$.20
$500–$1999	$7.50	$.20
$2000–$4999	$5.00	$.10
$5000 or more	0	0

EXAMPLE 1

Finding the Checking-Account Service Charge

Find the monthly service charge for the following business accounts.

(a) Pittsburgh Glass, 38 checks written, average balance $883

According to the preceding table, an account with an average balance between $500 and $1999 has a $7.50 maintenance charge for the month. In addition, there is a per-debit (check) charge of $.20. Since 38 checks were written, find the service charge as follows:

$$\$7.50 + 38(\$.20) = \$7.50 + \$7.60 = \$15.10$$

(b) Fargo Western Auto, 87 checks written, average balance $2367

Since the average balance is between $2000 and $4999, the maintenance charge for the month is $5.00 plus $.10 per debit (check). The monthly service charge is

$$\$5.00 + 87(\$.10) = \$5.00 + \$8.70 = \$13.70$$

The calculator solutions to this example use chain calculations, with the calculator observing the order of operations.

(a) 7.5 [+] 38 [×] .2 [=] 15.1 **(b)** 5 [+] 87 [×] .1 [=] 13.7

Note: Refer to Appendix C for calculator basics.

QUICK CHECK 1

Find the monthly service charge for the following business accounts.

(a) Towne Florist, 76 checks written, average balance $2180
(b) On-Line Books, 58 checks written, average balance $1850

Quick Check Answers

1. (a) $12.60
(b) $19.10

OBJECTIVE 4 Identify the parts of a deposit slip. Money, either cash or checks, is placed in a checking account with a **deposit slip**, or **deposit ticket** (see the following sample). The account number is printed at the bottom in magnetic ink. The slip contains blanks for entering any currency (bills) or coin (change) as well as any checks that are to be deposited.

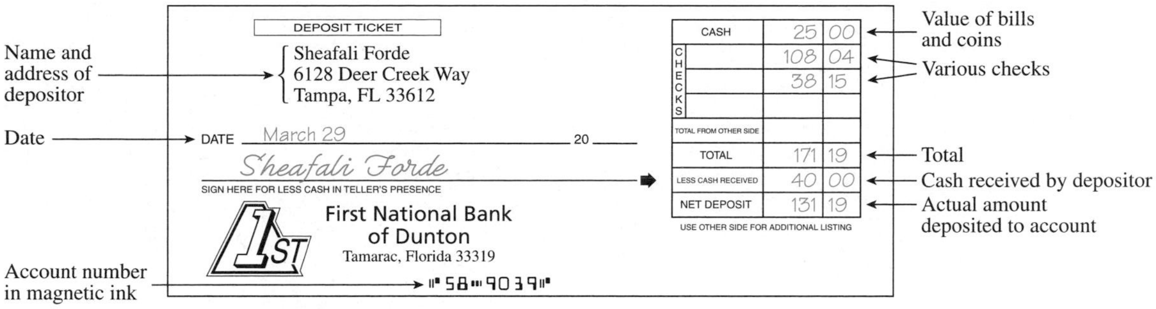

When a check is deposited, it should have "for deposit only" and either the depositor's signature or the company stamp placed on the back within 1.5 inches of the trailing edge (as seen in the following figure). In this way, if a check is lost or stolen before it is deposited, it will be worthless to anyone finding it. Such an endorsement, which limits the ability to cash a check, is called a **restricted endorsement**. An example of a restricted endorsement is shown below along with two other types of endorsements. The most common endorsement by individuals is the **blank endorsement**, where only the name of the person being paid is signed. This endorsement should be used only at the moment of cashing the check. The **special endorsement**, used to pass on the check to someone else, might be used to pay a bill on another account.

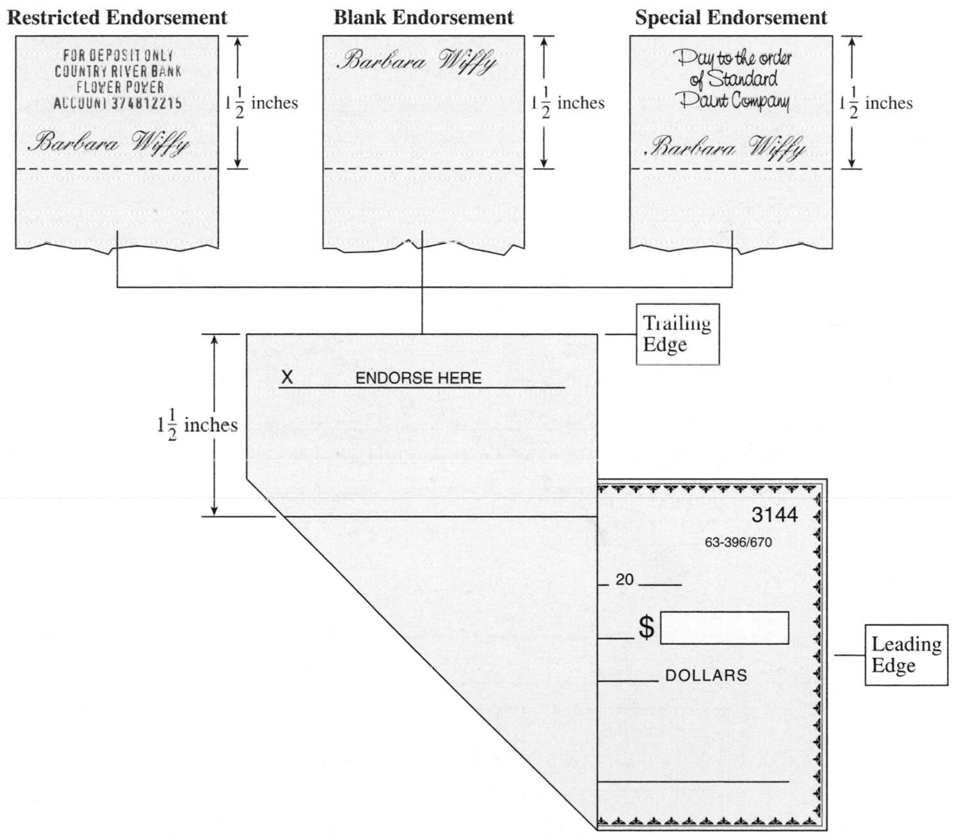

After the check is endorsed, it is normally cashed or deposited at a bank. The payee is either given cash or receives a credit in his or her account for the amount of the check. The check is then routed to a Federal Reserve Bank, which forwards the check to the payer's bank. After going through this procedure, known as **processing**, the check is **cancelled** and returned to the payer. The check will now have additional processing information on its back as follows.

The date that the bank debited (deducted) the payer's account.

The date and bank where the check was deposited are important proof against claims that a check was late or was never received.

Restricted endorsement for deposit only

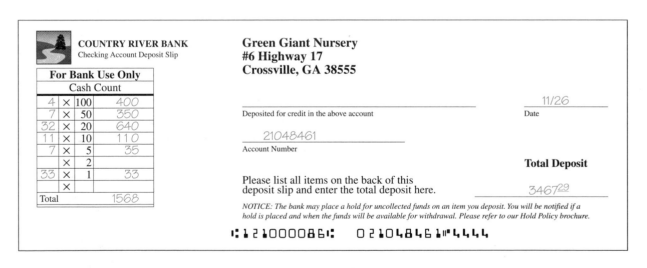

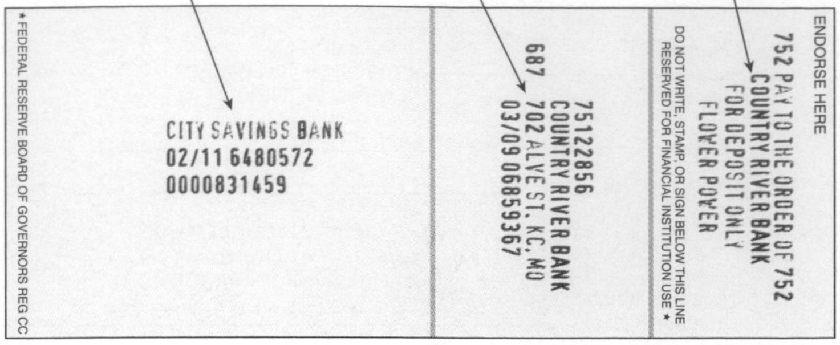

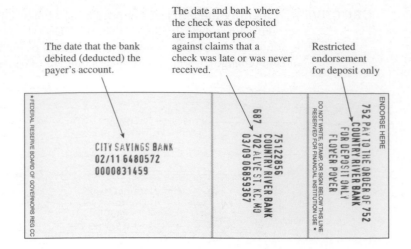

QUICK TIP A federal law known as **Check 21** took effect in October 2004. Check 21, short for the 21st Century Act, resulted in several changes in the handling of checking-account transactions. These changes in the federal banking laws allow banks to take electronic photos (images) of all cancelled checks and to exchange checks electronically. The bank then retains the photos and the cancelled checks are destroyed instead of returned to the payer. The one-to-five-day window between the time you write a check and the time your money is withdrawn from your account (known as "float") is reduced greatly.

A two-sided commercial deposit slip is shown in the figure below. Notice that much more space is given for an itemized list of customers' checks that are being deposited to the business account. Many financial institutions require that the bank and Federal Reserve district numbers be shown in the description column of the deposit slip. These numbers appear near the upper right-hand corner of the check and are identified in the sample check shown on page 144.

COUNTRY RIVER BANK
Checking Account Deposit Slip

For Bank Use Only			
Cash Count			
4	×	100	400
7	×	50	350
32	×	20	640
11	×	10	110
7	×	5	35
	×	2	
33	×	1	33
	×		
Total			1568

Green Giant Nursery
#6 Highway 17
Crossville, GA 38555

Deposited for credit in the above account — Date: 11/26

Account Number: 21048461

Total Deposit

Please list all items on the back of this deposit slip and enter the total deposit here. 3467^{29}

NOTICE: The bank may place a hold for uncollected funds on an item you deposit. You will be notified if a hold is placed and when the funds will be available for withdrawal. Please refer to our Hold Policy brochure.

⑆121000086⑆ 021048461⑈444

Please list each check separately
Specify by number the bank on which each check is drawn

Description	Dollars	Cents
Currency	1568	00
Coin	135	00
Checks - List Below		
1 90 - 7030/1	38	18
2 11 - 8	462	53
3 119	79	24
4 2208	57	14
5 514	118	32
6 111	68	76
7 35/8	25	14
8 721	9	05
9 76 - 218	188	29
10 4421	8	56
11 119	220	15
12 218	79	86
13 90 - 725	26	19
14 90 - 725	18	74
15 71 - 668	134	55
16 119	156	24
17 721	73	35
18		
19		
20		
21		
22		
23		
24		
25		
26		
27		
28		
29		
30		
31		
32		
33		
34		
35		
36		
TOTAL	3467	29

Please enter total on front of this slip

OBJECTIVE 5 Identify the parts of a check stub. A record must be kept of all deposits made and all checks written. Business firms normally do this with a **check stub** for *each* check. These check stubs provide room to list the date, the person or firm to whom the check is paid, and the purpose of the check. Also, the check stub provides space to record the balance in the account after the last check was written (called the **balance brought forward**, abbreviated "Bal. Bro't. For'd." on the stub) and any sums deposited since the last check was written. The balance brought forward and amount deposited are added to provide the current balance in the checking account. The amount of the current check is then subtracted and a new balance is found. This **balance forward** from the bottom of the check stub should be written on the next check stub. A typical check stub is shown below.

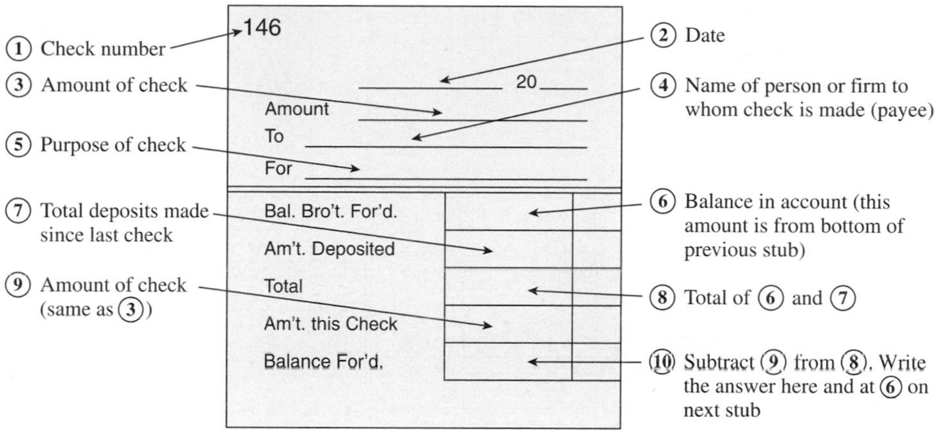

EXAMPLE 2

Completing a Check Stub

Check number 2724 was made out on June 8 to Lillburn Utilities as payment for water and power. Assume that the check was for $182.15, that the balance brought forward is $4245.36, and that deposits of $337.71 and $193.17 have been made since the last check was written. Complete the check stub.

SOLUTION

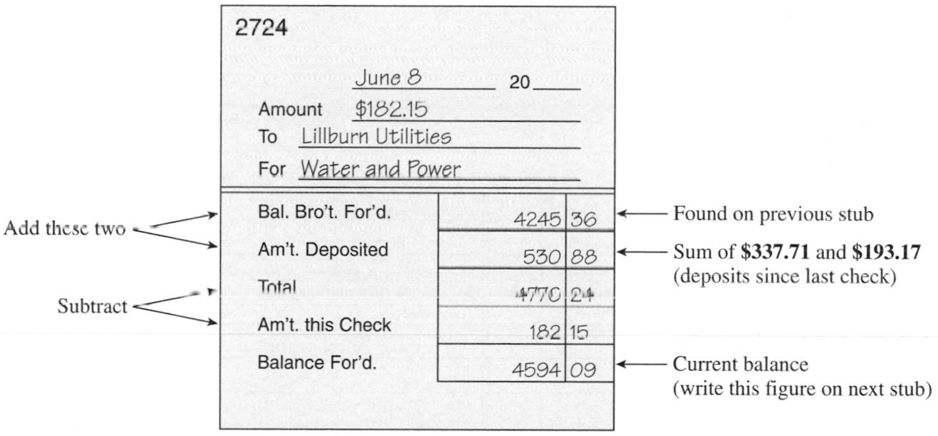

QUICK CHECK 2

Use the check stub to find the balance forward. Check number 3502 is made out on April 4 to City Hall for $273.28. The balance brought forward was $6750.17 and deposits of $1876.22 and $879.65 have been made since the last check was written.

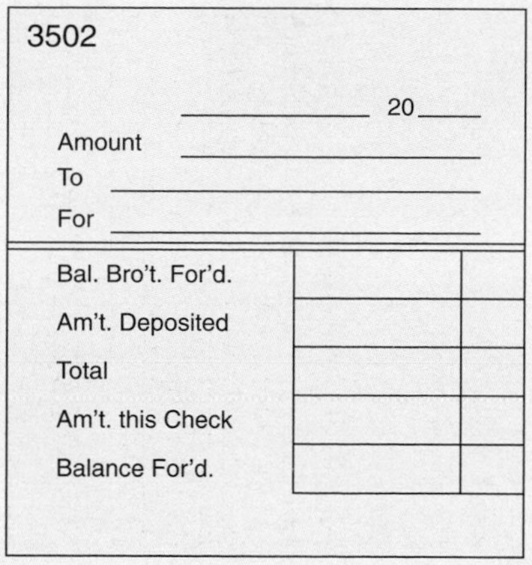

Quick Check Answer

2. $9232.76

Banks offer many styles of checkbooks. Notice that the following two styles shown offer two stubs and may be used for payroll. The stub next to the check can be used as the employee's record of earnings and deductions. The second style provides space on the check itself for listing a group of invoices or bills that are being paid with that same check.

Check stub **Check**

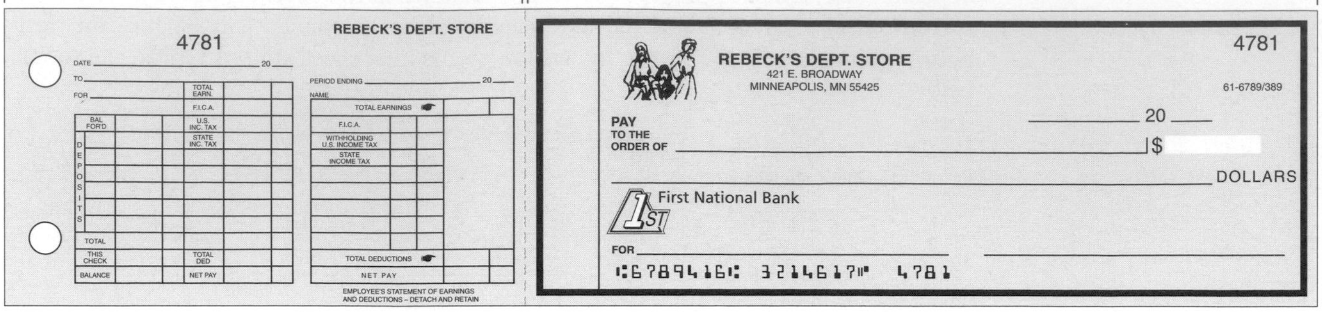

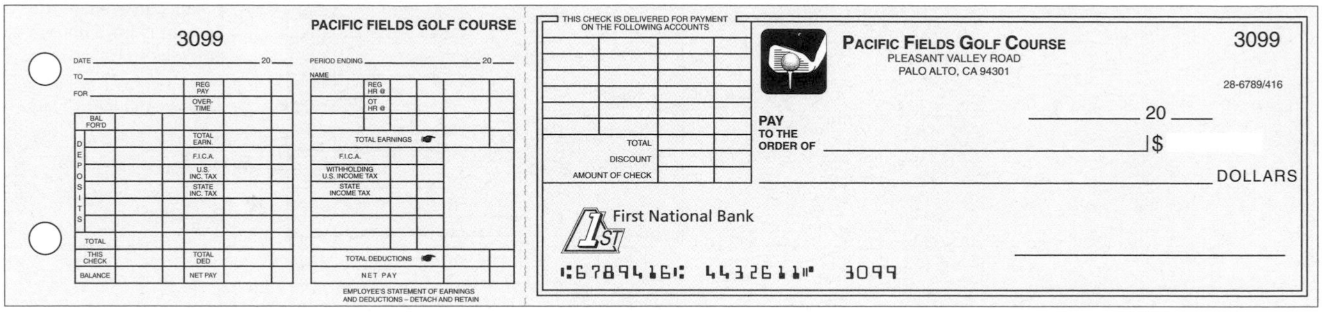

OBJECTIVE 6 Complete the parts of a check register (transaction register). Some depositors prefer a check register to check stubs, while others use both. A **check register**, also called a **transaction register**, is shown below. It lists the checks written and deposits made at a glance. The column headed with a check mark is used to record each check after it has cleared or when it is received back from the bank.

QUICK TIP ATM transactions for cash withdrawals, purchases and any ATM fees must be entered on check stubs or in the check register. The transaction amount and the charge for each transaction must then be subtracted to maintain an accurate balance.

CHECK NO.	DATE	CHECK ISSUED TO	AMOUNT OF CHECK		✓	DATE OF DEP.	AMOUNT OF DEPOSIT		BALANCE	
		BALANCE BROUGHT FORWARD →							3518	72
1435	5/8	Swan Brothers	378	93					3139	79
1436	5/8	Class Acts	25	14					3114	65
1437	5/9	Mirror Lighting	519	65					2595	00
		Deposit				5/10	3821	17	6416	17
1438	5/10	Woodlake Auditorium	750	00					5666	17
		Deposit				5/12	500	00	6166	17
1439	5/12	Rick's Clowns	170	80					5995	37
1440	5/14	Y.M.C.A.	219	17					5776	20
	5/14	ATM	120	00					5656	20
		Deposit				5/15	326	15	5982	35
1441	5/16	Stage Door Playhouse	825	00					5157	35
1442	5/17	Gilbert Eckern	1785	00					3372	35
		Deposit				5/19	1580	25	4952	60

4.1 EXERCISES

FOR EXTRA HELP

MyMathLab

MathXL PRACTICE

WATCH

DOWNLOAD

READ

REVIEW

The QUICK START *exercises in each section contain solutions to help you get started.*

CHECKING CHARGES *Use the table on page 146 to find the monthly checking-account service charge for the following accounts. (See Example 1.)*

QUICK START

1. Green Giant Nursery, 92 checks, average balance \$4618 — **1.** \$14.20

$\$5.00 + (92 \times \$.10) = \$5.00 + \$9.20 = \$14.20$

2. Fresh Choice Restaurant, 114 checks, average balance \$3318 — **2.** \$16.40

$\$5.00 + (114 \times \$.10) = \$5.00 + \$11.40 = \$16.40$

3. Pest-X, 40 checks, average balance \$491 — **3.** ____________

4. Kent's Keys, Inc., 76 checks, average balance \$468 — **4.** ____________

5. Budget Dry Cleaning, 48 checks, average balance \$1763 — **5.** ____________

6. Direct Connection, 272 checks, average balance \$8205 — **6.** ____________

7. Software and More, 72 checks, average balance \$516 — **7.** ____________

8. Mart & Bottle, 74 checks, average balance \$875 — **8.** ____________

C indicates an exercise that is related to the Case in Point feature.

C *MAINTAINING BANK RECORDS* *Use the following information to complete each check stub. (See Example 2.)*

	Date	To	For	Amount	Bal. Bro't. For'd.	Deposits
9.	Mar. 8	Nola Akala	Tutoring	$380.71	$3971.28	$79.26
10.	Oct. 15	Corinn Berman	Rent	$850.00	$2973.09	$1853.24
11.	Dec. 4	Paul's Pools	Chemicals	$37.52	$1126.73	______

9. 857

______ 20____
Amount ______
To ______
For ______

Bal. Bro't. For'd.		
Am't. Deposited		
Total		
Am't. this Check		
Balance For'd.		

10. 1248

______ 20____
Amount ______
To ______
For ______

Bal. Bro't. For'd.		
Am't. Deposited		
Total		
Am't. this Check		
Balance For'd.		

11. 735

______ 20____
Amount ______
To ______
For ______

Bal. Bro't. For'd.		
Am't. Deposited		
Total		
Am't. this Check		
Balance For'd.		

12. List and explain at least six parts of a check. Draw a sketch showing where these parts appear on a check. (See Objective 1.)

13. Explain at least two advantages and two possible disadvantages of using an ATM card. (See Objective 2.)

14. Write an explanation of two types of check endorsements. Describe where these endorsements must be placed. (See Objective 4.)

15. Explain in your own words the factors that determine the service charges on a business checking account. (See Objective 3.)

COMPLETING CHECK STUBS *Using the information provided, complete the following check stubs for Green Giant Nursery.* ***The balance brought forward for check stub 5311 is $7223.69.*** *(See Example 2.)*

Checks Written

Number	Date	To	For	Amount
5311	Oct. 7	Julie Davis	Seeds	$1250.80
5312	Oct. 10	County Clerk	License	$39.12
5313	Oct. 15	United Parcel	Shipping	$356.28

Deposits Made

Date	Amount
Oct. 8	$752.18
Oct. 9	$23.32
Oct. 13	$1025.45

16. 5311

______ 20___

Amount ______

To ______

For ______

Bal. Bro't. For'd.		
Am't. Deposited		
Total		
Am't. this Check		
Balance For'd.		

17. 5312

______ 20___

Amount ______

To ______

For ______

Bal. Bro't. For'd.		
Am't. Deposited		
Total		
Am't. this Check		
Balance For'd.		

18. 5313

______ 20___

Amount ______

To ______

For ______

Bal. Bro't. For'd.		
Am't. Deposited		
Total		
Am't. this Check		
Balance For'd.		

BANK BALANCES *In Exercises 19–22, complete the balance column in the following company check registers after each check or deposit transaction. (See Objective 6.)*

19. Green Giant Nursery

CHECK NO.	DATE	CHECK ISSUED TO	AMOUNT OF CHECK		✓	DATE OF DEP.	AMOUNT OF DEPOSIT		BALANCE	
		BALANCE BROUGHT FORWARD →							9628	35
1221	10/4	Delta Contractors	215	71						
1222	10/5	Hand Fabricating	573	78						
1223	10/5	Photo Specialties	112	15						
		Deposit				10/6	753	28		
		Deposit				10/8	1475	69		
1224	10/9	Young Marketing	426	55						
1225	10/11	Wholesale Supply	637	93						
	10/11	ATM (fuel)	65	62						
1226	10/14	Light and Power Utilities	248	17						
		Deposit				10/16	335	85		
1227	10/16	License Board	450	50						

20. Ontime Marketing

CHECK NO.	DATE	CHECK ISSUED TO	AMOUNT OF CHECK		✓	DATE OF DEP.	AMOUNT OF DEPOSIT		BALANCE	
		BALANCE BROUGHT FORWARD →							1629	86
861	7/3	Ahwahnee Hotel	250	45						
862	7/5	Willow Creek	149	00						
863	7/5	Void								
		Deposit				7/7	117	73		
864	7/9	Del Campo High School	69	80						
		Deposit				7/10	329	86		
		Deposit				7/12	418	30		
865	7/14	Big 5 Sporting Goods	109	76						
866	7/14	Dr. Yates	614	12						
867	7/16	Greyhound	32	18						
		Deposit				7/16	520	95		

21. Stencils by Loree

CHECK NO.	DATE	CHECK ISSUED TO	AMOUNT OF CHECK		✓	DATE OF DEP.	AMOUNT OF DEPOSIT		BALANCE	
		BALANCE BROUGHT FORWARD →							832	15
1121	3/17	AirTouch Cellular	257	29						
1122	3/18	Curry Village	190	50						
		Deposit				3/19	78	29		
		Deposit				3/21	157	42		
1123	3/22	San Juan District	38	76						
1124	3/23	Macy's Gourmet	175	88						
		Deposit				3/23	379	28		
1125	3/24	Class Video	197	20						
1126	3/24	Water World	25	10						
1127	3/25	Bel Air Market	75	00						
		Deposit				3/28	722	35		

22. Roy's Handyman Services

CHECK NO.	DATE	CHECK ISSUED TO	AMOUNT OF CHECK		✓	DATE OF DEP.	AMOUNT OF DEPOSIT		BALANCE	
		BALANCE BROUGHT FORWARD →							3852	48
2308	12/6	Web Masters	143	16						
2309	12/7	Water and Power	118	40						
		Deposit				12/8	286	32		
	12/10	ATM (cash)	80	00						
2310	12/11	Ann Kuick	986	22						
2311	12/11	Account Temps	375	50						
		Deposit				12/14	1201	82		
2312	12/14	Central Chevrolet	735	68						
2313	12/15	Miller Mining	223	94						
		Deposit				12/17	498	01		
2314	12/18	Federal Parcel	78	24						

4.2 CHECKING SERVICES AND CREDIT-CARD TRANSACTIONS

OBJECTIVES

1. Identify bank services available to customers.
2. Understand interest-paying checking plans.
3. Determine deposits with credit-card transactions.
4. Calculate the discount fee on credit-card deposits.

OBJECTIVE 1 **Identify bank services available to customers.** Most business checking-account charges are determined by either the average balance or the minimum balance in the account, together with specific charges for each service performed by the bank. Some of the services provided by banks, along with the *typical charges*, are listed here.

Undergrads Love Their Plastic

Undergrads with a credit card	78%
Average number of cards owned	3
Average student card debt	$2748
Students with four or more cards	32%
Balances of $3000 to $7000	13%
Balances over $7000	9%
Pay off card balance in full each month	39%

Source: Nellie Mae (college loan provider)

ATM cards are used as debit cards when making point-of-sale purchases. The fee for purchases varies from $.10 per transaction to $1 per month for unlimited transactions. When the card is used at the ATM machine, there is usually no fee at any branch of your bank, a fee as high as $2.50 at other banks, and an international fee as high as $5.

An **overdraft** occurs when a check is written for which there are **nonsufficient funds (NSF)** in the checking account and the customer has no overdraft protection, also referred to as *bouncing a check*. The typical charge to the writer of the "bad" check is $20 to $35 per bad check. The same charge occurs when a check is returned because it was improperly completed.

Overdraft protection is given when an account balance is insufficient to cover the amount of a check and an overdraft occurs. Charges for overdraft protection vary among banks.

A **returned-deposit item** is a check that was deposited and then returned to the bank, usually because of lack of funds in the account of the person or firm writing the check. A common charge to the depositor of the check is $25. At least one bank in New York charges $35.

A **stop-payment order** is a request by a depositor that the bank not honor a check the depositor has written ($25 per request).

A **cashier's check** is a check written by the financial institution itself and is viewed as being as good as cash ($8 per check).

A **money order** is a purchased instrument that is often used in place of cash and is sometimes required instead of a personal or business check ($4 each).

A **notary service** (official certification of a signature on a document) is a service that is required on certain business documents. Occasionally this service is free to customers, but there is usually a charge ($10).

Online banking or banking on the Internet allows customers to perform many banking functions from their home or place of business. This service is occasionally free, but there is often a charge ($5–$10 per month).

OBJECTIVE 2 **Understand interest-paying checking plans.** Federal banking regulations allow both personal and business interest-paying checking plans. Some of the plans combine two accounts, a savings account and a checking account, while others are simply checking accounts that collect interest on the average daily balance.

QUICK TIP The credit-card information above gives some credit-card facts for undergraduate college students. Graduate students owned an average of six credit cards, with 95% having at least one card. The average credit-card balance for graduate students is $4676.

While paying for purchases with checks remains popular, customer shopping habits have been changing as new payment options, such as debit cards, begin to take hold. The bar graph at the side shows the number and types of cards that the average household has.

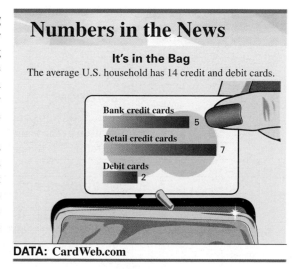

Numbers in the News

It's in the Bag

The average U.S. household has 14 credit and debit cards.

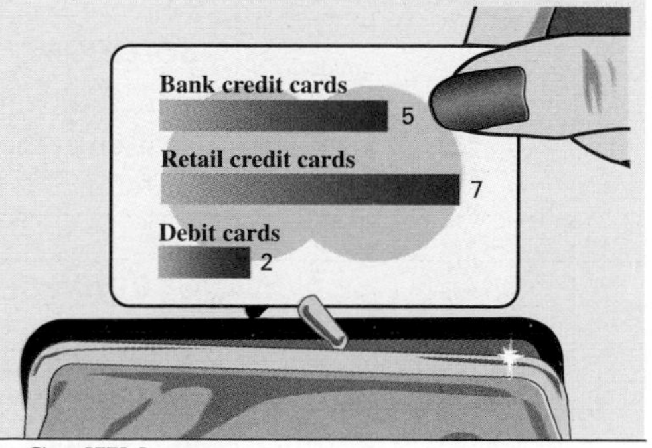

DATA: CardWeb.com

OBJECTIVE 3 Determine deposits with credit-card transactions. With the continuing growth in electronic commerce, more and more **credit-card transactions** are being completed electronically by the retailer. This results in a direct deposit to the merchant's bank account and eliminates the need for a paper transaction. The largest retail stores use a terminal at the cash register as a credit-card authorization terminal. The credit card is swiped through the terminal by either the store employee or the customer. The terminal very quickly approves (or denies) the purchase and then adds the amount charged to the bank account of the store. However, many small retailers continue to process their credit-card sales mechanically. These credit-card sales are deposited into a business checking account with a **merchant batch header ticket** such as the one in Example 1. This form is used with Visa or MasterCard credit-card deposits. Notice that the form lists both sales slips and credit slips (refunds). Entries in each of these categories are totaled, and the total credits are subtracted from the total sales to give the net amount of deposit.

The merchant batch header ticket is a triplicate form. The *bank copy* along with the charge slips, credit slips, and a printed calculator tape showing the itemized deposits and credits are deposited in the business checking account.

EXAMPLE 1

Calculating Deposits with Credit-Card Transactions

Green Giant Nursery had the following credit-card sales and refunds. Complete a merchant batch header ticket.

Sales		Refunds (Credits)
$82.31	$146.50	$13.83
$38.18	$78.80	$25.19
$65.29	$63.14	$78.56
$178.22	$208.67	

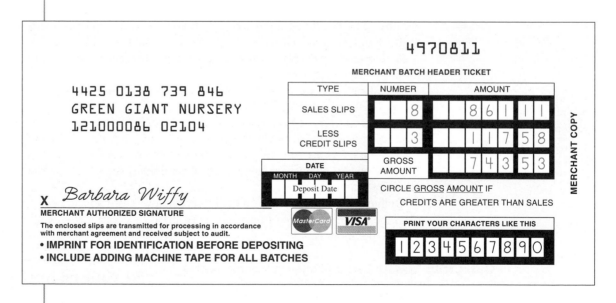

4970811

MERCHANT BATCH HEADER TICKET

4425 0138 739 846
GREEN GIANT NURSERY
121000086 02104

TYPE	NUMBER	AMOUNT
SALES SLIPS	8	861 11
LESS CREDIT SLIPS	3	117 58
GROSS AMOUNT		743 53

DATE: MONTH DAY YEAR — Deposit Date

CIRCLE GROSS AMOUNT IF CREDITS ARE GREATER THAN SALES

MERCHANT COPY

X *Barbara Wiffy*
MERCHANT AUTHORIZED SIGNATURE

The enclosed slips are transmitted for processing in accordance with merchant agreement and received subject to audit.

- IMPRINT FOR IDENTIFICATION BEFORE DEPOSITING
- INCLUDE ADDING MACHINE TAPE FOR ALL BATCHES

MasterCard VISA

PRINT YOUR CHARACTERS LIKE THIS
1 2 3 4 5 6 7 8 9 0

SOLUTION

All credit slips and sales slips must be totaled. The number of each of these and the totals are written at the right on the form. The sales slips total $861.11 and the credit slips total $117.58. The difference is the gross amount; here $743.53 is the gross amount of the deposit.

QUICK CHECK 1

Fair Oaks Auto Repair had credit card sales of $218.68, $468.17, $106.18, $75.96, $524.36, $416.35, $62.15, and $38.20. During the same period it had returns of $73.82 and $132.36. Find the amount of the gross deposit.

Quick Check Answer

1. $1703.87

Some banks offer credit cards to new customers as a way to promote business in an increasingly competitive market. The table below shows the major credit-card issuers, their dollars outstanding, and their percent of the total credit card market.

Numbers in the News

Pick a Card

The top five card issuers control 70% of the general purpose credit card market, by dollars outstanding.

Issuer	Dollars (in billions)	Market share
Bank of America	$149.2	20.2%
JPMorgan Chase	$140.1	19.0%
Citigroup	$111.9	15.1%
American Express	$72.6	9.8%
Capital One	$53.9	7.3%
Discover	$44.3	6.0%
HSBC	$27.2	3.7%
Washington Mutual	$20.0	2.7%
Wells Fargo	$17.4	2.4%
U.S. Bancorp	$11.2	1.5%
Total GP Cards	$738.6	87.7%

DATA: *Nilson Report*

The newspaper article below shows the expanding use of plastic in the fast-food industry as a way to boost sales.

HERE & NOW

McDonald's Joins Pay-With-Plastic Trend

By Bruce Horovitz
USA TODAY

Hold the mayo. Hold the pickles. Hold the cash.

The $105 billion fast-food industry – searching for quick-n-easy ways to boost sales – is finally embracing the one thing it snubbed for years: the credit card.

But Ronald McDonald isn't the only one eyeing your plastic. Wendy's accepts credit cards – where cashless purchases average 35% higher than cash. Burger King also is moving into the cashless fray.

Driving the fast-food industry's move to credit cards: Average purchases are higher and, yes, quicker. Many chains don't require signatures on credit card purchases, cutting way back on wait time.

The fast foodies also have observed the success of the prepaid and reloadable Starbucks card, which encourages frequent customers to sip without cash.

"We've been evolving into a cashless society for a long time," says John Glass, restaurant industry analyst at CIBC World Markets. "Fast food is finally catching up."

OBJECTIVE 4 Calculate the discount fee on credit-card deposits. The bank collects a fee (a percent of the credit-card sales) from the merchant. The bank also collects an interest charge from the card user on all accounts not paid in full at the first billing. Although credit-card transactions are deposited frequently by a business, the bank calculates the discount fee on the gross amount of the credit-card deposits since the last bank statement date. The fee paid by the merchant varies from 2% to 5% of the sales slip amount and is determined by the type of processing used (electronic or manual), the dollar volume of credit-card usage by the merchant, and the average amount of the sale at the merchant's store. All credit-card deposits for the month are added, and the fee is subtracted from the total at the statement date.

EXAMPLE 2

Finding the Discount and the Credit Given on a Credit-Card Deposit

If the deposit in Example 1 represented total credit-card deposits for the month, find the discount fee charged and the credit given to the merchant at the statement date if Green Giant Nursery pays a 3% fee.

SOLUTION

Since the total credit-card deposit for Green Giant Nursery is \$743.53 and the fee is 3%, the discount fee charged is

$$\$743.53 \times .03 = \mathbf{\$22.31} \quad \text{discount fee charge (rounded)}$$

Out of a deposit of \$743.53, the merchant will receive a credit of \$743.53 − **\$22.31** = **\$721.22**.

The calculator solution to this example is \$743.53 [−] 3 [%] [=] 721.2241

QUICK CHECK 2

The gross deposit in Quick Check 1 represents total credit-card deposits for the month. Find the fee charged and the credit given to the merchant at the statement date if Fair Oaks Auto Repair pays a $2\frac{1}{2}$% fee.

Quick Check Answer

2. \$42.60 fee (rounded); \$1661.27 credit

Case Studies

Jackson & Perkins

www.jacksonandperkins.com

- 1872: Founded
- 1901: Marketed the first of their hybridized roses
- 1978: Roses selected for special-issue stamp by the U.S. Postal Service
- 2004: Developed 110 hybrid rose varieties
- 2007: Had sales of over 10 million plants
- 2007: Cultivated over 5000 acres of rose plants
- 2007: Shipped over 3 million roses and other plants to customers annually

The Jackson & Perkins Company was founded in 1872 by Charles Perkins and A. E. Jackson. Beginning as a small company wholesaling strawberry and grape plants, it soon began selling hybrid roses as its main product. In those early days, when you bought a garden plant from Charles Perkins, he would always say, "If it doesn't grow for you, let me know." If the plant didn't grow, he would provide either a replacement or a refund. To this day, every Jackson & Perkins plant is guaranteed to grow.

Today, Jackson & Perkins sells a complete variety of roses and other plants and gardening accessories. Located in Medford, Oregon, the company distributes a full-color catalog of products, which are sold through mail-order or by a toll-free telephone number. Most recently, Jackson & Perkins has started using the Internet so customers can buy products online.

1. If Jackson & Perkins pays a monthly checking-account fee of \$5 plus \$.10 per check, find the total checking-account charge for a month when 836 checks were written.

2. The total credit-card sales for Jackson & Perkins during a certain period were \$837,422, while credit-card returns for the same period were \$28,225. Find **(a)** the gross amount of the credit-card deposit and **(b)** the amount of credit given to Jackson & Perkins after a fee of 2% is subtracted.

3. List and explain three advantages and three disadvantages of buying your merchandise on the Internet.

4. By asking your classmates, coworkers, and friends, find someone who has purchased items on the Internet. What was that person's experience like? Did he or she save money? Get a better selection? Get quick delivery? Would the person recommend this method of purchase to others?

4.2 EXERCISES

FOR EXTRA HELP

MyMathLab

MathXL PRACTICE

WATCH

DOWNLOAD

READ

REVIEW

The **QUICK START** *exercises in each section contain solutions to help you get started.*

CREDIT-CARD DEPOSITS *Mak's Tune and Smog accepts cash, checks, and credit cards from customers for auto repair and the sale of parts. The following credit-card transactions occurred during a recent period. Complete a merchant batch header ticket.*

Sales		Credits
$ 66.68	$ 18.95	$ 62.16
$119.63	$496.28	$106.62
$ 53.86	$ 21.85	$ 38.91
$178.62	$242.78	
$219.78	$176.93	

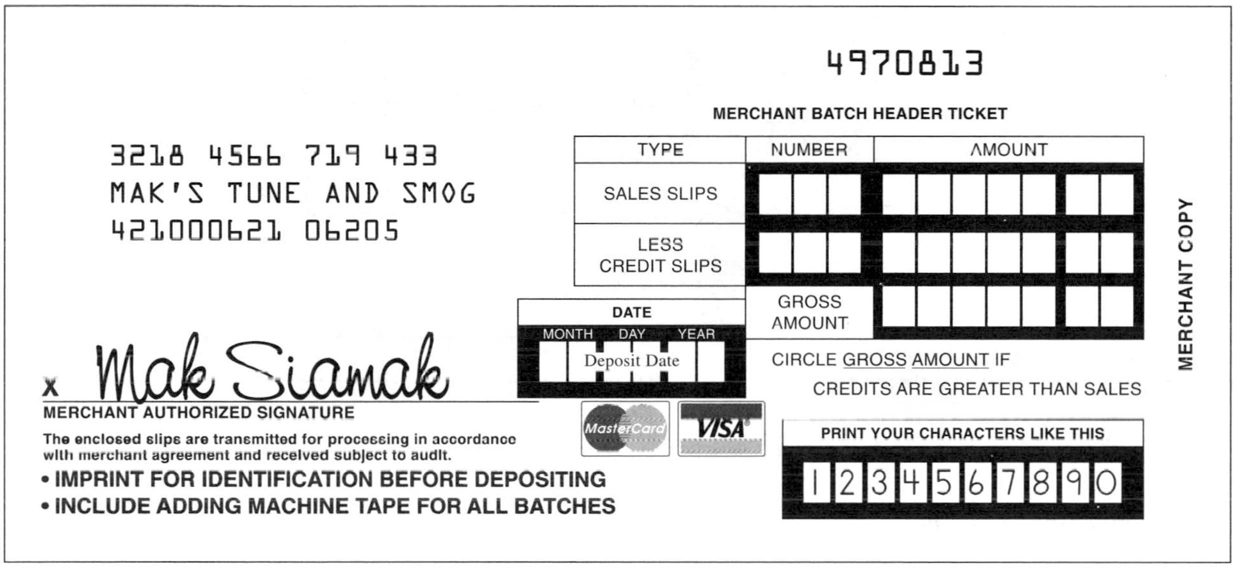
4970813

MERCHANT BATCH HEADER TICKET

3218 4566 719 433
MAK'S TUNE AND SMOG
421000621 06205

TYPE	NUMBER	AMOUNT
SALES SLIPS		
LESS CREDIT SLIPS		
	GROSS AMOUNT	

DATE
MONTH DAY YEAR
Deposit Date

CIRCLE GROSS AMOUNT IF CREDITS ARE GREATER THAN SALES

X Mak Siamak
MERCHANT AUTHORIZED SIGNATURE

The enclosed slips are transmitted for processing in accordance with merchant agreement and received subject to audit.

- IMPRINT FOR IDENTIFICATION BEFORE DEPOSITING
- INCLUDE ADDING MACHINE TAPE FOR ALL BATCHES

MasterCard VISA

PRINT YOUR CHARACTERS LIKE THIS
1 2 3 4 5 6 7 8 9 0

MERCHANT COPY

QUICK START

1. What is the total amount of the sales slips? — 1. $1595.36

   $66.68 + $119.63 + $53.86 + $178.62 + $219.78 + $18.95 + $496.28 + $21.85 + $242.78 + $176.93 = $1595.36

2. Find the total of the credit slips. — 2. $207.69

   $62.16 + $106.62 + $38.91 = $207.69

3. Find the gross deposit when the sales and credits are deposited. — 3. ________

4. If the fee paid by the business is 4%, find the amount of the charge at the statement date. — 4. ________

5. Find the amount of the credit given to Mak's Tune and Smog after the fee is subtracted. — 5. ________

C indicates an exercise that is related to the Case in Point feature.

CONCEPTS	EXAMPLES
	(c) Find gross deposit. $\$207.48 - \$41.48 = \$166$ **(d)** Given a 3% fee, find the amount of the charge. $\$166 \times .03 = \$4.98$ **(e)** Find the amount of credit given to the business. $\$166 - \$4.98 = \$161.02$
4.3 Reconciliation of a checking account A checking-account customer must periodically reconcile checking-account records with those of the bank or financial institution. The bank statement is used for this.	The accuracy of all checks written, deposits made, service charges incurred, and interest paid is checked and verified. The customer's checkbook balance and bank balance must be the same for the account to reconcile, or balance.

CHAPTER 4 SUMMARY EXERCISE

The Banking Activities of a Retailer

Barbara Wiffy owns and operates Green Giant Nursery. The nursery sells outdoor trees and shrubs, vegetable plants and fruit trees, indoor plants, and gardening accessories. Many of her customers use credit cards for their purchases, and her credit-card sales during a recent week were \$8752.40. During the same period, she had \$573.94 in credit slips and Wiffy pays a credit-card fee of $2\frac{1}{2}\%$.

When Wiffy received her bank statement, the balance was \$4228.34. The checks outstanding were found to be \$758.14, \$38.37, \$1671.88, \$120.13, \$2264.75, \$78.11, \$3662.73, \$816.25, and \$400. Wiffy had credit-card and bank deposits of \$458.23, \$771.18, \$235.71, \$1278.55, \$663.52, and \$1475.39 that were not recorded.

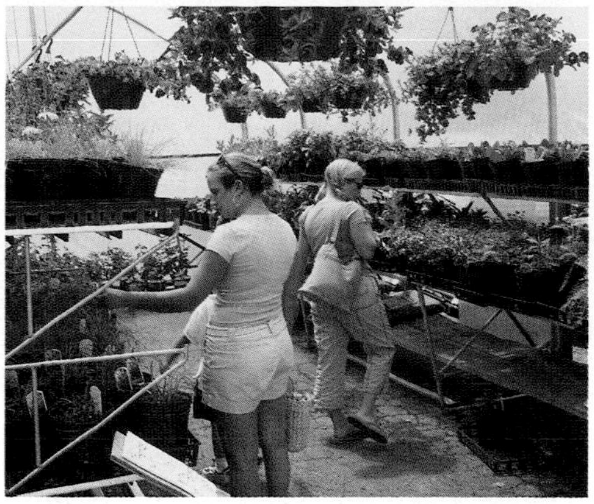

(a) Find the gross deposit when the credit-card sales and credits are deposited. **(a)** ________________

(b) Find the amount of the credit given to Wiffy after the fee is subtracted. **(b)** ________________

(c) What is the total of the checks outstanding? **(c)** ________________

(d) Find the total of the deposits that were not recorded. **(d)** ________________

(e) Find the current balance in Wiffy's checking account. **(e)** ________________

INVESTIGATE

Contact three banks or credit unions (other than your own) and ask about their charges for a personal checking account. Compare these fees with what you or your family members or friends pay for their checking accounts. Is there a way for you to get free checking? Name three considerations other than cost that are important to you in selecting a bank. Based on what you have learned, would it be a good idea for you to change banks?

CHAPTER 4 TEST

To help you review, the numbers in brackets show the section in which the topic was discussed.

Use the table on page 146 to find the monthly checking-account service charge for the following accounts. **[4.1]**

1. Tino's Italian Grocery, 62 checks, average balance $1834 **1.** ____________

2. Gifts Galore, 44 checks, average balance $2398 **2.** ____________

3. Batista Tile Works, 27 checks, average balance $418 **3.** ____________

Complete the following three check stubs for Advertising Specialists. Find the balance forward at the bottom of each stub. **[4.1]**

Checks Written

Number	Date	To	For	Amount
2261	Aug. 6	WBC Broadcasting	Airtime	$6892.12
2262	Aug. 8	Lakeland Weekly	Space buy	$1258.36
2263	Aug. 14	W. Wilson	Freelance art	$416.14

Deposits made: $1572 on Aug. 7, $10,000 on Aug. 10.

4. 2261

_______ 20___
Amount _______
To _______
For _______

Bal. Bro't. For'd.	$16,409	82
Am't. Deposited		
Total		
Am't. this Check		
Balance For'd.		

5. 2262

_______ 20___
Amount _______
To _______
For _______

Bal. Bro't. For'd.		
Am't. Deposited		
Total		
Am't. this Check		
Balance For'd.		

6. 2263

_______ 20___
Amount _______
To _______
For _______

Bal. Bro't. For'd.		
Am't. Deposited		
Total		
Am't. this Check		
Balance For'd.		

John Hendrick owns Outdoor Machines. The shop sells new and used jet skis, snowmobiles, and other outdoor recreation equipment. The following credit-card transactions occurred during a recent period. **[4.2]**

Sales		Credits
$218.68	$135.82	$45.63
$37.84	$67.45	$36.36
$33.18	$461.82	
$20.76	$116.35	
$12.72	$23.78	
$8.97	$572.18	

7. Find the total amount of sales slips for the store. **7.** ________

8. What is the total amount of the credit slips? **8.** ________

9. Find the gross amount of the deposit. **9.** ________

10. Assuming that the bank charges the retailer a $3\frac{1}{2}\%$ discount charge, find the amount of the discount charge at the statement date. **10.** ________

11. Find the amount of the credit given to Outdoor Machines after the fee is subtracted. **11.** ________

12. Weddings by Bobbi is a regular customer of Green Giant Nursery. Use the information in the following table to reconcile her checking account on the form that follows. **[4.3]** **12.** ________

Balance from bank statement		$4721.30
Checks outstanding	3221	$82.74
(check number is given first)	3229	$69.08
	3230	$124.73
	3232	$51.20
Deposits not yet recorded		$758.06
		$32.51
		$298.06
Bank charge		$2.00
Interest credit		$9.58
Checkbook balance		$5474.60
Current balance		________

Checks Outstanding		
Number	Amount	
Total		

Compare the list of checks paid by the bank with your records. List and total the checks not yet paid.

(1) Enter new balance from bank statement: ________

(2) List any deposits made by you and not yet recorded by the bank: + ________ + ________ + ________ + ________

(3) Add all numbers from lines above. Total: ________

(4) Write total of checks outstanding: − ________

(5) Subtract (4) from (3). This is adjusted bank balance: ________

To reconcile your records:

(6) List your checkbook balance: ________

(7) Write the total of any fees or charges deducted by the bank and not yet subtracted by you from your checkbook: − ________

(8) Subtract line (7) from line (6). ________

(9) Enter interest credit: (Add to your checkbook) + ________

(10) Add line (9) to line (8). Adjusted checkbook balance. ________

New balance of your account; this number should be same as (5).

CHAPTER 5

Payroll

CHAPTER CONTENTS

By the year 2007, Starbucks had opened stores in thirty-six countries outside the United States. It had grown to over 14,000 store locations and sold its products around the world.

CASE *in* POINT

Sarah Brynski worked part time for Starbucks Coffee while in college and became a full-time employee after graduation. She was recently promoted to manager of her own Starbucks Coffee location. As a store manager with over thirty-five employees, it is her responsibility to prepare the payroll. This chapter provides the essential information on calculating and working with payroll.

Preparing the payroll is one of the most important jobs in any business. Payroll records must be accurate, and the payroll must be prepared on time so that the necessary checks can be written.

5.1 GROSS EARNINGS: WAGES AND SALARIES

OBJECTIVES

1. Understand the methods of calculating gross earnings for salaries and wages.
2. Find overtime earnings for over 40 hours of work per week.
3. Use the overtime premium method of calculating gross earnings.
4. Find overtime earnings for over 8 hours of work per day.
5. Understand double time, shift differentials, and split-shift premiums.
6. Find equivalent earnings for different pay periods.
7. Find overtime for salaried employees.

CASE *in* POINT Starbucks hires most of its employees as part-time workers and pays them on an hourly basis. Sarah Brynski, the manager, will occasionally ask part-time and full-time employees to work overtime (over 8 hours in one day). When employees work more than 8 hours in one day they are paid time and a half. Having a thorough understanding of payroll helps a manager operate a business more efficiently and results in improved employee relations.

The first step in preparing the payroll is to determine the **gross earnings** (the total amount earned). There are many methods used to find gross earnings, and several of these are discussed in this chapter. A number of **deductions** may be subtracted from gross earnings to arrive at the **net pay**, the amount the employee actually receives. These various deductions also are discussed in this chapter. Finally, the employer must keep records to maintain an efficient business and to satisfy legal requirements. Many businesses use the services of a company such as Automatic Data Processing (ADP) to professionally prepare their payroll. Other businesses use computer software such as QuickBooks to help them complete this task.

OBJECTIVE 1 Understand the methods of calculating gross earnings for salaries and wages. Several methods are used for finding an employee's pay. Two of these methods (salaries and wages) are discussed in this section; two additional methods (piecework and commission) are discussed in the next section. Many employees live from paycheck to paycheck. Understanding how your total pay is calculated can eliminate the unwanted surprises that come with living from one paycheck to the next. The bar graph on page 181 shows how unprepared many workers are to cope with a period of unemployment.

In many businesses, the first step in preparing the payroll is to look at the **time card** maintained for each employee. The following time card shows the dates of the pay period; the employee's name and other personal information; the days, times, and hours worked; the total number of hours worked; and the signature of the employee as verification of the accuracy of the card. While the card shown is filled in by hand, many companies use a time clock that automatically stamps days, dates, and times on the card. The information on these cards is then transferred to a **payroll ledger** (a chart showing all payroll information) such as the one shown in Example 1.

Katie Nopper, whose payroll card is shown, is a shift manager at Starbucks and is paid an **hourly wage** of \$14.80. Her gross earnings can be calculated with the following formula.

$$\text{Gross earnings} = \text{Number of hours worked} \times \text{Rate per hour}$$

For example, if Nopper works 7 hours at \$14.80 per hour, her gross earnings are

$$\text{Gross earnings} = 7 \times \$14.80 = \$103.60$$

Numbers in the News

Living on the Edge?

While being worried about being laid off, 40 percent of workers are not prepared financially for a potential layoff. Current bank savings would last:

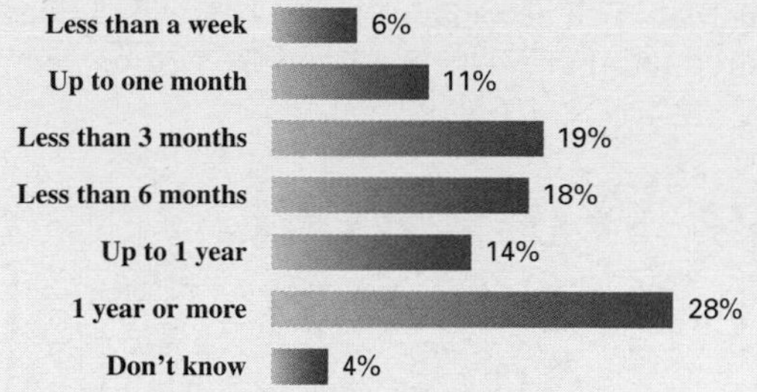

DATA: KRC Research and Consulting for Prudential Securities

PAYROLL CARD

NO TIME CLOCK REQUIRED

EMPL. NO. 1375 CARD NO. ______

FULL NAME Katie Nopper AGE (IF UNDER 18)

ADDRESS 412 Fawndale Drive SOCIAL SECURITY NO. 123-45-6789

DATE EMPLOYED POSITION Shift MGR RATE $14.80

PAY PERIOD STARTING 7/23 ENDING 7/27

DATE	REGULAR TIME IN	OUT	IN	OUT	DAILY TOTALS	OVER TIME IN	OUT	DAILY TOTALS
7/23	8:00	11:50	12:20	4:30	8	4:30	6:30	2
7/24	7:58	12:00	12:30	4:30	8	5:00	7:30	2.5
7/25	8:00	12:00	12:30	4:32	8			
7/26	7:58	12:05	12:35	4:30	8	4:30	5:00	.5
7/27	8:01	12:00	1:00	5:00	8			
APPROVED BY PD			TOTAL REGULAR TIME		40			5

REGULAR DAYS WORKED 5 @ 8 HRS. @ EARNINGS 14.80 $ 592.00

ADDITIONAL COMPENSATION: VALUE OF MEALS, LODGING, GIFTS, ETC. AMOUNT $

COMMISSIONS, FEES, BONUSES, GOODS, ETC. OT 5 @ 22.20 AMOUNT $ 111.00

OTHER REMUNERATIONS (KIND) $

DEDUCTIONS: TOTAL EARNINGS $ 703.00

I CERTIFY THE FOREGOING TO BE A CORRECT ACCOUNT OF THE TIME WORKED AND WAGES RECEIVED:

SIGNATURE DATE PAID

EXAMPLE 1

Completing a Payroll Ledger

Sarah Brynski is doing the payroll for two employees, Nelson and Orr. The first thing she must do is complete a payroll ledger.

Employee	Hours Worked S	M	T	W	Th	F	S	Total Hours	Rate	Gross Earnings
Nelson, L.	—	2	4	8	6	3	—		$8.40	
Orr, T.	—	3.5	3	7	6.75	7	—		$9.12	

SOLUTION

First, find the total number of hours worked by each person.

Nelson: $2 + 4 + 8 + 6 + 3 = 23$ **hours**

Orr: $3.5 + 3 + 7 + 6.75 + 7 = 27.25$ **hours**

Then multiply the number of hours worked by the rate per hour to find the gross earnings.

Nelson:	Orr:
23	27.25
× $8.40	× $9.12
$193.20	**$248.52**

The payroll ledger can now be completed.

Employee	Hours Worked S	M	T	W	Th	F	S	Total Hours	Rate	Gross Earnings
Nelson, L.	—	2	4	8	6	3	—	**23**	$8.40	**$193.20**
Orr, T.	—	3.5	3	7	6.75	7	—	**27.25**	$9.12	**$248.52**

QUICK CHECK 1

Ellie Kugler worked 6 hours on Monday, 4.5 hours on Tuesday, 4 hours on Wednesday, 5.75 hours on Thursday, and 3 hours on Friday. If she is paid $10.18 per hour, find her gross earnings for the week.

Workers' pay varies around the world. The list at the side shows how long it takes an average worker around the world to earn enough to buy a Big Mac. The newspaper article below describes how long American workers spend on the job compared to other workers around the world.

Numbers in the News

Where to Buy a Big Mac Fast

Here is a new way to measure economic health. The UBS Bank calculated how long it takes an average worker around the world to earn enough to buy a Big Mac.

Tokyo	10 minutes
New York	13 minutes
London	16 minutes
Hong Kong	17 minutes
Paris	21 minutes
Moscow	25 minutes
Rome	39 minutes
Beijing	44 minutes
Manila	81 minutes
Jakarta	86 minutes

DATA: *Parade Magazine*

A 40-hour Workweek Any Way You Cut It

By Chad Graham
DES MOINES REGISTER

While on vacation in Los Angeles, a lovely couple from Manchester, England, bellied up next to me at the bar. They'd spent the final day of their "holiday" in Hollywood.

"When did you leave for vacation?" I asked.

"October," they said.

"You've been in la-la land for the past two months?" I asked, eyebrow raised.

Oh no, they said. This was an around-the-world trip: Singapore, Borneo, New Zealand and then the States.

Those wacky Europeans and their vacations.

According to the Bureau of Labor Statistics, Italians get on average 42 days of paid vacation a year. The French get 37, the Germans get 35 and the British get 28. U.S. workers get a measly 16, but they tend to take only 14.

In addition American workers are on the job an average of 49 hours a week, 350 more hours a year than their European counterparts.

OBJECTIVE 2 **Find overtime earnings for over 40 hours of work per week.** The **Fair Labor Standards Act**, which covers the majority of full-time employees in the United States, establishes a workweek of 40 hours and sets the minimum hourly wage. The law states that an **overtime** wage (a higher-than-normal wage) must be paid for all hours worked over 40 hours per workweek. Also, many companies not covered by the Fair Labor Standards Act have voluntarily followed the practice of paying a **time-and-a-half rate** ($1\frac{1}{2}$ or 1.5 times the normal rate) for any work over 40 hours per week. With the time-and-a-half rate, gross earnings are found with the following formula.

Gross earnings = Earnings at regular rate + Earnings at time-and-a-half rate

EXAMPLE 2

Completing a Payroll Ledger with Overtime

Complete the following payroll ledger.

	Hours Worked							Total Hours			Gross Earnings		
Employee	**S**	**M**	**T**	**W**	**Th**	**F**	**S**	**Reg.**	**O.T.**	**Reg. Rate**	**Reg.**	**O.T.**	**Total**
Lanier, D.	6	9	8.25	8	9	4.5	—			$8.30			
Morse, T.	—	10	6.75	9	6.25	10	4.25			$9.48			

Quick Check Answer

1. $236.69 (rounded)

SOLUTION

First, find the total number of hours worked.

Lanier: $6 + 9 + 8.25 + 8 + 9 + 4.5 = $ **44.75 hours**
Morse: $10 + 6.75 + 9 + 6.25 + 10 + 4.25 = $ **46.25 hours**

Both employees worked more than 40 hours. Gross earnings at the regular rate can now be found as discussed earlier. Lanier earned 40 × \$8.30 = \$332 at the regular rate, and Morse earned 40 × \$9.48 = \$379.20 at the regular rate. To find overtime earnings, first find the number of overtime hours worked by each employee.

Lanier: 44.75 − **40** = **4.75 overtime hours**
Morse: 46.25 − **40** = **6.25 overtime hours**

The regular rate given for each employee can be used to find the time-and-a-half rate.

Lanier: **1.5** × \$8.30 = \$12.45
Morse: **1.5** × \$9.48 = \$14.22

Now find the overtime earnings.

Lanier: 4.75 hours × **\$12.45** per hour = **\$59.14** (rounded to the nearest cent)
Morse: 6.25 hours × **\$14.22** per hour = **\$88.88** (rounded)

The ledger can now be completed.

Employee	Hours Worked							Total Hours		Reg. Rate	Gross Earnings		
	S	M	T	W	Th	F	S	Reg.	O.T.		Reg.	O.T.	Total
Lanier, D.	6	9	8.25	8	9	4.5	—	40	4.75	\$8.30	\$332	\$59.14	\$391.14
Morse, T.	—	10	6.75	9	6.25	10	4.25	40	6.25	\$9.48	\$379.20	\$88.88	\$468.08

QUICK CHECK 2

Joseph Monti works 5 hours on Monday, 10 hours on Tuesday, 9.5 hours on Wednesday, 8.25 hours on Thursday, 6 hours on Friday, and 7.5 hours on Saturday. Monti is paid \$9.85 per hour and time and a half for all hours over 40 per week. Find his gross earnings.

The following newspaper clipping discusses the number of workers who depend on overtime so that they can enjoy middle-class lives.

HERE & NOW

Making Ends Meet: Overtime to the Rescue

Carmela and Alberto Gonzalez have created their version of the American dream: their own home, a daughter in college with her eye on a teaching career, and another in parochial school. But, theirs is a time-and-a-half dream, funded by the overtime both work whenever they can.

"If I didn't have overtime, it would be terrible," said Carmela, a 37-year-old mother of three. "My daughter's at university. I pay a babysitter, and I pay for school for my other daughter."

Many families are using overtime to finance middle-class lives. Although pilots, nurses, telephone operators, and paramedics are protesting forced overtime, other workers are taking second jobs or volunteering—even competing—for every hour of work they can get.

The preservation of overtime pay was a key issue that propelled Los Angeles area bus and rail operators to walk off their jobs in a strike that ran from Sept. 16 through Oct. 17.

"To maintain a standard of living, people are working longer hours. Most people don't like it but feel forced to do it," said Art Pulaski, executive secretary-treasurer for the California Labor Federation.

Source: *Los Angeles Times.*

Quick Check Answer

2. \$486.34 (rounded)

OBJECTIVE 3 Use the overtime premium method of calculating gross earnings. Gross earnings with overtime is sometimes calculated with the **overtime premium method**. This method produces the same result as the method used in Example 2. Add the total hours at the regular rate to the overtime hours at one-half the regular rate to arrive at gross earnings.

Overtime Premium Method

Straight-time earnings	⟵	total hours worked × regular rate
+ Overtime premium	⟵	overtime hours worked × $\frac{1}{2}$ regular rate
Gross earnings		

EXAMPLE 3

Using the Overtime Premium Method

This week, Holly Kelly worked 40 regular hours and 12 overtime hours. Her regular rate of pay is \$17.40 per hour. Find her total gross pay, using the overtime premium method.

SOLUTION

Kelly's total hours are 40 + 12 = 52, and her overtime premium rate is .5 × \$17.40 = \$8.70.

52 hours × \$17.40 =	\$904.80	regular rate earnings
12 overtime hours × \$8.70 =	\$104.40	overtime premium
	\$1009.20	gross earnings

QUICK TIP Many companies prefer the overtime premium method, since it readily identifies the extra cost of overtime labor. Quite often, excessive use of overtime indicates inefficiencies in management.

The calculator solution uses the order of operations to find the regular earnings and the overtime earnings, and then adds these together.

52 [×] 17.4 [+] 12 [×] 17.4 [×] .5 [=] 1009.2

Note: Refer to Appendix C for calculator basis.

QUICK CHECK 3

Tabitha Garinger worked 40 regular hours and 10 overtime hours this week. If her regular pay is \$12.10 per hour, find her gross earning using the overtime premium method.

OBJECTIVE 4 Find overtime earnings for over 8 hours of work per day. Some companies pay the time-and-a-half rate for all time worked over 8 hours in any one day no matter how many hours are worked in a week. This **daily overtime** is shown in the next example.

EXAMPLE 4

Finding Overtime Each Day

Peter Harris worked 10 hours on Monday, 5 hours on Tuesday, 7 hours on Wednesday, and 12 hours on Thursday. His regular rate of pay is \$10.10. Find his gross earnings for the week.

	S	M	T	W	Th	F	S	Total Hours
Reg.	—	8	5	7	8	—	—	28
O.T.	—	2	—	—	4	—	—	6

SOLUTION

Harris worked more than 8 hours on Monday and Thursday. On Monday, he had 10 − 8 = 2 hours of overtime, with 12 − 8 = 4 hours of overtime on Thursday. In total, he earns 2 + 4 = 6 hours of overtime. His regular hours are 8 on Monday, 5 on Tuesday, 7 on Wednesday, and 8 on Thursday, for a total of

8 + 5 + 7 + 8 = 28

Quick Check Answer

3. \$665.50 gross earnings

hours at the regular rate. His hourly earnings are $10.10. At the regular rate he earns

$$28 \times \$10.10 = \$282.80$$

If the regular rate is $10.10, the time-and-a-half rate is

$$\$10.10 \times 1.5 = \$15.15$$

He earned time and a half for 6 hours.

$$6 \times \$15.15 = \$90.90$$

His gross earnings are

$$\underbrace{\$282.80}_{\text{total regular pay}} + \underbrace{\$90.90}_{\text{total overtime}} = \underbrace{\$373.70}_{\text{gross earnings}}$$

QUICK TIP Many careers require unusual work schedules and do not pay overtime for over 40 hours worked in one week or over 8 hours worked in one day. An obvious example is the work schedule of a firefighter, who may work 24 hours and then get 48 hours off.

QUICK CHECK 4

Luke Stansbury is paid $9.60 per hour and time and a half for all hours over 8 worked per day. He worked 9 hours on Monday, 6 hours on Tuesday, 12 hours on Wednesday, and 3 hours on Friday. Find his gross earning for the week.

OBJECTIVE 5 **Understand double time, shift differentials, and split-shift premiums.** In addition to premiums paid for overtime, other **premium payment plans** include **double time** for holidays and, in some industries, Saturdays and Sundays. A **shift differential** is often given to compensate employees for working less-desirable hours. For example, an additional amount per hour or per shift might be paid to swing shift (4:00 P.M. to midnight) and graveyard shift (midnight to 8:00 A.M.) employees.

Restaurant employees and nursing home employees often receive a **split-shift premium**. Hours are staggered so that the employees are on the job during only the busiest times. For example, an employee may work 4 hours, be off 4 hours, and then work another 4 hours. The employee is paid a premium because of this less-desirable schedule.

Some employers offer **compensatory time**, or **comp time**, for overtime hours worked. Instead of additional money, an employee is given time off from the regular work schedule as compensation for overtime hours already worked. Quite often, the compensatory time is calculated at $1\frac{1}{2}$ times the overtime hours worked. For example, 12 hours might be given as compensation for 8 hours of previously worked overtime. Occasionally, an employee is given a choice of overtime pay or comp time. Many companies reserve the use of compensatory time for their supervisory or managerial employees. Also, compensatory time is very common in government agencies.

OBJECTIVE 6 **Find equivalent earnings for different pay periods.** The second common method of finding gross earnings uses a **salary**, a fixed amount given as so much per **pay period** (time between paychecks). Common pay periods are weekly, biweekly, semimonthly, and monthly.

QUICK TIP One person's salary might be a certain amount per month, while another person might earn a certain amount every 2 weeks. Many people receive an annual salary, divided among shorter pay periods.

Common Pay Periods

Monthly	12 paychecks each year
Semimonthly	Twice each month; 24 paychecks each year
Biweekly	Every 2 weeks; 26 paychecks each year
Weekly	52 paychecks each year

Quick Check Answer

4. $312

EXAMPLE 5

Determining Equivalent Earnings

You are a career counselor and want to compare the earnings of four clients you have helped to find jobs. Scott Perrine receives a weekly salary of $546, Tonya McCarley receives a biweekly salary of $1686, Julie Circle receives a semimonthly salary of $736, and Bill Leonard receives a monthly salary of $1818. For each worker, find the following: **(a)** earnings per year, **(b)** earnings per month, and **(c)** earnings per week.

SOLUTION

Scott Perrine:

(a) $546 × 52 = $28,392 per year
(b) $28,392 ÷ 12 = $2366 per month
(c) $546 per week

Tonya McCarley:

(a) $1686 × 26 = $43,836 per year
(b) $43,836 ÷ 12 = $3653 per month
(c) $1686 ÷ 2 = $843 per week

Julie Circle:

(a) $736 × 24 = $17,664 per year
(b) $736 × 2 = $1472 per month
(c) $17,664 ÷ 52 = $339.69 per week

Bill Leonard:

(a) $1818 × 12 = $21,816 per year
(b) $1818 per month
(c) $21,816 ÷ 52 = $419.54 per week

QUICK CHECK 5

Glen Lewis receives a weekly salary of $852. Find his **(a)** earnings per year, **(b)** earnings per month, and **(c)** semimonthly earnings.

HERE & NOW

Many careers require a four-year college degree. The newspaper clipping below at the left describes some of the advantages of having this degree. However, the clipping at the right shows that there are still excellent careers that do not require the four-year college degree. Notice that many of these careers do require special training or an associate degree.

Jobs for College Grads Plentiful

Hiring reaches four-year high

By Stephanie Armour
USA TODAY

College graduates are experiencing the best job market in four years as a stronger economy leads more employers to ramp up hiring.

Employers expect to hire 17.4% more new college graduates in 2006 and 2007 than in 2005 and 2006, according to a new survey by the Bethlehem, Pa.-based National Association of Colleges and Employers (NACE).

Signing bonuses range from $1,000 to $10,000, with the average at $3,568. And employers reported plans to boost their starting salary offers by 4.6% over last year, nearly a full percentage point higher than increases for the classes of 2006 and 2005.

No Degree? Apply Here

Four years of college may be your best ticket to a high-paying career, but these solid jobs don't require an undergraduate degree:

Profession	Median Annual Earnings
Air traffic controller	**$87,930**
Nuclear power reactor operator	**60,180**
Dental hygienist*	**54,700**
Elevator installer/repairer	**51,630**
Real estate broker	**51,380**
Commercial pilot (non-airline)	**47,410**
Electrical power line installer/repairer	**47,210**
Locomotive engineer	**46,540**
Telecom equipment installer/repairer*	**46,390**
Funeral director*	**42,010**
Aircraft mechanic*	**41,990**
Brick mason	**41,590**
Police officer	**40,970**
Electrician	**40,770**
Flight attendant	**40,600**
Court reporter*	**40,410**
Real estate appraiser*	**38,950**

*Requires associate's degree or vocational diploma

Source: *U.S. Department of Labor.*

OBJECTIVE 7 **Find overtime for salaried employees.** A salary is ordinarily paid for the performance of a certain job, regardless of the number of hours worked. However, the Fair Labor Standards Act requires that employees in certain salaried positions receive additional compensation for overtime. Like a wage earner, such salaried workers are paid time and a half for all hours worked over 40 hours per week.

Quick Check Answers

5. (a) $44,304 **(b)** $3692 **(c)** $1846

EXAMPLE 6

Finding Overtime for Salaried Employees

Monica Wilson is paid \$936 a week as an executive assistant. If her normal workweek is 40 hours, find her gross earnings for a week in which she works 45 hours.

SOLUTION

The executive assistant's salary has an hourly equivalent of

$$\frac{\$936}{\textbf{40 hours}} = \$23.40 \text{ per hour}$$

Since she must be paid overtime at the rate of $1\frac{1}{2}$ times her regular pay, she will get $1.5 \times \$23.40$, or \$35.10 per hour for overtime. Her gross earnings for the week are

\$936.00	salary for 40 hours
+ \$175.50	overtime for 5 hours ($5 \times \$35.10$)
\$1111.50	weekly gross earnings

The calculator solution to this example is

936 [+] 936 [÷] 40 [×] 1.5 [×] 5 [=] 1111.5

QUICK CHECK 6

Elinor Nunes has a normal workweek of 35 hours and is paid \$675.50 each week. What are her gross earnings in a week in which she works 42 hours?

HERE & NOW

Over the years, more and more women have become a part of the workforce. The percents of women in the workforce for selected countries are shown below. Many of these women are working mothers.

The following bar graph shows the work schedules of U.S. women with and without children.

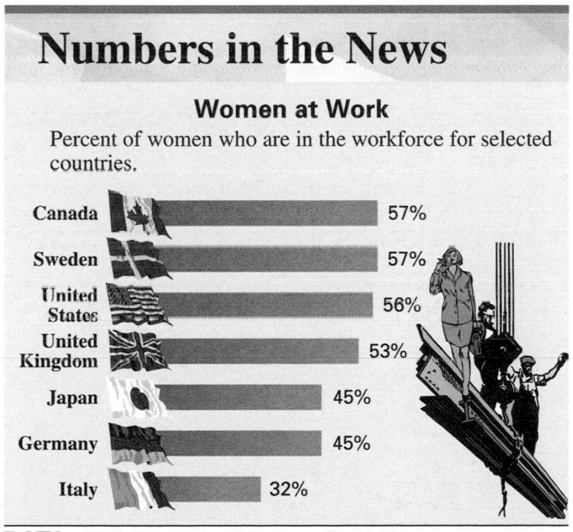

DATA: U.S. Bureau of Labor Statistics

DATA: AFL–CIO

Quick Check Answer

6. \$878.15

5.1 EXERCISES

FOR EXTRA HELP

MyMathLab

MathXL PRACTICE

WATCH

DOWNLOAD

READ

REVIEW

The QUICK START *exercises in each section contain solutions to help you get started.*

Find the number of regular hours and the overtime hours (any hours over 40) for each employee. Then calculate the overtime rate (time and a half) for each employee. (See Examples 1 and 2.)

QUICK START

Employee	S	M	T	W	Th	F	S	Reg. Hrs.	O.T. Hours	Reg. Rate	O.T. Rate
1. Burke, E.	—	7	4	7	10	8	4	40	0	$8.10	$12.15
2. Elbern, J.	—	6.5	9	7.5	8	9.5	7			$8.24	
3. Kling, J.	3	5	8.25	9	8.5	5	—			$18.70	
4. Scholz, K.	8.5	9	7.5	8	10	8.25	—			$9.50	
5. Tomlin, M.	—	9.5	7	9	9.25	10.5	—			$11.48	

Using the information from Exercises 1–5, find the earnings at the regular rate, the earnings at the overtime rate, and the gross earnings for each employee. Round to the nearest cent. (See Example 2.)

QUICK START

Employee	Earnings at Reg. Rate	Earnings at O.T. Rate	Gross Earnings
6. Burke, E.	$324	$0	$324
7. Elbern, J.			
8. Kling, J.			
9. Scholz, K.			
10. Tomlin, M.			

Find the overtime rate, the amount of earnings at regular pay, the amount at overtime pay, and the total gross wages for each employee. Round to the nearest cent. (See Example 2.)

QUICK START

	Total Hours				Gross Earnings		
Employee	Reg.	O.T.	Reg. Rate	O.T. Rate	Regular	Overtime	Total
11. Deining, M.	39.5	—	$8.80	$13.20	$347.60	$0	$347.60
12. Demaree, D.	36.25	—	$10.20				
13. Snow, P.	40	4.5	$14.40				
14. Taylor, O.	40	6.75	$12.08				
15. Weyers, C.	40	4.25	$9.18				

C indicates an exercise that is related to the Case in Point feature.

Some companies use the overtime premium method to determine gross earnings. Use this method to complete the following payroll ledger. Overtime is paid at the time-and-a-half rate for all hours over 40. (See Example 3.)

QUICK START

	Hours Worked											Gross Earnings		
Employee	**S**	**M**	**T**	**W**	**Th**	**F**	**S**	**Total Hours**	**Reg. Rate**	**O.T. Hours**	**O.T. Premium Rate**	**Reg.**	**O.T.**	**Total**
16. Averell, B.	10	9	8	5	12	7	—	51	$11.40	11	$5.70	$581.40	$62.70	$644.10
17. Brownlee, K.	7.75	10	5	9.75	8	10	—		$9.50					
18. Carter, M.	—	12	11	8	8.25	11	—		$8.60					
19. Parks, K.	—	8.5	5.5	10	12	10.5	7		$12.50					
20. Parr, J.	—	10	9.75	9	11.5	10	—		$10.20					

Some companies pay overtime for all time worked over 8 hours in a given day. Use this method to complete the following payroll ledger. Overtime is paid at the time-and-a-half rate. (See Example 4.)

QUICK START

	Hours Worked							Total Hours				Gross Earnings		
Employee	**S**	**M**	**T**	**W**	**Th**	**F**	**S**	**Reg.**	**O.T.**	**Reg. Rate**	**O.T. Rate**	**Reg.**	**O.T.**	**Total**
21. Bailey, M.	—	10	9	11	6	5	—	35	6	$9.40	$14.10	$329.00	$84.60	$413.60
22. Campbell, C.	—	9	8.75	7	8.5	10	—			$7.60				
23. Ruhkala, B.	—	7.5	8	9	10.75	8	—			$10.80				
24. Salorin, B.	—	9	10	8	6	9.75	—			$17.20				
25. Warren, L.	—	9.5	8.5	7.75	8	9.5	—			$21.50				

26. Explain what premium payment plans are in your own words. Select a premium payment plan and describe it. (See Objective 5.)

27. If you were given a choice of overtime pay or compensatory time, which would you choose? Why? (See Objective 5.)

Find the equivalent earnings for each of the following salaries as indicated. (See Example 5.)

QUICK START

	Earnings				
	Weekly	Biweekly	Semimonthly	Monthly	Annual
28.	$496	$992	$1074.67	$2149.33	$25,792
29.	$443.08	$886.15	$960	$1920	$23,040
30.		$852			
31.				$2410	
32.					$26,100
33.	$830				
34.					$27,600

Find the weekly gross earnings for the following people who are on salary and normally work a 40-hour week. Overtime is paid at the time-and-a-half rate. (See Example 6.)

	Employee	Weekly Salary	Hours Worked	Weekly Gross Earnings
35.	Beckenstein, J.	$360	42	
36.	de Bouchel, V.	$468	45	
37.	Feist-Milker, R.	$420	43	
38.	Johnson, J.	$520	56	
39.	Mader, C.	$640	48	

Solve the following application problems.

QUICK START

40. RETAIL EMPLOYMENT Last week, Frank Nicolazzo worked 48 hours at Starbucks. Find his gross earnings for the week if he is paid $8.40 per hour and earns time and a half for all hours over 40 worked in a week.

48 − 40 = 8 overtime hours
1.5 × $8.40 = $12.60 overtime rate
40 × $8.40 = $336 regular
8 × $12.60 = $100.80 overtime
$336 + $100.80 = $436.80

40. $436.80

41. INSIDE SALES Sheila Spinney is an inside salesperson and is paid $13.60 per hour for straight time and time and a half for all hours over 40 worked in a week. Find her gross earnings for a week in which she worked 52 hours.

41. ______

42. DESK CLERK Jamie Commissaris, a receptionist, earns $12.80 per hour and is paid time and a half for all time over 8 hours worked on a given day. Find her gross earnings for a week in which she works the following hours: Monday 9.5, Tuesday 7, Wednesday 10.75, Thursday 4.5, and Friday 8.75 hours.

42. ________________

43. OFFICE ASSISTANT Michelle Small is an office assistant and worked 10 hours on Monday, 9.75 hours on Tuesday, 5.5 hours on Wednesday, 12 hours on Thursday, and 7.25 hours on Friday. Her regular rate of pay is $11.50 an hour, with time and a half paid for all hours over 8 worked in a given day. Find her gross earnings for the week.

43. ________________

44. INSURANCE OFFICE MANAGER Alicia Klein is paid $728 a week as an insurance office manager. Her normal workweek is 40 hours. She gets paid time and a half for overtime. Find her gross earnings for a week in which she works 46 hours.

44. ________________

45. OFFICE EMPLOYEE An office employee earns $630 weekly. Find the equivalent earnings if the employee is paid **(a)** biweekly, **(b)** semimonthly, **(c)** monthly, and **(d)** annually.

(a) ________________
(b) ________________
(c) ________________
(d) ________________

C **46.** STORE MANAGER Michelle Renda manages a Starbucks Coffee shop and is paid $42,900 annually. Find the equivalent earnings if this amount is paid **(a)** weekly, **(b)** biweekly, **(c)** semimonthly, and **(d)** monthly.

(a) ________________
(b) ________________
(c) ________________
(d) ________________

47. Semimonthly pay periods result in 24 paychecks per year. Biweekly pay periods result in 26 paychecks per year. Which of these pay periods results in three checks in two months of the year? Will it always be the same two months? Explain.

48. Which would you prefer: a monthly pay period or a weekly pay period? What special budgetary issues might you consider regarding the pay period that you choose?

5.2 GROSS EARNINGS: PIECEWORK AND COMMISSIONS

OBJECTIVES

1. Find the gross earnings for piecework.
2. Determine the gross earnings for differential piecework.
3. Find the gross pay for piecework with a guaranteed hourly wage.
4. Calculate the overtime earnings for piecework.
5. Find the gross earnings using commission rate times sales.
6. Determine a commission using the variable commission rate.
7. Find the gross earnings with a salary plus commission.

OBJECTIVE 1 Find the gross earnings for piecework. The salaries and wages of the preceding section are **time rates** because they depend only on the actual time an employee is on the job. The methods described in this section are **incentive rates** because they are based on production and pay an employee for actual performance on the job. The ten help-wanted ads from the classified section of the newspaper are for jobs offering incentive rates of pay. The ad for lathers and stucco construction workers offers piecework and hourly compensation, while the ad for truck drivers lists piece rates of 32 cents per mile (cpm). The ads for bill collectors and commercial roofing, health insurance, Better Business Bureau membership, automobile, swimming pool, and home security system sales positions pay on a commission plan.

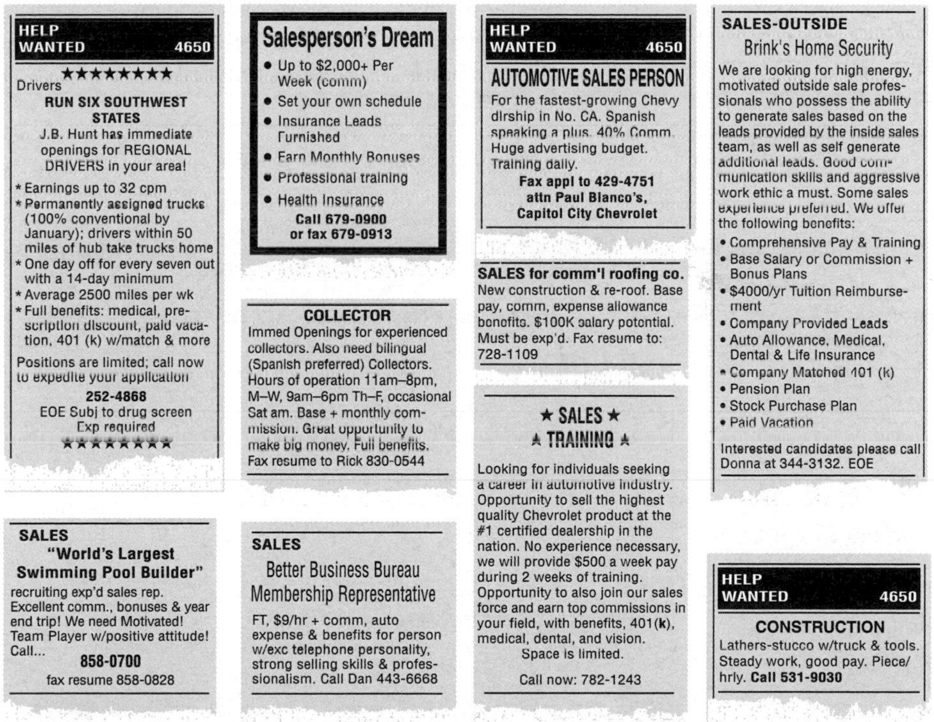
HELP WANTED 4650
★★★★★★★★
Drivers
RUN SIX SOUTHWEST STATES
J.B. Hunt has immediate openings for REGIONAL DRIVERS in your area!
* Earnings up to 32 cpm
* Permanently assigned trucks (100% conventional by January); drivers within 50 miles of hub take trucks home
* One day off for every seven out with a 14-day minimum
* Average 2500 miles per wk
* Full benefits: medical, prescription discount, paid vacation, 401 (k) w/match & more
Positions are limited; call now to expedite your application
252-4868
EOE Subj to drug screen
Exp required
★★★★★★★★

Salesperson's Dream
• Up to $2,000+ Per Week (comm)
• Set your own schedule
• Insurance Leads Furnished
• Earn Monthly Bonuses
• Professional training
• Health Insurance
Call 679-0900
or fax 679-0913

COLLECTOR
Immed Openings for experienced collectors. Also need bilingual (Spanish preferred) Collectors. Hours of operation 11am–8pm, M–W, 9am–6pm Th–F, occasional Sat am. Base + monthly commission. Great opportunity to make big money. Full benefits. Fax resume to Rick 830-0544

SALES
"World's Largest Swimming Pool Builder"
recruiting exp'd sales rep. Excellent comm., bonuses & year end trip! We need Motivated! Team Player w/positive attitude! Call...
858-0700
fax resume 858-0828

SALES
Better Business Bureau Membership Representative
FT, $9/hr + comm, auto expense & benefits for person w/exc telephone personality, strong selling skills & professionalism. Call Dan 443-6668

HELP WANTED 4650
AUTOMOTIVE SALES PERSON
For the fastest-growing Chevy dlrship in No. CA. Spanish speaking a plus. 40% Comm. Huge advertising budget. Training daily.
Fax appl to 429-4751
attn Paul Blanco's,
Capitol City Chevrolet

SALES for comm'l roofing co.
New construction & re-roof. Base pay, comm, expense allowance benefits. $100K salary potential. Must be exp'd. Fax resume to: 728-1109

★ SALES ★
★ TRAINING ★
Looking for individuals seeking a career in automotive industry. Opportunity to sell the highest quality Chevrolet product at the #1 certified dealership in the nation. No experience necessary, we will provide $500 a week pay during 2 weeks of training. Opportunity to also join our sales force and earn top commissions in your field, with benefits, 401(k), medical, dental, and vision.
Space is limited.
Call now: 782-1243

SALES-OUTSIDE
Brink's Home Security
We are looking for high energy, motivated outside sale professionals who possess the ability to generate sales based on the leads provided by the inside sales team, as well as self generate additional leads. Good communication skills and aggressive work ethic a must. Some sales experience preferred. We offer the following benefits:
• Comprehensive Pay & Training
• Base Salary or Commission + Bonus Plans
• $4000/yr Tuition Reimbursement
• Company Provided Leads
• Auto Allowance, Medical, Dental & Life Insurance
• Company Matched 401 (k)
• Pension Plan
• Stock Purchase Plan
• Paid Vacation
Interested candidates please call Donna at 344-3132. EOE

HELP WANTED 4650
CONSTRUCTION
Lathers-stucco w/truck & tools. Steady work, good pay. Piece/hrly. Call 531-9030

A **piecework rate** pays an employee a given amount per item produced. Gross earnings are found with the following formula.

$$\text{Gross earnings} = \text{Pay per item} \times \text{Number of items}$$

For example, a truck driver who drives 680 miles and is paid a piecework rate of \$.32 per mile has total gross earnings as follows.

$$\text{Gross earnings} = \$.32 \times 680 = \$217.60$$

EXAMPLE 1

Finding Gross Earnings for Piecework

Stacy Arrington is paid $.73 for sewing a jacket collar, $.86 for a sleeve with cuffs, and $.94 for a lapel. One week she sewed 318 jacket collars, 112 sleeves with cuffs, and 37 lapels. Find her gross earnings.

SOLUTION

Multiply the rate per item by the number of that type of item.

Item	Rate		Number		Total
Jacket collars	$.73	×	318	=	$232.14
Sleeves with cuffs	$.86	×	112	=	$96.32
Lapels	$.94	×	37	=	$34.78

Find the gross earnings by adding the three totals from the table.

$232.14 + $96.32 + $34.78 = **$363.24**

QUICK CHECK 1

A production worker is paid $.58 for assembling a ceiling lamp, $1.23 for assembling a ceiling fan, and $.86 for assembling a box fan. One week a worker assembled 220 ceiling lamps, 318 ceiling fans, and 174 box fans. Find the worker's gross earnings.

OBJECTIVE 2 **Determine the gross earnings for differential piecework.** There are many variations to the straight piecework rate just described. For example, some rates have **quotas** that must be met, with a premium for each item produced beyond the quota. These plans offer an added incentive within an incentive. A typical **differential piece rate** plan is one where the rate paid per item depends on the number of items produced.

EXAMPLE 2

Using Differential Piecework

QUICK TIP With differential piecework, the highest amount paid applies to only the last units produced. In Example 2, $2.10 is paid for units 1–100, $2.25 is paid for units 101–150, and $2.40 is paid on only those units beyond unit 150, which, in this case, is 64 units.

Suppose Metro Electric pays assemblers as follows:

1–100 units	$2.10 each
101–150 units	$2.25 each
151 or more units	$2.40 each

Find the gross earnings of a worker producing **214 units**.

SOLUTION

214	⟵ total units	
− 100	⟵ first 100 units ⟶	100 units at $2.10 each = $210.00
114		
− 50	⟵ next 50 units ⟶	50 units at $2.25 each = $112.50
64	⟵ number over 150 ⟶	64 units at $2.40 each = $153.60
		214 total units = $476.10

The gross earnings are $476.10.

QUICK CHECK 2

Scooter Frame Company pays welders as follows: 1–150 frames, $2.85 each; 151–250, $3.20 each; and 251 or more, $3.45 each. Find the gross earnings of a worker who welds 282 frames.

Quick Check Answers

1. $668.38

2. $857.90

OBJECTIVE 3 Find the gross pay for piecework with a guaranteed hourly wage. The piecework and differential piecework rates are frequently modified to include a guaranteed hourly pay rate. This is often necessary to satisfy federal and state laws concerning minimum wages. With this method, the employer must pay either the minimum wage or the piecework earnings, whichever is higher.

EXAMPLE 3

Finding Earnings with a Guaranteed Hourly Wage

QUICK TIP The worker *cannot* earn less than \$10.50 per hour or \$84 (\$10.50 × 8) for the day. Since the piecework earnings on Tuesday and Thursday in Example 3 fall below the hourly minimum, the hourly rate, or \$84 for the day, is paid on those days.

A tire installer at the Tire Center is paid \$10.50 per hour for an 8-hour day or \$1.15 per tire installed, whichever is higher. Find the weekly earnings for an employee having the following rate of production.

Monday	85 tires
Tuesday	70 tires
Wednesday	88 tires
Thursday	68 tires
Friday	82 tires

SOLUTION

The hourly earnings for an 8-hour day are **\$84** (8 × \$10.50). The larger of hourly earnings or the piecework earnings is paid each day.

Monday	85 × \$1.15 = \$97.75 piece rate
Tuesday	~~70 × \$1.15~~ = **\$84 hourly** (**piece rate is \$80.50**)
Wednesday	88 × \$1.15 = \$101.20 piece rate
Thursday	~~68 × \$1.15~~ = **\$84 hourly** (**piece rate is \$78.20**)
Friday	82 × \$1.15 = \$94.30 piece rate
	\$461.25 weekly earnings

QUICK CHECK 3

A cabinet door finisher is paid \$14.70 per hour for an 8-hour day or \$.95 per cabinet door finished, whichever is higher. Find the gross earnings for a worker who finished 106 doors on Monday, 127 doors on Tuesday, 152 doors on Wednesday, 120 doors on Thursday, and 138 doors on Friday.

OBJECTIVE 4 Calculate the overtime earnings for piecework. Piecework employees, like other workers, are paid time and a half for overtime. It is common for the overtime rate to be $1\frac{1}{2}$ times the regular rate per piece.

EXAMPLE 4

Calculating Earnings with Overtime Piecework

Eugene Smith is paid \$.98 per child's tricycle assembled. During one week, he assembled 480 tricycles on regular time and 104 tricycles during overtime hours. Find his gross earnings for the week if time and a half per assembly is paid for overtime.

SOLUTION

$$\begin{aligned}\text{Gross earnings} &= \text{Earnings at regular piece rate} + \text{Earnings at overtime piece rate}\\ &= (480 \times \$.98) + 104 \times (1.5 \times \$.98)\\ &= \$470.40 + \$152.88\\ &= \mathbf{\$623.28}\end{aligned}$$

QUICK CHECK 4

An assembler is paid \$.84 for each child car seat assembled. During a recent week, she assembled 400 car seats on regular time and 138 car seats during overtime hours. If time and a half is paid for each overtime assembly, find the gross earnings for the week.

Quick Check Answers

3. \$631.35
4. \$509.88

Have you ever wondered what time of the day workers think is most productive? The following bar graph is the result of a survey asking workers that exact question.

Numbers in the News

Workers' Most Productive Time of the Day

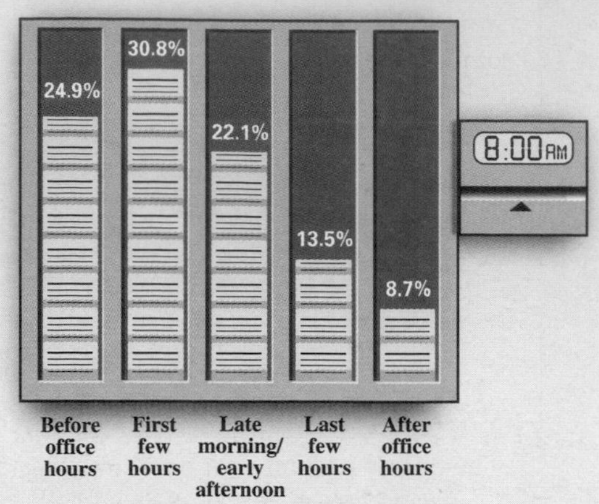

DATA: At-A-Glance survey of 1,385 office workers.

A **commission rate** pays a salesperson either a fixed percent of sales or a fixed amount per item sold. Commissions are designed to produce maximum output from the salesperson, since pay is directly dependent on sales. All of the types of sales commission arrangements are discussed here.

OBJECTIVE 5 Find the gross earnings using commission rate times sales. With **straight commission**, the salesperson is paid a fixed percent of sales. Gross earnings are found with the following formula.

$$\text{Gross earnings} = \text{Commission rate} \times \text{Amount of sales}$$

EXAMPLE 5 Determining Earnings Using Commission

A real estate broker charges a 6% commission. Find the commission on a house selling for \$268,500.

SOLUTION

The commission is 6% × \$268,500 = **.06** × \$268,500 = \$16,110. The 6% is called the commission rate, or the **rate of commission**.

QUICK CHECK 5

An advertising sales representative is paid a 20% commission. Find the commission earned on sales of \$2368.40.

Before the commission is calculated, any **returns** from customers, or any **allowances**, such as discounts, must be subtracted from sales.

EXAMPLE 6 Subtracting Returns When Using Commission

Amanda Roach, a food-supplements sales representative, had sales of \$10,230 one month, with returns and allowances of \$1120. If her commission rate is 12%, find her gross earnings.

SOLUTION

The returns and allowances must first be subtracted from gross sales. Then multiply the difference, net sales, by the commission rate.

$$\begin{aligned}\text{Gross earnings} &= (\$10{,}230 \text{ gross sales} - \$1120 \text{ returns and allowances}) \times 12\% \\ &= \$9110 \text{ net sales} \times .12 \\ &= \$1093.20 \text{ gross earnings}\end{aligned}$$

Quick Check Answer

5. \$473.68

QUICK TIP Before the commission is calculated, all items returned are subtracted from the amount of sales. The company will not pay a commission on sales that are not completed.

QUICK CHECK 6

Nate Sellers, an Avon salesperson, had sales of $45,350 one month, with returns and allowances of $432. If his commission rate is 18%, find his gross earnings.

OBJECTIVE 6 **Determine a commission using the variable commission rate.** The **sliding scale**, or **variable commission**, is a method of pay designed to retain top-producing salespeople. Under such a plan, a higher rate of commission is paid as sales get larger and larger.

EXAMPLE 7

Finding Earnings Using a Variable Commission

Maureen O'Connor sells food and bakery products to businesses, such as Starbucks, and is paid as follows.

Sales	Rate
Up to $10,000	6%
$10,001–$20,000	8%
$20,001 and up	9%

Find O'Connor's earnings if she has sales of $32,768 one month.

SOLUTION

$32,768	← total sales		
− 10,000	← first $10,000 →	$10,000 at 6%	= $600.00
$22,768			
− 10,000	← next $10,000 →	$10,000 at 8%	= $800.00
$12,768	← over $20,000 →	$12,768 at 9%	= $1149.12
		$32,768 total sales	**$2549.12 total commissions**

QUICK CHECK 7

Timmy Heslin sells office copiers to businesses and is paid a variable commission rate. His commission rate on sales up to $20,000 is 2%; sales of $20,001 to $30,000, 2.5%, and sales of $30,001 and up, 3%. If he has sales of $38,400, find the commission earned.

OBJECTIVE 7 **Find the gross earnings with a salary plus commission.** With a **salary plus commission**, the salesperson is paid a fixed sum per pay period, plus a commission on all sales. This method of payment is commonly used by large retail stores. Gross earnings with salary plus commission are found with the following formula.

Gross earnings = Fixed amount per pay period + Amount earned on commission

Many salespeople like this method. It is especially attractive to beginning salespeople who lack selling experience. While providing an incentive, it offers the security of a guaranteed income to cover basic living costs. Occasionally, this income is an earnings advance or a **draw**, which is a loan against future commissions. This loan is paid back when future commissions are earned.

Quick Check Answers

6. $8085.24
7. $902

EXAMPLE 8

Adding Commission to a Salary

Jaime Bailey is paid $325 per week by Beverly's Creations, plus 3% on all sales over $500. During a certain week, her total sales were $2972. Find her gross earnings.

SOLUTION

$$\text{Gross earnings} = \text{Weekly salary} + 3\% \text{ on sales above } \$500$$
$$= \$325 + .03\,(\$2972 - \$500)$$
$$= \$325 + (.03 \times \$2472)$$
$$= \$325 + \$74.16$$
$$= \$399.16$$

QUICK CHECK 8

Sanford Howard is paid a salary of $290 a week, plus a 4% commission on all sales over $750. Find his gross earnings for a week in which his total sales were $1870.

EXAMPLE 9

Subtracting a Draw to Find Earnings

QUICK TIP

Commission-based earning plans may be a strong deterrent to attracting new salespeople. Many companies offer the salary plus commission and draw plans to help fill sales positions.

Craig Johnson has office product sales of $36,850 for the month and is paid an 8% commission on all sales. He had draws of $850 for the month. Find his gross earnings after repaying the drawing account.

SOLUTION

$$\text{Gross earnings} = \text{Commissions} - \text{Draw}$$
$$= (.08 \times \$36,850) - \$850$$
$$= \$2948 - \$850$$
$$= \$2098$$

QUICK CHECK 9

Bob Smith has toy train sales of $18,540 for the month and is paid a 10% commission on all sales. If he had draws of $975 for the month, find his gross earnings after repaying the drawing account.

The list at the left shows the "Hot Jobs" in 2008 and beyond. At the right are the median weekly wages for a variety of careers.

Hot Jobs
In 2008 *and Beyond:*

International advertising & promotions managers: $33,760 to $145,000+

Pharmacists: $62,780 to $112,530

Personal financial planners: $31,340 to $108,740

Loan officers: $24,090 to $102,830

Physical therapists: $42,910 to $89,830

Nurses: $24,910 to $77,170

Electricians: $25,730 to $70,200

Source for average manual range of salaries: Challenger, Gray & Christmas, with data provided by the Bureau of Labor Statistics.

Quick Check Answers

8. $334.80
9. $879

Numbers in the News

Median Weekly Wages

Career	Wage
Petroleum engineers	$1,923
Actuaries	$1,639
Lawyers	$1,609
Economists	$1,569
Chiropractors	$1,531
Aerospace engineers	$1,362
Medical and health-service managers	$1,089
Meeting and convention planners	$912
Loan counselors and officers	$861
Elementary schoolteachers	$826
Funeral directors	$768
Social workers	$700
Pest-control workers	$508
Animal trainers	$482
Actors	$481
Child-care workers	$332
Dishwashers	$296

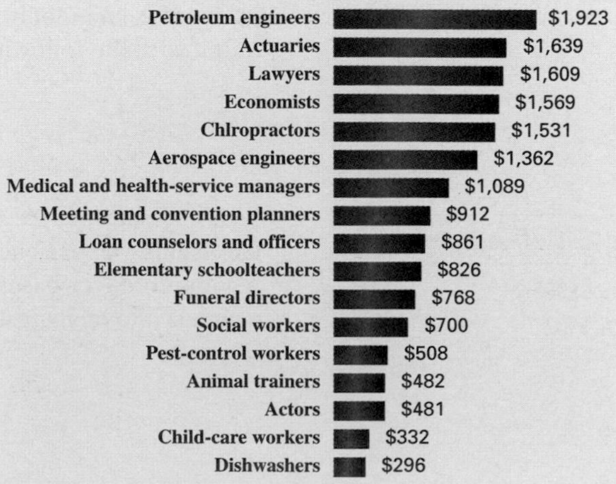

DATA: Bureau of Labor Statistics

5.2 EXERCISES

FOR EXTRA HELP

MyMathLab

MathXL PRACTICE

WATCH

DOWNLOAD

READ

REVIEW

The **QUICK START** *exercises in each section contain solutions to help you get started.*

RECYCLING *Earth Plus pays workers $.48 per container for sorting recyclable materials. Find the gross earnings for each worker. (See Example 1.)*

QUICK START

Employee	Number of Containers	Gross Earnings	Employee	Number of Containers	Gross Earnings
1. Crossett, J.	194	**$93.12**	**2.** Biron, C.	292	______
194 × $.48 = $93.12					
3. Campbell, K.	320	______	**4.** Halcomb, J.	243	______

AGRICULTURAL WORKERS *Find the daily gross earnings for each employee. (See Example 2.) Suppose that avocado pickers are paid as follows.*

1–500 avocados	$.05 each
501–700 avocados	$.07 each
Over 700 avocados	$.09 each

QUICK START

Employee	Number of Avocados	Gross Earnings	Employee	Number of Avocados	Gross Earnings
5. Hoch, R.	695	**$38.65**	**6.** Leonard, M.K.	907	______
(500 × $.05) + (195 × $.07) = $38.65					
7. Matysek, J.	852	______	**8.** Pannunzio, K.	1108	______

9. Wages and salaries are known as *time rates*, while commissions are called *incentive rates of pay*. Explain in your own words the difference between these payment methods. (See Objective 5.)

10. Explain in your own words the difference between a piecework rate and differential piece rate. (See Objective 2.)

GUARANTEED HOURLY WORK *Find the gross earnings for each employee by first finding the daily hourly earnings and then finding the daily piecework earnings. Each employee has an 8-hour workday and is paid $.75 for each unit of production or the hourly rate, whichever is higher. (See Example 3.)*

QUICK START

	Units Produced						
Employee	**M**	**T**	**W**	**Th**	**F**	**Hourly Rate**	**Gross Earnings**
11. Coughlin, S.	66	75	58	72	68	$6.18	**$260.19**
12. Bahary, N.	62	78	79	80	81	$7.20	______
13. Shea, D.	98	92	102	96	106	$8.80	______
14. Ward, M.	98	104	95	110	108	$9.10	______

$49.50 + $56.25 + $49.44 (hourly) + $54 + $51 = $260.19

C indicates an exercise that is related to the Case in Point feature.

PIECEWORK WITH OVERTIME *Find the gross earnings for each employee. Overtime is 1.5 times the normal rate per piece. (See Example 4.)*

QUICK START

	Units Produced		Rate per Unit	Gross Earnings
Employee	Reg.	O.T.		
15. Shannon, B.	430	62	$.76	$397.48
16. Mc Donald, M.	530	58	$.74	_____
17. Jennings, A.	470	70	$.82	_____
18. O'Brien, K.	504	36	$.80	_____

COMMISSION WITH RETURNS *Find the gross earnings for each of the following salespeople. (See Examples 5 and 6.)*

QUICK START

Employee	Total Sales	Returns and Allowances	Rate of Commission	Gross Earnings
19. Mares, E.	$3210	$129	10%	$308.10

$(\$3210 - \$129) \times 10\% = \$3081 \times .1 = \308.10

Employee	Total Sales	Returns and Allowances	Rate of Commission	Gross Earnings
20. Peterson, J.	$5734	$415	7%	_____
21. Remington, J.	$2875	$64	15%	_____
22. Kling, J.	$3806	$108	20%	_____

VARIABLE-COMMISSION PAYMENT *Find the gross earnings for each of the following employees. (See Example 7.) Livingston's Concrete pays its salespeople the following commissions.*

6% on first $7500 in sales
8% on next $7500 in sales
10% on any sales over $15,000

QUICK START

Employee	Total Sales	Gross Earnings	Employee	Total Sales	Gross Earnings
23. Christensen, C.	$18,550	$1405	**24.** Hubbard, P.	$11,225	_____

$(\$7500 \times .06) + (\$7500 \times .08) + (\$3550 \times .10) = \1405

Employee	Total Sales	Gross Earnings	Employee	Total Sales	Gross Earnings
25. Steed, F.	$10,480	_____	**26.** Goldstein, S.	$25,860	_____

SALARY PLUS COMMISSION *Stockdale Marine pays salespeople as follows: $452 per week plus a commission of .9% on sales above $15,000 through $25,000 with 1.1% paid on sales in excess of $25,000. Find the gross earnings for each of the following salespeople. (No commission is paid on the first $15,000 of sales.) (See Example 8.)*

QUICK START

Employee	Total Sales	Gross Earnings	Employee	Total Sales	Gross Earnings
27. West, S.	$17,900	$478.10	**28.** Barnes, A.	$36,300	_____

$\$452 + \$2900 \times .009 = \$478.10$

Employee	Total Sales	Gross Earnings	Employee	Total Sales	Gross Earnings
29. Feathers, C.	$32,874	_____	**30.** Maguire, J.	$14,946	_____

5.3 SOCIAL SECURITY, MEDICARE, AND OTHER TAXES

OBJECTIVES

1. Understand FICA.
2. Find the maximum FICA tax paid by an employee in one year.
3. Understand Medicare tax.
4. Find FICA tax and Medicare tax.
5. Determine the FICA tax and the Medicare tax paid by a self-employed person.
6. Find state disability insurance deductions.

CASE in POINT After finding the gross earnings of each employee at Starbucks, all deductions for each employee must be subtracted. Two deductions taken from employees, no matter what they earn, are FICA (Social Security) and Medicare. As Sarah Brynski does the payroll, she must be certain that she has deducted the correct amounts from each employee's gross earnings.

Finding gross earnings is only the first step in preparing a payroll. The employer must then subtract all required deductions from gross earnings. For most employees, these deductions include Social Security tax, Medicare tax, federal income tax withholding, and state income tax withholding. Other deductions may include state disability insurance, union dues, retirement, vacation pay, credit union savings or loan payments, purchase of bonds, uniform expenses, group insurance plans, and charitable contributions. Subtracting these deductions from gross earnings results in **net pay**, the amount the employee receives.

OBJECTIVE 1 Understand FICA. The **Federal Insurance Contributions Act (FICA)** was passed into law in the 1930s in the middle of the Great Depression. This plan, now called **Social Security**, was originally designed to give monthly benefits to retired workers and their survivors. As the number of people receiving benefits has increased along with the individual benefit amounts, people paying into Social Security have had to pay a larger amount of earnings into this fund each year. From 1937 through 1950, an employee paid 1% of income into Social Security, up to a maximum of $30 per year. This amount has increased over the years until an employee in 2008 paid 6.2% of income to FICA and 1.45% to **Medicare**, which together can total $7803 or more per year.

	Social Security Tax		Medicare Tax	
Year	Social Security Tax Rate	Employee Earnings Subject to the Tax	Medicare Tax Rate	Employee Earnings Subject to the Tax
1994	6.2%	$59,600	1.45%	all
1995	6.2%	$61,200	1.45%	all
1996	6.2%	$62,700	1.45%	all
1997	6.2%	$65,400	1.45%	all
1998	6.2%	$68,400	1.45%	all
1999	6.2%	$72,600	1.45%	all
2000	6.2%	$76,200	1.45%	all
2001	6.2%	$80,400	1.45%	all
2002	6.2%	$84,900	1.45%	all
2003	6.2%	$87,000	1.45%	all
2004	6.2%	$87,900	1.45%	all
2005	6.2%	$90,000	1.45%	all
2006	6.2%	$94,200	1.45%	all
2007	6.2%	$97,500	1.45%	all
2008	6.2%	$102,000	1.45%	all
2009				
2010				

QUICK TIP Congress sets the tax rates and the maximum employee earnings subject to both Social Security tax and Medicare tax each year. Because these maximum employee earnings change often, **we will use 6.2% of the first $105,000 that the employee earns in a year** for Social Security tax. For Medicare tax, **we will use 1.45% of everything that the employee earns in a year.** These figures are used in all examples and exercises in this chapter.

For many years both the Social Security tax rate and the Medicare tax rate were combined; however, since 1991 these tax rates have been expressed individually. The table on page 201 shows the tax rates and the maximum earnings on which Social Security and Medicare taxes are paid by the employee. The employer pays the same rate as the employee, *matching dollar for dollar* all employee contributions. Self-employed people pay almost double the amount paid by those who are employees, since they are paying for both employee and employer.

Each employee, whether a U.S. citizen or not, must have a Social Security card. Most post offices have applications for the cards. All money set aside for an individual is credited to his or her account according to the Social Security number. Each year, the Social Security Administration sends out a Social Security statement that shows workers how Social Security fits into their future. The statements are sent three months before the employee's birthday, but only to workers who are 25 years of age and older. However, anyone may submit a **Request for Earnings and Benefit Estimate Statement** like the one shown below. Since mistakes do occur, it is important to check the statements very carefully. There is a limit of about three years, after which errors may not be corrected. To obtain one of the forms and other information about Social Security, you may phone 800-772-1213 or go on the World Wide Web to www.socialsecurity.gov.

Request for *Social Security Statement*

☐ Please check this box if you want to get your *Statement* in Spanish instead of English.

Please print or type your answers. When you have completed the form, fold it and mail it to us. If you prefer to send your request using the Internet, contact us at *www.socialsecurity.gov.*

1. Name shown on your Social Security card:

First Name ________ Middle Initial ____

Last Name Only ________

2. Your Social Security number as shown on your card:

☐☐☐-☐☐-☐☐☐☐

3. Your date of birth (Mo.-Day-Yr.)

☐☐-☐☐-☐☐☐☐

4. Other Social Security numbers you have used:

☐☐☐-☐☐-☐☐☐☐

☐☐☐-☐☐-☐☐☐☐

5. Your Sex: ☐ Male ☐ Female

For items 6 and 8 show only earnings covered by Social Security. Do NOT include wages from state, local or federal government employment that are NOT covered by Social Security or that are covered ONLY by Medicare.

6. Show your actual earnings (wages and/or net self-employment income) for last year and your estimated earnings for this year.

A. Last year's actual earnings: *(Dollars Only)*

$☐☐☐,☐☐☐.0 0

B. This year's estimated earnings: *(Dollars Only)*

$☐☐☐,☐☐☐.0 0

7. Show the age at which you plan to stop working:

☐☐ *(Show only one age)*

8. Below, show the average yearly amount (not your total future lifetime earnings) that you think you will earn between now and when you plan to stop working. Include performance or scheduled pay increases or bonuses, but not cost-of-living increases.

If you expect to earn significantly more or less in the future due to promotions, job changes, part-time work, or an absence from the work force, enter the amount that most closely reflects your future average yearly earnings.

If you don't expect any significant changes, show the same amount you are earning now (the amount in 6B).

Future average yearly earings: *(Dollars Only)*

$☐☐☐,☐☐☐.0 0

9. Do you want us to send the *Statement:*
- To you? Enter your name and mailing address.
- To someone else (your accountant, pension plan, etc.)? Enter your name with "c/o" and the name and address of that person or organization.

"C/O" or Street Address (Include Apt. No., P.O. Box, Rural Route)

Street Address

Street Address (If Foreign Address, enter City, Province, Postal Code)

U.S. City, State, ZIP code (If Foreign Address, enter Name of Country only)

NOTICE:
I am asking for information about my own Social Security record or the record of a person I am authorized to represent. I declare under penalty of perjury that I have examined all the information on this form, and on any accompanying statements or forms, and it is true and correct to the best of my knowledge. I authorize you to use a contractor to send the *Social Security Statement* to the person and address in item 9.

▶

Please sign your name (Do Not Print)

Date ________ (Area Code) Daytime Telephone No.

Form SSA-7004-SM

OBJECTIVE 2 Find the maximum FICA tax paid by an employee in one year. Remember that Social Security tax is paid on only the first $105,000 (see the quick tip above) of gross earnings in our examples. An employee earning $105,000 during the first 10 months of a year pays no more Social Security tax on any additional earnings that year. The maximum Social Security tax to be paid by an employee is $\$105{,}000 \times 6.2\% = \$105{,}000 \times .062 = \$6510$.

QUICK TIP Only 7% of all income earners are affected by the Social Security maximum.

OBJECTIVE 3 Understand Medicare tax. Medicare tax is paid on all earnings. The total earnings are multiplied by 1.45%.

OBJECTIVE 4 Find FICA tax and Medicare tax. When finding the amounts to be withheld for Social Security tax and Medicare tax, the employer must use the current rates and the current maximum earnings amount.

EXAMPLE 1

Finding FICA Tax and Medicare Tax

Imagine that you are Sarah Brynski, the manager of a Starbucks. Find the Social Security tax and the Medicare tax that must be withheld from the gross earnings of Kelleher and Kimbrel.

(a) Kelleher: \$362.40 gross earnings **(b)** Kimbrel: \$194.02 gross earnings

SOLUTION

(a) The Social Security tax is found by multiplying gross earnings by 6.2%.

$$\$362.40 \times 6.2\% = \$362.40 \times .062 = \$22.47 \text{ (rounded)}$$

The Medicare tax is found by multiplying gross earnings by **1.45%**.

$$\$362.40 \times 1.45\% = \$362.40 \times .0145 = \$5.25 \text{ (rounded)}$$

(b) The Social Security tax is

$$\$194.02 \times 6.2\% - \$194.02 \times .062 = \$12.03 \text{ (rounded)}$$

The Medicare tax is

$$\$194.02 \times 1.45\% = \$194.02 \times .0145 = \$2.81 \text{ (rounded)}$$

QUICK CHECK 1

Find **(a)** the Social Security tax and **(b)** the Medicare tax that must be withheld from gross earnings of \$418.50.

EXAMPLE 2

Finding FICA Tax

Shannon Woolums has earned \$102,634.05 so far this year. Her gross earnings for the current pay period are \$5224.03. Find her Social Security tax.

SOLUTION

Social Security tax is paid on only the first \$105,000 earned in a year. Woolums has already earned \$102,634.05. Subtract \$102,634.05 from \$105,000 to find that she has to pay Social Security tax on only \$2365.95 of her earnings for the current pay period.

\$105,000.00	maximum earnings subject to Social Security tax
− \$102,634.05	earnings to date
\$2,365.95	earnings on which tax is due

The Social Security tax on \$2365.95 is \$146.69 (\$2365.95 × 6.2%) (rounded). Therefore, Woolums pays \$146.69 for the current pay period and no additional Social Security tax for the rest of the year.

QUICK CHECK 2

Mary Single has earned \$103,750.10 so far this year. If her gross earnings are \$3080 this week, find the Social Security tax to be withheld.

Quick Check Answers

1. **(a)** \$25.95 (rounded)
   (b) \$6.07 (rounded)
2. \$77.49 (rounded)

The table below compares the contributions to social programs (Social Security and Medicare) in selected countries around the world. How do U.S. workers' (employee) contributions compare with those of other countries?

Social insurance contributions as a percent of total gross earnings

Country	Employee	Employer
Italy	10.26	48.00
France	20.66	42.57
Sweden	33.00	7.00
Belgium	14.24	32.73
Mexico	22.00	3.00
Germany	21.12	21.12
Netherlands	7.04	13.05
Japan	11.00	12.00
Ireland	5.52	10.54
U.K.	7.08	10.00
Switzerland	6.55	8.37
Canada	5.00	8.00
U.S.A.	7.65	7.65

Source: *Benefits Report* Europe, USA, and Canada; Watson Wyatt Worldwide, and Knight Ridder Tribune.

The following bar graph shows where people 25 to 69 years of age think they will get their retirement income.

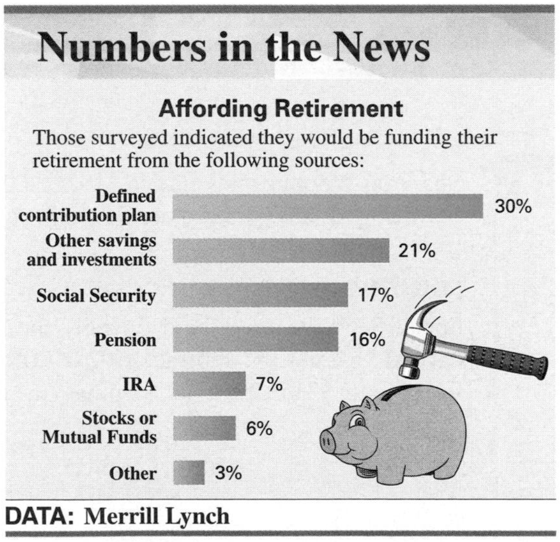

OBJECTIVE 5 Determine the FICA tax and the Medicare tax paid by a self-employed person. People who are self-employed pay higher Social Security tax and higher Medicare tax than people who work for others. There is no employer to match the employee contribution, so the self-employed person pays a rate that is double that of an employee. The gross earnings of the self-employed person are first multiplied by 92.35% (.9235) to find the adjusted earnings. These adjusted earnings are then multiplied by the current rates. In our examples, the self-employed person pays 12.4% of adjusted earnings for Social Security tax and 2.9% of adjusted earnings for Medicare tax.

EXAMPLE 3

Finding FICA and Medicare Tax for the Self-Employed

Find the Social Security tax and the Medicare tax paid by Ta Shon Williams, a self-employed Web designer who had adjusted earnings of $53,820 this year.

SOLUTION

$$\text{Social Security tax} = \$53{,}820 \times 12.4\% = \$53{,}820 \times .124 = \$6673.68$$

$$\text{Medicare tax} = \$53{,}820 \times 2.9\% = \$53{,}820 \times .029 = \$1560.78$$

QUICK TIP All employers and those who are self-employed should have the current tax rates for both Social Security and Medicare. These can always be found in **Circular E, Employer's Tax Guide**, which is available from the Internal Revenue Service.

QUICK CHECK 3

Find **(a)** the Social Security tax and **(b)** the Medicare tax for a self-employed auto mechanic who had adjusted earnings of $73,875 this year.

Have you ever wondered why we haven't run out of Social Security numbers? Marilyn Vos Savant answers this question for a reader in her weekly column in *Parade* magazine. The reader's question and her answers are shown below.

HERE & NOW

Ask Marilyn

Why haven't we run out of Social Security numbers yet? With only 999,999,999 combinations available, the total U.S. population plus all those deceased should have used them up by now.

—Gregory Rhodes, Modesto, Calif.

Actually, only 400 million of those combinations have been issued since November 1936, when Social Security began. (Note: Numbers are not reassigned after a person dies.) Only 6 million new numbers are issued each year, so we have enough for several more generations.

Source: *PARADE magazine.*

OBJECTIVE 6 **Find state disability insurance deductions.** Many states have a state disability insurance (SDI) program. Qualifying employees must pay a portion of their earnings to the program. If an employee is injured and unable to work, the program pays the employee during the period of disability. A typical program requires an **SDI deduction** of 1% of gross earnings on the first $31,800 earned each year, with no payment on earnings above this amount.

EXAMPLE 4

Finding State Disability Insurance Deductions

Find the state disability insurance deduction for an employee at Comet Auto Parts with gross earnings of $418 this pay period. The SDI rate is 1%, and the employee has not earned $31,800 this year.

SOLUTION

The state disability insurance deduction is $4.18 ($418 × .01).

Quick Check Answers

3. (a) $9160.50
(b) $2142.38 (rounded)
4. $5.26 (rounded)

QUICK CHECK 4

An employee has gross earnings of $525.80 this week. The employee has not earned $31,800 this year and the SDI rate is 1%. What is the state disability insurance deduction?

EXAMPLE 5

Knowing SDI Maximum Deductions

Jenoa Perkins has earned \$29,960 so far this year. Find the SDI deduction if gross earnings this pay period are \$2872. Use an SDI rate of 1% on the first \$31,800.

SOLUTION

The SDI deduction will be taken on \$1840 of the current gross earnings.

\$31,800	maximum earnings subject to SDI
− \$29,960	earnings this year
\$1,840	earnings subject to SDI

The SDI deduction is \$18.40 (\$1840 × .01).

QUICK TIP Those involved in payroll work must always be up to date on the current rates and the maximum annual earning amounts against which FICA, Medicare, and SDI payroll deductions are taken.

QUICK CHECK 5

Linda Shirley has earned \$30,780 so far this year. Her earnings this pay period are \$3289. Find the SDI deduction using an SDI rate of 1% on the first \$31,800.

The federal minimum wage amount will be \$7.25 per hour in 2009. Some states have minimum wages that are higher than the federal rate. The accompanying newspaper clipping discusses minimum wage changes and says that ten states have minimum wage rates that are automatically tied to inflation.

HERE & NOW

Minimum-Wage Voting Nears

Six states to consider inflation adjustments on basic pay level.

By David A. Lieb
ASSOCIATED PRESS

JEFFERSON CITY, MO. When residents of Missouri and five other states vote Tuesday on an increase in their minimum wage, they will essentially be deciding whether to raise their pay not once, but again and again and again.

That's because the ballot measures include not only a one-time increase in the minimum wage, but also an automatic annual adjustment to keep up with inflation.

If all of the measures pass, the number of states with minimum wages tied to inflation will reach 10.

Supporters view the automatic cost-of-living adjustments as the best way to get around the political resistance that has kept the federal minimum wage unchanged for nearly a decade.

Business leaders warn that tying wages to the consumer price index could make labor costs prohibitive and lead to layoffs, inflation and business closings.

Quick Check Answer

5. \$10.20

5.3 EXERCISES

FOR EXTRA HELP

MyMathLab

MathXL PRACTICE

WATCH

DOWNLOAD

READ

REVIEW

The **QUICK START** *exercises in each section contain solutions to help you get started.*

Find the Social Security tax and the Medicare tax for each of the following amounts of gross earnings. Assume a 6.2% FICA rate and a 1.45% Medicare tax rate. (See Example 1.)

QUICK START

1. $324.72	**$20.13**	**$4.71**	**2.** $207.25	**$12.85**	**$3.01**	**3.** $463.24	______	______
4. $606.35	______	______	**5.** $854.71	______	______	**6.** $683.65	______	______

SOCIAL SECURITY TAX *Find the Social Security tax for each employee for the current pay period. Assume a 6.2% FICA rate up to a maximum of $105,000. (See Example 2.)*

QUICK START

Employee	Gross Earnings This Year (So Far)	Earnings Current Pay Period	Social Security Tax
7. Dandridge, T.	$101,945.32	$6218.48	**$189.39**
8. Hale, R.	$102,438.75	$5200.00	**$158.80**
9. Hall, T.	$100,016.22	$7260.00	______
10. Maurin, J.	$103,971.95	$4487.52	______
11. Saraniti, S.	$104,329.75	$3053.73	______
12. De Bouchel, V.	$103,974.08	$6160.86	______

PAYROLL DEDUCTIONS *Find the regular earnings, overtime earnings, gross earnings, Social Security tax (6.2%), Medicare tax (1.45%), and state disability insurance deduction (1%) for each employee. Assume that no employee will have earned more than the FICA or SDI maximum at the end of the current pay period. Assume that time and a half is paid for any overtime in a 40-hour week. (See Examples 1–4.)*

QUICK START

Employee	Hours Worked	Regular Rate	Regular Earnings	Overtime Earnings	Gross Earnings	Social Security Tax	Medicare Tax	SDI Deduction
13. Garrett, R.	45.5	$9.22	**$368.80**	**$76.07**	**$444.87**	**$27.58**	**$6.45**	**$4.45**
14. Harcos, W.	47.75	$7.52	______	______	______	______	______	______
15. Plescia, P.	45	$6.58	______	______	______	______	______	______
16. Eckern, G.	45	$10.20	______	______	______	______	______	______
17. McIntosh, R.	47	$11.68	______	______	______	______	______	______
18. Wright, R.	46.75	$8.24	______	______	______	______	______	______

Solve the following application problems. Round to the nearest cent.

QUICK START

C **19.** SOCIAL SECURITY AND MEDICARE Maria Ortega worked 43.5 hours last week at Starbucks. She is paid $8.58 per hour, plus time and a half for all hours over 40 per week. Find her **(a)** Social Security tax and **(b)** Medicare tax for the week.

(a) **$24.07**
(b) **$5.63**

Gross income is $(40 \times \$8.58) + (3.5 \times 1\frac{1}{2}) \times \$8.58 = \$388.25$

(a) Social Security tax is $.062 \times \$388.25 = \$24.07$

(b) Medicare tax is $.0145 \times \$388.25 = \$5.63$

C indicates an exercise that is related to the Case in Point feature.

20. SOCIAL SECURITY AND MEDICARE Chriscelle Merquillo receives 7% commission on all sales. Her sales on Monday of last week were $1412.20, with $1928.42 on Tuesday, $598.14 on Wednesday, $1051.12 on Thursday, and $958.72 on Friday. Find her **(a)** Social Security tax and **(b)** Medicare tax for the week.

(a) ________
(b) ________

21. STATE DISABILITY INSURANCE DEDUCTION Donna Laughman is paid an 8% commission on sales. During a recent pay period, she had sales of $19,482 and returns and allowances of $193. Find the amount of **(a)** her Social Security tax, **(b)** her Medicare tax, and **(c)** her state disability insurance deduction for this pay period. (The FICA rate is 6.2%, the Medicare rate is 1.45%, the SDI rate is 1%, and earnings will not exceed $31,800.)

(a) ________
(b) ________
(c) ________

22. STATE DISABILITY INSURANCE DEDUCTION Peter Phelps is a representative for Delta International Machinery and is paid $675 per week plus a commission of 2% on sales. His sales last week were $17,240. Find the amount of **(a)** his Social Security tax, **(b)** his Medicare tax, and **(c)** his state disability insurance deduction for the pay period. (The FICA rate is 6.2%, the Medicare rate is 1.45%, the SDI rate is 1%, and earnings will not exceed $31,800.)

(a) ________
(b) ________
(c) ________

SELF-EMPLOYMENT DEDUCTIONS The following problems refer to self-employed individuals. These people pay a Social Security tax of 12.4% and Medicare tax of 2.9%. Find both of the taxes on the following annual adjusted earnings. (See Example 3.)

23. Tony Romano, owner of The Cutlery, earned $58,238.74. **23.** ________

24. Rachel Leach, an interior designer, earned $36,724.72. **24.** ________

25. Krystal McClellan, cosmetics consultant, earned $29,104.80. **25.** ________

26. Ron Morris, a Chic-Filet franchise owner, earned $78,007.14. **26.** ________

27. Peggy Kelleher, shop owner, earned $26,843.60. **27.** ________

28. Sadie Chambers, senior account executive, earned $92,748.32. **28.** ________

29. A young person who has just received her first paycheck is puzzled by the amounts that have been deducted from gross earnings. Briefly explain both the FICA and Medicare deductions to this person. (See Objectives 1–4.)

30. Describe the difference between the FICA paid by an employee and FICA paid by a self-employed person. (See Objective 5.)

5.4 INCOME TAX WITHHOLDING

OBJECTIVES

1. Understand the Employee's Withholding Allowance Certificate.
2. Find the federal withholding tax using the wage bracket method.
3. Find the federal withholding tax using the percentage method.
4. Find the state withholding tax using the state income tax rate.
5. Find net pay when given gross wages, taxes, and other deductions.
6. Find the quarterly amount owed to the Internal Revenue Service.
7. Understand additional employer responsibilities and employee benefits.

CASE in POINT After completing the payroll at Starbucks, Sarah Brynski must be certain that all FICA taxes, Medicare taxes, and federal withholding taxes withheld from employees are sent to the Internal Revenue Service. Additionally, it's essential that Brynski keeps current with all of the changes in the tax codes that affect withholding.

The **personal income tax** is the largest single source of money for the federal government. The law requires that the bulk of the tax owed by an individual be paid as the income is earned. For this reason, employers must deduct money from the gross earnings of almost every employee. These deductions, called **income tax withholdings**, are sent periodically to the Internal Revenue Service. Most recently, the Internal Revenue Service has introduced EFTPS, an electronic funds transfer payment system, which allows employers to transfer these funds electronically. The amount of money withheld from employees depends on several factors.

Marital status. Generally, the withholding tax for a married person is less than the withholding tax for a single person making the same income.

OBJECTIVE 1 **Understand the Employee's Withholding Allowance Certificate.** Each employee must file a W-4 form, as shown, with his or her employer. On this form, the employee states the number of **withholding allowances** being claimed along with additional information so that the employer can withhold the proper amount for income tax.

Form **W-4**
Department of the Treasury
Internal Revenue Service

Employee's Withholding Allowance Certificate

▶ **Whether you are entitled to claim a certain number of allowances or exemption from withholding is subject to review by the IRS. Your employer may be required to send a copy of this form to the IRS.**

OMB No. 1545-0074
200X

1 Type or print your first name and middle initial. | Last name | 2 Your social security number

Home address (number and street or rural route) | 3 ☐ Single ☐ Married ☐ Married, but withhold at higher Single rate.
Note. If married, but legally separated, or spouse is a nonresident alien, check the "Single" box.

City or town, state, and ZIP code | 4 **If your last name differs from that shown on your social security card, check here. You must call 1-800-772-1213 for a replacement card.** ▶ ☐

5 Total number of allowances you are claiming (from line **H** above **or** from the applicable worksheet on page 2) 5

6 Additional amount, if any, you want withheld from each paycheck . . . . 6 $

7 I claim exemption from withholding for 200X, and I certify that I meet **both** of the following conditions for exemption.
- Last year I had a right to a refund of **all** federal income tax withheld because I had **no** tax liability **and**
- This year I expect a refund of **all** federal income tax withheld because I expect to have **no** tax liability.

If you meet both conditions, write "Exempt" here . . . . ▶ 7

Under penalties of perjury, I declare that I have examined this certificate and to the best of my knowledge and belief, it is true, correct, and complete.
Employee's signature
(Form is not valid
unless you sign it.) ▶ **Date** ▶

8 Employer's name and address (Employer: Complete lines 8 and 10 only if sending to the IRS.) | 9 Office code (optional) | 10 Employer identification number (EIN)

For Privacy Act and Paperwork Reduction Act Notice, see page 2. Cat. No. 10220Q Form **W-4**

44. TRAVEL-AGENCY SALES Scott Salman, a travel agent, is paid on a variable commission, is married, and claims four withholding allowances. He receives 3% of the first $20,000 in sales, 4% of the next $10,000 in sales, and 6% of all sales over $30,000. This week he has sales of $45,550 and the following deductions: FICA, Medicare, federal withholding, state disability insurance, state withholding, a retirement contribution of $45, a savings bond of $50, and charitable contributions of $20. Find his net pay after subtracting all of his deductions.

44. ________________

45. HEATING-COMPANY REPRESENTATIVE Evelyn Beaton, a commission sales representative for Alternative Heating Company, is paid a monthly salary of $4200 plus a bonus of 1.5% on monthly sales. She is married and claims three withholding allowances. Her deductions include FICA, Medicare, federal withholding, state disability insurance, no state withholding, credit union savings of $150, charitable contributions of $25, and a savings bond of $50. Find her net pay for a month in which her sales were $42,618. The state in which Beaton works has no state income tax.

45. ________________

46. RIVER RAFT MANAGER River Raft Adventures pays its manager, Kathryn Speers, a monthly salary of $2880 plus a commission of .8% based on total monthly sales volume. In May, River Raft Adventures has total sales of $86,280. Speers is married and claims five withholding allowances. Her deductions include FICA, Medicare, federal withholding, state disability insurance, state withholding of $159.30, credit union payment of $300, March of Dimes contribution of $20, and savings bonds of $250. Find her net pay for May.

46. ________________

CHAPTER 5 QUICK REVIEW

CHAPTER TERMS *Review the following terms to test your understanding of the chapter. For each term you do not know, refer to the page number found next to that term.*

CONCEPTS	EXAMPLES

5.1 Gross earnings

Gross earnings = Hours worked × Rate per hour

40 hours worked at \$8.40 per hour
Gross earnings = 40 × \$8.40 = \$336

5.1 Gross earnings with overtime

First, find the regular earnings. Then, determine overtime pay at overtime rate. Finally, add regular and overtime earnings.

Gross earnings =
Earnings at regular rate + Earnings at time-and-half rate

40 regular hours at \$8.40 per hour
10 overtime hours at time and a half
Gross earnings =

$$(40 \times \$8.40) + (10 \times 8.40 \times 1.5)$$
$$= \$336 + \$126 = \$462$$

5.1 Common pay periods

Pay Period	Paychecks Per Year
Monthly	12
Semimonthly	24
Biweekly	26
Weekly	52

Find the earnings equivalent of \$2800 per month for other pay periods.

$$\text{Semimonthly} = \frac{2800}{2} = \$1400$$
$$\text{Biweekly} = \frac{2800 \times 12}{26} = \$1292.31$$
$$\text{Weekly} = \frac{2800 \times 12}{52} = \$646.15$$

5.1 Overtime for salaried employees

First, find the hourly equivalent. Next, multiply the hourly equivalent rate by the overtime hours by 1.5. Finally, add overtime earnings to the salary.

Salary is \$648 per week for 40 hours. Find the earnings for 46 hours.

$$\$648 \div 40 = \$16.20 \text{ per hour}$$
$$\$16.20 \times 6 \times 1.5 = \$145.80 \text{ overtime}$$
$$\$648 + \$145.80 = \$793.80$$

5.2 Gross earnings for piecework

Gross earnings = Pay per item × Number of items

Items produced, 175; pay per item, \$.65; find the gross earnings.

$$\$.65 \times 175 = \$113.75$$

CONCEPTS	EXAMPLES
5.2 Gross earnings for differential piecework The rate paid per item produced varies with level of production.	1–100 items, \$.75 each 101–150 items, \$.90 each 151 or more items, \$1.04 each Find the gross earnings for producing 214 items. 100 × \$.75 = \$75.00 first 100 units 50 × \$.90 = \$45.00 next 50 units 64 × \$1.04 = \$66.56 number over 150 214 total items \$186.56 total earnings
5.2 Overtime earnings on piecework Gross earnings = Earnings at regular rate + Earnings at overtime rate	Items produced on regular time, 530; items produced on overtime, 110; piece rate \$.34; find the gross earnings. Gross earnings = (530 × \$.34) + 110 (1.5 × \$.34) = \$180.20 + \$56.10 = \$236.30
5.2 Straight commission Gross earnings = Commission rate × Amount of sales	Sales of \$25,800; commission rate is 5%. .05 × \$25,800 = \$1290
5.2 Variable commission Commission rate varies at different sales levels.	Up to \$10,000, 6% \$10,001–\$20,000, 8% \$20,001 and up, 9% Find the commission on sales of \$32,768. .06 × \$10,000 = \$600.00 first \$10,000 .08 × \$10,000 = \$800.00 next \$10,000 .09 × \$12,768 = \$1149.12 amount over \$20,000 \$32,768 \$2549.12 total commission
5.2 Salary and commission Gross earnings = Fixed earnings + Commission	Salary, \$250 per week; commission rate, 3%; find the gross earnings on sales of \$6848. Gross earnings = \$250 + (.03 × \$6848) = \$250 + \$205.44 = \$455.44
5.2 Commission with a drawing account Gross earnings = Commission − Draw	Sales for month, \$28,560; commission rate, 7%; draw, \$750 for month; find the gross earnings. Gross earnings = (.07 × \$28,560) − \$750 = \$1999.20 − \$750 = \$1249.20
5.3 FICA; Social Security tax The gross earnings are multiplied by the tax rate. When the maximum earnings are reached, no additional FICA is withheld that year.	Gross earnings, \$458; Social Security tax rate, 6.2%; find the Social Security tax. \$458 × .062 = \$28.40
5.3 Medicare tax The gross earnings are multiplied by the Medicare tax rate. Medicare tax is paid on all earnings.	Gross earnings, \$458; Medicare tax rate, 1.45%; find the Medicare tax. \$458 × .0145 = \$6.64

CONCEPTS	EXAMPLES
5.3 State disability insurance deductions Multiply the gross earnings by the SDI tax rate. When the maximum earnings are reached, no additional taxes are paid in that year.	Gross earnings, \$2880; SDI tax rate, 1%; find SDI tax. $\$2880 \times .01 = \$28.80$
5.4 Federal withholding tax Tax is paid on total earnings. No maximum as with FICA.	Single employee with 3 allowances; weekly earnings of \$338; find the federal withholding tax. From the wage bracket amount "at least \$330, but less than \$340," withholding is \$9. Use the percentage method to find the withholding tax. $\$338 - (\$51 \times 3) = \$185$ $\$185 - \$51 = \$134$ $\$134 \times .1 = \$13.40$
5.4 State withholding tax Tax is paid on total earnings. No maximum as with FICA.	Married employee with weekly earnings of \$692; find the state withholding tax given a state withholding tax rate of 4.5%. $4.5\% \times \$692 = .045 \times \$692 = \$31.14$
5.4 Quarterly report, Form 941 Filed each quarter; FICA and federal withholding are sent to the IRS (FICA + Medicare) × 2 (employer matches) + federal withholding tax.	If quarterly FICA withheld from employees is \$5269, Medicare tax is \$1581, and federal withholding tax is \$14,780, find the total owed to the IRS by the employer. $(\$5269 + \$1581) \times 2 + \$14,780 = \$28,480$

CHAPTER 5 SUMMARY EXERCISE

Payroll: Finding Your Take-Home Pay

Sarah Brynski, the manager of a Starbucks Coffee shop, receives an annual salary of \$42,536, which is paid weekly. Her normal workweek is 40 hours, and she is paid time and a half for all overtime. She is single and claims one withholding allowance. Her deductions include FICA, Medicare, federal withholding, state disability insurance, state withholding, credit union payments of \$125, retirement deductions of \$75, association dues of \$12, and a Diabetes Association contribution of \$25. Find each of the following for a week in which she works 52 hours.

(a) Regular weekly earnings **(a)** ____________

(b) Overtime earnings **(b)** ____________

(c) Total gross earnings **(c)** ____________

(d) FICA **(d)** ____________

(e) Medicare **(e)** ____________

(f) Federal withholding using the percentage method **(f)** ____________

(g) State disability insurance deduction **(g)** ____________

(h) State withholding (Assume that the state income tax rate is 4.4%.) **(h)** ____________

(i) Net pay **(i)** ____________

INVESTIGATE

Look at the statement that you received with your last paycheck. Be certain that your gross earnings are correct. Understand and check all of the deductions made by your employer. Subtract all deductions from your gross earnings to be certain that your net pay is accurate.

CHAPTER 5 TEST

To help you review, the numbers in brackets show the section in which the topic was discussed.

Complete the following payroll ledger. Find the total gross earnings for each employee. Time and a half is paid on all hours over 40 in one week. **[5.1]**

Employee	Hours Worked	Reg. Hrs.	O.T. Hrs.	Reg. Rate	Gross Earnings
1. Bianchi	46.5	___	___	$10.80	_______
2. Hanna	47.5	___	___	$8.60	_______

Solve the following application problems.

3. Judy Martinez is paid $34,060 annually. Find the equivalent earnings if this amount is paid **(a)** weekly, **(b)** biweekly, **(c)** semimonthly, and **(d)** monthly. **[5.1]**

(a) ______________
(b) ______________
(c) ______________
(d) ______________

4. At Jalisco Electronics, assemblers are paid according to the following differential piece rate scale: 1–20 units in a day, $4.50 each; 21–30 units, $5.50 each; and $7 each for every unit over 30. Adrian Ortega assembled 35 units in one week. Find his gross pay. **[5.2]**

4. ______________

5. Rheonna Winston receives a commission of 6% for selling a $235,500 house. One-half of the commission goes to the broker and one-half of the remainder to another salesperson. Winston gets the rest. Find the amount she receives. **[5.2]**

5. ______________

An employee is paid a salary of $9300 per month. If the current FICA rate is 6.2% on the first $105,000 of earnings, and the Medicare tax rate is 1.45% of all earnings, how much should be withheld for (a) FICA tax and (b) Medicare tax during the following months? **[5.3]**

6. March: **(a)** ______ **(b)** ______ **7.** December: **(a)** ______ **(b)** ______

Find the federal withholding tax using the wage bracket method for each of the following employees. **[5.4]**

8. Ahearn: 2 withholding allowances, single, $315.82 weekly earnings — **8.** ______________

9. Zanotti: 2 withholding allowances, married, $675.25 weekly earnings — **9.** ______________

10. Allgier: 3 withholding allowances, married, $3210.55 monthly earnings — **10.** ______________

11. Yeoman: 4 withholding allowances, single, $1859.62 monthly earnings — **11.** ______________

12. Benner: 6 withholding allowances, married, $2864.47 monthly earnings — **12.** ______________

Find the net pay for each of the following employees after FICA, Medicare, federal withholding tax, state disability insurance, and other deductions have been taken out. Assume that none has earned over $105,000 so far this year. Assume a FICA rate of 6.2%, Medicare rate of 1.45%, and a state disability insurance rate of 1%. Use the percentage method of withholding. **[5.3 and 5.4]**

13. Tran: $1852.75 monthly earnings, 1 withholding allowance, single, $37.80 in other deductions **13.** ________

14. Blumka: $522.11 weekly earnings, 4 withholding allowances, married, state withholding of $15.34, credit union savings of $20, educational television contribution of $7.50 **14.** ________

15. Comar: $677.92 weekly earnings, 6 withholding allowances, married, state withholding of $22.18, union dues of $14, charitable contribution of $15 **15.** ________

Solve the following application problems.

16. Joseph Flores is paid $452 per week plus a commission of 2% on all sales. Flores sold $712 worth of goods on Monday, $523 on Tuesday, $1002 on Wednesday, $391 on Thursday, and $609 on Friday. Returns and allowances for the week were $114. Find the employee's **(a)** Social Security tax (6.2%), **(b)** Medicare tax (1.45%), and **(c)** state disability insurance deduction (1%) for the week. **[5.3 and 5.4]**

(a) ________
(b) ________
(c) ________

17. Neta Fitzgerald earned $102,375.60 so far this year. This week she earned $2649.78. Find her **(a)** FICA tax and **(b)** Medicare tax for this week's earnings. **[5.3]**

(a) ________
(b) ________

For Exercises 18 and 19, find (a) the Social Security tax and (b) the Medicare tax for each of the following self-employed people. Use a FICA tax rate of 12.4% and a Medicare tax rate of 2.9%. **[5.3]**

18. Kirby: $36,714.12

(a) ________
(b) ________

19. Biondi: $42,380.62

(a) ________
(b) ________

20. The employees of Quick-Lube paid a total of $418.12 in Social Security tax last month, $96.48 in Medicare tax, and $1217.34 in federal withholding tax. Find the total amount that the employer must send to the Internal Revenue Service. **20.** ________

CHAPTER 6

Mathematics of Buying

CHAPTER CONTENTS

Ryan Andrews owns Kitchen Crafters, a specialty store that carries many unique and hard-to-find kitchen, houseware, and gift items.

CASE *in* POINT

The store purchases its inventory from a variety of suppliers at a retailer's discounted price (trade discount) and then receives an invoice from the supplier. When the invoice is paid, it is common for another discount (cash discount) to be taken. Andrews realizes how important these discounts are in contributing to the profitability of his business.

Retail businesses make a profit by purchasing items and then selling them for more than they cost. There are several steps in this process: **manufacturers** buy raw materials and component parts and assemble them into products that can be sold to other manufacturers or **wholesalers**. The wholesaler, often called a "middleman," buys from manufacturers or other wholesalers and sells to the retailer. **Retailers** sell directly to the ultimate user, the **consumer**.

Documents called **invoices** help businesses keep track of sales, while various types of discounts help them buy products at lower costs so that they can increase profits. Recent technology has enabled businesses to replace much of their paper-based business processes with electronic solutions, known collectively as **electronic commerce (EC)**. Expect to see further changes in how business is conducted in the future. This chapter covers the mathematics needed for working with invoices and discounts—the mathematics of buying.

6.1 INVOICES AND TRADE DISCOUNTS

OBJECTIVES

1. Complete an invoice.
2. Understand common shipping terms.
3. Identify invoice abbreviations.
4. Calculate trade discounts and understand why they are given.
5. Differentiate between single and series discounts.
6. Calculate each series discount separately.
7. Use complements to calculate series discounts.
8. Use a table to find the net cost equivalent of series discounts.

CASE in POINT Ryan Andrews, owner of Kitchen Crafters, must have a thorough understanding of invoices, trade discounts, and cash discounts. As the owner of a small, independent store, he must carry top-quality items, buy at the best price, and take all earned discounts.

An invoice is a printed record of a purchase and sale. For the seller, it is a **sales invoice** that records a sale. For the buyer, it is a **purchase invoice** that records a purchase. The invoice identifies the seller and the buyer, describes the items purchased, states the quantity purchased, and provides the unit price of each item. In addition, the invoice shows the *extension total* (the number of items purchased times the price per unit) any discounts, the shipping and insurance charges, and the *total invoice amount*.

OBJECTIVE 1 Complete an invoice. The document on the next page serves as a sales invoice for J. B. Sherr Company and as a purchase invoice for Kitchens Galore. The numbers in the **units shipped** column multiplied by the **unit price** give the **amount**, or **extension total**, for each item. The **invoice total** is the sum of the extension totals.

Trade and cash discounts, discussed later in this chapter, ***are never applied to shipping and insurance charges***. For this reason, shipping and insurance charges are often not included in the invoice total, so the purchaser must add them to the invoice total to find the total amount due. In the J. B. Sherr Company invoice, the freight (shipping) charges of $19.45 are included in the INVOICE TOTAL space.

OBJECTIVE 2 Understand common shipping terms. The shipping term **FOB (free on board)**, followed by the words **shipping point** or **destination**, commonly appears on invoices. The term *FOB shipping point* means that the *buyer* pays for shipping and that ownership of the merchandise passes to the purchaser prior to shipment. The term *FOB destination* means that the *seller* pays the shipping charges and retains ownership until the goods reach the destination. This becomes very important in the event that the merchandise is lost or damaged during shipment.

The shipping term **COD** means **cash on delivery**. When goods are sent COD, the shipper delivers to the purchaser upon receipt of enough cash to pay for the goods. When goods are moved over water, the shipping term **FAS**, which means **free alongside ship**, is common. Goods shipped this way are delivered to the dock with all freight charges paid to that point by the seller.

J. B. SHERR Co.

SHOWROOM AND WAREHOUSE
1704 ROLLINS ROAD
BURLINGAME, CA 94010
TELEPHONE: (650) 697-3430
TO ORDER 1-800-660-1422

INVOICE

SOLD TO
KITCHENS GALORE OAK007
10100 FAIR OAKS BLVD.
FAIR OAKS CA 95628

PAGE NO. 1 OF

SHIP TO
KITCHENS GALORE
10100 FAIR OAKS BLVD.
FAIR OAKS CA 95628

INVOICE DATE	INVOICE NO.
03/17	0002271-IN

TERMS 1% 15 DAYS, NET 30

SALESMAN	ENTRY NUMBER	ENTRY DATE	SHIPPING DATE	SHIPPED VIA	CUSTOMER ORDER NO./DEPT.
0008	0002280	03/17		UPS	3-13

TAG #	QTY. ORD.	SHIPPED	UNIT	STOCK NUMBER	DESCRIPTION	SUGG. RETAIL	UNIT PRICE	AMOUNT
1	12	12	EACH	736-080	IMPT NATURAL SEA SPONGE	.00	2.400	28.80
2	1	0	EA	267-6682	ACRYLIC BUTTER DISH	6.39	3.760	.00
3	1	1	EA	267-6683	ACRYLIC CREAM & SUGAR S	6.39	3.760	3.76
4	1	1	EA	267-6684	ACRYLIC NAPKIN HOLDER	5.29	3.140	3.14
5	6	6	EACH	694-322	IMPT WENOL METAL POLISH	7.79	4.650	27.90
6	6	6	EACH	694-353	IMPTRED BEAR POLISH	7.39	4.370	26.22
7	1	1	EA	274-10012	FRIENDSHIP MIXING BOWL	31.50	18.750	18.75
8	1	0	EACH	274-10014	FRIENDSHIP MIXING BOWL	44.90	26.500	.00
9	2	2	EA	589-31008	FLEXIBLE CHOPPING MATS	3.93	2.360	4.72
10	1	1	EA	589-22153	CORNER SINK SHELF W/SUC	2.79	1.600	1.60
11	6	0	EACH	281-7950	GEMCO JUICER W/GLASS JA	4.59	2.730	.00
12	2	2	EACH	54-611	ARDEN WAFFLE TOWEL-BLUE	3.19	1.900	3.80
13	2	2	EACH	54-612	ARDEN WAFFLE TOWEL-GREE	3.19	1.900	3.80
14	2	2	EACH	60-6	ASHLAND TIRE MAT 18.5 X	18.75	11.250	22.50
15	2	2	EACH	998-713	3 HALF/RD DRAGON 18 X 30	.00	5.200	10.40
16	2	2	EACH	998-143	3 WELCOME MAT 18 X 30	.00	6.910	13.82
17	3	3	EACH	998-303	3 MB PLAIN MAT 18 X 30	.00	8.640	25.92
18	2	2	EACH	998-504	4 HALF/RD MB PLAIN 20 X 3	.00	10.550	21.10
19								
20								

NON-TAX TOTAL	TAXABLE TOTAL	SALES TAX	FREIGHT	MISC.	INVOICE TOTAL
216.23	.00	.00	19.45		235.68

ALL ITEMS NOT SHIPPED ARE CANCELLED. PLEASE REORDER

PLEASE PAY FROM THIS INVOICE

ALL ORDERS SUBJECT TO CREDIT ACCEPTANCE. PRICES SUBJECT TO CHANGE WITHOUT NOTICE. SHORTAGES MUST BE REPORTED WITHIN 10 DAYS. NO RETURNS ACCEPTED WITHOUT PRIOR AUTHORIZATION. PAST DUE ACCOUNTS SUBJECT TO INTEREST (1½% PER MO.) PLUS COLLECTION CHARGES.

CUSTOMER'S COPY

OBJECTIVE 3 **Identify invoice abbreviations.** A number of abbreviations are used on invoices to identify measurements, quantities of merchandise, shipping terms, and additional discounts. The most common ones are found in the following table.

Invoice Abbreviations

ea.	each	drm.	drum
doz.	dozen	cs.	case
gro.	gross (144 items)	bx.	box
gr gro.	great gross (12 gross)	sk.	sack
qt.	quart	pr.	pair
gal.	gallon (4 quarts)	C	Roman numeral for 100
bbl.	barrel	M	Roman numeral for 1000
mL	milliliter	cwt.	per hundredweight
cL	centiliter	cpm.	cost per thousand
L	liter	@	at
in.	inch	lb.	pound
ft.	foot	oz.	ounce
yd.	yard	g	gram
mm	millimeter	kg	kilogram
cm	centimeter	ROG	receipt of goods
m	meter	ex. or x	extra dating
km	kilometer	FOB	free on board
ct.	crate	EOM	end of month
cart	carton	COD	cash on delivery
ctn.	carton	FAS	free alongside ship

OBJECTIVE 4 **Calculate trade discounts and understand why they are given.** **Trade discounts** are often given to businesses or individuals who buy an item for resale or produce an item that will then be sold. The seller usually gives the price of an item as its **list price** (the suggested price at which the item can be sold to the public). Then the seller gives a trade discount that is subtracted from the list price. The result is the **net cost** or **net price**, which is the amount paid by the buyer. Find the net cost with the following formula.

QUICK TIP The terms *net cost* and *net price* both refer to the amount paid by the buyer. However, *net cost* is the preferred term, since this is the cost of an item to the business.

Finding the Net Cost

Net cost = List price − Trade discount or

List price
− Trade discount
Net cost

EXAMPLE 1

Calculating a Single Trade Discount

The list price of a KitchenAid Artisan Stand Mixer is \$298.80, and the trade discount is 25%. Find the net cost.

SOLUTION

First, find the amount of the trade discount by finding 25% of \$298.80.

$$\begin{array}{ccccc} R \times B & & & = & P \\ 25\% \times \$298.80 & = & .25 \times \$298.80 & = & \$74.70 \end{array}$$

Subtract \$74.70 from the list price of \$298.80.

\$298.80	list price
− 74.70	**trade discount**
\$224.10	net cost

The net cost of the mixer is \$224.10.

QUICK CHECK 1

A wine refrigerator has a list price of \$589.99 and a trade discount of 35%. Find the net cost.

OBJECTIVE 5 **Differentiate between single and series discounts.** In Example 1, a **single discount** of 25% was offered. Sometimes two or more discounts are combined into a **series** or **chain discount**. A series discount is written, for example, as 20/10, which means that a 20% discount is subtracted from the list price, and *from this difference* another 10% discount is subtracted. Another discount of 15% could be attached to the series discount of 20/10, giving a new series discount of 20/10/15.

Why Trade Discounts Change

Price changes may cause trade discounts to be raised or lowered.
As the *quantity purchased* increases, the discount offered may increase.
The buyer's position in *marketing channels* (manufacturer → wholesaler → retailer → consumer) may determine the amount of discount offered. For example, a wholesaler would receive a larger discount than a succeeding retailer.
Geographic location may influence the trade discount. An additional discount may be offered to increase sales in a particular area.
Seasonal fluctuations in sales may influence the trade discounts offered.
Competition from other companies may cause the raising or lowering of trade discounts.

Quick Check Answer

1. \$383.49 (rounded)

The following advertisement indicates that the retail store received some very large trade discounts so that it is able to offer customers as much as 25%–60% off the list price. These high discounts may have resulted from very large quantities of merchandise purchased, or perhaps it was the end of the season or the last of a production cycle for the manufacturer.

SAT. ONLY, STARTS 7 A.M.!
TAKE AN EXTRA
25% OFF
CLEARANCE-PRICED

ENTIRE STOCK
50–60% OFF
**MEN'S & YOUNG MEN'S
FALL & HOLIDAY SWEATERS**

SATURDAY ONLY
30–50% OFF
**MISSES' COLLECTIONS
FROM CRAZYHORSE®
& FAMOUS NEW YORK MAKER**

OBJECTIVE ⑥ **Calculate each series discount separately.** Three methods can be used to calculate a series discount and net cost. The first of these is **calculating discounts separately**.

EXAMPLE 2

Calculating Series Trade Discounts

QUICK TIP Single discounts in a series are *never* added together. For example, a series discount of 20/10 is *not the same* as a discount of 30%.

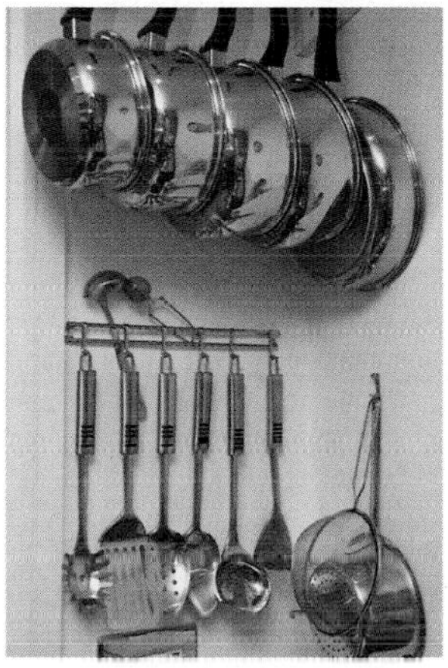

Kitchen Crafters is offered a series discount of 20/10 on a Cooking with Calphalon stainless steel cookware set with a list price of $150. Find the net cost after the series discount.

SOLUTION

First, multiply the decimal equivalent of 20% (.2) by $150. Then subtract the product ($30) from $150, getting $120. Multiply the decimal equivalent of the second discount, 10% (.1), by $120. Finally, subtract the product ($12) from $120, getting $108. The result is the net cost.

$$
\begin{array}{ll}
\$150 & \text{list price} \qquad \text{discount: 20/10} \\
-\ \ \ 30 & (.2 \times \$150) \longleftarrow \\
\hline
\$120 & \\
-\ \ \ 12 & (.1 \times \$120) \longleftarrow \\
\hline
\$108 & \text{net cost}
\end{array}
$$

After the first discount, each discount is applied to the balance remaining after the preceding discount or discounts have been subtracted. This method demonstrates how trade discounts are applied, but this is usually *not* the preferred method for finding the invoice amount.

QUICK CHECK 2

A 12-place setting of stainless steel flatware is list priced at $249.99. If a series discount of 10/15 is offered, what is the net cost after the series discount is taken?

Quick Check Answer

2. $191.24 (rounded)

OBJECTIVE ⑦ **Use complements to calculate series discounts.** Using this second method of finding the net cost, first find the **complement** (with respect to 1, or 100%) of each single discount. The complement is the number that must be added to a given discount to get 1. For example, the complement (with respect to 1) of 10%, or .1, is .9 since .1 + .9 = 1. The complement (with respect to 1) of 40%, or .4, is .6. Other typical complements (with respect to 1) are as follows.

Discount	Complement with Respect to 100%	Decimal Equivalent of Discount	Complement with Respect to 1
10%	90%	.1	.9
15%	85%	.15	.85
20%	80%	.2	.8
25%	75%	.25	.75
30%	70%	.3	.7
35%	65%	.35	.65
50%	50%	.5	.5

The complement of the discount is the portion actually paid. For example, 10% discount means 90% is paid, 25% discount means 75% is paid, and 50% discount means 50% is paid.

Multiply each of the complements of the single discounts to get the **net cost equivalent**. The net cost equivalent is the percent paid. Then multiply the net cost equivalent (percent paid) by the list price to obtain the net cost.

EXAMPLE 3

Using Complements to Find the Net Cost

Kitchen Crafters is offered a series discount of 20/10 on a George Foreman Grilling Machine with a list price of \$150. Find the net cost after the series discount.

SOLUTION

For a series discount of 20/10, the complements (with respect to 1) of 20% and 10% are .8 and .9. Multiplying the complements gives $.8 \times .9 = .72$, the net cost equivalent. In other words, receiving a series discount of 20/10 is the same as paying 72% of the list price. Find the net cost by multiplying .72 by the list price of \$150, to get \$108 as the net cost. The calculation is shown as follows.

STEP 1	Series discount	20 / 10
		↓ ↓
STEP 2	Find complements with respect to 1.	.8 .9
		↓ ↓
STEP 3	Multiply complements.	$.8 \times .9 = \mathbf{.72}$ net cost equivalent

$$\begin{array}{rl} \$150 & \text{list price} \\ \times\quad .72 & \textbf{net cost equivalent} \\ \hline 300 & \\ 1050 & \\ \hline \$108.00 & \textbf{net cost} \end{array}$$

Find the amount of the discount by subtracting the net cost from the list price.

$$\begin{array}{rl} \$150 & \text{list price} \\ -\ 108 & \textbf{net cost} \\ \hline \$\ 42 & \text{amount of discount} \end{array}$$

On many calculators, you can subtract the discount percents from the list price in a series calculation.

150 [−] 20 [%] [−] 10 [%] [=] 108

Note: Refer to Appendix C for calculator basics.

QUICK CHECK 3

A supplier offers a series discount of 25/15 on a waffle iron. If the list price of the waffle iron is \$135, use the complements with respect to 1 of each of the single discounts to find **(a)** the net cost and **(b)** the amount of the discount.

Quick Check Answers

3. (a) \$86.06 (rounded)
(b) \$48.94

EXAMPLE 4

Using Complements to Solve Series Discounts

The list price of a Heartland 30-inch combination gas and electric stove is $3095. Find the net cost after a series discount of 20/10/10.

SOLUTION

Start by finding the complements with respect to 1 of each discount.

series discount ⟶ 20/10/10

Find complements with respect to 1. ⟶ .8 .9 .9

Multiply complements. ⟶ $.8 \times .9 \times .9 = \mathbf{.648}$ net cost equivalent

	$3095	list price
×	**.648**	**net cost equivalent**
	$2005.56	net cost

QUICK TIP **Never round the net cost equivalent.** Doing so will often result in a net cost that is incorrect.

QUICK CHECK 4

A 22.2-cubic-foot bottom-freezer refrigerator is list priced at $2249.99. What is the net cost after a series discount of 15/20/5?

OBJECTIVE 8 **Use a table to find the net cost equivalent of series discounts.** A third method is used by people who work with series discounts every day. A table is used to find the net cost equivalents for various series discounts. The number from the table is then multiplied by the list price to find the net cost. For example, the following table shows that the net cost equivalent for a series discount of 20/10/10 is .648, the number located both to the right of 10/10 and below 20%.

Because changing the order in which numbers are multiplied does not change the answer, the order of the discounts in a series does not change the net cost equivalent. A 10/20 series is the same as a 20/10 series, and a 15/10/20 is identical to a 20/15/10 or to a 15/20/10.

Net Cost Equivalents of Series Discounts

	5%	10%	15%	20%	25%	30%	35%	40%
5	.9025	.855	.8075	.76	.7125	.665	.6175	.57
10	.855	.81	.765	.72	.675	.63	.585	.54
10/5	.81225	.7695	.72675	.684	.64125	.5985	.55575	.513
10/10	.7695	.729	.6885	.648	.6075	.567	.5265	.486
15	.8075	.765	.7225	.68	.6375	.595	.5525	.51
15/10	.72675	.6885	.65025	.612	.57375	.5355	.49725	.459
20	.76	.72	.68	.64	.6	.56	.52	.48
20/15	.646	.612	.578	.544	.51	.476	.442	.408
25	.7125	.675	.6375	.6	.5625	.525	.4875	.45
25/20	.57	.54	.51	.48	.45	.42	.39	.36
25/25	.534375	.50625	.478125	.45	.421875	.39375	.365625	.3375
30	.665	.63	.595	.56	.525	.49	.455	.42
40	.57	.54	.51	.48	.45	.42	.39	.36

EXAMPLE 5

Using a Table of Net Cost Equivalents

Using the table of net cost equivalents, find the net cost equivalent of the following series discounts.

(a) 10/10 **(b)** 20/10 **(c)** 25/25/5 **(d)** 35/20/15

SOLUTION

(a) .81 **(b)** .72 **(c)** .534375 **(d)** .442

QUICK CHECK 5

Use the table of net cost equivalents to find the net cost equivalents of the following series discounts: **(a)** 30/5, **(b)** 10/40, **(c)** 20/15/10, **(d)** 10/5/5.

Quick Check Answers

4. $1453.49
5. (a) .665 **(b)** .54 **(c)** .612 **(d)** .81225

New and improved technology is helping small businesses keep better records of purchases and discounts, sales, and expenses. Less costly software programs have helped small businesses achieve this goal. The next article shows that greater tech spending by small and medium-sized businesses has attracted the attention of the software giants.

HERE & NOW

Software Giants Think Small

IBM, Microsoft move into niche markets

By Byron Acohido
USA TODAY

SEATTLE – Not long after sales at his Houston-area Krispy Kreme operation began to soar, Jason Gordon discovered that his $200 Intuit accounting software couldn't keep up.

So two years ago, the small-business owner nearly shelled out $100,000 for high-powered accounting software. At the last minute, Gordon learned that Intuit was about to roll out a juiced-up product for $2,500. He jumped on it and hasn't looked back. Intuit, the dominant supplier of bookkeeping software for very small firms, savors the win.

It had better.

That's because small and midsize businesses, or SMBs, loom as the tech industry's key to growth amid anemic spending by big companies. IBM and Microsoft, the two biggest tech companies, are squaring off to dominate the still-fragmented market. In doing so, they're forcing thousands of independent tech resellers, specialty software makers and tech consultants – the middlemen who sell to small firms – to pick sides.

Numbers in the News

Up with Spending

Spending on technology products and services by small and medium-size businesses is projected to almost double over a seven-year period.

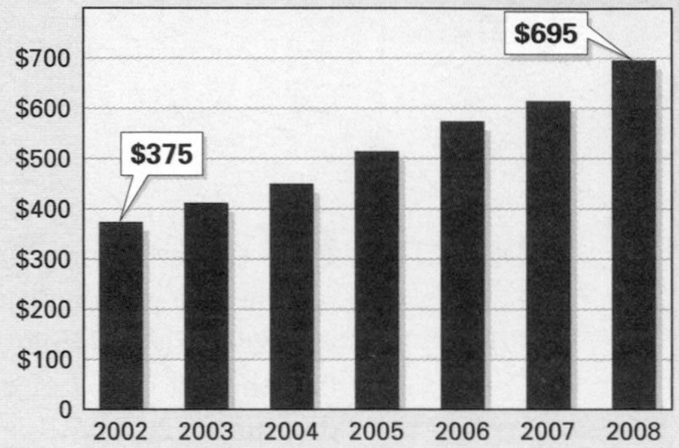

DATA: AMI-Partners

6.1 EXERCISES

FOR EXTRA HELP

MyMathLab

MathXL PRACTICE

WATCH

DOWNLOAD

READ

REVIEW

The QUICK START *exercises in each section contain solutions to help you get started.*

USING INVOICES *Compute the extension totals and the invoice total for the following invoices.*

QUICK START

HOME ACCESSORIES WHOLESALERS

Sold to: Kitchen Crafters
10100 Fair Oaks Blvd.
Fair Oaks, CA 95628

Date: June 10
Order. No.: 796152
Shipped by: UPS
Terms: Net

	Quantity	Order No./Description	Unit Price	Extension Total
1.	6 doz.	pastry brush, wide	$37.80 doz.	$226.80
2.	3 gro.	napkins, cotton	$12.60 gro.	$37.80
3.	9 doz.	cherry pitters	$14.04 doz.	
4.	8	food processors (3 qt.)	$106.12 ea.	
5.	53 pr.	stainless tongs	$68.12 pr.	
6.			**Invoice Total**	
			Shipping and Insurance	$37.45
7.			**Total Amount Due**	

J & K'S MUSTANG PARTS
New and Used

Sold to: Dave's Auto Body & Paint
4443-B Auburn Blvd.
York, PA 17402

Date: July17
Order. No.: 100603
Shipped by: Emery
Terms: Net

	Quantity	Order No./Description	Unit Price	Extension Total
8.	24	filler tube gaskets	$2.25 ea.	
9.	12 pr.	taillight lens gaskets	$4.75 pr.	
10.	6 pr.	taillight bezels to body	$10.80 pr.	
11.	2 gr.	door panel fasteners	$14.20 gr.	
12.	18	bumper bolt kits	$16.50 ea.	
13.			**Invoice Total**	
			Shipping and Insurance	$23.75
14.			**Total Amount Due**	

ABBREVIATIONS ON INVOICES *What does each of the following abbreviations represent?*

QUICK START

15. ft. foot ______ **16.** sk. sack ______

17. pr. ______ **18.** gr. gro. ______

19. kg ______ **20.** qt. ______

21. cs. ______ **22.** gro. ______

23. drm. ______ **24.** yd. ______

25. L ______ **26.** cpm. ______

27. gal. ______ **28.** cwt. ______

29. COD ______ **30.** FOB ______

C indicates an exercise that is related to the Case in Point feature.

31. Name six items that appear on an invoice. Try to do this without looking at an invoice. (See Objective 1.)

32. Explain in your own words the difference between *FOB shipping point* and *FOB destination*. In each case, who pays for shipping? When does ownership of the merchandise transfer? (See Objective 2.)

Using complements (with respect to 1) of the single discounts, find the net cost equivalents for each of the following discounts. Do not round. (See Examples 3 and 4.)

QUICK START

33. 10/20 $.9 \times .8 = .72$ **34.** 20/20 $.8 \times .8 = .64$

35. 10/10/10 $.9 \times .9 \times .9 = .729$ **36.** 15/20/25 $.85 \times .8 \times .75 = .51$

37. 25/5 ________ **38.** 5/15 ________

39. 40/30/20 ________ **40.** 20/20/10 ________

41. 50/10/20/5 ________ **42.** 25/10/20/10 ________

Find the net cost of each of the following list prices. Round to the nearest cent. (See Examples 1–4.)

QUICK START

43. $418 less 20/20 **$267.52** **44.** $148 less 25/10 **$99.90**

45. $16.40 less 5/10 ________ **46.** $860 less 20/40 ________

47. $1260 less 15/25/10 ________ **48.** $8.80 less 40/10/20 ________

49. $380 less 20/10/20 ________ **50.** $2008 less 10/5/20 ________

51. $22 less 10/15 ________ **52.** $25 less 30/20 ________

53. $980 less 10/10/10 ________ **54.** $8220 less 30/5/10 ________

55. $2000 less 10/40/10 ________ **56.** $1630 less 10/5/10 ________

57. $1250 less 20/20/20 ________ **58.** $1410 less 10/20/5 ________

59. Identify and explain four reasons that might cause series trade discounts to change. (See Objective 5.)

60. Explain the difference between a single trade discount and a series or chain trade discount.

61. Explain what a complement (with respect to 1 or 100%) is. Give an example. (See Objective 7.)

62. Using complements, explain how to find the net cost equivalent of a 25/20 series discount. Explain why a 25/10/10 series discount is not the same as a 25/20 discount. (See Objective 7.)

Solve the following application problems in trade discount. Round to the nearest cent.

QUICK START

63. VIDEO PLAYER The list price of a Zune 30 GB MP3/Video Player is \$299.99. If the series discount offered is 10/10/25, what is the net cost after trade discounts?

$.9 \times .9 \times .75 = .6075$
$\$299.99 \times .6075 = \$182.243 = \$182.24$

63. \$182.24

64. NURSING-CARE PURCHASES Roger Wheatley, a restorative nursing assistant (RNA), finds that the list price of one dozen adjustable walkers is \$1680. Find the cost per walker if a series discount of 40/25 is offered.

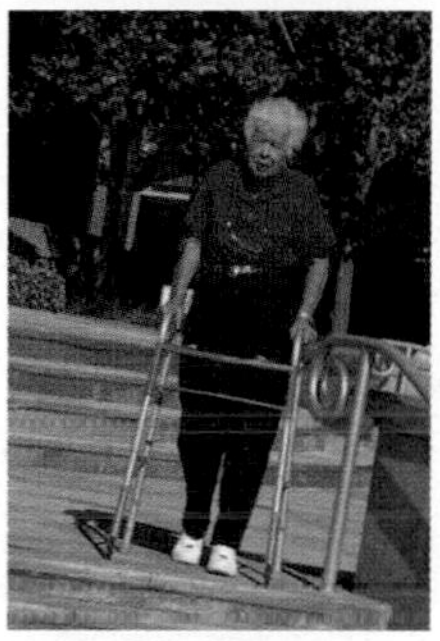

64. ______________

65. KITCHEN ISLAND Kitchen Crafters purchases a tile-topped wooden kitchen island list priced at \$480. It is available at either a 10/15/10 discount or a 20/15 discount. **(a)** Which discount gives the lower price? **(b)** Find the difference in net cost.

(a) ______________
(b) ______________

66. HARDWARE PURCHASE Oaks Hardware purchases an extension ladder list priced at \$120. It is available at either a 10/10/10 discount or a 15/15 discount. **(a)** Which discount gives the lower price? **(b)** Find the difference.

(a) ______________
(b) ______________

67. TRIPOD PURCHASE The list price of an aluminum tripod is \$65. It is available at either a 15/10/10 discount or a 15/20 discount. **(a)** Which discount gives the lower price? **(b)** Find the difference.

(a) ______________
(b) ______________

68. LIQUID FERTILIZER Continental Fertilizer Supply offers a series discount of 10/20/20 on major purchases. If a 58,000-gallon tank (bulk) of liquid fertilizer is list priced at \$27,200, what is the net cost after trade discounts?

68. ______________

69. HOME BEVERAGE FOUNTAINS Kitchen Crafters receives a 10/5/20 series trade discount from a supplier. If they purchase 4 dozen Bella Home beverage fountains list priced at \$468 per dozen, find the net cost.

69. ______________

70. WHOLESALE AUTO PARTS Kimara Swenson, an automotive mechanics instructor, is offered mechanics' net prices on all purchases at Foothill Auto Supply. If mechanics' net prices mean a 10/20 discount, how much will Swenson spend on a dozen sets of metallic brake pads that are list priced at $648 per dozen?

70. ________________

71. BULK CHEMICALS Brazilian Chemical Supply offers a series discount of 5/20/5 on all bulk purchases. A tank (bulk) of industrial solvent is list priced at $78,500. What is the net cost after trade discounts?

71. ________________

72. DANCE SHOES How much will Giselle, a dance instructor, pay for three dozen pairs of dance shoes if the list price is $144 per dozen and a series discount of 10/25/30 is offered?

72. ________________

73. TRADE-DISCOUNT COMPARISON The Door Store offers a series trade discount of 30/20 to its builder customers. Robert Gonzalez, a new employee in the billing department, understood the 30/20 terms to mean 50% and computed this trade discount on a list price of $5440. How much difference did this error make in the amount of the invoice?

73. ________________

74. FIBER OPTICS Pam Gondola has a choice of two suppliers of fiber optics for her business. Tyler Suppliers offers a 20/10/25 discount on a list price of $5.70 per unit. Irving Optics offers a 30/20 discount on a list price of $5.40 per unit. **(a)** Which supplier gives her the lower price? **(b)** Find the amount saved if she buys 12,500 units from the lower-priced supplier. (*Hint:* Do not round.)

(a) ________________
(b) ________________

6.2 SERIES DISCOUNTS AND SINGLE DISCOUNT EQUIVALENTS

OBJECTIVES

1. Express a series discount as an equivalent single discount.
2. Find the net cost by multiplying the list price by the complements of the single discounts in a series.
3. Find the list price given the series discount and the net cost.

OBJECTIVE 1 **Express a series discount as an equivalent single discount.** Series or chain discounts are often expressed as a single discount rate. Find a **single discount equivalent** to a series discount by multiplying the complements (with respect to 1 or 100%) of the individual discounts. As in the preceding section, the result is the net cost equivalent. Then subtract the net cost equivalent from 1 (1 = 100%). The result is the single discount that is equivalent to the series discount. *The single discount equivalent is expressed as a percent.*

Finding the Single Discount Equivalent

Single discount equivalent = 1 − Net cost equivalent

EXAMPLE 1

Finding a Single Discount Equivalent

If the Optimum Energy Company offered a 20/10 discount to wholesale accounts on all heating, ventilation, and cooling systems, what was the single discount equivalent?

SOLUTION

series discount ⟶ 20/10

Find complements with respect to 1. ⟶ .8   .9

Multiply complements. ⟶ .8 × .9 = .72 net cost equivalent

	1.00	base (100%)
−	**.72**	**net cost equivalent (remains)**
	.28	or 28% was discounted

The single discount equivalent of a 20/10 series discount is 28%.

QUICK CHECK 1

Baltimore Wholesale Electric offers a 30/20 discount on wholesale purchases of all small appliances. What is the single discount equivalent?

OBJECTIVE 2 **Find the net cost by multiplying the list price by the complements of the single discounts in a series.** Net cost can be found by multiplying the list price by the complements of each of the single discounts in a series, as shown in the next example.

Quick Check Answer

1. 44%

6.2 EXERCISES

FOR EXTRA HELP

MyMathLab

MathXL PRACTICE

WATCH

DOWNLOAD

READ

REVIEW

The **QUICK START** *exercises in each section contain solutions to help you get started.*

Find the net cost equivalent and the single discount equivalent of each of the following series discounts. Do not round net cost equivalents or single discount equivalents. (See Example 1.)

QUICK START

Series Discount	*Net Cost Equivalent*	*Single Discount Equivalent*
1. 10/20	**.72**	**28%**
.9 × .8 = .72; 1.00 − .72 = 28%		
2. 10/10	**.81**	**19%**
.9 × .9 = .81; 1.00 − .81 = 19%		
3. 20/15	________	________
4. 25/25	________	________
5. 10/30/20	________	________
6. 5/10/15	________	________
7. 20/10/10/20	________	________
8. 25/10/5/20	________	________

9. Using complements, show that the single discount equivalent of a 25/20/10 series discount is 46%. (See Objective 1.)

10. Suppose that you own a business and are offered a choice of a 10/20 trade discount or a 20/10 trade discount. Which do you prefer? Why? (See Objective 1.)

Find the list price, given the net cost and the series discount. (See Examples 3 and 4.)

QUICK START

11. Net cost $518.40; trade discount 20/10 — **11.** **$720**

.8 × .9 = .72; $518.40 ÷ .72 = $720

12. Net cost $813.75; trade discount 30/25 — **12.** ________

C indicates an exercise that is related to the Case in Point feature.

13. Net cost \$1559.52; trade discount 5/10/20 — **13.** ____

14. Net cost \$2697.30; trade discount 10/10/10 — **14.** ____

Solve the following application problems in trade discount. Round to the nearest cent.

QUICK START

15. COMPARING DISCOUNTS A S'mores Maker Kit has a list price of \$39.95 and is offered to wholesalers with a series discount of 20/10/10. The same appliance is offered to Kitchen Crafters (a retailer) with a series discount of 20/10. **(a)** Find the wholesaler's price. **(b)** Find Kitchen Crafters' price. **(c)** Find the difference between the two prices.

(a) $.8 \times .9 \times .9 = .648$; $\$39.95 \times .648 = \$25.887 = \$25.89$ wholesale
(b) $.8 \times .9 = .72$; $\$39.95 \times .72 = \$28.764 = \$28.76$ retailer's price
(c) $\$28.76 - \$25.89 = \$2.87$

(a) \$25.89 wholesale
(b) \$28.76 retailer's price
(c) \$2.87

16. STAINLESS STEEL GRILL A stainless steel gas grill is list priced at \$495. The manufacturer offers a series discount of 25/20/10 to wholesalers and a 25/20 series discount to retailers. **(a)** What is the wholesaler's price? **(b)** What is the retailer's price? **(c)** What is the difference between the prices?

(a) ____
(b) ____
(c) ____

17. COMPARING DISCOUNTS Express Video offers a series discount of 20/20/20, while States Video offers a series discount of 40/10/5. **(a)** Which discount is higher? **(b)** Find the difference.

(a) ____
(b) ____

18. COMPARING COST Rheonna Winston is offered an oak stair railing by The Turning Point for \$1370 less 30/10. Sierra Stair Company offers the same railing for \$1220 less 10/10. **(a)** Which offer is better? **(b)** How much does Winston save by taking the better offer?

(a) ____
(b) ____

19. PRICING INDOOR PLANTS Irene's Plant Place paid a net price of \$207.20 for a shipment of indoor plants after a trade discount of 30/20 from the list price. Find the list price. — **19.** ____

20. VITAMIN SUPPLEMENTS SJ's Nutrition Center received a shipment of vitamins, minerals, and diet supplements at a net cost of \$1125. This cost was the result of a trade discount of 25/20 from the list price. Find the list price of this shipment. — **20.** ____

21. SINGLE TRADE DISCOUNT A Craftsman dual-state 5.5-HP snow thrower with a list price of \$799.99 is sold by a wholesaler at a net cost of \$559.99. Find the single trade discount rate being offered. Round to the nearest tenth of a percent. — **21.** ____

22. SINGLE TRADE DISCOUNT Modern Glassware offers crystal wine glasses to Kitchen Crafters at a net cost of \$864 per gross. If the list price of the wine glasses is \$1350 per gross, find the single trade discount rate. — **22.** ____

6.3 CASH DISCOUNTS: ORDINARY DATING METHODS

OBJECTIVES

1. Calculate net cost after discounts.
2. Use the ordinary dating method.
3. Determine whether cash discounts are earned.
4. Use postdating when calculating cash discounts.

CASE in POINT At Kitchen Crafters, Ryan Andrews pays close attention to all invoices received from suppliers. Besides the fact that invoices can frequently have errors on them, he wants to be certain that all of these invoices are paid early enough to receive any additional cash discounts that are offered. He prides himself that he has never missed a final due date and has said, "I'm never overdue on an account."

OBJECTIVE 1 Calculate net cost after discounts. **Cash discounts** are offered by sellers to encourage prompt payment by customers. In effect, the seller is saying, "Pay me quickly and receive a discount." Businesses often borrow money for their day-to-day operation. Immediate cash payments from customers decrease the need for borrowed money.

To find the net cost when a cash discount is offered, begin with the list price and subtract any trade discounts. From the result, subtract the cash discount. Use the following formula.

QUICK TIP A cash discount is never allowed on shipping and insurance charges. If an invoice amount includes shipping and insurance charges, subtract these charges before a cash discount is taken. These charges are then added back to find net cost after the cash discount is subtracted.

Finding the Net Cost

$$\text{Net cost} = (\text{List price} - \text{Trade discount}) - \text{Cash discount}$$

The type of cash discount appears on the invoice, under TERMS, which can be found in the bottom right-hand corner of the Hershey invoice on the next page. Many companies using automated billing systems state the exact amount of the cash discount on the invoice. This eliminates all calculations on the part of the buyer. The Hershey invoice is an example of an invoice stating the exact amount of the cash discount. This exact amount is found at the bottom of the invoice. Not all businesses do this, however, so it is important to know how to determine cash discounts.

OBJECTIVE 2 Use the ordinary dating method. There are many methods for finding cash discounts, but nearly all of these are based on the **ordinary dating method**. The methods discussed here and in the next section are the most common in use today. The ordinary dating method of cash discount, for example, is expressed on an invoice as

2/10, n/30 or **2/10, net 30**

and is read "two ten, net thirty." The first digit is the rate of discount (2%), the second digit is the number of days allowed to take the discount (10 days), and n/30 (net 30) is the total number of days given to pay the invoice in full if the buyer does not use the cash discount. If this invoice is paid within 10 days from the date of the invoice, a 2% discount is subtracted from the amount owed. If payment is made between the 11th and 30th days from the invoice date, the entire amount of the invoice is due. After 30 days from the date of the invoice, the invoice is considered overdue and may be subject to a late charge.

Hershey Chocolate U.S.A.
Hershey Foods Corporation
Hershey, Pennsylvania 17033-0819 U.S.A.

04 98 921006 00

CLAIMS FOR LOSS, DAMAGE, SHORTAGE MUST BE PROMPTLY FILED AND FORWARDED TO:
HERSHEY CHOCOLATE U.S.A.
ATTN: CREDIT DEPARTMENT
HERSHEY, PA 17033

INVOICE NO.	DATE
00003	10/06
1956003	

CHARGE TO:
HANCOCK & OBRIEN
309 SPRING RD
TREMONT PA
17981

SHIP TO:
HANCOCK & OBRIEN
309 SPRING RD
TREMONT PA

0

COPY OF INVOICE TO CREDIT ON ALL
MISC/CASH SALES
INVOICE TO ART GINGRICH FOR MAILING

HERSHEY CHOC CO. HERSHEY, PA 17033

PLEASE RETURN DUPLICATE COPY WITH PAYMENT TO

REGION/DIST.	CL BILL	WHSE NO.	CT	CARRIER CODS	SALES REP NO.	ORDER DATE	CUSTOMER ORDER NUMBER	SCN.	DATE SHIPPED	PLEASE REFER TO THIS NUMBER WHEN REMITTING — ACCOUNT NUMBER
9091	04		09	HEST		10 06	3406	5	10 06	088500 0091

QTY. SHIPPED	UNIT	UPC CASH CODE	VER	CUSTOMER STOCK NO.	DESCRIPTION	PACK	RETAIL UNIT UPC	QTY. BILLED	UNIT PRICE	ALLOW	NET UNIT PRICE	AMOUNT
		34000		MANUFACTURER ID FOR THE FOLLOWING ITEMS:								
2	CS	11614			RE PCS368X12			2	6845		6845	13690
2	CS	15500			5TH AVE REG CT			2	12320		12320	24640
2	CS	48400			REESE 4-CUP24/6			2	7020		7020	14040
2	CS	22600			KITKAT KING 6/24			2	7020		7020	14040
2	CS	31800			STRWBRY SYP 22OZ			2	1603		1603	3206
2	CS	37014			SKOR 36BX12			2	12320		12320	24640
2	CS	24100			ALMOND 36CT12			2	12320		12320	24640
2	CS	06630			YORK MINT 200/8			2	8580		8580	17160
2	CS	22200			KRACKL KNG 18/12			2	10530		10530	21060
2	CS	24000			MILK 36CT12			2	12320		12320	24640

TOTAL PCS	GROSS WT.		
20	846	ITM HAS QTY HAS	243458 20

2/10 N30
TERMS 2% DISCOUNT OF $36.35 IF PAID BY 10/16
NET 30 DAYS

181756

PAY LAST AMOUNT IF DISCOUNT IS NOT EARNED

To find the due date of an invoice, use the number of days in each month, given in the following chart.

The Number of Days in Each Month

30-Day Months	31-Day Months		Exception
April	January	August	February
June	March	October	(28 days normally;
September	May	December	29 days in leap year)
November	July		

QUICK TIP Leap years occur every 4 years. They are the same as Summer Olympic years and presidential-election years in the United States. If a year is evenly divisible by the number 4, it is a leap year. The years 2012, 2016, and 2020 are all leap years because they are evenly divisible by 4.

The number of days in each month of the year can also be remembered using the following rhyme and "knuckle" methods:

Rhyme Method:
30 days hath September,
April, June, and November.
All the rest have 31, except February,
which has 28 and in a leap year 29.

Knuckle Method:

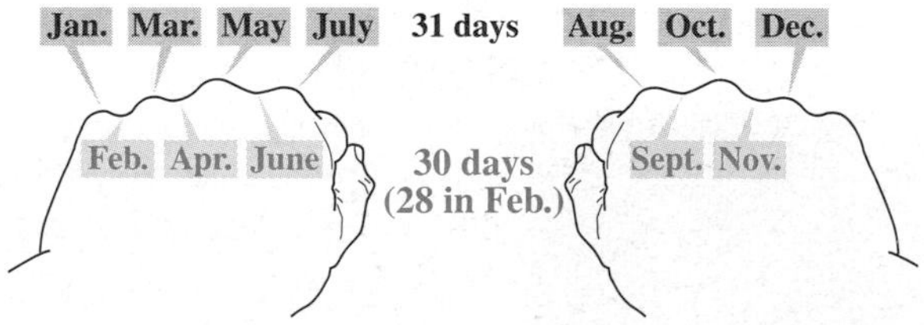

OBJECTIVE 3 Determine whether cash discounts are earned. Find the date that an invoice is due by counting from the next day after the date of the invoice. The date of the invoice is never counted. Another way to determine due dates is to add the given number of days to the starting date. For example, to determine 10 days from April 7, add the number of days to the date $(7 + 10 = 17)$. The due date, or 10 days from April 7, is April 17.

When the discount date or net payment date falls in the next month, the number of days remaining in the current month is found by subtracting the invoice date from the number of days in the month. Then find the number of days in the next month needed to equal the discount period or net payment period. For example, determine the date that is 15 days from October 20.

31	days in October
− 20	the beginning date is October 20
11	days remaining in October
15	total number of days
− 11	days remaining in October
4	November (future date)

Therefore, November 4 is 15 days from October 20.

EXAMPLE 1

Finding Cash Discount Dates

A Hershey invoice is dated January 2 and offers terms of 2/10, net 30. Find **(a)** the last date on which the 2% discount may be taken and **(b)** the net payment date.

SOLUTION

(a) Beginning with the invoice date, January 2, the last date for taking the discount is January 12 (2 + 10).

(b) The net payment date is February 1 (31 − 2 = 29 days remaining in January plus 1 day in February.)

QUICK CHECK 1

An invoice is dated June 8 and offers terms of 3/15, net 30. Find **(a)** the last date on which the 3% discount may be taken and **(b)** the net payment date.

EXAMPLE 2

Finding the Amount Due on the Invoice

An invoice received by Kitchen Crafters for $840 is dated July 1 and offers terms of 2/10, n/30. If the invoice is paid on July 8 and the shipping and insurance charges, which were FOB shipping point, are $18.70, find the total amount due.

SOLUTION

STEP 1 The invoice was paid 7 days after its date (8 − 1 = 7); therefore, the 2% cash discount is taken.

STEP 2 The 2% cash discount is found on $840. The discount to be taken is $840 × .02 = **$16.80.**

STEP 3 The cash discount is subtracted from the invoice amount to determine the amount due.

$840 invoice amount − **$16.80 cash discount** (**2%**) = $823.20 amount due

STEP 4 The shipping and insurance charges are added to find the total amount due.

$823.20 amount due + **$18.70 shipping and insurance** = $841.90 total amount due

QUICK TIP When the terms of an invoice are 2/10, a 2% discount is taken. Only 98% (100% − 2%) of the invoice must be paid if the invoice is paid during the first 10 days. In Example 2, the amount due may be found as follows.

$840 × .98 = $823.20

(invoice amount × complement of 2% = amount due)

QUICK CHECK 2

An invoice is received for $2830.15, is dated March 21, and offers 3/15, n/30. If the invoice is paid on April 4 and the shipping and insurance charges are $124.96, find the amount due.

OBJECTIVE 4 **Use postdating when calculating cash discounts.** In the ordinary dating method, the cash discount date and net payment date are both counted from the date of the invoice. Occasionally, an invoice is **postdated**. This may be done to give the purchaser more time to take the cash discount on the invoice or maybe to more closely fit the accounting practices of the seller. The seller

Quick Check Answers

1. (a) June 23 **(b)** July 8
2. $2870.21 (rounded)

QUICK TIP A cash discount is never taken on shipping and insurance charges. Be certain that shipping and insurance charges are excluded from the invoice amount before calculating the cash discount. Shipping and insurance charges must then be added back in to find the total amount due.

places a date that is after the actual invoice date, sometimes labeling it **AS OF**. For example, the following Levi Strauss invoice is dated 07/25 AS OF 08/01. Both the cash discount period and the net payment date are counted from 08/01 (August 1). This results in giving additional time for the purchaser to pay the invoice and receive the discount.

L INVOICE NO ▶ 92-903

PLEASE SEND REMITTANCE ONLY TO:
LEVI STRAUSS & CO.
LEVI PLAZA
1155 BATTERY P.O.BOX 7215
SAN FRANCISCO, CA 94120

DATE 07/25 AS OF 08/01

SHIPPED FROM: Florence, KY
SHIPMENT NO:

BILL TO: Renee Miller Swenson
1155 Laurel Place
San Francisco, CA 94111

SHIP TO: The Rustic Ribbon
310 Union Street
San Rafael, CA 94901
MARK FOR T. Cooper

YOUR ORDER NUMBER	STORE/DEPT. NO.	SHIPPED	CARRIER	NO. CTNS	WEIGHT	NO. INV.	TERMS:	NO ANTICIPATION
72523	368	COLLECT	SPRINGRIGHT	4	210		8% /10 EOM	

DESCRIPTION		TOTAL QUANTITY	UNIT PRICE	EXTENDED AMOUNT
54111-1919	L/S Navy Cardigan	24	13.12	314.88
45159-2161	S/S Camp Shirt	6	10.50	63.00
45199-8119	S/S Shirt w/ Logo	12	10.50	126.00
35158-8019	Sausalito Skort	10	10.50	105.00
25248-8019	Sausalito Pant	18	10.50	189.00
45151-5861	Vest w/ Black Tie	6	14.00	84.00
54198-6319	L/S Banded Polo	6	15.50	93.00
54220-5551	L/S Cardigan Sweater	6	28.00	168.00

NET/10 EOM + TERMS DISCOUNT = INVOICE TOTAL ▶ $1,142.88

REMITTANCE COPY
PLEASE RETURN THIS COPY WITH YOUR REMITTANCE

DUE ▶ 9/10

EXAMPLE 3

Using Postdating AS OF with Invoices

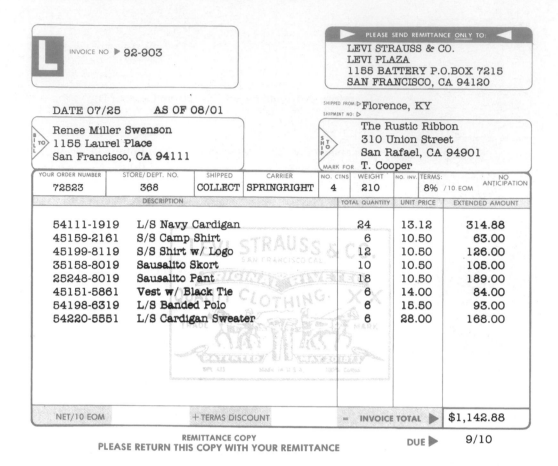

ONLY 199.99
HENKELS PREMIER CLASSIC 15-PIECE SET
Includes five kitchen knives, six steak knives, fork, shears, steel, and block

An invoice for a shipment of Henkels cutlery from Germany is dated October 21 AS OF November 1 with terms of 3/15, n/30. Find **(a)** the last date on which the cash discount may be taken and **(b)** the net payment date.

SOLUTION

(a) Beginning with the postdate (AS OF) of November 1, the last date for taking the discount is November 16 $(1 + 15)$.

(b) The net payment date is December 1 **(29 days remaining in November and 1 day in December)**.

QUICK CHECK 3

An invoice for Waterford Crystal from Ireland is dated August 24 AS OF September 1 with terms of 1/10, n/30. Find **(a)** the last date on which the cash discount may be taken and **(b)** the net payment date.

Quick Check Answers

3. **(a)** September 11
(b) October 1

Business customers, as well as consumers, look for the best prices and the best discounts. A greater number of discounts resulting in lower costs allows the business to operate more efficiently, which results in higher profits. The following newspaper article reminds us that even businesses must comparison shop to save money.

HERE & NOW

QUICK TIP Sometimes, a sliding scale of cash discounts is offered. For example, with the cash discount 3/10, 2/20, 1/30, n/60, a discount of 3% is given if payment is made within 10 days, 2% if paid from the 11th through the 20th day, and 1% if paid from the 21st through the 30th day. The entire amount (net) must be paid no later than 60 days from the date of the invoice.

Businesses Turn to Smart Shopping

NEW YORK—Being a savvy business owner means being a smart shopper—deciding which retailers and service establishments provide the best deal. That means shopping like a consumer—and at times, buying in the same places a consumer does.

Whether you're looking for mundane items like office supplies or bigger investments such as computer equipment or telephone service, you'll do better if you comparison shop.

If your business is very small, chances are you won't be able to negotiate a volume discount with an office supplies wholesaler or distributor. So your first thought might be to head to a big superstore chain such as Staples, Office Depot or OfficeMax that tend to have lower prices than independent retailers.

But you might find you'll do better at a local warehouse retailer such as Sam's Wholesale Club or Costco, which have business memberships.

(***Source:*** *Sacramento Bee.*)

EXAMPLE 4

Determining Cash Discount Due Dates for a Sliding Scale

An invoice from Cellular Products is dated May 18 and offers terms of 4/10, 3/25, 1/40, n/60. Find **(a)** the three final dates for each cash discount and **(b)** the net payment date.

SOLUTION

(a) The three final cash discount dates are

4% if paid by May 28	10 days from May 18
3% if paid by June 12	25 days from May 18
1% if paid by June 27	40 days from May 18

(b) The net payment date is July 17 (20 days beyond the cash discount period).

QUICK CHECK 4

An invoice is dated April 14 and offers terms of 3/10, 2/30, 1/40, n/60. Find **(a)** the three final dates for each cash discount and **(b)** the net payment date.

Quick Check Answers

4. (a) April 24; May 14; May 24

(b) June 13

Never take more than one of the cash discounts. *With all methods of giving cash discounts, if the net payment period is not given, the net payment due date is assumed to be 20 days beyond the cash discount period.* After that date, the invoice is considered overdue. If either the final discount date or the net payment date is on a Sunday or holiday, the next business day is used. Many companies insist that payment is made when the payment is received. In non-retail transactions, payment is considered to be made when it is mailed.

Case Studies

George Foreman

www.igrillwithgeorge.com

- 1949: Born January 10th
- 1968: Wins Olympic gold medal for boxing
- 1973: Defeats Joe Frazier to become world heavyweight champion
- 1974: Loses heavyweight title to Muhammad Ali
- 1994: Wins heavyweight title at age of 45 from Michael Moore, age 26
- 1995: Partners with Salton to promote the George Foreman Lean Mean Grilling Machine
- 1999: Crowned King of the Grill after selling over 10 million grills
- 2007: Over 75 million machines sold

George E. Foreman was born on January 10, 1949 in Marshal, Texas. He grew up on the tough streets of Houston's Fifth Ward area, and as a young kid he was always getting into trouble. He joined the Job Corps and his life changed. One of the counselors noticed that he was always into fights, so he decided that George should put all of his energy into something positive. This started his boxing career. Since 1995 Foreman has been a partner with Salton in promoting the George Foreman cooking grills and other barbecue products. Today, "if there is one thing George Foreman knows, it's good cooking."

1. Kitchen Crafters purchased George Foreman Super Searing Grills that were list priced at $149.99. If the supplier offered a trade discount of 20/20, find the cost of one dozen grilling machines.

2. The list price of a George Foreman Next Grilleration Contact Grill is $119.99. The manufacturer gives a 25/10 trade discount and offers a cash discount of 3/15, net/30. Find the cost to Kitchen Crafters if both discounts are earned and taken.

3. The list price of a *George Foreman Knock-Out-the-Fat Barbecue and Grilling Cookbook* is $16.95. If the cookbook is offered at a reduced price of $13.95 when purchased on the Internet, what is the percent of markdown? Round to the nearest tenth of a percent.

4. Many celebrities and athletes use their popularity to promote the products of various companies. However, George Foreman has his own line of products. Name four other well-known people who don't just promote the products of others, but have their own line of products.

6.3 EXERCISES

FOR EXTRA HELP

MyMathLab

MathXL PRACTICE

WATCH

DOWNLOAD

READ

REVIEW

The QUICK START *exercises in each section contain solutions to help you get started.*

Find the final discount date and the net payment date for each of the following. (See Examples 1 and 3.)

QUICK START

	Invoice Date	AS OF	Terms	Final Discount Date	Net Payment Date
1.	May 4		2/10, n/30	**May 14**	**June 3**
2.	Apr. 12		3/10, net 30	**April 22**	**May 12**
3.	June 30	July 10	3/15, n/60	______	______
4.	Nov. 7	Nov. 18	3/10, n/40	______	______
5.	Sept. 11		4/20, n/30	______	______
6.	July 31		2/15, net 20	______	______

Solve for the amount of discount and the total amount due on each of the following invoices. Add shipping and insurance charges if given. (See Examples 2 and 4.)

QUICK START

	Invoice Amount	Invoice Date	Terms	Date Invoice Paid	Shipping and Insurance	Amount of Discount	Total Amount Due
7.	$85.18	Nov. 2	2/10, net 30	Nov. 11	$8.72	**$1.70**	**$92.20**
	$85.18 − $1.70 + $8.72 = $92.20						
8.	$66.10	Mar. 8	6/10, n/30	Mar. 14	$4.39	**$3.97**	**$66.52**
	$66.10 − $3.97 + $4.39 = $66.52						
9.	$78.07	May 5	net 30	June 1	$3.18	______	______
10.	$294	Apr. 5	net 30	May 2	$16.20	______	______
11.	$1080	July 8	5/10, 2/20, n/30	July 26	$62.15	______	______
12.	$1282	July 1	4/15, net 40	July 7	$21.40	______	______

13. Describe the difference between a trade discount and a cash discount. Why are cash discounts offered? (See Objective 1.)

14. Using 2/10, n/30 as an example, explain what an ordinary dating cash discount means. (See Objective 2.)

C indicates an exercise that is related to the Case in Point feature.

Solve the following application problems. Round to the nearest cent.

QUICK START

15. CATERING COMPANY Kitchen Crafters offers cash discounts of 4/10, 2/20, net 30 to all catering companies. An invoice is dated June 18 amounting to $4635.40 and is paid on July 7. Find the amount needed to pay the invoice.

June 18 to July 7 = (30 − 18) + 7 = 19 days
Discount is 2%; $4635.40 × .98 = $4542.69

15. $4542.69

16. RUSSIAN ELECTRICAL SUPPLIES A shipment of electrical supplies is received from the Lyskovo Electrotechnical Works. The invoice is dated March 8, amounts to $6824.58, and has terms of 2/15, 1/20 AS OF March 20. Find the amount needed to pay the invoice on April 2.

16. ______________

17. PETROCHEMICAL PRODUCTS Century Petrochemical Products offers customers a trade discount of 10/20/5 on all products, with terms of net 30. Find the customer's price for products with a total list price of $2630 if the invoice was paid within 30 days.

17. ______________

18. GEORGE FOREMAN GRILL A George Foreman Rotisserie Grill is list priced at $59.99 with a trade discount of 20/5/10 and terms of 4/10, n/30. Find the cost to Kitchen Crafters assuming that both discounts are earned.

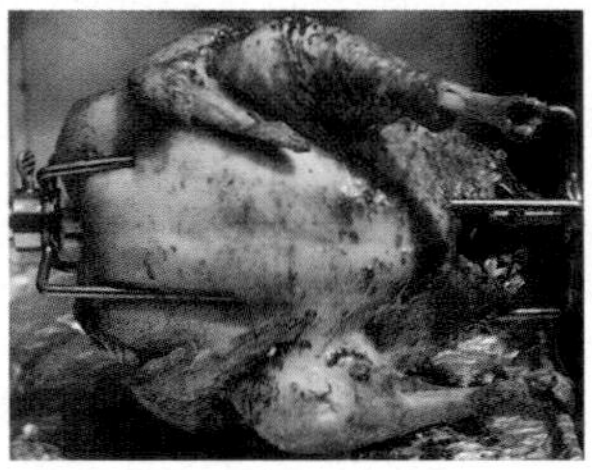

18. ______________

19. FINDING DISCOUNT DATES An invoice is dated January 18 and offers terms of 6/10, 4/20, 1/30, n/50. Find **(a)** the three final discount dates and **(b)** the net payment date.

(a) ______________
(b) ______________

20. FINDING DISCOUNT DATES An invoice with terms of 4/15, 3/20, 1/30, n/60 is dated September 4. Find **(a)** the three final discount dates and **(b)** the net payment date.

(a) ______________
(b) ______________

21. AS OF DATING An invoice is dated March 28 AS OF April 5 with terms of 4/20, n/30. Find **(a)** the final discount date and **(b)** the net payment date.

(a) ______________
(b) ______________

22. AS OF DATING An invoice is dated May 20 AS OF June 5 with terms of 2/10, n/30. Find **(a)** the final discount date and **(b)** the net payment date.

(a) ______________
(b) ______________

23. How do you remember the number of days in each month of the year? List the months and the number of days in each. (See Objective 2.)

24. Explain in your own words how AS OF dating (postdating) works. Why is it used? (See Objective 4.)

6.4 CASH DISCOUNTS: OTHER DATING METHODS

OBJECTIVES

1. Solve cash discount problems with end-of-month dating.
2. Use receipt-of-goods dating to solve cash discount problems.
3. Use extra dating to solve cash discount problems.
4. Determine credit given for partial payment of an invoice.

CASE in POINT In addition to the ordinary dating method of cash discounts, several other cash discount methods are in common use. Ryan Andrews of Kitchen Crafters must be able to understand and use each of these.

OBJECTIVE 1 Solve cash discount problems with end-of-month dating. This section discusses several other methods of finding cash discounts. **End-of-month** and **proximo** dating, abbreviated **EOM** and **prox.**, are treated the same. For example, both

SALE 59.99
OSTER TOASTER OVEN/BROILER
6-slice capacity, four heat settings and continuous-clean interior, #6232. Reg. 69.99
Muffins not included.

3/10 EOM and **3/10 prox.**

mean that 3% may be taken as a cash discount if payment is made by the 10th of the month that follows the sale. The 10 days are counted from the *end of the month* in which the invoice is dated. For example, an invoice dated July 14 with terms of 3/10 EOM would have a discount date 10 days from the end of the month, or the 10th of August (August 10).

Since this is a method of increasing the length of time during which a discount may be taken, it has become common business practice to add an extra month when the date of an invoice is the 26th of the month or later. For example, if an invoice is dated March 25 and the discount offered is 3/10 EOM, the last date on which the discount may be taken is April 10. ***However, if the invoice is dated March 26 (or any later date in March) and the cash discount offered is 3/10 EOM, then the last date on which the discount may be taken is May 10.***

QUICK TIP The practice of adding an extra month when the invoice is dated the 26th of a month or after is used *only* with the end-of-month (proximo) dating cash discount. It does *not* apply to any of the other cash discount methods.

EXAMPLE 1 Using End-of-Month Dating

If an invoice from Oster is dated June 10 with terms of 3/20 EOM, find **(a)** the final date on which the cash discount may be taken and **(b)** the net payment date.

SOLUTION

(a) The discount date is July 20 (20 days after the end of June).

(b) When no net payment due date is given, common business practice is to allow 20 days after the last discount date. The net payment date is August 9, which is **20 days** after the last discount date (July 20), since no net payment date is given.

QUICK CHECK 1

An invoice from Pearson Education, Inc., is dated February 15 with terms of 2/10 EOM. Find **(a)** the final date on which the discount may be taken and **(b)** the net payment date.

Quick Check Answers

1. (a) March 10
(b) March 30

EXAMPLE 2

Using Proximo Dating

Find the amount due on an invoice of $782 for some Black and Decker Belgian waffle makers dated August 3, if terms are 1/10 prox. and the invoice is paid on September 4.

SOLUTION

The last date on which the discount may be taken is September 10 (**10 days** after the end of August). September 4 is within the discount period, so the discount is earned. The 1% cash discount is computed on $782, the amount of the invoice. Subtract the discount ($782 × **.01** = $7.82) from the invoice amount to find the amount due.

$782.00	invoice amount
− **7.82**	**cash discount (1%)**
$774.18	amount due

QUICK TIP With all methods of cash discounts, if the net payment period is not given, the net payment due date is assumed to be ***20 days beyond the cash discount date.***

QUICK CHECK 2

An invoice for some gourmet cookbooks is for $1475 and dated October 17. Find the amount due if the invoice terms are 3/20 proximo and the invoice is paid on November 18.

OBJECTIVE 2 **Use receipt-of-goods dating to solve cash discount problems.** **Receipt-of-goods dating**, abbreviated **ROG**, offers cash discounts determined from the date on which goods are actually received. This method is often used when shipping time is long. The invoice might arrive overnight by mail, but the goods may take several weeks. Under the ROG method of cash discount, the buyer is given the time to receive and inspect the merchandise and then is allowed to benefit from a cash discount. For example, the discount

3/15 ROG

allows a 3% cash discount if the invoice is paid within 15 days from receipt of goods. The date that goods are received is determined by the delivery date. If the invoice was dated March 5 and goods were received on April 7, the last date to take the 3% cash discount would be April 22 (April 7 plus 15 days). The net payment date, since it is not stated, is 20 days after the last discount date, or May 12 (April 22 plus 20 days).

EXAMPLE 3

Using Receipt-of-Goods Dating

Kitchen Crafters received an invoice dated December 12, with terms of 2/10 ROG. The goods were received on January 2. Find **(a)** the final date on which the cash discount may be taken and **(b)** the net payment date.

SOLUTION

(a) The discount date is January 12 (**10 days** after receipt of goods, January 2 plus **10 days**).
(b) The net payment date is February 1 (**20 days** after the last discount date).

QUICK CHECK 3

An invoice from Silver Specialties is dated June 4, with terms of 4/15 ROG. The merchandise was received on July 25. Find **(a)** the final date on which the cash discount may be taken and **(b)** the net payment date.

Quick Check Answers

2. $1430.75
3. (a) August 9
(b) August 29

EXAMPLE 4

Working with ROG Dating

Find the amount due to Sir Speedy on an invoice of $285 for some printing services, with terms of 3/10 ROG, if the invoice is dated June 8, the goods are received June 18, and the invoice is paid June 30.

SOLUTION

The last date to take the 3% cash discount is June 28, 10 days after June 18. Since the invoice is paid on June 30, 2 days after the last discount date, **no cash discount may be taken**. The entire amount of the invoice must be paid.

	$285	invoice amount
−	0	**no cash discount**
	$285	amount due

QUICK CHECK 4

Find the amount due on an invoice of $896, with terms of 4/20 ROG, if the invoice is dated March 10, the goods are received April 28, and the invoice is paid on May 15.

OBJECTIVE 3 Use extra dating to solve cash discount problems. **Extra dating (extra, ex., or x)** gives the buyer additional time to take advantage of a cash discount. For example, the discount

2/10–50 extra or **2/10–50 ex.** or **2/10–50 x**

allows a 2% cash discount if the invoice is paid within 10 + 50 = 60 days from the date of the invoice. The discount is expressed as 2/10–50 ex. (rather than 2/60) to show that the 50 days are *extra*, or in addition to the normal 10 days offered.

There are several reasons for using extra dating. A supplier might extend the discount period during a slow sales season to generate more sales or to gain a competitive advantage. For example, the seller might offer Christmas merchandise with extra dating to allow the buyer to take the cash discount after the holiday selling period.

EXAMPLE 5

Using Extra Dating

An invoice for Oster blenders is dated November 23 with terms of 2/10–50 ex. Find **(a)** the final date on which the cash discount may be taken and **(b)** the net payment date.

SOLUTION

(a) The discount date is January 22 (**7 days** remaining in November + 31 days in December = 38; thus, **22 more days** are needed in January to total 60).

(b) The net payment date is February 11 (**20 days** after the last discount date).

Quick Check Answers

4. $860.16

5. (a) September 15

(b) October 5

QUICK CHECK 5

An invoice is dated July 7 with terms of 1/10–60 ex. Find **(a)** the final date on which the cash discount may be taken and **(b)** the net payment date.

EXAMPLE 6

Understanding Extra Dating

An invoice from KitchenAid is dated August 5, amounts to $8180, offers terms of 3/10–30 x, and is paid on September 12. Find the net payment.

SOLUTION

STEP 1 The last day to take the 3% cash discount is September 14 (**August 5 + 40 days = September 14**). Since the invoice is paid on September 12, the **3%** discount may be taken.

STEP 2 The **3%** cash discount is computed on $8180, the amount of the invoice. The discount to be taken is $245.40.

STEP 3 Subtract the cash discount from the invoice amount to determine the amount of payment.

$8180.00	invoice amount
− $245.40	**3% cash discount**
$7934.60	amount of payment

QUICK CHECK 6

An invoice for $5412 is dated May 22 and offers terms of 2/20–40 x. If the invoice is paid on July 15, what is the amount of payment due?

QUICK TIP In Example 6, the amount of payment may be found by multiplying the invoice amount by 100% − 3%, or 97%. Here, $8180 × .97 = $7934.60 is the amount of payment.

OBJECTIVE 4 Determine credit given for partial payment of an invoice. Occasionally, a customer may pay only a portion of the total amount due on an invoice. If this **partial payment** is made within a discount period, the customer is entitled to a discount on the portion of the invoice that is paid.

If the terms of an invoice are 3%, 10 days, then only 97% (100% − 3%) of the invoice amount must be paid during the first 10 days. So, for each $.97 paid, the customer is entitled to $1.00 of credit. When a partial payment is made, the credit given for the partial payment (base) is found by dividing the partial payment by the complement of the cash discount percent. Then, to find the balance due, subtract the credit given from the invoice amount. The cash discount is found by subtracting the partial payment from the credit given.

EXAMPLE 7

Finding Credit for Partial Payment

Dave's Body and Paint receives an invoice for $1140 dated March 8 that offers terms of 2/10 prox. A partial payment of $450 is made on April 5. Find **(a)** the amount credited for the partial payment, **(b)** the balance due on the invoice, and **(c)** the cash discount earned.

SOLUTION

(a) The cash discount is earned on the $450 partial payment made on April 5 (April 10 was the last discount date). The amount paid ($450) is part of the base (amount for which credit is given).

$$100\% - 2\% = 98\%$$

The rate 98% is used to solve for base using the formula Base $= \frac{\text{Part}}{\text{Rate}}$.

$$B = \frac{P}{R}$$

$$B = \frac{450}{98\%} = \frac{450}{.98} = \$459.18 \text{ (rounded)}$$

The amount credited for partial payment is $459.18.

(b) Balance due = Invoice amount − Credit given
Balance due = $1140 − **$459.18** = $680.82

(c) Cash discount = Credit given − Partial payment
Cash discount = **$459.18** − $450 = $9.18

Quick Check Answer

6. $5303.76

QUICK TIP Cash discounts are important, and a business should make the effort to pay invoices early to earn the cash discounts. In many cases, the money saved through cash discounts has a great effect on the profitability of a business. Often, companies will borrow money to enable them to take advantage of cash discounts. The mathematics of this type of loan is discussed in **Section 8.1**, Simple Interest.

A calculator solution to this example includes these three steps.

STEP 1 First, find the amount of credit given.

450 ÷ .98 = 459.18 (rounded)

STEP 2 Now, store the amount of credit and subtract this amount from the invoice amount to find the balance due.

STO 1140 − RCL = 680.82 (rounded)

STEP 3 Finally, subtract the partial payment from the amount of credit given to find the cash discount.

RCL − 450 = 9.18 (rounded)

QUICK CHECK 7

Central Parts receives an invoice for $1082 dated September 14 that offers terms of 2/20 prox. A partial payment of $590 is paid on October 15. Find **(a)** the amount credited for the partial payment, **(b)** the balance due on the invoice, and **(c)** the cash discount earned.

QUICK TIP The cash discounts discussed in this chapter are normally not used when selling to foreign customers or purchasing from foreign suppliers. Instead, other types of discounts may be offered to reduce the price of goods sold to foreign buyers. These discounts may be given as allowances for tariffs paid (import duties) by the customer, reimbursement for shipping and insurance paid by the customer, or advertising allowances.

Retail store owners are always looking for the lowest cost on products that they purchase. This enables them to offer good value to their customers. The newspaper article below introduces the $14.98 Starbury One basketball shoes promoted by NBA star Stephon Marbury, who plays for the New York Knicks. Marbury insists that the shoes are comparable to $150-plus high-end basketball shoes. He says, "It's the same shoe."

HERE & NOW

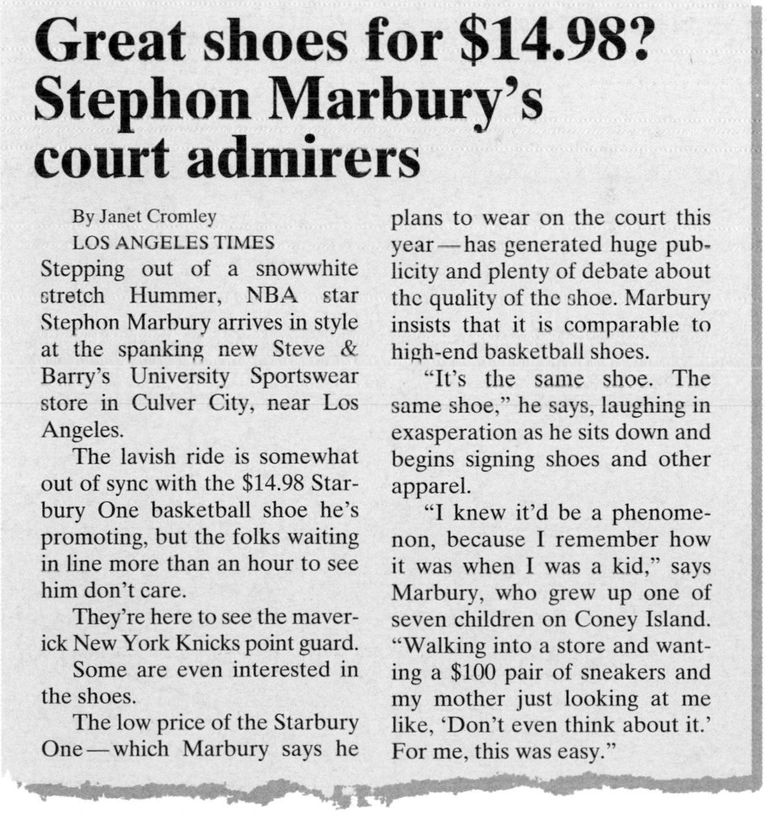
Great shoes for $14.98? Stephon Marbury's court admirers

By Janet Cromley
LOS ANGELES TIMES

Stepping out of a snowwhite stretch Hummer, NBA star Stephon Marbury arrives in style at the spanking new Steve & Barry's University Sportswear store in Culver City, near Los Angeles.

The lavish ride is somewhat out of sync with the $14.98 Starbury One basketball shoe he's promoting, but the folks waiting in line more than an hour to see him don't care.

They're here to see the maverick New York Knicks point guard.

Some are even interested in the shoes.

The low price of the Starbury One—which Marbury says he plans to wear on the court this year—has generated huge publicity and plenty of debate about the quality of the shoe. Marbury insists that it is comparable to high-end basketball shoes.

"It's the same shoe. The same shoe," he says, laughing in exasperation as he sits down and begins signing shoes and other apparel.

"I knew it'd be a phenomenon, because I remember how it was when I was a kid," says Marbury, who grew up one of seven children on Coney Island. "Walking into a store and wanting a $100 pair of sneakers and my mother just looking at me like, 'Don't even think about it.' For me, this was easy."

The Nike Air Max 360, left, retails for $160. Stephon Marbury's Starbury One, the two on the right, retail for $14.98.

Quick Check Answers

7. **(a)** $602.04 (rounded)
(b) $479.96
(c) $12.04

6.4 EXERCISES

FOR EXTRA HELP

MyMathLab

MathXL PRACTICE

WATCH

DOWNLOAD

READ

REVIEW

The QUICK START *exercises in each section contain solutions to help you get started.*

Find the discount date and net payment date for each of the following. (The net payment date is 20 days after the final discount date. See Examples 1, 3, and 5.)

QUICK START

	Invoice Date	Terms	Date Goods Received	Final Discount Date	Net Payment Date
1.	Feb. 8	3/10 EOM		**Mar. 10**	**Mar. 30**
2.	July 14	2/15 ROG	Sept. 3	**Sept. 18**	**Oct. 8**
3.	Nov. 22	1/10–20 x		______	______
4.	July 6	2/10 EOM		______	______
5.	Apr. 12	3/15–50 ex.		______	______
6.	Jan. 15	3/15 ROG	Feb. 5	______	______

Solve for the amount of discount and the amount due on each of the following invoices. Round to the nearest cent. (See Examples 2, 4, and 6.)

QUICK START

	Invoice Amount	Invoice Date	Terms	Date Goods Received	Date Invoice Paid	Amount of Discount	Amount Due
7.	$682.28	June 4	3/20 ROG	July 25	Aug. 10	**$20.47**	**$661.81**
	$20.47 discount; $682.28 − $20.47 = $661.81 due						
8.	$356.20	May 17	3/15 prox.		June 12	**$10.69**	**$345.51**
	10.686 = $10.69 discount; $356.20 − $10.69 = $345.51 due						
9.	$785.64	Sept. 8	2/10–20 x		Oct. 14	______	______
10.	$12.38	Mar. 29	2/15 ROG	Apr. 15	Apr. 30	______	______
11.	$11,480	Apr. 6	2/15 prox.		Apr. 30	______	______
12.	$1380	May 28	1/15 EOM		June 10	______	______
13.	$23.95	Aug. 2	3/10–20 extra		Sept. 1	______	______
14.	$3250.60	Oct. 17	3/15–20 ex.		Oct. 20	______	______

C indicates an exercise that is related to the Case in Point feature.

15. Quite often there is no mention of a net payment date on an invoice. Explain the common business practice when no net payment date is given. (See Objective 1.)

16. Describe why ROG dating is offered to customers. Use an example in your description. (See Objective 2.)

Solve the following application problems. Round to the nearest cent.

QUICK START

17. NOSTALGIC KITCHEN APPLIANCES Nostalgia Electronics, a manufacturer of Nostalgic Kitchen appliances, offers terms of 2/10–30 ex. to stimulate slow sales in the winter months. Kitchen Crafters purchased $2382.58 worth of appliances and was offered the above terms. If the invoice was dated November 3, find **(a)** the final date on which the cash discount may be taken and **(b)** the amount paid if the discount was earned.

(a) Dec. 13
(b) $2334.93

(a) 27 days remain in November
+ 13 days in December
40 days is December 13

(b) $2382.58 × .02 = 47.651 = $47.65 discount
$2382.58 − $47.65 = $2334.93 paid

18. CANADIAN FOOD PRODUCTS Vanitha Evans, a wholesaler of Canadian food products, offers terms of 4/15–40 ex. to encourage the sales of her products. In a recent order, a retailer purchased $9864.18 worth of Canadian foods and was offered the above terms. If the invoice was dated March 10, find **(a)** the final date on which the cash discount may be taken and **(b)** the amount paid if the discount was earned.

(a) ______
(b) ______

19. GLOBAL POSITIONING SYSTEMS A recent invoice for 24 Magellan Roadmate 2000 auto GPS systems amounting to $6720.50 was dated February 20 and offered terms of 2/20 ROG. If the equipment was received on March 20 and the invoice was paid on April 8, find the amount due.

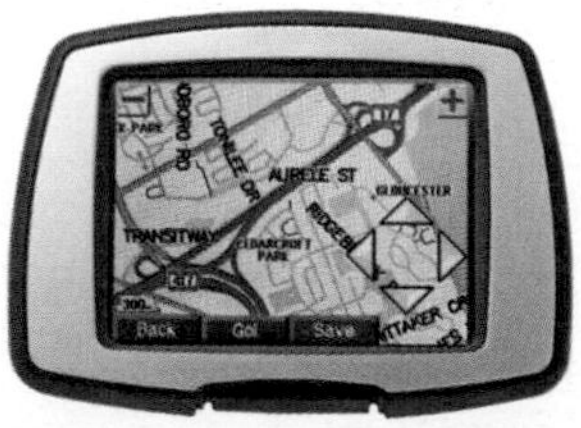

19. ______

20. WHEELS WITH BLING Scott Ryder purchased some 21-inch and 23-inch custom wheels for his performance auto parts store and was offered a cash discount of 2/10 EOM. The invoice amounted to $7218.80 and was dated June 2. The wheels were received 7 days later, and the invoice was paid on July 7. Find the amount necessary to pay the invoice in full.

20. ______

21. ENGLISH SOCCER EQUIPMENT An invoice dated December 8 is received with a shipment of soccer equipment from England on April 18 of the following year. The list price of the equipment is $2538, with allowed series discounts of 25/10/10. If cash terms of sale are 3/15 ROG, find the amount necessary to pay in full on April 21.

21. ____________

C **22.** CRYSTAL FROM IRELAND Kitchen Crafters receives an invoice for Waterford crystal from Ireland amounting to $5382.40 and dated May 17. The terms of the invoice are 5/20–90 x and the invoice is paid on September 2. Find the amount necessary to pay the invoice in full.

22. ____________

23. PARTIAL INVOICE PAYMENT PetSmart receives an invoice amounting to $2016.90 with terms of 8/10, net 30 and dated August 20 AS OF September 1. If a partial payment of $1350 is made on September 8, find **(a)** the credit given for the partial payment and **(b)** the balance due on the invoice.

(a) ____________
(b) ____________

24. FROZEN YOGURT Yogurt for You receives an invoice amounting to $263.40 with terms of 2/20 EOM and dated September 6. If a partial payment of $150 is made on October 15, find **(a)** the credit given for the partial payment and **(b)** the balance due on the invoice.

(a) ____________
(b) ____________

C **25.** DISCOUNT DATES An invoice received by Kitchen Crafters is dated May 12 with terms of 2/10 prox. Find **(a)** the final date on which the discount may be taken and **(b)** the net payment date.

(a) ____________
(b) ____________

26. DISCOUNT DATES An invoice from Dollar Distributors is dated November 11 with terms of 3/20 ROG, and the goods are received on December 3. Find **(a)** the final date on which the cash discount may be taken and **(b)** the net payment date.

(a) ____________
(b) ____________

27. INVOICE AMOUNT DUE Find the amount due on an invoice of $1525 with terms of 1/20 ROG. The invoice is dated October 20, goods are received December 1, and the invoice is paid on December 20.

27. ____________

28. PAYMENT DUE Find the payment that should be made on an invoice dated September 28, amounting to $4680, offering terms of 2/10–50 x and paid on November 25.

28. ____________

29. PARTIAL INVOICE PAYMENT An invoice received for Spode china has terms of 3/15–30 x and is dated May 20. The amount of the invoice is $4402.58, and a partial payment of $3250 is made on July 1. Find **(a)** the credit given for the partial payment and **(b)** the balance due on the invoice.

(a) ____________
(b) ____________

30. AUTOMOTIVE Orange County Choppers makes a partial payment of $8726 on an invoice of $17,680.38. If the invoice is dated April 14 with terms of 4/20 prox. and the partial payment is made on May 13, find **(a)** the credit given for the partial payment and **(b)** the balance due on the invoice.

(a) ____________
(b) ____________

31. Write a short explanation of partial payment. Why would a company accept a partial payment? Why would a customer make a partial payment? (See Objective 4.)

32. Of all the different types of cash discounts presented in this section, which type seemed most interesting to you? Explain your reasons.

CHAPTER 6 QUICK REVIEW

CHAPTER TERMS *Review the following terms to test your understanding of the chapter. For each term you do not know, refer to the page number found next to that term.*

amount **[p. 232]**
AS OF **[p. 252]**
cash discount **[p. 249]**
chain discount **[p. 234]**
COD (cash on delivery) **[p. 232]**
complement **[p. 235]**
consumer **[p. 232]**
electronic commerce (EC) **[p. 232]**
end of month (EOM) **[p. 257]**
extension total **[p. 232]**
extra dating (extra, ex., x) **[p. 259]**
FAS (free alongside ship) **[p. 232]**
FOB (free on board) **[p. 232]**
invoice **[p. 232]**
invoice total **[p. 232]**
list price **[p. 234]**
manufacturers **[p. 232]**
net cost **[p. 234]**
net cost equivalent **[p. 236]**
net price **[p. 234]**
ordinary dating method **[p. 249]**
partial payment **[p. 260]**
postdated "AS OF" **[p. 252]**
prox. **[p. 257]**
proximo **[p. 257]**
purchase invoice **[p. 232]**
receipt-of-goods dating **[p. 258]**
retailer **[p. 232]**
ROG **[p. 258]**
sales invoice **[p. 232]**
series discount **[p. 234]**
single discount **[p. 234]**
single discount equivalent **[p. 243]**
trade discounts **[p. 234]**
unit price **[p. 232]**
units shipped **[p. 232]**
wholesalers **[p. 232]**

CONCEPTS	EXAMPLES
6.1 Trade discount and net cost First find the amount of the trade discount. Then use the formula for net cost. **Net cost = List price − Trade discount**	List price, \$28; trade discount, 25%; find the net cost. \$28 × .25 = \$7 Net cost = \$28 − \$7 = \$21
6.1 Complements with respect to 1 (100%) The complement is the number that must be added to a given discount to get 1 or 100%.	Find the complement with respect to 1 (100%) for each of the following. **(a)** 10% 10% + ________ = 100% or 100% − 10% = 90% **(b)** 50% complement = 50% **(c)** 5% complement = 95%
6.1 Complements and series discounts The complement of a discount is the percent paid. Multiply the complements of the series discounts to get the *net cost equivalent.*	Series discount, 10/20/10; find the net cost equivalent. 10/ 20/ 10 ↓ ↓ ↓ .9 × .8 × .9 = .648
6.1 Net cost equivalent (percent paid) and net cost Multiply the net cost equivalent (percent paid) by the list price to get the net cost.	List price, \$280; series discount, 10/30/20; find the net cost. 10/ 30/ 20 ↓ ↓ ↓ .9 × .7 × .8 = .504 percent paid .504 × \$280 = \$141.12
6.2 Single discount equivalent to a series discount Often needed to compare one series discount to another, the single discount equivalent is found by multiplying the complements of the individual discounts to get the net cost equivalent, then subtracting from 1. **1 − Net cost equivalent = Single discount equivalent**	What single discount is equivalent to a 10/20/20 series discount? 10/ 20/ 20 ↓ ↓ ↓ .9 × .8 × .8 = .576 1 − .576 = .424 = 42.4%
6.2 Net cost, using complements of individual discounts **Net cost = List price × Complements of individual discounts**	List price, \$510; series discount, 30/10/5; find the net cost. 30/ 10/ 5 ↓ ↓ ↓ \$510 × .7 × .9 × .95 = \$305.24 (rounded)

CONCEPTS | **EXAMPLES**

6.2 Finding list price, given the series discount and the net cost

First, find the net cost equivalent, percent paid. Then use the standard percent formula to find the list price (base).

$$B = \frac{P}{R}$$

Net cost; $224; series discount, 20/20; find list price.

$$\begin{array}{cc} 20/ & 20 \\ \downarrow & \downarrow \\ .8 \times & .8 = .64 \end{array}$$

$$B = \frac{P}{R} = \frac{224}{.64} = \$350 \text{ list price}$$

6.3 Number of days and dates

30-Day Months	*31-Day Months*
April	All the rest
June	except February with
September	28 days (29 days in leap year)
November	

Date, July 24; find 10 days from date.

July 31 − 24 = 7 days remaining in July

$$\begin{array}{rl} 10 & \text{total number of days} \\ -\ 7 & \text{days remaining in July} \\ \hline \text{August } 3 & (\text{future date}) \end{array}$$

6.3 Ordinary dating and cash discounts

With ordinary dating, count days from the date of the invoice. Remember:

$$\begin{array}{cccc} 2/ & 10, & n/ & 30 \\ \downarrow & \downarrow & \downarrow & \downarrow \\ \% & \text{days,} & \text{net} & \text{days} \end{array}$$

Invoice amount $182; terms 2/10, n/30; find the cash discount and amount due.

Cash discount: $182 × .02 = $3.64

Amount due: $182 − $3.64 = $178.36

6.4 Cash discounts with end-of-month dating (EOM or proximo dating)

The final discount date and the net date are counted from the end of the month. If the invoice is dated the 26th or after, add the entire following month when determining the dates. If not stated, the net date is 20 days beyond the discount date.

Terms, 2/10 EOM; invoice date, Oct. 18; find the final discount date and the net payment date.

Final discount date:
November 10, which is 10 days from the end of October

Net payment date:
November 30, which is 20 days beyond the discount date

6.4 Receipt-of-goods (ROG) dating and cash discounts

Time is counted from the date goods are received to determine the final cash discount date and the net payment date. If not stated, the net date is 20 days beyond the discount date.

Terms, 3/10 ROG; invoice date, March 8; goods received, May 10; find the final discount date and the net payment date.

Final discount date:
May 20 (May 10 + 10 days)

Net payment date:
June 9 (May 20 + 20 days)

6.4 Extra dating and cash discounts

Extra dating adds extra days to the usual cash discount period, so 3/10–20 x means 3/30. If not stated, the net date is 20 days beyond the discount date.

Terms, 3/10–20 x, invoice date, January 8; find the final discount date and the net payment date.

Final discount date:
February 7 (23 days in January + 7 days in February = 30)

Net payment date:
February 27 (February 7 + 20 days)

6.4 Partial payment credit

When only a portion of an invoice amount is paid within the cash discount period, credit will be given for the partial payment. Use the standard percent formula

$$B = \frac{P}{R}$$

where the credit given is the base, the partial payment is the part, and (100% − cash discount) is the rate.

Invoice, $400; terms, 2/10, n/30; invoice date, Oct. 10; partial payment of $200 on Oct. 15; find credit given for partial payment and the balance due on the invoice.

$$B = \frac{P}{R} = \frac{\$200}{100\% - 2\%} = \frac{\$200}{.98}$$

Credit = $204.08 (rounded)

Balance due = $400 − $204.08 = $195.92

CHAPTER 6 SUMMARY EXERCISE

The Retailer: Invoices, Trade Discounts, and Cash Discounts

Ryan Andrews of Kitchen Crafters buys much of his merchandise from Gourmet Kitchen Wholesalers. In early September, he ordered kitchen flatware, dinnerware, and cutlery having a total list price of $9748, and appliances and cookware having a list price of $17,645. Gourmet Kitchen Wholesalers offers trade discounts of 20/10/10 on these items and charges for shipping.

The invoice for this order arrived a few days later, is dated September 4, has terms of 3/15 EOM, and shows a shipping charge of $748.38.

Kitchen Crafters will need to know all of the following. Round to the nearest cent.

(a) The total amount of the invoice excluding shipping **(a)** ____________

(b) The final discount date **(b)** ____________

(c) The net payment date **(c)** ____________

(d) The amount necessary to pay the invoice in full on October 11, including the shipping **(d)** ____________

(e) Suppose that on October 11 the invoice is not paid in full, but a partial payment of $10,000 is made instead. Find the credit given for the partial payment and the balance due on the invoice including shipping. **(e)** ____________ ____________

INVESTIGATE

Talk with business owners or store managers. Ask what kinds of trade and cash discounts are standard in their particular line of business. Do they take their earned discounts? Are these discounts important to them? Who is responsible for making sure that discounts are taken? Do they do any of their purchasing electronically? How does their electronic purchasing work?

CHAPTER 6 TEST

To help you review, the numbers in brackets show the section in which the topic was discussed.

Find the net cost (invoice amount) for the following. Round to the nearest cent. **[6.1]**

1. List price: $348.22 less 10/20/10 **1.** ________

2. List price: $1308 less 20/25 **2.** ________

Find (a) the net cost equivalent and (b) the single discount equivalent for the following series discounts. **[6.2]**

3. 30/10 **(a)** ________ **(b)** ________

4. 20/10/20 **(a)** ________ **(b)** ________

Find the final discount date for the following. **[6.4]**

	Invoice Date	*Terms*	*Date Goods Received*	*Final Discount Date*
5.	Feb. 10	4/15 EOM	Feb. 16	________
6.	May 8	2/10 ROG	May 20	________
7.	Dec. 8	4/15 prox.	Jan. 5	________
8.	Oct. 20	2/20–40 extra	Oct. 31	________

9. The following invoice was paid on November 15. Find **(a)** the invoice total, **(b)** the amount that should be paid after the cash discount, and **(c)** the total amount due, including shipping and insurance. **[6.1–6.4]** **(a)** ________ **(b)** ________ **(c)** ________

GOURMET KITCHEN WHOLESALER

Terms: 2/10, 1/15, n/60 **November 6**

Quantity	Description	Unit Price	Extension Total
16	tablecloths, linen	@ 17.50 ea.	
8	rings, napkin	@ 3.25 ea.	
4	cups, ceramic	@ 12.65 ea.	
12	bowls, 1 qt. stainless	@ 3.15 ea.	
		(a) Invoice Total	
		Cash Discount	
		(b) Due after Cash Discount	
		Shipping and Insurance	$11.55
		(c) Total Amount Due	

Solve the following application problems involving cash and trade discounts. Round to the nearest cent.

10. The Toy Train Store made purchases at a net cost of $46,746 after a series discount of 20/20/20. Find the list price. **[6.2]**

10. ________________

11. An invoice of $3168 from Scottish Importers has cash terms of 4/20 EOM and is dated June 5. Find **(a)** the final date on which the cash discount may be taken and **(b)** the amount necessary to pay the invoice in full if the cash discount is earned. **[6.4]**

(a) ________________
(b) ________________

12. Mel's Diner purchased paper products list priced at $696 less series discounts of 10/20/10, with terms of 3/10–50 extra. If the retailer paid the invoice within 60 days, find the amount paid. **[6.4]**

12. ________________

13. The Fireside Shop offers chimney caps for $120 less 25/10. The same chimney cap is offered by Builders Supply for $111 less 25/5. Find **(a)** the firm that offers the lower price and **(b)** the difference in price. **[6.1]**

(a) ________________
(b) ________________

14. The amount of an invoice from Cloverdale Creamery is $1780 with terms of 2/10, 1/15, net 30. The invoice is dated March 8. **(a)** What amount should be paid on March 20? **(b)** What amount should be paid on April 3? **[6.3]**

(a) ________________
(b) ________________

15. Diamond Consulting receives an invoice dated November 23 for $2514 with terms of 3/15 EOM. If the invoice is paid on December 14, find the amount necessary to pay the invoice in full. **[6.4]**

15. ________________

16. Jim Havey receives an invoice amounting to $2916 with cash terms of 3/10 prox. and dated June 7. If a partial payment of $1666 is made on July 8, find **(a)** the credit given for the partial payment and **(b)** the balance due on the invoice. **[6.4]**

(a) ________________
(b) ________________

CHAPTER 7

Mathematics of Selling

CHAPTER CONTENTS

CASE in POINT

Olympic Sports carries a full line of sports equipment, sportswear, and athletic shoes for the entire family. The store is best known for its quality and selection of merchandise, but it is also competitive in its pricing.

All offered business discounts are taken to keep the costs of merchandise down. The company must also adjust the markups on various merchandise to keep prices "in the ballpark" relative to competition. Olympic Sports reduces prices on merchandise on a regular basis, using these sale opportunities to clear out existing merchandise and make room for incoming orders.

The success of a business depends on many things. One of the most important is the price it charges for goods and services. The difference between the amount a business pays for an item (cost) and the price at which the item is sold is called the **markup**. For example, if Olympic Sports buys Swiss Military "Sierra" watches for $46 and sells them for $59, the markup is $13. This chapter discusses (1) the two standard methods of calculating markup as a percent of cost and as a percent of selling price, (2) converting markups from one method to the other, (3) markdown, and (4) turnover and valuation of inventory.

7.1 MARKUP ON COST

OBJECTIVES

1. Recognize the terms used in selling.
2. Use the basic formula for markup.
3. Calculate markup based on cost.
4. Apply percent to markup problems.

CASE in POINT Last week, Olympic Sports received a shipment of fishing tackle boxes. Store manager Alyssa Romano must determine the selling price of each tackle box by using a basic markup formula. She knows her regular monthly operating expenses. She also knows that she will be sending out an advertising flyer soon. She must price all merchandise with just enough markup that it is still attractive to customers, while at the same time generating enough revenue to attain the store's profit goals.

OBJECTIVE 1 Recognize the terms used in selling. The terms used in markup are summarized here.

Cost is the amount paid to the manufacturer or supplier after trade and cash discounts have been taken. Shipping and insurance charges are included in cost.

Selling price is the price at which merchandise is offered for sale to the public.

Markup, **margin**, or **gross profit** is the difference between the cost and the selling price. These three terms are often used interchangeably.

Operating expenses, or **overhead**, include the expenses of operating the business, such as wages and salaries of employees, rent for buildings and equipment, utilities, insurance, and advertising. Even an expense like postage can add up. Mailing costs average from 6.2% of operating expenses for small companies to as high as 9.2% for the largest companies. Notice in the chart at the side how postal rates have changed during the last thirty-six years.

U.S. Postal Rates Since 1971

May 16, 1971	8 cents
March 2, 1974	10 cents
Dec. 31, 1975	13 cents
May 29, 1978	15 cents
March 22, 1981	18 cents
Nov. 1, 1981	20 cents
Feb. 17, 1985	22 cents
April 3, 1988	25 cents
Feb. 3, 1991	29 cents
Jan. 1, 1995	32 cents
Jan. 1, 1999	33 cents
Jan. 1, 2001	34 cents
June 30, 2002	37 cents
Jan. 8, 2006	39 cents
May 14, 2007	41 cents

Net profit (net earnings) is the amount (if any) remaining for the business after operating expenses and the cost of goods have been paid. (Income tax is computed on net profit.)

Most manufacturers, many wholesalers, and some retailers calculate markup as a percent of cost (**markup on cost**). Manufacturers usually express inventories in terms of cost, a method most consistent with their operations. Retailers, on the other hand, usually compute **markup on selling price**, since retailers compare most areas of their business operations to sales revenue. Such items of expense as sales commissions, sales taxes, and advertising are expressed as a percent of sales. It is reasonable, then, for the retailer to express markup as a percent of sales. Wholesalers use either cost or selling price.

Having the right product selection available at the right time of the year is necessary to meet the needs of the customer. The bar graph at the left shows consumer spending by holiday season in the United States. The bar graph at the right shows when consumers start shopping for the winter holidays.

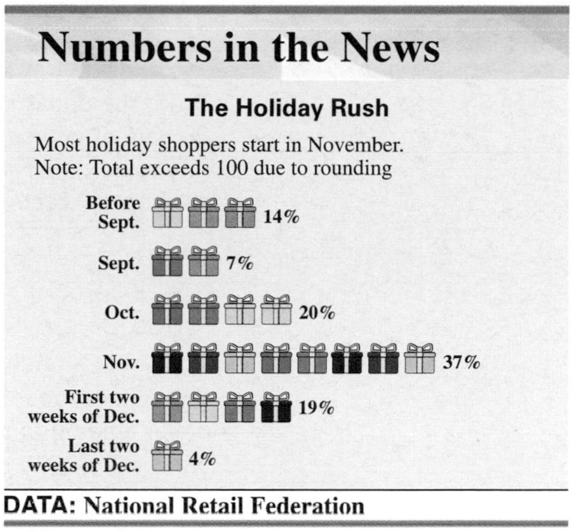

OBJECTIVE 2 **Use the basic formula for markup.** Whether markup is based on cost or on selling price, the same basic **markup formula** is always used.

Basic Markup Formula

$$C + M = S \quad \text{or} \quad \begin{array}{r} \text{Cost} \\ +\ \text{Markup} \\ \hline \text{Selling price} \end{array} \quad \text{or} \quad \begin{array}{r} C \\ +\ M \\ \hline S \end{array}$$

This markup formula is shown by the following diagram.

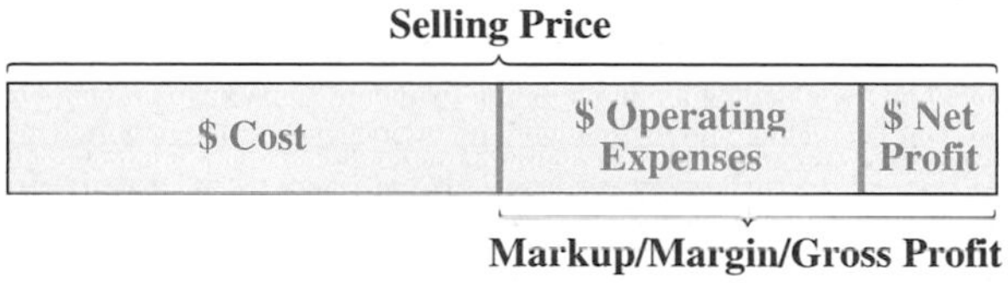

EXAMPLE 1 Using the Basic Markup Formula

Most markup problems give two of the items in the formula and ask you to find the third. Olympic Sports purchased roof prism binoculars. Determine the selling price, markup, and cost of the binoculars in the following problems.

(a) $\begin{array}{rr} C & \$10 \\ +M & \$\ 5 \\ \hline S & \$ \end{array}$ **(b)** $\begin{array}{rr} C & \$10 \\ +M & \$ \\ \hline S & \$15 \end{array}$ **(c)** $\begin{array}{rr} C & \$ \\ +M & \$\ 5 \\ \hline S & \$15 \end{array}$

SOLUTION

(a) $\begin{array}{rr} C & \$10 \\ +M & \$\ 5 \\ \hline S & \$15 \end{array}$ **(b)** $\begin{array}{rr} C & \$10 \\ +M & \$\ 5 \\ \hline S & \$15 \end{array}$ **(c)** $\begin{array}{rr} C & \$10 \\ +M & \$\ 5 \\ \hline S & \$15 \end{array}$

QUICK CHECK 1

Find the selling price in part (a), the markup in (b), and the cost in (c).

(a) $\begin{array}{rr} C & \$25 \\ +M & \$\ 8 \\ \hline S & \$ \end{array}$ **(b)** $\begin{array}{rr} C & \$72 \\ +M & \$ \\ \hline S & \$98 \end{array}$ **(c)** $\begin{array}{rr} C & \$ \\ +M & \$\ 35 \\ \hline S & \$118 \end{array}$

Quick Check Answers

1. (a) \$33 **(b)** \$26 **(c)** \$83

OBJECTIVE 3 **Calculate markup based on cost. Markup based on cost** is expressed as a percent of cost. As shown in the discussion of percent in **Section 3.5**, the base is always 100%. Therefore, cost has a value of 100%. Markup and selling price also have percent values found by comparing their dollar values to the dollar value of the cost. Solve markup problems with the basic formula.

$$C + M = S \quad \text{or} \quad \begin{array}{r} C \\ +\,M \\ \hline S \end{array}$$

Write the dollar values of cost, markup, and selling price on the right of the formula, and place the rate or percent value for each of these on the left of the formula.

Suppose that an item costs \$2 and sells for \$3, and that markup is **based on cost**. To find markup, percent of markup on cost, and selling price as a percent of cost, begin as follows.

100%	*C*	**\$2**
%	*M*	\$
%	*S*	**\$3**

The dollar amounts of cost and selling price have been written in their corresponding positions to the right of the formula, and **100%** has been written to the left of cost, **since cost *is* the base**. The dollar amount of markup is the difference between cost and selling price.

100%	*C*	\$2	base
%	*M*	**\$1**	
%	*S*	\$3	

QUICK TIP With markup on cost, the base is cost and the markup and selling price are parts.

Next, find the percent of markup based on cost. Do this by comparing the amount of markup, \$1, to the cost, \$2. The comparison of 1 to 2 is $\frac{1}{2}$, or **50%**.

	100%	*C*	\$2	base
rate	**50%**	*M*	\$1	part
	%	*S*	\$3	part

QUICK TIP **Cost plus markup always equals selling price,** with both dollar amounts and rate (percents).

Finally, add 100% and 50%.

100%	*C*	\$2	base
+ **50%**	*M*	\$1	part
150%	*S*	\$3	part

OBJECTIVE 4 **Apply percent to markup problems.** Knowledge of percent is used to solve markup problems.

EXAMPLE 2

Solving for Percent of Markup on Cost

The manager of the shoe department bought some hiking boots manufactured in Mexico for \$30 a pair and will sell them for \$37.50 a pair. Find the percent of markup based on cost.

SOLUTION

Set up the problem using the basic markup formula.

	100%	*C*	\$30.00	**base**
rate	**?%**	*M*	\$	**part**
	%	*S*	\$37.50	

The dollar amounts of markup is the difference between \$37.50 and \$30.00, or \$7.50.

100%	*C*	\$30.00
?%	*M*	**\$ 7.50**
%	*S*	\$37.50

The cost, \$30.00, is the base—it is identified by the 100%. There are two rates and two corresponding parts. Find percent of markup (a rate) by using the part corresponding to markup, \$7.50. Identify the components in this example as follows.

	100%	*C*	\$30.00	**base**
rate	?%	*M*	\$ 7.50	**part**
rate	%	*S*	\$37.50	**part**

Find the percent of markup based on cost, using the formula for rate.

$$\text{Rate} = \frac{\text{Part}}{\text{Base}} = \frac{\$7.50}{\$30.00} = .25 = 25\% \text{ markup based on cost}$$

Complete the problem by adding the rate for cost to the rate for markup and arriving at a rate for selling price.

100%	C	$30.00
+ 25%	M	$ 7.50
125%	S	$37.50

The calculator solution to this example is as follows.

(37.5 − 30) ÷ 30 = .25

Note: Refer to Appendix C for calculator basics.

QUICK CHECK 2

A retail buyer purchased some pedometers at a cost of $12 and will sell them for $16. What is the percent of markup based on cost?

This method can be used for solving all problems involving markup, as shown in the next few examples.

EXAMPLE 3

Finding Cost When Cost Is Base

Olympic Sports places a markup on a 100-lb iron barbell set of $16, which is 50% based on cost. Find the cost and the selling price.

SOLUTION

Set up the problem.

100%	C	$?
50%	M	$16
%	S	$

Identify the components.

	100%	C	$?	base
rate	50%	M	$16	part
rate	150%	S	$	part

The rate of markup, 50%, and the corresponding part, $16, are used in the formula to find the base. Solve for base.

$$\text{Base} = \frac{\text{Part}}{\text{Rate}} = \frac{\$16}{.5} = \$32 \text{ cost}$$

The cost of the weight set is $32.

Now find the selling price by adding the cost and the markup.

100%	C	$32
50%	M	$16
150%	S	$48

The selling price of the weight set is $48.

Quick Check Answers

2. 33.3% (rounded)

3. $240 cost; $324 selling price

QUICK CHECK 3

A 6-foot billiard table has a markup of $84, which is 35% based on cost. Find the cost and the selling price.

EXAMPLE 4

Finding the Markup and the Selling Price

Find the markup and the selling price for an Adidas hooded sweatshirt if the cost is $23.60 and the markup is 25% of cost.

SOLUTION

Set up the problem.

100%	*C*	$23.60
25%	*M*	$?
%	*S*	$

Identify the components.

	100%	*C*	$23.60	base
rate	25%	*M*	$?	part
rate	125%	*S*	$	part

If the rate for selling price, 125%, is used in the formula, the resulting part is the selling price. Since markup is to be found, use the rate for markup in the formula. Solve for the markup part.

$$\text{Part} = \text{Base} \times \text{Rate} = \$23.60 \times .25 = \$5.90 \text{ markup}$$

The markup is $5.90.

Now solve for the selling price by adding cost and markup.

100%	*C*	$23.60
25%	*M*	$ 5.90
125%	*S*	$29.50

The selling price of the hooded sweatshirt is $29.50.

This calculator solution uses the percent add-on feature found on many calculators.

23.6 [+] 25 [%] [=] 29.5

QUICK TIP Be certain that you use the corresponding rate and part when working with markup problems. If 125% was used as the rate in Example 4, the answer (part) would have been the selling price. This would work, but you would have to remember to subtract the cost from the selling price ($29.50 − $23.60) to get the markup of $5.90.

QUICK CHECK 4

The cost of some women's running shoes is $45. If the markup is 22% of cost, find the markup and the selling price.

EXAMPLE 5

Finding Cost When Cost Is Base

Olympic Sports sells a Wilson baseball glove for $42 in order to be competitive. If the markup is 40% on cost, how much can Olympic Sports afford to pay for each glove (cost)?

SOLUTION

Set up the problem.

100%	*C*	$?
%	*M*	$
140%	*S*	$42

Identify the elements.

	100%	*C*	$?	base
rate	40%	*M*	$	
rate	140%	*S*	$42	part

The rate for markup, 40%, *cannot* be used in the formula because there is no corresponding part. Solve for base using the *corresponding* rate and part.

$$\text{Base} = \frac{\text{Part}}{\text{Rate}} = \frac{\$42}{1.4} = \$30 \text{ cost}$$

Olympic Sports can afford to pay $30. Check: .40 × $30 = **$12** (markup); then $30 + **$12** = $42.

QUICK CHECK 5

Olympic sports wants to sell a 2-pack of thermal socks for $4.99. If the markup is 30% on cost, how much can they afford to pay for the socks (cost)?

Quick Check Answers

4. $9.90 markup; $54.90 selling price

5. $3.84 (rounded)

EXAMPLE 6

Finding the Cost and the Markup

The retail (selling) price of a Lifetime 50-inch portable basketball system is $549.99. If the markup is 35% of cost, find the cost and the markup.

SOLUTION

Set up the problem.

100%	*C*	$?
35%	*M*	$
%	*S*	$549.99

Identify the elements.

	100%	*C*	$?	base
rate	35%	*M*	$	part
rate	135%	*S*	$549.99	part

The rate of markup, 35%, *cannot* be used in the formula, since there is no corresponding part. Instead, solve for base using the *corresponding* rate and part.

$$\text{Base} = \frac{\text{Part}}{\text{Rate}} = \frac{\$549.99}{1.35} = \$407.40 \text{ cost}$$

The cost of the system is $407.40.

Now solve for the markup by subtracting cost from selling price.

100%	*C*	$407.40
35%	*M*	$142.59
135%	*S*	$549.99

The markup is $142.59 ($549.99 − $407.40).

QUICK TIP Remember, when calculating markup on cost, *cost is always the base* and 100% always goes next to cost.

QUICK CHECK 6

The selling price of a telescope is $64.99. If the markup is $40% of cost, find the cost and the markup.

Longer retail store hours and deep discounts are often used by businesses to compete with their discount business rivals. The newspaper article below reports the recent success of mall merchants in their holiday sales.

Pre-dawn sales give mall stores the edge

By Michael Barbaro
New York Times

The clock struck midnight. Then the mall struck back.

Early openings, deep discounts and resurgent department stores appeared to give merchants at the mall an edge over discount retailers during the holiday weekend, a reversal of fortune from last year.

Retail analysts and industry executives credited the strong performance of mall stores to an unusually aggressive posture this season. Badly beaten last year, they stole a page from their discount rivals, pushing up their openings by as much as six hours, to midnight, and offering bigger early-morning deals.

The tactics succeeded in drawing crowds but could haunt the chains if consumers snatched up the bargains and skipped over the full-priced merchandise.

Quick Check Answer

6. $46.42 cost (rounded); $18.57 markup (rounded)

7.1 EXERCISES

FOR EXTRA HELP

MyMathLab

MathXL PRACTICE

WATCH

DOWNLOAD

READ

REVIEW

The **QUICK START** *exercises in each section contain solutions to help you get started.*

Solve for the missing numbers. Markup is based on cost. Round dollar amounts to the nearest cent. (See Examples 1–6.)

QUICK START

1.

100%	C	$12.40
40%	M	**$ 4.96**
140%	S	**$17.36**

2.

100%	C	**$5.40**
25%	M	$1.35
125%	S	**$6.75**

3.

%	C	$
%	M	$
120%	S	$32.60

4.

%	C	$
50%	M	$ 50.00
%	S	$

5.

%	C	$
30%	M	$ 50.40
%	S	$

6.

100%	C	$78.00
%	M	$17.94
%	S	$

Find the missing numbers. Round rates to the nearest tenth of a percent and dollar amounts to the nearest cent. (See Examples 1–6.)

QUICK START

	Cost Price	*Markup*	*% Markup on Cost*	*Selling Price*
7.	$9.00	**$2.70**	30%	**$11.70**
8.	**$36.00**	$7.20	**20%**	$43.20
9.	$12.00	$7.20	______	______
10.	______	______	100%	$68.98
11.	$153.60	______	______	$215.04
12.	______	$54.38	50%	______
13.	______	$8.45	______	$42.25
14.	$7.75	______	28%	______

15. Markup may be calculated on cost or on selling price. Explain why most manufacturers use cost as base when calculating markup. (See Objective 1.)

16. Write the markup formula in vertical form. Define each term. (See Objective 2.)

Solve the following application problems, using cost as a base. Round rates to the nearest tenth of a percent and dollar amounts to the nearest cent.

QUICK START

17. EXERCYCLE Olympic Sports pays $330.30 for a ProForm Exercycle, and the markup is 45% of cost. Find the markup.

	100%	**C**	**$330.30**	**base**
	45%	**M**	**$?**	
rate	**145%**	**S**	**$**	**part**

P = B × R = $330.30 × .45 = 148.635 = $148.64

17. **$148.64**

C indicates an exercise that is related to the Case in Point feature.

18. SKI JACKETS Olympic Sports offers ski jackets, sizes S, M, and L, for $138. If the markup is 35% of cost, find the cost.

18. ________

19. TAIWAN TOOL PRODUCTS The cost of some socket-wrench sets from Taiwan is $10.36 per set. Harbor Tool decides to use a markup of 25% on cost. Find the selling price of the socket wrench set.

19. ________

20. WEIGHT-TRAINING BOOKS Gold's Gym sells weight-training books for $15.60 per copy. If this includes a markup of 50% on cost, find the cost.

20. ________

21. PRICING TABLE TENNIS TABLES Olympic Sports purchases TIGA table tennis tables at a cost of $180 each. If the company's operating expenses are 16% of cost, and a net profit of 7% of cost is desired, find the selling price of one basketball system.

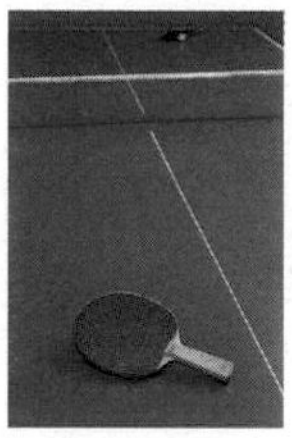

21. ________

22. PRICING MERCHANDISE Barstools are purchased by Factory Outlet Stores at a cost of $59 each. If the company's operating expenses are 12% of cost, and a net profit of 9% of cost is needed, find the selling price of six barstools.

22. ________

23. OUTDOOR LIGHTING Patios Plus sold an outdoor lighting set for $119.95. The markup on the set was $23.99. Find **(a)** the cost, **(b)** the markup percent on cost, and **(c)** the selling price as a percent of cost.

(a) ________
(b) ________
(c) ________

24. GOLF CLUBS Olympic Sports had a markup of $46.64 on golf clubs sold for $222.64. Find **(a)** the cost, **(b)** the markup percent on cost, and **(c)** the selling price as a percent of cost.

(a) ________
(b) ________
(c) ________

25. TRACTOR PARTS Bismark Tractor put a markup of 26% on cost on some parts for which they paid $4.50. Find **(a)** the selling price as a percent of cost, **(b)** the selling price, and **(c)** the markup.

(a) ________
(b) ________
(c) ________

26. CUSTOM-MADE JEWELRY A jewelry dealer sold custom-made necklaces at a selling price that was 250% of his cost. If the markup is $135, find **(a)** the markup percent on cost, **(b)** the cost, and **(c)** the selling price.

(a) ________
(b) ________
(c) ________

7.2 MARKUP ON SELLING PRICE

OBJECTIVES

1. Understand the phrase *markup based on selling price.*
2. Solve markup problems when selling price is the base.
3. Use the markup formula to solve variations of markup problems.
4. Determine the percent markup on cost and the equivalent percent markup on selling price.
5. Convert markup percent on cost to selling price.
6. Convert markup percent on selling price to cost.
7. Find the selling price for perishables.

CASE in POINT Olympic Sports faces stiff competition from companies like Sportmart. Sportmart has placed a newspaper ad about its baseball equipment specifically aimed at teams that buy in large quantities. Sportmart offers to pay customers double the difference if the customer finds any item for a lower price at another store. Olympic Sports must compete by buying its merchandise at the lowest possible price and keeping markups at a minimum.

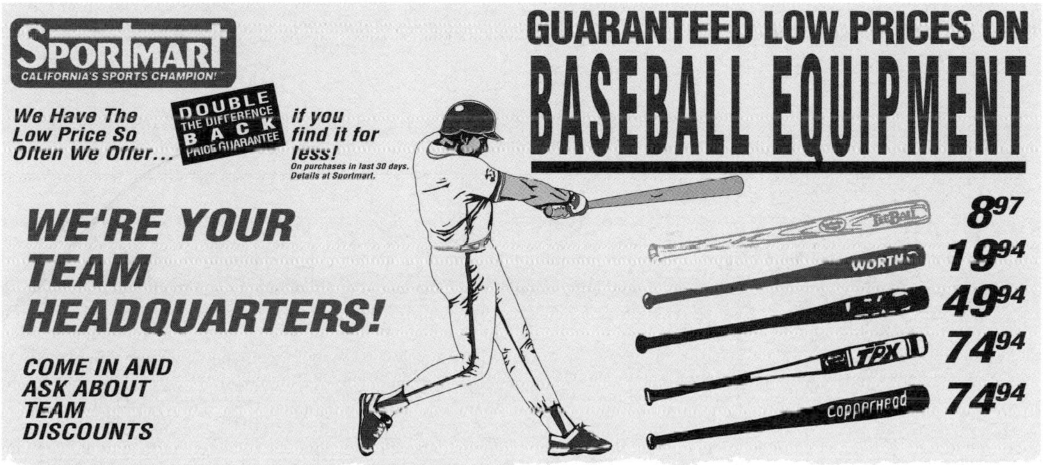

OBJECTIVE 1 **Understand the phrase *markup based on selling price.*** As mentioned in **Section 7.1**, wholesalers sometimes calculate markup based on cost and other times calculate markup based on selling price. In retailing, it is common to calculate markup based on selling price. In each method, markup is stated as being "on cost" or "on selling price." If markup is based on selling price, then selling price is the base.

When **markup on selling price** is calculated, the same basic markup formula is used.

$$C + M = S \quad \text{or} \quad \begin{array}{rcl} \% & C & \$ \\ \% & +\,M & \$ \\ \hline \% & S & \$ \end{array}$$

OBJECTIVE 2 **Solve markup problems when selling price is the base.** The dollar amounts for cost, markup, and selling price are still written to the right of the formula, and the rate amounts for each of these are still written to the left of the formula. However, the base is now the selling price.

Since the selling price is the base, which is always 100%, place 100% next to the selling price on the left-hand side.

%	C	$	
%	M	$	
100%	S	$	base

EXAMPLE 1

Solving for Markup on Selling Price

To remain competitive, Olympic Sports must sell Body Glove Sunglasses for $39.99. They pay $35 for each pair and calculate markup on selling price. Find the amount of markup, the percent of markup on selling price, and the percent of cost on selling price.

SOLUTION

Set up the problem.

?%	C	$35.00
?%	M	$?
100%	S	$39.99

Solve for markup.

?%	C	$35.00
?%	M	$ 4.99
100%	S	$39.99

Identify the components.

rate	?%	C	$35.00	part
rate	?%	M	$ 4.99	part
	100%	S	$39.99	base

Solve for either of the rates, and subtract the result from 100% to find the other. Solve for markup rate.

$$\text{Rate} = \frac{\textbf{Part}}{\textbf{Base}} = \frac{4.99}{39.99} = .1247 = 12.5\% \text{ markup on selling price (rounded)}$$

The percent of markup on selling price is 12.5%, and the percent of cost on selling price is 87.5% (100% − 12.5% = 87.5%). The result is shown below.

87.5%	C	$35.00
12.5%	M	$ 4.99
100%	S	$39.99

QUICK TIP Remember that *part* and *rate* must *always correspond*. If you use the markup part in the formula, the resulting rate will be the markup rate. If you use the cost part in the formula, the resulting rate will be the cost rate.

QUICK CHECK 1

The cost of a two-piece exercise suit is $13.50 and the selling price is $19.99. Find **(a)** the amount of markup, **(b)** the percent of markup on selling price, and **(c)** the percent of cost on selling price.

Markups vary widely from industry to industry and from business to business. This variation is a result of different costs of merchandise. operating costs, levels of profit margin, and local competition. The next table shows average markups for different types of retail stores.

Average Markups for Retail Stores (Markup on Selling Price)

Type of Store	Markup	Type of Store	Markup
General merchandise stores	29.97%	Furniture and home furnishings	35.75%
Grocery stores	22.05%	Bars	52.49%
Other food stores	27.31%	Restaurants	56.35%
Motor vehicle dealers (new)	12.83%	Drug and proprietary stores	30.81%
Gasoline service stations	14.47%	Liquor stores	20.19%
Other automotive dealers	29.57%	Sporting goods and bicycle shops	29.72%
Apparel and accessories	37.64%	Gift, novelty, and souvenir shops	41.86%

Source: Sole-proprietorship income tax returns, U.S. Treasury Dept., Internal Revenue Service, Statistics Division.

Quick Check Answers

1. **(a)** $6.49
   (b) 32.5% (rounded)
   (c) 67.5% (rounded)

OBJECTIVE 3 Use the markup formula to solve variations of markup problems. As with problems where markup is based on cost, this basic formula may be used for all markup problems in which selling price is the base. In each of these examples, the selling price has a percent value of 100%.

EXAMPLE 2
Finding Cost When Selling Price Is Base

An Olympic Sports employee needs a 35% markup on selling price in order to have a markup of \$5.16 on a pair of "PRO CLASSIC" Batting Gloves. How much can Olympic Sports afford to pay for each pair of gloves?

SOLUTION

Set up the problem.

%	*C*	\$?
35%	*M*	\$5.16
100%	*S*	\$

Identify the components.

rate	65%	*C*	\$?	
rate	35%	*M*	\$5.16	part
	100%	*S*	\$?	base

Now solve for base (selling price), and subtract the markup from the selling price to find the cost. Solve for base using the *corresponding* rate and part.

$$\text{Base} = \frac{\textbf{Part}}{\textbf{Rate}} = \frac{5.16}{.35} = \textbf{\$14.74} \text{ selling price (rounded)}$$

Solve for cost.

$$\text{Selling price} - \text{Markup} = \text{Cost}$$
$$\textbf{\$14.74} - \$5.16 = \$9.58$$

The cost is \$9.58.

65%	*C*	\$ 9.58
35%	*M*	\$ 5.16
100%	*S*	\$14.74

QUICK CHECK 2

The manager of a golf pro shop wants a 15% markup on selling price so that she can have a markup of \$13.50 on a "Tiger Lies" fairway wood golf club. How much can she afford to pay for each club?

EXAMPLE 3
Finding Markup When Selling Price Is Given

Marilyn Westby, an employee at Olympic Sports, must calculate the markup on a Wilson youth tennis racket. The selling price of the tennis racket is \$15.99, and the markup is 20% of selling price. Find the markup.

SOLUTION

Set up the problem.

%	*C*	\$
20%	*M*	\$?
100%	*S*	\$15.99

Identify the components.

	80%	*C*	\$	
rate	20%	*M*	\$?	part
	100%	*S*	\$15.99	base

Solve for part.

$$\text{Part} = \textbf{Base} \times \textbf{Rate} = \$15.99 \times .2 = 3.198 = \$3.20 \text{ markup (rounded)}$$

The markup is \$3.20.

Quick Check Answer

2. \$76.50

QUICK TIP If the rate for cost, 80%, had been used in the formula, the result would have been the cost.

QUICK CHECK 3

The selling price of a three-pack of tennis balls is $3.95, and the markup is 25% of selling price. Find the markup.

EXAMPLE 4

Finding Markup When Cost Is Given

Find the markup on a dartboard made in England if the cost is $27.45 and the markup is 25% of selling price.

SOLUTION

Set up the problem.

%	*C*	$27.45
25%	*M*	$?
100%	*S*	$

Identify the components.

rate	75%	*C*	$27.45	part
rate	25%	*M*	$?	part
	100%	*S*	$	base

Solve for base, using the rate and part that go together. In this example, use the rate and part for cost.

$$\text{Base} = \frac{\text{Part}}{\text{Rate}} = \frac{\$27.45}{.75} = \mathbf{\$36.60} \text{ selling price}$$

Selling price − Cost = Markup
$36.60 − $27.45 = $9.15

75%	*C*	$27.45
25%	*M*	$ 9.15
100%	*S*	$36.60

QUICK TIP Remember, when calculating markup on selling price, *selling price is always the base* and 100% always goes next to selling price.

QUICK CHECK 4

What is the markup on a sleeping bag if the cost is $40.80 and the markup is 32% of selling price?

OBJECTIVE 4 Determine the percent markup on cost and the equivalent percent markup on selling price. Sometimes a markup based on cost must be compared with a markup based on selling price. For example, a salesperson who sells to both manufacturers who use markup on cost and to retailers who use markup on selling price might have to make quick conversions from one markup method to the other. Such a conversion might also be necessary for a manufacturer who thinks in terms of cost and who wants to understand a wholesaler or retail customer. Or perhaps a retailer or wholesaler might convert markup on selling price to markup on cost to better understand the manufacturer.

Make these comparisons by computing first the markup on cost and then the markup on selling price.

EXAMPLE 5

Determining Equivalent Markups

Awanata Jackson sells fishing lures to both fishing-equipment wholesalers and sporting-goods stores. If a lure costs her $4.20 and she sells it for $5.25, what is the percent of markup on cost? What is the percent of markup on selling price?

SOLUTION

First, compute the rate of **markup on cost**. Set up the problem.

100%	*C*	$4.20
?%	*M*	$
%	*S*	$5.25

Quick Check Answers

3. $.99 (rounded)
4. $19.20

Identify the components.

	100%	C	$4.20	base
rate	?%	M	$1.05	part
rate	%	S	$5.25	part

Solve for rate.

$$\text{Rate} = \frac{\text{Part}}{\text{Base}} = \frac{\$1.05}{\$4.20} = .25 = 25\% \text{ markup on cost}$$

The markup on cost is 25%.

Next, compute the rate of **markup on selling price**. Set up the problem.

%	C	$4.20
?%	M	$
100%	S	$5.25

Identify the components.

rate	%	C	$4.20	part
rate	?%	M	$1.05	part
	100%	S	$5.25	base

Solve for rate.

$$\text{Rate} = \frac{\text{Part}}{\text{Base}} = \frac{\$1.05}{\$5.25} = .20 = 20\% \text{ markup on selling price}$$

The markup on selling price is 20%.

The results in this example show that a 25% markup on cost is equivalent to a 20% markup on selling price.

QUICK TIP In Example 5, the markup on cost was determined first (25%). The problem was then reworked with the same dollar amounts but with the selling price as base. The result was 20%.

QUICK CHECK 5

The cost of a Razor A-3 Kick Scooter is $45 and it sells for $59.99. What is **(a)** the percent of markup on cost and **(b)** the percent of markups on selling price?

OBJECTIVE 5 **Convert markup percent on cost to selling price.** Another method for markup comparisons is to use **conversion formulas**. Convert markup percent on cost to markup percent on selling price with the following formula.

$$\frac{\%\text{ markup on cost}}{100\% + \%\text{ markup on cost}} = \%\text{ markup on selling price}$$

EXAMPLE 6

Converting Markup on Cost to Markup on Selling Price

Convert a markup of 25% on cost to its equivalent markup on selling price.

SOLUTION

Use the formula for converting markup on cost to markup on selling price.

$$\frac{\%\text{ markup on cost}}{100\% + \%\text{ markup on cost}} = \%\text{ markup on selling price}$$

$$\frac{25\%}{100\% + 25\%} = \frac{25\%}{125\%} = \frac{.25}{1.25} = .20 = 20\%$$

As shown, a markup of 25% on cost is equivalent to a markup of 20% on selling price.

The markup on cost (25%) is divided by 100% plus the markup on cost. The parentheses keys are used here.

25 [%] [÷] [(] 100 [%] [+] 25 [%] [)] [=] 0.2

QUICK CHECK 6

Convert a markup of 100% on cost to a markup on selling price.

Quick Check Answers

5. **(a)** 33.3% (rounded)
(b) 25% (rounded)
6. 50%

OBJECTIVE 6 **Convert markup percent on selling price to cost.** Convert markup percent on selling price to markup percent on cost with the following formula.

$$\frac{\%\text{ markup on selling price}}{100\% - \%\text{ markup on selling price}} = \%\text{ markup on cost}$$

EXAMPLE 7

Converting Markup on Selling Price to Markup on Cost

Convert a markup of 20% on selling price to its equivalent markup on cost.

SOLUTION

Use the formula for converting markup on selling price to markup on cost.

$$\frac{\%\text{ markup on selling price}}{100\% - \%\text{ markup on selling price}} = \%\text{ markup on cost}$$

$$\frac{20\%}{100\% - 20\%} = \frac{20\%}{80\%} = \frac{.2}{.8} = .25 = 25\%$$

A markup of 20% on selling price is equivalent to a markup of 25% on cost.

QUICK CHECK 7

Convert a markup of 40% on selling price to a markup on cost.

The following table shows common markups expressed as percent on cost and as percent on selling price. A table like this is helpful to anyone using markup equivalents on a regular basis.

Markup Equivalents

Markup on Cost	Markup on Selling Price
20%	$16\frac{2}{3}\%$
25%	20%
$33\frac{1}{3}\%$	25%
50%	$33\frac{1}{3}\%$
$66\frac{2}{3}\%$	40%
75%	$42\frac{6}{7}\%$
100%	50%

OBJECTIVE 7 **Find the selling price for perishables.** When a business sells items that are perishable (such as baked goods, fruits, or vegetables), the fact that some items will spoil and cannot be sold must be considered when determining the selling price of each item that is sold.

Quick Check Answer

7. 66.7% (rounded)

The bar graph below shows the top 10 retailers in the United States. Which of these companies do you think considers perishables as part of their business operations? It appears that half of them sell groceries as part of the product line.

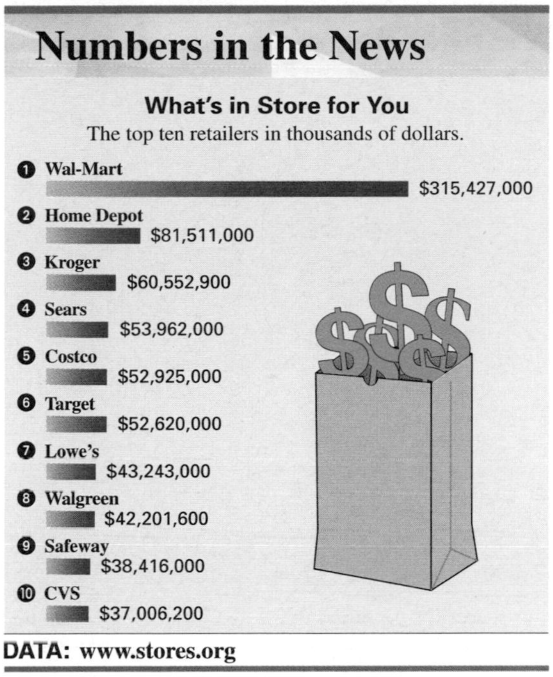

EXAMPLE 8

Finding Selling Price for Perishables

The Bagel Boy bakes 60 dozen bagels at a cost of \$2.16 per dozen. If a markup of 50% on selling price is needed and 5% of the bagels remain unsold and will be donated to a shelter, find the selling price per dozen bagels.

SOLUTION

STEP 1 Find the cost of the bagels.

$$\text{Cost} = 60 \text{ dozen} \times \$2.16 = \$129.60$$

STEP 2 Find the selling price, using a markup of 50% of selling price.

rate	50%	C	\$129.60	part
	50%	M	\$	
	100%	S	\$?	base

$$\text{Base} = \frac{\text{Part}}{\text{Rate}} = \frac{\$129.60}{.5} = \$259.20$$

The total selling price is \$259.20.

STEP 3 Find the number of dozen bagels that will be sold. Since 5% will not be sold, 95% (100% − 5%) will be sold.

$$95\% \times 60 \text{ dozen} = 57 \text{ dozen bagels sold}$$

The selling price of \$259.20 must be received from the sale of 57 dozen bagels.

STEP 4 Find the selling price per dozen bagels by dividing the total selling price by the number of bagels sold.

$$\frac{\$259.20}{57} = \$4.55 \text{ selling price per dozen (rounded)}$$

A selling price of \$4.55 per dozen gives the desired markup of 50% on selling price while allowing for 5% of the bagels to be unsold.

QUICK CHECK 8

The Cookie Jar bakes 80 dozen cookies at a cost of \$1.08 per dozen. If a markup of 60% on selling price is needed and 10% of the cookies remain unsold and will be donated, find the selling price per dozen cookies.

Quick Check Answer

8. \$3 per dozen

7.2 EXERCISES

FOR EXTRA HELP

MyMathLab

MathXL PRACTICE

WATCH

DOWNLOAD

READ

REVIEW

The **QUICK START** *exercises in each section contain solutions to help you get started.*

Solve for the missing numbers. Markup is based on selling price. Round dollar amounts to the nearest cent. (See Examples 1–4.)

QUICK START

1.	**75%**	*C*	**$21.00**
	25%	*M*	$ 7.00
	100%	*S*	**$28.00**

2.	**60%**	*C*	**$18.60**
	40%	*M*	$12.40
	100%	*S*	$31.00

3.		*C*	$145.00
		M	
	100%	*S*	$250.00

4.	$66\frac{2}{3}\%$	*C*	
		M	$ 89.00
		S	

5.	50%	*C*	$2025
		M	
		S	

6.	65%	*C*	
		M	$ 527.80
		S	

Find the missing quantities by first computing the markup on one base and then computing the markup on the other. Round rates to the nearest tenth of a percent and dollar amounts to the nearest cent. (See Example 5.)

QUICK START

	Cost	Markup	Selling Price	% Markup on Cost	% Markup on Selling Price
7.	**$1920**	$480.00	**$2400.00**	25%	20%
8.	**$357.52**	$78.48	$436.00	**22%**	**18%**
9.	$13.80	_______	_______	_______	38%
10.	$33.75	_______	$67.50	_______	_______
11.	_______	$300.00	_______	40%	_______
12.	$5.15	_______	$15.45	_______	_______

Find the equivalent markups on either cost or selling price using the appropriate formula. Round to the nearest tenth of a percent. (See Examples 6 and 7.)

QUICK START

	Markup on Cost	Markup on Selling Price
13.	100%	**50%**
15.	18%	_______

$$\frac{100\%}{100\% + 100\%} = \frac{1}{2} = .5 = 50\%$$

	Markup on Cost	Markup on Selling Price
14.	_______	20%
16.	50%	_______

17. Use the table on page 284 to find the three types of retail stores with the lowest markups. Why do markups differ so much from one type of retail store to another?

18. To have a markup of 100% or greater, the markup must be calculated on cost. Show why this is always true. (See Objective 6.)

C indicates an exercise that is related to the Case in Point feature.

10. DOUBLE-PANE WINDOWS Eastern Building Supply pays $3808 for all the double-pane windows needed for a 3-bedroom, 2-bath home. If the markup on the windows is 15% on selling price, what is **(a)** the cost as a percent of selling price, **(b)** the selling price, and **(c)** the markup?

(a) ____________
(b) ____________
(c) ____________

11. COMMUNICATION EQUIPMENT A discount store purchased DVD players at a cost of $288 per dozen. If the store needs 20% of cost to cover operating expenses and 15% of cost for the net profit, what are **(a)** the selling price of a DVD player and **(b)** the percent of markup on selling price?

(a) ____________
(b) ____________

12. BOWLING EQUIPMENT The Bowlers Pro-Shop determines that operating expenses are 23% of selling price and desires a net profit of 12% of selling price. If the cost of a team shirt is $29.25, what are **(a)** the selling price and **(b)** the percent of markup on cost?

(a) ____________
(b) ____________

C **13.** MOUNTAIN BIKE SALES Olympic Sports advertises mountain bikes for $199.90. If the store's cost is $2100 per dozen, what are **(a)** the markup per bicycle, **(b)** the percent of markup on selling price, and **(c)** the percent of markup on cost?

(a) ____________
(b) ____________
(c) ____________

14. COMPUTER FLASH DRIVE Office Depot advertises 2 GB USB 2.0 flash drives for $49.99. Their cost is $449.91 per dozen. Find **(a)** the markup per flash drive, **(b)** the percent of markup on selling price, and **(c)** the percent of markup on cost.

(a) ____________
(b) ____________
(c) ____________

15. LONG-STEMMED ROSES Farmers Flowers purchased 12 gross of long-stemmed roses at a cost of $945. If 25% of the roses cannot be sold and a markup of 100% on cost is needed, find the regular selling price per dozen roses.

15. ____________

C **16.** SPORTSWEAR Olympic Sports buys 2000 baseball caps at $2.50 per hat. If a markup of 50% on selling price is needed and 5% of the caps are damaged and cannot be sold, what is the selling price of each cap?

16. ____________

7.3 MARKDOWN

OBJECTIVES

1. Define the term *markdown* when applied to selling.
2. Calculate markdown, reduced price, and percent of markdown.
3. Define the terms associated with loss.
4. Determine the break-even point and operating loss.
5. Determine the amount of a gross or absolute loss.

CASE in POINT Alyssa Romano, the manager of Olympic Sports, keeps a close eye on inventory. This January, some winter ski parkas are still on the shelves and she has decided to mark them down in order to sell them. Monitoring inventory is an important management function. Slow-selling and outdated merchandise must be moved out of the store to make room for new, more profitable merchandise.

Markdowns are used to stimulate sales volume. The newspaper clipping shows how slashed prices have stimulated the sales of electronics items for holiday gift giving. When retailers discounted high-profile products, "men took the opportunity to stock up on their own entertainment centers." The bar graph in the clipping shows where shoppers did their shopping.

HERE & NOW

Men shop early in rush for bargains

Deals on electronics trump stereotypes

By Mindy Fetterman
USA TODAY

Early clues about how the holiday shopping season will go this year show two clear trends: Electronics are selling, and men are buying them.

Men outspent women by 38% over the weekend, the official start of the holiday season, the National Retail Federation (NRF) says.

Lured by price-slashing "door-buster" deals on consumer electronics—including flat-screen TVs, laptop computers and cell phones—men woke from post-Thanksgiving-meal naps to head to the mall.

They spent an average of $420.37 compared with $304.30 spent by women, according to the NRF survey of 3,090 shoppers Thursday through Saturday. Nearly 40% of men bought consumer electronics, and half bought books, CDs, DVDs, videos or video games.

Historically, men are last-minute holiday shoppers. Nearly 20% don't start until mid-December, and 10% wait until as late as Christmas Eve, according to a survey of 13,399 adults by Deloitte & Touche, a financial services firm.

Men typically don't do a lot of shopping on the day after Thanksgiving, says Ellen Davis of the NRF. But with retailers discounting high-profile products this year, "men took the opportunity to stock up their own entertainment centers."

Numbers in the News

Where Shoppers Shop

Traffic at discount department stores Thursday through Saturday was down from last year, when more than 60% shopped there. This year's breakdown:

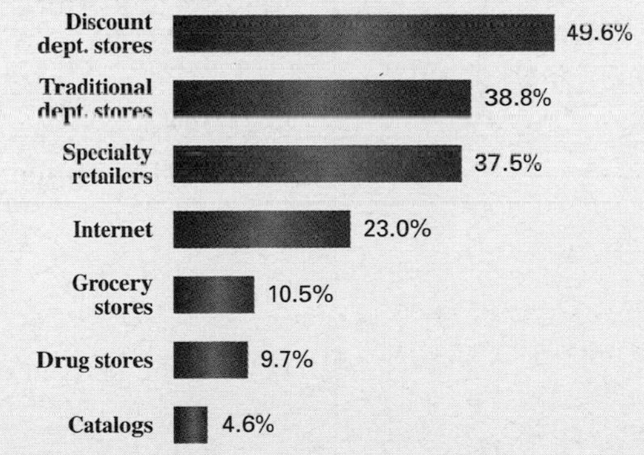

DATA: National Retail Federation survey of 3,090 consumers

OBJECTIVE 1 Define the term *markdown* when applied to selling. When merchandise does not sell at its marked price, the price is often reduced. The difference between the original selling price and the reduced selling price is called the **markdown**, with the selling price after the markdown called the **reduced price, sale price**, or **actual selling price**. The basic **formula for markdown** is as follows.

$$\text{Reduced price} = \text{Original price} - \text{Markdown}$$

EXAMPLE 1

Finding the Reduced Price

QUICK TIP The original selling price is always the base or 100%, and the percent of markdown is always calculated on the original selling price.

Olympic Sports has marked down an Atlas Home Fitness Center. Find the reduced price if the original price was \$2879 and the markdown is 30%.

SOLUTION

The markdown is 30% of \$2879, or $.3 \times \$2879 = \$863.70$. Find the reduced price as follows.

OBJECTIVE 2 Calculate markdown, reduced price, and percent of markdown.

\$2879.00	original price
− 863.70	markdown (.30 × \$2879)
\$2015.30	reduced price (70% of original price)

The calculator solution to this example uses the complement, with respect to 1, of the discount.

\$2879 [×] [(] 1 [−] .3 [)] [=] 2015.3

QUICK CHECK 1

Ski boots originally priced at \$289.99 were marked down 40%. Find the reduced price.

The next example shows how to find a **percent of markdown**.

EXAMPLE 2

Calculating the Percent of Markdown

The total inventory of coffee mugs at the local bookstore has a retail value of \$785. If the mugs were sold at reduced prices that totaled \$530, what is the percent of markdown on the original price?

SOLUTION

First find the amount of the markdown.

\$785	original price
− 530	reduced price
\$255	markdown

Finding the percent of the original price that is the markdown is a rate problem. (See **Chapter 3**.)

$$\text{Rate} = \frac{\textbf{Part}}{\textbf{Base}} = \frac{\textbf{255}}{\textbf{785}} = .3248 = 32\% \text{ markdown rounded to the nearest whole percent}$$

The mugs were sold at a markdown of 32%.

QUICK CHECK 2

The entire inventory of decorations remaining after Christmas has a retail value of \$1836. If the decorations are sold at reduced prices totaling \$459, what is the percent of markdown on the original price?

Quick Check Answers

1. \$173.99 (rounded)
2. 75%

EXAMPLE 3

Finding the Original Price

Bouza's Baby News offers a child's car seat at a reduced price of \$63 after a 25% markdown from the original price. Find the original price.

SOLUTION

After the 25% markdown, the reduced price of \$63 represents 75% of the original price. The original price, or base, must be found.

$$\text{Base} = \frac{\text{Part}}{\text{Rate}} = \frac{63}{.75} = \$84 \text{ original price}$$

The original price of the car seat was \$84.

Check the answer by subtracting 25% of \$84 from \$84: $\$84 - (.25 \times \$84) = \$63$.

QUICK CHECK 3

Men's and women's winter gloves are sold at a reduced price of \$17.99 after a markdown of 40% from the original price. Find the original price.

QUICK TIP In Example 3, notice that 75% is used in the formula rather than 25%. The reduced price, \$63, is represented by 75%.

OBJECTIVE 3 **Define the terms associated with loss.** The amount of a markdown must be large enough to sell the merchandise while providing as much profit as possible. Merchandise that is marked down will result in a **reduced net profit**, **breaking even**, an **operating loss**, or a **gross** or **absolute loss**.

The following diagram illustrates the meaning of these terms.

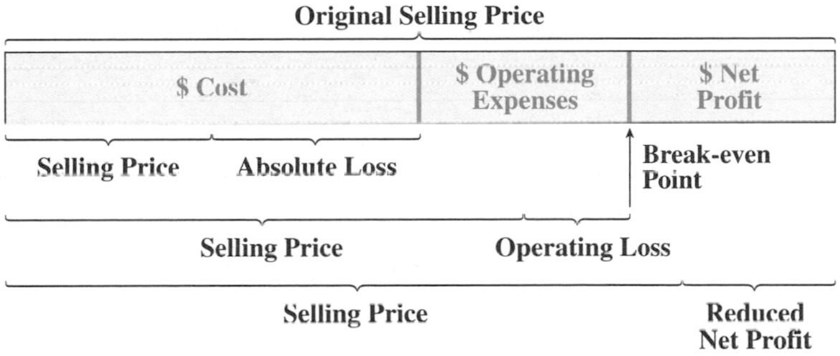

Reduced net profit results when the reduced price is still within the net profit range—is greater than the cost plus operating expenses.

OBJECTIVE 4 **Determine the break-even point and operating loss.** The **break-even point** is the point at which the reduced price just covers cost plus overhead (operating expenses). An **operating loss** occurs when the reduced price is less than the break-even point. The operating loss is the difference between the break-even point and the reduced selling price.

OBJECTIVE 5 **Determine the amount of an absolute or gross loss.** An **absolute loss** or **gross loss** is the result of a reduced price that is below the cost of the merchandise alone. The absolute or gross loss is the difference between the cost and the reduced selling price.

The following formulas are helpful when working with markdowns.

$$\text{Break-even point} = \text{Cost} + \text{Operating expenses}$$
$$\text{Operating loss} = \text{Break-even point} - \text{Reduced selling price}$$
$$\text{Absolute loss} = \text{Cost} - \text{Reduced selling price}$$

Quick Check Answer

3. \$29.98 (rounded)

EXAMPLE 4

Determining a Profit or a Loss

Appliance Giant paid $1600 for a 40-inch LCD HDTV. If operating expenses are 30% of cost and the television is sold for $2000, find the amount of profit or loss.

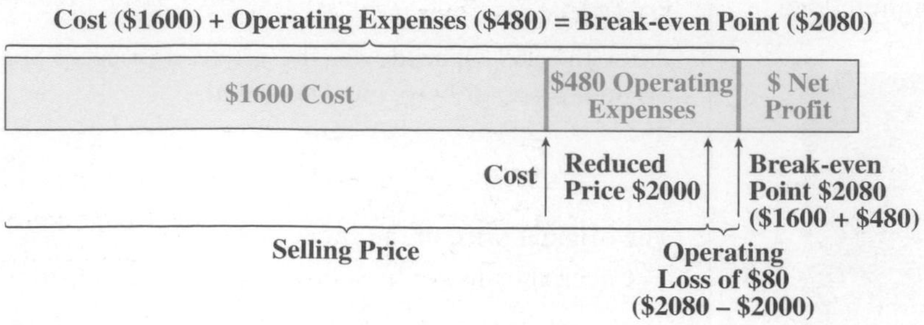

SOLUTION

Operating expenses are 30% of cost.

$$\text{Operating expenses} = .30 \times \$1600 = \$480$$

The break-even point for the LCD HDTV is

$$\text{Cost} + \text{Operating expenses} = \text{Break-even point}$$

$$\$1600 + (.3 \times \$1600) = \$1600 + \$480 = \$2080 \text{ break-even point}$$

Since the break-even point is $2080 and the selling price is $2000, there is a loss of

$$\$2080 - \$2000 = \$80$$

The $80 loss is an operating loss, since the selling price is less than the break-even point but greater than the cost.

The calculator solution to this example follows.

1600 [+] [(] .3 [×] 1600 [)] [−] 2000 [=] 80

QUICK CHECK 4

Big Chime Electronics paid $480 for a flat-screen television set. If operating expenses are 35% of cost and the television is sold for $600, find the amount of the operating loss.

EXAMPLE 5

Determining the Operating Loss and the Absolute Loss

A game table normally selling for $360 at Olympic Sports is marked down 30%. If the cost of the game table is $260 and the operating expenses are 20% of cost, find **(a)** the operating loss and **(b)** the absolute loss.

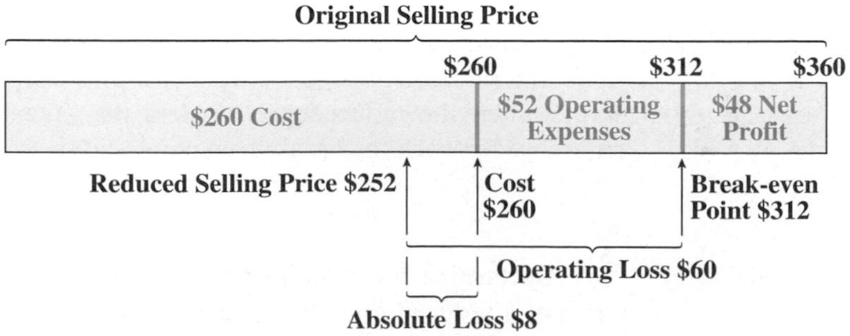

SOLUTION

(a) The break-even point (cost + operating expenses) is $312: $\$260 + (.2 \times \$260) = \$260 + \$52$.

$$\text{Reduced price} = \$360 - (.3 \times \$360) = \$360 - \$108 = \$252$$

$$\text{Operating loss} = \$312 \text{ break-even point} - \$252 \text{ reduced price} = \$60$$

(b) The absolute or gross loss is the difference between the cost and the reduced price.

$$\$260 \text{ cost} - \$252 \text{ reduced price} = \$8 \text{ absolute loss}$$

Quick Check Answer

4. $48 operating loss

QUICK CHECK 5

A propane forced-air heater normally selling for $290 is marked down 25%. If the cost of the heater is $220 and the operating expenses are 15% of cost, find **(a)** the operating loss and **(b)** the absolute loss.

The following bar graph shows the percent of adults who get an emotional high from making certain purchases. Customers love buying things—especially when they are on sale. This is valuable information to manufacturers, retailers, and all merchandisers.

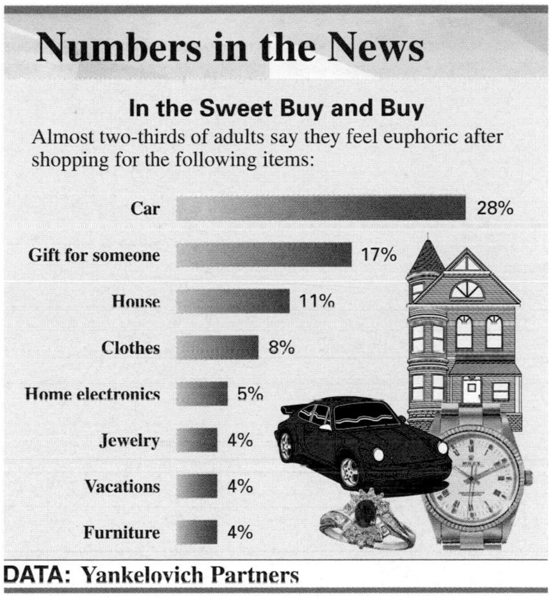

Quick Check Answers

5. **(a)** $35.50 operating loss
(b) $2.50 absolute loss

7.3 EXERCISES

FOR EXTRA HELP

MyMathLab

MathXL PRACTICE

WATCH

DOWNLOAD

READ

REVIEW

The **QUICK START** *exercises in each section contain solutions to help you get started.*

Find the missing quantities. Round rates to the nearest whole percent and dollar amounts to the nearest cent. (See Examples 1–3.)

QUICK START

	Original Price	% Markdown	$ Markdown	Reduced Price
1.	$860	25%	$215	$645
	$R = \frac{P}{B} = \frac{215}{860} = .25 = 25\%$; $\$860 - \$215 = \$645$			
2.	$240	40%	$96	$144
	$B = \frac{P}{R} = \frac{144}{.6} = \$240$; $\$240 - \$144 = \$96$			
3.	$61.60	_____	_____	$43.12
4.	_____	$66\frac{2}{3}\%$	_____	$3.10
5.	$6.50	_____	$1.30	_____
6.	_____	50%	$65.25	_____

Complete the following. If there is no operating loss or absolute loss, write "none." (See Examples 4 and 5.)

QUICK START

	Cost	Operating Expense	Break-even Point	Reduced Price	Operating Loss	Absolute Loss
7.	$96	$24	$120	$100	$20	none
	$\$96 + \$24 = \$120$; $\$120 - \$100 = \$20$					
8.	$25	$8	$33	$22	$11	$3
	$\$25 + \$8 = \$33$; $\$33 - \$22 = \$11$; $\$25 - \$22 = \$3$					
9.	$50	16	$66	$44	22	6
10.	$12.50	_____	$16.50	$11	_____	_____
11.	$310	$75	385	_____	$135	_____
12.	$156	$44	_____	_____	$60	_____

C indicates an exercise that is related to the Case in Point feature.

13. Give five reasons a store will mark down the price of merchandise to get it sold.

14. As a result of a markdown, there are three possible results: reduced net profit, operating loss, and absolute loss. As a business owner, which would concern you the most? Explain. (See Objectives 4 and 5.)

Solve the following application problems. Round rates to the nearest whole percent and dollar amounts to the nearest cent.

QUICK START

15. GPS SYSTEMS Best Buy prices its entire inventory of Tom Tom portable in-car Global Positioning Systems at \$133,509. If the original price of the inventory was \$226,284, find the percent of markdown on the original price.

$\$226{,}284 - \$133{,}509 = \$92{,}775;\ R = \frac{P}{B} = \frac{92{,}775}{226{,}284} = .409 = 41\%$

15. 41%

16. OAK DESK An oak desk originally priced at \$837.50 is reduced to \$686.75. Find the percent of markdown on the original price.

16. ____________

17. ELLIPTICAL TRAINER Olympic Sports paid \$360 for a ProForm 850 elliptical trainer. The operating expenses are $33\frac{1}{3}\%$ of cost. If they sell the elliptical trainer at a clearance price of \$449.99, find the amount of profit or loss.

17. ____________

18. EXERCISE BICYCLES Olympic Sports has an end-of-season sale during which it sells a ProForm Upright Bike for \$265. If the cost was \$198 and the operating expenses were 25% of cost, find the amount of profit or loss.

18. ____________

19. TRUCK ACCESSORIES Pep Boys Automotive paid \$208.50 for a pickup truck bedliner. The original selling price was \$291.90, but this was marked down 35%. If operating expenses are 28% of the cost, find **(a)** the operating loss and **(b)** the absolute loss.

(a) ____________
(b) ____________

20. ANTIQUES American Antiques paid \$153.49 for a fern stand. The original selling price was \$208.78, but this was marked down 46% in order to make room for incoming merchandise. If operating expenses are 14.9% of cost, find **(a)** the operating loss and **(b)** the absolute loss.

(a) ____________
(b) ____________

7.4 TURNOVER AND VALUATION OF INVENTORY

OBJECTIVES

1. Determine average inventory.
2. Calculate stock turnover.
3. Use uniform product codes.
4. Use the specific identification method to value inventory.
5. Determine inventory value using the weighted-average method.
6. Use the FIFO method to value inventory.
7. Use the LIFO method to value inventory.
8. Estimate inventory value using the retail method.

CASE in POINT Many of the items stocked and sold by Olympic Sports are ordered year round. One example is the Explorer internal frame backpack. Alyssa Romano, the manager, wants to make sure that her products are turning over (selling) so that the store does not have too much cash tied up in stock that is not selling. She also wants to be sure that the store has enough of the most popular products.

OBJECTIVE 1 Determine average inventory. The average time for merchandise to sell is a common measure of a business's efficiency. The number of times that the merchandise sells during a certain period of time is called the **inventory turnover** or the **stock turnover**. A business such as a florist shop or produce stand has a very fast turnover of merchandise, perhaps just a few days. On the other hand, a furniture store normally has a much slower turnover, perhaps several months.

Find stock turnover by first calculating **average inventory**. The average inventory for a certain period is found by adding the inventories taken during the time period and then dividing the total by the number of times that the inventory was taken.

EXAMPLE 1 Determining Average Inventory

Inventory at Olympic Sports was $285,672 on April 1 and $198,560 on April 30. What was the average inventory?

SOLUTION

First add the inventory values.

$285,672	**April 1**
+ 198,560	**April 30**
$484,232	

Then divide by the number of times inventory was taken.

$$\frac{\$484{,}232}{2} = \$242{,}116$$

The average inventory was $242,116.

QUICK TIP To find the average inventory for a period of time, an inventory must always be taken at the beginning of the period and at the end of the period. For example, to find average inventory for a full year, businesses commonly find inventory on the first day of each month and on the last day of the last month. They then find the average inventory by adding 13 inventory amounts and dividing by 13, the number of inventories taken.

QUICK CHECK 1

Inventory on September 1 was $76,822 and on September 30 it was $43,280. Find the average inventory.

Quick Check Answer

1. $60,051

Keeping a close watch on inventory is an ongoing concern of management. The following newspaper advertisement is promoting a year-end sale with no money to be paid until June of the following year. This sale should have a major impact in reducing the store's inventory.

MONDAY–FRIDAY 10AM–9PM SATURDAY 10AM-8PM & SUNDAY 11AM–6PM. PRICES GOOD 'TIL TUESDAY!
GET HUGE STOREWIDE SAVINGS!
YEAR-END SALE!
No Money Down, No Interest & No Payment 'til June
...On Every Item ...On Every Room!
Same As Cash Option. On Approved Credit With No Down Payment, Interest Accrues From Delivery Date if not Paid in Full by June
NO DOWN PAYMENT, NO INTEREST & NO PAYMENTS 'TIL JUNE ON 8-WAY, HAND-TIED LEATHER

Turnover is the number of times that the value of the merchandise or inventory in the store has sold during a period of time.

OBJECTIVE 2 **Calculate stock turnover.** Businesses value inventory either at retail or at cost. For this reason, **stock turnover** is found by using either of these formulas.

$$\text{Turnover at retail} = \frac{\text{Retail sales}}{\text{Average inventory at retail}}$$

$$\text{Turnover at cost} = \frac{\text{Cost of goods sold}}{\text{Average inventory at cost}}$$

The turnover ratio may be identical by using either method. The variation that often exists is caused by stolen merchandise (called *inventory shrinkage*) or merchandise that has been marked down or has become unsellable. Normally, turnover at retail is slightly lower than turnover at cost. For this reason, many businesses prefer this more conservative figure.

EXAMPLE 2

Finding Stock Turnover at Retail

During May, Red Lolly Pop Children's Apparel has retail sales of $64,064 and an average retail inventory of $19,712. Find the stock turnover at retail.

SOLUTION

$$\text{Turnover at retail} = \frac{\text{Retail sales}}{\text{Average inventory at retail}} = \frac{\$64{,}064}{\$19{,}712} = \mathbf{3.25\ at\ retail}$$

On average, the store turned over or sold the value of its entire inventory 3.25 times during the month.

QUICK CHECK 2

In July, Painters Supply has an average retail inventory of $26,528 and retail sales of $183,308. Find the stock turnover at retail.

EXAMPLE 3

Finding Stock Turnover at Cost

If the average inventory value at cost for Red Lolly Pop Children's Apparel in Example 2 was $11,826 and the cost of goods sold was $38,792, find the stock turnover at cost.

SOLUTION

$$\text{Turnover at cost} = \frac{\text{Cost of goods sold}}{\text{Average inventory at cost}} = \frac{\$38{,}792}{\$11{,}826} = \mathbf{3.28\ at\ cost\ (rounded)}$$

Quick Check Answer

2. 6.91 at retail (rounded)

QUICK CHECK 3

If the cost of goods sold by Painters Supply in Quick Check 2 was $150,348 and the average inventory at cost was $21,820, find the stock turnover at cost.

The stock turnover is useful for comparison purposes only. Many trade organizations publish such operating statistics to permit businesses to compare their operation with the industry as a whole. In addition to this, management uses these rates to compare turnover from period to period and from department to department.

It is not always easy to place a value on each of the items in inventory. Many large companies keep a **perpetual inventory** by using a computer. As new items are received, the quantity, size, and cost of each are entered in the computer. Sales clerks enter uniform product codes into the cash register automatically using an optical scanner.

OBJECTIVE 3 **Use uniform product codes.** **Uniform product codes (UPC)** are the black stripes that appear on the packaging for most items sold in stores. Each product and product size is assigned its own code number. These UPCs are a great help in keeping track of inventory.

A Cracker Jack box is shown at the left. The UPC number on the package is 3000002914. The checkout clerk in a retail store passes the coded lines over an optical scanner. The numbers are picked up by a computer, which recognizes the product by its code. The computer then forwards the price of the item to the cash register. At the same time the price is being recorded, the computer is subtracting the item automatically from inventory. After all the items being purchased have passed over the scanner, the customer receives a detailed cash-register receipt that gives a description of each item, the price of each item, and the total amount of the purchase.

Since the computer keeps track of stock on hand and is programmed to respond when inventory gets low, it provides more accurate inventory control and lower labor costs for the store.

Most businesses take a **physical inventory**, which is an actual count of each item in stock at a given time at regular intervals. For example, inventory may be taken monthly, quarterly, semiannually, or just once a year. An inventory taken at regular intervals is called a **periodic inventory**.

There are four major methods used for inventory valuation: the specific identification method; the weighted-average method; the first-in, first-out method; and the last-in, first-out method.

OBJECTIVE 4 **Use the specific identification method to value inventory.** The **specific identification method** is useful when items are easily identified and costs do not fluctuate. Each item is cost coded with either numerals or letters. These costs are then added to find ending inventory.

Since the cost of many items changes with time, there may be several of the same item in stock that were purchased at different costs. For this reason, many businesses prefer taking inventory at retail. The retail value of all identical items is the same.

OBJECTIVE 5 **Determine inventory value using the weighted-average method.** The **weighted average (average cost)** of inventory involves finding the average cost of an item and then multiplying the number of items remaining by the average cost per item.

EXAMPLE 4

Using Weighted Average (Average Cost) Inventory Valuation

Suppose Olympic Sports made the following purchases of the Explorer internal frame backpack during the year.

Beginning inventory	20 backpacks at $70
January	50 backpacks at $80
March	100 backpacks at $90
July	60 backpacks at $85
October	40 backpacks at $75

At the end of the year, there are 75 backpacks in inventory. Use the weighted-average method to find the inventory value.

SOLUTION

Find the total cost of all the backpacks.

Beginning inventory	$20 \times \$70 = \$1400$
January	$50 \times \$80 = \$4000$
March	$100 \times \$90 = \$9000$

Quick Check Answer

3. 6.89 at cost (rounded)

July	60 × \$85 = \$5100	
October	40 × \$75 = \$3000	
Total	270	\$22,500

Find the average cost per backpack by dividing this total cost by the number purchased.

$$\frac{\$22{,}500}{270} = \$83.33 \text{ (rounded)}$$

Since the average cost is \$83.33 and 75 backpacks remain in inventory, the weighted-average method gives the inventory value of the remaining backpacks as \$83.33 × 75 = \$6249.75.

The calculator solution to this example has several steps. First, find the total number of backpacks purchased and place the total in memory.

20 [+] 50 [+] 100 [+] 60 [+] 40 [=] 270 [STO]

Next, find the total cost of all the backpacks purchased and divide by the number stored in memory. This gives the average cost per backpack.

20 [×] 70 [+] 50 [×] 80 [+] 100 [×] 90 [+] 60 [×] 85 [+]
40 [×] 75 [=] [÷] [RCL] [=] 83.3333

Finally, round the average cost to the nearest cent and multiply by the number of backpacks in inventory to get the weighted average inventory value.

83.33 [×] 75 [=] 6249.75

QUICK CHECK 4

Olympic Sports made the following purchases of the Iron Horse BMX bicycle during the year.

Beginning inventory	20 bicycles at \$115
February	30 bicycles at \$95
April	50 bicycles at \$100
June	40 bicycles at \$110
August	80 bicycles at \$105
November	60 bicycles at \$130

At the end of the year, there are 85 bicycles in inventory. Use the weighted-average method to find the inventory value.

The cost of items purchased by the retailer is one of the greatest influences on the final retail price. The factors affecting cost include the quality of the product, the quantity purchased, and the geographic location of the purchaser. The following graphic shows the average price paid for a tennis racket in various countries around the world.

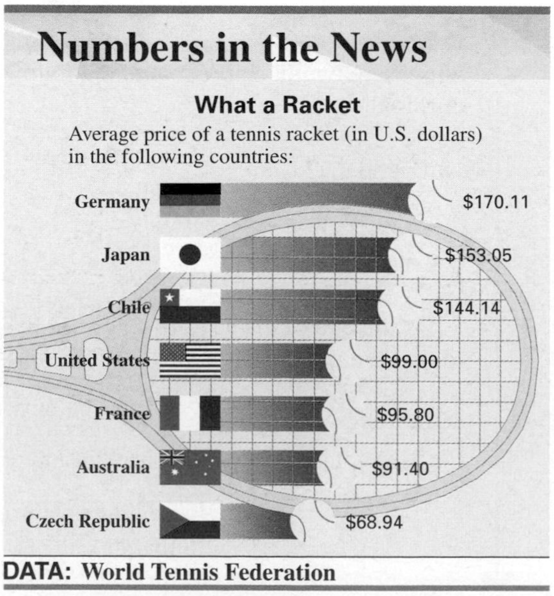

Quick Check Answer

4. \$9334.70 weighted average (rounded)

OBJECTIVE 6 **Use the FIFO method to value inventory.** The **first-in, first-out (FIFO) method** of inventory valuation assumes a natural flow of goods through the inventory. The first goods to arrive are the first goods to be sold, so the last items purchased are the items remaining in inventory.

EXAMPLE 5

Using FIFO to Determine Inventory Valuation

Use the FIFO method to find the inventory value of the 75 backpacks from Olympics Sports in Example 4.

SOLUTION

With the FIFO method, the 75 remaining backpacks are assumed to consist of the 40 backpacks bought in October and 35 $(75 - 40 = 35)$ backpacks from the previous purchase in July. The value of the inventory is:

October	40 backpacks at $75 = $3000	value of last 40
July	35 backpacks at $85 = $2975	value of previous 35
	75 valued at $5975	

The value of the backpack inventory is $5975 using the FIFO method.

QUICK CHECK 5

Use the FIFO method to find the inventory value of the 85 bicycles from Olympic Sports in Quick Check 4.

OBJECTIVE 7 **Use the LIFO method to value inventory.** The **last-in, first-out (LIFO) method** of inventory valuation assumes a flow of goods through the inventory that is just the opposite of the FIFO flow. With LIFO, the goods remaining in inventory are those goods that were first purchased.

EXAMPLE 6

Using LIFO to Determine Inventory Valuation

Use the LIFO method to value the 75 backpacks in inventory at Olympic Sports in Example 4.

SOLUTION

The calculation starts with the beginning inventory and moves through the year's purchases, resulting in 75 backpacks still in stock. The beginning inventory and January purchases come to 70 backpacks, so the cost of 5 more $(75 - 70 = 5)$ backpacks from the March purchase is needed.

Beginning inventory	20 backpacks at $70 = $1400	value of first 20
January	50 backpacks at $80 = $4000	value of next 50
March	5 backpacks at $90 = $ 450	value of last 5
Total	75 valued at $5850	

The value of the backpack inventory is $5850 using the LIFO method.

QUICK TIP Although the FIFO method of inventory evaluation is the most commonly used method, accepted accounting practice insists that the method used to evaluate inventory be stated on the company's financial statements.

QUICK CHECK 6

Use the LIFO method to value the 85 bicycles in inventory at Olympic Sports in Quick Check 4.

Depending on the method of valuing inventories that is used, Olympic Sports may show the inventory value of the 75 backpacks as follows.

Average cost method	$6249.75
FIFO	$5975
LIFO	$5850

The preferred inventory valuation method would be determined by Olympic Sports, perhaps on the advice of an accountant.

Quick Check Answers

5. $10,425 FIFO
6. $8650 LIFO

OBJECTIVE 8 **Estimate inventory value using the retail method.** An estimate of the value of inventory may be found using the **retail method of estimating inventory**. With this method, the cost of goods available for sale is found as a percent of the retail value of the goods available for sale during the same period. This percent is then multiplied by the retail value of inventory at the end of the period. The result is an estimate of the inventory at cost.

EXAMPLE 7

Estimating Inventory Value Using the Retail Method

The inventory on December 31 at Olympic Sports was $129,200 at cost and $171,000 at retail. Purchases during the next three months were $165,400 at cost, $221,800 at retail, and net sales were $168,800. Use the retail method to estimate the value of inventory at cost on March 31.

SOLUTION

STEP 1 Find the value of goods available for sale (inventory) at cost and at retail.

	At cost	At retail	
	$129,200	$171,000	beginning inventory
	+ 165,400	+ 221,800	purchases
	$294,600	$392,800	goods available for sale
STEP 2 Find the retail value of current inventory.		− 168,800	net sales
		$224,000	March 31 inventory at retail

STEP 3 Now find the percent of the value of goods available for sale at cost to goods available for sale at retail (cost ratio).

$$\frac{\mathbf{\$294{,}600} \text{ goods available for sale at cost}}{\mathbf{\$392{,}800} \text{ goods available for sale at retail}} = \mathbf{.75} = 75\% \text{ (cost ratio)}$$

STEP 4 Finally, the estimated inventory value at cost on March 31 is found by multiplying inventory at retail on March 31 by 75% (cost ratio).

$$\text{Ending inventory at retail} \times \% \text{ (cost ratio)} = \text{Inventory at cost}$$

$$\$224{,}000 \times \mathbf{.75} = \$168{,}000 \text{ March 31 inventory at cost}$$

QUICK CHECK 7

At the end of June, Solar Solutions had an inventory of $87,500 at cost and $125,000 at retail. During the next three months, there were purchases of $103,200 at cost, $147,600 at retail, and net sales were $185,000. Use the retail method to estimate the value of inventory at cost at the end of September.

Companies selling on the Internet often will be able to have products shipped directly from a manufacturer or wholesaler to their customers. This could result in decreased inventory requirements in the supply chain. The graph shows projected sales growth in the fastest-growing online sales categories.

Numbers in the News

Computers, Not Carts

Researchers estimate the fastest-growing online sales categories (in billions):

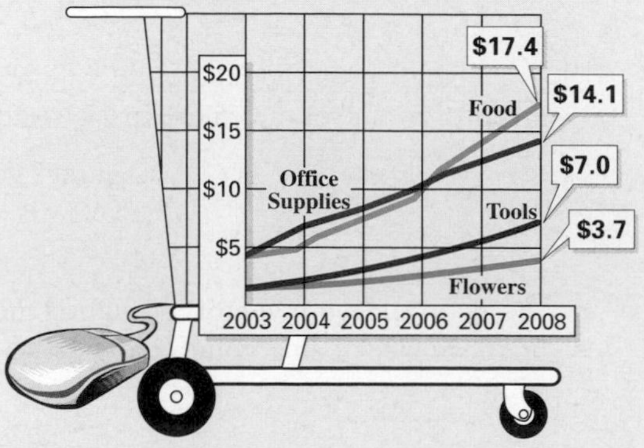

DATA: Forrester Research

Quick Check Answer

7. $61,320 inventory at cost

The newspaper clipping below shows the increasing use and the growing confidence that shoppers have when making luxury purchases on the Internet. The bar graph shows the forecast for Internet sales of jewelry and luxury goods, in billions of dollars.

Internet diamond sales are glittering

By Lorrie Grant
USA TODAY

Buying diamonds sight unseen on the Internet might seem an odd concept, but it's one that's gaining popularity.

A signal of the Internet's legitimacy for diamond sales is the pending initial stock offer of Blue Nile (www.bluenile.com). Blue Nile, launched in 1999, is one of several diamond e-tailers among hardy survivors of the dot-com crash.

Behind the increased sales are several factors. Consumers have become increasingly comfortable buying luxury goods online. And with diamonds, the Web offers easy access to a breadth of information about the features of a diamond, as well as the ability to easily and quickly compare prices.

The sites also have improved their displays. Earlier, "product images were grainy, and you couldn't zoom in. But today, the image is sharp, and technology has let consumers get close by 3D, zoom technology, good photography and rotation," says Kate Delhagen, retail analyst at Forrester.

But one expert says what has helped seal the big-ticket sales of diamonds is assurance they are authentic.

Numbers in the News

Sales that Sparkle

Online retail sales forecast of jewelry/luxury goods:

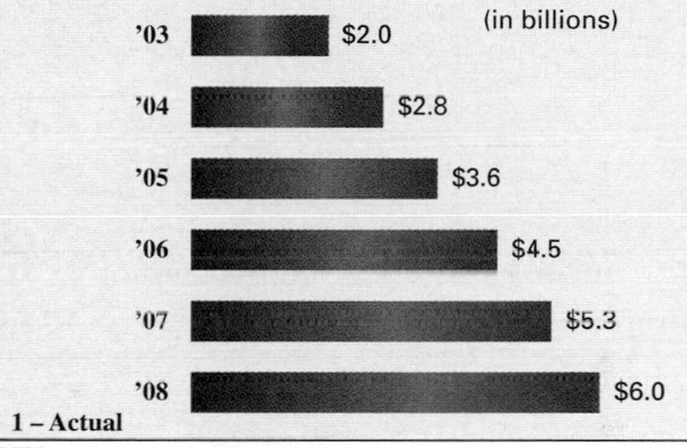

DATA: Forrester Research

"People are shopping online for diamonds because of one thing: certification. The certificate tells you what you're buying," says Ken Gassman, research analyst for the Jewelry Industry Research Institute. "Because they're certified, you know the quality. No other jewelry is certified."

7.4 EXERCISES

FOR EXTRA HELP

MyMathLab

MathXL PRACTICE

WATCH

DOWNLOAD

READ

REVIEW

The QUICK START *exercises in each section contain solutions to help you get started.*

Find the average inventory in each of the following. (See Example 1.)

QUICK START

	Date	Inventory Amount at Retail	Average Inventory		Date	Inventory Amount at Retail	Average Inventory
1.	July 1	\$18,300		**2.**	January 1	\$42,312	
	October 1	\$26,580			July 1	\$38,514	
	December 31	\$23,139	**\$22,673**		December 31	\$30,219	**\$37,015**
	\$68,019 total of inv. ÷ 3 = \$22,673				**\$111,045 total of inv. ÷ 3 = \$37,015**		
3.	January 1	\$65,430		**4.**	January 31	\$69,480	
	April 1	\$58,710			April 30	\$55,860	
	July 1	\$53,410			July 31	\$80,715	
	October 1	\$78,950			October 31	\$88,050	
	December 31	\$46,340	______		January 31	\$63,975	______

Find the stock turnover at cost and at retail in each of the following. Round to the nearest hundredth. (See Examples 2 and 3.)

QUICK START

	Average Inventory at Cost	Average Inventory at Retail	Cost of Goods	Retail Sales	Turnover at Cost	Turnover at Retail
5.	\$17,830	\$35,390	\$50,394	\$99,450	**2.83**	**2.81**
	\$50,394 ÷ \$17,830 = 2.83 at cost; \$99,450 ÷ \$35,390 = 2.81 at retail					
6.	\$15,140	\$24,080	\$67,408	\$106,193	**4.45**	**4.41**
	\$67,408 ÷ \$15,140 = 4.45 at cost; \$106,193 ÷ \$24,080 = 4.41 at retail					
7.	\$72,120	\$138,460	\$259,123	\$487,379	______	______
8.	\$38,074	\$48,550	\$260,420	\$330,060	______	______
9.	\$180,600	\$256,700	\$846,336	\$1,196,222	______	______
10.	\$411,580	\$780,600	\$1,905,668	\$3,559,536	______	______

C indicates an exercise that is related to the Case in Point feature.

Find the inventory values using (a) the weighted-average method, (b) the FIFO method, and (c) the LIFO method for each of the following. Round to the nearest cent if necessary. (See Examples 4–6.)

QUICK START

Purchases	Now in Inventory	Weighted-Average Method	FIFO Method	LIFO Method
11. Beginning inventory: 10 units at $8 June: 25 units at $9 August: 15 units at $10	20 units	$182	$195	$170

($455 purchases ÷ 50) × 20 = $9.10 × 20 = $182 average cost method

15 × $10 =	$150	10 × $8 =	$ 80
+ 5 × $ 9 =	$ 45	+ 10 × $9 =	$ 90
20	$195 FIFO	20	$170 LIFO

Purchases	Now in Inventory	Weighted-Average Method	FIFO Method	LIFO Method
12. Beginning inventory: 80 units at $14.50 July: 50 units at $15.80 October: 70 units at $13.90	90 units	_______	_______	_______
13. Beginning inventory: 50 units at $30.50 March: 70 units at $31.50 June: 30 units at $33.25 August: 40 units at $30.75	75 units	_______	_______	_______
14. Beginning inventory: 700 units at $1.25 May: 400 units at $1.75 August: 500 units at $2.25 October: 600 units at $3.00	720 units	_______	_______	_______

15. Identify three types of businesses that you think would have a high turnover. Identify three types of businesses that you think would have a low turnover.

16. Which departments in a grocery store do you think have the highest turnover? Which ones have the lowest turnover? Why do you think this is true?

Solve the following application problems. Round stock turnover to the nearest hundredth.

QUICK START

17. STOCK TURNOVER AT COST The Glass Works has an average inventory at cost of $15,730, and cost of goods sold for the same period is $85,412. Find the stock turnover at cost.

$\frac{\$85,412}{\$15,730} = 5.43$ turnover at cost

17. 5.43 turnover at cost

18. STOCK TURNOVER AT RETAIL Jumbo Market has an average canned-fruit inventory of $2320 at retail. Retail sales of canned fruit for the year were $98,669. Find the stock turnover at retail.

18. ________

19. SPRAY-PAINT INVENTORY The Graphic Hobby House made purchases of assorted colors of spray paint during the year as follows.

(a) ________
(b) ________
(c) ________

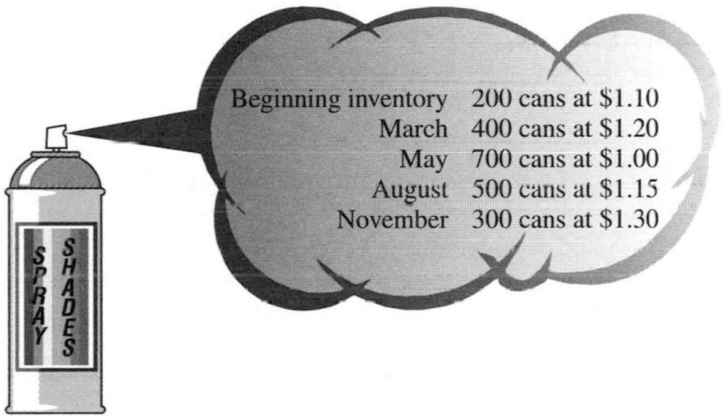

At the end of the year, they had 450 cans of spray paint in stock.

(a) Find the inventory value using the weighted-average method.
(b) Find the inventory value using the FIFO method.
(c) Find the inventory value using the LIFO method.

20. SPORT T-SHIRTS Olympic Sports made the following purchases of sport T-shirts made in Taiwan: beginning inventory was 650 shirts at $3.80 each; June, 500 shirts at $4.20 each; September, 450 shirts at $3.95 each; and December, 600 shirts at $4.05 each. An inventory at the end of the year shows that 775 T-shirts remain. **(a)** Find the inventory value using the weighted-average method. **(b)** Find the inventory value using the FIFO method. **(c)** Find the inventory value using the LIFO method.

(a) ________
(b) ________
(c) ________

21. ATHLETIC SOCKS Olympic Sports made the following purchases of 3-pair packages of athletic socks.

(a) ________
(b) ________
(c) ________

Beginning inventory	200 packages at $3.10
May	250 packages at $3.50
August	300 packages at $4.25
October	280 packages at $4.50

An inventory at the end of October shows that 320 packages remain. **(a)** Find the inventory value using the weighted-average method. **(b)** Find the inventory value using the FIFO method. **(c)** Find the inventory value using the LIFO method.

22. AUTOMOBILE MUFFLERS Marco Muffler Wholesalers made purchases of automobile mufflers through the year as follows.

(a) ______
(b) ______
(c) ______

Beginning inventory	300 units at $21.60
March	400 units at $24.00
August	450 units at $24.30
November	350 units at $22.50

An inventory at the end of December shows that 530 mufflers remain. **(a)** Find the inventory value using the weighted-average method. **(b)** Find the inventory value using the FIFO method. **(c)** Find the inventory value using the LIFO method.

23. PIANO REPAIR The September 30 inventory at Liverpool Piano Repair was $43,750 at cost and $62,500 at retail. Purchases during the next three months were $51,600 at cost, $73,800 at retail, and net sales were $92,500. Use the retail method to estimate the value of the inventory at cost on December 31.

23. ______

24. EVALUATING INVENTORY Cell Phones Plus had an inventory of $27,000 at cost and $45,000 at retail on March 31. During the next three months, they made purchases of $108,000 at cost and $180,000 at retail and had net sales of $162,000. Use the retail method to estimate the value of inventory at cost on June 30.

24. ______

25. In your opinion, what are the benefits to a merchant who is using uniform product codes (UPCs)?

26. Which of the three inventory valuation methods discussed in this section is most interesting to you? Explain how this method determines inventory value.

CHAPTER 7 QUICK REVIEW

CHAPTER TERMS *Review the following terms to test your understanding of the chapter. For each term you do not know, refer to the page number found next to that term.*

absolute loss **[p. 297]**
actual selling price **[p. 296]**
average inventory **[p. 303]**
break-even point **[p. 297]**
breaking even **[p. 297]**
conversion formulas **[p. 287]**
cost **[p. 274]**
first-in, first-out (FIFO) method **[p. 307]**
formula for markdown **[p. 296]**
gross loss **[p. 297]**
gross profit **[p. 274]**
inventory turnover **[p. 303]**
last-in, first-out (LIFO) method **[p. 307]**
margin **[p. 274]**
markdown **[p. 296]**
markup **[p. 274]**
markup based on cost **[p. 276]**
markup formula **[p. 275]**
markup on cost **[p. 274]**
markup on selling price **[p. 274]**
net earnings **[p. 274]**
net profit **[p. 274]**
operating expenses **[p. 274]**
operating loss **[p. 297]**
overhead **[p. 274]**
percent of markdown **[p. 296]**
periodic inventory **[p. 305]**
perpetual inventory **[p. 305]**
physical inventory **[p. 305]**
reduced net profit **[p. 297]**
reduced price **[p. 296]**
retail method of estimating inventory **[p. 308]**
sale price **[p. 296]**
selling price **[p. 274]**
specific identification method **[p. 305]**
stock turnover **[p. 303]**
uniform product code (UPC) **[p. 305]**
weighted-average (average cost) method **[p. 305]**

CONCEPTS	EXAMPLES
7.1 Finding the markup on cost 100% Cost base % + **Markup ? part** % Selling price Cost is base. Use the basic percent formula. $P = B \times R$	100% *C* $160 **base** **rate** 25% *M* $? **part** % *S* $ $P = B \times R$ $P = \$160 \times .25$ $P = \$40$ markup
7.1 Calculating the percent of markup 100% *C* $ base **rate** ?% *M* $ % *S* $ Solve for rate.	100% *C* $420 base **rate** ?% *M* $ part % *S* $546 part $546 − $420 = $126 markup $R = \frac{P}{B} = \frac{126}{420}$ $R = 30\%$
7.1 Finding the cost and the selling price 100% *C* $? **base** % *M* $ % *S* $? **part** Solve for base.	100% *C* $? **base** rate 50% *M* $56 % *S* $? **part** $B = \frac{P}{R} = \frac{56}{.5}$ $B = \$112$ cost $112 + $56 = $168 selling price
7.2 Finding the markup on selling price % *C* $ % *M* $? **part** 100% *S* $ base Solve for part.	% *C* $ rate 25% *M* $? **part** 100% *S* $6.00 base $P = B \times R$ $P = \$6.00 \times .25$ $P = \$1.50$
7.2 Finding the cost % *C* $? **part** % *M* $ 100% *S* $	% *C* $? **part** rate 35% *M* $87.50 part 100% *S* $ base $B = \frac{P}{R} = \frac{87.5}{.35} = \$250$ selling price $250 − $87.50 = $162.50 cost

CONCEPTS	EXAMPLES
7.2 Calculating the selling price and the markup % C \$ % M \$? part 100% S \$? base	rate % C \$150 part 25% M \$? part 100% S \$? base 100% − 25% = 75% cost $B = \frac{P}{R} = \frac{150}{.75} = \$200$ selling price \$200 − \$150 = \$50 markup
7.2 Converting markup on cost to markup on selling price Use the formula $\text{\% markup on selling price} = \frac{\text{\% markup on cost}}{100\% + \text{\% markup on cost}}$	Convert 25% markup on cost to markup on selling price. $\text{\% markup on selling price} = \frac{25\%}{100\% + 25\%}$ $= \frac{.25}{1.25} = .2 = 20\%$
7.2 Converting markup on selling price to markup on cost Use the formula $\text{\% markup on cost} = \frac{\text{\% markup on selling price}}{100\% - \text{\% markup on selling price}}$	Convert 20% markup on selling price to markup on cost. $\text{\% markup on cost} = \frac{20\%}{100\% - 20\%}$ $= \frac{.2}{.8} = .25 = 25\%$
7.2 Finding the selling price for perishables **1.** Find total cost and selling price. **2.** Subtract the quantity not sold to find the number that are sold. **3.** Divide the remaining sales by the number of sellable units to get selling price per unit.	60 doughnuts cost 25¢ each; 10 are not sold; 50% markup on selling price; find selling price per doughnut. Cost = 60 × \$.25 = \$15 (rate) 50% C \$15 part 50% M \$ 100% S \$? base $B = \frac{P}{R} = \frac{15}{.5} = \$30$ 60 − 10 = 50 doughnuts sold \$30 ÷ 50 = \$.60 per doughnut
7.3 Finding the percent of markdown Markdown is always a percent of the original price. Use the formula $R = \frac{P}{B}$ $\text{Markdown percent} = \frac{\text{Markdown amount}}{\text{Original price}}$	Original price, \$76; markdown, \$19; find the percent of markdown. $R = \frac{P}{B} = \frac{19}{76} = .25$ $R = 25\%$ markdown
7.3 Calculating the break-even point The cost plus operating expenses equals the break-even point.	Cost, \$54; operating expenses, \$16; find the break-even point. \$54 cost + \$16 operating expenses = \$70 break-even point
7.3 Finding operating loss The difference between the break-even point and the reduced price (when below the break-even point) is the operating loss.	Break-even point, \$70; reduced price, \$58; find the operating loss. \$70 break-even point − \$58 reduced price \$12 operating loss
7.3 Finding absolute loss (gross loss) When the reduced price is below cost, the difference between the cost and reduced price is the absolute loss.	Cost, \$54; reduced price, \$48; find the absolute loss. \$54 cost − \$48 reduced price = \$6 absolute loss

CONCEPTS	EXAMPLES
7.4 Determining average inventory Inventory is taken two or more times. Totals are added together, then divided by the number of inventories taken to get the average.	Inventories, \$22,635, \$24,692, and \$18,796; find the average inventory. $\frac{\$22{,}635 + \$24{,}692 + \$18{,}796}{3}$ $= \frac{\$66{,}123}{3} = \$22{,}041$ average inventory
7.4 Finding turnover at retail Use the formula $\text{Turnover} = \frac{\text{Retail sales}}{\text{Average inventory at retail}}$	Retail sales, \$78,496; average inventory at retail, \$18,076; find turnover at retail. $\frac{\$78{,}496}{\$18{,}076} = 4.34$ at retail (rounded)
7.4 Finding turnover at cost Use the formula $\text{Turnover} = \frac{\text{Cost of goods sold}}{\text{Average inventory at cost}}$	Cost of goods sold, \$26,542; average inventory at cost, \$6592; find turnover at cost. $\frac{\$26{,}542}{\$6592} = 4.03$ at cost (rounded)
7.4 Using specific identification to value inventory Each item is cost coded, and the cost of each of the items is added to find total inventory.	Individual cost of each item in inventory is: item 1, \$593; item 2, \$614; item 3, \$498; find total value of inventory. \$593 + \$614 + \$498 = \$1705 total value of inventory
7.4 Using weighted-average (average cost) method of inventory valuation This method values items in an inventory at the average cost of buying them.	Beginning inventory of 20 at \$75; purchases of 15 at \$80; 25 at \$65; 18 at \$70; 22 remain in inventory. Find the inventory value. 20 × \$75 = \$1500 15 × \$80 = \$1200 25 × \$65 = \$1625 18 × \$70 = \$1260 Total 78 \$5585 $\frac{\$5585}{78} = \$71.60$ average cost (rounded) \$71.60 × 22 = \$1575.20 weighted-average method inventory value
7.4 Using first-in, first-out (FIFO) method of inventory valuation The first items in are the first sold. Inventory is based on cost of last items purchased.	Beginning inventory of 25 items at \$40; purchased on August 7, 30 items at \$35; 35 remain in inventory. Find the inventory. 30 × \$35 = \$1050 value of last 30 5 × \$40 = \$ 200 value of previous 5 35 \$1250 value of inventory FIFO method
7.4 Using last-in, first-out (LIFO) method of inventory valuation The items remaining in inventory are those items that were first purchased.	Beginning inventory of 48 items at \$20 each; purchase on May 9, 40 items at \$25 each; 55 remain in inventory. Find the inventory value. 48 × \$20 = \$ 960 value of first 48 7 × \$25 = \$ 175 value of last 7 55 \$1135 value of inventory LIFO method
7.4 Estimating inventory value using the retail method $\frac{\text{Goods available for sale at cost}}{\text{Goods available for sale at retail}} = \%\ (\text{cost ratio})$ $\text{Ending inventory at retail} \times \%\ (\text{cost ratio}) = \text{Inventory at cost}$	Use the retail method to estimate the inventory value at cost. (see table below)

	Cost	Retail
beginning inventory	\$9,000	\$15,000
purchases	+ 36,000	+ 60,000
goods available for sale	\$45,000	\$75,000
net sales		− 54,000
ending inventory		\$21,000

$\frac{\$45{,}000 \text{ goods available for sale at cost}}{\$75{,}000 \text{ goods available for sale at retail}} = .6 = 60\%$

\$21,000 × .6 = \$12,600 inventory value at cost

CHAPTER 7 SUMMARY EXERCISE

Markdown: Reducing Prices to Move Merchandise

Olympic Sports purchased two dozen pairs of 5th Element Adult Aggresive in-line skates at a cost of \$1950. Operating expenses for the store are 25% of cost, while total markup on this type of product is 35% of selling price. Only 6 pairs of the skates sell at the original price, and the manager decides to mark down the remaining skates. The price is reduced 25% and 6 more pairs sell. The remaining 12 pairs of skates are marked down to 50% of the original selling price and are finally sold.

(a) Find the original selling price of each pair of skates. **(a)** ______________

(b) Find the total of the selling prices of all the skates. **(b)** ______________

(c) Find the operating loss. **(c)** ______________

(d) Find the absolute loss. **(d)** ______________

INVESTIGATE

Talk with the manager of a retail store. Does the store calculate markup based on cost or retail? Does the store use markdowns to promote the sale or liquidation of merchandise? How does the management decide how much to mark down merchandise? Ask the manager for an example of a product that had to be marked down so much that a gross loss resulted.

Case Studies

REI

www.rei.com

- 1938: Established by a group of 23 mountaineers
- 2007: more than 3 million members
- 90 stores in 26 states
- 9000 employees nationwide
- Has been on the "100 Best Companies to Work For" list by *Fortune* magazine every year since the list began
- Has contributed over $20 million to outdoor and conservation groups

REI was formed in 1938 by a group of 23 mountain climbers from Seattle, Washington. The company wanted the finest-quality climbing equipment and formed a buying cooperative (membership group) in order to find the best prices for their equipment. Today, anyone may shop at REI, but members—those who pay a one-time $15 fee to join—share in the company's profits through an annual patronage refund. In 2006, company-wide sales reached $1 billion and patronage refunds were more than $50 million.

REI's easy-to-navigate Internet store provides access to more than 40,000 outdoor products and offers a variety of interactive education opportunities for outdoor enthusiasts. In addition to selecting from thousands of products and securely placing online orders, customers can use gear checklists, interact with gear experts, and learn basic outdoor skills by accessing educational clinics.

1. REI purchased one dozen Jansport backpacks at a cost of $504. If the company uses a markup of 25% on selling price, find the selling price of each backpack.

2. A two-person dome tent with a full rain fly has a wholesale price of $78. If the store has operating expenses of 24.5% of cost and managers desire a net profit of 10.5% of cost, find the selling price.

3. Do you have a special activity, sport, or hobby for which it is sometimes difficult to get the right kind and quality of equipment or supplies? Would you consider buying what you need by mail-order catalog or over the Internet? Why or why not?

4. List five possible advantages and five possible disadvantages of buying through the Internet. How could the disadvantages be eliminated or reduced? Do you see a time when you will be making half or more of your purchases through the Internet?

CHAPTER 7 TEST

To help you review, the numbers in brackets show the section in which the topic was discussed.

Solve for (a), (b), and (c). **[7.1 and 7.2]**

1.

100%	*C*	$64.00
(a)%	*M*	$12.80
(b)%	*S*	$(c)

2.

100%	*C*	$(b)
38%	*M*	$(c)
(a)%	*S*	$504.39

3.

(a)%	*C*	$134.40
(b)%	*M*	$(c)
100%	*S*	$168.00

4.

(a)%	*C*	$(c)
(b)%	*M*	$ 6.15
100%	*S*	$24.60

Find the equivalent markup on either cost or selling price, using the appropriate formula. Round to the nearest tenth of a percent. **[7.2]**

	Markup on Cost	*Markup on Selling Price*
5.	25%	_______
6.	100%	_______

Complete the following. If there is no operating loss or absolute loss, write "none." **[7.3]**

	Cost	*Operating Expense*	*Break-even Point*	*Reduced Price*	*Operating Loss*	*Absolute Loss*
7.	$160	$40	_______	$186	_______	_______
8.	$225	_______	$297	$198	_______	_______

Find the stock turnover at cost and at retail in the following. Round to the nearest hundredth. **[7.4]**

	Average Inventory at Cost	*Average Inventory at Retail*	*Cost of Goods Sold*	*Retail Sales*	*Turnover at Cost*	*Turnover at Retail*
9.	$14,120	$25,572	$81,312	$146,528	_______	_______

Solve the following application problems.

10. Olympic Sports buys jogging shorts manufactured in Indonesia for $97.50 per dozen pair. Find the selling price per pair if the retailer maintains a markup of 35% on selling price. **[7.2]** **10.** _______________

11. Restaurant Supply sells a walk-in refrigerator for $5250 while using a markup of 25% on cost. Find the cost. **[7.1]** **11.** _______________

12. The Computer Service Center sells a DeskJet print cartridge for $18.75. If the print cartridge costs the store $11.25, find the markup as a percent of selling price. **[7.2]** **12.** _______________

13. Olympic Sports offers an inflatable boat for $199.95. If the boats cost $1943.52 per dozen, find **(a)** the markup, **(b)** the percent of markup on selling price, and **(c)** the percent of markup on cost. Round to the nearest tenth of a percent. **[7.1 and 7.2]**

(a) ____________
(b) ____________
(c) ____________

14. A motorcycle originally priced at $13,875 is marked down to $9990. Find the percent of markdown on the original price. **[7.3]**

14. ____________

15. Leslie's Pool Supply, a retailer, pays $285 for a diving board. The original selling price was $399, but it was marked down 40%. If operating expenses are 30% of cost, find **(a)** the operating loss and **(b)** the absolute loss. **[7.3]**

(a) ____________
(b) ____________

16. Carpets Plus had an inventory of $117,328 on January 1, $147,630 on July 1, and $125,876 on December 31. Find the average inventory. **[7.4]**

16. ____________

Round to the nearest dollar amount.

17. Craighead Products made the following purchases of fuel tanks during the year: 25 at $270 each, 40 at $330 each, 15 at $217 each, and 30 at $284 each. An inventory shows that 45 fuel tanks remain. Find the inventory value using the weighted-average method. **[7.4]**

17. ____________

18. Find the value of the inventory listed in Exercise 17 using **(a)** the FIFO method and **(b)** the LIFO method. **[7.4]**

(a) ____________
(b) ____________

CHAPTER 7 CUMULATIVE REVIEW

Chapters 4–7

The following credit-card transactions were made at the Patio Store. Answer Exercises 1–5 using this information. Round to the nearest cent. **[4.2]**

Sales			Credits
$428.80	$733.18	$22.51	$76.15
$316.25	$38.00	$162.15	$118.44
$68.95	$188.36		$13.86

1. Find the total amount of the sales slips. **1.** ________

2. What is the total amount of the credit slips? **2.** ________

3. Find the total amount of the deposit. **3.** ________

4. Assuming that the bank charges the retailer a $3\frac{1}{4}$% discount charge, find the amount of the discount charge at the statement date. **4.** ________

5. Find the amount of the credit given to the retailer after the fee is subtracted. **5.** ________

Solve the following application problems.

6. Shaundra Brown worked 7 hours on Monday, 10 hours on Tuesday, 8 hours on Wednesday, 9 hours on Thursday, and 10 hours on Friday. Her regular hourly pay is $12.80. Find her gross earnings for the week if Brown is paid time and a half for all hours over 8 worked in a day. **[5.1]** **6.** ________

7. The employees of Feather Farms paid a total of $968.50 in Social Security tax last month, $223.50 in Medicare tax, and $1975.38 in federal withholding tax. Find the total amount the employer must send to the Internal Revenue Service. **[5.4]** **7.** ________

Find the net cost (invoice amount) for each of the following. Round to the nearest cent. **[6.1]**

8. List price $475.50, less 20/20 ________

9. List price $375, less 25/10/5 ________

Find the single discount equivalent for each of the following series discounts. **[6.2]**

10. 10/20 ________

11. 30/40/10 ________

Find the discount date and the net payment date for each of the following. The net payment date is 20 days after the final discount date. **[6.4]**

	Invoice Date	Terms	Date Goods Received	Final Discount Date	Net Payment Date
12.	May 27	2/10 ROG	June 5	_______	_______
13.	Oct. 9	3/15 EOM		_______	_______
14.	June 24	4/10–30 ex.		_______	_______

Complete the following. If there is no operating loss or absolute loss, write "none." **[7.3]**

	Cost	Operating Expense	Break-even Point	Reduced Price	Operating Loss	Absolute Loss
15.	$312	$88	_______	_______	$120	_______
16.	_______	_______	_______	$220	$112	$32

Solve the following application problems.

17. The list price of an Iron Horse BMX bike at Olympic Sports is $149.99. Find the dealer's cost if given a 20/20 trade discount and a 3/20, n/30 cash discount. Assume that the dealer earns the maximum cash discount. **[6.1 and 6.3]**

17. _______________

18. Computer Towne purchases mouse pads for $43.20 per box of 3 dozen. If the store wants a markup of 52% on the selling price, find the selling price per mouse pad. **[7.2]**

18. _______________

19. The Retro-Fit Window Company has an average inventory of $18,784 at cost. If the cost of goods sold for the year was $241,938, find the stock turnover at cost. Round to hundredths. **[7.4]**

19. _______________

20. Inventory at a local store was taken at retail value four times and was found to be $53,820; $49,510; $60,820; and $56,380. Sales during the same period were $252,077. Find the stock turnover at retail. Round to hundredths. **[7.4]**

20. _______________

21. Thunder Manufacturing made the following purchases of rivet drums during the year: 25 at $135 each, 40 at $165 each, 15 at $108.50 each, and 30 at $142 each. An inventory shows that 45 rivet drums remain. Find the inventory value, using the weighted-average method. **[7.4]**

21. _______________

22. Refer to Exercise 21. Find the inventory value using **(a)** the FIFO method and **(b)** the LIFO method. **[7.4]**

(a) _______________
(b) _______________

CHAPTER 8

Simple Interest

CHAPTER CONTENTS

Many years ago Jane Benson, with the support of an encouraging banker, was one of the first women to open an automobile dealership. Benson Automotive frequently borrows large amounts of money from a bank to finance its inventory of new vehicles. Benson must clearly understand interest and notes, since these represent a significant cost to her business, literally the difference between profit and loss.

CASE in POINT

Interest is a fee charged to borrow money. Ancient clay tablets show that interest was being charged 5000 years ago. Banks, corporations, states, cities, countries, partnerships, and individuals borrow money. Large, financially strong corporations such as Microsoft and McDonald's borrow at the most favorable interest rate called the **prime rate**. The remainder of us must pay higher rates when we borrow to buy a car, a house, or to charge items to our charge cards.

The graph below shows the fluctuations in both new housing starts and prime interest rates. Since interest costs on homes are important to both builders and buyers, higher interest rates tend to slow new home construction, while lower rates tend to encourage it.

Simple interest applies only to the **principal**, or the original amount borrowed, and it is usually used for loans lasting less than 1 year. Simple interest is discussed in this chapter. **Compound interest** requires interest to be paid on the principal and *also* on previously earned interest. Compound interest is covered in **Chapter 9**.

8.1 BASICS OF SIMPLE INTEREST

OBJECTIVES

1. Solve for simple interest.
2. Calculate maturity value.
3. Use a table to find the number of days from one date to another.
4. Use the actual number of days in a month to find the number of days from one date to another.
5. Find exact and ordinary interest.
6. Define the basic terms used with notes.
7. Find the due date of a note.

CASE in POINT Benson liked the new automobile models that just came out and thought she could sell a lot of them if her dealership had a good selection available. So Benson Automotive borrowed $1,350,000 from a bank to finance its inventory of new models. Benson hoped to borrow the money at 8%, but wasn't sure what rate the banker would charge her. She noted with relief that at least interest rates weren't as high as in the 1980s.

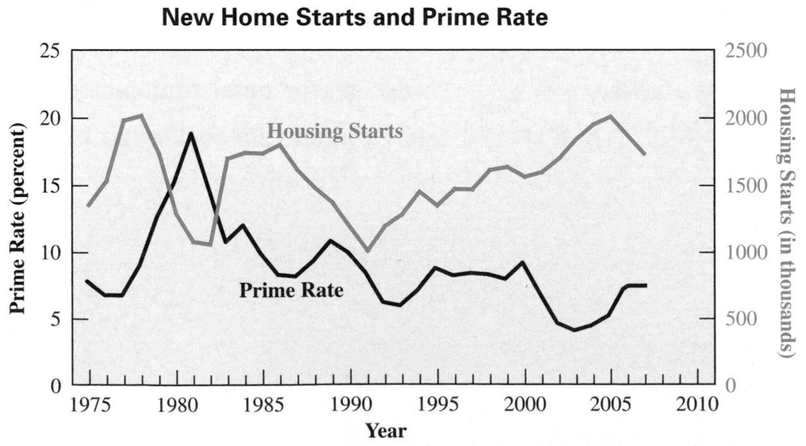

OBJECTIVE 1 Solve for simple interest. Simple interest is interest charged on the entire principal for the entire length of the loan. It is found using the formula shown in the following box. **Principal** is the loan amount, **rate** is the interest rate, and **time** is the length of the loan *in years*.

QUICK TIP **Rate *(R)*** must be changed to a decimal or fraction before being substituted into $I = PRT$. For example, change 8% to .08 or $\frac{8}{100}$ before substituting into the formula in place of rate.

Simple interest = Principal × Rate × Time

$$I = P \times R \times T$$

QUICK TIP **Time *(T)*** must be converted to years *before* being substituted into $I = PRT$. For example, convert 7 months to $\frac{7}{12}$ of a year before substituting in place of time.

EXAMPLE 1

Finding Simple Interest

Benson Automotive borrowed $1,350,000 at 8.5% to help purchase 75 new automobiles and SUVs. Benson borrowed the money for 9 months, anticipating that most of the vehicles would be sold by then and that she would have funds to pay back the loan with interest. One bank offered her 8.5%, and a second offered her 10%. Find the interest **(a)** at 8.5% and **(b)** at 10%. **(c)** Then find the interest she saved by going with the lower interest rate.

SOLUTION

(a) Substitute the values into $I = PRT$ and solve for simple interest.

$$I = PRT$$

$$I = \$1{,}350{,}000 \times .085 \times \frac{9}{12} \quad \text{9 months} = \tfrac{9}{12} \text{ of a year}$$

$$I = \$86{,}062.50 \quad \text{simple interest}$$

(b) Change the interest rate to 10% and find simple interest using $I = PRT$.

$$I = PRT$$

$$I = \$1{,}350{,}000 \times .10 \times \frac{9}{12}$$

$$I = \$101{,}250 \quad \text{simple interest}$$

(c) Difference = $101,250 − $86,062.50 = $15,187.50.

Benson noted that the difference in interest saved is more than she would earn from selling five vehicles! She resolved to keep interest costs low.

The calculator solution for part **(a)** follows:

1350000 [×] 8.5 [%] [×] 9 [÷] 12 [=] 86062.5

Note: Refer to Appendix C for calculator basics.

QUICK CHECK 1

Find the interest on a loan of $14,680 for 6 months at 9%.

OBJECTIVE 2 **Calculate maturity value.** The amount that must be repaid when the loan is due is the **maturity value** of the loan. Find this value by adding principal and interest.

Maturity value = Principal + Interest

$$M = P + I$$

EXAMPLE 2

Finding Maturity Value

Tom Swift needs to borrow $7200 to remodel his bookstore so that he can serve coffee to customers as they browse or sit and read. He borrows the funds from his uncle for 10 months at an interest rate of 9.25%. Find the interest due on the loan and the maturity value at the end of 10 months.

Quick Check Answer

1. $660.60

QUICK TIP The lender is making an investment when making a loan. The lender expects to get more back at the end of the loan than when the money was loaned out.

SOLUTION

Interest due is found using $I = PRT$, where T must be in years $\left(10 \text{ months} = \frac{10}{12} \text{ year}\right)$.

$$\textit{Interest} = PRT$$

$$I = \$7200 \times .0925 \times \frac{10}{12} = \$555$$

$$\textit{Maturity value} = P + I$$

$$M = \$7200 + \$555 = \$7755$$

QUICK CHECK 2

Find the maturity value of a loan of $25,000 at 9% for 8 months.

OBJECTIVE 3 **Use a table to find the number of days from one date to another.** Up to this point, the period of the loan was given in months, but it can also be given in days. Or a loan may be due at a fixed date, such as April 17, and we may have to figure out the number of days until the loan must be paid off. One way to do this is to number the days of the year as in the table on the next page. Note that this table is also on the inside of the back cover of the book.

QUICK TIP Leap years are years with one additional day in February. If it is a leap year, June 11 is day 163 and December 25 is day 360. There are still 197 days from June 11 to December 25.

For example, suppose it is June 11 and you want to know how many days until Christmas. In the table, June 11 is day 162 of the year and December 25 is day 359 of the year. Subtract to find the number of days until Christmas.

December 25 is day	359
June 11 is day	− 162
	197 days from June 11 to December 25

There are 197 days from June 11 to December 25.

EXAMPLE 3 Finding the Number of Days from One Date to Another, Using a Table

Use the table on the next page to find the number of days from **(a)** March 24 to July 22, **(b)** April 4 to October 10, **(c)** November 8 to February 17 of the following year, and **(d)** December 2 to January 17 of the following year. Assume that it is not a leap year.

SOLUTION

(a)

July 22 is day	203
March 24 is day	− 83
	120 days from March 24 to July 22

(b)

October 10 is day	283
April 4 is day	− 94
	189 days from April 4 to October 10

(c) November 8 is day 312, so there are 365 − 312 = 53 days from November 8 to the end of the year. Add days until the end of the year plus days into the next year to find the total.

November 8 to end of year	53
February 17 is day	+ 48
	101 days from November 8 to February 17 of next year

(d) December 2 is day 336, so there are 365 − 336 = 29 days to the end of the year. Add days until the end of the year plus days into the next year to find the total.

December 2 to end of year	29
January 17 is day	+ 17
	46 days from December 2 to January 17 of the next year

QUICK CHECK 3

Find the number of days from **(a)** July 7 to November 7 and **(b)** August 25 to January 20 of the following year.

Quick Check Answers

2. $26,500
3. **(a)** 123 days
(b) 148 days

The Number of Each of the Days of the Year*

Day of Month	Jan.	Feb.	Mar.	Apr.	May	June	July	Aug.	Sept.	Oct.	Nov.	Dec.	Day of Month
1	1	32	60	91	121	152	182	213	244	274	305	335	1
2	2	33	61	92	122	153	183	214	245	275	306	336	2
3	3	34	62	93	123	154	184	215	246	276	307	337	3
4	4	35	63	94	124	155	185	216	247	277	308	338	4
5	5	36	64	95	125	156	186	217	248	278	309	339	5
6	6	37	65	96	126	157	187	218	249	279	310	340	6
7	7	38	66	97	127	158	188	219	250	280	311	341	7
8	8	39	67	98	128	159	189	220	251	281	312	342	8
9	9	40	68	99	129	160	190	221	252	282	313	343	9
10	10	41	69	100	130	161	191	222	253	283	314	344	10
11	11	42	70	101	131	162	192	223	254	284	315	345	11
12	12	43	71	102	132	163	193	224	255	285	316	346	12
13	13	44	72	103	133	164	194	225	256	286	317	347	13
14	14	45	73	104	134	165	195	226	257	287	318	348	14
15	15	46	74	105	135	166	196	227	258	288	319	349	15
16	16	47	75	106	136	167	197	228	259	289	320	350	16
17	17	48	76	107	137	168	198	229	260	290	321	351	17
18	18	49	77	108	138	169	199	230	261	291	322	352	18
19	19	50	78	109	139	170	200	231	262	292	323	353	19
20	20	51	79	110	140	171	201	232	263	293	324	354	20
21	21	52	80	111	141	172	202	233	264	294	325	355	21
22	22	53	81	112	142	173	203	234	265	295	326	356	22
23	23	54	82	113	143	174	204	235	266	296	327	357	23
24	24	55	83	114	144	175	205	236	267	297	328	358	24
25	25	56	84	115	145	176	206	237	268	298	329	359	25
26	26	57	85	116	146	177	207	238	269	299	330	360	26
27	27	58	86	117	147	178	208	239	270	300	331	361	27
28	28	59	87	118	148	179	209	240	271	301	332	362	28
29	29		88	119	149	180	210	241	272	302	333	363	29
30	30		89	120	150	181	211	242	273	303	334	364	30
31	31		90		151		212	243		304		365	31

**Add 1 to each date after February 29 for a leap year.*

OBJECTIVE 4 Use the actual number of days in a month to find the number of days from one date to another. The number of days between specific dates can be found using the number of days in each month of the year as shown in the table.

Number of Days in Each Month

31 Days		30 Days	28 Days
January	August	April	February
March	October	June	(29 days in leap year)
May	December	September	
July		November	

Two other ways of remembering the number of days in each month are the rhyme method and the knuckle method, as seen below.

Rhyme Method:
30 days hath September
April, June, and November.
All the rest have 31, except
February, which has 28 and
in a leap year 29.

Knuckle Method:

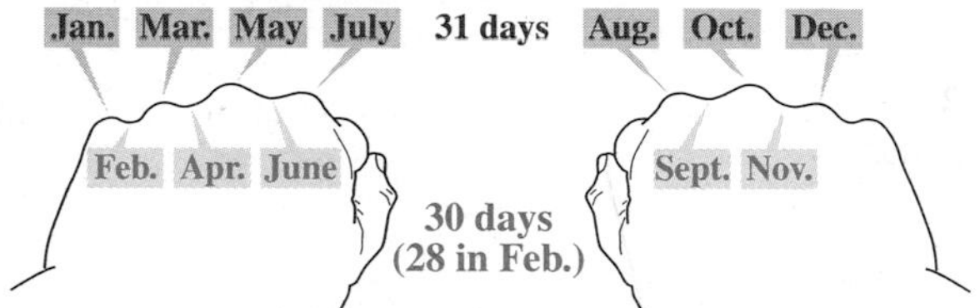

EXAMPLE 4

Finding the Number of Days from One Date to Another, Using Actual Days

Find the number of days from **(a)** June 3 to August 14 and **(b)** November 4 to February 21.

SOLUTION

(a) June has 30 days, so there are 30 − 3 = 27 days from June 3 to the end of June.

June 3 to the end of June	27
31 days in July	31
14 days in August	+ 14
	72 days from June 3 to August 14

(b) November has 30 days, so there are 30 − 4 = 26 days from November 4 to the end of November.

November 4 to end of November	26
31 days in December	31
31 days in January	31
21 days in February	+ 21
	109 days from November 4 to February 21

QUICK TIP To find the number of days from one date to another, do not count the day the loan was made, but do count the day the loan is paid.

QUICK CHECK 4

Find the number of days from March 14 to September 9.

OBJECTIVE 5 **Find exact and ordinary interest.** A simple interest rate is given as an annual rate, such as 7% per year. Since the rate is per year, time must also be given in years or fraction of a year when using $I = PRT$. If time is given in number of days, first change it to a fraction of a year.

$$T = \frac{\text{Number of days in the loan period}}{\text{Number of days in a year}}$$

Exact interest calculations require the use of the exact number of days in the year, 365 or 366 if a leap year. **Ordinary interest**, or **banker's interest**, calculations require the use of 360 days. Banks commonly used 360 days in a year for interest calculations before calculators and computers became widely available. Today, many institutions, the government, and the Federal Reserve Bank use the exact number of days in a year in interest calculations. However, some banks and financial institutions still use 360 days. You need to be able to use both.

For exact interest: Use 365 days (or 366 days if a leap year).

$$T = \frac{\text{Number of days in a loan period}}{365}$$

For ordinary, or banker's, interest: Use 360 days for the number of days.

$$T = \frac{\text{Number of days in a loan period}}{360}$$

Example 5 shows that **ordinary interest produces more interest** for the lending institution than does exact interest.

Quick Check Answer

4. 179 days

EXAMPLE 5

Finding Exact and Ordinary Interest

QUICK TIP Ordinary interest results in slightly more interest than exact interest. Thus ordinary interest favors those banks that use it when calculating loans.

Radio station KOMA borrowed $28,300 on May 12 with interest due on August 27. If the interest rate is 10%, find the interest on the loan using **(a)** exact interest and **(b)** ordinary interest.

SOLUTION

Either the table method or the method of the number of days in a month can be used to find that there are 107 days from May 12 to August 27.

(a) The **exact interest** is found from $I = PRT$ with $P = \$28{,}300$, $R = .1$, and $T = \frac{107}{365}$.

$$I = PRT$$

$$I = \$28{,}300 \times .1 \times \frac{\mathbf{107}}{\mathbf{365}} \quad \text{Use 365 days.}$$

$$I = \$829.62 \text{ (rounded)}$$

(b) Find **ordinary interest** with the same formula and values, except $T = \frac{107}{360}$.

$$I = PRT$$

$$I = \$28{,}300 \times .1 \times \frac{\mathbf{107}}{\mathbf{360}} \quad \text{Use 360 days.}$$

$$I = \$841.14 \text{ (rounded)}$$

In this example, the ordinary interest is $841.14 − $829.62 = $11.52 more than the exact interest.

QUICK CHECK 5

Find the exact and ordinary interest for a 200-day loan of $19,500 at 9% to the nearest cent. Then find the difference between the two interest amounts.

Use ordinary or banker's interest throughout the remainder of the book unless stated otherwise.

OBJECTIVE 6 **Define the basic terms used with notes.** A **promissory note** is a *legal document* in which one person or firm agrees to pay a certain amount of money, on a specific day in the future, to another person or firm. An example of a promissory note follows.

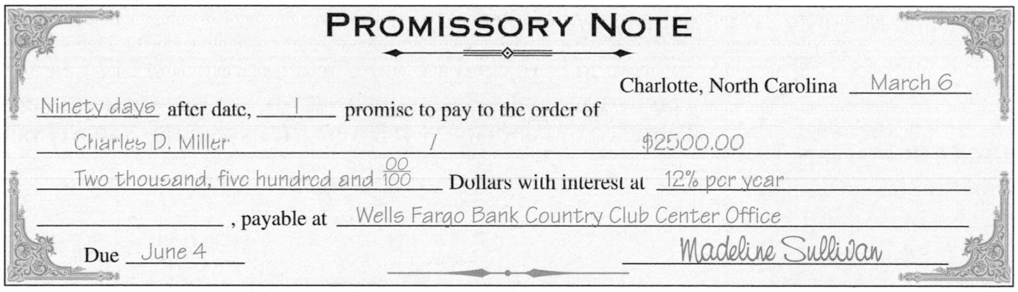
PROMISSORY NOTE

Charlotte, North Carolina March 6

Ninety days after date, I promise to pay to the order of

Charles D. Miller / $2500.00

Two thousand, five hundred and 00/100 Dollars with interest at 12% per year

, payable at Wells Fargo Bank Country Club Center Office

Due June 4 Madeline Sullivan

This type of promissory note is called a **simple interest note**, since simple interest calculations involving $I = PRT$ are used. Here are the terms of a simple interest promissory note.

Maker or **payer:** The person borrowing the money. (Madeline Sullivan in the sample note)
Payee: The person who loaned the money and who will receive the payment (Charles D. Miller in the sample note)
Term: The length of time until the note is due (90 days in the sample note)
Face value or **principal:** The amount being borrowed ($2500 in the sample note)
Maturity value: The face value plus interest, also the amount due at maturity
Maturity date or **due date:** The date the loan must be paid off with interest (June 4 in the sample note)

Quick Check Answer

5. $961.64 exact interest; $975 ordinary interest; difference of $13.36

Find the interest and the maturity value on the loan in the sample note on the previous page.

$$\textbf{Interest} = \textbf{Face value} \times \textbf{Rate} \times \textbf{Time}$$

$$\text{Interest} = \$2500 \times .12 \times \frac{90}{360} = \$75$$

$$\textbf{Maturity value} = \textbf{Face value} + \textbf{Interest}$$

$$\text{Maturity value} = \$2500 + \$75 = \$2575$$

Madeline Sullivan must pay $2575 to Charles D. Miller on June 4, the maturity date of the note.

Banks and financial institutions lend money only to individuals and firms they believe will repay the loan with interest. Even then, banks often require **collateral** or assets such as an automobile or stock in order to make a loan. If the loan is not repaid, the bank **forecloses** on the collateral, takes ownership, and sells or liquidates it. Funds from the sale of the collateral are first used to pay off the note and the expenses of the foreclosure. Any excess is returned to the maker of the note.

OBJECTIVE 7 Find the due date of a note. Time is in months in some promissory notes. When this occurs, the loan is due after the given number of months has passed but on the same day of the month as the original loan was made. For example, a 4-month note made on May 25 is due 4 months later on the 25th of September. Other examples follow.

Date Made	Length of Loan	Date Due
March 12	5 months	August 12
April 24	7 months	November 24
October 7	9 months	July 7
January 31	3 months	April 30

A loan made on January 31 for 3 months would normally be due on April 31. However, there are only 30 days in April, so the loan is due on April 30. Whenever a due date does not exist, such as February 30 or November 31, use the last day of the month (February 28 or November 30 in these examples).

EXAMPLE 6

Finding Due Date, Interest, and Maturity Value

Find the due date, interest, and maturity value for a $600,000 loan made to Benson Automotive on July 31 for 7 months at 7.5% interest.

SOLUTION

Interest and principal are due 7 months from July 31 or February 31, which *does not* exist. Since February has only 28 days (unless it is a leap year), interest and principal are due on the last day of February, or February 28. If it were a leap year, the maturity value would be due on February 29.

$$I = PRT = \$600{,}000 \times .075 \times \frac{7}{12} = \$26{,}250$$

$$M = P + I = \$600{,}000 + \$26{,}250 = \$626{,}250$$

A total of $626,250 must be repaid on February 28.

QUICK TIP Do not convert the period of a loan from months to days to find the due date.

QUICK CHECK 6

Find the due date for a 6-month loan made on March 31.

Quick Check Answer

6. September 30

8.1 EXERCISES

FOR EXTRA HELP

MyMathLab

MathXL PRACTICE

WATCH

DOWNLOAD

READ

REVIEW

The QUICK START *exercises in each section contain solutions to help you get started.*

Find simple interest and maturity value to the nearest cent. (See Examples 1 and 2.)

QUICK START

	Interest	Maturity Value
1. \$3800 at 11% for 6 months	\$209	\$4009
$I = \$3800 \times .11 \times \frac{6}{12} = \$209$		
$M = \$3800 + \$209 = \$4009$		
2. \$10,200 at 9.5% for 10 months	______	______
3. \$5500 at 8% for 1 year	______	______
4. \$800 at 6% for $2\frac{1}{2}$ years	______	______

Find the exact number of days from the first date to the second. (See Examples 3 and 4.)

QUICK START

5. February 15 to April 24 — **5.** 68

From the table, February 15 is day 46; April 24 is day 114

Number of days = 114 − 46 = 68 days

6. May 22 to August 30 — **6.** ______

7. December 1 to March 10 of the following year — **7.** ______

8. October 12 to February 22 of the following year — **8.** ______

C indicates an exercise that is related to the Case in Point feature.

Find (a) the exact interest and (b) the ordinary interest for each of the following to the nearest cent. Then find (c) the amount by which the ordinary interest is larger. (See Example 5.)

QUICK START

9. \$52,000 at $8\frac{3}{4}\%$ for 200 days

(a) Exact interest = \$52,000 × .0875 × $\frac{200}{365}$ = \$2493.15

(b) Ordinary interest = \$52,000 × .0875 × $\frac{200}{360}$ = \$2527.78

(c) Ordinary is larger by \$2527.78 − \$2493.15 = \$34.63

(a) \$2493.15
(b) \$2527.78
(c) \$34.63

10. \$185,000 at 7.5% for 180 days

(a) ______
(b) ______
(c) ______

11. \$29,500 at $11\frac{1}{4}\%$ for 120 days

(a) ______
(b) ______
(c) ______

12. \$52,610 at $8\frac{1}{2}\%$ for 82 days

(a) ______
(b) ______
(c) ______

Identify each of the following from the promissory note shown. (See Objective 6.)

PROMISSORY NOTE

Jackson, Mississippi October 27

Ninety days after date, I promise to pay to the order of

Donna Sharp / \$750.00

Seven hundred fifty and $\frac{00}{100}$ Dollars with interest at 12% per year

, payable at Crocker–Citizens Bank, Oak Park Branch

Due January 25 Helen Spence

13. Maker ______ **14.** Payer ______

15. Payee ______ **16.** Face value ______

17. Term of loan ______ **18.** Date loan was made ______

19. Date loan is due ______ **20.** Maturity value ______

Find the date due, the amount of interest (rounded to the nearest cent if necessary), and the maturity value. (See Example 6.)

QUICK START

	Date Loan Was Made	*Face Value*	*Term of Loan*	*Rate*	*Date Loan Is Due*	*Maturity Value*
21.	Mar. 12	\$4800	220 days	9%	Oct. 18	\$5064
22.	Jan. 3	\$12,000	100 days	9.8%	______	______

For 21: I = \$4800 × .09 × $\frac{220}{360}$ = \$264; M = \$4800 + \$264 = \$5064

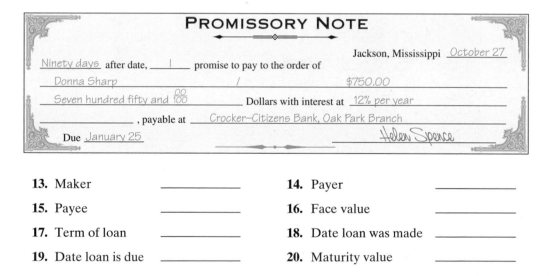

	Date Loan Was Made	*Face Value*	*Term of Loan*	*Rate*	*Date Loan Is Due*	*Maturity Value*
23.	Nov. 10	$6300	180 days	$9\frac{1}{4}\%$	________	________
24.	July 14	$6800	90 days	$11\frac{3}{4}\%$	________	________

Solve the following application problems. Round dollar amounts to the nearest cent.

QUICK START

25. INVENTORY Benson Automotive borrows $2,000,000 at $9\frac{1}{4}\%$ from a bank to buy land to build a building for a new dealership. Given that the loan is for 9 months, find **(a)** the interest and **(b)** the maturity value.

(a) $138,750
(b) $2,138,750

(a) $I = \$2{,}000{,}000 \times .0925 \times \frac{9}{12} = \$138{,}750$

(b) $M = \$2{,}000{,}000 + \$138{,}750 = \$2{,}138{,}750$

26. LOANS BETWEEN BANKS A bank in New York City borrows $25,000,000 at 9% for 90 days from a bank in Chicago. Find **(a)** the interest and **(b)** the maturity value.

(a) ________
(b) ________

27. ROAD PAVING Gilbert Construction Company needs to borrow $280,000 to build a short, paved road and install all utilities in a subdivision. The company decides to borrow the funds at 10% for 180 days. In 1980, the same note would have been at a rate of 22%. Find the difference in the interest charges based on the two rates.

27. ________

28. INTERNATIONAL BUSINESS Lesly Pacas borrows 300,000 pesos for 90 days at 18% per year to remodel her hair salon. She lives in Guadalajara, Mexico, where the rate would have been 35% a few years earlier. Find the difference in the interest charges based on the different rates.

28. ________

29. CAPITAL IMPROVEMENT Elizabeth Barton borrowed $6850 to install a small rock fountain and fish pond in front of her flower shop. She signed a 90-day note on July 5 at $9\frac{1}{4}\%$ interest. Find **(a)** the due date and **(b)** the maturity value of the note.

(a) ________
(b) ________

30. COMPUTER STORE ComputerTown signed a promissory note to a bank with a face value of $32,500 on September 10. The 90-day note is at 11% interest. Find **(a)** the due date and **(b)** the maturity value of the note.

(a) ________
(b) ________

31. HEALTH FOOD On March 10, the owner of The Granary borrowed $80,000 on a 180-day promissory note at 10.5% interest. Find **(a)** the due date and **(b)** the maturity value of the note.

(a) ________
(b) ________

32. CORPORATE FINANCE On October 15, IBM borrows $45,000,000 at 8% from a bank in San Francisco and agrees to repay the loan in 120 days using ordinary interest. Find **(a)** the due date and **(b)** the maturity value.

(a) ________
(b) ________

33. PENALTY ON UNPAID PROPERTY TAX Joe Simpson's property tax is $3416.05 and is due on April 15. He does not pay until July 23. The county adds a penalty of 9.3% simple interest on his unpaid tax. Find the penalty using exact interest.

33. ________

34. PENALTY ON UNPAID INCOME TAX On January 5, Helen Terry made an income tax payment that was due on September 15. The penalty was 11% simple interest on the unpaid tax of $2100. Find the penalty using exact interest.

34. ________

35. EQUIPMENT SUPPLY Fireman's Supply borrowed $48,000 on January 31 to remodel the front of their store. The 8.75% simple interest note was due in 8 months. Find **(a)** the due date and **(b)** the maturity value of the note.

(a) ________
(b) ________

36. LOAN TO EMPLOYEE On the last day in November, Terry Thompson loaned one of his employees $1600 for 3 months at 10% interest. Find **(a)** the due date and **(b)** the maturity value.

(a) ________
(b) ________

37. Explain the difference between exact interest and ordinary, or banker's, interest. (See Objective 5.)

38. List three companies that you have purchased products or services from in the past. List two reasons each of the companies may have needed to borrow money in the past.

8.2 FINDING PRINCIPAL, RATE, AND TIME

OBJECTIVES

1. Find the principal.
2. Find the rate.
3. Find the time.

Principal (P), rate (R), and time (T) were given for all problems in **Section 8.1**, and we calculated interest. In this section, interest is given, and we solve for principal, rate, or time.

OBJECTIVE 1 Find the principal. The principal (P) is found by dividing both sides of the simple interest equation $I = PRT$ by RT. See Appendix A for a review of algebra if needed.

QUICK TIP For simplicity, use banker's interest with 360 days for all problems in this section.

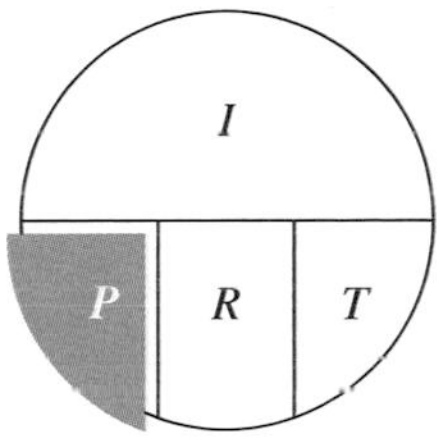

$P = \frac{I}{RT}$

$$I = PRT$$

$$\frac{I}{RT} = \frac{P\cancel{RT}}{\cancel{RT}} \quad \text{Divide both sides by } RT.$$

$$\frac{I}{RT} = P \quad \text{or} \quad P = \frac{I}{RT}$$

The various forms of the simple interest equation can be remembered using the circle sketch shown above. In the sketch, I (interest) is in the top half of the circle, with P (principal), R (rate), and T (time) in the bottom half of the circle. Find the formula for any one variable by covering that letter in the circle and then read the remaining letters, noticing their position. For example, cover P and you are left with $\frac{I}{RT}$.

$$\text{Principal} = \frac{\text{Interest}}{\text{Rate} \times \text{Time (in years)}} \quad \text{or} \quad P = \frac{I}{RT}$$

EXAMPLE 1

Finding Principal Given Interest in Days

Gilbert Construction Company borrows funds at 10% for 54 days to build a home. Find the principal that results in interest of $780.

SOLUTION

Write the rate as .10, the time as $\frac{54}{360}$, and then use the formula for principal.

$$P = \frac{I}{RT}$$

$$P = \frac{\$780}{.10 \times \frac{54}{360}}$$

$$.10 \times \frac{54}{360} = .015 \quad \text{Simplify the denominator.}$$

$$P = \frac{\$780}{.015} = \$52{,}000 \quad \text{Divide.}$$

QUICK TIP Remember that time must be in years or fraction of a year.

The principal is $52,000.

Check the answer using $I = PRT$. The principal is $52,000, the rate is 10%, and the time is $\frac{54}{360}$ year. The interest should be, and is, $780.

$$I = \$52{,}000 \times .10 \times \frac{54}{360} = \mathbf{\$780}$$

The calculator approach to finding the principal uses parentheses so that the numerator is divided by the entire denominator.

780 [÷] [(] .10 [×] 54 [÷] 360 [)] [=] 52000

QUICK CHECK 1

A 90-day loan with a rate of 12% results in interest of $285. Find the principal.

EXAMPLE 2

Finding Principal Given Length of Loan

Frank Thomas took out a loan to pay his college tuition on February 2. The loan is due to be repaid on April 15 when Thomas expects to receive an income tax refund. The interest on the loan is $37.80 at a rate of 10.5%. Find the principal.

SOLUTION

First find the number of days.

26	days remaining in February
31	March
+ 15	April
72	days from February 2 to April 15

$$T = \frac{72}{360}$$

Next find the principal.

$$P = \frac{I}{RT}$$

$$P = \frac{\$37.80}{.105 \times \frac{72}{360}} \quad \text{Substitute values into the formula.}$$

$$.105 \times \frac{72}{360} = .021 \quad \text{Simplify the denominator.}$$

$$P = \frac{\$37.80}{.021} = \$1800 \quad \text{Divide.}$$

The principal is $1800. Check the answer using the formula for simple interest.

$$I = \$1800 \times .105 \times \frac{72}{360} = \mathbf{\$37.80}$$

QUICK CHECK 2

A loan made on May 12 must be repaid on December 18. Find the principal given that the rate is 9% and the interest at maturity is $1551.

OBJECTIVE 2 **Find the rate.** Solve the formula $I = PRT$ for rate (R) by dividing both sides of the equation by PT. The rate found in this manner will be the annual interest rate. See Appendix A for a review of algebra if needed.

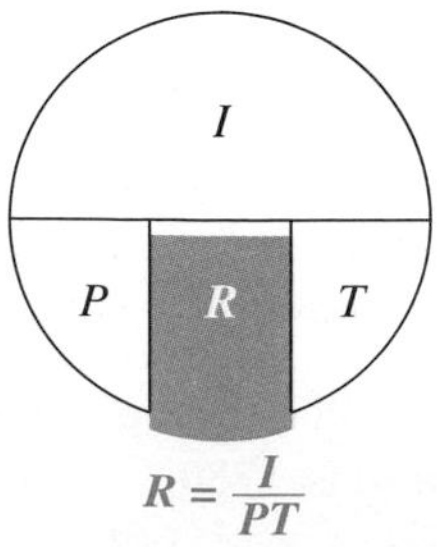

$$I = PRT$$

$$\frac{I}{PT} = \frac{\cancel{P}R\cancel{T}}{\cancel{P}\cancel{T}} \quad \text{Divide both sides by } PT.$$

$$\frac{I}{PT} = R \quad \text{or} \quad R = \frac{I}{PT}$$

$$\text{Rate} = \frac{\text{Interest}}{\text{Principal} \times \text{Time (in years)}} \quad \text{or} \quad R = \frac{I}{PT}$$

Quick Check Answers

1. $9500
2. $28,200

EXAMPLE 3

Finding Rate Given Length of Loan

An exchange student from the United States living in Brazil deposits \$2500 in U.S. currency in a Brazilian bank for 45 days. Find the rate if the interest is \$37.50 in U.S. currency.

SOLUTION

$$\text{Rate} = \frac{I}{PT}$$

$$R = \frac{\$37.50}{\$2500 \times \frac{45}{360}}$$

$$\$2500 \times \frac{45}{360} = \$312.50 \qquad \text{Simplify the denominator.}$$

$$R = \frac{\$37.50}{\$312.50} = .12 \qquad \text{Divide.}$$

Convert .12 to a percent to get 12%. Check the answer using the simple interest formula.

QUICK CHECK 3

A 120-day loan for \$15,000 has interest of \$412.50. Find the rate to the nearest tenth of a percent.

EXAMPLE 4

Finding Rate Given Length of Loan

Benson Automotive kept extra cash of \$86,500 in an account from June 1 to August 16. Find the rate if the company earned \$365.22 in interest during this period of time.

SOLUTION

Find the number of days using the table on page 329.

August 16 is day	228
June 1 is day	− 152
	76 days

There are 76 days from June 1 to August 16.

$$T = \frac{76}{360}$$

$$\text{Rate} = \frac{I}{PT}$$

$$R = \frac{\$365.22}{\$86{,}500 \times \frac{76}{360}} = .02 \text{ (rounded)}$$

The rate of interest is 2%.

QUICK CHECK 4

A loan of \$37,000 made on February 4 results in interest of \$770.83. If the loan is due on May 15, find the rate to the nearest tenth of a percent.

OBJECTIVE 3 Find the time. The time (T) is found by dividing both sides of the simple interest equation $I = PRT$ by PR. Note that time will be in years or fraction of a year. See Appendix A for a review of algebra if needed.

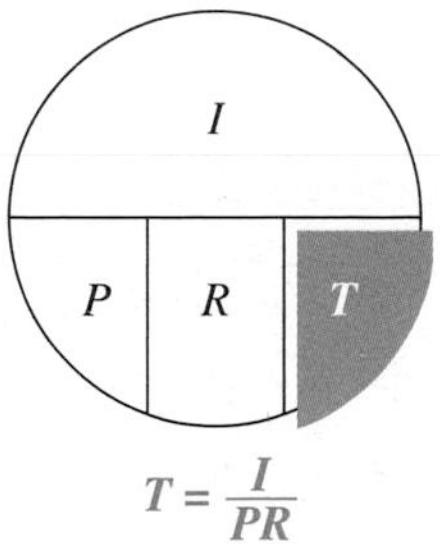

$T = \frac{I}{PR}$

$$I = PRT$$

$$\frac{I}{PR} = \frac{PRT}{PR} \qquad \text{Divide both sides by } PR.$$

$$\frac{I}{PR} = T \quad \text{or} \quad T = \frac{I}{PR}$$

Quick Check Answers

3. 8.3%
4. 7.5%

$$\text{Time (in years)} = \frac{\text{Interest}}{\text{Principal} \times \text{Rate}} \quad \text{or} \quad T = \frac{I}{PR}$$

This formula gives time in years, but we often need time in days. Convert time in years to time in days by multiplying the time in years by 360. For example, $\frac{1}{2}$ year is $\frac{1}{2} \times 360 = 180$ days.

$$\text{Time in days} = \frac{I}{PR} \times 360$$

Similarly, use the following if time is needed in months.

$$\text{Time in months} = \frac{I}{PR} \times 12$$

EXAMPLE 5

Finding Time in Days Given Principal and Rate

Roberta Sanchez deposited \$6200 in an account paying 3% and she earned \$72.33 in interest. Find the number of days that the deposit earned interest. Round to a whole number of days.

SOLUTION

$$T \text{ in days} = \frac{I}{PR} \times 360$$

$$T = \frac{\$72.33}{\$6200 \times .03} \times 360 = 140 \text{ days (rounded)}$$

The money was on deposit for 140 days.

Use parentheses around the denominator of the fraction to make sure that the calculations are done in the correct order. Round to the nearest day.

72.33 [÷] [(] 6200 [×] .03 [)] [×] 360 [=] 140

QUICK CHECK 5

A loan for \$22,000 results in interest of \$1283.33 at 10.5%. Find the time to the nearest day.

Summary

Interest	$I = PRT$	All of these are modifications of the formula $I = PRT$.
Principal	$P = \frac{I}{RT}$	
Rate	$R = \frac{I}{PT}$	
Time	$T \text{ (in years)} = \frac{I}{PR}$	
	$T \text{ (in months)} = \frac{I}{PR} \times 12$	
	$T \text{ (in days)} = \frac{I}{PR} \times 360$	

Quick Check Answer

5. 200 days

8.2 | EXERCISES

The **QUICK START** exercises in each section contain solutions to help you get started.

Find the principal in each of the following. Round to the nearest cent. (See Example 1.)

QUICK START

	Rate	Time (in days)	Interest	Principal
1.	$7\frac{3}{4}\%$	90	$271.25	**$14,000**

$$P = \frac{\$271.25}{.0775 \times \frac{90}{360}} = \$14,000$$

	Rate	Time (in days)	Interest	Principal
2.	9.5%	120	$63.79	**$2014.42**

$$P = \frac{\$63.79}{.095 \times \frac{120}{360}} = \$2014.42$$

	Rate	Time (in days)	Interest	Principal
3.	10%	80	$11.20	_____
4.	6%	24	$6.24	_____
5.	$8\frac{1}{2}\%$	120	$306	_____
6.	10.5%	140	$87.20	_____

Find the rate in each of the following. Round to the nearest tenth of a percent. (See Example 3.)

QUICK START

	Principal	Time	Interest	Rate
7.	$7600	200 days	$498.22	**11.8%**

$$R = \frac{\$498.22}{\$7600 \times \frac{200}{360}} = 11.8\%$$

	Principal	Time	Interest	Rate
8.	$15,600	90 days	$312	_____
9.	$42,800	60 days	$677.67	_____

▼ indicates an exercise that is related to the Case in Point feature.

	Principal	Time	Interest	Rate
10.	$2000	90 days	$62.50	______
11.	$8000	4 months	$200	______
12.	$4800	5 months	$197.60	______

Find the time in each of the following. In Exercises 13–16, round to the nearest day; in Exercises 17 and 18, round to the nearest month. (See Example 5.)

QUICK START

	Principal	Rate	Interest	Time
13.	$74,000	9.5%	$2343.33	120 days

$$T = \frac{\$2343.33}{\$74{,}000 \times .095} \times 360 = 119.9998 \text{ or } 120 \text{ days}$$

	Principal	Rate	Interest	Time
14.	$3600	9%	$58.50	______
15.	$2400	11%	$45.47	______
16.	$20,000	8%	$1200	______
17.	$3500	$10\frac{1}{4}\%$	$143.50	______
18.	$8400	$7\frac{1}{4}\%$	$357	______

In each of the following application problems, find principal to the nearest cent, rate to the nearest tenth of a percent, or time to the nearest day.

QUICK START

19. MONEY MARKET Liz Nault earned $196.88 interest in 9 months from a money market account paying 3.5% interest. Find the amount initially invested.

19. $7500.19

$$P = \frac{\$196.88}{.035 \times \frac{9}{12}} = \$7500.19$$

20. BANK LOAN Citizens Bank earned $12,250 interest in 45 days from a short-term investment that paid 5.6% interest. Find the amount initially invested.

20. ______

21. INVESTING IN BONDS Joan Gretz invested $3600 in a mutual fund containing bonds. Find the rate if she earned $237.50 in interest in 250 days.

21. ______

22. LAW ENFORCEMENT The Smith County Police Department borrowed $120,000 for 135 days to purchase new radar-detection equipment to detect speeders. Find the rate if the interest was $4050.

22. ____________

C 23. INVENTORY Benson Automotive was offered a discount on all new models that were purchased within 15 days. Jane Benson worked out an agreement with her bank to borrow $180,000 with interest charges of $6300 in 140 days. Find the rate.

23. ____________

24. SAVING FOR RETIREMENT Mike Jordan deposited $2000 into a Roth Individual Retirement Account (IRA) investing in a mutual fund containing corporate bonds. Find the rate if he has $2192.50 in the account 15 months later.

24. ____________

25. RETIREMENT ACCOUNT Over a period of 300 days, Shawna Johnson earned $450 interest in a retirement account paying interest at a rate of 5%. Find **(a)** the principal at the beginning of the 300 days and **(b)** the amount in the account at the end of 300 days.

(a) ____________
(b) ____________

26. INTEREST EARNINGS Patterson Plumbing had an account that earned $214.67 interest in 280 days. If the interest rate was 4%, find **(a)** the principal at the beginning of the 280 days and **(b)** the amount in the account at the end of the 280 days.

(a) ____________
(b) ____________

C 27. TIME OF DEPOSIT Benson Automotive earned $69.46 interest on a $9400 deposit in an account paying 3.5%. Find the number of days that the funds were on deposit.

27. ____________

28. TIME OF DEPOSIT Find how long Quinlan Enterprises must deposit $7500 at 6% in order to earn $243.75 interest.

28. ____________

29. RATE OF INTEREST Ti Lee earns $223.03 in interest in 320 days after making a deposit of $6272.73. Find the interest rate.

29. ____________

30. PENALTY ON LATE PAYMENT Smithville Used Toyota lets an $1800 mortgage payment go 70 days overdue and is charged a penalty of $59.50. Find the rate of interest that was charged as a penalty. (*Note:* Penalty rates are frequently quite high.)

30. ____________

31. COMPUTER PURCHASE Ideal Computers purchased 10 computers from a Chinese computer manufacturer. Ideal paid the bill after 45 days, paying a finance charge of $150. If the Chinese company charges 10% interest, find **(a)** the cost of the 10 computers excluding the interest and **(b)** the cost per computer.

(a) ____________
(b) ____________

32. LAWN-MOWER PURCHASE Yard Mowers, Inc., bought 15 self-propelled, 22-inch lawn mowers from Green Lawns, Ltd. The company paid after 90 days and was charged an annual finance charge of 12% or $126. Find **(a)** the cost of the 15 lawn mowers excluding the interest and **(b)** the cost per mower.

(a) ____________
(b) ____________

33. PROMISSORY NOTE Jan Rice signed a promissory note for $640 at $11\frac{1}{2}\%$ interest with interest charges of $42.52. Find the term of the note to the nearest day.

33. ____________

34. TIME OF DEPOSIT The Frampton Chamber of Commerce earns $682.71 interest on a $16,385 investment at 5.5%. Find the length of time of the investment to the nearest day.

34. ____________

35. HOME CONSTRUCTION Gilbert Construction Company needs to borrow $220,000 for 1 year for materials needed to build three homes. They can borrow from either of two banks. Interest charges from Bank One would amount to $23,650, whereas interest charges from First National Bank would amount to $25,000. Find the interest rates associated with a loan from **(a)** Bank One and **(b)** First National Bank.

(a) ____________
(b) ____________

36. INVENTORY PURCHASE Forest Nursery needs to borrow $9500 on February 1 to buy additional inventory and will repay the loan on July 15. Interest charges for State Bank and First National Bank are $480 and $443.60, respectively. Find the rate for **(a)** the State Bank loan and **(b)** the First National Bank loan.

(a) ____________
(b) ____________

37. A retired couple receives $14,000 per year from Social Security and an additional $18,000 in interest from retirement plans and lifetime savings. They need all of their income to pay expenses including medical bills. What will happen will if the interest rate on their retirement plans and lifetime savings decreases significantly?

38. How would the formula for calculating time in days (given principal, interest, and rate) change if exact interest were used rather than ordinary interest?

8.3 SIMPLE DISCOUNT NOTES

OBJECTIVES

1. Define the basic terms used with simple discount notes.
2. Find the bank discount and proceeds.
3. Find the face value.
4. Find the effective interest rate.
5. Understand U.S. Treasury bills.

CASE *in* POINT In the past, Benson Automotive often borrowed funds to purchase new automobiles to place on its car lot. It wasn't that owner Jane Benson liked debt. In fact, she strongly disliked debt and was very careful with it. However, the cost of new cars was so high that she commonly had to borrow. Benson knows that interest rates change and that higher rates result in higher costs and lower profits. To help minimize interest costs and determine whether to borrow, she tries to understand the direction in which interest rates are moving.

HERE & NOW

Economists Differ

All eyes are on the Fed chairman while economists wait for the outcome of the next meeting. Economists differ in the direction they expect interest rates to go from here. Some expect the Fed to increase interest rates slightly next year, but others think rates will remain the same or decrease slightly.

In this section, we discuss **simple discount notes**, which are simply a different way to set up a promissory note based on simple interest calculations. Any note that uses simple interest calculations with a lump-sum payment can be set up *either* as a simple interest note or as a simple discount note. One type of note is *not* better than the other type of note. They merely represent two different ways to discuss the same thing. We study both because some banks use simple interest notes while others use simple discount notes.

QUICK TIP College students sometimes borrow money from the government using **Stafford loans**, which are simple discount notes.

OBJECTIVE 1 Define the basic terms used with simple discount notes. As we saw in **Section 8.2**, simple interest notes involve principal (face value or loan amount), interest rate, time, interest, and maturity value. Simple discount notes involve **proceeds (loan amount), discount rate, time, bank discount, (interest)** and **face value** (or **maturity value**). Face value in a simple interest note is the amount loaned to the borrower, but it is the maturity value in a simple discount note. Simple discount notes are also called **interest-in-advance notes**, since interest is subtracted before funds are given to the borrower. A basic difference between the two types of notes is that simple interest is calculated based on principal, whereas simple discount is calculated based on maturity value, as shown in the table.

QUICK TIP Simple interest is calculated on the *principal*, while simple discount is calculated on the *maturity value*.

Simple Interest versus Simple Discount Notes

Type of Note	Loan Amount		Interest		Repayment Amount
Simple interest	Face value **(Principal)**	+	Interest	=	Maturity value
Simple discount	Proceeds	+	Discount **(Interest)**	=	Face value **(Maturity value)**

OBJECTIVE 2 Find the bank discount and proceeds. The formula for finding the bank discount is a form of the basic percent equation of Chapter 3. The formula is similar to the one used to calculate simple interest, but different letters are used since the ideas differ slightly.

QUICK TIP Simple interest rate *applies to the principal* of a simple interest note. Simple discount rate *applies to the face value or maturity value* of a simple discount note.

Calculating Bank Discount

Bank discount = Face value × Discount rate × Time or $B = MDT$

where

B = Bank discount
M = Face value (maturity value)
D = Discount rate
T = Time (in years)

Then, if P is the proceeds,

Proceeds (loan amount) = Face value − Bank discount or $P = M - B$

Stated in another way,

Face value = Proceeds (loan amount) + Bank discount or $M = P + B$

EXAMPLE 1

Finding Discount and Proceeds

Jim Peterson signs a simple discount note with a face value of $35,000 so that he can purchase a truck with plow for his snow removal business. The banker discounts the 10-month note at 9%. Find the amount of the discount and the proceeds.

SOLUTION

First use $B = MDT$, to find the bank discount, where $M = \$35{,}000$, $D = 9\%$, and $T = \frac{10}{12}$, or $\frac{5}{6}$.

$$\textit{Bank discount} = M \times D \times T$$
$$B = \$35{,}000 \times .09 \times \frac{5}{6} = \$2625$$

The discount of $2625 is the interest charge on the loan. The proceeds that Peterson actually receives when making the loan is found using $P = M - B$.

$$\mathbf{P = M - B}$$
$$P = \$35{,}000 - \$2625 = \$32{,}375$$

Peterson signs the discount note with a face value of $35,000, but receives $32,375. Ten months later he must pay $35,000 to the bank.

QUICK CHECK 1

A simple discount loan has a maturity value of $15,800, discount rate of 9%, and time of 180 days. Find the bank discount and proceeds.

EXAMPLE 2

Finding the Proceeds

To finance a new electronic sign to put in front of its retail store, Mustang Auto Sales signs a 6-month, simple discount note with a face value of $4500. Find the proceeds if the discount rate is 10.5%.

SOLUTION

The bank discount (B) is not known, but we do know that $B = MDT$. Therefore, we can substitute MDT in place of B.

$$P = M - B$$
$$P = M - MDT \qquad \text{Substitute } MDT \text{ in place of } B.$$
$$P = \$4500 - \left(\$4500 \times .105 \times \frac{6}{12}\right) \qquad \text{Substitute values.}$$
$$P = \$4263.75$$

Mustang Auto Sales receives $4263.75 but must pay back $4500 in 6 months.

Quick Check Answer

1. $711; $15,089

QUICK CHECK 2

A 220-day loan with a face value of $40,000 has a discount rate of 12%. Find the proceeds.

OBJECTIVE 3 **Find the face value.** If the loan amount (proceeds) of a simple discount note is known, use the following formula to find the corresponding face value.

Calculating Face Value to Achieve Desired Proceeds

$$M = \frac{P}{1 - DT}$$

where

M = Face value of the simple discount note
P = Proceeds received by the borrower
D = Discount rate used by the bank
T = Time of the loan (in years)

NOTE: The symbol D is the discount *rate*, not the bank discount.

EXAMPLE 3

Finding the Face Value

Bill Thompson needs $4000 for 180 days to rebuild his 1956 Oldsmobile. His banker agrees to lend him the money at a 10% discount rate. Find the face value of the simple discount note that would result in proceeds of $4000 to Thompson.

SOLUTION

Use the formula.

$$M = \frac{P}{1 - DT}$$

Replace P with $4000, D with .10, and T with $\frac{180}{360}$.

$$M = \frac{\$4000}{1 - \left(.10 \times \frac{180}{360}\right)} = \$4210.53 \text{ (rounded)}$$

The face value of the note is $4210.53. Thompson receives $4000 in proceeds on signing the note and 180 days later must repay $4210.53 to the bank.

The problem

$$\frac{\$4000}{1 - \left(.10 \times \frac{180}{360}\right)}$$

can be solved using a calculator by first thinking of the problem as shown below with brackets to set off the denominator.

$$\$4000 \div \left[1 - \left(.10 \times \frac{180}{360}\right)\right]$$

The parentheses inside the brackets are not really needed due to order of operations. The problem is then solved as follows.

4000 [÷] [(] 1 [−] .10 [×] 180 [÷] 360 [)] [=] 4210.53 (rounded)

Quick Check Answers

2. $37,066.67
3. $51,798.56

QUICK CHECK 3

A 300-day note has proceeds of $48,000 and a discount rate of 8.8%. Find the maturity value.

27. RACE HORSES Robert Johnson owns a farm and breeds race horses. To purchase three thoroughbreds, he signs a 180-day note with a maturity value of $265,000 and proceeds of $253,737.50. Find **(a)** the discount and **(b)** the true rate.

(a) ____________
(b) ____________

28. PIZZA To remodel the restaurant, Two Brothers Pizza signs a 250-day note with proceeds of $63,159.72 and a maturity value of $68,000. Find **(a)** the discount and **(b)** the APR.

(a) ____________
(b) ____________

The following exercises apply to U.S. Treasury bills, discussed at the end of this section. (Assume 52 weeks per year for each exercise, and round to the nearest hundredth of a percent.) (See Example 6.)

29. PURCHASE OF T-BILLS A large British investment firm purchases $25,000,000 in U.S. T-bills at a 6% discount rate for 13 weeks. Find **(a)** the purchase price of the T-bills, **(b)** the maturity value of the T-bills, **(c)** the interest earned, and **(d)** the effective rate.

(a) ____________
(b) ____________
(c) ____________
(d) ____________

30. T-BILLS Nina Horn buys a $50,000 T-bill at a 5.8% discount rate for 26 weeks. Find **(a)** the purchase price of the T-bill, **(b)** the maturity value, **(c)** the interest earned, and **(d)** the effective rate of interest.

(a) ____________
(b) ____________
(c) ____________
(d) ____________

31. Explain the main differences between simple interest notes and simple discount notes. (See Objective 1.)

32. As a borrower, would you prefer a simple interest note with a rate of 11% or a simple discount note at a rate of 11%? Explain using an example. (See Example 4.)

8.4 DISCOUNTING A NOTE BEFORE MATURITY

OBJECTIVES

1. Understand the concept of discounting a note.
2. Find the proceeds when discounting simple interest notes.
3. Find the proceeds when discounting simple discount notes.

FINANCIAL

#1 U.S. Buyer—First National
Pays the most for notes & contracts. Free Quote. Close in 10 days. 800-555-2324

ARE YOU RECEIVING MORTGAGE Payments? Cash for your note. FREE Quotes. 800-555-9510

Slay Cashes Notes
1st Liens on Real Estate
1-800-555-9400

A note is a *legal responsibility* for one individual or firm to pay a specific amount on a specific date to another individual or firm. Notes can be bought and sold just like a tangible item, such as an automobile can be bought and sold. The clipping taken from a newspaper shows firms that buy notes. This section shows how to find the value of a note that is sold before its maturity date.

OBJECTIVE 1 Understand the concept of discounting a note. Businesses sometimes help their customers purchase products or services by accepting a promissory note rather than requiring an immediate cash payment. For example, a company that manufactures boats, a retailer that sells the boats, and a bank may do business as follows:

1. Boat manufacturer sells boats to a retailer and accepts a promissory note instead of cash.
2. Boat manufacturer needs cash and sells the note to a bank before it matures.
3. Retailer pays the maturity value of the note to the bank when due.

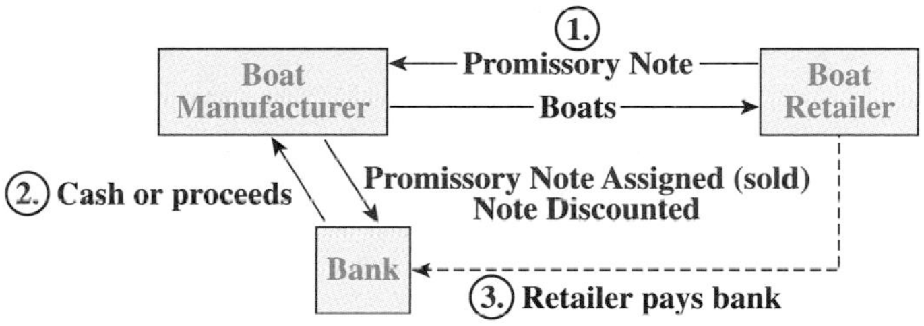

QUICK TIP Both simple interest notes and simple discount notes can be discounted before they mature.

The bank deducts a fee from the maturity value of the note when it buys the note from the manufacturer. The fee is interest for the number of days, called the **discount period**, that the bank will hold the note until it is due. The fee charged by the bank is the **bank discount** or just **discount**. The **discount rate** is the percent used by the bank to find the discount. The process of finding the value of the note on a specific date before it matures is **discounting the note**.

OBJECTIVE 2 Find the proceeds when discounting simple interest notes. The amount of cash actually received by the boat manufacturer on the sale of a promissory note is the **proceeds**. The bank then collects the maturity value from the maker of the note, the retailer, when it is due. These notes are usually sold with **recourse**. This means that the bank receives reimbursement from the manufacturer if the retailer does not pay the bank when the note matures. Thus the bank is protected against loss. Many banks refuse to buy these types of notes unless they have recourse.

The figure on the next page shows the Federal rate that is set by the government. It is used to influence economic activity by changing the cost of borrowing money. The figure shows that interest rates change frequently. As a result, it is common for the rate at which a note is discounted to differ from the original rate of the loan.

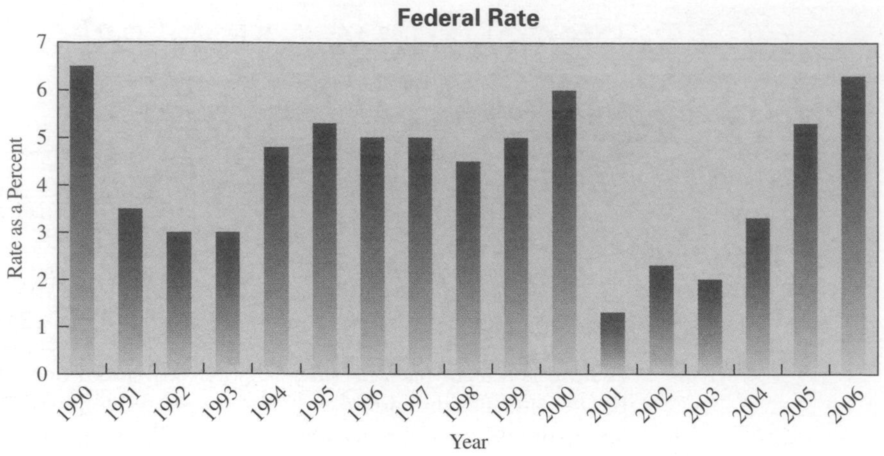

Calculate the Proceeds When Discounting a Simple Interest Note

1. First, understand the simple interest note by finding:
   (a) the **due date** of the original note and
   (b) the **maturity value** of the original note ($M = P + I$, where $I = PRT$).
2. Then discount the simple interest note.
   (a) Find the **discount period**, which is the time (e.g., number of days) from the sale of the note to the maturity date of the note.
   (b) Find the **discount** using the formula

$$B = M \times D \times T$$
$$= \text{Maturity value} \times \textit{Discount rate} \times \textit{Discount period}$$

   (c) Find the **proceeds** after discounting the original note using $P = M - B$.

EXAMPLE 1

Finding Proceeds

QUICK TIP A company that sells a note before it matures receives less money than if it waits until the loan matures. However, the firm will receive funds earlier than if it waits.

Jameson Plumbing takes a simple interest, 180-day note from a contractor with a face value of \$64,750 and a rate of 10.5%. The company sells the note 50 days later at a discount rate of 12%. Find the proceeds to the plumbing company.

SOLUTION

STEP 1 ***Find the maturity value.*** The face value equals the proceeds, since this is a simple interest note.

$$\text{Maturity value} = \text{Principal} + \text{Interest on the simple interest note}$$
$$\text{Maturity value} = \$64{,}750 + PRT$$
$$\text{Maturity value} = \$64{,}750 + \$64{,}750 \times .105 \times \frac{180}{360} = \$68{,}149.38 \text{ (rounded)}$$

STEP 2 The note is discounted after 50 days, so the discount period is 180 − 50 = 130 days. This means that the buyer of the note will own it for 130 days before the note is paid off.

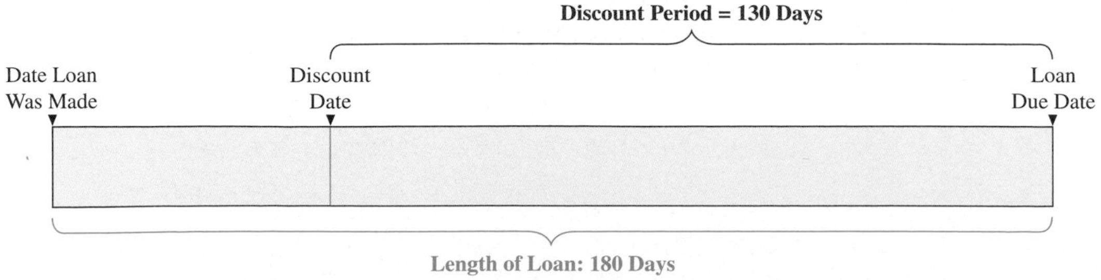

$$\text{Bank discount} = MDT = \$68{,}149.38 \times .12 \times \frac{130}{360} = \$2953.14$$
$$\text{Proceeds} = \text{Maturity value of simple interest note} - \text{Bank discount}$$
$$\text{Proceeds} = \$68{,}149.38 - \$2953.14 = \$65{,}196.24$$

QUICK CHECK 1

A simple interest note has a face value of $14,000, a rate of 9%, and a time to maturity of 240 days. It is discounted after 80 days at a rate of 11%. Find the maturity value of the simple interest note and the proceeds at the time of the discount.

EXAMPLE 2

Finding Proceeds

Blues Recording holds a 200-day simple interest note from a rock group that agreed to pay them to record an album and produce 1000 CDs. The 12% simple interest note is dated March 24 and has a face value of $4800. Blues Recording wishes to convert the note to cash, so they sell it to a bank on August 15. If there is a discount rate of 12.5%, find the proceeds to the recording studio.

SOLUTION

Go through the four steps of discounting a note.

STEP 1 ***Find the maturity value.*** The note is dated March 24 and is due in 200 days. The due date is found as follows.

$$\text{day } 83 \text{ (March 24)} + 200 \text{ days} = \text{day } 283 \text{ (October 10)}$$

Since this is a simple interest note, the proceeds are given but the maturity value must be found. First find the **interest** on the note if held until maturity.

$$I = PRT = \$4800 \times .12 \times \frac{200}{360} = \$320$$

The **maturity value** is $4800 + $320 = $5120.

STEP 2 Now discount this simple interest note.

(a) ***Find the discount period.*** The **discount period** is the number of days from August 15, which is the date the note is discounted (sold) to the bank, to the due date of the note (October 10).

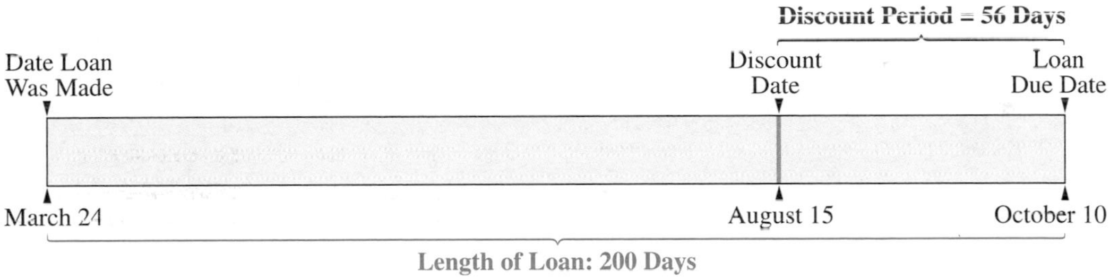

October 10 is day	283
August 15 is day	− 227
Discount period	56 days

Blues Recording holds the 200-day note for 200 − 56 = 144 days before they sell it. The buyer of the note holds it for 56 days before the rock group must pay off the note.

QUICK TIP When finding the bank discount, be sure to use the maturity value of the original note.

(b) ***Find the bank discount.*** Find the **discount** by using the formula $B = MDT$, where $M = \$5120$, $D = 12.5\%$, and T is $\frac{56}{360}$.

$$B = MDT = \$5120 \times .125 \times \frac{56}{360} = \$99.56 \text{ (rounded)}$$

The bank discount is $99.56.

(c) ***Find the proceeds.*** **Proceeds** are found by subtracting the bank discount from the maturity value.

$$P = M - B$$
$$P = \$5120 - \$99.56 = \$5020.44$$

Date	Transaction
March 24	Rock group signs 200-day simple interest note for $4800.
August 15	Blues Recording sells note to bank for $5020.44.
October 10	Bank receives $5120 from payer (rock group).

Quick Check Answer

1. $14,840; $14,114.49

QUICK CHECK 2

On March 27, Dayton Finance loans Jorge Rivera $9200 for 150 days at 11% simple interest. The finance company sells the note to a private investor on April 24. Find the maturity value of the simple interest note and the proceeds to Dayton Finance if the note is sold at a discount rate of 12%.

It is also common for a business needing cash to sell part of its accounts receivable (money owed to the company) before it is due. The process is called **factoring**, and those who buy the accounts receivable are called **factors**. The calculations involved in factoring are the same as those for finding the discount discussed in this section.

OBJECTIVE 3 Find the proceeds when discounting simple discount notes.

Calculate the Proceeds When Discounting a Simple Discount Note

1. First, understand the simple discount note by finding:
   (a) the **due date** of the original note,
   (b) the **discount** of the original note using $B = MDT$, and
   (c) the **proceeds** from the original note using $P = M - B$.
   The **maturity value (face value)** of the note is written on the note itself and is the value needed in step 2(b) below.
2. Then discount the simple discount note.
   (a) Find the **discount period**, which is the time (e.g., number of days) from the sale of the note to the maturity date of the note.
   (b) Find the **discount** using the formula $B = MDT$.
   (c) Find the **proceeds** after discounting the original note using $P = M - B$.

QUICK TIP There are two different discounts in problems of this type. The first occurs when the original note is signed. The second discount occurs when this note is sold before maturity.

The steps for finding the proceeds at the time of sale are shown for a U.S. Treasury bill in Example 3. The calculations to find the proceeds are the same for any simple discount note.

EXAMPLE 3

Finding the Proceeds

Benson Automotive used excess cash to purchase a $100,000 Treasury bill with a term of 26 weeks at a 6.5% simple discount rate. However, the firm needs cash exactly 8 weeks later and sells the T-bill. During the 8 weeks, market interest rates moved up slightly so that the bill was sold at a 7% discount rate. Find **(a)** the initial purchase price of the T-bill, **(b)** the proceeds received by the firm at the subsequent sale of the T-bill, and **(c)** the effective interest rate received by Benson Automotive.

SOLUTION

(a) ***Find the discount and proceeds.*** The discount that Benson Automotive receives when buying the T-bill is found as follows.

$$B = MDT = \$100{,}000 \times .065 \times \frac{26}{52} = \$3250$$

The cost to the company is the maturity value minus the discount.

$$P = M - B = \$100{,}000 - \$3250 = \$96{,}750$$

Therefore, the U.S. government receives $96,750 from the sale of the T-bill.

Quick Check Answer

2. $9621.67; $9230.39

(b) ***Find the discount period, discount, and proceeds.*** Now follow the steps in the table on the previous page to find the proceeds Benson Automotive receives for selling the T-bill 8 weeks later. The discount period is 18 weeks, since the T-bill is sold 26 − 8 = 18 weeks before its due date.

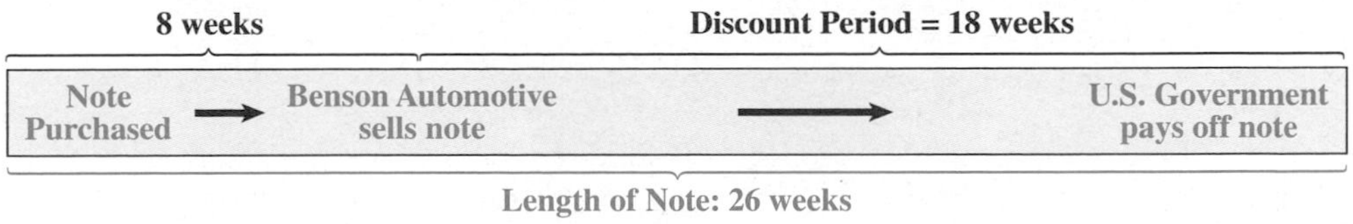

The discount at the time of the sale is as follows.

$$B = MDT = \$100{,}000 \times .07 \times \frac{18}{52} = \$2423.08$$

Finally, the proceeds equal the maturity value of the T-bill ($100,000) less the discount at the time of the sale.

$$P - M - B = \$100{,}000 - \$2423.08 = \$97{,}576.92$$

(c) Benson Automotive paid $96,750 to buy the T-bill and received $97,576.92 for it 8 weeks later.

$$\text{Interest received} = \$97{,}576.92 - \$96{,}750 = \$826.92$$

$$R = \frac{\$826.92}{\$96{,}750 \times \frac{8}{52}} = 5.56\% \text{ (rounded)}$$

The company would have earned 6.5% on the T-bill had it left the Treasury bill invested until maturity. Instead, the company sold it after market interest rates rose, but before the T-bill matured. This caused the company to end up with an effective interest rate somewhat less than 6.5%.

QUICK CHECK 3

A 240-day discount note has a maturity value of $24,000 and a discount rate of 8%. It is sold after 100 days at a discount rate of 10.5%. Find the maturity value of the original discount note and the proceeds at the time of the sale.

Quick Check Answer

3. $24,000; $23,020

Case Studies

General Motors

www.gm.com

- 1908 General Motors founded
- 1952 Power steering is offered by Cadillac, Oldsmobile, and Buick
- 2005–2006 GM lays off thousands of workers
- 80 miles per gallon vehicles may be possible in 10–15 years
- 2007 GM ends 2-day worker's strike

General Motors (GM) has been in business for 100 years. You may recognize some of the brand names that it produces: Buick, Cadillac, Chevrolet, GMC, Holden, HUMMER, Opel, Pontiac, Saab, Saturn, and Vauxhall. Additionally, it markets automobiles made by GM Daewoo, Isuzu, Subaru, and Suzuki.

GM has operations in 33 countries and sells vehicles in 190 countries. It sold more than 9 million cars and trucks in 2006 and had about 15% of the total worldwide market. The company owns part of GMAC, a large financial services company that lends money to individuals to purchase cars or homes, but also lends to businesses. The 2006 total revenue for GM exceeded $190 billion.

1. Assume that GM sells 2.7 million trucks and sport utility vehicles (SUVs) at an average price of $32,140 in 1 year. Find the total revenue.

2. Assume that GM borrows $850 million for 216 days from Bank of America. Find the interest and the maturity value if the rate is 6%.

3. Bank of America sells the above note after 96 days to the Bank of New York. Find the discount period and the proceeds to Bank of America if the discount rate is 6.3%.

4. Use the World Wide Web to find GM's Total Revenue (from GM's Income Statement) and Total Current Liabilities (from its Balance Sheet) for the most recent year.

8.4 EXERCISES

FOR EXTRA HELP

MyMathLab

MathXL PRACTICE

WATCH

DOWNLOAD

READ

REVIEW

The **QUICK START** *exercises in each section contain solutions to help you get started.*

Find the discount period for each of the following. (See Examples 2 and 3, Step 2.)

QUICK START

	Date Loan Was Made	Length of Loan	Date of Discount	Discount Period
1.	Apr. 29	200 days	July 31	**107 days**
2.	July 28	120 days	Sept. 20	________
3.	May 28	74 days	June 18	________
4.	Sept. 17	130 days	Jan. 13	________

Find the proceeds to the nearest cent when each of the following is discounted. (Hint: The maturity value is given.) (See Examples 1 and 2.)

QUICK START

	Maturity Value	Discount Rate	Discount Period	Proceeds
5.	$10,400	8.5%	90 days	**$10,179**
	$B = \$10{,}400 \times .085 \times \frac{90}{360} = \$221$; $P = \$10{,}400 - \$221 = \$10{,}179$			
6.	$4800	10.3%	200 days	________
7.	$2500	9%	30 days	________
8.	$3000	11%	60 days	________

Find the maturity value of each of the following simple interest notes. Each note is then discounted at 12%. Find the discount period, the discount, and the proceeds after discounting. (See Examples 1 and 2.)

QUICK START

	Date Loan Was Made	Face Value	Length of Loan	Rate	Maturity Value	Date of Discount	Discount Period	Discount	Proceeds
9.	Feb. 7	$6200	90 days	$10\frac{1}{2}\%$	**$6362.75**	Apr. 1	**37 days**	**$78.47**	**$6284.28**

$I = \$6200 \times .105 \times \frac{90}{360} = \$162.75$; $M = \$6200 + \$162.75 = \$6362.75$

Feb. 7 is day 38; Apr. 1 is day 91; 91 − 38 = 53

Discount period = 90 − 53 = 37 days

$B = \$6362.75 \times .12 \times \frac{37}{360} = \$78.47$

Proceeds = $6362.75 − $78.47 = $6284.28

C indicates an exercise that is related to the Case in Point feature.

Date Loan Was Made	Face Value	Length of Loan	Rate	Maturity Value	Date of Discount	Discount Period	Discount	Proceeds
10. June 15	$9200	140 days	12%	_____	Oct. 22	_____	_____	_____
11. July 10	$2000	72 days	11%	_____	Aug. 2	_____	_____	_____
12. May 29	$5500	80 days	10%	_____	July 8	_____	_____	_____

First, find the initial proceeds of each of the following simple discount notes. Each note is then discounted at 11%. Find the discount period, the discount, and the proceeds after discounting. (See Example 3.)

QUICK START

Date Loan Was Made	Maturity Value	Length of Loan	Rate	Initial Proceeds	Date of Discount	Discount Period	Discount	Proceeds at Time of Sale
13. Jan. 12	$17,800	90 days	10%	**$17,355**	Mar. 1	**42 days**	**$228.43**	**$17,571.57**

$B = MDT = \$17,800 \times .10 \times \frac{90}{360} = \$445; \; P = M - B = \$17,800 - \$445 = \$17,355$

Jan. 12 is day 12; Due date is 12 + 90 = 102 or Apr. 12

Mar. 1 is day 60; Discount period is 102 − 60 = 42 days

$B = MDT = \$17,800 \times .11 \times \frac{42}{360} = \228.43

$P = M - B = \$17,800 - \$228.43 = \$17,571.57$

14. Aug. 4	$24,000	120 days	10.5%	_____	Oct. 8	_____	_____	_____
15. May 4	$32,100	150 days	9.5%	_____	July 10	_____	_____	_____

	Date Loan Was Made	*Maturity Value*	*Length of Loan*	*Rate*	*Initial Proceeds*	*Date of Discount*	*Discount Period*	*Discount*	*Proceeds at Time of Sale*
16.	Apr. 30	$22,000	200 days	9%	______	July 12	______	______	______

Solve the following application problems. Round interest and discount to the nearest cent.

QUICK START

17. ROCK CRUSHER First Bank loaned $360,000 for 180 days to a company purchasing a rock-crushing machine. The bank sold the 7% simple interest note 120 days later at an 8% discount rate. Find **(a)** the bank discount and **(b)** the proceeds.

(a) $4968
(b) $367,632

(a) $M = \$360{,}000 + \left(\$360{,}000 \times .07 \times \frac{180}{360}\right) = \$372{,}600$ (b) $P = \$372{,}600 - \$4968 = \$367{,}632$

Discount period = 180 days − 120 days = 60 days

$B = \$372{,}600 \times .08 \times \frac{60}{360} = \$4968$

18. TRACTOR PURCHASE Cook and Daughters Farm Equipment accepts a $5800 simple interest note at 12% for 100 days, for a small used tractor. The note is dated May 12. On June 17, the firm discounts the note at the bank, at a 13% discount rate. Find **(a)** the bank discount and **(b)** the proceeds.

(a) ______
(b) ______

19. AUTOMOBILE DEALERSHIP Benson Automotive signed a 180-day simple discount note with a face value of $250,000 and a rate of 9% on March 19. The lender sells the note at an 8% discount rate on June 14. Find **(a)** the proceeds of the original note to the dealership, **(b)** the discount period, **(c)** the discount, and **(d)** the proceeds at the sale of the note on June 14.

(a) ______
(b) ______
(c) ______
(d) ______

20. SEWING CENTER Kathy Bates, owner of Marie's Sewing Center, agreed to a 10% simple discount note with a maturity value of $18,500 on July 30. She planned to add to her inventory of sewing machines with the funds. The 120-day note is sold by the lender at a 12% discount rate on September 2. Find **(a)** the proceeds of the original note to Bates, **(b)** the discount period, **(c)** the discount, and **(d)** the proceeds at the sale of the note on September 2.

(a) ______
(b) ______
(c) ______
(d) ______

21. FINANCING CONSTRUCTION To build a new building for its body shop, Benson Automotive signed a $300,000 simple interest note at 9% for 150 days with National Bank on November 20. On February 6, National Bank sold all of its notes to Bank One. Find **(a)** the maturity value of the note and **(b)** the proceeds to National Bank given a discount rate of 10.5%.

(a) ______________
(b) ______________

22. BATTERY STORE An NTB outlet borrowed $48,500 on a 200-day simple interest note to expand the battery store. The note was signed on December 28 and carried an interest rate of 9.8%. The note was then sold on March 17 at a discount rate of 10%. Find **(a)** the maturity value of the note and **(b)** the proceeds to the seller of the note on May 17.

(a) ______________
(b) ______________

23. PURCHASE OF A T-BILL Elizabeth Barton bought a $25,000, 26-week T-bill at a discount rate of 6.8% on August 7. She sold it 10 weeks later at a discount rate of 7%. Find **(a)** Barton's purchase price, **(b)** the discount 10 weeks later when she sold it, **(c)** the proceeds to Barton, and **(d)** the effective interest rate rounded to the nearest hundredth of a percent for the time Barton held the note.

(a) ______________
(b) ______________
(c) ______________
(d) ______________

24. PURCHASE OF A T-BILL Tina Klein bought a $10,000, 7.5%, 52-week T-bill on June 29 and sold it 26 weeks later at a discount rate of 8%. Find Klein's **(a)** purchase price for the T-bill, **(b)** the discount at time of sale, **(c)** the proceeds to Klein, and **(d)** the effective interest rate rounded to the nearest hundredth of a percent.

(a) ______________
(b) ______________
(c) ______________
(d) ______________

25. Explain the procedure used to determine the bank discount and the proceeds for a note. (See Objective 2.)

26. Explain the effect of a rise in general market interest rates on an investor who is holding notes. Give an example. (See Example 3.)

SUPPLEMENTARY APPLICATION EXERCISES ON SIMPLE INTEREST AND SIMPLE DISCOUNT

The **QUICK START** *exercises in each section contain solutions to help you get started.*

There are similarities and differences between simple interest and simple discount calculations. This exercise set compares these two important concepts. First, the key similarities between the two are as follows.

1. Both types of notes involve lump sums repaid with a single payment at the end of a stated period of time.
2. The length of time is generally 1 year or less.

The following table compares simple interest and simple discount notes.

	Simple Interest Note	**Simple Discount Note**
Variables	I = Interest	B = Discount
	P = Principal (face value)	P = Proceeds
	R = Rate of interest	D = Discount rate
	T = Time, in years or fraction of a year	T = Time, in years or fraction of a year
	M = Maturity value	M = Maturity value (face value)
Face value	Stated on note	Same as maturity value
Interest charge	$I = PRT$	$B = MDT$
Maturity value	$M = P + I$	Same as face value
Amount received by borrower	Face value or principal	Proceeds: $P = M - B$
Identifying phrases	Interest at a certain rate	Discount at a certain rate
	Maturity value greater than face value	Proceeds
		Maturity value equal to face value
Effective interest rate	Same as stated rate, R	Greater than stated rate, D

QUICK TIP The variable P is used for *principal or face value* in simple interest notes, but P is used for *proceeds* in simple discount notes. P represents the amount received by the borrower.

Solve the following application problems. Round rates to the nearest tenth of a percent, time to the nearest day, and money to the nearest cent.

QUICK START

1. The owner of Redwood Furniture, Inc., signed a 120-day note for $18,000 at 11% simple interest. Find **(a)** the interest and **(b)** the maturity value.

   (a) $I = PRT = \$18{,}000 \times .11 \times \frac{120}{360} = \$660$

   (b) $M = \$18{,}000 + \$660 = \$18{,}660$

   (a) $660 **(b)** $18,660

2. Bill Travis signed a note for $18,500 with his uncle to start an auto repair shop on Commerce Street. The note is due in 300 days and has a discount rate of 14%. Travis hopes that a bank will refinance the note for him at a lower rate after he has been in business for 300 days. Find the proceeds.

   $B = \$18{,}500 \times .14 \times \frac{300}{360} = \$2158.33$; $P = \$18{,}500 - \$2158.33 = \$16{,}341.67$

   2. $16,341.67

C indicates an exercise that is related to the Case in Point feature.

3. James Watkins signed a note with a 10% simple interest rate, interest of $2400, and time of 180 days. Find the principal.

3. ________________

4. Bill Abel signed a simple interest note at a rate of only 6% because he had excellent collateral—a $200,000 CD at the same bank. If the loan matures in 300 days and the interest is $9000, find the principal.

4. ________________

5. Benson Automotive signed a $150,000 note at a simple discount rate of 10.5% and a discount of $8750. Find the length of the loan in days.

5. ________________

6. A loan to a German bank was for $1,290,000 with a maturity value of $1,327,410 and a rate of 6%. Find the time.

6. ________________

7. Jane Benson of Benson Automotive loaned her nephew $20,000 for 150 days at 9% simple interest. Find **(a)** the interest and **(b)** the maturity value.

(a) ________________
(b) ________________

8. John O'Neill borrowed $24,000 for 250 days at 7% simple interest. Find **(a)** the interest and **(b)** the maturity value.

(a) ________________
(b) ________________

9. BlueWater Pools signed a 5-month, $145,000 note at an 11.5% discount rate. Find the effective rate of interest.

9. ________________

10. First Bank signed an 80-day, $82,000 note at a 12% discount rate. Find the effective rate of interest.

10. ________________

11. On October 14, Citibank loaned $10,000,000 to Fleet Mortgage Company for 180 days at a 10.5% discount rate. Find **(a)** the due date and **(b)** the proceeds.

(a) ________________
(b) ________________

12. On December 24, Junella Martin signed a 100-day note for $80,000 for a new Jaguar. Given a discount rate of 11%, find **(a)** the due date and **(b)** the proceeds.

(a) ________________
(b) ________________

13. Lupe Galvez has a serious problem: two of her more energetic preschoolers keep getting out of the yard of her child-care center. She signs a note with interest charges of $670.83 to reinforce the fence around the entire yard. The simple interest note is for 140 days at 11.5%. Find the principal to the nearest dollar.

13. ____________

14. Quality Furnishings accepted a 270-day, $8000 note on May 25. The interest rate on the note is 12% simple interest. The note was then discounted at 14% on August 7. Find the proceeds.

14. ____________

15. On November 19, a firm accepts an $18,000, 150-day note with a simple interest rate of 9%. The firm discounts the note at 12% on February 2. Find the proceeds.

15. ____________

16. Barton's Flowers accepted a $16,000, 150-day note from Wedded Bliss Catering. The note had a simple interest rate of 11% and was accepted on May 12. The note was then discounted at 13% on July 20. Find the proceeds to Barton's Flowers.

16. ____________

17. Leon Herbert signed a 220-day, 10% simple interest note with a face value of $28,000. In turn, the bank he borrowed the money from sold the note 90 days later at an 11% discount rate. Find **(a)** the interest, **(b)** the maturity value, **(c)** the discount period, **(d)** the discount, and **(e)** the proceeds to the bank.

(a) ____________
(b) ____________
(c) ____________
(d) ____________
(e) ____________

18. Janice Dart signed a 140-day simple discount note at a rate of 9.9% with a maturity value of $82,000. The bank she borrowed the funds from sold the note 40 days later at a 10% discount rate. Find **(a)** the discount on the original note, **(b)** the proceeds of the original note, **(c)** the discount period, **(d)** the discount at the time of sale, and **(e)** the proceeds to the bank at the time of sale.

(a) ____________
(b) ____________
(c) ____________
(d) ____________
(e) ____________

19. James and Tiffany Paterson need a 220-day loan for $68,000 to open Adventure Sports Unlimited. Bank One agrees to a simple interest note with a loan amount of $68,000 at $9\frac{1}{4}$% interest. Union Bank agrees to a simple discount note with proceeds of $68,000 and a 9.5% simple discount rate. Find **(a)** the interest for the simple interest note, **(b)** the maturity value of the discount note, **(c)** the interest for the discount note, and **(d)** the savings in interest charges of the simple interest note over the discount note.

(a) ____________
(b) ____________
(c) ____________
(d) ____________

20. Gilbert Construction Company needs to borrow $380,000 for $1\frac{1}{2}$ years to purchase some land to subdivide. One bank offers the firm a simple interest note with a principal of $380,000 and a rate of 12%. A second bank offers the company a discount note with proceeds of $380,000 and an 11% discount rate. **(a)** Which note produces the lower interest charges? **(b)** What is the difference in interest?

(a) ____________
(b) ____________

21. Show with an example that the effective interest rate is higher than the discount rate stated on a note.

22. Explain the difference in the meaning of the variable *P* (principal) in a simple interest note and the variable *P* (proceeds) in a simple discount note.

23. What is interest? Why is interest used?

24. Why might a bank use ordinary interest rather than exact interest?

CHAPTER 8 QUICK REVIEW

CHAPTER TERMS *Review the following terms to test your understanding of the chapter. For each term you do not know, refer to the page number found next to that term.*

annual percentage rate (APR) **[p. 348]**
bank discount **[p. 345]**
banker's interest **[p. 330]**
collateral **[p. 331]**
compound interest **[p. 326]**
discount **[p. 355]**
discounting the note **[p. 355]**
discount period **[p. 355]**
discount rate **[p. 345]**
due date **[p. 331]**
effective rate of interest **[p. 348]**
exact interest **[p. 330]**
face value **[p. 331]**
factoring **[p. 358]**
factors **[p. 358]**
foreclose **[p. 331]**
interest **[p. 326]**
interest-in-advance notes **[p. 345]**
loan amount **[p. 345]**
maker of a note **[p. 331]**
maturity date **[p. 331]**
maturity value **[p. 327]**
nominal rate **[p. 348]**
ordinary interest **[p. 330]**
payee of a note **[p. 331]**
payer of a note **[p. 331]**
prime rate **[p. 326]**
principal **[p. 326]**
proceeds of a note **[p. 345]**
promissory note **[p. 331]**
rate **[p. 326]**
recourse **[p. 355]**
simple discount note **[p. 345]**
simple interest **[p. 326]**
simple interest note **[p. 331]**
Stafford loan **[p. 345]**
stated rate **[p. 348]**
T-bills **[p. 349]**
term of a note **[p. 331]**
time **[p. 326]**
true rate of interest **[p. 348]**
Truth in Lending Act **[p. 348]**
U.S. Treasury bills **[p. 349]**

CONCEPTS	EXAMPLES
8.1 Finding the simple interest when time is expressed in years **1.** Use the formula $I = PRT$. **2.** Express R in decimal form. **3.** Express time in years. **4.** Substitute values for P, R, and T and multiply.	A loan of \$5900 is made for $1\frac{3}{4}$ years at 10% per year. Find the simple interest. $I = PRT$ $I = \$5900 \times .10 \times 1.75 = \$1032.50$ The simple interest is \$1032.50.
8.1 Finding the simple interest when time is expressed in months **1.** Use the formula $I = PRT$. **2.** Express R in decimal form. **3.** Express time in years by dividing the number of months by 12. **4.** Substitute values for P, R, and T and multiply.	Find the simple interest on \$24,000 for 8 months at 10%. $I = PRT$ $I = \$24{,}000 \times .10 \times \frac{8}{12} = \$1600$ The simple interest is \$1600.
8.1 Finding the maturity value of a loan **1.** Find I using the formula $I = PRT$. **2.** Find the maturity value using the formula $M = P + I$.	A loan of \$8500 is made for 1 year at 9%. Find the maturity value of the loan. $I = PRT$ $I = \$8500 \times .09 \times 1 = \$765$ $M = P + I$ $M = \$8500 + \$765 = \$9265$ The maturity value is \$9265.
8.1 Finding the number of days from one date to another using a table **1.** Find the day corresponding to the final date using the table. **2.** Find the day corresponding to the initial date. **3.** Subtract the smaller number from the larger number.	Find the number of days from February 15 to July 28. **1.** July 28 is day 209. **2.** Feb. 15 is day 46. **3.** Number of days is **209** **− 46** **163** There are 163 days from February 15 to July 28.
8.1 Finding the number of days from one date to another using actual number of days in a month Add the actual number of days in each month or partial month from initial date to final date.	Find the number of days from April 20 to June 27. April 20 to April 30 **10 days** May **31 days** June **27 days** **68 days**

CONCEPTS	EXAMPLES

8.1 Finding the exact interest

Use the formula

$$I = PRT$$

$$\text{with } T = \frac{\text{Number of days of loan}}{365}$$

Find the exact interest on a \$9000 loan at 8% for 140 days.

$$I = PRT$$

$$I = \$9000 \times .08 \times \frac{140}{365} = \$276.16$$

The exact interest is \$276.16.

8.1 Finding the ordinary, or banker's, interest

Use the formula

$$I = PRT$$

$$\text{with } T = \frac{\text{Number of days of loan}}{360}$$

Find the ordinary interest on a loan of \$14,000 at 7% for 120 days.

$$I = PRT$$

$$I = \$14{,}000 \times .07 \times \frac{120}{360} = \$326.67$$

The ordinary, or banker's, interest is \$326.67.

8.1 Finding the due date, interest, and maturity value of a simple interest promissory note when the term of the loan is in months

1. Add the number of months in the term of the note to the initial date of note.
2. Use the formula $I = PRT$ to find interest.
3. Find the maturity value as follows.
   Maturity value = Principal + Interest

Find the due date, the interest, and the maturity value of a loan made on February 15 for 7 months at 8% with a face value of \$9400.

September 15 is 7 months from February 15, so note is due on September 15.

$$I = PRT$$

$$I = \$9400 \times .08 \times \frac{7}{12} = \$438.67$$

$$M = \text{Principal} + \text{Interest}$$

$$M = \$9400 + \$438.67 = \$9838.67$$

8.1 Finding the due date of a promissory note when the term of the loan is expressed in days

Use either a table or the actual number of days in each month.

A loan is made on August 14 and is due in 80 days. Find the due date.

August 14 to August 31	17 days
September	30 days
October	31 days
	78 days

The loan is for 80 days, which is 2 days more than 78. Therefore, the loan is due on November 2.

8.2 Finding the principal given the interest, interest rate, and time

Use the formula

$$P = \frac{I}{RT}$$

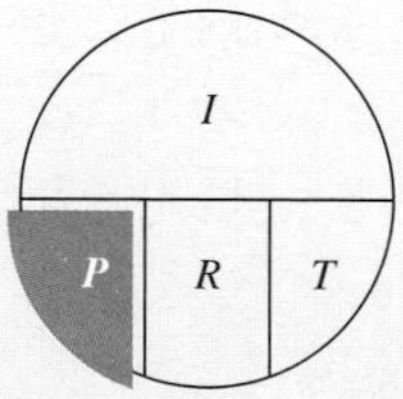

$$P = \frac{I}{RT}$$

Find the principal that produces interest of \$240 at 9% for 60 days.

$$P = \frac{I}{RT}$$

$$P = \frac{\$240}{.09 \times \frac{60}{360}} = \$16{,}000$$

The principal is \$16,000.

8.2 Finding the rate of interest given the principal, interest, and time

Use the formula

$$R = \frac{I}{PT}$$

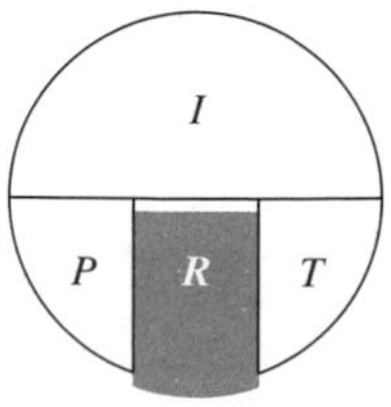

$$R = \frac{I}{PT}$$

A principal of \$8000 deposited for 45 days earns interest of \$75. Find the rate of interest.

$$R = \frac{I}{PT}$$

$$R = \frac{\$75}{\$8000 \times \frac{45}{360}} = .075$$

Rate of interest = 7.5%.

CONCEPTS	EXAMPLES

8.2 Finding the time given the principal, rate of interest, and interest

To find the time in days, use the formula

$$T\ (\text{in days}) = \frac{I}{PR} \times 360$$

To find the time in months, use the formula

$$T\ (\text{in months}) = \frac{I}{PR} \times 12$$

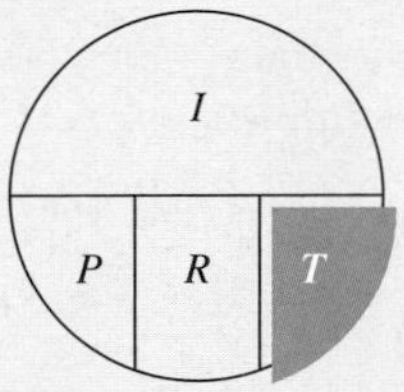

$T = \frac{I}{PR}$

Tom Jones invested $4000 at 8% and earned interest of $160. Find the number of days.

$$T = \frac{I}{PR} \times 360$$

$$T = \frac{\$160}{\$4000 \times .08} \times 360 = 180 \text{ days}$$

The loan was for 180 days.

8.3 Finding the proceeds of a simple discount note

Calculate the bank discount using the formula $B = MDT$. Then calculate the proceeds or loan amount using the formula $P = M - B$.

Karen Pattern borrows $6000 for 120 days at a discount rate of 9%. Find the proceeds.

$$B = MDT$$

$$B = \$6000 \times .09 \times \frac{120}{360} = \$180$$

$$P = M - B$$

$$P = \$6000 - \$180 = \$5820$$

8.3 Finding the face value of a simple discount note

Use the formula

$$M = \frac{P}{1 - DT}$$

Sam Spade needs $15,000 for new equipment for his restaurant. Find the face value of a note that will provide the $15,000 in proceeds if he plans to repay the note in 180 days and the bank charges an 11% discount rate.

$$M = \frac{P}{1 - DT}$$

$$M = \frac{\$15{,}000}{1 - \left(.11 \times \frac{180}{360}\right)} = \$15{,}873.02 \text{ (rounded)}$$

8.3 Finding the effective interest rate

Find the interest (B) from the formula

$$B = MDT$$

Find proceeds from the formula

$$P = M - B$$

Then use the formula

$$R = \frac{I}{PT}$$

A 150-day, 11% simple discount note has a face value of $12,400. Find the effective rate to the nearest tenth of a percent.

$$B = \$12{,}400 \times .11 \times \frac{150}{360} = \mathbf{\$568.33}$$

$$P = \$12{,}400 - \mathbf{\$568.33} = \mathbf{\$11{,}831.67}$$

$$R = \frac{\$568.33}{\mathbf{\$11{,}831.67} \times \frac{150}{360}} = 11.5\% \text{ (rounded)}$$

CONCEPTS

EXAMPLES

8.4 Finding the proceeds to an individual or firm that discounts a simple interest note

1. If necessary, find
- **(a)** the **due date** of the original note and
- **(b)** the **maturity value** of the original note ($M = P + I$, where $I = PRT$).

2. (a) Find the **discount period**, which is the time (e.g., number of days) from the sale of the note to the maturity date of the note.
- **(b)** Find the **discount** using the formula $B = MDT$.
- **(c)** Find the **proceeds** using $P = M - B$.

Moe's Ice Cream holds a 150-day note dated March 1 with a face value of $15,000 and a simple interest rate of 9%. Moe sells the note at a discount on June 1. Assume a discount rate of 11%. Find the proceeds.

1. Due date = day 60 (March 1) + 150 days = day 210 or July 29

$$I = PRT = \$15{,}000 \times .09 \times \frac{150}{360} = \$562.50$$

$$M = P + I = \$15{,}000 + \$562.50 = \mathbf{\$15{,}562.50}$$

2. (a) The discount period is 58 days.

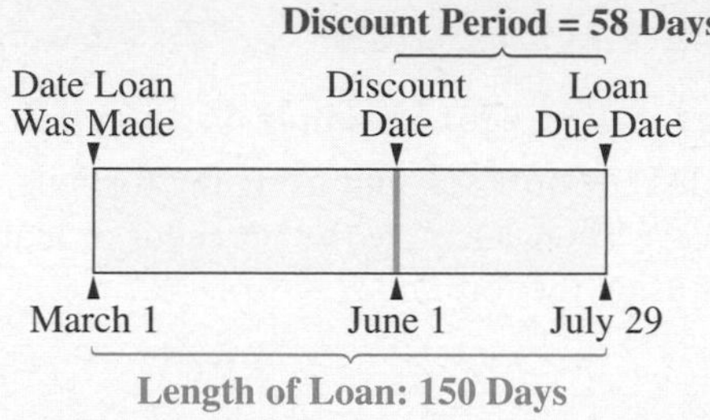

(b) Bank discount = MDT

$$B = \mathbf{\$15{,}562.50} \times .11 \times \frac{58}{360} = \$275.80$$

(c) Proceeds = $M - B$

$$D = \mathbf{\$15{,}562.50} - \$275.80 = \$15{,}286.70$$

8.4 Finding the proceeds to an individual or firm that discounts a simple interest note

1. If necessary, find
- **(a)** the **due date** of the original note,
- **(b)** the **discount** of the original note using $B = MDT$, and
- **(c)** the **proceeds** from the original note using $P = M - B$.

The **maturity value (face value)** of the note is written on the note itself.

2. (a) Find the **discount period**, which is the time (e.g., number of days) from the sale of the note to the maturity date of the note.
- **(b)** Find the **discount** using the formula $B = MDT$.
- **(c)** Find the **proceeds** using $P = M - B$.

On May 10, Applecrest Farm Orchards signed a 120-day note for $22,000 at a simple discount rate of 10%. The note was sold on June 30 at a discount rate of 10.5%. Find **(a)** the proceeds from the original note and **(b)** the proceeds at the time of sale.

(a) Due date is day 130 (May 10) + 120 days = day 250 or Sept. 7

$$B = MDT = \$22{,}000 \times .10 \times \frac{120}{360} = \$733.33$$

$$P = M - B = \$22{,}000 - \$733.33 = \$21{,}266.67$$

(b) June 30 is day 181
Discount period is 250 − 181 = 69 days

$$B = MDT = \$22{,}000 \times .105 \times \frac{69}{360} = \mathbf{\$442.75}$$

(c) $P = M - B = \$22{,}000 - \mathbf{\$442.75} = \$21{,}557.25$

CHAPTER 8 SUMMARY EXERCISE

Banking in a Global World: How Do Large Banks Make Money?

Bank of America borrowed $80,000,000 at 5% interest for 180 days from a Japanese investment house. At the same time, the bank made the following loans, each for the exact same 180-day period:

1. A 7% *simple interest note* for $38,000,000 to a Canadian firm that extracts oil from Canadian tar sands;
2. An 8.2% *simple discount note* for $27,500,000 to a European contractor building a factory in South Africa; and
3. An 8% *simple discount note* for $14,500,000 to a Louisiana company building minesweepers in New Orleans for the British government.

(a) Find the difference between interest received and interest paid by the bank on these funds.

(a) ____________________

(b) The bank did not loan out all $80,000,000. Find the amount it actually loaned out.

(b) ____________________

(c) Find the effective rate of interest to the nearest hundredth of a percent.

(c) ____________________

This seems like a low rate; however, this is the amount the bank earned over and above that paid out to the Japanese investment house on the same funds.

INVESTIGATE

The very idea of interest is not acceptable in some third-world countries. Here a bank takes partial ownership of a company when it lends to a company, at least until funds are repaid. Even in countries that do allow interest, interest rates vary considerably. Use financial newspapers, magazines, or the World Wide Web to find interest rates in three different countries and compare them to similar rates in the United States.

CHAPTER 8 TEST

To help you review, the numbers in brackets show the section in which the topic was discussed.

Find the simple interest for each of the following. Round to the nearest cent. **[8.1]**

1. \$12,500 at $10\frac{1}{2}\%$ for 280 days **1.** ______

2. \$8250 at $9\frac{1}{4}\%$ for 8 months **2.** ______

3. A loan of \$6000 at 11% made on June 8 and due August 22 **3.** ______

4. A promissory note for \$4500 at 10.3% made on November 13 and due March 8 **4.** ______

5. Joan Davies signed a 140-day simple interest note for \$12,500 with a bank that uses *exact* interest. If the rate is 10.7%, find the maturity value. **[8.1]** **5.** ______

6. Chez Bazan Bakery borrowed \$24,300 for new ovens and other equipment. The simple interest loan was repaid in 6 months at $10\frac{1}{2}\%$. Find the amount of the repayment. **[8.1]** **6.** ______

7. Glenda Pierce plans to borrow \$14,000 for a new hot tub and deck for her home. She has decided on a term of 200 days at 10.5% simple interest. However, she has a choice of two lenders. One calculates interest using a 360-day year and the other uses a 365-day year. Find the amount of interest Pierce will save by using the lender with the 365-day year. **[8.1]** **7.** ______

8. Lupe Gonzalez has \$6500 in her retirement account. Find the interest rate required for the fund to grow to \$7247.50 in 15 months. **[8.2]** **8.** ______

9. Hilda Heinz lends \$1200 to her sister Olga at a rate of 9%. Find how long it will take for her investment to earn \$100 in interest. (Round to the nearest day.) **[8.2]** **9.** ______

10. A woman invested money received from an insurance settlement for 7 months at 5% interest. If she received \$1254.17 interest on her investment during this time, find the amount that she invested. (Round to the nearest dollar.) **[8.2]** **10.** ______

11. Mike Fagan needs \$25,000 to expand his flower shop. Find the face value of a simple discount note that will provide the \$25,000 in proceeds if he plans to repay the note in 240 days and the bank charges a 9% discount rate. **[8.3]** **11.** ______

Find the discount and the proceeds for the following simple discount notes. **[8.3]**

	Face Value	Discount Rate	Time (Days)	Discount	Proceeds
12.	$9800	11%	120	________	________
13.	$10,250	9.5%	60	________	________

14. Barbara Waters signed a simple discount note for $15,000 for 120 days at a rate of 9%. Find **(a)** the proceeds and **(b)** the effective interest rate based on the proceeds received by Waters. **[8.3]**

(a) ________
(b) ________

15. Lizabeth Neault needed funds to open a law office. She borrowed $28,400 at 8.5% simple interest for 150 days on July 7. The bank she borrowed from sold the note at a 9% discount on August 20. Find the proceeds to the bank. **[8.4]**

15. ________

16. A 90-day simple discount promissory note for $9200 with a simple discount rate of 11% was signed on January 25. It was discounted on March 2 at 12%. Find the proceeds at the time of the sale. **[8.4]**

16. ________

17. A $20,000 T-bill is purchased at a 3.75% discount rate for 13 weeks. Find **(a)** the purchase price of the T-bill, **(b)** the maturity value, **(c)** the interest earned, and **(d)** the effective rate of interest to the nearest hundredth of a percent. **[8.3]**

(a) ________
(b) ________
(c) ________
(d) ________

The following note was discounted at $12\frac{1}{2}\%$. *Find the discount period, the discount, and the proceeds.* **[8.4]**

	Date Loan Was Made	Face Value	Length of Loan	Rate	Date of Discount	Discount Period	Discount	Proceeds
18.	Jan. 25	$9200	90 days	10%	Mar. 12	________	________	________

19. Jan Guerra lends $9000 to her second cousin using a 180-day 10% simple interest note that was signed on October 30. Guerra subsequently has a car accident and desperately needs money, so she sells the note at a discount of 15% on January 3 to an investor. Find **(a)** the discount, **(b)** the proceeds, and **(c)** the amount of money Guerra gains or loses. **[8.4]**

(a) ________
(b) ________
(c) ________

CHAPTER 9

Compound Interest

CHAPTER CONTENTS

Bank of America is one of the largest banks in the world with over 13,000 automated teller machines (ATMs). It also offers

CASE in POINT

online banking so that computer-savvy customers can pay bills, apply for loans and credit cards, balance check books, and transfer money at any time of the day using their computer.

As we saw in **Chapter 8**, interest is calculated only once on **simple interest** loans. These short-term loans are typically for one year or less. Bank loans to businesses are often simple interest loans.

In contrast, **compound interest** loans require interest to be calculated more than once during the life of the loan. Every time compound interest is calculated, it is added to the principal before interest is calculated again. Thus, compound interest is found based on principal plus any interest previously credited. Compound interest is used to find interest for savings accounts, money market accounts, certificates of deposits, and retirement accounts.

9.1 COMPOUND INTEREST

OBJECTIVES

1. Use the formula $I = PRT$ to calculate compound interest.
2. Identify interest rate per compounding period and number of compounding periods.
3. Use the formula $M = P(1 + i)^n$ to find compound amount.
4. Use the table to find compound amount.

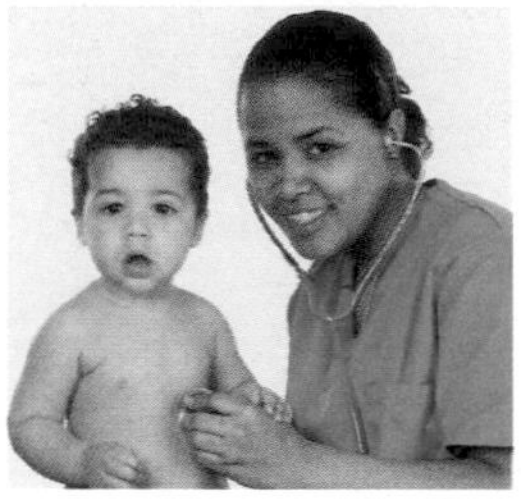

CASE in POINT Regina Foster worked overtime as a nurse and earned an extra $2000. She banks at Bank of America and wonders what the difference would be between a 6-year investment earning 5% offered by her bank and one earning 8% that the bank paid her father some years ago.

The **future amount** is the amount at the end of the loan or investment. It is also called **compound amount** or **future value**. The future value of an investment depends on:

1. The interest rate
2. The length of the investment
3. Whether interest is found using simple interst or compound interest

The table and graph show the effects of these factors on a $10,000 investment.

Investment	*Term*	*Annual Rate*	*Interest*	*Future Value*
1. Simple interest	6 years	5%	$3,000	$13,000
2. Compound interest	6 years	5%	$3,401	$13,401
3. Compound interest	6 years	8%	$5,869	$15,869
4. Compound interest	10 years	8%	$11,589	$21,589

Investments 1 and 2 show that compound interest generates more interest than simple interest. Investments 2 and 3 show that a higher interest rate results in more interest. Finally, investments 3 and 4 show that the length of an investment adds significantly to the future value.

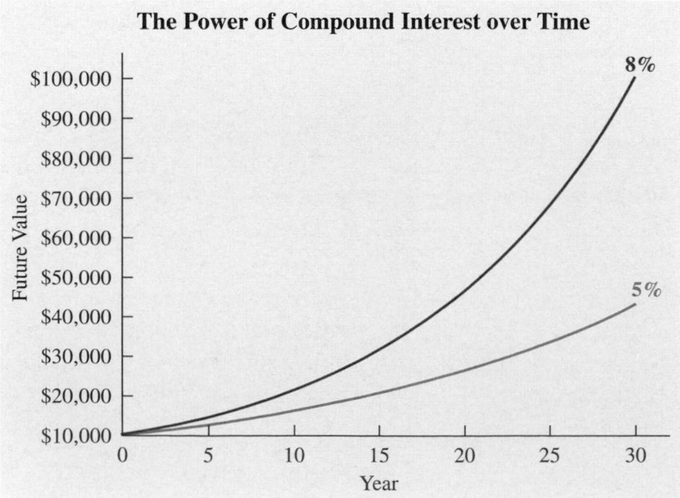

OBJECTIVE 1 Use the formula $I = PRT$ to calculate compound interest. **Compound interest** is interest calculated on previously credited interest in addition to the original principal. Compound interest calculations require that interest be calculated and credited to an account many times each year. The simple interest formulas ($I = PRT$ and $M = P + I$) are used each time compound interest is calculated.

EXAMPLE 1

Comparing Simple to Compound Interest

Regina Foster wants to compare simple interest to compound interest on a \$2000 investment.

(a) Find the interest if funds earn 6% simple interest for 1 year.
(b) Find the interest if funds earn 6% interest compounded every 6 months for 1 year.
(c) Find the difference between the two.

SOLUTION

(a) Simple interest on \$2000 at 6% *for 1 year* is found as follows.

$$I = PRT = \$2000 \times .06 \times 1 = \$120$$

(b) Interest compounded every 6 months means that interest must be calculated at the end of each 6-months using $I = PRT$. Interest must then be added to principal before going on to the next 6-month interval.

$$\text{Interest for first 6 months} = PRT = \$2000 \times .06 \times \tfrac{1}{2} = \$60$$

$$\text{Principal at end of first 6 months} = \text{Original principal} + \text{Interest}$$
$$= \$2000 + \$60 = \mathbf{\$2060}$$

QUICK TIP Round interest amounts to the nearest cent each time interest is calculated.

The new principal of \$2060 earns interest for the second 6 months.

$$\text{Interest for second 6 months} = PRT = \mathbf{\$2060} \times .06 \times \tfrac{1}{2} = \$61.80$$
$$\text{Principal at end of 1 year} = \$2060 + \$61.80 = \$2121.80$$

The interest earned in the second 6 months (\$61.80) is greater than that earned in the first 6 months (\$60). This occurs because the interest earned in the first 6 months becomes principal and it also earns interest during the second 6 months.

$$\text{Total compound interest} = \$60 + \$61.80 = \$121.80$$

QUICK TIP Relatively small differences in interest rates can add up to large differences in compound amounts over time.

(c) Difference in interest = \$121.80 − \$120 = \$1.80.

More interest is earned using compound interest calculations. The difference of \$1.80 over a year does not seem like much, but ***compound interest leads to huge differences*** when applied to larger sums of money over long time periods.

QUICK CHECK 1

\$15,000 is invested for 1 year. Find the future value based on **(a)** simple interest of 8% and **(b)** 8% interest compounded every 6 months. **(c)** Then find the difference between the future values.

EXAMPLE 2

Finding Compound Interest

The Peters hope to have \$5000 in 4 years for a down payment on their first new car. They invest \$3800 in an account that pays 6% interest at the end of each year, on previous interest in addition to principal. **(a)** Find the excess of compound interest over simple interest after 4 years. **(b)** Will they have enough money at the end of 4 years to meet their goal of a down payment?

SOLUTION

For each year, first calculate interest using $I = PRT$ and round to the nearest cent. Then find the new principal by adding the interest earned to the preceding principal.

(a)

Year	*P* × *R* × *T*	*Interest*	*P* + *I*	*Compound Amount*
1	\$3800.00 × .06 × 1 =	\$228.00	\$3800.00 + **\$228.00** =	\$4028.00
2	\$4028.00 × .06 × 1 =	\$241.68	\$4028.00 + **\$241.68** =	\$4269.68
3	\$4269.68 × .06 × 1 =	\$256.18	\$4269.68 + **\$256.18** =	\$4525.86
4	\$4525.86 × .06 × 1 =	\$271.55	\$4525.86 + **\$271.55** =	\$4797.41

Quick Check Answers

1. (a) \$16,200 **(b)** \$16,224 **(c)** \$24

$$\text{Compound interest} = \$4797.41 - \$3800 = \$997.41$$
$$\text{Simple interest} = \$3800 \times .06 \times 4 = \$912$$
$$\text{Difference} = \$997.41 - \$912 = \$85.41$$

(b) No, they will be short of their goal by $5000 − $4797.41 = **$202.59**.

QUICK CHECK 2

Find the future amount at the end of 2 years for an $80,000 investment that earns 7% at the end of each year.

OBJECTIVE 2 Identify interest rate per compounding period and number of compounding periods. Compound interest results in interest calculations more than once per year depending on the **compounding period**. The *interest rate per compounding period* is the annual rate divided by the number of compounding periods per year. The numbers of *compounding periods in one year* are listed in the table.

Interest Compounded	Compound at the End of Every	Number of Compounding Periods in 1 Year
Semiannually	6 months	2
Quarterly	3 months	4
Monthly	1 month	12
Daily	1 day	365*

*Leap year has 366 compounding periods.

The number of compounding periods in an investment is *the number of years multiplied by the number of compounding periods per year.*

EXAMPLE 3

Finding the Interest Rate per Compounding Period and the Number of Compounding Periods

Find the interest rate per compounding period and the number of compounding periods over the life of each loan.

(a) 8% compounded semiannually, 3 years
(b) 12% per year, compounded monthly, $2\frac{1}{2}$ years
(c) 9% per year, compounded quarterly, 5 years

SOLUTION

(a) 8% compounded semiannually is $\frac{8\%}{2} = 4\%$ credited at the end of each 6 months. There are 3 years × 2 periods per year = 6 compounding periods in 3 years.
(b) 12% per year, compounded monthly, results in $\frac{12\%}{12} = 1\%$ credited at the end of each month. There are 2.5 years × 12 periods per year = 30 compounding periods in 2.5 years.
(c) 9% per year, compounded quarterly, results in $\frac{9\%}{4} = 2.25\%$ credited at the end of each quarter. There are 5 years × 4 periods per year = 20 compounding periods in 5 years.

QUICK TIP The interest rate per compounding period is the annual rate times the fraction of a year over which compounding occurs. For 10% compounded quarterly, the interest rate per compounding period = $10\% \times \frac{1}{4} = 2.5\%$ per quarter.

QUICK CHECK 3

A loan requires that the 8% interest be compounded quarterly for 6 years. Find the interest rate per compounding period and the number of compounding periods.

Quick Check Answers

2. $91,592
3. 2%; 24 periods

OBJECTIVE 3 Use the formula $M = P(1 + i)^n$ to find compound amount. The **formula for compound interest** uses **exponents**, which is a short way of writing repeated products. For example,

Exponent: 3 tells how many times the base **2** is multiplied by itself.

$$2 \times 2 \times 2 = 2^3$$

base

Also, $4^2 = 4 \times 4 = 16$, and $5^4 = 5 \times 5 \times 5 \times 5 = 625$.

Assume that P dollars are deposited at a rate of interest i per compounding period for n periods. Then the compound amount and the interest are found as follows.

QUICK TIP It is important to keep in mind that *i is the interest rate per compounding period*, not per year. Also, *n is the total number of compounding periods.*

Formula for Compounding Interest

Maturity value $= M = P(1 + i)^n$
Interest $= I = M - P$

where
P = initial investment
n = total number of compounding periods
i = interest rate per compounding period

EXAMPLE 4

Finding Compound Interest

An investment at Bank of America pays 7% interest per year compounded semiannually. Given an initial deposit of $2500, **(a)** use the formula to find the compound amount after 3 years, and **(b)** find the compound interest.

SOLUTION

(a) Interest is compounded at $\frac{7\%}{2} = 3.5\%$ every 6 months for 3 years $\times$ 2 periods per year = 6 periods. Therefore, 3.5% is the interest rate per compounding period (i) and 6 is the number of compounding periods (n).

$$\begin{aligned} M &= P(1 + i)^n \\ &= \$2500 \times (1 + .035)^6 \\ &= \$2500 \times (1.035)^6 \\ &= \$3073.14 \text{ rounded} \end{aligned}$$

The compound amount is $3073.14.

(b)
$$\begin{aligned} I &= M - P \\ &= \$3073.14 - \$2500 = \$573.14 \end{aligned}$$

The interest is $573.14.

The calculator solution for part (a) is as follows.

2500 [×] [(] 1 [+] .035 [)] [y^x] 6 [=] $3073.14 (rounded)

Note: Refer to Appendix C for calculator basics.

QUICK CHECK 4

Use the formula for maturity value to find the compound amount and interest on a $9000 investment at 6% compounded semiannually for 5 years.

Quick Check Answer

4. $12,095.25; $3095.25

Compound Interest Table

Period	1%	$1\frac{1}{2}\%$	2%	$2\frac{1}{2}\%$	3%	4%	5%	6%	8%	10%	Period
	Interest Rate per Compounding Period										
1	1.01000	1.01500	1.02000	1.02500	1.03000	1.04000	1.05000	1.06000	1.08000	1.10000	1
2	1.02010	1.03023	1.04040	1.05063	1.06090	1.08160	1.10250	1.12360	1.16640	1.21000	2
3	1.03030	1.04568	1.06121	1.07689	1.09273	1.12486	1.15763	1.19102	1.25971	1.33100	3
4	1.04060	1.06136	1.08243	1.10381	1.12551	1.16986	1.21551	1.26248	1.36049	1.46410	4
5	1.05101	1.07728	1.10408	1.13141	1.15927	1.21665	1.27628	1.33823	1.46933	1.61051	5
6	1.06152	1.09344	1.12616	1.15969	1.19405	1.26532	1.34010	1.41852	1.58687	1.77156	6
7	1.07214	1.10984	1.14869	1.18869	1.22987	1.31593	1.40710	1.50363	1.71382	1.94872	7
8	1.08286	1.12649	1.17166	1.21840	1.26677	1.36857	1.47746	1.59385	1.85093	2.14359	8
9	1.09369	1.14339	1.19509	1.24886	1.30477	1.42331	1.55133	1.68948	1.99900	2.35795	9
10	1.10462	1.16054	1.21899	1.28008	1.34392	1.48024	1.62889	1.79085	2.15892	2.59374	10
11	1.11567	1.17795	1.24337	1.31209	1.38423	1.53945	1.71034	1.89830	2.33164	2.85312	11
12	1.12683	1.19562	1.26824	1.34489	1.42576	1.60103	1.79586	2.01220	2.51817	3.13843	12
13	1.13809	1.21355	1.29361	1.37851	1.46853	1.66507	1.88565	2.13293	2.71962	3.45227	13
14	1.14947	1.23176	1.31948	1.41297	1.51259	1.73168	1.97993	2.26090	2.93719	3.79750	14
15	1.16097	1.25023	1.34587	1.44830	1.55797	1.80094	2.07893	2.39656	3.17217	4.17725	15
16	1.17258	1.26899	1.37279	1.48451	1.60471	1.87298	2.18287	2.54035	3.42594	4.59497	16
17	1.18430	1.28802	1.40024	1.52162	1.65285	1.94790	2.29202	2.69277	3.70002	5.05447	17
18	1.19615	1.30734	1.42825	1.55966	1.70243	2.02582	2.40662	2.85434	3.99602	5.55992	18
19	1.20811	1.32695	1.45681	1.59865	1.75351	2.10685	2.52695	3.02560	4.31570	6.11591	19
20	1.22019	1.34686	1.48595	1.63862	1.80611	2.19112	2.65330	3.20714	4.66096	6.72750	20
21	1.23239	1.36706	1.51567	1.67958	1.86029	2.27877	2.78596	3.39956	5.03383	7.40025	21
22	1.24472	1.38756	1.54598	1.72157	1.91610	2.36992	2.92526	3.60354	5.43654	8.14027	22
23	1.25716	1.40838	1.57690	1.76461	1.97359	2.46472	3.07152	3.81975	5.87146	8.95430	23
24	1.26973	1.42950	1.60844	1.80873	2.03279	2.56330	3.22510	4.04893	6.34118	9.84973	24
25	1.28243	1.45095	1.64061	1.85394	2.09378	2.66584	3.38635	4.29187	6.84848	10.83471	25
26	1.29526	1.47271	1.67342	1.90029	2.15659	2.77247	3.55567	4.54938	7.39635	11.91818	26
27	1.30821	1.49480	1.70689	1.94780	2.22129	2.88337	3.73346	4.82235	7.98806	13.10999	27
28	1.32129	1.51722	1.74102	1.99650	2.28793	2.99870	3.92013	5.11169	8.62711	14.42099	28
29	1.33450	1.53998	1.77584	2.04641	2.35657	3.11865	4.11614	5.41839	9.31727	15.86309	29
30	1.34785	1.56308	1.81136	2.09757	2.42726	3.24340	4.32194	5.74349	10.06266	17.44940	30

OBJECTIVE 4 **Use the table to find compound amount.** The value of $(1 + i)^n$ can be looked up in the compound interest table above. The interest rate i at the top of the table is the interest rate *per compounding period*. The value of n down the far left (or far right) column of the table is *the total number of compounding periods*. The value in the body of the table is the compound amount, or maturity value, for each $1 in principal.

Compound amount = Principal × Number from compound interest table

EXAMPLE 5

Finding Compound Interest

In each case, find the interest earned on a $2000 deposit.

(a) For 3 years, compounded annually at 4%
(b) For 5 years, compounded semiannually at 6%
(c) For 6 years, compounded quarterly at 8%
(d) For 2 years, compounded monthly at 12%

SOLUTION

(a) In 3 years, there are $3 \times 1 = 3$ compounding periods. The interest rate per compounding period is $4\% \div 1 = 4\%$. Look across the top of the compound interest table above for 4% and down the side for 3 periods to find 1.12486.

$$\text{Compound amount} = M = \$2000 \times 1.12486 = \mathbf{\$2249.72}$$
$$\text{Interest earned} = I = \mathbf{\$2249.72} - \$2000 = \$249.72$$

QUICK TIP Example 1 in Appendix D shows how a financial calculator can be used to solve this same type of problem.

(b) In 5 years, there are $5 \times 2 = 10$ semiannual compounding periods. The interest rate per compounding period is $6\% \div 2 = 3\%$. In the compound interest table, look at 3% at the top and 10 periods down the side to find **1.34392**.

$$\text{Compound amount} = M = \$2000 \times 1.34392 = \mathbf{\$2687.84}$$
$$\text{Interest earned} = I = \mathbf{\$2687.84} - \$2000 = \$687.84$$

(c) Interest compounded quarterly is compounded 4 times a year. In 6 years, there are $4 \times 6 =$ 24 quarters, or 24 periods. Interest of 8% per year is $\frac{8\%}{4} = 2\%$ per quarter. In the compound interest table, locate 2% across the top and 24 periods at the left, finding the number **1.60844**.

$$\text{Compound amount} = M = \$2000 \times 1.60844 = \mathbf{\$3216.88}$$
$$\text{Interest earned} = I = \mathbf{\$3216.88} - \$2000 = \$1216.88$$

(d) In 2 years, there are $2 \times 12 = 24$ monthly periods. Interest of 12% per year is $\frac{12\%}{12} = 1\%$ per month. Look in the compound interest table for 1% and 24 periods, finding the number **1.26973**.

$$\text{Compound amount} = M = \$2000 \times 1.26973 = \mathbf{\$2539.46}$$
$$\text{Interest earned} = I = \mathbf{\$2539.46} - \$2000 = \$539.46$$

QUICK CHECK 5

Find the interest earned on a $5000 deposit for 4 years at 6% compounded semiannually.

The more often interest is compounded, the greater the amount of interest earned. Using a financial calculator, a compound interest table more complete than the compound interest table on page 382, or the compound interest formula will give the results of interest on $1000 shown in the following table. (Leap years were ignored in finding daily interest.)

Compounding makes a BIG difference!

Interest on $1000 at 8% per Year for 10 Years

Compounded	Interest
Not at all (simple interest)	$ 800.00
Annually	$1158.92
Semiannually	$1191.12
Quarterly	$1208.04
Monthly	$1219.64
Daily	$1225.35

EXAMPLE 6

Finding Compound Interest

John Smith inherited $15,000, which he deposited in a retirement account that pays interest compounded semiannually. How much will he have after 15 years if the funds grow at

(a) 6%? **(b)** 8%? **(c)** 10%?

SOLUTION

In 15 years, there are $15 \times 2 = 30$ semiannual periods. The semiannual interest rates are

(a) $\frac{6\%}{2} = 3\%$ **(b)** $\frac{8\%}{2} = 4\%$ **(c)** $\frac{10\%}{2} = 5\%$

Using factors from the table:

(a) $15,000 × **2.42726** = $36,408.90
(b) $15,000 × **3.24340** = $48,651
(c) $15,000 × **4.32194** = $64,829.10

Quick Check Answer

5. $1333.85

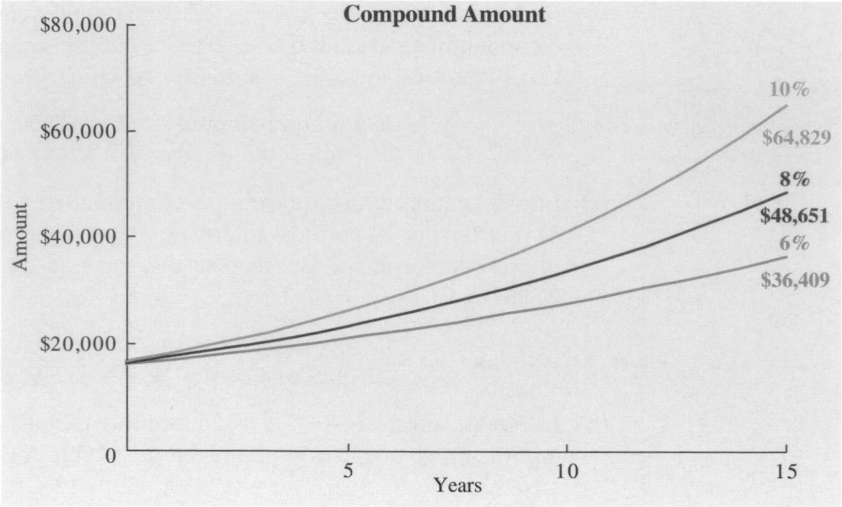

The graph shows the growth at the different interest rates over time.

QUICK TIP Compound interest rate calculations are indicated by phrases such as *compounded quarterly, 2% per quarter*, or *compounded daily*.

QUICK CHECK 6

A bank offers a certificate of deposit that earns 6% compounded quarterly for 3 years. Find the compound amount for an investment of $3500.

Parents believe that their children should study personal finance. The following pie chart indicates when parents believe this education should begin.

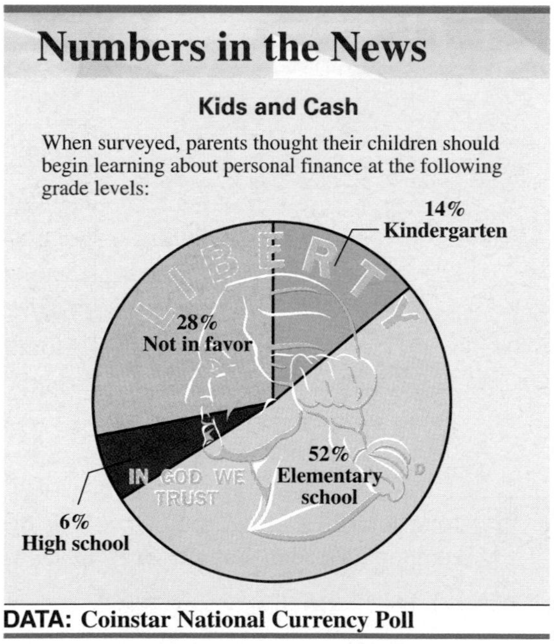

Quick Check Answer

6. $4184.67

9.1	EXERCISES

The QUICK START exercises in each section contain solutions to help you get started.

Use the formula for compound amount, not the table, to find the compound amount and interest. Round to the nearest cent. (See Examples 3 and 4.)

		Compound Amount	Interest
QUICK START			
1.	$12,000 at 8% compounded annually for 4 years	$16,325.87	$4325.87

Compound interest is 8% per year for 4 years.
$$M = \$12{,}000 \times (1 + .08)^4 = \$12{,}000 \times 1.08 \times 1.08 \times 1.08 \times 1.08 = \$16{,}325.87$$
$$I = \$16{,}325.87 - \$12{,}000 = \$4325.87$$

2.	$14,800 at 6% compounded semiannually for 4 years	_____	_____
3.	$28,000 at 10% compounded quarterly for 1 year	_____	_____
4.	$20,000 at 5% compounded quarterly for $\frac{3}{4}$ year	_____	_____

Use values from the compound interest table on page 382 to find both the compound amount and the compound interest. Round the compound amount to the nearest cent. (See Examples 3–6.)

		Compound Amount	Interest
QUICK START			
5.	$32,350 at 6% compounded annually for 4 years	$40,841.23	$8491.23

Compound interest is 6% per year for 4 years.
$$M = \$32{,}350 \times 1.26248 = \$40{,}841.23; \quad I = \$40{,}841.23 - \$32{,}350 = \$8491.23$$

6.	$19,400 at 8% compounded quarterly for 3 years	_____	_____
7.	$14,500 at 10% compounded quarterly for 7 years	_____	_____
8.	$12,500 at 8% compounded quarterly for 5 years	_____	_____

C indicates an exercise that is related to the Case in Point feature.

9. $45,000 at 6% compounded semiannually for 5 years __________ __________

10. $82,000 at 8% compounded semiannually for 4 years __________ __________

Find the simple interest for the period indicated. Then use table values to find the compound interest. Finally, find the difference between compound interest and simple interest. Round each to the nearest cent. (Interest is compounded annually.)

QUICK START

	Principal	Rate	Number of Years	Simple Interest	Compound Interest	Difference
11.	$5400	6%	4	$1296	$1417.39	$121.39
12.	$9200	5%	6	__________	__________	__________
13.	$1200	8%	15	__________	__________	__________
14.	$4625	4%	12	__________	__________	__________

Use the table to solve the following application problems. Round to the nearest cent.

QUICK START

15. CREDIT UNION Bill Jensen deposits $8500 with Bank of America in an account paying 5% compounded semiannually. Find **(a)** the compound amount and **(b)** the interest in 6 years.

(a) $11,431.57
(b) $2931.57

Compound interest is $\frac{5\%}{2}$ = 2.5% and there are 2 × 6 = 12 compounding periods.

(a) M = $8500 × 1.34489 = $11,431.57; (b) I = $11,431.57 − $8500 = $2931.57

16. SAVINGS Vickie Ewing deposits her savings of $2800 in an account paying 6% compounded quarterly and she leaves it there for 7 years. Find **(a)** the compound amount and **(b)** the interest.

(a) __________
(b) __________

17. SAVINGS Tom Blasting invested $4500 in an account paying 8% compounded quarterly for 3 years. Find **(a)** the compound amount and **(b)** the interest.

(a) __________
(b) __________

18. INVESTMENT John Crandall deposited $6000 in an account at a bank that pays 5% compounded semiannually for 4 years. Find **(a)** the compound amount and **(b)** the interest.

(a) __________
(b) __________

19. INTERNATIONAL FINANCE Chi Tang, a businessperson from Taiwan, deposits 25,000 yen in a Hong Kong branch of Bank of America that pays 6% compounded semiannually. Find **(a)** the balance in the account after 4 years and **(b)** the interest.

(a) __________
(b) __________

20. APPLIANCE STORE AAA Appliance places \$42,000 in an account paying 6% compounded quarterly and leaves it there as collateral for a loan. Find **(a)** the balance in the account after one year and **(b)** the interest.

(a) ______
(b) ______

21. INVESTMENT DECISION Bill Baxter has \$25,000 to invest for a year. He can lend it to his sister, who has agreed to pay 10% simple interest for the year. Or, he can invest it with a bank at 8% compounded quarterly for a year. How much additional interest would the simple interest loan to his sister generate?

21. ______

C **22.** MAXIMIZING INTEREST Bank of America has \$850,000 to lend for 9 months. It can lend it to a local contractor at a simple interest rate of 12%, or it can lend it to a small business that will pay 12% compounded monthly. How much additional interest would the compound interest loan to the small business generate?

22. ______

23. INTERNATIONAL FINANCE Barton's Ltd. lends \$1,400,000 for 2 years at 12% compounded monthly to an Egyptian company that manufactures tug boats. Find **(a)** the future value and **(b)** the interest.

(a) ______
(b) ______

24. CORPORATE FINANCE Key Bank lends \$4,500,000 for $1\frac{1}{2}$ years at 8% compounded quarterly to Rengen Biomedical to fund a clinical trial on a new cancer drug. Find **(a)** the future value and **(b)** the interest.

(a) ______
(b) ______

25. INVESTING Bob Williams has \$25,000 to invest and believes that he will earn 6% compounded semiannually. Find the compound amount if he invests **(a)** for 2 years and **(b)** for 8 years. **(c)** Then find the additional amount earned due to the longer period.

(a) ______
(b) ______
(c) ______

26. WHICH INVESTMENT? Jan Reus sold her home and has \$18,000 to invest. She believes she can earn 8% compounded quarterly. Find the compound amount if she invests for **(a)** 3 years and **(b)** 6 years. **(c)** Then find the additional amount earned due to the longer time period.

(a) ______
(b) ______
(c) ______

27. TIME OR RATE? Becky Hilton has a choice for her investment of \$7500. She can invest it **(a)** at 8% compounded quarterly for 2 years or **(b)** at 6% compounded semiannually for 5 years. Find the future value of both. **(c)** Which is larger?

(a) ______
(b) ______
(c) ______

28. TIME OR RATE? Manager Isat Riyadh has a choice to make regarding short-term, excess corporate cash of $330,000. He can invest it **(a)** at 6% compounded quarterly for 6 months or **(b)** at 5% compounded semiannually for 1 year. Find the future amount of both. **(c)** Which is larger?

(a) ________________
(b) ________________
(c) ________________

29. Explain the difference between simple interest and compound interest. (See Objectives 1 and 3.)

30. Explain the difference between 8% compounded monthly for 1 year and 8% simple interest for 1 year. If you were lending money, which type of interest would you specify? Why?

31. Show the effect of both the interest rate and the period on an original investment of $2500. Decide on your own rates and time periods.

32. List three institutions that work with simple interest. List three others that use compound interest.

9.2 INTEREST-BEARING BANK ACCOUNTS AND INFLATION

OBJECTIVES

1. Define passbook, savings, and other interest-bearing accounts.
2. Find interest compounded daily.
3. Define time deposit accounts.
4. Define inflation and the consumer price index.
5. Examine the effect of inflation on spendable income.
6. Understand the role of the government related to inflation.

CASE in POINT Individuals, businesses, and even countries have money on deposit at Bank of America. These deposits can be in many forms, including checking accounts, savings accounts, money market accounts, and time deposits, such as certificates of deposits.

Banks make money by charging *higher interest on funds they lend out* to customers than they pay out on funds they have on deposit at the bank. They also make money from fees for services such as safe deposit boxes, money transfers from one place to another, use of the ATM, and checking accounts.

People sometimes think that banks have huge vaults of stored cash, but that is rarely the case. Banks usually have only enough cash to meet customers' needs for cash during the next few days. Most bank assets are in the loans to their many customers, rather than in cash.

OBJECTIVE 1 Define passbook, savings, and other interest-bearing accounts. **Savings accounts, passbook accounts, money market accounts**, and other interest-bearing accounts are offered by banks and credit unions and can be a safe place to deposit money. These accounts are commonly insured by the Federal Deposit Insurance Corporation (FDIC) on deposits up to $100,000. Many of these accounts require a minimum balance. Interest rates paid on these accounts range from below 1% to over 5%, and the interest is often compounded daily. The Truth in Savings Act of 1991 resulted in Regulation DD, which requires that interest on savings accounts be paid based on the *exact* number of days.

Interest-bearing checking accounts are also offered by many banks and credit unions. These accounts often have a minimum balance, such as $1500, that must be maintained, but they have the advantage that checks can be written on the account. They can be a good way to earn interest on your money as long as your balance does not fall too low, in which case the bank commonly charges a fee. Even though interest rates on these accounts tend to be very low, many people use them to pay bills either electronically or using checks, since they want to maximize the interest earned each year.

OBJECTIVE 2 Find interest compounded daily. Interest on savings accounts, passbook accounts, and other interest-bearing checking accounts is found using compound interest. It is common for banks to pay interest **compounded daily** so that interest is credited for every day that the money is on deposit.

The formula for daily compounding is *exactly* the same as the formula given in **Section 9.1.** However, because the annual interest rate must be divided by 365 (for daily compounding), the arithmetic is tedious. To avoid this, use the following special tables that give the necessary numbers for 1 to 90 days, as well as for 1 to 4 ninety-day quarters, assuming $3\frac{1}{2}\%$ interest compounded daily. Even with daily compounding, interest is often credited to an account *only at the end of each quarter* to make record keeping easier for the bank.

QUICK TIP Interest rates vary widely. No one, including the authors of this textbook, knows what interest rates will be in the future. Thus, the interest rate in this section is $3\frac{1}{2}\%$, or close to the historical average for accounts of this type.

Interest by Quarter for $3\frac{1}{2}\%$ Compounded Daily Assuming 90-Day Quarters

Number of Quarters	Value of $(1 + i)^n$
1	1.008667067
2	1.017409251
3	1.026227205
4	1.035121585

The four quarters in a year begin on January 1, April 1, July 1, and October 1. Although some quarters have 91 or 92 days in them, we assume 90-day quarters for convenience in calculation. Assuming daily compounding and a compounding period expressed in days or quarters, compound amount and interest are found as follows.

Compound amount = Principal × Number from table
Interest = Compound amount − Principal

Find the value from the table below if the number of days of the deposit is 90 days or less. Use the smaller table at the side if time is given in number of quarters.

Values of $(1 + i)^n$ for $3\frac{1}{2}\%$ Compounded Daily

Number of Days n	Value of $(1 + i)^n$	n	Value of $(1 + i)^n$	n	Value of $(1 + i)^n$	n	Value of $(1 + i)^n$	n	Value of $(1 + i)^n$
1	1.000095890	19	1.001823491	37	1.003554076	55	1.005287650	73	1.007024219
2	1.000191790	20	1.001919556	38	1.003650307	56	1.005384048	74	1.007120783
3	1.000287699	21	1.002015631	39	1.003746548	57	1.005480454	75	1.007217357
4	1.000383617	22	1.002111714	40	1.003842797	58	1.005576870	76	1.007313939
5	1.000479544	23	1.002207807	41	1.003939056	59	1.005673296	77	1.007410531
6	1.000575480	24	1.002303909	42	1.004035324	60	1.005769730	78	1.007507132
7	1.000671426	25	1.002400021	43	1.004131602	61	1.005866174	79	1.007603742
8	1.000767381	26	1.002496141	44	1.004227888	62	1.005962627	80	1.007700362
9	1.000863345	27	1.002592271	45	1.004324184	63	1.006059089	81	1.007796990
10	1.000959318	28	1.002688410	46	1.004420489	64	1.006155560	82	1.007893628
11	1.001055300	29	1.002784558	47	1.004516803	65	1.006252041	83	1.007990276
12	1.001151292	30	1.002880716	48	1.004613127	66	1.006348531	84	1.008086932
13	1.001247293	31	1.002976882	49	1.004709460	67	1.006445030	85	1.008183598
14	1.001343303	32	1.003073058	50	1.004805802	68	1.006541538	86	1.008280273
15	1.001439322	33	1.003169243	51	1.004902153	69	1.006638056	87	1.008376958
16	1.001535350	34	1.003265438	52	1.004998513	70	1.006734583	88	1.008473651
17	1.001631388	35	1.003361641	53	1.005094883	71	1.006831119	89	1.008570354
18	1.001727435	36	1.003457854	54	1.005191262	72	1.006927665	90	1.008667067

Note: The value of $(1 + i)^n$ for $3\frac{1}{2}\%$ compounded daily for a quarter with 91 days is 1.008763788 and for a quarter with 92 days is 1.008860519.

EXAMPLE 1

Finding Daily Interest

Becky Gonzales received $12,500 from the sale of a piece of real estate. She wants to use the money for a downpayment on a new Toyota Camry, but decides to wait 60 days until the new models are out. She decides to place her money in a savings account earning $3\frac{1}{2}\%$ interest compounded daily for the 60 days. Find the amount of interest she will earn.

SOLUTION

The table value for 60 days is 1.005769730.

Compound amount = $12,500 × 1.005769730 = **$12,572.12**
Interest = **$12,572.12** − $12,500 = $72.12

The additional $72.12 isn't much money to Gonzales, but she is happy to earn some interest.

QUICK CHECK 1

Find the interest if $1200 is invested in a money market account earning 3.5% compounded daily for 90 days.

Quick Check Answer

1. $10.40

The next two examples show how interest is calculated when there are several deposits and/or withdrawals within a short period of time.

EXAMPLE 2

Finding Interest on Multiple Deposits

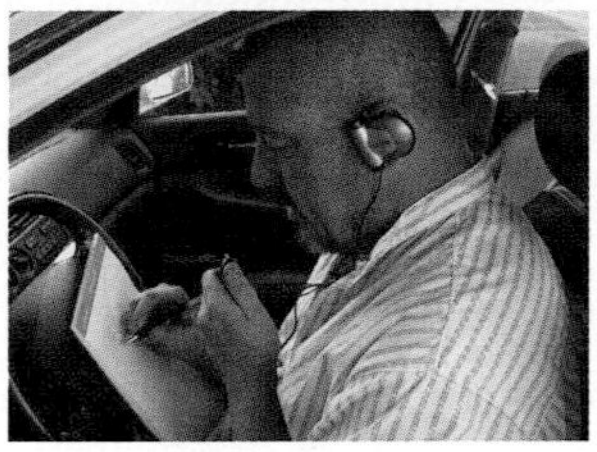

Tom Blackmore is a private investigator who keeps his extra cash in a savings account to earn interest. On January 10, he deposited \$2463 in a savings account paying $3\frac{1}{2}\%$ compounded daily. He deposited an additional \$1320 on February 18 and \$840 on March 3. Find the interest earned through April 10.

SOLUTION

Treat each deposit separately. The \$2463 was in the account for 90 days (21 days in January, 28 days in February, 31 days in March, and 10 days in April). The value for 90 days from the table is **1.008667067**.

Compound amount = \$2463 × **1.008667067** = \$2484.35   first deposit plus interest

The \$1320 deposited on February 18 was in the account for 51 days (10 days in February, 31 days in March, and 10 days in April).

Compound amount = \$1320 × **1.004902153** = \$1326.47   second deposit plus interest

The \$840 was in the account for 38 days (28 days in March and 10 days in April).

Compound amount = \$840 × **1.003650307** = \$843.07   final deposit plus interest

The total amount in the account on April 10 is found by adding the three compound amounts.

Total in account = \$2484.35 + \$1326.47 + \$843.07 = **\$4653.89**

The interest earned is the total amount in the account less the deposits.

Interest earned = **\$4653.89** − (\$2463 + \$1320 + \$840) = \$30.89

QUICK CHECK 2

A money market account is opened with an \$8500 deposit on April 10, and another \$1500 is deposited on May 5. Find the total in the account on June 30 if funds earn $3\frac{1}{2}\%$ compounded daily. Also find the interest earned.

EXAMPLE 3

Finding Interest for the Quarter

Beth Gardner owns Blacktop Paving, Inc. She needs a place to keep extra cash, a place that will earn interest but that will allow her to get funds when needed. She opened a money market account on July 20 with a \$24,800 deposit. She then withdrew \$3800 on August 29 for an unexpected truck repair, and she made another withdrawal of \$8200 on September 29 for payroll. Find the interest earned through October 1, given interest at $3\frac{1}{2}\%$ compounded daily.

QUICK TIP See **Appendix C** for financial calculator solutions that do not require the use of a table.

SOLUTION

Of the original \$24,800, a total of \$24,800 − \$3800 − \$8200 = \$12,800 earned interest from July 20 to October 1 or for 274 − 201 = 73 days. Find the factor **1.007024219** from the table.

Compound amount = \$12,800 × **1.007024219** = \$12,889.91
Interest = \$12,889.91 − \$12,800 = \$89.91

The withdrawn \$3800 earned interest from July 20 to August 29 or for 241 − 201 = 40 days.

Compound amount = \$3800 × **1.003842797** = \$3814.60
Interest = \$3814.60 − \$3800 = \$14.60

Finally, the withdrawn \$8200 earned interest from July 20 to September 29 or for 272 − 201 = 71 days.

Compound amount = \$8200 × **1.006831119** = \$8256.02
Interest = \$8256.02 − \$8200 = \$56.02

The total interest earned is (\$89.91 + \$14.60 + \$56.02) = **\$160.53.** The total in the account on October 1 is found as follows.

Deposits + Interest − Withdrawals = Balance on October 1
\$24,800 + **\$160.53** − (\$3800 + \$8200) = \$12,960.53

Quick Check Answer

2. \$10,074.35; \$74.35

QUICK CHECK 3

An account is opened with a deposit of \$4000, but \$3000 is withdrawn 40 days later. Find the amount in the account and the interest earned at the end of 90 days from the original deposit if interest is $3\frac{1}{2}\%$ compounded daily.

OBJECTIVE 3 **Define time deposit accounts.** Banks pay higher interest rates on funds left on deposit for *longer time periods* in **time deposits.** A **certificate of deposit (CD)** requires a minimum amount of money, such as \$1000, to be on deposit for a minimum period of time, such as 1 year. Find the compound amount of a time deposit as follows.

Compound amount = Principal × Number from the table
Interest = Compound amount − Principal

QUICK TIP This compound interest table assumes daily compounding. The compound interest table on page 382 of **Section 9.1** *does not.*

Compound Interest for Time Deposit Accounts Compounded Daily

Number of Years	3%	4%	5%	6%	7%	Number of Years
1	1.03045326	1.04080849	1.05126750	1.06183131	1.07250098	1
2	1.06183393	1.08328232	1.10516335	1.12748573	1.15025836	2
3	1.09417024	1.12748944	1.16182231	1.19719965	1.23365322	3
4	1.12749129	1.17350058	1.22138603	1.27122408	1.32309429	4
5	1.16182708	1.22138937	1.28400343	1.34982553	1.41901993	5
10	1.34984217	1.49179200	1.64866481	1.82202895	2.01361756	10

EXAMPLE 4

Finding Interest and Compound Amount for Time Deposits

Tony Sanchez plans to purchase three machines for his auto-repair shop. Bank of America requires \$20,000 in collateral before making the loan. Therefore, Tony deposits \$20,000 with the bank in a 2-year certificate of deposit yielding 4% compounded daily. Find the compound amount and interest.

SOLUTION

Look at the table for 4% and 2 years, finding 1.08328232.

Compound amount = \$20,000 × 1.08328232 = **\$21,665.65** rounded
Interest = **\$21,665.65** − \$20,000 = \$1665.65

QUICK CHECK 4

Find the compound amount and interest on \$10,000 invested in a 4-year CD earning 6% compounded daily.

OBJECTIVE 4 **Define inflation and the consumer price index.** **Inflation** results in a continual rise in the prices of goods and services. In other words, the value of a dollar falls every year. It makes sense to earn interest when you can to make up for loss due to inflation. Look at the newspaper clipping on the next page to see how difficult inflation can make it for some to attain a middle-class lifestyle.

The **consumer price index (CPI** or **cost of living index)** is calculated by the government each year and is used to track inflation. It measures the average change in prices from one year to the next for a common select group of goods and services, including food, housing, fuel, utilities, apparel, transportation, insurance, health care, and even pet care. Go to the Bureau of Labor Statistics Web site (http://www.bls.gov/) to see the effect of inflation over time.

QUICK TIP If inflation averages 3% a year, an automobile costing \$25,000 today will cost about \$45,000 in 20 years.

Quick Check Answers

3. \$1020.20; \$20.20
4. \$12,712.24; \$2712.24

Low inflation rate? Some Consumers Beg to Differ

"Typical" middle-class life harder to attain for many

By John Waggoner
USA TODAY

Ask most economists about inflation, and they'll tell you it's low. Ask the average consumer, and you might get a very different answer.

Sean Taylor, 34, an information technology consultant in Trenton, N.J., ticks off the changes in his bills in the past nine years: property taxes, now $9,000 a year, up 105%; heating oil, $238, up 109%. His wife, Carrie, a state employee, pays $87 a month for health care; nine years ago, it was free. His income varies from year to year. Her salary is $75,000, up from $45,000 or 67%.

"And she's been promoted twice," he says.

OBJECTIVE 5 Examine the effect of inflation on spendable income. Inflation reduces the buying power of a family. Example 5 shows what happens to purchasing power when a 2% pay raise is received in a year with 4.8% inflation. It isn't pretty!

EXAMPLE 5

Estimating the Effects of Inflation

Inflation from one year to the next was 4.8% as measured by the CPI.

(a) Find the effect of the increase on a family with an annual income and budget of $39,600 (after taxes).

(b) What is the overall effect if the family members receive only a 2% (after tax) increase in pay for the year?

SOLUTION

(a) This is a percent problem. The cost of the goods and services that this family buys, if they buy the common bundle of goods and services, went up by 4.8% as measured by the CPI.

$$.048 \times \$39{,}600 = \mathbf{\$1900.80}$$

Therefore next year these same goods and services will cost the family

$$\$39{,}600 + \mathbf{\$1900.80} = \$41{,}500.80$$

(b) The family's income went up 2% after taxes, or by

$$.02 \times \$39{,}600 = \mathbf{\$792}$$

Thus, their new income is $39,600 + $792 = $40,392. In effect, the family loses $41,500.80 − $40,392 = $1108.80 in purchasing power without considering taxes.

QUICK TIP Example 5 can also be solved as follows.

Inflation rate	4.8%
− Raise	2.0%
Loss	2.8%

2.8% × $39,600 = $1108.80

QUICK CHECK 5

A family with an income of $32,000 receives a raise of 1.5% in a year when inflation is 3.5%. Find the decrease in purchasing power.

Quick Check Answer

5. $640 loss

Example 5 shows that inflation can slowly erode purchasing power. Imagine the effect of losing purchasing power every year for 10 years. Inflation can erode purchasing power even though pay raises are received every year. Retired people are particularly concerned with inflation, since they live off of Social Security payments and their estate. Some retired people have had to go back to work because they did not plan appropriately for inflation.

EXAMPLE 6

Estimating the Effects of Inflation

Joan Davies has \$14,650 in a savings account paying $3\frac{1}{2}\%$ compounded daily. Ignoring taxes, what is her gain or loss in purchasing power in a year in which the CPI index increases by 4.2%?

SOLUTION

Use the interest-by-quarter table on page 390 to find that the compound amount factor for 4 quarters is **1.035121585**.

$$\text{Compound amount at end of year} = \$14{,}650 \times \mathbf{1.035121585} = \mathbf{\$15{,}164.53}$$

To keep up with inflation, Davies needs to earn 4.2% on her investment.

$$\text{Needed to keep up with inflation} = \$14{,}650 \times 1.042 = \mathbf{\$15{,}265.30}$$

The difference of \$15,265.30 − \$15,164.53 = \$100.77 is the loss in purchasing power. The purchasing power of Davies's savings actually went *down*, even though she earned interest for the year and her account balance grew. The problem worsens if Davies has to pay taxes on interest earned, since she will end up with even less interest.

QUICK CHECK 6

Tador Roofing deposits \$50,000 in an account earning $3\frac{1}{2}\%$ compounded daily for 1 year. Find the loss in purchasing power in a year with an increase in the CPI of 4%.

OBJECTIVE 6 **Understand the role of the government related to inflation.** Since inflation can be harmful to families and businesses, the Federal Reserve Bank (the Fed) works to control inflation. To slow the economy when it is growing too fast and inflation is rising, the Fed increases interest rates. It lowers interest rates when the economy is growing slowly and inflation is low. The graph below shows the inflating tuition costs of college education.

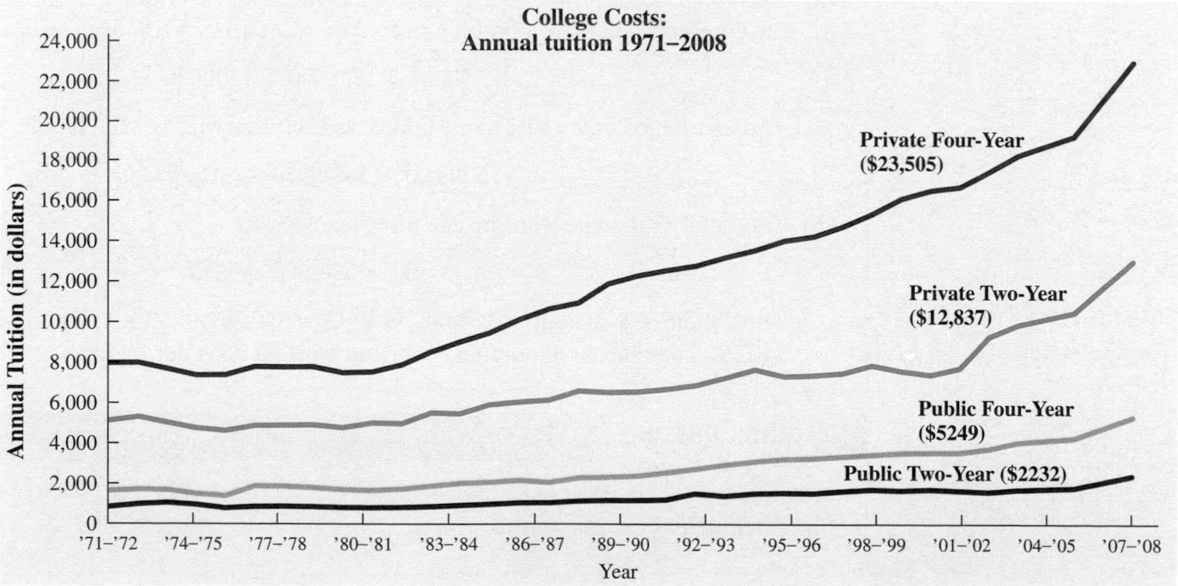

Quick Check Answer

6. \$243.92

9.2 EXERCISES

The QUICK START exercises in each section contain solutions to help you get started.

Find the interest earned by the following. Assume $3\frac{1}{2}$% interest compounded daily. (See Examples 1–3.)

QUICK START

	Amount	Date Deposited	Date Withdrawn	Interest Earned
1.	$4800	July 6	September 30	$39.75

There are $(31 - 6) + 31 + 30 = 86$ days.
Interest is $4800 \times 1.008280273 - $4800 = 39.75.

	Amount	Date Deposited	Date Withdrawn	Interest Earned
2.	$3850	January 5	February 9	$12.94

There are $(31 - 5) + 9 = 35$ days.
Interest is $3850 \times 1.003361641 - $3850 = 12.94.

	Amount	Date Deposited	Date Withdrawn	Interest Earned
3.	$8200	October 4	December 7	_____
4.	$2830	May 4	June 23	_____
5.	$17,958	September 9	November 7	_____
6.	$12,000	December 3	February 20	_____

Find the compound amount for each of the following certificates of deposit. Assume daily compounding. (See Example 4.)

QUICK START

	Amount Deposited	Interest Rate	Time in Years	Compound Amount
7.	$3900	5%	4	$4763.41

$3900 \times 1.22138603 = 4763.41

	Amount Deposited	Interest Rate	Time in Years	Compound Amount
8.	$8000	4%	1	_____
9.	$12,900	3%	10	_____
10.	$3600.40	6%	10	_____

 indicates an exercise that is related to the Case in Point feature.

Case Studies

Bank of America Corporation

www.bankofamerica.com

- More than 55 million customers and 17,000 ATMs
- 20 million active online users
- 2005: Revenues of $84 billion
- 2006: Contributed $200 million to charities

Bank of America Corporation is one of the largest financial institutions in the world, having offices in more than 30 countries and serving customers in more than 175 countries. It has the largest talking ATM network in the world, and the online banking system is compatible with both Quicken and Microsoft Money for those who bank online.

1. Assume that one week the bank has 1.1 million customers who pay a total of $258,500,000 in bills online. Find the average amount per bill paid online for the month.

2. Assume that Bank of America Corporation borrows a total of $80,000,000 from a European bank at 4% interest for 1 year. It then lends out $65,000,000 of this amount at 8% compounded quarterly for 1 year. Find the difference between interest earned and interest paid out by the bank. (Use the compound interest table.)

3. List three advantages and three disadvantages of banking with a very large bank.

9.3 PRESENT VALUE AND FUTURE VALUE

OBJECTIVES

1. Define the terms *future value* and *present value.*
2. Use tables to calculate present value.
3. Use future value and present value to estimate the value of a business.

OBJECTIVE 1 Define the terms *future value* and *present value*. **Future value** is the amount available at a specific date in the future. It is the amount available after an investment has earned interest. All of the values found in **Sections 9.1 and 9.2** were future values.

In contrast, **present value** is the amount needed today so that the desired future value will be available when needed. For example, an individual may need to know the present value that must be invested today in order to have a down payment for a new car in 3 years. Or a firm may need to know the present value that must be invested today in order to have enough money to purchase a new computer system in 20 months. The bar chart shows present value as the value today and future value as the value at a future date.

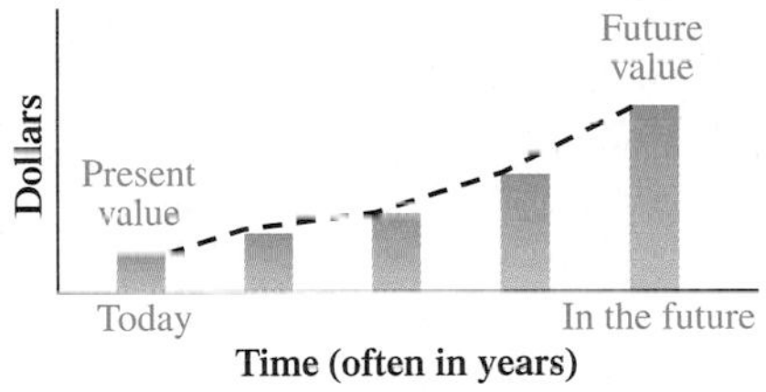

In this section, the future value, interest rate, and term are given and the present value that must be invested today to reach the future value is calculated.

OBJECTIVE 2 Use tables to calculate present value. First, find the interest rate per compounding period (i) and the total number of compounding periods (n) of the investment. Then use these values to find the appropriate value in the present value of a dollar table. Finally, use the formula to find present value.

QUICK TIP n is the number of compounding periods of the investment. The interest rate per compounding period (i) is found by dividing the annual interest rate by the number of compounding periods per year.

$$\text{Present value } (P) = \text{Future value} \times \text{Table value}$$

EXAMPLE 1 Finding Present Value

Betty Clark needs to replace the pumps at her gas station in 3 years at an estimated cost of $12,000. What lump sum deposited today at 5% compounded annually must she invest to have the needed funds? How much interest will she earn?

SOLUTION

STEP 1 The interest rate is 5% per compounding period for 3 compounding periods (years in this case). Look across the top of the table for 5% and down the left column for 3 to find .86384.

$$\text{Present value} = \$12{,}000 \times .86384 = \mathbf{\$10{,}366.08}$$

STEP 2 Interest earned = $12,000 − **$10,366.08** = $1633.92.

STEP 3 Check the answer by finding the future value of an investment of $10,366.08 in an account earning 5% compounded annually for 3 years. Use the table on page 382 to find 1.15763.

$$\text{Future value} = \$10{,}366.08 \times 1.15763 = \$12{,}000.09$$

The reason it is not exactly $12,000 is rounding in the table value.

QUICK CHECK 1

Find the lump sum that must be deposited today to have a future value of $25,000 in 5 years if funds earn 6% compounded annually.

Quick Check Answer

1. $18,681.50

Present Value of a Dollar Table

	Interest Rate per Period										
Period	**1%**	**$1\frac{1}{2}$%**	**2%**	**$2\frac{1}{2}$%**	**3%**	**4%**	**5%**	**6%**	**8%**	**10%**	**Period**
1	.99010	.98522	.98039	.97561	.97087	.96154	.95238	.94340	.92593	.90909	1
2	.98030	.97066	.96117	.95181	.94260	.92456	.90703	.89000	.85734	.82645	2
3	.97059	.95632	.94232	.92860	.91514	.88900	.86384	.83962	.79383	.75131	3
4	.96098	.94218	.92385	.90595	.88849	.85480	.82270	.79209	.73503	.68301	4
5	.95147	.92826	.90573	.88385	.86261	.82193	.78353	.74726	.68058	.62092	5
6	.94205	.91454	.88797	.86230	.83748	.79031	.74622	.70496	.63017	.56447	6
7	.93272	.90103	.87056	.84127	.81309	.75992	.71068	.66506	.58349	.51316	7
8	.92348	.88771	.85349	.82075	.78941	.73069	.67684	.62741	.54027	.46651	8
9	.91434	.87459	.83676	.80073	.76642	.70259	.64461	.59190	.50025	.42410	9
10	.90529	.86167	.82035	.78120	.74409	.67556	.61391	.55839	.46319	.38554	10
11	.89632	.84893	.80426	.76214	.72242	.64958	.58468	.52679	.42888	.35049	11
12	.88745	.83639	.78849	.74356	.70138	.62460	.55684	.49697	.39711	.31863	12
13	.87866	.82403	.77303	.72542	.68095	.60057	.52032	.46884	.36770	.28966	13
14	.86996	.81185	.75788	.70773	.66112	.57748	.50507	.44230	.34036	.26333	14
15	.86135	.79985	.74301	.69047	.64186	.55526	.48102	.41727	.31524	.23939	15
16	.85282	.78803	.72845	.67362	.62317	.53391	.45811	.39365	.29189	.21763	16
17	.84438	.77639	.71416	.65720	.60502	.51337	.43630	.37136	.27027	.19784	17
18	.83602	.76491	.70016	.64117	.58739	.49363	.41552	.35034	.25025	.17986	18
19	.82774	.75361	.68643	.62553	.57029	.47464	.39573	.33051	.23171	.16351	19
20	.81954	.74247	.67297	.61027	.55368	.45639	.37689	.31180	.21455	.14864	20
21	.81143	.73150	.65978	.59539	.53755	.43883	.35894	.29416	.19866	.13513	21
22	.80340	.72069	.64684	.58086	.52189	.42196	.34185	.27751	.18394	.12285	22
23	.79544	.71004	.63416	.56670	.50669	.40573	.32557	.26180	.17032	.11168	23
24	.78757	.69954	.62172	.55288	.49193	.39012	.31007	.24698	.15770	.10153	24
25	.77977	.68921	.60953	.53939	.47761	.37512	.29530	.23300	.14602	.09230	25
26	.77205	.67902	.59758	.52623	.46369	.36069	.28124	.21981	.13520	.08391	26
27	.76440	.66899	.58586	.51340	.45019	.34682	.26785	.20737	.12519	.07628	27
28	.75684	.65910	.57437	.50088	.43708	.33348	.25509	.19563	.11591	.06934	28
29	.74934	.64936	.56311	.48866	.42435	.32065	.24295	.18456	.10733	.06304	29
30	.74192	.63976	.55207	.47674	.41199	.30832	.23138	.17411	.09938	.05731	30
31	.73458	.63031	.54125	.46511	.39999	.29646	.22036	.16425	.09202	.05210	31
32	.72730	.62099	.53063	.45377	.38834	.28506	.20987	.15496	.08520	.04736	32
33	.72010	.61182	.52023	.44270	.37703	.27409	.19987	.14619	.07889	.04306	33
34	.71297	.60277	.51003	.43191	.36604	.26355	.19035	.13791	.07305	.03914	34
35	.70591	.59387	.50003	.42137	.35538	.25342	.18129	.13011	.06763	.03558	35
36	.69892	.58509	.49022	.41109	.34503	.24367	.17266	.12274	.06262	.03235	36
37	.69200	.57644	.48061	.40107	.33498	.23430	.16444	.11579	.05799	.02941	37
38	.68515	.56792	.47119	.39128	.32523	.22529	.15661	.10924	.05369	.02673	38
39	.67837	.55953	.46195	.38174	.31575	.21662	.14915	.10306	.04971	.02430	39
40	.67165	.55126	.45289	.37243	.30656	.20829	.14205	.09722	.04603	.02209	40
41	.66500	.54312	.44401	.36335	.29763	.20028	.13528	.09172	.04262	.02009	41
42	.65842	.53509	.43530	.35448	.28896	.19257	.12884	.08653	.03946	.01826	42
43	.65190	.52718	.42677	.34584	.28054	.18517	.12270	.08163	.03654	.01660	43
44	.64545	.51939	.41840	.33740	.27237	.17805	.11686	.07701	.03383	.01509	44
45	.63905	.51171	.41020	.32917	.26444	.17120	.11130	.07265	.03133	.01372	45
46	.63273	.50415	.40215	.32115	.25674	.16461	.10600	.06854	.02901	.01247	46
47	.62646	.49670	.39427	.31331	.24926	.15828	.10095	.06466	.02686	.01134	47
48	.62026	.48936	.38654	.30567	.24200	.15219	.09614	.06100	.02487	.01031	48
49	.61412	.48213	.37896	.29822	.23495	.14634	.09156	.05755	.02303	.00937	49

EXAMPLE 2

Finding Present Value

The local Harley-Davidson shop has seen business grow rapidly. The owners plan to double the size of their 6000-square-foot shop in one year at a cost of \$280,000. How much should be invested in an account paying 6% compounded semiannually to have the funds needed?

SOLUTION

The interest rate per compounding period is $\frac{6\%}{2} = 3\%$, and the number of compounding periods is 1 year × 2 periods per year = 2. Use the table to find .94260.

$$\text{Present value} = \$280{,}000 \times .94260 = \$263{,}928$$

A deposit of \$263,928 today at 6% compounded semiannually will provide \$280,001.22 in one year. The difference is due to rounding.

QUICK CHECK 2

In 5 years, Great Lakes Dairy estimates it will need \$350,000 for a down payment to purchase a nearby farm. Find the amount that should be invested today to meet the down payment if funds earn 8% compounded quarterly.

EXAMPLE 3

Applying Present Value

QUICK TIP See Appendix D for financial calculator solutions that do not require the use of a table.

Radiux Inc. wishes to partner with a Korean company to purchase a satellite in 3 years. Radiux plans to make a cash down payment of 40% of its anticipated \$8,000,000 cost and borrow the remaining funds from a bank. Find the amount Radiux should invest today in an account earning 6% compounded annually to have the down payment needed in 3 years.

SOLUTION

First find the down payment to be paid in 3 years.

$$\text{Down payment} = .40 \times \$8{,}000{,}000 = \$3{,}200{,}000$$

This is the future value needed exactly 3 years from now. Using the present value of a dollar table on page 400 with 3 periods and 6% per period gives

$$\$3{,}200{,}000 \times .83962 = \$2{,}686{,}784$$

Radiux must invest \$2,686,784 today at 6% interest compounded annually to have the required down payment of \$3,200,000 in 3 years.

QUICK CHECK 3

Mom and Pop Jenkins plan to buy a new car in 2 years and want to make a down payment of 25% of the estimated purchase price of \$32,000. Find the amount they need to invest to make the down payment if funds earn 6% compounded quarterly.

OBJECTIVE 3 **Use future value and present value to estimate the value of a business.** Sometimes a business has such a strong growth opportunity that it is valued at more than it would be if it had normal growth. In this case, the strong growth opportunity increases the market price of the business. To estimate the value of a business with strong growth, first find the future value of the business 2 to 5 years in the future as projected. Then find the present value of this amount using the appropriate discount rate.

Quick Check Answers

2. \$235,539.50
3. \$7101.68

EXAMPLE 4

Evaluating a Business

Brianna Delfs and Tanya Zoban own Extreme Sports, Inc., whose value is $120,000 today assuming normal growth. However, the partners believe the value will grow at 15% per year for the next four years. They want to take this rapid growth into consideration when valuing the business for a potential sale.

(a) Find the future value of the business in 4 years.
(b) Estimate the value of the retail store by finding the present value of the amount found in part **(a)** at 6% compounded quarterly.

SOLUTION

(a) The partners expect the business to grow at 15% per year for the next 4 years. There is no 15% column in the compound interest table of **Section 9.1,** so we use the formula $(1 + i)^n$, where $i = .15$ and $n = 4$.

$$\text{Future value} = \$120{,}000 \times (1 + i)^n$$
$$= \$120{,}000 \times (1 + .15)^4 = \mathbf{\$209{,}881}\ (\textbf{rounded})$$

This is an estimate of the value of the store in 4 years.

(b) Now find the present value of $209,881 assuming 6% compounded quarterly for 4 years or at $\frac{6\%}{4} = 1.5\%$ per quarter for $4 \times 4 = 16$ compounding periods. The value from the present value of a dollar table on page 400 is **.78803**.

$$\text{Present value} = \$209{,}881 \times \mathbf{.78803} = \$165{,}393\ (\textbf{rounded})$$

Thus, the partners should ask about $165,400 for their business. The rapid growth rate adds about $165,400 − $120,000 = $45,400 to the value of the business.

QUICK CHECK 4

Assuming normal growth, a clothing store is worth $100,000. But the owners believe it will grow at 9% per year for the next three years. Estimate a reasonable selling price for the business by finding the present value at 5% per year compounded semiannually.

Quick Check Answer

4. $111,670.35

9.3 EXERCISES

FOR EXTRA HELP

MyMathLab

MathXL PRACTICE

WATCH

DOWNLOAD

READ

REVIEW

The QUICK START *exercises in each section contain solutions to help you get started.*

Find the present value of the following. Round to the nearest cent. Also, find the amount of interest earned. (See Examples 1 and 2.)

QUICK START

	Amount Needed	*Time (Years)*	*Interest*	*Compounded*	*Present Value*	*Interest Earned*
1.	$12,300	3	8%	annually	$9764.11	$2535.89
	$P = \$12{,}300 \times .79383 = \$9764.11$; $I = \$12{,}300 - \$9764.11 = \$2535.89$					
2.	$14,500	$2\frac{1}{2}$	8%	quarterly	$11,895.08	$2604.92
	$P = \$14{,}500 \times .82035 = \$11{,}895.08$; $I = \$14{,}500 - \$11{,}895.08 = \$2604.92$					
3.	$9350	4	5%	semiannually	________	________
4.	$850	10	8%	semiannually	________	________
5.	$18,853	11	6%	quarterly	________	________
6.	$20,984	9	10%	quarterly	________	________

Solve the following application problems.

QUICK START

7. DIVORCE SETTLEMENT The Prestons are getting a divorce, and part of the divorce settlement involves setting aside money for college tuition for their daughter who enters college in 7 years. They estimate that the cost of four years' tuition, food, and lodging at the state university their daughter will attend will be $40,000. Find **(a)** the lump sum that must be invested at 6% compounded semiannually and **(b)** the amount of interest earned.

(a) $26,444.80
(b) $13,555.20

(a) Lump sum $= P = \$40{,}000 \times .66112 = \$26{,}444.80$
(b) $I = \$40{,}000 - \$26{,}444.80 = \$13{,}555.20$

8. SELF-EMPLOYMENT Janet Becker wishes to start her own day-care business in 4 years and estimates that she will need $25,000 to do so. **(a)** What lump sum should be invested today at 5%, compounded semiannually, to produce the needed amount? **(b)** How much interest will be earned?

(a) ________
(b) ________

9. FINANCING COLLEGE EXPENSES Mrs. Lorez wants all of her grandchildren to go to college and decides to help financially. How much must she give to each child at birth if they are to have $10,000 on entering college 18 years later, assuming 6% interest compounded annually?

9. ________

10. TIRE STORE Felipe Bazan recently immigrated to the United States from Mexico. He has a little cash and hopes to open a small tire store in 3 years. How much must he deposit today if his credit union pays 6% compounded quarterly and if he needs $15,000 to open the store?

10. ________________

11. EXPANDING MANUFACTURING OPERATIONS Quantum Logic recently expanded its computer-chip assembly operations at a cost of $450,000. Management expects that the value of the investment will grow at a rate of 12% per year compounded annually for the next 5 years. **(a)** Find the future value of the investment. **(b)** Find the present value of the amount found in part **(a)** at a rate of 6% compounded annually. Round to the nearest dollar at each step.

(a) ________________
(b) ________________

12. BUSINESS EXPANSION Village Hardware expands its business at a cost of $20,000. They expect that the investment will grow at a rate of 10% per year compounded annually for the next 4 years. **(a)** Find the future value of the investment. **(b)** Find the present value of the amount found in part **(a)** at a rate of 6% compounded annually. Round to the nearest dollar at each step.

(a) ________________
(b) ________________

13. VALUE OF A BUSINESS Jessie Marquette believes her hair salon is worth $20,000 and estimates that its value will grow at 10% per year compounded annually for the next 3 years. If she sells the business, the funds will be invested at 8% compounded quarterly. **(a)** Find the future value if she holds onto the business. **(b)** What price should she insist on now if she sells the business?

(a) ________________
(b) ________________

14. VALUE OF A BUSINESS John Fernandez figures his bike shop is worth $88,000 if sold today and that it will grow in value at 8% per year compounded annually for the next 6 years. If he sells the business, the funds will be invested at 5% compounded semiannually. **(a)** Find the future value of the shop. **(b)** What price should he insist on at this time if he sells the business?

(a) ________________
(b) ________________

15. Explain the difference between future value and present value. (See Objective 1.)

16. Explain how and when to use both the compound interest table in **Section 9.1** and the present value table in this section.

CHAPTER 9 QUICK REVIEW

CHAPTER TERMS *Review the following terms to test your understanding of the chapter. For each term you do not know, refer to the page number found next to that term.*

CD **[p. 392]**
CPI **[p. 392]**
certificate of deposit **[p. 392]**
compound amount **[p. 378]**
compound interest **[p. 378]**
compounded daily **[p. 389]**
compounding period **[p. 380]**
consumer price index **[p. 392]**
cost of living index **[p. 392]**
exponents **[p. 381]**
formula for compounding interest **[p. 381]**
future amount **[p. 378]**
future value **[p. 378]**
inflation **[p. 392]**
interest-bearing checking accounts **[p. 389]**
money market accounts **[p. 389]**
passbook accounts **[p. 389]**
present value **[p. 399]**
savings accounts **[p. 389]**
simple interest **[p. 378]**
time deposit **[p. 392]**

CONCEPTS	EXAMPLES
9.1 Finding compound amount and compound interest Find the number of compounding periods (n) and the interest rate per period (i). Use the compound interest table to find the interest on $1. Multiply the table value by the principal to obtain the compound amount. Subtract principal from compound amount to obtain the interest.	Tom Jones invested $3000 at 6% compounded quarterly for 7 years. There are $7 \times 4 = 28$ quarters or compounding periods in 7 years. Interest of 6% per year $= \frac{6\%}{4} = 1\frac{1}{2}\%$ per period. Find $1\frac{1}{2}\%$ across the top of the compound interest table and 28 down the left side to find 1.51722. Compound amount = $3000 × 1.51722 = $4551.66 Interest = $4551.66 − $3000 = $1551.66
9.2 Finding the interest earned when the interest is compounded daily Find the number of days that the deposit earns interest. Use the 90-day or 1-quarter table to calculate interest on $1. Find compound amount using the formula Compound amount = Principal × Table value Find interest earned using the formula Interest = Compound amount − Principal	Mary Carver deposits $1000 at $3\frac{1}{2}\%$ compounded daily on May 15. She withdraws the money on July 17. Find the compounded amount and interest earned. May 15–May 31: 16 days June: 30 days July 1–July 17: 17 days **63 days** Table value = **1.006059089** Compound amount = $1000 × **1.006059089** = **$1006.06** Interest = **$1006.06** − $1000 = $6.06
9.2 Finding the interest on time deposits Use the compound interest for time deposit accounts table to find the interest on $1 compounded daily. Find the compound amount using the formula Compound amount = Principal × Table value Find interest using the formula Interest = Compound amount − Principal	Susan Barbee invests $50,000 in a certificate of deposit paying 5% compounded daily. Find the amount after 4 years. Table value for 4 years at 5% = **1.22138603** Compound amount = $50,000 × **1.22138603** = $61,069.30 Interest = $61,069.30 − $50,000 = $11,069.30
9.2 Finding the effect of inflation on a pay raise Find the new salary by multiplying the old salary by (1 + percent increase). Find the salary needed to offset inflation by multiplying the old salary by (1 + inflation rate). Find the gain or loss by subtracting.	Leticia Jaramillo earns $45,000 per year as a computer programmer. She gets a raise of 3.5% in a year in which inflation is 5%. Ignoring taxes, find the effect on her purchasing power. New salary = $45,000 × 1.035 = **$46,575** Salary needed to offset inflation = $45,000 × 1.05 = **$47,250** Loss in purchasing power = $47,250 − $46,575 = $675

CONCEPTS	EXAMPLES
9.3 Finding the present value of a future amount Determine the number of compounding periods (n). Determine the interest per compounding period (i). Use the values of n and i to determine the table value from the present value table. Find present value from the following formula. Present value = Future value × Table value	Sue York must pay a lump sum of \$4500 in 6 years. What lump sum deposited today at 6% compounded quarterly will amount to \$4500 in 6 years? Number of compounding periods = 6 × 4 = 24 Interest per compounding period $= \frac{6\%}{4} = 1\frac{1}{2}\%$ **per period** Table value = **.69954** Present value = \$4500 × **.69954** = \$3147.93

CHAPTER 9 SUMMARY EXERCISE

Valuing a Chain of McDonald's Restaurants

James and Mary Watson own a small chain of McDonald's restaurants that is valued at \$2,300,000. They believe that the chain will grow in value at 12% per year compounded annually for the next 5 years. If they sell the chain, the funds will be invested at a rate of 6% compounded semiannually. They expect inflation to be 4% per year for the next 5 years. Ignore taxes, and answer the following, rounding answers to the nearest dollar at each step.

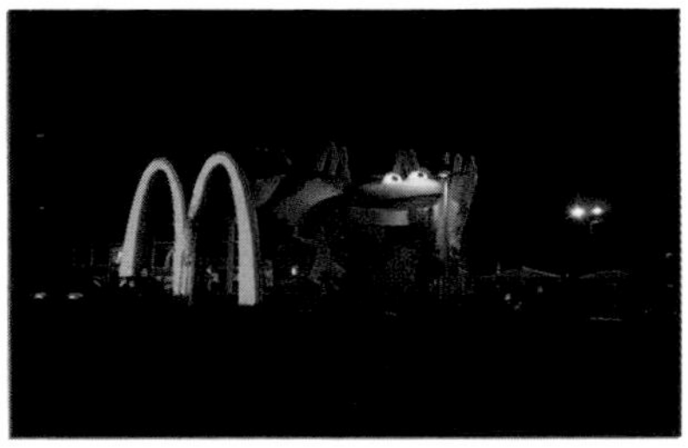

(a) Find the future value of the chain after 5 years. Then find the price they should sell the chain for if they wish to have the same future value at the end of 5 years.

(a) ____________

(b) Find the future value of the chain if it grows at only 2% per year for 5 years. Then find the price they should ask for the chain given a 2% growth rate per year.

(b) ____________

(c) What future value would the chain be worth if it grew at their expected rate of inflation? Find the price they should ask for the chain if it grows at the rate of inflation.

(c) ____________

(d) Complete the following table.

Growth Rate	Future Value	Market Value Today
2%	________	________
4% (inflation)	________	________
12%	________	________

The value of the chain varies by more than one million dollars, depending on the rate of growth assumed for the business for the next 5 years.

INVESTIGATE

The interest rates that a bank pays depend on whether the money is in a checking account, money market account, savings account, or time deposit. Visit a local bank, and find the different interest rates that the bank will pay. Identify the conditions such as the minimum amount in an account, the minimum deposit, and the length of time the money must be on deposit to earn each interest rate.

10.1 ANNUITIES AND RETIREMENT ACCOUNTS

OBJECTIVES

1. Define the basic terms involved with annuities.
2. Find the amount of an annuity.
3. Find the amount of an annuity due.
4. Understand different retirement accounts and find the amount of a retirement account.

CASE in POINT The benefits coordinator at the college asked Roman Rodriguez if he preferred an annuity paying a guaranteed interest or one invested in a mutual fund containing stocks. Rodriguez knew that he needed to be careful, since it was his financial future they were discussing.

OBJECTIVE 1 Define the basic terms involved with annuities. In **Chapter 9**, we discussed lump sums that were invested for periods of time. In this chapter, we talk about an **annuity** or a series of equal payments made at regular intervals. Monthly mortgage payments, quarterly payments by a company into an employee retirement account, and monthly checks paid by an insurance company to a retired couple are examples of annuities. The graph below shows why people buy annuities. Here are some definitions you need to know.

Ordinary annuity: annuity in which payments are made *at the end of each period*
Payment period: the time between payments
Term of the annuity: the time from the first payment through the last payment

Interest calculations for annuities are made using compound interest. Consider regular monthly investments into a retirement account. Each payment earns compound interest until the annuity ends. The total amount in the account at the end is the **amount, compound amount**, or **future value of the annuity**.

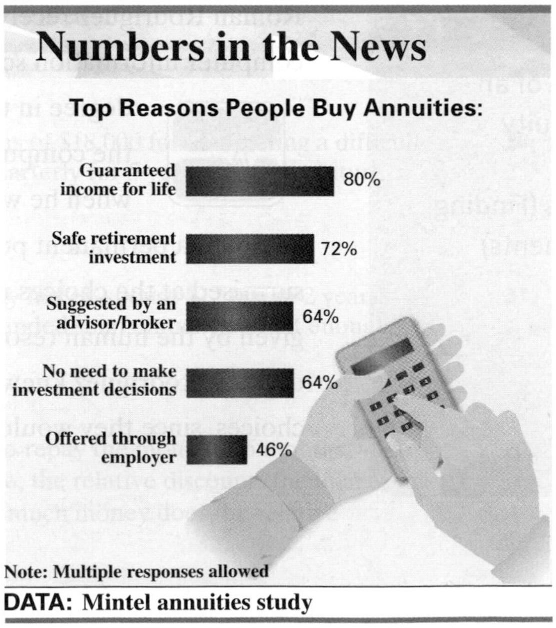

A company uses an annuity when it saves money to purchase a new vehicle. Assume the company makes deposits of $3000 *at the end of each year* for 6 years into an account earning 8% compounded annually. The first deposit is made at the end of year 1 and earns interest for 5 years. Use the compound interest table in **Section 9.1** (page 382) for 5 years and 8% to find the future value of the first payment.

$$\$3000 \times \mathbf{1.46933} = \$4407.99$$

The future value of the annuity is *the sum* of the compound amounts of all six payments.

QUICK TIP The annuity ends on the day of the last payment. Therefore, the last payment, which is made at the end of year 6, earns no interest.

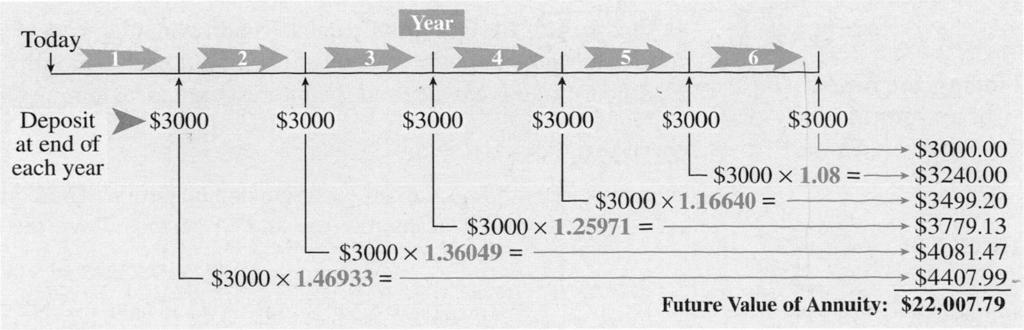

OBJECTIVE 2 **Find the amount of an annuity.** The amount of an annuity can also be found using the amount of an annuity table on page 417. The number from the table is the amount or future value of an annuity with a payment of $1. The amount of an annuity with any payment is found as follows.

Amount = Payment × Number from amount of an annuity table

As a check, reconsider the annuity of $3000 at the end of each year for 6 years at 8% compounded annually. Locate 8% at the top of the table on page 417 and 6 periods in the far left (or far right) column to find 7.33593.

Amount = $3000 × 7.33593 = $22,007.79

This amount is identical to the amount calculated earlier.

EXAMPLE 1

Finding the Value of an Annuity and Interest Earned

The community college will match Roman Rodriguez's contribution into his retirement plan, but only up to 5% of his salary. In other words, the community college will put one dollar into his retirement plan for every dollar that Rodriguez puts into it, but they will not contribute more than 5% of his $32,000 yearly salary. Rodriguez immediately decides to put 5% of his salary into the retirement plan. Using quarterly calculations, find the future value in 8 years **(a)** if the account earns 4% compounded quarterly and **(b)** if the account earns 8% compounded quarterly. **(c)** Then find the difference between the two future values.

SOLUTION

Salary per quarter	= $32,000 ÷ 4 = $8000			
Total contributions	=	Rodriguez's contributions	+	Employer's matching contributions
	=	.05 × $8000	+	.05 × $8000
	=	$400	+	$400
	= $800 invested per quarter			

(a) Interest of $\frac{4\%}{4}$ = 1% is earned per quarter for 8 × 4 = 32 quarters. Look across the top of the table for 1% and down the side for 32 periods to find 37.86901.

Amount = $800 × 37.86901 = **$30,295.21** (rounded)

(b) Interest of $\frac{8\%}{4}$ = 2% is earned per quarter for 8 × 4 = 32 quarters. Look across the top of the table for 2% and down the side for 32 periods to find 44.22703.

Amount = $800 × 44.22703 = **$35,381.62** (rounded)

(c) Difference = $35,381.62 − $30,295.21 = $5086.41

QUICK CHECK 1

At the end of every quarter, $2000 is put into a retirement plan that earns 6% compounded quarterly. Find the future value in 5 years.

Quick Check Answer

1. $46,247.34

EXAMPLE 2

Finding the Amount of an Annuity and Interest Earned

QUICK TIP Example 2 in Appendix D shows how a financial calculator can be used to solve these same types of problems.

At the birth of her grandson, Junella Smith commits to help pay for his college education. She decides to make deposits of $600 at the end of each 6 months into an account for 17 years. Find the amount of the annuity and the interest earned, assuming 6% compounded semiannually.

SOLUTION

Interest of $\frac{6\%}{2} = 3\%$ is earned each semiannual period. There are $2 \times 17 = 34$ semiannual periods in 17 years. Find 3% across the top and 34 periods down the side of the table for **57.73018**.

$$\text{Amount} = \$600 \times 57.73018 = \$34{,}638.11$$

$$\text{Interest} = \$34{,}638.11 - (\mathbf{34} \times \mathbf{\$600}) = \$14{,}238.11\text{(rounded)}$$

Smith knows that a college education will cost a lot more in 17 years than it does now, but she also knows that $34,638.11 will be of great help to her grandson.

QUICK CHECK 2

Bob Nelson deposits $250 into a retirement account at the end of every month for 30 months. The fund holds international stocks and Nelson optimistically thinks it may yield 12% compounded monthly. Find the future amount.

OBJECTIVE 3 **Find the amount of an annuity due.** Payments were made at the *end of each period* in the ordinary annuities discussed previously. In contrast, an annuity in which payments are made at the *beginning of each time period* is called an **annuity due**. To find the amount of an annuity due, treat each payment as if it were made at *the end of the preceding period*, then

STEP 1 Add 1 to the number of periods.

STEP 2 Find: Amount = Payment × Number from amount of an annuity table.

STEP 3 Subtract 1 payment.

EXAMPLE 3

Finding the Amount of an Annuity Due

QUICK TIP For an annuity due, be sure to add 1 period to the number of compounding periods and subtract 1 payment from the amount calculated.

Mr. and Mrs. Thompson set up an investment program using an *annuity due* with payments of $500 at the *beginning of each quarter*. Find **(a)** the amount of the annuity and **(b)** the interest if they make payments for 7 years into an investment account expected to pay 8% compounded quarterly.

SOLUTION

(a) STEP 1: Interest of $\frac{8\%}{4} = 2\%$ is earned each quarter. There are $4 \times 7 = 28$ periods in 7 years. Since it is an annuity due, add 1 period to 28, making 29 periods.

STEP 2: Look across the top of the table for 2% and down the side for 29 periods to find **38.79223**.

$$\$500 \times 38.79223 = \mathbf{\$19{,}396.12}\text{ (rounded)}$$

STEP 3: Now subtract one payment to find the amount of the annuity due.

$$\text{Amount of annuity due} = \mathbf{\$19{,}396.12} - \$500 = \$18{,}896.12$$

(b) Subtract the 28 payments (7 years × 4 payments per year) of $500 each to find the interest.

$$\text{Interest} = \$18{,}896.12 - (\mathbf{28} \times \mathbf{\$500}) = \$4896.12$$

The calculator solution to finding the interest in part **(b)** follows.

18896.12 [−] 28 [×] 500 [=] 4896.12

Note: Refer to Appendix C for calculator basics.

QUICK CHECK 3

If $1000 is deposited at the beginning of every six months into an account that earns 5% compounded semiannually, find the amount after 8 years.

Quick Check Answers

2. $8696.22
3. $19,864.73

Amount of an Annuity Table

Period					Interest Rate per Period							Period
n	1%	$1\frac{1}{2}$%	2%	$2\frac{1}{2}$%	3%	4%	5%	6%	8%	10%	12%	n
1	1.00000	1.00000	1.00000	1.00000	1.00000	1.00000	1.00000	1.00000	1.00000	1.00000	1.00000	1
2	2.01000	2.01500	2.02000	2.02500	2.03000	2.04000	2.05000	2.06000	2.08000	2.10000	2.12000	2
3	3.03010	3.04522	3.06040	3.07562	3.09090	3.12160	3.15250	3.18360	3.24640	3.31000	3.37440	3
4	4.06040	4.09090	4.12161	4.15252	4.18363	4.24646	4.31013	4.37462	4.50611	4.64100	4.77933	4
5	5.10101	5.15227	5.20404	5.25633	5.30914	5.41632	5.52563	5.63709	5.86660	6.10510	6.35285	5
6	6.15202	6.22955	6.30812	6.38774	6.46841	6.63298	6.80191	6.97532	7.33593	7.71561	8.11519	6
7	7.21354	7.32299	7.43428	7.54743	7.66246	7.89829	8.14201	8.39384	8.92280	9.48717	10.08901	7
8	8.28567	8.43284	8.58297	8.73612	8.89234	9.21423	9.54911	9.89747	10.63663	11.43589	12.29969	8
9	9.36853	9.55933	9.75463	9.95452	10.15911	10.58280	11.02656	11.49132	12.48756	13.57948	14.77566	9
10	10.46221	10.70272	10.94972	11.20338	11.46388	12.00611	12.57789	13.18079	14.48656	15.93742	17.54874	10
11	11.56683	11.86326	12.16872	12.48347	12.80780	13.48635	14.20679	14.97164	16.64549	18.53117	20.65458	11
12	12.68250	13.04121	13.41209	13.79555	14.19203	15.02581	15.91713	16.86994	18.97713	21.38428	24.13313	12
13	13.80933	14.23683	14.68033	15.14044	15.61779	16.62684	17.71298	18.88214	21.49530	24.52271	28.02911	13
14	14.94742	15.45038	15.97394	16.51895	17.08632	18.29191	19.59863	21.01507	24.21492	27.97498	32.39260	14
15	16.09690	16.68214	17.29342	17.93193	18.59891	20.02359	21.57856	23.27597	27.15211	31.77248	37.27971	15
16	17.25786	17.93237	18.63929	19.38022	20.15688	21.82453	23.65749	25.67253	30.32428	35.94973	42.75328	16
17	18.43044	19.20136	20.01207	20.86473	21.76159	23.69751	25.84037	28.21288	33.75023	40.54470	48.88367	17
18	19.61475	20.48938	21.41231	22.38635	23.41444	25.64541	28.13238	30.90565	37.45024	45.59917	55.74971	18
19	20.81090	21.79672	22.84056	23.94601	25.11687	27.67123	30.53900	33.75999	41.44626	51.15909	63.43968	19
20	22.01900	23.12367	24.29737	25.54466	26.87037	29.77808	33.06595	36.78559	45.76196	57.27500	72.05244	20
21	23.23919	24.47052	25.78332	27.18327	28.67649	31.96920	35.71925	39.99273	50.42292	64.00250	81.69874	21
22	24.47159	25.83758	27.29898	28.86286	30.53678	34.24797	38.50521	43.39229	55.45676	71.40275	92.50258	22
23	25.71630	27.22514	28.84496	30.58443	32.45288	36.61789	41.43048	46.99583	60.89330	79.54302	104.60289	23
24	26.97346	28.63352	30.42186	32.34904	34.42647	39.08260	44.50200	50.81558	66.76476	88.49733	118.15524	24
25	28.24320	30.06302	32.03030	34.15776	36.45926	41.64591	47.72710	54.86451	73.10594	98.34706	133.33387	25
26	29.52563	31.51397	33.67091	36.01171	38.55304	44.31174	51.11345	59.15638	79.95442	109.18177	150.33393	26
27	30.82089	32.98668	35.34432	37.91200	40.70963	47.08421	54.66913	63.70577	87.35077	121.09994	169.37401	27
28	32.12910	34.48148	37.05121	39.85980	42.93092	49.96758	58.40258	68.52811	95.33883	134.20994	190.69889	28
29	33.45039	35.99870	38.79223	41.85630	45.21885	52.96629	62.32271	73.63980	103.96594	148.63093	214.58275	29
30	34.78489	37.53868	40.56808	43.90270	47.57542	56.08494	66.43885	79.05819	113.28321	164.49402	241.33268	30
31	36.13274	39.10176	42.37944	46.00027	50.00268	59.32834	70.76079	84.80168	123.34587	181.94342	271.29261	31
32	37.86901	40.68829	44.22703	48.15028	52.50276	62.70147	75.29883	90.88978	134.21354	201.13777	304.84772	32
33	38.86901	42.29861	46.11157	50.35403	55.07784	66.20953	80.06377	97.34316	145.95062	222.25154	342.42945	33
34	40.25770	43.93309	48.03380	52.61289	57.73018	69.85791	85.06696	104.18375	158.62667	245.47670	384.52098	34
35	41.66028	45.59209	49.99448	54.92821	60.46208	73.65222	90.32031	111.43478	172.31680	271.02437	431.66350	35

OBJECTIVE 4 Understand different retirement accounts and find the amount of a retirement account. The newspaper clipping below shows that it can be difficult to know how much is needed to retire, but the consequences of having too little can be serious. The important thing is to begin saving as soon as possible and to save regularly. A great benefit of retirement plans is that an employed person can save for decades without paying taxes on gains or interest until the money is actually withdrawn. This makes it easier to accumulate large amounts of money. Retirement plans are for everyone, *including those who just graduated from college.*

HERE & NOW

Retired Without Enough Income

Tom Wheat retired in 2003 thinking that his Social Security check of $1040 per month and income from his savings would be enough to support his lifestyle. However, he subsequently developed diabetes, increasing his medical expenses to significantly more than he anticipated. Now, at 73 years of age, he can no longer work and must get by on a limited fixed income. He may have to sell his small home so that he can use the equity. But where would he live?

An employed person can set up an **individual retirement account (IRA)** at a bank or brokerage firm. Each person in a married couple can contribute to a regular IRA even if only one of them works. Deposits to a **regular IRA** are usually excluded from federal income taxes. For example, an individual making $50,000 per year has to pay income taxes on only $46,000 if he or she makes a $4000 contribution to a regular IRA. Funds in a regular IRA grow tax-free, but income taxes must be paid at the time the funds are withdrawn. There is a penalty for taking money out of an IRA before age $59\frac{1}{2}$ unless funds are related to extreme medical expenses, first-time home purchases, or death.

Another type of IRA is a **Roth IRA**. Deposits to a Roth IRA *are not excluded from federal taxes in the year paid*, so they do not reduce current income taxes. However, the deposits and interest grow tax-free. In addition, withdrawals from a Roth IRA at retirement **are not subject to income taxes** when withdrawn. This offers you a great opportunity to save money for retirement without having to pay taxes as you withdraw the funds. The following table may help you.

Roth IRA

WHICH IRA IS BEST FOR YOU?

	DEDUCTIBLE IRA	ROTH IRA
Tax deductible?	If you qualify	No
Taxable at withdrawal?	Yes	No
Penalty for early withdrawal?	Yes, prior to age 59.5	Yes*
Mandatory withdrawal age?	70.5	None
Penalty-free withdrawals?	$10,000 for first-time home buyers; unlimited for education	$10,000 for first-time home buyers, after five-year wait; unlimited for education

*Never any penalty for withdrawing your own contributions, but a penalty applies to withdrawal of any gains within five years of opening the account and/or before turning 59.5.

Allowable IRA Contribution

	Age	
Year	**Under 50**	**50 and over**
2008	$5000	$6000
after 2008	Limits adjusted depending on inflation	

The following figure shows some of the many reasons companies offer retirement plans to full-time employees. There are several different types of company-sponsored retirement plans. Two common plans are the **401(k)** plan for individuals working for private-sector companies and the **403(b)** plan for employees of public schools and certain tax-exempt organizations. The names 401(k) and 403(b) refer to sections of the Internal Revenue Service code that define these plans. Each of these plans allows an employer to deduct a certain amount of money from your paycheck *before* taxes are calculated and to invest those funds in the plan. Companies also sometimes match all or part of the contribution of an employee.

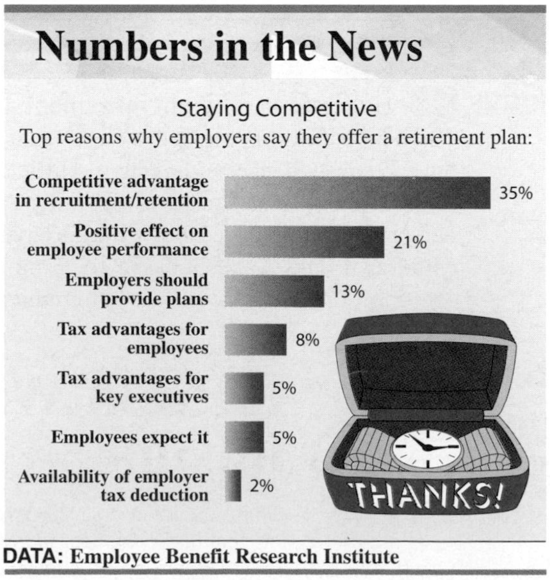

QUICK TIP Individuals who pay FICA (Social Security) taxes are eligible for monthly payments from the Social Security system at retirement. Social Security benefits are in addition to any income from IRAs or company retirement plans.

Regular contributions into either an IRA or a company-sponsored retirement plan are an annuity. The amount of the annuity is found using the same methods discussed earlier in this section. Payments are at the end of each period in an ordinary annuity, and payments are at the beginning of each period in an annuity due.

EXAMPLE 4

Finding the Value of an IRA

At 27, Joann Gretz sets up an IRA with Merrill Lynch where she plans to deposit \$2000 at the end of each year until age 60. Find the amount of the annuity if she invests in **(a)** a bond fund that has historically yielded 6% compounded annually versus **(b)** a stock fund that has historically yielded 10% compounded annually. Assume that future yields equal historical yields.

SOLUTION

Age 60 is $60 - 27 = 33$ years away, so she will make deposits at the end of each year for 33 years.

(a) Bond fund: Look down the left column of the amount of an annuity table on page 417 at 33 years and across the top for 6% to find 97.34316.

$$\text{Amount} = \$2000 \times 97.34316 = \$194{,}686.32 \text{ (rounded)}$$

(b) Stock fund: Look down the left column of the table for 33 years and across the top for 10% to find 222.25154.

$$\text{Amount} = \$2000 \times 222.25154 = \$444{,}503.08$$

The differences in the two investments are shown in the figure. Gretz wants the larger amount, but she is worried she might lose money in the stock fund. See *Exercise 20* at the end of this section to find her investment choice.

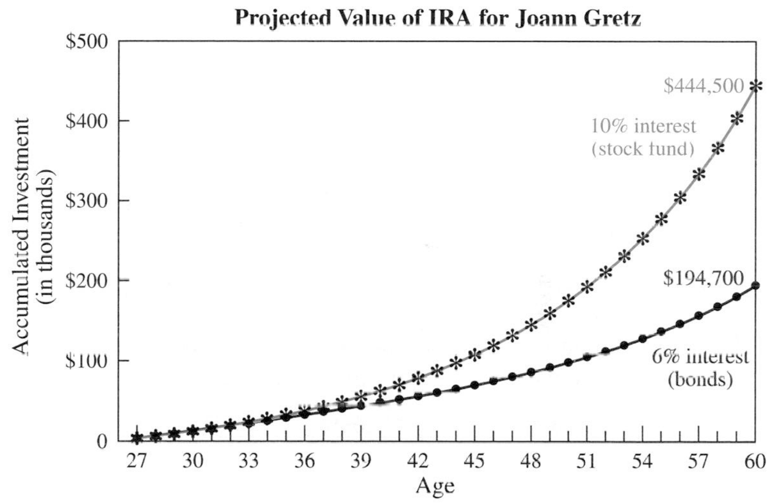

QUICK CHECK 4

Bill James plans to deposit \$2500 in a regular IRA at the end of six months for the next 17 years until he retires. Find the future value if funds earn **(a)** 5% compounded semiannually and **(b)** 8% compounded semiannually.

Quick Check Answers

4. (a) \$131,532.23
(b) \$174,644.78

Now find the present value needed at the beginning of year 1 to accumulate $188,416.50 by the end of year 5, which is the same as the beginning of year 6. Use the present value of a dollar table in **Section 9.3** (page 400) with $\frac{6\%}{2} = 3\%$ per compounding period and $5 \times 2 = 10$ compounding periods.

Present value needed at beginning of year 1 = $188,416.50 × **.74409** = $140,198.83

A lump sum of $140,198.83 deposited today will grow to $188,416.50 in 5 years, which will fund 16 semiannual payments of $15,000 each during the following 8 years.

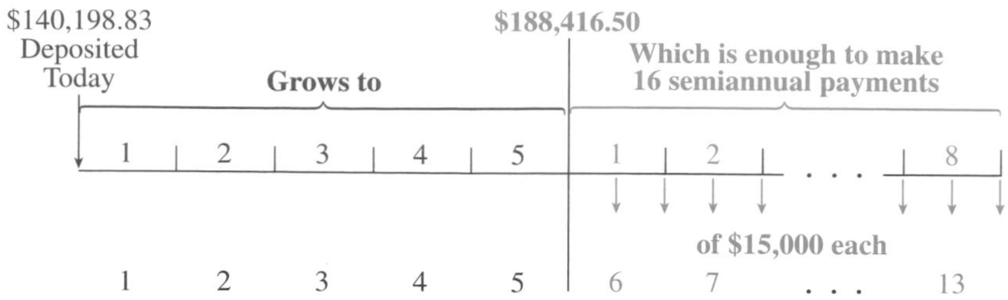

QUICK CHECK 3

A project manager signs a contract that will pay him a bonus of $20,000 at the end of each year for 5 years, beginning in 4 years. Assuming 4% per year, find the amount that must be set aside today to fund this benefit.

EXAMPLE 4

Determining Retirement Income

Tish Baker plans to retire from nursing at age 65 and hopes to withdraw $25,000 per year until she is 90. **(a)** If money earns 8% per year compounded annually, how much will she need at age 65? **(b)** If she deposits $2000 per year into her retirement plan beginning at age 32, and if the retirement plan earns 8% per year compounded annually, will her retirement account have enough for her to meet her goals? Ignore taxes.

SOLUTION

(a) The amount needed at age 65 is the present value of an annuity of $25,000 per year for $90 - 65 = 25$ years with interest of 8% compounded annually. The present value of an annuity table is used to find the following.

Present value = $25,000 × **10.67478** = $266,869.50

Baker will need $266,869.50 at age 65. This sum, at 8% compounded annually, will permit withdrawals of $25,000 per year until age 90.

(b) Baker makes payments of $2000 at the end of each year for $65 - 32 = 33$ years, at 8% compounded annually. These payments form a regular annuity. The amount of an annuity table in **Section 10.1** is used to find the following.

Future value = $2000 × **145.95062** = $291,901.24

The value in the retirement account at 65 (**$291,901.24**) exceeds the amount needed to fund 25 yearly withdrawals of $25,000 each (**$266,869.50**). Therefore, Tish Baker will have more than enough money.

QUICK TIP Example 7 in Appendix D shows how a financial calculator can be used to solve a problem similar to Example 4.

QUICK CHECK 4

The Smiths want to plan for retirement using an annual income of $35,000 at the end of each year for 25 years based on a rate of 5% per year. **(a)** Find the present value needed when they retire to generate this income. **(b)** If they save $20,000 at the end of each year for 15 years, will they have enough?

Quick Check Answers

3. $76,108.31

4. (a) $493,287.90

(b) no, short by $61,716.70

OBJECTIVE 3 **Find the equivalent cash price of an ordinary annuity.** Payments made at different times cannot be compared directly to one another to see which is better. Rather, we first find the present value of each payment, which is called the **equivalent cash price**. Then compare the two present values to identify the better of the two.

EXAMPLE 5

Comparing Methods of Investment

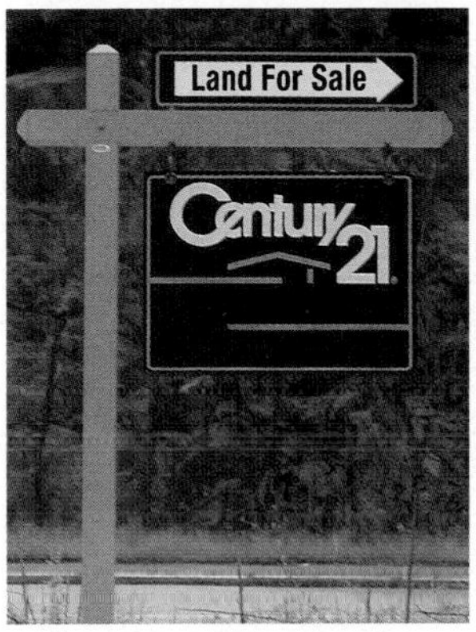

Jean Braddock is offering to sell a piece of property to two different real estate developers. Kapton Homes offers $200,000 in cash today for the land. RealProperty offers $80,000 now as a down payment and payments of $10,000 at the end of each quarter for 4 years. Assume that money can be invested at 8% per year compounded quarterly. Which offer should Braddock accept?

SOLUTION

Since payments from the two real estate developers occur over different time periods, the present value of each offer must be found to determine which is better.

The present value of Kapton Homes' offer is **$200,000**, since that payment is made now.

The present value of RealProperty's offer is the sum of the down payment plus the present value of the series of payments. Use $\frac{8\%}{4} = 2\%$ per compounding period for 4 years × 4 quarters per year = 16 compounding periods. Use the present value of an annuity table to find 13.57771.

Present value of payments = $10,000 × 13.57771 =	$135,777.10
Down payment	+ $80,000.00
Present value of RealProperty's offer	**$215,777.10**

Therefore, $215,777.10 is the **equivalent cash price** to $80,000 down plus 16 quarterly payments of $10,000 each.

RealProperty's offer is the better of the two by the following amount.

$215,777.10 − $200,000 = $15,777.10

QUICK CHECK 5

Ben James has two different offers for a lot that he owns: (1) $48,000 cash and (2) $12,000 down and $2659 per quarter for 12 quarters. Assuming 6% compounded quarterly, find the present value of both and determine the better of the two.

As shown in the next example, we can use the concepts in this section to estimate the present value of Social Security payments at the time of retirement. To do so, first simplify the problem by assuming that payments are made at the end of each year and that the payments remain constant. Note that increases in Social Security payments are due to inflation, so Social Security payments effectively do remain constant in terms of buying power.

EXAMPLE 6

Finding the Present Value of Social Security Payments

Debra Shorter expects to receive $20,940 per year in Social Security payments. Assume that she receives these payments for 28 years and use a rate of 6% per year. Find the present value of her retirement payments.

SOLUTION

Use the present value of an annuity table with 28 years and 6% per year to find 13.40616.

Present value = $20,940 × 13.40616 = $280,724.99

Her Social Security retirement payments have a present value of $280,724.99. In other words, the Social Security payments equate to having cash of $280,724.99 at the time of retirement.

QUICK CHECK 6

Benjamin Thomason decides to wait until age 70 to begin receiving Social Security benefits, since it will result in higher payments. Find the present value of his estimated $26,000 per year in payments assuming 5% per year and payments until his 85th birthday.

Quick Check Answers

5. $48,000; $41,003.07; $48,000 cash is the better offer

6. $269,871.16

10.2 EXERCISES

FOR EXTRA HELP

MyMathLab

MathXL PRACTICE

WATCH

DOWNLOAD

READ

REVIEW

The **QUICK START** *exercises in each section contain solutions to help you get started.*

Find the present value of the following annuities. Round to the nearest cent. (See Examples 1–3.)

QUICK START

	Amount per Payment	*Payment at End of Each*	*Time (Years)*	*Rate of Investment*	*Compounded*	*Present Value*
1.	$1800	year	18	10%	annually	**$14,762.54**
	Present value = $1800 × 8.20141 = $14,762.54					
2.	$4100	year	7	6%	annually	**$22,887.76**
	Present value = $4100 × 5.58238 = $22,887.76					
3.	$2000	6 months	12	8%	semiannually	______
4.	$1700	6 months	14	5%	semiannually	______
5.	$894	quarter	6	4%	quarterly	______
6.	$7500	quarter	5	10%	quarterly	______

7. Explain the difference between the two ways to think of the present value of an annuity. (See Objective 1.)

8. Explain the meaning of equivalent cash price. (See Objective 3.)

Solve the following application problems. Round to the nearest cent.

QUICK START

9. INJURY LAWSUIT The court ruled that Bakon Corporation was liable in the death of an employee. The settlement called for the company to pay the employee's widow $65,000 at the end of each year for 20 years. Find the amount the company must set aside today to satisfy this annuity assuming 5% compounded annually.

Present value of annuity = $65,000 × 12.46221 = $810,043.65

9. **$810,043.65**

10. COMPUTER REPLACEMENT The community college where Roman Rodriguez works sets aside an annual payment of $35,000 per year for 5 years so it will have funds to replace the personal computers, servers, and printers in the computer labs when needed. Assuming 5% compounded annually, what lump sum deposited today would result in the same future value?

10. ______

11. COLLEGE EXPENSES Jason Clendenen needs $7000 every 6 months for living expenses and tuition at the University of Texas at Austin. As an engineering major, he will take 5 years to earn his college degree. Find **(a)** the lump sum that must be deposited to meet this need and **(b)** the interest earned assuming 8% per year, compounded semiannually.

(a) ______
(b) ______

C indicates an exercise that is related to the Case in Point feature.

12. DISASTER RELIEF After a terrible flood in Bangladesh, an international disaster relief organization agreed to help support families in a small city who lost everything with a payment of $25,000 every quarter for 5 years. Find **(a)** the lump sum that must be deposited to meet this need and **(b)** the interest earned assuming 6% per year, compounded quarterly.

(a) ______________
(b) ______________

13. PAYING FOR COLLEGE Tom Potter estimates that his daughter's college needs, beginning in 8 years, will be $3600 at the end of each quarter for 4 years. **(a)** Find the total amount needed in 8 years assuming 8% compounded quarterly. **(b)** Will he have enough money available in 8 years if he invests $700 at the end of each quarter for the next 8 years at 8% compounded quarterly?

(a) ______________
(b) ______________

14. VAN PURCHASE In 4 years, Jennifer Videtto will need a delivery van, for her office-supply store, that will require a down payment of $10,000 with payments of $1200 per month for 36 months. **(a)** Find the total amount needed in 4 years assuming 12% compounded monthly. **(b)** Will she have enough money available if she invests $1000 at the end of each month for the next 4 years at 12% compounded monthly?

(a) ______________
(b) ______________

15. SELLING A BUSINESS Anna Stanley has two offers for her business. The first offer is a cash payment of $85,000, and the second is a down payment of $25,000 with payments of $3500 at the end of each quarter for 5 years. **(a)** Identify the better offer assuming 8% compounded quarterly. **(b)** Find the difference in the present values.

(a) ______________
(b) ______________

16. GROCERY STORE Adolf Hegman has two offers for his Canadian grocery company. The first offer is a cash payment of $540,000, and the second is a down payment of $240,000 with payments of $65,000 at the end of each semiannual period for 4 years. **(a)** Identify the better offer assuming 10% compounded semiannually. **(b)** Find the difference in the present values.

(a) ______________
(b) ______________

17. SOCIAL SECURITY Jessica Thames expects to receive $18,400 per year based on her deceased husband's contributions to Social Security. Assume that she receives payments for 14 years and a rate of 8% per year, and find the present value of this annuity.

17. ______________

18. SOCIAL SECURITY Warren and Bernice White's combined Social Security payments add up to $35,400 per year. Assume payments for 20 years and a rate of 6% per year, and find the present value.

18. ______________

10.3 SINKING FUNDS (FINDING ANNUITY PAYMENTS)

OBJECTIVES

1. Understand the basics of a sinking fund.
2. Set up a sinking fund table.

CASE in POINT Roman Rodriguez is excited. The president of the college has decided to set up a sinking fund to accumulate funds needed in 5 years for a new building that will include a gymnasium and an indoor 50-meter swimming pool, which Rodriguez plans to use.

OBJECTIVE 1 Understand the basics of a sinking fund. Individuals and businesses often need to raise a certain amount of money for use *at some fixed time in the future*. For example, Paul Pence needs \$28,000 to purchase a truck in 3 years. Using 8% compounded quarterly and the amount of an annuity table in **Section 10.1**, one can guess the required payment at the end of each quarter needed to accumulate the \$28,000.

Guess of quarterly payment	*From table*	*Future value*	*The guess is*
\$1500	\$1500 × 13.41209 =	\$20,118.14	too low
\$2800	\$2800 × 13.41209 =	\$37,553.85	too high

Clearly this method is awkward. The exact payment in this example can be found by dividing the future value of \$28,000 by 13.41209, or by using the table and methods provided in this section. In summary, this section shows how to find the periodic payment needed to achieve a specific future value at a specific date.

A fund set up to receive periodic payments is called a **sinking fund**. Sinking funds are used to provide money *to pay off a loan* in one lump sum *or to accumulate money* to build new factories, buy equipment, and so on. Large corporations and some government agencies use a form of debt called a **bond**, which is a promise to pay a fixed amount of money at some stated time in the future. Bonds are discussed in detail in **Section 10.5**. This section covers only the use of a sinking fund to pay off a bond when it is due.

The amount of the periodic payment needed, at the end of each period, to accumulate a fixed amount at a future date is found as follows.

Payment = Future value × Number from sinking fund table

EXAMPLE 1

Finding Periodic Payments

The president of a community college wants to set up a sinking fund to accumulate funds needed in 5 years for a new sports complex. The cost that includes a gymnasium and an indoor 50-meter swimming pool is estimated to be \$16,500,000. The school board decides to make end-of-quarter deposits into a fund earning 6% compounded quarterly. Find **(a)** the amount of each quarterly payment and **(b)** the interest earned.

SOLUTION

(a) Use $\frac{6\%}{4} = 1.5\%$ per compounding period for 4×5 years = 20 compounding periods in the sinking fund table on page 433 to find .04325.

$$\text{Quarterly payment} = \$16{,}500{,}000 \times .04325 = \mathbf{\$713{,}625}$$

Twenty end-of-quarter payments of \$713,625 at 6% compounded quarterly will grow to \$16,501,629 using the table in **Section 10.1**.

(b) Interest is the future value minus the payments.

$$\text{Interest} = \$16{,}501{,}629 - (20 \times \mathbf{\$713{,}625}) = \$2{,}229{,}129 \text{ (rounded)}$$

QUICK CHECK 1

A utility company needs \$600 million in 6 years to build a coal-fired power plant. What amount does it need to deposit at the end of each quarter into a sinking fund, if funds earn 8% compounded quarterly?

Quick Check Answer

1. \$19.722 million or \$19,722,000

EXAMPLE 2

Finding the Periodic Payments

First Christian Church sold $100,000 worth of bonds that must be paid off in 8 years. It now must set up a sinking fund to accumulate the necessary $100,000 to pay off the debt. Find the amount of each payment into a sinking fund if the payments are made at the end of each year and the fund earns 10% compounded annually. Find the amount of interest earned.

SOLUTION

Look along the top of the sinking fund table for 10% and down the side for 8 periods to find .08744.

$$\text{Payment} = \$100{,}000 \times .08744 = \$8744$$

The church must deposit $8744 at the end of each year for 8 years into an account paying 10% compounded annually to accumulate $100,000. The interest earned is the future value less all payments.

$$\text{Interest} = \$100{,}000 - (8 \times \$8744) = \$30{,}048$$

QUICK CHECK 2

A charter airline sold $1,000,000 in bonds to buy a new aircraft. It chose to make end-of-semiannual-period deposits to accumulate the funds needed to pay off the bonds in 4 years. Use 5% compounded semiannually and find **(a)** the payment and **(b)** the interest.

OBJECTIVE 2 **Set up a sinking fund table.** A **sinking fund table** is used to show the interest earned and the accumulated amount of a sinking fund at the end of each period.

EXAMPLE 3

Setting up a Sinking Fund Table

First Christian Church in Example 2 deposited $8744 at the end of each year for 8 years into a sinking fund that earned 10% compounded annually. Set up a sinking fund table for these deposits. After each calculation, round each answer to the nearest cent before proceeding.

QUICK TIP The interest rate a company earns on sinking fund investments frequently differs from the interest rate it must pay on debts such as bonds.

SOLUTION

The sinking fund account contains no money until the end of the first year, when a single deposit of $8744 is made. Since the deposit is made at the end of the year, no interest is earned.

At the end of the second year, the account contains the original $8744 plus the interest earned by this money. This interest is found by the formula for simple interest.

$$I = \$8744 \times .10 \times 1 = \$874.40$$

An additional deposit is also made at the end of the second year, so that the sinking fund then contains the following total.

$$\$8744 + \$874.40 + \$8744 = \mathbf{\$18{,}362.40}$$

Continue this work to get the following sinking fund table.

	Beginning of Period		End of Period	
Period	Accumulated Amount	Periodic Deposit	Interest Earned	Accumulated Amount
1	$0	$8744.00	$0	$8744.00
2	$8744.00	$8744.00	$874.40	$18,362.40
3	$18,362.40	$8744.00	$1836.24	$28,942.64
4	$28,942.64	$8744.00	$2894.26	$40,580.90
5	$40,580.90	$8744.00	$4058.09	$53,382.99
6	$53,382.99	$8744.00	$5338.30	$67,465.29
7	$67,465.29	$8744.00	$6746.53	$82,955.82
8	$82,955.82	$8748.60	$8295.58	$100,000.00

QUICK TIP Normally the last payment is adjusted as needed so that the future value exactly equals the desired amount. We assume this is true from this point forward.

Quick Check Answers

2. **(a)** $114,470
(b) $84,240

The last payment differs from the earlier payments by $4.60, since the final amount needs to be exactly $100,000 to pay off the bonds.

Sinking Fund Table

Period	1%	$1\frac{1}{2}$%	2%	$2\frac{1}{2}$%	3%	4%	5%	6%	8%	10%	Period
					Interest Rate per Period						
1	1.00000	1.00000	1.00000	1.00000	1.00000	1.00000	1.00000	1.00000	1.00000	1.00000	1
2	.49751	.49628	.49505	.49383	.49261	.49020	.48780	.48544	.48077	.47619	2
3	.33002	.32838	.32675	.32514	.32353	.32035	.31721	.31411	.30803	.30211	3
4	.24628	.24444	.24262	.24082	.23903	.23549	.23201	.22859	.22192	.21547	4
5	.19604	.19409	.19216	.19025	.18835	.18463	.18097	.17740	.17046	.16380	5
6	.16255	.16053	.15853	.15655	.15460	.15076	.14702	.14336	.13632	.12961	6
7	.13863	.13656	.13451	.13250	.13051	.12661	.12282	.11914	.11207	.10541	7
8	.12069	.11858	.11651	.11447	.11246	.10853	.10472	.10104	.09401	.08744	8
9	.10674	.10461	.10252	.10046	.09843	.09449	.09069	.08702	.08008	.07364	9
10	.09558	.09343	.09133	.08926	.08723	.08329	.07950	.07587	.06903	.06275	10
11	.08645	.08429	.08218	.08011	.07808	.07415	.07039	.06679	.06608	.05396	11
12	.07885	.07668	.07456	.07249	.07046	.06655	.06283	.05928	.05270	.04676	12
13	.07241	.07024	.06812	.06605	.06403	.06014	.05646	.05296	.04652	.04078	13
14	.06690	.06472	.06260	.06054	.05853	.05467	.05102	.04758	.04130	.03575	14
15	.06212	.05994	.05783	.05577	.05377	.04994	.04634	.04296	.03683	.03147	15
16	.05794	.05577	.05365	.05160	.04961	.04582	.04227	.03895	.03298	.02782	16
17	.05426	.05208	.04997	.04793	.04595	.04220	.03870	.03544	.02963	.02466	17
18	.05098	.04881	.04670	.04467	.04271	.03899	.03555	.03236	.02670	.02193	18
19	.04805	.04588	.04378	.04176	.03981	.03614	.03275	.02962	.02413	.01955	19
20	.04542	.04325	.04116	.03915	.03722	.03358	.03024	.02718	.02185	.01746	20
21	.04303	.04087	.03878	.03679	.03487	.03128	.02800	.02500	.01983	.01562	21
22	.04086	.03870	.03663	.03465	.03275	.02920	.02597	.02305	.01803	.01401	22
23	.03889	.03673	.03467	.03270	.03081	.02731	.02414	.02128	.01642	.01257	23
24	.03707	.03492	.03287	.03091	.02905	.02559	.02247	.01968	.01498	.01130	24
25	.03541	.03326	.03122	.02928	.02743	.02401	.02095	.01823	.01368	.01017	25
26	.03387	.03173	.02970	.02777	.02594	.02257	.01956	.01690	.01251	.00916	26
27	.03245	.03032	.02829	.02638	.02456	.02124	.01829	.01570	.01145	.00826	27
28	.03112	.02900	.02699	.02509	.02329	.02001	.01712	.01459	.01049	.00745	28
29	.02990	.02778	.02578	.02389	.02211	.01888	.01605	.01358	.00962	.00673	29
30	.02875	.02664	.02465	.02278	.02102	.01783	.01505	.01265	.00883	.00608	30
31	.02768	.02557	.02360	.02174	.02000	.01686	.01413	.01179	.00811	.00550	31
32	.02667	.02458	.02261	.02077	.01905	.01595	.01328	.01100	.00745	.00497	32
33	.02573	.02364	.02169	.01986	.01816	.01510	.01249	.01027	.00685	.00450	33
34	.02484	.02276	.02082	.01901	.01732	.01431	.01176	.00960	.00630	.00407	34
35	.02400	.02193	.02000	.01821	.01654	.01358	.01107	.00897	.00580	.00369	35
36	.02321	.02115	.01923	.01745	.01580	.01289	.01043	.00839	.00534	.00334	36
37	.02247	.02041	.01851	.01674	.01511	.01224	.00984	.00786	.00492	.00303	37
38	.02176	.01972	.01782	.01607	.01446	.01163	.00928	.00736	.00454	.00275	38
39	.02109	.01905	.01717	.01544	.01384	.01106	.00876	.00689	.00419	.00249	39
40	.02046	.01843	.01656	.01484	.01326	.01052	.00828	.00646	.00386	.00226	40
41	.01985	.01783	.01597	.01427	.01271	.01002	.00782	.00606	.00356	.00205	41
42	.01928	.01726	.01542	.01373	.01219	.00954	.00739	.00568	.00329	.00186	42
43	.01873	.01672	.01489	.01322	.01170	.00909	.00699	.00533	.00303	.00169	43
44	.01820	.01621	.01439	.01273	.01123	.00866	.00662	.00501	.00280	.00153	44
45	.01771	.01572	.01391	.01227	.01079	.00826	.00626	.00470	.00259	.00139	45
46	.01723	.01525	.01345	.01183	.01036	.00788	.00593	.00441	.00239	.00126	46
47	.01677	.01480	.01302	.01141	.00996	.00752	.00561	.00415	.00221	.00115	47
48	.01633	.01437	.01260	.01101	.00958	.00718	.00532	.00390	.00204	.00104	48
49	.01591	.01396	.01220	.01062	.00921	.00686	.00504	.00366	.00189	.00095	49
50	.01551	.01357	.01182	.01026	.00887	.00655	.00478	.00344	.00174	.00086	50

QUICK CHECK 3

The payments into a sinking fund are $2400 at the end of each quarter for 1 year. Assume interest of 6% compounded quarterly and construct a sinking fund table.

Frequently, an item costs more if its purchase is delayed a few years. The next example shows how to estimate the cost of a large purchase at a future date, and then how to find the payment needed to accumulate the necessary funds.

EXAMPLE 4

Finding Periodic Payments and Interest Earned

Lee Bareli manages a small coal mine that uses a Caterpillar tractor. She estimates that the tractor would cost $850,000 today but that the cost will increase at 5% per year for 4 years until she plans the purchase. If she earns 8% compounded quarterly in a sinking fund, find the quarterly payments needed to accumulate the funds for the purchase.

SOLUTION

First, find the cost of the tractor in 4 years. Use 5% per compounding period and 4 compounding periods in the compound interest table on page 382 to find 1.21551.

$$\text{Cost in 4 years} = \$850{,}000 \times 1.21551 = \$1{,}033{,}183.50$$

This is the amount that must be accumulated in the sinking fund. The required quarterly payment is found using 4 years × 4 quarters per year = 16 compounding periods and $\frac{8\%}{4} = 2\%$ per compounding period in the sinking fund table for a value of .05365.

$$\text{Quarterly payment} = \$1{,}033{,}183.50 \times .05365 = \$55{,}430.29 \text{ (rounded)}$$

Payments of $55,430.29 at the end of each quarter for 4 years will result in the needed funds to purchase the tractor.

QUICK CHECK 4

The $19,000 cost of a compressor is increasing by 5% per year. First find the amount needed to buy the compressor in 3 years. Then find the necessary semiannual payments into a sinking fund for the purchase if funds earn 10% compounded semiannually.

Two different interest rates are involved in Example 4. The price is increasing at 5% per year compounded annually, but deposits in the sinking fund earn 8% compounded quarterly. **Interest rate spreads** such as this are common in business. For example, banks use an interest rate spread between what they pay for funds on deposit and what they charge on loans to customers.

Quick Check Answers

3.

	Beginning of Period		End of Period	
Period	**Accumulated Amount**	**Periodic Deposit**	**Interest Earned**	**Accumulated Amount**
1	$0.00	$2400.00	$0.00	$2400.00
2	$2400.00	$2400.00	$36.00	$4836.00
3	$4836.00	$2400.00	$72.54	$7308.54
4	$7308.54	$2400.00	$109.63	$9818.17

4. $21,994.97; $3233.70

10.3 EXERCISES

FOR EXTRA HELP

MyMathLab

MathXL PRACTICE

WATCH

DOWNLOAD

READ

REVIEW

The QUICK START *exercises in each section contain solutions to help you get started.*

Find the amount of each payment needed to accumulate the indicated amount in a sinking fund. Round to the nearest cent. (See Examples 1–3.)

QUICK START

1. $12,000, money earns 5% compounded annually, 4 years — **1.** $2784.12

Payment = $12,000 × .23201 = $2784.12

2. $125,000, money earns 6% compounded annually, 25 years — **2.** $2278.75

Payment = $125,000 × .01823 = $2278.75

3. $8200, money earns 6% compounded semiannually, 5 years — **3.** ______

4. $12,000, money earns 10% compounded semiannually, 3 years — **4.** ______

5. $50,000, money earns 4% compounded quarterly, 5 years — **5.** ______

6. $32,000, money earns 6% compounded quarterly, 3 years — **6.** ______

7. $7894, money earns 12% compounded monthly, 3 years — **7.** ______

8. $29,804, money earns 12% compounded monthly, 2 years — **8.** ______

9. Explain the difference between a sinking fund (see Objective 1) and the present value of an annuity discussed in **Section 10.2**.

10. What is a sinking fund table? Who would use one? (See Objective 2.)

Solve each application problem. Round to the nearest cent.

QUICK START

C **11.** STUDENT UNION A community college needs $920,000 in 3 years to remodel the student union. It decides to make payments into a sinking fund at the end of each semiannual period.
(a) Find the amount of each payment assuming 5% per year compounded semiannually. **(b)** Find the total interest earned.

(a) $144,026
(b) $55,844

(a) Payment = $920,000 × .15655 = $144,026
(b) Interest = $920,000 − (6 × $144,026) = $55,844

C indicates an exercise that is related to the Case in Point feature.

12. SCUBA DIVING The owner of Emerald Diving plans to buy all new scuba diving equipment to rent to divers in 5 years at a cost of $34,000. He believes that he can earn 8% compounded quarterly. Find **(a)** the amount of each of the quarterly payments needed and **(b)** the total interest earned.

(a) ____________
(b) ____________

13. ACCUMULATING $1 MILLION Jessica Smith wants to know if she can accumulate $1,000,000 in her lifetime. She feels that she can earn 10% per year for 50 years if she invests in stocks. Find **(a)** the amount of each of the annual payments needed and **(b)** the total interest earned.

(a) ____________
(b) ____________

14. ALLIGATOR HUNTING Cajun Jack needs $45,000 in 4 years for boats used to hunt alligators.
(a) Find the amount of each payment if payments are made at the end of each quarter with interest at 6% compounded quarterly.
(b) Find the total amount of interest earned.

(a) ____________
(b) ____________

15. NEW MACHINERY Smith Dry Cleaning must buy a new cleaning machine in 7 years for $120,000. The firm sets up a sinking fund for this purpose. Find the payment into the fund at the end of each year if money in the fund earns 10% compounded annually.

15. ____________

16. NEW AUDITORIUM The membership of the Green Fields Baptist Church is large and growing rapidly. The leaders of the church are planning to build a new auditorium with special features for their televised broadcasts at a cost of $2,800,000 in 5 years. The membership has set up a sinking fund with the idea of making a payment at the end of each quarter. Find the payment needed if money earns 8% compounded quarterly.

16. ____________

17. A NEW SHOWROOM A Ford dealership wants to build a new showroom costing $2,300,000. It set up a sinking fund with end-of-the-month payments in an account earning 12% compounded monthly. Find the amount that should be deposited in this fund each month if the dealership wishes to build the showroom in **(a)** 3 years and **(b)** 4 years.

(a) ____________
(b) ____________

18. AIRPORT IMPROVEMENTS A city near Chicago sold $9,000,000 in bonds to pay for improvements to an airport. It sets up a sinking fund with end-of-the-quarter payments in an account earning 8% compounded quarterly. Find the amount that should be deposited in this fund each quarter if the city wishes to pay off the bonds in **(a)** 7 years and **(b)** 12 years.

(a) ____________
(b) ____________

19. LAND SALE Helen Spence sells a lot in Nevada. She will be paid a lump sum of $60,000 in 4 years. Until then, the buyer pays 8% simple interest every quarter. **(a)** Find the amount of each quarterly interest payment. **(b)** The buyer sets up a sinking fund so that enough money will be present to pay off the $60,000. The buyer wants to make semiannual payments into the sinking fund. The account pays 8% compounded semiannually. Find the amount of each payment into the fund. **(c)** Prepare a table showing the amount in the sinking fund after each deposit.

(a) ______________

(b) ______________

Payment Number	Amount of Deposit	Interest Earned	Total in Account

20. RARE STAMPS Jeff Reschke bought a rare stamp for his collection. He agreed to pay a lump sum of $4000 after 5 years. Until then, he pays 6% simple interest every 6 months. **(a)** Find the amount of each semiannual interest payment. **(b)** Reschke sets up a sinking fund so that money will be available to pay off the $4000. He wants to make annual payments into the fund. The account pays 8% compounded annually. Find the amount of each payment into the fund. **(c)** Prepare a table showing the amount in the sinking fund after each deposit.

(a) ______________

(b) ______________

Payment Number	Amount of Deposit	Interest Earned	Total in Account

21. SPORTS COMPLEX Prepare a sinking fund table for the first four payments for the community college sports complex described in Example 1.

Payment Number	Amount of Deposit	Interest Earned	Total in Account

22. COMMERCIAL BUILDING Joan Miller plans to make a down payment of $70,000 on a commercial building for her plumbing company in 5 years. Construct a sinking fund table given semiannual payments of $6106.10 at the end of each period and an interest rate of 6% compounded semiannually.

Payment Number	Amount of Deposit	Interest Earned	Total in Account

23. SAVING FOR COLLEGE Barbara Funicello hopes to go to a private college where tuition is $22,500 per year. She believes that tuition will increase at 8% for the 4 years until she plans to enter college. Find the end-of-quarter payments needed to accumulate funds to pay the first year's tuition if funds earn 6% compounded quarterly. Round to the nearest dollar.

23. ____________

24. FIRE TRUCK A volunteer fire department anticipates purchasing a fire truck in 3 years. Today it would cost $175,000, but the cost is increasing at 10% per year. Find the semiannual payments needed to accumulate funds to purchase the truck if funds earn 8% compounded semiannually. Round to the nearest dollar.

24. ____________

25. NEW ROOF The manager of an apartment complex estimates she will need a new roof on one of the buildings in 5 years. Today it would cost $52,000 to reroof the building, but the cost is increasing at 8% per year. Find the semiannual payments needed to accumulate the necessary funds at 5% compounded semiannually.

25. ____________

26. NEW KITCHEN A restaurant manager believes he will need all new kitchen appliances in 2 years. The cost today is $48,800, but costs are going up at 10% per year. Find the semiannual payments needed if funds earn 5% compounded semiannually.

26. ____________

SUPPLEMENTARY APPLICATION EXERCISES ON ANNUITIES AND SINKING FUNDS

Solve the following application problems. Round to the nearest cent.

QUICK START

1. Bill Carrier deposits $500 at the end of each quarter for 6 years into a mutual fund that he believes will grow at 8% compounded quarterly. Find **(a)** the future value and **(b)** the interest.

(a) $15,210.93
(b) $3210.93

(a) Future value = $500 × 30.42186 = $15,210.93
(b) Interest = $15,210.93 − (24 × $500) = $3210.93

2. For 6 years, Jessica Savage deposits $1000 at the end of each quarter into an account earning 8% per year compounded quarterly. Find **(a)** the future value and **(b)** the interest.

(a) ________
(b) ________

3. Mr. and Mrs. Thompson deposit $2000 at the beginning of each year for 20 years into a retirement account earning 6% compounded annually. Find **(a)** the future value and **(b)** the interest

(a) ________
(b) ________

4. Jaime Navarro deposits $1000 at the end of every 6 months into a Roth IRA for 8 years at 10% compounded semiannually. Find **(a)** the future value and **(b)** the interest.

(a) ________
(b) ________

5. Solectron needs to purchase new equipment for its production line in 3 years. The company has been advised to deposit $135,000 at the end of each quarter into an account that managers believe will yield 10% per year compounded quarterly. Find the lump sum that could be deposited today that will grow to the same future value.

5. ________

6. Abel Plumbing saves $12,000 at the end of every semiannual period in an account earning 6% compounded semiannually to replace several of its trucks in 5 years. Find the lump sum that could be deposited today that will grow to the same future value.

6. ________

7. Kitty Wysong was in a car accident and needs $3200 per month to live on for the next 3 years. Find the lump sum her insurance company must deposit into a fund earning 12% per year compounded monthly to make these payments.

7. ________

8. Carl and Amy Glaser recently divorced. As part of the divorce settlement, Carl must pay Amy $1000 at the end of every quarter for 8 years. Find the lump sum he must deposit into an account earning 8% per year compounded quarterly to make the payments.

8. ________

9. Ajax Coal sets up a sinking fund to purchase a new industrial bulldozer in 3 years at a price of $870,000. Find the annual payment the firm must make if funds are deposited into an account earning 8% compounded annually. Then set up a sinking fund table.

Payment Number	Amount of Deposit	Interest Earned	Total in Account

10. Swift Petrochemicals wishes to purchase a new corporate jet costing $3,200,000 in 2 years. Find the semiannual payment the company must make into a sinking fund account earning 6% compounded semiannually. Then set up a sinking fund table.

Payment Number	Amount of Deposit	Interest Earned	Total in Account

11. Ben Jamison is 45. He wants to retire at age 65 and draw $25,000 per year until he turns 85. He assumes that he can earn 8% per year *before* retiring but that he would invest more conservatively and earn 6% per year *after retiring*. **(a)** Find the amount needed at 65 to fund his retirement. **(b)** Then find the end-of-the-year payment into a sinking fund needed to accumulate this amount.

(a) ________________
(b) ________________

12. A chief executive officer agrees to try to rescue a company from bankruptcy and signs a contract to work there for 5 years. The contract also specifies that at the end of his 5 years of service, he will receive $90,000 at the end of the following 3 years. Assume funds earn 6% compounded annually. **(a)** Find the amount needed at the end of his 5 years of service to fund the payments. **(b)** Find the end-of-year payment into a sinking fund needed to accumulate this amount.

(a) ________________
(b) ________________

10.4 STOCKS

OBJECTIVES

1. Define the types of stock.
2. Read stock tables.
3. Find the current yield on a stock.
4. Find the stock's PE ratio.
5. Define the Dow Jones Industrial Average and the NASDAQ Composite Index.
6. Define a mutual fund.

CASE *in* POINT When Roman Rodriguez began his new job, he was given the choice of investing his retirement funds in a fixed interest fund or in a fund containing stocks and/or bonds. Which should he choose? Which would you choose? Why?

Almost all large businesses and also many smaller ones are set up as **corporations**. For example, companies that we refer to as Microsoft, Intel, Nike, McDonald's, and Toyota are actually corporations. **Publicly held corporations** are those owned by the public; their stocks are traded daily in markets called stock markets. **Privately held corporations** are owned by one or a few individuals, and their stock is not traded on a market. For example, your medical doctor or plumber may have organized a small business as a privately held corporation.

A corporation is a form of business that gives the owners (the stockholders) **limited liability**. You do not have to worry that lawsuits will be filed against you or your family just because you own stock in General Motors, Inc. The owners of corporations have protection through the limited-liability laws and can never lose more than they have invested in the corporation.

A corporation is set up with money, or **capital**, raised through the sale of shares of **stock**. A share of stock represents partial ownership of a corporation. If one million shares of stock are sold to establish a new firm, the owner of one share will own one-millionth of the corporation. The ownership of stock is shown by either paper **stock certificates**, like the one shown here, or by regular statements that are generated by the brokerage firm that bought the stock on your behalf.

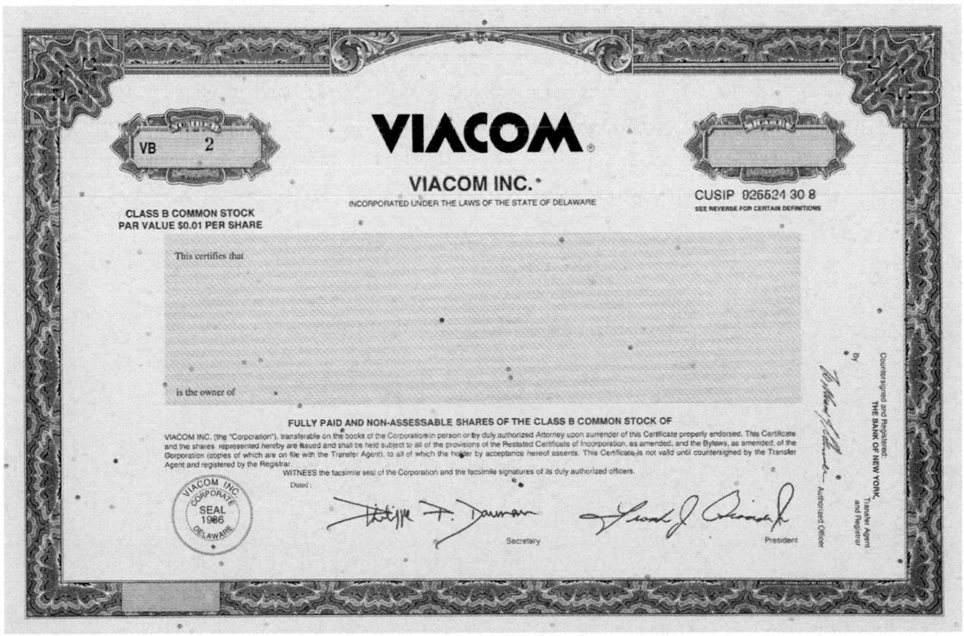

In most states, corporations are required to have an **annual meeting**. At this meeting, open to all **stockholders** (owners of stock), the management of the firm is open to questions from stockholders. The stockholders also elect a **board of directors**—a group of people who represent the stockholders. The board of directors hires the **executive officers** of the corporation, such as the president, vice-presidents, and so on. The board of directors also distributes a portion of any profits in the form of **dividends** that are paid to the stockholders.

OBJECTIVE 1 **Define the types of stock.** The two types of stock normally issued are **preferred stock** and **common stock**. As the name suggests, preferred stock *has certain rights* over common stock. For example, owners of preferred stock must be paid dividends *before* any dividends can be paid to owners of common stock. Also, corporate debt and preferred shareholders must be paid *before* common shareholders receive anything in the event that a corporation declares bankruptcy.

The shares of **publicly held corporations** are typically owned by many different individuals and institutions. Share prices of these firms are determined by supply and demand in public markets called **stock exchanges**. The New York Stock Exchange (NYSE) is the largest of the several exchanges in the United States. This exchange is located on Wall Street in New York City. Many foreign countries, including Japan, Taiwan, England, Canada, and Mexico, have their own stock exchanges. One of the most widely circulated financial newspapers in the country is *The Wall Street Journal*, which is published daily by Dow Jones & Company, Inc. It provides the reader with stock and bond quotes in addition to general business, marketing, and financial news.

OBJECTIVE 2 **Read stock tables.** Daily stock prices can easily be found on the World Wide Web, but many newspapers also print daily stock prices for at least some stocks. The format of the information given varies from one source of information to another, but we will use the format used by *Barron's,* which reports stock prices once each week.

EXAMPLE 1 Reading the Stock Table

After receiving his first paycheck from the community college, Roman Rodriguez went to Harley-Davidson to look at motorcycles. Analyze the information in the stock table about Harley-Davidson.

52 week			Tick	Vol			Week's		Earnings			Div
High	**Low**	**Name**	**Sym**	**100s**	**Yld**	**P/E**	**Last**	**Chg.**	**Latest Year**	**This Year**	**Next Year**	**Amt**
75.87	47.86	HarleyDav	HOG	37597	1.2	18	70.47	+0.27	3.41	3.92	4.36	.21
(a)	**(b)**		**(c)**	**(d)**	**(e)**	**(f)**	**(g)**	**(h)**		**(i)**		**(j)**

SOLUTION

(a) The highest price the stock sold for during the year was \$75.87.
(b) The lowest price the stock sold for during the year was \$47.86.
(c) The ticker symbol for Harley-Davidson is HOG.
(d) The volume of shares sold for the week was $100 \times 37597 = 3{,}759{,}700$ shares.
(e) The dividend yield is 1.2% of the current stock price.
(f) The ratio of the current stock price to earnings for the past 4 quarters is 18.
(g) The stock closed at \$70.47, which is the current (or closing) price of the stock.
(h) The stock price was up \$0.27 for the week.
(i) Harley-Davidson earned \$3.41 per share last year and is expected to earn \$3.92 per share this year and \$4.36 per share next year.
(j) The most recent quarterly dividend was \$.21.

QUICK CHECK 1

Analyze the information in the stock table about Hasbro.

Quick Check Answer

1. High for the year = \$27.69; low for the year = \$17; ticker symbol = HAS; vol. for week = 3,965,400 shares; 1.8% dividend yield; P/E ratio = 25; closed at \$27.25; change for the week = +\$.10; last year's earnings = \$1.22; expected earnings this year = \$1.30; expected earnings next year = \$1.50; quarterly dividend = \$.12

Individuals must use **stockbrokers** to trade publicly held stocks. Regular stockbrokers charge more, but they offer financial advice. Some people trade stocks using **discount brokers**, who offer less advice and a lower cost. Yet others trade stock over the Internet using E*Trade, Schwab, or Ameritrade, for example, where the costs of trading are very low. Some firms on the Internet will let you play a game of buying and selling stock to help you learn about trading stocks.

Mkt Sym	52-Wk High	Low	Name	Tick Sym	Vol. 100s	Yld	P/E	–Week's– Last	Chg.	---EARNINGS--- Latest Year	This Year	Next Year	Div Amt
	77.70	43.04	HDFC Bnk	HDB	9344	.5	...	75.48	+ 4.48	1.50	1.88	2.47	.359
	61.68	38.34	HNI	HNI	3323	1.6	18	44.41	− 0.27	2.55	2.52	2.84	.18
x	12.81	10.30	HRPT Prop	HRP	24190	6.8	12	12.35	+ 0.21	.60	.93	.45	.21
	98.56	80.85	HSBC ADS	HBC	11559	4.1	...	91.65	+ 0.75	6.75	7.73	8.05	.75
	55.71	40.66	Haemonetic	HAE	4503	...	22	45.02	+ 0.05	1.99	2.08	2.26	...
s	41.99	26.33	Hallibrtn	HAL	334249	1.0	12	31.05	− 0.41	1.60	2.14	2.57	.075
lf	4.75	2.51	HnckFabrcs	HKF	7606	...	dd	3.44	+ 0.35	.13	−.66	−.44	...
	13.48	6.50	Handleman	HDL	6675	4.7	dd	6.77	+ 0.07	.44	−.46	.17	.08
n	24.77	17.75	Hanesbrands	HBI	10047	...	...	23.62	+ 0.27	NA	1.67	2.08	...
	8.95	5.67	HangerOrtho	HGR	1353	...	dd	7.53	− 0.02	.38	.43	.57	...
	21.10	14.20	HanovrCmprsr	HC	22329	...	37	18.89	− 0.31	−.42	.40	.83	...
	54.43	40.72	Hanoverins	THG	5320	.6	11	48.80	− 0.15	1.31	3.64	4.23	.30
	76.50	54.74	Hanson ADS	HAN	846	2.5	...	75.69	+ 1.79	4.67	5.13	5.42	.6044
	51.25	33.10	Harland	JH	13866	1.4	18	50.20	+ 0.25	2.69	2.87	3.13	.175
	75.87	47.86	HarleyDav	HOG	37597	1.2	18	70.47	+ 0.27	3.41	3.92	4.36	.21
	115.85	74.65	Harmanint	HAR	13195	.1	26	99.91	+ 0.29	3.89	4.45	5.49	.0125
	18.84	11.90	HrmnyGld ADS	HMY	31892	...	...	15.75	+ 0.39	−.25	.57	.49	.0463
	84.25	58.22	HarrahEntn	HET	87995	1.9	45	82.72	+ 0.06	3.58	3.57	4.16	.40
	49.78	37.69	Harris	HRS	22946	1.0	24	45.86	+ 0.36	2.22	2.76	3.08	.11
	89.70	67.52	Harsco	HSC	7217	1.9	16	76.10	− 0.75	3.72	4.51	5.11	.355
	31.00	22.35	HarteHanks	HHS	7899	.9	20	27.71	+ 0.88	1.34	1.38	1.53	.06
	94.03	79.24	HrtfrdFnl	HIG	31532	2.1	12	93.31	+ 0.86	7.40	8.95	9.63	.50
	9.97	5.50	Hartmarx	HMX	4342	...	19	7.06	− 0.27	.63	.20	.50	...
x	33.50	21.70	HrvsErgyTr g	HTE	39101	...	9g	22.45	− 0.33	...	...	...	.38
	14.83	7.83	HarvstNatRes	HNR	11327	...	dd	10.63	+ 0.34	...	...	...	...
	27.69	17.00	Hasbro	HAS	39654	1.8	25	27.25	+ 0.10	1.22	1.30	1.50	.12
	17.15	12.66	HavrtyFurn	HVT	2703	1.8	17	14.80	− 0.11	.66	.73	.86	.0675
	17.01	12.93	HavrtyFum A	HVTA	74	1.7	17	14.86	− 0.16	...	...	...	.0625
	28.94	25.69	HawEllnd	HE	5701	4.6	17	27.15	− 0.25	1.57	1.53	1.63	.31
	4.76	2.90	Head	HED	314	8.6	...	3.70	− 0.09	...	...	...	.3168
	40.19	20.54	Headwaters	HW	18992	...	11	23.96	+ 0.27	2.19	1.73	1.46	...
	37.84	25.12	HlthCrProp	HCP	31395	4.6	28	36.82	+ 1.12	1.07	.80	.67	.425
	43.02	32.80	HlthCr Reit	HCN	12473	6.0	28	43.02	+ 1.58	1.15	1.38	1.43	.3409
	24.00	19.04	HlthMgt A	HMA	37849	1.1	16	21.11	+ 0.03	NA	1.24	1.34	.06
	54.11	37.10	HealthNet	HNT	25628	...	18	48.66	− 0.13	2.42	3.04	3.59	...
	42.83	31.25	HlthcrRlty	HR	5683	6.7	43	39.54	+ 1.49	1.09	.91	.97	.66
n	26.25	19.80	Hlthsouth	HLS	8040	...	...	22.65	− 0.45	NA	−.23	.13	...
n	24.19	15.41	HealthSpring	HS	7913	...	...	20.35	− 0.19	.28	1.46	1.60	...
	26.14	19.97	HearstArgyl	HTV	1647	1.1	36	25.50	− 0.11	.87	1.00	.77	.07
	29.90	21.22	HeartlndPymnt	HPY	1731	.2	41	28.25	− 0.04	.49	.78	1.05	.025
	7.95	3.93	HeclaMin	HL	80549	...	22	7.66	+ 0.41	−.22	.11	.44	...
	40.07	24.56	Heico	HEI	4648	.2	32	38.83	+ 1.03	1.20	1.39	1.60	.04
	33.01	19.73	Heico A	HEIA	1332	.2	27	32.58	+ 1.09	...	...	...	.04
	46.75	33.42	Heinz	HNZ	41017	3.1	23	45.01	− 0.11	2.17	2.38	2.56	.35
	45.61	27.55	HelixEnergy	HLX	53983	...	11	31.37	− 0.70	1.92	2.93	4.15	...
	15.80	9.88	Hellenic	OTE	662	...	...	15.15	− 0.30	−.65	.90	.80	.2135
s	40.24	21.26	HelmPayne	HP	36652	.7	9	24.47	− 0.30	2.63	3.44	3.93	.045
	41.34	27.73	Herbalife	HLF	4694	...	22	40.16	+ 0.18	1.52	2.03	2.47	...
	19.87	10.98	Hercules	HPC	33150	...	dd	19.31	+ 0.03	.85	1.17	1.36	...
	57.65	48.20	Hershey	HSY	24067	2.2	21	49.80	− 0.10	2.36	2.41	2.58	.27
n	17.48	14.55	HertzGlbHldgs	HTZ	20000	...	...	17.39	+ 0.34	NA	.64	.65	...

Mkt Sym	52-Wk High	Low	Name	Tick Sym	Vol. 100s	Yld	P/E	–Week's– Last	Chg.	---EARNINGS--- Latest Year	This Year	Next Year	Div Amt
	111.60	80.52	Ipsco g	IPS	16748	...	7g	93.87	+ 1.66	11.90	14.02	14.15	.20
	44.86	33.96	IronMtn	IRM	10019	...	46	41.34	− 0.45	.84	.94	1.12	...
	23.00	17.92	IrwinFnl	IFC	3459	1.9	cc	22.63	+ 0.15	...	...	...	.11
	68.84	55.65	iShrMSCIGrth	EFG	1375	1.0	...	68.23	+ 0.70	...	...	...	.6888
	72.88	57.05	iShrMSCIVal	EFV	5438	1.6	...	72.20	+ 0.85	...	...	...	1.1925
	48.93	35.41	iStarFnl	SFI	10910	6.4	17	47.82	+ 0.47	3.36	3.59	3.90	.77
	11.58	5.53	IvanhoeMn	IVN	14311	...	...	9.83	+ 0.26	−.41	−.27	−.22	...
			J										
n	43.56	24.00	JCrewGrp	JCG	27411	...	...	38.55	+ 0.85	NA	.98	1.21	...
x	21.57	14.85	JER InvTr	JRT	2733	8.1	18	20.67	+ 0.34	1.08	1.26	1.81	.42+.30
	49.00	37.88	JPMorgChas	JPM	269125	2.8	14	48.30	+ 0.41	2.95	3.70	3.97	.34
lf	43.70	22.01	JabilCircuit	JBL	80956	.9	18	24.55	+ 0.40	1.28	1.52	1.76	.07
	64.60	33.15	JackInTheBx	JBX	9584	...	20	61.04	+ 0.31	3.03	3.07	3.41	...
x	37.12	24.80	JcksnHewittTaxSvc	JTX	14427	1.4	23	33.97	− 0.08	1.67	1.92	2.24	.12
	93.27	67.80	JacobEngrg	JEC	7699	...	25	81.54	− 0.06	3.22	3.96	4.61	...
	12.76	7.55	JacuzziBrnd	JJZ	6321	...	24	12.43	+ 0.08	.56	.71	NA	...
	37.88	24.20	JamesHardie	JHX	96	1.2	dd	37.76	+ 1.85	1.39	2.16	2.11	.25
	24.20	15.50	JanusCapGrp	JNS	42789	.2	42	21.59	+ 0.20	.52	.65	.90	.04
	39.27	23.68	JardenCp	JAH	16653	...	31	34.79	+ 0.39	2.07	2.28	2.47	...
s	34.80	21.45	JefferiesGp	JEF	22306	1.9	19	26.82	+ 0.28	1.17	1.38	1.55	.125
	24.97	10.98	JoAnnStrs	JAS	14699	...	dd	24.60	+ 0.18	.18	−.18	.30	...
	69.41	56.65	JohnsJohns	JNJ	202248	2.3	18	66.02	+ 0.37	3.50	3.74	4.06	.375
	90.00	66.36	JohnsCtrl	JCI	18218	1.5	16	85.92	+ 0.71	5.23	6.05	6.98	.33
	36.10	27.30	JonesApparel	JNY	14162	1.7	21	33.43	− 0.07	2.48	2.20	2.49	.14
	95.00	49.62	JonsLngLaSal	JLL	4404	.7	19	92.17	+ 2.21	3.12	5.05	4.95	.35
	14.45	10.05	JournalComm A	JRN	5506	2.1	16	12.61	+ 0.15	.81	.82	.76	.065
	15.38	5.49	JmlRgstr	JRC	8558	1.1	9	7.30	+ 0.10	1.12	.87	.84	.02
			K										
	23.65	15.06	K&F IndHldg	KFI	5899	...	17	22.71	− 0.24	.77	1.29	1.54	...
lf	81.99	37.89	KB Home	KBH	48414	2.0	5	51.28	+ 1.14	9.53	8.05	4.27	.25
nl	27.63	20.50	KBR	KBR	11285	...	...	26.16	− 0.84	NA	1.41	1.26	...
n	30.40	25.51	KBW	KBW	2502	...	...	29.39	+ 1.02	NA	1.25	1.33	...
	36.40	30.70	KSeaTmsp	KSP	130	7.1	64	36.09	+ 0.59	1.31	1.55	1.52	.64
	26.67	19.71	KT Crp ADS	KTC	13298	...	...	25.35	− 0.85	2.27	2.71	2.74	.9732
lf	25.22	16.59	KV Pharm A	KVA	5477	...	28	23.78	− 0.03	...	...	...	...
lf	25.01	16.84	KV Pharm B	KVB	59	...	28	23.77	− 0.04	...	...	...	...
	14.45	9.80	K2	KTO	12985	...	dd	13.19	+ 0.23	.78	.87	.99	...
	27.98	17.95	KadantInc	KAI	1633	...	25	24.38	+ 0.17	.64	1.29	1.59	...
	30.26	21.85	KSCitySo	KSU	17480	...	45	28.98	+ 0.85	.07	1.01	1.40	...
h	3.75	1.85	KatyInd	KT	185	...	dd	2.68	+ 0.11	...	...	...	...
	44.33	31.53	Kaydon	KDN	5719	1.2	19	39.74	+ 0.69	1.57	2.15	2.38	.12
nx	24.95	21.56	KayneAndrsn	KED	9582	.9	...	23.94	+ 1.62	NA	.20	1.17	.22
	16.50	10.18	KeaneInc	KEA	5748	...	22	11.91	+ 0.15	.63	.69	.76	...
	16.10	10.77	KeithlyInstr	KEI	3644	1.1	26	13.15	+ 0.42	.61	.47	.59	.0375
	50.95	42.41	Kellogg	K	24378	2.3	20	50.06	− 0.05	2.36	2.51	2.75	.291
	34.84	23.20	Kellwood	KWD	9469	2.0	23	32.52	− 0.14	1.68	1.63	1.81	.16

QUICK TIP To help identify the particular stock in the table, the ticker symbol will be shown in parentheses following the name of the company.

EXAMPLE 2 Finding the Cost of Stocks

Ignoring commissions, find Roman Rodriguez's cost for the following purchases.

(a) 100 shares of KB Homes (KBH) at the closing price for the week.
(b) 200 shares of Johnson's Controls (JCl) at the high for the year.
(c) Then find the combined *annual* dividend these shares will pay.

SOLUTION

(a) $100 \times \$51.28 = \$5128$
(b) $200 \times \$90 = \$18{,}000$
(c) Per-share annual dividend for KBH $= \$.25 \times 4 = \$1.00$
Per-share annual dividend for JCL $= \$.33 \times 4 = \mathbf{\$1.32}$

Total annual dividend $= 100 \times \$1.00 + 200 \times \mathbf{\$1.32} = \$364$

QUICK CHECK 2

Ignore commissions and find the cost of 300 shares of Heico (HEI) at the low for the year. Then find the *annual* dividend these shares will pay.

Quick Check Answer

2. \$7368; \$48

OBJECTIVE 3 **Find the current yield on a stock.** There is no certain way of choosing stocks that will go up in price. However, two **stock ratios** that people commonly look at before buying shares of a company are the **current yield** and the **price–earnings ratio**. Although current yield is shown in the stock tables as Yld, we show how to find it here since you may not always have the tables available. It is used to compare the dividends paid by stocks selling at different prices. The result is commonly rounded to the nearest tenth of a percent.

$$\text{Current yield} = \frac{\text{Annual dividend per share}}{\text{Closing price per share}}$$

EXAMPLE 3

Finding the Current Yield

Find the current yield for **(a)** Harris (HRS) and **(b)** Iron Mountain (IRM) to the nearest tenth of a percent.

SOLUTION

(a) $\text{Current yield for Harris} = \frac{\text{Annual dividend}}{\text{Closing price}} = \frac{4 \times \$.11}{\$45.86} = 1.0\% \text{ (rounded)}$

(b) $\text{Current yield for Iron Mountain} = \frac{\text{Annual dividend}}{\text{Closing price}} = \frac{4 \times \$0}{\$41.34} = 0.0\% \text{ (rounded)}$

Iron Mountain pays no dividend, so the current yield is 0%.

QUICK CHECK 3

Find the current yield for Johnson and Johnson (JNJ) to the nearest tenth of a percent.

Note that a company such as Iron Mountain in Example 3 may not pay a dividend because

1. it is going through difficult financial times;
2. it needs the funds that would be paid out for research and development; or
3. it may be growing rapidly and needs the money to finance its growth.

OBJECTIVE 4 **Find the stock's PE ratio.** One number that some people use to help decide which stock to buy is the **price–earnings ratio**, also called the **PE ratio**. It is often rounded to the nearest whole number.

$$\text{PE ratio} = \frac{\text{Closing price per share}}{\text{Annual net income per share}}$$

EXAMPLE 4

Finding the PE Ratio

Find the PE ratio for each of the following corporations and round to the nearest whole number.

(a) Chevron (CVX) with a closing price of $70.28 and earnings of $7.91
(b) Target (TGT) with a closing price of $57.59 and earnings of $2.98

SOLUTION

(a) $\text{PE ratio for Chevron} = \frac{\$70.28}{\$7.91} = 9$

(b) $\text{PE ratio for Target} = \frac{\$57.59}{\$2.98} = 19$

QUICK CHECK 4

Pfizer Inc (PFE) has a closing price of $26.38 and earnings of $1.72. Find the PE ratio to the nearest whole number.

Quick Check Answers

3. 2.3%
4. 15

Investors may be willing to pay more for rapidly growing companies because these companies may generate yet more profit in the near future. As a result, the PE ratios of rapidly growing companies are often higher than those of slow-growing companies.

A low PE ratio may indicate that a company is growing slowly or that it is having financial problems. It is best to compare the PE ratios of similar companies, such as oil giants Exxon Mobil and Chevron. It usually is not worthwhile to compare the PE ratios of very different companies such as Wal-Mart and Exxon Mobil, since they have very different business environments.

OBJECTIVE 5 **Define the Dow Jones Industrial Average and the NASDAQ Composite Index.** Both the **Dow Jones Industrial Average** and the **NASDAQ Composite Index** are used as indicators of trends in stock prices. The Dow Jones Industrial Average refers to an average of 30 very large industrial companies. The NASDAQ Composite Index includes price information on over 5000 companies, many of which are involved with technology. Both of these indexes are commonly quoted by television and radio, in newsprint, and on the Internet.

The Dow Jones Industrial Average has been widely available for over 100 years, as you can see on the graph. The Great Depression from 1929 to 1939 devastated many investors, businesses, and families. Stock prices collapsed during the early years of the depression followed by many companies, including banks, going bankrupt. Many people were out of work and were unable to find a job. The entire world was mired in the depression until World War II, when war-related activity brought us out of the depression. However, stock prices did not recover to pre-depression levels until the 1950s.

In spite of the Great Depression and the many smaller recessions in the United States, you can clearly see that the trend of stock prices has been up over the past 100 years or so.

QUICK TIP Historically, stocks have consistently had a greater return on investment than savings accounts, certificates of deposit, or bonds. Most financial planners agree that stocks should be a part of any long-range investment plan.

Dow Jones Industrial Average since 1900

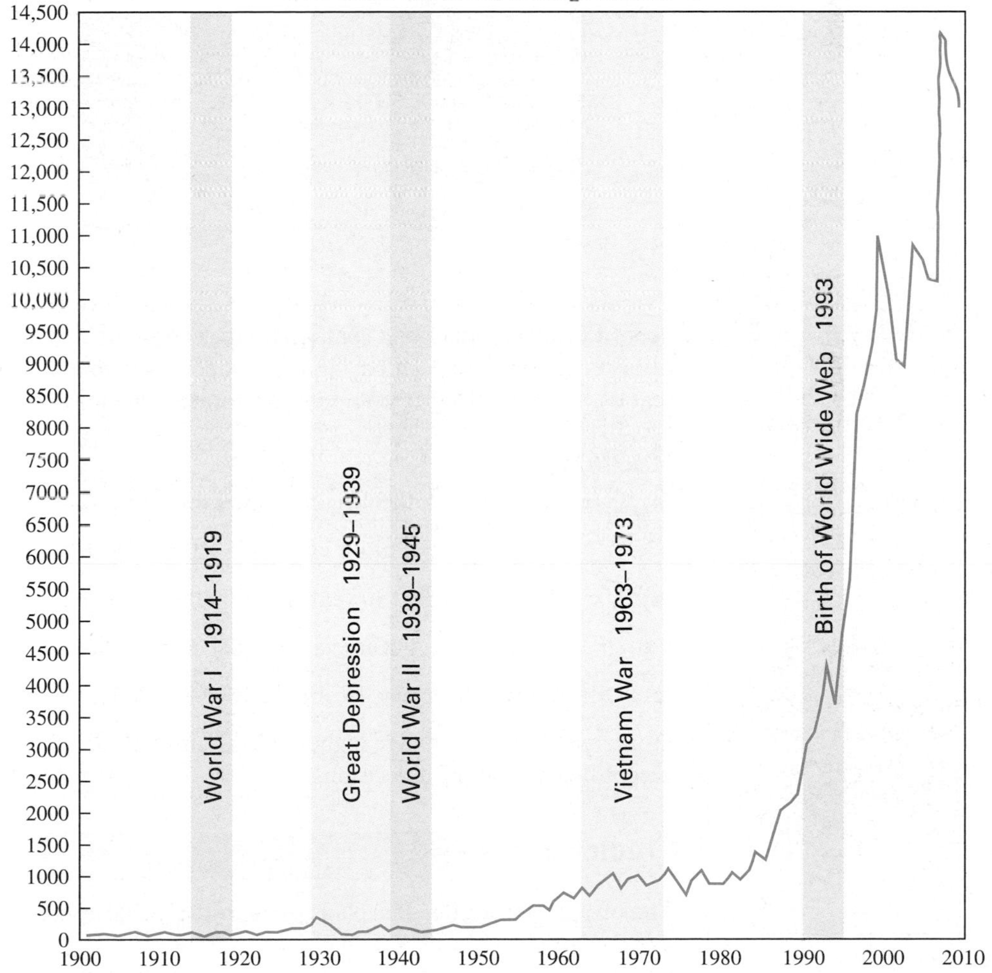

OBJECTIVE 6 **Define a mutual fund.** Ownership of shares in a single company *can be risky*—the company may suffer poor financial results causing the stock price to fall. This risk *can be reduced* by simultaneously investing in the stocks of several different companies, especially when they are in different industries.

One way to participate in the profits of successful corporations but to reduce risk is to purchase shares in a mutual fund that invests in stocks. A **mutual fund** receives money from many different investors and uses the money to purchase stocks or bonds in many different companies.

For example, a $1000 investment in a typical mutual fund that owns stock means that you own a very small piece of perhaps 100 different companies.

Most mutual funds are actively managed, meaning that managers are paid to buy and sell stock as they think best for investors in the fund. **Exchange-traded funds (ETFs)** are similar to mutual funds except that they tend not to be actively managed. They attempt to match the performance of an index such as the Dow Jones Averages, a market sector such as energy, or a commodity such as petroleum. Essentially, ETFs are a low-cost way to purchase a portfolio with some diversification.

The next table shows that some funds *specialize* by investing in the stocks *of different types* of publicly held companies. For example, mutual funds or exchange-traded funds may specialize in large-cap (large companies), small-cap (small companies), overseas (global), or specialty (real estate, oil, banking, etc.) stocks. Many financial planners say that *the first fund* you should invest in is an **index fund** that tracks a broad index such as Standard & Poors 500, which includes 500 of the largest and best-managed companies in the world. Funds that specialize in companies in one industry, such as biotechnology, or funds that specialize in international stock are usually more volatile or risky.

Numbers in the News

Going Global

By mixing just two or three of these low-priced exchange-traded funds, you can create a globally diversified portfolio

Exchange-traded fund (Ticker)	Invests in	Recent Price
Vanguard Total Stock Market VIPERs (VTI)	U.S. stocks, all sizes	$140.27
iShares S&P 500 (IVV)	Large-cap U.S. stocks	$142.00
iShares S&P Midcap 400 (IJH)	Mid-cap U.S. stocks	$80.61
Midcap SPDRs (MDY)	Mid-cap U.S. stocks	$147.29
iShares Russell 2000 (IWM)	Small-cap U.S. stocks	$78.40
iShares MSCI Japan (EWJ)	Japanese stocks	$14.25
iShares MSCI Pacific Ex-Japan (EPP)	Pacific Rim, but not Japan	$123.00
iShares MSCI EAFE (EFA)	Europe and Pacific Rim	$73.32
iShares MSCI Emerging Markets (EEM)	Emerging markets	$113.55

DATA: Finance.yahoo.com

EXAMPLE 5 Comparing Investment Alternatives

Cynthia Peck wants to know whether she should invest her retirement monies in certificates of deposit or in a mutual fund containing stock. Assume payments of $2000 per year for 30 years and **(a)** a certificate of deposit paying 4% compounded annually or **(b)** a mutual fund containing stock that has returned 8% per year. Find the future value for both and **(c)** compare the two investments.

QUICK TIP Neither the 4% on the certificate of deposit nor the 8% on the mutual fund is guaranteed for 30 years. Stocks may do better or worse than bank deposits in any year, but stocks tend to have higher returns over the long time periods required for retirement planning.

SOLUTION

(a) Use 4% per year and 30 years in the table in **Section 10.1** to find 56.08494.

$$\text{Future value} = \$2000 \times 56.08494 = \$112{,}169.88$$

(b) Use 8% per year and 30 years in the table in **Section 10.1** to find 113.28321.

$$\text{Future value} = \$2000 \times 113.28321 = \$226{,}566.42$$

(c) Difference = $226,566.42 − $112,169.88 = $114,396.54

Stocks yield more but have higher risk. Cynthia Peck will need to decide how much risk she will accept before making a decision.

QUICK CHECK 5

The owner of Termites Inc. plans to deposit $15,000 at the end of each year for 10 years into an investment account. A bank deposit would pay 5% per year, and he assumes a stock fund would continue to yield 10% per year. Find the future value of both.

Quick Check Answer

5. $188,668.35; $239,061.30

10.4 EXERCISES

FOR EXTRA HELP

MyMathLab

MathXL PRACTICE

WATCH

DOWNLOAD

READ

REVIEW

The **QUICK START** *exercises in each section contain solutions to help you get started.*

Find the following from the stock table on page 443. (See Example 1.)

QUICK START

1. Low for the year for Hasbro (HAS) **1.** $17
2. High for the year for Head (HED) **2.** $4.76
3. Most recent quarterly dividend for Kaydon (KDN) **3.** ________
4. Most recent quarterly dividend for Kellwood (KWD) **4.** ________
5. Volume for KBW (KBW) **5.** ________
6. Volume for Heinz (HNZ) **6.** ________
7. PE ratio for Hershey (HSY) **7.** ________
8. PE ratio for JP Morgan Chase (JPM) **8.** ________
9. Estimated earnings for this year for Harsco (HSC) **9.** ________
10. Estimated earnings for this year for Herbalife (HLF) **10.** ________
11. Dividend yield for Harland (JH) **11.** ________
12. Dividend yield for JER InvTr (JRT) **12.** ________
13. Estimated earnings for next year for K2 (KTO) **13.** ________
14. Estimated earnings for next year for HarrahEntn (HET) **14.** ________
15. Closing price for the week for Hanson ADS (HAN) **15.** ________
16. Closing price for the week for JardenCp (JAH) **16.** ________
17. Change from previous week for JonesApparel (JNY) **17.** ________
18. Change from previous week for Hallibrtn (HAL) **18.** ________

Find the cost for the following stock purchases at the closing price for the week. Then find the annual dividend that would have been paid for the year on that number of shares. (See Example 2.)

QUICK START

Stock	*Number of Shares*	*Cost*	*Dividend*
19. HavrtyFurn (HVT)	500	$7400	$135
$500 \times \$14.80 = \$7400$; $500 \times (4 \times \$.0675) = \$135$			
20. Kellogg (K)	300	________	________
21. Hallibrtn (HAL)	1000	________	________
22. JPMorgChas (JPM)	100	________	________
23. Heinz (HNZ)	700	________	________
24. Haemonetic (HAE)	250	________	________

25. Define and explain **(a)** current yield and **(b)** PE ratio. (See Objectives 3 and 4.)

26. Use the chart of the Dow Jones Industrial Average and estimate the years in which stocks fell by more than 10%. (See Objective 5.)

Find the current yield for each of the following stocks. Round to the nearest tenth of a percent. (See Example 3.)

QUICK START

Stock	*Current Price per Share*	*Annual Dividend*	*Current Yield*
27. Coca-Cola (KO)	$50.06	$1.24	2.5%
$1.24 ÷ $50.06 = 2.5%			
28. Microsoft (MSFT)	$29.81	$.40	______
29. McDonalds (MCD)	$43.54	$1.00	______
30. General Motors (GM)	$29.64	$1.00	______
31. Nike (NKE)	$98.67	$1.48	______
32. Wal-Mart (WMT)	$47.78	$.67	______

Find the PE ratio for each of the following. Round all answers to the nearest whole number. (See Example 4.)

QUICK START

Stock	*Current Price per Share*	*Annual Net Earnings per Share*	*PE Ratio*
33. Pepsi (PBG)	$30.43	$1.91	16
$30.43 ÷ $1.91 = 16			
34. Target (TGT)	$57.59	$2.71	______
35. General Electric (GE)	$37.75	$1.65	______
36. Exxon Mobil (XOM)	$72.72	$6.59	______
37. Dell (DELL)	$26.24	$1.20	______
38. Intel (INTL)	$21.19	$1.01	______

Stock prices on consecutive days for a stock are shown next. Find the increase (decrease) in the price of each stock as a number and the percent increase (decrease) rounded to the nearest tenth of a percent.

39. 34.35, 35.20

40. 46.50, 45.90

Solve the following application problems.

QUICK START

41. STOCK PURCHASE Patsy Bonner buys 200 shares of General Electric at \$56.30 and 100 shares of Safeway at \$38.60. Find the total cost ignoring commissions.

41. \$15,120

200 × \$56.30 + 100 × \$38.60 = \$15,120

42. WRITING A WILL In her will, Barbara Bains stated that the trustee should purchase 300 shares of Pfizer and 200 shares of Wal-Mart and give the stock to her grandson on his 25th birthday. If the stocks are selling for \$58.70 per share and \$52.20 per share, respectively, find the total amount paid, ignoring broker's commissions.

42. ______________

43. CDS OR GLOBAL STOCKS Stan Walker is comparing certificates of deposit currently yielding 5% compounded semiannually to a mutual fund with international stocks that he believes will yield 8% compounded semiannually. Find the future value of an annuity with deposits of \$600 every 6 months for 10 years for **(a)** the CDs and **(b)** the mutual fund. **(c)** Find the difference.

(a) ______________
(b) ______________
(c) ______________

44. FIXED RATE OR STOCKS Jesica Tate plans to contribute \$2500 per year to a retirement plan and is debating the use of a fund that pays 4% per year versus a stock fund that she believes will yield 10% per year. Find the future value after 12 years for **(a)** the fixed rate and **(b)** the stock fund. **(c)** Find the difference.

(a) ______________
(b) ______________
(c) ______________

Case Studies

American River College

www.arc.losrios.edu

- Founded in 1955
- 2007: Serves 32,640 students
- 2007: 41.8% of the students are under 25
- 2007: 22.5% of the students are over 40
- Offers on-line/TV and off-campus classes

Similar to many other community colleges across the country, American River College has continued to expand and diversify the programs of study that it offers. It now offers more than 60 different majors of study, including biology, engineering, hospitality management, mortuary science, collision repair, Japanese, and even fire technology. College personnel work very closely with students to help them find financial aid. Amazingly, about one-half of the students at American River College have some kind of financial aid.

1. American River College makes a contribution of \$3200 per year to Roman Rodriguez's retirement plan. Assume that the college continues to make this contribution to his plan for 25 years and that funds are in stocks that average 8% per year. Find the future value.

2. Find the annual cost if American River College makes an average retirement plan contribution of \$2400 per full-time employee, given that it has 860 full-time employees.

3. How many students at American River College have some kind of financial aid?

4. Assume that a wealthy donor has agreed to give American River College \$250,000 per year for the next five years. Find the present value of these gifts, assuming 6% per year.

5. What are the characteristics of a great instructor?

10.5 BONDS

OBJECTIVES

1. Define the basics of bonds.
2. Read bond tables.
3. Find the commission charge on bonds and the cost of bonds.
4. Understand how mutual funds containing bonds are used for monthly income.

CASE in POINT Roman Rodriguez has decided to include mutual funds holding stocks in his retirement plan, but he doesn't know about bonds. What are bonds? Should he invest in them?

OBJECTIVE 1 Define the basics of bonds. Corporations can sell shares of stock to raise funds. Shares represent ownership in the corporation. However, managers sometimes prefer to borrow money rather than issue stock. They borrow money for short-term needs from banks or insurance companies. Managers can also make long-term loans with banks, but they often prefer to borrow for the long term by issuing bonds. **Bonds** are legally binding promises (contracts) to repay borrowed money at a specific date in the future. Corporations commonly pay interest on each bond each year. Unlike shareholders, bondholders do not own part of the corporation. Other entities, including countries, cities, and even churches, also borrow money by using bonds.

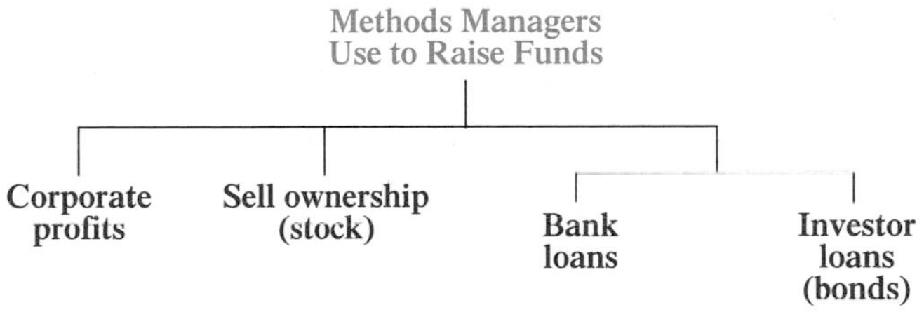

A company is said to go **bankrupt** if it can no longer meet its financial obligations to suppliers, banks, bondholders, and others. Bankruptcy is a complex process involving management, creditors, lawyers, and courts, but generally bankruptcy lawyers are paid first. Remaining assets are then used to pay off debt, including bonds. Shareholders *do not receive anything* unless there are assets remaining after all debts have been paid. Shareholders often receive very little or nothing from a bankruptcy, and bondholders often receive only a few cents on every dollar originally loaned.

Corporations frequently use substantial amounts of debt to build factories, expand operations, or buy other companies. The interest that must be paid on that debt is the *cost of having debt.* The larger the debt, the greater the amount of revenue the company must set aside to pay interest. As interest rates go higher, companies must set aside additional money to pay interest, leaving less for other purposes including profits. On the other hand, interest costs go down when interest rates go down. The article on the next page describes the increasing problems with government debt in the United States and suggests that Republicans and Democrats need to work together to solve the problems.

OBJECTIVE 2 Read bond tables. The **face value**, or **par value**, of a bond is *the original amount of money* borrowed by a company. Most public corporations issue bonds with a par value of $1000. Principal and any interest due must be paid when a bond **matures**. Suppose that a bond's owner needs money before the **maturity date** of the bond. In that event, the bond can be quickly sold through a bond dealer, such as Merrill Lynch. However, the price of the bond is determined, not by its initial price, but instead *by market conditions at the time of the sale.*

Market *interest rates fluctuate widely* from year to year, yet each bond pays exactly the same dollar amount of interest each year. If interest rates rise, investors will pay less for a bond because they want the new, higher interest yield. If interest rates fall, investors will pay more for a bond because they are satisfied with the lower yield. As a result, the price of a bond fluctuates in the opposite direction of interest rates. A bond may have a face value of $1000, but it often trades at a different value than $1000, as shown in Example 1.

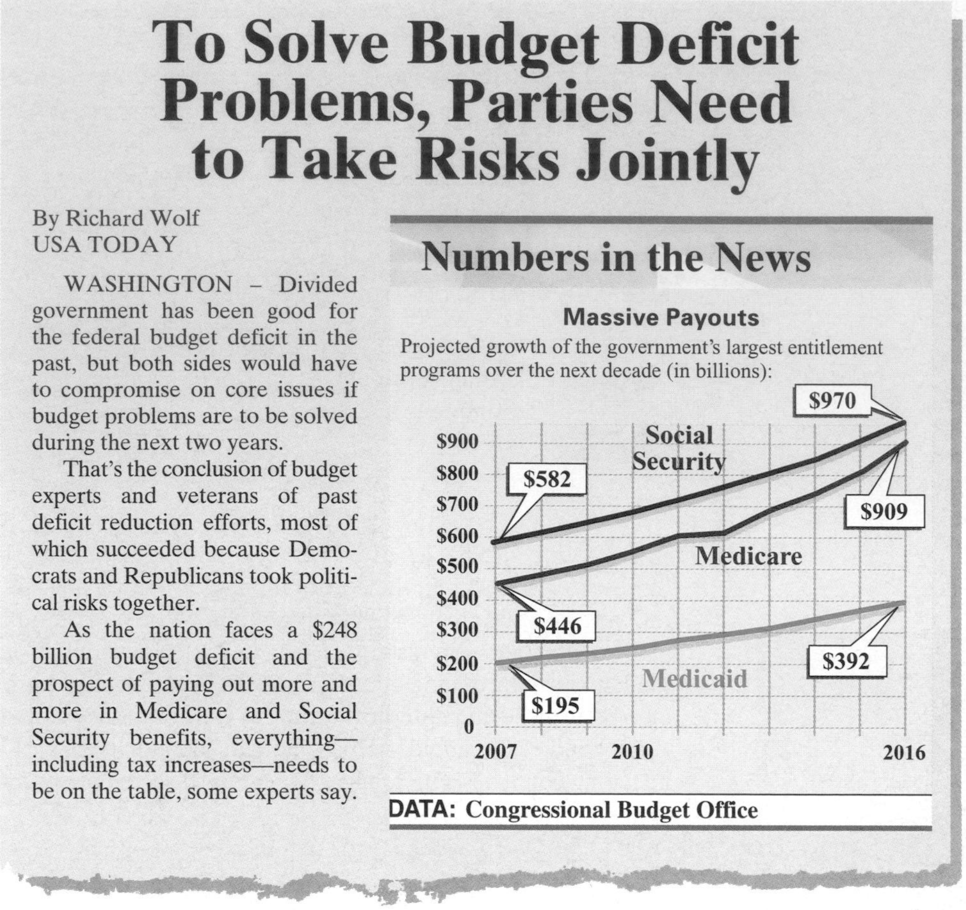

To Solve Budget Deficit Problems, Parties Need to Take Risks Jointly

By Richard Wolf
USA TODAY

WASHINGTON – Divided government has been good for the federal budget deficit in the past, but both sides would have to compromise on core issues if budget problems are to be solved during the next two years.

That's the conclusion of budget experts and veterans of past deficit reduction efforts, most of which succeeded because Democrats and Republicans took political risks together.

As the nation faces a $248 billion budget deficit and the prospect of paying out more and more in Medicare and Social Security benefits, everything—including tax increases—needs to be on the table, some experts say.

EXAMPLE 1

Working with the Bond Table

Brandy Barrett was in an automobile accident that put her in the hospital for 3 weeks and required months of rehabilitation. The other driver was at fault, and his insurance company paid Barrett the liability limits on his policy of $50,000. Barrett needs monthly income and is thinking about investing the funds in Hershey (HSY) bonds that mature in 2011. Analyze the data in the table.

Company (Ticker)	Coupon	Maturity	Last Price	Last Yield	Est $ Vol (000's)
Hershey Co* (HSY)	5.300	Sep 01, 2011	100.509	5.174	38,032
(a)	**(b)**	**(c)**	**(d)**	**(e)**	**(f)**

SOLUTION

(a) The ticker symbol for Hershey Company is HSY.

(b) Each of these bonds pays 5.300% of the $1000 face value of the bond each year.

$$\text{Annual interest paid} = 5.300\% \times \$1000 = \$53$$

(c) This bond matures and must be paid off on September 1, 2011.

(d) The last price the bond sold for was 100.509% of $1000.

$$\text{Last price} = 1.00509 \times \$1000 = \$1005.09$$

It sold for $5.09 more than the original loan to Hershey of $1000.

(e) An investor holding the bond to maturity would make 5.174% per year on his or her money.

(f) Est $ Vol is bond sales in dollars for the week.

$$38{,}032 \times \$1000 = \$38{,}032{,}000 \text{ in Hershey bonds sold during the week}$$

QUICK CHECK 1

Analyze the data in the bond table for Oracle (ORCL) bonds maturing in 2011.

Quick Check Answers

1. (a) ticker symbol ORCL
(b) annual interest = $50
(c) matures January 15, 2011
(d) last price = $990.97
(e) yield to maturity = 5.251%
(f) $48,511,000 in volume for the week

Corporate Bonds

Company (Ticker)	Coupon	Maturity	Last Price	Last Yield	Est $ Vol (000's)
Vodafone Group * (VOD)	7.750	Feb 15, 2010	106.561	5.430	86,045
General Electric Capital * (GE)	6.125	Feb 22, 2011	103.866	5.075	59,665
Johnson Controls (JCI)	5.500	Jan 15, 2016	98.242	5.752	56,452
Verizon Global Funding * (VZ)	7.250	Dec 01, 2010	106.793	5.302	55,040
General Electric Capital (GE)	5.875	Feb 15, 2012	102.846	5.232	50,579
Sprint Nextel (S)	6.000	Dec 01, 2016	97.558	6.334	49,503
Morgan Stanley * (MS)	4.000	Jan 15, 2010	96.654	5.206	49,274
Oracle (ORCL)	5.000	Jan 15, 2011	99.097	5.251	48,511
Embarq (EQ)	7.995	Jun 01, 2036	103.979	7.652	47,514
Sprint Nextel * (S)	6.875	Oct 31, 2013	101.375	6.535	45,071
Slm * (SLMA)	4.000	Jan 15, 2009	97.899	5.100	43,609
Kraft Foods * (KFT)	5.625	Nov 01, 2011	101.203	5.337	43,519
Halliburton Co * (HAL)	6.750	Feb 01, 2027	100.000	6.749	42,300
Constellation Energy Group (CEG)	7.600	Apr 01, 2032	117.702	6.202	39,025
Conocophillips Canada Funding Co I (COP)	5.625	Oct 15, 2016	100.700	5.530	38,460
Hershey Co * (HSY)	5.300	Sep 01, 2011	100.509	5.174	38,032
Home Depot (HD)	5.875	Dec 16, 2036	98.569	5.978	35,925
Prudential Financial (PRU)	5.700	Dec 15, 2036	97.283	5.894	35,410
Countrywide Home Loans * (CFC)	3.250	May 21, 2008	97.364	5.244	34,792
Sprint Nextel * (S)	7.375	Aug 01, 2015	102.750	6.666	34,246
HSBC Finance Corp (HSBC)	5.836	Feb 15, 2008	100.588	5.287	34,175
EI Du Pont De Nemours And Co (DD)	5.250	Dec 15, 2016	98.026	5.510	34,022
Merrill Lynch Inc * (MER)	6.050	May 16, 2016	103.659	5.543	33,671
Alltel * (AT)	7.000	Mar 15, 2016	103.144	6.530	33,318
General Electric Capital (GE)	5.250	Oct 27, 2009	100.391	5.096	32,543
Citigroup * (C)	6.500	Jan 18, 2011	104.665	5.204	32,271
General Electric Capital * (GE)	6.750	Mar 15, 2032	115.079	5.623	32,176
Washington Mutual Bank Fa * (WM)	6.875	Jun 15, 2011	105.734	5.407	30,999
Wells Fargo * (WFC)	4.875	Jan 12, 2011	99.330	5.060	30,674
Citigroup * (C)	3.625	Feb 09, 2009	97.239	5.023	30,407
Citigroup Global Markets Holdings * (C)	6.500	Feb 15, 2008	101.348	5.234	29,860

EXAMPLE 2

Using the Bond Table

Find the volume sold and the last sale price of the following bonds.

(a) Vodafone Group (VOD) maturing in 2010
(b) Halliburton (HAL) maturing in 2027
(c) Home Depot (HD) maturing in 2036

SOLUTION

	Company	Volume Sold	Last Sale Price per Bond
(a)	Vodafone Group	$86,045,000	$1065.61
(b)	Halliburton	$42,300,000	$1000
(c)	Home Depot	$35,925,000	$985.69

QUICK CHECK 2

Find the volume sold and the last sale price for Alltel (AT) bonds maturing in 2016.

OBJECTIVE 3 **Find the commission charge on bonds and the cost of bonds.** Commissions charged on bond sales vary among brokers. A common charge is $10 per bond, either to buy or to sell. However, commissions are lower for large volumes.

Quick Check Answer

2. $33,318,000; $1031.44

EXAMPLE 3

Finding the Cost to Buy Bonds

QUICK TIP The effective interest rate is not the same as the Last Yield. The Last Yield takes into consideration the cost of the bond, the maturity value of the bond, the time to maturity, and all interest payments.

Assume that the sales charge is $10 per bond, and find the following for Sprint Nextel (S) bonds maturing in 2015.

(a) The total cost of purchasing 20 bonds
(b) The total annual interest paid on these bonds
(c) The effective interest rate to the buyer including the cost of buying the bonds

SOLUTION

(a) Total cost = (Price per bond + Sales charge per bond) × Number of bonds
= (**$1027.50** + $10) × 20 = **$20,750**

(b) Annual interest = Coupon rate × Par value of bond × Number of bonds
= (**.07375** × $1000) × 20 = $1475

(c) $\text{Effective rate} = \dfrac{\text{Total interest}}{\text{Total cost of bonds}} = \dfrac{\$1475}{\mathbf{\$20{,}750}} = 7.1\%$ (rounded)

QUICK CHECK 3

Find the total cost, annual interest, and effective rate for 10 Prudential Financial (PRU) bonds maturing in 2036.

EXAMPLE 4

Finding the Net Amount from the Sale of Bonds

Find the amount received from the sale of 50 General Electric Capital (GE) bonds maturing in 2011.

SOLUTION

Amount received = (Sales price of a bond − Sales charge per bond) × Number of bonds
= (**$1038.66** − $10) × 50 = $51,433

QUICK CHECK 4

Find the amount received from the sale of 200 HSBC Finance Corp (HSBC) bonds maturing in 2008.

OBJECTIVE 4 **Understand how mutual funds containing bonds are used for monthly income.** A mutual fund can invest everything in stocks, everything in bonds, or part in stocks and part in bonds. Stock prices can be quite volatile, so financial planners recommend stock investments for people *who have a longer time horizon* over which to accumulate funds. Many planners recommend that *people invest in both stocks and bonds* during their lifetimes. Stocks may be a better investment *when investors are young*, since stocks have tended to have a higher return. Bonds may be a better investment *for investors close to retirement*, since there is less risk of losing principal in bonds and bonds pay regular interest.

EXAMPLE 5

Using a Bond Fund for Income

Brandy Barrett from Example 1 is undergoing rehabilitation and needs safety of principal. She also needs regular interest payments to help with medical expenses. She decides to place the $50,000 received from the insurance company in a mutual fund containing bonds. **(a)** Find her annual income if the fund yields 6.5% per year. **(b)** How much would Barrett need to invest in the fund to earn $10,000 per year?

SOLUTION

(a) Use the formula for simple interest: $I = PRT$.

Interest = $50,000 × **.065** = $3250

(b) Again use the formula for simple interest, but now the principal *(P)* is unknown. Divide both sides of $I = PRT$ by RT to find the following form of the equation.

$$\text{Principal} = P = \frac{I}{RT} = \frac{\$10{,}000}{.065 \times 1} = \$153{,}846.15$$

QUICK CHECK 5

James Corporation wants $80,000 per year in interest. Find the amount the firm must invest in a bond fund yielding 6.125% to attain this annual income.

Quick Check Answers

3. $9828.30; $570; 5.8%
4. $199,176
5. $1,306,122.45

10.5 EXERCISES

FOR EXTRA HELP

MyMathLab

MathXL PRACTICE

WATCH

DOWNLOAD

READ

REVIEW

The **QUICK START** *exercises in each section contain solutions to help you get started.*

Use the bond table in this section to find the following for Kraft Foods (KFT) maturing in 2011. (See Examples 1 and 2.)

QUICK START

1. Price per bond — 1. **\$1012.03**
2. Volume of bonds sold during the week — 2. ______
3. Date when bonds must be paid off by Kraft Foods — 3. ______
4. Annual interest paid — 4. ______
5. Last yield or yield to maturity — 5. ______
6. Price to buy 50 of these bonds including sales charge of \$10 per bond — 6. ______

Find the cost, including sales charges of \$10 per bond, for each of the following purchases. (See Example 3.)

QUICK START

	Bond	*Maturity*	*Number Purchased*	*Cost*
7.	Johnson Controls (JCL) **(\$982.42 + \$10) × 50 = \$49,621**	Jan. 15, 2016	50	**\$49,621**
8.	Merrill Lynch (MER)	May 16, 2016	100	______
9.	Slm (SLMA)	Jan. 15, 2009	350	______
10.	Morgan Stanley (MS)	Jan. 15, 2010	80	______
11.	Embarq (EQ)	June 01, 2036	250	______
12.	Alltel (AT)	Mar. 15, 2016	700	______

13. Explain the purpose of bonds. (See Objective 1.)

14. Explain how a bondholder can estimate the effective interest rate return on the total cost of the investment, including commissions. (See Example 3.)

C indicates an exercise that is related to the Case in Point feature.

Solve each application problem. Assume a sales commission of $10 per bond, unless indicated otherwise, and use the table in this section. Round the rate to the nearest tenth of a percent.

QUICK START

15. BOND PURCHASE Pete Chong bought 25 Constellation Energy Group (CEG) bonds maturing in 2032. Find **(a)** the total cost of the purchase including commissions, **(b)** the annual interest payment, and **(c)** the effective interest rate to total cost including commissions.

(a) Total cost $= (1.17702 \times \$1000 + \$10) \times 25 = \$29{,}675.50$

(b) Annual interest $= (.076 \times \$1000) \times 25 = \$1900$

(c) Effective interest rate $= \frac{\$1900}{\$29{,}675.50} = 6.4\%$

(a) $29,675.50
(b) $1900
(c) 6.4%

16. BOND PURCHASE New York City purchased 10,000 General Electric Capital (GE) bonds maturing in 2032. **(a)** Find the total cost of the purchase, including commissions (assume commissions of $1 per bond based on the large purchase). Then find **(b)** the annual interest payment and **(c)** the effective interest rate to total cost, including commissions.

(a) ______
(b) ______
(c) ______

17. BOND PURCHASE An investor bought 15 Countrywide Financial Corporation (CFC) bonds maturing in 2008. Find **(a)** the total cost of the purchase including commissions, **(b)** the annual interest payment, and **(c)** the effective interest rate using total cost including commissions.

(a) ______
(b) ______
(c) ______

18. RETIREMENT FUNDS The manager of a retirement account for United Pensions of America purchased 300 Conocophillips Canada Funding Co I (COP) bonds maturing in 2016. Find **(a)** the total cost of the purchase including commissions, **(b)** the annual interest payment, and **(c)** the effective interest rate using total cost including commissions.

(a) ______
(b) ______
(c) ______

19. BOND FUND Bernice Clarence places $45,000 in a bond fund that is currently yielding 8% compounded annually. **(a)** Find interest for the first year. **(b)** She decides to let all interest payments remain in the account. Find the amount in the account after 10 years if the fund continues to earn 8% compounded annually.

(a) ______
(b) ______

20. BOND FUND The community college where Roman Rodriguez works has an endowment funded by alumni and business owners in the community. The manager of the endowment invested $500,000 in a bond fund yielding 6% compounded semiannually. Find **(a)** the interest for the first year and **(b)** the future value of the account in 8 years.

(a) ______
(b) ______

CHAPTER 10 QUICK REVIEW

CHAPTER TERMS *Review the following terms to test your understanding of the chapter. For each term you do not know, refer to the page number found next to that term.*

401(k) **[p. 418]**
403(b) **[p. 418]**
amount of the annuity **[p. 414]**
annual meeting **[p. 441]**
annuity **[p. 414]**
annuity due **[p. 416]**
bankrupt **[p. 451]**
board of directors **[p. 441]**
bond **[p. 451]**
capital **[p. 441]**
common stock **[p. 442]**
compound amount of the annuity **[p. 414]**
corporation **[p. 441]**
current yield **[p. 444]**
discount brokers **[p. 442]**
dividends **[p. 441]**
Dow Jones Industrial Average **[p. 445]**
equivalent cash price **[p. 427]**
ETF **[p. 445]**
exchange-traded funds (ETFs) **[p. 445]**
executive officers **[p. 441]**
face value **[p. 451]**
future value of the annuity **[p. 414]**
index fund **[p. 446]**
individual retirement account (IRA) **[p. 418]**
interest rate spreads **[p. 438]**
IRA **[p. 418]**
limited liability **[p. 441]**
mature **[p. 451]**
maturity date **[p. 451]**
mutual fund **[p. 445]**
NASDAQ Composite Index **[p. 445]**
ordinary annuity **[p. 414]**
par value **[p. 451]**
payment period **[p. 414]**
PE ratio **[p. 444]**
preferred stock **[p. 442]**
present value of an annuity **[p. 423]**
price–earnings (PE) ratio **[p. 444]**
privately held corporation **[p. 441]**
publicly held corporation **[p. 441]**
regular IRA **[p. 418]**
Roth IRA **[p. 418]**
sinking fund **[p. 431]**
sinking fund table **[p. 432]**
stock **[p. 441]**
stockbrokers **[p. 442]**
stock certificates **[p. 441]**
stock exchanges **[p. 442]**
stockholders **[p. 441]**
stock ratios **[p. 444]**
term of the annuity **[p. 414]**

CONCEPTS	EXAMPLES
10.1 Finding the amount of an ordinary annuity Determine the number of periods in the annuity *(n)* and the interest rate per annuity period *(i)*. Use *n* and *i* in the annuity table to find the value of \$1 at the term of annuity. Find the value of an annuity using the formula. Amount = Payment × Number from table	Ed Navarro deposits \$800 at the end of each quarter for 7 years into an IRA. Given interest of 8% compounded quarterly, find the future value. $n = 7 \times 4 = 28$ periods; $i = \frac{8\%}{4} = 2\%$ per period Number from table is 37.05121. Amount = \$800 × 37.05121 = **\$29,640.97** (rounded)
10.1 Finding the amount of an annuity due Determine the number of periods in the annuity. Add 1 to the value and use this as the value of *n*. Determine the interest rate per annuity period, and use the table to find the value of \$1 at term of annuity. The amount of the annuity is Payment × Number from table − 1 payment	Find the amount of an annuity due if payments of \$700 are made at the beginning of each quarter for 3 years in an account paying 8% compounded quarterly. $n = 3 \times 4 + 1 = 13$; $i = \frac{8\%}{4} = 2\%$ Number from table is 14.68033. Amount = \$700 × 14.68033 − **\$700** = \$9576.23
10.2 Finding the present value of an annuity Determine the payment per period. Determine the number of periods in the annuity *(n)*. Determine the interest rate per period *(i)*. Use the values of *n* and *i* to find the number in the present value of an annuity table. The present value of an annuity is Present value = Payment × Number from table	What lump sum deposited today at 8% compounded annually will yield the same total as payments of \$600 at the end of each year for 10 years? Payment = \$600; $n = 10$ Interest = 8% Number from table is 6.71008. Present value = \$600 × 6.71008 = **\$4026.05**

CONCEPTS	EXAMPLES

10.2 Finding the equivalent cash price

Determine the amount of the annuity payment.

Determine the number of periods in the annuity (n).

Determine the interest rate per annuity period (i).

Use n and i in the present value of an annuity table.

Add the present value of the annuity to the down payment to obtain today's equivalent cash price.

A buyer offers to purchase a business for $75,000 down and payments of $4000 at the end of each quarter for 5 years. Money is worth 8% compounded quarterly. How much is the buyer actually offering for the business?

Payment = $4000; $n = 20$

Interest = $\frac{8\%}{4}$ = 2%

Number from table is 16.35143.

Present value = $4000 × 16.35143 = **$65,405.72**

Equivalent cash value = $75,000 + **$65,405.72**

= $140,405.72

10.3 Determining the payment into a sinking fund

Determine the number of payments (n). Determine the interest rate per period (i). Find the value of the payment needed to accumulate $1 from the sinking fund table.

Calculate the payment using

Payment = Future value × Number from table

No-Leak Plumbing plans to accumulate $500,000 in 4 years in a sinking fund for a new building. Find the amount of each semiannual payment if the fund earns 10% compounded semiannually.

$n = 4 \times 2 = 8$ periods; $i = \frac{10\%}{2} = 5\%$ per period

Number from table is **.10472**.

Payment = $500,000 × **.10472** = $52,360

10.3 Setting up a sinking fund table

Determine the required payment into the sinking fund.

Calculate the interest at the end of each period.

Add the previous total, next payment, and interest to determine the total.

Repeat these steps for each period.

A company wants to set up a sinking fund to accumulate $10,000 in 4 years. It wishes to make semiannual payments into the account, which pays 8% compounded semiannually. Set up a sinking fund table.

$n = 8$; $i = 4\%$

Number from table is **.10853**.

Payment = $10,000 × **.10853** = $1085.30

Payment	Amount of Deposit	Interest Earned	Total
1	$1085.30	$0	$1085.30
2	$1085.30	$43.41	$2214.01
3	$1085.30	$88.56	$3387.87
4	$1085.30	$135.51	$4608.68
5	$1085.30	$184.35	$5878.33
6	$1085.30	$235.13	$7198.76
7	$1085.30	$287.95	$8572.01
8	$1085.11	$342.88	$10,000.00

10.4 Reading the stock table

Use the stock table in **Section 10.4** to find the following information for Hartford Financial (HIG) and identify the values.

52 week High	52 week Low	Name	Vol 100s	Yld	P/E	Week's Last	Week's Chg.	Div Amt
94.03	79.24	HrtfrdFnl	31532	2.1	12	93.31	+0.86	.50
52-week high price	52-week low price		Volume for week	Dividend yield	Price–earnings ratio	Closing price	Change for the week	Last quarterly dividend

CONCEPTS	EXAMPLES
10.4 Finding the current yield on a stock To determine the current yield, use the formula $$\text{Current yield} = \frac{\text{Annual dividend}}{\text{Closing price}}$$	Find the current yield for a stock if the purchase price is \$35 and the annual dividend is \$.64. $$\text{Current yield} = \frac{\$.64}{\$35} = 1.8\%\ (\text{rounded})$$
10.4 Finding the price–earnings (PE) ratio To find the PE ratio, use the formula $$\text{PE ratio} = \frac{\text{Price per share}}{\text{Annual net income per share}}$$	Find the PE ratio for a stock priced at \$42.50 with earnings of \$2.11. $$\text{PE Ratio} = \frac{\$42.50}{\$2.11} = 20\ (\text{rounded})$$
10.5 Reading the bond table Locate the bond and determine the various quantities.	Use the bond table in **Section 10.5** to find the following. (see table below)
10.5 Determining the cost of purchasing bonds First locate the bond in the table. Then determine the price of the bond and multiply this value by \$1000 and the number of bonds purchased. Finally, add \$10 per bond to the total cost of bonds purchased.	Including sales charges of \$10 per bond, find the cost of 50 General Electric bonds that are selling at 111.898. $$(1.11898 \times 1000 + \$10) \times 50 = \$56{,}449$$
10.5 Determining the amount received from the sale of bonds First locate the bond in the table. Then determine the price of the bond and multiply this value by 1000 and the number of bonds sold. Finally, subtract \$10 per bond from the total selling price.	Find the amount received after the sales charge from the sale of 20 Bank of America bonds selling at 99.969. $$(.99969 \times \$1000 - \$10) \times 20 = \$19{,}793.80$$
10.5 Finding the effective yield of a bond Find the cost of the bond after commission. Find the interest paid on the bond using the coupon rate. Finally, divide the interest by the cost of the bond.	Find the effective interest rate, to the nearest tenth, for a bond with a coupon rate of 3.8% and selling at 98.25. Price of bond = .9825 × \$1000 + \$10 = \$992.50 Interest = .038 × \$1000 = \$38 $$\text{Effective rate} = \frac{\$38}{\$992.50} = 3.8\%\ (\text{rounded})$$

Bond table (10.5 example):

Company (Ticker)	Coupon	Maturity	Last Price	Last Yield	Est \$ Vol (000's)
Alltel (AT)	7.000	Mar 15, 2016	103.144	6.530	33,318
Pays 7% of \$1000 per year		Matures March 15, 2016	Closed at \$1031.44	Yield to maturity of 6.53%	Estimated volume of \$33,318,000 for week

CHAPTER 10 SUMMARY EXERCISE

Planning for Retirement

At age 37, Roman Rodriguez decides to plan for his retirement at age 67. He currently has a net worth of about $45,000 including the equity in his home. He assumes that his employer will contribute $3500 to his retirement plan at the end of each year for the next 30 years. He plans to put one-half of his money in a mutual fund containing stocks and the other one-half in a mutual fund containing bonds.

(a) Estimate Rodriguez's future accumulation if his net worth grows at 5% and the mutual funds with stocks and bonds grow at 10% and 6%, respectively.

(a) ________________

(b) Rodriguez is amazed that he will be able to accumulate over $600,000. However, he knows that inflation will increase his cost of living significantly in 30 years. He assumes 3% inflation and wants to find the income he needs at age 67 to have the same purchasing power as $40,000 today. (*Hint:* Look at inflation in **Section 9.2** and use the compound interest table in **Section 9.1.**)

(b) ________________

(c) Rodriguez has read newspaper articles stating that Social Security benefits will be reduced in the years ahead. After some thought, he decides to be conservative and assume that Social Security will pay only the first $30,000 of the annual income he needs at age 67. Find the remaining income he will need beginning at age 67.

(c) ________________

(d) Rodriguez decides to plan funding for his retirement for 20 years, from ages 67 to 87. If funds earn 8% compounded annually, find the present value of the annual income that he needs at 67 based on the income from part **(c).**

(d) ________________

(e) Will his expected savings fund his retirement?

(e) ________________

(f) What could go wrong with his plans?

(f) ________________

INVESTIGATE

There is some discussion about the ability of Social Security to pay retirement benefits. Do you think Social Security will be around to help you during your retirement? What percent of your retirement needs do you think Social Security will pay? Try to support your views with recent articles from newspapers, magazines, or the World Wide Web.

CHAPTER 10 TEST

To help you review, the numbers in brackets show the section in which the topic was discussed.

Find the amounts of the following annuities. **[10.1]**

	Amount of Each Deposit	Deposited	Rate per Year	Number of Years	Type of Annuity	Amount of Annuity
1.	$1000	annually	6%	8	ordinary	________
2.	$4500	semiannually	10%	9	ordinary	________
3.	$30,000	quarterly	8%	6	due	________
4.	$2600	semiannually	10%	12	due	________

5. James Rivera earned his degree in drafting at a community college and recently began his new career. He was happy to learn that his new employer will deposit $2000 into his 401(k) retirement account at the end of each year. Find the amount he will have accumulated in 15 years if funds earn 8% per year. **[10.1]** **5.** ________

6. James Rivera from Exercise 5 has also decided to invest $500 at the end of each quarter in an IRA that grows tax deferred. Find the amount he will have accumulated if he does this for 10 years and earns 8% compounded quarterly. **[10.1]** **6.** ________

Find the present value of the following annuities. **[10.2]**

	Amount per Payment	Payment at End of Each	Number of Years	Interest Rate	Compounded	Present Value
7.	$1000	year	9	6%	annually	________
8.	$4500	6 months	6	10%	semiannually	________
9.	$708	month	3	12%	monthly	________
10.	$14,000	quarter	6	8%	quarterly	________

11. Betty Yowski borrows money for a new swimming pool and hot tub. She agrees to repay the note with a payment of $1200 per quarter for 6 years. Find the amount she must set aside today to satisfy this capital requirement in an account earning 10% compounded quarterly. **[10.2]** **11.** ________

12. Dan and Mary Fisher just divorced. The divorce settlement included $650 a month payment to Dan for the 4 years until their son turns 18. Find the amount Mary must set aside today in an account earning 12% per year compounded monthly to satisfy this financial obligation. **[10.2]** **12.** ________

Find the amount of each payment into a sinking fund for the following. **[10.3]**

	Amount Needed	*Years Until Needed*	*Interest Rate*	*Interest Compounded*	*Amount of Payment*
13.	$100,000	9	6%	annually	________
14.	$250,000	10	8%	semiannually	________
15.	$360,000	11	6%	quarterly	________
16.	$800,000	12	10%	semiannually	________

Solve the following application problems.

17. The owner of Hickory Bar-B-Que plans to open a new restaurant in 4 years at a cost of $200,000. Find the required semiannual payment into a sinking fund if funds are invested in an account earning 6% per year compounded semiannually. **[10.3]**

17. ________________

18. Lupe Martinez will owe her retired mother $45,000 for a piece of land. Find the required quarterly payment into a sinking fund if Lupe pays it off in 4 years and the interest rate is 10% per year compounded quarterly. **[10.3]**

18. ________________

19. George Jones purchases 200 shares of Merck stock at $79.50 per share. Find **(a)** the total cost and **(b)** the annual dividend if the dividend per share is $1.36. **[10.4]**

(a) ________________
(b) ________________

20. Belinda Deal purchases 25 IBM bonds that mature in 2021 at 95.1. They have a coupon rate of 4.2%. Find **(a)** the total cost if commissions are $10 per bond, **(b)** the annual interest, and **(c)** the effective interest rate rounded to the nearest tenth. **[10.5]**

(a) ________________
(b) ________________
(c) ________________

21. Explain the following from the stock table. **[10.4]**

52 week							–Week's–		---- Earnings ----			
High	**Low**	**Name**	**Tick Sym**	**Vol 100s**	**Yld**	**P/E**	**Last**	**Chg.**	**Latest Year**	**This Year**	**Next Year**	**Div Amt**
54.43	40.72	HanoverIns	THG	5320	.6	11	48.80	−0.15	1.31	3.64	4.23	.30

22. Explain the following from the bond table. **[10.5]**

Company (Ticker)	Coupon	Maturity	Last Price	Last Yield	Est $ Vol (000's)
Halliburton (HAL)	6.750	Feb 01, 2027	100.000	6.749	42,300

CHAPTER 11

Business and Consumer Loans

CHAPTER CONTENTS

After Jackie Waterton received her degree in business, she went to work for Citigroup Inc. Citigroup is one of the largest banks in the world. Due to her interest in the Internet and electronic commerce, Jackie transferred to Citibank Direct, which is the online banking segment of Citigroup. She has been promoted and now manages a group that works with customers who have credit problems.

CASE *in* POINT

It is almost impossible in our society to pay cash for everything. People borrow for purchases at department stores, gas stations, furniture stores, and automobile dealerships. Other examples of using credit that we don't commonly think of include turning on the lights, using running water, and using our cell phone. Almost everyone borrows when they buy a home. This chapter looks at various methods of determining interest charges on purchases.

11.1 OPEN-END CREDIT AND CHARGE CARDS

OBJECTIVES

1. Define open-end credit.
2. Define revolving charge accounts.
3. Use the unpaid balance method.
4. Use the average daily balance method.
5. Define loan consolidation.

CASE in POINT Jackie Waterton has worked with many families who have serious debt problems. She often helps these families set up budgets and then tries to reduce their monthly debt payments by refinancing loans when possible.

The newspaper clipping shows that young adults commonly struggle with debt because they are often trying to start a household and pay for college at the same time.

HERE & NOW

Young People Struggle to Deal with Kiss of Debt

High price of college, soaring housing costs stack the deck

By Mindy Fetterman and Barbara Hansen USA TODAY

Thirty years ago, the "generation gap" reflected the cultural gulf between World War II-era parents and their children. Parents then just didn't get sex, drugs and rock 'n' roll.

Today, the gap is about debt.

This generation of twentysomethings is straining under the weight of college loans and other debt, a crushing load that separates it from every previous generation.

Nearly two-thirds carry some debt, and those with debt have taken on more in the past five years, according to an analysis of the credit records of 3 million twentysomethings that Experian, the credit-reporting agency, did for USA TODAY. Their late payments are rising, and they're more likely to be late than other Americans are.

Nearly half of twentysomethings have stopped paying a debit, forcing lenders to "charge off" the debt and sell it to a collection agency, or had cars repossessed or sought bankruptcy protection.

High debt loads are causing anxiety, too. A poll of twentysomethings by USA TODAY and the National Endowment for Financial Education (NEFE) found 60% feel they're facing tougher financial pressures than young people did in previous generations. And 30% say they worry frequently about their debt.

"I have nightmares," says Heather Schopp, 29, of Long Beach, Calif., who accrued $165,000 in student-loan debt to become a chiropractor. "I dream I'm on a hot-air balloon, hanging on for dear life."

Numbers in the News

What 20somethings Owe

Experian Group, a credit-reporting company, analyzed data from 3 million credit records of twentysomethings over five years. Here's how twentysomethings are doing:

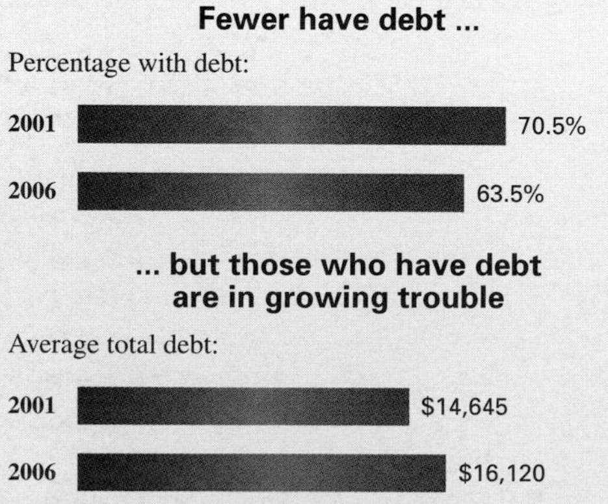

DATA: Experian analysis for USA TODAY of credit records of 3 million twentysomethings from Aug. 1, 2001, compared with Aug. 1, 2006

OBJECTIVE 1 **Define open-end credit.** A common way of buying on credit, called **open-end credit**, has no fixed payments. The customer continues making payments until no outstanding balance is owed. With open-end credit, additional credit is often extended before the initial amount is paid off. Examples of open-end credit include most department-store charge accounts and charge cards, including MasterCard and Visa. Individuals are given a **credit limit**, or a maximum amount that may be charged on these accounts. The lender determines the credit limit for each person based on his or her income, assets, other debts, and credit history.

QUICK TIP **Debit cards** do not involve credit, since their use results in an immediate debit.

A sale paid for with a **debit card** authorizes the retailer's bank to debit the purchaser's checking account immediately upon receipt. A Visa or MasterCard can be either a charge card or a debit card, depending on the bank and the card holder's preference.

OBJECTIVE 2 **Define revolving charge accounts.** With a typical department-store account or bank card, a customer might make several small purchases during a month. Such accounts are often *never paid off*, although a minimum amount must be paid each month, since new purchases are continually being made. Since the account may never be paid off, it is called a **revolving charge account**. Visa, MasterCard, Discover, and some oil-company cards use this method of extending credit. Sometimes there is an annual membership fee or a minimum monthly charge for the use of this service.

A sample copy of a credit card receipt is shown on the left. The graph below shows the rapid acceptance of credit and debit cards as people use them for purchases of less than $25.

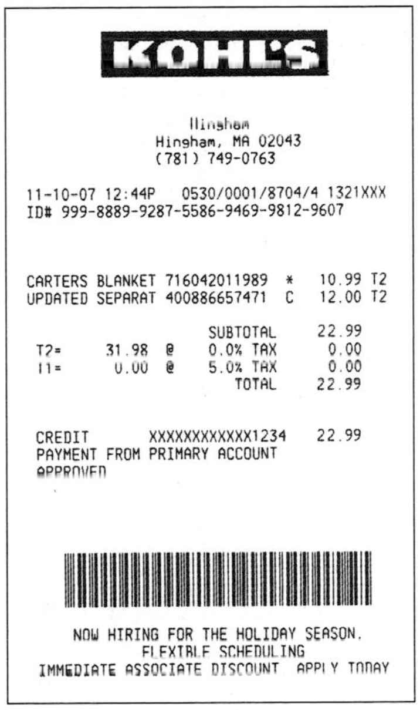

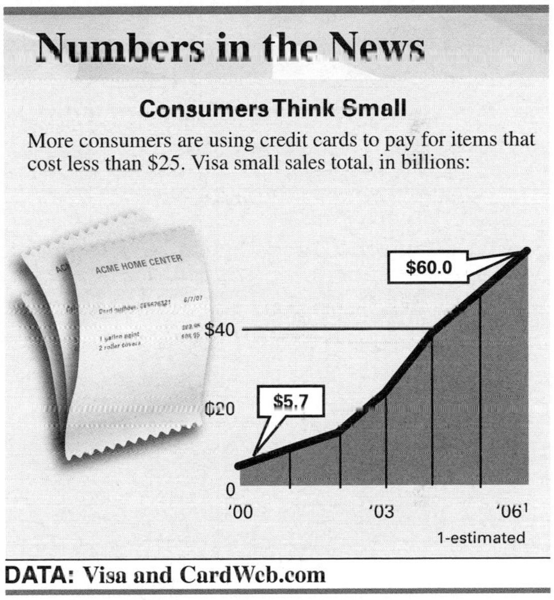

QUICK TIP The credit card business is very profitable for banks, so they compete to issue as many credit cards as possible to qualified consumers.

At the end of a billing period, the customer receives a statement of payments and purchases made. This statement typically takes one of two forms. **Country club billing** provides a carbon copy of all original charge receipts. **Itemized billing**, more and more common because of its lower cost to credit card companies, provides an itemized listing of all charges, without copies of each individual charge. A typical itemized statement is also shown on the next page.

Finance charges are interest charges beyond the cash price of an item and may include interest, credit life insurance, a time-payment differential, and carrying charges. Interest charges can be avoided if the total balance is paid by the end of the **grace period**. Grace periods range between 15 and 30 days depending on the company. Often, there is no grace period on cash advances, so that finance charges are assessed beginning immediately. Many lenders also charge **late fees** for payments that are received after the due date. **Over-the-limit fees** are charged by the lender when the borrower charges more than an approved maximum amount of debt.

QUICK TIP Both late fees and over-the-limit fees are high. Avoid them!

OBJECTIVE 3 **Use the unpaid balance method.** Finance charges on open-end credit accounts may be calculated using the **unpaid balance method**. This method calculates finance charges based on the unpaid balance at *the end of the previous month*. Any purchases or returns during the current month are not used in calculating the finance charge, as you can see in the next example.

AMERICA'S CHARGE CARD
★★★★★★★★

$ ______ WRITE IN THE AMOUNT OF YOUR PAYMENT

IMPORTANT! 1. Return this portion of your statement with your check; please do not fold or bend 2. Write your account number on the face of your check 3. Make checks payable to America's Charge Card

ACCOUNT NUMBER	BILLING DATE	PAYMENT DUE DATE	NEW BALANCE	MINIMUM PAYMENT DUE
5211-1234-5678	10-18	11-12	609.26	30.00

JOHN Q. CARDHOLDER
1000 MAIN STREET
ANYTOWN, USA 00000

52112345678 0060926003000

PLEASE BE SURE OUR MAILING ADDRESS ON THE REVERSE SIDE APPEARS IN THE WINDOW OF THE RETURN ENVELOPE

DO NOT INCLUDE INQUIRIES WITH PAYMENT. SEE REVERSE SIDE

PLEASE PRINT

FOR CHANGE OF ADDRESS	NEW STREET ADDRESS	APT. P.O. BOX NO.
	CITY	STATE	ZIP CODE

RETAIN THIS PORTION FOR YOUR RECORDS

Account Number	Credit Line	Available Credit	Past Due Amount	BILLING DATE
5211-1234-5678	1,000.00	390.74	.00	10-18

TRAN DATE	POSTING DATE	REFERENCE NUMBER	TRANSACTION DESCRIPTION			TRANSACTION AMOUNT
09 06	09 09	12009230	TURNSTYLE 702	CHICAGO	IL	25.17CR
09 07	09 13	55190432	POLK BROS	CHICAGO	IL	150.00
09 13	09 21	86235671	MINNESOTA FABRICS 32	NORRIDGE	IL	39.54
09 14	09 19	21345678	SPIEGELS, INC.	CHICAGO	IL	60.10
09 20	09 20	93703523	PAYMENT THANK YOU			110.00CR
09 21	09 26	86245671	MINNESOTA FABRICS 32	NORRIDGE	IL	42.64
09 25	09 28	12001051	TURNSTYLE 702	CHICAGO	IL	14.49

PREVIOUS BALANCE	AVERAGE DAILY BALANCE	FINANCE CHARGE	NEW BALANCE	Minimum Payment
432.64	501.80	5.02	609.26	30.00

For Customer Service Call	Charge Transactions	PAYMENTS	CREDITS	PAYMENT DUE DATE
	306.77	110.00	25.17CR	11-12

SEE ITEM NUMBER ON REVERSE SIDE FOR YOUR PERIODIC RATE(S). THE RANGE OF AVERAGE DAILY BALANCE(S) TO WHICH IT APPLIES AND THE CORRESPONDING **ANNUAL PERCENTAGE RATE**

Additional **FINANCE CHARGE** on purchases may be avoided if total NEW BALANCE is paid in full by PAYMENT DUE DATE

NOTICE: SEE REVERSE SIDE FOR IMPORTANT INFORMATION

YOU MAY AT ANY TIME PAY ALL OR PART OF THE BALANCE OWING ON YOUR ACCOUNT

EXAMPLE 1

Finding Finance Charge Using the Unpaid Balance Method

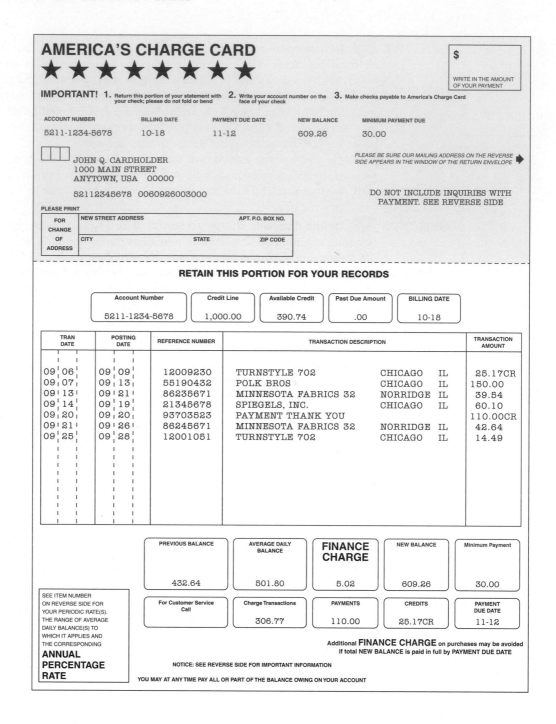

(a) Peter Brinkman's MasterCard account had an unpaid balance of \$870.40 on November 1. During November, he made a payment of \$100 and purchased a yellow Lab costing \$150 for his son using the card. Find the finance charge and the unpaid balance on December 1 if the bank charges 1.5% per month on the unpaid balance.

A finance charge of 1.5% per month on the unpaid balance would be

$$\$870.40 \times .015 = \$13.06 \text{ for the month}$$

Find the unpaid balance on December 1 as follows.

$$\underset{\text{previous balance}}{\$870.40} + \underset{\text{finance charge}}{\$13.06} + \underset{\text{purchases during month}}{\$150} - \underset{\text{payment}}{\$100} = \underset{\text{new balance}}{\$933.46}$$

(b) During December, Brinkman made a payment of \$50, charged \$240.56 for Christmas presents, returned \$35.45 worth of items, and took his family to dinner with charges of \$92.45. Find his unpaid balance on January 1.

The finance charge calculated on the unpaid balance is $933.46 × .015 = $14.00. The unpaid balance on January 1 follows.

$$\$933.46 + \mathbf{\$14.00} + \mathbf{\$240.56} + \mathbf{\$92.45} - \mathbf{\$35.45} - \mathbf{\$50} = \$1195.02$$

Month	Unpaid Balance at Beginning of Month	Finance Charge	Purchases During Month	Returns	Payment	Unpaid Balance at End of Month
November	$870.40	$13.06	$150.00	—	$100	$ 933.46
December	$933.46	$14.00	$333.01	$35.45	$ 50	$1195.02

The total finance charge during the 2-month period was $13.06 + $14.00 = $27.06.

(c) Brinkman knows that his debt is increasing. He moves the balance to another charge card that charges only .8% per month. Find his savings in finance charges for January.

$$\text{Savings} = \underbrace{(\$1195.02 \times .015)}_{\text{old charge card}} - \underbrace{(\$1195.02 \times .008)}_{\text{new charge card}} = \$8.37$$

QUICK CHECK 1

The unpaid balance on a Visa card was $284.37. During the month, a payment of $200 was made and charges of $357.54 were added. If the finance charge is 1.2% per month on the unpaid balance, find **(a)** the finance charge for the month and **(b)** the new balance at the end of the month.

Suppose you decide to purchase a $1000 digital television set and charge it to a Visa card with finance charges of 1.5% per month on the unpaid balance. Further suppose that you make payments of $50 every month and don't charge anything else on the card. As shown next, it will take you 24 months to pay off the television set. The $1000 television set will cost you an extra $197.83 in finance charges for a total cost of $1197.83.

Month	Unpaid Balance at Beginning of Month	Finance Charge	Payment	Unpaid Balance at End of Month
1	$1,000.00	$15.00	$50.00	$965.00
2	$965.00	$14.48	$50.00	$929.48
3	$929.48	$13.94	$50.00	$893.42
⋮	⋮	⋮	⋮	⋮
22	$143.53	$ 2.15	$50.00	$95.68
23	$ 95.68	$ 1.44	$50.00	$47.12
24	$ 47.12	$ 0.71	$47.83	$ 0.00
	Totals	$197.83	$1197.83	

QUICK TIP Notice that the unpaid balance decreases each month. Since the finance charge is based on the unpaid balance, it too decreases each month.

The cost of technology items often falls rapidly. If you had waited eight months and saved your money before buying, you might have been able to purchase the same television set for $700 cash rather than paying nearly $1200.

OBJECTIVE 4 **Use the average daily balance method.** Most revolving charge plans now calculate finance charges using the **average daily balance method**. First, the balance owed on the account is found at the end of each day during a month or billing period. All of these amounts are added, and the total is divided by the number of days in the month or billing period. The result is the average daily balance of the account, which is then used to calculate the finance charge.

Quick Check Answers

1. (a) $3.41 **(b)** $445.32

EXAMPLE 2

Finding the Average Daily Balance

Beth Hogan's balance on a Visa card was \$209.46 on March 3. Her activity for the next 30 days is shown in the table. **(a)** Find the average daily balance on April 3. Given finance charges based on $1\frac{1}{2}\%$ on the average daily balance, find **(b)** the finance charge for the month and **(c)** the balance owed on April 3.

Transaction Description		Transaction Amount
Previous balance \$209.46		
March 3	Billing date	
March 12	Payment	\$50.00 CR*
March 17	Clothes	\$28.46
March 20	Mail order	\$31.22
April 1	Auto parts	\$59.10

*CR represents *credit.*

SOLUTION

(a)

Date	Unpaid Balance	Number of Days Until Balance Changes
March 3	\$209.46	9
March 12	\$159.46 = \$209.46 − March 12 payment of \$50	5
March 17	\$187.92 = \$159.46 + March 17 charge of \$28.46	3
March 20	\$219.14 = \$187.92 + March 20 charge of \$31.22	12
April 1	\$278.24 = \$219.14 + April 1 charge of \$59.10	2
April 3	end of billing cycle . . .	31 total number of days in billing period

It is 9 days from March 3 to March 12, so the unpaid balance remains at \$209.46 for 9 days.

QUICK TIP The billing period in Example 2 is 31 days. Some billing periods are 30 days (or 28 or 29 days in February). Be sure to use the correct number of days for the month of the billing period.

There are 31 days in the billing period (March has 31 days). Find the average daily balance as follows:

STEP 1 Multiply each unpaid balance by the number of days for that balance.

STEP 2 Total these amounts.

STEP 3 Divide by the number of days in that particular billing cycle (month).

Step 1

Unpaid Balance		Days		Total Balance
\$209.46	×	9	=	\$1885.14
\$159.46	×	5	=	797.30
\$187.92	×	3	=	563.76
\$219.14	×	12	=	2629.68
\$278.24	×	2	=	556.48
				\$6432.36 ← Step 2

Step 3

$$\frac{\$6432.36}{31} = \$207.50 \text{ average daily balance}$$

Hogan will pay a finance charge based on the average daily balance of \$207.50.

(b) The finance charge is **.015** × **\$207.50** = \$3.11 (rounded).

(c) The amount owed on April 3 is the beginning unpaid balance less any returns or payments, plus new charges and the finance charge.

$$\underset{\text{previous balance}}{\$209.46} - \underset{\text{payment}}{\$50} + \underbrace{(\$28.46 + \$31.22 + \$59.10)}_{\text{new charges}} + \underset{\text{finance charge}}{\$3.11} = \$281.35$$

QUICK CHECK 2

The July 5 balance on a credit card was $494. A payment of $400 was made on July 22, and a charge of $258.67 was made on July 25. If the finance charge is based on $1\frac{1}{2}\%$, find **(a)** the average daily balance on August 5, **(b)** the finance charge for the month, and **(c)** the unpaid balance on August 5.

If the finance charges are expressed on a per-month basis, find the **annual percentage rate** by multiplying the monthly rate by 12, the number of months in a year. For example, $1\frac{1}{2}\%$ per month is the same as:

$$1\tfrac{1}{2}\% \times 12 = 1.5\% \times 12 = 18\% \text{ per year}$$

OBJECTIVE 5 **Define loan consolidation.** Credit is *very easy to get* for individuals who have a good credit history and a stable job. The clipping shows that too much spending and borrowing often creates problems. Below are some ways to help gain control of your finances.

HERE & NOW

Easy Credit Comes with Big Penalty

Young adults' free-spending ways set stage for bankruptcy.

By Margaret Webb Pressler
WASHINGTON POST

Christopher Siwy thinks he's pretty good with his finances, especially for a 23-year-old. Siwy just moved to Alexandria, Va., from Allentown, Pa., and with a starting job in information technology, he has no problem paying $160 on his student loan every month. He even saves a little bit out of each paycheck so that someday he can buy a condo.

But when Siwy wanted some wheels, he turned to the most popular financing plan for someone his age: a credit card.

Gaining Control of Your Finances

1. Increase your income by investing in yourself. Choose a career you enjoy, and get training and education.
2. Make a budget and stick to it.
3. Spend less. Here are some suggestions.
   (a) Make sure you can afford your rent or mortgage payment.
   (b) Eat out less often.
   (c) Drive that old automobile one or two more years.
   (d) Purchase a less expensive automobile or reduce the number of automobiles in your family by one.
   (e) Be careful with the amount you spend on entertainment, hobbies, and travel.
   (f) Don't buy on impulse. If you want something, write it down on a piece of paper and stick it on your refrigerator for 30 days. After 30 days, ask yourself if you actually need the item.
4. Try to pay cash for things the day you buy them rather than using credit.
5. Save more by paying yourself first. Do this by saving a certain amount every month before you spend money on other things.
6. Set some money aside for emergencies.
7. Contribute to a long-range retirement plan.

Have you ever found yourself in a position where you cannot make all of your monthly payments? If so, you may be able to **consolidate your loans** into a single loan with one lower monthly payment. The new loan may have a lower interest rate and also a longer term, meaning that payments must be made for a longer period of time. This process can help you afford your monthly payments rather than defaulting on debt. **Defaulting on your debt**, or not making your payments, can mean repossession of your automobile or furniture, eviction from your apartment or house, and/or court appearances. Defaulting on your debt also ruins your credit history and can make it difficult to borrow money to buy a car or a home for years into the future.

Quick Check Answers

2. **(a)** $405.14 **(b)** $6.08 **(c)** $358.75

EXAMPLE 3

Consolidating Loans

Bill and Jane Smith were married two years ago. Both were happy when they had their first child, but they needed to buy several things on credit. They now have the monthly payments shown below. The Smiths are having difficulties making the payments and they sometimes argue over money. They bank online at Citibank Direct and ask Jackie Waterton for help.

Revolving Accounts	Debt	Annual Percentage Rate	Minimum Monthly Payment
Sears	$3880.54	18%	$150
Dillards	$1620.13	16%	$ 60
MasterCard	$3140.65	14%	$100
Visa	$4920.98	18%	$200
	Total $13,562.30		Total $510

Other Payments	Monthly Payment
Rent	$800
Jane's car payment	$315
Bill's truck payment	$268
	Total $1383

SOLUTION

Jackie Waterton:

1. Put the Smiths on a **strict monthly budget**.
2. Consolidated their revolving account debts into one longer-term, low-interest loan (this required a loan guarantee from Bill's father).
3. Decreased one automobile payment by refinancing the loan over a longer term.

Here are their new monthly payments.

Account	Monthly Payment	New Status
Credit union loan for $13,562.30	$337.50	Revolving loans were consolidated
Rent	$800.00	Unchanged
Jane's car payment	$247.50	Refinanced using a longer term
Bill's truck payment	$268.00	Unchanged
	Total $1653.00	

$$\text{Reduction in payments} = (\$510 + \$1383) - \$1653 = \mathbf{\$240\ per\ month}$$

The Smiths should be all right as long as they do the following.

1. **Stay on their monthly budget.**
2. **Do not make additional credit purchases.**
3. **Continue to make all payments.**

The Smiths may end up with severe debt problems if they borrow more before the existing loan balances are significantly reduced. Borrowing more could force them to declare bankruptcy.

QUICK TIP Individuals who consolidate their loans and then borrow even more can get into very serious financial difficulties.

QUICK CHECK 3

A family refinanced the mortgage on their home, reducing the payment from $1269.45 to $1093.12. They also sold a car that had a monthly payment of $385.65 and negotiated a $50-per-month payment reduction on their second car. Find the decrease in monthly payments.

Quick Check Answer

3. $611.98

11.1 EXERCISES

FOR EXTRA HELP

MyMathLab

MathXL PRACTICE

WATCH

DOWNLOAD

READ

REVIEW

The **QUICK START** *exercises in each section contain solutions to help you get started.*

Find the finance charge on each of the following revolving charge accounts. Assume interest is calculated on the unpaid balance of the account. Round to the nearest cent. (See Example 1.)

QUICK START

	Unpaid Balance	*Monthly Interest Rate*	*Finance Charge*
1.	$6425.40	1.7%	**$109.23**
	$6425.40 × .017 = $109.23		
2.	$595.35	$1\frac{1}{2}\%$	______
3.	$1201.43	$1\frac{1}{4}\%$	______
4.	$2540.33	1.6%	______

Complete the following tables, showing the unpaid balance at the end of each month. Assume an interest rate of 1.4% on the unpaid balance. (See Example 1.)

	Month	*Unpaid Balance at Beginning of Month*	*Finance Charge*	*Purchases During Month*	*Returns*	*Payment*	*Unpaid Balance at End of Month*
5.	October	$437.18	______	$128.72	$27.85	$125	______
	November	______	______	$291.64	—	$175	______
	December	______	______	$147.11	$17.15	$150	______
	January	______	______	$27.84	$127.76	$225	______
6.	October	$255.40	______	$27.50	—	$50	______
	November	______	______	$59.60	$22.15	$45.50	______
	December	______	______	$85.45	$32.00	$125	______
	January	______	______	$325.68	—	$100	______

7. Compare the unpaid balance method and the average daily balance method for calculating interest on open-end credit accounts. (See Objectives 3 and 4.)

8. Explain how consolidating loans may be of some advantage to the borrower. What disadvantages can you think of? (See Objective 5.)

C indicates an exercise that is related to the Case in Point feature.

Find the finance charge for the following revolving charge accounts. Assume that interest is calculated on the average daily balance of the account. (See Example 2.)

QUICK START

	Average Daily Balance	*Monthly Interest Rate*	*Finance Charge*
9.	$1458.25	1.4%	**$20.42**
	$1458.25 × .014 = $20.42		
10.	$841.60	$1\frac{1}{2}$%	**$12.62**
	$841.60 × .015 = $12.62		
11.	$389.95	$1\frac{1}{4}$%	________
12.	$2235.46	1.6%	________
13.	$1235.68	1.4%	________
14.	$4235.47	$1\frac{3}{4}$%	________

Solve the following application problems.

15. HOT TUB PURCHASE Betty Thomas borrowed $6500 on her Visa card to install a hot tub with landscaping around it. The interest charges are 1.6% per month on the unpaid balance. **(a)** Find the interest charges. **(b)** Find the interest charges if she moves the debt to a credit card charging 1% per month on the unpaid balance. **(c)** Find the savings.

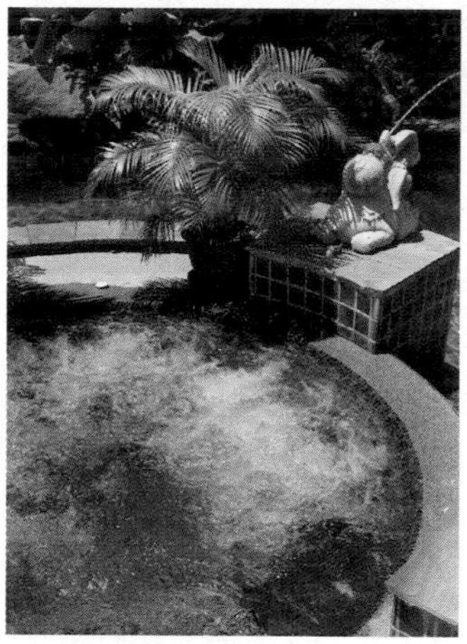

(a) ________
(b) ________
(c) ________

16. CREDIT CARD BALANCE Alphy Jurarim used a credit card from Citibank Direct to help pay for tuition expenses while in college and now owes $5232.25. The interest charges are 1.75% per month. **(a)** Find the interest charges. **(b)** Find the interest charges if he moves the debt to a credit card charging .8% per month on the unpaid balance. **(c)** Find the savings.

(a) ________
(b) ________
(c) ________

***(a)** Find the average daily balance for the following credit card accounts. Assume one month between billing dates using the proper number of days in the month. **(b)** Then find the finance charge if interest is 1.5% per month on the average daily balance. **(c)** Finally, find the new balance. (See Example 2.)*

QUICK START

17. Previous balance $139.56

September 12	Billing date	
September 20	Payment	$45
September 21	Athletic shoes	$37.25

(a) $132.64
(b) $1.99
(c) $133.80

Sept. 12 to Sept. 20 = 8 days at $139.56, gives $1116.48
Sept. 20 to Sept. 21 = 1 day at $139.56 − $45 = $94.56, gives $94.56
Sept. 21 to Oct. 12 = 21 days at $94.56 + $37.25 = $131.81, gives $2768.01
8 + 1 + 21 = 30 days
$1116.48 + $94.56 + $2768.01 = $3979.05

(a) Average daily balance $= \frac{\$3979.05}{30} = \$132.64$
(b) Finance charge = $132.64 × .015 = $1.99
(c) New balance = $139.56 + $1.99 + $37.25 − $45 = $133.80

18. Previous balance $228.95

January 27	Billing date	
February 9	Socks	$11.08
February 13	Returns	$26.54
February 20	Payment	$29
February 25	Restaurant	$71.19

(a) ______
(b) ______
(c) ______

19. Previous balance $312.78

June 11	Billing date	
June 15	Returns	$106.45
June 20	Watch	$115.73
June 24	Car rental	$74.19
July 3	Payment	$115

(a) ______
(b) ______
(c) ______

20. Previous balance $714.58

August 17	Billing date	
August 21	Mail order	$26.94
August 23	Returns	$25.41
August 27	Beverages	$31.82
August 31	Payment	$128.00
September 9	Returns	$71.14
September 11	Veterinarian	$110.00
September 14	Cash advance	$100.00

(a) ____________
(b) ____________
(c) ____________

21. Previous balance $355.72

March 29	Billing date	
March 31	Returns	$209.53
April 2	Auto parts	$28.76
April 10	Pharmacy	$14.80
April 12	Returns	$63.54
April 13	Returns	$11.71
April 20	Payment	$72.00
April 21	Flowers	$29.72

(a) ____________
(b) ____________
(c) ____________

11.2 INSTALLMENT LOANS

OBJECTIVES

1. Define installment loan.
2. Find the total installment cost and the finance charge.
3. Use the formula for approximate APR.
4. Use the table to find APR.

OBJECTIVE 1 **Define installment loan.** A loan is **amortized** if both principal and interest are paid off by a sequence of equal periodic payments. An example is the paying of $490 per month for 48 months on a car loan. This type of loan is called an **installment loan**. Installment loans are used for cars, boats, home improvements, and even for consolidating several smaller loans into one affordable payment. The graphic below shows the interest you might have to pay to finance a new automobile with an installment loan. Look on the World Wide Web to find competitive interest rates for car loans. Incidentally, you can also check the market value of an automobile on the Web.

Numbers in the News

Sticker Shock

What you'll pay for a $30,000 loan at 8% interest for a well-equipped SUV.

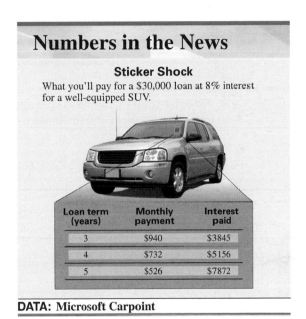

Loan term (years)	Monthly payment	Interest paid
3	$940	$3845
4	$732	$5156
5	$526	$7872

DATA: Microsoft Carpoint

The federal **Truth in Lending Act** (Regulation Z) of 1969 requires lenders to disclose their **finance charge** (the charge for credit) and **annual percentage rate (APR)** on installment loans. The federal government *does not* regulate rates. Each individual state sets the maximum allowable rates and charges.

The interest rate that is **stated** (in the newspaper, a marketing brochure, or a problem in a textbook) is also called the **nominal rate**. The nominal or stated rate can differ from the annual percentage rate or APR, which is based on the actual amount received by the borrower. The APR is the true effective annual interest rate for a loan. Information on two loans of $1000 each is shown below. An advertisement indicates a rate of 10% for each loan, and the actual interest is $100 for each. However, the terms differ.

	Stated Rate	Interest	Term	APR
Loan 1	10%	$100	1 year	$R = \frac{I}{PT} = \frac{\$100}{\$1000 \times 1} = 10\%$
Loan 2	10%	$100	9 months	$R = \frac{I}{PT} = \frac{\$100}{\$1000 \times \frac{9}{12}} = 13.3\%$

Wow! Look at the difference in the annual percentage rate between the two loans even though the stated rate, the principal, and the interest are the same. Why? Because *the term differs*. Which loan would you prefer?

Interest rate charges *vary significantly* from one loan source to another. The table below shows that the total finance charge for a $200 loan can be as high as $165 if the loan is rolled over a few times to extend it to six weeks. The finance charge also depends on the borrower's past credit history and income.

QUICK TIP It pays to shop and make comparisons based on APR values before you borrow!

Numbers in the News

The Cost of Immediate Money

While a "fee" of 20% of a loan's face value may seem small, when compounded over six weeks it adds up when compared to a cash advance on a credit card. *Rollover* means extending the loan for *another* short period.

$200 Pawn Shop Loan for Six Weeks

Payday advance loan	
Interest rate (20% of loan's face value)	$40
Setup charge (weeks 1 and 2)	$15
First rollover (weeks 3 and 4)	$55
Second rollover (weeks 5 and 6)	$55
TOTAL COST	**$165**
Effective APR	**715%**
Credit-card cash advance	
TOTAL COST	**$5**
APR	**21%**

DATA: *Fortune* **magazine**

OBJECTIVE 2 **Find the total installment cost and the finance charge.** The total **installment cost** (or the **deferred payment price**) and the **finance charge** on a loan are found as follows.

Finding the Total Installment Cost, Finance Charge, and Amount Financed

STEP 1 Find the total installment cost.

$$\text{Total installment cost} = \text{Down payment} + \text{Payment amount} \times \text{Number of payments}$$

STEP 2 Find the finance charge (interest).

$$\text{Finance charge} = \text{Total installment cost} - \text{Cash price}$$

STEP 3 Finally, find the amount financed (principal of loan).

$$\text{Amount financed} = \text{Cash price} - \text{Down payment}$$

QUICK TIP The finance charge includes interest and any fees the lender charges. The amount financed is the loan amount, or the principal.

EXAMPLE 1 Finding the Total Installment Cost

Frank Kimlicko recently received his master's degree and began work at a large community college as a music professor specializing in classical guitar. He purchased an exquisite-sounding classical guitar costing $3800 with $500 down and 36 monthly payments of $109.61 each. Find **(a)** the total installment cost, **(b)** the finance charge, and **(c)** the amount financed.

SOLUTION

(a) The total installment cost is the down payment plus the total of all monthly payments.

$$\text{Total installment cost} = \$500 + (\$109.61 \times 36) = \$4445.96$$

(b) The finance charge is the total installment cost less the cash price.

$$\text{Finance charge} = \$4445.96 - \$3800 = \$645.96$$

(c) The amount financed is $3800 − $500 = $3300.

QUICK TIP To determine the total installment cost, the down payment is added to the total of the monthly payments.

QUICK CHECK 1

Robert Chu purchased a new Toyota Prius costing $24,200, including taxes and licensing, with $4000 down and 48 payments of $488.25 each. Find **(a)** the total installment cost, **(b)** the finance charge, and **(c)** the amount financed.

Quick Check Answers

1. **(a)** $27,436
   (b) $3236
   (c) $20,200

Many students use an installment loan called a **Stafford loan** to help pay costs while in college. The government pays the interest on a *subsidized* Stafford loan while the student borrower is in school on at least a half-time basis. In contrast, the student is responsible for interest on *unsubsidized* Stafford loans. Repayment of a loan begins six months after the borrower ceases at least half-time enrollment. You can find information about Stafford loans at the financial aid office at your college or at a bank.

OBJECTIVE 3 **Use the formula for approximate APR.** The **approximate annual percentage rate (APR)** for a loan paid off in monthly payments can be found with the following formula.

$$\text{Approximate APR} = \frac{24 \times \text{Finance charge}}{\text{Amount financed} \times (1 + \text{Total number of payments})}$$

The formula is *only an estimate* of the APR. It is not accurate enough for the purposes of the federal Truth in Lending Act, which requires the use of tables.

EXAMPLE 2

Finding the Annual Percentage Rate

QUICK TIP The precise APR can be found using a financial calculator as shown in examples in Appendix D.

Ed Chamski decides to buy a used car for \$6400. He makes a down payment of \$1200 and monthly payments of \$169 for 36 months. Find the approximate annual percentage rate.

SOLUTION

Use the steps outlined on page 476.

$$\text{Total installment cost} = \$1200 + (\$169 \times 36 \text{ months}) = \$7284$$

$$\text{Finance charge} = \$7284 - \$6400 = \$884$$

$$\text{Amount financed} = \$6400 - \$1200 = \$5200$$

Use the formula for approximate APR. Replace the finance charge with \$884, the amount financed with \$5200, and the number of payments with 36.

$$\text{Approximate APR} = \frac{24 \times \text{Finance charge}}{\text{Amount financed} \times (1 + \text{Total number of payments})}$$

$$= \frac{24 \times \$884}{\$5200 \times (1 + 36)}$$

$$= \frac{\$21{,}216}{\$192{,}400}$$

$$= .110 \text{ or } 11\% \text{ approximate APR}$$

The approximate annual percentage rate on this loan is 11%. Example 3 shows how to find the actual APR for this loan.

QUICK CHECK 2

Bob Drake purchases a two-year old Harley-Davidson motorcycle costing \$26,500. He financed the purchase at his bank with a \$5000 down payment and payments of \$693.74 for 36 months. Estimate the annual percentage rate to the nearest tenth of a percent.

OBJECTIVE 4 **Use the table to find APR.** Special tables must be used to find annual percentage rates *accurate enough* to satisfy federal law. These tables are available from a Federal Reserve Bank or the Board of Governors of the Federal Reserve System, Washington, DC 20551. The table on page 479 shows a small portion of these tables. The APR is found from the APR table as follows.

QUICK TIP Federal law requires that a loan's annual percentage rate (APR) be stated to the nearest quarter of a percent.

Quick Check Answer

2. 10.5%

Finding the Annual Percentage Rate (APR)

STEP 1 Multiply the finance charge by \$100, and divide by the amount financed.

$$\frac{\text{Finance charge} \times \$100}{\text{Amount financed}}$$

The result is the finance charge per \$100 of the amount financed.

STEP 2 Read down the left column of the annual percentage rate table to the proper number of payments. Go across to the number closest to the number found in Step 1. Read the number at the top of that column to find the annual percentage rate.

EXAMPLE 3

Finding the Annual Percentage Rate

QUICK TIP When using the annual percentage rate table, select the column with the table number that is closest to the finance charge per $100 of amount financed.

In Example 2, a used car costing $6400 was financed at $169 per month for 36 months after a down payment of $1200. The total finance charge was $884, and the amount financed was $5200. Find the annual percentage rate.

SOLUTION

STEP 1 Multiply the finance charge by $100, and divide by the amount financed.

$$\frac{\$884 \times \$100}{\$5200} = \$17.00$$

Round to two decimal places for use in the table.

This gives the finance charge per $100 financed.

STEP 2 Read down the left column of the annual percentage rate table to the line for 36 months (the actual number of monthly payments). Follow across to the right to find the number closest to $17.00. Here, find $17.01. Read the number at the top of this column of figures to find the annual percentage rate, 10.50%.

In this example, 10.50% is the annual percentage rate that must be disclosed to the buyer of the car. In Example 2, the formula for the approximate annual percentage rate gave an answer of 11%, which is not accurate enough to meet the requirements of the law.

QUICK CHECK 3

A refrigerator costing $1450 was financed with $100 down and 20 monthly payments of $74.95 each. Find **(a)** the finance charge, **(b)** amount financed, and **(c)** the annual percentage rate.

EXAMPLE 4

Finding the Annual Percentage Rate

Two Brothers from Italy Pizza borrowed $48,000 to remodel their store. They agreed to a note with payments of $1565.78 per month for 36 months. They were able to do so with no down payment by putting up a CD for collateral. Find the annual percentage rate.

SOLUTION

$$\text{Total installment cost} = \$0 \text{ down payment} + \$1565.78 \times 36 = \$56{,}368.08$$

$$\text{Finance charge} = \$56{,}368.08 - \$48{,}000 = \$8368.08$$

$$\text{Amount financed} = \$48{,}000 - \$0 \text{ down payment} = \mathbf{\$48{,}000}$$

Now use the formula for the APR.

$$\frac{\$8368.08 \times \$100}{\mathbf{\$48{,}000}} = 17.4335$$

Find the row associated with 36 payments in the annual percentage rate table. Look to the right across that row to find the number closest to 17.4335, which is 17.43. Look to the top of that column to find 10.75%. This is the APR to the nearest quarter of a percent.

QUICK CHECK 4

An insurance agent borrowed $22,500 for new hardware and software for her growing business. She agreed to a note with payments of $858.10 per month for 30 months and put a CD up for collateral instead of making a down payment. Find the annual percentage rate.

Quick Check Answers

3. (a) $149
(b) $1350
(c) 12.25%
4. 10.75%

Annual Percentage Rate Table for Monthly Payment Plans

Annual Percentage Rate (Finance Charge per $100 of Amount Financed)

Number of Payments	10.00%	10.25%	10.50%	10.75%	11.00%	11.25%	11.50%	11.75%	12.00%	12.25%	12.50%	12.75%	13.00%	13.25%	13.50%	13.75%	Number of Payments
1	0.83	0.85	0.87	0.90	0.92	0.94	0.96	0.98	1.00	1.02	1.04	1.06	1.08	1.10	1.12	1.15	1
2	1.25	1.28	1.31	1.35	1.38	1.41	1.44	1.47	1.50	1.53	1.57	1.60	1.63	1.66	1.69	1.72	2
3	1.67	1.71	1.76	1.80	1.84	1.88	1.92	1.96	2.01	2.05	2.09	2.13	2.17	2.22	2.26	2.30	3
4	2.09	2.14	2.20	2.25	2.30	2.35	2.41	2.46	2.51	2.57	2.62	2.67	2.72	2.78	2.83	2.88	4
5	2.51	2.58	2.64	2.70	2.77	2.83	2.89	2.96	3.02	3.08	3.15	3.21	3.27	3.34	3.40	3.46	5
6	2.94	3.01	3.08	3.16	3.23	3.31	3.38	3.45	3.53	3.60	3.68	3.75	3.83	3.90	3.97	4.05	6
7	3.36	3.45	3.53	3.62	3.70	3.78	3.87	3.95	4.04	4.12	4.21	4.29	4.38	4.47	4.55	4.64	7
8	3.79	3.88	3.98	4.07	4.17	4.26	4.36	4.46	4.55	4.65	4.74	4.84	4.94	5.03	5.13	5.22	8
9	4.21	4.32	4.43	4.53	4.64	4.75	4.85	4.96	5.07	5.17	5.28	5.39	5.49	5.60	5.71	5.82	9
10	4.64	4.76	4.88	4.99	5.11	5.23	5.35	5.46	5.58	5.70	5.82	5.94	6.05	6.17	6.29	6.41	10
11	5.07	5.20	5.33	5.45	5.58	5.71	5.84	5.97	6.10	6.23	6.36	6.49	6.62	6.75	6.88	7.01	11
12	5.50	5.64	5.78	5.92	6.06	6.20	6.34	6.48	6.62	6.76	6.90	7.04	7.18	7.32	7.46	7.60	12
13	5.93	6.08	6.23	6.38	6.53	6.68	6.84	6.99	7.14	7.29	7.44	7.59	7.75	7.90	8.05	8.20	13
14	6.36	6.52	6.69	6.85	7.01	7.17	7.34	7.50	7.66	7.82	7.99	8.15	8.31	8.48	8.64	8.81	14
15	6.80	6.97	7.14	7.32	7.49	7.66	7.84	8.01	8.19	8.36	8.53	8.71	8.88	9.06	9.23	9.41	15
16	7.23	7.41	7.60	7.78	7.97	8.15	8.34	8.53	8.71	8.90	9.08	9.27	9.46	9.64	9.83	10.02	16
17	7.67	7.86	8.06	8.25	8.45	8.65	8.84	9.04	9.24	9.44	9.63	9.83	10.03	10.23	10.43	10.63	17
18	8.10	8.31	8.52	8.73	8.93	9.14	9.35	9.56	9.77	9.98	10.19	10.40	10.61	10.82	11.03	11.24	18
19	8.54	8.76	8.98	9.20	9.42	9.64	9.86	10.08	10.30	10.52	10.74	10.96	11.18	11.41	11.63	11.85	19
20	8.98	9.21	9.44	9.67	9.90	10.13	10.37	10.60	10.83	11.06	11.30	11.53	11.76	12.00	12.23	12.46	20
21	9.42	9.66	9.90	10.15	10.39	10.63	10.88	11.12	11.36	11.61	11.85	12.10	12.34	12.59	12.84	13.08	21
22	9.86	10.12	10.37	10.62	10.88	11.13	11.39	11.64	11.90	12.16	12.41	12.67	12.93	13.19	13.44	13.70	22
23	10.30	10.57	10.84	11.10	11.37	11.63	11.90	12.17	12.44	12.71	12.97	13.24	13.51	13.78	14.05	14.32	23
24	10.75	11.02	11.30	11.58	11.86	12.14	12.42	12.70	12.98	13.26	13.54	13.82	14.10	14.38	14.66	14.95	24
25	11.19	11.48	11.77	12.06	12.35	12.64	12.93	13.22	13.52	13.81	14.10	14.40	14.69	14.98	15.28	15.57	25
26	11.64	11.94	12.24	12.54	12.85	13.15	13.45	13.75	14.06	14.36	14.67	14.97	15.28	15.59	15.89	16.20	26
27	12.09	12.40	12.71	13.03	13.34	13.66	13.97	14.29	14.60	14.92	15.24	15.56	15.87	16.19	16.51	16.83	27
28	12.53	12.86	13.18	13.51	13.84	14.16	14.49	14.82	15.15	15.48	15.81	16.14	16.47	16.80	17.13	17.46	28
29	12.98	13.32	13.66	14.00	14.33	14.67	15.01	15.35	15.70	16.04	16.38	16.72	17.07	17.41	17.75	18.10	29
30	13.43	13.78	14.13	14.48	14.83	15.19	15.54	15.89	16.24	16.60	16.95	17.31	17.66	18.02	18.38	18.74	30
31	13.89	14.25	14.61	14.97	15.33	15.70	16.06	16.43	16.79	17.16	17.53	17.90	18.27	18.63	19.00	19.38	31
32	14.34	14.71	15.09	15.46	15.84	16.21	16.59	16.97	17.35	17.73	18.11	18.49	18.87	19.25	19.63	20.02	32
33	14.79	15.18	15.57	15.95	16.34	16.73	17.12	17.51	17.90	18.29	18.69	19.08	19.47	19.87	20.26	20.66	33
34	15.25	15.65	16.05	16.44	16.85	17.25	17.65	18.05	18.46	18.86	19.27	19.67	20.08	20.49	20.90	21.31	34
35	15.70	16.11	16.53	16.94	17.35	17.77	18.18	18.60	19.01	19.43	19.85	20.27	20.69	21.11	21.53	21.95	35
36	16.16	16.58	17.01	17.43	17.86	18.29	18.71	19.14	19.57	20.00	20.43	20.87	21.30	21.73	22.17	22.60	36
37	16.62	17.06	17.49	17.93	18.37	18.81	19.25	19.69	20.13	20.58	21.02	21.46	21.91	22.36	22.81	23.25	37
38	17.08	17.53	17.98	18.43	18.88	19.33	19.78	20.24	20.69	21.15	21.61	22.07	22.52	22.99	23.45	23.91	38
39	17.54	18.00	18.46	18.93	19.39	19.86	20.32	20.79	21.26	21.73	22.20	22.67	23.14	23.61	24.09	24.56	39
40	18.00	18.48	18.95	19.43	19.90	20.38	20.86	21.34	21.82	22.30	22.79	23.27	23.76	24.25	24.73	25.22	40
41	18.47	18.95	19.44	19.93	20.42	20.91	21.40	21.89	22.39	22.88	23.38	23.88	24.38	24.88	25.38	25.88	41
42	18.93	19.43	19.93	20.43	20.93	21.44	21.94	22.45	22.96	23.47	23.98	24.49	25.00	25.51	26.03	26.55	42
43	19.40	19.91	20.42	20.94	21.45	21.97	22.49	23.01	23.53	24.05	24.57	25.10	25.62	26.15	26.68	27.21	43
44	19.86	20.39	20.91	21.44	21.97	22.50	23.03	23.57	24.10	24.64	25.17	25.71	26.25	26.79	27.33	27.88	44
45	20.33	20.87	21.41	21.95	22.49	23.03	23.58	24.12	24.67	25.22	25.77	26.32	26.88	27.43	27.99	28.55	45
46	20.80	21.35	21.90	22.46	23.01	23.57	24.13	24.69	25.25	25.81	26.37	26.94	27.51	28.08	28.65	29.22	46
47	21.27	21.83	22.40	22.97	23.53	24.10	24.68	25.25	25.82	26.40	26.98	27.56	28.14	28.72	29.31	29.89	47
48	21.74	22.32	22.90	23.48	24.06	24.64	25.23	25.81	26.40	26.99	27.58	28.18	28.77	29.37	29.97	30.57	48
49	22.21	22.80	23.39	23.99	24.58	25.18	25.78	26.38	26.98	27.59	28.19	28.80	29.41	30.02	30.63	31.24	49
50	22.69	23.29	23.89	24.50	25.11	25.72	26.33	26.95	27.56	28.18	28.80	29.42	30.04	30.67	31.29	31.92	50
51	23.16	23.78	24.40	25.02	25.64	26.26	26.89	27.52	28.15	28.78	29.41	30.05	30.68	31.32	31.96	32.60	51
52	23.64	24.27	24.90	25.53	26.17	26.81	27.45	28.09	28.73	29.38	30.02	30.67	31.32	31.98	32.63	33.29	52
53	24.11	24.76	25.40	26.05	26.70	27.35	28.00	28.66	29.32	29.98	30.64	31.30	31.97	32.63	33.30	33.97	53
54	24.59	25.25	25.91	26.57	27.23	27.90	28.56	29.23	29.91	30.58	31.25	31.93	32.61	33.29	33.98	34.66	54
55	25.07	25.74	26.41	27.09	27.77	28.44	29.13	29.81	30.50	31.18	31.87	32.56	33.26	33.95	34.65	35.35	55
56	25.55	26.23	26.92	27.61	28.30	28.99	29.69	30.39	31.09	31.79	32.49	33.20	33.91	34.62	35.33	36.04	56
57	26.03	26.73	27.43	28.13	28.84	29.54	30.25	30.97	31.68	32.39	33.11	33.83	34.56	35.28	36.01	36.74	57
58	26.51	27.23	27.94	28.66	29.37	30.10	30.82	31.55	32.27	33.00	33.74	34.47	35.21	35.95	36.69	37.43	58
59	27.00	27.72	28.45	29.18	29.91	30.65	31.39	32.13	32.87	33.61	34.36	35.11	35.86	36.62	37.37	38.13	59
60	27.48	28.22	28.96	29.71	30.45	31.20	31.96	32.71	33.47	34.23	34.99	35.75	36.52	37.29	38.06	38.83	60

11.2 EXERCISES

FOR EXTRA HELP

MyMathLab

MathXL PRACTICE

WATCH

DOWNLOAD

READ

REVIEW

The **QUICK START** *exercises in each section contain solutions to help you get started.*

Find the finance charge (FC) and the total installment cost (TIC) for the following. (See Example 1.)

QUICK START

	Amount Financed	Down Payment	Cash Price	Number of Payments	Amount of Payment	Total Installment Cost	Finance Charge
1.	\$1400	\$400	\$1800	24	\$68.75	**\$2050**	**\$250**
	TIC = \$400 + (24 × \$68.75) = \$2050; FC = \$2050 − \$1800 = \$250						
2.	\$650	\$125	\$775	24	\$32	**\$893**	**\$118**
	TIC = \$125 + (24 × \$32) = \$893; FC = \$893 − \$775 = \$118						
3.	\$150	none	\$150	12	\$15	______	______
4.	\$1200	none	\$1200	20	\$70	______	______
5.	\$2525	\$375	\$2900	18	\$176	______	______
6.	\$6388	\$380	\$6768	60	\$136	______	______

Find the approximate annual percentage rate using the approximate annual percentage rate formula. Round to the nearest tenth of a percent. (See Example 2.)

QUICK START

	Amount Financed	Finance Charge	No. of Monthly Payments	Approximate APR
7.	\$11,500	\$1200	30	**8.1%**
	Approx. APR $= \dfrac{24 \times \$1200}{\$11{,}500 \times (1 + 30)} = 8.1\%$			
8.	\$2200	\$434	36	______
9.	\$7542	\$1780	48	______
10.	\$4500	\$650	36	______
11.	\$132	\$11	12	______
12.	\$8046	\$973	24	______

C indicates an exercise that is related to the Case in Point feature.

Find the annual percentage rate using the annual percentage rate table. (See Example 3.)

QUICK START

	Amount Financed	Finance Charge	No. of Monthly Payments	APR
13.	$1400	$185.68	24	12.25%
14.	$345	$24.62	12	____
15.	$442	$28.68	14	____
16.	$4690	$1237.22	48	____
17.	$145	$13.25	18	____
18.	$650	$73.45	24	____

(Solution for 13:) $\frac{FC \times \$100}{AF} = \frac{\$185.68 \times \$100}{\$1400} = 13.26$; from 24-payment row, APR = 12.25%

19. Explain the difference between open-end credit and installment loans. (See **Section 11.1** and Objective 1 of this section.)

20. Make a list of all of the items that you have bought on an installment loan. Make another list of things you plan to buy in the next 2 years on an installment loan. (See Objective 1.)

Solve the following application problems. Use the formula on page 477 to estimate the APR, and round rates to the nearest tenth of a percent.

QUICK START

21. METAL LATHE Benson Fabrication purchased a new precision metal lathe for $74,800. The company made a down payment of 20% and financed the balance using 36 monthly payments of $1916.85. Find **(a)** the amount financed, **(b)** the total installment cost, and **(c)** the finance charge. **(d)** Then estimate the APR.

(a) Down payment = .2 × $74,800 = $14,960
Amount financed = $74,800 − $14,960 = $59,840
(b) Total installment cost = $14,960 + 36 × $1916.85 = $83,966.60
(c) Finance charge = $83,966.60 − $74,800 = $9166.60
(d) Approximate APR = $\frac{24 \times \$9166.60}{\$59,840 \times (1 + 36)} = 9.9\%$

(a) $59,840
(b) $83,966.60
(c) $9166.60
(d) 9.9%

22. PLAYSET Tom and Jane Franklin bought a backyard playset with a trampoline for their grandchildren for $9400. They paid 10% down and financed the balance with 24 monthly payments of $398.24. Find **(a)** the amount financed, **(b)** the total installment cost, and **(c)** the finance charge. **(d)** Then estimate the APR.

(a) ____________
(b) ____________
(c) ____________
(d) ____________

23. ELECTRIC GUITAR Yanni Benjamin purchased an electric guitar with amplifier and financed \$3600 over 12 months. The finance charge was \$260. **(a)** Estimate the APR, then **(b)** find the exact APR using the table.

(a) ____________
(b) ____________

24. CANNING MACHINE Aluminum Cans Inc. purchased a new machine to press aluminum into cans and financed \$385,000 over 30 months. The finance charge was \$54,411. **(a)** Estimate the APR, then **(b)** find the exact APR using the table.

(a) ____________
(b) ____________

Solve the following application problems and use the table to find the annual percentage rate.

QUICK START

25. CHIP FABRICATION A Chinese computer chip manufacturer borrowed \$84 million worth of Chinese yuan to purchase some sophisticated equipment. The note required 24 monthly payments of \$3.88 million each. Find the annual percentage rate.

25. 10.00%

FC = 24 × \$3.88 million − \$84 million = \$9.12 million

$$\frac{\text{FC} \times \$100}{\text{AF}} = \frac{\$9.12 \times \$100}{\$84 \text{ million}} = 10.86; \text{ from 24-payment row, APR} = 10.00\%$$

26. REFRIGERATOR PURCHASE Sears offers a refrigerator for \$1600 with no down payment, \$294.06 in interest charges, and 30 equal payments. Find the annual percentage rate.

26. ____________

27. AUTO PURCHASE Pat Waller bought a new Toyota Corolla for \$20,800 including taxes and license. She made a down payment of \$2000 and agreed to make 60 payments to Citibank of \$404 each. Find **(a)** the amount financed, **(b)** the total installment cost, **(c)** the total interest paid, and **(d)** the APR.

(a) ____________
(b) ____________
(c) ____________
(d) ____________

28. SKI BOAT James Berry purchased a ski boat costing \$12,800 with \$500 down and loan payments to Citibank of \$399 per month for 36 months. Find **(a)** the amount financed, **(b)** the total installment cost, **(c)** the total interest paid, and **(d)** the APR.

(a) ____________
(b) ____________
(c) ____________
(d) ____________

29. COMPUTER SYSTEM A contractor in Mexico City purchased a computer system for 650,000 pesos. After making a down payment of 100,000 pesos, he agreed to make payments of 26,342.18 pesos per month for 24 months. Find **(a)** the total installment cost and **(b)** the annual percentage rate.

(a) ____________
(b) ____________

30. TRACTOR PURCHASE An electrical contractor in Hiroshima, Japan with poor credit, purchased a tractor costing 2,700,000 yen. He made a down payment of 1,000,000 yen and agreed to monthly payments of 54,855 yen for 36 months. Find **(a)** the total installment cost and **(b)** the annual percentage rate.

(a) ________________
(b) ________________

31. PECAN TREES Josefina Torres and her husband need $85,000 to plant pecan trees on their small farm. They pay $20,000 down and finance the balance with 40 payments of $1942.24. Find **(a)** the total installment cost and **(b)** the annual percentage rate.

(a) ________________
(b) ________________

32. GOAT CHEESE Toni Smith wants to produce goat cheese and needs $120,000 to purchase 400 goats. He pays $30,000 down and finances the balance with 24 monthly payments of $4253.44. Find **(a)** the total installment cost and **(b)** the annual percentage rate.

(a) ________________
(b) ________________

33. Should businesses be able to charge interest rates of over 20% to customers with poor credit histories? Why or why not?

34. Explain why it is important for the government to regulate the way in which interest rates are stated.

11.3 EARLY PAYOFFS OF LOANS

OBJECTIVES

1. Use the United States Rule for an early payment.
2. Find the amount due on the maturity date using the United States Rule.
3. Use the Rule of 78 when prepaying a loan.

OBJECTIVE 1 Use the United States Rule for an early payment. It is common for a payment to be made on a loan *before it is due*. This may occur when a person receives extra money or refinances a debt at a lower interest rate somewhere else. Prepayments of loans are discussed in this section.

The first method for calculating early loan payment is the **United States Rule**, and it is used by the U.S. government as well as most states and financial institutions. Under the United States Rule, any payment is first applied to any interest owed. The balance of the payment is then used to reduce the principal amount of the loan.

Using the United States Rule

STEP 1 Find the simple interest due from the date the loan was made until the date the partial payment is made. Use the formula $I = PRT$.

STEP 2 Subtract this interest from the amount of the payment.

STEP 3 Any difference is used to reduce the principal.

STEP 4 Treat additional partial payments in the same way, always finding interest on *only* the unpaid balance after the last partial payment.

STEP 5 The remaining principal plus interest on this unpaid principal is then due on the due date of the loan.

QUICK TIP We will continue to use 360-day years in the calculations of this section.

OBJECTIVE 2 Find the amount due on the maturity date using the United States Rule. If the partial payment is not large enough to pay the interest due, the payment is simply held until enough money is available to pay the interest due. This means that a partial payment smaller than the interest due offers no advantage to the borrower—the lender just holds the partial payment until enough money is available to pay the interest owed.

EXAMPLE 1

Finding the Amount Due

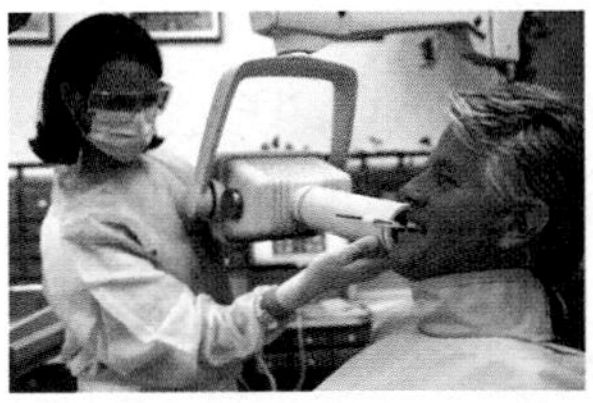

On August 14, Dr. Jane Ficker signed a 180-day note for $28,500 for an x-ray machine for her dental office. The note has an interest rate of 10% compounded annually. On October 25, a payment of $8500 is made. **(a)** Find the balance owed on the principal after the payment. **(b)** If no additional payments are made, find the amount due at maturity of the loan.

SOLUTION

(a) STEP 1 Find interest from August 14 to October 25 $(298 - 226 = 72 \text{ days})$* using $I = PRT$.

$$\text{Interest} = \$28{,}500 \times .10 \times \frac{72}{360} = \mathbf{\$570}$$

STEP 2 Subtract interest from the October 25 payment to find the amount of the payment to be applied to principal.

$$\text{Applied to principal} = \$8500 - \mathbf{\$570} = \$7930$$

STEP 3 Reduce the original principal by this amount.

$$\text{New principal} = \$28{,}500 - \$7930 = \mathbf{\$20{,}570}$$

(b) STEP 4 Since there are no additional partial payments, go on to Step 5.

*The chart for the number of days of the year is inside the back cover of the book.

STEP 5 The note was originally for 180 days, but the partial payment was made after 72 days. Interest on the new principal of \$20,570 will be charged for 180 − 72 = 108 days.

$$\text{Interest} = \$20{,}570 \times .10 \times \frac{108}{360} = \$617.10$$

$$\text{Amount due at maturity} = \mathbf{\$20{,}570} + \$617.10 = \$21{,}187.10$$

QUICK CHECK 1

A 200-day note, signed on April 7 for \$48,300, has a rate of 9% compounded annually. A payment of \$12,000 was made on June 25. Find **(a)** the balance owed on the principal on June 25 and **(b)** the amount due at maturity.

EXAMPLE 2

Finding the Interest Paid and Amount Due

On March 1, Boston Dairy signs a promissory note for \$38,500 to repair milking equipment for their Holsteins. The note is for 180 days at a rate of 10%. The dairy makes the following partial payments: \$6000 on June 9 and \$3500 on July 11. Find the interest paid on the note and the amount due on the due date of the note.

SOLUTION

The first partial payment is on June 9 or, using the number of days in each month, after (30 + 30 + 31 + 9) = 100 days.

$$\text{Interest for 100 days} = \$38{,}500 \times .10 \times \frac{100}{360} = \$1069.44 \text{ (rounded)}$$

First partial payment	\$6000.00
Portion going to interest	−1069.44
Portion going to reduce debt	**\$4930.56**

Debt on June 9 *after 1st partial payment* = \$38,500 − **\$4930.56** = \$33,569.44

The second partial payment occurs 21 + 11 = 32 days later.

$$\text{Interest for 32 days} = \$33{,}569.44 \times .10 \times \frac{32}{360} = \$298.40 \text{ (rounded)}$$

Second partial payment	\$3500.00
Portion going to interest	−298.40
Portion going to reduce debt	**\$3201.60**

Debt on July 11 *after 2nd partial payment* = \$33,569.44 − **\$3201.60** = \$30,367.84

The first partial payment is made after 100 days, and the second partial payment is made after an additional 32 days. Thus, the due date of the note is 180 − 100 − 32 = 48 days after the second partial payment.

$$\text{Interest for the last 48 days} = \$30{,}367.84 \times .10 \times \frac{48}{360} = \$404.90 \text{ (rounded)}$$

Amount due *at maturity* = \$30,367.84 + \$404.90 = \$30,772.74

Date Payment Made	Amount of Payment	Applied to Interest	Applied to Principal	Remaining Balance
June 9	\$6,000.00	\$1069.44	\$4,930.56	\$33,569.44
July 11	\$3,500.00	\$298.40	\$3,201.60	\$30,367.84
At maturity	\$30,772.74	\$404.90	\$30,367.84	\$0
Total	\$40,272.74	\$1772.74	\$38,500.00	

QUICK CHECK 2

A 120-day note has a face value of \$7500 and a rate of 11.5%. A partial payment of \$1700 is made after 40 days. Find **(a)** the balance owed on the principal after the partial payment and **(b)** the amount due at maturity.

Quick Check Answers

1. (a) \$37,253.93
(b) \$38,380.86

2. (a) \$5895.83
(b) \$6046.50

OBJECTIVE 3 **Use the Rule of 78 when prepaying a loan.** A variation of the United States Rule, called the **Rule of 78**, is still used by many lenders for installment loans. This rule allows a lender *to earn more of the finance charge during the early months* of the loan compared with the United States Rule. Lenders typically use this rule *to protect against* early payoffs on small loans. Effectively, the lender will earn a higher rate of interest in the event of an early payoff under the Rule of 78 than under the United States Rule.

The Rule of 78 gets its name based on a loan of 12 months—the sum of the months $1 + 2 + 3 + \cdots + 12 = 78$. The finance charge for the first month is $\frac{12}{78}$ of the total charge, with $\frac{11}{78}$ in the second month, $\frac{10}{78}$ in the third month, and so on with $\frac{1}{78}$ in the final month. The Rule of 78 can be applied to loans *with terms other than 12 months*. For example, the sum of the months in a 6-month contract is $1 + 2 + 3 + 4 + 5 + 6 = 21$. The finance charge for the first month is $\frac{6}{21}$; $\frac{5}{21}$ for the second month; and so on. Similarly, the sum of the months in a 15-month contract is $1 + 2 + \cdots + 15 = 120$. The finance charge for the first month of a 15-month contract is $\frac{15}{120}$ or $\frac{1}{8}$, and so on.

Monthly Finance Charges

Term of Loan	Month 1	Month 2	Month 3	Month 4	Month 5	Month 6	Month 7	Month 8	Month 9	Month 10	Month 11	Month 12
12 months	$\frac{12}{78}$	$\frac{11}{78}$	$\frac{10}{78}$	$\frac{9}{78}$	$\frac{8}{78}$	$\frac{7}{78}$	$\frac{6}{78}$	$\frac{5}{78}$	$\frac{4}{78}$	$\frac{3}{78}$	$\frac{2}{78}$	$\frac{1}{78}$
6 months	$\frac{6}{21}$	$\frac{5}{21}$	$\frac{4}{21}$	$\frac{3}{21}$	$\frac{2}{21}$	$\frac{1}{21}$						

The total finance charge on an installment loan is calculated when a loan is first made. Early payoff of a loan results in a lower finance charge. The portion of the finance charge that is *not earned* by the lender under the Rule of 78, called **unearned interest** or **refund**, is found using the following formula.

Finding unearned interest

$$U = F\left(\frac{N}{P}\right)\left(\frac{1 + N}{1 + P}\right)$$

where

U = unearned interest F = finance charge

N = number of payments remaining P = original number of payments

QUICK TIP Unearned interest is interest that has not been earned by the lender.

EXAMPLE 3

Finding Unearned Interest and Balance Due

Adrian Ortega borrowed \$6000, which he is paying back in 24 monthly payments of \$295 each. With 9 payments remaining, he decides to repay the loan in full. Find **(a)** the amount of unearned interest and **(b)** the amount necessary to repay the loan in full. Use the Rule of 78.

SOLUTION

(a) Total of all payments = 24 payments × \$295 = \$7080

Amount borrowed

Finance charge = \$7080 − \$6000 = **\$1080**

Find the amount of unearned interest as follows. The finance charge is \$1080, the scheduled number of payments is 24, and the loan is paid off with 9 payments left. Solve as follows.

$$\text{Unearned interest} = \mathbf{\$1080} \times \frac{9}{24} \times \frac{(1 + 9)}{(1 + 24)} = \$162$$

(b) When Ortega decides to pay off the loan, he has 9 payments of \$295 left.

Sum of remaining payments = 9 payments × \$295 = **\$2655**

Ortega saves the unearned interest of \$162 by paying off the loan early. Therefore, the amount needed to pay the loan in full is the sum of the remaining payments minus the unearned interest.

Amount needed to repay the loan in full = Remaining payments − Unearned interest

= **\$2655** − \$162 = \$2493

QUICK CHECK 3

Simplot Maps has signed a note with a face value of $24,000 that requires 20 monthly payments of $1307.76. The manager pays the debt in full after 12 payments. Find **(a)** the finance charge, **(b)** the amount of unearned interest, and **(c)** the amount needed to repay the loan in full using the Rule of 78.

EXAMPLE 4

Finding Unearned Interest and Balance Due

Matt Thompson borrows $1200 for a new washer and dryer and agrees to make 18 monthly payments of $74.30 each. After the 10th payment, he pays the loan in full. Find **(a)** the amount of unearned interest and **(b)** the amount needed to repay the loan in full using the Rule of 78.

SOLUTION

(a)

$$\text{Sum of payments} = 18 \text{ payments} \times \$74.30 = \mathbf{\$1337.40}$$

$$\text{Finance charge} = \mathbf{\$1337.40} - \$1200 = \$137.40$$

Since there are $(18 - 10) =$ **8 payments remaining** when he pays the loan off, the unearned interest is found as follows.

$$\text{Unearned interest} = \$137.40 \times \frac{8}{18} \times \frac{(1 + 8)}{(1 + 18)} = \$28.93 \text{ (rounded)}$$

(b) The amount needed to pay the loan in full is the sum of the remaining payments less the unearned interest.

$$\text{Sum of remaining 8 payments} = 8 \text{ payments} \times \$74.30 = \mathbf{\$594.40}$$

$$\text{Amount needed to repay the loan in full} = \mathbf{\$594.40} - \$28.93 = \mathbf{\$565.47}$$

QUICK CHECK 4

Tim O'Murphy borrows $2100 to buy a riding lawn mower and agrees to make 12 monthly payments of $186.58 each. He pays the debt in full after 6 months. Find **(a)** the finance charge, **(b)** the amount of unearned interest, and **(c)** the amount needed to repay the loan in full using the Rule of 78.

Quick Check Answers

3. (a) $2155.20 **(b)** $369.46 **(c)** $10,092.62

4. (a) $138.96 **(b)** $37.41 **(c)** $1082.07

11.3 EXERCISES

FOR EXTRA HELP

MyMathLab

MathXL PRACTICE

WATCH

DOWNLOAD

READ

REVIEW

The **QUICK START** *exercises in each section contain solutions to help you get started.*

Find the balance due on the maturity date of the following notes. Find the total amount of interest paid on each note. Use the United States Rule. (See Examples 1 and 2.)

QUICK START

	Principal	Interest	Time (Days)	Partial Payments	Balance Due	Total Interest Paid
1.	$9800	$8\frac{1}{2}\%$	150	$1800 on day 50	**$8307.31**	**$307.31**

Interest for 50 days = $9800 × .085 × $\frac{50}{360}$ = $115.69
Amount of 1st payment applied to reduce debt = $1800 − $115.69 = $1684.31
Debt after 1st payment = $9800 − $1684.31 = $8115.69
Interest due at end of 150-day note = $8115.69 × .085 × $\frac{100}{360}$ = $191.62
Balance due on maturity date = $191.62 + $8115.69 = $8307.31
Total interest paid = $115.69 + $191.62 = $307.31

	Principal	Interest	Time (Days)	Partial Payments	Balance Due	Total Interest Paid
2.	$5800	12%	120	$2000 on day 45	______	______
3.	$15,000	10.5%	200	$6500 on day 100	______	______
4.	$76,900	11%	180	$31,250 on day 75	______	______
5.	$18,457	12%	120	$5978 on day 34 $3124 on day 55	______	______
6.	$39,864	9%	105	$8458 on day 43 $11,354 on day 88	______	______

Each of the following loans is paid in full before the date of maturity. Find the amount of unearned interest. Use the Rule of 78. (See Example 3.)

QUICK START

	Finance Charge	Total Number of Payments	Remaining Number of Payments When Paid in Full	Unearned Interest
7.	$1050	24	11	**$231**

$1050 × $\frac{11}{24}$ × $\frac{(1 + 11)}{(1 + 24)}$ = $231

	Finance Charge	Total Number of Payments	Remaining Number of Payments When Paid in Full	Unearned Interest
8.	$422	30	16	______
9.	$881	36	12	______
10.	$325	24	22	______

C indicates an exercise that is related to the Case in Point feature.

	Finance Charge	*Total Number of Payments*	*Remaining Number of Payments When Paid in Full*	*Unearned Interest*
11.	$900	36	6	________
12.	$1250	60	12	________

13. Explain why banks prefer the Rule of 78 to the United States Rule in the event of prepayment. (See Objective 3.)

14. Describe a situation in which a bank might prefer a loan to be prepaid.

Solve the following application problems using the United States Rule.

QUICK START

15. LANDSCAPING Andrew Raring borrowed $8900 from Citibank to landscape his yard. The 240-day note had an interest rate of 12% compounded annually. He repaid the note in 140 days with his income tax refund. Find **(a)** the interest due and **(b)** the total amount due.

(a) $415.33
(b) $9315.33

(a) Loan is for 140 days
Interest $= \$8900 \times .12 \times \frac{140}{360} = \$415.33$

(b) Amount due $= \$8900 + \$415.33 = \$9315.33$

16. COMPUTER CONSULTANT The computer system at Genome Therapy crashed several times last year. On January 10, the company borrowed $125,000 at 11% compounded annually for 250 days to pay a consultant to work on the Novell network. However, they decide to pay the loan in full on July 1. Find **(a)** the interest due and **(b)** the total amount due.

(a) ________
(b) ________

17. PARTIAL PAYMENT Thompson Packaging borrowed $92,000 on May 7, signing a note due in 90 days at 11.25% interest. On June 24, the company made a partial payment of $24,350. Find **(a)** the amount due on the maturity date of the note and **(b)** the interest paid on the note.

(a) ________
(b) ________

18. REMODELING The Second Avenue Butcher Shop financed a remodeling program by giving the builder a note for $32,500. The note was made on September 14 and is due in 120 days. Interest on the note is 9.75%. On December 9, the firm makes a partial payment of $9000. Find **(a)** the amount due on the

(a) ________
(b) ________

maturity date of the note and **(b)** the interest paid on the note.

19. INVENTORY Wholesale Paper orders large quantities of basic paper goods every 4 months to save on freight charges. For its last order, the firm signed a note on February 18, maturing on May 15. The face value of the note was $104,500, with interest of 11%. The firm made a partial payment of $38,000 on March 20 and a second partial payment of $27,200 on April 16. Find **(a)** the amount due on the maturity date of the note and **(b)** the amount of interest paid on the note.

(a) ________
(b) ________

20. SURVEILLANCE CAMERAS To help detect trespassers at night, a small security firm purchased some high-technology cameras using a note from Citibank for $32,000. The note was signed on July 26 and was due on November 20. The interest rate is 13%. The firm made a partial payment of $6000 on August 31 and a second partial payment of $11,700 on October 4. Find **(a)** the amount due on the maturity date of the note and **(b)** the interest paid on the note.

(a) ________
(b) ________

Solve the following application problems using the Rule of 78. (See Example 3.)

QUICK START

21. ENGAGEMENT RING Tom Stowe purchased a diamond engagement ring for $1150. He paid $100 down and agreed to 12 monthly payments of $95 each. After making 7 payments, he paid the loan in full. Find **(a)** the unearned interest and **(b)** the amount necessary to pay the loan in full.

(a) Finance charge $= \$100 + (\$95 \times 12) - \$1150 = \$90$
$U = \$90 \times \frac{5}{12} \times \frac{6}{13} = \$17.31$ (rounded)
(b) $(5 \times \$95) - \$17.31 = \$457.69$

(a) $17.31
(b) $457.69

22. GARBAGE TRUCK Haul-it-Away, Inc., purchased a dump truck for $62,000. The owners made a down payment of $22,000 and financed the remainder with 36 payments of $1328.57 each. They paid off the note with 12 payments remaining. Find **(a)** the amount of unearned interest and **(b)** the amount necessary to pay the loan in full.

(a) ________
(b) ________

C **23.** PRINTING BlackTop Printing made a $5000 down payment on a special copy machine costing $23,800. The loan agreement with Citibank called for 20 monthly payments of $1025 each. Find **(a)** the finance charge, **(b)** the unearned interest, and **(c)** the amount necessary to pay the loan in full after the 14th payment.

(a) ________
(b) ________
(c) ________

24. MOVIE PROJECTORS Movie 6, Inc., purchased two movie projectors at a total cost of $12,200 with a down payment of $1500. The company agreed to make 12 monthly payments of $945 each. Find **(a)** the finance charge, **(b)** the unearned interest, and **(c)** the amount necessary to pay the loan in full after the 8th payment.

(a) ________
(b) ________
(c) ________

25. WEB DESIGN Blackstone Web Design needed $76,800 to purchase computers, software, and network equipment. The owners paid $15,000 down and financed the balance with 30 monthly payments of $2423.89 each. Find **(a)** the total installment cost, **(b)** the finance charge, **(c)** the unearned interest, and **(d)** the amount needed to pay the loan in full after the 10th payment.

(a) ________
(b) ________
(c) ________
(d) ________

26. ASPHALT CRUMB Binston Asphalt borrowed $850,000 to purchase a machine that converts old tires into asphalt crumb for use as a base material under sports arenas. The company paid $200,000 of the cost up-front and financed the balance with 36 monthly payments of $20,821.42 each. Find **(a)** the total installment cost, **(b)** the finance charge, **(c)** the unearned interest, and **(d)** the amount needed to pay the loan in full after the 25th payment.

(a) ________
(b) ________
(c) ________
(d) ________

11.4 PERSONAL PROPERTY LOANS

OBJECTIVES

1. Define personal property and real estate.
2. Use the formula for amortization to find payment.
3. Set up an amortization schedule.
4. Find monthly payments.

CASE in POINT Before she worked at Citibank, Jackie Waterton made personal property loans for a neighborhood bank. Every day she would receive many loan applications showing income, assets, and debt, as well as employment information. She would then carefully check the creditworthiness of each applicant.

OBJECTIVE 1 Define personal property and real estate. Items that can be moved from one location to another, such as an automobile, a boat, or a stereo, are called **personal property**. In contrast, land and homes cannot be moved and are called **real estate** or **real property**. Personal property loans are discussed in this section, and real estate loans are discussed in the next section.

Banks, credit unions, finance companies, and many other types of companies make money through personal property loans. Typically, these loans are repaid, or **amortized**, using monthly payments. Sometimes, a buyer is not able to make the payments as promised. In that event, the lender must **repossess** the personal property and sell it to someone else. Financial companies charge a slightly higher interest rate to everyone to make up for loans on which they never fully recover their money. Interest rates for personal property loans vary significantly from lender to lender and from year to year. Be sure to shop carefully before borrowing.

OBJECTIVE 2 Use the formula for amortization to find payment. The periodic payment needed at the end of each period to amortize a loan with interest i per period, over n periods, is found by using the following formula.

$$\text{Payment} = \text{Loan amount} \times \text{Number from amortization table}$$

EXAMPLE 1 Amortizing a Loan

Sven Yarborough earned his degree, at a community college, and is now a mechanic at a Ford dealership. He was so impressed with the quality of Fords that he purchased an SUV at a cost of $29,400, including tax, title, and license, after the rebate. He made a down payment of $3500 and was able to finance the balance at a special incentive rate of 6% per year for 4 years. Find **(a)** the monthly payment, **(b)** the portion of the first payment that is interest, **(c)** the balance due after one payment, **(d)** the interest owed for the second month, and **(e)** the balance after the second payment.

SOLUTION

(a) Amount financed = \$29,400 − \$3500 = \$25,900.

Use $\frac{6\%}{12}$ = .5% per month and 4 years × 12 = 48 months in the table to find **.02349**.

Monthly payment = \$25,900 × **.02349** = \$608.39 (rounded)

(b) Interest for month = $I = PRT$ = \$25,900 × .06 × $\frac{1}{12}$ = **\$129.50**

Amount of 1st payment applied to principal = \$608.39 − **\$129.50** = **\$478.89**

(c) Balance after 1st payment = \$25,900 − **\$478.89** = \$25,421.11.

(d) Interest for 2nd month = PRT = \$25,421.11 × .06 × $\frac{1}{12}$ = **\$127.11** (rounded)

Amount of 2nd payment applied to principal = \$608.39 − **\$127.11** = \$481.28

(e) Balance after 2nd payment = \$25,421.11 − \$481.28 = **\$24,939.83**.

QUICK CHECK 1

Marine Ltd. paid \$300,000 down on a tugboat costing \$1,800,000. The firm financed the balance at 12% per year for 4 years. Find **(a)** the monthly payment and **(b)** the balance after the first payment.

OBJECTIVE 3 Set up an amortization schedule.

EXAMPLE 2

Creating an Amortization Table

Clarence Thomas purchased new commercial-grade washers and dryers for his laundromat at a cost of \$22,300. He made a down payment of \$5000 and agreed to pay the balance off in quarterly payments over 2 years at 12% compounded quarterly. **(a)** Find the quarterly payment, and **(b)** show the first four payments in a table called an **amortization schedule**.

SOLUTION

(a) The amount financed is \$22,300 − \$5000 = \$17,300. Find the factor from the table using 2 × 4 = 8 quarters and $\frac{12\%}{4}$ = 3% per quarter. Then multiply the amount financed by the factor to find the payment.

Payment = \$17,300 × **.14246** = \$2464.56 (rounded)

(b)

Amortization Schedule

Payment Number	Amount of Payment	Interest for Period	Portion to Principal	Principal at End of Period
0	—	—	—	\$17,300.00
1	\$2464.56	\$519.00	\$1945.56	\$15,354.44
2	\$2464.56	\$460.63	\$2003.93	\$13,350.51
3	\$2464.56	\$400.52	\$2064.04	\$11,286.47
4	\$2464.56	\$338.59	\$2125.97	\$9,160.50

QUICK TIP Notice that interest is large at first when the debt is high but it decreases with every payment as the debt goes down. The last payment varies slightly from the regular monthly payments due to rounding.

QUICK CHECK 2

BlueLake Marina purchased a party barge costing \$85,700 with a down payment of \$20,000 and financed the balance at 8% for 4 quarters. Find the payment and construct an amortization schedule for the first 2 quarters.

Quick Check Answers

1. (a) \$39,495 **(b)** \$1,475,505

2.

Payment Number	Amount of Payment	Interest for Period	Portion to Principal	Principal at End of Period
0	—	—	—	\$65,700.00
1	\$17,254.13	\$1,314.00	\$15,940.13	\$49,759.87
2	\$17,254.13	\$995.20	\$16,258.93	\$33,500.94

Amortization Table

	Interest Rate per Period										
Period	$\frac{1}{2}$%	1%	$1\frac{1}{2}$%	2%	$2\frac{1}{2}$%	3%	4%	6%	8%	10%	Period
1	1.00500	1.01000	1.01500	1.02000	1.02500	1.03000	1.04000	1.06000	1.08000	1.10000	1
2	.50375	.50751	.51128	.51505	.51883	.52261	.53020	.54544	.56077	.57619	2
3	.33667	.34002	.34338	.34675	.35014	.35353	.36035	.37411	.38803	.40211	3
4	.25313	.25628	.25944	.26262	.26582	.26903	.27549	.28859	.30192	.31547	4
5	.20301	.20604	.20909	.21216	.21525	.21835	.22463	.23740	.25046	.26380	5
6	.16960	.17255	.17553	.17853	.18155	.18460	.19076	.20336	.21632	.22961	6
7	.14573	.14863	.15156	.15451	.15750	.16051	.16661	.17914	.19207	.20541	7
8	.12783	.13069	.13358	.13651	.13947	.14246	.14853	.16104	.17401	.18744	8
9	.11391	.11674	.11961	.12252	.12546	.12843	.13449	.14702	.16008	.17364	9
10	.10277	.10558	.10843	.11133	.11426	.11723	.12329	.13587	.14903	.16275	10
11	.09366	.09645	.09929	.10218	.10511	.10808	.11415	.12679	.14008	.15396	11
12	.08607	.08885	.09168	.09456	.09749	.10046	.10655	.11928	.13270	.14676	12
13	.07964	.08241	.08524	.08812	.09105	.09403	.10014	.11296	.12652	.14078	13
14	.07414	.07690	.07972	.08260	.08554	.08853	.09467	.10758	.12130	.13575	14
15	.06936	.07212	.07494	.07783	.08077	.08377	.08994	.10296	.11683	.13147	15
16	.06519	.06794	.07077	.07365	.07660	.07961	.08582	.09895	.11298	.12782	16
17	.06151	.06426	.06708	.06997	.07293	.07595	.08220	.09544	.10963	.12466	17
18	.05823	.06098	.06381	.06670	.06967	.07271	.07899	.09236	.10670	.12193	18
19	.05530	.05805	.06088	.06378	.06676	.06981	.07614	.08962	.10413	.11955	19
20	.05267	.05542	.05825	.06116	.06415	.06722	.07358	.08718	.10185	.11746	20
21	.05028	.05303	.05587	.05878	.06179	.06487	.07128	.08500	.09983	.11562	21
22	.04811	.05086	.05370	.05663	.05965	.06275	.06920	.08305	.09803	.11401	22
23	.04613	.04889	.05173	.05467	.05770	.06081	.06731	.08128	.09642	.11257	23
24	.04432	.04707	.04992	.05287	.05591	.05905	.06559	.07968	.09498	.11130	24
25	.04265	.04541	.04826	.05122	.05428	.05743	.06401	.07823	.09368	.11017	25
26	.04111	.04387	.04673	.04970	.05277	.05594	.06257	.07690	.09251	.10916	26
27	.03969	.04245	.04532	.04829	.05138	.05456	.06124	.07570	.09145	.10826	27
28	.03836	.04112	.04400	.04699	.05009	.05329	.06001	.07459	.09049	.10745	28
29	.03713	.03990	.04278	.04578	.04889	.05211	.05888	.07358	.08962	.10673	29
30	.03598	.03875	.04164	.04465	.04778	.05102	.05783	.07265	.08883	.10608	30
31	.03490	.03768	.04057	.04360	.04674	.05000	.05686	.07179	.08811	.10550	31
32	.03389	.03667	.03958	.04261	.04577	.04905	.05595	.07100	.08745	.10497	32
33	.03295	.03573	.03864	.04169	.04486	.04816	.05510	.07027	.08685	.10450	33
34	.03206	.03484	.03776	.04082	.04401	.04732	.05431	.06960	.08630	.10407	34
35	.03122	.03400	.03693	.04000	.04321	.04654	.05358	.06897	.08580	.10369	35
36	.03042	.03321	.03615	.03923	.04245	.04580	.05289	.06839	.08534	.10334	36
37	.02967	.03247	.03541	.03851	.04174	.04511	.05224	.06786	.08492	.10303	37
38	.02896	.03176	.03472	.03782	.04107	.04446	.05163	.06736	.08454	.10275	38
39	.02829	.03109	.03405	.03717	.04044	.04384	.05106	.06689	.08419	.10249	39
40	.02765	.03046	.03343	.03656	.03984	.04326	.05052	.06646	.08386	.10226	40
41	.02704	.02985	.03283	.03597	.03927	.04271	.05002	.06606	.08356	.10205	41
42	.02646	.02928	.03226	.03542	.03873	.04219	.04954	.06568	.08329	.10186	42
43	.02590	.02873	.03172	.03489	.03822	.04170	.04909	.06533	.08303	.10169	43
44	.02538	.02820	.03121	.03439	.03773	.04123	.04866	.06501	.08280	.10153	44
45	.02487	.02771	.03072	.03391	.03727	.04079	.04826	.06470	.08259	.10139	45
46	.02439	.02723	.03025	.03345	.03683	.04036	.04788	.06441	.08239	.10126	46
47	.02393	.02677	.02980	.03302	.03641	.03996	.04752	.06415	.08221	.10115	47
48	.02349	.02633	.02938	.03260	.03601	.03958	.04718	.06390	.08204	.10104	48
49	.02306	.02591	.02896	.03220	.03562	.03921	.04686	.06366	.08189	.10095	49
50	.02265	.02551	.02857	.03182	.03526	.03887	.04655	.06344	.08174	.10086	50

OBJECTIVE 4 Find monthly payments. The loan payoff table below can be used as an alternative to the amortization table on the preceding page. The table on this page shows some higher interest rates and longer terms than the previous table. Personal property loans sometimes have higher interest rates, since people are more likely to default on a loan for an expensive plasma television set than, say, on the loan on their home.

This table has a different format from the table on the preceding page. The APR is down the left column, and the number of months is across the top of this table.

Payment = Loan amount × Number from loan payoff table

Loan Payoff Table

	Number of Months								
APR	**18**	**24**	**30**	**36**	**42**	**48**	**54**	**60**	**APR**
8%	.05914	.04523	.03688	.03134	.02738	.02441	.02211	.02028	8%
9%	.05960	.04568	.03735	.03180	.02785	.02489	.02259	.02076	9%
10%	.06006	.04615	.03781	.03227	.02832	.02536	.02307	.02125	10%
11%	.06052	.04661	.03828	.03274	.02879	.02585	.02356	.02174	11%
12%	.06098	.04707	.03875	.03321	.02928	.02633	.02406	.02225	12%
13%	.06145	.04754	.03922	.03369	.02976	.02683	.02456	.02275	13%
14%	.06192	.04801	.03970	.03418	.03025	.02733	.02507	.02327	14%
15%	.06238	.04849	.04018	.03467	.03075	.02783	.02558	.02379	15%
16%	.06286	.04896	.04066	.03516	.03125	.02834	.02610	.02432	16%
17%	.06333	.04944	.04115	.03565	.03176	.02885	.02662	.02485	17%
18%	.06381	.04993	.04164	.03615	.03226	.02937	.02715	.02539	18%
19%	.06428	.05041	.04213	.03666	.03278	.02990	.02769	.02594	19%
20%	.06476	.05090	.04263	.03716	.03330	.03043	.02823	.02649	20%

EXAMPLE 3

Finding Amortization Payments

After a trade-in, Vickie Ewing owes $17,400 on a new Harley-Davidson motorcycle and wishes to pay the loan off in 60 months. She has found that she can finance the loan at 9% per year if she has a good credit history, but at 14% per year if she has a poor credit history.

(a) Find the monthly payment at both interest rates.
(b) Find the total finance charge at both interest rates.
(c) Find the extra cost of having poor credit.

SOLUTION

(a) Monthly payment at 9% = $17,400 × .02076 = $361.22 (rounded).
Monthly payment at 14% = $17,400 × .02327 = $404.90 (rounded).

(b) The finance charge is the sum of all of the payments minus the amount financed.

number of payments

Finance charge at 9% = 60 × $361.22 − $17,400 = **$4273.20**

Finance charge at 14% = 60 × $404.90 − $17,400 = **$6894**

(c) Extra cost of poor credit = **$6894** − **$4273.20** = $2620.80.

Clearly, having a poor credit history can be very costly.

QUICK CHECK 3

After his down payment, Josh Crandall needs to borrow $12,800 for 48 months to buy a truck. He can finance it at 8% per year if he has excellent credit but, at 15% per year if he has poor credit. Find **(a)** the monthly payment at both interest rates, **(b)** the total finance charge for both rates, and **(c)** the extra cost of having poor credit.

Quick Check Answers

3. (a) $312.45; $356.22
(b) $2197.60; $4298.56
(c) $2100.96

11.4 EXERCISES

FOR EXTRA HELP

MyMathLab

MathXL PRACTICE

WATCH

DOWNLOAD

READ

REVIEW

The QUICK START *exercises in each section contain solutions to help you get started.*

Find the payment necessary to amortize the following loans using the amortization table. Round to the nearest cent if needed. (See Example 1.)

QUICK START

	Amount of Loan	*Interest Rate*	*Payments Made*	*Number of Years*	*Payment*
1.	$6800	8%	annually	5	**$1703.13**
	Payment = $6800 × .25046 = $1703.13				
2.	$7500	10%	annually	6	**$1722.08**
	Payment = $7500 × .22961 = $1722.08				
3.	$4500	8%	semiannually	$7\frac{1}{2}$	________
4.	$12,000	6%	semiannually	8	________
5.	$96,000	8%	quarterly	$7\frac{3}{4}$	________
6.	$210,000	12%	quarterly	8	________
7.	$4876	12%	monthly	3	________
8.	$6800	6%	monthly	3	________

Use the loan payoff table to find the monthly payment (MP) and finance charge (FC) for each of the following loans. (See Example 3.)

QUICK START

	Amount Financed	*Number of Months*	*APR*	*Monthly Payment*	*Finance Charge*
9.	$5300	42	9%	**$147.61**	**$899.62**
	MP = $5300 × .02785 = $147.61; FC = (42 × $147.61) − $5300 = $899.62				
10.	$4800	24	12%	**$225.94**	**$622.56**
	MP = $4800 × .04707 = $225.94; FC = (24 × $225.94) − $4800 = $622.56				

C indicates an exercise that is related to the Case in Point feature.

	Amount Financed	*Number of Months*	*APR*	*Monthly Payment*	*Finance Charge*
11.	$12,000	48	13%	_______	_______
12.	$8102	48	8%	_______	_______
13.	$11,750	60	11%	_______	_______
14.	$16,000	60	10%	_______	_______

15. Explain the process of amortizing a loan. (See Objective 2.)

16. Explain why a loan officer at a bank might look at a credit report on someone before making a loan. What would you do if your credit report was inaccurate?

Solve the following application problems using the amortization table.

QUICK START

17. ROAD GRADER After a large down payment, Revis Construction borrows $62,400 to purchase a grader to prepare roads before paving. The loan has a rate of 12% per year and requires 40 monthly payments. Find **(a)** the monthly payment and **(b)** the total interest paid.

(a) Monthly payment = $62,400 × .03046 = $1900.70

(b) Total interest = (40 × $1900.70) − $62,400 = $13,628

(a) $1900.70
(b) $13,628

18. OPENING A RESTAURANT Chuck and Judy Nielson opened a restaurant at a cost of $340,000. They paid $40,000 of their own money and agreed to pay the remainder in quarterly payments over 7 years at 12%. Find **(a)** the quarterly payment and **(b)** the total amount of interest paid over 7 years.

(a) ____________
(b) ____________

19. PRINTER An insurance firm pays $4000 for a new high-speed color printer. It amortizes the loan for the printer in 4 annual payments at 8%. Prepare an amortization schedule for this machine.

Payment Number	Amount of Payment	Interest for Period	Portion to Principal	Principal at End of Period

20. TRACTOR PURCHASE Long Haul Trucking purchases a used tractor for pulling eighteen-wheel trailers on interstate highways at a cost of $72,000. It agrees to pay for it with a loan from Citibank that will be amortized over 9 annual payments at 8% interest. Prepare an amortization schedule for the truck.

Payment Number	Amount of Payment	Interest for Period	Portion to Principal	Principal at End of Period

Solve the following application problems. Use the loan payoff table. (See Objective 3.)

21. ELECTRONIC EQUIPMENT An engineering firm purchases 7 new workstations with laser printers for $3500 each. The firm makes a down payment of $10,000 and amortizes the balance with monthly loan payments to Citibank of 11% for 4 years. Prepare an amortization schedule showing the first 5 payments.

Payment Number	Amount of Payment	Interest for Period	Portion to Principal	Principal at End of Period

22. AMORTIZING A LOAN Rebecca Reed just graduated from dental school and borrows $120,000 from Citibank to purchase equipment for her own business. She agreed to amortize the loan with monthly payments at 10% for 4 years. Prepare an amortization schedule for the first 5 payments.

Payment Number	Amount of Payment	Interest for Period	Portion to Principal	Principal at End of Period

23. CELL PHONE Ben Watson needs $50,000 to set up his own cell phone booth at a local mall. He has $15,000 and financed the balance at a high rate of 14% for 36 months, since he did not have much credit history. Prepare an amortization schedule showing the first 5 payments.

Payment Number	Amount of Payment	Interest for Period	Portion to Principal	Principal at End of Period

24. SKI EQUIPMENT Jessica Chien needed $280,000 for inventory for a second ski shop that she was opening. She had $40,000, and the bank loaned her the balance at 11% for 30 months. Prepare an amortization schedule showing the first 5 payments.

Payment Number	Amount of Payment	Interest for Period	Portion to Principal	Principal at End of Period

11.5 REAL ESTATE LOANS

OBJECTIVES

1. Determine monthly payments on a home.
2. Prepare a repayment schedule.
3. Define escrow accounts.
4. Define fixed and variable rate loans.
5. Understand your credit score.

CASE in POINT Jackie Waterton's position at Citibank requires her to work with customers who have difficulty paying their bills. Since the house payment is often the largest expense for a family, she often looks to see if she can reduce the monthly payment on the mortgage.

QUICK TIP You can obtain mortgages from many financial institutions, including banks and mortgage companies.

OBJECTIVE 1 Determine monthly payments on a home. A home is *one of the most expensive purchases* that a person makes in his or her lifetime. The monthly payment for a home **mortgage** depends on the amount borrowed, the interest rate, and the term of the loan.

The bar graph shows that home **mortgage rates** have fallen from a high of over 15% in 1981 to about 6% in 2007. Interest rates are a very important factor in determining the monthly payment and therefore the affordability of a particular home. If interest rates fall, people **refinance** their home loans at lower rates to reduce their monthly payments. Sometimes, people are able to get cash out of the equity in their home when they refinance. The interest on a home loan may also be tax deductible, which can help people afford homes by reducing their income taxes.

Numbers in the News

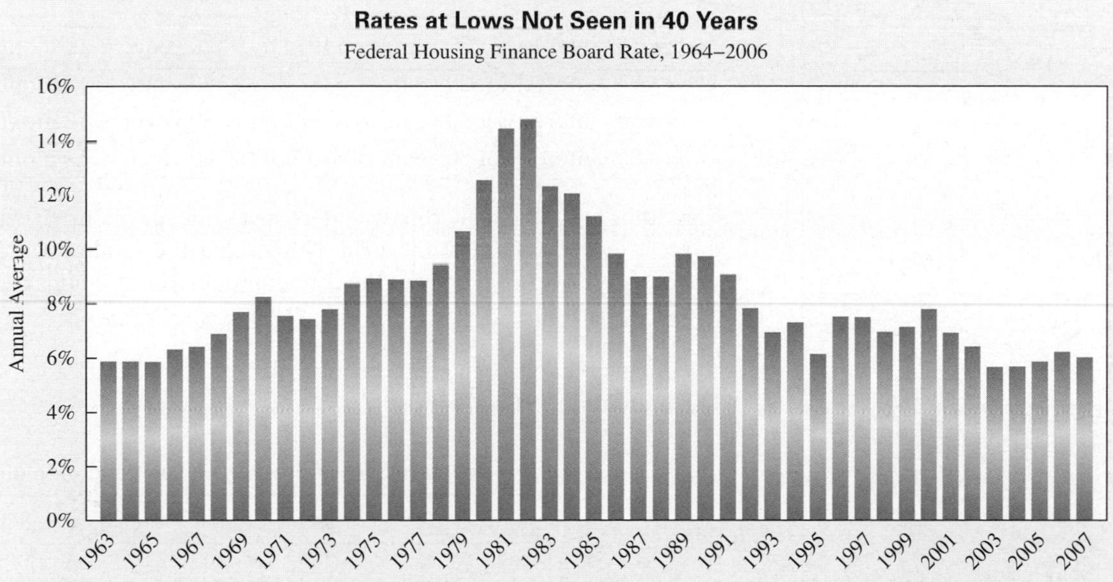

The amount of the monthly payment is found by the methods given in **Section 11.4,** but special tables are used for real estate loans because of the long repayment periods. The real estate amortization table on the next page shows the monthly payment necessary to repay a $1000 loan for differing interest rates and lengths of repayment. To use the table, first find the amount to be financed in thousands by dividing the total amount to be borrowed by $1000. Then multiply this value by the appropriate number from the table.

Real Estate Amortization Table (Principal and Interest per Thousand Dollars Borrowed)

Terms in Years	6%	$6\frac{1}{4}$%	$6\frac{1}{2}$%	$6\frac{3}{4}$%	7%	$7\frac{1}{4}$%	$7\frac{1}{2}$%	$7\frac{3}{4}$%	8%	$8\frac{1}{4}$%	$8\frac{1}{2}$%	9%	Terms in Years
10	11.10	11.23	11.35	11.48	11.62	11.75	11.88	12.01	12.14	12.27	12.40	12.67	10
15	8.44	8.57	8.71	8.85	8.99	9.13	9.28	9.42	9.56	9.71	9.85	10.15	15
20	7.16	7.31	7.46	7.60	7.76	7.91	8.06	8.21	8.37	8.53	8.68	9.00	20
25	6.44	6.60	6.75	6.91	7.07	7.23	7.39	7.56	7.72	7.89	8.06	8.40	25
30	6.00	6.16	6.32	6.49	6.65	6.83	7.00	7.17	7.34	7.52	7.69	8.05	30

EXAMPLE 1

Understanding the Effects of Rate and Term

The Stringers make a 10% down payment but still need to borrow \$140,000 to purchase a condominium. They want to know the effect of the interest rate and term of the loan on cost. **(a)** Find the monthly payment for both 20 and 30 years at $6\frac{1}{2}$% and at 8%. Then find **(b)** the total cost of the home with each loan and **(c)** the finance charge for each loan.

SOLUTION

(a) The amount to be financed in thousands = \$140,000 ÷ \$1000 = 140. Multiply this value by the appropriate factor from the real estate amortization table.

	Monthly Payment
$6\frac{1}{2}$% interest for 20 years = 140 × 7.46 =	**\$1044.40**
8% interest for 20 years = 140 × 8.37 =	**\$1171.80**
$6\frac{1}{2}$% interest for 30 years = 140 × 6.32 =	**\$ 884.80**
8% interest for 30 years = 140 × 7.34 =	**\$1027.60**

Monthly payments range from \$884.80 to \$1171.80, depending on rate and term. The lower payment of \$884.80 may look good to you at first, but look at part **(b)**.

(b) The total cost of financing the home is the sum of all payments.

	Monthly Payment		Total Cost
$6\frac{1}{2}$% interest for 20 years =	\$1044.40	× 20 years × 12 month/yr =	**\$250,656**
8% interest for 20 years =	\$1171.80	× 20 years × 12 month/yr =	**\$281,232**
$6\frac{1}{2}$% interest for 30 years =	\$ 884.80	× 30 years × 12 month/yr =	**\$318,528**
8% interest for 30 years =	\$1027.60	× 30 years × 12 month/yr =	**\$369,936**

Spreading out the loan repayment reduces the payment, BUT it results in much more interest over the term of the loan. Notice that the total cost of the condominium is much more than the original price of the condominium. Interest adds *a lot of cost* to the purchase as shown in part **(c)**.

(c) The finance charge or interest cost of each of the loans is the total cost found in part **(b)** minus the amount financed of \$140,000.

Interest Cost of Purchasing the Condominium

		$6\frac{1}{2}$%	8%
Term of Loan	20 years	\$110,656	\$141,232
	30 years	\$178,528 (cheapest)	\$229,936 (most costly)

Clearly, higher interest rates and longer terms add **HUGE** amounts to the interest that must be paid to purchase a property.

QUICK TIP You can reduce your long-term cost of a mortgage by paying more than the required payment every month. Even an extra \$60 per month can make a big difference over the long run.

QUICK CHECK 1

A couple plans to borrow \$220,000 for 30 years to purchase a home. Find both the payment and the total 30-year cost assuming **(a)** a 6.5% rate and **(b)** a 7.25% rate.

Quick Check Answers

1. **(a)** \$1390.40; \$500,544
(b) \$1502.60; \$540,936

QUICK TIP Be sure to divide the loan amount by \$1000 before calculating the monthly payment.

Mortgage payoffs of 25 or 30 years have been common in the past. However, **accelerated mortgages**, with payoffs of 15 or 20 years, are becoming more common for the reason pointed out in Example 1—lower total costs. Mortgages with shorter terms also tend to have slightly lower interest rates.

OBJECTIVE 2 **Prepare a repayment schedule.** Many lenders use a computer to calculate an **amortization schedule**, also called a **repayment schedule**. This schedule separates each payment into the portion going to interest and the portion reducing the debt (principal payment).

EXAMPLE 2 Preparing a Repayment Schedule

The Zinks purchase a house by borrowing \$195,000 at 7% for 30 years. Prepare a loan repayment schedule for this loan.

SOLUTION

First find the monthly payment, then use simple interest calculations for the first two months. Be sure to round to the nearest cent at each step.

$$\text{Monthly payment} = \$195 \times 6.65 = \$1296.75$$

First month:

Interest = PRT = **\$195,000 × .07 ×** $\frac{1}{12}$ = \$1137.50

monthly payment → ; ← 1st month's interest

Amount that payment reduces principal = \$1296.75 − \$1137.50 = **\$159.25**

Remaining debt at end of 1st month = \$195,000 − **\$159.25** = \$194,840.75

Every time a payment is made, interest is first subtracted from the payment. As a result, only a small portion of the first payment is applied to reduce the principal.

Second month:

Interest = PRT = **\$194,840.75 × .07 ×** = **\$1136.57**

Amount that payment reduces principal = \$1296.75 − \$1136.57 = **\$160.18**

Remaining debt at end of 2nd month = \$194,840.75 − **\$160.18** = \$194,680.57

These and other results are shown in the table. Notice that at first the amount applied to interest is large and the amount applied to reduce principal is small. But every month, the debt goes down, resulting in lower interest the following month, and more of each payment is applied to reduce the principal. It requires 262 months (nearly 22 years) to pay off half of the debt and only 98 months (just over 8 years) to pay off the other half of the loan.

Loan Repayment Schedule

Loan: $195,000; Term: 30 years; Rate 7%; Payment $1296.75

Payment Number	Interest Payment	Principal Payment	Remaining Balance	Payment Number	Interest Payment	Principal Payment	Remaining Balance
0	—	—	$195,000.00	258	$586.73	$710.02	$99,872.80
1	$1137.50	$159.25	$194,840.75	259	$582.59	$714.16	$99,158.64
2	$1136.57	$160.18	$194,680.57	260	$578.43	$718.32	$98,440.32
3	$1135.64	$161.11	$194,519.46	261	$574.24	$722.51	$97,717.81
4	$1134.70	$162.05	$194,357.41	262	$570.02	$726.73	$96,991.08
5	$1133.75	$163.00	$194,194.41	.	.	.	.
6	$1132.80	$163.95	$194,030.46	.	.	.	.
7	$1131.84	$164.91	$193,865.55	.	.	.	.
8	$1130.88	$165.87	$193,699.68	359	$19.14	$1277.61	$2,004.17
9	$1129.91	$166.84	$193,532.84	360	$11.69	$2004.17*	$0.00

*Due to rounding, the last payment needs to be a little larger to bring the debt to exactly $0.

QUICK CHECK 2

After making a 20% down payment, a couple purchases a home using a mortgage of $155,000 at $6\frac{3}{4}\%$ for 20 years. First find the monthly payment, then prepare a loan repayment schedule for the first 3 months.

OBJECTIVE 3 **Define escrow accounts.** To prevent losses from unpaid taxes or uninsured damages, many lenders require **escrow accounts** (also called **impound accounts**) for people taking out a mortgage. With an escrow account, buyers pay $\frac{1}{12}$ of the total estimated property tax and insurance each month. The lender holds these funds until the taxes and insurance fall due and then *pays the bills for the borrower*. Many consumer groups oppose this practice, since the lender earns interest on the money while waiting for payments to come due. In fact, a few states require that interest be paid on escrow accounts on any homes located in those states.

EXAMPLE 3

Finding the Total Monthly Payment

Susan Beckman received a $75,000 loan for 25 years at $7\frac{1}{4}\%$ to purchase a summer cabin. Annual insurance and taxes on the property are $654 and $1329, respectively. Find the total monthly payment.

SOLUTION

Use the real estate amortization table to find $7.23. Add monthly insurance and taxes to the payment amount.

principal and interest; insurance; taxes

$$\text{Monthly payment} = (75 \times \$7.23) + \left(\frac{\$654 + \$1329}{12}\right)$$

$$= \$542.25 + \$165.25 = \$707.50$$

Quick Check Answers

2. Monthly payment = $1178

Payment Number	Interest Payment	Principal Payment	Remaining Balance
0	—	—	$155,000.00
1	$871.88	$306.12	$154,693.88
2	$870.15	$307.85	$154,386.03
3	$868.42	$309.58	$154,076.45

QUICK CHECK 3

A 20-year mortgage is taken out with a debt of \$147,000 and a rate of $6\frac{1}{2}\%$. Taxes are estimated to be \$2400 per year, and a homeowner's insurance policy costs \$647 per year. Find the total monthly payment.

QUICK TIP Managers of banks and mortgage companies seriously and continuously think about the effects of an increase or decrease in interest rates on company profits.

OBJECTIVE 4 **Define fixed and variable rate loans.** Home loans with fixed, stated interest rates are called **fixed-rate loans**. Many borrowers prefer fixed-rate loans, since they know that the principal and interest portion of their monthly payments will be fixed until they either sell the house or pay off the debt. In particular, it is good for a borrower (but bad for the lender) if he or she locks in a fixed-rate loan before interest rates go up. If interest rates fall after a person has borrowed money for a home, the person can usually refinance at a lower interest rate.

Another type of loan is the **adjustable rate mortgage (ARM)**, also called **variable interest rate loan**, as shown in the clipping below. The interest rate on this type of loan is periodically adjusted either up or down depending on the movement of interest rates in general. Usually, there is a maximum limit in the increase in the rate from one year to the next.

With this type of mortgage, monthly payments increase if the interest rate is increased. Payments decrease if the rate is decreased. Thus, a borrower's monthly payment is not fixed but changes from time to time. The advantage of an adjustable rate mortgage is that it will originally have a lower interest rate than a fixed rate loan and thus a lower monthly payment. However, the clipping shows one potential disadvantage of ARMs: When interest rates rise, the payment may go up to the point where the home is unaffordable. Some people avoid ARMs for this reason.

Foreclosures Biting More Homeowners

- **Number so far this year in county is already higher than for all of last year**

BY PURVA PATEL

HOUSTON CHRONICLE

Billy Addison could soon join the thousands of area homeowners who've catapulted Harris County foreclosures past last year's numbers.

As of Oct. 3, the county had 7,339 foreclosures, which eclipses last year's total of 7,132, according to Woodlands-based Foreclosure Information & Listing Service.

That's 23 percent higher than the same period last year.

The reasons, according to experts, include overextended borrowers, lax lending practices and rising interest rates.

Numbers in the News

Trouble at Home

Foreclosures in Harris County have been rising for the last few years.

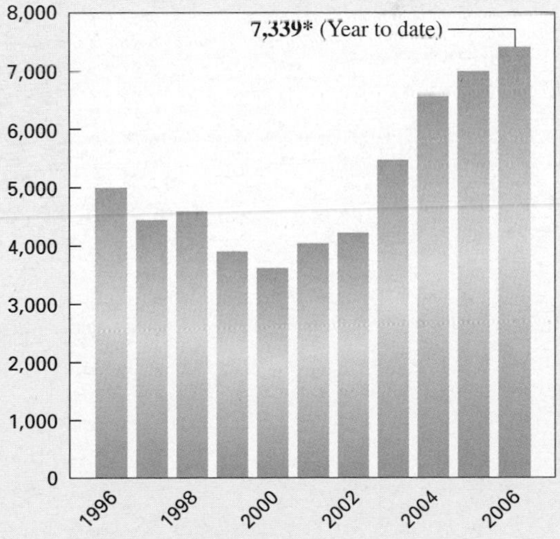

*Through Oct. 3. Foreclosures are counted on the first Tuesday of every month.

DATA: Foreclosure Information & Listing Service

Quick Check Answer

3. \$1350.54

OBJECTIVE 5 Understand your credit score. Mortgage companies, banks, and other lending institutions determine your creditworthiness using a FICO® score. This **credit score** was established by **FICO** (Fair Isaac Corporation) in 1989, and it is based on numerical values ranging from 300 to 850. The higher the score, the higher the creditworthiness; the lower the score, the more difficult it is to get a loan at a good interest rate. Three national credit-reporting agencies have databases that contain financial information about you: Equifax, TransUnion, and Experian. Each calculates a FICO score for you. The three scores may differ slightly from one agency to the next, since they do not always have the same information about you.

QUICK TIP It is a good idea to contact at least one of the three credit reporting agencies annually to examine your credit history.

Here is how one large lender uses FICO scores:

FICO Score	Creditworthiness
above 730	excellent
700–729	good
670–699	increased scrutiny
585–669	higher credit risk
below 585	high credit risk

QUICK TIP Higher FICO scores result in lower interest rates, whether on a personal property loan or on a home mortgage.

Your FICO score is based on a weighted average of the following factors:

1. payment history,
2. amount owed,
3. length of credit history,
4. new credit, and
5. types of credit in use.

QUCIK TIP Charging rates that depend on creditworthiness helps a lender ensure that its portfolio of loans remains profitable.

The largest weights in the FICO score are applied to the first two factors: payment history and amounts owed. You can control both of these factors, but you do not have control over the third factor (length of credit history), since that is partly based on age. New credit refers to the amount of new credit you have recently been given.

To raise your FICO score, first make sure the credit agencies do not have any false information on your records. They handle billions of pieces of information monthly, so it is easy for them to make mistakes. Your credit rating will be hurt by late payments, too many sources of credit, and high debt compared to your income. To raise your score, correct any mistakes on your financial records at the agencies, close accounts you no longer use, pay off existing balances, and always make payments on time.

11.5 EXERCISES

The **QUICK START** *exercises in each section contain solutions to help you get started.*

Use the real estate amortization table to find the monthly payment for the following loans. (See Example 1.)

QUICK START

	Amount of Loan	*Interest Rate*	*Term of Loan*	*Monthly Payment*
1.	\$310,000	$6\frac{1}{4}\%$	20 years	**\$2266.10**
	Payment = 310 × \$7.31 = \$2266.10			
2.	\$149,000	$7\frac{3}{4}\%$	20 years	**\$1223.29**
	Payment = 149 × 8.21 = \$1223.29			
3.	\$112,800	$8\frac{1}{2}\%$	15 years	________
4.	\$132,000	$6\frac{1}{2}\%$	25 years	________
5.	\$92,400	$6\frac{3}{4}\%$	30 years	________
6.	\$280,000	6%	15 years	________

7. Explain how different interest rates can make a large difference in interest charges over a number of years. (See Example 1.)

8. Explain how interest can result in a total cost that is over twice the original loan amount when a home is financed over 30 years. (See Example 1.)

Find the total monthly payment, including taxes and insurance, for the following loans. Round to the nearest cent. (See Example 3.)

QUICK START

	Amount of Loan	*Interest Rate*	*Term of Loan*	*Annual Taxes*	*Annual Insurance*	*Monthly Payment*
9.	\$98,000	7%	30 years	\$1250	\$560	**\$802.53**
	98 × \$6.65 = \$651.70; \$651.70 + $\frac{\$1250 + \$560}{12}$ = \$802.53					
10.	\$75,400	$8\frac{1}{2}\%$	20 years	\$1177	\$520	**\$795.89**
	75.4 × \$8.68 = \$654.47; \$654.47 + $\frac{\$1177 + \$520}{12}$ = \$795.89					

	Amount of Loan	Interest Rate	Term of Loan	Annual Taxes	Annual Insurance	Monthly Payment
11.	$58,600	8%	30 years	$745	$380	________
12.	$68,400	9%	30 years	$1256	$350	________
13.	$91,580	$8\frac{1}{4}$%	25 years	$1326	$489	________
14.	$173,000	$6\frac{1}{2}$%	30 years	$2800	$920	________

Solve the following application problems.

QUICK START

15. HOME PURCHASE The Potters want to buy a cottage costing $127,000 with annual insurance and taxes of $720 and $2300, respectively. They have saved $10,000 for a down payment, and they can get a $7\frac{1}{2}$%, 30-year mortgage from Citibank. They are qualified for a home loan as long as the total monthly payment does not exceed $1200. Are they qualified?

Loan amount = $127,000 − $10,000 = $117,000

Monthly payment = 117 × $7.00 = $819

Total payment = $819 + $\frac{\$720 + \$2300}{12}$ = $1070.67; Yes, qualified

15. Yes, qualified

16. CONDOMINIUM PURCHASE The Polinki family wants to buy a condominium that costs $225,000 with annual insurance and taxes of $850 and $3200, respectively. They plan to pay $20,000 down and amortize the balance at 8% per year for 25 years. They are qualified for a loan as long as the payments do not exceed $1800. Are they qualified for the loan?

16. ________

17. HOME LOAN June and Bill Able borrow $122,500 on their home at $7\frac{1}{2}$% for 15 years. Prepare a repayment schedule for the first two payments. (See Example 2.)

Payment Number	Total Payment	Interest Payment	Principal Payment	Balance of Principal

18. ELDERLY HOUSING Tom Ajax purchases a tiny home for his elderly mother. After a large down payment, he finances $44,300 at $7\frac{1}{4}$% for 10 years. Prepare a repayment schedule for the first two payments. (See Example 2.)

Payment Number	Total Payment	Interest Payment	Principal Payment	Balance of Principal

CHAPTER 11 QUICK REVIEW

CHAPTER TERMS *Review the following terms to test your understanding of the chapter. For each term you do not know, refer to the page number found next to that term.*

CONCEPTS	EXAMPLES

11.1 Finding the finance charge on a revolving charge account, using the unpaid balance method

Start with the unpaid balance of the previous month. Then find the finance charge on the unpaid balance. Next, add the finance charge and any purchases. Finally, subtract any payments made.

Debbie Mahoney's MasterCard account had an unpaid balance of $385.65 on March 1. During March, she made a $100 payment and charged $68.92. Find the finance charge and the unpaid balance on April 1 if the bank charges 1.25% per month on the unpaid balance.

Finance charge = $385.65 × .0125 = $4.82

previous balance		finance charge		purchases		payment		new balance
$385.65	+	$4.82	+	$68.92	−	$100	=	$359.39

11.1 Finding the finance charge on a revolving charge account, using the average daily balance method

First find the unpaid balance on each day of the month. Then add up the daily unpaid balances.

Next divide the total of the daily unpaid balances by the number of days in the billing period.

Finally, calculate the finance charge by multiplying the average daily balance by the finance charge.

The following is a summary of a credit card account.

Previous balance		$115.45
November 1	Billing date	
November 15	Payment	$35.00
November 22	Charge	$45.00

Find the average daily balance and the finance charge if interest is 2% per month on the average daily balance.

Balance on Nov. 1 = $115.45

Nov. 1 − 15 = 14 days at $115.45

14 × $115.45 = **$1616.30**

Payment on Nov. 15 = $35.00

Balance on Nov. 15 = $115.45 − $35 = $80.45

Nov. 15 − Nov. 22 = 7 days at $80.45

7 × $80.45 = **$563.15**

Charge on Nov. 22 of $45.00

Balance on Nov. 22 = $80.45 + $45 = $125.45

Nov. 22 − Dec. 1 = 9 days at $125.45

9 × $125.45 = **$1129.05**

Daily balances

$1616.30 + **$563.15** + **$1129.05** = **$3308.50**

Average daily balance = $\frac{\$3308.50}{30}$ = $110.28

Finance charges = $110.28 × .02 = $2.20

CONCEPTS	EXAMPLES

11.2 Finding the total installment cost, finance charge, and amount financed

Total installment cost
= Down payment
+ (Amount of each payment × Number of payments)

Finance charge (interest)
= Total installment cost − Cash price

Amount financed (principal of loan)
= Cash price − Down payment

Joan Taylor bought a leather coat for $1580. She put $350 down and then made 12 payments of $115 each. Find the total installment cost, the finance charge, and the amount financed.

Total installment cost = $350 + ($115 × 12) = $1730

Finance charge = $1730 − $1580 = $150

Amount financed = $1580 − $350 = $1230

11.2 Determining the approximate APR using a formula

First determine the finance charge. Then find the amount financed. Next calculate approximate APR using the formula.

Approximate APR

$$= \frac{24 \times \text{Finance charge}}{\text{Amt. fin.} \times (1 + \text{Total number of payments})}$$

Tom Jones buys a motorcycle for $8990. He makes a down payment of $1800 and then makes monthly payments of $230 for 36 months. Find the approximate APR.

Total installment cost = $1800 + ($230 × 36) = $10,080

Finance charge = $10,080 − $8990 = **$1090**

Amount financed = $8990 − $1800 = $7190

$$\textbf{Approximate APR} = \frac{24 \times \mathbf{\$1090}}{\$7190 \times (1 + 36)} = 9.8\% \text{ (rounded)}$$

11.2 Finding the APR using a table

First determine the finance charge per $100 of amount financed, using the formula

$$\frac{\text{Finance charge} \times \$100}{\text{Amount financed}}$$

Then read down the left column of the annual percentage rate table to the proper number of payments. Go across to the number closest to the number found above. Look to the top of the column to find the annual percentage rate.

Lupe Torres buys a used car for $6500. She makes a down payment of $1000 and agrees to make 24 monthly payments of $260.83. Use the table to find the APR.

Finance charge = $1000 + ($260.83 × 24) − $6500
= $759.92

Amount financed = $5500

Finance charge per $100

$$\frac{\$759.92 \times \$100}{\$5500} = \mathbf{13.817} \text{ (rounded)}$$

Use the 24-payment row in the table to find APR = 12.75%

11.3 Finding the amount due on the maturity date using the United States Rule

First determine the simple interest due from the date the loan was made until the date of the partial payment.

Then subtract this interest from the amount of the payment and reduce the principal by the difference.

Next find the interest from the date of partial payment to the due date of the note, and add the unpaid balance and interest to find the amount due.

Sam Wiley signs a 90-day note on August 1 for $5000 at an interest rate of 12%. On September 15, he makes a payment of $1800. Find the balance owed on the principal. If no additional payments are made, find the amount due on the maturity date of the loan.

From August 1 to September 15, there are 30 + 15 = 45 days.

$$I = \$5000 \times .12 \times \frac{45}{360} = \mathbf{\$75} \text{ interest due}$$

	$1800	payment
−	**75**	interest due
	$1725	applied to principal reduction

	$5000	amount owed
−	1725	principal reduction
	$3275	**balance owed**

Note is for 90 days; a partial payment was made after 45 days. Interest on $3275 will be charged for 90 − 45 = 45 days.

$$I = \$3275 \times .12 \times \frac{45}{360} = \mathbf{\$49.13}$$

	$3275.00	principal owed
+	**49.13**	interest
	$3324.13	**amount due**

CONCEPTS	EXAMPLES
11.3 Finding the unearned interest using the Rule of 78 First calculate the finance charge. Then find the unearned interest using the formula $U = F\left(\frac{N}{P}\right)\left(\frac{1+N}{1+P}\right)$ where U = unearned interest F = finance charge N = number of payments remaining P = total number of payments Next find the total of the remaining payments. Finally, subtract the unearned interest to find the balance remaining.	Tom Fish borrows \$1500, which he is paying back in 36 monthly installments of \$52.75 each. With 10 payments remaining, he decides to pay the loan in full. Find **(a)** the amount of unearned interest and **(b)** the amount necessary to pay the loan in full. 36 payments of \$52.75 each for a total repayment of 36 × \$52.75 = \$1899. Finance charge = \$1899 − \$1500 = \$399 Unearned interest = $\$399 \times \frac{10}{36} \times \frac{(1+10)}{(1+36)}$ = **\$32.95** 10 payments of \$52.75 are left. These payments total \$52.75 × 10 = \$527.50 \$527.50 − **\$32.95** = \$494.55 This is the amount needed to pay the loan in full.
11.4 Finding the periodic payment for amortizing a loan First determine the number of periods for the loan and the interest rate per period. The payment is found by multiplying the loan amount by the number from the amortization table.	Bob Smith agrees to pay \$12,000 for a used car. The amount will be repaid in monthly payments over 3 years at an interest rate of 12%. Find the amount of each payment. 12 × 3 = **36 periods (payments)** $\frac{12\%}{12}$ = **1% per period** Number from table is .03321. Payment = \$12,000 × .03321 = \$398.52
11.4 Setting up an amortization schedule First find the periodic payment. Then calculate the interest owed in the first period using the formula $I = PRT$. Next subtract the value of I from the periodic payment. This is the amount applied to the reduction of the principal. Then find the balance after the first periodic payment by subtracting the value of the debt reduction from the original amount. Now repeat the above steps until the original loan is amortized (paid off).	Terri Meyer borrows \$1800. She will repay this amount in 2 years with semiannual payments at an interest rate of 8%. Set up an amortization schedule. **4 periods (payments); 4% per period** Number from table is .27549 Payment = \$1800 × .27549 = \$495.88 $I = PRT$ Interest owed = $\$1800 \times .08 \times \frac{1}{2}$ = \$72 Debt reduction = \$495.88 − \$72 = \$423.88 Balance of loan = \$1800 − \$423.88 = \$1376.12

Payment Number	Amount of Payment	Interest for Period	Portion to Principal	Principal at End of Period
0	—	—	—	\$1800.00
1	\$495.88	\$72.00	\$423.88	\$1376.12
2	\$495.88	\$55.04	\$440.84	\$ 935.28
3	\$495.88	\$37.41	\$458.47	\$ 476.81
4	\$495.88	\$19.07	\$476.81	\$ 0.00

CONCEPTS	EXAMPLES
11.4 Finding monthly payments, total amount paid, and finance charge First multiply the amount to be financed by the number from the amortization table or the loan payoff table to find the periodic payment. Then find the total amount repaid by multiplying the periodic payment by the number of payments. Finally, subtract the amount financed from the total amount repaid to obtain the finance charge.	Ben Apostolides purchased a new Toyota Camry and owes \$16,400 after the trade-in. He decides on a term with 50 monthly payments. Assume an interest rate of 12% compounded monthly and find the amount of each payment and the finance charge. Monthly payment = \$16,400 × .02551 = **\$418.36** Finance charge = 50 × **\$418.36** − \$16,400 = \$4518
11.5 Finding the amount of monthly home loan payments and total interest charges over the life of a home loan Using the number of years and the interest rate, find the amortization value per thousand dollars from the real estate amortization table. Next multiply the table value by the number of thousands in the principal to obtain the monthly payment. Then find the total amount of the payments and subtract the original amount owed from the total payments to obtain interest paid.	Lou and Rose Waters bought a house at the beach. After a large down payment, they owe \$75,000. Find the monthly payment at $8\frac{1}{2}\%$ and the total interest charges over the life of a 25-year loan. $n = 25 \quad i = 8\frac{1}{2}\%$ **Table value** = \$8.06 There are $\frac{\$75{,}000}{1000} = 75$ thousands in \$75,000. **Monthly payment** = 75 × \$8.06 = **\$604.50** There are 25 × 12 = 300 payments. **Total payment** = 300 × **\$604.50** = \$181,350 **Interest paid** = \$181,350 − \$75,000 = \$106,350

CHAPTER 11 SUMMARY EXERCISE

Consolidating Loans

John and Kathy MacGruder are struggling to make their monthly payments. Kathy works one job and takes care of their two small children. The interest rates on their numerous debts are high, since they have historically had a poor credit history. However, John has taken on a second job and they have somehow managed to make their payments regularly for a little over a year.

(a) Find the monthly payments on each of the following purchases and the total monthly payment.

Purchase	Original Loan Amount	Interest Rate	Term of Loan	Monthly Payment
Honda Accord	$18,800	12%	4 years	______
Ford truck	$14,300	18%	4 years	______
Home	$96,500	$8\frac{1}{2}$%	15 years	______
2nd mortgage on home	$4,500	12%	3 years	______
			Total	______

(b) These monthly expenses do not include car insurance ($215 per month), health insurance ($120 per month), or real estate taxes on their home ($2530 per year), among other expenses. Find their total monthly outlay for all of these expenses.

Expense	Monthly Outlay
Payments on debt from **(a)**	______
Car insurance	______
Health insurance	______
Real estate taxes on home	______
Total	______

(c) After discussing things with Jackie Waterton at Citibank, the MacGruders have learned that they can (1) refinance the remaining $14,900 amount on the Honda Accord at 12% over 4 years, (2) refinance the remaining $8600 loan amount on the Ford truck at 12% over 3 years, (3) refinance the remaining $94,800 loan amount on their home at 8% over 30 years, and (4) reduce their car insurance payments by $28 per month. Complete the following table.

Item	Current Loan Amount	New Interest Rate	New Term of Loan	New Monthly Payment
Honda Accord				________
Ford truck				________
Home				________
2nd mortgage on home				________
Car insurance				________
Health insurance				________
Real estate taxes on home				________
				________

(d) Find the reduction in their monthly payments. **(d)** ____________________

Part of the savings in the monthly payment came from reducing the interest rates. The remainder of the savings came from extending the loans further into the future.

INVESTIGATE

The interest rate that you are charged for borrowing money differs depending on the bank you go to for a loan. Find current interest rates for financing a 2-year-old car from at least two banks in the area in which you live. Then go onto the World Wide Web and look for a lower interest rate.

Case Studies

Citigroup Inc.

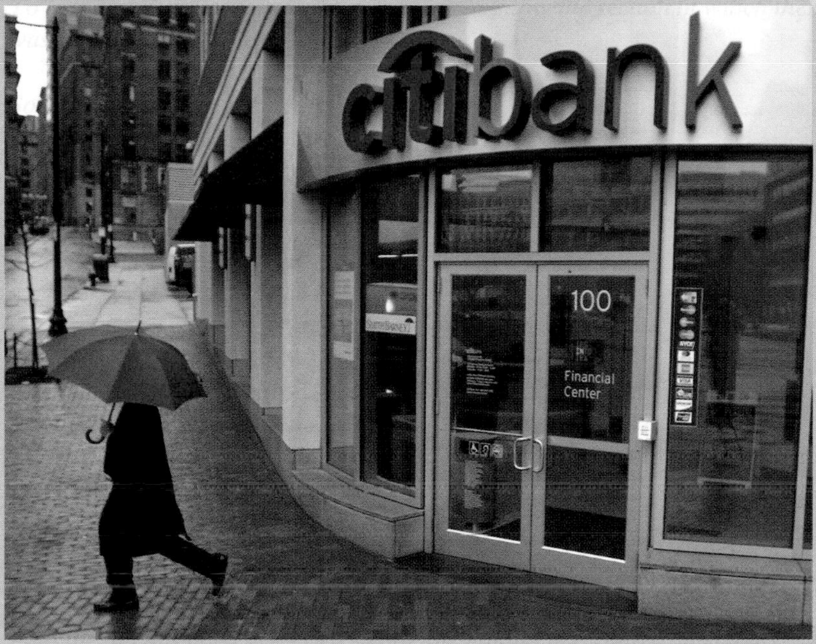

www.citigroup.com

- 1812: Founded in New York City
- 1914: Opened branch in Argentina
- 1998: Merged with Travelers Insurance Group
- 2005: 299,000 full-time employees
- 2007: Operates in over 100 countries

Citigroup Inc. provides various banking, lending, insurance, and investment services to consumers and corporate customers worldwide. It operates over 7200 branches, nearly 7000 automated teller machines, and even 682 automated lending machines. Through various subsidiaries, the firm offers credit cards, banking, loans and mortgages, asset management, bill-paying services, and international banking.

1. In one year, assume Citigroup Inc. finances 372,000 automobiles with an average loan amount of $23,200. Find the total loan amount.

2. Assume the average interest rate earned in one year was 7.29%. Find the annual interest on every $1 billion in loans.

3. Loan officer Jackie Waterton helped Betsy Faber finance a $69,800 loan for a new Jaguar. If the interest rate is 6% and the loan is for 48 months, find the monthly payment.

4. Go to Citigroup Inc.'s Web site and find five countries not in North America in which the company has branches.

Find the amount of each payment necessary to amortize the following loans. **[11.4]**

8. Jenson SawLogs borrows $34,500 to buy a new electric generator. The company agrees to make quarterly payments for 2 years at 10% per year. Find the amount of the quarterly payment.

8. ________________

9. Pizza for You has its building remodeled for $36,000. It pays $6000 down and pays off the balance in payments made at the end of each quarter for 5 years. Interest is 10% compounded quarterly. Find the amount of each payment so that the loan is fully amortized.

9. ________________

Find the monthly payment necessary to amortize the following home mortgages. **[11.5]**

10. $123,500, $7\frac{1}{2}$%, 30 years

10. ________________

11. $134,560, 7%, 15 years

11. ________________

Work the following application problems. **[11.5]**

12. Mr. and Mrs. Zagorin plan to buy a $90,000 one-room cabin, paying 20% down and financing the balance at 8% for 30 years. The taxes are $960 per year, with fire insurance costing $252 per year. Find the monthly payment (including taxes and insurance).

12. ________________

13. Billiards Galore purchases a commercial building for $680,000, pays 20% down, and finances the balance at $7\frac{1}{4}$% for 15 years. Taxes and insurance are $14,500 and $3200 per year, respectively. **(a)** Find the monthly payment. **(b)** Assume that insurance and taxes do not increase, and find the total cost of owning the building for 15 years, including the down payment.

(a) ________________
(b) ________________

14. Jerome Watson, owner of Watson Welding, purchases a storage building for his business and makes a $25,000 down payment. He finances the balance of $122,500 for 20 years at 8%. **(a)** Find the total monthly payment given taxes of $3200 per year and insurance of $1275 per year. **(b)** Assume that insurance and taxes do not increase, and find the total cost of owning the building for 20 years (including the down payment).

(a) ________________
(b) ________________

CHAPTER 11 CUMULATIVE REVIEW

Chapters 10 and 11

Round money amounts to the nearest cent and rates to the nearest tenth of a percent.

Find the amount and interest earned of each of the following ordinary annuities. **[10.1]**

	Amount of Each Deposit	Deposited	Rate	Time (Years)	Amount of Annuity	Interest Earned
1.	$1000	annually	4%	8	______	______
2.	$2000	quarterly	6%	5	______	______

Find the amount of each annuity due and the interest earned. **[10.1]**

	Amount of Each Deposit	Deposited	Rate	Time (Years)	Amount of Annuity	Interest Earned
3.	$2500	annually	5%	6	______	______
4.	$1800	semiannually	8%	5	______	______

Find the present value of the following annuities. **[10.2]**

	Amount per Payment	Payment at End of Each	Time (Years)	Rate of Investment	Compounded	Present Value
5.	$925	6 months	11	8%	semiannually	______
6.	$27,235	quarter	8	8%	quarterly	______

Find the required payment into a sinking fund. **[10.3]**

	Future Value	Interest Rate	Compounded	Time (Years)	Payment
7.	$3600	8%	annually	7	______
8.	$4500	10%	quarterly	7	______

Solve the following application problems using 360-day years where applicable.

9. At 58, Thomas Jones knows that he must start saving for his retirement. He decides to invest $300 per quarter in an account paying 10% compounded quarterly. Find the accumulated amount **(a)** at age 65 and **(b)** at age 70. **[10.1]**

(a) ______________
(b) ______________

10. A public utility needs $60 million in 5 years for a major capital expansion. What annual payment must the firm place into a sinking fund earning 10% per year in order to accumulate the required funds? **[10.3]**

10. ______________

11. Jerry Walker purchased 100 shares of stock at $23.45 per share. The company had earnings of $1.56 and a yearly dividend of $.35. Find **(a)** the cost of the purchase ignoring commissions, **(b)** the price–earnings ratio to the nearest whole number, and **(c)** the dividend yield. **[10.4]**

(a) ______
(b) ______
(c) ______

12. Martin Wicker buys 9000 GM bonds due in 2020 at 104.38 for the pension fund he manages. The coupon rate is 6.4%. Find **(a)** the cost to purchase the bonds if the commission is $1 per bond, **(b)** the annual interest from all of the bonds, and **(c)** the effective interest rate. **[10.5]**

(a) ______
(b) ______
(c) ______

13. James Thompson purchased a large riding lawnmower costing $2800 with $500 down and payments of $108.27 per month for 24 months. Find **(a)** the total installment cost, **(b)** the finance charge, and **(c)** the amount financed. **(d)** Then use the table to find the annual percentage rate to the nearest quarter of a percent. **[11.2]**

(a) ______
(b) ______
(c) ______
(d) ______

14. Abbie Spring's unpaid balance on her Visa card on July 8 was $204.37. She made a payment of $100 on July 14 and had charges of $34.95 on July 16 and $95.12 on July 30. Assume an interest rate of 1.6% per month and find the balance on August 8 using **(a)** the unpaid balance method and **(b)** the average daily balance method. **[11.1]**

(a) ______
(b) ______

15. Mayberry Pets borrows to purchase a van to transport animals and supplies. They agree to make quarterly payments on the $22,400 debt for 3 years at a rate of 8% compounded quarterly. Find **(a)** the quarterly payment and **(b)** the total amount of interest paid. **[11.4]**

(a) ______
(b) ______

16. The Hodges purchase an older 4-bedroom home for $195,000 with 5% down. They finance the balance at $7\frac{1}{2}$% per year for 30 years. If insurance is $720 per year and taxes are $2940 per year, find the monthly payment. **[11.5]**

16. ______

17. On January 10, Bob Jones signed a 200-day note for $24,000 to finance some work on a commercial building. The note was at 9% per year simple interest. Due to an unexpected income tax refund, he was able to repay $10,000 on April 15. Use the United States Rule and **(a)** find the balance owed on the principal after the partial payment. **(b)** Then find the amount due at maturity of the loan. **[11.3]**

(a) ________
(b) ________

18. Karoline Jacobs borrowed $2200 for new kitchen appliances. She agreed to pay the loan back with 8 payments of $290.69 each. After 3 payments, she decides to go ahead and pay off the loan in full. Use the Rule of 78 to find **(a)** the amount of unearned interest and **(b)** the amount needed to repay the loan in full. **[11.3]**

(a) ________
(b) ________

19. Waterford Landscaping lost a lawsuit and must pay the injured party $3500 at the end of each quarter for 1 year. If funds earn 8% compounded quarterly, find the amount that needs to be set aside today to fulfill this obligation. **[10.2]**

19. ________

20. James Booker signs an employment contract that guarantees him $35,000 at the end of each year for 3 years when he retires in 4 years. If funds earn 8% per year, find the present value needed today to meet the eventual payment stream. **[9.3 and 10.2]**

20. ________

21. Explain the terms *present value*, *future value*, and *annuity*.

22. Describe stocks and bonds, explaining similarities and differences.

CHAPTER 12

Taxes and Insurance

CHAPTER CONTENTS

CASE in POINT

Martha Spencer owns The Doll House. She sells dolls from around the world and specializes in buying and selling Barbie dolls, both collectible and newer ones. Her Web page has allowed her to do a lot of business over the Internet, much of which is from other countries. Spencer owns the building in which her business is located and she has several employees. As a result, she must keep up with changes in the laws related to taxes and insurance.

Both **taxes** and **insurance** are facts of life. In one form or another, we pay taxes to many different entities, including the federal government, states, counties, school districts, and cities. Supreme Court Justice Oliver Wendell Holmes, Jr., said, "Taxes are the price we pay to live in a civilized society." The figure shows the number of days per year the "average worker" works to pay various taxes. Property taxes and federal income taxes are discussed in this chapter.

Average Number of Days Worked to Pay Taxes by Type of Tax and Level of Government

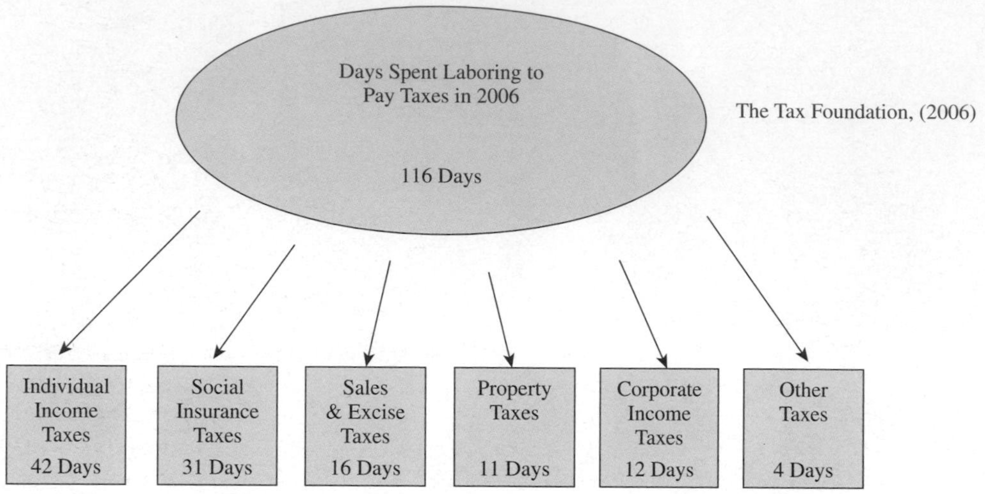

Individuals buy insurance to protect from catastrophic losses to their homes and automobiles and also to pay medical expenses or to pay expenses at the time of death of a family member. Companies buy insurance to protect from potential losses to buildings and property, losses due to workers injured on the job, or even lawsuits from customers. Three common types of insurance are discussed in this chapter.

12.1 PROPERTY TAX

OBJECTIVES

1. Define *fair market value* and *assessed value.*
2. Find the tax rate.
3. Use the formula for property tax.
4. Express tax rate in percent, in dollars per $100, in dollars per $1000, and in mills.
5. Find taxes given the assessed value and the tax rate.

CASE *in* POINT Martha Spencer was surprised by the amount of the property tax on her business this year. Her taxes went up significantly and she was determined to find out why. She also wanted to know where the money was going.

In virtually every area of the nation, owners of real property (such as buildings and land) must pay property tax. The money raised by this tax is used to provide services needed by the local community, such as police and fire protection, roads, schools, and other city and county services. The figure on the next page shows that the average property tax per person has generally increased over the years.

America's Rising Property Tax Burden

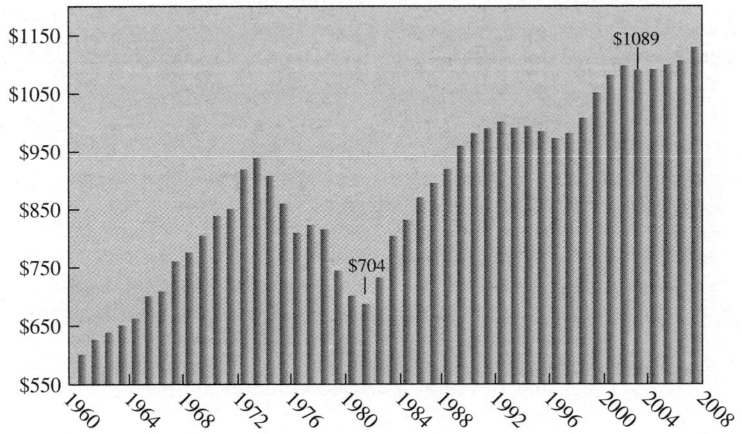

Annual Property Taxes per Person, in Inflation-Adjusted Dollars

DATA: The Tax Foundation

OBJECTIVE 1 Define *fair market value* and *assessed value*. A local tax assessor estimates the market value of all the land and buildings in an area. The **fair market value** is the price at which a property can reasonably be expected to be sold. The **assessed value** of each property is found by multiplying the fair market value by a percent called the **assessment rate**. The assessment rate varies widely from one area to another, but normally remains constant within a state.

In some states, assessed value is 25% of fair market value. In other states, the assessed value is 40% to 60%, or even 100%, of fair market value. Using an assessed value rate that is a percent of fair market value has become an accepted practice over the years.

EXAMPLE 1

Finding the Assessed Valuation of Property

Find the assessed value for the following pieces of property owned by Martha Spencer.

(a) Home: fair market value $185,300; assessment rate 35%
(b) Business property: fair market value $328,500; assessment rate 35%
(c) Commercial lot located in a different state: fair market value $123,800; assessment rate 60%

SOLUTION

Multiply the fair market value by the assessment rate.

(a) $185,300 × .35 = $64,855
(b) $328,500 × .35 = $114,975
(c) $123,800 × .60 = $74,280

QUICK TIP Just because the assessment rate is higher in one area than another does not necessarily mean that the taxes are higher. The assessed value of the property must be multiplied by the tax rate to find the tax. (See Objective 3.)

QUICK CHECK 1

A commercial building has a fair market value of $1,480,000. If the assessment rate is 70%, find the assessed value.

OBJECTIVE 2 Find the tax rate. A taxing authority uses the following steps to find the **property tax rate**.

STEP 1 Identify the amount of money needed.

STEP 2 Find the total fair market value of all real properties in the area.

STEP 3 Find the total assessed value of all real properties in the area.

STEP 4 Property tax rate = Total amount needed ÷ Total assessed value.

$$\text{Tax rate} = \frac{\text{Total tax amount needed}}{\text{Total assessed value}}$$

Quick Check Answer

1. $1,036,000

EXAMPLE 2

Finding the Tax Rate

Find the tax rate for the following school districts, rounded to the nearest tenth of a percent.

(a) Amount needed = \$14,253,000; total assessed value = \$575,890,000
(b) Amount needed = \$8,490,000; total assessed value = \$663,270,000

SOLUTION

(a) \$14,253,000 ÷ \$575,890,000 = 2.5% (rounded)
(b) \$8,490,000 ÷ \$663,270,000 = 1.3% (rounded)

QUICK CHECK 2

A large community college district needs \$22,350.000. The taxing authority has determined that the total assessed value of all the real estate in the district is \$2.48 billion. Find the property tax rate.

OBJECTIVE 3 **Use the formula for property tax.** Property tax rates are expressed in different ways in different parts of the country. However, property tax is always found with this formula:

QUICK TIP The market value of a piece of property usually differs considerably from the assessed value, which is used only to calculate taxes.

Tax = Tax rate × Assessed value

OBJECTIVE 4 **Express tax rate in percent, in dollars per \$100, in dollars per \$1000, and in mills.**
Percent. Some areas express tax rates as a percent of assessed value. The tax on a piece of property with an assessed value of \$74,000 at a tax rate of 9.42% follows.

Tax = .0942 × \$74,000 = \$6970.80

Dollars per \$100. In some areas, the tax rate is expressed as a number of dollars per \$100 of assessed value. In this event, find the tax on a piece of land by first finding the number of hundreds in the assessed value and then multiplying the number of hundreds by the tax rate. For example, assume an assessed value of \$56,300 and a tax rate of \$11.42 per \$100 of assessed value and find taxes as follows.

\$56,300 ÷ 100 = **563 hundreds** Divide by 100 by moving the decimal point 2 places to the left.

Tax = 563 × \$11.42 = **\$6429.46** Multiply by the tax rate to find tax.

Dollars per \$1000. In other areas, the tax rate is expressed as a number of dollars per \$1000 of assessed value. If the tax rate is \$98.12 per \$1000, a piece of property having an assessed value of \$197,000 would be taxed as follows.

\$197,000 = **197 thousands** Move the decimal point 3 places to the left to divide by 1000.

Tax = \$98.12 × 197 = **\$19,329.64**

Mills. Other taxing authorities express tax rates in mills or one-thousandths of a dollar. For example, a tax rate might be expressed as 46 mills. Divide the 46 mills by 1000 to find \$.046 per dollar of assessed value. Assuming a tax rate of 46 mills, the tax on a house assessed at \$81,000 is found as follows.

→ 46 mills = \$.046
Tax = **.046** × \$81,000 = **\$3726**

Quick Check Answer

2. .9% (rounded)

QUICK TIP Although expressed differently, the rates in each row of this chart are equivalent tax rates.

The following chart shows the same tax rates written in the four different systems.

Percent	Per $100	Per $1000	In Mills
12.52%	$12.52	$125.20	125.2
3.2%	$3.20	$32	32
9.87%	$9.87	$98.70	98.7

OBJECTIVE 5 **Find taxes given the assessed value and the tax rate.** Property taxes are found by multiplying the tax rate by the assessed value, as shown in the following example.

EXAMPLE 3 Finding the Property Tax

Find the taxes on each of the following pieces of property. Assessed values and tax rates are given.

(a) $58,975; 8.4% **(b)** $875,400; $7.82 per $100
(c) $129,600; $64.21 per $1000 **(d)** $221,750; 94 mills

QUICK TIP Some states give a special tax break to homeowners called a *homeowner's exemption*. This feature allows homeowners to deduct a certain amount (varying from state to state) from the assessed value of their home before the taxes are calculated. This results in a lower tax.

SOLUTION

Multiply the tax rate by the assessed value.

(a) 8.4% = **.084**

Tax = Tax rate × Assessed value
Tax = **.084** × $58,975 = $4953.90

(b) $875,400 = **8754 hundreds**

Tax = $7.82 × **8754** = $68,456.28

(c) $129,600 = **129.6 thousands**

Tax = $64.21 × **129.6** = $8321.62

(d) 94 mills = **.094**

Tax = **.094** × $221,750 = $20,844.50

QUICK CHECK 3

A home is assessed at $65,000. Find the property tax if the tax rate is **(a)** 3.4%, **(b)** $4.50 per $100, **(c)** $38.40 per $1000, and **(d)** 48.2 mills.

EXAMPLE 4 Comparing Tax Rates

As Ben Waller decides where to build a 30-unit apartment complex that he estimates will have a market value of $1,400,000, he considers property tax. In one county, property is assessed at 50% of market value with a tax rate of 3.2%. In a second county, property is assessed at 80% with a tax rate of 35 mills. **(a)** Find the county with the lower tax. **(b)** Find the amount saved by building in the county with the lower tax.

SOLUTION

(a) Property tax 1st county = $1,400,000 × .5 × .032 = **$22,400**
Property tax 2nd county = $1,400,000 × .8 × .035 = **$39,200**

The first county has the lower tax.

(b) Amount saved = **$39,200** − **$22,400** = $16,800 per year

QUICK CHECK 4

One county has a tax rate of $2.40 per $100, and a second county has a tax rate of $26.60 per $1000. A planned home will have an assessed value of $290,000. **(a)** Find the county with the lower tax. **(b)** Find the amount saved by building in the county with the lower tax.

Quick Check Answers

3. **(a)** $2210 **(b)** $2925 **(c)** $2496 **(d)** $3133
4. **(a)** first county **(b)** $754 per year

12.1 EXERCISES

FOR EXTRA HELP

MyMathLab

MathXL PRACTICE

WATCH

DOWNLOAD

READ

REVIEW

The **QUICK START** *exercises in each section contain solutions to help you get started.*

Find the assessed value for each of the following pieces of property. (See Example 1.)

QUICK START

Fair Market Value	Rate of Assessment	Assessed Value	Fair Market Value	Rate of Assessment	Assessed Value
1. $85,000	40%	$34,000	**2.** $68,000	60%	$40,800
$85,000 × .4 = $34,000			$68,000 × .6 = $40,800		
3. $142,300	50%	______	**4.** $98,200	42%	______
5. $1,300,500	25%	______	**6.** $2,450,000	80%	______

Find the tax rate for the following. Write the tax rate as a percent, rounded to the nearest tenth. (See Example 2.)

QUICK START

Total Tax Amount Needed	Total Assessed Value	Tax Rate	Total Tax Amount Needed	Total Assessed Value	Tax Rate
7. $18,300,000	$60,150,000	30.4%	**8.** $7,600,000	$39,280,000	19.3%
$18,300,000 ÷ $60,150,000 = .30424 = 30.4% (rounded)			$7,600,000 ÷ $39,280,000 = .19348 = 19.3% (rounded)		
9. $1,580,000	$19,750,000	______	**10.** $2,175,000	$54,375,000	______
11. $1,224,000	$40,800,000	______	**12.** $2,941,500	$81,700,000	______

Complete the following list comparing tax rates. (See Example 3.)

QUICK START

	Percent	Per $100	Per $1000	In Mills
13.	4.84%	**(a)** $4.84	**(b)** $48.40	**(c)** 48.4
14.	**(a)** ______	$6.75	**(b)** ______	**(c)** ______
15.	**(a)** ______	**(b)** ______	$70.80	**(c)** ______
16.	**(a)** ______	**(b)** ______	**(c)** ______	28

C indicates an exercise that is related to the Case in Point feature.

17. What is the difference between fair market value and assessed value? How is the assessment rate used when finding the assessed value? (See Objective 1.)

18. Select any tax rate and express it as a percent. Write this tax rate in three additional equivalent forms, and explain what each form means. (See Objective 4.)

Find the property tax for the following. (See Example 3.)

QUICK START

	Assessed Value	*Tax Rate*	*Tax*		*Assessed Value*	*Tax Rate*	*Tax*
19.	$86,200	$6.80 per $100	**$5861.60**	**20.**	$41,300	$46.40 per $1000	______
	862 × $6.80 = $5861.60						
21.	$128,200	42 mills	______	**22.**	$37,250	3.4%	______

Solve the following application problems.

QUICK START

23. REAL ESTATE TAXES Martha Spencer owns the real estate used by The Doll House. The property has a fair market value of $328,500, the assessment rate is 35%, and the local tax rate is 5.2%. Find the tax.

$328,500 × .35 = $114,975; $114,975 × .052 = $5978.70

23. **$5978.70**

24. APARTMENT OWNER Chad LeCompte owns a four-unit apartment building with a fair market value of $248,000. Property in the area is assessed at 40% of market value, and the tax rate is 5.5%. Find the amount of the property tax.

24. ______

25. COMMERCIAL PROPERTY TAX A new FM radio station broadcasts from a building having a fair market value of $334,400. The building is in an area where property is assessed at 25% of market value, and the tax rate is $75.30 per $1000 of assessed value. Find the property tax.

25. ______

26. OFFICE COMPLEX Huron Development just purchased a modern office complex for $12,380,000. The county assesses the property at 60% of market value and has a property tax of $18.40 per $1000 of assessed value. Find the property tax.

26. ______________

27. OFFICE COMPLEX The Savon Park office complex has a fair market value of $1,350,000. Property in the area is assessed at 40% of fair market value, and the tax rate is $7.40 per $100 of assessed value. Find the property tax.

27. ______________

28. MOTORCYCLES Harley-Davidson of Lincoln has property with a fair market value of $518,600. The property is located in an area that is assessed at 35% of market value. The tax rate is $7.35 per $100. Find the property tax.

28. ______________

29. COMPARING PROPERTY TAX RATES In one parish (county), property is assessed at 40% of market value, with a tax rate of 32.1 mills. In a second parish, property is assessed at 24% of market value, with a tax rate of 50.2 mills. A telephone company is trying to decide where to place a small storage building with a fair market value of $95,000. **(a)** Which parish would charge the lower property tax? **(b)** Find the annual amount saved.

(a) ______________
(b) ______________

30. PROPERTY TAXES In one county, property is assessed at 30% of market value, with a tax rate of 45.6 mills. In a second county, property is assessed at 48% of market value, with a tax rate of 29.3 mills. If Henry Hernandez is trying to decide where to build a $140,000 house, **(a)** find which county would charge the lower property tax and **(b)** find the annual amount saved.

(a) ______________
(b) ______________

12.2 PERSONAL INCOME TAX

OBJECTIVES

1. List the four steps that determine income tax liability.
2. Find the adjusted gross income.
3. Know the standard deduction amounts.
4. Find the taxable income and income tax.
5. List possible deductions.
6. Determine a balance due or a refund from the Internal Revenue Service.
7. Prepare a 1040A and a Schedule 1 federal tax form.

CASE in POINT As a business owner, Martha Spencer has her income taxes prepared by a qualified accountant. Still, she must keep track of all her financial information throughout the year for the time when preparing her taxes arrives. Even though she does not prepare her own taxes, Martha Spencer is still responsible for the accuracy of all the information contained on her personal income tax forms.

Income taxes are calculated based on income. They are a source of revenue for the federal government, most states, and many local governments. The pie charts below show the major categories of income and outlays for the U.S. government. Notice that personal income taxes generate 43% of federal revenues, whereas corporate income taxes generate 13% of federal revenues. The three largest outlays of the government are Medicare and other retirement, Social Security, and the Department of Defense/military.

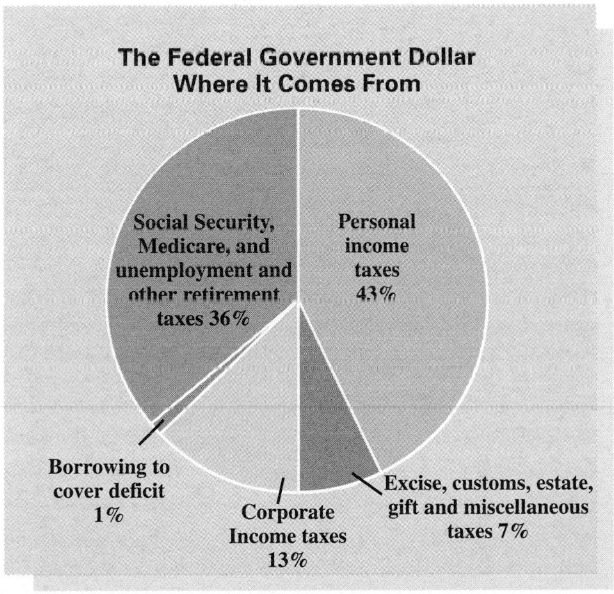

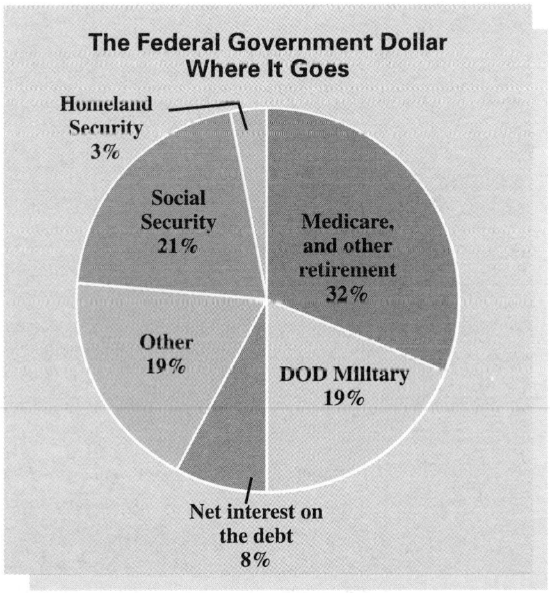

DATA: Internal Revenue Service

Some believe that wealthy individuals do not pay income tax, but that is not true as shown in the following table. The top 1% of earners pay 33.7% of all personal income taxes, and the top 50% of earners pay over 96% of all personal income taxes.

Projected Share of Individual Income Taxes and Income (U.S. Treasury Estimate)

	Top 1%	Top 5%	Top 10%	Top 25%	Top 50%	Bottom 50%
Percent of Income Taxes	33.7	54.1	65.8	83.6	96.4	3.6
Percent of Income	16.5	31.0	42.1	64.7	86.1	13.9

DATA: Tax Foundation (Internal Revenue Service)

Most working adults are required to file an income tax return with the federal government every year. Married couples often submit one income tax return that shows income and deductions for both spouses. Forms for filing income taxes can be found at **Internal Revenue Service (IRS)** offices or at the IRS Web site, www.irs.gov. The IRS is the branch of the government responsible for collecting income taxes. Last year, more than 73 million tax returns were filed electronically, with more than 20 million filed using home computers.

There are thousands of rules about income tax preparation and many different forms, each with its own instructions. However, many people have relatively simple income tax returns that do not require professionals to complete. No matter whether you use a professional to file your income tax return or do it yourself, you should carefully save all records related to income and expenses. These records should be kept until the statute of limitations runs out, which is 3 years from the date the tax return was filed or 2 years from the date the tax was paid, whichever is later. The IRS can audit you during this period and it requires proof of income and deductions. Many accountants recommend that you keep records for 7 years, but you should keep records on property such as your home as long as they are needed, often longer than 3 years.

QUICK TIP Filing electronically results in a quick refund.

OBJECTIVE 1 **List the four steps that determine income tax liability.** There are four basic steps in finding total tax liability. They are listed here and described one at a time in the remainder of this section.

QUICK TIP It can be very complex to find the income tax for some people. This section introduces only the basic concepts.

Determine Your Income Tax Liability

STEP 1 Find the adjusted gross income (AGI) for the year.
STEP 2 Find the taxable income.
STEP 3 Find the tax.
STEP 4 Check to see if a refund is due or if money is owed to the government.

OBJECTIVE 2 **Find the adjusted gross income.** The first step in finding personal income tax is to find **adjusted gross income**. Adjusted gross income is the total of all income less certain adjustments. Employers are required to send out **W-2 forms** showing wages paid, federal income taxes withheld, Social Security tax withheld, and Medicare tax withheld. Other types of income such as interest, dividends, and self-employment income are shown on **1099 forms**, which are also mailed to each individual. Sample W-2 and 1099-INT forms are shown on the next page.

Finding Adjusted Gross Income

STEP 1 Add amounts from all W-2 and 1099 forms along with dividends, capital gains, unemployment compensation, and tips or other employee compensation.
STEP 2 From this sum, subtract adjustments such as contributions to a *regular* **individual retirement account (IRA)** or alimony payments.

EXAMPLE 1

Finding Adjusted Gross Income (AGI)

As an assistant manager at The Doll House, Jennifer Crum earned $24,738.41 last year and $1624.01 in interest from her credit union (see her W-2 and 1099 forms). She had $1500 in regular IRA contributions. Find her adjusted gross income.

SOLUTION

$$\begin{aligned}\text{Adjusted gross income} &= \text{Wages} + \text{Interest} - \textbf{IRA contribution}\\ &= \$24{,}738.41 + \$1624.01 - \mathbf{\$1500}\\ &= \$24{,}862.42\end{aligned}$$

QUICK TIP When you file your income tax return, a copy of all W-2 forms is sent to the Internal Revenue Service along with the completed tax forms. However, the IRS does not require copies of 1099 forms to be sent unless income tax was withheld.

QUICK CHECK 1

Last year, Marelli Food Distribution paid marketing manager Beth Hogan $95,000. Hogan also earned $6450 in interest and contributed $2500 to an IRA. Find her adjusted gross income.

Quick Check Answer

1. $98,950

a Control number	22222	Void ☐	For Official Use Only ► OMB No. 1545-0008

b Employer identification number: 94-1287319	1 Wages, tips, other compensation: $24,738.41	2 Federal income tax withheld: $3275.60
c Employer's name, address, and ZIP code: The Doll House, 1568 Liberty Heights Ave., Baltimore, MD 21230	3 Social security wages: $24,738.41	4 Social security tax withheld: $1533.78
	5 Medicare wages and tips: $24,738.41	6 Medicare tax withheld: $358.71
	7 Social security tips	8 Allocated tips
d Employee's social security number: 123-45-6789	9 Advance EIC payment	10 Dependent care benefits
e Employee's first name and initial: Jennifer; Last name: Crum	11 Nonqualified plans	12a See instructions for box 12 (Code)
2136 Old Road, Towson, MD 21285	13 Statutory employee ☐ Retirement plan ☐ Third-party sick pay ☐	12b (Code)
	14 Other	12c (Code)
f Employee's address and ZIP code		12d (Code)

15 State	Employer's state ID number	16 State wages, tips, etc.	17 State income tax	18 Local wages, tips, etc.	19 Local income tax	20 Locality name
MD	600-5076					

Form **W-2** Wage and Tax Statement — Department of the Treasury—Internal Revenue Service

9292 ☐ VOID ☐ CORRECTED

PAYER'S name, street address, city, state, ZIP code, and telephone no.: Employees Credit Union, 2572 Brookhaven Drive, Dundalk, MD 21222	Payer's RTN (optional)	OMB No. 1545-0112; 200_; Form 1099-INT	**Interest Income**
PAYER'S Federal identification number: 94-1287319 / RECIPIENT'S identification number: 123-45-6789	1 Interest income not included in box 3: $ 1624.01		**Copy A For Internal Revenue Service Center** File with Form 1096. For Privacy Act and Paperwork Reduction Act Notice, see the **200X General Instructions for Forms 1099, 1098, 5498, and W-2G.**
RECIPIENT'S name: Jennifer Crum	2 Early withdrawal penalty: $	3 Interest on U.S. Savings Bonds and Treas. obligations: $	
Street address (including apt. no.): 2136 Old Road	4 Federal income tax withheld: $	5 Investment expenses: $	
City, state, and ZIP code: Towson, MD 21285	6 Foreign tax paid: $	7 Foreign country or U.S. possession	
Account number (optional) / 2nd TIN not. ☐			

Form **1099-INT** Cat. No. 14410K Department of the Treasury - Internal Revenue Service

OBJECTIVE 3 **Know the standard deduction amounts.** Most people are almost finished at this point. A taxpayer next subtracts the larger of either the itemized deductions or the standard deduction from adjusted gross income. Itemized deductions are described in Objective 5 in this section and are associated with several limitations based on adjusted gross income. The **standard deduction** amount is based on the taxpayer's filing status as follows.

Finding Standard Deduction

$5150 for single taxpayers

$10,300 for married taxpayers filing jointly or qualifying widow(er)

$5150 for married taxpayers filing separately

$7550 for head of household

A **head of household** is an unmarried person who provides a home for other people, such as a dependent child or even a dependent parent of the taxpayer.

Additional standard deductions are given for taxpayers and dependents who are blind or 65 years of age or older. The standard deduction amounts commonly change from one year to the next. The most current amounts can be obtained from the IRS.

The next step is to find the number of **personal exemptions**. One exemption is allowed for yourself, another for your spouse if filing a joint return, and yet another exemption for each child or other dependent. A **dependent** is a child, spouse, parent, or certain other relative to whom the primary taxpayer contributes all or a major portion of necessary financial support. The number of exemptions does not depend on whether the filing status is single or married. The deduction for personal exemptions is \$3300 times the number of exemptions. Here are some examples.

Filing Status and Exemptions	Total Deduction
Single individual (1 exemption)	$1 \times \$3300 = \$3300$
Married with 3 children (5 exemptions)	$5 \times \$3300 = \$16{,}500$
Single, head of household, 2 children (3 exemptions)	$3 \times \$3300 = \$9900$

Taxable income is found by subtracting the standard deduction amount and personal exemptions from adjusted gross income. Taxes are then calculated based on taxable income as shown next.

OBJECTIVE 4 **Find the taxable income and income tax.** Taxable income is used along with data from the tax rate schedule shown next to find the income tax. As you can see from the tax rate schedules, individual income tax rates range from a low of 10% to a high of 35% depending on income and filing status. Assume a single filer has a taxable income of \$37,300. Use the table for single filer below to find:

$$\begin{aligned}\text{Federal Income Tax} &= \$4220 + \mathbf{25\%\ of\ excess\ over\ \$30{,}650} \\ &= \$4220 + \mathbf{.25 \times (\$37{,}300 - \$30{,}650) = \$5882.50}\end{aligned}$$

The 25% tax rate applied only to the amount above \$30,650 and not to the entire taxable income.

2006 Federal Tax Rate Schedules
Schedule X—Single

If taxable income is over–	But not over–	The tax is:
\$0	\$7,550	10% of the amount over \$0
\$7,550	\$30,650	\$755 plus 15% of the amount over \$7,550
\$30,650	\$74,200	\$4,220.00 plus 25% of the amount over \$30,650
\$74,200	\$154,800	\$15,107.50 plus 28% of the amount over \$74,200
\$154,800	\$336,550	\$37,675.50 plus 33% of the amount over \$154,800
\$336,550	no limit	\$97,653.00 plus 35% of the amount over \$336,550

Schedule Y-1—Married Filing Jointly or Qualifying Widow(er)

If taxable income is over–	But not over–	The tax is:
\$0	\$15,100	10% of the amount over \$0
\$15,100	\$61,300	\$1,510.00 plus 15% of the amount over \$15,100
\$61,300	\$123,700	\$8,440.00 plus 25% of the amount over \$61,300
\$123,700	\$188,450	\$24,040.00 plus 28% of the amount over \$123,700
\$188,450	\$336,550	\$42,170.00 plus 33% of the amount over \$188,450
\$336,550	no limit	\$91,043.00 plus 35% of the amount over \$336,550

Schedule Y-2—Married Filing Separately

If taxable income is over–	But not over–	The tax is:
$0	$7,550	10% of the amount over $0
$7,550	$30,650	$755.00 plus 15% of the amount over $7,550
$30,650	$61,850	$4,220.00 plus 25% of the amount over $30,650
$61,850	$94,225	$12,020.00 plus 28% of the amount over $61,850
$94,225	$168,275	$21,085.00 plus 33% of the amount over $94,225
$168,275	no limit	$45,521.50 plus 35% of the amount over $168,275

Schedule Z—Head of Household

If taxable income is over–	But not over–	The tax is:
$0	$10,750	10% of the amount over $0
$10,750	$41,050	$1,075.00 plus 15% of the amount over $10,750
$41,050	$106,000	$5,620.00 plus 25% of the amount over $41,050
$106,000	$171,650	$21,857.50 plus 28% of the amount over $106,000
$171,650	$336,550	$40,239.50 plus 33% of the amount over $171,650
$336,550	no limit	$94,656.50 plus 35% of the amount over $336,550

EXAMPLE 2

Find Taxable Income and the Income Tax Amount

Find the taxable income and income tax for each of the following.

(a) Herbert White, married filing jointly, 5 daughters, adjusted gross income $48,300
(b) Onita Fields, single, no dependents, adjusted gross income $28,400
(c) Imogene Griffin, single, head of household, 2 children, adjusted gross income $74,500
(d) Jeffy Norwood, married filing separately, 1 child, adjusted gross income $145,000

SOLUTION

(a) Herbert White + spouse + 5 daughters, or 7 exemptions total

Taxable income = $48,300 − $10,300 (standard deduction) − (7 × $3300) (deduction for exemptions) = **$14,900** (taxable income)

The tax rate for married filing jointly with less than $15,100 in taxable income is 10%.

Income tax = .10 × **$14,900** (taxable income) = $1490

(b) Onita Fields has no other exemptions, or 1 exemption total

Taxable income = $28,400 − $5150 (standard deduction) − (1 × $3300) (deduction for exemptions) = $19,950 (taxable income)

Income tax = $755 + **15% of excess over $7550**
= $755 + **.15** × (**$19,950** − **$7550**) = **$2615**

(c) Imogene Griffin + 2 children, or 3 exemptions

Taxable income = $74,500 − $7550 (standard deduction) − (3 × $3300) (deduction for exemptions) = $57,050 (taxable income)

Income tax = $5620 + **25% of excess over $41,050**
= $5620 + **.25** × (**$57,050** − **$41,050**) = **$9620**

(d) Jeffy Norwood + 1 child, or 2 exemptions

Taxable income = $145,000 − $5150 (standard deduction) − (2 × $3300) (deduction for exemptions) = $133,250 (taxable income)

Income tax = $21,085 + **33% of excess over $94,225**
= $21,085 + **.33** × (**$133,250** − **$94,225**) = **$33,963.25**

QUICK CHECK 2

John O'Neill files jointly with his wife. They have 1 child and an adjusted gross income of \$62,300. Find their taxable income and income tax.

OBJECTIVE 5 **List possible deductions.** Actually, taxpayers may deduct *the larger of* **itemized deductions** *or* the standard deduction from their adjusted gross income *before* finding taxable income. This is particularly applicable to individuals who are paying interest on a home loan, but sometimes others can use this to their advantage. The most common **tax deductions** are listed next.

QUICK TIP The taxpayer can take the larger of the standard deduction, or the itemized deduction, although limitations may apply if the adjusted gross income is over a certain amount. Rent and utilities are not tax deductible.

Medical and dental expenses: Only medical and dental expenses exceeding 7.5% of adjusted gross income may be deducted. This deduction is effectively limited to catastrophic illnesses for most taxpayers. Expenses reimbursed by an insurance company are not deductible.
Taxes: State and local income taxes, real estate taxes, and personal property taxes may be deducted (but not federal income or gasoline taxes).
Interest: Deductible interest includes interest on a home morgage and qualified interest on other real estate. Other personal interest is not deductible.
Casualty or theft losses: Losses due to a casualty (e.g., fire) or theft are deductible if not reimbursed by insurance.
Contributions: Contributions to most charities may be deducted.
Unreimbursed job expenses, tax preparation, and **miscellaneous deductions:** These expenses are deductible only if the total exceeds 2% of the taxpayer's adjusted gross income.

EXAMPLE 3

Using Itemized Deductions to Find Taxable Income and Income Tax

Kristina Kelly is single, has 1 child, and had an adjusted gross income of \$58,700 last year. She paid \$3240 in real estate taxes, \$7280 in home mortgage interest, and donated \$1200 to her church. Find her taxable income and her income tax.

SOLUTION

$$\text{Itemized deductions} = \$3240 + \$7280 + \$1200 = \$11{,}720$$

Her itemized deductions of \$11,720 exceed the standard deduction of \$5150 for a single person, so she uses the itemized deduction amount.

$$\text{Taxable income} = \$58{,}700 - \underbrace{\$11{,}720}_{\text{itemized deductions}} - \underbrace{(2 \times \$3300)}_{\text{personal exemptions}} = \mathbf{\$40{,}380}$$

$$\text{Income tax} = \$4220 + 25\% \text{ of the amount over } \$30{,}650$$

$$= \$4220 + .25 \times (\mathbf{\$40{,}380} - \$30{,}650) = \$6652.50$$

QUICK CHECK 3

Tom Garcia and his wife file jointly. They have no children, earned an adjusted gross income of \$48,200, and paid the following: \$2350 in other taxes, \$6807.45 in home mortgage interest, and \$500 to the Red Cross. Find their taxable income and income tax.

OBJECTIVE 6 **Determine a balance due or a refund from the Internal Revenue Service.** A taxpayer may have paid more to the IRS than is due. Add up the total amount of income tax paid using the W-2 forms. Usually, no taxes are withheld on 1099 forms. If the amount withheld is greater than the tax owed, the taxpayer is entitled to a refund. If the amount withheld is less than the tax owed, then the taxpayer must send the difference along with the tax return to the IRS.

Quick Check Answers

2. \$42,100; \$5560
3. \$31,300; \$3940

EXAMPLE 4

Determining Tax Due or Refund

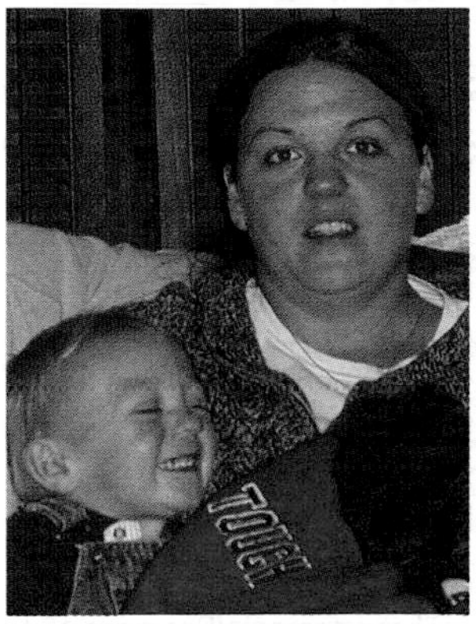

Tim Owen works as an attorney and his wife stays at home with their young son. Last year Tim had an adjusted gross income of $87,300, and $573.50 was withheld from his paycheck every month for federal income taxes. The Owens file a joint return and use the standard deduction. Find either the additional amount of income taxes they owe or the amount they overpaid.

SOLUTION

Adjusted gross income	$87,300	
Standard deduction	− 10,300	married filing jointly
Personal exemptions	− 9,900	3 exemptions × $3300
Taxable income	$67,100	

$$\text{Income tax} = \$8440 + 25\% \times \text{of excess over } \$61{,}300$$
$$= \$8440 + .25 \times (\$67{,}100 - \$61{,}300) = \$9890$$

$$\text{Amount withheld last year} = \$573.50 \times 12 = \mathbf{\$6882}$$

$$\text{Amount owed to IRS} = \$9890 - \$6882 = \mathbf{\$3008}$$

The Owens must send an additional **$3008** with their federal income tax return.

QUICK CHECK 4

James Benson files as head of household and has 2 children. His adjusted gross income is $59,200, and he uses the standard deduction. Last year, his employer held $280 out of every bimonthly paycheck. Find **(a)** his taxable income, **(b)** tax due, **(c)** amount withheld by his employer last year, and **(d)** either the additional amount of income taxes he owes or the amount he overpaid.

QUICK TIP Every year, many of the rules related to the calculation of income taxes change. Always use the most current information and forms from the Internal Revenue Service when preparing your taxes.

Use the simplest IRS form possible when filing your income taxes. Here are basic guidelines starting with the simplest form. Be sure to check with the IRS before choosing the tax form—the rules change often!

1040EZ (general guidelines)

1. Single or married filing jointly with no dependents
2. No adjustments to income
3. Cannot itemize
4. Limited sources of income and use of tax credits
5. Under age 65 with taxable income less than $100,000

1040A (general guidelines)

1. Sources of income limited to wages, interest, capital gains, and other categories
2. Limited adjustments to income and use of tax credits
3. Cannot itemize
4. Taxable income less than $100,000

QUICK TIP When completing income tax forms and calculations, notice that all amounts may be rounded to the nearest dollar.

If neither the 1040EZ nor the 1040A form applies, then you must use the 1040 form. Partnerships and corporations require a completely different set of forms.

OBJECTIVE 7 **Prepare a 1040A and a Schedule 1 federal tax form.** The next example shows how to complete an income tax return using **Form 1040A** and **Schedule 1 (Form 1040A)**.

Quick Check Answers

4. **(a)** $41,750
(b) $5795
(c) $6720
(d) overpaid by $925

Schedule 1 (Form 1040A)

Department of the Treasury—Internal Revenue Service

Interest and Ordinary Dividends for Form 1040A Filers

(99) OMB No. 1545-0074

Name(s) shown on Form 1040A	Your social security number
Jennifer Crum	123 45 6789

Part I Interest

(See back of schedule and the instructions for Form 1040A, line 8a.)

Note. If you received a Form 1099-INT, Form 1099-OID, or substitute statement from a brokerage firm, enter the firm's name and the total interest shown on that form.

			Amount
1	List name of payer. If any interest is from a seller-financed mortgage and the buyer used the property as a personal residence, see back of schedule and list this interest first. Also, show that buyer's social security number and address.		
	Employees Credit Union	1	$1,624
2	Add the amounts on line 1.	2	$1,624
3	Excludable interest on series EE and I U.S. savings bonds issued after 1989. Attach Form 8815.	3	
4	Subtract line 3 from line 2. Enter the result here and on Form 1040A, line 8a.	4	$1,624

Part II Ordinary dividends

(See back of schedule and the instructions for Form 1040A, line 9a.)

Note. If you received a Form 1099-DIV or substitute statement from a brokerage firm, enter the firm's name and the ordinary dividends shown on that form.

			Amount
5	List name of payer.	5	
6	Add the amounts on line 5. Enter the total here and on Form 1040A, line 9a.	6	

For Paperwork Reduction Act Notice, see Form 1040A instructions. Cat. No. 12075R **Schedule 1 (Form 1040A)**

12.2 EXERCISES

FOR EXTRA HELP

MyMathLab

MathXL PRACTICE

WATCH

DOWNLOAD

READ

REVIEW

The QUICK START *exercises in each section contain solutions to help you get started.*

Find the adjusted gross income for each of the following people. (See Example 1.)

QUICK START

	Name	Income from Jobs	Interest	Misc. Income	Dividend Income	Adjustments to Income	Adjusted Gross Income
1.	R. Jacob	$22,840	$234	$1209	$48	$1200	**$23,131**
	$22,840 + $234 + $1209 + $48 − $1200 = $23,131						
2.	K. Chandler	$68,156	$285	$73	$542	$317	**$68,739**
	$68,156 + $285 + $73 + $542 − $317 = $68,739						
3.	The Hanks	$21,380	$625	$139	$184	$618	________
4.	The Jazwinskis	$33,650	$722	$375	$218	$473	________
5.	The Brashers	$38,643	$1020	$3820	$1050	$0	________
6.	The Ameens	$41,379	$1174	$536	$186	$2258	________

Find the amount of taxable income and the tax owed for each of the following people. Use the tax rate schedule. The letter following the names indicates the marital status, and all married people are filing jointly. (See Examples 2 and 3.)

QUICK START

	Name	Number of Exemptions	Adjusted Gross Income	Total Deductions	Taxable Income	Tax Owed
7.	R. Rodriguez, S	1	$32,400	$2398	**$23,950**	**$3215**
	$32,400 − $5150 − $3300 = $23,950; $755 + .15 × ($23,950 − $7550) = $3215					
8.	L. Pacos, S	1	$22,700	$898	**$14,250**	**$1760**
	$22,700 − $5150 − $3300 = $14,250; $755 + .15 × ($14,250 − $7550) = $1760					
9.	The Cooks, M	3	$38,751	$5968	________	________
10.	The Loveridges, M	7	$52,532	$6972	________	________

C indicates an exercise that is related to the Case in Point feature.

Name	Number of Exemptions	Adjusted Gross Income	Total Deductions	Taxable Income	Tax Owed
11. The Jordans, M	5	$71,800	$12,400	________	________
12. G. Clarke, S	1	$64,200	$8300	________	________
13. D. Collins, S	2	$35,350	$6240	________	________
14. K. Tang, Head of Household	2	$93,240	$5480	________	________
15. B. Kammerer, S	1	$43,526	$6800	________	________
16. G. Nation, M	3	$143,420	$15,240	________	________
17. B. Albert, Head of Household	2	$132,800	$9800	________	________
18. B. Nelson, Head of Household	4	$58,630	$6290	________	________

Find the tax refund or tax due for the following people. The letter following the names indicates the marital status. Assume a 52-week year and that married people are filing jointly. (See Example 4.)

QUICK START

Name	Taxable Income	Federal Income Tax Withheld from Checks	Tax Refund or Tax Due
19. L. Karecki, S	$78,500	$1516 monthly	**$1880.50 tax refund**
$18,192 − $16,311.50 = $1880.50			
20. K. Turner, S	$32,060	$347.80 monthly	________
21. M. Hunziker, S	$23,552	$72.18 weekly	________
22. The Fungs, M	$38,238	$119.27 weekly	________
23. The Todds, M	$202,100	$3200 monthly	________
24. The Bensons, M	$140,400	$510 weekly	________

25. List four sources of income for which an individual might receive W-2 and 1099 forms. (See Objective 2.)

26. List four possible tax deductions, and explain the effect that a tax deduction will have on taxable income and on income tax due. (See Objective 5.)

Find the tax in the following application problems.

27. MARRIED—INCOME TAX The Tobins had an adjusted gross income of $98,700 last year. They had deductions of $2820 for state income tax, $490 for city income tax, $4400 for property tax, $5800 in mortgage interest, and $1450 in contributions. They file a joint return and claim 5 exemptions.

27. ____________

C **28.** SINGLE—INCOME TAX Diane Bolton works at The Doll House and had an adjusted gross income of $34,975 last year. She had deductions of $971 for state income tax, $564 for property tax, $3820 in mortgage interest, and $235 in contributions. Bolton claims one exemption and files as a single person.

28. ____________

29. SINGLE—INCOME TAX Martha Crutchfield has an adjusted gross income of $79,300 and files as as single person with only one exemption. Her deductions amounted to $4630.

29. ____________

30. MARRIED—INCOME TAX The Hernandez family had an adjusted gross income of $48,260 last year. They had deductions of $1078 for state income tax, $253 for city income tax, $3240 for property tax, $5218 in mortgage interest, and $386 in contributions. They claim three exemptions and file a joint return.

30. ____________

31. HEAD OF HOUSEHOLD Martha Spencer, owner of The Doll House, had wages of $73,800, dividends of $385, interest of $1672, and adjustments to income of $1058 last year. She had deductions of $877 for state income tax, $342 for city income tax, $4986 for property tax, $5173 in mortgage interest, and $1800 in contributions. She claims four exemptions and files as head of household. **31.** ____________

32. HEAD OF HOUSEHOLD John Walker had wages of $48,200, other income of $2892, dividends of $340, interest of $651, and a regular IRA contribution of $2000 last year. He had deductions of $1163 for taxes, $5350 in mortgage interest, and $540 in contributions. Walker claims two exemptions and files as head of household. **32.** ____________

33. MARRIED John and Vicki Karsten had combined wages and salaries of $64,280, other income of $5283, dividend income of $324, and interest income of $668. They have adjustments to income of $2484. Their itemized deductions are $7615 in mortgage interest, $2250 in state income tax, $3300 in real estate taxes, and $1219 in charitable contributions. The Karstens filed a joint return and claimed 6 exemptions. **33.** ____________

34. HEAD OF HOUSEHOLD Eleanor Joyce is single and claims one exemption. As a television news reporter, her salary last year was $74,300, and she had other income of $2800 and interest income of $8400. She has an adjustment to income of $2200 for an Individual Retirement Account (IRA) contribution. Her itemized deductions are $5807 in mortgage interest, $2800 in state income tax, $4230 in real estate taxes, and $4690 in charitable contributions. **34.** ____________

12.3 FIRE INSURANCE

OBJECTIVES

1. Define the terms *policy, coverage, face value*, and *premium*.
2. Find the annual premium for fire insurance.
3. Use the coinsurance formula.
4. Understand multiple-carrier insurance.
5. List additional types of insurance coverage.

CASE in POINT Martha Spencer owns the building in which The Doll House is located. A fire in that building could leave her in financial ruin. Although she hopes that there is never a fire, she carries fire insurance to protect her business in the event there is one.

Insurance protects against risk. For example, there is only a slight chance that a particular building will be damaged by fire in any year. However, the financial loss from a fire could be devastating to the owner. Therefore, people or companies pay a small fee each year to an insurance company to protect them against catastrophic losses. The insurance company collects money from many different people and companies that buy insurance and pays money to the few who suffer damages. The following graph shows that most fires in homes begin in the kitchen. Perhaps that is why many recommend that you keep a fire extinguisher in your kitchen. The clipping in the margin shows who is most at risk of fire death and also the common causes of fires in homes.

At Risk: Fire Deaths

- Seniors over age 70 and children under 5
- Men twice as much as women
- Blacks and Native Americans, whose fire death rates are higher than the national average

What Causes Fires

- Cooking
- Careless smoking
- Heating systems
- Arson

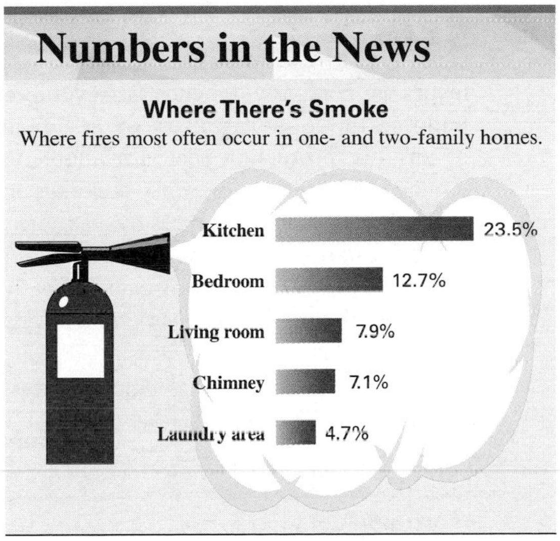

QUICK TIP Lenders almost always require fire insurance on any property that they use as collateral for a loan.

Individuals buy insurance to protect against losses due to fire, theft, illness or health problems, disability, car wrecks, lawsuits, and even death. Companies buy insurance to protect against losses due to fire, automobile accidents, employee illnesses, lawsuits, and worker accidents on the job.

OBJECTIVE 1 Define the terms *policy, coverage, face value,* and *premium*. The contract between the owner of a building and an insurance company is called a **policy** or an **insurance policy**. A basic fire policy provides **coverage** or protection for both the owner of the building and the company that holds the mortgage on the building. The owner of a building can also purchase coverage on the contents of the building and liability insurance in the event someone is injured while on the property. Homeowners purchase a **homeowner's policy**, which includes all of these coverages. The line graph on the next page shows that the cost of homeowner's insurance continues to increase.

The dollar value of the insurance coverage provided on a building itself is called the **face value** of the policy. The annual charge for the policy is called the **premium**. The premium is usually calculated based on factors such as age of the building, materials used in the construction of the building, crime rate of the neighborhood, presence of any safety features such as a sprinkler system, security system, and history of previous insurance claims on the property.

QUICK TIP Much of the increase in the cost of homeowner's insurance shown in the graph is simply due to inflation, although insurance costs have increased slightly more rapidly than inflation during the time period shown.

Numbers in the News

The Rising Price of Protection

Annual homeowner's insurance premiums continue to climb.

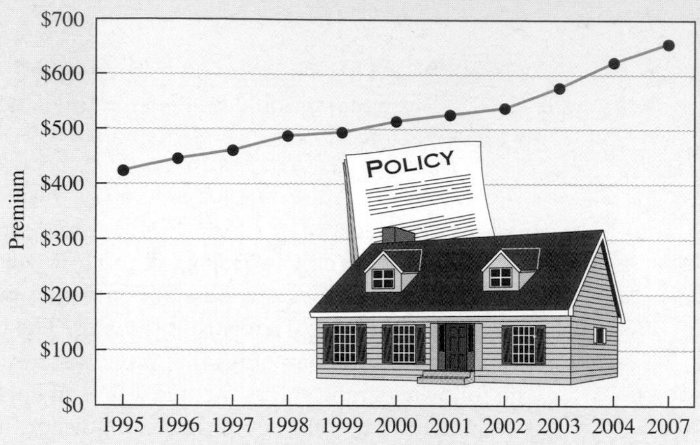

DATA: National Association of Insurance Commissioners; and Insurance Information Institute

OBJECTIVE 2 **Find the annual premium for fire insurance.** The amount of the premium charged by the insurance company depends on several factors. Among them are the type of construction of the building, the contents and use of the building, the location of the building, and the type and location of any fire protection that is available. Wood frame buildings generally are more likely to be damaged by fire than masonry buildings and thus require a higher premium. Building classifications are assigned to building types by insurance company employees called **underwriters**. These building categories are usually designated by letters such as A, B, and C. Underwriters also assign ratings called **territorial ratings** to each area that describe the quality of fire protection in the area. Although fire insurance rates vary from state to state, the rates in the following table are typical.

Annual Rates for Each $100 of Insurance

	Building Classification					
	A		B		C	
Territorial Rating	Building	Contents	Building	Contents	Building	Contents
1	$.25	$.32	$.36	$.49	$.45	$.60
2	$.30	$.44	$.45	$.55	$.54	$.75
3	$.37	$.46	$.54	$.60	$.63	$.80
4	$.50	$.52	$.75	$.77	$.84	$.90
5	$.62	$.58	$.92	$.99	$1.05	$1.14

EXAMPLE 1 Finding the Annual Fire Insurance Premium

The Doll House is in a building rated class C. It is in territory 4. Find the annual premium if the replacement cost of the building is $640,000 and the contents are valued at $186,500.

SOLUTION

Building:

$$\text{Replacement cost in hundreds} = \$640{,}000 \div 100 = 6400$$
$$\text{Insurance premium for the building} = 6400 \times \$.84 = \$5376$$

Contents:

Replacement cost in hundreds = $186,500 ÷ 100 = **1865**
Insurance premium for contents = **1865** × $.90 = $1678.50

Total premium: $5376 + $1678.50 = **$7054.50**

QUICK CHECK 1

A commercial building has a replacement cost of $1,480,000 and contents valued at $110,000. It has a classification of B and a territory rating of 5. Find the annual premium.

OBJECTIVE 3 **Use the coinsurance formula.** Most fires damage only a portion of a building and the contents. Since complete destruction of a building is rare, many owners save money by buying insurance for only a portion of the value of the building and contents. Realizing this, insurance companies place a **coinsurance clause** in almost all fire insurance policies. Effectively, the business assumes part of the risk of a loss under coinsurance.

An 80% coinsurance clause in the policy requires that the amount of insurance carried by the owner of a building be at least 80% of the **replacement cost** of the building, where replacement cost is the cost to rebuild the entire building. Replacement cost is often higher than fair market value on older buildings. If the amount of insurance is less than 80% of the replacement cost, the insurance company pays only a portion of any loss, as shown in the following formula.

QUICK TIP The insurance company never pays more than the face value of the policy, nor more than the amount of the loss. Buying too much insurance is a waste of money.

Finding Amount Insurance Will Pay

$$\text{Amount insurance company will pay (assuming 80\% coinsurance)} = \text{Amount of loss} \times \frac{\text{Amount of policy}}{\text{80\% of replacement cost}}$$

EXAMPLE 2

Using the Coinsurance Formula

Buster Stetson owns a commercial building with a replacement cost of $760,000. His fire insurance policy has an 80% coinsurance clause and a face value of $570,000. The building suffers a fire loss of $144,000. Find the amount of the loss that the insurance company will pay.

SOLUTION

The policy must have a face value of at least 80% of $760,000 or $608,000 in order to receive the payment for the entire loss. Since the face value of $570,000 is less than 80% of the replacement cost, the company will pay only the following portion of the loss.

$$\text{Amount insurance company pays} = \$144{,}000 \times \frac{\mathbf{\$570{,}000}}{\mathbf{\$608{,}000}} = \$135{,}000$$

$$\text{Amount not paid by insurance company} = \$144{,}000 - \$135{,}000 = \$9000$$

Stetson is responsible for $9000.

The calculator solution to this example uses chain calculations and parentheses to set off the denominator. The result is then subtracted from the fire loss.

144,000 [×] 570,000 [÷] [(] 80 [%] [×] 760,000 [)] [=] 135,000

144,000 [−] 135,000 [=] 9000

Note: Refer to Appendix C for calculator basics.

QUICK CHECK 2

A real estate investment trust owns an apartment complex with a replacement cost of $8,400,000 that is insured for $5,600,000. Find the amount of the loss paid for by the insurance company if a fire causes $2,300,000 in losses and the policy has an 80% coinsurance feature.

Quick Check Answers

1. $14,705
2. $1,916,666.67

EXAMPLE 3

Finding the Amount of Loss Paid by the Insurance Company

A Swedish investment group owns a warehouse with a replacement cost of \$3,450,000. The company has a fire insurance policy with a face value of \$3,400,000. The policy has an 80% coinsurance feature. If the firm has a fire loss of \$233,500, find the part of the loss paid by the insurance company.

SOLUTION

$$80\% \text{ of replacement cost} = .80 \times \$3{,}450{,}000 = \$2{,}760{,}000$$

The business has a fire insurance policy with a face value of more than 80% of the value of the store. Therefore, the insurance company pays the entire \$233,500 loss.

QUICK CHECK 3

A plumbing company owns its own building with a replacement cost of \$1,600,000. A fire results in damages of \$445,000. Find the amount the insurance company will pay if the company has \$1,400,000 in insurance coverage.

OBJECTIVE 4 **Understand multiple-carrier insurance.** A business may have fire insurance policies with several companies at the same time. Perhaps additional insurance coverage was purchased over a period of time, as new additions were made to a factory or building complex. Or perhaps the building is so large that one insurance company does not want to take the entire risk by itself, so several companies each agree to take a portion of the insurance coverage and thereby share the risk. In either event, the insurance coverage is divided among **multiple carriers**. When an insurance claim is made against multiple carriers, each insurance company pays its fractional portion of the total claim on the property.

EXAMPLE 4

Understanding Multiple-Carrier Insurance

Youngblood Apartments has an insured loss of \$1,800,000 while having insurance coverage beyond its coinsurance requirement. The insurance is divided among Company A with \$5,900,000 coverage, Company B with \$4,425,000 coverage, and Company C with \$1,475,000 coverage. Find the amount of the loss paid by each of the insurance companies.

SOLUTION

Start by finding the total face value of all three policies.

$$\$5{,}900{,}000 + \$4{,}425{,}000 + \$1{,}475{,}000 = \$11{,}800{,}000 \text{ total face value}$$

$$\text{Company A pays } \frac{\$5{,}900{,}000}{\$11{,}800{,}000} = \frac{1}{2} \text{ of the loss}$$

$$\text{Company B pays } \frac{\$4{,}425{,}000}{\$11{,}800{,}000} = \frac{3}{8} \text{ of the loss}$$

$$\text{Company C pays } \frac{\$1{,}475{,}000}{\$11{,}800{,}000} = \frac{1}{8} \text{ of the loss}$$

Since the insurance loss is \$1,800,000, the amount paid by each of the multiple carriers is

$$\text{Company A } \frac{1}{2} \times \$1{,}800{,}000 = \$900{,}000$$

$$\text{Company B } \frac{3}{8} \times \$1{,}800{,}000 = \$675{,}000$$

$$\text{Company C } \frac{1}{8} \times \$1{,}800{,}000 = \underline{\$225{,}000}$$

$$\text{Total loss} = \$1{,}800{,}000$$

QUICK CHECK 4

A fully insured bank has \$780,000 in fire damage. The coverage is divided between Company A (\$1,200,000) and Company B (\$800,000). Find the amount of the loss paid by each company.

Quick Check Answers

3. \$445,000

4. Company A—\$468,000; Company B—\$312,000

12.3 EXERCISES

The QUICK START *exercises in each section contain solutions to help you get started.*

Find the total annual premium for each of the following. Use the table on page 548. (See Example 1.)

QUICK START

	Territorial Rating	Building Classification	Building Value	Contents Value	Total Annual Premium
1.	2	B	$280,000	$80,000	$1700
2.	5	A	$220,500	$105,000	$1976.10
3.	1	C	$285,000	$152,000	_____
4.	2	B	$272,500	$111,500	_____
5.	5	B	$782,600	$212,000	_____
6.	3	A	$596,400	$206,700	_____

Find the amount to be paid by the insurance company in the following problems. Assume that each policy includes an 80% coinsurance clause. (See Examples 2 and 3.)

QUICK START

	Replacement Cost of Building	Face Value of Policy	Amount of Loss	Amount Paid
7.	$1,450,000	$850,000	$96,000	$70,344.83

$1,450,000 \times .8 = \$1,160,000\ (80\%);\ \frac{\$850,000}{\$1,160,000} \times \$96,000 = \$70,344.83$

8.	$187,400	$140,000	$10,850	$10,132.07

$187,400 \times .8 = \$149,920\ (80\%);\ \frac{\$140,000}{\$149,920} \times \$10,850 = \$10,132.07$

9.	$287,000	$232,500	$19,850	_____
10.	$780,000	$585,000	$10,400	_____
11.	$218,500	$195,000	$36,500	_____
12.	$750,000	$500,000	$56,000	_____

V indicates an exercise that is related to the Case in Point feature.

If the coinsurance requirement is not met, first find the total amount of the loss paid by the insurers. Then find the amount paid by each, as shown in Example 5.

EXAMPLE 5

Understanding Partial Coverage and Multiple Carriers

The fire damage to a small shopping center with a replacement cost of $4,800,000 was limited to $140,000 thanks to an advanced sprinkler system. The insurance coverage is divided between Company A ($2,000,000) and Company B ($1,200,000). Find the amount of the loss paid by each, assuming management had full coverage.

SOLUTION

80% of $4,800,000 = $3,840,000

Total insurance coverage = $2,000,000 + $1,200,000 = $3,200,000

Since the total insurance coverage is less than 80% of the replacement cost of the building, the insurance companies will pay only a portion of the total damages.

Amount paid by insurance: $140,000 \times \frac{\$3,200,000}{\$3,840,000} = \$116,666.67$

Paid by Company A: $\frac{\$2,000,000}{\$3,200,000} \times \$116,666.67 = \$72,916.67$

Paid by Company B: $\frac{\$1,200,000}{\$3,200,000} \times \$116,666.67 = \$43,750$

QUICK CHECK 5

An office building with a replacement cost of $800,000 has fire damage of $100,000. The insurance coverage is divided between Company 1 ($300,000) and Company 2 ($200,000). First **(a)** find the amount covered by insurance, then **(b)** find the amount paid by each company.

The amount of money paid for insurance premiums by businesses is often small compared with other business expenses. Likewise, the average household pays only a small portion of its budget for insurance premiums. The following chart shows the percent of total household spending going to pay for insurance coverage.

Numbers in the News

Small Price to Pay

Homeowner's insurance accounts for less than 1% of household spending and is carried by 95% of homeowners.

Percent of Household Budget

Housing 31%
Health care 3%
Entertainment 4.9%
Clothing 5.2%
Homeowner's 0.7%
Life 1.2%
Auto 2.2%
Transportation 16.9%
Health 2.6%
All Insurance 6.7%
Food 13.9%
Other 10.3%
Retirement 8.1%

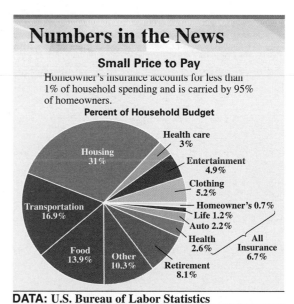

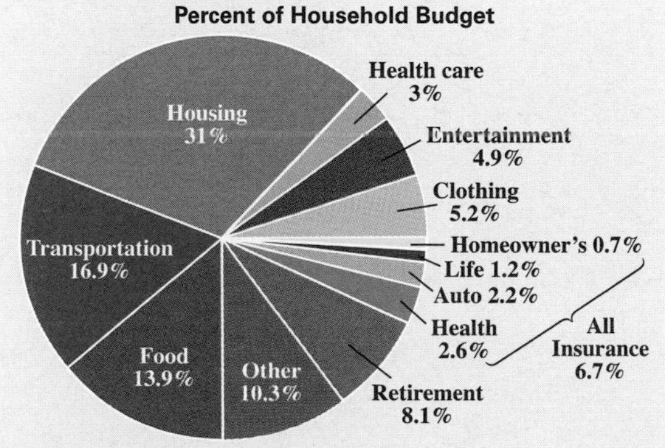

DATA: U.S. Bureau of Labor Statistics

Quick Check Answers

5. (a) $78,125
 (b) Company 1—$46,875
 Company 2—$31,250

OBJECTIVE 5 List additional types of insurance coverage. There are many other types of insurance coverages available as you can see.

QUICK TIP A renter without insurance on contents will not be paid for damages to contents in the event of a fire.

Disability: pays monthly payments in the event of disability
Homeowner: protects a homeowner against fire and theft, but can also cover losses on stolen credit cards and medical costs for guests
Liability: pays in the event of an injury to someone or to property
Long-term care: pays the long-term costs of a nursing home
Medical: pays for medical expenses
Renter: protects a renter against loss of personal property
Worker's compensation: pays employees for injuries while on the job

Liability/Auto

Commercial

Homeowners

Find the amount paid by each insurance company in the following problems involving multiple carriers. Assume that the coinsurance requirement is met. (See Example 4.)

QUICK START

	Insurance Loss	*Companies*	*Coverage*	*Amount Paid*
13.	$80,000	Company 1	$750,000	$60,000
		Company 2	$250,000	$20,000

$\frac{750{,}000}{1{,}000{,}000} \times \$80{,}000 = \$60{,}000$; $\frac{250{,}000}{1{,}000{,}000} \times \$80{,}000 = \$20{,}000$

	Insurance Loss	*Companies*	*Coverage*	*Amount Paid*
14.	$360,000	Company A	$1,200,000	________
		Company B	$800,000	________
15.	$650,000	Company 1	$1,350,000	________
		Company 2	$1,200,000	________
		Company 3	$450,000	________
16.	$1,600,000	Company A	$4,800,000	________
		Company B	$800,000	________
		Company C	$2,400,000	________

Find the annual fire insurance premium in each of the following application problems. Use the table on page 548.

QUICK START

17. FURNITURE STORE FIRE INSURANCE Billings Furniture owns a building with a replacement cost of $1,400,000 and with contents of $360,000. The building is class C with a territorial rating of 5. **17.** $18,804

$14{,}000 \times 1.05 = \$14{,}700$; $3600 \times \$1.14 = \$4104$
$\$14{,}700 + \$4104 = \$18{,}804$

18. FIRE INSURANCE PREMIUM Martha Spencer, owner of The Doll House, owns a class-B building with a replacement cost of $165,400. Contents are valued at $128,000. The territorial rating is 3. **18.** ________

19. INDUSTRIAL FIRE INSURANCE Valley Crop Dusting owns a class-B building with a replacement cost of $107,500. Contents are worth $39,800. The territorial rating is 2. **19.** ________

20. INDUSTRIAL BUILDING INSURANCE London's Dredging Equipment is in a class-C building with a territorial rating of 4. The building has a replacement cost of $305,000 and the contents are worth $682,000. **20.** ________

21. Describe three factors that determine the premium charged for fire insurance. (See Objective 2.)

22. Explain the coinsurance clause and describe how coinsurance works. (See Objective 3.)

In the following application problems, find the amount of the loss paid by (a) the insurance company and (b) the insured. Assume an 80% coinsurance clause.

QUICK START

23. FIRE LOSS The Doll House is located in a building with a replacement cost of $328,500, but Martha Spencer insured it for only $200,000 in order to save money on insurance premiums. An electrical short causes a fire that results in $180,000 in damage.

(a) $\$328{,}500 \times .8 = \$262{,}800;\ \frac{\$200{,}000}{\$262{,}800} \times \$180{,}000 = \$136{,}986.30$
(b) $\$180{,}000 - \$136{,}986.30 = \$43{,}013.70$

(a) $136,986.30
(b) $43,013.70

24. GIFT-SHOP FIRE LOSS Indonesian Wonder gift shop has a replacement cost of $395,000. The shop is insured for $280,000. Fire loss is $22,500.

(a) ______
(b) ______

25. SALVATION ARMY LOSS The main office of the Salvation Army suffers a loss from fire of $45,000. The building has a replacement cost of $550,000 and is insured for $300,000.

(a) ______
(b) ______

26. APARTMENT FIRE LOSS Kathy Stephenson owns a duplex with a replacement cost of $185,000 and insured for $111,000. Fire loss is $28,000.

(a) ______
(b) ______

In the following application problems, find the amount paid by each of the multiple carriers. Assume that the coinsurance requirement has been met.

QUICK START

27. COINSURED FIRE LOSS C. Wood Plumbing had an insured fire loss of $548,000. It has insurance coverage as follows: Company A, $600,000; Company B, $400,000; and Company C, $200,000.

A: $\frac{600{,}000}{1{,}200{,}000} \times \$548{,}000 = \$274{,}000$
B: $\frac{400{,}000}{1{,}200{,}000} \times \$548{,}000 = \$182{,}666.67$
C: $\frac{200{,}000}{1{,}200{,}000} \times \$548{,}000 = \$91{,}333.33$

A: $274,000
B: $182,666.67
C: $91,333.33

28. COINSURED FIRE LOSS The Cycle Centre had an insured fire loss of $68,500. It has insurance as follows: Company 1, $60,000; Company 2, $40,000; and Company 3, $30,000.

1: ______
2: ______
3: ______

QUICK TIP Claims following a car accident can be quite large. For example, imagine the loss of income of a surgeon who was disabled for life in a car accident.

QUICK TIP Drivers who have several speeding tickets or have been involved in accidents often have much higher premiums. This is especially true if the driver is young.

OBJECTIVE 2 Define liability insurance. **Liability** or **bodily injury insurance** protects the insured in case he or she injures someone with a car. Many states have minimum amounts of liability insurance coverage set by law. The amount of liability insurance is expressed as a fraction, such as 15/30. The fraction 15/30 means that the insurance company will pay up to $15,000 for injury to one person, and a total of $30,000 for injury to two or more persons in the same accident.

The following table shows typical premium rates for various amounts of liability coverage. Included in the cost of the liability insurance is **medical insurance** for the driver and passengers in case of injury. For example, the table column 15/30 shows that the insured can also receive reimbursement for up to $1000 of his or her own medical expenses in an accident. Insurance companies divide the nation into territories based on past claims in all areas. Four territories are shown here. All tables in this section show annual premiums.

Liability (Bodily Injury) and Medical Insurance (Per Year)

	Liability and Medical Expense Limits				
Territory	15/30 $1000	25/50 $2000	50/100 $3000	100/300 $5000	250/500 $10,000
1	$207	$222	$253	$282	$308
2	269	302	341	378	392
3	310	314	375	398	459
4	216	218	253	284	310

EXAMPLE 1 Finding the Liability and Medical Premium

Martha Spencer, owner of The Doll House, is in territory 2 and wants 100/300 liability coverage. Find the amount of the premium for this coverage and the amount of medical coverage included.

SOLUTION

Look up territory 2 and 100/300 coverage in the liability and medical insurance table to find an annual premium of $378. This cost includes $5000 medical coverage.

QUICK CHECK 1

Find the annual cost, for a person living in territory 4, for 250/500 liability coverage with $10,000 in medical insurance.

QUICK TIP In some states, drivers can get a discount on their insurance if they have a good driving record, an antitheft system, good grades, or even if they take a defensive driving class. Contact your insurance agent to see if you are eligible for any discounts.

OBJECTIVE 3 Define property damage insurance. Liability coverage pays if you injure someone. **Property damage coverage** pays if you damage someone else's property such as an automobile or a building. The following table shows the annual cost for various **policy limits** on property damage. You are responsible for damages above the policy limit.

Property Damage Insurance (Per Year)

	Property Damage Limits			
Territory	$10,000	$25,000	$50,000	$100,000
1	$88	$93	$97	$103
2	168	192	223	251
3	129	134	145	158
4	86	101	112	124

Quick Check Answer

1. $310

EXAMPLE 2

Finding the Premium for Property Damage

Find the premium if Martha Spencer, in territory 2, wants property damage coverage of $50,000.

SOLUTION

Property damage coverage of $50,000 in territory 2 requires a premium of $223.

QUICK CHECK 2

Find the premium for $50,000 in property damage coverage for a person living in territory 3.

OBJECTIVE 4 Describe comprehensive and collision insurance. **Comprehensive insurance** pays for damages to the insured's vehicle caused by a fire, by theft of the automobile, by vandalism (e.g., someone purposefully scratches off paint), by a tree falling onto the automobile, and by other similar events. In general, comprehensive insurance pays for damages that are not covered by collision insurance.

Collision coverage pays for repairs to the insured's vehicle when it is involved in a collision with another object. For example, collision insurance would pay for damages to your automobile should you lose control during an ice storm and run into a tree. Common collision insurance and **deductibles** are $100, $250, $500, and $1000. You pay the deductible, and then the collision coverage pays for damages to the vehicle as shown below. The higher the deductible, the lower the insurance premium, but of course you are responsible for the deductible in the event of an accident. Suppose your deductible is $500 but the damage to your automobile is $3280. The amount paid by the insurance company is found as follows.

Damages to your automobile	$3280
Deductible must be paid by you	– $500
Insurance company pays	$2780

QUICK TIP States require liability insurance but not comprehensive or collision. Lenders require comprehensive and collision coverages. If your car is paid for, it is your choice whether or not to purchase comprehensive and collision coverages. It may or may not be worthwhile on older vehicles.

The following table shows some typical rates for comprehensive and collision insurance. Rates are determined not only by territories but also by age group and symbol. Here, age group refers to the age of the *vehicle*, not the driver. Age group 1 is a vehicle that is less than 2 years of age. Age group 2 is a vehicle that is at least 2, but less than 3, years of age. Age group 6 is a vehicle 6 years of age or older. Symbol is determined by the *cost* of the vehicle.

Comprehensive and Collision Insurance (Per Year)

		Comprehensive			Collision ($500 Deductible)		
		Symbol			Symbol		
Territory	**Age Group**	**6**	**7**	**8**	**6**	**7**	**8**
1	1	$58	$64	$90	$153	$165	$184
	2, 3	50	56	82	135	147	171
	4, 5	44	52	76	116	128	147
	6	34	44	64	92	110	128
2	1	$26	$28	$40	$89	$95	$104
	2, 3	22	24	36	80	86	98
	4, 5	20	24	34	71	77	86
	6	16	20	28	60	68	77
3	1	$70	$78	$108	$145	$157	$174
	2, 3	60	66	90	128	139	162
	4, 5	52	64	92	111	122	139
	6	20	22	32	66	74	81
4	1	$42	$46	$66	$97	$104	$124
	2, 3	36	40	58	87	94	107
	4, 5	32	38	54	77	84	94
	6	26	32	46	64	74	84

QUICK TIP Higher deductibles result in lower premiums. However, higher deductibles also mean that the insured may have to pay more in the event of an accident.

Quick Check Answer

2. $145

EXAMPLE 3

Finding the Comprehensive and Collision Premiums

Martha Spencer, owner of The Doll House, is in territory 2 and has a 2-year-old minivan that has a symbol of 8. Use the comprehensive and collision insurance table to find the cost for **(a)** comprehensive coverage and **(b)** collision coverage.

SOLUTION

(a) The cost of comprehensive coverage is $36.
(b) The cost of collision coverage is $98.

QUICK CHECK 3

Find the premium for **(a)** comprehensive and **(b)** collision coverage for a 3-year-old vehicle in territory 4 and symbol 8.

OBJECTIVE 5 **Define no-fault and uninsured motorist insurance.** Some states have **no-fault** laws. Under no-fault insurance, all medical expenses and costs associated with an accident are paid to each individual by *his or her own insurance company*, no matter who is at fault. Legislators and insurance companies argue that no-fault insurance removes lawyers, courts, and juries from the process and results in quicker, less costly settlements. Others (including trial lawyers) argue that no-fault insurance leaves accident victims unable to recover all of their damages.

Uninsured Motorist Insurance (Per Year)

Territory	Basic Limit
1	$66
2	$44
3	$76
4	$70

Most states do not have no-fault laws, thereby requiring the insurance company of the person at fault to pay for damages. A potential problem in these states is that the motorist who caused an accident either has no insurance at all or has too little insurance for the damages that occurred. **Uninsured motorist insurance** protects a vehicle owner from financial liability when hit by a driver with no insurance. **Underinsured motorist insurance** provides protection to a vehicle owner when hit by a driver who has *too little* insurance. Typical costs for uninsured motorist insurance are shown in the table at the left.

EXAMPLE 4

Determining the Premium for Uninsured Motorist Coverage

Martha Spencer, in territory 2, wants uninsured motorist coverage. Find the premium in the uninsured motorist insurance table.

SOLUTION

The premium for uninsured motorist coverage in territory 2 is $44.

QUICK CHECK 4

Find the annual cost of uninsured motorist coverage in territory 1.

OBJECTIVE 6 **Apply youthful-operator factors.** Sometimes young people think they are being charged *far too much* for automobile insurance. Insurance companies base their rates on probabilities calculated from statistical data. The graph on the next page shows that drivers under 25 are more likely to be involved in a fatal automobile accident than drivers 25 or older. Therefore, insurance companies charge higher rates for **youthful** compared to **adult** drivers. The age at which a youth becomes an adult varies from company to company. Generally, drivers under 25 are considered youthful drivers, and drivers 25 or older are considered adults.

Quick Check Answers

3. (a) $58 **(b)** $107
4. $66

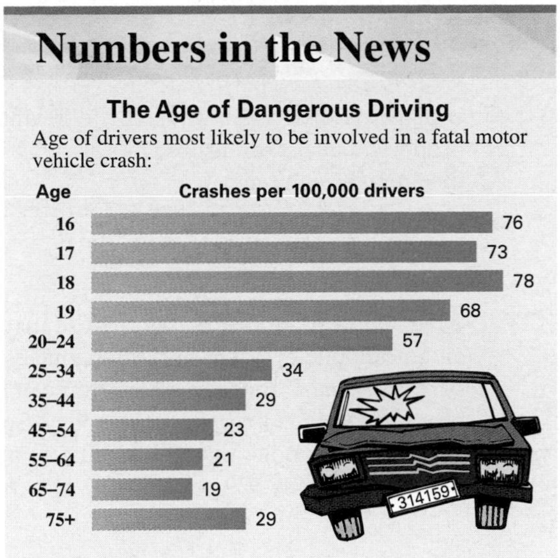

DATA: National Safety Council

The following table shows typical youthful-operator factors based on age and on whether or not the operator has taken driver's training. You can see that the factors are much higher for youthful operators who have not taken driver's training. The steps to apply these factors follow.

1. Determine the total premium for **all coverages** desired.
2. Multiply the total premium by the youthful-operator factor from the table.

Youthful-Operator Factor

Age	With Driver's Training	Without Driver's Training
20 or less	1.55	1.75
21–25	1.15	1.40

EXAMPLE 5

Using the Youthful-Operator Factor

Janet Ito lives in territory 4, is 22 years old, has had driver's training, has never received a ticket or been involved in an accident, and drives a 5-year-old car with a symbol of 7. She wants a 25/50 liability policy, a $10,000 property damage policy, a comprehensive and collision policy, and uninsured motorist coverage. Find her annual insurance premium using the tables in this section.

SOLUTION

1. Determine the total premium for all coverages desired.

25/50 liability insurance	$218
$10,000 property damage	86
Comprehensive insurance	38
Collision	84
Uninsured motorist	+ 70
Subtotal	$496

2. Multiply the premium by the youthful-operator factor from the table.

$$\$496 \times \mathbf{1.15} = \$570.40$$

The calculator solution to this example uses parentheses and chain calculations.

(218 + 86 + 38 + 84 + 70) × 1.15 = 570.4

QUICK CHECK 5

Scott Burch is 20, lives in territory 3, has not had driver's training, and drives a 3-year-old car with a symbol of 6. He wants the following coverages: 100/300 liability, $5000 medical, $50,000 property damage, uninsured motorist, and both comprehensive and collision insurance. Find the annual premium.

QUICK TIP Remember, the limits on the insurance policy are the maximum that the insurance company will pay.

OBJECTIVE 7 Find the amounts paid by the insurance company and the insured. If you are at fault in an automobile accident and the damages *exceed the limits* on your insurance policy, you *may be personally liable* for the excess. You can help avoid this situation if you increase the liability and property damage limits on your policy. Sometimes, it does not cost much to increase your liability limits. For example, the additional cost of increasing liability coverage in territory 1 from 50/100 to 100/300 is only $29 per year ($282 − $253).

EXAMPLE 6 Finding the Amounts Paid by the Insurance Company and the Insured

Eric Liwanag has 25/50 liability limits, $25,000 property damage limits, and $500 deductible collision insurance. While on vacation, he was at fault in an accident that caused $5800 damage to his car, $3380 in damage to another car, and severe injuries to the other driver and his passenger. A subsequent lawsuit for injuries resulted in a judgment of $45,000 and $35,000, respectively, to the other parties. Find the amounts that the insurance company will pay for **(a)** repairing Liwanag's car, **(b)** repairing the other car, and **(c)** paying the court judgment resulting from the lawsuit. **(d)** How much will Liwanag have to pay the injured parties?

SOLUTION

(a) The insurance company will pay $5300 (**$5800 − $500 deductible**) to repair Liwanag's car.

(b) Repairs on the other car will be paid to the property damage limits ($25,000). Here, the total repairs of $3380 are paid.

(c) Since more than one person was injured, the insurance company pays the limit of $50,000 ($25,000 to each of the two injured parties).

(d) Liwanag is liable for $30,000 (**$80,000 − $50,000**), the amount awarded over the insurance limits.

QUICK CHECK 6

Janet Yahn has the following coverages: 50/100 liability, $3000 medical, $25,000 property damage, and $500 deductible collision. She runs through a stop sign and hits a van with a value of $12,200. The van is destroyed and the cost to repair Yahn's car is $8600. The driver of the van had medical costs of $68,000 and Yahn had medical costs of $2800. Find each cost Yahn must pay.

Quick Check Answers

5. $1412.25

6. $500 to repair her own car; $18,000 for medical expenses of other driver

12.4 EXERCISES

FOR EXTRA HELP

MyMathLab

MathXL PRACTICE

WATCH

DOWNLOAD

READ

REVIEW

The QUICK START *exercises in each section contain solutions to help you get started.*

Find the annual premium for the following. (See Examples 1–5.)

QUICK START

	Name	Territory	Age	Driver Training?	Liability	Property Damage	Comprehensive Collision Age Group	Symbol	Uninsured Motorist?	Annual Premium
1.	Smyth	3	42	No	50/100	\$25,000	2	7	Yes	\$790
	\$375 + \$134 + \$66 + \$139 + \$76 = \$790									
2.	Morrissey	1	20	Yes	25/50	\$25,000	4	7	No	\$767.25
	\$222 + \$93 + \$52 + \$128 + \$0 = \$495 × 1.55 = \$767.25									
3.	Shraim	3	52	No	250/500	\$50,000	2	8	Yes	______
4.	Waldron	2	67	No	50/100	\$100,000	1	6	Yes	______

5. Describe four factors that determine the premium on an automobile insurance policy. (See Objective 1.)

6. Explain in your own words the difference between liability (bodily injury) and property damage. (See Objectives 2 and 3.)

Solve the following application problems.

QUICK START

7. ADULT AUTO INSURANCE Bill Poole is 47 years old, lives in territory 4, and drives a 2-year-old car with a symbol of 7. He wants 250/500 liability limits, \$100,000 property damage limits, comprehensive and collision insurance, and uninsured motorist coverage. Find his annual insurance premium.

\$310 + \$124 + \$40 + \$94 + \$70 = \$638

7. \$638

C indicates an exercise that is related to the Case in Point feature.

8. ADULT AUTO INSURANCE Martha Spencer, owner of The Doll House, is thinking about moving from a house in territory 2 to a house in territory 3 and wants to know the effect on the insurance costs for her new car. She currently lives in territory 2 and the car has symbol 7. Her coverages are 250/500 for liability, $100,000 for property damage, comprehensive, collision, and uninsured motorist. She is 53 years old. Find the change in annual cost.

8. ________________

9. YOUTHFUL-OPERATOR AUTO INSURANCE Brandy Barrett is 23 years old, took a driver's education course, lives in territory 1, and drives a 4-year-old vehicle with a symbol of 6. She wants 50/100 liability limits, $25,000 property damage limits, comprehensive and collision insurance, and uninsured motorist coverage. Find her annual insurance premium.

9. ________________

10. YOUTHFUL OPERATOR—NO DRIVER'S TRAINING Karen Roberts' father gave her a new Honda Accord to use at college under the condition she pay her own insurance. She is 17, has not had driver's training, lives in territory 1, and her vehicle has a symbol of 6. She wants 50/100 liability limits, $25,000 property damage limits, comprehensive and collision insurance, and uninsured motorist coverage. Find her annual insurance premium.

10. ________________

11. BODILY INJURY INSURANCE Suppose your bodily injury policy has limits of 25/50 and you injure a person on a bicycle. The judge awards damages of $36,500 to the cyclist. **(a)** How much will the company pay? **(b)** How much will you pay?

(a) ________________
(b) ________________

12. BODILY INJURY INSURANCE Three years ago Martha Spencer, owner of The Doll House, lost control of her car while trying to find her cell phone and forced another driver off the road. The court awarded $28,000 to the driver of the other car and $8000 to a passenger of the other car. Spencer had limits of 15/30. **(a)** Find the amount the insurance company paid. **(b)** Find the amount Spencer had to pay.

(a) ________________
(b) ________________

13. MEDICAL EXPENSES AND PROPERTY DAMAGE Wes Hanover accidentally backed into a parked car. He caused $4300 in damage to the car, and Hanover's passenger needed stitches in her forehead, which cost $850. Hanover had 15/30 liability limits, $1000 medical expense, and property damage of $10,000. Find the amount paid by the insurance company for **(a)** damages to the automobile and **(b)** medical expenses.

(a) ________________
(b) ________________

14. MEDICAL EXPENSES AND PROPERTY DAMAGE Jessica Wallace backed into a new Mercedes and caused $12,800 in damage to the car. She also injured the vertebrae in her neck, requiring surgery costing $48,200. She had 50/100 liability limits, $10,000 in property damage, and $3000 in medical expense coverage. Find the amount paid by the insurance company for **(a)** damages to the automobile and **(b)** medical expenses.

(a) ________________
(b) ________________

15. INSURANCE COMPANY PAYMENT A reckless driver caused Sandy Silva to collide with a car in another lane. Silva had 50/100 liability limits, $25,000 property damage limits, and collision coverage with a $100 deductible. Silva's car had damage of $1878, while the other car suffered $6936 in damages. The resulting lawsuit gave injury awards of $60,000 and $55,000, respectively, in damages for personal injury to the two people in the other car. Find the amount that the insurance company will pay for **(a)** repairing Silva's car, **(b)** repairing the other car, and **(c)** personal injury damages. **(d)** How much must Silva pay beyond her insurance coverage, including the collision deductible?

(a) ________
(b) ________
(c) ________
(d) ________

16. INSURANCE PAYMENT Bob Armstrong lost control of his car and crashed into another car. He had 15/30 liability limits, $10,000 property damage limits, and collision coverage with a $100 deductible. Damage to Armstrong's car was $2980; the other car, with a value of $22,800, was totaled. The results of a lawsuit awarded $75,000 and $45,000, respectively, in damages for personal injury to the two people in the other car. Find the amount that the insurance company will pay for **(a)** repairing Armstrong's car, **(b)** repairing the other car, and **(c)** personal injury damages. **(d)** How much must Armstrong pay beyond his insurance coverage?

(a) ________
(b) ________
(c) ________
(d) ________

17. Explain why insurance companies charge a higher premium for auto insurance sold to a youthful operator. Do you think that this higher premium is a good idea or not? (See Objective 6.)

18. Property damage pays for damage caused by you to the property of others. Since the average cost of a new car today is over $20,000, what amount of property damage coverage would you recommend to a friend who owns her own business?

12.5 LIFE INSURANCE

OBJECTIVES

1. Understand life insurance that does not accumulate cash value (term and decreasing term).
2. Understand life insurance that accumulates cash value (whole life, universal life, variable life, limited payment, and endowment).
3. Find the annual premium for life insurance.
4. Use premium factors with different modes of premium payment.

CASE in POINT Martha Spencer owns and manages The Doll House and makes a living for herself and her two children. Recently divorced, Spencer worries about what would happen to her children if she became disabled or died. For this reason, she carries disability insurance in addition to $200,000 in life insurance on herself. She also has medical insurance on the entire family.

There is no doubt about it: Insurance is expensive! Yet, most of us need insurance (car, home, medical, disability, and life insurance). The graph on the left below shows that about one-fifth of adults have found themselves in a situation where they wished they had more insurance. The figure on the right illustrates that many adults are insured through either their employer or their spouse's employer.

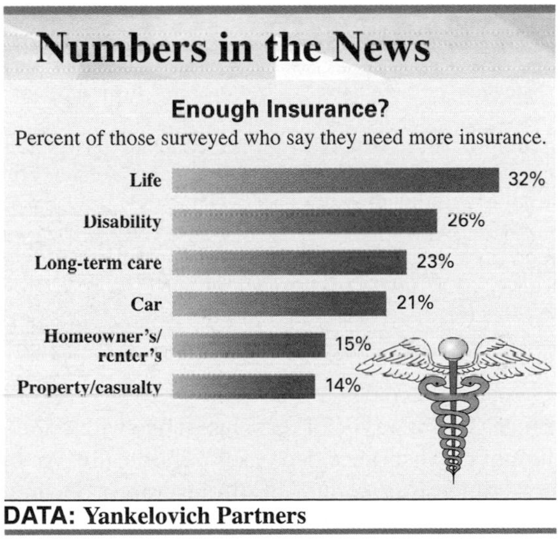

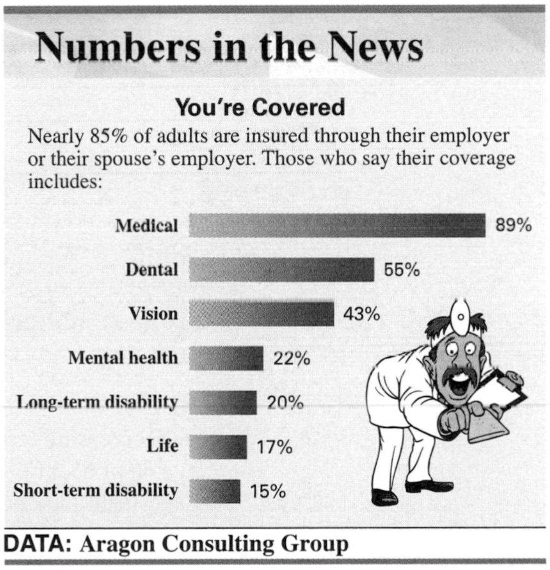

People buy **life insurance** to pay for their own burial expenses, to pay off a home mortgage or a car loan, to provide for a spouse and/or children, or to pay for their children's future college expenses. Some forms of life insurance build up a cash retirement value; other forms do not. Life insurance can also be important for the owner(s) of a business. Upon the death of the business owner, life insurance proceeds can provide a company with enough money to continue until it can be sold. Alternatively, life insurance proceeds can be used by one partner of a firm to buy out the ownership interest of a deceased partner.

QUICK TIP Proceeds from a life insurance policy are generally free of income taxes.

OBJECTIVE 1 Understand life insurance that does not accumulate cash value (term and decreasing term). Term insurance. Term insurance is the least expensive type of life insurance. It provides the most insurance per dollar spent, but it does not build up any cash values for retirement. This type of insurance coverage is usually renewable until some age, such as 70, when the insured is no longer allowed to renew it. As a result, most people discontinue term insurance before they die. However, term insurance is an excellent way to provide funds in the event of death.

The premium on some term policies increases each year as the insured ages. Premiums on this type of policy become very expensive by the time a person is 60 years of age or so. As a result, many people prefer **level premium** term policies. Initially, these policies require a higher premium than policies with annually increasing premiums. However, the premium on a level premium policy is constant for a period of time such as 10 years or 20 years. Thereafter, the premiums increase significantly. The graph shows that 20-year level term insurance costs have decreased significantly since 1991. The clipping below shows one reason why: We are living longer.

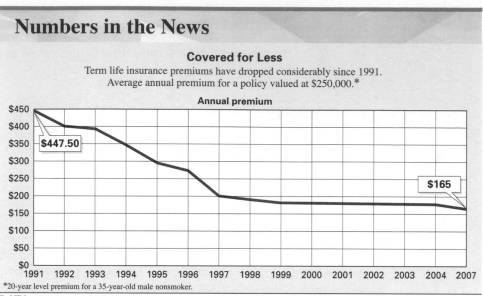

Numbers in the News

Covered for Less

Term life insurance premiums have dropped considerably since 1991.
Average annual premium for a policy valued at $250,000.*

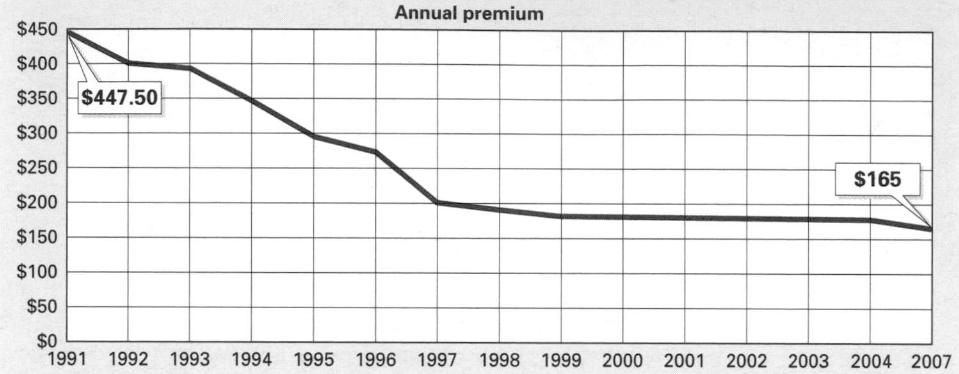

*20-year level premium for a 35-year-old male nonsmoker.

DATA: Insurance information based on analysis of more than 600 companies

HERE & NOW

Insuring longer lives

We're living longer these days.

The evidence goes beyond the big jump in centenarians. (There are 50,000 centenarians nationally, and the numbers are expected to double each decade.)

The evidence now extends to insurance companies such as USAA Life Insurance of San Antonio, Texas.

The company has established lower premiums for its term life insurance products in 39 states, including California.

The new rates incorporate a decrease of 10 to 30 percent, on average.

Decreasing term insurance. This is a type of term insurance with fixed premiums commonly to age 60 or 65, but the amount of life insurance decreases periodically. An example of this is a mortgage insurance policy on a home. The amount of life insurance on the owner decreases as the amount owed to the mortgage company decreases. Many large companies provide decreasing term insurance to employees as a benefit. The table provides an example of the benefits of one particular decreasing term policy.

Death Benefits for a Decreasing Term Policy with a Premium of $11 per Month

Age	Amount of Life Insurance
Under 29	$40,000
30–34	$35,000
35–39	$30,000
40–44	$25,000
45–49	$18,000
50–54	$11,000
55–59	$7,000
60–66	$4,000
67 and over	$0

QUICK TIP Mortgage insurance is sometimes much more expensive than a regular term insurance policy. Compare prices before you buy.

Nation's Top Killers

The 10 leading causes of death in the United States, ranked according to the number of lives lost:

1. Heart disease
2. Cancer
3. Stroke
4. Lung disease
5. Accidents
6. Diabetes
7. Alzheimer's disease
8. Influenza and pneumonia
9. Kidney disease
10. Bacterial infections

Source: National Center for Health Statistics

The list on the left gives the nation's leading causes of death, and the graph on the right shows the increase in life expectancy in the United States.

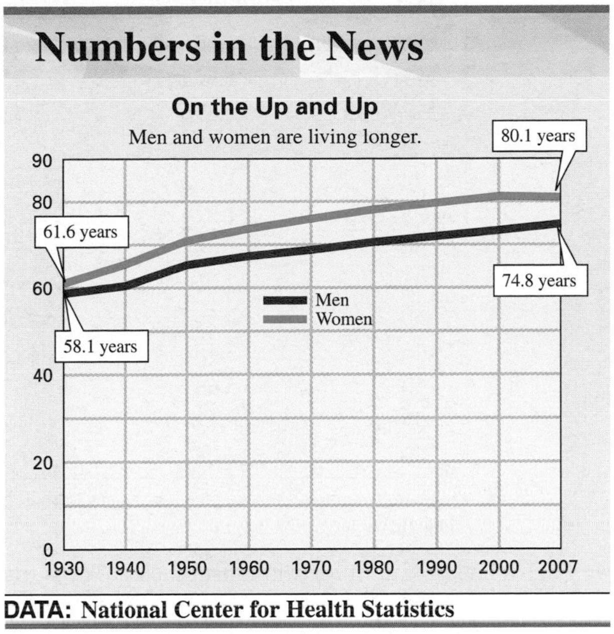

OBJECTIVE 2 **Understand life insurance that accumulates cash value (whole life, universal life, variable life, limited payment, and endowment).**

QUICK TIP Scientists believe that diabetes will be much more common in North America during the coming decades. Therefore, this cause of death may eventually be ranked higher than the 6th leading cause of death.

Whole life (also called **straight life, ordinary life**, or **permanent**). This type of insurance provides a death benefit and a savings plan. The insured commonly pays a constant premium until death or retirement, whichever occurs first. If the policy is in force at the time of death, a death benefit is paid. Alternatively, the insured may choose to convert the accumulated **cash value** to a retirement benefit after paying the premium for many years.

Universal life. This type of insurance provides the life insurance protection of term insurance plus a tax-deferred way to accumulate assets. It sometimes allows people to establish a permanent policy at a lower premium than they would have to pay under a whole life policy, and it gives the insured more flexibility. For example, universal life can help a family obtain more insurance when young children are at home and then help accumulate savings later after the children are grown. The portion of the premium going into retirement benefits receives money market interest rates and often has a guaranteed minimum rate of return regardless of what happens to market rates.

QUICK TIP Variable life policies accounted for only 7% of all life insurance policies sold in 1990 but have since grown to over 55% of all life insurance policies sold.

Variable life. This type of insurance allows the policyholder to make choices among a number of different investment options. It places the investment risk on the shoulders of the policyholder by allowing the insured to invest in any of the following: money market funds, bond funds, stock funds, or a combination of the three.

Limited-payment life insurance. Limited-payment life is similar to whole life insurance, except that premiums are paid for only a fixed number of years, such as 20. This type of insurance is thus often called 20-pay life, representing payments for 20 years. The premium for limited-payment life is higher than that for whole life policies. Limited-payment life is most appropriate for athletes, actors, and others whose income is likely to be high for several years and then decline.

Endowment policies are the most expensive type of policy. These policies guarantee payment of a fixed amount of money to a given individual, whether or not the insured lives. Endowment policies might be taken out by parents to guarantee a sum of money for their children's college education. Because of the high premiums, this is one of the least popular types of policies today.

OBJECTIVE 3 **Find the annual premium for life insurance.** Calculation of life insurance rates by **actuaries** is based on statistical data involving death rates, interest rates, and other factors. Women tend to live a few years longer than men, so a woman pays a lower life insurance premium than a man of the same age. Incidentally, women are more likely to be disabled than men and therefore have higher disability insurance rates than men. Use the actual age of a man to find the premium factor in the table on the next page. However, subtract 5 from the age of a woman before finding the premium factor in the table.

QUICK TIP Individuals with health problems must pay substantially more for life insurance than healthy individuals. Other factors that increase life insurance premiums include smoking and even some hobbies such as scuba diving or bungee jumping.

Annual Premium Rates* Per $1000 of Life Insurance

Age	10-Year Level Premium Term	Whole Life	Universal Life	20-Pay Life
20	1.60	4.07	3.48	12.30
21	1.65	4.26	3.85	12.95
22	1.69	4.37	4.10	13.72
23	1.73	4.45	4.56	14.28
24	1.78	4.68	4.80	15.95
25	1.82	5.06	5.11	16.60
30	1.89	5.66	6.08	18.78
35	2.01	7.68	7.45	21.60
40	2.56	12.67	10.62	24.26
45	3.45	19.86	15.24	28.16
50	5.63	26.23	21.46	32.59
55	8.12	31.75	28.38	38.63
60	14.08	38.42	36.72	45.74

*For women, subtract 5 years from the actual age. For example, rates for a 30-year-old woman are shown for age 25 in the table.

QUICK TIP Life insurance rates differ significantly from one company to the next. As always, compare before you buy, but be sure to ask agents for proof that the quotes are from financially sound companies.

The premium for a life insurance policy is found with the following formula.

$$\text{Annual premium} = \text{Number of thousands} \times \text{Rate per } \$1000$$

EXAMPLE 1 Finding the Life Insurance Premium

Martha Spencer became the primary source of income for her family at age 35 after her divorce. At that time, she decided that she needed $200,000 in life insurance to pay off the mortgage on her home, to repay some loans at her business, and to provide for her children. Find her annual premium for **(a)** a 10-year level premium term policy, **(b)** a whole life policy, **(c)** a universal life policy, and **(d)** a 20-pay life plan.

QUICK TIP Use the actual age of a man when using the table of premiums. However, subtract 5 from the age of a woman before using the table.

SOLUTION

First, divide the desired amount of life insurance by $1000 to find the number of thousands.

$$\$200{,}000 \div \$1000 = 200 \text{ thousands}$$

Since Spencer is a woman, subtract 5 from her actual age before using the table $(35 - 5 = 30)$. Look in the table at age 30 for the rates for each type of insurance.

(a) 10-year level premium term $200 \times 1.89 = \$378$
(b) Whole life $200 \times 5.66 = \$1132$
(c) Universal life $200 \times 6.08 = \$1216$
(d) 20-pay life $200 \times 18.78 = \$3756$

Spencer wanted to buy universal life because of the savings feature, which would help her save for retirement. However, she purchased the level premium term instead, since her income was limited.

QUICK CHECK 1

James Liberty is 50 and wants to buy $250,000 in life insurance. Find the annual cost for **(a)** 10-year level premium term, **(b)** whole life, **(c)** universal life, and **(d)** 20-pay life.

OBJECTIVE 4 **Use premium factors with different modes of premium payment.** The annual life insurance premium is not always paid in a single payment. Many companies give the insured the option of paying the premium semiannually, quarterly, or monthly. For this convenience, the policyholder *pays an additional amount* that is determined by a **premium factor**. The following table shows typical premium factors.

Quick Check Answers

1. **(a)** $1407.50 **(b)** $6557.50 **(c)** $5365 **(d)** $8147.50

Premium Factors

Mode of Payment	Premium Factor
Semiannually	.51
Quarterly	.26
Monthly	.0908

EXAMPLE 2

Using a Premium Factor

The annual insurance premium on a $200,000 10-year level premium term life policy for Martha Spencer is $378. Use the premium factors table to find the amount of premium and the total annual cost if she pays **(a)** semiannually, **(b)** quarterly, or **(c)** monthly.

SOLUTION

	Premium	Annual Cost
(a) Semiannually:	$378 × .51 = $192.78	$192.78 × 2 payments/year = $385.56
(b) Quarterly:	$378 × .26 = $98.28	$98.28 × 4 payments/year = $393.12
(c) Monthly:	$378 × .0908 = $34.32 (rounded)	$34.32 × 12 payments/year = $411.84

QUICK CHECK 2

The annual premium on a life insurance policy is $470. Find the premium if payments are made **(a)** semiannually, **(b)** quarterly, and **(c)** monthly.

EXAMPLE 3

Pricing Life Insurance

Shauna Jones has decided to buy $200,000 in life insurance to make sure that her kids will have funds if something happens to her. Jones is 28 and in good health. Find the monthly premium for **(a)** 10-year level premium term and **(b)** universal life.

SOLUTION

(a) 10-year level premium term:

premium factor for monthly payment

$$\text{Monthly premium} = (\$200 \times 1.73) \times .0908 = \$31.42$$

(b) Universal life:

premium factor for monthly payment

$$\text{Monthly premium} = (\$200 \times 4.56) \times .0908 = \$82.81$$

QUICK CHECK 3

Darryl Foster is 40 years old and wants to buy $400,000 of whole life insurance. Find the quarterly premium.

Quick Check Answers

2. (a) $239.70 **(b)** $122.20 **(c)** $42.68

3. $1317.68

Case Studies

Mattel Inc.

www.mattel.com

- 1945: Founded by Elliot and Ruth Handler
- 1959: Barbie doll introduced
- 1968: Established Hot Wheels brand
- 2004: Over one billion Barbie dolls sold since 1959
- 2007: Sales of over $5 billion

Antique dolls representing adults from the 17 and 18 centuries have been found, but they are very rare. Individual craftsmen in England made most of these earliest dolls. The craftsmen carved the dolls of wood, painted their features, and also designed the costumes for the dolls. Some of these earliest dolls are valued at over $40,000.

The Barbie doll is the most popular fashion doll ever created. If all the Barbie dolls that have been sold since 1959 were placed head-to-toe, the dolls would circle the earth more than seven times. The most popular Barbie ever sold was the Totally Hair Barbie, which was introduced in 1992. With hair from the top of her head to her toes, more than 10 million of these dolls were sold, resulting in revenue of $100 million. With annual retail sales at an estimated $3.6 billion, Barbie is the #1 brand of doll for girls.

1. In 2005, Mattel Inc. paid $235,030,000 in income taxes on an operating income of $664,529,000. Find the percent of operating income that went to income taxes, to the nearest tenth of a percent.

2. Assume Mattel Inc. owns a building with a replacement cost of $1,450,000 in an area with an assessment rate of 35% and a tax rate of 9%. Find the property tax on the building.

3. Mattel Inc. does some manufacturing in Mexico. Why do you think they do this?

4. Why do you think Barbie has been so popular?

12.5 EXERCISES

FOR EXTRA HELP

MyMathLab

MathXL PRACTICE

WATCH

DOWNLOAD

READ

REVIEW

The QUICK START *exercises in each section contain solutions to help you get started.*

Find the annual premium, the semiannual premium, the quarterly premium, and the monthly premium for each of the following. (Note: Subtract 5 years for women.) Round to the nearest cent.

QUICK START

	Face Value of Policy	Age of Insured	Sex of Insured	Type of Policy	Annual Premium	Semi-annual Premium	Quarterly Premium	Monthly Premium
1.	$100,000	45	F	Term	$256	$130.56	$66.56	$23.24
	100 × $2.56 = $256; $256 × .51 = $130.56; $256 × .26 = $66.56; $256 × .0908 = $23.24							
2.	$60,000	30	M	Whole life	$339.60	$173.20	$88.30	$30.84
	60 × $5.66 = $339.60; $339.60 × .51 = $173.20; $339.60 × .26 = $88.30; $339.60 × .0908 = $30.84							
3.	$35,000	40	M	20-pay life				
4.	$60,000	50	F	20-pay life				
5.	$85,000	30	M	Universal life				
6.	$150,000	60	M	Term				
7.	$75,000	21	M	Whole life				
8.	$80,000	35	F	Term				
9.	$65,000	60	M	20-pay life				
10.	$50,000	45	F	Universal life				

11. Compare level premium term insurance to universal life insurance. Which would you prefer for yourself? Why? (See Objectives 1 and 2.)

C indicates an exercise that is related to the Case in Point feature.

12. Describe premium factors and how they are used. How often do you prefer paying an insurance premium: annually, semiannually, quarterly, or monthly? (See Objective 4.)

Solve the following application problems.

QUICK START

13. LEVEL PREMIUM Tom Peters purchased a $200,000 10-year, level premium policy on his 40th birthday. Find the annual premium.

200 × $2.56 = $512

13. **$512**

14. WHOLE LIFE INSURANCE Jessica Smith buys a whole life policy with a face value of $100,000 at age 35. Find the annual premium.

14. ________

C 15. KEY EMPLOYEE INSURANCE Martha Spencer owns the Doll House and has a 35-year-old key male employee whom she wants to insure for $50,000. Find the annual premium **(a)** for 10-year level term and **(b)** for whole life.

(a) ________
(b) ________

16. 20-PAY LIFE POLICY Luan Lee buys a $100,000, 20-pay life policy at age 45. Her son Bryan is the beneficiary and will collect the face value of the policy. **(a)** Find the annual premium. **(b)** How much will Bryan get if his mother dies after making payments for 12 years?

(a) ________
(b) ________

17. WHOLE LIFE INSURANCE Find the total premium paid over 30 years for a whole life policy with a face value of $20,000. Assume that the policy is taken out by a 25-year-old man.

17. ________

18. UNIVERSAL LIFE INSURANCE Richard Gonsalves takes out a universal life policy with a face value of $50,000. He is 40 years old. Find the monthly premium.

18. ________

19. PREMIUM FACTORS The annual premium for a whole life policy is $872. Using premium factors, find **(a)** the semiannual premium, **(b)** the quarterly premium, and **(c)** the monthly premium.

(a) ________
(b) ________
(c) ________

20. PREMIUM FACTORS A universal life policy has an annual premium of $2012. Use premium factors to find **(a)** the semiannual premium, **(b)** the quarterly premium, and **(c)** the monthly premium.

(a) ________
(b) ________
(c) ________

CHAPTER 12 QUICK REVIEW

CHAPTER TERMS *Review the following terms to test your understanding of the chapter. For each term you do not know, refer to the page number found next to that term.*

1099 forms **[p. 534]**
actuaries **[p. 557]**
adjusted gross income **[p. 534]**
adult operator **[p. 560]**
assessed value **[p. 525]**
assessment rate **[p. 525]**
bodily injury coverage **[p. 558]**
cash value **[p. 569]**
casualty or theft losses **[p. 538]**
coinsurance clause **[p. 549]**
collision insurance **[p. 559]**
comprehensive insurance **[p. 559]**
contributions **[p. 538]**
coverage **[p. 547]**
decreasing term insurance **[p. 568]**
deductible **[p. 559]**
dependent **[p. 536]**
disability coverage **[p. 552]**
dollars per \$100 **[p. 526]**
dollars per \$1000 **[p. 526]**
endowment policies **[p. 569]**
face value **[p. 548]**
fair market value **[p. 525]**
Form 1040A **[p. 539]**
head of household **[p. 536]**
homeowner's policy **[p. 547]**
income tax **[p. 533]**
Individual Retirement Account (IRA) **[p. 534]**
insurance **[p. 524]**
interest **[p. 538]**
Internal Revenue Service **[p. 534]**
IRS **[p. 534]**
itemized deductions **[p. 538]**
level premium **[p. 568]**
liability coverage **[p. 552]**
life insurance **[p. 567]**
limited-payment life insurance **[p. 569]**
long-term care coverage **[p. 552]**
medical and dental expenses **[p. 538]**
medical insurance **[p. 552]**
mills **[p. 526]**
miscellaneous deductions **[p. 538]**
multiple carriers **[p. 550]**
no-fault insurance **[p. 560]**
ordinary life insurance **[p. 569]**
permanent life insurance **[p. 569]**
personal exemptions **[p. 536]**
policy **[p. 547]**
policy limits **[p. 558]**
premium **[p. 548]**
premium factor **[p. 570]**
property damage insurance **[p. 558]**
property tax rate **[p. 525]**
renter's coverage **[p. 552]**
replacement cost **[p. 549]**
Schedule 1 (Form 1040A) **[p. 539]**
standard deduction **[p. 535]**
straight life insurance **[p. 569]**
tax deduction **[p. 538]**
tax preparation **[p. 538]**
taxable income **[p. 536]**
taxes **[p. 524]**
term insurance **[p. 567]**
territorial ratings **[p. 548]**
underinsured motorist insurance **[p. 560]**
underwriters **[p. 548]**
uninsured motorist insurance **[p. 560]**
universal life policy **[p. 569]**
unreimbursed job expenses **[p. 538]**
variable life policy **[p. 569]**
W-2 forms **[p. 534]**
whole life insurance **[p. 569]**
worker's compensation **[p. 552]**
youthful operator **[p. 560]**

CONCEPTS	EXAMPLES
12.1 Fair market value and assessed value The value of property is multiplied by a given percent to arrive at the assessed value. Assessed value = **Assessment rate** × Market value	The assessment rate is 30%; fair market value is \$115,000; find the assessed value. **30%** × \$115,000 = \$34,500
12.1 Tax rate The tax rate formula is $\text{Tax rate} = \dfrac{\text{Total tax amount needed}}{\textbf{Total assessed value}}$	Tax amount needed: \$3,864,400; total assessed value: \$107,345,000; find the tax rate. $\dfrac{\$3,864,400}{\$107,345,000} = .036 = 3.6\%\ (\text{rounded})$
12.1 Tax rates in different forms 1. **Percent**: multiply by assessed value. 2. **Dollars per \$100**: move decimal point 2 places to the left in assessed value and multiply. 3. **Dollars per \$1000**: move decimal point 3 places to the left in assessed value and multiply. 4. **Mills**: move decimal point 3 places to the left in rate and multiply by assessed value. Use the formula Property tax = Assessed value × **Tax rate**	Assessed value, \$90,000; tax rate, 2.5%: \$90,000 × **2.5%** = \$2250 Tax rate, **\$2.50** per \$100: 900 × **\$2.50** = \$2250 Tax rate, **\$25** per \$1000: 90 × **\$25** = \$2250 Tax rate, **25 mills**: \$90,000 × **.025** = \$2250

CONCEPTS	EXAMPLES
12.2 Adjusted gross income Adjusted gross income includes wages, salaries, tips, dividends, and interest. Subtract IRA contributions and alimony.	Salary, \$32,540; interest income, \$875; dividends, \$315; find adjusted gross income. \$32,540 + \$875 + \$315 = \$33,730
12.2 Standard deduction amounts The majority of taxpayers use the standard deduction allowed by the IRS.	\$5150 for single taxpayers \$10,300 for married taxpayers filing jointly or qualifying widow(er) \$5150 for married taxpayers filing separately \$7550 for head of household
12.2 Taxable income The larger of either the total of itemized deductions or the standard deduction is subtracted from adjusted gross income along with \$3300 for each personal exemption.	Single taxpayer, adjusted gross income, \$38,500; itemized deductions, \$3850; find taxable income. Note that itemized deductions are less than the standard deduction of \$5150 and the personal exemption is \$3300. Taxable income = \$38,500 − \$5150 − \$3300 = \$30,050
12.2 Tax rates There are six tax rates: 10%, 15%, 25%, 28%, 33%, and 35%.	Single: 10%; 15% over \$7550; 25% over \$30,650; 28% over \$74,200; 33% over \$154,800; 35% over \$336,550 Married filing jointly or qualifying widow(er): 10%; 15% over \$15,100; 25% over \$61,300; 28% over \$123,700; 33% over \$188,450; 35% over \$336,550 Married filing separately: 10%; 15% over \$7550; 25% over \$30,650; 28% over \$61,850; 33% over \$94,225; 35% over \$168,275 Head of household: 10%; 15% over \$10,750; 25% over \$41,050; 28% over \$106,000; 33% over \$171,650; 35% over \$336,550
12.2 Balance due or a refund from the IRS If the total amount withheld by employers is greater than the tax owed, a refund results. If the tax owed is the greater amount, a balance is due.	Tax owed, \$1253; tax withheld, \$113 per month for 12 months. Find balance due or refund. \$113 withheld × 12 = \$1356 withheld \$1356 withheld − \$1253 owed = \$103 refund
12.3 Annual premium for fire insurance The building and territorial ratings are used to find the premiums per \$100 for the building and contents. The two are added.	Building value, \$180,000; contents, \$35,000. Premiums are: building, \$.75 per \$100; contents, \$.77 per \$100. Find the annual premium. Building: 1800 (hundreds) × \$.75 = \$1350 Contents: 350 (hundreds) × \$.77 = \$269.50 Total premium: \$1350 + \$269.50 = \$1619.50
12.3 Coinsurance formula Part of the risk of fire is taken by the insured. An 80% coinsurance clause is common. $\text{Loss paid by insurance company} = \text{Amount of loss} \times \dfrac{\text{Policy amount}}{\text{80\% of replacement cost}}$	Replacement cost, \$125,000; policy amount, \$75,000; fire loss, \$40,000; 80% coinsurance clause; find the amount of loss paid by insurance company. $\$40{,}000 \times \dfrac{\$75{,}000}{\$100{,}000} = \$30{,}000$ (amount insurance company pays)

CONCEPTS	EXAMPLES
12.3 Multiple carriers Several companies insure the same property, which limits the risk of the insurance company, with each paying its fractional portion of any claim.	Insured loss, \$500,000 Insurance is Company A with \$1,000,000; Company B with \$750,000; Company C with \$250,000; find the amount of loss paid by each company. Total insurance: \$1,000,000 + \$750,000 + \$250,000 = \$2,000,000 Company A: $\frac{1{,}000{,}000}{2{,}000{,}000} \times \$500{,}000 = \$250{,}000$ Company B: $\frac{750{,}000}{2{,}000{,}000} \times \$500{,}000 = \$187{,}500$ Company C: $\frac{250{,}000}{2{,}000{,}000} \times \$500{,}000 = \$62{,}500$
12.4 Annual auto insurance premium Most drivers are legally required to purchase automobile insurance. The premium is determined by the types of coverage selected, the type of car, geographic territory, past driving record, and other factors.	Determine the premium: territory, 2; liability, 50/100; property damage, \$50,000; comprehensive and collision, 3-year-old car with a symbol of 8; uninsured motorist coverage; driver is age 23 with driver's training. \$341 liability \$223 property damage 36 comprehensive 98 collision 44 uninsured motorist **\$742 × 1.15** youthful-operator factor = **\$853.30**
12.5 Annual life insurance premium There are several types of life policies. Use the table and multiply by the number of \$1000s of coverage. Subtract 5 years from the age of women. Premium = Number of thousands × **Rate per \$1000**	Find the premiums on a \$50,000 policy for a 30-year-old man. **(a)** 10-year level premium term: 50 × **\$1.89** = \$94.50 **(b)** Whole life: 50 × **\$5.66** = \$283 **(c)** Universal life: 50 × **\$6.08** = \$304 **(d)** 20 pay life: 50 × **\$18.78** − \$939
12.5 Premium factors Life insurance premiums may be paid semiannually, quarterly, or monthly. The annual premium is multiplied by the premium factor to determine the premium amount.	The annual life insurance premium is \$740. Use the table to find the **(a)** semiannual, **(b)** quarterly, and **(c)** monthly premiums. **(a)** Semiannual: \$740 × **.51** = \$377.40 **(b)** Quarterly: \$740 × **.26** = \$192.40 **(c)** Monthly: \$740 × **.0908** = \$67.19

CHAPTER 12 SUMMARY EXERCISE

Financial Planning for Taxes and Insurance

Baker's Pottery manufactures and sells ceramic pots of all types, shapes, and styles. Planning ahead, the company set aside \$53,500 to pay property taxes, fire insurance premiums, and life insurance premiums on the company president. All of these premiums happen to be due in the same month. Find each of the following.

(a) The company property has a fair market value of \$1,990,000 and is assessed at 75% of this value. If the tax rate is \$7.90 per \$1000 of assessed value, find the annual property tax.

(a) ________________

(b) The building occupied by the company is a class-B building with a replacement cost of \$1,730,000. The contents are worth \$3,502,000 and the territorial rating is 4. Find the annual fire insurance premium.

(b) ________________

(c) The president of the company is a 50-year-old woman who lost the use of her legs in an automobile accident. She needs life insurance and the company buys a \$250,000, 10-year level premium life insurance policy on her. Find the semiannual premium.

(c) ________________

(d) Find the total amount needed to pay property taxes, the fire insurance premium, and the semiannual life insurance premium.

(d) ________________

(e) How much more than the amount needed had the company set aside to pay these expenses?

(e) ________________

INVESTIGATE

A recent article in *Consumer Reports* listed thirty Web sites that offer to help a person shop for term life insurance. The article also lists dial-up services that offer a similar service. Use the Web to find information and prices for term life insurance to meet your personal life insurance needs and look at several types of life insurance products.

CHAPTER 12 TEST

To help you review, the numbers in brackets show the section in which the topic was discussed.

Find the following property tax rates. **[12.1]**

	Percent	*Per $100*	*Per $1000*
1.	5.76%	______	______
2.	______	______	$93.50

Find the taxable income and the tax for each of the following people. The letter following the names indicates the marital status. **[12.2]**

Name	*Number of Exemptions*	*Adjusted Gross Income*	*Total Deductions*	*Taxable Income*	*Tax*
3. J. Spalding, S	2	$68,295	$4870	______	______
4. The Bensons, M	4	$43,487	$8315	______	______

Find the tax owed in the following problems.

5. Bradkin's Toggery owns property with a fair market value of $104,600. Property in the area is assessed at 30% of fair market value with a tax rate of 3.65%. Find the annual tax. **[12.1]** **5.** ______

6. The Blakely family has an adjusted gross income of $82,316. They are married and file jointly with five exemptions and deductions of $6200. **[12.2]** **6.** ______

7. Kari Heen had an adjusted gross income of $44,600 last year. She had deductions of $1280 for state income tax, $2408 for property tax, $3540 in mortgage interest, and $343 in contributions. Heen claims one exemption and files as a single person. **[12.2]** **7.** ______

Find the annual fire insurance premium for the following. Use the table on page 548. **[12.3]**

8. Southside Plating owns a class-B building with a replacement cost of $780,000. Contents are valued at $128,600. The territorial rating is 5. **8.** ______

9. A fourplex is valued at $220,000. The fire insurance policy (with an 80% coinsurance clause) has a face value of $150,000. If the building has a fire loss of $50,000, find the amount of the loss that the insurance company will pay. **9.** ______

10. Dave's Body and Paint has an insurable loss of $72,000, while having insurance coverage beyond coinsurance requirements. The insurance is divided among Company A with $250,000 coverage, Company B with $150,000 coverage, and Company C with $100,000 coverage. Find the amount of the loss paid by each of the insurance companies.

A: ______
B: ______
C: ______

Find the annual motor-vehicle insurance premium for the following people. **[12.4]**

Name	Territory	Age	Driver Training?	Liability	Property Damage	Comprehensive Collision Age Group	Symbol	Uninsured Motorist?	Annual Premium
11. Ramos	3	18	Yes	15/30	$10,000	5	7	Yes	______
12. Larik	1	42	No	50/100	$100,000	1	8	Yes	______

Find the annual premium, the semiannual premium, the quarterly premium, and the monthly premium for each of the following life insurance policies. Use the tables in Section 12.5. **[12.5]**

	Annual	Semiannual	Quarterly	Monthly
13. Irene Chong, whole life, $28,000 face value, age 35	______	______	______	______
14. Gil Eckern, 20-pay life, $80,000 face value, age 40	______	______	______	______

Solve the following.

15. Betsy Monikens (age 28) and Jim Faber (age 30) recently married and need to buy both a car and life insurance. They have one car, 4 years old, with symbol 7 and live in territory 2. Auto: 50/100 liability with $3000 in medical expense limits, $25,000 in property damage, comprehensive, $500 deductible collision, and uninsured motorist. Life: $100,000 10-year level term on Jim and $50,000 universal life on Betsy. Find the annual cost of **(a)** the auto insurance and **(b)** the life insurance. **[12.4 and 12.5]**

(a) ______
(b) ______

16. Jessie Hernandez's truck spun out of control on an icy road, causing an accident with another driver. Damages to his truck were $6400, damages to the other driver's vehicle were $8200, and the other driver had medical expenses of $12,900. Hernandez was not hurt and his policy showed that he had liability limits of 15/30, medical expenses of $1000, property damage of $10,000, no comprehensive or collision, and no uninsured motorist. Identify each of the costs he must pay. **[12.4]**

16. ______

CHAPTER 13

Depreciation

CHAPTER CONTENTS

Capital Curb and Concrete is owned and managed by John Goodby. The company does concrete work for building contractors and for the owners of new and existing residential and commercial properties. The company builds curbs and sidewalks, driveways and walkways, retaining walls, patios, and concrete mowing strips. To perform these services, Capital Curb and Concrete has purchased many pieces of equipment, including trucks, trailers, tractors, backhoes, trenchers, and concrete-pumping equipment.

CASE *in* POINT

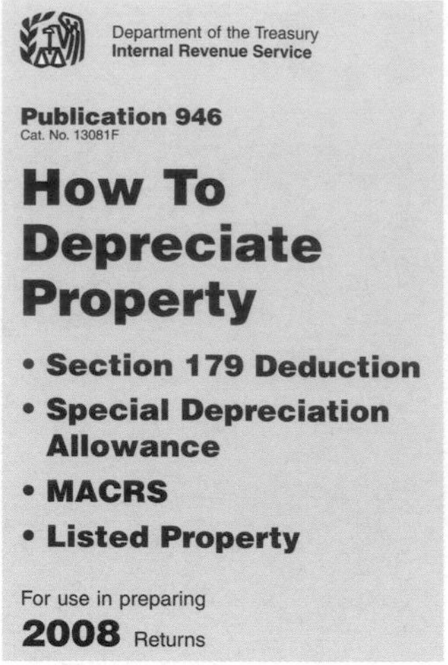
Department of the Treasury
Internal Revenue Service

Publication 946
Cat. No. 13081F

How To Depreciate Property

- Section 179 Deduction
- Special Depreciation Allowance
- MACRS
- Listed Property

For use in preparing
2008 Returns

Business expenses such as salaries, rent, and utilities must be subtracted from company revenues to determine net income. Other expenses including the cost of buildings, machinery, and fixtures are not subtracted all in one year. Since these items usually last several years, the cost of these purchases must be spread over the length of their useful life. This procedure is called **depreciation**.

Over the years, several methods of computing depreciation have been used, including **straight-line, declining-balance, sum-of-the-years'-digits**, and **units-of-production**. These methods are used in keeping company accounting records and, in many states, preparing state income tax returns. Items purchased after 1981 are depreciated for federal income tax returns with the **accelerated cost recovery system** or the **modified accelerated cost recovery system**, discussed later. The use of depreciation for federal income tax purposes is detailed in an Internal Revenue Service publication. The complete title of this publication is shown at the side.

A company need not use the same method of depreciation for all of its various assets. For example, the straight-line method of depreciation might be used on some assets and the declining-balance method on others. Furthermore, the depreciation method used in preparing a company's financial statement may be different from the method used in preparing income tax returns.

13.1 DEPRECIATION: STRAIGHT-LINE METHOD

OBJECTIVES

1. Understand the terms used in depreciation.
2. Use the straight-line method of depreciation to find the amount of depreciation each year.
3. Use the straight-line method to find the book value of an asset.
4. Use the straight-line method to prepare a depreciation schedule.

CASE in POINT John Goodby and his accountant decide on which method of depreciation to use for the depreciable assets of Capital Curb and Concrete. The most commonly used method for both accounting and tax purposes is the straight-line method of depreciation.

OBJECTIVE 1 **Understand the terms used in depreciation.** The physical assets of a company such as machinery, trucks, cars, and computers are **tangible assets**. Assets such as patents and copyrights, franchise fees, and customer lists are **intangible assets**. In general, either type of asset may be depreciated, as long as its useful life can be determined. The key terms in depreciation are summarized below.

Cost is the basis for determining depreciation. It is the total amount paid for the asset.

Useful life is the period of time during which the asset will be used. The Internal Revenue Service has guidelines for estimating the life of an asset used in a particular trade or business. However, useful life depends on the use of the asset, the repair policy, the replacement policy, obsolescence, and other factors.

Salvage value or **scrap value** (sometimes called **residual value**) is the estimated value of an asset when it is retired from service, traded in, disposed of, or exhausted. An asset may have a salvage value of zero, or **no salvage value**.

Accumulated depreciation is the amount of depreciation taken so far, a running balance of depreciation to date.

Book value is the cost of an asset minus the total depreciation to date. The book value at the end of an asset's life is equal to the salvage value. The book value can never be less than the salvage value.

OBJECTIVE 2 **Use the straight-line method of depreciation to find the amount of depreciation each year.** The simplest method of depreciation, **straight-line depreciation**, assumes that assets lose an equal amount of value during each year of life. For example, suppose a heavy equipment trailer is purchased by Capital Curb and Concrete at a cost of \$14,100. The trailer has a useful life of 8 years and a salvage value of $2100. Find the amount to be depreciated (**depreciable amount**) using the following formula.

$$\text{Amount to be depreciated} = \text{Cost} - \text{Salvage value}$$

Here, the amount to be depreciated over the 8-year period is:

$14,100	cost
− 2,100	**salvage value**
$12,000	amount to be depreciated

With the straight-line method, an equal amount of depreciation is taken each year over the 8-year life of the trailer. The annual depreciation for this trailer is

$$\text{Depreciation} = \frac{\text{Depreciable amount}}{\text{Years of life}} = \frac{\$12{,}000}{8} = \$1500$$

Each year during the 8-year life of the trailer, the annual depreciation will be $1500, or $\frac{1}{8}$ of the depreciable amount. The annual rate of depreciation is $12\frac{1}{2}\%$ $\left(\frac{1}{8} = 12\frac{1}{2}\%\right)$.

OBJECTIVE 3 **Use the straight-line method to find the book value of an asset.** The book value, or remaining value, of an asset at the end of a year is the original cost minus the depreciation up to and including that year (**accumulated depreciation**). With the trailer, the book value at the end of the first year is found as follows.

$14,100	cost
− 1,500	**first year's depreciation**
$12,600	book value at end of the first year

Book value is found with the following formula.

$$\text{Book value} = \text{Cost} - \text{Accumulated depreciation}$$

Subtract the second year's depreciation from the book value at the end of year 1 to find the book value at the end of year 2, and so on.

EXAMPLE 1

Finding First-Year Depreciation and Book Value

KFC purchased a new low-fat chicken cooker at a cost of $26,500. The estimated life of the fryer is 5 years, with a salvage value of $3500. Find **(a)** the annual rate of depreciation, **(b)** the annual amount of depreciation, and **(c)** the book value at the end of the first year.

SOLUTION

(a) The annual rate of depreciation is 20% (5-year life = $\frac{1}{5}$ **per year = 20%**).

(b)

$26,500	cost
− 3,500	**salvage value**
$23,000	depreciable amount

This $23,000 will be depreciated evenly over the 5-year life for an annual depreciation of $4600 ($23,000 × 20% = $4600).

(c) Since the annual depreciation is $4600, the book value at the end of the first year will be

$26,500	cost
− 4,600	**depreciation in the first year**
$21,900	book value at the end of the first year

To solve Example 1 using a calculator, first use parentheses to find the depreciable amount. Next, divide to find depreciation. Finally, find the book value.

(26,500 − 3500) ÷ 5 = 4600

26,500 − 4600 = 21,900

Note: Refer to Appendix C for calculator basics.

QUICK TIP Find the book value at the end of any year by multiplying the annual amount of straight-line depreciation by the number of years and subtracting this result, the depreciation to date, from the cost.

QUICK CHECK 1

Class Printers purchased a new printing press at a cost of $18,400. The estimated life of the printing press is 8 years, with a salvage value of $3600. Find **(a)** the annual rate of depreciation, **(b)** the annual amount of depreciation, and **(c)** the book value at the end of the first year.

If an asset is expected to have **no salvage value** at the end of its expected life, the entire cost will be depreciated over its life. In Example 1, if the chicken cooker had been expected to have no salvage value at the end of 5 years, the annual amount of depreciation would have been $5300 ($26,500 × 20% = $5300).

EXAMPLE 2

Finding the Book Value at the End of Any Year

A lighted display case at Bead Works cost $3400, has an estimated life of 10 years, and has a salvage value of $800. Find the book value at the end of 6 years.

SOLUTION

The annual rate of depreciation is 10% (10-year life is $\frac{1}{10}$ or 10%).

$3400	cost
− 800	**salvage value**
$2600	depreciable amount

Since $2600 is depreciated evenly over the 10-year life of the case, the annual depreciation is $260 (**$2600 × 10% = $260**).

The accumulated depreciation over the 6-year period is

$260 × **6 years** = $1560 accumulated depreciation (6 years)

Find the book value at the end of 6 years by subtracting the accumulated depreciation from the cost.

$3400	cost
− 1560	**accumulated depreciation (6 years)**
$1840	book value at the end of 6 years

After 6 years, this display case would be carried on the firm's books with a value of $1840.

QUICK TIP The book value helps the owner of a business estimate the value of the business, which is important when the owner is borrowing money or trying to sell the business.

QUICK CHECK 2

Brothers Wheel Alignment bought a new wheel alignment system for $15,900. If the salvage value of the equipment is $4500 and the estimated life is 12 years, find the book value at the end of 8 years.

OBJECTIVE 4 **Use the straight-line method to prepare a depreciation schedule.** A **depreciation schedule** is often used to show the annual depreciation, accumulated depreciation, and book value over the useful life of an asset. As an aid in comparing three of the methods of depreciation discussed in the text, the depreciation schedule of Example 3 and the schedules shown for the double-declining-balance (see **Section 13.2**) and sum-of-the-years'-digits methods (see **Section 13.3**) use the same pickup truck.

Quick Check Answers

1. **(a)** 12.5% rate
   (b) $1850 depreciation
   (c) $16,550 book value
2. $8300

EXAMPLE 3

Preparing a Depreciation Schedule

Capital Curb and Concrete bought a new pickup truck for $21,500. The truck is estimated to have a useful life of 5 years, at which time it will have a salvage value (trade-in value) of $3500. Prepare a depreciation schedule using the straight-line method of depreciation.

SOLUTION

The annual rate of depreciation is 20% (5-year life = $\frac{1}{5}$ **per year = 20%**). Find the depreciable amount as follows.

$21,500	cost
− **3,500**	**salvage value**
$18,000	depreciable amount

This $18,000 will be depreciated evenly over the 5-year life for an annual depreciation of $3600 ($18,000 × **20%** = $3600).

This depreciation schedule includes a year zero that represents the initial purchase of the truck.

Year	Computation	Amount of Depreciation	Accumulated Depreciation	Book Value
0	—	—	—	$21,500
1	**(20% × $18,000)**	$3600	$3,600	$17,900
2	**(20% × $18,000)**	$3600	$7,200	$14,300
3	**(20% × $18,000)**	$3600	$10,800	$10,700
4	**(20% × $18,000)**	$3600	$14,400	$7,100
5	**(20% × $18,000)**	$3600	$18,000	$3,500

The depreciation is $3600 each year, the accumulated depreciation at the end of 5 years is equal to the depreciable amount, and the book value at the end of 5 years is equal to the salvage value.

QUICK TIP If the rate is a repeating decimal, use the fraction that is equivalent to the decimal. Instead of 33.3%, use the fraction $\frac{1}{3}$. Instead of 16.7%, use the fraction $\frac{1}{6}$.

QUICK CHECK 3

A concrete extruding machine is purchased at a cost of $4300. The machine has a useful life of 4 years and a salvage value of $700. Prepare a depreciation schedule using the straight-line method of depreciation to find the book value at the end of each year of the asset's life.

Depreciation is used with assets having a useful life of *more than one year*. The asset to be depreciated must have a predictable life. A truck can be depreciated because its useful life can be estimated, but land cannot be depreciated because its life is considered to be indefinite. For example, the graph below shows the remaining value of the pickup truck in Example 3 as it is depreciated over its useful life.

QUICK TIP Sometimes the remaining value (book value) corresponds closely to the actual market value. Sometimes it does not.

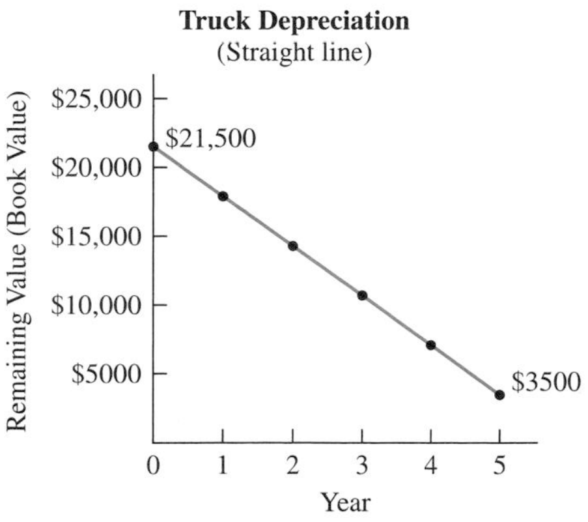

Quick Check Answer

3. year 0 = $4300
year 1 = $3400
year 2 = $2500
year 3 = $1600
year 4 = $ 700

31. Develop a single formula that will show how to find annual depreciation using the straight-line method of depreciation. (See Objective 1.)

32. Explain the procedure used to calculate depreciation when there is no salvage value. Why will the book value always be zero at the end of the asset's life?

33. BARGE DEPRECIATION A Dutch petroleum company purchased a barge for $1,300,000. The estimated life is 20 years, at which time it will have a salvage value of $200,000. Find **(a)** the annual amount of depreciation using the straight-line method and **(b)** the book value at the end of 5 years.

(a) ________
(b) ________

34. DEPRECIATING COMPUTER EQUIPMENT The new computer equipment at Capital Curb and Concrete has a cost of $14,500, an estimated life of 8 years, and a scrap value of $2100. Find **(a)** the annual depreciation and **(b)** the book value at the end of 4 years using the straight-line method of depreciation.

(a) ________
(b) ________

35. DEPRECIATING MACHINERY A bottle-capping machine costs $88,000, has an estimated life of 8 years, and has a scrap value of $16,000. Use the straight-line method of depreciation to find **(a)** the annual rate of depreciation, **(b)** the annual amount of depreciation, and **(c)** the book value at the end of the first year.

(a) ________
(b) ________
(c) ________

36. WAREHOUSE SHELVING Levinson Supply purchased new warehouse shelving for $37,500. The estimated life is 10 years, with a salvage value of $7500. Use the straight-line method of depreciation to find **(a)** the annual rate of depreciation, **(b)** the annual amount of depreciation, and **(c)** the book value at the end of 5 years.

(a) ________
(b) ________
(c) ________

13.2 DEPRECIATION: DECLINING-BALANCE METHOD

OBJECTIVES

1. Describe the declining-balance method of depreciation.
2. Find the double-declining-balance rate.
3. Use the double-declining-balance method to find the amount of depreciation and the book value for each year.
4. Use the double-declining-balance method to prepare a depreciation schedule.

CASE in POINT Straight-line depreciation assumes that an asset loses an equal amount of value each year of its life. This is not realistic for most of the machinery and equipment owned by Capital Curb and Concrete. For example, a new tractor loses much more value during its first year of life than during its fifth year of life.

OBJECTIVE 1 Describe the declining-balance method of depreciation. Methods of **accelerated depreciation** are used to more accurately reflect the rate at which assets actually lose value. One of the more common accelerated methods of depreciation is the **double-declining-balance method** or **200% method**. With this method, the **double-declining-balance rate** is first established. This rate is multiplied by last year's book value to get this year's depreciation. Since the book value declines from year to year, the annual depreciation also declines, giving the origin of the name of this method.

OBJECTIVE 2 Find the double-declining-balance rate. Calculate depreciation using the double-declining-balance method by first finding the straight-line rate of depreciation. Then adjust the straight-line rate to the desired declining-balance rate of 200% of the straight-line rate.

EXAMPLE 1 Finding the 200% Declining-Balance Rate

Find the straight-line rate and the double-declining-balance (200%) rate for each of the following years of life.

SOLUTION

Years of Life	Straight-Line Rate	Double-Declining-Balance Rate
3	33.33% $(\frac{1}{3})$	$\times 2 =$ 66.67% $(\frac{2}{3})$
4	25%	$\times 2 =$ 50%
5	20%	$\times 2 =$ 40%
8	12.5%	$\times 2 =$ 25%
10	10%	$\times 2 =$ 20%
20	5%	$\times 2 =$ 10%
25	4%	$\times 2 =$ 8%
50	2%	$\times 2 =$ 4%

QUICK CHECK 1

Find the straight-line rate and the double-declining-balance rate (200%) for **(a)** 40 years, **(b)** 6 years, **(c)** 15 years, and **(d)** 25 years.

Quick Check Answers

1. (a) $2\frac{1}{2}\%$, 5%
(b) $16\frac{2}{3}\%$, $33\frac{1}{3}\%$
(c) $6\frac{2}{3}\%$, $13\frac{1}{3}\%$
(d) 4%, 8%

13.2 EXERCISES

FOR EXTRA HELP

MyMathLab

MathXL PRACTICE

WATCH

DOWNLOAD

READ

REVIEW

The QUICK START *exercises in each section contain solutions to help you get started.*

Find the annual double-declining-balance (200% method) rate of depreciation, given the following estimated lives. (See Example 1.)

QUICK START

Life	Annual Rate	Life	Annual Rate
1. 5 years **20% × 2 = 40%**	**40%**	**2.** 20 years **5% × 2 = 10%**	**10%**
3. 8 years	______	**4.** 25 years	______
5. 15 years	______	**6.** 4 years	______
7. 10 years	______	**8.** 30 years	______
9. 6 years	______	**10.** 40 years	______
11. 50 years	______	**12.** 100 years	______

Find the first year's depreciation for the following, using the double-declining-balance method of depreciation. (See Example 2.)

QUICK START

13. Cost: $15,000
Estimated life: 10 years
Estimated scrap value: $3000
Depreciation (year 1): **$3000**

$15,000 × 20% = $3000

14. Cost: $10,800
Estimated life: 20 years
Estimated scrap value: None
Depreciation (year 1): **$1080**

$10,800 × 10% = $1080

15. Cost: $22,500
Estimated life: 5 years
Estimated scrap value: $500
Depreciation (year 1): ______

16. Cost: $38,000
Estimated life: 40 years
Estimated scrap value: $5000
Depreciation (year 1): ______

17. Cost: $3800
Estimated life: 4 years
Estimated scrap value: None
Depreciation (year 1): ______

18. Cost: $1140
Estimated life: 6 years
Estimated scrap value: $350
Depreciation (year 1): ______

C indicates an exercise that is related to the Case in Point feature.

Find the book value at the end of the first year for the following, using the double-declining-balance method of depreciation. Round to the nearest dollar. (See Examples 1 and 2.)

QUICK START

19. Cost: $4200
Estimated life: 10 years
Estimated scrap value: $1000
Book value: $3360

$4200 × 20% = $840
$4200 − $840 = $3360 book value

20. Cost: $2500
Estimated life: 6 years
Estimated scrap value: $400
Book value: ______

21. Cost: $1620
Estimated life: 8 years
Estimated scrap value: None
Book value: ______

22. Cost: $11,280
Estimated life: 5 years
Estimated scrap value: $1600
Book value: ______

Find the book value at the end of 3 years for the following, using the double-declining-balance method of depreciation. Round to the nearest dollar. (See Examples 1 and 2.)

QUICK START

23. Cost: $16,200
Estimated life: 8 years
Estimated scrap value: $1500
Book value: $6834

$16,200 × 25% = $4050 dep. year 1
$16,200 − $4050 = $12,150
$12,150 × 25% = $3038 dep. year 2
$12,150 − $3038 = $9112
$9112 × 25% = $2278 dep. year 3
$9112 − $2278 = $6834 book value year 3

24. Cost: $8500
Estimated life: 10 years
Estimated scrap value: $1100
Book value: ______

25. Cost: $6000
Estimated life: 3 years
Estimated scrap value: $750
Book value: ______

26. Cost: $75,000
Estimated life: 50 years
Estimated scrap value: None
Book value: ______

Solve the following application problems.

QUICK START

27. WEIGHT-TRAINING EQUIPMENT Gold's Gym selects the double-declining-balance method of depreciation for some weight-training equipment costing $14,400. If the estimated life of the equipment is 4 years and the salvage value is zero, prepare a depreciation schedule.

Year	Computation	Amount of Depreciation	Accumulated Depreciation	Book Value
0	—	—	—	$14,400
1	(50% × $14,400)	$7200	$7,200	$7,200
2	(50% × $7,200)	$3600	$10,800	$3,600
3	(50% × $3,600)	$1800	$12,600	$1,800
4		$1800*	$14,400	$0

*To depreciate to $0 scrap value

28. STUDIO SOUND SYSTEM A studio sound system costing $11,760 has a 3-year life and a scrap value of $1400. Prepare a depreciation schedule using the double-declining-balance method of depreciation.

Year	Computation	Amount of Depreciation	Accumulated Depreciation	Book Value
0	—	—	—	$11,760
1				
2				
3				$1,400

29. CONVEYOR SYSTEM Use the double-declining-balance method of depreciation to prepare a depreciation schedule for a new conveyor system installed at Camblin Steel. Cost = $14,000; estimated life = 5 years; estimated scrap value = $2500. (Round to the nearest dollar.)

Year	Computation	Amount of Depreciation	Accumulated Depreciation	Book Value
0	—	—	—	$14,000
1				
2				
3				
4				
5				$2,500

30. ELECTRONIC ANALYZER Neilo Lincoln-Mercury decides to use the double-declining-balance method of depreciation on a Barnes Electronic Analyzer that was acquired at a cost of $25,500. If the estimated life of the analyzer is 8 years and the estimated scrap value is $3500, prepare a depreciation schedule. (Round to the nearest dollar.)

Year	Computation	Amount of Depreciation	Accumulated Depreciation	Book Value
0	—	—	—	$25,500
1				
2				
3				
4				
5				
6				
7				
8				$3,500

31. Another name for the double-declining-balance method of depreciation is the 200% method. Explain why the straight-line method of depreciation is often called the 100% method. (See Objective 2.)

32. Explain why the amount of depreciation taken in the last year of an asset's life may be zero when using the double-declining-balance method of depreciation. (See Objective 4.)

Case Studies

Ford Motor Company

www.ford.com

- 1925: First Ford truck built
  —Price: $281
- 1936: Ford had already sold 3 million trucks
- 1950s: Moved to more car-like comfort and styling in their trucks
- 2003: Ford celebrates 100th anniversary
- 1983–2007: Ford F-150 best-selling full-size pickup truck
- 2007: A three-time 5 best trucks winner

In 1903, with $28,000 in cash, Henry Ford started Ford Motor Company, which is now one of the world's largest companies. Ford's greatest contribution to automobile manufacturing was the moving assembly that allowed individual workers to stay in one place and perform the same task on each vehicle as it passed by. Today, Ford Motor Company is a family of automotive brands, including Ford, Lincoln, Mercury, Mazda, Jaguar, Land Rover, Aston Martin, and Volvo.

Capital Curb and Concrete purchased another Ford F-150 XLT pickup truck for $26,500. The useful life of the truck is 5 years, and the estimated salvage value is $4500.

1. Using the information above, find the book value of the pickup truck after 3 years using the straight-line method of depreciation.

2. Find the book value of the truck at the end of 3 years using the double-declining-balance method of depreciation.

3. List four factors that affect how fast a pickup truck is used up or wears out. Does the book value of an asset necessarily reflect the true value (resale value) of that asset? Explain.

4. Talk to some business owners and list a few of the assets that they are depreciating. If a business had a choice of depreciating gradually over the life of an asset (straight-line) or more rapidly using an accelerated depreciation method, what factors would business owners consider when making their decisions?

13.4 EXERCISES

FOR EXTRA HELP

MyMathLab

MathXL PRACTICE

WATCH

DOWNLOAD

READ

REVIEW

The **QUICK START** *exercises in each section contain solutions to help you get started.*

Find the depreciation per unit in the following. Round to the nearest thousandth of a dollar. (See Example 1.)

QUICK START

	Cost	*Salvage Value*	*Estimated Life*	*Depreciation per Unit*
1.	$16,800	$1800	20,000 units	**$.75**
	$16,800 − $1800 = $15,000; $15,000 ÷ 20,000 = $.75			
2.	$22,500	$1500	60,000 units	________
3.	$3750	$250	120,000 units	________
4.	$7500	$500	15,000 miles	________
5.	$37,500	$7500	125,000 miles	________
6.	$300,000	$25,000	4000 hours	________
7.	$175,000	$25,000	5000 hours	________
8.	$125,000	$20,000	500,000 miles	________

Find the amount of depreciation in each of the following. (See Example 1.)

QUICK START

	Depreciation per Unit	*Units Produced*	*Amount of Depreciation*
9.	$.46	55,000	**$25,300**
	55,000 × $.46 = $25,300		
10.	$.18	275,000	**$49,500**
	275,000 × $.18 = $49,500		
11.	$.54	32,000	________
12.	$.73	16,500	________
13.	$.185	15,000	________

C indicates an exercise that is related to the Case in Point feature.

	Depreciation per Unit	*Units Produced*	*Amount of Depreciation*
14.	$.032	73,000	______
15.	$.14	22,200	______
16.	$.075	110,000	______

17. In your own words, describe the conditions in which the units-of-production method of depreciation is most applicable.

18. Use an example of your own to demonstrate how the annual depreciation amount is found using the units-of-production method of depreciation. (See Objective 3.)

Solve the following application problems. Round to the nearest dollar.

QUICK START

19. DEEP FRYER McDonald's purchased a new grilling station at a cost of $6800. The expected life is 5000 hours of production, at which time it will have a salvage value of $500. Using the units-of-production method, prepare a depreciation schedule given the following production: year 1: 1350 hours; year 2: 1820 hours; year 3: 730 hours; year 4: 1100 hours.

Year	Computation	Amount of Depreciation	Accumulated Depreciation	Book Value
0	—	—	—	$6800
1	(1350 × $1.26)	$1701	$1701	$5099
2	(1820 × $1.26)	$2293	$3994	$2806
3	(730 × $1.26)	$920	$4914	$1886
4	(1100 × $1.26)	$1386	$6300	$500

20. HEAVY-DUTY TRUCK Capital Curb and Concrete purchased a Kenworth truck at a cost of $87,000. It estimates that the truck will have a life of 300,000 miles and a salvage value of $15,000. Use the units-of-production method to prepare a depreciation schedule given the following production: year 1: 108,000 miles; year 2: 75,000 miles; year 3: 117,000 miles.

Year	Computation	Amount of Depreciation	Accumulated Depreciation	Book Value
0	—	—	—	$87,000

13.5 DEPRECIATION: MODIFIED ACCELERATED COST RECOVERY SYSTEM

OBJECTIVES

1. Understand the modified accelerated cost recovery system (MACRS).
2. Determine the recovery period of different types of property.
3. Find the depreciation rate, given the recovery period and recovery year.
4. Use the MACRS to find the amount of depreciation.
5. Prepare a depreciation schedule using the MACRS.

CASE in POINT Several different methods of depreciation may have been used by Capital Curb and Concrete for the company's accounting and state tax purposes. However, the accountant tells the company owner, John Goodby, that the modified accelerated cost recovery system (MACRS) must be used for federal income tax purposes. This means that every depreciable asset owned by the company must have a MACRS depreciation schedule and that the owner must also have an understanding of MACRS.

OBJECTIVE 1 **Understand the modified accelerated cost recovery system (MACRS).** A depreciation method known as the **accelerated cost recovery system (ACRS)** originated as part of the Economic Recovery Tax Act of 1981. It was later modified by the Tax Equity and Fiscal Responsibility Act of 1982 and again by the Tax Reform Act of 1984. The Tax Reform Act of 1986 brought the most recent and significant overhaul to the accelerated cost recovery system (ACRS) and applies to all property placed in service after 1986. The new method is known as the **modified accelerated cost recovery system (MACRS)**. The result is that there are now three systems for computing depreciation for *federal tax purposes*.

QUICK TIP Occasionally the IRS will allow additional depreciaton in the first year of an asset's life. Currently, Section 179 of the IRS Tax Code allows this additional depreciation. However, qualifying under Section 179 is difficult due to the many restrictions and limitations.

Federal Tax Depreciation Methods

1. The MACRS method of depreciation is used for all property placed in service after 1986.
2. The ACRS method of depreciation will continue to be used for all property placed in service from 1981 through 1986.
3. The straight-line, declining-balance, and sum-of-the-years'-digits methods continue to be used for property placed in service before 1981.

Keep two things in mind about the MACRS: First, the system is designed for tax purposes (it is sometimes called the **income tax method**), and businesses often use some alternative method of depreciation (in addition to MACRS) for financial accounting purposes. Second, some states do not allow the modified accelerated cost recovery system of depreciation for finding state income tax liability. This means that businesses must use the *MACRS* on the *federal tax return* and one of the other methods on the *state tax return*.

OBJECTIVE 2 **Determine the recovery period of different types of property.** Under the modified accelerated cost recovery system, assets are placed in one of nine **recovery classes**, depending on whether the law assumes a 3-, 5-, 7-, 10-, 15-, 20-, 27.5-, 31.5-, or 39-year life for the asset. These lives, or **recovery periods**, are determined as follows.

MACRS Recovery Classes

3-year property	Tractor units for use over-the-road, any racehorse that is over 2 years old, any other horse that is over 12 years old, and qualified rent-to-own property
5-year property	Automobiles, taxis, trucks, buses, computers and peripheral equipment, office machinery (typewriters, calculators), copiers, and research equipment, breeding cattle, and dairy cattle
7-year property	Office furniture and fixtures (desks, files, safes), and any property not designated by law to be in any other class
10-year property	Vessels, barges, tugs, and similar water transportation equipment
15-year property	Improvements made directly to land, such as shrubbery, fences, roads, bridges, and any single-purpose agricultural or horticultural structure, and any tree or vine bearing fruits or nuts
20-year property	Certain farm buildings such as a storage shed
27.5-year property	Residential rental real estate such as rental houses, apartments, and mobile homes
31.5-year property	Nonresidential rental real estate such as office building, stores, and warehouses if placed in service before May 13, 1993
39-year property	Nonresidential property placed in service after May 12, 1993

EXAMPLE 1

Finding the Recovery Period for Property

Capital Curb and Concrete owns the following assets. Determine the recovery period for each of them.

(a) computer equipment **(b)** an industrial warehouse (after May 12, 1993)
(c) a pickup truck **(d)** office furniture **(e)** a farm building (storage shed)

SOLUTION

Use the MACRS Recovery Classes list above.

(a) 5 years **(b)** 39 years **(c)** 5 years **(d)** 7 years **(e)** 20 years

QUICK CHECK 1

Determine the recovery period for each of the following assets using the MACRS recovery classes.

(a) a drilling barge **(b)** a taxi cab **(c)** office landscaping **(d)** an apartment building

OBJECTIVE 3 **Find the depreciation rate, given the recovery period and recovery year.** With MACRS, salvage value is ignored, so that *depreciation is based on the entire original cost of the asset.* The depreciation rates are determined by applying the double-declining-balance (200%) method to the 3-, 5-, 7-, and 10-year class properties, the 150% declining-balance method to the 15- and 20-year class properties, and the straight-line (100%) method to the 27.5-, 31.5-, and 39-year class properties. Since these calculations are repetitive and require additional knowledge, the Internal Revenue Service provides tables that show the depreciation rates. The rates are shown as **percents** in the table on the following page. To determine the rate of depreciation for any year of life, find the recovery year in the left-hand column and then read across to the allowable recovery period.

Notice that the number of recovery years is one greater than the class life of the property. This is because only a half-year of depreciation is allowed for the first year the property is placed in service, regardless of when the property is placed in service during the year. This is known as the **half-year convention** and is used by most taxpayers. A complete coverage of depreciation, including all depreciation tables, is included in the **Internal Revenue Service**, **Publication 946**, and may be obtained by contacting the IRS Forms Distribution Center or by going to www.irs.gov. This publication (946) lists several items that the taxpayer or tax preparer might find useful. This list is shown at the side.

Modified Accelerated Cost Recovery System (MACRS)

Useful Items
You may want to see:

Publication
- ☐ **225** Farmer's Tax Guide
- ☐ **463** Travel, Entertainment, and Gift Expenses
- ☐ **544** Sales and Other Dispositions of Assets
- ☐ **551** Basis of Assets
- ☐ **587** Business Use of Your Home

Quick Check Answers

1. (a) 10 years
(b) 5 years
(c) 15 years
(d) 27.5 years

MACRS Depreciation Rates

Recovery Year	Applicable Percent for the Class of Property								
	3-Year	5-Year	7-Year	10-Year	15-Year	20-Year	27.5-Year	31.5-Year	39-Year
1	33.33	20.00	14.29	10.00	5.00	3.750	3.485	3.042	2.461
2	44.45	32.00	24.49	18.00	9.50	7.219	3.636	3.175	2.564
3	14.81	19.20	17.49	14.40	8.55	6.677	3.636	3.175	2.564
4	7.41	11.52	12.49	11.52	7.70	6.177	3.636	3.175	2.564
5		11.52	8.93	9.22	6.93	5.713	3.636	3.175	2.564
6		5.76	8.92	7.37	6.23	5.285	3.636	3.175	2.564
7			8.93	6.55	5.90	4.888	3.636	3.175	2.564
8			4.46	6.55	5.90	4.522	3.636	3.175	2.564
9				6.56	5.91	4.462	3.636	3.174	2.564
10				6.55	5.90	4.461	3.637	3.175	2.564
11				3.28	5.91	4.462	3.636	3.174	2.564
12					5.90	4.461	3.637	3.175	2.564
13					5.91	4.462	3.636	3.174	2.564
14					5.90	4.461	3.637	3.175	2.564
15					5.91	4.462	3.636	3.174	2.564
16					2.95	4.461	3.637	3.175	2.564
17						4.462	3.636	3.174	2.564
18						4.461	3.637	3.175	2.564
19						4.462	3.636	3.174	2.564
20						4.461	3.637	3.175	2.564
21						2.231	3.636	3.174	2.564
22							3.637	3.175	2.564
23							3.636	3.174	2.564
24							3.637	3.175	2.564
25							3.636	3.174	2.564
26							3.637	3.175	2.564
27							3.636	3.174	2.564
28							1.97	3.175	2.564
29								3.174	2.564
30								3.175	2.564
31								3.174	2.564
32								1.720	2.564
33–39									2.564
40									0.107

EXAMPLE 2

Finding the Rate of Depreciation with MACRS

Find the rate of depreciation given the following recovery years, and recovery periods.

	(a)	(b)	(c)	(d)
Recovery Year	3	4	2	12
Recovery Period	3 years	10 years	5 years	27.5 years

SOLUTION

(a) 14.81% **(b)** 11.52% **(c)** 32.00% **(d)** 3.637%

QUICK TIP MACRS is the federal income tax method of depreciation, and three important points should be remembered.

1. No salvage value is used.
2. The life of the asset is determined by using the recovery periods assigned to different types of property.
3. A depreciation rate is usually found for each year by referring to a MACRS table of depreciation rates.

QUICK CHECK 2

Find the rate of depreciation given the following recovery years and recovery periods.

	(a)	(b)	(c)	(d)
Recovery Year	4	2	20	7
Recovery Period	7	20	31.5	15

OBJECTIVE 4 Use the MACRS to find the amount of depreciation. No salvage value is subtracted from the cost of property under the MACRS method, and the depreciation rate multiplied by the original cost determines the depreciation amount.

EXAMPLE 3

Finding the Amount of Depreciation with MACRS

Capital Curb and Concrete bought a new pickup truck for $21,500. Find the amount of depreciation for the pickup truck in the fourth year.

SOLUTION

A pickup truck has a recovery period of 5 years. From the table on page 619, the depreciation rate in the fourth year of recovery of 5-year property is 11.52%. Multiply this rate by the full cost of the property to determine the amount of depreciation.

$$11.52\% \times \$21{,}500 = \$2476.80 = \$2477 \text{ (rounded)}$$

The amount of depreciation is $2477.

QUICK CHECK 3

Find the depreciation in year 2 for the pickup truck in Example 3.

EXAMPLE 4

Preparing a Depreciation Schedule with MACRS

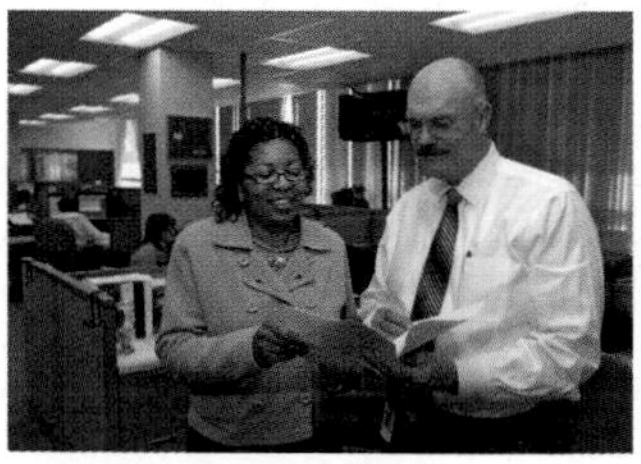

Omaha Insurance Company has purchased new office furniture at a cost of $24,160. Prepare a depreciation schedule using the modified accelerated cost recovery system.

SOLUTION

No salvage value is used with MACRS. Office desks and chairs have a 7-year recovery period. The annual depreciation rates for 7-year properties are as follows.

Recovery Year	Recovery Percent (Rate)
1	14.29%
2	24.49%
3	17.49%
4	12.49%
5	8.93%
6	8.92%
7	8.93%
8	4.46%

Quick Check Answers

2. (a) 12.49%
(b) 7.219%
(c) 3.175%
(d) 5.90%
3. $6880

OBJECTIVE 5 Prepare a depreciation schedule using the MACRS. For the furniture in Example 4, multiply the appropriate percents by $24,160 to get the results shown in the following depreciation schedule.

Year	Computation	Amount of Depreciation	Accumulated Depreciation	Book Value
0	—	—	—	$24,160
1	(14.29% × $24,160)	$3452	$3,452	$20,708
2	(24.49% × $24,160)	$5917	$9,369	$14,791
3	(17.49% × $24,160)	$4226	$13,595	$10,565
4	(12.49% × $24,160)	$3018	$16,613	$7,547
5	(8.93% × $24,160)	$2157	$18,770	$5,390
6	(8.92% × $24,160)	$2155	$20,925	$3,235
7	(8.93% × $24,160)	$2157	$23,082	$1,078
8	(4.46% × $24,160)	$1078	$24,160	$0

QUICK CHECK 4

Airport Transit purchased a new bus at a cost of $128,000. Use the MACRS method of depreciation to find the book value at the end of the fourth year.

Quick Check Answer

4. $22,118

The MACRS method of depreciation allows a rapid rate of investment recovery and at the same time results in less complicated computations. By eliminating the necessity for estimating the life of an asset and the need for using a salvage value, the tables provide a more direct method of calculating depreciation.

13.5 EXERCISES

FOR EXTRA HELP

MyMathLab

MathXL PRACTICE

WATCH

DOWNLOAD

READ

REVIEW

The **QUICK START** *exercises in each section contain solutions to help you get started.*

Use the MACRS depreciation rates table to find the recovery percent (rate), given the following recovery years and recovery periods. (See Examples 1 and 2.)

QUICK START

	Recovery Year	Recovery Period	Recovery Percent (Rate)		Recovery Year	Recovery Period	Recovery Percent (Rate)
1.	3	5-year	**19.2%**	**2.**	5	7-year	**8.93%**
3.	9	10-year	______	**4.**	1	3-year	______
5.	1	5-year	______	**6.**	5	20-year	______
7.	15	27.5-year	______	**8.**	11	31.5-year	______
9.	6	5-year	______	**10.**	4	27.5-year	______
11.	14	39-year	______	**12.**	4	31.5-year	______

Find the first year's depreciation for each of the following using the MACRS method of depreciation and the MACRS depreciation rates table. Round to the nearest dollar. (See Example 3.)

QUICK START

13. Cost: $12,250
Recovery period: 7 years
Depreciation (year 1): **$1751**

14.29% rate
$12,250 × .1429 = $1751 depreciation

14. Cost: $8790
Recovery period: 5 years
Depreciation (year 1): **$1758**

20% rate
$8790 × .20 = $1758 depreciation

15. Cost: $430,500
Recovery period: 10 years
Depreciation (year 1): ______

16. Cost: $72,300
Recovery period: 20 years
Depreciation (year 1): ______

17. Cost: $48,000
Recovery period: 10 years
Depreciation (year 1): ______

18. Cost: $12,340
Recovery period: 3 years
Depreciation (year 1): ______

Find the book value at the end of the first year for each of the following using the MACRS method of depreciation and the MACRS depreciation rates table. Round to the nearest dollar. (See Example 4.)

QUICK START

19. Cost: $9380
Recovery period: 3 years
Book value: **$6254**

$9380 × .3333 = $3126
$9380 − $3126 = $6254 book value

20. Cost: $68,700
Recovery period: 5 years
Book value: ______

C indicates an exercise that is related to the Case in Point feature.

Use the MACRS depreciation rates table in the following application problems. Round to the nearest dollar.

33. COMMERCIAL FISHING BOAT Reef Fisheries purchased a new fishing boat (10-year property) for $74,125. Find the depreciation in year 8 using the MACRS method of depreciation.

33. ________________

34. SHOPPING CENTER A new parking lot was added to the Oak Shopping Center at a cost of $118,000. Find the depreciation in year 12 using the MACRS method of depreciation (15-year property).

34. ________________

C **35.** LAPTOP COMPUTERS Capital Curb Concrete purchased laptop computers for the office for $1700. Find the book value at the end of the third year using the MACRS method of depreciation.

35. ________________

36. DENTAL OFFICE FURNITURE Dr. Jill Owens Family Dentistry purchased new furniture for its patient reception area at a cost of $27,400. Find the book value at the end of the fifth year using the MACRS method of depreciation.

36. ________________

37. BOOKKEEPING BUSINESS Jim Bralley, owner of Interlink Financial Services, purchased an office building at a cost of $860,000. Find the amount of depreciation for each of the first five years using the MACRS method of depreciation (39-year property).

Year 1: ________________
Years 2–5: ________________

38. INDEPENDENT BOOKSTORE OWNERSHIP Maretha Roseborough, owner of the Barnstormer Bookstore, bought a building to use for her business. The cost of the building was $620,000. Find the amount of depreciation for each of the first five years using the MACRS method of depreciation (39-year property).

Year 1: ________________
Years 2–5: ________________

CHAPTER 13 QUICK REVIEW

CHAPTER TERMS *Review the following terms to test your understanding of the chapter. For each term you do not know, refer to the page number found next to that term.*

CONCEPTS	EXAMPLES
13.1 Straight-line method of depreciation The depreciation is the same each year. $\text{Depreciation} = \dfrac{\textbf{Depreciable amount}}{\textbf{Years of life}}$	Cost, \$500; scrap value, \$100; life, 8 years; find the annual amount of depreciation. \$500 cost − 100 scrap \$400 depreciable amount $\dfrac{\$400}{8} = \$50$ depreciation each year
13.1 Book value Book value is the remaining value at the end of the year. **Book value = Cost − Accumulated depreciation**	Cost, \$400; scrap value, \$100; life, 3 years; find the book value at the end of the first year. \$400 cost − 100 scrap value \$300 depreciable amount $\dfrac{\$300}{3} = \$100$ depreciation \$400 cost − 100 depreciation \$300 book value year 1
13.2 Double-declining-balance rate First find the straight-line rate, and then adjust it. For the 200% method, **multiply by 2**.	The life of an asset is 10 years. Find the double-declining-balance (200%) rate. $10 \text{ years} = 10\%\left(\dfrac{1}{10}\right)$ straight-line $2 \times 10\% = 20\%$ per year
13.2 Double-declining-balance depreciation method First find the double-declining-balance rate, and then multiply by the cost in year 1. The rate is then multiplied by the declining book value in the following years. **Depreciation = Double-declining-balance rate × Declining balance**	Cost, \$1400; life, 5 years; find the depreciation in years 1 and 2. $2 \times 20\%$ (straight-line rate) = 40% Year 1: 40% × \$1400 = \$560 depreciation year 1 \$1400 − \$560 = \$840 book value year 1 Year 2: 40% × \$840 = \$336 depreciation year 2

CONCEPTS	EXAMPLES
13.3 Sum-of-the-years'-digits depreciation fraction Add the years' digits to get the denominator. The numerator is the number of years of life remaining. The shortcut formula for finding the denominator is: $\frac{n(n+1)}{2}$	Useful life is 4 years. Find the depreciation fraction for each year. $1 + 2 + 3 + 4 = 10$ **Year** — **Depreciation Fraction** 1 — $\frac{4}{10}$ 2 — $\frac{3}{10}$ 3 — $\frac{2}{10}$ 4 — $\frac{1}{10}$
13.3 Sum-of-the-years'-digits depreciation method First find the depreciation fraction, and then multiply by the depreciable amount. **Depreciation = Depreciation fraction × Depreciable amount**	Cost, \$2500; salvage value, \$400; life, 6 years; find depreciation in year 1. Depreciation fraction $= \frac{6}{21}$ Depreciable amount = \$2100 (**\$2500 − \$400**) Depreciation $= \frac{6}{21} \times \$2100 = \$600$
13.4 Units-of-production depreciation amount per unit Use the following formula. $\text{Depreciation per unit} = \frac{\text{Depreciable amount}}{\text{Units of life}}$	Cost, \$10,000; salvage value, \$2500; useful life, 15,000 units; find depreciation per unit. \$10,000 − \$2500 = \$7500 depreciable amount $\text{Depreciation per unit} = \frac{\$7500 \text{ depreciable amount}}{15{,}000 \text{ units of life}} = \$.50$
13.4 Units-of-production depreciation method Multiply the number of units (hours) of production by the depreciation per unit (per hour). **Depreciation = Number of units (hours) × Depreciation per unit (hour)**	Cost, \$25,000; salvage value, \$2000; useful life, 100,000 units; production in year 1, 22,300 units; find the first year's depreciation. **1.** \$25,000 − **\$2000** = \$23,000 depreciable amount **2.** $\frac{\$23{,}000}{100{,}000}$ = \$.23 depreciation per unit **3.** 22,300 × **\$.23** = \$5129 depreciation year 1
13.5 Modified accelerated cost recovery system (MACRS) Established in 1986 for federal income tax purposes. No salvage value. Recovery periods are: 3-year, 5-year, 7-year 10-year, 15-year, 20-year 27.5-year, 31.5-year, 39-year Find the proper rate from the table and then multiply by the cost to find depreciation.	Use the table, finding the recovery period column at the top of the table and the recovery year in the left-hand column. Cost, \$4850; recovery period, 5 years; recovery year, 3; find the depreciation. Rate is **19.20%** from table. \$4850 × **.192** = \$931 depreciation

CHAPTER 13 SUMMARY EXERCISE

Comparing Depreciation Methods: A Business Application

Trader Joe's purchased freezer cases at a cost of $285,000. The estimated life of the freezer cases is 5 years, at which time they will have no salvage value. The company would like to compare allowable depreciation methods and decides to prepare depreciation schedules for the fixtures using the straight-line, double-declining-balance, and sum-of-the-years'-digits methods of depreciation. Using depreciation schedules, find the answers to these questions for Trader Joe's.

(a) What is the book value at the end of 3 years using the straight-line depreciation method? **(a)** ____________

(b) Using the double-declining-balance method of depreciation, what is the book value at the end of the third year? **(b)** ____________

(c) With the sum-of-the-years'-digits method of depreciation, what is the accumulated depreciation at the end of 3 years? **(c)** ____________

(d) What amount of depreciation will be taken in year 4 with each of the methods? **(d)** ____________

____

____

INVESTIGATE

Identify a store or business with which you are familiar and list six of its depreciable assets. Examples could be such items as buildings, computer equipment, vehicles, and fixtures. Using the information on the MACRS method of depreciation, give the recovery period and the first-year depreciation rate for each of the six depreciable assets you listed.

CHAPTER 13 TEST

To help you review, the numbers in brackets show the section in which the topic was discussed.

Find the annual straight-line and double-declining-balance rates (percents) of depreciation and the sum-of-the-years'-digits fraction for the first year for each of the following estimated lives. **[13.1–13.3]**

Life	Straight-Line Rate	Double-Declining-Balance Rate	Sum-of-the-Years'-Digits Fraction
1. 4 years	______	______	______
2. 5 years	______	______	______
3. 8 years	______	______	______
4. 20 years	______	______	______

Solve the following application problems. Round to the nearest dollar.

5. Cloverdale Creamery purchased a soft-serve ice cream maker at a cost of $12,400. The machine has an estimated life of 10 years and a scrap value of $3000. Use the straight-line method of depreciation to find the annual depreciation. **[13.1]**

5. ________________

6. Capital Curb and Concrete purchased a new dump truck for $38,000. If the estimated life of the dump truck is 8 years, find the book value at the end of 2 years using the double-declining-balance method of depreciation. **[13.2]**

6. ________________

7. The Feather River Youth Camp purchased a diesel generator for $8250. Use the sum-of-the-years'-digits method of depreciation to determine the amount of depreciation to be taken during *each of the 4 years* on the diesel generator that has a 4-year life and a scrap value of $1500. **[13.3]**

Year 1: ________________
Year 2: ________________
Year 3: ________________
Year 4: ________________

8. A private road costs $56,000 and has a 15-year recovery period. Find the depreciation in the third year using the MACRS method of depreciation. **[13.5]**

8. ________________

9. The water filtration system at Micro Brew costs $74,000, has an estimated life of 20 years, and has an estimated scrap value of $12,000. Use the straight-line method of depreciation to find the book value of the machinery at the end of 10 years. **[13.1]**

9. ________________

10. Karl Schmidt, owner of Toy Train Hobby Shop, has added paging and intercom features to the communication systems of his 4 stores at a cost of $2800 per store. The estimated life of the systems is 10 years, with no expected salvage value. Using the sum-of-the-years'-digits method of depreciation, find the total book value of all the systems at the end of the third year. **[13.3]**

10. ____________

11. Table Fresh Foods purchased a machine to package its presliced garden salads. The machine costs $20,100 and has an estimated life of 30,000 hours and a salvage value of $1500. Use the units-of-production method of depreciation to find **(a)** the annual amount of depreciation and **(b)** the book value at the end of each year, given the following use information: year 1: 7800 hours; year 2: 4300 hours; year 3: 4850 hours; year 4: 7600 hours. **[13.4]**

(a) ____________

(b) ____________

12. The Rice Growers Cooperative paid $2,800,000 to build a new rice-drying plant. The recovery period is 39 years. Use the MACRS method of depreciation to find the book value of the rice-drying plant at the end of the fifth year. **[13.5]**

12. ____________

CHAPTER 14

Financial Statements and Ratios

CHAPTER CONTENTS

CASE in POINT

The Hershey Company (ticker symbol: HSY) is the largest manufacturer of chocolate and nonchocolate candies in North America. You may have seen or tasted some of their delicious brand-name products: HERSHEY'S® milk chocolate, REESE'S® peanut butter cups, KIT KAT wafer bars, HERSHEY'S KISSES, JOLLY RANCHER candies, and ICE BREAKERS chewing gum and mints. Recent financial statements for The Hershey Company are reviewed in this chapter.

Managers must keep careful records of expenses and income in order to operate the business, communicate with others about the business, provide information to lenders, and prepare tax returns. **Accountants** track the income and expenses of the firm. They are concerned with issues such as meeting payroll, paying suppliers, estimating and paying taxes, and estimating and receiving revenues. This chapter looks at some tools used in business to gauge the financial health of a firm.

14.1 THE INCOME STATEMENT

OBJECTIVES

1. Understand the terms on an income statement.
2. Prepare an income statement.

CASE in POINT As a publicly held corporation, The Hershey Company must prepare and distribute quarterly reports and an annual report showing income, expenses, assets, and liabilities. In turn, managers and investors must be able to analyze and understand these financial reports in order to make a judgment about the company's financial performance and chances for future growth.

OBJECTIVE 1 Understand the terms on an income statement. An **income statement** is used to summarize all income and expenses for a given period of time, such as a month, a quarter, or a year. Here are some important definitions related to financial statements.

Gross sales, or **total revenue**, is the total amount of money received from customers.
Returns are returns by customers (usually used by smaller companies and not large ones).
Net sales is the value of goods and services bought and kept by customers.

Net sales = Gross sales − Returns

Cost of goods sold is the amount paid by the firm for items sold to customers.
Gross profit, or **gross profit on sales**, is the money left over after a firm pays for the cost of goods it sells.

Gross profit = Net sales − Cost of goods sold

QUICK TIP You can find information about The Hershey Company (ticker symbol: HSY) at the Web site (www.hersheys.com) or on many financial Web sites.

Operating expenses, or **overhead**, is the firm's cost to run the business.
Net income before taxes is the amount earned by the firm before taxes are paid.
Net income, or **net income after taxes**, is the income remaining after income taxes are paid.

Net income before taxes = Gross profit − Operating expenses
Net income = Net income before taxes − Income taxes

EXAMPLE 1 Finding Net Income

A portion of the 2006 income statement for The Hershey Company is shown, with all numbers in millions. Thus net sales of \$4944 actually means net sales of \$4,944,000,000 or four billion, nine hundred forty-four million dollars. Five billion represents a lot of candy! Check to make sure the income statement balances.

QUICK TIP Bankers and investors pore over the financial statements of publicly held corporations to determine their credit-worthiness and whether they would be good investments.

SOLUTION

The Hershey Company
Consolidated Statement of Income
Year Ending December 31, 2006
(in millions of dollars)

Gross Sales	$4944
Returns	− 0
Net Sales	$4944
Cost of Goods Sold	−3077
Gross Profit	$1867
Operating Expenses	− 990
Net Income before Taxes	$ 877
Income Taxes	− 318
Net Income	$ 559

In 2006, the company had no returns from customers and paid income taxes of about $318,000,000. The after-tax profit was $559 million.

$$\underbrace{\$3077}_{\text{cost of goods sold}} + \underbrace{\$990}_{\text{operating expenses}} + \underbrace{\$318}_{\text{income taxes}} + \underbrace{\$559}_{\text{net income}} = \$4944$$

The income statement checks.

QUICK CHECK 1

A firm has gross sales of $5.2, cost of goods sold of $3.7, operating expenses of $.7, and income taxes of $.2, all in millions of dollars. Find the net income after taxes.

OBJECTIVE 2 **Prepare an income statement.** Example 1 gave the value for the cost of goods sold, but this amount would normally need to be calculated. The cost of goods sold can be found using the following formula. **Initial inventory** is the value of all goods on hand for sale at the beginning of the period. **Ending inventory** is the value of all goods on hand for sale at the end of the period.

Value of initial inventory
+ Cost of goods purchased during time period
+ Freight
− Value of ending inventory
Cost of goods sold

EXAMPLE 2 Preparing an Income Statement

In the first year of business, Timber Lake Building Supplies had $452,700 in gross sales, with returns of $38,100. Inventory at the beginning of the year was $48,800, with a cost of goods purchased of $253,700 and freight of $7430. Inventory at the end of the year was $89,090. Expenses were as follows: salaries $104,300; rent $38,800; advertising $24,300; utilities $11,600; taxes on inventory and payroll $9400; and miscellaneous expenses $13,350. They paid no income taxes because they had a slight loss in their first year. Complete an income statement using the following steps.

Quick Check Answer

1. $.6 million or $600,000

Preparing an Income Statement

STEP 1 Enter gross sales and returns. Subtract returns from gross sales to find net sales. Net sales in this example were $414,600.

STEP 2 Enter the cost of goods purchased and the freight. Add these two numbers.

STEP 3 Add the inventory on January 1 and the total cost of goods purchased.

STEP 4 Subtract the inventory on December 31 from the result of step 3. This gives the cost of goods sold.

STEP 5 Subtract the cost of goods sold from net sales, which were found in step 1. The result is the gross profit.

STEP 6 Enter all expenses and add them to get the total expenses.

STEP 7 Subtract the total expenses from the gross profit to find the net income before taxes.

STEP 8 Subtract income taxes from net income before taxes to find net income (net income after taxes).

SOLUTION

Timber Lake Building Supplies
Income Statement
Year Ending December 31

Gross Sales			① Subtract.	$452,700
Returns				$38,100
Net Sales				$414,600
Inventory, January 1		$48,800		
Cost of Goods Purchased	$253,700		② Add. ③ Add.	
Freight	$7,430			
Total Cost of Goods Purchased		$261,130	⑤ Subtract.	
Total of Goods Available for Sale		$309,930		
Inventory, December 31		$89,090	④ Subtract.	
Cost of Goods Sold				$220,840
Gross Profit				$193,760
Expenses				
Salaries and Wages		$104,300		
Rent		$38,800		
Advertising		$24,300		
Utilities		$11,600	⑥ Add.	
Taxes on Inventory, Payroll		$9,400		
Miscellaneous Expenses		$13,350		
Total Expenses				$201,750
Net Income before Taxes			⑦ Subtract.	−$7,990
Income Taxes				$0
Net Income			⑧ Subtract.	−$7,990

QUICK CHECK 2

Find the net income for a firm given the following information, in millions of dollars: Gross Sales $10.2; Returns $.1; Beginning Inventory $.3; Cost of Goods Purchased including freight $6.9; Ending Inventory $.6; Total Expenses $1.8; and Income Taxes $.5.

Quick Check Answer

2. $1.2 million

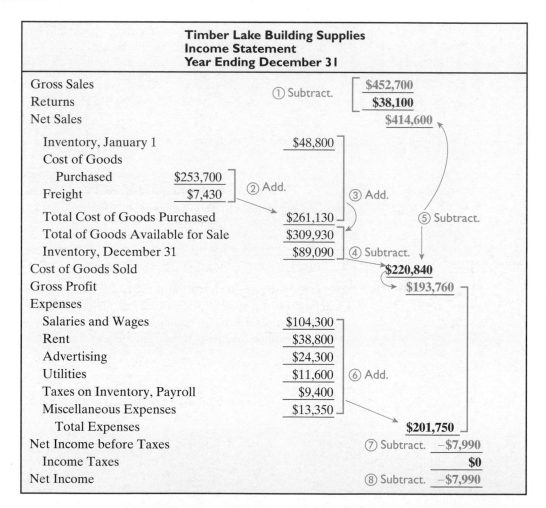

14.1 EXERCISES

FOR EXTRA HELP

MyMathLab

MathXL PRACTICE

WATCH

DOWNLOAD

READ

REVIEW

The **QUICK START** *exercises in each section contain solutions to help you get started.*

Find (a) the gross profit, (b) the net income before taxes, and (c) the net income after taxes for each firm. (See Example 1.)

QUICK START

1. GIFT SHOP Janis Jacobs opened a small candle and gift shop in the mall three years ago. Last year, the cost of goods sold was $367,200, operating expenses were $228,300, income taxes were $22,700, gross sales were $685,900, and returns were $2350.

   (a) $316,350
   (b) $88,050
   (c) $65,350

   (a) Gross profit = $685,900 − $2350 − $367,200 = $316,350

   (b) Net income before taxes = $316,350 − $228,300 = $88,050

   (c) Net income after taxes = $88,050 − $22,700 = $65,350

2. ICE CREAM SHOP Ben's Ice Cream had net sales of $281,400, operating expenses (including wages) of $119,380, a cost of goods sold of $103,800, and paid $7240 in taxes.

   (a) ________
   (b) ________
   (c) ________

3. ELECTRONICS Amber Electronics had gross sales of $852,300 last year, with returns of $42,800. The inventory on January 1 was $174,690. A total of $345,790 worth of goods was purchased with freight of $18,107. The inventory on December 31 was $158,200. Wages and salaries were $168,240; rent was $48,200; advertising was $24,300; utilities were $11,600; taxes on inventory and payroll totaled $13,880; miscellaneous expenses totaled $21,900; and income taxes were $34,800. Complete the following income statement.

Pure Bliss	Income Statement	Year Ending December 31	
Gross Sales			________
Returns			________
Net Sales			________
Inventory, January 1		________	
Cost of Goods Purchased	________		
Freight	________		
Total Cost of Goods Purchased		________	
Total of Goods Available for Sale		________	
Inventory, December 31		________	
Cost of Goods Sold			________
Gross Profit			________
Expenses			
Salaries and Wages		________	
Rent		________	
Advertising		________	
Utilities		________	
Taxes on Inventory, Payroll		________	
Miscellaneous Expenses		________	
Total Expenses			________
Net Income before Taxes			________
Income Taxes			________
Net Income			________

4. Explain why a lender and an investor would want to look at an income statement before making a loan or an investment. (See Objective 1.)

5. Explain why a banker would look at your personal income statement before approving you for a loan. (See Objective 1.)

6. DENTAL-SUPPLY COMPANY New England Dental Supply is a regional wholesaler that had gross sales last year of $2,215,000. Returns totaled $26,000. Inventory on January 1 was $215,000. Goods purchased during the year totaled $1,123,000. Freight was $4000. Inventory on December 31 was $265,000. Wages and salaries were $326,000, rent was $59,000, advertising was $11,000, utilities were $12,000, taxes on inventory and payroll totaled $28,200, and miscellaneous expenses were $18,800. In addition, income taxes for the year amounted to $197,800. Complete the following income statement for this firm. (See Example 2.)

New England Dental Supply
Income Statement
Year Ending December 31

Gross Sales			_____	
Returns			_____	
Net Sales				_____
Inventory, January 1		_____		
Cost of Goods Purchased	_____			
Freight	_____			
Total Cost of Goods Purchased		_____		
Total of Goods Available for Sale		_____		
Inventory, December 31		_____		
Cost of Goods Sold				_____
Gross Profit				_____
Expenses				
Salaries and Wages		_____		
Rent		_____		
Advertising		_____		
Utilities		_____		
Taxes on Inventory, Payroll		_____		
Miscellaneous Expenses		_____		
Total Expenses				_____
Net Income before Taxes				_____
Income Taxes				_____
Net Income				_____

14.2 ANALYZING THE INCOME STATEMENT

OBJECTIVES

1. Compare income statements using vertical analysis.
2. Compare income statements to published charts.
3. Compare income statements using horizontal analysis.

CASE in POINT It is important that you look carefully at the income statement of The Hershey Company, or any other company, before investing in the stock of that company. Invest only if you are convinced the company will be profitable.

OBJECTIVE 1 **Compare income statements using vertical analysis.** A firm can find its net income for a given period of time by going through the steps presented in the preceding section. A question that might then be asked is "What happened to each part of the sales dollar?" The first step toward answering this question is to list each of the important items on the income statement as a percent of net sales. This process is called a **vertical analysis** of the income statement.

In a vertical analysis, each item on the income statement is found as a percent of the net sales.

$$R = \frac{P}{B} \quad \text{or} \quad R = \frac{\text{Particular item}}{\text{Net sales}}$$

For example, we can use data from the 2006 income statement for The Hershey Company on page 635.

$$\text{Percent cost of goods sold} = \frac{\$3077}{\$4944} = 62.2\%$$

In 2006, The Hershey Company spent slightly more than 62% of the total revenue for the cost of goods used in manufacturing processes. A few companies may have little or no cost of goods. For example, Microsoft Corporation writes computer software. The cost of labor to produce the software is very high (operating expense), but the cost of goods such as optical disks on which software is written is very low. So this ratio would be tiny for Mircosoft.

A **comparative income statement** is used to compare results from two or more years. It can be used to show how the company is doing over time.

EXAMPLE 1 Performing a Vertical Analysis

First perform a vertical analysis of the 2005 and 2006 income statements shown for The Hershey Company. Then construct a comparative income statement by showing the results in a table.

The Hershey Company
Consolidated Statement of Income
(in millions of dollars)

Year Ending December 31	2005	2006
Gross Sales	$4820	$4944
Returns	− 0	− 0
Net Sales	$4820	$4944
Cost of Goods Sold	− 2957	− 3077
Gross Profit	$1863	$1867
Operating Expenses	− 1097	− 990
Net Income before Taxes	$766	$877
Income Taxes	− 277	− 318
Net Income	$489	$559

SOLUTION

Calculate each value in the column labeled 2005 as a percent of 2005 sales rounded to the nearest tenth of a percent. Then do the same for 2006.

Comparative Income Statement	2005	2006
Percent Cost of Goods Sold	$\frac{\$2957}{\$4820} = 61.3\%$	$\frac{\$3077}{\$4944} = 62.2\%$
Percent Gross Profit	$\frac{\$1863}{\$4820} = 38.7\%$	$\frac{\$1867}{\$4944} = 37.8\%$
Percent Operating Expenses	$\frac{\$1097}{\$4820} = 22.8\%$	$\frac{\$990}{\$4944} = 20.0\%$
Percent Net Income before Taxes	$\frac{\$766}{\$4820} = 15.9\%$	$\frac{\$877}{\$4944} = 17.7\%$

The cost of goods sold increased from 61.3% of net sales in 2005 to 62.2% of net sales in 2006. The company's costs seem to be going up, which is not a good trend. However, they were able to offset this by reducing operating expenses from 22.8% of net sales to 20.0% of net sales. As a result, their net income increased from 15.9% of net sales to 17.7% of net sales.

QUICK TIP Before deciding to invest in a company, prudent investors want to know much more about a company than what is shown in the preceding example.

QUICK CHECK 1

A 2007 income statement shows the following figures in millions: Net Sales $23.5, Returns $.5, Cost of Goods sold $12.9, and Operating Expenses $3.8. Do a vertical analysis and round each percent to the nearest tenth.

OBJECTIVE 2 **Compare income statements to published charts.** If you own a business or are considering investing in a business, you would be wise to compare the financial figures for that business to industry averages. Published charts of industry averages can be obtained from the federal government.

Type of Business	Cost of Goods	Gross Profit	Total Expenses*	Net Income	Wages	Rent	Advertising
Supermarkets	82.7%	17.3%	13.9%	3.4%	6.5%	.8%	1.0%
Men's and women's apparel	67.0%	33.0%	21.2%	11.8%	8.0%	2.5%	1.9%
Women's apparel	64.8%	35.2%	23.4%	11.7%	7.9%	4.9%	1.8%
Shoes	60.3%	39.7%	24.5%	15.2%	10.3%	4.7%	1.6%
Furniture	68.9%	31.2%	21.7%	9.6%	9.5%	1.8%	2.5%
Appliances	66.9%	33.1%	26.0%	7.2%	11.9%	2.4%	2.5%
Drugs	67.9%	32.1%	23.5%	8.6%	12.3%	2.4%	1.4%
Restaurants	48.4%	51.6%	43.7%	7.9%	26.4%	2.8%	1.4%
Service stations	76.8%	23.2%	16.9%	6.3%	8.5%	2.3%	.5%

* Total Expenses represents the total of all expenses involved in running the firm. These expenses include, but are not limited to, wages, rent, and advertising.

Quick Check Answer

1. Returns 2.1%; Cost of Goods sold 54.9%; Operating Expenses $16.2%

EXAMPLE 2

Comparing Business Ratios

Gina Burton wishes to compare the business ratios of her shoe store, Burton's Shoes, to industry averages. Figures from her store and industry averages for shoe stores are shown in the table.

	Cost of Goods	Gross Profit	Total Expenses	Net Income	Wages	Rent	Advertising
Burton's Shoes	58.2%	41.8%	28.3%	13.5%	11.7%	5.6%	2.8%
Shoes (from previous chart)	60.3%	39.7%	24.5%	15.2%	10.3%	4.7%	1.6%

SOLUTION

Burton's expenses are higher than the average for other shoe stores and her net income is lower. Wages are higher—perhaps because her store is located in an area with high wages or perhaps the store is not large enough to efficiently utilize its employees. Burton also spends a higher percent than average for advertising. Perhaps she can reduce her advertising expenses without lowering sales.

QUICK CHECK 2

A furniture store has total expenses of 21.3% and cost of goods of 72%. Compare to averages.

OBJECTIVE 3 **Compare income statements using horizontal analysis.** Another way to analyze an income statement is to prepare a **horizontal analysis**. A horizontal analysis finds the percent of change (either increases or decreases) between the current time period and a previous time period. This comparison can expose unusual changes, such as a rapid increase in expenses or decline in net sales or profits.

Do a horizontal analysis by finding the amount of change from the previous year to the current year in dollars and as a percent. For example, the income statement of The Hershey Company on page 639 shows that net sales increased from \$4820 (in millions) in 2005 to \$4944 (in millions) in 2006. The increase in net sales was \$4944 − \$4820 = \$124 million.

$$\text{Percent increase in net sales} = \frac{\$124}{\$4820} = 2.6\%$$

net sales for 2005 ↑

Net sales grew slowly during this period, at about the same rate as inflation. The following graph shows how the stock price for The Hershey Company (HSY) compares to the Dow Jones Industrial Average (DJIA).

Numbers in the News

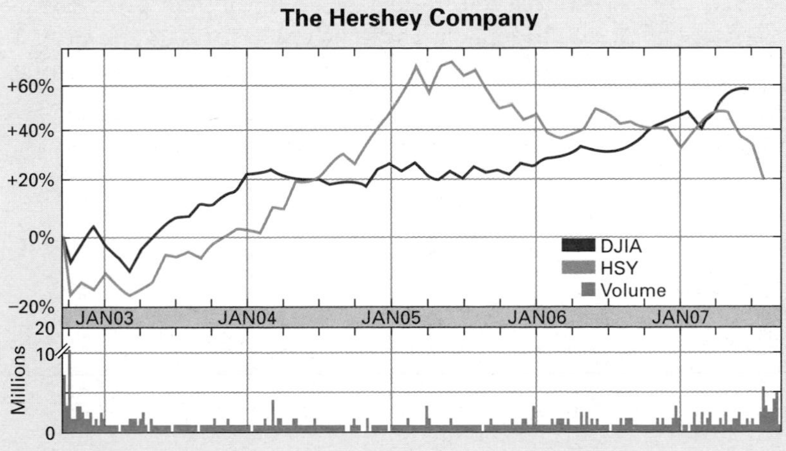

DATA: Yahoo! Finance

Quick Check Answer

2. Total Expenses are below average of 21.7%; Cost of Goods is above average of 68.9%

To emphasize,

$$\% \text{ of change} = \frac{\text{Change}}{\text{Previous year's amount}}$$

Always use *last year* as the base.

EXAMPLE 3

Performing a Horizontal Analysis

Calculate a horizontal analysis for the 2005 and 2006 income statements for The Hershey Company using the data given in Example 1.

SOLUTION

Find the increase by subtracting the 2005 figure from the 2006 figure. Then divide by the 2005 figure to find the percent increase (decrease) to the nearest tenth of a percent.

The Hershey Company
Consolidated Statement of Income
Year Ending December 31
(in millions of dollars)

	2005	2006	Increase	Percent
Net Sales	\$4820	\$4944	\$124	2.6%
Gross Profit	\$1863	\$1867	\$4	.2%
Net Income before Taxes	\$766	\$877	\$111	14.5%
Net Income	\$489	\$559	\$70	14.3%

QUICK TIP During the past 25 years, many companies have moved manufacturing jobs to third-world countries to decrease labor costs. Now there is evidence that some technology and professional jobs are being moved to third-world countries for the same reasons. Education is one of the basic ways to help protect yourself and your family from the job displacement brought by this trend.

The very small increase in net sales and gross profit indicates that the company is not growing. However, both net income before taxes and net income after taxes were up by a significant 14% or so. But, the net incomes were up because the operating expenses were down. Effectively, the company increased profit by cutting costs and not by growing sales. A company can cut costs only to a point without damaging operations. Beyond that, a company must increase sales to grow. Before investing, an investor might want to figure out why The Hershey Company is growing so slowly.

Here are a few actions The Hershey Company might be able to take to increase revenue and decrease costs:

1. Increase sales outside of the United States.
2. Develop additional products to sell.
3. Increase marketing efforts.
4. Decrease costs by doing some manufacturing in foreign countries.

QUICK CHECK 3

Partial 2007 results for a company are: Gross Sales \$58.6 million and Operating Expenses \$12.1 million. The same results for 2008 are: Gross Sales \$61.2 million and Operating Expenses \$12.9 million. Do a *horizontal comparison*.

Quick Check Answer

3. Gross Sales increased 4.4%; Operating Expenses increased 6.6%

14.2 EXERCISES

FOR EXTRA HELP

MyMathLab

MathXL PRACTICE

WATCH

DOWNLOAD

READ

REVIEW

The QUICK START *exercises in each section contain solutions to help you get started.*

Prepare a vertical analysis for each of the following firms. Round percents to the nearest tenth of a percent. (See Example 1.)

QUICK START

1. SCUBA SHOPPE Reef Scuba, Inc., had net sales of $439,000, operating expenses of $143,180, and a cost of goods sold of $198,400.

Percent cost of goods sold $= \frac{\$198{,}400}{\$439{,}000} = 45.2\%$

Percent operating expenses $= \frac{\$143{,}180}{\$439{,}000} = 32.6\%$

1. 45.2%; 32.6%

2. COFFEE SHOP Tatum's Coffee and Books had operating expenses of $198,400, a cost of goods sold of $287,104, and net sales of $589,250.

2. ______________

3. GUITAR SHOP In 2009, Classic Guitars had a cost of goods sold (mostly guitars) of $243,570, operating expenses of $140,450, and net sales of $480,300.

3. ______________

4. COIN SHOP Traver's Coin Shop, Inc., had net sales of $294,380, operating expenses of $68,650, and a cost of goods sold of $163,890.

4. ______________

The following charts show some figures from income statements. In each case, prepare a vertical analysis by expressing each item as a percent of net sales. Then write in the appropriate average percent from the table in the book. (See Objective 2.)

5. **Gooden Drugs**

	Amount	Percent	Average Percent
Net Sales	$850,000	100%	100%
Cost of Goods Sold	$570,350	_____	_____
Gross Profit	$279,650	_____	_____
Wages	$106,250	_____	_____
Rent	$21,250	_____	_____
Advertising	$12,750	_____	_____
Total Expenses	$209,100	_____	_____
Net Income before Taxes	$70,550	_____	_____

6. **Ellis Restaurant**

	Amount	Percent	Average Percent
Net Sales	$600,000	100%	100%
Cost of Goods Sold	$280,000	_____	_____
Gross Profit	$320,000	_____	_____
Wages	$160,600	_____	_____
Rent	$15,000	_____	_____
Advertising	$8,000	_____	_____
Total Expenses	$255,000	_____	_____
Net Income before Taxes	$65,000	_____	_____

7. Compare a vertical analysis to a horizontal analysis. (See Objectives 1 and 3.)

8. Why would a lender want to use both vertical and horizontal analyses before making a long-term loan to a firm?

9. Complete the comparative income statement. Round to the nearest tenth of a percent.

Hernandez Nursery Comparative Income Statement

	This Year		Last Year	
	Amount	**Percent**	**Amount**	**Percent**
Gross Sales	$1,856,000	______	$1,692,000	______
Returns	$6,000	______	$12,000	______
Net Sales	______	100.0%	______	100.0%
Cost of Goods Sold	$1,102,000	______	$950,000	______
Gross Profit	$748,000	______	$730,000	______
Wages	$252,000	______	$248,000	______
Rent	$82,000	______	$78,000	______
Advertising	$111,000	______	$122,000	______
Utilities	$32,000	______	$17,000	______
Taxes on Inv., Payroll	$17,000	______	$18,000	______
Miscellaneous Expenses	$62,000	______	$58,000	______
Total Expenses	$556,000	______	$541,000	______
Net Income before Taxes	______	______	______	______

10. Complete the horizontal analysis for the Hernandez Nursery comparative income statement given in Exercise 9. Round to the nearest tenth of a percent.

Hernandez Nursery Horizontal Analysis

			Increase or (Decrease)	
	This Year	**Last Year**	**Amount**	**Percent**
Gross Sales	$1,856,000	$1,692,000	______	______
Returns	$6,000	$12,000	______	______
Net Sales	$1,850,000	$1,680,000	______	______
Cost of Goods Sold	$1,102,000	$950,000		
Gross Profit	$748,000	$730,000	______	______
Wages	$252,000	$248,000	______	______
Rent	$82,000	$78,000	______	______
Advertising	$111,000	$122,000	______	______
Utilities	$32,000	$17,000		
Taxes on Inv., Payroll	$17,000	$18,000	______	______
Miscellaneous Expenses	$62,000	$58,000	______	______
Net Income before Taxes	$192,000	$189,000	______	______

The following table gives the percents for various items from the income statements of firms in two businesses. Complete these tables by including the appropriate percents from the table on page 640. Identify any areas that might require attention by management.

Type of Store	Cost of Goods	Gross Profit	Total Operating Expenses	Net Income	Wages	Rent	Advertising
11. Women's apparel	66.4%	33.6%	25.3%	8.3%	8.4%	6.5%	1.9%
	_____	_____	_____	_____	_____	_____	_____
12. Drug store	71.2%	28.8%	26.5%	2.3%	12.9%	5.3%	2.0%
	_____	_____	_____	_____	_____	_____	_____

13. Update the graph on page 641 using data from the Internet.

14. Use the Internet to find a graph of the stock-price history of a company you are familiar with.

14.3 THE BALANCE SHEET

OBJECTIVES

1 Understand the terms on a balance sheet.

2 Prepare a balance sheet.

CASE *in* POINT You also need to look at the balance sheet before deciding to buy stock in a company. The income statement shows information during an interval of time, such as a quarter or a year. In contrast, the balance sheet shows information at one point in time, such as the amount of cash The Hershey Company had on a specific day.

OBJECTIVE 1 Understand the terms on a balance sheet. An income statement summarizes the financial affairs of a business firm for a given period of time, such as a year. In contrast, a **balance sheet** describes the financial condition of a firm *at one point in time*, such as the last day of a year. A balance sheet shows the **assets** of a firm, which is the total value of everything owned by a business at a particular time. Assets include property, equipment, money owed to the company, cash, and securities owned. A balance sheet also shows the amounts owed by the business to others, called **liabilities**.

Both assets and liabilities are divided into two categories, **long-term** and **current (short-term)**. Long-term generally applies to assets or liabilities with a life of more than a year. Short-term applies when the time involved is less than a year.

Assets

Current assets—cash or items that can be converted into cash within a short period of time such as a year

Cash—amount in checking and savings accounts and money market instruments
Accounts receivable—funds owed by customers of the firm
Notes receivable—value of all notes owed to the firm
Inventory—cost of merchandise that the firm has for sale

Plant and equipment—assets that are expected to be used for more than one year (also called **fixed assets** or **plant assets**)

Land—book value of any land owned by the firm
Buildings—book value of any buildings owned by the firm
Equipment—book value of equipment, store fixtures, furniture, and similar items owned by the firm

Liabilities

Current liabilities—items that must be paid by the firm within a short period of time, usually one year

Accounts payable—amounts that must be paid to other firms
Notes payable—value of all notes owed by the firm

Long-term liabilities—items that will be paid after one year

Mortgages payable—total due on all mortgages
Long-term notes payable—total of all other debts of the firm

The difference between the total of all assets and the total of all liabilities is called the **owners' equity**, which is also referred to as **net worth** or, for a corporation, **stockholders' equity**. The relationship among owners' equity, assets, and liabilities is shown in the fundamental formula below.

Owners' equity = Assets − Liabilities

or

Assets = Liabilities + Owners' equity

OBJECTIVE 2 Prepare a balance sheet.

EXAMPLE 1 Preparing a Balance Sheet

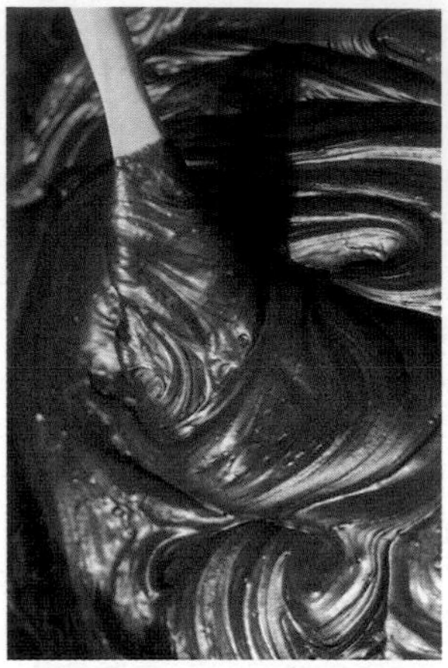

On December 31, 2006, The Hershey Company's balance sheet showed the following assets, in millions of dollars: cash and short-term investments, $97; accounts receivable and other, $672; inventory, $649; net plant and property, $1651; other assets, $1089. It also showed the following liabilities, in millions of dollars: loans and accounts payable, $1000; other current liabilities, $454; long-term debt, $1248; other long-term liabilities, $773. Complete a balance sheet and find the stockholders' equity.

SOLUTION

The Hershey Company
Consolidated Balance Sheet
Year Ending December 31, 2006
(in millions of dollars)

Current Assets:		
Cash and short-term investments	$97	
Accounts receivable and other	$672	
Inventory	$649	
Total Current Assets	$1418	sum of all current assets
Other Assets:		
Net plant and property	$1651	
Other assets	$1089	
Total Assets	$4158	total current and other assets
Current Liabilities:		
Loans and accounts payable	$1000	
Other current liabilities	$454	
Total Current Liabilities	$1454	sum of all current liabilities
Other Liabilities:		
Long-term debt	$1248	
Other long-term liabilities	$773	
Total Liabilities	$3475	total current and other liabilities
Stockholders' Equity:	**$683**	**Total assets − Total liabilities**
Total Liabilities and Equity	$4158	

On December 31, 2006, The Hershey Company had about $97,000,000 in cash and other short-term investments that could quickly be converted to cash. This amount could be very different on another day. The balance sheet gives no information abount assets or liabilities on any date other than December 31, 2006.

The Hershey Company had a lot of inventory on December 31, 2006: $649,000,000. This includes supplies needed to make candy, candy in the process of being made, and also finished candy ready to be shipped from their manufacturing plants.

QUICK CHECK 1

A plumbing contractor's balance sheet shows the following assets (in thousands): Cash, $398; Accounts Receivable and other, $789; Inventory, $481, Net Plant and Property, $1047; Other Assests, $212. The liabilities were: Loans and Accounts Payable, $659; Other Current Liabilities, $241; Long-term Debt, $384, Other Long-term Liabilities, $412. Find the Stockholders' Equity.

QUICK TIP Bankruptcy usually happens when a firm's stockholders' equity is negative.

Remember this important relationship:

Stockholders' equity = Total assets − Total liabilities.

Quick Check Answer

1. $1,231,000

14.3 EXERCISES

FOR EXTRA HELP

MyMathLab

MathXL PRACTICE

WATCH

DOWNLOAD

READ

REVIEW

Complete the balance sheets for the following business firms. (See Example 1.)

1. GROCERY CHAIN Brookshire's Grocery (all figures in millions): fixtures, \$28; buildings, \$290; land, \$466; cash, \$273; notes receivable, \$312; accounts receivable, \$264; inventory, \$180; notes payable, \$312; mortgages payable, \$212; accounts payable, \$63; long-term notes payable, \$55.

Brookshire's Grocery Balance Sheet December 31 (in millions)

ASSETS			
Current Assets			
Cash	____		
Notes Receivable	____		
Accounts Receivable	____		
Inventory	____		
Total Current Assets		____	
Plant Assets			
Land	____		
Buildings	____		
Fixtures	____		
Total Plant Assets		____	
Total Assets			____
LIABILITIES			
Current Liabilities			
Notes Payable	____		
Accounts Payable	____		
Total Current Liabilities		____	
Long-Term Liabilities			
Mortgages Payable	____		
Long-Term Notes Payable	____		
Total Long-Term Liabilities		____	
Total Liabilities			____
OWNERS' EQUITY			
Owners' Equity			____
Total Liabilities and Owners' Equity			____

2. LOPEZ MANUFACTURING Land is $8750; accounts payable total $49,230; notes receivable are $2600; accounts receivable are $37,820; cash is $14,800; buildings are $21,930; notes payable are $3780; owners' equity is $54,320; long-term notes payable are $18,740; mortgages payable total $26,330; inventory is $49,680; fixtures are $16,820 (all figures in thousands).

Lopez Manufacturing Balance Sheet—December 31 (in thousands)

ASSETS			
Current Assets			
Cash	_______		
Notes Receivable	_______		
Accounts Receivable	_______		
Inventory	_______		
Total Current Assets		_______	
Plant Assets			
Land	_______		
Buildings	_______		
Fixtures	_______		
Total Plant Assets		_______	
Total Assets			_______
LIABILITIES			
Current Liabilities			
Notes Payable	_______		
Accounts Payable	_______		
Total Current Liabilities		_______	
Long-Term Liabilities			
Mortgages Payable	_______		
Long-Term Notes Payable	_______		
Total Long-Term Liabilities		_______	
Total Liabilities			_______
OWNERS' EQUITY			
Owners' Equity			_______
Total Liabilities and Owners' Equity			_______

3. Compare a balance sheet to an income statement.

4. Use the World Wide Web to find the amount of cash and equivalents at the end of the most recent fiscal year for GM and the Coca-Cola Company. Which company has more? Why do you suppose it has as much as it does?

14.4 ANALYZING THE BALANCE SHEET

OBJECTIVES

1. Compare balance sheets using vertical analysis.
2. Compare balance sheets using horizontal analysis.
3. Find financial ratios.

OBJECTIVE 1 **Compare balance sheets using vertical analysis.** A balance sheet can be analyzed in much the same way as an income statement. In a **vertical analysis**, each item on the balance sheet is expressed as a percent of total assets. A **comparative balance sheet** shows the vertical analysis for two different years.

EXAMPLE 1

Comparing Balance Sheets

First, do a vertical analysis for the 2005 and the 2006 balance sheets for The Hershey Company by calculating each value as a percent of the total assets for the respective year. Round percents to the nearest tenth. Then compare the percents to identify changes from 2005 to 2006.

SOLUTION

The Hershey Company
Consolidated Statement of Income
Year Ending December 31
(in millions of dollars)

	2005		2006	
ASSETS:	**Amount**	**Percent**	**Amount**	**Percent**
Current Assets:				
Cash and short-term investments	$67	1.6%*	$97	2.3%
Accounts receivable and Other	$674	15.8%	$672	16.2%
Inventory	$635	14.9%	$649	15.6%
Total Current Assets	$1376	32.3%	$1418	34.1%
Other Assets:				
Net plant and property	$1659	38.9%	$1651	39.7%
Other assets	$1228	28.8%	$1089	26.2%
Total Assets	$4263	100.0%	$4158	100.0%
LIABILITIES:	**Amount**	**Percent**	**Amount**	**Percent**
Current Liabilities:				
Loans and accounts payable	$987	23.2%	$1000	24.1%
Other current liabilities	$503	11.8%	$454	10.9%
Total Current Liabilities	$1490	35.0%	$1454	35.0%
Other Liabilities:				
Long term debt	$943	22.1%	$1248	30.0%
Other long-term liabilities	$813	19.1%	$773	18.6%
Total Liabilities	$3246	76.2%	$3475	83.6%
Stockholders' Equity:	$1017	23.9%	$683	16.4%
Total Liabilities and Equity	$4263	100.1%	$4158	100.0%

*Percents were added to find total percents.

Notice that stockholders' equity fell from $1017 to $683 (in millions) or from 23.9% of total assets to 16.4% of total assets. This indicates that some kind of a significant problem occurred in 2006. Current assets increased from $1376 to $1418 (in millions), which is moving in the right direction. Investors and lenders want sufficient current assets because that supports a company's ability to handle unforeseen problems. Long-term debt went from $943 (22.1% of total assets) to $1248 (30% of total assets), which was a large increase. For some reason, the company took on significant long-term debt and stockholders' equity decreased sharply. Investors and lenders would want to know full details before lending money to the company or buying the stock of the company.

Then the ratio of net income after taxes to average owners' equity is found.

$$\text{Ratio of net income after taxes to average owners' equity} = \frac{\text{Net income after taxes}}{\text{Average owners' equity}}$$

EXAMPLE 5

Finding the Return on Average Equity

Find the 2006 ratio of net income after taxes to average owners' equity for The Hershey Company.

SOLUTION

Stockholders' equity fell from \$1017 to \$683 (in millions) from the end of 2005 to the end of 2006.

$$\text{Average owners' equity} = \frac{\$1017 + \$683}{2} = \$850 \text{ (in millions)}$$

Use the net income after taxes in 2006 from the income statement in **Section 14.1** on page 635 to find the ratio.

$$\text{Ratio of net income after taxes to average owners' equity} = \frac{\$559}{\$850} = \mathbf{65.8\%} \text{ (rounded)}$$

QUICK TIP All of the ratios discussed in this section become more meaningful when a company is compared with a company in the same industry. For example, compare The Hershey Company to Cadbury Schweppes. Cadbury Schweppes is a large British manufacturer of confectionary drinks that competes worldwide with The Hershey Company.

QUICK CHECK 5

Stockholders' equity for a firm increased from \$3456 at the end of 2006 to \$3720 at the end of 2007, and net income after taxes during the year was \$402 (all figures in thousands). Find the ratio of net income after taxes to average owners' equity.

The ratio of net income after taxes to average owners' equity should be significantly higher than the interest rate paid on savings accounts or even government bonds. Otherwise, the capital represented by these assets should be deposited in a bank account or in government bonds. After all, government bonds have *less risk* than an investment in a company. Generally, investments with a higher risk must give more reward to investors to encourage them to invest. Thus, increased risk should result in a higher return to the investor than a risk-free savings account. The ratio for The Hershey Company far exceeds the rate paid on government bonds. In fact, it is unusually high—perhaps partly because stockholders' equity fell so much from 2005 to 2006. At any rate, this illustrates that it is very difficult to truly understand how well a company is doing from a few financial ratios.

The financial ratios of this section can be summarized as follows.

QUICK TIP The ratio of net income after taxes to average owners' equity is the only ratio of the three we have looked at that requires you to look at both the income statement and the balance sheet.

Summary of Ratios

$$\text{Current ratio} = \frac{\text{Current assets}}{\text{Current liabilities}} \qquad \text{Acid-test ratio} = \frac{\text{Liquid assets}}{\text{Current liabilities}}$$

$$\text{Ratio of net income after taxes to average owners' equity} = \frac{\text{Net income after taxes}}{\text{Average owners' equity}}$$

Quick Check Answer

5. 11.2%

14.4 EXERCISES

FOR EXTRA HELP

MyMathLab

MathXL PRACTICE

WATCH

DOWNLOAD

READ

REVIEW

1. YACHT CONSTRUCTION Complete this balance sheet using vertical analysis. Round to the nearest tenth of a percent. (See Example 1.)

Comparative Balance Sheet for Pleasure Yacht, Inc. (in thousands of dollars)

	Amount This Year	Percent This Year	Amount Last Year	Percent Last Year
ASSETS				
Current Assets				
Cash	$52,000	_____	$42,000	_____
Notes Receivable	$8,000	_____	$6,000	_____
Accounts Receivable	$148,000	_____	$120,000	_____
Inventory	$153,000	_____	$120,000	_____
Total Current Assets	_____	_____	_____	_____
Plant Assets				
Land	$10,000	_____	$8,000	_____
Buildings	$14,000	_____	$11,000	_____
Fixtures	$15,000	_____	$13,000	_____
Total Plant Assets	_____	_____	_____	_____
TOTAL ASSETS	_____	100%	_____	100%
LIABILITIES				
Current Liabilities				
Accounts Payable	$3,000	_____	$4,000	_____
Notes Payable	$201,000	_____	$152,000	_____
Total Current Liabilities	_____	_____	_____	_____
Long-Term Liabilities				
Mortgages Payable	$20,000	_____	$16,000	_____
Long-Term Notes Payable	$58,000	_____	$42,000	_____
Total Long-Term Liabilities	_____	_____	_____	_____
TOTAL LIABILITIES	_____	_____	_____	_____
Owners' Equity	$118,000	_____	$106,000	_____
TOTAL LIABILITIES AND OWNERS' EQUITY	_____	_____	_____	_____

2. RETAIL STORE Complete the following horizontal analysis for a portion of the balance sheet for the Dollar Value chain of retail stores. Note that figures are shown in thousands of dollars. Round to the nearest tenth of a percent. (See Example 1.)

Dollar Value, Inc. (in thousands)

			Increase or (Decrease)	
	This Year	**Last Year**	**Amount**	**Percent**
ASSETS				
Current Assets				
Cash	$52,000	$42,000	_____	_____
Notes Receivable	$8,000	$6,000	_____	_____
Accounts Receivable	$148,000	$120,000	_____	_____
Inventory	$153,000	$120,000	_____	_____
Total Current Assets	$361,000	$288,000	_____	_____
Plant Assets				
Land	$10,000	$8,000	_____	_____
Buildings	$14,000	$11,000	_____	_____
Fixtures	$15,000	$13,000	_____	_____
Total Plant Assets	$39,000	$32,000	_____	_____
TOTAL ASSETS	$400,000	$320,000	_____	_____

In Exercises 3–6, find (a) the current ratio and (b) the acid-test ratio. Round each ratio to the nearest hundredth. (c) Do the ratios suggest that the company is financially healthy, according to the guidelines given in the text? (See Examples 3 and 4.)

3. Dollar Value, Inc., has the balance sheet given above and current liabilities of $204,000.

(a) ________
(b) ________
(c) ________

4. PLUMBING COMPANY Tekla Plumbing has current liabilities of $356,800, cash of $32,800, notes and accounts receivable of $248,500, and an inventory valued at $82,400.

(a) ________
(b) ________
(c) ________

5. CADILLAC DEALER Wagner Cadillac has current assets of $2,210,350, current liabilities of $1,232,500, total cash of $480,500, notes and accounts receivable of $279,050, and an inventory of $1,450,800.

(a) ________
(b) ________
(c) ________

6. OXYGEN SUPPLY BlueTex Oxygen Supply has current assets of $2,234,000, current liabilities of $840,000, total cash of $339,000, notes and accounts receivable of $1,215,000, and an inventory of $680,000.

(a) ________
(b) ________
(c) ________

A portion of a comparative balance sheet is shown next. First complete the chart, and then find the current ratio and the acid-test ratio for the indicated year. Round each ratio to the nearest hundredth.

West Coast Auto & Truck Auction (in thousands)

	Amount This Year	Percent This Year	Amount Last Year	Percent Last Year
Current Assets				
Cash	$12,000	______	$15,000	______
Notes Receivable	$4,000	______	$6,000	______
Accounts Receivable	$22,000	______	$18,000	______
Inventory	$26,000	______	$24,000	______
Total Current Assets	$64,000	80%	$63,000	84%
Total Plant Assets	$16,000	______	$12,000	______
TOTAL ASSETS	______	100.0%	______	100.0%
Total Current Liabilities	$30,000	______	$25,000	______

7. This year ________

8. Last year ________

Find the ratio of net income after taxes to average owners' equity for the following. (See Example 5.) Round to the nearest tenth of a percent.

9. INTERNATIONAL AIRLINE Stockholders' equity in TNA Airline, a small start-up international airline that uses small airplanes to move freight to and from Mexico, is $845,000 at the beginning of the year and $928,500 at the end of the year. Net income after taxes for the year was $54,400. **9.** ________________

10. TRANSMISSION REPAIR Owners' equity at Amgen Transmission was $372,600 at the beginning of the year and $402,100 at the end of the year. Net income after taxes for the year was $55,003. **10.** ________________

Calculate the current ratio and the acid-test ratio for the following companies. Are the companies healthy, based on the guidelines given in the text?

11. Akron Hardware: **11.** ________________

Current assets:	$268,700
Current liabilities:	$294,200
Liquid assets:	$109,900

12. Janson Hair Salon: **12.** ________________

Current assets:	$54,750
Current liabilities:	$17,200
Liquid assets:	$24,650

13. Explain why the acid-test ratio is a better measure of the financial health of a firm than the current ratio. (See Objective 3.)

14. Explain why increased risk requires a higher return on investment. (See Objective 3.)

CHAPTER 14 QUICK REVIEW

CHAPTER TERMS *Review the following terms to test your understanding of the chapter. For each term you do not know, refer to the page number found next to that term.*

accountant **[p. 634]**
acid test **[p. 652]**
acid-test ratio **[p. 652]**
assets **[p. 647]**
average owners' equity **[p. 653]**
balance sheet **[p. 647]**
banker's ratio **[p. 652]**
comparative balance sheet **[p. 651]**
comparative income statement **[p. 639]**
cost of goods sold **[p. 634]**
current assets **[p. 647]**
current liabilities **[p. 647]**
current ratio **[p. 652]**
ending inventory **[p. 635]**
financial ratios **[p. 652]**
fixed assets **[p. 647]**
gross profit **[p. 634]**
gross profit on sales **[p. 634]**
gross sales **[p. 634]**
horizontal analysis **[p. 652]**
income statement **[p. 634]**
initial inventory **[p. 635]**
liabilities **[p. 647]**
liquid assets **[p. 652]**
liquidity **[p. 652]**
long-term liabilities **[p. 647]**
net income **[p. 634]**
net income after taxes **[p. 634]**
net income before taxes **[p. 634]**
net sales **[p. 634]**
net worth **[p. 647]**
operating expenses **[p. 634]**
overhead **[p. 634]**
owners' equity **[p. 647]**
plant and equipment **[p. 647]**
plant assets **[p. 647]**
quick ratio **[p. 652]**
ratio of net income after taxes to average owners' equity **[p. 653]**
returns **[p. 634]**
short-term liabilities **[p. 647]**
stockholders' equity **[p. 647]**
total revenue **[p. 634]**
vertical analysis **[p. 651]**

CONCEPTS	EXAMPLES
14.1 Finding the gross profit and net income 1. Find the net sales. 2. Determine the cost of goods sold. 3. Find gross profit from the formula. **Gross profit = Net sales − Cost of goods sold** 4. Find the operating expenses. 5. Find the net income from the formula. **Net income = Gross profit − Operating expenses**	Candy-You-Love had a cost of goods sold of \$218,509, operating expenses of \$103,217, gross sales of \$432,119, and no returns. Find the gross profit and net income before taxes. **Gross profit** = *Gross sales* − *Returns* − *Cost of goods sold* = \$432,119 − \$0 − \$218,509 = **\$213,610** **Net income before taxes = Gross profit** − Operating expenses = \$213,610 − \$103,217 = \$110,393
14.2 Finding the percent of net sales of individual items 1. Determine net sales using the formula. **Net sales = Gross sales − Returns** 2. Use the formula $\text{Percent of net sales} = \dfrac{\text{Particular item}}{\text{Net sales}}$ for each item.	Bill's Appliances lists the following information. Gross sales = \$340,000 Salaries and wages = \$19,000 Returns = \$15,000 Rent = \$8000 Cost of goods sold = \$210,000 Advertising = \$12,000 Express each item as a percent of net sales. Round to the nearest tenth of a percent. Net sales = \$340,000 − \$15,000 = **\$325,000** Gross profit = \$325,000 − \$210,000 = **\$115,000** Total expenses = \$19,000 + \$8000 + \$12,000 = **\$39,000** Net income = \$115,000 − \$39,000 = **\$76,000** Find all the desired percents to the nearest tenth of a percent by dividing each item by net sales. $\text{Percent gross sales} = \dfrac{\$340{,}000}{\$325{,}000} = 104.6\%$ $\text{Percent return} = \dfrac{\$15{,}000}{\$325{,}000} = 4.6\%$ $\text{Percent cost of goods sold} = \dfrac{\$210{,}000}{\$325{,}000} = 64.6\%$ $\text{Percent gross profit} = \dfrac{\$115{,}000}{\$325{,}000} = 35.4\%$ $\text{Percent expenses} = \dfrac{\$39{,}000}{\$325{,}000} = 12\%$

CONCEPTS	EXAMPLES

$$\text{Percent salaries and wages} = \frac{\$19{,}000}{\$325{,}000} = 5.8\%$$

$$\text{Percent net income} = \frac{\$76{,}000}{\$325{,}000} = 23.4\%$$

$$\text{Percent rent} = \frac{\$8{,}000}{\$325{,}000} = 2.5\%$$

$$\text{Percent advertising} = \frac{\$12{,}000}{\$325{,}000} = 3.7\%$$

14.2 Comparing income statements with published charts

In one chart, list the percent of items from a published chart and from the particular company.

From the preceding example, prepare a vertical analysis of Bill's Appliances.

Bill's Appliances

	Cost of Goods	Gross Profit	Total Expenses	Net Income	Wages	Rent	Advertising
Bill's Appliances	64.6%	35.4%	12%	23.4%	5.8%	2.5%	3.7%
Published Data	66.9%	33.1%	26%	7.2%	11.9%	2.4%	2.5%

14.2 Preparing a horizontal analysis chart

1. List last year's and this year's values for each item.
2. Calculate the amount of the increase or decrease of each item.
3. Calculate the percent increase or decrease by dividing the change by last year's amount.

The results of a horizontal analysis of the portion of a business is given. Calculate the percent increase or decrease in each item.

Ocean Salvage

	This Year	Last Year	Increase or (Decrease) Amount	Increase or (Decrease) Percent
Gross Sales	$735,000	$700,000	$35,000	5%
Returns	$5,000	$10,000	($5,000)	(50%)
Net Sales	$730,000	$690,000	$40,000	5.8%
Cost of Goods Sold	$530,000	$540,000	($10,000)	(1.9%)
Gross Profit	$200,000	$150,000	$50,000	33.3%

14.3 Constructing a balance sheet

List all of the current assets, other assets, current liabilities, and other liabilities on one page.

Subtract total liabilities from total assets to find stockholders' equity.

A cell phone kiosk in a local mall has cash of $28,300, accounts receivable of $49,250, and inventories of $4900. Other assets consist of equipment and a truck with a total value of $24,300. Accounts payable are $9300, and loans total $12,200. There is no long-term debt. Other liabilities amount to $12,400.

Balance Sheet

Current Assets:		**Current Liabilities:**	
Cash and Equivalents	$28,300	Accounts Payable	$9,300
Accounts Receivable	$49,250	Loans and Notes Payable	$12,200
Inventories	$4,900	***Total Current Liabilities***	$21,500
Total Current Assets	$82,450	**Other Liabilities:**	$12,400
Other Assets:		***Total Liabilities***	$33,900
Equipment and Truck	$24,300		
Total Assets	$106,750	***Stockholders' Equity***	$72,850
		Total Liabilities and Equity	$106,750

CONCEPTS	EXAMPLES
14.4 Determining the value of the current ratio **1.** Determine the current assets. **2.** Find the current liabilities. **3.** Divide current assets by current liabilities.	The Circle Tour Agency has \$250,000 in current assets and \$110,000 in current liabilities. Find the current ratio. $\text{Current ratio} = \dfrac{\text{Current assets}}{\text{Current liabilities}}$ $= \dfrac{\$250,000}{\$110,000} = \textbf{2.27 (rounded)}$
14.4 Finding the value of the acid-test ratio **1.** Determine the liquid assets. **2.** Find the current liabilities. **3.** Divide liquid assets by liabilities.	If the Circle Tour Agency has \$125,000 in liquid assets, find the acid-test ratio. $\text{Acid-test ratio} = \dfrac{\text{Liquid assets}}{\text{Current liabilities}}$ $= \dfrac{\$125,000}{\$110,000} = \textbf{1.14 (rounded)}$
14.4 Determining the ratio of net income after taxes to the average owners' equity **1.** Find the net income after taxes. **2.** Determine the average owners' equity for the year using the formula. $\text{Average owners' equity} = \dfrac{\text{Owners' equity at beginning} + \text{Owners' equity at end}}{2}$ **3.** Divide the net income by the average owners' equity.	At the beginning of the year, the Circle Tour Agency had owners' equity of \$140,000. At the end of the year, owners' equity was \$180,000. The net income after taxes for the agency was \$25,000. Find the ratio of net income after taxes to average owners' equity. Net income after taxes = \$25,000 Average owners' equity $= \dfrac{\$140,000 + \$180,000}{2} = \textbf{\$160,000}$ Ratio of net income after taxes to average owners' equity $= \dfrac{\$25,000}{\textbf{\$160,000}} = \textbf{15.6\% (rounded)}$

CHAPTER 14 SUMMARY EXERCISE

Owning Your Own Business

Tom Walker wants to expand his start-up, one-person bicycle shop and has gone to a bank for a loan. The commercial loan officer asks Walker for his most recent income statement and balance sheets.

Gross Sales	$212,000	Salaries and Wages	$37,000
Returns	$12,500	Rent	$12,000
Inventory on January 1	$44,000	Advertising	$2,000
Cost of Goods Purchased	$75,000	Utilities	$3,000
Freight	$8,000	Taxes on Inventory, Payroll	$7,000
Inventory on December 31	$26,000	Miscellaneous Expenses	$4,500
		Income taxes	$4,320

(a) Prepare an income statement.

Walker's Bicycle Shop
Income Statement
Year Ending December 31

Gross Sales			______
Returns			______
Net Sales			______
Inventory, January 1		______	
Cost of Goods Purchased	______		
Freight	______		
Total Cost of Goods Purchased		______	
Total of Goods Available for Sale		______	
Inventory, December 31		______	
Cost of Goods Sold			______
Gross Profit			______
Expenses			
Salaries and Wages		______	
Rent		______	
Advertising		______	
Utilities		______	
Taxes on Inventory, Payroll		______	
Miscellaneous Expenses		______	
Total Expenses			______
Net Income before Taxes			______
Income Taxes			______
NET INCOME AFTER TAXES			______

(b) Express the following items as a percent of net sales. Round to nearest tenth of a percent.

Gross Sales	_____	Salaries and Wages	____
Returns	_____	Rent	____
Cost of Goods Sold	_____	Utilities	____

(c) After the year is completed, Walker has $62,000 in cash, $2500 in notes receivable, $8200 in accounts receivable, and $26,000 in inventory. He has land worth $7600 and buildings and improvements worth $41,500. He also has $4500 in notes payable and $27,000 in accounts payable, mortgages for $15,000, long-term notes payable of $8000, and owners' equity of $93,300. Prepare a balance sheet.

Walker's Bicycle Shop **Balance Sheet** **December 31**			
ASSETS			
Current Assets			
Cash	______		
Notes Receivable	______		
Accounts Receivable	______		
Inventory	______		
Total Current Assets		______	
Plant Assets			
Land	______		
Buildings and Improvements	______		
Total Plant Assets		______	
Total Assets			______
LIABILITIES			
Current Liabilities			
Notes Payable	______		
Accounts Payable	______		
Total Current Liabilities		______	
Long-Term Liabilities			
Mortgages Payable	______		
Long-Term Notes Payable	______		
Total Long-Term Liabilities		______	
Total Liabilities			______
OWNERS' EQUITY			
Owners' Equity	______		
TOTAL LIABILITIES AND OWNERS' EQUITY			______

(d) Find the current ratio and the acid-test ratio for Walker's business. (Round to the nearest hundredths.) ______

(e) If you were the commercial loan officer, would you approve Walker's requested loan? Why or why not?

INVESTIGATE

Publicly held companies must publish their financial statements and make them available to anyone who wishes to look at them. Choose a publicly held company that you are familiar with and obtain its financial statements using the World Wide Web. Calculate the financial ratios introduced in the last section of this chapter for the company you choose (current ratio, acid-test ratio, and ratio of net income after taxes to average owners' equity).

Case Studies

The Hershey Company

www.hersheys.com

- 1893: Founded
- 1940s: Created Ration D chocolate bar for U.S. military
- 1963: Purchased H. B. Reese Candy Co.
- 1968: First advertised nationwide
- 2007: More than 13,000 employees

The Hershey Company has been satisfying customers' desire for chocolate and sweets since 1893. During World War II, the company was asked by the U.S. military to construct and produce a ration bar that weighed about 4 ounces, would not melt at high temperatures, was high in food energy value, but did *not* taste very good. The military wanted a bar that soldiers would be tempted to eat only during an emergency. By the end of the war, The Hershey Company was producing 24 million of these bars every week.

The Hershey Company and its subsidiaries market products under all of the following brands: HERSHEY'S, REESE'S, HERSHEY'S KISSES, KIT KAT, Almond Joy, Mounds, JOLLY RANCHER, TWIZZLERS, ICE BREAKERS, Mauna Loa, Take 5, HERSHEY'S Cookies, HERSHEY'S cocoa, HERSHEY'S syrup, and Scharffen Berger.

1. Total assets for The Hershey Company on December 31, 2006, were about \$4.2 billion. Estimate assets at the end of 2008 assuming growth of 5% per year.

2. Assume the total liabilities for The Hershey Company at the end of 2008 are \$3.97 billion and find the stockholders' equity.

3. Assume the following for The Hershey Company on a recent balance sheet: total current assets, \$1510; total inventory, \$743; total current liabilities, \$1649. Find the current ratio and the acid-test ratio.

4. Use the World Wide Web to find a graph showing The Hershey Company's (HSY) stock price over the past year.

CHAPTER 14 TEST

To help you review, the numbers in brackets show the section in which the topic was discussed.

1. Benni's Catfish Distribution, Inc., had gross sales of $756,300 with returns of $285. The inventory on January 1 was $92,370, and the cost of goods purchased during the year was $465,920. Freight costs during the year were $1205. Total inventory on December 31 was $82,350. Salaries and wages totaled $84,900, advertising was $2800, rent was $42,500, utilities were $18,950, taxes on inventory and payroll were $4500, and miscellaneous expenses totaled $18,400. Income taxes were $25,450. Complete the following income statement. **[14.1]**

Benni's Catfish Distribution, Inc. Income Statement Year Ending December 31			
Gross Sales			______
Returns			______
Net Sales			______
Inventory, January 1		______	
Cost of Goods Purchased	______		
Freight	______		
Total Cost of Goods Purchased		______	
Total of Goods Available for Sale		______	
Inventory, December 31		______	
Cost of Goods Sold			______
Gross Profit			______
Expenses			
Salaries and Wages		______	
Rent		______	
Advertising		______	
Utilities		______	
Taxes on Inventory and Payroll		______	
Miscellaneous Expenses		______	
Total Expenses			______
Net Income before Taxes			______
Income Taxes			______
Net Income after Taxes			______

2. Complete a horizontal analysis for the following portion of an income statement. Round to the nearest tenth of a percent. **[14.2]**

China Imports, Inc.
Comparative Income Statement
(in thousands)

	This Year	Last Year	Increase or (Decrease) Amount	Increase or (Decrease) Percent
Net Sales	$95,000	$60,000	______	______
Cost of Goods Sold	$63,000	$40,000	______	______
Gross Profit	$16,000	$12,000	______	______

3. Complete the following chart for Alberta Heights Service Station. Express each item as a percent of net sales, and then write in the appropriate average percent from the chart on page 640. Round to the nearest tenth of a percent. **[14.2]**

Alberta Heights Service Station

	Amount (in thousands)	Percent	Average Percent
Net Sales	$1200	100%	100%
Cost of Goods Sold	_____	_____	_____
Gross Profit	$325	_____	_____
Net Income	$112	_____	_____
Wages	$129	_____	_____
Rent	$72	_____	_____
Total Expenses	$213	_____	_____

Find (a) the current ratio and (b) the acid-test ratio for each firm. (Round to the nearest hundredth.) **[14.4]**

4. Bonfry Bridge Construction:

Current assets:	$2,482,500
Current liabilities:	$1,800,200
Cash:	$850,000
Notes and accounts receivable:	$680,100
Inventory:	$952,400

(a) ________________
(b) ________________

5. Ben Franklin Tobacco:

Current assets:	$154,000
Current liabilities:	$146,500
Cash:	$22,000
Note and accounts receivable:	$32,500
Inventory:	$99,500

(a) ________________
(b) ________________

Find the ratio of net income after taxes to average owners' equity for each of the following firms. (Round to the nearest tenth of a percent.) **[14.4]**

6. Talisman Imports:

Net income after taxes:	$148,200
Owners' equity	
beginning of year:	$472,600
end of year:	$514,980

6. ________________

7. Baker Drilling Co.:

Net income after taxes:	$8,465,000
Owners' equity	
beginning of year:	$28,346,000
end of year:	$36,450,000

7. ________________

CHAPTER 15

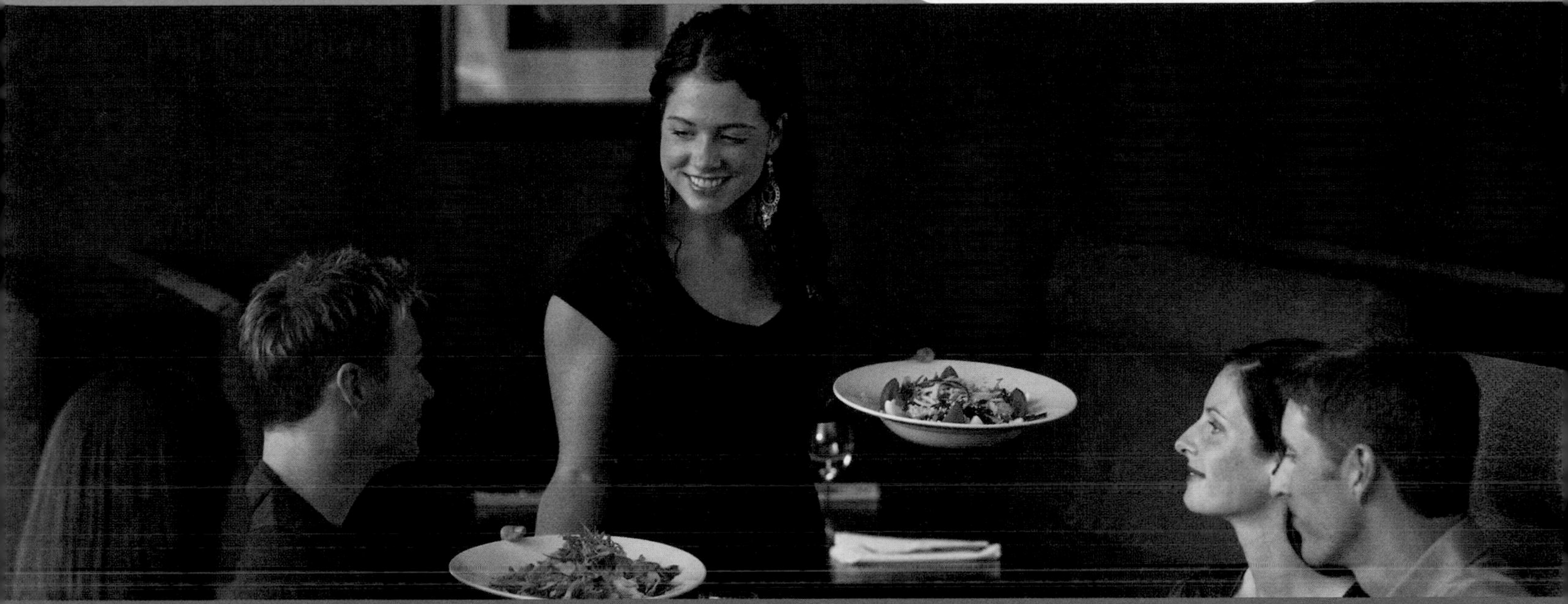

Business Statistics

CHAPTER CONTENTS

CASE *in* POINT

Gina Harden began working in a restaurant at age 16 and managed one for several years. As an exchange student in France during college, she loved the sidewalk cafes in Paris and decided that one day she would open her own. Using money she had saved and additional funds borrowed from her brother, Gina opened Gina's Bistro. She uses statistics to help her evaluate her business.

The word **statistics** comes from words that mean *state numbers*, or data gathered by the government, such as numbers of births and deaths. Today, the word *statistics* is used in a much broader sense to include data from business, economics, and many other fields. Statistics is a powerful and commonly used tool in business. Large companies such as General Motors and The Hershey Company use statistics to understand their markets and forecast demand, as well as many other purposes.

15.1 FREQUENCY DISTRIBUTIONS AND GRAPHS

OBJECTIVES

1. Construct and analyze a frequency distribution.
2. Make a bar graph.
3. Make a line graph.
4. Draw a circle graph.

CASE in POINT Gina's Bistro uses only the freshest ingredients in its gourmet sandwiches and is already building a reputation for delicious soups and salads. The cafe has been open for only six months, and Harden has to watch sales very carefully, since most restaurants fail within their first year.

OBJECTIVE 1 Construct and analyze a frequency distribution. It can be difficult to interpret or find patterns in a large group of numbers. One way of analyzing the numbers is to organize them in a table that shows the frequency of occurrence of the various numbers. This type of table is called a **frequency distribution**.

EXAMPLE 1

Constructing a Frequency Distribution

Gina Harden is analyzing sales activity over the past 24 weeks at Gina's Bistro. The weekly sales data shown next are in thousands of dollars. Read down the columns, beginning with the left column, for successive weeks of the year.

\$3.9	\$4.0	\$4.3	\$4.6	\$5.1	\$5.6
\$3.2	\$4.2	\$4.8	\$4.9	\$4.8	\$4.8
\$3.3	\$4.1	\$4.1	\$5.2	\$5.0	\$5.3
\$3.5	\$3.9	\$4.8	\$5.0	\$5.3	\$5.3

Construct a table that shows each value of sales. Then go through the data and place a **tally mark** (|) next to each corresponding value, thereby creating a frequency distribution table.

SOLUTION

Sales (thousands)	Tally	Frequency	Sales (thousands)	Tally	Frequency	Sales (thousands)	Tally	Frequency
\$3.2	|	1	\$4.2	|	1	\$5.1	|	1
\$3.3	|	1	\$4.3	|	1	\$5.2	|	1
\$3.5	|	1	\$4.6	|	1	\$5.3	|||	3
\$3.9	||	2	\$4.8	||||	4	\$5.6	|	1
\$4.0	|	1	\$4.9	|	1			
\$4.1	||	2	\$5.0	||	2			

This frequency distribution shows that the most common weekly sales amount was \$4800, although there were three weeks with sales of \$5300.

QUICK CHECK 1

To the nearest thousand, weekly sales in the spring at a nursery were: \$21, \$23, \$21, \$25, \$23, and \$21. Construct a frequency distribution.

Quick Check Answer

1. \$21, 3; \$23, 2; \$25, 1

The frequency distribution given in the preceding example contains a great deal of information, perhaps more than is needed. It can be simplified by combining weekly sales into groups, forming the following grouped data.

QUICK TIP The number of groups in the left column of the grouped data table is arbitrary and usually varies between 5 and 15.

Gina's Bistro Grouped Data

Sales (thousands)	Frequency (number of weeks)
\$3.1–\$3.5	3
\$3.6–\$4.0	3
\$4.1–\$4.5	4
\$4.6–\$5.0	8
\$5.1–\$5.5	5
\$5.6–\$6.0	1

EXAMPLE 2

Analyzing a Frequency Distribution

Based on the data from Gina's Bistro, answer the following questions.

(a) Harden can take no salary, and the business still loses money when sales are less than or equal to \$4000 per week. During how many weeks did this occur?

(b) Harden can take a small salary from the company when sales go above \$5000 per week. During how many weeks did this occur?

SOLUTION

(a) The first two classes in the grouped data table represent weeks in which sales were equal to or less than \$4000. Thus, Harden took no salary and the restaurant lost money for **6 weeks**.

(b) The last two classes in the grouped data table are the numbers of weeks during which sales were above \$5000, or 6 weeks. Therefore, Harden took a small salary for **6 weeks**.

QUICK CHECK 2

Gina's Bistro needs sales of \$4600 per week in order to break even so that all expenses can be paid from sales. Use the grouped data table for Gina's Bistro to find the number of weeks during which the restaurant broke even.

OBJECTIVE 2 **Make a bar graph.** The next step in analyzing these data is to use them to make a **graph**. A graph is a visual presentation of numerical data. One of the most common graphs is a **bar graph**, where the height of a bar represents the frequency of a particular value. A bar graph for the sales data follows.

Sales for Gina's Bistro

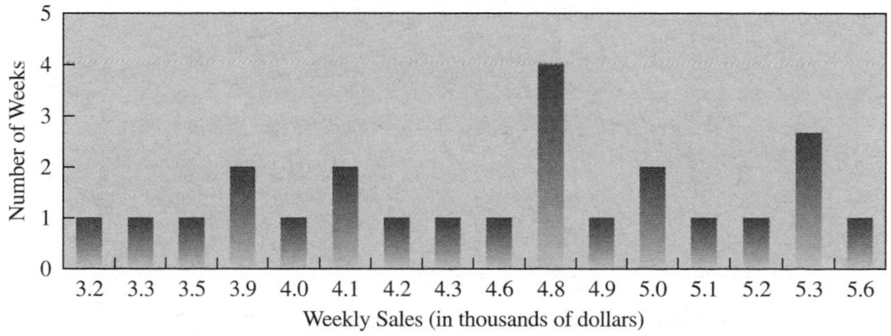

Quick Check Answer

2. 14 weeks

The information from the grouped data is shown in the following bar graph. This graph shows that weekly sales of between \$4600 and \$5000 were the most common. Notice that this graph *does not* show any trend that may be occurring over time.

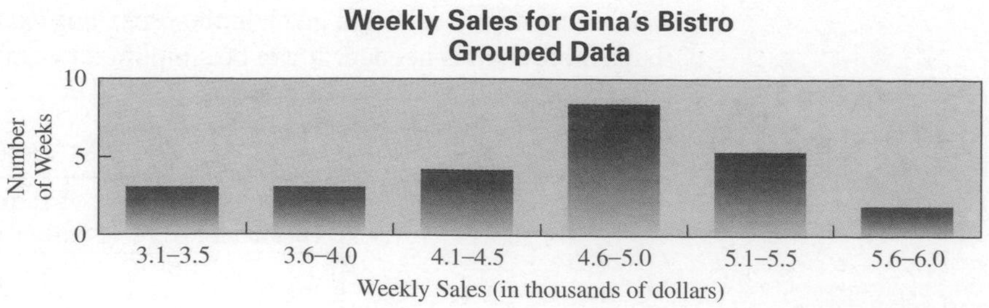

OBJECTIVE **Make a line graph.** Bar graphs show which numbers occurred and how many times, but do not necessarily show the order in which the numbers occurred. To discover any trends that may have developed, draw a **line graph**.

EXAMPLE 3

Drawing a Line Graph

Show the progression of sales at Gina's Bistro through the year using a line graph. Do this by totaling the first 4 weeks (the first column) of data in Example 1 for the first data point. Similarly, total the second 4 weeks (second column) of data for the next data point, and so on.

SOLUTION

The total for the first four weeks is $3.9 + $3.2 + $3.3 + $3.5 = $13.9 or $13,900 in sales for the first four weeks. The total for the second four weeks is $4.0 + $4.2 + $4.1 + $3.9 = $16.2, or $16,200 in sales. The six data points of the graph are $13.9, $16.2, $18, $19.7, $20.2, and $21, in thousands of dollars.

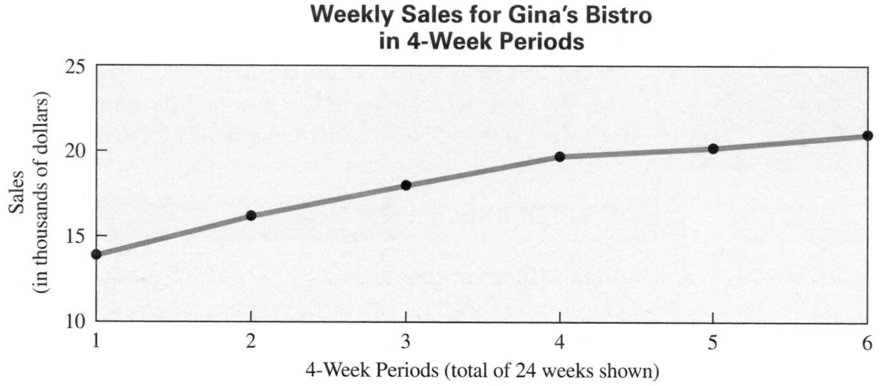

It is apparent from the line graph that weekly sales are growing. Gina Harden is excited about this trend. She is determined to continue improving the business, since her livelihood depends on the restaurant. She plans to work very hard over the next few months to further increase sales.

QUICK CHECK 3

Gina's Bistro breaks even (sufficient sales to pay all expenses) with sales of $18,400 per 4-week period. Use the line graph in Example 3 to estimate the first 4-week period in which the restaurant breaks even.

One advantage of line graphs is that two or more sets of data can be shown on the same graph. For example, suppose the manager of a local Radio Shack wants to compare total sales, profits, and overhead using the following historical data.

Year	Total Sales	Overhead	Profit
2006	$740,000	$205,000	$83,000
2007	$860,000	$251,000	$102,000
2008	$810,000	$247,000	$21,000
2009	$1,040,000	$302,000	$146,000

Separate lines can be made on a line graph for each category so that necessary comparisons can be made. A graph such as this is called a **comparative line graph**.

Quick Check Answer

3. 4th

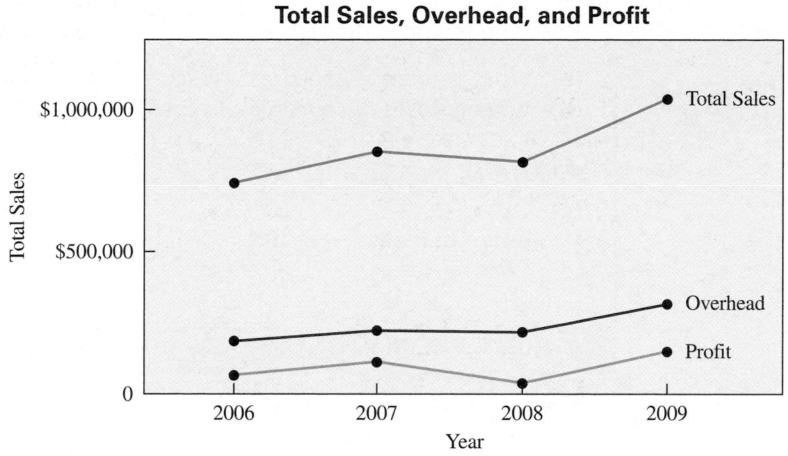

OBJECTIVE 4 **Draw a circle graph.** Suppose a sales manager for Genome Pharmaceutical Company makes a record of the expenses involved in keeping a sales force on the road. After finding the total expenses, she could convert each expense into a percent of the total, with the following results. Notice that the percents add to 100%.

Sales Force Expenses

Item	Percent of Total
Travel	30%
Lodging	25%
Food	15%
Entertainment	10%
Sales meetings	10%
Other	10%

The sales manager can show these percents by using a **circle graph**, sometimes called a **pie chart**. A circle has 360 degrees (360°). The 360° represents the total expenses, or 100%. Since entertainment is 10% of the total expenses, she used

$$360^\circ \times 10\% = 360^\circ \times .10 = 36^\circ$$

to represent her entertainment expense. Since lodging is **25%** of the total expenses, she used

$$360^\circ \times \mathbf{25\%} = 360^\circ \times \mathbf{.25} = 90^\circ$$

to represent lodging. After she found the degrees that represent each of her expenses, she drew the circle graph shown here.

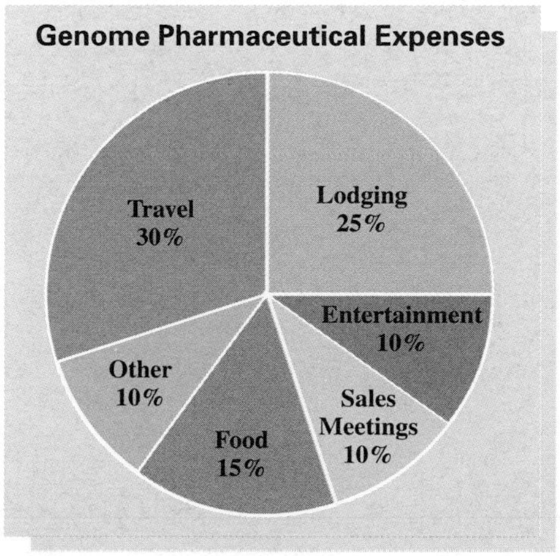

Circle graphs can be used to show comparisons *when one item is very small compared to another*. In the circle graph shown here, an item representing 1% of the total could be drawn as a very small but noticeable slice. Such a small item would hardly show up in a line graph.

EXAMPLE 4

Interpreting a Circle Graph

Based on the preceding circle graph of expenses, answer the following questions.

(a) What percent of expenses was spent on travel and entertainment?
(b) What percent of expenses was spent on food and lodging?

SOLUTION

(a) Travel	30%		**(b)** Food	15%
Entertainment	+ 10%		Lodging	+ 25%
Total spent	**40%**		**Total spent**	**40%**

QUICK CHECK 4

Use the pie chart that precedes Example 4 to find the total percent spent on sales meetings and entertainment combined.

Business people use graphs to communicate ideas. The graph on the left below shows that, on average, student credit-card debt increases as a student goes through college. The figure on the right is a colorful way to show the percent of adults between ages 50 and 64 who do not have health insurance. States with the highest percent of uninsured include those along the Mexican border from California to Texas, as well as Vermont, Florida, Louisiana, Arkansas, Oklahoma, Colorado, and Utah.

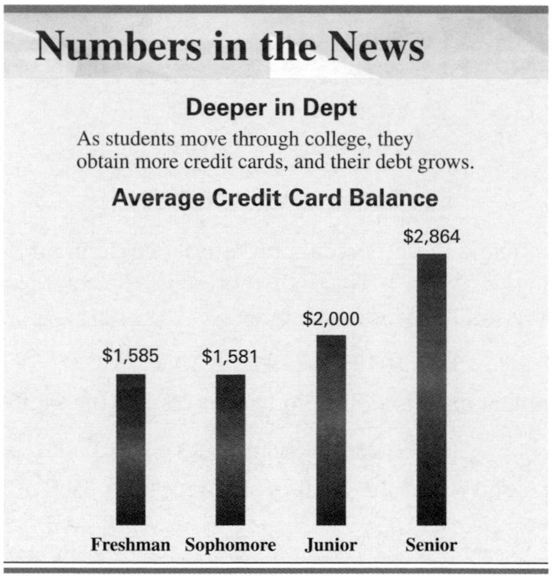

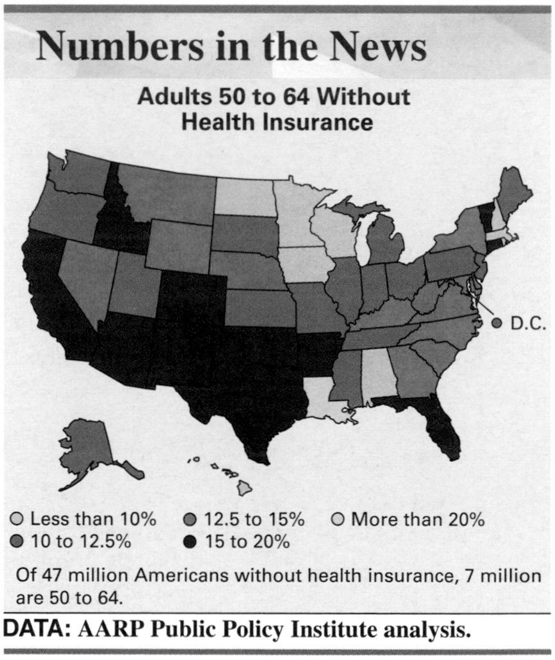

Quick Check Answer

4. 20%

15.1 EXERCISES

FOR EXTRA HELP

MyMathLab

MathXL PRACTICE

WATCH

DOWNLOAD

READ

REVIEW

The QUICK START *exercises in each section contain solutions to help you get started.*

Answer Exercises 1–3 using the bar graph on population growth. Answer Exercises 4–6 using the line graph on people who live together.

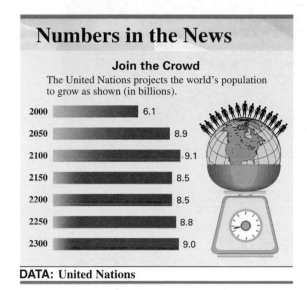

Numbers in the News

Join the Crowd

The United Nations projects the world's population to grow as shown (in billions).

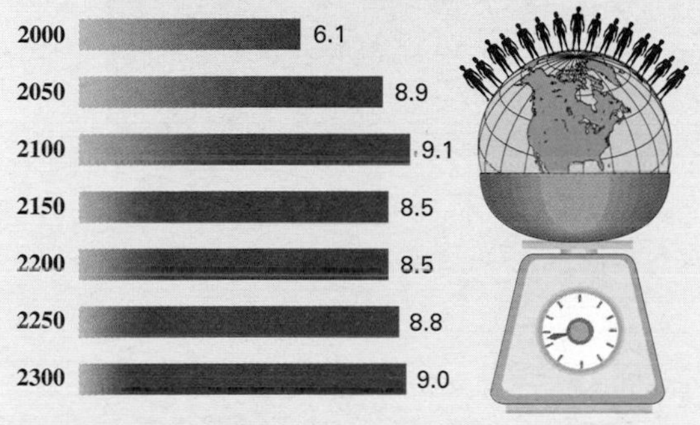

DATA: United Nations

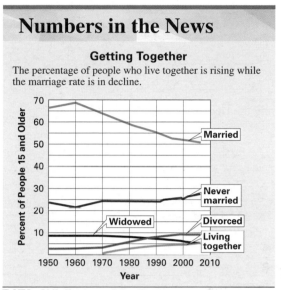

Numbers in the News

Getting Together

The percentage of people who live together is rising while the marriage rate is in decline.

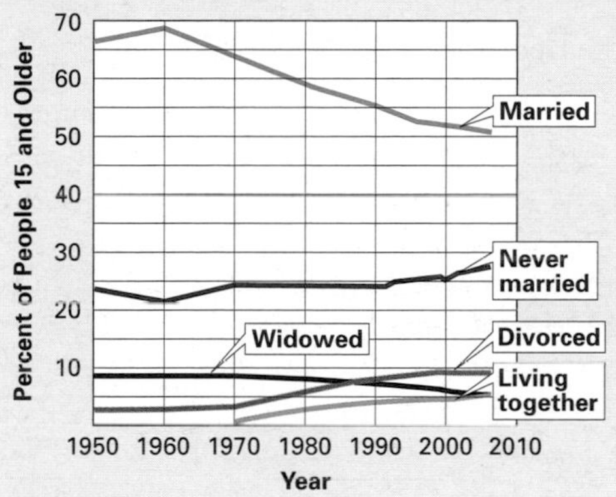

DATA: U.S. Bureau of the Census

QUICK START

1. When is world population expected to reach its peak, and what is the estimated population? **1.** 2100; 9.1 billion

2. Find the percent increase in world population from 2000 to 2050 to the nearest tenth of a percent. **2.** ________

3. In 2050, assume that 24% of the world's population are Chinese and 4% of the world's population are Americans. Estimate the number of Chinese and the number of Americans. **3.** ________

4. Approximately what percent of the U.S. population was married in 1950 and in 2008? **4.** ________

5. What has happened with the percent of people divorced during the past 50+ years? **5.** ________

6. Estimate the percent of widowed people in 2008. **6.** ________

The following list gives the numbers of college credits completed by 30 employees of the Franklin Bank.

College Credits
Franklin Bank Employees

74	133	4	127	20	30
103	27	139	118	138	121
149	132	64	141	130	76
42	50	95	56	65	104
4	140	12	88	119	64

Use these numbers to complete the following table. (See Examples 1 and 2.)

QUICK START

Number of Credits	Number of Employees
7. 0–24	4
8. 25–49	______
9. 50–74	______
10. 75–99	______
11. 100–124	______
12. 125–149	______

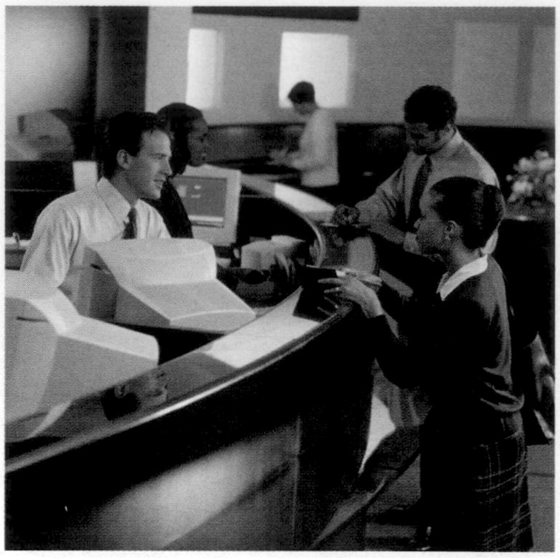

13. Make a line graph using the frequencies that you found.

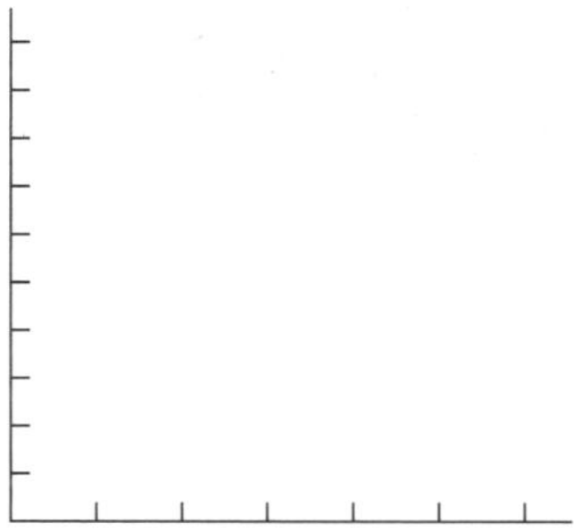

QUICK START

14. How many employees completed fewer than 25 credits? **14.** 4

15. How many employees completed 50 or more credits? **15.** ______

16. How many employees completed from 50 to 124 credits? **16.** ______

17. How many employees completed from 0 to 49 credits? **17.** ______

Six months' data on weekly sales (in thousands of dollars) for a chain of Wendy's restaurants follow. The numbers are in chronological order going down the columns. For example, sales for the first and fourth weeks, respectively, are $302,000 and $304,000.

302	304	318	301	330	337	335	348	339
265	275	279	283	322	349	330	325	334
315	288	299	326	325	342	328	347	

Use the numbers to complete the following table. (See Example 1.)

QUICK START

Sales (in thousands)	Frequency	Sales (in thousands)	Frequency
18. 260–269	1	**19.** 270–279	2
20. 280–289	______	**21.** 290–299	______
22. 300–309	______	**23.** 310–319	______
24. 320–329	______	**25.** 330–339	______
26. 340–349	______		

27. Make a bar graph using your answers to Exercises 18–26.

28. Make a line graph using the original numbers.

29. How many weeks did sales equal or exceed $300,000? **29.** ________

30. How many weeks did sales fall below $270,000? **30.** ________

The following numbers show the scores of 80 students on a marketing test.

79	60	74	59	55	98	61	67	83	71
71	46	63	66	69	42	75	62	71	77
78	65	87	57	78	91	82	73	94	48
87	65	62	81	63	66	65	49	45	51
69	56	84	93	63	60	68	51	73	54
50	88	76	93	48	70	39	76	95	57
63	94	82	54	89	64	77	94	72	69
51	56	67	88	81	70	81	54	66	87

Use these numbers to complete the following table. (See Example 1.)

QUICK START

Score	*Frequency*	*Score*	*Frequency*
31. 30–39	1	**32.** 40–49	6
33. 50–59	______	**34.** 60–69	______
35. 70–79	______	**36.** 80–89	______
37. 90–99	______		

38. Make a bar graph showing your answers to Exercises 31–37.

39. How many students passed the marketing test (passing is 70)? **39.** ________

40. If a grade of B is given for a score of 80 or higher, how many students received a B or better? **40.** ________

41. How many students failed the test (scored below 70)? **41.** ________

42. How many students scored from 60 to 79? **42.** ________

During one recent period Angela Rueben, a student, had \$1400 in expenses, as shown in the following table. Find all numbers missing from the table in Exercises 43–48. (See Objective 4.)

QUICK START

Item	Dollar Amount	Percent of Total	Degrees of a Circle	Item	Dollar Amount	Percent of Total	Degrees of a Circle
43. Rent	\$280	**20%**	72°	**44.** Clothing	\$210	**15%**	**54°**
$\frac{72°}{360°} = .20 = 20\%$				$\frac{\$210}{\$1400} = .15 = 15\%;\ .15 \times 360° = 54°$			
45. Books	\$140	10%	____	**46.** Entertainment	\$210	____	54°
47. Savings	\$70	____	____	**48.** Other	____	____	36°

49. Draw a circle graph using Rueben's information. (See Objective 4.)

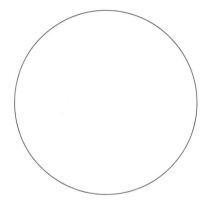

50. What percent did Rueben spend on food and rent? **50.** ____________

51. What percent did Rueben spend on savings and entertainment? **51.** ____________

Solve the following application problems.

QUICK START

52. FURNITURE Annual sales at Antique Furnishings are divided into five categories as follows.

Item	**Annual Sales**
Finishing materials	\$25,000
Desks	\$80,000
Bedroom sets	\$120,000
Dining room sets	\$100,000
Other	\$75,000

Make a circle graph showing this distribution. (See Example 4.)

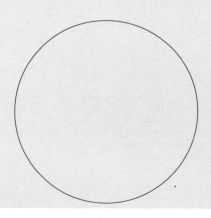

53. BOOK PUBLISHING Armstrong Publishing Company had 25% of its sales in mysteries, 10% in biographies, 15% in cookbooks, 15% in romance novels, 20% in science, and the rest in business books. Draw a circle graph with this information. (See Example 4.)

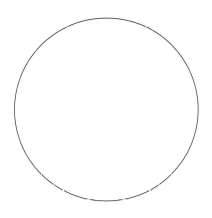

54. FAST FOOD The market shares of the different types of fast-food chains are shown in the figure at the right. Show this information in a circle graph. After making calculations, round degrees to the nearest whole degree and percents to the nearest whole percent.

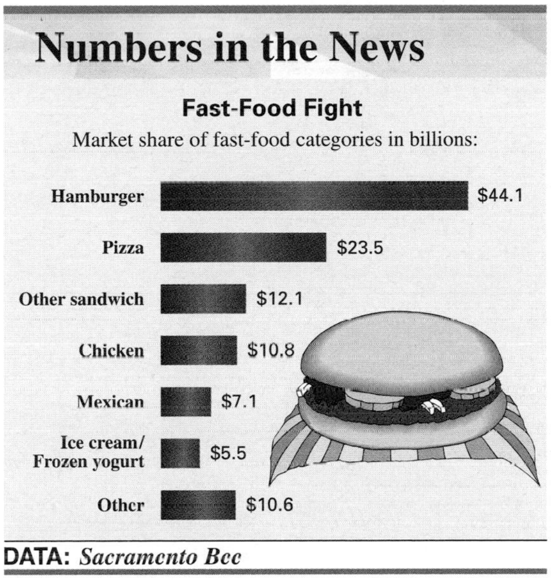

55. MUSIC DOWNLOADS The following graphic shows the amount spent to download individual songs from the Web, along with forecasts. Show the data using a bar chart.

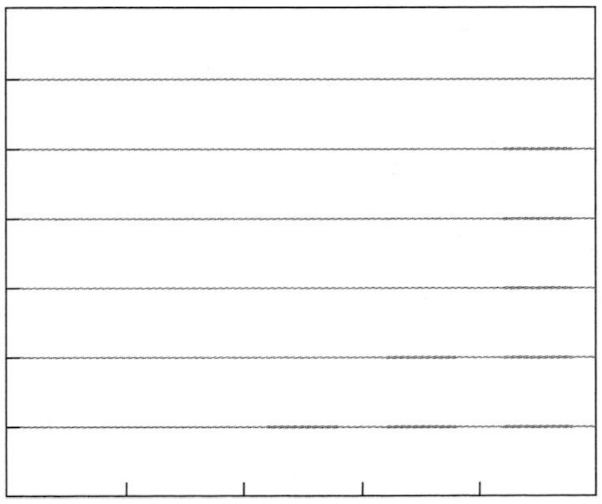

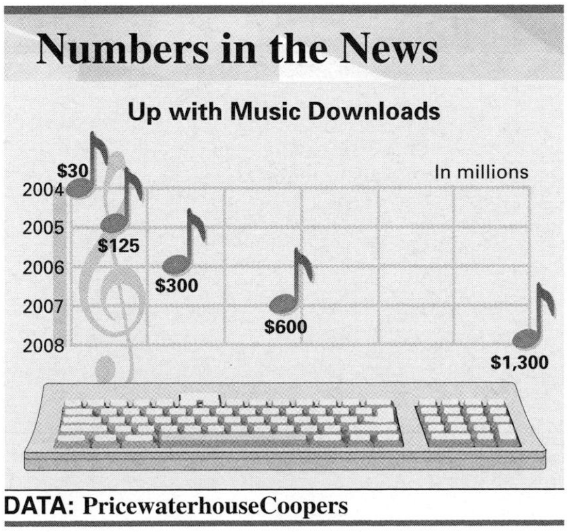

56. List the advantages of using a graph over a table when looking for trends.

57. Cut out three graphs from newspapers or magazines and tape them to your homework assignment. Be sure to explain the data in each case.

15.2 MEAN, MEDIAN, AND MODE

OBJECTIVES

1. Find the mean of a list of numbers.
2. Find the weighted mean.
3. Find the median.
4. Find the mode.

OBJECTIVE 1 Find the mean of a list of numbers. Businesses are often faced with the problem of analyzing a mass of raw data. Reports come in from many different branches of a company, or salespeople send in a large number of expense claims, for example. In analyzing all these data, one of the first things to look for is a **measure of central tendency**—a single number that is designed to represent the entire list of numbers. One such measure of central tendency is the **mean**, which is just the **average** of a collection of numbers or data.

$$\text{Mean} = \frac{\text{Sum of all values}}{\text{Number of values}}$$

For example, suppose milk sales at a local 7-Eleven for each of the days last week were \$86, \$103, \$118, \$117, \$126, \$158, and \$149. The mean sales of milk (rounded to the nearest cent) follows.

$$\text{Mean} = \frac{86 + 103 + 118 + 117 + 126 + 158 + 149}{7} = \$122.43$$

One criticism of the mean is that its value *can be distorted* by one very large (or very small) value, as shown in the next example. A better measure of central tendency in cases with one abnormally large (or small) value is shown later in this section. (See Objective 3.)

EXAMPLE 1
Finding the Mean

Gina Harden has promised seven of her employees at Gina's Bistro that they will all work about the same number of hours. One employee commented that she worked considerably more hours than the other employees last month. The number of hours worked by each of the seven employees during the past month are given. Find the mean to the nearest hour.

75, 63, 76, 82, 70, 81, 149

SOLUTION

Add the numbers and divide by 7, since there are 7 numbers. Check that the sum of the numbers is 596.

distorted by 1 large number

$$\text{Mean} = \frac{596}{7} = 85 \text{ (rounded)}$$

The mean of 85 seems a bit large, since one employee worked a lot more hours than the other six employees. The mean without this value of 149 is the sum of the remaining 6 numbers divided by 6.

$$\text{Mean} = \frac{447}{6} = 75 \text{ (rounded)}$$

This value seems more in line with the average number of hours worked. Perhaps there was an unusual reason the one employee worked 149 hours (e.g., someone else was sick).

QUICK CHECK 1

First find the mean of the following numbers: 24, 65, 25, 24, and 28. Then eliminate the largest value and find the mean of the remaining numbers.

Quick Check Answer

1. 33.2; 25.25

Averages are commonly used. The graph at the left on the next page shows that people today are waiting longer to get married than in the 1960s. The data are based on the average age at which people marry. The bar graph on the right shows average medical costs for individuals living in several different countries. Notice that the United States has, by far, the highest medical costs. Also notice that costs in neighboring Canada and Mexico are much lower than in the United States.

Numbers in the News

Older Brides and Grooms

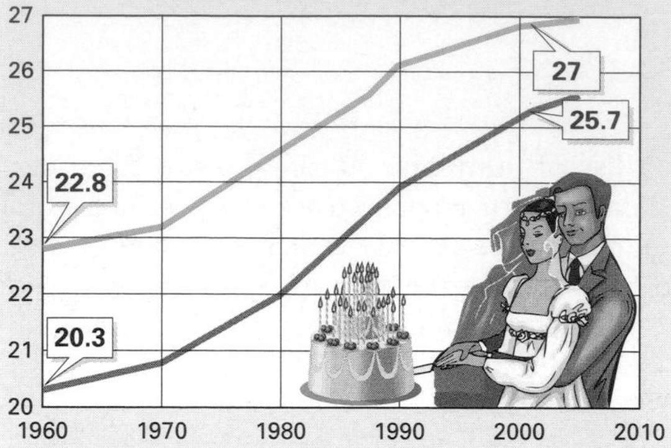

DATA: U.S. Bureau of the Census

Numbers in the News

Medical Costs

Spending on health, per person, for selected countries.

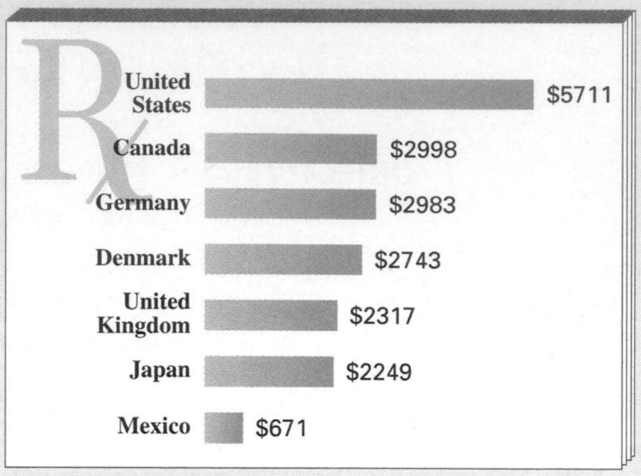

DATA: Organization for Economic Cooperation and Development

OBJECTIVE 2 Find the weighted mean. Some of the items in a list might appear more than once. In this case, it is necessary to find the weighted mean or weighted average, where each value is the product of the number itself and the number of times it occurs.

EXAMPLE 2 Finding the Weighted Mean

Find the weighted mean of the numbers given in the following table.

Value	Frequency
3	4
5	2
7	1
8	5
9	3
10	2
12	1
13	2

SOLUTION

According to this table, the value 5 occurred 2 times, 8 occurred 5 times, 12 occurred 1 time, and so on. To find the mean, multiply each value by the frequency for that value. Then add the products. Finally, add the values in the Frequency column to find the total number of values.

Value	Frequency	Product
3	4	12
5	2	10
7	1	7
8	5	40
9	3	27
10	2	20
12	1	12
13	2	26
Totals	**20**	**154**

$$\text{Weighted mean} = \frac{154}{20} = 7.7$$

QUICK CHECK 2

Find the weighted mean of the following sample of average family income in three lower-income neighborhoods: 12 families, \$15,300/year; 15 families, \$19,700/year; and 22 families, \$22,450/year.

Quick Check Answer

2. \$19,857.14

A weighted average is used to find a student's grade point average, as shown in the next example.

EXAMPLE 3

Finding the Grade Point Average

Mark Benson earned the following grades last semester. Find his grade point average to the nearest tenth. Assume A = 4, B = 3, C = 2, D = 1, and F = 0.

Course	Credits	Grade	Grade × Credits
Business Mathematics	3	A (=4)	**4 × 3 = 12**
Retailing	4	C (=2)	**2 × 4 = 8**
English	3	B (=3)	**3 × 3 = 9**
Biology	2	A (=4)	**4 × 2 = 8**
Biology Lab	2	D (=1)	**1 × 2 = 2**
Totals	14		39

SOLUTION

The grade point average for Benson is $\frac{39}{14} = 2.79 = 2.8$.

This problem is solved using a scientific calculator as follows.

(4 × 3 + 2 × 4 + 3 × 3 + 4 × 2 + 1 × 2) ÷ (3 + 4 + 3 + 2 + 2) = 2.8
↑
(rounded)

Note: Refer to Appendix C for calculator basics.

QUICK TIP It is common to round grade point averages to the nearest tenth as we have done in the preceding example.

QUICK CHECK 3

Becky Johnson received an A in English, a C in History, and a C in Biology. All three classes are three-credit classes. An A is 4 points, a B is 3 points, and a C is 2 points. Find her grade point average to the nearest tenth.

OBJECTIVE 3 **Find the median.** As we saw in Example 1, the mean is a poor indicator of central tendency when there is one very large or one very small number. This effect can be avoided by using another measure of central tendency called the **median**. The median divides a group of numbers in half—half the numbers lie at or above the median, and half lie at or below the median.

The process to find the median depends on whether the list has an odd number of numbers or an even number of numbers. Find the median as follows.

1. List the numbers from smallest to largest as an **ordered array**.
2. Find the median.
   - **(a)** If there are an odd number of numbers, then the median is the number in the middle. Find it by dividing the total number of numbers by 2. Use the next larger whole number in the array.
   - **(b)** If there are an even number of numbers, then the median is the average of the two numbers in the middle. Find it by dividing the total number of numbers by 2. The median is the average of this number and the next larger number.

EXAMPLE 4

Finding the Median

Find the median of the following weights (in pounds).

(a) 30 lb, 25 lb, 28 lb, 23 lb, 24 lb
(b) 14 lb, 18 lb, 17 lb, 10 lb, 15 lb, 19 lb, 18 lb, 20 lb

SOLUTION

(a) First list the numbers from smallest to largest.

23, 24, 25, 28, 30 ordered array

There are 5 numbers, so divide 5 by 2 to get 2.5. The next larger whole number is 3, so the median is the third number, **or 25**. The numbers 23 and 24 are less than 25, and the numbers 28 and 30 are greater than 25.

(b) First list the numbers from smallest to largest.

10, 14, 15, 17, 18, 18, 19, 20 ordered array

Quick Check Answer
3. 2.7

There are 8 numbers, so divide 8 by 2 to get 4. The median is the mean of the numbers in the 4th and 5th positions.

$$\text{Median} = \frac{\mathbf{17 + 18}}{\mathbf{2}} = 17.5$$

QUICK CHECK 4

The heights of the students in one club at an elementary school are: 48, 41, 49, 47, and 51 inches. Find the median height.

The following figure shows the median household income in 2005 by race. Notice the large differences in median incomes. It is important to note that the median was used to represent these data rather than the mean, since it better represents the situation. This is because a relative few people with very large incomes of over $10,000,000 would cause the mean to be higher than the median.

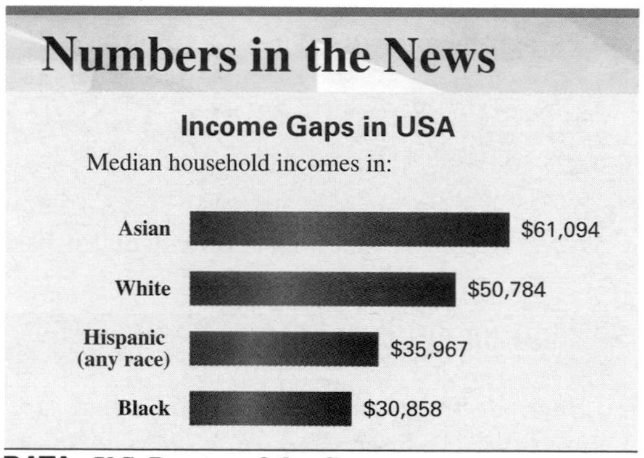

DATA: U.S. Bureau of the Census

OBJECTIVE 4 **Find the mode.** The last important statistical measure is called the **mode**. The mode is the number that occurs most often. For example, if 10 students earned scores of

74, 81, 38, 74, 82, 80, 100, 92, 74, 85

on a business law examination, then the mode is 74. This is because more students obtained this score than any other score.

A data set in which every number occurs the same number of times is said to have *no mode*. A data set in which two different numbers occur the same number of times, with each occurring more often than any other number in the data set, is said to be bimodal. The prefix "bi" means two and the root "modal" refers to modes, so **bimodal** means *two modes.*

EXAMPLE 5

Finding the Mode

Professor Miller gave the same test to both his day and evening sections of Business Math at American River College. Find the mode of the tests given in each class. Which class has the lower mode?

(a) Day Class: 85, 92, 81, 73, 78, 80, 83, 80, 74, 69, 80, 65, 71,
65, 80, 93, 54, 78, 80, 45, 70, 76, 73, 80, 71, 68

(b) Evening Class: 68, 73, 59, 76, 79, 73, 85, 90, 73, 69, 73,
75, 93, 73, 76, 70, 73, 68, 82, 84, 77

QUICK TIP It is not necessary to place the numbers in numerical order when looking for the mode, but it helps with a large set of numbers.

SOLUTION

(a) The number 80 is the mode for the day class because it occurs more often than any other number.

(b) The number 73 is the mode for the evening class because it occurs more often than any other number.

The evening class has the lower mode.

QUICK CHECK 5

Five economists were asked to forecast the growth rate of the gross domestic product (GDP) for the following year. Find the mode of their forecasts: 3.7%, 3.4%, 4.1%, 3.5%, and 3.4%.

Quick Check Answers

4. 48 inches
5. 3.4%

15.2 EXERCISES

FOR EXTRA HELP

MyMathLab

MathXL PRACTICE

WATCH

DOWNLOAD

READ

REVIEW

The QUICK START *exercises in each section contain solutions to help you get started.*

Find the mean for the following lists of numbers. Round to the nearest tenth. (See Example 1.)

QUICK START

1. Gallons of spoiled milk: 3.5, 1.1, 2.8, .8, 4.1 — **1.** 2.5

$$\frac{3.5 + 1.1 + 2.8 + .8 + 4.1}{5} = 2.5$$

2. Weeks premature: 2, 3, 1, 4, 5, 2 — **2.** 2.8

$$\frac{2 + 3 + 1 + 4 + 5 + 2}{6} = 2.8$$

3. Guests at board meetings: 40, 51, 59, 62, 68, 73, 49, 80 — **3.** ____________

4. Algebra quiz scores: 32, 26, 30, 19, 51, 46, 38, 39 — **4.** ____________

5. Number attending games: 21,900, 22,850, 24,930, 29,710, 28,340, 40,000 — **5.** ____________

6. Annual salaries: $38,500, $39,720, $42,183, $21,982, $43,250 — **6.** ____________

7. Avcragc numbcr of dcfccts pcr spool: 10.6, 12.5, 11.7, 9.6, 10.3, 9.6, 10.9, 6.4, 2.3, 4.1 — **7.** ____________

8. Weight of dogs (pounds): 30.1, 42.8, 91.6, 51.2, 88.3, 21.9, 43.7, 51.2 — **8.** ____________

9. When is it better to use the median, rather than the mean, for a measure of central tendency? Give an example. (See Objective 3.)

10. List some situations in which the mode is the best measure of central tendency to use to describe the data. (See Objective 4.)

Find the weighted mean for the following. Round to the nearest tenth. (See Example 2.)

QUICK START

11.

Value	*Frequency*
9	3
12	4
18	2

12.3

$9 \times 3 = 27$
$12 \times 4 = 48$
$18 \times 2 = 36$
$\quad 9 \quad 111$

$\frac{111}{9} = 12.3$

12.

Value	*Frequency*
9	3
12	5
15	1
18	1

12

$9 \times 3 = 27$
$12 \times 5 = 60$
$15 \times 1 = 15$
$18 \times 1 = 18$
$\quad 10 \quad 120$

$\frac{120}{10} = 12$

13.

Value	*Frequency*
12	4
13	2
15	5
19	3
22	1
23	5

____

14.

Value	*Frequency*
25	1
26	2
29	5
30	4
32	3
33	5

____

15.

Value	*Frequency*
104	6
112	14
115	21
119	13
123	22
127	6
132	9

____

16.

Value	*Frequency*
243	1
247	3
251	5
255	7
263	4
271	2
279	2

____

Find the grade point averages for the following students. Assume that A = 4, B = 3, C = 2, D = 1, and F = 0. Round to the nearest tenth. (See Example 3.)

17.

Credits	*Grade*
4	B
2	A
5	C
1	F
3	B

____

18.

Credits	*Grade*
3	A
3	B
4	B
2	C
4	D

____

Find the median for the following lists of numbers. (See Example 4.)

QUICK START

19. Number of virus attacks on a network: 140, 85, 122, 114, 98

85, 98, 114, 122, 140

↑ Median

19. 114

20. Cost of new computers: $1400, $850, $975, $1045, $1190

20. _______

21. Number of books loaned: 125, 100, 114, 150, 135, 172

21. _______

22. Calories in menu items: 346, 521, 412, 515, 501, 528, 298, 621

22. _______

23. Number of students taking business math: 37, 63, 92, 26, 44, 32, 75, 50, 41

23. _______

24. Number of orders: 1072, 1068, 1093, 1042, 1056, 1005, 1009

24. _______

Find the mode or modes for each of the following lists of numbers. (See Example 5.)

QUICK START

25. Porosity of soil samples: 21%, 18%, 21%, 28%, 22%, 21%, 25% **25.** 21%

If the data are listed according to how many times each number appears,

18%, 21%, 22%, 25%, 28%

21%

21%

↑ 21% is the mode since 21% is listed more than any other number.

26. Number of students graduating with honors: 85, 69, 72, 69, 103, 81, 98 **26.** ________

27. Age of retirees: 80, 72, 64, 64, 72, 53, 64 **27.** ________

28. Number of pages read: 86, 84, 83, 84, 83, 86, 86 **28.** ________

29. Number of fifth-grade students: 32, 38, 32, 36, 38, 34, 35, 30, 39 **29.** ________

30. Number of people on flights from Chicago to Denver: 178, 104, 178, 150, 165, 165, 82 **30.** ________

A quality-control inspector in a plant that manufactures electric motors measured the following shaft diameters (in thousandths of an inch).

35, 33, 32, 34, 35, 34, 35, 35, 34

Using these numbers, find each of the following. (Round to the nearest hundredth.)

31. The mean ________ **32.** The median ________

The quality-control inspector subsequently determined that he had made a mistake when he wrote 32 thousandths of an inch. Eliminate this number from the list above and find each of the following.

33. The mean ________ **34.** The median ________

35. If you want to avoid a single extreme value having a large effect on the average, would you use the mean or the median? Explain your answer.

36. Does an employer look at the mean, median, or mode grade on a college transcript when considering hiring a new employee? Which do you think the employer should look at? Explain.

CHAPTER 15 QUICK REVIEW

CHAPTER TERMS *Review the following terms to test your understanding of the chapter. For each term you do not know, refer to the page number found next to that term.*

CONCEPTS / EXAMPLES

15.1 Constructing a frequency distribution from raw data

1. Construct a table listing each value and the number of times this value occurs.
2. Combine the pieces of data into groups.

Construct a frequency distribution for weekly sales, in thousands, at a small concrete plant.

$22, $20, $22, $25, $18, $19, $22, $24, $24, $29, $19

Data	Tally	Frequency
$18	I	1
$19	II	2
$20	I	1
$22	III	3
$24	II	2
$25	I	1
$29	I	1

Class	Frequency
$18–$20	4
$21–$23	3
$24–$26	3
$27–$29	1

15.1 Constructing a bar graph from a frequency distribution

Draw a bar for each class using the frequency of the class as the height of the bar.

Construct a bar graph from the frequency distribution of the preceding example.

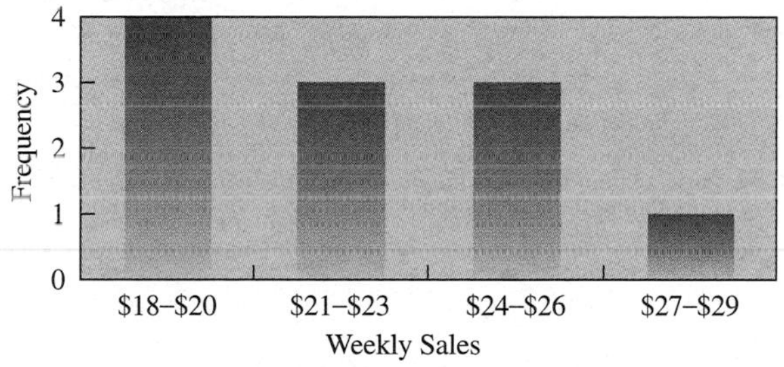

15.1 Constructing a line graph

1. Plot each year on the horizontal axis.
2. For each year, find the value of sales, and plot a point at that value.
3. Connect all points with straight lines.

Construct a line graph for the following sales data.

Year	Total Sales
2005	$850,000
2006	$920,000
2007	$875,000
2008	$975,000

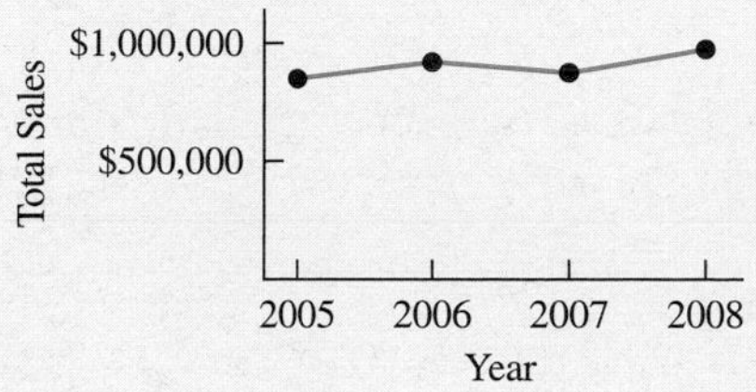

CONCEPTS	EXAMPLES

15.1 Constructing a circle graph

1. Determine the percent of the total for each item.
2. Find the number of degrees of a circle that each percent represents.
3. Draw the circle.

Construct a circle graph for the following table which lists expenses for a business trip.

Item	Amount
Car	\$200
Lodging	\$300
Food	\$250
Entertainment	\$150
Other	\$100
	\$1000

Item	Amount	Percent of Total
Car	\$200	$\frac{\$200}{\$1000} = \frac{1}{5} = 20\%;\ 360° \times 20\% = 360 \times .20 = \mathbf{72°}$
Lodging	\$300	$\frac{\$300}{\$1000} = \frac{3}{10} = 30\%;\ 360° \times 30\% = 360 \times .30 = \mathbf{108°}$
Food	\$250	$\frac{\$250}{\$1000} = \frac{1}{4} = 25\%;\ 360° \times 25\% = 360 \times .25 = \mathbf{90°}$
Entertainment	\$150	$\frac{\$150}{\$1000} = \frac{3}{20} = 15\%;\ 360° \times 15\% = 360 \times .15 = \mathbf{54°}$
Other	\$100	$\frac{\$100}{\$1000} = \frac{1}{10} = 10\%;\ 360° \times 10\% = 360 \times .10 = \mathbf{36°}$

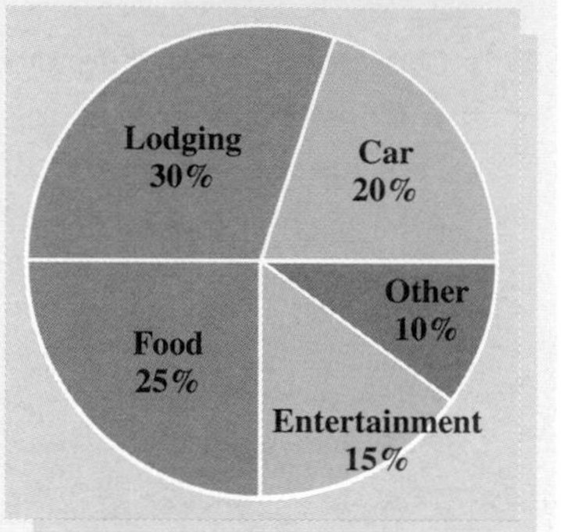

15.2 Finding the mean of a set of numbers

1. Add all numbers to obtain the total.
2. Divide the total by the number of pieces of data.

The quiz scores for Pat Phelan in her business math course were as follows:

85 79 93 91 78 82 87 85

Find Pat's quiz average.

$$\text{Mean} = \frac{85 + 79 + 93 + 91 + 78 + 82 + 87 + 85}{8} = \mathbf{85}$$

15.2 Finding the median of a set of numbers

1. Arrange the data in numerical order from lowest to highest.
2. Select the middle value or the average of the two middle values.

Find the median for Pat Phelan's grades from the preceding example. The data arranged from the lowest to highest are

78 79 82 85 85 87 91 93

The middle two values are 85 and 85. The average of these two values is

$$\frac{85 + 85}{2} = \mathbf{85}$$

15.2 Finding the mode of a set of values

Determine the most frequently occurring value.

Find the mode for Pat Phelan's grades in the preceding example. The most frequently occurring score is 85 (it occurs twice), so the mode is 85.

CHAPTER 15 SUMMARY EXERCISE

Watching the Growth of a Small Business

Jeremy Clark decided to call his business The Soft Touch, and he opened his first kiosk selling candles and other gifts in a nearby mall on February 1. In June, he opened a second kiosk selling the same gifts. Sales at the two kiosks (stores) are shown in thousands of dollars.

	Feb.	Mar.	Apr.	May	June	July	Aug.	Sept.	Oct.
Store 1	6.5	6.8	7.0	6.9	7.5	7.8	8.0	7.6	8.2
Store 2	—	—	—	—	8.2	6.2	8.2	8.7	9.6

(a) Find the median, mean, and mode sales for each store to the nearest tenth.

(b) Plot sales for both stores on the same line graph, with month on the horizontal axis and sales on the vertical axis.

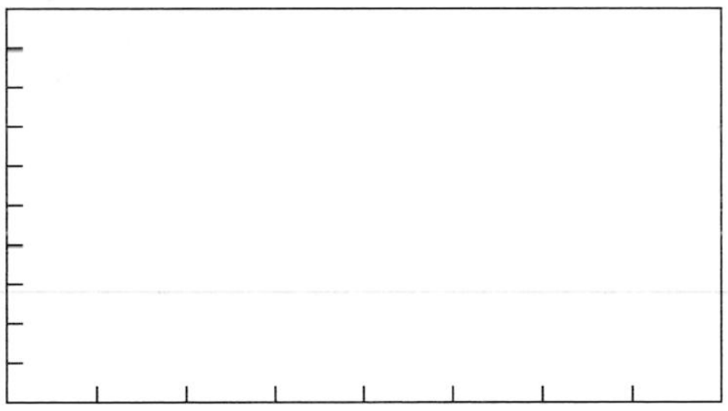

(c) What trends are apparent from the preceding line graph?

INVESTIGATE

Cut at least three graphs and charts out of recent newspapers or magazines. Then explain each of them in writing. Graphs and charts can be great tools for communicating with customers, fellow workers, or even your boss. How can you make sure that a graph or chart clearly communicates the message that you wish it to convey?

Case Studies

Bobby Flay

www.bobbyflay.com

- 1991: Opened Mesa Grill in New York
- 1996: First time on Food Network
- 2004: Published his fifth cookbook
- 2007: "Boy Meets Grill" on TV several times each week

Bobby Flay opened Mesa Grill in New York City in 1991 with "a new twist on southwestern cuisine." He owns several restaurants in the New York area and also one in Las Vegas. Flay prides himself on creating a working environment in which his employees are able to express their creativity and grow professionally. His organization currently offers a $30,000 scholarship to one high school senior who plans to attend the French Culinary Institute. His most recent book, *Grilling for Life,* is about great food and healthy choices.

Go to Mesa Grill in New York for Sunday brunch and you will find mouth-watering dishes such as spicy chicken sweet potato hash with poached eggs and green chili hollandaise. For dinner, you might find New Mexican spice-rubbed pork tenderloin with bourbon ancho chile sauce and sweet potato tamale. You may even be tempted by caramel apple shortcake with autumn-fruit compote or other desserts at the end of your meal.

1. Assume recent weekly sales leading up to and including Thanksgiving week at a small bistro called Avenue Bistro are: $22.5, $21.7, $23.8, $27.2, $28.6, and $32.9, in thousands of dollars. Find the mean, median, and mode rounded to the nearest tenth of a thousand.

2. Show the sales data above in a line graph—be sure to label appropriately.

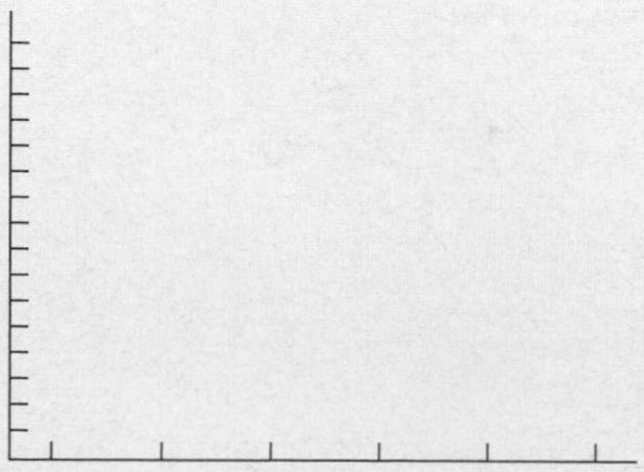

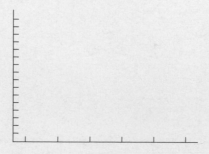

CHAPTER 15 TEST

To help you review, the numbers in brackets show the section in which the topic was discussed.

1. The following are the numbers of cases of motor oil sold per week, by a regional distributor on the East Coast, for each of the past 20 weeks.

12,450	11,300	12,800	10,850	14,100
14,900	12,300	11,600	12,400	12,900
13,300	12,500	13,390	12,800	12,500
15,100	13,700	12,200	11,800	12,600

Use these numbers to complete the following table. **[15.1]**

Cases of Motor Oil	Number of Weeks
10,000–10,999	____
11,000–11,999	____
12,000–12,999	____
13,000–13,999	____
14,000–14,999	____
15,000–15,999	____

2. How many weeks had sales of 13,000 cases or more? **[15.1]** **2.** ____________

3. Use the numbers in the table above to draw a bar graph. Be sure to put a title and labels on the graph. **[15.1]**

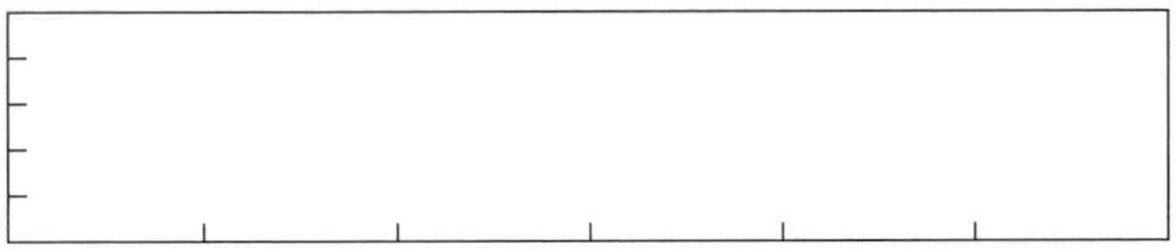

4. During a 1-year period, the campus newspaper at Dallas Community College had the following expenses. Find all numbers missing from the table. **[15.1]**

Item	*Dollar Amount*	*Percent of Total*	*Degrees of a Circle*
Newsprint	$12,000	20%	____
Ink	$6,000	____	36°
Wire service	$18,000	30%	____
Salaries	$18,000	30%	____
Other	$6,000	10%	____

5. Draw a circle graph using the information in test question 4. **[15.1]**

6. What percents of the expenses were for newsprint, ink, and wire service? **[15.1]** **6.** ________

Find the means for the following. Round to the nearest tenth if necessary. **[15.2]**

7. Number attending classical music recitals: 220, 275, 198, 212, 233, 246 **7.** ________

8. Length of boards (centimeters): 12, 18, 14, 17, 19, 22, 23, 25 **8.** ________

9. Weekly commission ($): 458, 432, 496, 491, 500, 508, 512, 396, 492, 504 **9.** ________

10.

Volume (quarts)	***Frequency***
6	7
10	3
11	4
14	2
19	3
24	1

____

11.

Sales ($)	***Frequency***
150	15
160	17
170	21
180	28
190	19
200	7

____

Find the median for the following lists of numbers. Do not round. **[15.2]**

12. Numbers of actors trying out for a part: 22, 18, 15, 25, 20, 19, 7 **12.** ________

13. Number of telephone calls received per hour: 41, 39, 45, 47, 38, 42, 51, 38 **13.** ________

14. Hours worked per day: 7.6, 9.3, 11.8, 10.4, 4.2, 5.3, 7.1, 9.0, 8.3 **14.** ________

15. Trees planted: 58, 76, 91, 83, 29, 34, 51, 92, 38, 41 — **15.** ________

Find the mode or modes for the following lists of numbers. **[15.2]**

16. Contestants' ages: 51, 47, 48, 32, 47, 71, 82, 47 — **16.** ________

17. Customers served: 32, 51, 74, 19, 25, 43, 75, 82, 98, 100 — **17.** ________

18. Defectives per batch: 96, 104, 103, 104, 103, 104, 91, 74, 103 — **18.** ________

Solve the following application problems.

19. Stein's Fine Furnishings had the following sales (in thousand of dollars).

Year	Sales
2005	$754
2006	$782
2007	$853
2008	$592
2009	$680

The geographic area in which Stein's operates had a serious business recession (economic slow down) in 2008. Do you think the recession may have affected the business? Support your view by drawing a line graph.

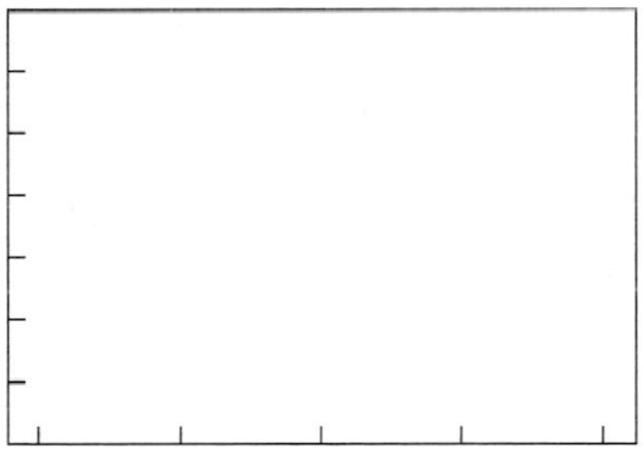

20. Ted Smith sells stocks and bonds at Merrill Lynch and receives a base salary and a commission based on performance. His wife developed a serious illness at the beginning of 2008 and her condition slowly improved through the balance of the year. Do you think his personal problems may have influenced his work performance?

	Quarterly Commissions			
Year	**Quarter 1**	**Quarter 2**	**Quarter 3**	**Quarter 4**
2006	$14,250	$12,375	$15,750	$13,682
2007	$13,435	$14,230	$11,540	$15,782
2008	$8,207	$7,350	$10,366	$11,470

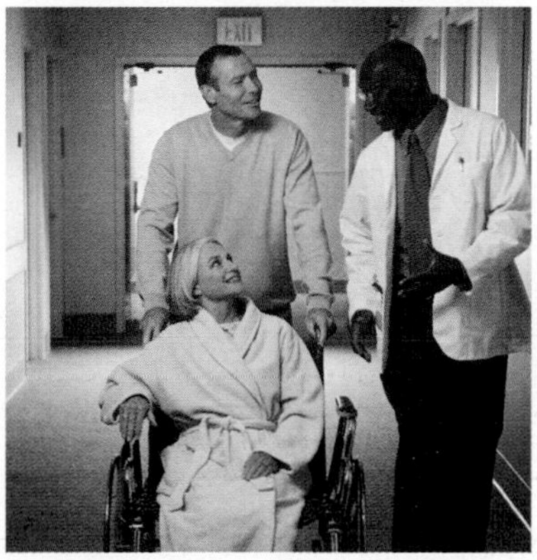

Support your view by drawing a line graph. Be sure to label the quarter in which Mrs. Smith became ill.

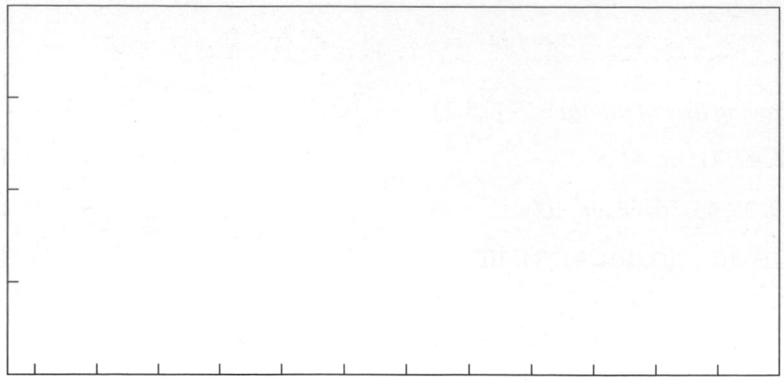

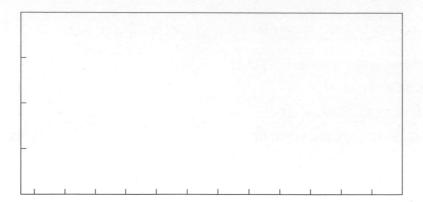

Appendix A

Equations and Formula Review

A.1 EQUATIONS

OBJECTIVES

1. Learn the basic terminology of equations.
2. Use basic rules to solve equations.
3. Solve equations requiring more than one operation.
4. Combine like terms in equations.
5. Use the distributive property to simplify equations.

OBJECTIVE 1 Learn the basic terminology of equations. An equation is a statement that says two expressions are equal. For example, in the equation

$$x + 5 = 9$$

the expression $x + 5$ and the number 9 are equal to each other. The letter x is just a name for a value that is not yet known. Clearly, x must be 4 in order for $x + 5$ to be equal to 9. So $x = 4$ is the **solution** to the equation. Some other terminology used when working with equations follows.

QUICK TIP In the expression $x + 5$, x is the same thing as $+1x$, or 1 times x.

Equation Terminology

The letter x is called a **variable**; it is a letter that represents a number. Any letter can be used for a variable.

A **term** is a single letter, a single number, or the product of a number and a letter. In $x + 5 = 9$, the variable x as well as the numbers 5 and 9 are terms. In the expression $3y - 14.5$, both $3y$ and 14.5 are terms.

In $x + 5 = 9$, the expression $x + 5$ is the **left side** of the equation, and 9 is the **right side**.

A **solution** to the equation is any number that can replace the variable and result in a true statement. The solution for this equation is the number 4, since the replacement of the variable x with the number 4 results in a true statement.

$$x + 5 = 9$$
$$4 + 5 = 9 \quad \text{Let } x = 4.$$
$$9 = 9 \quad \text{True}$$

The check shows an example of **substitution**; the number 4 was substituted for the variable x.

OBJECTIVE 2 Use basic rules to solve equations. In solving equations, the object is to find a number that can be used to replace the variable so that the equation is a true statement. This is done by changing the equation so that all the terms containing a variable are on one side of the equation and all numbers are on the other side. An equation states that two expressions are equal to each other. As long as both sides of an equation are changed in exactly the same way, the expressions are still equal to each other. Look at the following two rules, which can be used when solving equations.

Rules for Solving Equations

Addition Rule The same number may be added or subtracted on both sides of an equation.

Multiplication Rule Both sides of an equation may be multiplied or divided by the same nonzero number.

EXAMPLE 1

Solving a Linear Equation Using Addition

Solve $x - 9 = 15$.

SOLUTION

To solve this equation, x must be alone on one side of the equal sign and all numbers collected on the other side. To change the $x - 9$ to x, perform the opposite operation to "undo" what was done. The opposite of subtraction is addition, so add 9 to both sides.

$$\begin{aligned} x - 9 &= 15 \\ x - 9 + 9 &= 15 + 9 \quad \text{Add 9 to both sides.} \\ x + 0 &= 24 \\ x &= 24 \end{aligned}$$

To check this answer, substitute 24 for x in the original equation.

$$\begin{aligned} x - 9 &= 15 \quad \text{Original equation} \\ 24 - 9 &= 15 \quad \text{Let } x = 24. \\ 15 &= 15 \quad \text{True} \end{aligned}$$

The answer of $x = 24$ checks.

QUICK TIP Remember these two things when solving equations:

1. What you do to one side of an equation, you must also do to the other side.
2. Solve equations using the opposite math operation from those used in the equation.

QUICK CHECK 1

Solve $y - 22 = 45$.

EXAMPLE 2

Solving a Linear Equation Using Subtraction

Solve $k + 7 = 18$.

SOLUTION

To isolate k on the left side, do the opposite of adding 7, which is *subtracting* 7.

$$\begin{aligned} k + 7 &= 18 \\ k + 7 - 7 &= 18 - 7 \quad \text{Subtract 7.} \\ k &= 11 \end{aligned}$$

QUICK CHECK 2

Solve $m + 19 = 32$.

EXAMPLE 3

Solving a Linear Equation Using Division

Solve $5p = 60$.

SOLUTION

The term $5p$ indicates the multiplication of 5 and p. Since division is the inverse of multiplication, solve the equation by *dividing* both sides by 5.

$$\begin{aligned} 5p &= 60 \\ \frac{5p}{5} &= \frac{60}{5} \quad \text{Divide by 5.} \\ p &= 12 \end{aligned}$$

Check by substituting 12 for p in the original equation.

QUICK CHECK 3

Solve $17g = 153$.

Sometimes we put slash or cancel marks through the numbers used to divide both sides. Slash marks would be used in Example 3 as follows.

$$\begin{aligned} 5p &= 60 \\ \frac{\cancel{5}p}{\cancel{5}} &= \frac{60}{5} \\ p &= 12 \end{aligned}$$

Quick Check Answers

1. $y = 67$
2. $m = 13$
3. $g = 9$

EXAMPLE 4

Solving a Linear Equation Using Multiplication

Solve $\frac{y}{3} = 9$.

SOLUTION

The bar in $\frac{y}{3}$ means to divide, so solve the equation by multiplying both sides by 3. (The opposite of division is multiplication.) As in the following solution, it is common to use a dot to indicate multiplication.

$$\frac{y}{3} = 9$$
$$\frac{y}{3} \cdot 3 = 9 \cdot 3 \quad \text{Multiply by 3.}$$
$$y = 27$$

QUICK CHECK 4

Solve $\frac{t}{4} = 28$.

Example 5 shows how to solve an equation using a reciprocal. To get the **reciprocal** of a nonzero fraction, exchange the numerator and the denominator. For example, the reciprocal of $\frac{7}{9}$ is $\frac{9}{7}$. The product of two reciprocals is 1.

$$\frac{\overset{1}{\cancel{7}}}{\underset{1}{\cancel{9}}} \cdot \frac{\overset{1}{\cancel{9}}}{\underset{1}{\cancel{7}}} = 1$$

EXAMPLE 5

Solving a Linear Equation Using Reciprocals

Solve $\frac{3}{4}z = 9$.

SOLUTION

Solve this equation by multiplying both sides by $\frac{4}{3}$, the reciprocal of $\frac{3}{4}$. This process will give $1z$, or just z, on the left.

$$\frac{3}{4}z = 9$$
$$\frac{3}{4}z \cdot \frac{4}{3} = 9 \cdot \frac{4}{3} \quad \text{Multiply both sides by } \tfrac{4}{3}.$$
$$z = 12$$

QUICK CHECK 5

Solve $\frac{1}{2}z = 99$.

OBJECTIVE 3 Solve equations requiring more than one operation. The equation in Example 6 requires two steps to solve.

EXAMPLE 6

Solving a Linear Equation Using Several Steps

Solve $2m + 5 = 17$.

SOLUTION

To solve equations that require more than one step, first isolate the terms involving the unknown (or variable) on one side of the equation and the constants (or numbers) on the other side by using addition and subtraction.

$$2m + 5 = 17$$
$$2m + 5 - 5 = 17 - 5 \quad \text{Subtract 5 from both sides.}$$
$$2m = 12$$

Now divide both sides by 2.

$$\frac{2m}{2} = \frac{12}{2} \quad \text{Divide by 2.}$$
$$m = 6$$

As before, check by substituting 6 for m in the original equation.

Quick Check Answers

4. $t = 112$
5. $z = 198$

The unknown can be on either side of the equal sign. $6 = m$ is the same as $m = 6$. The number is the solution when the equation has the variable by itself on either the left or the right side of the equation.

QUICK CHECK 6

Solve $3y + 9 = 45$.

EXAMPLE 7

Solving a Linear Equation Using Several Steps

Solve $3y - 12 = 52$.

SOLUTION

$$3y - 12 = 52$$
$$3y - 12 + 12 = 52 + 12 \quad \text{Add 12 to both sides.}$$
$$3y = 64$$
$$\frac{3y}{3} = \frac{64}{3} \quad \text{Divide both sides by 3.}$$
$$y = 21\frac{1}{3}$$

QUICK CHECK 7

Solve $9q - 14 = 58$.

OBJECTIVE 4 Combine like terms in equations. Some equations have more than one term with the same variable. Terms with the same variables can be *combined* by adding or subtracting the coefficients, as shown.

$$5y + 2y = (5 + 2)y = 7y$$
$$11k - 8k = (11 - 8)k = 3k$$
$$12p - 5p + 2p = (12 - 5 + 2)p = 9p$$
$$2z + z = 2z + 1z = (2 + 1)z = 3z$$

Terms with different variables in them *cannot* be combined into a single term. For example, $12y + 5x$ cannot be combined to make one term, since y and x are different variables and may have different values.

EXAMPLE 8

Solving a Linear Equation Using Several Steps

Solve $8y - 6y + 4y = 24$.

SOLUTION

Start by combining terms on the left: $8y - 6y + 4y = 2y + 4y = 6y$. This gives the simplified equation $6y = 24$.

$$8y - 6y + 4y = 24$$
$$(8 - 6 + 4)y = 24 \quad \text{Combine like terms.}$$
$$6y = 24$$
$$\frac{6y}{6} = \frac{24}{6} \quad \text{Divide by 6.}$$
$$y = 4$$

QUICK CHECK 8

Solve $17z - 12z = 42$.

Quick Check Answers

6. $y = 12$
7. $q = 8$
8. $z = 8.4$

EXAMPLE 9

Solving a Linear Equation

Solve $7z - 3z + .5z = 15$.

SOLUTION

$$\begin{aligned} 7z - 3z + .5z &= 15 \\ (7 - 3 + .5)z &= 15 && \text{Combine like terms.} \\ 4.5z &= 15 \\ \frac{4.5z}{4.5} &= \frac{15}{4.5} && \text{Divide both sides by 4.5.} \\ z &= 3\frac{1}{3} \end{aligned}$$

QUICK CHECK 9

Solve $3t - .5t = 17$.

OBJECTIVE 5 **Use the distributive property to simplify equations.** Some of the more advanced formulas used in this book involve a number in front of terms in parentheses. These formulas often require use of the *distributive property*. According to the **distributive property**, a number on the outside of the parentheses can be multiplied by each term inside the parentheses, as shown here.

$$a(b + c) = ab + ac$$

The following diagram may help in remembering the distributive property.

Multiply a by b and c.

$$a(b + c) = ab + ac$$

The a is *distributed* over the b and the c, as in the following examples.

Multiply 2 by m and 7.

$$\begin{aligned} 2(m + 7) &= 2m + 2 \cdot 7 = 2m + 14 \\ 8(k - 5) &= 8k - 8 \cdot 5 = 8k - 40 \end{aligned}$$

EXAMPLE 10

Solving a Linear Equation Using the Distributive Property

Solve $8(t - 5) = 16$.

SOLUTION

First use the distributive property on the left to remove the parentheses.

$$\begin{aligned} 8(t - 5) &= 16 \\ 8t - 40 &= 16 \\ 8t - 40 + 40 &= 16 + 40 && \text{Add 40 to both sides.} \\ 8t &= 56 \\ \frac{8t}{8} &= \frac{56}{8} && \text{Divide by 8.} \\ t &= 7 \end{aligned}$$

QUICK CHECK 10

Solve $9(s - 16) = 135$.

Quick Check Answers

9. $t = 6.8$
10. $s = 31$

Use the following steps to solve an equation.

Solving an Equation

STEP 1 Remove all parentheses on both sides of the equation using the distributive property.

STEP 2 Combine all like terms on both sides of the equation.

STEP 3 Place all terms containing a variable on the same side of the equation and all terms not containing a variable on the other side of the equation. Do this by adding or subtracting terms from both sides of the equation as needed.

STEP 4 Multiply or divide the variable term by numbers as needed to produce a term with a coefficient of 1 in front of the variable. Do the same on the other side of the equation by multiplying or dividing by the same value.

EXAMPLE 11

Solving a Linear Equation Using the Distributive Property

Solve $5r - 2 = 2(r + 5)$.

SOLUTION

$5r - 2 = 2(r + 5)$	Use the distributive property on the right side.
$5r - 2 = 2r + 10$	
$5r - 2 + \mathbf{2} = 2r + 10 + \mathbf{2}$	Add 2 to both sides to get all numbers on the right side.
$5r = 2r + 12$	
$5r - \mathbf{2r} = 2r + 12 - \mathbf{2r}$	Subtract $2r$ from both sides to get all variables on the left side.
$5r - 2r = 12$	Combine like terms on the left side.
$3r = 12$	
$\frac{3r}{\mathbf{3}} = \frac{12}{\mathbf{3}}$	Divide both sides by 3.
$r = 4$	

Check by substituting 4 for r in the original equation.

QUICK TIP Be sure to check the answer in the *original* equation, not in any other step.

QUICK CHECK 11

Solve $5(s - 4) = 3(s + 9)$.

EXAMPLE 12

Solving a Linear Equation Using the Distributive Property

Solve $3(t - .8) = 14 + t$.

SOLUTION

$3(t - .8) = 14 + t$	
$3t - 2.4 = 14 + t$	Use the distributive property.
$3t - 2.4 - t = 14 + t - t$	Subtract t from both sides.
$2t - 2.4 = 14$	Combine like terms.
$2t - 2.4 + \mathbf{2.4} = 14 + \mathbf{2.4}$	Add 2.4 to both sides.
$2t = 16.4$	
$\frac{2t}{\mathbf{2}} = \frac{16.4}{\mathbf{2}}$	Divide both sides by 2.
$t = 8.2$	

QUICK TIP You may wish to solve Exercises 1–24 at the end of this appendix before proceeding to the next section.

QUICK CHECK 12

Solve $12u - 8 = 8(u + 4)$.

Quick Check Answers

11. $s = 23.5$
12. $u = 10$

A.2 BUSINESS APPLICATIONS OF EQUATIONS

OBJECTIVES

1. Translate phrases into mathematical expressions.
2. Write equations from given information.
3. Solve application problems.

OBJECTIVE 1 Translate phrases into mathematical expressions. Most problems in business are expressed in words. Before these problems can be solved, they must be converted into mathematical language.

Word problems tend to have certain phrases that occur again and again. The key to solving word problems is to correctly translate these expressions into mathematical expressions. The next few examples illustrate this process.

EXAMPLE 1

Translating Verbal Expressions Involving Addition

Write the following verbal expressions as mathematical expressions. Use x to represent the unknown quantity. Note that other letters can also be used to represent this unknown quantity.

SOLUTION

Verbal Expression	Mathematical Expression	Comments
(a) 5 plus a number	$5 + x$	x represents the number, and *plus* indicates **addition**
(b) Add 20 to a number	$x + 20$	x represents the number, and *add* indicates **addition**
(c) The sum of a number and 12	$x + 12$	x represents the number, and *sum* indicates **addition**
(d) 6 more than a number	$x + 6$	x represents the number, and *more than* indicates **addition**

QUICK CHECK 1

Write a number plus 7 as a mathematical expression using y for the unknown.

EXAMPLE 2

Translating Verbal Expressions Involving Subtraction

Write each of the following verbal expressions as a mathematical expression. Use p as the variable.

SOLUTION

Verbal Expression	Mathematical Expression	Comments
(a) 3 less than a number	$p - 3$	p represents the number, and *less than* indicates **subtraction**
(b) A number decreased by 14	$p - 14$	p represents the number, and *decreased by* indicates **subtraction**
(c) 10 fewer than p	$p - 10$	p represents the number, and *fewer than* indicates **subtraction**

QUICK CHECK 2

Use s for the unknown, and write a mathematical expression for 19 minus an unknown.

Quick Check Answers

1. $y + 7$
2. $19 - s$

EXAMPLE 3

Translating Verbal Expressions Involving Multiplication and Division

Write the following verbal expressions as mathematical expressions. Use y as the variable.

SOLUTION

Verbal Expression	Mathematical Expression	Comments
(a) The product of a number and 3	$3y$	y represents the number, and *product* indicates **multiplication**
(b) Four times a number	$4y$	y represents the number, and *times* indicates **multiplication**
(c) Two-thirds of a number	$\frac{2}{3}y$	y represents the number, and *of* indicates **multiplication**
(d) The quotient of a number and 2	$\frac{y}{2}$	y represents the number, and *quotient* indicates **division**
(e) The sum of 3 and a number is multiplied by 5	$5(3 + y)$ or $5(y + 3)$	This requires **parentheses.**
(f) 7 is multiplied by the difference of an unknown number and 14	$7(y - 14)$	This requires **parentheses.**

QUICK TIP In addition and multiplication, the order of the variable and the number doesn't matter. For example,

$$3 + x = x + 3$$
and
$$5 \cdot y = y \cdot 5$$

The order *cannot* be reversed in subtraction (or division).

For example, $8 - y$ is *not* the same as $y - 8$, and $6 \div z$ is *not* the same as $z \div 6$.

QUICK CHECK 3

Use t for the variable, and write an expression for the product of 7 and the sum of 9 plus an unknown.

OBJECTIVE 2 **Write equations from given information.** Since equal mathematical expressions represent the same number, any words that mean *equals* or *same* translate into an =. The = sign produces an equation that can usually be solved.

EXAMPLE 4

Writing an Equation from Words

Translate "the product of 5 and a number decreased by 8 is 100" into an equation. Use y as the variable. Solve the equation.

SOLUTION

Translate as follows.

The product of 5		and a number	decreased by	8	is	100.
↓	↓	↓	↓	↓		↓
5	·	(y	−	8)	=	100

Simplify and complete the solution of the equation.

$$5 \cdot (y - 8) = 100$$
$$5y - 40 = 100 \quad \text{Apply the distributive property.}$$
$$5y = 140 \quad \text{Add 40 to both sides.}$$
$$y = 28 \quad \text{Divide by 5.}$$

QUICK CHECK 4

Write "ninety-four is the product of 12 and the sum of a number and 2.5" as an equation, using p for the variable.

Quick Check Answers

3. $7(9 + t)$
4. $94 = 12(p + 2.5)$

EXAMPLE 5

Writing an Equation from Words

Write "The sum of an unknown and 6, when divided by 15, is equal to 7" as an equation, using r as the variable.

SOLUTION

The sum of an unknown and 6	when divided by 15	is equal to	7.
↓	↓	↓	↓
$(r + 6)$	$\div 15$	$=$	7

Simplify and solve the equation.

$$(r + 6) \div 15 = 7$$

$$(r + 6) \div 15 \cdot \mathbf{15} = 7 \cdot \mathbf{15} \quad \text{Multiply both sides by 15.}$$

$$r + 6 = 105$$

$$r + 6 - \mathbf{6} = 105 - \mathbf{6} \quad \text{Subtract 6 from both sides.}$$

$$r = 99$$

QUICK CHECK 5

Write "the quantity 17 minus an unknown, divided by 12, is equal to 14" as an equation, using r as the variable.

OBJECTIVE 3 **Solve application problems.** Now that statements have been translated into mathematical expressions, you can use this knowledge to solve problems. The following steps represent a systematic approach to solving application problems.

Solving Application Problems: A Systematic Approach

STEP 1 Read the problem very carefully. Reread the problem to make sure that its meaning is clear.

STEP 2 Figure out what is not known. Choose a variable to represent the unknown number.

STEP 3 Identify the knowns. Use the given information to write an equation describing the relationship given in the problem.

STEP 4 Solve the equation.

STEP 5 Answer the question asked in the problem.

STEP 6 Check the solution by using the original words of the problem.

QUICK TIP Always check to see whether your answer to a word problem needs to be expressed in units such as dollars, gallons, ounces, or whatever. Your answer is incomplete unless you have the correct units.

Step 3 is often the most difficult. To write an equation from the information given in the problem, convert the facts stated in words into mathematical expressions. These expressions are used to build a *mathematical model* of the situation.

EXAMPLE 6

Solving a Business Problem

A restaurant manager found that she has 18 more women than men scheduled to work next week. The total number scheduled to work next week is 64. Find the number of women.

SOLUTION

Let m represent the number of men. Then $(m + 18)$ is the number of women. The number of men plus the number of women is equal to 64, which is the total number scheduled to work. Write this using an equation.

Number of men	plus	number of women	equals	total scheduled.
↓	↓	↓	↓	↓
m	$+$	$(m + 18)$	$=$	64
m	$+$	$m + 18$	$=$	64

Quick Check Answer

5. $\frac{(17 - r)}{12} = 14$

Solve the equation for the number of men.

$$2m + 18 = 64$$
$$2m + 18 - \mathbf{18} = 64 - \mathbf{18} \quad \text{Subtract 18 from each side.}$$
$$2m = 46$$
$$\frac{2m}{2} = \frac{46}{2} \quad \text{Divide by 2.}$$
$$m = 23 \quad \text{There are 23 men scheduled.}$$

Now find the number of women using $(m + 18) = (23 + 18) = 41$ women.

QUICK CHECK 6

A professor was taking 28 students to Guadalajara, Mexico, on a two-week, travel-study program. If there were 14 more women than men, find the number of men and the number of women.

EXAMPLE 7

Applying Equation Solving

A mattress is on sale for \$200, which is $\frac{4}{5}$ of its original price. Find the original price.

SOLUTION

Let p represent the original price, \$200 is the sale price, and the sale price is $\frac{4}{5}$ of the original price. Use all this information to write the equation.

Sale price	is	$\frac{4}{5}$	of	original price.
↓	↓	↓	↓	↓
\$200	=	$\frac{4}{5}$	×	p

Solve the equation.

$$200 = \frac{4}{5} \cdot p$$
$$\frac{5}{4} \cdot 200 = \frac{5}{4} \cdot \frac{4}{5} \cdot p \quad \text{Multiply by reciprocal.}$$
$$\frac{1000}{4} = \mathbf{1} \cdot p$$
$$250 = p$$

The original price was \$250.

QUICK CHECK 7

Fearful of bankruptcy, the top manager of a company laid off enough people so that the workforce was only 2/3 of the original workforce. Find the original number of employees if there were 34 employees after the layoff.

EXAMPLE 8

Solving a Business Problem

The Eastside Nursery ordered 27 tree seedlings. Some of the seedlings were elms, costing \$17 each. The remainder of the seedlings were maples at \$11 each. The total cost of the seedlings was \$375. Find the number of elms and the number of maples.

SOLUTION

Let x represent the number of elm seedlings in the shipment. Since the shipment contained 27 seedlings, the number of maples is found by subtracting the number of elms from 27.

$$27 - x = \text{number of maples}$$

If each elm seedling costs \$17, then x elm seedlings will cost $17x$ dollars. Also, the cost of $(27 - x)$ maple seedlings at \$11 each is $11(27 - x)$. The total cost of the shipment was \$375.

A table can be very helpful in identifying the knowns and unknowns.

	Number of Seedlings	Cost per Seedling	Total Cost
Elms	x	\$17	$17x$
Maples	$(27 - x)$	\$11	$11(27 - x)$
Totals	27		375

Quick Check Answers

6. 7 men, 21 women
7. 51 employees

The information in the table is used to develop the following equation.

$$\textbf{Cost of elms} + \textbf{Cost of maples} = \textbf{Total cost}$$
$$17x + 11(27 - x) = 375$$

Now solve this equation. First use the distributive property.

$$17x + 297 - 11x = 375$$
$$6x + 297 = 375 \quad \text{Combine terms.}$$
$$6x = 78 \quad \text{Subtract 297 from each side.}$$
$$x = 13 \quad \text{Divide each side by 6.}$$

There were $x = 13$ elm seedlings and $(27 - 13) = 14$ maple seedlings.

QUICK CHECK 8

A beer-bottling company ordered 2100 more 12-ounce bottles than 1-quart bottles. The cost of the 12-ounce bottles was \$.08 each, and the cost of the 1-quart bottles was \$.11 each. The total cost was \$310.50 not including shipping. Find the number of each type of bottle ordered.

EXAMPLE 9

Solving Investment Problems

Laurie Zimmerman has \$15,000 to invest. She places a portion of the funds in a passbook account and \$3000 more than twice this amount in a retirement account. How much is put into the passbook account? How much is placed in the retirement account?

SOLUTION

Let z represent the amount invested in the passbook account. To find the amount invested in the retirement account, translate as follows.

3000	more than	2 times the amount
↓	↓	↓
3000	+	$2z$

Since the sum of the two investments must be \$15,000, an equation can be formed as follows.

Amount invested in passbook	+	Amount invested in retirement account	=	Total amount invested
z	+	$(3000 + 2z)$	=	\$15,000

Now solve the equation.

QUICK TIP You may wish to work Exercises 61–70 at the end of this appendix before proceeding to the next section.

$$z + (3000 + 2z) = 15{,}000$$
$$3z + 3000 = 15{,}000$$
$$3z = 12{,}000 \quad \text{Subtract 3000.}$$
$$z = 4000 \quad \text{Divide by 3.}$$

The amount invested in the passbook account is z, or \$4000. The amount invested in the retirement account is $3000 + 2z$ or $3000 + 2(4000) = \$11{,}000$.

QUICK CHECK 9

A mutual fund company has \$24 million to invest. They place part of the funds in the bonds of a utility company and \$4 million more than three times that amount in New York City bonds. Find the amount placed in utility bonds and the amount in New York City bonds.

Quick Check Answers

8. 2850 12-ounce bottles; 750 1-quart bottles
9. Utility bonds, \$5 million; New York City bonds, \$19 million

A.3 BUSINESS FORMULAS

OBJECTIVES

1. Evaluate formulas for given values of the variables.
2. Solve formulas for a specific variable.
3. Use standard business formulas to solve word problems.
4. Evaluate formulas containing exponents.

OBJECTIVE 1 Evaluate formulas for given values of the variables. Many of the most useful rules and procedures in business are given as **formulas**: equations showing how one number is found from other numbers. One of the single most useful formulas in business is the one for simple interest.

$$\text{Interest} = \text{Principal} \times \text{Rate} \times \text{Time}$$

When written out in words, as shown, a formula can take up too much space and be hard to remember. For this reason, it is common to *use letters as variables for the words* in a formula. Many times the first letter in each word of a formula is used, to make it easier to remember the formula. By this method, the formula for simple interest is written as follows.

$$\text{Interest} = \text{Principal} \times \text{Rate} \times \text{Time}$$
$$I = PRT$$

By using letters to express the relationship among interest, principal, rate, and time, we have generalized the relationship so that any value can be substituted into the formula. Once, three values are substituted into the formula, we can find the value of the remaining variable.

EXAMPLE 1

Evaluating a Formula

Use the formula $I = PRT$ and find I if $P = 7000$, $R = .09$, and $T = 2$.

SOLUTION

Substitute 7000 for P, .09 for R, and 2 for T in the formula $I = PRT$. Remember that writing P, R, and T together as PRT indicates the product of the three letters.

$$I = PRT$$
$$I = 7000(.09)(2)$$

Multiply on the right to get the solution.

$$I = 1260$$

QUICK CHECK 1

Use $F = ma$ to find F if $m = 1700$ and $a = 9.8$.

EXAMPLE 2

Evaluating a Formula

Use the formula $I = PRT$ and find P if $I = 5760$, $R = .16$, and $T = 3$.

SOLUTION

Substitute the given numbers for the letters of the formula.

$$I = PRT$$
$$5760 = P(.16)(3)$$
$$5760 = .48P \quad P(.16)(3) = .48P$$
$$\frac{5760}{.48} = \frac{.48P}{.48} \quad \text{Divide both sides by .48.}$$
$$12{,}000 = P$$

QUICK CHECK 2

Use the formula $I = PRT$ to find T if $I = \$3000$, $P = \$40{,}000$, and $R = 0.75$.

Quick Check Answers

1. $F = 16{,}660$
2. $T = 0.1$

EXAMPLE 3

Evaluating a Formula

Solve for rate (R) given $M = \$12{,}540$, $P = \$12{,}000$, and $T = .5$ in the equation $M = P(1 + RT)$.

SOLUTION

$$
\begin{aligned}
M &= P(1 + RT) \\
\$12{,}540 &= \$12{,}000(1 + R \cdot .5) \\
12{,}540 &= 12{,}000 + 12{,}000 \cdot R \cdot .5 && \text{Use the distributive property.} \\
12{,}540 &= 12{,}000 + 6000 \cdot R \\
12{,}540 - \mathbf{12{,}000} &= 12{,}000 + 6000 \cdot R - \mathbf{12{,}000} && \text{Subtract 12,000 from each side.} \\
540 &= 6000 \cdot R \\
\frac{540}{\mathbf{6000}} &= \frac{6000 \cdot R}{\mathbf{6000}} && \text{Divide by 6000.} \\
.09 &= R
\end{aligned}
$$

Rate is .09 or 9%.

QUICK CHECK 3

Solve for rate (R) if $M = \$8300$, $P = \$8000$, and $T = .5$ in the equation $M = P(1 + RT)$.

OBJECTIVE 2 **Solve formulas for a specific variable.** In Example 2, we found the value of P when given the values of I, R, and T. If several problems of this type must be solved, it may be better to rewrite the formula $I = PRT$ so that P is alone on one side of the equation. Do this with the rules of equations given earlier. Since P is multiplied by RT, get P alone by dividing both sides of the equation by RT.

QUICK TIP The process of rearranging a formula is sometimes called solving a formula for a specific variable.

$$
\begin{aligned}
I &= PRT \\
\frac{I}{RT} &= \frac{P\cancel{RT}}{\cancel{RT}} && \text{Divide by } RT. \\
\frac{I}{RT} &= P
\end{aligned}
$$

EXAMPLE 4

Solving a Formula for a Specific Variable

Solve for T in the formula $M = P(1 + RT)$. This formula gives the maturity value (M) of an initial amount of money (P) invested at a specific rate (R) for a certain period of time (T).

SOLUTION

Start by using the distributive property on the right side.

$$
\begin{aligned}
M &= P(1 + RT) \\
M &= P + PRT
\end{aligned}
$$

Now subtract P from both sides.

$$
\begin{aligned}
M - P &= P + PRT - P \\
M - P &= PRT
\end{aligned}
$$

Divide each side by PR.

$$
\begin{aligned}
\frac{M - P}{PR} &= \frac{\cancel{PR}T}{\cancel{PR}} \\
\frac{M - P}{PR} &= T
\end{aligned}
$$

The original formula is now solved for T.

QUICK CHECK 4

Solve $S = (kT - 12)$ for T.

Quick Check Answers

3. $R = 7.5\%$

4. $T = \dfrac{(S + 12)}{k}$

EXAMPLE 5

Solving a Formula for a Specific Variable

Solve for T in the formula $D = \frac{B}{MT}$.

SOLUTION

This formula gives the discount rate (D) of a note in terms of the face value (B), the time of a note (T), and the maturity value (M). Solve for T.

$$D = \frac{B}{MT}$$

$$DMT = \frac{B}{\cancel{MT}}\cancel{MT} \quad \text{Multiply by } MT.$$

$$DMT = B$$

$$\frac{\cancel{DM}T}{\cancel{DM}} = \frac{B}{DM} \quad \text{Divide by } DM.$$

$$T = \frac{B}{DM}$$

QUICK CHECK 5

Solve $T = \frac{R}{JK}$ for J.

OBJECTIVE 3 **Use standard business formulas to solve word problems.** In the following examples, application problems that use some common business formulas are solved.

EXAMPLE 6

Finding Gross Sales

Find the gross sales amount from selling 481 fishing lures at \$2.65 each.

SOLUTION

The formula for gross sales is $G = NP$, where N is the number of items sold and P is the price per item. To find the gross sales from selling 481 fishing lures at \$2.65 each, use the formula.

$$G = NP$$

$$G = 481(\$2.65)$$

$$G = \mathbf{\$1274.65}$$

The gross sales will be \$1274.65.

QUICK CHECK 6

Find the gross revenue from selling 27 cases of wine at \$156 each.

EXAMPLE 7

Finding Selling Price

A retailer purchased a personal computer with a microphone to digitize voice at a cost of \$1265. He then adds a markup of \$150 before placing it on the shelf to sell. Find the selling price.

SOLUTION

The selling price is found by adding the cost of the item and the markup.

$$S = C + M$$

The variable C is the cost and M is the markup, which is the amount added to the cost to cover expenses and profit. The selling price is found as shown.

$$S = \$1265 + \$150$$

$$S = \mathbf{\$1415}$$

The selling price is \$1415.

QUICK CHECK 7

A discount Web retailer buys software packages for \$26.92 each and marks them up by \$8.07 each. Find the selling price.

Quick Check Answers

5. $J = \frac{R}{KT}$

6. \$4212

7. \$34.99

OBJECTIVE 4 Evaluate formulas containing exponents. Exponents are used to show repeated multiplication of a quantity called the *base*. For example,

Exponent: the number of times the base appears as a factor

$$x^2 = x \cdot x$$

Base: the quantity being multiplied.

Similarly,

$$z^3 = z \cdot z \cdot z \qquad \text{and} \qquad 5^4 = 5 \cdot 5 \cdot 5 \cdot 5 = 625$$

EXAMPLE 8

Finding Monthly Sales

Trinity Sporting Goods has found that monthly sales can be approximated using

$$\text{Sales} = 40 + 1.6 \times (\text{Advertising})^2$$

as long as advertising is less than \$4000. All of the figures in the equation above are in thousands. Estimate sales for a month with \$3500 in advertising.

SOLUTION

Place 3.5 in the equation for the number of thousands of dollars of advertising and find sales.

$$\text{Sales} = 40 + 1.6(3.5)^2$$
$$\text{Sales} = 40 + 1.6(12.25)$$
$$\text{Sales} = 40 + 19.6$$
$$\text{Sales} = 59.6$$

Sales are projected to be \$59,600 for the month.

QUICK TIP Try solving Exercises 25–40 on page A-21 before starting Section A.4.

QUICK CHECK 8

Stress on a suspension cable on a bridge can be estimated using $S = 7.2(\text{weight})^2 + 3480$. Find the stress if the weight is 29 tons.

Quick Check Answer

8. 9535.2

A.4 RATIO AND PROPORTION

OBJECTIVES

1. Define a ratio.
2. Set up a proportion.
3. Solve a proportion for unknown values.
4. Use proportions to solve problems.

OBJECTIVE 1 Define a ratio. A **ratio** is a quotient of two quantities that can be used to *compare* the quantities. The ratio of the number a to the number b is written in any of the following ways.

$$a \text{ to } b, \qquad a{:}b, \qquad \frac{a}{b}$$

All pronounced "a to b" or "a is to b". This last way of writing a ratio is most common in mathematics, while $a{:}b$ is perhaps most common in business.

EXAMPLE 1

Writing Ratios

Write a ratio in the form $\frac{a}{b}$ for each word phrase. Notice in each example that the number mentioned first is always the numerator.

SOLUTION

(a) The ratio of 5 hours to 3 hours is $\frac{5}{3}$.

(b) To find the ratio of 5 hours to 3 days, *first convert* 3 *days* to *hours*. Since there are 24 hours in 1 day, **3 days** $= 3 \cdot 24 =$ **72 hours**. Then the ratio of 5 hours to 3 days is the quotient of 5 and 72.

$$\frac{5}{72}$$

(c) The ratio of \$700,000 in sales to \$950,000 in sales is written this way.

$$\frac{\$700{,}000}{\$950{,}000}$$

Write this ratio in lowest terms.

$$\frac{\$700{,}000}{\$950{,}000} = \frac{14}{19}$$

QUICK CHECK 1

Write 40 sheep to 15 goats as a ratio.

EXAMPLE 2

Writing Ratios

Burger King sold the following items in a one-hour period last Friday afternoon.

70 bacon cheeseburgers
15 plain hamburgers
30 salad combos
45 chicken sandwiches
40 fish sandwiches

Write ratios for the following items sold:

(a) bacon cheeseburgers to fish sandwiches
(b) salad combos to chicken sandwiches
(c) plain hamburgers to salad combos
(d) fish sandwiches to total items sold

SOLUTION

(a) $\frac{\text{bacon cheeseburgers}}{\text{fish sandwiches}} = \frac{70}{40} = \frac{7}{4}$

(b) $\frac{\text{salad combos}}{\text{chicken sandwiches}} = \frac{30}{45} = \frac{2}{3}$

(c) $\frac{\text{plain hamburgers}}{\text{salad combos}} = \frac{15}{30} = \frac{1}{2}$

(d) $\frac{\text{fish sandwiches}}{\text{total items sold}} = \frac{40}{200} = \frac{1}{5}$

QUICK CHECK 2

Use the data from Example 2 to write a ratio for the sum of bacon cheeseburgers and plain hamburgers, to salad combos.

OBJECTIVE 2 **Set up a proportion.** A ratio is used to compare two numbers or amounts. A **proportion** says that two ratios are equal, as in the following example.

$$\frac{3}{4} = \frac{15}{20}$$

This proportion says that the ratios $\frac{3}{4}$ and $\frac{15}{20}$ are equal.

To see whether a proportion is true, use the method of **cross-products**.

Method of Cross-Products

The proportion

$$\frac{a}{b} = \frac{c}{d}$$

is true if the cross-products $a \cdot d$ and $b \cdot c$ are equal (that is, if $ad = bc$).

Quick Check Answers

1. 8:3
2. 17:6

EXAMPLE 3

Determining If a Proportion Is True

Decide whether the following proportions are true.

(a) $\frac{3}{5} = \frac{12}{20}$ **(b)** $\frac{2}{3} = \frac{9}{16}$

SOLUTION

(a) Find each cross-product.

$$\frac{3}{5} = \frac{12}{20}$$
$$3 \times 20 = 5 \times 12$$
$$60 = 60$$

Since the cross-products are equal, the proportion is true.

(b) Find the cross-products.

$$\frac{2}{3} = \frac{9}{16}$$
$$2 \times 16 = 3 \times 9$$
$$32 \neq 27$$

This proportion is false, so $\frac{2}{3} \neq \frac{9}{16}$.

QUICK TIP The symbol $\neq$ means "not equal to."

QUICK CHECK 3

Decide whether the following proportion is true: $\frac{2}{9} = \frac{8}{18}$.

OBJECTIVE 3 Solve a proportion for unknown values. The method of cross-products is just a shortcut version of solving an equation. To see how, start with the proportion

$$\frac{a}{b} = \frac{c}{d}$$

and multiply both sides by the product of the two denominators, *bd*.

$$\text{bd} \cdot \frac{a}{b} = \text{bd} \cdot \frac{c}{d}$$

or

$$ad = bc$$

The expressions *ad* and *bc* are the cross-products, and this solution shows that they are equal.

Four numbers are used in a proportion. If any three of these numbers are known, the fourth can be found.

EXAMPLE 4

Solving a Proportion

(a) Find x in this proportion.

$$\frac{3}{5} = \frac{x}{40}$$

SOLUTION

(a) In a proportion, the cross-products are equal. The cross-products in this proportion are $3 \cdot 40$ and $5 \cdot x$. Setting these equal gives the following equation.

$$3 \cdot 40 = 5 \cdot x$$
$$120 = 5x$$

Divide both sides by 5 to find the solution.

$$24 = x$$

(b) Solve the following proportion to find k.

$$\frac{3}{10} = \frac{5}{k}$$

Find the two cross-products and set them equal.

$$3k = 10 \cdot 5$$
$$3k = 50$$
$$k = \frac{50}{3}$$

Quick Check Answer

3. false

Write the answer as the mixed number $16\frac{2}{3}$ if desired.

QUICK CHECK 4

Find y in the following proportion: $\frac{7}{y} = \frac{84}{228}$.

EXAMPLE 5
Solving Proportions

A food wholesaler charges a restaurant chain \$83 for 3 crates of fresh produce. How much should it charge for 5 crates of produce?

SOLUTION

Let x be the cost of 5 crates of produce. Set up a proportion with one ratio the number of crates and the other ratio the costs. Use this pattern.

$$\frac{\text{Crates}}{\text{Crates}} = \frac{\text{Cost}}{\text{Cost}}$$

Now substitute the given information.

$$\frac{3}{5} = \frac{83}{x}$$

3 crates cost \$83

Use the cross-products to solve the proportion.

$$3x = 5(83)$$
$$3x = \$415$$
$$x = \$138.33 \quad \text{(rounded to the nearest cent)}$$

The 5 crates cost \$138.33.

QUICK CHECK 5

A fish wholesaler sells 40 pounds of fresh salmon for \$232. Estimate the cost of 300 pounds of salmon.

OBJECTIVE 4 Use proportions to solve problems. Proportions are used in many practical applications, as shown in the next two examples.

EXAMPLE 6
Solving Applications

A firm in Hong Kong and one in Thailand agree to jointly develop an engine-control microchip to be sold to North American auto manufacturers. They agree to split the development costs in a ratio of 8:3 (Hong Kong firm to Thailand firm), resulting in a cost of \$9,400,000 to the Hong Kong firm. Find the cost to the Thailand firm.

SOLUTION

Let x represent the cost to the Thailand firm, then

$$\frac{8}{3} = \frac{9{,}400{,}000}{x}$$
$$8x = 3 \cdot 9{,}400{,}000 \quad \text{Cross multiply.}$$
$$8x = 28{,}200{,}000$$
$$x = 3{,}525{,}000 \quad \text{Divide by 8.}$$

The Thailand firm's share of the costs is \$3,525,000.

Quick Check Answers

4. $y = 19$
5. \$1740

QUICK CHECK 6

Two real estate developers agree to a project estimated to cost $17.6 million. They decide to split costs in a ratio of 7:4. Find the cost to each.

EXAMPLE 7

Solving Applications

Bill Thomas wishes to estimate the amount of timber on some forested land that he owns. One value he needs to estimate is the average height of the trees. One morning, Thomas notices that his own 6-foot body casts an 8-foot shadow at the same time that a typical tree casts a 34-foot shadow. Find the height of the tree.

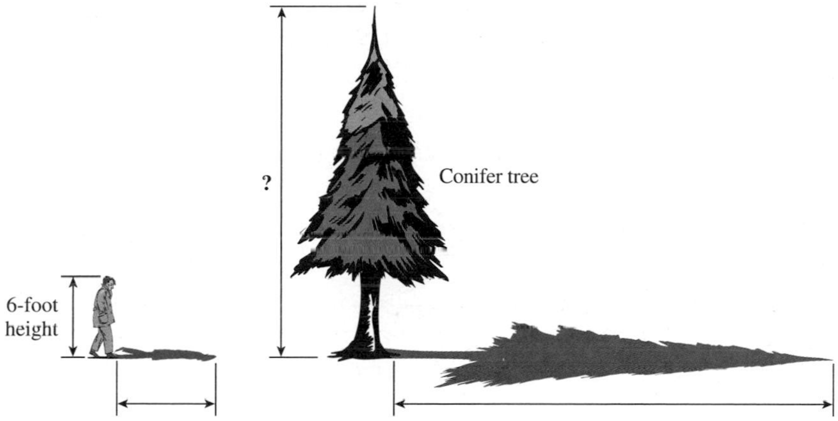

SOLUTION

Set up a proportion in which the height of the tree is given the variable name x.

$$\frac{6}{8} = \frac{x}{34}$$

$$6 \cdot 34 = 8 \cdot x \quad \text{Cross multiply.}$$

$$\frac{204}{8} = \frac{8 \cdot x}{8} \quad \text{Divide by 8.}$$

$$x = 25.5 \text{ feet}$$

The height of the tree is 25.5 feet.

QUICK CHECK 7

Late afternoon one day, a 20-foot flagpole casts a 32-foot shadow. Find the shadow cast by a boy 4 feet tall.

Quick Check Answers

6. $11.2 million and $6.4 million

7. 6.4 feet

Appendix A EXERCISES

In Exercises 1–24, solve each equation for the variable. **[A.1]**

1. $s + 12 = 15$ ______

2. $k + 15 = 22$ ______

3. $b - 7 = 24$ ______

4. $P - 13 = 52$ ______

5. $12 = b + 9$ ______

6. $7 = m - 3$ ______

7. $8k = 56$ ______

8. $3q = 120$ ______

9. $60 = 30m$ ______

10. $94 = 2z$ ______

11. $\frac{m}{5} = 6$ ______

12. $\frac{r}{7} = 1$ ______

13. $\frac{2}{3}a = 5$ ______

14. $\frac{3}{4}m = 18$ ______

15. $\frac{9}{5}r = 18$ ______

16. $2x = \frac{5}{3}$ ______

17. $3m + 5 = 17$ ______

18. $2y - 5 = 39$ ______

19. $4r + 3 = 9$ ______

20. $2p + \frac{1}{2} = \frac{3}{2}$ ______

21. $11r - 5r + 6r = 84$ ______

22. $5m + 6m - 2m = 72$ ______

23. $3x + 12 = 3(2x + 3)$ ______

24. $4z + 2 = 2(z + 2)$ ______

In Exercises 25–34, a formula is given, along with the values of all but one of the variables in the formula. Find the value of the variable that is not given. **[A.3]**

25. $I = PRT$; $P = 2800$, $R = .09$, $T = 2$ ______

26. $S = C + M$; $C = 275$, $M = 49$ ______

27. $G = NP$; $N = 840$, $P = 3.79$ ______

28. $M = P(1 + RT)$; $P = 420$, $R = .07$, $T = 2\frac{1}{2}$ ______

29. $R = \frac{D}{1 - DT}$; $D = .04$, $T = 5$ ______

30. $A = \frac{S}{1 + RT}$; $S = 12{,}600$, $R = .12$, $T = \frac{5}{12}$ ______

31. $T = \frac{D}{S}$; $T = 100$, $S = 2$ ______

32. $\frac{I}{PR} = T$; $P = 100$, $R = .02$, $T = 500$ ______

33. $d = rt$; $r = .07$, $t = 12$ ______

34. $I = PRT$; $P = 500$, $R = .08$, $T = 3$ ______

In Exercises 35–40, solve for the indicated variables. **[A.3]**

35. $A = LW$; for W ______

36. $d = rt$; for r ______

37. $I = PRT$; for T ______

38. $P = 1 + RT$; for R ______

39. $A = P + PRT$; for T ______

40. $R(1 - DT) = D$; for R ______

In Exercises 41–46, write the ratio in lowest terms. **[A.4]**

41. 250 pesos to 1250 pesos ______

42. 45 women to 110 men ______

43. \$1.20 to 75¢ ______

44. 20 hours to 5 days 1/6

45. 35 dimes to 6 dollars ______

46. 30 inches to five yards 1/6

In Exercises 47–52, decide whether the proportions are true or false. **[A.4]**

47. $\frac{2}{3} = \frac{42}{63}$ ______

48. $\frac{6}{9} = \frac{36}{52}$ ______

49. $\frac{18}{20} = \frac{56}{60}$ ______

50. $\frac{12}{18} = \frac{8}{12}$ ______

51. $\frac{420}{600} = \frac{14}{20}$ ______

52. $\frac{7.6}{10} = \frac{76}{100}$ ______

In Exercises 53–60, solve the proportions. **[A.4]**

53. $\frac{y}{35} = \frac{25}{5}$ ______

54. $\frac{15}{s} = \frac{45}{117}$ ______

55. $\frac{a}{25} = \frac{4}{20}$ ______

56. $\frac{6}{x} = \frac{4}{18}$ ______

57. $\frac{z}{20} = \frac{80}{200}$ ______

58. $\frac{25}{100} = \frac{8}{m}$ ______

59. $\frac{1}{2} = \frac{r}{7}$ ______

60. $\frac{2}{3} = \frac{5}{s}$ ______

Solve the following application problems.

61. The sum of an unknown and eight is twenty. Find the unknown. **[A.2]** **61.** ______

62. The sum of four plus an unknown equals fifty-one. Find the unknown. **[A.2]** **62.** ______

63. An unknown times thirty equals one thousand eight hundred. Find the unknown. **[A.2]** **63.** ______

64. Twenty-four equals three times an unknown. Find the unknown. **[A.2]** **64.** ______

65. Three times an unknown plus five is equal to fifty. Find the unknown. **[A.2]** **65.** ______

66. Four plus seven times an unknown is eighteen. Find the unknown. **[A.2]** **66.** ______

67. The sum of two consecutive whole numbers is equal to ninety-one. Find the numbers. **[A.2]** **67.** ______

68. The sum of two consecutive odd whole numbers is equal to two hundred forty. Find both numbers. **[A.2]** **68.** ______

69. Tom throws some coins onto a table. His twin brother Joe throws coins worth twice as much onto the table. The total value of the coins on the table is $2.61. How much money did Joe place on the table? **[A.2]**

69. ______

70. A business math class has 47 students, with 9 more women than men. Find the number of men and women in the class. **[A.2]**

70. ______

71. Cajun Boatin' Inc. bought 5 small boats and 3 skiffs for $14,878. A small boat costs $1742. Find the cost of a skiff. **[A.2]**

71. ______

72. Mike Anderson bought a 4-unit apartment house for $172,000. Use ratios to find the cost of a 10-unit apartment house. **[A.4]**

72. ______

73. The tax on a $40 item is $3. Find the tax on a $160 item. **[A.4]**

73. ______

74. Sam bought 17 table-model television sets for $1942.25. Find the cost of one set. **[A.4]**

74. ______

75. The bookstore at Hudson Community College has a markup that is $\frac{1}{4}$ its cost on a book. Find the cost to the bookstore of a paperback book selling for $20. **[A.3]**

75. ______

76. An unknown principal (P) invested at 8% for $1\frac{3}{4}$ years yields a maturity value (M) of $1368. Use $M = P(1 + RT)$ to find the principal. **[A.3]**

76. ______

77. Explain why all terms with a variable should be placed on one side of the equation, and all terms without a variable should be placed on the other side, when solving an equation. **[A.1]**

78. In your own words, explain the terms *formula, ratio,* and *proportion.* **[A.3–A.4]**

Appendix B

The Metric System

Today, the **metric system** is used just about everywhere in the world. In the United States, many industries are switching over to this improved system. The metric system is being taught in elementary schools, and it may eventually replace the current system.

A table on the **English system** is included here to refresh your memory. Notice that the time relationships are the same in both the English and metric systems.

Length		**Weight**	
1 foot	= 12 inches (in.)	1 pound (lb)	= 16 ounces (oz)
1 yard (yd)	= 3 feet (ft)	1 ton (T)	= 2000 pounds (lb)
1 mile (mi)	= 5280 feet (ft)		
Capacity		**Time**	
1 cup (c)	= 8 fluid ounces	1 week (wk)	= 7 days
1 pint (pt)	= 2 cups	1 day	= 24 hours (hr)
1 quart (qt)	= 2 pints (pt)	1 hour (hr)	= 60 minutes (min)
1 gallon (gal)	= 4 quarts (qt)	1 minute (min)	= 60 seconds (sec)

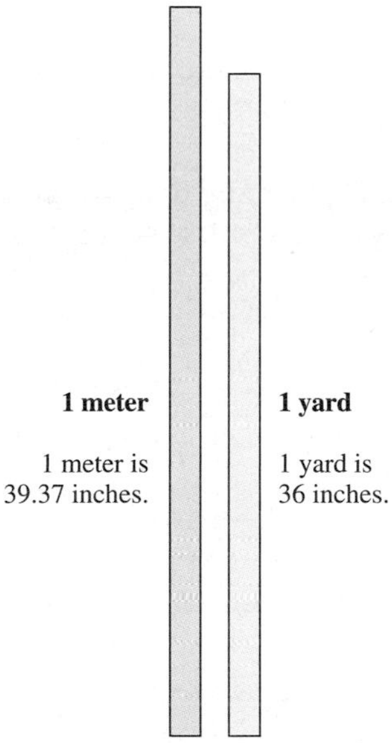

OBJECTIVES

1. Learn the metric system.
2. Learn how to convert from one system to the other.

Recall the metric units for length, volume, weight, and temperature.

Prefixes in the Metric System	
deca-	= 10 times
kilo-	= 1000 times
deci-	= $\frac{1}{10}$ times
centi-	= $\frac{1}{100}$ times
milli-	= $\frac{1}{1000}$ times

OBJECTIVE 1 Learn the metric system. The basic unit of length in the metric system is the **meter**. A meter is a little longer than a yard. For shorter lengths, the units **centimeter** and **millimeter** are commonly used. The prefix "centi" means hundredth, so 1 centimeter is one-hundredth of a meter. Thus

$$100 \text{ centimeters} = 1 \text{ meter}$$

The prefix "milli" means thousandth, so 1 millimeter means one-thousandth of a meter. Thus

$$1000 \text{ millimeters} = 1 \text{ meter}$$

"Meter" is abbreviated m, "centimeter" is cm, and "millimeter" is mm.

Convert from centimeters to millimeters to meters by moving the decimal point, as shown in the following example.

EXAMPLE 1

Converting Length Measurements

Convert the following measurements:

(a) 6.4 m to cm
(b) .98 m to mm
(c) 34 cm to m

SOLUTION

(a) A centimeter is a small unit of measure (a centimeter is about $\frac{1}{2}$ the diameter of a penny) and a meter is a large unit (a little over 3 feet), so many centimeters make a meter. Therefore, *multiply* by **100** to convert meters to centimeters.

$$6.4 \text{ m} = 6.4 \times 100 = 640 \text{ cm}$$

(b) Multiply by 1000 to convert meters to millimeters.

$$.98\text{ m} = .98 \times 1000 = 980\text{ mm}$$

(c) A meter is a large unit of measure, and a centimeter is a smaller unit, so 34 cm is equivalent to a smaller number of meters. Thus, *divide* by 100 to convert centimeters to meters.

$$34\text{ cm} = \frac{34}{100} = .34\text{ m}$$

QUICK CHECK 1

Convert 6 meters to millimeters and 3 centimeters to meters.

Long distances are measured in **kilometer** (km) units. The prefix "kilo" means one thousand. Thus,

$$1\text{ kilometer} = 1000\text{ meters}$$

1 liter 1 quart

A liter equals 1.06 quarts.

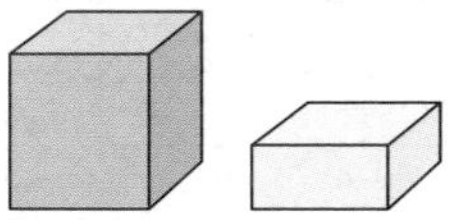

1 kilogram 1 pound

A kilogram equals 2.2 pounds.

Since a meter is about a yard, 1000 meters is about 1000 yards, or 3000 feet. Therefore, 1 kilometer is about 3000 feet. One mile is 5280 feet, so 1 kilometer is about 3000/5280 of a mile. Divide 3000 by 5280 to find that 1 kilometer is about .6 mile.

The basic unit of volume in the metric system is the **liter** (L), which is a little more than a quart. You may have noticed that Coca Cola is sometimes sold in 2-liter plastic bottles. Again the prefixes "milli" and "centi" are used. Thus,

$$1\text{ liter} = 100\text{ centiliters}$$
$$1\text{ liter} = 1000\text{ milliliters}$$

Milliliter (mL) and **centiliter** (cL) are such small volumes that they find their main uses in science. In particular, drug doses are often expressed in milliliters.

Weight is measured in **grams** (g). A nickel weighs about 5 grams. **Milligrams** (mg; one-thousandth of a gram) and **centigrams** (cg; one-hundredth of a gram) are so small that they are used mainly in science. A more common measure is the **kilogram** (kg), which is 1000 grams. A kilogram weighs about 2.2 pounds.

$$1000\text{ grams} = 1\text{ kilogram}$$

EXAMPLE 2

Converting Weight Measurements

Convert the following measurements.

(a) 650 g to kg
(b) 9.4 L to cL
(c) 4350 mg to g

SOLUTION

(a) A gram is a small unit, and a kilogram is a larger unit. Thus, *divide* by 1000 to convert grams to kilograms.

$$650\text{ g} = \frac{650}{1000} = .65\text{ kg}$$

(b) *Multiply* by 100 to convert liters to centiliters.

$$9.4\text{ L} = 9.4 \times 100 = 940\text{ cL}$$

(c) *Divide* by 1000 to convert milligrams to grams.

$$4350\text{ mg} = \frac{4350}{1000} = 4.35\text{ g}$$

QUICK CHECK 2

Convert 2 kilograms to grams and 700 centiliters to liters.

Quick Check Answers

1. 6000 mm; .03 m
2. 2000 g; 7L

OBJECTIVE 2 Learn how to convert from one system to the other. Most Americans do not think in the metric system as easily as in the English system of feet, quarts, pounds, and so on. So, they find it necessary to convert from one system to the other. Approximate conversion can be made with the aid of the next table.

English-Metric Conversion Table

From Metric	To English	Multiply By	From English	To Metric	Multiply By
Meters	Yards	1.09	Yards	Meters	.914
Meters	Feet	3.28	Feet	Meters	.305
Meters	Inches	39.37	Inches	Meters	.0254
Kilometers	Miles	.62	Miles	Kilometers	1.609
Grams	Pounds	.00220	Pounds	Grams	454
Kilograms	Pounds	2.20	Pounds	Kilograms	.454
Liters	Quarts	1.06	Quarts	Liters	.946
Liters	Gallons	.264	Gallons	Liters	3.785

EXAMPLE 3

Converting Metric to English

Convert the following measurements.

(a) 15 meters to yards
(b) 39 yards to meters
(c) 47 meters to inches
(d) 87 kilometers to miles
(e) 598 miles to kilometers
(f) 12 quarts to liters

SOLUTION

(a) Look at the table for converting meters to yards and find the number **1.09**. Multiply 15 meters by **1.09**.

$$15 \times \mathbf{1.09} = 16.35 \text{ yards}$$

(b) Read the yards-to-meters row of the table. The number **.914** appears. Multiply 39 yards by **.914**.

$$39 \times \mathbf{.914} = 35.646 \text{ meters}$$

(c) 47 meters = 47 × **39.37** = 1850.39 inches
(d) 87 kilometers = 87 × **.62** = 53.94 miles
(e) 598 miles = 598 × **1.609** = 962.182 kilometers
(f) 12 quarts = 12 × **.946** = 11.352 liters

QUICK CHECK 3

Convert a speed limit of 70 miles per hour to kilometers per hour, and convert 3 pounds to grams.

Temperature in the metric system is measured in degrees **Celsius** or **centigrade** (abbreviated C). In the Celsius scale, water freezes at 0°C and boils at 100°C. This is more sensible than degrees **Fahrenheit** (abbreviated F) in use now, in which a mixture of salt and water freezes at 0°F, and 100°F represents the temperature inside the individual Gabriel Fahrenheit's mouth.

Converting from Fahrenheit to Celsius

STEP 1 Subtract 32.
STEP 2 Multiply by 5.
STEP 3 Divide by 9.

These steps can be expressed by the following formula.

$$C = \frac{5(F - 32)}{9}$$

Quick Check Answer

3. 112.63 km per hour; 1362 g

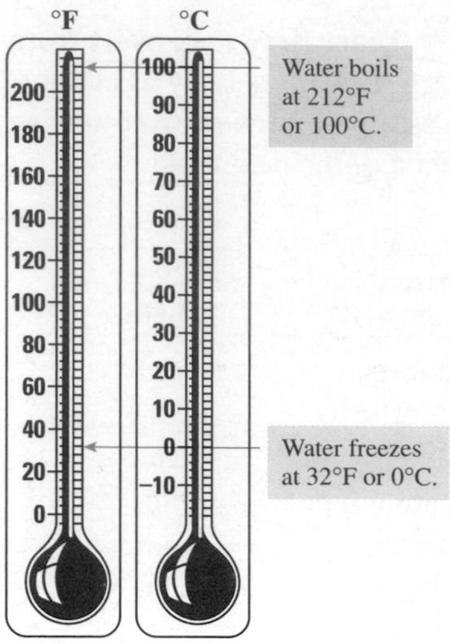

EXAMPLE 4

Converting Fahrenheit to Celsius

Convert 68°F to Celsius.

SOLUTION

Use the steps on the previous page.

STEP 1 Subtract 32: $68 - 32 = 36$

STEP 2 Multiply by 5: $36 \times 5 = 180$

STEP 3 Divide by 9: $\frac{180}{9} = 20$

Thus, 68°F = 20°C.

QUICK CHECK 4

Convert 85°F to Celsius.

Converting from Celsius to Fahrenheit

STEP 1 Multiply by 9.

STEP 2 Divide by 5.

STEP 3 Add 32.

These steps can be expressed by the following formula.

$$F = \frac{9 \times C}{5} + 32$$

EXAMPLE 5

Converting Celsius to Fahrenheit

Convert 11°C to Fahrenheit.

SOLUTION

Use the steps above.

STEP 1 Multiply by 9: $9 \times 11 = 99$

STEP 2 Divide by 5: $99 \div 5 = 19.8$

STEP 3 Add 32: $19.8 + 32 = 51.8$°F

Thus, 11°C = 51.8°F.

QUICK CHECK 5

Convert 35°C to Fahrenheit.

Quick Check Answers

4. 29.4°C (rounded)

5. 95°F

Appendix B EXERCISES

Convert the following measurements.

1. 68 cm to m ____________

2. 934 mm to m ____________

3. 4.7 m to mm ____________

4. 7.43 m to cm ____________

5. 8.9 kg to g ____________

6. 4.32 kg to g ____________

7. 39 cL to L ____________

8. 469 cL to L ____________

9. 46,000 g to kg ____________

10. 35,800 g to kg ____________

11. .976 kg to g ____________

12. .137 kg to g ____________

Convert the following measurements. Round to the nearest tenth.

13. 36 m to yards ____________

14. 76.2 m to yards ____________

15. 55 yards to m ____________

16. 89.3 yards to m ____________

17. 4.7 m to feet ____________

18. 1.92 m to feet ____________

19. 3.6 feet to m ____________

20. 12.8 feet to m ____________

21. 496 km to miles ____________

22. 138 km to miles ____________

23. 768 miles to km ____________

24. 1042 miles to km ____________

25. 683 g to pounds ____________

26. 1792 g to pounds ____________

27. 4.1 pounds to g ____________

28. 12.9 pounds to g ____________

29. 38.9 kg to pounds ____________

30. 40.3 kg to pounds ____________

31. One nickel weighs 5 grams. How many nickels are in 1 kilogram of nickels? **31.** ________

32. Seawater contains about 3.5 grams of salt per 1000 milliliters of water. How many grams of salt do 5 liters of seawater contain? **32.** ________

33. Helium weighs about .0002 gram per milliliter. A balloon contains 3 liters of helium. How much does the helium weigh? **33.** ________

34. About 1500 grams of sugar can be dissolved in 1 liter of warm water. How much sugar can be dissolved in 1 milliliter of warm water? **34.** ________

35. Find your height in centimeters. **35.** ________

36. Find your height in meters. **36.** ________

Convert the following Fahrenheit temperatures to Celsius. Round to the nearest degree.

37. 104°F ________

38. 86°F ________

39. 536°F ________

40. 464°F ________

41. 98°F ________

42. 114°F ________

Convert each of the following Celsius temperatures to Fahrenheit.

43. 35°C ________

44. 100°C ________

45. 10°C ________

46. 25°C ________

47. 135°C ________

48. 215°C ________

In most cases today, medical measurements are given in the metric system. In each of the following problems, a doctor's prescription is given. Decide whether the dosage is or is not reasonable.

49. 1940 grams of Kaopectate after each meal **49.** ________

50. 76.8 centiliters of cough syrup every 2 hours **50.** ________

51. 943 milliliters of antibiotic every 6 hours **51.** ________

52. 1.4 kilograms of vitamins every 3 hours **52.** ________

Appendix C

Basic Calculators

OBJECTIVES

1. Learn the basic calculator keys.
2. Understand the [C], [CE], and [ON/C] keys.
3. Understand the floating decimal point.
4. Use the [%] and [1/x] keys.
5. Use the [x^2], [y^x], and [$\sqrt{\ }$] keys.
6. Use the [$a^{b/c}$] key.
7. Solve problems with negative numbers.
8. Use the calculator memory function.
9. Solve chain calculations using order of operations.
10. Use the parentheses keys.
11. Use the calculator for problem solution.

QUICK TIP The various calculator models differ significantly. *Use the instruction booklet that came with your calculator* for specifics about that calculator if your answers differ from those in this section.

Calculators are among the more popular inventions of the last four decades. Each year, better calculators are developed and their cost drops. The first all-transistor desktop calculator was introduced to the market in 1966. It weighed 55 pounds, cost $2500, and was slow. Today, these same calculations are performed quite well on a calculator costing less than $10, and today's $200 pocket calculators have more ability to solve problems than some of the early computers.

Many instructors allow their students to use calculators in business mathematics courses. Some require calculator use. Many types of calculators are available, from the inexpensive basic calculator to the more complex **scientific**, **financial**, and **graphing** calculators.

In this appendix, we discuss the basic calculator, which has a percent key, reciprocal key, exponent keys, square-root key, memory function, order of operations, and parentheses keys. In Appendix D, the financial calculator with its associated financial keys is discussed.

OBJECTIVE 1 **Learn the basic calculator keys.** Most calculators use **algebraic logic**. Some problems can be solved by entering number and function keys in the same order as you would solve a problem by hand. Other problems require a knowledge of the order of operations when entering the problem.

EXAMPLE 1

Using the Basic Keys

Perform the following operations.

(a) 12 + 25 **(b)** 456 ÷ 24

SOLUTION

(a) The problem 12 + 25 would be entered as

[1] [2] [+] [2] [5] [=]

and 37 would appear as the answer.

(b) Enter 456 ÷ 24 as

[4] [5] [6] [÷] [2] [4] [=]

and 19 appears as the answer.

QUICK CHECK 1

Find 279.04 ÷ 12.8.

OBJECTIVE 2 **Understand the [C] [CE], and [ON/C] keys.** Most calculators have a [C] key. Pressing this key erases everything in most calculators and prepares them for a new problem. Some calculators have a [CE] key. Pressing this key erases only the number displayed, thus allowing for the correction of a mistake without having to start the problem over. Many calculators combine the [C] key and [CE] key and have an [ON/C] key. This key turns the calculator on and is also used to erase the calculator display. If the [ON/C] is pressed after the [=] key, or after one of the operation keys ([+], [−], [×], [÷]), everything in the calculator is erased. If the wrong operation key is pressed, simply press the correct key and the error is corrected. For example, in 7 [+] [−] 3 [=] 4, pressing the [−] key cancels out the previous [+] key entry.

OBJECTIVE 3 **Understand the floating decimal point.** Most calculators have a **floating decimal** that locates the decimal point in the final result.

EXAMPLE 2

Calculating with Decimal Numbers

Jennifer Videtto purchased 55.75 square yards of vinyl floor covering at $18.99 per square yard. Find her total cost.

SOLUTION

Proceed as follows.

55.75 [×] 18.99 [=] 1058.6925

The decimal point is automatically placed in the answer. Since money answers are usually rounded to the nearest cent, the answer is $1058.69.

QUICK CHECK 2

Find the cost of 7 boxes of paper costing $24.87 each.

To use a machine with a floating decimal, enter the decimal point as needed. For example, enter $47 as

[4] [7]

with no decimal point, but enter $.95 as follows.

[.] [9] [5]

One problem in utilizing a floating decimal is shown by the following example.

EXAMPLE 3

Placing the Decimal Point in Money Answers

Add $21.38 and $1.22.

SOLUTION

21.38 [+] 1.22 [=] 22.6

The final 0 is left off. Remember that the problem deals with dollars and cents, and write the answer as $22.60.

QUICK CHECK 3

Add 95.07 and 100.33.

Quick Check Answers

1. 21.8
2. $174.09
3. 195.4

OBJECTIVE 4 Use the [%] and [1/x] keys. The [%] key moves the decimal point two places to the left when used following multiplication or division.

EXAMPLE 4

Using the [%] Key

Find 8% of $4205.

SOLUTION

4205 [×] 8 [%] [=] 336.4 = $336.40

QUICK CHECK 4

Find the real estate commission of 6% on a home sold for $235,000.

The [1/x] key replaces a number with the reciprocal of that number.

EXAMPLE 5

Using the [1/x] Key

Find the inverse or reciprocal of 40.

SOLUTION

40 [1/x] .025

QUICK CHECK 5

Find the inverse of 80.

OBJECTIVE 5 Use the [x^2], [y^x], and [√] keys. The product of 3 × 3 can be written as follows.

exponent

3^2

base

The exponent (2 in this case) shows how many times the base is multiplied by itself (multiply 3 by itself or 3 × 3). The [x^2] key can be used to quickly find the square of a number.

EXAMPLE 6

Using the [x^2] Key

Find 5^2 and 8.5^2.

SOLUTION

5 [x^2] 25 and 8.5 [x^2] 72.25

Pushing [=] is usually not necessary when using the [x^2] key.

QUICK CHECK 6

Find 25^2.

The [y^x] key raises any base number y to a power x. Use as follows.

1. Enter the base number first.
2. [y^x]
3. Enter the exponent.
4. [=]

Quick Check Answers

4. $14,100
5. .0125
6. 625

EXAMPLE 7

Using the y^x Key

Find 5^3.

SOLUTION

$$5 \boxed{y^x}\ 3 \boxed{=}\ 125$$

QUICK CHECK 7

Find 4.8^3.

Since $3^2 = 9$, the number 3 is called the **square root** of 9. Square roots of numbers are written with the symbol $\sqrt{\ }$.

$$\sqrt{9} = 3$$

EXAMPLE 8

Using the $\sqrt{\ }$ Key

Find each square root.

(a) $\sqrt{144}$ **(b)** $\sqrt{20}$

SOLUTION

(a) Enter

$$144 \boxed{\sqrt{x}}$$

and 12 appears in the display. The square root of 144 is 12.

(b) The square root of 20 is

$$20 \boxed{\sqrt{x}}\ 4.472136$$

which may be rounded to the desired position.

QUICK CHECK 8

Find the square root of 729.

OBJECTIVE 6 Use the $\boxed{a^{b/c}}$ key. Many calculators have an $\boxed{a^{b/c}}$ key that can be used for problems containing fractions and mixed numbers. A mixed number is a number with both a whole number and a fraction, such as $7\frac{3}{4}$, which equals $7 + \frac{3}{4}$. The rules for adding, subtracting, multiplying, and dividing both fractions and mixed numbers are given in Chapter 2. Here, we simply show how these operations are done on a calculator.

EXAMPLE 9

Using the $\boxed{a^{b/c}}$ Key with Fractions

QUICK TIP The calculator automatically shows fractions in lowest terms and as mixed numbers when possible.

Solve the following.

(a) $\frac{6}{11} + \frac{3}{4}$

(b) $\frac{3}{8} \div \frac{5}{6}$

SOLUTION

(a) $6 \boxed{a^{b/c}}\ 11 \boxed{+}\ 3 \boxed{a^{b/c}}\ 4 \boxed{=}\ 1\frac{13}{44}$

(b) $3 \boxed{a^{b/c}}\ 8 \boxed{\div}\ 5 \boxed{a^{b/c}}\ 6 \boxed{=}\ \frac{9}{20}$

QUICK CHECK 9

Solve $\frac{7}{8} + \frac{9}{16}$.

Quick Check Answers

7. 110.592
8. 27
9. $1\frac{7}{16}$

EXAMPLE 10

Using the [a b/c] Key

Solve the following.

(a) $4\frac{7}{8} \div 3\frac{4}{7}$ **(b)** $\frac{5}{3} \div 27.5$ **(c)** $65.3 \times 6\frac{3}{4}$

SOLUTION

(a) 4 [a b/c] 7 [a b/c] 8 [÷] 3 [a b/c] 4 [a b/c] 7 [=] $1\frac{73}{200}$

(b) 5 [a b/c] 3 [÷] 27.5 [=] 0.060606061

(c) 65.3 [×] 6 [a b/c] 3 [a b/c] 4 [=] 440.775

QUICK CHECK 10

Solve $5\frac{3}{4} \div 4\frac{1}{2}$.

OBJECTIVE 7 **Solve problems with negative numbers.** There are several calculations in business that result in a **negative number**, or **deficit amount**.

EXAMPLE 11

Working with Negative Numbers

The amount in the advertising account last month was $4800, while $5200 was actually spent. Find the balance remaining in the advertising account.

SOLUTION

Enter the numbers in the calculator.

4800 [−] 5200 [=] −400

The minus sign in front of the 400 indicates that there is a deficit or negative amount. This value can be written as −$400 or sometimes as ($400), which indicates a negative amount. Some calculators place the minus sign after the number, as 400−.

QUICK CHECK 11

The following transactions were made to a checking account with a balance of $1482.05: a deposit of $185, an electronic bill payment of $122.17, and a withdrawal of $100 at an ATM machine. Find the new balance.

Negative numbers may be entered into the calculator by using the [−] key before entering the number. For example, if $3000 is now added to the advertising account in Example 11, the new balance is calculated as follows.

[−] 400 [+] 3000 [=] 2600

The new account balance is $2600.

The [+/−] key can be used to change the sign of a number that has already been entered. For example, 520 [+/−] changes +520 to −520.

OBJECTIVE 8 **Use the calculator memory function.** Many calculators feature memory keys, which are a sort of electronic scratch paper. These **memory keys** are used to store intermediate steps in a calculation. On some calculators, a key labeled [M] or [STO] is used to store the numbers in the display, with [MR] or [RCL] used to recall the numbers from memory.

Other calculators have [M+] and [M−] keys. The [M+] key adds the number displayed to the number already in memory. For example, if the memory contains the number 0 at the beginning of a problem, and the calculator display contains the number 29.4, then pushing [M+] will cause

Quick Check Answers

10. $1\frac{5}{18}$
11. $1444.88

29.4 to be stored in the memory (the result of adding 0 and 29.4). If 57.8 is then entered into the display, pushing **M+** will cause

$$29.4 + 57.8 = 87.2$$

to be stored. If 11.9 is then entered into the display, with **M−** pushed, the memory will contain

$$87.2 - 11.9 = 75.3$$

The **MR** key is used to recall the number in memory as needed, with **MC** used to clear the memory.

Scientific calculators typically have one or more **memory registers** in which to store numbers. These memory keys are usually labeled **STO** for store and **RCL** for recall. For example, 32.5 can be stored in memory register 1 by

32.5 **STO** 1

or it can be stored in memory register 2 by 32.5 **STO** 2, and so forth. Values are retrieved from a particular memory register by using the **RCL** key followed by the number of the register. For example, **RCL** 2 recalls the contents of memory register 2.

With a scientific calculator, a number stays in memory until it is replaced by another number or until the memory is cleared. The contents of the memory are saved even when the calculator is turned off.

QUICK TIP Always clear the memory before starting a problem; not doing so is a common error.

EXAMPLE 12

Using the Memory Registers

An elevator technician counted the number of people entering an elevator and also measured the weight of each group of people. Find the average weight per person.

Number of People	Total Weight
6	839 pounds
8	1184 pounds
4	640 pounds

SOLUTION

First find the weight of all three groups and store in memory register 1.

839 **+** 1184 **+** 640 **=** 2663 **STO** 1

Then find the total number of people.

6 **+** 8 **+** 4 **=** 18

Finally, divide the contents of memory register 1 by the 18 people.

RCL 1 **÷** 18 **=** 147.94444 pounds

This value can be rounded as needed.

QUICK CHECK 12

The following animals were brought to the market: 7 calves with a total weight of 2989 pounds; 10 calves with a total weight of 4490 pounds; and 17 calves with a total weight of 6953 pounds. Find the average weight of a calf to the nearest tenth of a pound.

OBJECTIVE 9 **Solve chain calculations using order of operations.** Long calculations involving several operations (adding, subtracting, multiplying, and dividing) must be done in a specific sequence called the **order of operations** and are called **chain calculations**. The logic of the following order of operations is built into most scientific calculators and can help us work problems without having to store a lot of intermediate values.

Quick Check Answer

12. 424.5 pounds (rounded)

Order of Operations

STEP 1 Do all operations inside parentheses first.
STEP 2 Simplify any expressions with exponents and find any square roots.
STEP 3 Multiply and divide from left to right.
STEP 4 Add and subtract from left to right.

EXAMPLE 13

Using the Order of Operations

Solve the following.

(a) $3 + 7 \times 9\frac{3}{4}$ **(b)** $42.1 \times 5 - 90 \div 4$

SOLUTION

The calculator automatically keeps track of the order of operations for us.

(a) 3 [+] 7 [×] 9 [a b/c] 3 [a b/c] 4 [=] $71\frac{1}{4}$

(b) 42.1 [×] 5 [−] 90 [÷] 4 [=] 188

QUICK CHECK 13

Solve $9^2 + 2.7 \cdot 14$.

OBJECTIVE 10 **Use the parentheses keys.** The parentheses keys can be used to help establish the order of operations in a more complex chain calculation. For example, $\frac{4}{5+7}$ can be written as $\frac{4}{(5+7)}$, which can be solved as follows.

left-parenthesis key

4 [÷] [(] 5 [+] [7] [)] [=] 0.3333333

right-parenthesis key

EXAMPLE 14

Using Parentheses

Solve the following problem.

$$\frac{16 \div 2.5}{39.2 - 29.8 \times .6}$$

SOLUTION

Think of this problem as follows:

$$\frac{(16 \div 2.5)}{(39.2 - 29.8 \times .6)}$$

Using parentheses to set off the numerator and denominator will help you minimize errors.

[(] 16 [÷] 2.5 [)] [÷] [(] 39.2 [−] 29.8 [×] .6 [)] [=] 0.3001876

QUICK CHECK 14

Solve $\frac{5^3 - 16}{253 - 4^2 \cdot 9}$

OBJECTIVE 11 **Use the calculator for problem solution.** Scientific calculators are great tools to help you solve problems.

Quick Check Answers

13. 118.8
14. 1

EXAMPLE 15

Finding Sale Price

A compact-disc player with an original price of $560 is on sale at 10% off. Find the sale price.

SOLUTION

If the discount from the original price is 10%, then the sale price is 100% − 10% of the original price.

560 [×] [(] 100 [−] 10 [)] [%] [=] 504

On some calculators the following keystrokes will also work.

560 [−] 10 [%] [=] 504

The sale price is $504.

QUICK CHECK 15

Find the price of a new home that was originally priced at $239,000 if the price was reduced by 15%.

EXAMPLE 16

Applying Calculator Use to Problem Solving

A home buyer borrows $86,400 at 10% on a cottage, for 30 years. The monthly payment on the loan is $8.78 per $1000 borrowed. Annual taxes are $780, and fire insurance is $453 a year. Find the total monthly payment including taxes and insurance.

SOLUTION

The monthly payment is the *sum* of the monthly payment on the loan *plus* monthly taxes *plus* monthly fire insurance costs. The monthly payment on the loan is the number of thousands in the loan (86.4) times the monthly payment per $1000 borrowed (8.78).

monthly taxes

86400 [÷] 1000 [×] 8.78 [+] 780 [÷] 12 [+] 453 [÷] 12 [=] 861.342

monthly fire insurance premium

To the nearest cent, this amount rounds to $861.34.

QUICK CHECK 16

An investor borrows $1,200,000 on a piece of commercial property. The monthly payment on the loan is $8.43 per $1000 of debt. Annual taxes and insurance are $28,200 and $6240, respectively. Find the monthly payment.

EXAMPLE 17

Applying Calculator Use to Problem Solving

A Japanese company produces robotic dogs for the retail market. The dogs talk, cock their heads, bark, and walk. The company sells the robotic dogs to distributors for $256.80 each.

(a) Find the revenue to the manufacturer if the company sells 26,340 robotic dogs.
(b) Find the final price to the customer if the robotic dogs are marked up an average of 87% on cost.

SOLUTION

(a) Revenue = Number sold × Price of each

26340 [×] 256.80 [=] 6764112 or $6,764,112

(b) Sales price = Cost × (1 + Markup percent)

256.80 [×] 1.87 [=] 480.216 or $480.22

QUICK CHECK 17

It cost a manufacturer an average of $38.20 per pair for each of the 180,400 shoes produced in one month. The markup on the shoes is 35% based on cost. Find the total revenue to the company from the sale of the month's production.

Quick Check Answers

15. $203,150
16. $12,986
17. $9,303,228

Appendix C EXERCISES

Solve the following problems on a calculator. Round each answer to the nearest hundredth.

1. $\begin{array}{r} 384.92 \\ 407.61 \\ 351.14 \\ +\ 27.93 \\ \hline \end{array}$

2. $\begin{array}{r} 85.76 \\ 21.94 \\ +\ 39.89 \\ \hline \end{array}$

3. $\begin{array}{r} 6850 \\ 321 \\ +\ 4207 \\ \hline \end{array}$

4. $\begin{array}{r} 781.42 \\ 304.59 \\ +\ 261.35 \\ \hline \end{array}$

5. $\begin{array}{r} 4270.41 \\ -\ 365.09 \\ \hline \end{array}$

6. $\begin{array}{r} 3000.07 \\ -\ 48.12 \\ \hline \end{array}$

7. $\begin{array}{r} 384.96 \\ -\ 129.72 \\ \hline \end{array}$

8. $36.84 - 12.17$

9. $\begin{array}{r} 365 \\ \times\ 43 \\ \hline \end{array}$

10. $\begin{array}{r} 27.51 \\ \times\ 1.18 \\ \hline \end{array}$

11. 3.7×8.4

12. 62.5×81

13. $\dfrac{375.4}{10.6}$

14. $\dfrac{9625}{400}$

15. $96.7 \div 3.5$

16. $103.7 \div .35$

Solve the following chain calculations. Round each answer to the nearest hundredth.

17. $\dfrac{9 \times 9}{2 \times 5}$

18. $\dfrac{15 \times 8 \times 3}{11 \times 7 \times 4}$

19. $\dfrac{87 \times 24 \times 47.2}{13.6 \times 12.8}$

20. $\dfrac{2 \times (3 + 4)}{6 + 10}$

21. $\dfrac{2 \times 3 + 4}{6 + 10}$

22. $\dfrac{4200 \times .12 \times 90}{365}$

23. $\dfrac{640 - .6 \times 12}{17.5 + 3.2}$

24. $\dfrac{16 \times 18 \div .42}{95.4 \times 3 - .8}$

25. $\dfrac{14^2 - 3.6 \times 6}{95.2 \div .5}$

26. $\dfrac{9^2 + 3.8 \div 2}{14 + 7.5}$

Solve the following problems. Reduce any fractions to lowest terms or round to the nearest hundredth.

27. $7\frac{5}{8} \div \left(1 + \frac{3}{8}\right)$

28. $\left(5\frac{1}{4}\right)^2 \times 3.65$

29. $\left(\frac{3}{4} \div \frac{5}{8}\right)^3 \div 3\frac{1}{2}$

30. $\sqrt{6} \times \dfrac{3^2 + 2\frac{1}{2}}{7 \times \frac{5}{6}}$

31. Describe in your own words the order of operations to be used when solving chain calculations. (See Objective 9.)

32. Explain how the parentheses keys are used when solving chain calculations. (See Objective 10.)

Solve the following application problems on a calculator. Round each answer to the nearest cent.

33. Bucks County Community College Bookstore bought 397 used copies of a computer science book at a net cost of $46.40 each; 125 used copies of an accounting book at $38.40 each; and 740 used copies of a real estate text at $28.30 each. Find the total paid by the bookstore. **33.** ____________

34. Judy Martinez needs to file her expense account claims. She spent 5 nights at the Macon Holiday Inn at $104.19 per night and 4 nights at the Charlotte Super 8 motel at $86.80 per night. She then rented a car for 8 days at $36.40 per day. She drove the car 916 miles with a charge of $.28 per mile. Find her total expenses. **34.** ____________

35. In Virginia City, the sales tax is 6.5%. Find the tax on each of the following items: **(a)** a new car costing $17,908.43 and **(b)** a computer costing $1463.58. **(a)** ____________ **(b)** ____________

36. Marja Strutz bought a two-year-old commercial fishing boat equipped for sardine fishing at a cost of $78,250. Additional safety equipment was needed at a cost of $4820, and sales tax of $7\frac{1}{4}$% was due on the boat and safety equipment. In addition she was charged a licensing fee of $1135 and a Coast Guard registration fee of $428. Strutz will pay $\frac{1}{3}$ of the total cost as a down payment and will borrow the balance. How much must she borrow? **36.** ____________

37. Becky Agnosti and her husband bought a small townhouse for $155,000. They paid $8000 down and agreed to make payments of $1002.80 per month for 30 years. By how much does the down payment and the sum of the monthly payments exceed the purchase price? **37.** ____________

38. Linda Smelt purchased a 20-unit apartment house for $620,000. She made a down payment of $150,000, which she had inherited from her parents, and agreed to make monthly payments of $5050 for 15 years. By how much does the sum of her down payment and all monthly payments exceed the original purchase price?

38. ________________

39. Ben Hurd wishes to open a small repair shop but has only $32,400 in cash. He estimates that he will need $15,000 for equipment, $2800 for the first month's rent on a building, and about $28,000 operating expenses until the business is profitable. How much additional funding does he need?

39. ________________

40. Koplan Kitchens wishes to expand their retail store. In order to do so, they must first purchase the $52,000 parcel of land next door to them. They then anticipate $240,000 in construction costs plus an additional $57,000 for additional inventory. They have $100,000 in cash and must borrow the balance from a bank. How much must they borrow?

40. ________________

41. A college bookstore buys a used textbook for $24.50 at the end of a semester and sells it at the beginning of the next semester for $60. Find the percent of markup on selling price to the nearest percent.

41. ________________

42. A homebuilder spent the following when building a home: $37,800 for a cleared parcel of land with utility hookups, $59,600 for materials, and $24,300 for labor and other expenses. He then sold the home for $136,500. Find the percent markup over cost to the nearest percent.

42. ________________

Appendix D

Financial Calculators

OBJECTIVES

1. Learn the basic conventions used with cash flows.
2. Learn the basic financial keys.
3. Understand which keys to use for a particular problem.
4. Use the calculator to solve financial problems.

Calculators are among the more popular inventions of recent times. The power and capability of calculators have increased significantly even as their cost has continued to fall. Today, programmable calculators costing less than $100 have more ability to solve problems than some of the early computers.

OBJECTIVE 1 **Learn the basic conventions used with cash flows.** There is a need to separate inflows of cash (cash received) from outflows of cash (cash paid out). The following convention is commonly used for this purpose and will be used throughout this appendix.

1. Inflows of cash (cash received) are **positive**.
2. Outflows of cash (cash paid out) are **negative**.

For example, assume that you are making regular investments into an account. Your payments are *outflows* of cash and should be considered *negative* numbers. The future value of your savings will eventually be returned to you as an inflow of cash, thereby as a positive number.

OBJECTIVE 2 **Learn the basic financial keys.** **Financial calculators** have special functions that allow the user to solve financial problems involving time, interest rates, and money. Many of the compound interest problems presented in this text can be solved using a financial calculator. Most financial calculators have financial keys similar to those shown below.

QUICK TIP Different financial calculators look and work somewhat differently from one another. You *must look at the instruction book* that came with your calculator to determine how the keys are used with that particular calculator.

[n] [i] [PV] [PMT] [FV]

These keys represent the following functions (see Chapter 9 for a full definition of each term).

[n]—The number of compounding periods

[i]—The interest rate *per compounding period*

[PV]—Present value, the value in *today's* dollars

[PMT]—The amount of a level payment (for example, $625 per month); this is used for annuity type problems.

[FV]—Future value, the value at *some future date*

OBJECTIVE 3 **Understand which keys to use for a particular problem.** Most simple financial problems require only four of the five financial keys described earlier. Both the number of compounding periods [n] and the interest rate per compounding period [i] *are needed for each financial problem*—these two keys will always be used. Which two of the remaining three financial keys ([PV], [PMT], and [FV]) are used depends on the particular problem. Using the convention described under Objective 1, one of these values will be negative and one will be positive. The process of solving a financial problem is to enter values for the three variables that are known, *then press the key for the unknown*, fourth variable.

QUICK TIP Different financial calculators sometimes give slightly different answers to the same problems due to rounding.

QUICK TIP Be sure to enter a cash inflow as a positive number or a cash outflow as a negative number. Also be sure to clear all values from the memory of your calculator before working a problem.

For example, if you wish to know the future value of a series of known, equal payments, enter the specific values for [n], [i], and [PMT]. Then press [FV] for the result. Or, if you wish to know how long it will take for an investment to grow to some specific value at a given interest rate, enter values for [PV], [i], and [FV]. Then press [n] to find the required number of compounding periods.

OBJECTIVE 4 Use the calculator to solve financial problems.

EXAMPLE 1

Finding *FV*, given *n*, *i*, and *PV*

Barbara and Ivan Cushing invest $2500 that they received from the sale of the old family car in a stock mutual fund that has recently paid 12% compounded quarterly. Find the future value in 5 years if the fund continues to do as well.

SOLUTION

The present value of $2500 (a cash outflow is entered as a negative number) is compounded at 3% per quarter $(12\% \div 4 = 3\%)$ for 20 quarters $(4 \times 5 = 20)$. Enter values for [PV], [i], and [n].

−2500 [PV] 3 [i] 20 [n]

Then press [FV] to find the compound amount at the end of 5 years.

[FV] $4515.28, which is the future value

QUICK CHECK 1

A lump sum of $28,000 is deposited in a retirement account paying 10% compounded quarterly. Find the future value in 10 years.

EXAMPLE 2

Finding *FV*, given *n*, *i*, and *PMT*

Joan Jones plans to invest $100 at the end of each month in a mutual fund that she believes will grow at 9% per year compounded monthly. Find the future value at her retirement in 20 years.

SOLUTION

Two hundred forty payments $(12 \times 20 = 240)$ of $100 each (cash outflows entered as a negative number) are made into an account earning .75% per month $(9\% \div 12 = .75\%)$. Enter values for [n], [PMT], and [i].

240 [n] −100 [PMT] .75 [i]

Press [FV] for the result.

[FV] $66,788.69, which is the future value

QUICK TIP The order in which data are entered into the calculator does not matter—just remember to press the financial key for the unknown value last.

QUICK CHECK 2

Benjamin Delton deposits $2500 at the end of each year into a retirement account paying 8% per year. Find the future value in 45 years.

Quick Check Answers

1. $75,181.79
2. $966,264.04

Any one of the four values used to solve a particular financial problem *can be unknown*. Look at the next three examples in which the number of compounding periods [n], the payment amount [PMT], and the interest rate per compounding period [i], respectively, are unknown.

EXAMPLE 3

Finding n, given i, PMT, and FV

Mr. Trebor needs $140,000 for a new tractor. He can invest $8000 at the end of each month in an account paying 6% per year compounded monthly. How many monthly payments are needed?

SOLUTION

The $8000 monthly payment (cash outflow) will grow at .5% per compounding period (6% ÷ 12 = .5%) until a future value of $140,000 (cash inflow at a future date) is accumulated. Enter values for **PMT**, **i**, and **FV**.

−8000 **PMT** .5 **i** 140000 **FV**

Press **n** to determine the number of payments.

n 17 monthly payments of $8000 each are needed

Actually, 17 payments of $8000 each into an account earning .5% per month will grow to slightly more than $140,000.

−8000 **PMT** .5 **i** 17 **n**

Press **FV** to determine the future value.

FV $141,578.41, which is the future value

The 17th payment would need to be only

$8000 − ($141,578.41 − $140,000) = $6421.59

to accumulate exactly $140,000.

QUICK CHECK 3

Black Coal, Inc., needs $1,280,000 for a new dredge. The firm can invest $21,200 at the end of each quarter in a fund earning 2% per quarter. Find the number of quarters needed to save up the required funds.

EXAMPLE 4

Finding PMT, given n, i, and FV

Jane Abel wishes to have $1,000,000 at her retirement in 40 years. Find the payment she must make at the end of each quarter into an account earning 10% compounded quarterly to attain her goal.

SOLUTION

One hundred sixty payments (40 × 4 = 160) are made into an account earning 2.5% per quarter (10% ÷ 4 = 2.5%) until a future value of $1,000,000 (cash inflow at a future date) is accumulated. Enter values for **n**, **i**, and **FV**.

160 **n** 2.5 **i** 1000000 **FV**

Press **PMT** for the quarterly payment.

PMT − $490.41, which is the required quarterly payment of cash

One hundred sixty payments of $490.41 at the end of each quarter into an account earning 10% compounded quarterly will grow to $1,000,000.

QUICK CHECK 4

Bill Watson has only 13 years until he retires and he wants to have $1 million at that time. He decides to make payments into a mutual fund at the end of each year, one that he hopes will earn 12% per year. Find the yearly payment needed.

Quick Check Answers

3. 40 quarters
4. $35,677.20

EXAMPLE 5

Finding *i*, given *n*, *PV*, and *FV*

Tom Fernandez bought 200 shares of stock in an oil company at \$33.50 per share. Exactly three years later, he sold the stock at \$41.25 per share. Find the annual rate, rounded to the nearest tenth of a percent, that Mr. Fernandez earned on this investment.

SOLUTION

In three years, the per-share price increased from a present value of \$33.50 to a future value of \$41.25. The purchase of the stock is a cash outflow, and the eventual sale of the stock is a cash inflow. It is not necessary to multiply the stock price by the number of shares—the interest rate indicating the return on the investment is the same whether 1 share or 200 shares are used. Enter values for [n], [PV], and [FV].

3 [n] −33.50 [PV] 41.25 [FV]

Press [i] for the annual interest rate.

[i] 7.18%, or about 7.2% per year

Mr. Fernandez's return on his original investment compounded at 7.2% per year.

QUICK CHECK 5

Fang Hzu bought a commercial lot for \$148,400 and sold it six years later for \$245,000. Find the annual interest rate to the nearest tenth of a percent.

Interest rates can have a great influence on both individuals and businesses. Individuals borrow for homes, cars, and other personal items, whereas firms borrow to buy real estate, expand operations, or cover operating expenses. A small difference in interest rates can make *a large difference* in costs over time, as shown in the next example.

EXAMPLE 6

Comparing Monthly House Payments

John and Leticia Adams wish to borrow \$62,000 on a 30-year home loan. Find the monthly payment at interest rates of **(a)** 8% and **(b)** 9%. Show **(c)** the monthly savings at the lower rate and **(d)** the total savings in monthly payments over the 30 years.

SOLUTION

(a) Enter a present value of \$62,000 (cash inflow) with 360 compounding periods (30 × 12 = 360) and a rate of .666667% per month (8% ÷ 12 = .666667, rounded) and press [PMT] to find the monthly payment.

62000 [PV] 360 [n] .666667 [i]

[PMT] −\$454.93 is the monthly payment at 8% per year, rounded

(b) Enter the values again using the new interest rate of .75% (9% ÷ 12 = .75%).

62000 [PV] 360 [n] .75 [i]

[PMT] −\$498.87 is the monthly payment at 9% per year, again, rounded

(c) The difference in the monthly payments follows.

\$498.87 − \$454.93 = \$43.94

(d) The total difference saved over 30 years (30 × 12 = 360 payments) is

\$43.94 × 360 payments = \$15,818.40

The lower amount will reduce the Adams' mortgage payments by a total of \$15,818.40 over 30 years.

QUICK CHECK 6

Bernie Slotsky borrowed \$168,000 for 30 years. Find the monthly payment at interest rates of **(a)** 6.5% and **(b)** 7.5%. **(c)** Then find the difference in the monthly payments.

Quick Check Answers

5. 8.7%
6. (a) \$1061.87
(b) \$1174.68
(c) \$112.81

EXAMPLE 7

Planning for Retirement

Courtney and Nathan Wright plan to retire in 25 years and need $3500 per month for 20 years.

(a) Find the amount needed at retirement to fund the monthly retirement payments, assuming the funds earn 9% compounded monthly while payments are being made.

(b) Find the amount of the quarterly payment they must make for the next 25 years to accumulate the necessary funds, assuming earnings of 12% compounded quarterly during the accumulation period.

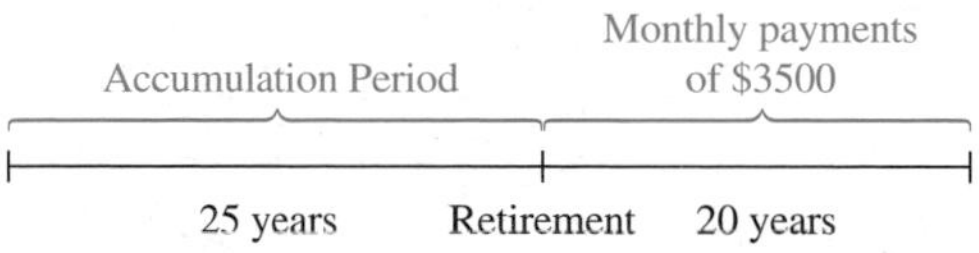

SOLUTION

(a) The accumulated funds at the end of 25 years are, at their retirement, a present value that must generate a cash inflow to the Wrights of $3500 per month for 240 months $(20 \times 12 = 240)$ assuming earnings of .75% per month $(9\% \div 12 = .75\%)$. Enter values for [n], [i], and [PMT].

240 [n] .75 [i] 3500 [PMT]

Press [PV] to find the amount needed at the end of 25 years.

[PV] **$389,007.34** is the amount they must accumulate

(b) The Wrights have 25 years of quarterly payments (100 payments that are cash outflows) in an account earning 3% per quarter $(12\% \div 4 = 3\%)$ to accumulate a future value of $389,007.34. The question is what quarterly payment is required. Enter values for [n], [i], and [FV].

100 [n] 3 [i] 389007.34 [FV]

Press [PMT] to find the quarterly payment needed.

[PMT] **−$640.57** is the required quarterly payment

Thus, the Wrights must make 100 end-of-quarter deposits of $640.57 each into an account earning 3% per quarter in order to subsequently receive 20 years of payments of $3500 per month, assuming 9% per year during the time that payments are made.

QUICK CHECK 7

Tom and Jane Blackstone plan to retire in 20 years. At that time, they believe they will need $60,000 per year for 25 years, not including income from Social Security. **(a)** If funds earn 7% per year during retirement, find the amount needed to fund their retirement when they retire, to the nearest dollar. **(b)** Find the end-of-the-year payment they must make for the next 20 years to have the needed amount at retirement, assuming funds earn 8% per year.

Quick Check Answers

7. (a) $699,215
(b) $15,279.39

Appendix D EXERCISES

Using a financial calculator, solve the following problems for the missing quantity. Round dollar answers to the nearest cent, interest rates to the nearest hundredth of a percent, and number of compounding periods to the nearest whole number. Assume that any payments are made at the end of the period.

	n	*i*	*PV*	*PMT*	*FV*
1.	20	10%	$5800	—	________
2.	7	8%	$8900	—	________
3.	10	3%	________	—	$12,000
4.	16	4%	________	—	$8200
5.	7	8%	—	$300	________
6.	25	2%	—	$1000	________
7.	30	________	—	$319.67	$12,000
8.	50	________	—	$4718.99	$285,000
9.	360	1%	$83,500	________	—
10.	180	.5%	$125,000	________	—
11.	________	4%	$85,383	$5600	—
12.	________	2%	$3822	$100	—

Solve each of the following application problems.

13. Juanipa Manglimont inherited $23,500 from her father. She placed the money in a 5-year certificate of deposit earning 6% compounded quarterly. Find the future value at the end of 5 years. **13.** ________________

14. At the end of each month, Tina Ramirez has $50 taken out of her paycheck and invested in an account paying .5% per month. Find the future value at the end of 14 years. **14.** ________________

15. After a large down payment, Mr. and Mrs. Thrash borrowed $86,500 on a 30-year home loan at 9% per year. Find the monthly payment.

15. ______________

16. Terrance Walker wishes to have $20,000 in 10 years when his son begins college. What payment must he make at the end of each quarter into an investment earning 10% compounded quarterly?

16. ______________

17. The *Daily Gazette* needs $340,000 for a new printing press. The *Gazette* can invest $12,000 per month in an account paying .8% per month. Find the number of payments that must be paid before reaching the goal. Round to the nearest whole number.

17. ______________

18. Cathy Cockrell anticipates that she will need $70,000 when her son Sam enters college. She can save $500 per month and earn 7% per year compounded monthly. How long will it take her to save the needed funds?

18. ______________

19. Mr. and Mrs. Peters wish to build a home and must borrow $110,000 on a 30-year mortgage to do so. Find the highest acceptable annual interest rate, to the nearest tenth of a percent, if they cannot afford a monthly payment above $845.

19. ______________

20. Jim Blalock needs to borrow $28,000 for a new work truck but cannot afford a payment of more than $700 per month. If a bank will finance the truck for 4 years, find the maximum interest rate Blalock can afford.

20. ______________

Answers to Selected Exercises

Chapter 1

Section 1.1 Exercises (Page 11)

1. seven thousand, forty **3.** thirty-seven thousand, nine hundred one **5.** seven hundred twenty-five thousand, nine **7.** 2070; 2100; 2000 **9.** 46,230; 46,200; 46,000 **11.** 106,050; 106,100; 106,000 **15.** 210 **17.** 2186 **19.** 1396 **21.** 983,493 **23.** 668 **25.** 2877 **27.** 21,546 **29.** 6,088,899 **31.** Totals vertically: \$293,267; \$387,795; \$426,869; \$373,100; \$1,481,031; Totals horizontally: \$269,761; \$267,502; \$206,932; \$246,587; \$244,616; \$245,633; \$1,481,031 **33.** 9374 **35.** 117,552 **37.** 1,696,876 **39.** 8,107,899 **41.** Estimate: 12,760; Exact: 12,605 **43.** Estimate: 600; Exact: 545 **45.** Estimate: 30,000; Exact: 29,986 **47.** $37 \times 18 = 666$; 66,600 **49.** $376 \times 6 = 2256$; 22,560,000 **51.** $1241\frac{1}{4}$ **53.** $458\frac{21}{43}$ **57.** $2385\frac{5}{18}$ **59.** $58\frac{4}{13}$ **61.** twenty-four million, three hundred seventy-five thousand, three hundred **63.** three million, two hundred thousand **65.** 854,795 boxes **67.** 55,572,633 **69.** 200,000 chips **71.** 500 items per hour **73.** \$2408 **75.** 293,387 acres **77.** 24,235 acres **79.** 4500 stores **81.** 6000 stores **83.** 500 stores

Section 1.2 Exercises (Page 21)

1. 5208 sandwiches **3.** 467 passengers **5.** 511,000 veterans **7.** 8589 pounds **9.** \$29,544 **11.** 6,098,400 square feet **13.** \$378 **15.** \$20,961 **17.** \$375 **19.** 20 seats

Section 1.3 Exercises (Page 27)

1. thirty-eight hundredths **3.** five and sixty-one hundredths **5.** seven and four hundred eight thousandths **7.** thirty-seven and five hundred ninety-three thousandths **9.** four and sixty-two ten-thousandths **13.** 438.4 **15.** 97.62 **17.** 1.0573 **19.** 3.5827 **21.** \$6.00 **23.** \$.58 **25.** \$1.17 **27.** 3.5; 3.52; 3.522 **29.** 2.5; 2.55; 2.548 **31.** 27.3; 27.32; 27.325 **33.** 36.5; 36.47; 36.472 **35.** .1; .06; .056 **37.** \$5.06 **39.** \$32.49 **41.** \$382.01 **43.** \$42.14 **45.** \$.00 **47.** \$1.50 **49.** \$2.00 **51.** \$752.80 **53.** \$26 **55.** \$0 **57.** \$12,836 **59.** \$395 **61.** \$4700 **63.** \$379 **65.** \$722

Section 1.4 Exercises (Page 31)

1. $40 + 20 + 9 = 69$; 68.46 **3.** $6 + 4 + 5 + 7 + 2 = 24$; 23.82 **5.** $2000 + 5 + 3 + 7 = 2015$; 2171.414 **7.** $6000 + 500 + 20 + 8 = 6528$; 6666.061 **9.** $2000 + 70 + 500 + 600 + 400 = 3570$; 3451.446 **11.** 173.273 **13.** 59.3268 **17.** \$15,138.19 **19.** \$5.73 per pound **21.** $20 - 7 = 13$; 13.16 **23.** $50 - 20 = 30$; 31.507 **25.** $300 - 90 = 210$; 240.034 **27.** $8 - 3 = 5$; 4.848 **29.** $5 - 2 = 3$; 3.0198 **31.** \$43,815.81

Section 1.5 Exercises (Page 39)

1. $100 \times 4 = 400$; 406.56 **3.** $30 \times 7 = 210$; 231.88 **5.** $40 \times 2 = 80$; 89.352 **7.** 1.9152 **9.** 9.3527 **11.** .002448 **13.** \$152.63 **15.** \$418.10 **17.** 8.075 **19.** 27.442 **21.** 57.977 (rounded) **25.** \$14,790 **27.** 25.1 mpg **29.** 27 months **31. (a)** .43 inch **(b)** 4.3 inches **33.** \$129.25 **35. (a)** \$70.05 **(b)** \$25.80

Summary Exercise (Page 45)

(a) \$30,166 **(b)** \$5998 **(c)** 203 guests; \$38 left over **(d)** \$73.33 **(e)** 162 guests; \$6 left over **(f)** 66 guests; \$10 left over **(g)** \$644.25

Chapter 1 Test (Page 47)

1. 840 **2.** 22,000 **3.** 672,000 **4.** 50,000 **5.** 900,000 **6.** \$606 **7.** \$8399 **8.** \$21.06 **9.** \$364.35 **10.** \$7246 **11.** 181.535 **12.** 498.795 **13.** 133.6 **14.** 3.7947 **15.** 15.8256 **16.** 8.0882 **17.** 11.56 **18.** 23.8 **19.** 4.25 **20.** \$125.18 **21.** \$3942.90 (rounded) **22.** 14,454 gallons saved **23.** \$17.31 **24.** \$.79 per pound (rounded) **25.** 253 seedlings

Chapter 2

Section 2.1 Exercises (Page 55)

1. $\frac{29}{8}$ **3.** $\frac{17}{4}$ **5.** $\frac{38}{3}$ **7.** $\frac{183}{8}$ **9.** $\frac{55}{7}$ **11.** $\frac{364}{23}$ **13.** $3\frac{1}{4}$ **15.** $2\frac{2}{3}$ **17.** $3\frac{4}{5}$ **19.** $3\frac{7}{11}$ **21.** $1\frac{62}{63}$ **23.** $7\frac{8}{25}$ **27.** $\frac{1}{2}$ **29.** $\frac{5}{8}$ **31.** $\frac{3}{5}$ **33.** $\frac{11}{12}$ **35.** 1 **37.** $\frac{7}{12}$ **41.** √ x √ x x √ x x **43.** √ √ √ √ √ x x √ **45.** √ √ x √ √ x √ √ **47.** √ x √ x x x x x

Section 2.2 Exercises (Page 61)

1. 16 **3.** 36 **5.** 48 **7.** 42 **9.** 24 **11.** 180 **13.** 480 **15.** 2100 **17.** 360 **21.** $\frac{2}{3}$ **23.** $\frac{1}{2}$ **25.** $\frac{17}{48}$ **27.** $1\frac{23}{36}$ **29.** $\frac{13}{14}$ **31.** $2\frac{1}{13}$ **33.** $2\frac{11}{36}$ **35.** $1\frac{13}{30}$ **37.** $\frac{9}{20}$ **39.** $\frac{7}{24}$ **43.** $\frac{23}{24}$ cubic yard **45.** $\frac{47}{60}$ inch **47.** $\frac{7}{24}$ of the contents **49.** $\frac{19}{24}$ of the debt **51.** $\frac{3}{16}$ inch **53.** $\frac{7}{24}$ **55.** work and travel; $\frac{1}{2}$ **57.** $\frac{1}{2}$ inch **59.** $\frac{1}{12}$ mile

Section 2.3 Exercises (Page 67)

1. $97\frac{4}{5}$ **3.** $80\frac{3}{4}$ **5.** $97\frac{7}{40}$ **7.** $53\frac{17}{24}$ **9.** $105\frac{107}{120}$ **11.** $7\frac{1}{8}$ **13.** $162\frac{1}{6}$ **15.** $9\frac{1}{24}$ **17.** $46\frac{23}{30}$ **19.** $\frac{7}{10}$ **23.** $116\frac{1}{2}$ inches **25.** 130 feet **27.** $1\frac{5}{8}$ cubic yards **29.** $22\frac{7}{8}$ hours

Section 2.4 Exercises (Page 73)

1. $\frac{3}{10}$ **3.** $\frac{99}{160}$ **5.** $\frac{9}{32}$ **7.** $4\frac{3}{8}$ **9.** $9\frac{1}{3}$ **11.** $\frac{1}{3}$ **13.** $4\frac{7}{12}$ **15.** $1\frac{7}{9}$ **17.** $\frac{3}{5}$ **19.** $1\frac{1}{2}$ **21.** $\frac{2}{3}$ **23.** $2\frac{2}{3}$ **25.** $\frac{3}{20}$ **27.** $8\frac{2}{5}$ **31.** \$12 **33.** \$18.75 **37.** 6¢ **39.** 36 yards **41.** 12 homes **43.** $2632\frac{1}{2}$ inches **45.** 2480 anchors **47.** 471 gallons **49.** 88 dispensers **51.** 60 trips

Section 2.5 Exercises (Page 79)

1. $\frac{3}{4}$ **3.** $\frac{6}{25}$ **5.** $\frac{73}{100}$ **7.** $\frac{17}{20}$ **9.** $\frac{17}{50}$ **11.** $\frac{111}{250}$ **13.** $\frac{5}{8}$ **15.** $\frac{161}{200}$ **17.** $\frac{12}{125}$ **19.** $\frac{3}{80}$ **21.** $\frac{3}{16}$ **23.** $\frac{1}{625}$ **27.** .25 **29.** .375 **31.** .667 (rounded) **33.** .778 (rounded) **35.** .636 (rounded) **37.** .88 **39.** .883 (rounded) **41.** .993 (rounded) **43. (a)** .667 **(b)** 123 patients

Summary Exercise (Page 83)

(a) \$144,000 **(b)** $\frac{5}{12}$; $\frac{1}{4}$; $\frac{1}{12}$; $\frac{1}{16}$; $\frac{1}{16}$; $\frac{1}{8}$ **(c)** Miscellaneous: $\frac{1}{8}$; Insurance: $\frac{1}{16}$; Advertising: $\frac{1}{16}$; Utilities: $\frac{1}{12}$; Rent: $\frac{1}{4}$; Salaries: $\frac{5}{12}$ **(d)** 150°; 90°; 30°; 22.5°; 22.5°; 45° **(e)** 360°; a full circle is 360°

Chapter 2 Test (Page 85)

1. $\frac{5}{6}$ **2.** $\frac{7}{8}$ **3.** $\frac{7}{11}$ **4.** $8\frac{1}{8}$ **5.** $4\frac{2}{3}$ **6.** $2\frac{2}{3}$ **7.** $\frac{31}{4}$ **8.** $\frac{94}{5}$ **9.** $\frac{147}{8}$ **10.** 30 **11.** 120 **12.** 72 **13.** $\frac{7}{8}$ **14.** $15\frac{1}{16}$ **15.** $36\frac{5}{16}$ **16.** 36 **17.** $1\frac{1}{2}$ **18.** $24\frac{1}{8}$ pounds **19.** \$340 **20.** $35\frac{7}{8}$ gallons **21.** 36 screen sections **22.** $\frac{5}{8}$ **23.** $\frac{41}{50}$ **24.** .25 inch **25.** .875 inch

Chapter 3

Section 3.1 Exercises (Page 93)

1. 25% **3.** 72% **5.** 203.4% **7.** 362.5% **9.** 87.5% **11.** .05% **13.** 345% **15.** 3.08% **17.** .625 **19.** .65 **21.** .125 **23.** .125 **25.** .0025 **27.** .8475 **29.** 1.75 **31.** .5; 50% **33.** $\frac{7}{8}$; 87.5% **35.** $\frac{1}{125}$; .008 **37.** 10.5; 1050% **39.** $\frac{13}{20}$; 65% **41.** $\frac{1}{200}$; .5% **43.** $.33\overline{3}$; $33\frac{1}{3}$% **45.** $2\frac{1}{2}$; 250% **47.** $\frac{17}{400}$; .0425 **49.** .015; 1.5% **51.** $10\frac{3}{8}$; 10.375 **53.** $\frac{1}{400}$; .25% **55.** $\frac{3}{8}$; .375

Section 3.2 Exercises (Page 101)

1. 62 homes **3.** $604 **5.** 4.8 feet **7.** 10,185 miles **9.** 182 cell phones **11.** 148.44 yards **13.** $5366.65 **17.** 264 adults **19.** $429.92 **21.** 44 females **23.** 8.95 ounces **25.** 4853 accidents **27.** **(a)** 28.6% female **(b)** 313,099 female **29.** $239.25 **31.** 2156 products **33.** 860,907 units **35.** $51,844.20 **37.** $6296.40 **39.** $199.89 **41.** $87.58

Section 3.3 Exercises (Page 109)

1. 2120 **3.** 325 **5.** 2000 **7.** 4800 **9.** 44,000 **11.** 20,000 **13.** $90,320 **15.** 1080 **17.** 312,500 **19.** 65,400 **21.** 40,000 **25.** 107.1 million households **27.** 7761 students **29.** $4500 **31.** 1055 people **33.** 1749 owners **35.** $185,500

Supplementary Exercises (Page 111)

1. 16 ounces **3.** $288,150 **5.** 478,175 Mustangs **7.** 162 calories **9.** $39,000 **11.** 230 companies **13.** 55 companies

Section 3.4 Exercises (Page 117)

1. 10 **3.** 50 **5.** 28.3 **7.** 76 **9.** 4.1 **11.** 5.9 **13.** 1.3 **15.** 250 **17.** 27.8 **21.** 6.2% **23.** 2% **25.** 8.7% **27.** 35.9% **29.** 20%

Supplementary Exercises (Page 119)

1. 97 people **3.** 40% **5.** 1100 boaters **7.** $396.05 **9.** $134 **11.** $568.80 **13.** 4% **15.** 4 million riders **17.** 9.6% **19.** 12.5% **21.** 5.5% **23.** 5760 items **25.** $10,098 **27.** 11.6% **29.** 5742 deaths **31.** **(a)** 36% **(b)** 64%

Section 3.5 Exercises (Page 129)

1. $375 **3.** $27.91 **5.** $25 **7.** $854.50 **11.** $195,500 **13.** **(a)** $950 **(b)** $76 **15.** 842,857 restaurants **17.** 22,000 people **19.** 1,299,886 subscribers **21.** 120.5 billion **23.** $3864 **25.** $145.24 million **27.** 51.2 million **29.** 30,000 students **31.** 695 deaths **33.** 18,195 homes

Summary Exercise (Page 135)

Amazon.com, 52.4%; DaimlerLG, $59.13; Gateway Computer, $3.14; Krispy Kreme, 117.4%; McDonald's, 32.3%; Merck, $27.98; Pepsi Bottling, $31.91; NetFlix Inc., $18.12; Wal-Mart, $46.47; Yahoo, 20.9%

Chapter 3 Test (Page 137)

1. 300 home sales **2.** 12 open houses **3.** 1100 shippers **4.** 2.5% **5.** $3.15 **6.** $\frac{6}{25}$ **7.** 1920 purchase orders **8.** $\frac{7}{8}$ **9.** 8.5% **10.** $\frac{1}{200}$ **11.** $2.28 **12.** 224,000 units **13.** $9090; $41,410 **14.** 307.7 million people **15.** **(a)** 11% **(b)** $4488 per year **16.** 75% **17.** $280.50 **18.** 1200 backpacks **19.** 6.2% **20.** $1.47 billion

Cumulative Review Chapters 1–3 (Page 139)

1. 65,500 **3.** 78.4 **5.** 3609 **7.** 24,092 **9.** 85 **11.** 35.174 **13.** 12.218 **15.** $198 **17.** $31,658.27 **19.** $\frac{8}{9}$ **21.** $7\frac{2}{15}$ **23.** $13\frac{13}{24}$ **25.** 3 **27.** $12\frac{1}{2}$ square feet **29.** 130 feet **31.** $\frac{13}{20}$ **33.** 87.5% **35.** 2170 home loans **37.** 25% **39.** 38.5% **41.** 97,757 copies **43.** 45,000% **45.** **(a)** 83% **(b)** 1.909 billion pounds **47.** .69 billion pounds

Chapter 4

Section 4.1 Exercises (Page 151)

1. $14.20 **3.** $20.00 **5.** $17.10 **7.** $21.90 **9.** Mar. 8; $380.71; Nola Akala; Tutoring; 3971.28; 79.26; 4050.54; 380.71; 3669.83 **11.** Dec. 4; $37.52; Paul's Pools; Chemicals; 1126.73; 1126.73; 37.52; 1089.21 **17.** Oct. 10; $39.12; County Clerk; License; 5972.89; 752.18; 23.32; 6748.39; 39.12; 6709.27 **19.** 9412.64; 8838.86; 8726.71; 9479.99; 10,955.68; 10,529.13; 9891.20; 9825.58; 9577.41; 9913.26; 9462.76 **21.** 574.86; 384.36; 462.65; 620.07; 581.31; 405.43; 784.71; 587.51; 562.41; 487.41; 1209.76

Section 4.2 Exercises (Page 161)

1. $1595.36 **3.** $1387.67 **5.** $1332.16 **7.** $203.86 **9.** $66.48 **11.** $1064.72 **13.** $991.89 **15.** $962.13 **17.** $60.21 **19.** $59.25

Section 4.3 Exercises (Page 169)

1. $4870.24 **3.** $7690.62 **5.** $18,314.72 **11.** 421, $371.52; 424, $429.07; 427, $883.69; 429, $35.62; $1719.90; $6875.09; 701.56; 421.78; 689.35; 8687.78; 1719.90; $6967.88; $6965.92; 8.75; 6957.17; 10.71; $6967.88 **13.** 767, $63.24; 771, $135.76; $199.00; $5636.51; 220.16; 5856.67; 199.00; $5657.67; $5858.85; 209.30; 5649.55; 8.12; $5657.67

Summary Exercise (Page 175)

(a) $8178.46 gross deposit **(b)** $7974 credit **(c)** $9810.36 total of checks outstanding **(d)** $4882.58 deposits not recorded **(e)** $7274.56 balance

Chapter 4 Test (Page 177)

1. $19.90 **2.** $9.40 **3.** $17.40 **4.** Aug. 6; $6892.12; WBC Broadcasting; Airtime; $16,409.82; 16,409.82; 6892.12; 9517.70 **5.** Aug. 8; $1258.36; Lakeland Weekly; Space buy; 9517.70; 1572.00; 11,089.70; 1258.36; 9831.34 **6.** Aug. 14; $416.14; W. Wilson; Freelance Art; 9831.34; 10,000.00; 19,831.34; 416.14; 19,415.20 **7.** $1709.55 **8.** $81.99 **9.** $1627.56 **10.** $56.96 **11.** $1570.60 **12.** $5482.18 current balance

Chapter 5

Section 5.1 Exercises (Page 189)

1. 40; 0; $12.15 **3.** 38.75; 0; $28.05 **5.** 40; 5.25; $17.22 **7.** $329.60; $92.70; $422.30 **9.** $380; $160.31; $540.31 **11.** $13.20; $347.60; $0; $347.60 **13.** $21.60; $576.00; $97.20; $673.20 **15.** $13.77; $367.20; $58.52; $425.72 **17.** 50.5; 10.5; $4.75; $479.75; $49.88; $529.63 **19.** 53.5; 13.5; $6.25; $668.75; $84.38; $753.13 **21.** 35; 6; $14.10; $329.00; $84.60; $413.60 **23.** 39.5; 3.75; $16.20; $426.60; $60.75; $487.35 **25.** 39.75; 3.5; $32.25; $854.63; $112.88; $967.51 **29.** $443.08; $886.15; $1920; $23,040 **31.** $556.15; $1112.31; $1205; $28,920 **33.** $1660; $1798.33; $3596.67; $43,160 **35.** $387 **37.** $467.25 **39.** $832 **41.** $788.80 **43.** $556.32 **45.** **(a)** $1260 biweekly **(b)** $1365 semimonthly **(c)** $2730 monthly **(d)** $32,760 annually

Section 5.2 Exercises (Page 199)

1. $93.12 **3.** $153.60 **5.** $38.65 **7.** $52.68 **11.** $260.19 **13.** $371.90 **15.** $397.48 **17.** $471.50 **19.** $308.10 **21.** $421.65 **23.** $1405 **25.** $688.40 **27.** $478.10 **29.** $628.61

Section 5.3 Exercises (Page 207)

1. $20.13; $4.71 **3.** $28.72; $6.72 **5.** $52.99; $12.39 **7.** $189.39 **9.** $308.99 **11.** $41.56 **13.** $368.80; $76.07; $444.87; $27.58; $6.45; $4.45 **15.** $263.20; $49.35; $312.55; $19.38; $4.53; $3.13 **17.** $467.20; $122.64; $589.84; $36.57; $8.55; $5.90 **19.** **(a)** $24.07 **(b)** $5.63 **21.** **(a)** $95.67 **(b)** $22.38 **(c)** $15.43 **23.** $7221.60; $1688.92 **25.** $3609; $844.04 **27.** $3328.61; $778.46

Section 5.4 Exercises (Page 221)

1. $180 **3.** $38 **5.** $47 **7.** $45 **9.** $27 **11.** $81 **13.** $6.87 **15.** $28.00 **17.** $69.11 **19.** $35.73; $8.36; $21.83; $510.36 **21.** $155.78; $36.43; $279.48;

$2040.84 **23.** $141.16; $33.01; $210.07; $1892.59 **25.** $184.21; $43.08; $264.71; $2479.06 **27.** $232.70; $54.42; $717.74; $2748.32 **29.** $110.76; $25.90; $362.11; $1287.67 **35.** $8748.05 **37.** $53,332.52 **39.** $44,323.10 **41.** $664.21 **43.** $546.15 **45.** $3733.24

Summary Exercise (Page 228)

(a) $818 **(b)** $368.10 **(c)** $1186.10 **(d)** $73.54 **(e)** $17.20 **(f)** $204.43 **(g)** $11.86 **(h)** $52.19 **(i)** $589.88

Chapter 5 Test (Page 229)

1. 40; 6.5; $537.30 **2.** 40; 7.5; $440.75 **3. (a)** $655 weekly **(b)** $1310 biweekly **(c)** $1419.17 semimonthly **(d)** $2838.33 monthly **4.** $180 **5.** $3532.50 **6. (a)** $576.60 **(b)** $134.85 **7. (a)** $167.40 **(b)** $134.85 **8.** $13 **9.** $44 **10.** $192 **11.** $51 **12.** $49 **13.** $1474.18 **14.** $417.70 **15.** $546.31 **16. (a)** $31.90 **(b)** $7.46 **(c)** $5.14 **17. (a)** $162.71 **(b)** $38.42 **18. (a)** $4552.55 **(b)** $1064.71 **19. (a)** $5255.20 **(b)** $1229.04 **20.** $2246.54

Chapter 6

Section 6.1 Exercises (Page 239)

1. $226.80 **3.** $126.36 **5.** $3610.36 **7.** $4887.73 **9.** $57.00 **11.** $28.40 **13.** $501.20 **15.** foot **17.** pair **19.** kilogram **21.** case **23.** drum **25.** liter **27.** gallon **29.** cash on delivery **33.** .9 × .8 = .72 **35.** .9 × .9 × .9 = .729 **37.** .75 × .95 = .7125 **39.** .6 × .7 × .8 = .336 **41.** .5 × .9 × .8 × .95 = .342 **43.** $267.52 **45.** $14.02 **47.** $722.93 **49.** $218.88 **51.** $16.83 **53.** $714.42 **55.** $972 **57.** $640 **63.** $182.24 **65. (a)** 20/15 **(b)** $4.08 **67. (a)** 15/20 **(b)** $.55 **69.** $1280.45 **71.** $56, 677 **73.** $326.40 undercharged

Section 6.2 Exercises (Page 247)

1. .72; 28% **3.** .68; 32% **5.** .504; 49.6% **7.** .5184; 48.16% **11.** $720 **13.** $2280 **15. (a)** $25.89 **(b)** $28.76 **(c)** $2.87 **17. (a)** 20/20/20 is higher **(b)** .1% **19.** $370 **21.** 30.0%

Section 6.3 Exercises (Page 255)

1. May 14; June 3 **3.** July 25; Sept. 8 **5.** Oct. 1; Oct. 11 **7.** $1.70; $92.20 **9.** $0; $81.25 **11.** $21.60; $1120.55 **15.** $4542.69 **17.** $1798.92 **19. (a)** Jan. 28; Feb. 7; Feb. 17 **(b)** Mar. 9 **21. (a)** Apr. 25 **(b)** May 5

Section 6.4 Exercises (Page 263)

1. Mar. 10; Mar. 30 **3.** Dec. 22; Jan. 11 **5.** June 16; July 6 **7.** $20.47; $661.81 **9.** $0; $785.64 **11.** $229.60; $11,250.40 **13.** $.72; $23.23 **17. (a)** Dec. 13 **(b)** $2334.93 **19.** $6586.09 **21.** $1495.58 **23. (a)** $1467.39 **(b)** $549.51 **25. (a)** June 10 **(b)** June 30 **27.** $1509.75 due **29. (a)** $3350.52 **(b)** $1052.06

Summary Exercise (page 269)

(a) $17,750.66 **(b)** October 15 **(c)** November 4 **(d)** $17,966.52 **(e)** $10,309.28; $8189.76

Chapter 6 Test (Page 271)

1. $225.65 **2.** $784.80 **3. (a)** .63 **(b)** 37% **4. (a)** .576 **(b)** 42.4% **5.** Mar. 15 **6.** May 30 **7.** Jan. 15 **8.** Dec. 19 **9. (a)** $394.40 invoice total **(b)** $386.51 after discount **(c)** $398.06 total amt due **10.** $91,300.78 **11. (a)** July 20 **(b)** $3041.28 **12.** $437.48 **13. (a)** Builders Supply **(b)** $1.91 **14. (a)** $1762.20 **(b)** $1780 full amount **15.** $2438.58 **16. (a)** $1717.53 **(b)** $1198.47

Chapter 7

Section 7.1 Exercises (Page 281)

1. 140%; $4.96; $17.36 **3.** 100%; 20%; $27.17; $5.43 **5.** 100%; 130%; $168.00; $218.40 **7.** $2.70; $11.70 **9.** 60%; $19.20 **11.** $61.44; 40% **13.** $33.80; 25% **17.** $148.64 markup **19.** $12.95 selling price **21.** $221.40 selling price **23. (a)** $95.96 **(b)** 25% **(c)** 125% **25. (a)** 126% **(b)** $5.67 selling price **(c)** $1.17 markup

Section 7.2 Exercises (Page 291)

1. 75%; $21.00; $28.00 **3.** 58%; 42%; $105.00 **5.** 50%; 100%; $2025; $4050 **7.** $1920; $2400.00 **9.** $8.46; $22.26; 61.3% **11.** $750; $1050; 28.6% **13.** 50% **15.** 15.3% **19. (a)** $1250 selling price **(b)** $812.50 cost **(c)** 65% **21. (a)** $4990 total received **(b)** $2710 markup **(c)** 54.3% **(d)** 118.9% **23.** $.57

Supplementary Exercises (Page 293)

1. $180 markup **3.** 19.1% **5.** $6.98 **7.** $119 **9. (a)** 76% **(b)** $130 **(c)** $31.20 **11. (a)** $32.40 **(b)** 25.9% **13. (a)** $24.90 **(b)** 12.5% **(c)** 14.2% **15.** $17.50

Section 7.3 Exercises (Page 301)

1. 25%; $645 **3.** 30%; $18.48 **5.** 20%; $5.20 **7.** $120; $20; none **9.** $16; $22; $6 **11.** $385; $250; $60 **15.** 41% **17.** $30.01 operating loss **19. (a)** $77.15 operating loss **(b)** $18.77 absolute loss

Section 7.4 Exercises (Page 311)

1. $22,673 **3.** $60,568 **5.** 2.83; 2.81 **7.** 3.59; 3.52 **9.** 4.69; 4.66 **11.** $182; $195; $170 **13.** $2352; $2385; $2312.50 **17.** 5.43 turnover at cost **19. (a)** $508.50 weighted-average method **(b)** $562.50 FIFO **(c)** $520 LIFO **21. (a)** $1251.20 weighted-average method **(b)** $1430 FIFO **(c)** $1040 LIFO **23.** $30,660

Summary Exercise (Page 319)

(a) $125 original selling price **(b)** $2062.50 total selling price **(c)** $375 operating loss **(d)** none

Chapter 7 Test (Page 321)

1. (a) 20 **(b)** 120 **(c)** 76.80 **2. (a)** 138 **(b)** 365.50 **(c)** 138.89 **3. (a)** 80 **(b)** 20 **(c)** 33.60 **4. (a)** 75 **(b)** 25 **(c)** 18.45 **5.** 20% **6.** 50% **7.** $200; $14; none **8.** $72; $99; $27 **9.** 5.76; 5.73 **10.** $12.50 selling price per pair **11.** $4200 **12.** 40% **13. (a)** $37.99 **(b)** 19.0% (rounded) **(c)** 23.5% **14.** 28% **15. (a)** $131.10 operating loss **(b)** $45.60 absolute loss **16.** $130,278 average inventory **17.** $12,978 weighted-average method **18. (a)** $11,775 FIFO **(b)** $13,350 LIFO

Cumulative Review Chapters 4–7 (Page 323)

1. $1958.20 **3.** $1749.75 **5.** $1692.88 **7.** $4359.38 **9.** $240.47 **11.** 62.2% **13.** Nov. 15; Dec. 5 **15.** $400; $280; $32 **17.** $93.11 (rounded) **19.** 12.88 turnover at cost **21.** $6489 weighted-average method

Chapter 8

Section 8.1 Exercises (Page 333)

1. $209; $4009 **3.** $440; $5940 **5.** 68 **7.** 99 **9. (a)** $2493.15 **(b)** $2527.78 **(c)** $34.63 **11. (a)** $1091.10 **(b)** $1106.25 **(c)** $15.15 **13.** Helen Spence **15.** Donna Sharp **17.** 90 days **19.** Jan. 25 **21.** Oct. 18; $5064 **23.** May 9; $6591.38 **25. (a)** $138,750 **(b)** $2,138,750 **27.** $16,800 **29. (a)** Oct. 3 **(b)** $7008.41 **31. (a)** Sept. 6 **(b)** $84,200 **33.** $86.17 **35. (a)** Sept. 30 **(b)** $50,800

Section 8.2 Exercises (Page 341)

1. $14,000 **3.** $504 **5.** $10,800 **7.** 11.8% **9.** 9.5% **11.** 7.5% **13.** 120 days **15.** 62 days **17.** 5 months **19.** $7500.19 **21.** 9.5% **23.** 9% **25. (a)** $10,800 **(b)** $11,250 **27.** 76 days **29.** 4% **31. (a)** $12,000 **(b)** $1200 **33.** 208 days **35. (a)** 10.75% **(b)** 11.4%

Section 8.3 Exercises (Page 351)

1. $234; $7566 **3.** $950; $18,050 **5.** $408.33; $21,991.67 **7.** Jun. 20; $6248 **9.** Dec. 9; $957.29 **11.** Feb. 8; $23,600 **13. (a)** $220 **(b)** $5780 **15.** 200 days **17.** 9.5% **19.** $7891.30 **21. (a)** $3780 **(b)** 13.3% **23.** 105 days **25. (a)** 166,107.38 yen **(b)** 8.1% **27. (a)** $11,262.50 **(b)** 8.9% **29. (a)** $24,625,000 **(b)** $25,000,000 **(c)** $375,000 **(d)** 6.09%

Section 8.4 Exercises (Page 361)

1. 107 days **3.** 53 days **5.** $10,179 **7.** $2481.25 **9.** $6362.75; 37 days; $78.47; $6284.28 **11.** $2044; 49 days; $33.39; $2010.61 **13.** $17,355; 42 days; $228.43; $17,571.57 **15.** $30,829.37; 83 days; $814.09; $31,285.91 **17. (a)** $4968 **(b)** $367,632 **19. (a)** $238,750 **(b)** 93 days **(c)** $5166.67 **(d)** $244,833.33 **21. (a)** $311,250 **(b)** $304,713.75 **23. (a)** $24,150 **(b)** $538.46 **(c)** $24,461.54 **(d)** 6.71%

Supplementary Exercises (Page 365)

1. (a) $660 **(b)** $18,660 **3.** $48,000 **5.** 200 days **7. (a)** $750 **(b)** $20,750 **9.** 12.1% **11.** Apr. 12; $9,475,000 **13.** $15,000 **15.** $18,208.12 **17. (a)** $1711.11 **(b)** $29,711.11 **(c)** 130 days **(d)** $1180.19 **(e)** $28,530.92 **19. (a)** $3843.89 **(b)** $72,191.09 **(c)** $4191.09 **(d)** $347.20

Summary Exercise (Page 373)

3. (a) $1,037,500 **(b)** $78,292,500 **(c)** 2.65%

Chapter 8 Test (Page 375)

1. $1020.83 **2.** $508.75 **3.** $137.50 **4.** $148.06 **5.** $13,013.01 **6.** $25,575.75 **7.** $11.19 **8.** 9.2% **9.** 333 days **10.** $43,000 **11.** $26,595.74 **12.** $359.33; $9440.67 **13.** $162.29; $10,087.71 **14. (a)** $14,550 **(b)** 9.3% **15.** $28,626.58 **16.** $9034.40 **17. (a)** $19,812.50 **(b)** $20,000 **(c)** $187.50 **(d)** 3.79% **18.** 44 days; $144.07; $9285.93 **19. (a)** $452.81 **(b)** $8997.19 **(c)** loses $2.81

Chapter 9

Section 9.1 Exercises (Page 385)

1. $16,325.87; $4325.87 **3.** $30,906.76; $2906.76 **5.** $40,841.23; $8491.23 **7.** $28,949.25; $14,449.25 **9.** $60,476.40; $15,476.40 **11.** $1296; $1417.39; $121.39 **13.** $1440; $2606.60; $1166.60 **15. (a)** $11,431.57 **(b)** $2931.57 **17. (a)** $5707.08 **(b)** $1207.08 **19. (a)** 31,669.25 yen **(b)** 6669.25 yen **21.** $439.25 **23. (a)** $1,777,622 **(b)** $377,622 **25. (a)** $28,137.75 **(b)** $40,117.75 **(c)** $11,980 **27. (a)** $8787.45 **(b)** $10,079.40 **(c)** second is larger

Section 9.2 Exercises (Page 395)

1. $39.75 **3.** $50.48 **5.** $101.88 **7.** $4763.41 **9.** $17,412.96 **13. (a)** $3284.75 **(b)** $24.75 **15. (a)** $11,638.49 **(b)** $118.49 **17.** $4420.65; $4647.29 **19. (a)** $901,988.58 **(b)** $101,988.58 **21.** $4700 **23.** Loss of $397.50

Section 9.3 Exercises (Page 403)

1. $9764.11; $2535.89 **3.** $7674.01; $1675.99 **5.** $9792.06; $9060.94 **7. (a)** $26,444.80 **(b)** $13,555.20 **9.** $3503.40 **11. (a)** $793,054 **(b)** $592,618 **13. (a)** $26,620 **(b)** $20,989.60

Summary Exercise (Page 407)

(a) $4,053,386; $3,016,084 **(b)** $2,539,384; $1,889,530 **(c)** $2,798,295; $2,082,183 **(d)** $2,539,384; $1,889,530; $2,798,295; $2,082,183; $4,053,386; $3,016,084

Chapter 9 Test (Page 409)

1. $18,649.23; $9949.23 **2.** $16,127.04; $4127.04 **3.** $13,170.42; $3370.42 **4.** $18,556.38; $6056.38 **5.** $50.52 **6.** $530.60 **7.** $286.28 **8.** $7509.25 **9.** $10,380.83 **10.** $38,291.99 **11.** $16,077.25 **12.** $4120.01 **13.** $5399.30 **14.** $38,680.72 **15.** Loss of $676 **16.** Loss of $1625 **17. (a)** $4408.99 **(b)** $3801.87 **18. (a)** $15,173.40 **(b)** $13,481.41 **19. (a)** $283,233.48 **(b)** $206,955.87 **20. (a)** $59 million **(b)** $93 million

Cumulative Review: Chapters 8–9 (Page 411)

1. $272 **3.** $2400.17 **5.** 9.7% **7.** 80 days **9.** $270; $8730 **11.** $4875 **13.** $1947.90 **15.** $86.07; $12,686.07 **17.** $583.49; $416.51 **19.** $1250; $23,750 **21.** $10,871.40 **23.** $20.01

Chapter 10

Section 10.1 Exercises (Page 421)

1. $25,319.14; $9119.14 **3.** $201,527.78; $51,527.78 **5.** $139,509.30; $41,509.30 **7.** $7603.12; $1603.12 **9.** $207,485.32; $36,485.32 **11.** $51,985.25; $6385.25 **15. (a)** $423,452.16 **(b)** $290,452.16 **17. (a)** $11,277.89 **(b)** $3277.89 **19.** $44,502

Section 10.2 Exercises (Page 429)

1. $14,762.54 **3.** $30,493.92 **5.** $18,991.59 **9.** $810,043.65 **11. (a)** $56,776.30 **(b)** $13,223.70 **13. (a)** $48,879.76 **(b)** No **15. (a)** First offer **(b)** $2769.99 **17.** $151,694.02

Section 10.3 Exercises (Page 435)

1. $2784.12 **3.** $715.29 **5.** $2271 **7.** $183.22 **11. (a)** $144,026 **(b)** $55,844 **13. (a)** $860 **(b)** $957,000 **15.** $12,649.20 **17. (a)** $53,383 **(b)** $37,559 **19. (a)** $1200 **(b)** $6511.80

(c)

Payment Number	Amount of Deposit	Interest Earned	Total in Account
1	$6511.80	$0	$6511.80
2	$6511.80	$260.47	$13,284.07
3	$6511.80	$531.36	$20,327.23
4	$6511.80	$813.09	$27,652.12
5	$6511.80	$1106.08	$35,270.00
6	$6511.80	$1410.80	$43,192.60
7	$6511.80	$1727.70	$51,432.10
8	$6510.62	$2057.28	$60,000.00

21.

Payment Number	Amount of Deposit	Interest Earned	Total in Account
1	$713,625	$0	$713,625.00
2	$713,625	$10,704.38	$1,437,954.38
3	$713,625	$21,569.32	$2,173,148.70
4	$713,625	$32,597.23	$2,919,370.93

23. $1707 **25.** $6819.92

Supplementary Exercises (Page 439)

1. (a) $15,210.93 **(b)** $3210.93 **3. (a)** $77,985.46 **(b)** $37,985.46 **5.** $1,384,797.60 **7.** $96,344.03 **9.** $267,986.10

Payment Number	Amount of Deposit	Interest Earned	Total in Account
1	$267,986.10	$0	$267,986.10
2	$267,986.10	$21,438.89	$557,411.09
3	$267,996.02	$44,592.89	$870,000.00

11. (a) $286,748 **(b)** $6265.44

Section 10.4 Exercises (Page 447)

1. $17 **3.** $.12 **5.** 250,200 **7.** 21 **9.** $4.51 **11.** 1.4% **13.** $.99 **15.** $75.69 **17.** −$.07 **19.** $7400; $135 **21.** $31,050; $300 **23.** $31,507; $980 **27.** 2.5% **29.** 2.3% **31.** 1.5% **33.** 16 **35.** 23 **37.** 22 **39.** .85, 2.5% **41.** $15,120 **43. (a)** $15,326.80 **(b)** $17,866.85 **(c)** $2540.05

Section 10.5 Exercises (Page 455)

1. $1012.03 **3.** November 1, 2011 **5.** 5.337% **7.** $49,621 **9.** $346.146.50 **11.** $262,447.50 **15. (a)** $29,675.50 **(b)** $1900 **(c)** 6.4% **17. (a)** $14,754.60 **(b)** $487.50 **(c)** 3.3% **19. (a)** $3600 **(b)** $97,151.40

Summary Exercise (Page 460)

(a) $620,703.67 **(b)** $97,090.40 **(c)** $67,090.40 **(d)** $658,703.61 **(e)** Almost, about $38,000 short. **(f)** Answers will vary.

Chapter 10 Test (Page 461)

1. $9897.47 **2.** $126,595.71 **3.** $930,909 **4.** $121,490.46 **5.** $54,304.22 **6.** $30,200.99 **7.** $6801.69 **8.** $39,884.63 **9.** $21,316.12 **10.** $264,795.02 **11.** $21,461.99 **12.** $24,683.07 **13.** $8702 **14.** $8395 **15.** $5835.60 **16.** $17,976 **17.** $22,492 **18.** $2322 **19. (a)** $15,900 **(b)** $272 **20. (a)** $24,025 **(b)** $1050 **(c)** 4.4% **21.** Highest and lowest prices the stock sold for during the year were $54.43 and $40.72. Weekly volume is $532,000. Dividend yield is .6% of current price. PE ratio is 11. Stock closed at $48.80. The stock price was down $0.15 for the week. Earnings were $1.31 last year and are expected to be $3.64 this year and $4.23 next year. Last quarterly dividend was $.30. **22.** Pays 6.75% of $1000 per year. Matures February 1, 2027. Closed at $1000. Yield to maturity 6.749%. Weekly volume sold $42,300,000.

Chapter 11

Section 11.1 Exercises (Page 471)

1. $109.23 **3.** $15.02 **5.** October, $6.12; $419.17; November, $419.17, $5.87, $541.68; December, $541.68, $7.58, $529.22; January, $529.22, $7.41, $211.71 **9.** $20.42 **11.** $4.87 **13.** $17.30 **15. (a)** $104 **(b)** $65 **(c)** $39 **17. (a)** $132.64 **(b)** $1.99 **(c)** $133.80 **19. (a)** $312.91 **(b)** $4.69 **(c)** $285.94 **21. (a)** $139.71 **(b)** $2.10 **(c)** $74.32

Section 11.2 Exercises (Page 481)

1. $2050; $250 **3.** $180; $30 **5.** $3543, $643 **7.** 8.1% **9.** 11.6% **11.** 15.4% **13.** 12.25% **15.** 10.25% **17.** 11.25% **21. (a)** $59,840 **(b)** $83,966.60 **(c)** $9166.60 **(d)** 9.9% **23. (a)** 13.3% **(b)** 13% **25.** 10.00% **27. (a)** $18,800 **(b)** $26,240 **(c)** $5440 **(d)** 10.50% **29. (a)** 732,212.32 pesos **(b)** 13.75% **31. (a)** $97,689.60 **(b)** 10.75%

Section 11.3 Exercises (Page 489)

1. $8307.31; $307.31 **3.** $9198.18; $698.18 **5.** $9862.15; $507.15 **7.** $231 **9.** $103.18 **11.** $28.38 **15. (a)** $415.33 **(b)** $9315.33 **17. (a)** $69,936.02 **(b)** $2286.02 **19. (a)** $41,176.11 **(b)** $1876.11 **21. (a)** $17.31 **(b)** $457.69 **23. (a)** $1700 **(b)** $170 **(c)** $5980 **25. (a)** $87,716.70 **(b)** $10,916.70 **(c)** $4930.12 **(d)** $43,547.68

Section 11.4 Exercises (Page 497)

1. $1703.13 **3.** $404.73 **5.** $4185.60 **7.** $161.93 **9.** $147.61; $899.62 **11.** $321.96; $3454.08 **13.** $255.45; $3577 **17. (a)** $1900.70 **(b)** $13,628

19.

Payment Number	Amount of Payment	Interest for Period	Portion to Principal	Principal at End of Period
0	—		—	$4000.00
1	$1207.68	$320.00	$887.68	$3112.32
2	$1207.68	$248.99	$958.69	$2153.63
3	$1207.68	$172.29	$1035.39	$1118.24
4	$1207.70	$89.46	$1118.24	$0

21.

Payment Number	Amount of Payment	Interest for Period	Portion to Principal	Principal at End of Period
0	—	—	—	$14,500.00
1	$374.83	$132.92	$241.91	$14,258.09
2	$374.83	$130.70	$244.13	$14,013.96
3	$374.83	$128.46	$246.37	$13,767.59
4	$374.83	$126.20	$248.63	$13,518.96
5	$374.83	$123.92	$250.91	$13,268.05

23.

Payment Number	Amount of Payment	Interest for Period	Portion to Principal	Principal at End of Period
0	—	—	—	$35,000.00
1	$1196.30	$408.33	$787.97	$34,212.03
2	$1196.30	$399.14	$797.16	$33,414.87
3	$1196.30	$389.84	$806.46	$32,608.41
4	$1196.30	$380.43	$815.87	$31,792.54
5	$1196.30	$370.91	$825.39	$30,967.15

Section 11.5 Exercises (Page 507)

1. $2266.10 **3.** $1111.08 **5.** $599.68 **9.** $802.53 **11.** $523.87 **13.** $873.82 **15.** Yes, qualified

17. Monthly payment = 122.5 × $9.28 = $1136.80

Payment Number	Total Payment	Interest Payment	Principal Payment	Balance of Principal
0	—	—	—	$122,500.00
1	$1136.80	$765.63	$371.17	$122,128.83
2	$1136.80	$763.31	$373.49	$121,755.34

Summary Exercise (Page 513)

(a) $495.00; $419.94; $950.53; $149.45; $2014.97 **(b)** $2014.97; $215.00; $120.00; $210.83; $2560.80 **(c)** $392.32; $285.61; $695.83; $149.45; $187.00; $120.00; $210.83; $2041.04 **(d)** $519.76

Chapter 11 Test (Page 517)

1. $20,900 **2.** $932.56 **3.** 11.75% **4.** 12.25% **5.** 11% **6.** $4364.31 **7. (a)** $235.51 **(b)** $2502.17 **8.** $4811.72 **9.** $1924.50 **10.** $864.50 **11.** $1209.69 **12.** $629.48 **13. (a)** $6441.72 **(b)** $1,295,509.60 **14. (a)** $1398.24 **(b)** $360,577.60

Cumulative Review Chapters 10–11 (Page 519)

1. $9214.23; $1214.23 **3.** $17,855.03; $2855.03 **5.** $13,367.29 **7.** $403.45 **9. (a)** $11,957.94 **(b)** $27,257.87 **11. (a)** $2345 **(b)** 15 **(c)** 1.5% **13. (a)** $3098.48 **(b)** $298.48 **(c)** $2300 **(d)** 12.00% **15. (a)** $2118.14 **(b)** $3017.68 **17. (a)** $14,570 **(b)** $14,952.46 **19.** $13,327.06

Chapter 12

Section 12.1 Exercises (Page 529)

1. $34,000 **3.** $71,150 **5.** $325,125 **7.** 30.4% **9.** 8% **11.** 3% **13. (a)** $4.84 **(b)** $48.40 **(c)** 48.4 **15. (a)** 7.08% **(b)** $7.08 **(c)** 70.8 **19.** $5861.60 **21.** $5384.40 **23.** $5978.70 **25.** $6295.08 **27.** $39,960 **29. (a)** The second parish **(b)** $75.24

Section 12.2 Exercises (Page 543)

1. $23,131 **3.** $21,710 **5.** $44,533 **7.** $23,950; $3215 **9.** $18,551; $2027.65 **11.** $42,900; $5680 **13.** $22,510; $2999 **15.** $33,426; $4914 **17.** $116,400; $24,769.50 **19.** $1880.50 tax refund **21.** $598.06 tax refund **23.** $8274.50 due **27.** $9925 **29.** $14,270 **31.** $7462.75 **33.** $4328.05

Section 12.3 Exercises (Page 553)

1. $1700 **3.** $2194.50 **5.** $9298.72 **7.** $70,344.83 **9.** $19,850 **11.** $36,500 **13.** $60,000; $20,000 **15.** $292,500; $260,000; $97,500 **17.** $18,804 **19.** $702.65 **23. (a)** $136,986.30 **(b)** $43,013.70 **25. (a)** $30,681.82 **(b)** $14,318.18 **27. A:** $274,000 **B:** $182,666.67 **C:** $91,333.33 **29. 1:** $125,000 **2:** $41,666.67 **3:** $83,333.33 **31. (a)** $218,750 **(b) A:** $87,500; **B:** $131,250

Section 12.4 Exercises (Page 563)

1. $790 **3.** $932 **7.** $638 **9.** $657.80 **11. (a)** $25,000 **(b)** $11,500 **13. (a)** $4300 **(b)** $850 **15. (a)** $1778 **(b)** $6936 **(c)** $100,000 **(d)** $15,100

Section 12.5 Exercises (Page 573)

1. $256; $130.56; $66.56; $23.24 **3.** $849.10; $433.04; $220.77; $77.10 **5.** $516.80; $263.57; $134.37; $46.93 **7.** $319.50; $162.95; $83.07; $29.01 **9.** $2973.10; $1516.28; $773.01; $269.96 **13.** $512 **15. (a)** $100.50 **(b)** $384 **17.** $3036 **19. (a)** $444.72 **(b)** $226.72 **(c)** $79.18

Summary Exercise (Page 578)

(a) $11,790.75 **(b)** $39,940.40 **(c)** $439.88 **(d)** $52,171.03 **(e)** $1328.97

Chapter 12 Test (Page 579)

1. \$5.76; \$57.60 **2.** 9.35%; \$9.35 **3.** \$56,545; \$10,693.75 **4.** \$19,987; \$2243.05 **5.** \$1145.37 **6.** \$7572.40 **7.** \$4989.75 **8.** \$8449.14 **9.** \$42,613.64 **10. A:** \$36,000 **B:** \$21,600 **C:** \$14,400 **11.** \$1086.55 **12.** \$696 **13.** \$158.48; \$80.82; \$41.20; \$14.39 **14.** \$1940.80; \$989.81; \$504.61; \$176.22 **15. (a)** \$678 **(b)** \$417 **16.** \$6400 to repair his truck

Chapter 13

Section 13.1 Exercises (Page 587)

1. 20% **3.** 12.5% **5.** 5% **7.** $6\frac{2}{3}$% **9.** 1.25% **11.** 2% **13.** \$450 **15.** \$800 **17.** \$840 **19.** \$2850 **21.** \$5000 **23.** \$2775 **25.** \$73,000

27.

Year	Computation	Amount of Depreciation	Accumulated Depreciation	Book Value
0	—	—	—	\$12,000
1	($33\frac{1}{3}$% × \$9000)	\$3000	\$3000	\$9000
2	($33\frac{1}{3}$% × \$9000)	\$3000	\$6000	\$6000
3	($33\frac{1}{3}$% × \$9000)	\$3000	\$9000	\$3000

29.

Year	Computation	Amount of Depreciation	Accumulated Depreciation	Book Value
0	—	—	—	\$51,200
1	($16\frac{2}{3}$% × \$37,200)	\$6,200	\$6,200	\$45,000
2	($16\frac{2}{3}$% × \$37,200)	\$6,200	\$12,400	\$38,800
3	($16\frac{2}{3}$% × \$37,200)	\$6,200	\$18,600	\$32,600
4	($16\frac{2}{3}$% × \$37,200)	\$6,200	\$24,800	\$26,400
5	($16\frac{2}{3}$% × \$37,200)	\$6,200	\$31,000	\$20,200
6	($16\frac{2}{3}$% × \$37,200)	\$6,200	\$37,200	\$14,000

33. (a) \$55,000 depreciation **(b)** \$1,025,000 book value **35. (a)** 12.5% **(b)** \$9000 **(c)** \$79,000

Section 13.2 Exercises (Page 595)

1. 40% **3.** 25% **5.** $13\frac{1}{3}$% **7.** 20% **9.** $33\frac{1}{3}$% **11.** 4% **13.** \$3000 **15.** \$9000 **17.** \$1900 **19.** \$3360 **21.** \$1215 **23.** \$6834 **25.** \$750

27.

Year	Computation	Amount of Depreciation	Accumulated Depreciation	Book Value
0	—	—	—	\$14,400
1	(50% × \$14,400)	\$7200	\$7,200	\$7,200
2	(50% × \$7,200)	\$3600	\$10,800	\$3,600
3	(50% × \$3,600)	\$1800	\$12,600	\$1,800
4		\$1800*	\$14,400	\$0

*To depreciate to 0 scrap value.

29.

Year	Computation	Amount of Depreciation	Accumulated Depreciation	Book Value
0	—	—	—	\$14,000
1	(40% × \$14,000)	\$5600	\$5,600	\$8,400
2	(40% × \$8,400)	\$3360	\$8,960	\$5,040
3	(40% × \$5,040)	\$2016	\$10,976	\$3,024
4		\$524*	\$11,500	\$2,500
5		\$0	\$11,500	\$2,500

*To depreciate to \$2500 scrap value.

33. \$1153 **35.** \$8476 **37. (a)** 25% **(b)** \$1450 **(c)** \$4425 **(d)** \$1375

Section 13.3 Exercises (Page 603)

1. $\frac{4}{10}$ **3.** $\frac{6}{21}$ **5.** $\frac{7}{28}$ **7.** $\frac{10}{55}$ **9.** \$1640 **11.** \$10,000 **13.** \$7500 **15.** \$7700 **17.** \$2700 **19.** \$890 **21.** \$2400

23.

Year	Computation	Amount of Depreciation	Accumulated Depreciation	Book Value
0	—	—	—	\$3900
1	($\frac{3}{6}$ × \$3420)	\$1710	\$1710	\$2190
2	($\frac{2}{6}$ × \$3420)	\$1140	\$2850	\$1050
3	($\frac{1}{6}$ × \$3420)	\$570	\$3420	\$480

25.

Year	Computation	Amount of Depreciation	Accumulated Depreciation	Book Value
0	—	—	—	\$10,800
1	($\frac{6}{21}$ × \$8400)	\$2400	\$2400	\$8,400
2	($\frac{5}{21}$ × \$8400)	\$2000	\$4400	\$6,400
3	($\frac{4}{21}$ × \$8400)	\$1600	\$6000	\$4,800
4	($\frac{3}{21}$ × \$8400)	\$1200	\$7200	\$3,600
5	($\frac{2}{21}$ × \$8400)	\$800	\$8000	\$2,800
6	($\frac{1}{21}$ × \$8400)	\$400	\$8400	\$2,400

29. \$3000 depreciation **31.** \$4887 **33. (a)** \$7200 **(b)** \$6000 **35. (a)** $\frac{8}{36}$ **(b)** \$2360 **(c)** \$10,620 **(d)** \$4750

Supplementary Exercise (Page 607)

1. \$2,050,000 **3.** \$7400 **5.** \$1242 **7.** \$3760 **9.** \$63,180 **11.** \$13,680; \$10,260; \$6840; \$3420 **13.** \$37,575 **15.** \$10,080 **17. (a)** \$5580 **(b)** \$5220

Section 13.4 Exercises (Page 615)

1. \$.75 **3.** \$.029 **5.** \$.24 **7.** \$30 **9.** \$25,300 **11.** \$17,280 **13.** \$2775 **15.** \$3108

19.

Year	Computation	Amount of Depreciation	Accumulated Depreciation	Book Value
0	—	—	—	\$6800
1	(1350 × \$1.26)	\$1701	\$1701	\$5099
2	(1820 × \$1.26)	\$2293	\$3994	\$2806
3	(730 × \$1.26)	\$920	\$4914	\$1886
4	(1100 × \$1.26)	\$1386	\$6300	\$500

Section 13.5 Exercises (Page 623)

1. 19.2% **3.** 6.56% **5.** 20% **7.** 3.636% **9.** 5.76% **11.** 2.564% **13.** \$1751 **15.** \$43,050 **17.** \$4800 **19.** \$6254 **21.** \$16,920 **23.** \$2756 **25.** \$122,084

27.

Year	Computation	Amount of Depreciation	Accumulated Depreciation	Book Value
0	—	—	—	\$10,980
1	(33.33% × \$10,980)	\$3660	\$3,660	\$7,320
2	(44.45% × \$10,980)	\$4881	\$8,541	\$2,439
3	(14.81% × \$10,980)	\$1626	\$10,167	\$813
4	(7.41% × \$10,980)	\$813*	\$10,980	\$0

*due to rounding in prior years

29.

Year	Computation	Amount of Depreciation	Accumulated Depreciation	Book Value
0	—	—	—	$122,700
1	(10% × $122,700)	$12,270	$12,270	$110,430
2	(18% × $122,700)	$22,086	$34,356	$88,344
3	(14.4% × $122,700)	$17,669	$52,025	$70,675
4	(11.52% × $122,700)	$14,135	$66,160	$56,540
5	(9.22% × $122,700)	$11,313	$77,473	$45,227
6	(7.37% × $122,700)	$9,043	$86,516	$36,184
7	(6.55% × $122,700)	$8,037	$94,553	$28,147
8	(6.55% × $122,700)	$8,037	$102,590	$20,110
9	(6.56% × $122,700)	$8,049	$110,639	$12,061
10	(6.55% × $122,700)	$8,037	$118,676	$4,024
11	(3.28% × $122,700)	$4,024*	$122,700	$0

*due to rounding in prior years

33. $4855 **35.** $490 **37. Year 1:** $21,165; **Years 2–5:** $22,050

Summary Exercise (Page 629)

(a) $114,000 **(b)** $61,560 **(c)** $228,000 **(d)** $57,000 straight-line; $24,624 double-declining-balance, $38,000 sum-of-the-years'-digits

Chapter 13 Test (Page 631)

1. 25%; 50%; $\frac{4}{10}$ **2.** 20%; 40%; $\frac{5}{15}$ **3.** $12\frac{1}{2}$%; 25%; $\frac{8}{36}$ **4.** 5%; 10%; $\frac{20}{210}$ **5.** $940 **6.** $21,375 **7. Year 1:** $2700; **Year 2:** $2025; **Year 3:** $1350; **Year 4:** $675 **8.** $4788 **9.** $43,000 **10.** $5702 **11. (a)** Year 1: $4836; Year 2: $2666; Year 3: $3007; Year 4: $4712 **(b)** Year 1: $15,264; Year 2: $12,598; Year 3: $9591; Year 4: $4879 **12.** $2,443,924

Chapter 14

Section 14.1 Exercises (Page 637)

1. (a) $316,350 **(b)** $88,050 **(c)** $65,350 **3.** Gross Sales, $852,300; Returns, $42,800; Net Sales, $809,500; Inventory, January 1, $174,690; Cost of Goods Purchased, $345,790; Freight, $18,107; Total Cost of Goods Purchased, $363,897; Total of Goods Available for Sale, $538,587; Inventory, December 31, $158,200; Cost of Goods Sold, $380,387; Gross Profit, $429,113; Salaries and Wages, $168,240; Rent, $48,200; Advertising, $24,300; Utilities, $11,600; Taxes on Inventory, Payroll, $13,880; Miscellaneous Expenses, $21,900; Total Expenses, $288,120; Net Income before Taxes, $140,993; Income Taxes, $34,800; Net Income, $106,193

Section 14.2 Exercises (Page 643)

1. 45.2%; 32.6% **3.** 50.7%; 29.2% **5.** Cost of Goods Sold, 67.1%, 67.9%; Gross Profit, 32.9%, 32.1%; Wages, 12.5%, 12.3%; Rent, 2.5%, 2.4%; Advertising, 1.5%, 1.4%; Total Expenses, 24.6%, 23.5%; Net Income before Taxes, 8.3%, 8.6% **9.** Gross Sales, 100.3%, 100.7%; Returns, .3%, .7%; Net Sales, $1,850,000, $1,680,000; Cost of Goods Sold, 59.6%, 56.5%; Gross Profit, 40.4%, 43.4%; Wages, 13.6%, 14.8%; Rent, 4.4%, 4.6%; Advertising, 6.0%, 7.3%; Utilities, 1.7%, 1.0%; Taxes on Inv., Payroll, .9%, 1.1%; Miscellaneous Expenses, 3.4%, 3.5%; Total Expenses, 30.1%, 32.2%; Net Income before Taxes, $192,000, 10.4%, $189,000, 11.3% **11.** 64.8%, 35.2%, 23.4%, 11.7%, 7.9%, 4.9%, 1.8%

Section 14.3 Exercises (Page 649)

1. Cash, $273; Notes Receivable, $312; Accounts Receivable, $264; Inventory, $180; Total Current Assets, $1029; Land, $466; Buildings, $290; Fixtures, $28; Total Plant Assets, $784; Total Assets, $1813; Notes Payable, $312; Accounts Payable, $63; Total Current Liabilities, $375; Mortgages Payable, $212; Long-Term Notes Payable, $55; Total Long-Term Liabilities, $267; Total Liabilities, $642; Owners' Equity, $1171; Total Liabilities and Owners' Equity, $1813

Section 14.4 Exercises (Page 655)

1. Cash, 13%, 13.1%; Notes Receivable, 2%, 1.9%; Accounts Receivable, 37%, 37.5%; Inventory, 38.3%, 37.5%; Total Current Assets, $361,000, 90.3%, $288,000, 90%; Land, 2.5%, 2.5%; Buildings, 3.5%, 3.4%; Fixtures, 3.8%, 4.1%; Total Plant Assets, $39,000, 9.8%, $32,000, 10%; Total Assets, $400,000, $320,000; Accounts Payable, .8%, 1.3%; Notes Payable, 50.3%, 47.5%; Total Current Liabilities, $204,000, 51%, $156,000, 48.8%; Mortgages Payable, 5%, 5%; Long-Term Notes Payable, 14.5%, 13.1%; Total Long-Term Liabilities, $78,000, 19.5%, $58,000, 18.1%; Total Liabilities, $282,000, 70.5%, $214,000, 66.9%; Owners' Equity, 29.5%, 33.1%; Total Liabilities and Owners' Equity, $400,000, 100%, $320,000, 100% **3. (a)** 1.77 **(b)** 1.02 **(c)** No, current ratio is low **5. (a)** 1.79 **(b)** .62 **(c)** No, acid-test ratio is low **7.** 2.13; 1.27 **9.** 6.1% **11.** .91; .37; not healthy; very low liquidity

Summary Exercise (Page 662)

(a) Gross Sales, $212,000; Returns, $12,500; Net Sales, $199,500; Inventory, January 1, $44,000; Cost of Goods Purchased, $75,000; Freight, $8,000; Total Cost of Goods Purchased, $83,000; Total of Goods Available for Sale, $127,000; Inventory, December 31, $26,000; Cost of Goods Sold, $101,000; Gross Profit, $98,500; Salaries and Wages, $37,000; Rent, $12,000; Advertising, $2,000; Utilities, $3,000; Taxes on Inventory, Payroll, $7,000; Miscellaneous Expenses, $4,500; Total Expenses, $65,500; Net Income before Taxes, $33,000; Income Taxes, $4,320; Net Income after Taxes, $28,680 **(b)** Gross Sales, 106.3% (rounded); Returns, 6.3%; Cost of Goods Sold, 50.6%; Salaries and Wages, 18.5%; Rent, 6%; Utilities, 1.5% **(c)** Cash, $62,000; Notes Receivable, $2,500; Accounts Receivable, $8,200; Inventory, $26,000; Total Current Assets, $98,700; Land, $7,600; Buildings and Improvements, $41,500; Total Plant Assets, $49,100; Total Assets, $147,800; Notes Payable, $4,500; Accounts Payable $27,000; Total Current Liabilities, $31,500; Mortgages Payable, $15,000; Long-Term Notes Payable, $8,000; Total Long-Term Liabilities, $23,000; Total Liabilities, $54,500; Owners' Equity, $93,300; Total Liability and Owners' Equity, $147,800 **(d)** 3.13; 2.31

Chapter 14 Test (Page 665)

1. Gross Sales, $756,300; Returns, $285; Net Sales, $756,015; Inventory, January 1, $92,370; Cost of Goods Purchased, $465,920; Freight, $1,205; Total Cost of Goods Purchased, $467,125; Total of Goods Available for Sale, $559,495; Inventory, December 31, $82,350; Cost of Goods Sold, $477,145; Gross Profit, $278,870; Salaries and Wages, $84,900; Rent, $42,500; Advertising, $2,800; Utilities, $18,950; Taxes on Inventory and Payroll, $4,500; Miscellaneous Expenses, $18,400; Total Expenses, $172,050; Net Income Before Taxes, $106,820; Income Taxes, $25,450; Net Income After Taxes, $81,370 **2.** Net Sales, $35,000, 58.3%; Cost of Goods Sold, $23,000, 57.5%; Gross Profit, $4,000, 33.3% **3.** Cost of Goods Sold, $875, 72.9%, 76.8%; Gross Profit, 27.1%, 23.2%; Net Income, 9.3%, 6.3%; Wages, 10.8%, 8.5%; Rent, 6%, 2.3%; Total Expenses, 17.8%, 16.9% **4. (a)** 1.38 **(b)** .85 **5. (a)** 1.05 **(b)** .37 **6.** 30.0% **7.** 26.1%

Chapter 15

Section 15.1 Exercises (Page 673)

1. 2100; 9.1 billion **3.** 2.136 billion Chinese; .356 billion Americans **5.** It is increasing. **7.** 4 **9.** 6 **11.** 5

13.

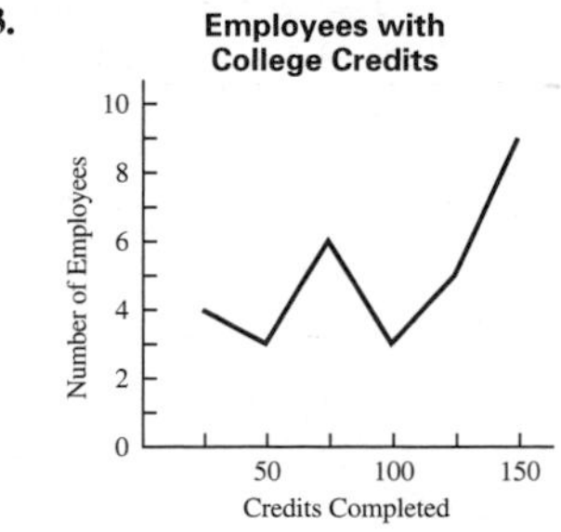

15. 23 **17.** 7 **19.** 2 **21.** 1 **23.** 2 **25.** 6

27.

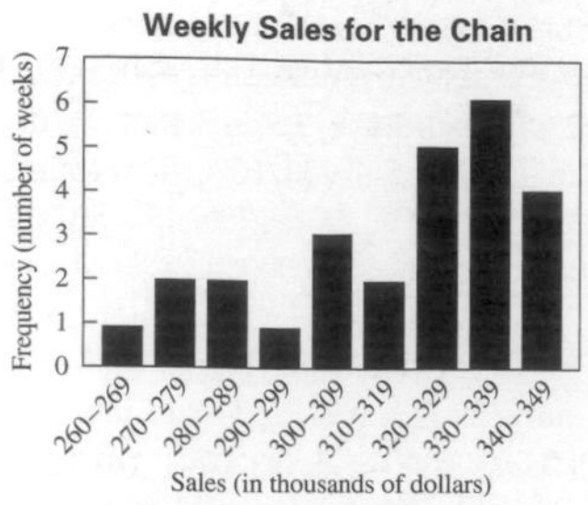

29. 20 **31.** 1 **33.** 13 **35.** 17 **37.** 8 **39.** 38 **41.** 42 **43.** 20% **45.** 36° **47.** 5%, 18°

49.

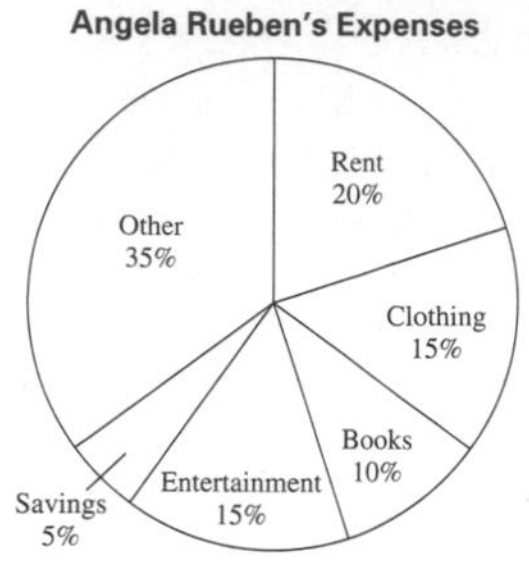

51. 20%

53.

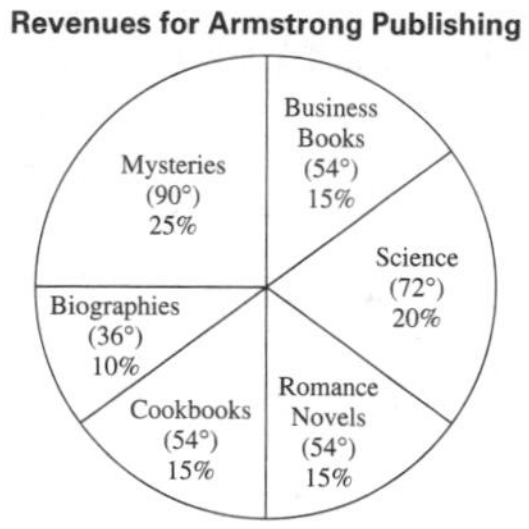

55.

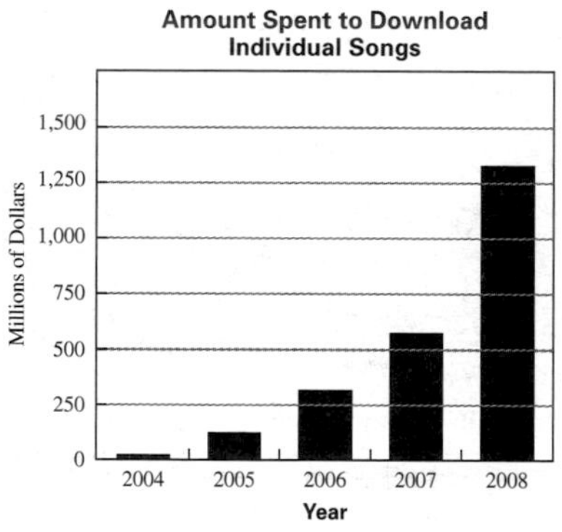

Section 15.2 Exercises (Page 683)

1. 2.5 **3.** 60.3 **5.** 27,955 **7.** 8.8 **11.** 12.3 **13.** 17.2 **15.** 118.8 **17.** 2.6 **19.** 114 **21.** 130 **23.** 44 **25.** 21% **27.** 64 **29.** Bimodal with modes 32 and 38 **31.** 34.11 **33.** 34.38

Summary Exercise (Page 689)

(a) Store 1 mean = \$7.4; Store 2 mean = \$8.2; Store 1 median = \$7.5; Store 2 median = \$8.2; Store 1 has no mode; Store 2 mode = \$8.2

(b)

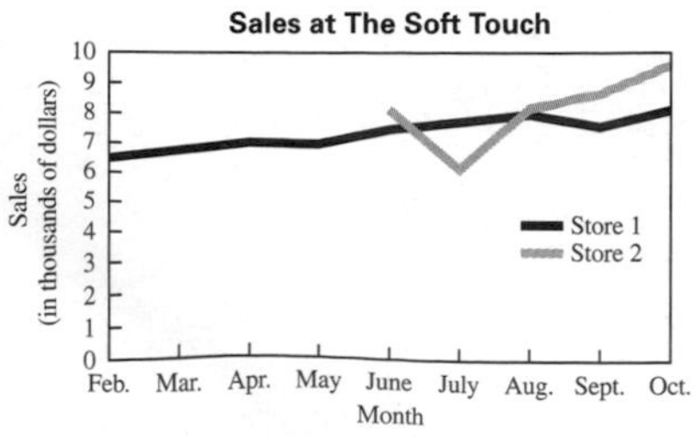

(c) Sales at Store 2 are growing faster than at Store 1.

Chapter 15 Test (Page 691)

1. 1, 3, 10, 3, 2, 1 **2.** 6

3.

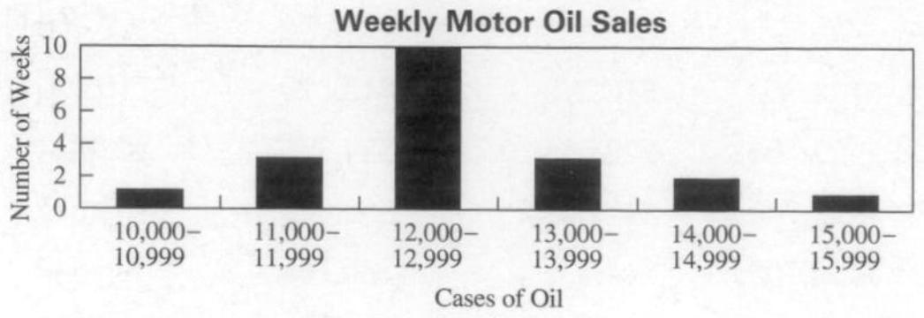

4. Newsprint, 72°; Ink, 10%; Wire Service, 108°; Salaries, 108°; Other, 36°

5.

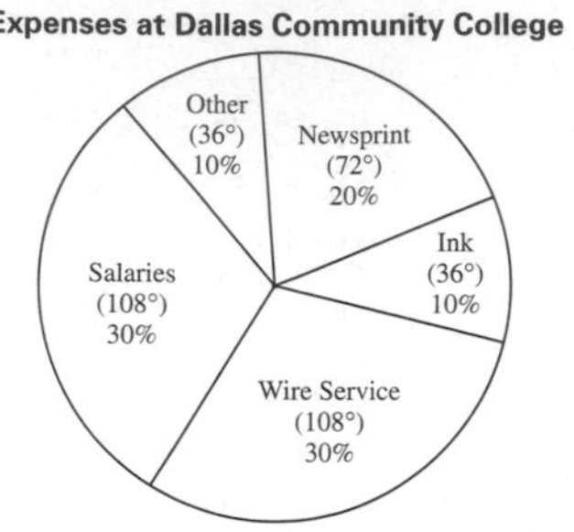

6. 60% **7.** 230.7 **8.** 18.8 centimeters **9.** \$478.90 **10.** 11.3 **11.** 173.7 **12.** 19 **13.** 41.5 **14.** 8.3 **15.** 54.5 **16.** 47 **17.** No mode **18.** bimodal, 103 and 104

19.

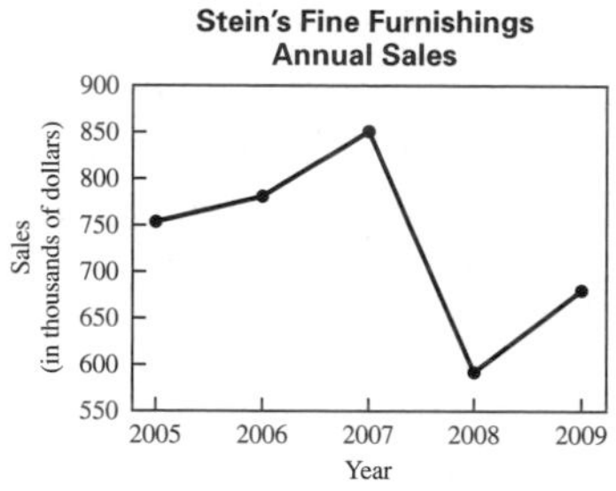

It appears that the recession had an effect on the business.

20.

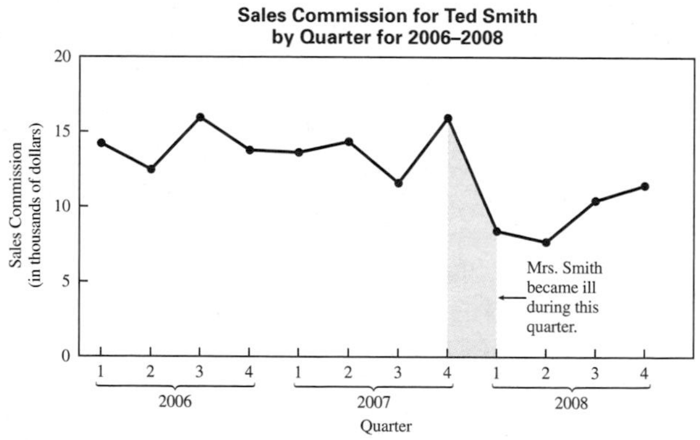

It appears that Mr. Smith's work was affected.

Appendices

Appendix A Exercises (Page A–21)

1. 3 **3.** 31 **5.** 3 **7.** 7 **9.** 2 **11.** 30 **13.** 7.5 **15.** 10 **17.** 4 **19.** $\frac{3}{2}$ or 1.5 **21.** 7 **23.** 1 **25.** $I = 504$ **27.** $G = 3183.6$ **29.** $R = .05$ **31.** $D = 200$ **33.** $d = .84$ **35.** $\frac{A}{L}$ **37.** $\frac{I}{PR}$ **39.** $\frac{A-P}{PR}$ **41.** $\frac{1}{5}$ **43.** $\frac{8}{5}$ **45.** $\frac{7}{12}$ **47.** true **49.** false **51.** true **53.** 175 **55.** 5 **57.** 8 **59.** $\frac{7}{2}$ **61.** 12 **63.** 60 **65.** 15 **67.** 45; 46 **69.** $1.74 **71.** $2056 **73.** $12 **75.** $16

Appendix B Exercises (Page B–5)

1. .68 m **3.** 4700 mm **5.** 8900 g **7.** .39 L **9.** 46 kg **11.** 976 g **13.** 39.2 yards **15.** 50.3 m **17.** 15.4 feet **19.** 1.1 m **21.** 307.5 miles **23.** 1235.7 km **25.** 1.5 pounds **27.** 1861.4 g **29.** 85.6 pounds **31.** 200 nickels **33.** .6 g **37.** 40°C **39.** 280°C **41.** 37°C **43.** 95°F **45.** 50°F **47.** 275°F **49.** Not reasonable **51.** Not reasonable

Appendix C Exercises (Page C–9)

1. 1171.60 **3.** 11,378 **5.** 3905.32 **7.** 255.24 **9.** 15,695 **11.** 31.08 **13.** 35.42 **15.** 27.63 **17.** 8.1 **19.** 566.1397059 = 566.14 (rounded) **21.** .625 = .63 (rounded) **23.** 30.57004831 = 30.57 (rounded) **25.** 0.915966387 = .92 (rounded) **27.** $5\frac{6}{11}$ **29.** .493714286 = .49 (rounded) **33.** $44,162.80 **35.** **(a)** $1164.05 rounded **(b)** $95.13 rounded **37.** $214,008 **39.** $13,400 **41.** 59%

Appendix D Exercises (Page D–7)

1. $39,019.50 **3.** $8929.13 **5.** $2676.84 **7.** 1.5% **9.** $858.89 **11.** 24 **13.** FV = $31,651.09 **15.** PMT = $696 **17.** $n = 26$ **19.** $i = 8.5\%$

Glossary

401 (k): A retirement plan for individuals working for private-sector companies.

403 (b): A retirement plan for employees of public schools and certain tax-exempt organizations.

A

Absolute, or gross, loss: The loss resulting when the selling price is less than the cost.

Accelerated depreciation: A technique to increase the depreciation taken during the early years of an asset's useful life.

Accelerated mortgages: Mortgages with payoffs of less than 30 years, such as 15, 20, or 25 years.

Accountant: A person who maintains financial data for a firm or individual and then prepares the income tax return.

Accounts payable: A business debt that must be paid.

Accumulated depreciation: A running balance or total of the depreciation to date on an asset.

Acid-test ratio: The sum of cash, notes receivable, and accounts receivable, divided by current liabilities.

ACRS (Accelerated cost recovery system): A depreciation method introduced as part of the Economic Recovery Tax Act of 1981.

Actual rate of interest: The true annual percentage rate that can be used to compare loans.

Actuary: A person who determines insurance premiums.

Addends: The numbers added in an addition problem.

Addition rule: The same number may be added or subtracted on both sides of an equation.

Adjustable rate mortgage: A home loan where the interest rate is adjusted up or down depending on a benchmark interest rate.

Adjusted bank balance: The actual current balance of a checking account after reconciliation.

Adjusted gross income: An individual's or family's income for a year, including all sources of income, and after subtracting certain expenses, such as moving expenses and sick pay.

Algebraic logic: Rules used by most calculators for entering and evaluating arithmetic expressions.

Allowances: The number of allowances claimed by a taxpayer affects the amount withheld for income taxes.

American Express: A widely accepted credit card that requires an annual fee.

Amortization table: A table showing the level (unchanging) payment necessary to pay in full a loan for a specific amount of money including interest over a specific length of time.

Amortize: The process of paying off a loan with a sequence of periodic payments over a period of time.

Amount of an annuity: The future value of the annuity.

Amount of depreciation: The dollar amount of depreciation taken. This is usually an annual figure.

Annual meeting: Corporations have annual meetings for stockholders.

Annual percentage rate (APR): The true annual percentage rate which can be used to compare loans. The federal Truth-in-Lending Act requires lenders to state the APR.

Annual percentage rate table: A table used to find the annual percentage rate (APR) on a loan or installment purchase.

Annual rate of depreciation: The percent or fraction of the depreciable amount or declining balance to be depreciated each individual year of an asset's useful life.

Annuity: Periodic payments of a given, fixed amount of money.

Annuity due: An annuity whose payments are made at the beginning of a time period.

APR (Annual percentage rate): The true annual percentage rate that can be used to compare loans. It is required by the federal Truth-in-Lending Act.

"AS OF": A later date that appears on an invoice. The given sales terms may start at this time.

Assessed value: The value of a piece of property. Set by the county assessor, assessed value is used in figuring property taxes.

Assessment rate: The assessed valuation of a property is found by multiplying the fair market value by the assessment rate.

Asset: An item of value owned by a firm.

ATM (Automated teller machine): A machine that allows bank customers to make deposits, withdrawals, and fund transfers.

Automatic savings transfer account: A bank account that automatically transfers funds from one account to another.

Average: *See* mean.

Average cost method: An inventory valuation method whereby the cost of all purchases during a time period is divided by the number of units purchased.

Average daily balance method: A method used to calculate interest on open-end credit accounts.

Average inventory: The sum of all inventories taken divided by the number of times inventory was taken.

Average owner's equity: Sum of owner's equity at the beginning and end of the year divided by 2.

B

Bad checks: A check that is not honored because there are insufficient funds in the checking account.

Balance brought forward (Current balance): The amount left in a checking account after previous checks written have been subtracted.

Balanced: In agreement. When the bank statement amount and the depositor's checkbook balance agree, they are balanced.

Balance sheet: A summary of the financial condition of a firm at one point in time.

Bank discount: A bank fee charged on a note. It is subtracted from the face value to find the proceeds loaned.

Banker's interest: A method used to calculate interest by dividing exact days by 360.

Banker's ratio: *See* current ratio.

Bank statement: A monthly statement prepared by a bank that lists all charges and deposits to a checking account. Historically banks mailed the statements, but many people now look at their monthly statements on the web.

Bankrupt: A company or individual whose liabilities exceed assets can declare bankruptcy, which is a legal process of working with debtors to pay off debts.

Bar graph: A graph using bars to compare various numbers.

Base: The starting point or reference point or that to which something is being compared.

bbl.: Abbreviation for *barrel.*

Bimodal: A set of data with two modes.

Blank endorsement: A signature on the back of a check by the person to whom the check is made.

Board of directors: A group of people who represent the stockholders of a corporation.

Bodily injury insurance: A type of automobile insurance that protects a driver in case he or she injures someone with a car.

Bond: A contractual promise by a corporation, government entity, or church to repay borrowed money at a specified rate and time.

Book value: The cost of an asset minus depreciation to date.

Break-even point: The cost of an item plus the operating expenses associated with the item. Above this amount a profit is made; below it, a loss is incurred.

Broker: A person who sells stocks, bonds, and other investments owned by others.

Business account: The type of checking account used by businesses.

bx.: Abbreviation for *box.*

C

C: Roman numeral for 100.

Canceled check: A check is canceled after the amount of the check has been transferred from the payer's bank account into the account of the receiver of the check.

Cancellation: A process used to simplify multiplication and division of fractions.

Capital: The amount of money originally invested in a firm. The difference between the total of all the assets and the total of all the liabilities is called the capital or net worth.

Capital gains: Profits made on investments such as stocks or real estate.

cart.: Abbreviation for *carton.*

Cash discount: A discount offered by the seller allowing the buyer to take a discount if payment is made within a specified period of time.

Cashier's check: A check written by a financial institution, such as a bank, that is guaranteed by the institution.

Cash value: Money that has built up in an ordinary life insurance policy.

Casualty or theft loss: Loss due to a casualty (e.g., fire) or theft that is deductible on a personal income tax return.

Centi-: A prefix used in the metric system meaning hundredth. (For example, a centiliter is one one-hundredth of a liter.)

Centimeter: One one-hundredth of a meter. There are 2.54 centimeters to an inch.

Central tendency: The middle of a set of data.

Certificate of deposit (CD): A savings account in which a minimum amount of money must be deposited and left for a minimum period of time.

Chain calculations: Long calculations done on a calculator.

Chain discount: Two or more discounts that are combined into one discount.

Check 21 Act: A federal law that took effect in October 2004 and allows banks to take electronic photos of all cancelled checks and exchange checks electronically, so the banks no longer have to mail cancelled checks.

Check register: A table usually found in a checkbook that is used by the check writer to list all checks written, deposits and withdrawals made, and ATM transactions.

Checks outstanding: Checks written that have not reached and cleared the bank as of the statement date.

Check stub: A stub attached to the check and retained as a record of checks written.

Circle graph: A circle divided into parts that are labeled and often colored or shaded to show data.

COD: A method of shipping goods that requires cash on delivery of goods.

Coinsurance: The portion of a loss that must be paid by the insured.

Collateral: Assets foreclosed on by a lender should the borrower default on payments.

Collision insurance: A form of automobile insurance that pays for car repairs in case of an accident.

Commission: A fee charged by a broker for buying and selling either stocks or bonds.

Commissions: Payments to an employee that represent a certain percent of the total sales produced by the employee's efforts.

Common denominator: Two or more fractions with the same denominator are said to have common denominators.

Common stock: Ownership of a corporation, held in portions called shares.

Comparative balance sheet: An analysis for two or more periods that compares asset categories such as cash.

Comparative income statement: A vertical analysis for two or more years that compares incomes or balance sheet items for each year analyzed.

Comparison graph (Comparative line graph): One graph that shows how several things relate.

Compensatory time (Comp time): Time off given to an employee to compensate for previously worked overtime.

Compound amount: The future value of an investment.

Compounding period: The interval of time at which interest is added to the account. For example, interest compounded quarterly results in interest being added to the account every quarter.

Compound interest: Interest charged or received on both principal and interest.

Comprehensive insurance: A form of automobile insurance that pays for damage to a car caused by fire, theft, vandalism, and weather.

Consolidated statement: A financial statement showing the combined results of all subsidiaries of a firm.

Consumer price index (CPI): A measure of the cost of living calculated by the government and used to estimate inflation.

Conventional loan: A loan made by a bank, savings and loan, or other lending agency that is not guaranteed or insured by the federal government.

Corporation: A form of business that gives the owners limited liability.

Cost: The total cost of an item, including shipping, insurance, and other charges. Most often, the cost is the basis for calculating depreciation of an asset.

Cost (Cost price): The price paid to the manufacturer or supplier after trade and cash discounts have been taken. This price includes transportation and insurance charges.

Cost of goods sold: The amount paid by a firm for the goods it sold during the time period covered by an income statement.

Cost of living index: A measure of the cost of living calculated by the government and used to estimate inflation. It is the same as the consumer price index or CPI.

Country club billing method: A billing method that provides copies of original charge receipts to the customer.

cpm.: Abbreviation for *cost per thousand*.

Credit card (transactions): The purchase or sale of goods or services using a credit card in place of cash or a check.

Credit score: Three national credit-reporting agencies (Equifax, TransUnion, and Experian) keep financial records on U.S. citizens and calculate a credit score on each indicating the credit-worthiness of that individual. Also called a FICO score.

Credit union: A financial institution similar to a bank, except that it is owned by its member customers.

Credit union share draft account: A credit union account that may be used as a checking account.

Cross-products: The equal products obtained when each numerator of a proportion is multiplied by the opposite denominator.

cs.: Abbreviation for *case*.

ct.: Abbreviation for *crate*.

ctn. Abbreviation for *carton*.

Current assets: Cash or items that can be converted into cash within a given period of time, such as a year.

Current liability: Debts that must be paid by a firm within a given period of time, such as a year.

Current ratio: The quotient of current assets and current liabilities.

Current yield: The annual dividend per share of stock divided by the current price per share.

cwt.: Abbreviation for *per hundredweight* or *per one hundred pounds*.

D

Daily interest charge: The amount of interest charged per day on a loan.

Daily overtime: The amount of overtime worked in a day.

Debit card: A card that results in a debit to a bank account when the card is used for a purchase.

Decimal: A number written with a decimal point, such as 4.3 or 7.22.

Decimal equivalent: A decimal that has the same value as a fraction.

Decimal point: The starting point in the decimal system (.).

Decimal system: The numbering system based on powers of 10 and using the 10 one-place numbers 0, 1, 2, 3, 4, 5, 6, 7, 8, and 9, which are called *digits*.

Declining-balance depreciation: An accelerated depreciation method.

(200%) Declining-balance method: An accelerated method of depreciation using twice, or 200% of, the straight-line rate.

Decrease problem (Difference problem): A percentage problem in which something is taken away from the base. It may require you to find the base.

Decreasing term insurance: A form of life insurance in which the insured pays a fixed premium until age 60 or 65, with the amount of life insurance decreasing periodically.

Deductible: An amount paid by the insured, with the balance of the loss paid by the insurance company.

Deductions: Amounts that are subtracted from the gross earnings of an employee to arrive at the amount of money the employee actually receives.

Defaulting on debt: Failure to pay back a debt.

Dependents: An extra deduction is allowed on income taxes for each dependent.

Deposits in transit: Deposits that have been made but have not yet been recorded by a bank.

Deposit slip: A slip for listing all currency and checks that are part of a deposit into a bank account.

Denominator: The number below the line in a fraction. For example, in the fraction $\frac{7}{9}$, 9 is the denominator.

Depreciable amount: The amount of an asset's value that can be depreciated.

Depreciation: The decrease in value of an asset caused by normal use, aging, or obsolescence.

Depreciation schedule: A schedule or table showing the depreciation rate, amount of depreciation, book value, and accumulated depreciation for each year of an asset's life.

Difference (Remainder): The answer in a subtraction problem.

Differential piece rate: A rate paid per item that depends on the number of items produced.

Digits: One-place numbers in the decimal system. They are 0, 1, 2, 3, 4, 5, 6, 7, 8, and 9.

Disability coverage: Insurance coverage in the event of a disability.

Discount: (1) To reduce the price of an item. (2) The amount subtracted from the face value of a note to find the proceeds loaned.

Discount broker: A stockbroker who charges a reduced fee to customers (and, generally, reduced services).

Discount date: The last date on which a cash discount may be taken.

Discounting a note: Cashing or selling a note at a bank before the note is due from the maker.

Discount method of interest: A method of calculating interest on a loan by subtracting the interest from the amount of the loan. The borrower receives the amount borrowed less the discounted interest.

Discount period: The discount period is the period from the time of sale of a note to the note's due date.

Discount rate: The discount rate is a percent that is multiplied by the face value and time to find bank discount.

Discover: A credit card that sometimes pays the card holder back a percentage of the amount charged.

Distributive property: The property that states the product of the sum of two numbers equals the sum of the individual products; that is $a(b + c) = ab + ac$.

Dividend: (1) The number being divided by another number in a division problem. (2) A return on an investment; money paid by a company to the holders of stock.

Divisor: The number doing the dividing in a division problem.

Double-declining balance: A method of accelerated depreciation that doubles depreciation in the early years compared to straight-line depreciation.

Double time: Twice the regular hourly rate. A premium often paid for working holidays and Sunday.

Dow Jones Industrial Average: A frequently quoted average price of the stocks of 30 large industrial companies.

doz.: Abbreviation for *dozen.*

Draw: A draw is an advance on future earnings.

Drawing account: An account from which a salesperson can receive payment against future commissions.

drm.: Abbreviation for *drum.*

E

ea.: Abbreviation for *each.*

Effective rate: The true rate of interest.

Effective rate of interest: The true annual percentage rate that can be used to compare loans. It is required by the federal Truth-in-Lending Act.

Electronic banking: Banking activities that take place over a network, such as the World Wide Web.

Electronic commerce: Purchases that take place over a network, such as the World Wide Web.

Electronic funds transfer: Moving money electronically over a network, such as the World Wide Web.

End-of-month dating (EOM): A system of cash discounts in which the time period begins at the end of the month the invoice is dated. *Proximo* and *prox.* have the same meaning.

Endowment policy: A life insurance policy guaranteeing the payment of a fixed amount of money to a given individual whether or not the insured person lives.

Equation: Two algebraic expressions that are equal to one another.

Escrow account into which monies are paid: *See* impound account.

Exact interest: A method of calculating interest based on 365 days per year.

Exchange traded funds (ETFs): These funds are similar to mutual funds except they are not as actively managed. A particular ETF tries to match the performance of an index such as the Dow Jones Averages or perhaps a market sector such as energy.

Executive officers: The top few officers in a corporation.

Expenses: The costs a firm must pay to operate and sell its goods or services.

Extension total: The number of items purchased times the price per unit.

Extra dating (ex., x): Extra time allowed in determining the net payment date of a cash discount.

F

Face value: The amount shown on the face of a note.

Face value of a bond (Par value of a bond): The amount the company has promised to repay.

Face value of a policy: The amount of insurance provided by the insurance company.

Factoring: The process of selling accounts receivable for cash.

Factors: Companies that buy accounts receivable.

Fair Labor Standards Act: A federal law that sets the minimum wage and also a 40-hour workweek.

Fair market value: The price for which a piece of property could reasonably be expected to be sold in the market.

FAS (Free alongside ship): A method of shipping goods in which the seller of goods pays for transportation of the goods to the port from which they will be shipped. The buyer of the goods must pay for all costs in moving the goods from the shipping port to his facility.

Federal Insurance Contributions Act (FICA): An emergency measure passed by Congress in the 1930s that established the so-called social security tax. *See* FICA tax.

Federal Reserve Bank: Today, all banks are part of the Federal Reserve system. The Federal Reserve is our national bank.

Federal Truth-in-Lending Act: An act passed in 1969 that requires all interest rates to be given as comparable percents.

Federal Unemployment Tax Act (FUTA): An unemployment insurance tax paid entirely by employers to the federal government for administrative costs of federal and state unemployment programs.

FHA loan: A real estate loan that is insured by the Federal Housing Administration, an agency of the federal government.

FICA tax (Social Security tax): The amount of money deducted from the paychecks of almost all employees, used by the federal government to pay pensions to retired people, survivors' benefits, and disability.

FICO: Three national credit-reporting agencies (Equifax, TransUnion, and Experian) keep financial records on U.S. citizens and calculate a credit score on each indicating the creditworthiness of that individual. Also called a credit score.

FIFO: A method of inventory accounting in which the first items received are considered to be the first ones shipped.

Finance charge: The difference between the cost of something paid for in installments and the cash price.

Financial ratio: A number found using financial data that is used to compare different companies within the same industry.

Fixed assets: Assets owned by a firm that will not be converted to cash within a year.

Fixed liabilities: Items that will not be paid off within a year.

Fixed-rate loan: A loan made at a fixed, stated rate of interest.

Flat-fee checking account: A checking account in which the bank supplies check printing, a bank charge card, and other services for a fixed charge per month.

Floating decimal: A feature on most calculators that positions the decimal point where it should be in the final answer.

FOB (Free on board): A notation sometimes used on an invoice. "Free on board shipping point" means the buyer pays for shipping. "Free on board destination" means the seller pays for shipping.

Foreclose: The process by which a lender takes back the property when payments are not made.

Form 941: The Employer's Quarterly Federal Tax Return form that must be filed by the employer with the Internal Revenue Service.

Form 1040A: The form used by most federal income tax payers.

Form 1040EZ: A simplified version of the 1040A federal income tax form.

Fraction: An indication of a part of a whole. (For example, $\frac{3}{4}$ means that the whole is divided into 4 parts, of which 3 are being considered.)

Frequency distribution table: A table showing the number of times one or more events occur.

Fringe benefits: Benefits offered by an employer, not including salary, that can include medical, dental, life insurance, and day care for employee's children.

Front-end rounding: Rounding so that all digits are changed to zero except the first digit.

Future amount: The value of an investment at a future date. It is the same as future value.

Future value: The value, at some future date, of an investment.

G

GI (VA) loan: A loan guaranteed by the Veterans Administration and available only to qualified veterans.

Grace period: The period between the due date of a payment and the time the lending institution assesses a penalty for the payment being late, usually a few days after the payment is due.

Gram: The unit of weight in the metric system. (A nickel weighs about 5 grams.)

Graph: A visual presentation of numerical data.

Gr. gro. (Great gross): Abbreviation for 12 gross ($144 \times 12 = 1728$).

Gro.: Abbreviation for *gross*.

gross: A dozen dozen, or 144 items.

Gross earnings: The total amount of money earned by an employee before any deductions are taken.

Gross loss: *See* absolute loss.

Gross profit: The difference between the amount received from customers for goods and what the firm paid for the goods.

Gross profit on sales: *See* gross profit.

Gross sales: The total amount of money received from customers for the goods or services sold by the firm.

H

Half-year convention: Method of depreciation used for the first year the property is placed in service.

Head of household: An unmarried person who has dependents can use the head of household category when filing income taxes.

High: The highest price reached by a stock during the day.

Homeowner's policy: An insurance policy that covers a home against fire, theft, and liability.

Horizontal analysis: An analysis that shows the amount of any change from last year to the current year, both in dollars and as a percent.

I

Impound account (Escrow account): An account at a lending institution into which taxes and insurance are paid on a monthly basis by a borrower on real estate. The lender then pays the tax and insurance bills from this account when they become due.

Improper fraction: A fraction with a numerator larger than the denominator. (For example, $\frac{7}{5}$ is an improper fraction; $\frac{1}{9}$ is not.)

Incentive rate: A payment system based on the amount of work completed.

Income statement: A summary of all the income and expenses involved in running a business for a given period of time.

Income tax: The tax based on income that both individuals and corporations are required to pay to the federal government and sometimes to a state.

Income tax withholding: Federal income tax that the employer withholds from gross earnings.

Income-to-monthly-payment ratio: A ratio used to determine from an income standpoint whether a prospective borrower meets the lender's qualifications.

Increase problem (Amount problem): A percentage problem in which something has been added to the base. Usually the base must be found.

Index fund: A mutual fund that holds the stocks that are in a particular market index such as the Dow Jones Industrial Average.

Indicator words: Key words that help indicate whether to add, subtract, multiply, or divide.

Individual retirement account (IRA): An account designed to help people prepare for future retirement.

Inflation: Inflation results in a continuing rise in the cost of goods and services. *See* consumer price index (CPI).

Installment loan: A loan that is paid off with a sequence of periodic payments.

Insurance: Individuals and firms purchase insurance from insurance companies to protect them in the event of an unexpected loss.

Insured: A person or business that has purchased insurance.

Insurer: The insurance company.

Intangible assets: Assets such as patents, copyrights, or customer lists that have a value that cannot be immediately converted to cash, unlike jewelry or stocks.

Interest: A charge paid for borrowing money or a fee received for lending money.

Interest-bearing checking account: A checking account that earns interest.

Interest-in-advance notes: *See* simple discount note.

Interest rate spread: The difference between the interest rate paid to depositors and the rates charged to borrowers by the same lender.

Internal Revenue Service: The branch of the U.S. federal government responsible for collecting taxes.

Inventory: The value of the merchandise that a firm has for sale on the date of balance sheet.

Inventory-to-net-working-capital ratio: Inventory divided by working capital, where working capital is current assets minus current liabilities.

Inventory turnover: The number of times during a certain time period that the average inventory is sold.

Invoice: A printed record of a purchase and sales transaction.

Invoice amount: List price minus trade discounts.

Invoice date: The date an invoice is printed.

Itemized billing method: A billing method that provides an itemization of the customer's charge purchases, but not copies of the original charge receipts.

Itemized deductions: Tax deductions, such as interest, taxes, and medical expenses, that are listed individually on a tax return in order to affect the total amount of taxes payable at the end of the year.

J

Joint return: An income tax return filed by both husband and wife.

K

Kilo-: A prefix used in the metric system to represent 1000.

Kilogram: A unit of weight in the metric system meaning 1000 grams. One kilogram is about 2.2 pounds.

Kilometer: One thousand meters. A kilometer is about .6 mile.

L

Late fees: Fees required because payments were made after a specific due date.

Least common denominator: The smallest whole number that all the denominators of two or more fractions evenly divide into. (For example, the least common denominator of $\frac{3}{4}$ and $\frac{5}{6}$ is 12.)

Level premium: A level premium insurance policy is one with a level premium throughout its life.

Liability: An expense that must be paid by a firm.

LIFO: A method of inventory accounting in which the most recent items received are considered to be the first ones shipped.

Like fractions: Fractions with the same denominator.

Limited liability: A form of protection that shields a company and its shareholders from having to pay large sums of money in the event that the company loses a lawsuit.

Limited-pay life insurance: Life insurance for which premiums are paid for only a fixed number of years.

Line graph: A graph that uses lines to compare numbers.

Liquid assets: Cash or items that can be converted to cash quickly.

Liquidity: The ability of a firm or individual to raise cash quickly without being forced to sell assets at a loss.

List price: The suggested retail price or final consumer price given by the manufacturer or supplier.

Liter: A measure of volume in the metric system. One liter is a little more than one quart.

Loan amount: The amount of a loan.

Loan reduction schedule: *See* repayment schedule.

Long-term care coverage: Insurance that pays for long-term care such as nursing home expenses.

Long-term liabilities: Money owed by a firm that is not expected to be paid off within a year.

Long-term notes payable: The total of all debts of a firm, other than mortgages, that will not be paid within a year.

Low: The lowest price reached by a stock during the day.

Lowest terms: The form of a fraction if no number except the number 1 divides evenly into both the numerator and denominator.

M

M: Roman numeral for 1000.

MACRS (Modified accelerated cost recovery system): A depreciation method introduced as part of the Tax Reform Act of 1986.

Maintenance charge per month: The charge to maintain a checking account (usually determined by the minimum balance in the account).

Maker of a note: A person borrowing money from another person.

Manufacturers: Businesses that buy raw materials and component parts and assemble them into products that can be sold.

Margin: The difference between cost and selling price.

Marital status: An individual can claim married, single, or head of household when filing income taxes.

Markdown: A reduction from the original selling price. It may be expressed as a dollar amount or as a percent of the original selling price.

Marketing channels: The path of products and services beginning with the manufacturer and ending with the consumer.

Markup (Margin, Gross profit): The difference between the cost and the selling price.

Markup on cost: Markup that is calculated as a percent of cost.

Markup on selling price: Markup that is calculated as a percent of selling price.

Markup with spoilage: The calculation of markup including deduction for spoiled or unsaleable merchandise.

MasterCard: A credit-card plan (formerly known as Master-Charge).

Maturity value: The amount that a borrower must repay on the maturity date of a note.

Mean: The sum of all the numbers divided by the number of numbers.

Median: A number that represents the middle of a group of numbers.

Medical insurance: Insurance providing medical protection in the event of accident or injury.

Medicare tax: The amount of money deducted from the paychecks of almost all employees, used by the federal government to pay for Medicare.

Memory function: A feature on some calculators that stores results internally in the machine for retrieval and future use.

Merchant batch header ticket: The bank form used by businesses to deposit credit-card transactions.

Meter: A unit of length in the metric system that is slightly longer than 1 yard.

Metric system: A system of weights and measures based on decimals, used throughout most of the world. It is gradually being adopted in the United States.

Milli-: A prefix used in the metric system meaning thousandth. (For example, a milligram is one one-thousandth of a gram.)

Millimeter: One one-thousandth of a meter. There are 25.4 millimeters to an inch.

Mills: A way of expressing a real estate tax rate that is based on thousandths of a dollar.

Minuend: The number from which another number (the subtrahend) is subtracted.

Mixed number: A number written as a whole number and a fraction. (For example $1\frac{3}{4}$ and $2\frac{5}{9}$ are mixed numbers.)

Mode: The number that occurs most often in a group of numbers.

Modified accelerated cost recovery system: *See* MACRS.

Money market account: An interest-bearing account offered by many banks, savings and loans, and brokerage firms. These accounts pay interest but allow the user to draw funds out without penalty.

Money order: A document that looks similar to a check and is issued by a bank, other financial institution, or a retail store that is often used in place of cash.

Mortgage: A loan on a home.

Mortgages payable: The balance due on all mortgages owed by a firm.

Multiple carrier insurance: The sharing of risk by several insurance companies.

Multiplicand: A number being multiplied.

Multiplication rule: The same nonzero number may be multiplied or divided on both sides of an equation.

Multiplier: A number doing the multiplying.

Mutual fund: A mutual fund accepts money from many different investors and uses it to purchase stocks or bonds of numerous companies.

N

NASDAQ composite index: A commonly quoted stock index composed of the stock prices of several technology companies.

Negative numbers: Numbers that are the opposite of positive numbers.

Net cost: The cost or price after allowable discounts have been taken. *See* net price.

Net cost equivalent: The decimal number derived from the complement of the single trade discount. This number multiplied by the list price gives the net cost.

Net earnings: The difference between gross margin and expenses. After the cost of goods and operating expenses are subtracted from total sales, the remainder is net profit.

Net income: The difference between gross margin and expenses.

Net pay: The amount of money actually received by an employee after deductions are taken from gross pay.

Net payment date: The date by which an invoice must be paid.

Net price: The list price less any discounts. *See* net cost.

Net proceeds: The amount received from the bank for a discounted note.

Net profit: *See* net earnings.

Net sales: The value of goods bought by customers after the value of goods returned is subtracted.

Net worth (Capital, Stockholder's equity, Owner's equity): The difference between assets and liabilities.

No-fault insurance: A guarantee of reimbursement (provided by the insured's own insurance company) for medical expenses and costs associated with an accident no matter who is at fault.

Nominal rate: The interest rate stated in connection with a loan. It may differ from the annual percentage rate.

Nonsufficient funds (NSF): When a check is written on an account for which there is an insufficient balance, the check is returned to the depositor for nonsufficient funds.

No scrap value: The value of an item is assumed to be zero at the end of its useful life.

Notes payable: The value of all notes owed by a firm.

Notes receivable: The value of all notes owed to a firm.

NOW account (Negotiable order or withdrawal): Technically a savings account with special withdrawal privileges. It looks the same and is used the same as a checking account.

Numerator: The number above the line in a fraction. (For example, in the fraction $\frac{5}{8}$, 5 is the numerator.)

O

Odd lot: Fewer than 100 shares of stock.

Open-end-credit: Credit with no fixed number of payments. The consumer continues making payments until no outstanding balance is owed.

Operating expenses (Overhead): Expenses of operating a business. Wages, salaries, rent, utilities, and advertising are examples.

Operating loss: The loss resulting when the selling price is less than the break-even point.

Ordered array: A list of numbers arranged from smallest to largest.

Order of operations: The rules that are used when evaluating long arithmetic expressions.

Ordinary annuity: An annuity whose payments are made at the end of a given period of time.

Ordinary dating: A method for calculating the discount date and the net payment date. Days are counted from the date of the invoice.

Ordinary interest: A method of calculating interest, assuming 360 days per year. *See* banker's interest.

Ordinary life insurance (Whole life insurance, Straight life insurance): A form of life insurance whereby the insured pays a constant premium until death or retirement, whichever occurs sooner. Upon retirement, monthly payments are made by the company to the insured until the death of the insured.

Other expenses: Certain expenses that are deductible on a personal income tax return.

Overdraft: An event that results when there is not enough money in a bank account to cover a check that is written from that account.

Overhead: Expenses involved in running a firm. *See* operating expenses.

Over-the-limit fees: Fees charged when the balance on a credit-card account exceeds the account's credit limit.

Overtime: The number of hours worked by an employee in excess of 40 hours per week.

Owner's equity: *See* net worth.

P

Part: The result of multiplying the base times the rate.

Partial payment: A payment made on an invoice that is less than the full amount of the invoice.

Partial product: Part of the process of getting the answer in a multiplication problem.

Par value of a bond: *See* face value of a bond.

Passbook account: A type of savings account for day-in and day-out savings.

Payee: The person who lends money and will receive repayment on a note.

Payer of a note: A person borrowing money from another person. *See* maker of a note.

Payroll: A record of the hours each employee of a firm worked and the amount of money due each employee for a given pay period.

Payroll card: A card maintained by employers showing the name of employee, dates of pay period, days, times, and hours worked.

Payroll ledger: A chart showing all payroll information.

Percent (Rate): Some parts of a whole: hundredths, or parts of a hundred. (For example, a percent is one one-hundredth. Two percent means two parts of a hundred, or $\frac{2}{100}$.)

Percentage method: A method of calculating income tax withholding that is based on percentages.

Per debit charge: A charge per check (usually continues regardless of the number of checks written).

Periodic inventory: A physical inventory taken at regular intervals.

Permanent life insurance: Life insurance that can be continued until death, no matter the age at the time of death.

Perpetual inventory: A continuous inventory system normally involving a computer.

Personal account: The type of checking account used by individuals.

Personal exemption (Exemption): A deduction allowed each taxpayer for each dependent and the taxpayer himself or herself.

Personal identification number (PIN): A lettered or numbered code that allows a person with a credit or debit card to gain access to credit or cash.

Personal property: Property such as a boat, a car, or a stereo.

Piecework: A method of pay by which an employee receives so much money per item produced or completed.

Plant assets: *See* fixed assets.

Point-of-sale terminal: A machine that allows a customer to make purchases using a credit or debit card.

Policy: A contract outlining the insurance agreement between an insured and an insurance company.

Policy limits: The maximum amount that an insurance company will pay as defined in the policy.

Postdating: Dating in the future; on an invoice, "AS OF" dating.

pr.: Abbreviation for *pair*.

Preferred stock: A type of stock that offers investors certain rights over holders of common stock.

Premium: The amount of money charged for insurance policy coverage.

Premium factor: A factor used to adjust an annual insurance premium to semiannually, quarterly, or monthly.

Premium payment plan: An additional payment for extra service such as overtime.

Present value: The amount that must be deposited today to generate a specific amount at a specific date in the future.

Price-earnings (PE) ratio: The price per share divided by the annual net income per share of stock.

Prime interest rate: The interest rate banks charge their largest and most financially secure borrowers.

Prime number: A number that can be divided without remainder by exactly two distinct numbers: itself and 1.

Principal: The amount of money either borrowed or deposited.

Privately held corporation: A corporation that has relatively few owners, or perhaps a single owner. Its stock is not traded on a large exchange such as the New York Stock Exchange.

Proceeds: The amount of money a borrower receives after subtracting the discount from the face value of a note.

Product: The answer in a multiplication problem.

Promissory note: A business document in which one person agrees to repay money to another person within a specified amount of time and at a specified rate of interest in exchange for money borrowed.

Proper fraction: A fraction in which the numerator is smaller than the denominator. (For example, $\frac{2}{3}$ is a proper fraction; $\frac{9}{5}$ is not.)

Property damage insurance: A type of automobile insurance that pays for damages that the insured causes to the property of others.

Proportion: A mathematical statement that two ratios are equal.

Proprietorship: Stockholder's equity.

Proximo (Prox.): *See* end-of-month dating.

Publicly held corporations: Corporations that are owned by the public and have stock that trades freely.

Purchase invoice: A list of items purchased, prices charged for the items, and payment terms.

Q

Qualifying for a loan: A person applying for a loan is said to qualify if his or her credit history, income, and financial statement satisfy the requirements of the lending institution.

Quick ratio: The quotient of liquid assets and current liabilities.

Quota: An expected level of production. A premium may be paid for surpassing quota.

Quotient: The answer in a division problem.

R

Rate: Parts of a hundred. *See* percent.

Rate of interest: The percent of interest charged on a loan for a certain time period.

Ratio: A comparison of two (or more) numbers, frequently indicated by a common fraction.

Real estate: Real property such as a home or a parcel of land.

Receipt-of-goods dating (ROG): A method of determining cash discounts in which time is counted from the date that goods are received.

Reciprocal: A fraction formed from a given fraction by interchanging the numerator and denominator.

Reconciliation: The process of checking a bank statement against the depositor's own personal records.

Recourse: Should the maker of a note not pay, the bank may have recourse to collect from the seller of the note.

Recovery classes: Classes used to determine depreciation under the modified accelerated cost recovery system.

Recovery period: The life of property depreciated under the accelerated cost recovery system.

Recovery year: The year of life of an asset when using the MACRS method of depreciation.

Reduced net profit: The situation that occurs when a markdown decreases the selling price to a point that is still above the break-even point.

Refinance: A borrower can go to a lender and refinance their existing loan with a different interest rate, period, and payment.

Regulation DD: A Federal Reserve System document that specifies how interest paid to savers is to be calculated.

Regulation Z: A Federal Reserve System document that implements the Truth-in-Lending Act.

Renter's coverage: Insurance that covers only the possessions of a renter and not the house or apartment in which the possessions are kept.

Repayment schedule: A schedule showing the amount of payment going toward interest and principal and the balance of principal remaining after each payment is made.

Repeating decimals: Decimal numbers that do not terminate, but that contain numbers that repeat themselves.

Replacement cost: The cost of replacing a property that is completely destroyed.

Repossess: The taking back of property by a lender when payments have not been made to the lender.

Residual value: *See* scrap value.

Restricted endorsement: A signature or imprint on the back of a check that limits the ability to cash the check.

Retailer: A business that buys from the wholesaler and sells to the consumer.

Retail method: A method used to estimate inventory value at cost that utilizes both cost and retail amounts.

Returned check: A check that was deposited and then returned due to lack of funds in the payer's account.

Return on average total assets: Net income divided by average total assets.

Returns: The total value of all goods returned by customers.

Revolving charge account: A charge account that never has to be paid off.

Roth IRA: Contributions to a Roth Individual Retirement Account (Roth IRA) are not deductible when made. However, funds in the account grow tax free and withdrawals are not taxed once the account holder reaches a certain age.

Rounding off: The reduction of a number with more decimals to a number with fewer decimals.

Rounding whole numbers: Reduction of the number of nonzero digits in a whole number.

Round lot: A multiple of 100 shares of stock.

Rule of 78: A method of calculating a partial refund of interest that has already been added to the amount of a loan. This calculation is done when the loan is paid off early.

S

Salary: A fixed amount of money per pay period.

Salary plus commission: Earnings based on a fixed salary plus a percent of all sales.

Sale price: The price of an item after markdown.

Sales invoice: *See* purchase invoice.

Sales tax: A tax placed on sales to the final consumer. The tax is collected by the state, county, or local government.

Salvage value: *See* scrap value.

Savings account: An interest-paying account that allows day-to-day savings and withdrawals.

Schedule 1: The part of the 1040A federal tax form that is used to list all interest and dividends.

Scrap value (Salvage value): The value of an asset at the end of its useful life. For depreciation purposes, this is often an estimate.

SDI deduction: State disability insurance pays the employee in the event of disability and is paid for by the employee.

Self-employed people: People who work for themselves instead of for the government or for a private company.

Series discount: *See* chain discount.

Shift differential: A premium paid for working a less desirable shift, such as the swing shift or the graveyard shift.

Simple discount note: A note in which the interest is deducted from the face value in advance.

Simple interest: Interest received on only the principal.

Simple interest note: A note in which interest $=$ principal $\times$ interest rate $\times$ time in years.

Single discount equivalent: A series, or chain, discount expressed as a single discount.

Single return: An income tax return filed by a single person.

Sinking fund: A fund set up to receive periodic payments in order to pay off a debt at some time in the future.

sk.: Abbreviation for *sack*.

Sliding scale: Commissions that are paid at increasing levels as sales increase.

Social Security tax: *See* FICA tax.

Special endorsement: A signature on the back of a check that passes the ownership of the check to someone else.

Specific identification method: An inventory valuation method that identifies the cost of each item.

Split-shift premium: A premium paid for working a split shift, for example, for an employee who is on 4 hours, off 4 hours, and then on 4 hours.

Square root: One of two equal positive factors of a number.

Stafford loan: A loan taken out by college students to help pay tuition.

Standard deduction: A tax preparer may use the higher of the itemized deductions or the standard deduction established by the government.

Stated rate: The interest rate stated in connection with a loan. It may differ from the annual percentage rate.

State income tax: An income tax that is paid to a state government on income earned in that state.

Statement: Usually sent out monthly by the bank, a list of all charges and deposits made against and to a checking account.

Statistics: Refers both to data and to the techniques used in analyzing data.

Stock: A form of ownership in a corporation that is measured in units called *shares*.

Stockbroker: A person who buys and sells stock at the stock exchange.

Stock exchange: An institution where stock shares are bought and sold.

Stockholders: Individuals who own stock in a particular company.

Stockholder's equity: *See* net worth.

Stock ratios: Ratios calculated from the financial statements of a company—used to determine the financial health of the firm.

Stock turnover: *See* inventory turnover.

Stop payment: A request from a depositor that the bank not honor a check that the depositor has written.

Straight commission: A salary that is a fixed percent of sales.

Straight life insurance: *See* ordinary life insurance.

Straight-line depreciation: A depreciation method in which depreciation is spread evenly over the life of the asset.

Substitution: Method for checking the solution to an equation.

Subtrahend: The number being subtracted or taken away in a subtraction problem.

Sum: The total amount; the answer in addition.

Sum-of-the-years'-digits method: An accelerated depreciation method that results in larger amounts of depreciation taken in earlier years of an asset's life.

T

Tangible assets: Assets such as a car, machinery, or computers.

Taxable income: Adjusted income subject to taxation.

Tax deduction: Any expense that the Internal Revenue Service allows taxpayers to subtract from adjusted gross income.

Taxes: Individuals and corporations must pay taxes to government entities such as schools, cities, counties, states, and the federal government. Here are a few of the many types of taxes: sales taxes, property taxes, gasoline taxes, income taxes, and estate taxes.

Tax preparation: The preparation of an income tax return which is then sent to the Internal Revenue Service.

T-bill: A short-term note issued by the federal government that pays interest to the note holder. Issuing T-bills allows the federal government to raise cash without having to borrow the money from a bank and pay interest.

Telephone transfer account: An interest-bearing checking account into which funds may be transferred by the customer over the telephone.

Term insurance: A form of life insurance providing protection for a fixed length of time.

Term of an annuity: The length of time that an annuity is in effect.

Term of a note: The length of time between the date a note is written and the date the note is due.

Terms: The area of an invoice where cash discounts are indicated if any are offered. The words "terms discount" are often used in place of "cash discount."

Territorial ratings: Ratings used by insurance companies that describe the quality of fire protection in a specific area.

Time-and-a-half rate: One and one-half times the normal rate of pay for any hours worked in excess of 40 per week.

Time card: A card filled out by an employee that shows the number of hours worked by that employee.

Time deposit account: A savings account in which the depositor agrees to leave money on deposit for a certain period of time.

Time rate: Earnings based on hours worked, not for work accomplished.

Total installment cost: Includes the down payment plus the sum of all payments.

Total revenue: The total of all revenue from all sources.

Trade discount: A discount offered to businesses. This discount is expressed either as a single discount (like 25%) or a series discount (like 20/10) and is subtracted from the list price.

Transaction register: Shows the checks written and deposits made on a checking account.

True rate of interest: *See* effective rate of interest.

Turnover at cost: The cost of goods sold, divided by the average inventory at cost.

Turnover at retail: Sales, divided by the average inventory at retail.

U

Underinsured motorist: A motorist who does not carry enough insurance to cover the costs of an accident.

Underwriters: Term applied to any insurer. Usually associated with an insurance company.

Unearned interest: Interest that a company has received but has not yet earned so that it is not shown in revenues.

Uniform product code (UPC): The series of black vertical stripes seen on products in stores that cashiers scan. Also called the *bar code.*

Uninsured motorist insurance: Insurance coverage that covers the insured when involved in an accident with a driver who is not insured.

United States Rule: The rule by which a loan payment is first applied to the interest owed, with the balance used to reduce the principal amount of the loan.

Unit price: The cost of one item.

Units-of-production: A depreciation method by which the number of units produced determines the depreciation allowance.

Universal life policy: A policy whose premiums flow into a general account from which the insurance company makes investments.

Unlike fractions: Fractions with different denominators.

Unpaid-balance method: A method used to calculate interest on open-end credit accounts.

Unreimbursed job expenses: Certain expenses that are deductible on a personal income tax return.

Useful life: The estimated life of an asset. The Internal Revenue Service gives guidelines of useful life for depreciation purposes.

V

Valuation of inventory: Determining the value of merchandise in stock. Four common methods are specific-identification, average cost, FIFO, and LIFO.

Variable: A letter that stands for a number.

Variable commission: A commission whose rate depends on the total amount of the sales.

Variable interest rate loan: A loan on which the interest rate can go up or down.

Variable life policy: A life insurance policy that allows the owner to invest the funds within the policy in different types of investments.

Verbal form: Word form (the form of numbers expressed in words).

Vertical analysis: The listing of each important item on an income statement as a percent of total net sales or each item on a balance sheet as a percent of total assets.

Visa: A credit-card plan (formerly known as Bank Americard).

W

Wage: A rate of pay expressed as a certain amount of dollars per hour.

Wage bracket method: A method of calculating income tax withholding that is based on tables that list income ranges.

Weighted average method: A method for calculating the arithmetic mean for data where each value is weighted (or multiplied) according to its importance.

Whole life insurance: *See* ordinary life insurance.

Whole number: A number made up of digits to the left of the decimal point.

Wholesaler: A business that buys directly from the manufacturer or other wholesalers and sells to the retailer.

Withholding allowance: An allowance for the employee, spouse, and dependents that determines the amount of withholding tax taken from gross earnings.

Withholding tax: The money withheld from an employee's paycheck and deposited to the account of the employee with the federal or state government to cover the amount of income tax owed by the employee.

With recourse: An understanding that the seller of a note is responsible for payment of the note if the original maker of the note does not make payment. The note is sold with recourse.

Worker's compensation: Insurance purchased by companies to cover employees against work-related injuries.

W-2 form: The wage and tax statement given to the employee each year by the employer.

W-4 form: A form usually completed at the time of employment, on which an employee states the number of withholding allowances being claimed.

Y

Youthful operator: A driver of a motor vehicle who is under a certain age, usually 25.

Index

Acknowledgments

Page xxi, group of students studying/Getty Royalty Free
Page 1, Subway sandwich shop/Beth Anderson
Page 6, Subway drink cup/Beth Anderson
Page 7, Ford Escape/Stan Salzman
Page 14, parachute jumpers/PhotoDisc
Page 15, rafters on river/Shutterstock
Page 16, Walmart supercenter/Beth Anderson
Page 20, Jared Fogle with big pants/AP Wideworld Photo
Page 20, Subway napkin/Beth Anderson
Page 21, Subway sandwiches/Beth Anderson
Page 21, Iwo Jima flag/Joe Rosenthal/Corbis
Page 21, Army WWII/Beth Anderson
Page 23, radio station call letters/Shutterstock
Page 23, two candy bars (not Milky way)/Beth Anderson
Page 27, brand name soda 12-pack/Shutterstock
Page 28, frozen-type pizza/iStockphoto
Page 30, Subway deposit slip/iStockphoto
Page 32, Circuit City product purchases/Purestock/Getty Royalty Free
Page 32, 4-year-olds at day car/Stockbyte/Getty Royalty Free
Page 40, Cadillac Escalade big rims and tires/iStockphoto
Page 42, Subway/Beth Anderson
Page 49, Home Depot storefront/Don Smetzer/Photo Edit
Page 50, built-in microwave oven/iStockphoto
Page 54, Home Depot/PhotoDisc
Page 56, gold bracelet and earrings/iStockphoto
Page 57, kitchen cabinets/Shutterstock
Page 70, chocolate/Oat-Chip cookie/Shutterstock
Page 74, woman using hairdryer/Shutterstock
Page 86, 6-unit apartment building/iStockphoto
Page 87, Century 21 sign/Beth Anderson
Page 90, woman making business presentation/Shutterstock
Page 95, $210K home/Stan Salzman
Page 99, pizza maker/PhotoDisc
Page 102, woman lawyer/courtesy of Stan Salzman
Page 103, GM sales in China/STR/AFP/Getty Images
Page 103, NFL Superbowl ad cost/Digital Vision
Page 104, Country Store household items/iStockphoto
Page 110, voting registration/Comstock Royalty Free
Page 111, Haagen-Dazs ice cream pint/Shutterstock
Page 114, portable DVD player/iStockphoto
Page 115, running around Lake Tahoe/iStockphoto
Page 118, women in military/AP Wideworld Photo
Page 118, woman on motorcycle/iStockphoto
Page 120, athletic shoe store/Corbis Royalty Free
Page 120, motorcycle helmet/Digital Vision
Page 122, totaled car/Shutterstock
Page 128, Case Study Century 21/Beth Anderson
Page 130, family restaurant/Shutterstock
Page 132, Chiquita banana with label/Beth Anderson
Page 132, CVS store sign/Beth Anderson
Page 138, Cadillac Escalade/iStockphoto
Page 140, shark cage/Shutterstock
Page 143, Green Giant Nursery/Shutterstock
Page 159, Jackson&Perkins Roses/iStockphoto
Page 161, auto repair shop/iStockphoto
Page 162, plants at nursery/Shutterstock
Page 164, studio family portrait/iStockphoto
Page 175, nursery with customers/Shutterstock
Page 179, Starbucks store/Beth Anderson
Page 197, bakery products sold in Starbucks/iStockphoto
Page 212, W-4 tax return/iStockphoto
Page 219, Social Security/Silver BurdettGinn
Page 231, Kitchen Crafters kitchen items/Digital Vision
Page 235, stainless steel cookware in store/Shutterstock
Page 236, George Foreman and grill/Jeremy O'Donnell/Getty Images
Page 241, Zune MP3 video player/iStockphoto
Page 241, walker/Shutterstock
Page 241, home beverage fountain/iStockphoto
Page 249, hour glass/Shutterstock
Page 251, Hershey products/Beth Anderson
Page 253, Razor video phone/Beth Anderson
Page 254, George Foreman/Anthony Harvey/Getty Images
Page 256, rotisserie grill/iStockphoto
Page 260, Kitchen Aid mixer/Shutterstock
Page 260, auto body shop/iStockphoto

Page 261, Nike Air Max360 and Steve Marbury Starbury One//GNU free documentation license

Page 264, GPS Magellan Roadmate 2000 for car/Shutterstock

Page 264, custom car wheels/Shutterstock

Page 266, custom chopped motorcycle/iStockphoto

Page 273, Olympic Sports equipment store/Robin Nelson/PhotoEdit

Page 274, Swiss Military sports watch/Shutterstock

Page 276, hiking boots in store/Shutterstock

Page 278, woman in hooded sweatshirt/iStockphoto

Page 281, Exercycle/Shutterstock

Page 282, custom-made necklaces/iStockphoto

Page 282, ping pong table/Shutterstock

Page 284, Body Glove sunglasses/Shutterstock

Page 285, tennis racket/Shutterstock

Page 292, Italian silk ties/Shutterstock

Page 292, treadmill/Shutterstock

Page 293, air hockey table/iStockphoto

Page 294, several dozen long-stemmed roses/Shutterstock

Page 298, 40" LCD HDTV/Shutterstock

Page 302, GPS for car/Shutterstock

Page 304, children's apparel store/Shutterstock

Page 305, Cracker Jack box/Beth Anderson

Page 314, Razor phones and latest cell phones/iStockphoto

Page 320, REI/Jeff Greenbeg/PhotoEdit

Page 324, Iron Horse BMX bike/iStockphoto

Page 325, car dealership/PhotoDisc Red

Page 325, car dealership/PhotoDisc Red

Page 335, hair salon/Shutterstock

Page 335, rock fountain and fish pond/Shutterstock

Page 337, home under construction/Shutterstock

Page 340, woman at bank/Shutterstock

Page 343, Toyota dealer/iStockphoto

Page 344, trees in nursery/Shutterstock

Page 346, smaller truck with plow/iStockphoto

Page 353, Malaysia/iStockphoto

Page 355, sailboat retailer-single boat/Beth Anderson

Page 357, recording studio/iStockphoto

Page 360, GM/iStockphoto

Page 363, retail sewing machine/Beth Anderson, courtesy of Marie's Sewing Center

Page 377, Bank of America ATM/courtesy of Joe Vetere

Page 378, female nurse/Shutterstock

Page 389, bank vault with cash/iStockphoto

Page 390, Toyota Camry/Shutterstock

Page 396, printing shop/iStockphoto

Page 398, Bank of America/Beth Anderson

Page 399, gas pumps/Shutterstock

Page 401, Harley Davidson motorcycle/Shutterstock

Page 403, day care business/iStockphoto

Page 413, community college computer lab job/Photodisc

Page 415, young male office worker/Shutterstock

Page 422, man and grandson fishing/Photodisc

Page 426, job in Saudi Arabia/iStockphoto

Page 426, female nurse/Shutterstock

Page 427, older woman teaching/iStockphoto

Page 429, attorney/iStockphoto

Page 431, sports complex/Shutterstock

Page 432, church building/Shutterstock

Page 434, large coal mine tractor/iStockphoto

Page 436, boat in swamp/Shutterstock

Page 438, fire truck/Shutterstock

Page 439, woman in wheelchair/Shutterstock

Page 441, stock certificate/Silver Burditt Ginn

Page 442, Harley Davidson shop/Beth Anderson

Page 444, Target Store/Beth Anderson

Page 444, soldier with Harris equipment/iStockphoto

Page 448, Pepsi/Beth Anderson

Page 450, American River College/Shutterstock

Page 451, church construction/Beth Anderson

Page 452, Hershey chocolates/Beth Anderson

Page 456, NYC/Photodisc

Page 463, Citbank Direct/Mario Tama/Getty Images

Page 466, yellow lab/Shutterstock

Page 467, large digital TV/Shutterstock

Page 472, hot tub and landscaping/iStockphoto

Page 473, restaurant/iStockphoto

Page 474, flower arrangement/Shutterstock

Page 475, SUV/Shutterstock

Page 477, used car/Beth Anderson

Page 478, inside a pizza restaurant/PhotoDisc Red

Page 483, new Toyota Corolla/AP Wideworld Photo

Page 486, Holstein cows/Shutterstock

Page 488, new washer and dryer/Shutterstock

Page 481, butcher shop/Shutterstock

Page 481, diamond engagement ring/Shutterstock

Page 492, computer network in design business/Shutterstock

Page 494, Ford SUV/iStockphoto

Page 500, ski shop/Shutterstock

Page 503, modest home/Shutterstock

Page 508, small cottage/Shutterstock

Page 513, couple and two young kids/iStockphoto

Page 515, Citigroup case study/AP Photo/Josh Reynolds

Page 523, doll business/Beth Anderson

Page 526, high school/Shutterstock

Page 530, 4-unit apartment building/iStockphoto

Page 538, woman and child/Shutterstock

Page 545, couple and child/iStockphoto

Page 549, fire and smoke in commercial building/Shutterstock

Page 551, smoke damage in mall/Shutterstock

Page 552, mosaic damage covered by insurance/Shutterstock

Page 555, firemen fighting business fire/Shutterstock

Page 559, car wreck on icy road/iStockphoto

Page 564, car collision/Shutterstock

Page 569, bungee jumper/iStockphoto

Page 571, woman and 2 young children/Shutterstock

Page 572, Mattell/Beth Anderson

Page 574, 45-year-old woman/Shutterstock

Page 578, distinguished woman in wheelchair/Stockbyte/Getty Royalty Free

Page 580, wrecked pickup on icy road/iStockphoto

Page 581, Capital Curb and Concrete/courtesy of Stan Salzman

Page 583, KFC cooking chicken/iStockphoto

Page 585, 2007 Ford work pickup/Corbis

Page 588, loader/courtesy of Stan Salzman

Page 590, warehouse/Shutterstock

Page 593, 2007 Ford work pickup/Corbis

Page 597, auto analysis at car dealer/iStockphoto

Page 598, dump truck/courtesy of Stan Salzman

Page 601, 2007 Ford work pickup/Corbis

Page 608, walk-in bank safe/Digital Vision

Page 609, car wash/Shutterstock

Page 610, deli display case/Corbis

Page 611, stump chipper/courtesy of Stan Salzman

Page 612, new heavy truck/Shutterstock

Page 614, Ford Truck/Reuters/Corbis

Page 616, McDonald's grilling station/Wolfgang Spunbarg/PhotoEdit

Page 620, 2007 Ford work pickup/Corbis

Page 620, business discussion/iStockphoto

Page 627, 2007 Ford work pickup/Corbis

Page 629, freezer case/Shutterstock

Page 631, dump truck being loaded/Shutterstock

Page 633, candy/Beth Anderson

Page 635, Hershey bar/Beth Anderson

Page 637, electronics store/Corbis

Page 639, chocolate syrup/Shutterstock

Page 643, scuba/Shutterstock

Page 648, Hershey's manufacturing chocolate/Shutterstock

Page 651, Chocolate Factory/Shutterstock

Page 652, Hershey kisses/Beth Anderson

Page 653, chocolate candy display/Beth Anderson

Page 655, yacht/Beth Anderson

Page 662, bicycle shop/Photodisc

Page 664, Case Study Hershey's/Beth Anderson

Page 666, tobacco shop/Shutterstock

Page 667, Bistro-style restaurant/Photodisc

Page 668, Bistro-style restaurant/Shutterstock

Page 669, artistic plate of food/Shutterstock

Page 674, bank employees/Photodisc

Page 675, marketing professor in class/Digital Vision

Page 683, dog/Shutterstock

Page 685, new laptop/Shutterstock

Page 689, mall gift kiosk (The Soft Touch)/Shutterstock

Page 690, Bobby Flay/AP Wideworld Photo

Page 693, man and wife/Digital Vision

Page C-8, robotic dog/Tom Strattman/Getty Images

Percent Formula Part = Base × Rate or $P = B \times R$ or $P = BR$

Markup Formula Cost + Markup = Selling price or $C + M = S$

Converting Markup Percent on Cost to Selling Price

$$\text{Markup on selling price} = \frac{\text{Markup on cost}}{100\% + \text{Markup on cost}}$$

Converting Markup Percent on Selling Price to Cost

$$\text{Markup on cost} = \frac{\text{Markup on selling price}}{100\% - \text{Markup on selling price}}$$

Terms Associated with Loss

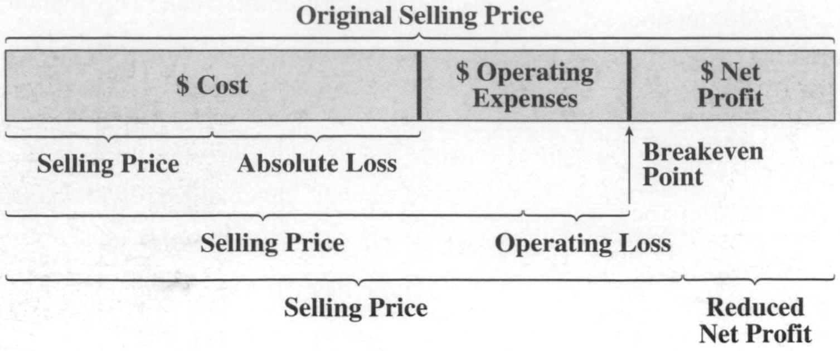

Stock Turnover

$$\text{Turnover at retail} = \frac{\text{Retail sales}}{\text{Average inventory at retail}} \qquad \text{Turnover at cost} = \frac{\text{Cost of goods sold}}{\text{Average inventory at cost}}$$

Simple Interest The *simple interest*, I, on a principal of P dollars at a rate of interest R per year for T years is given by $I = PRT$.

Number of Days in Each Month

31 Days		30 Days	28 Days
January	August	April	February
March	October	June	(29 days in leap year)
May	December	September	
July		November	

Types of Interest The method for forming the *time fraction* used for T in the formula $I = PRT$ is summarized as follows:

The *numerator* is the *exact number* of days in a loan period.
The *denominator* is one of the following:

- *exact interest* assumes 365 days in a year and uses 365 as denominator.
- *ordinary*, or *banker's interest* assumes 360 days in a year and uses 360 as denominator.

Interest, Principal, Rate, and Time Formulas

Interest: $I = PRT$ Principal: $P = \frac{I}{RT}$ Rate: $R = \frac{I}{PT}$

Time: Time in days $= \frac{I}{PR} \times 360$ Time in years $= \frac{I}{PR}$

Maturity Value The *maturity value* M of a loan having a principal P and interest I is given by $M = P + I$.

Simple Interest and Simple Discount

	Simple Interest Note	Simple Discount Note
	I = Interest P = Principal (face value) R = Rate of interest T = Time, in years or fraction of a year M = Maturity value	B = Discount P = Proceeds D = Discount rate T = Time, in years or fraction of a year M = Maturity value
Face value	Stated on note	Same as maturity value
Interest charge	$I = PRT$	$B = MDT$
Maturity value	$M = P + I$	Same as face value
Amount received by borrower	Face value or principal	Proceeds: $P = M - B$
Identifying phrases	Interest at a certain rate Maturity value greater than face value	Discounted at a certain rate Proceeds Maturity value equal to face value
True annual interest rate	Same as stated rate R	Greater than stated rate D

Compound Interest If P dollars are deposited at a rate of interest i per period for n periods, then the *compound amount* M, or the final amount of deposit, is

$$M = P(1 + i)^n$$

The interest earned I is

$$I = M - P$$

(Use the compound interest table.)

Tab Your Way to Success

Use these tabs to mark important pages of your textbook for quick reference and review.

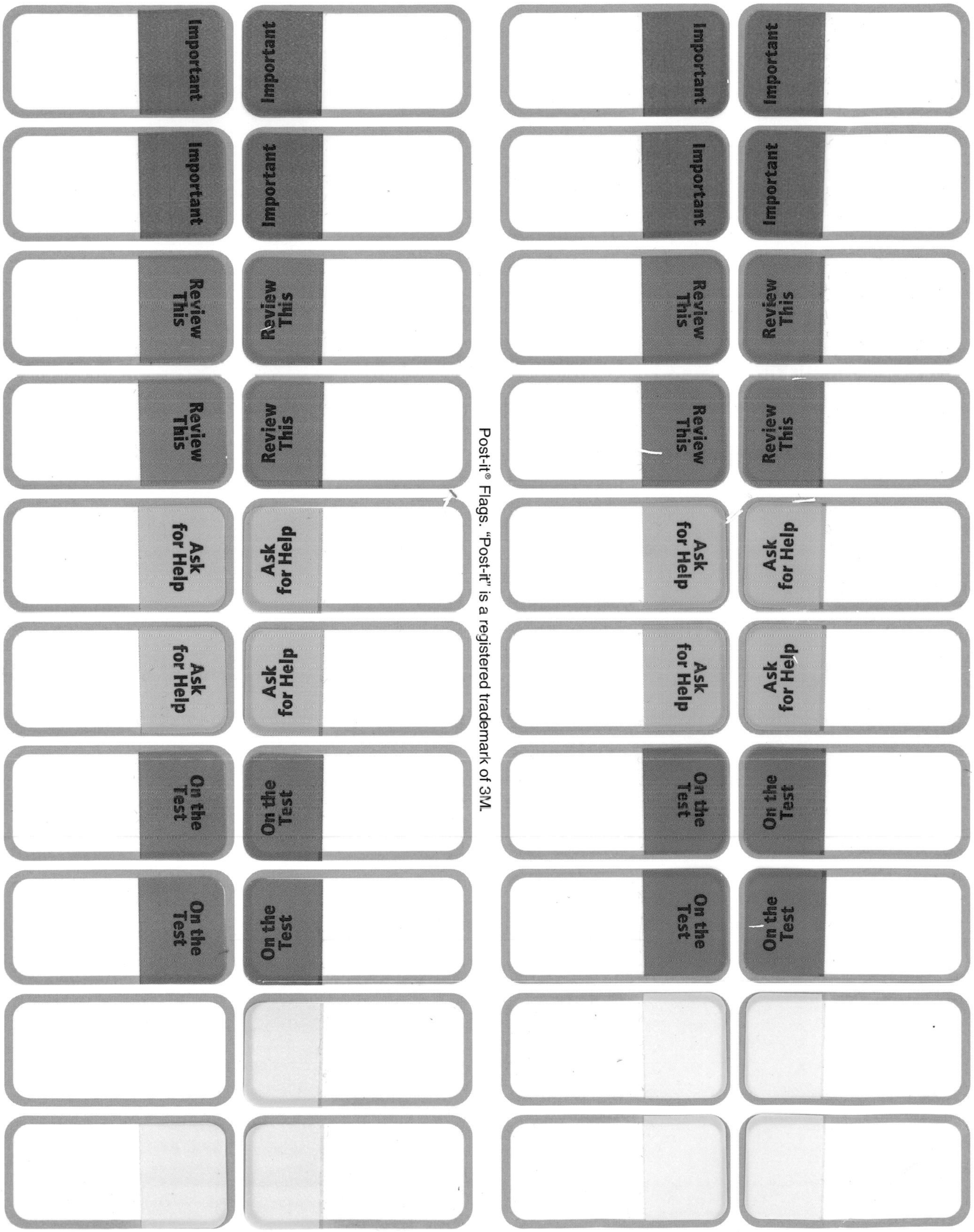

Using the Tabs

Customize Your Textbook and Make It Work for You!

These removable and reusable tabs offer you five ways to be successful in your math course by letting you bookmark pages with helpful reminders.

Important	Use these tabs to flag anything your instructor indicates is important.
Review This	Mark important definitions, procedures, or key terms to review later.
Ask for Help	Not sure of something? Need more instruction? Place these tabs in your textbook to address any questions with your instructor during your next class meeting or with your tutor during your next tutoring session.
On the Test	If your instructor alerts you that something will be covered on a test, use these tabs to bookmark it.
	Write your own notes or create more of the preceding tabs to help you succeed in your math course.

ISBN-13: 978-0-321-53635-8
ISBN-10: 0-321-53635-5
EAN
9 780321 536358 90000